CICA Research Studies

W9-BVD-107

Canadian
Advanced Financial
Accounting

anthony grewal.

Canadian
Advanced Financial
Accounting
Second Edition

Thomas H. Beechy
York University

Holt, Rinehart and Winston of Canada, Limited
Toronto

Canadian Cataloguing in Publication Data

Beechy, Thomas H., 1937-
    Canadian advanced financial accounting

2nd ed.
Includes index.
ISBN 0-03-922676-X

1. Accounting   I. Title

HF5635.B43 1990   657'.048   C89-094660-4

Publisher: *David Collinge*
Acquisitions Editor: *Warren Laws*
Developmental Editor: *Susan Bindernagel*
Publishing Services Manager: *Karen Eakin*
Editorial Co-ordinator: *Marcel Chiera*
Copy Editors: *Greg Ioannou and Lynne Missen/The Editorial Centre*
Interior Design: *Jack Steiner Graphic Design*
Cover Design: *Landgraff Design Associates Ltd.*
Cover Photograph: *George Calef/Masterfile*
Typesetting and Assembly: *Q Composition Inc.*
Printing and Binding: *John Deyell Company*

Printed in Canada

1 2 3 4 5   94 93 92 91 90

Preface

This volume is the second edition of the first "all-Canadian" advanced accounting text. Like its predecessor, it is written with the specific needs of Canadian professional accountants and accounting educators in mind.

The development of accounting education in Canada has tended to emphasize the professional component of accounting, the need to develop those skills of analysis and synthesis that distinguish the professional accountant from a highly skilled bookkeeper. This need has illuminated the preparation of this text. Rather than simply presenting a summary of accounting practices as they are currently proclaimed in professional pronouncements, the text discusses the range of alternatives from which recent practice has evolved, thereby helping the student to understand how we have arrived at our present situation and to grasp future evolutions in accounting.

The second edition maintains the basic thrust of the first edition, and in fact, strengthens the professional judgment aspect. Chapter 1, for example, includes a more extensive discussion of the meaning and role of professional judgement in accounting, drawing from the recent CICA research study by Gibbins and Mason, while the following chapters emphasize the elements of accounting practice that require the exercise of professional judgment.

As in the first edition, students are provided with an opportunity to hone their professional judgement skills through the analysis of cases. There is a total of 70 cases, an increase of almost 50% over the first edition. Some have been drawn from professional examinations, but most are original. These cases give students invaluable practice in sorting out objectives, alternatives, and outcomes, practice that cannot be achieved by the use of problems alone. The cases in this book can be supplemented by cases from other sources; the instructor's manual contains suggestions for suitable additional case material.

Two enhancements in this edition will assist students in their learning of complex material. The first is the addition of self-study problems at the end of most of the more technical chapters. There are sixteen self-study problems, the full solutions to which are provided at the end of the text, following Chapter 18.

The second enhancement is the availability of a computerized student manual containing a disk for most of the consolidation problem material. By using this manual and the accompanying template, students can drastically cut the amount of pencil-pushing that is necessary to solve these problems, thereby increasing the efficiency of their study time. In addition, instructors will be able to assign more problems to provide more practice without placing unreasonable demands on students' time. This student manual, prepared by Dr. Pierre Vézina of Université Laval, also contains fully worked out solutions for much of the illustrative material in the consolidation chapters using the direct approach exclusively; as well, complete solutions (with explanatory calculations) for the Practical Corporation-Silly Inc. series of problems that follows chapters, 8, 9, and 10 are also included. By using the manual and template along with the textbook, students have available the most comprehensive illustrative material provided in an advanced accounting text. (Problems on disk are identified in the text with this symbol: ⌨.)

Part 1 of the text focuses on the broad issues of financial reporting. Chapter 1 discusses the meaning of GAAP, the extent to which GAAP is reflected in professional pronouncements, and the meaning and role of professional judgment in financial reporting. Chapter 2 is a discussion of the objectives of financial reporting for business enterprises, and the ways in which the objectives are affected by the nature of the business organization and the users of the financial statements. In this edition, the discussion of objectives highlights the potentially differing objectives of users and preparers, and the circumstances under which the objectives of one group may take precedence over the other. Chapter 2 also discusses the qualitative characteristics of accounting information and the impact of these criteria on the choice of accounting measurements.

Chapter 3 illustrates the ways in which objectives and qualitative characteristics shape accounting and reporting practices in specific industries. Here the concepts raised in Chapter 2 are applied in reference to two very different industries: extractive companies and mutual funds. The chapter is not designed as a treatise on these two industries, but rather as an example of the application of fundamental concepts of financial reporting. An interesting research project or term paper would be for students to select an industry and perform a similar analysis of the ways in which accounting and financial reporting have developed in response to the special characteristics of that industry. The instructor's manual contains more explicit suggestions in this regard.

Having dealt with financial reporting for business enterprises in Chapters 2 and 3, we turn our attention to nonbusiness organizations in Chapters 4 and 5. These chapters have been extensively rewritten in this edition to reflect the rapid rate of development of accounting in nonprofit organizations. Chapter 4 discusses the objectives for financial reporting of nonprofit organizations, governments, and governmental units. Separate attention is devoted to the Public Sector Accounting Standards. Considerable reference is made to the research studies in this area that have been released in recent years, especially those of the CICA and of the CGA Research Foundation. The major reporting issues are highlighted, and increased use is made of current examples of reporting by nonprofit organizations, especially in the development of programmatic reporting of operations.

Chapter 5 deals with the characteristics of fund accounting, and the ways in which fund accounting is adapted to suit the needs of the organization. Illustrations are given of the application of fund accounting to different types of organizations.

Part 2 of the text is concerned with that basic core area of any advanced accounting text, intercorporate investments. Chapters 6 through 13 present an overview of this important topic, but with some differences, compared with the treatment in other texts.

First, alternatives to existing practice are presented and explained, in order to provide a context for the recommendations contained in the *CICA Handbook*.

Secondly, attention is focused on the major issues of accounting for intercorporate investments and of consolidations, rather than on the many intriguing but relatively minor issues. Many aspects of the subject, such as reciprocal shareholdings, are interesting to contemplate but are not essential to understanding the basic concepts. We have chosen not to concern ourselves with these many subsidiary issues.

Third, we have resisted the temptation to quote extensively from the *CICA Handbook*. Students must be aware of the recommendations of the *Handbook*, but they should be responsible for reading this important source directly, rather than in excerpted form in a text. What this text attempts to do is to present the issues and concepts in original wording, so that students will have two explanations rather than just one.

Fourth, the discussion of consolidations emphasizes consolidated financial *statements*, not just the balance sheet. Consolidated statements are prepared at the date of acquisition only once in the lifetime of a business combination; thereafter, consolidation always involves an income statement and a statement of changes in financial position. Our discussion reflects this reality.

The second edition has updated this material. There have been no major changes in the *CICA Handbook* relating to business combinations or consolidations, but there is a continuing evolution of accounting practice and presentation, and a continuing evolution of business practices. As a result, we have added sections on important topics such as leveraged buy-outs, reverse takeovers, and push-down accounting. Also, in response to user requests, we have expanded our discussion of joint ventures and of intercorporate bond investments.

The core of the discussion is contained in Chapters 6 through 10. Elaborations and major ancillary issues are presented in Chapters 11, 12, and 13. The chapters contain a logical progression of the material, from the most fundamental and least complicated to the more complex aspects. Coverage of intercorporate investments can be discontinued after any chapter, if time is limited, without leaving specific issues up in the air.

Chapter 6 contains an overview of accounting and financial reporting for intercorporate investments, including newly added material on portfolio investments. The basic concepts of subsidiaries and consolidation, and of significant influence and equity reporting, are presented. Preparation of a consolidated balance sheet and income statement in a simple situation is illustrated.

Chapter 7 discusses different forms of business combinations, and explains the reasons for using the purchase method for reporting the results of an acquisition of shares. The alternative approaches of pooling and new entity are also illustrated. This chapter deals with combinations and with consolidation at the date of acquisition, when the acquisition is of 100% of the acquired company's shares. The additional complexities that are introduced when a minority interest exists are deferred to Chapter 9.

Chapter 8 discusses consolidation and equity reporting subsequent to the date of acquisition for wholly owned subsidiaries. The concepts of unrealized profits and of amortization of fair-value increments and goodwill are emphasized.

Chapters 9 and 10 extend the discussion of the preceding two chapters to non-wholly owned subsidiaries. We discuss the alternative ways of viewing minority interest when preparing consolidated statements. We introduce the concept of income tax effects arising from unrealized profits. Proportionate consolidation for joint ventures is also discussed.

Chapter 11 explores the issues and methods of pooling, and also draws the distinction between pooling as a way of reporting intercorporate investments and pooling as the outcome of corporate reorganizations. In addition to being repositioned from the first edition, the discussion in this chapter has been slightly expanded. While pooling is seldom encountered in Canada in public companies as a method of reporting business combinations, its use is much more common among private corporations, wherein shareholder agreements define the extent of control of the various shareholders and provide a different basis for evaluating a business combination. In addition, many U.S. companies use pooling, and students will frequently encounter financial statements of U.S. companies.

Chapter 12 elaborates upon four issues that were touched on at a basic level in the preceding five chapters. For the sake of clarity, the discussion of unrealized profits in Chapters 8 through 10 is limited largely to inventories. The first part of Chapter 11 discusses the treatment of unrealized profits in more general terms, including unrealized profits in intercompany sales of depreciable assets. Chapter 11 also discusses extraordinary gains and losses of subsidiaries, income tax effects of consolidation, and intercorporate bond holdings.

Chapter 13 discusses additional aspects of ownership interests, including the effect of subsidiary preferred shares on the parent's interest, and increases or decreases in the parent's ownership interest.

After extensive discussion of the practice of consolidation, the book turns, in Chapter 14, to disaggregation. Chapter 14 discusses segmented reporting and interim reporting.

Part 3, Chapters 15-18, deals with the area of international accounting. Canada is a major international trader. Canadian companies are very active in international markets, and much of Canadian business is controlled by foreign investors. Thus, international business is relatively much more important in Canada than it is in the United States. The accounting issues that arise in international transactions and operations merit more attention than they traditionally have received in advanced accounting texts. This book devotes four chapters to this important topic.

Chapter 15 is a discussion of the dimensions of international accounting and the problems and issues that arise in attempting to report the results of international business.

Chapter 16 discusses the accounting for foreign-currency-denominated transactions by Canadian companies. Chapter 17 deals with the translation of financial results for foreign operations, and includes discussions of the concepts of accounting versus economic risk exposure, and of self-sustaining versus integrated operations. Chapter 18 is a somewhat technical chapter illustrating the process of consolidation and of equity reporting of foreign operations.

Many of the problems in this text have been drawn from the examinations of the three national professional accounting groups in Canada, the CAs, the CMAs, and the CGAs. A few have also been obtained from the Accountancy Admission Examinations of the Institute of Chartered Accountants of Ontario and from the CPA examination of the American Institute of Certified Public Accountants. I am indebted to these organizations for permitting the use of their copyrighted material. An acknowledgement appears at the end of each problem or case that was obtained from one of these four sources.

I am also deeply indebted to the many individuals who reviewed all or part of the manuscript and offered their valuable suggestions, most of which I have incorporated into the final text. While the reviewers can share none of the blame for anything that has gone wrong, they certainly can share much of the credit for whatever has come out right.

There are two special people to whom I am profoundly grateful. One is Lisa Gallant, who gallantly typed, edited, revised, and organized virtually the entire manuscript over the year that it has been in revision. The other is Brian McBurney, without whose understanding, support, and patience this book would not have been possible.

I can only hope that the efforts of all of these people have resulted in a text that will be helpful to the often beleaguered teachers of accountancy in this country.

PUBLISHER'S NOTE TO INSTRUCTORS AND STUDENTS

This textbook is a key component of your course. If you are the instructor of this course, you undoubtedly considered a number of texts carefully before choosing this as the one that would work best for your students and you. The authors and publishers of this book spent considerable time and money to ensure its high quality, and we appreciate your recognition of this effort and accomplishment.

If you are a student we are confident that this text will help you to meet the objectives of your course. You will also find it helpful after the course is finished as a valuable addition to your personal library.

As well, please do not forget that photocopying copyright work means the authors lose royalties that are rightfully theirs. This loss will discourage them from writing another edition of this text or other books; doing so would simply not be worth their time and effort. If this happens we all lose — students, instructors, authors, and publishers.

Since we want to hear what you think about this book, please be sure to send us the stamped reply card at the end of the text. This will help us to continue publishing high-quality books for your course.

Acknowledgements

Of the many individuals who have contributed to the development and ultimate success of this book, I am especially indebted to those who reviewed the manuscript and provided suggestions that often resulted in significant improvements. Some of the dedicated teachers and experienced professionals whose suggestions contibuted to the first edition are listed below:

Joan Conrod, University of Toronto
J.K. Courtis, University of Waterloo
Christina Drummond, Price Waterhouse
H.F.C. Graham, Clarkson Gordon
Jeffrey Kantor, University of Windsor
Don Lockwood, University of British Columbia
Alister Mason, Deloitte, Haskin and Sells
Mort Nelson, Wilfred Laurier University
L.S. Rosen, York University
Stephen Spector, CGA-Canada
Beverly Trifonidis, Simon Fraser University

I am also deeply grateful to those reviewers who provided valuable suggestions for the second edition. They include:

Martha Dunlop, University of Toronto
Paul Dunn, McGill University
Gail Fayerman, Concordia University
Robert Maher, University of New Brunswick, Fredericton
Jacques Maurice, Carleton University
J.R.E. Parker, Dalhousie University
Peter Secord, St. Mary's University
Raymonde Vachon, University of Waterloo
Pierre Vézina, Université Laval

Contents

PART

1

1

An Introduction to Advanced Accounting

This is a book on advanced accounting. The vast majority of students who take an advanced accounting course intend to pursue accounting as a career. Thus a book on advanced accounting must recognize the needs of the pre-professional accounting student.

In prior courses, students may have studied accounting as passive analyzers of data. They were presented with problems, given explicit directions on solving them, and expected to simply carry out the instructions. This is a passive approach to the study of accounting, because the student is not actively involved in identifying the accounting problems or in determining the general approach to solving them.

A professional accountant, whether employed in business, public practice, or the public or nonprofit sectors, must take an active role. It is the accountant who must point out accounting issues to managers, and who must devise ways to solve them. The accountant must identify the facts in the situation, determine how they potentially affect the financial reporting of the organization, and develop an approach to the problem that satisfies both managers and external users of the financial statements.

In the exercise of his or her profession, the accountant exists in a world of conflicting demands and multiple alternatives. Professional judgment is essential in choosing from among the available approaches to solving a problem. But the exercise of judgment requires the availability of benchmarks or explicit criteria by which to evaluate alternative approaches and alternative results. The use of professional judgment is not an application of arbitrariness. If choices were purely arbitrary, then there would be no difference between professional judgment and non-professional judgment; the professional would be in no better position to make a decision than would a lay person.

The first part of this text helps the advanced accounting student to develop professional judgment. A textbook can only be a guide; the development of judgmental skills requires practice through case analysis and practical experience, with review and evaluation by instructors and professional accountants.

What a textbook can do is to delineate the essential criteria and to provide guidelines for their application. In the remainder of this chapter and in the next, these criteria and guidelines are developed. Chapters 3 through 5 demonstrate their application to financial reporting in both business and nonbusiness organizations. In Chapters 6 through 18, specific topic areas are studied. These topics all involve alternative approaches and methodologies. To choose from among these alternatives, the student will have to use professional judgment. First, however, we should take a look at what constitutes the available range of accounting alternatives from which the accountant must recommend specific policies.

THE MEANING OF GAAP

Financial statements issued for external users are usually, although not always, prepared in accordance with **generally accepted accounting principles** or **GAAP**. Since GAAP defines the range of permissible alternatives in such reporting situations, we should pause to consider just what constitutes GAAP in Canada.

GAAP is sometimes viewed simply as the recommendations contained in the *CICA Handbook*. This view is reinforced by statute, such as the *Canada Business Corporations Act* (*CBCA*) regulations, which state that "the financial statements referred to . . . in the Act shall . . . be prepared in accordance with the standards, as they exist from time to time, of the Canadian Institute of Chartered Accountants set out in the *CICA Handbook*."[1]

While the *Handbook* recommendations certainly constitute a part of GAAP, they are only a small part. The *Handbook* contains recommendations on certain specific problem areas, such as intercorporate investments, foreign currency translation, earnings per share, leasing, and deferred taxes. These recommendations, being generally accepted, form a part of GAAP. But the *Handbook* has little to say on many of the major issues of accounting, including vast areas of revenue and expense recognition and income determination. Even asset valuation receives little attention. These are crucial areas in which professional accountants must make frequent decisions. The topics covered in the *Handbook*, while important, are not dominant in the scope of most accountants' day-to-day activities.

Even when the *Handbook* does contain recommendations on a specific topic, these are not gospel. The *Handbook*'s "Introduction to Accounting Recommendations" states quite explicitly that

> In issuing Recommendations, the Accounting Standards Committee recognizes that no rule of general application can be phrased to suit all circumstances or combination of circumstances that may arise, nor is there any substitute for the exercise of professional judgment in the determination of what constitutes fair presentation or good practice in a particular case.[2]

Thus the recommendations are not to be viewed as inviolable rules, but rather as guides to the exercise of professional judgment.

The *Handbook* frequently also provides alternatives within its recommen-

1 B.C. Regulation 402/81.
2 *CICA Handbook*, p. 9.

dations. For example, Section 3030, Inventories, discusses how *cost* should be defined *if* inventories are valued on the cost basis. The section does not rule out market-based valuation, which is common in some industries. If cost is used for manufactured products, "cost should include ... the applicable share of overhead expense properly chargeable to production." [para. 3030.06] There is, however, no definition of "applicable," so that overhead could include a wide range of possible amounts, from only variable factory overhead to a full allocation of all costs, including a portion of the president's salary. Thus, for inventory valuation, there are options within the *Handbook* when using a cost-based valuation, options outside of the *Handbook* in using market-based valuation, and options departing from the *Handbook* recommendations (for example, by including no overhead in "cost") that may be justified by the circumstances.

Since the *Handbook* recommendations and guidelines make up only a small part of GAAP, we must look elsewhere for the bulk of generally accepted accounting principles. The major source is general practice, as was implied by the inventory example. What is used and acceptable in practice is thereby generally accepted. The *CICA Handbook* states that

> The term generally accepted accounting principles encompasses not only specific rules, practices and procedures relating to particular circumstances but also broad principles and conventions of general application .... Specifically, generally accepted accounting principles comprise the Accounting Recommendations in the *Handbook* and, when a matter is not covered by a Recommendation, other accounting principles that either:
> (a) are generally accepted by virtue of their use in similar circumstances by a significant number of entities in Canada; or
> (b) are consistent with the Recommendations in the *Handbook* and are developed through the exercise of professional judgment .... [para. 1000.49]

Note that "generally accepted" does not mean used in the majority of cases; GAAP is the body of accounting practices or principles that are acceptable as the result of precedent or of expert opinion in particular circumstances. What is acceptable in one situation is not necessarily acceptable in another or even in the majority of situations.

For example, regulated public utilities capitalize a large variety of costs that pertain to assets not yet included in their rate base. Since the rate base consists of those assets upon which the utility is permitted to earn a return, no return is permitted by the regulators on assets that are not included in the rate base, and expenses relating to those assets are not considered in determining the revenue permitted to be earned. Since the assets and related costs are excluded, the costs are capitalized so that a return may be earned on those costs in the future when the assets do enter the rate base. These costs have a future benefit, since a return will be permitted in the future, so they may properly be included as assets on the balance sheet.

The fact that regulated public utilities can reasonably use this treatment does not mean that unregulated companies can necessarily follow the same practice. The determinants of the future benefit of costs are not so easily determinable in an unregulated environment, and costs such as interest are not so obviously recoverable. Therefore, the fact that there is precedent for capitalizing these costs in regulated utilities does not mean that the same accounting practice can automatically be used in other businesses.

Alternative accounting practices are acceptable because each practice serves a reporting need in a particular economic and legal environment. Individual practices are acceptable because they suit particular circumstances, not because they are used by many enterprises or are condoned by official pronouncements.

Authoritative support for particular accounting policies can be found in many sources other than the *Handbook*. From time to time, the CICA publishes research studies that describe accounting in specific industries (such as the real estate industry) or that describe accounting practices for particular types of problems (such as portfolio investments). Similar studies are published by the **American Institute of Certified Public Accountants (AICPA)** as *Industry Audit Guides* and *Industry Accounting Guides*. These studies aid in the exercise of professional judgment by describing the alternative accounting policies that suit certain industries or situations and the rationales underlying their use.

Another major source of authoritative support is professional pronouncements in other countries, particularly those in the United States. *Opinions of the Accounting Principles Board* or *Statements of Financial Accounting Standards* issued by the **Financial Accounting Standards Board (FASB)** are frequently cited in justifying the use of particular accounting methods. Canadian accountants often rely on U.S. pronouncements because of the strong economic ties between the two countries, and because quite a few Canadian companies raise funds in the United States and must satisfy the needs of their U.S. statement readers. The Canadian accountant must be careful, however, not to use foreign pronouncements as a substitute for professional judgment. The circumstances for which the pronouncements were designed are not necessarily the same as those for the accountant's employer or client.

International Accounting Standards (IAS) issued by the **International Accounting Standards Committee (IASC)** may also guide the accountant in determining acceptable accounting policies. The IASC standards are designed to promote harmonization of international financial reporting. A range of generally acceptable alternatives is given in the *IAS*s in order to satisfy the needs of differing economic and political environments.

Some accounting policies are specified by regulatory agencies or by statute. For example, the *Bank Act* contains specific requirements for accounting by the federally chartered banks. The banks themselves have little leeway on accounting matters that are specifically prescribed by the *Bank Act*.

One might expect that after all this time, there would be a succinct definition of what constitutes generally accepted accounting principles. However, definitions are very elusive in accounting. We do not even have good definitions of what constitutes an asset or a liability. In *SFAC (Statement of Financial Accounting Concepts) No. 3*, the FASB has attempted to provide some definitions that are reasonably clear and unambiguous. Nevertheless, different interpretations even of these definitions are possible. For example, two different authors have used the same FASB definition of a liability to argue whether or not the deferred tax credit balance is a liability.[3]

There have been some attempts to catalogue the alternatives available

---

3 J. A. Milburn has argued that deferred credits are a liability within the definition given in *SFAC No. 3*, while W. J. Kenley has argued just the opposite. J. A. Milburn, "Comprehensive Tax Allocation: Let's Stop Taking Some Misconceptions for Granted," *CA Magazine* (April 1982), pp. 41-42; W. J. Kenley, "Do We Need a Revision to or a Replacement of AAS 3?," *The Chartered Accountant in Australia* (November 1981), pp. 27-28.

under GAAP. The **Certified General Accountants' Association of Canada** has published a *GAAP Guide*, and the Vancouver-based **Accounting Standards Authority of Canada** (which is an independent body supported mainly by CGA-Canada) is publishing *Guidelines for Accounting Practice*. Both of these publications list many of the alternatives available under GAAP, but they are by no means complete, largely because they explicitly exclude accounting practices in "specialized" industries, and specialized industries make up most of the Canadian economy!

GAAP AS A CONSTRAINT

The fact that there are generally accepted accounting principles implies that there also are accounting principles that are not generally accepted. Non-GAAP alternatives can be of two types. The first type consists of practices that are contrary to specific *Handbook* recommendations. An example of such a practice is the use of the flow-through method of reporting income taxes, where the *Handbook* recommends the full allocation approach. The second type of non-GAAP practice is unusual practices that are not covered by the *Handbook* and that do not have general acceptance. An example would be the use of **NIFO** inventory valuation (i.e., **next-in-first-out**), a rare practice that has occasionally been used to avoid distorting cost of goods sold when an interruption in supply (such as by a labour strike against a major supplier) causes a temporary depletion in inventory levels. If **LIFO** is being used, the old inventory cost layers will flow through to cost of goods sold, possibly resulting in a serious distortion of operating results for the period. Both types of non-GAAP accounting policies are encountered in practice, and then the statements clearly are not presented in accordance with GAAP. The question therefore arises as to when GAAP is an effective constraint on accounting policy choices and what is the significance of non-GAAP financial statements.

The CBCA and the securities and corporations acts of the various provinces normally state that financial statements of each corporation shall be submitted annually to the appropriate provincial or federal minister and, in the case of public companies, to the appropriate securities commission. Six of the provincial corporations acts and four of the securities acts also state that the submitted financial statements shall be prepared in accordance with GAAP and that the companies' auditors shall report in accordance with GAAP. On the surface, therefore, it would appear that virtually all corporations in Canada are constrained to use GAAP. In practice, such is not the case. If all companies complied with the statutory requirements, there would be no such thing as a GAAP-qualified audit opinion, and yet we know that such opinions are used.

The one statutory requirement that is generally effective is that of GAAP compliance by public companies. Public companies are subject to scrutiny by the securities commissions, and questionable accounting practices can lead to a suspension of trading. The securities commissions therefore have an effective tool by which they can force compliance with the GAAP reporting requirements, if they so choose. Companies with securities traded on major exchanges will therefore almost always restrict their accounting policies to GAAP.

Even public companies, however, may depart from *Handbook* recommendations if the company and its auditors concur that a particular recommendation is not appropriate for the company under its specific circumstances. For example, a study of published financial statements revealed the following examples of instances where *Handbook* recommendations were not followed and no reservations were expressed in the auditors' opinions:

- A trust company departed from the *Handbook* method of computing deferred tax debits.
- An oil company did not follow the *Handbook* prescribed method in accounting for business combinations.
- A utility departed from the *Handbook* recommendations on accounting for foreign exchange in order to match revenues and costs and to conform with recommendations of the Board of Commissioners of Public Utilities.
- A mining company deferred a gain on sale of properties, contrary to the *CICA Handbook*, on the basis that the gain is unrealized and is contingent on the results of the purchaser's options.
- An oil company did not deduct incremental oil revenue tax in computing segment revenue, thus contravening the *Handbook* requirement.[4]

Departures from GAAP are much more common in private companies. The corporations acts generally state that each company will submit audited financial statements to its shareholders at the general annual meeting. However, the shareholders of a private company can waive the audit by unanimous consent. For example, the *British Columbia Company Act* states that "if all the members of a company that is not a reporting company [i.e., a public company] consent in writing to a resolution waiving the appointment of an auditor, the company is not required to appoint an auditor" [sec. 203(1)].

Some of the acts limit the availability of a waiver to companies that are below certain size thresholds. The thresholds under the CBCA, for example, are gross revenue of $10 million *or* total assets of $5 million. The provincial limits are less; for example, the Ontario limits are half of the CBCA amounts. In provinces where size tests exist, companies that are larger than these size limits should, in theory, submit their financial statements to audit and should comply with GAAP.

In fact, private companies may have little concern about the statutory requirements. Quite a few corporations that exceed the size tests do not have an audit, and many of those that do have an audit do not comply strictly with GAAP. The reason for the apparent non-compliance is that there is little basis for enforcing the statutory provisions on private companies of limited ownership. Since a waiver of an audit is done by consent of the shareholders, the shareholders have little basis for complaint if it turns out later that the financial statements were incorrect or the system of internal control was not operating properly. Outside financing of private companies is generally accomplished by means of bank loans, and bankers are assumed to be sophisticated users of financial information; if they rely on unaudited statements or on non-GAAP statements, they are presumed to know what they are doing and to have implicitly consented to the lack of an audit.

When a private company's financial statements are audited, the company's managers may still choose to use accounting policies that are outside of GAAP if they feel that non-GAAP policies best serve the reporting needs of

---

4 Michael Gibbins and Alister K. Mason, *Professional Judgment in Financial Reporting*, a CICA Research Study (CICA, 1988), p.120.

the enterprise. The auditors will, of course, qualify the audit opinion and insist on disclosure of the nature and impact of any non-GAAP policies, but the existence of non-GAAP policies need not cause external users of the statements undue concern.

Indeed, external users may well be more concerned about the particular accounting policies used rather than whether they are within GAAP. For example, for several years Wardair received a qualified audit report because the company did not provide for deferred income tax. This qualification caused no discernable concern amongst the shareholders or bankers of Wardair. In fact, the restrictive covenants placed by the bank on Wardair's operating results explicitly provided that the ratios be calculated using the taxes payable approach rather than the full allocation approach that is recommended in the *Handbook*. Therefore the needs of at least one major user of Wardair's statements were better served by not following GAAP than by following GAAP.

Non-compliance with GAAP usually means simply that one or two specific policies are at variance with the *Handbook*. The impact is measurable and reportable, and the readers of *audited* statements are told what the impacts are. An important concern for statement users is which specific accounting policy choices have been made by management, even within GAAP. A knowledgeable lender, for example, will not simply specify that the covenants in the loan agreement be determined in accordance with GAAP, because there are still many different accounting policies within GAAP; the manager could select an accounting policy that would result in better ratios than would that originally contemplated by the lender. Instead, the lender should specify major accounting policies to be used by the borrower (as with Wardair, above).

A less common but much more serious type of GAAP non-compliance arises when the deviation from GAAP permeates the financial statements and makes any attempt at quantification of the deviation's impact impossible. An example would be the failure to apply the matching principle in a business (as opposed to a nonprofit organization), wherein expenditures are treated as expenses regardless of whether corresponding revenues have been recognized or not. Such a non-GAAP policy would result in a denial of opinion by an auditor.

In summary, GAAP is a broad set of accounting alternatives that constitute a framework for financial reporting. Public companies are usually limited to using GAAP alternatives, and professional judgment is required for selecting from among the many available alternatives. In Canada, the vast majority of companies are private companies, not public. Private companies use GAAP as a frame of reference, but they have little incentive to stick strictly to GAAP as long as the shareholders and major lenders have no objection to specific deviations that suit (or at least do not hamper) their needs. Only for public companies is GAAP a real constraint, due to the power of the securities commissions to suspend trading.

THE MEANING OF PROFESSIONAL JUDGMENT

At the beginning of this chapter, we observed that professional judgment implies that there are criteria by which alternative approaches to financial reporting problems can be evaluated. These criteria make the exercise of professional judgment possible. One set of criteria has already been discussed: GAAP. Two other sets will be discussed at length in the next chapter: (1) objectives of financial reporting and (2) qualitative criteria. Before examining these additional sets of criteria, however, we should take a closer look at what constitutes professional judgment, and what distinguishes it from non-professional judgment.

In their research study, Gibbins and Mason recommend the following definition of professional judgment:

> The process of reaching a decision on a financial reporting issue can be described as "professional judgment" when it is analytical, based on experience and knowledge (including knowledge of one's own limitations and of relevant standards), objective, prudent and carried out with integrity and recognition of responsibility to those affected by its consequences. Such professional judgment is likely to be most valuable in complex, ill-defined or dynamic situations, especially where standards are incomplete, and should normally involve consultation with other knowledgeable people, identification of potential consequences and documentation of the analytical processes leading to the decision.[5]

Among the many components of professional judgment that are identified in this definition is the fact that professional judgment must be based on experience and on an understanding of relevant standards. Experience is important because it enables the accountant to draw parallels between a reporting problem that he or she is currently facing and similar problems faced in the past. Since no two problems are exactly alike, consultation with other professionals is frequently necessary in order to broaden the frame of reference. The interaction between precedents and current reporting issues is the primary force in the evolution of GAAP, and therefore experience plays an important part in the exercise of professional judgment.

Knowledge of standards is, of course, also an important component. It might appear that the promulgation of accounting standards (via the *CICA Handbook*) would eliminate the need for professional judgment, but such is definitely not the case. Standards do tend to reduce the options available for resolving a reporting issue, but only to the extent that the issue fits the circumstances envisioned in framing the standards in the first place. Determining whether the standards fit the current circumstances is one aspect of applying professional judgment. Furthermore, as we discussed earlier in connection with the *Handbook* recommendations on inventory valuation, judgment must be applied in selecting from amongst alternatives permitted by the standard. Judgment must also be exercised in interpreting the wording of the standards and especially words and phrases such as "normally," "significant," "substantial," "fair presentation," "good practice," "it may be appropriate," and "it is desirable". Even after judgments have been made as to (1) the applicability of a standard, (2) the interpretation of the wording, and (3) the selection from amongst alternatives, further judgment is required for measurement, i.e., the ubiquitous **accounting estimate**.

Gibbins and Mason comment quite extensively on the relationship between standards and judgment. In discussing the need for judgment in applying standards, they make the following points, among others:

> Even if it were thought desirable, writing standards to eliminate judgment

5 *Professional Judgment*, p. 133.

would be impractical because the targets of the standards keep changing as enterprises take actions which may be partly or wholly directed at the standards, or as the enterprises and their environment evolve and new business methods, financial instruments and resources develop. Judgments about whether the standards contemplate the new circumstances and judgments about "form versus substance" must be made continuously if financial reports are to meet the fairness criterion, so, like the case of materiality, the standards depend on such judgments if they are to work.

... Accounting and its environment evolve continuously, so standards which worked well at one point may cease to work, or gaps in the standards may appear. A standards' system which allowed for no judgment would soon become unworkable in these circumstances .... Professional judgment is important to the operation of the standards' system because it provides interim solutions out of which new standards can develop and it provides the general experimentation and variety that allow standards to be tested against changing circumstances, and innovations in general to arise and become accepted.[6]

One further facet of Gibbins and Mason's definition of professional judgment that should be noted is that professional judgment should be exercised with an understanding of the consequences for those affected by the financial statements. Both management and external users will be affected, and a recognition of the needs of these user groups is essential to the exercise of professional judgment. The next chapter will deal with the needs of internal and external users at length.

SUMMARY

We cannot rely on any ready definition of GAAP in order to make our job easier as accountants. The range of generally accepted accounting principles is suggested by the *CICA Handbook* recommendations, by accounting guidelines issued by the AcSC, by pronouncements in other countries, by standards issued by the IASC, by descriptive and research studies issued in Canada and the United States, and by practices established by regulative authorities or by statute. But the most important source for GAAP is simply prior practice. Official pronouncements deal with only a small portion of the problems encountered in the practice of accounting.

While GAAP would appear to be a constraint for almost all corporations in Canada, it really is an effective constraint only for public companies. For private corporations, it is up to the shareholders and/or the lenders to exercise their right to request statements that comply with GAAP should they so desire.

Modern business enterprises are constantly creating new and complex ways of doing business. Frequently, these innovations have no precedent, so that we cannot rely entirely on precedent in order to formulate accounting policy. The real challenge for the accountant is to develop suitable accounting approaches for innovative activities. To account for new types of business transactions or events, the accountant must use professional judgment. The accountant must determine whether standards exist and whether those standards are applicable in the specific situation, must interpret the wording

6 *Professional Judgment*, p. 32.

of any standards that do exist, must review her or his own past experience and consult with colleagues on precedents, must make a selection from amongst alternative solutions, and must make the many judgments involved in arriving at measurement estimates. These are all components of professional judgment.

The exercise of professional judgment also requires that the accountant determine the objectives of financial reporting for the enterprise, ascertain the facts of the situation, and use qualitative criteria to develop an accounting approach that will satisfy the objectives and the reporting constraints. Chapter 2 is devoted to a review of reporting objectives and qualitative criteria, necessary components of the judgmental process. It is the ability to make these judgments that distinguishes the professional accountant from the bookkeeper.

REVIEW QUESTIONS

1-1 What distinguishes **professional judgment** from ordinary judgment?

1-2 How much of the body of generally accepted accounting principles in Canada is contained in the *CICA Handbook*?

1-3 What is the largest single source of GAAP?

1-4 What are the authoritative sources of GAAP other than the *CICA Handbook*?

1-5 In order for a set of financial statements to be in accordance with GAAP, is it mandatory that the recommendations of the *CICA Handbook* be followed? Explain.

1-6 Must the recommendations of the *CICA Handbook* be followed in all circumstances? Explain.

1-7 In general, why might accounting principles that have been developed in some industries not be appropriate for use in other industries?

1-8 Is GAAP ever set by law? Explain.

1-9 When is GAAP most likely to be an effective constraint on a corporation's financial reporting?

1-10 Why are departures from GAAP more common for private companies than for public companies?

1-11 Does the existence of a *CICA Handbook* recommendation on a particular accounting issue eliminate the need for professional judgment on that issue? Explain.

1-12 What sorts of judgments must be made in applying GAAP to a particular situation?

Interprovincial Telephone Corporation   CASE 1-1

The Interprovincial Telephone Corporation (ITC) is a publicly held company that produces telephone equipment for independent sales (that is, not through Bell Canada or other telephone operating companies). The company had been a steady profit-earner and had paid high dividends for many years. However, legal battles in the early 1970s resulted in a restriction of ITC business to sales of equipment that would be used only in private communication systems and that could not be attached to Bell lines. As a result of this restriction, sales and profits fell drastically.

In 1979, it became apparent that the regulatory agencies were about to end Bell Canada's monopoly on equipment attached to Bell lines. ITC acquired large amounts of expensive production equipment in order to be able to produce the switching mechanisms, telephone handsets, and other equipment that they anticipated selling once the Bell Canada monopoly was ended. In total, ITC increased its fixed assets by almost 100%. To finance the purchase of the production equipment, ITC issued $250,000,000 in bonds to the general public. Some financial institutions (banks, insurance companies, etc.) bought substantial quantities of the bonds. The bonds carried interest of 13.75% per year, and also the restriction that

ITC must not issue dividends higher than 60% of each year's net income after taxes.

In 1980, the courts eliminated the final obstacles to free access to Bell lines. ITC immediately began to produce its new line of equipment and to fill the orders that had accumulated. The company encountered some production problems, however, and the initial output level was not as high as had been anticipated. ITC hoped to correct these problems within a year.

External security analysts began issuing reports that suggested that Bell Canada and its subsidiaries were poorly positioned to compete with companies such as ITC, and that ITC could expect to get large volumes of business for the next five years, until Bell's manufacturing subsidiary was able to get comparable equipment into production. Thereafter, the long reach of Bell was expected to affect substantially the profitability of independent telephone equipment manufacturers, including ITC.

Required:
Discuss the factors that should affect the selection of a depreciation policy for ITC's new production equipment.

CASE 1-2   Green Tree Farm

The Green Tree Farm is a small Ontario Christmas tree nursery comprising about 25,000 trees on twenty acres. Although the average consumer may be unaware of it, the value of a white pine Christmas tree is reckoned by the grower exclusively in terms of height. Since shape and thickness can be controlled by pruning, and colour is determined by spray dyes, these characteristics are not relevant to the pricing mechanism at the wholesale level. When planted, seedlings are about one foot tall. Stages of "production" are measured according to the height of the tree to the nearest foot. No tree is ever allowed to grow beyond ten feet tall.

The Christmas tree market is an almost classic example of pure competition. No supplier is able to affect the wholesale price for the product. Each year, a grower is faced with the decision of how many trees to harvest. The price is known and, as indicated, varies with height only. The decision may be based on the grower's expectations as to prices in future years, but is generally determined by cash flow requirements: how much of the crop the grower wishes to cash in on this year, as opposed to letting the crop grow more and cashing in later at a larger amount per tree.

The cost of growing the trees is quite predictable. The grower knows the cost of seedlings and the cost of tending the trees as they get older. Trees that are damaged or misshapen are scrapped as soon as their unsuitability becomes apparent. The normal scrappage rate is fairly predictable, barring natural calamities such as hurricanes.

Required:
Mr. Dean Greene, president of the Green Tree Farm, has hired you to write a report for him detailing the various ways in which he might value inventories and measure annual income for the farm. He would like your report to be divided into two sections: (1) methods of inventory valuation and income measurement that adhere to traditional measurement of historical cost, realization, and matching; and (2) methods that may deviate from the principle of historical cost for asset valuation, but still make some economic sense regarding realization and matching. He wants you to provide logical support for each of the methods you suggest, but he does not want you to make any recommendations. If measurement problems arise with any of the methods, be sure to point out the nature of the problem. (Note: Mr. Greene intensely dislikes verbosity in the reports he receives.)

Miltonics Potions Ltd. CASE 1-3

Miltonics Potions Ltd. (MPL) is a privately held Ontario corporation engaged in the development and marketing of patent medicines. In early 1984, the company's research chemists began working on a project to develop a patent remedy for certain strains of herpes. During the year, $80,000 was spent in research on this project without developing a useful product.

Work continued in 1985, with an additional $100,000 spent. By the end of 1985, an apparently feasible product had been developed and was being considered by MPL's top management for further development and exploitation. On February 14, 1986 (prior to completion and issuance of the 1985 financial statements), the managers reached the decision to proceed with further development, production, and marketing of the product, barring adverse medical results (i.e., unacceptable side effects) from tests then underway. Such adverse results were possible, but were considered unlikely since nothing untoward had occurred to date in the testing program.

During 1986, the product was refined and the mass production formulation was developed (at a cost of $60,000). Production facilities were prepared (at a cost of $30,000), and Patent Number 381-1003-86 was obtained on the product. Legal expenses totaled $12,000.

In early 1987, production and distribution began. Sales in the first year were modest, totaling only $150,000. However, $300,000 was spent on promotion, mainly in print media advertising and in sending free samples to doctors and clinics. Only in 1988 did the sales reach forecast levels, thereby indicating that MPL had a successful product.

However, the success of the product spawned an imitator, and in 1988, MPL sued a competitor for patent infringement. MPL demanded that the competitor cease production and marketing of the competing product and requested one million dollars in damages. Thirty thousand dollars in legal costs were incurred in this action in 1988; the case was still pending at the end of the year.

In July, 1989, after MPL had spent an additional $20,000 in legal fees, the case was dismissed in court, thereby rendering MPL's patent indefensible. Since the competitor was a well-known pharmaceutical firm, MPL's sales suffered considerably from the competition.

Required:
a. On a year-by-year basis, describe the alternative accounting methods that MPL could use for the costs incurred in developing, patenting, and defending the new product. Do not use hindsight.
b. Explain what additional information you would need and what criteria you would use to make a decision on which alternative to adopt.

Central Investments Ltd. CASE 1-4

Central Investments Ltd. (Central) is a large holding company with investments in a wide variety of stocks and bonds. The company has always accounted for its investments at cost; accordingly, it has recognized income only as dividends have been declared, although interest has been recorded as income on an accrual basis. Each of the equity investments the company holds constitutes less than 10% of the capital stock of the investee companies.

Central is controlled by a number of wealthy Canadian businessmen. However, they are no longer the exclusive owners, as some of the shares in the company have recently been sold to several major financial institutions.

Central's annual meeting for the year ended July 31, 1988, was held on September 15, 1988. This was the first meeting at which representatives of the new institutional investors were present. Some of these investors questioned the rates of return indicated by Central's financial statements. They pointed out that, although interest and dividends are still being received, the market values of many of the investments have declined in recent years. They expressed the view that some portion of the decline should be recognized in the financial statements. The president of Central responded by saying that the investments had been reviewed in detail during preparation of the financial statements, and that no write-down of asset values had been deemed necessary. He also pointed out that the auditor of the company had agreed with this conclusion.

The president then asked the auditor, who was at the meeting, to comment on the matter. The auditor said that he had indeed reviewed the work done by the company in valuing its investments and that he had found the work to be satisfactory. He said that this review had been an important part of his audit and that the statements had been prepared in accordance with generally accepted accounting principles, as indicated in his report.

A representative of one of the new investors said that she had no doubt this was true and that she was not questioning the adequacy of the audit. She said, however, that the policies used by many companies under the "umbrella" of generally accepted accounting principles in accounting for portfolio investments could be said to misstate the return on investment.

The representative went on to say that the return on investment is strongly influenced in many cases by the market value of the investments and that the cost method being used by Central gives no recognition to fluctuations in market value. She also said that for a few years her company has been using accounting methods for portfolio investments that do give appropriate recognition to market value fluctuations.

After the meeting, the president asked Central's controller to prepare a report for the next board meeting addressing the issues raised.

Required:
Prepare the report.
[CICA]

Financial Reporting by Business Enterprises

I n the first chapter, we suggested that the professional accountant is one who has the expertise to select or design accounting and reporting policies that are appropriate to the circumstances of the reporting enterprise. We emphasized the fact that in order to exercise the requisite professional judgment, the accountant must have internalized certain criteria by which to make his or her judgments. In this chapter, we discuss the most important of those criteria.

The first and most fundamental criteria are the objectives of financial reporting for a particular enterprise. Businesses vary considerably in size, ownership composition, sources of financing, management expertise, and nature of activity. In addition, there is great variation in the composition of the stakeholder group. A **stakeholder** is anyone who has a financial stake in the business and thus in its financial performance. Stakeholders include owners or investors, creditors, directors, managers, employees, government, customers, and suppliers.

Given the large differences among businesses and their stakeholders, it is not possible to assign a single objective to financial reporting, even if we restrict ourselves to **external** financial reporting. Therefore, the first task of the professional accountant is to identify the **reporting objectives** for each particular enterprise. Only by having these objectives firmly in mind can the accountant make decisions on how to report financial information in order to make it as useful as possible to the readers of the statements. Therefore, the first major section of this chapter will emphasize the objectives of financial reporting for business enterprises.

It is important not to confuse **financial reporting objectives** with **operating** or **business objectives**. Operating objectives relate to the way that the business is run rather than to the way in which the financial results are reported. Financial reporting objectives may support operating objectives, but not necessarily so. For example, a company may wish to maximize its profit from operations as a business objective, but may wish to minimize its income taxes as its financial reporting objective. In the following discussion of objectives, we are talking about objectives of financial reporting and not about business or operating objectives.

Once the reporting objectives have been determined, the possible accounting measurements (including GAAP) must be evaluated. The accountant evaluates these measurements using qualitative criteria. The second major portion of the chapter discusses the major qualitative criteria.

Our focus in this chapter is on business enterprises. Much of the discussion is also relevant to nonbusiness organizations. However, there are fundamental differences between business and nonbusiness organizations, and thus we will discuss nonbusiness organizations separately in Chapter 4.

OBJECTIVES OF FINANCIAL REPORTING

The Need for Objectives

The first task in developing financial accounting policies for an organization is to determine who will be using the financial statements, and what they will be using them for. The "right" information can be reported only if the accountant understands the uses to which that information will be put.

The need to establish the users and uses is not so obvious in financial accounting as it is in managerial accounting. In management accounting, if a manager asks the accountant what a certain product costs, the accountant should immediately inquire as to the purpose of the request. One cost figure may be needed if the objective is to value inventory on the balance sheet, a different figure may be required for long-run pricing decisions, and yet another estimate of cost is appropriate if the manager wishes to bid on incremental business using marginal cost.

In management accounting, the feedback loop is direct. That is, the accountants are providing managers with information upon which decisions are made. If the accountant gives the manager a cost figure that is inappropriate for the managerial task at hand, the manager may make the wrong decision. If enough wrong decisions are made, the manager should eventually become aware that something is wrong with the information being provided. She or he will either inquire of the accountant as to the appropriateness of the reported information, or else the accountant will simply be replaced by someone who can give better information.

Of course, it may take the manager a while to discover that the accounting information is deficient. Other factors will have to be analyzed, both within the company and in the external environment. But suppose, for example, that a manager routinely refuses to produce a product for private branding, because he or she believes that the price offered by the customer is not high enough to cover the production costs. Consequently, the business goes to competitors, who flourish as a result. The manager can see that the competitors are doing well on business that supposedly was unprofitable, and will inquire as to the appropriateness of the cost figures provided by the accountant. When the manager discovers that the accountant had supplied a full cost figure that included a large amount of allocated cost, he or she can take corrective action.

In financial accounting, the feedback loop is circuitous. Many of the people who make decisions based on accounting data are outside the company and must rely on the financial statements, or on financial information reported separately by the company and subsequently verified by the statements themselves, for their information. These users have no way of testing the appropriateness of the information by consultation with managers or accountants. If the information is inappropriate, it may nevertheless be self-fulfilling. For example, if the financial statements show a company to be unprofitable and debt-laden, then the company will have difficulty in obtaining financing and retaining customers, and may indeed fail. But if the problem was actually that the financial statements were ultraconservative and had undervalued assets and delayed the recognition of revenue, then the gloomy view actually prevailed, even though it was inaccurate at the time.

If investors make decisions to invest, not invest, or disinvest in a company at least partially on the basis of the reported financial results, it is very difficult for them to tell later whether the decision was correctly or incorrectly influenced by the accounting reports. There are so many intervening variables in the economy that affect the performance of a particular company that it becomes almost impossible to discern the appropriateness (or lack thereof) of any particular accounting information.

A countervailing force in the public securities markets is the specialized security analyst, who closely examines the accounting reports of companies in a particular industry that he or she knows well, and evaluates the adequacy of the companies' financial reporting. Thus some feedback is possible even in the open market. But in general, the lack of any direct feedback mechanism for the adequacy of financial statement reporting makes it more difficult to appreciate the importance of objectives in financial reporting.

It is commonly held that external financial statements are general in purpose, and that the information in the statements must be usable by a wide variety of users. Therefore, it is argued, there is no way in which external financial statements can recognize the needs of particular user groups. There is some truth in that assertion. Statements do frequently have to serve multiple users and uses, and compromises must be made in designing the accounting policies. This is particularly true for publicly traded companies, wherein the range of available accounting policies is more limited than for private companies but the range of potential users and uses is greater.

However, most Canadian companies are not public companies. The users of the statements of private companies are limited, and their needs can and must be taken into account in designing the accounting policies. Even for public companies, many alternatives available within GAAP would comply with the constraints of public reporting. Decisions must always be made as to how revenue and costs will be recognized, how fixed assets will be depreciated, how inventories will be valued, how bond discount or premium will be amortized, and so forth. If there are no objectives of reporting for public enterprises, then there are no criteria to use for making these decisions. One choice would be as good as another, and yet the reported results of the enterprise will vary considerably depending on the choices made.

Therefore, the notion of financial statements as unfocused, general purpose statements is not adequate. The statements may be general in purpose, but they must be prepared by focusing on the types of decisions that users will make. Without objectives, there are no criteria for making accounting policy decisions, and thus no way in which professional judgment can be exercised. Statements prepared without an eye to objectives are random collections of data, of little use to anyone.

Users vs. Preparers

Before we begin our discussion of specific financial reporting objectives, we should point out that there is a potential conflict between users and preparers of financial statements. Preparers means managers, since the financial statements are management's statements, not the accountant's and certainly not the auditor's. Financial statements are prepared in order to communicate financial information to users for their benefit in making decisions. The types of decisions or uses should be the primary determinant of the financial reporting objectives.

However, it frequently is in the self-interest of the preparers of the information to try to influence the perceptions and thus the decisions of the users of the statements, whether they be external users or internal users (i.e., other managers within the economic entity). Because of the different and possibly conflicting needs of users and preparers, we will examine both the reporting objectives that serve the needs of users (both external and internal) and the reporting objectives or motivations of preparers that are intended to influence the users.

USER OBJECTIVES

There is no definitive list of objectives for financial reporting. The FASB has developed a set of financial reporting objectives that they use as a guide to setting standards for their constituency in the United States, and we discuss that set of objectives later in this chapter. The AcSC has made a brief statement on objectives in Section 1000 of the *CICA Handbook*: "The objective of financial statements is to communicate information that is useful to investors, creditors and other users in making resource allocation decisions and/or assessing management stewardship" [para. 1000.12]. The AcSC has chosen in this statement to recognize only limited decision needs of financial statements users, although the AcSC believes that "financial statements prepared to satisfy these needs are often used by others who need external reporting of information about an entity" [para. 1000.09].

While the AcSC's objectives statement might be appropriate, it is too vague to be of much use as a criterion for selecting accounting policies. Indeed, there may well be differences in the information that is most useful for "resource allocation decisions" on the one hand and for "assessing management stewardship" on the other. Therefore we must attempt to be somewhat more specific in our discussion of financial reporting objectives that are relevant for the users of financial statements.

Three major objectives relate to the uses to which financial information will be put:

1. Cash flow prediction
2. Performance evaluation
3. Stewardship and contract compliance

To some extent these three objectives overlap, and the boundaries are not always clear. But in general, each of the three has different implications for the preparation of some financial statements. In addition, some of the objectives, especially the first and second, may have different implications, depending upon the nature of the user of the statements.

The objective of cash flow prediction has received much attention in recent years, particularly in the United States where it is the primary focus of the FASB's *Statement of Financial Accounting Concepts No. 1 (SFAC 1)* (1978) and of its predecessor, the AICPA's *Report of the Study Group on Objectives of Financial Statements* (1973), commonly referred to as the "Trueblood report" after its chairman, Robert M. Trueblood. In *SFAC 1*, the cash flow prediction objective is seen to be pervasive:

> Potential users of financial information most directly concerned with a particular business enterprise are generally interested in its ability to generate favorable cash flows because their decisions relate to amounts, timing, and uncertainties of expected cash flows. To investors, lenders, suppliers, and employees, a business enterprise is a source of cash in the form of dividends or interest and perhaps appreciated market prices, repayment of borrowing, payment for goods or services, or salaries or wages. They invest cash, goods, or services in an enterprise and expect to obtain sufficient cash in return to make the investment worthwhile. They are directly concerned with the ability of the enterprise to generate favorable cash flows and may also be concerned with how the market's perception of that ability affects the relative prices of its securities. To customers, a business enterprise is a source of goods or services, but only by obtaining sufficient cash to pay for the resources it uses and to meet its other obligations can the enterprise provide those goods or services. To managers, the cash flows of a business enterprise are a significant part of their management responsibilities, including their accountability to directors and owners. Many, if not most, of their decisions have cash flow consequences for the enterprise. Thus, investors, creditors, employees, customers, and managers significantly share a common interest in an enterprise's ability to generate favorable cash flows. Other potential users of financial information share the same interest, derived from investors, creditors, employees, customers or managers whom they advise or represent or derived from an interest in how those groups (and especially stockholders) are faring.[1]

The objective of a cash flow prediction objective is that the financial statements should convey information to users that will help them to predict future cash flows of the company based on past and current data. The statements should describe the current pattern of cash flows, and should indicate any expected alteration of those flows. Accounting policies will be affected in three ways:

1. Revenue will tend to be recognized earlier rather than later, since revenue is the accounting measure of cash inflow from operations.
2. Net income will tend to be measured in a way that indicates long-run cash flow from operations.
3. Notes will be used to describe future cash flows not indicated in the body of the statements themselves, including expected changes in those flows that are reported.

One important aspect of this objective is that the phrase "cash flow" should not be taken too literally. Cash flow from operations does not really mean just the net cash received for a specific period of time. The concept is really more of a longer-term view of how much cash will be returned to the enterprise as the result of current operations. Thus cash flow should be

Cash Flow Prediction

---

1 *Statement of Financial Concepts No. 1*, (FASB, 1978), para. 25.

viewed within the context of accrual accounting to include prepaid and accrued items. As *SFAC 1* puts it:

> [Users'] interest in an enterprise's future cash flows . . . leads primarily to an interest in information about its earnings rather than information directly about its cash flows. . . . Information about enterprise earnings and its components measured by accrual accounting generally provides a better indication of enterprise performance than information about current cash receipts and payments.[2]

When the objective of financial statements is to aid users in predicting future cash flows, revenue will tend to be recognized earlier in the earnings mincycle than under some alternative reporting objectives, such as the tax deferral objective (to be discussed later in the chapter). Users will be able to see the current level of revenue-generating activity by the firm and the costs associated with that level. In the absence of information to the contrary, the logical starting point for predicting future earnings is the level of current earnings. The more clearly the income statement discloses the current level of revenue and costs rather than deferring recognition until late in the earnings process, the better grasp users will have of the company's cash flow generation from current activities. Then the users can modify that information based on other factors, such as the predicted state of the economy.

The cash flow prediction objective is also furthered by measuring earnings in a way that most closely corresponds to accrual-basis cash flows. If a company uses a complex series of allocations of past costs and estimates of future costs in measuring earnings, the relationship between earnings and cash flow is unclear. When earnings relate closely to cash flows, prediction of future cash flows is easier than when earnings do not relate closely to cash flows.

Accountants are accustomed to the fact that periodic earnings measurement is different from cash flow measurement. Cash flow and net income are two different measures. In the long run, however, they are equal. An enterprise's lifetime net income is the net cash return on the investment. There is a clear relationship between cash flow and earnings, and earnings cannot be measured without direct reference to past, present, and future cash flows.

Financial analysts refer to earnings that do not correspond to cash flows as being of low quality. High-quality earnings, on the other hand, are those that are reflected readily in cash flows from operations. Since investors tend to be interested in cash flows, high-quality earnings are preferred to low-quality earnings, and this preference may show up in the market as higher share prices or a greater willingness by a bank to lend money.

Analysts' concern with the quality of earnings can be seen in an article on a computer software firm, in which one analyst was quoted as saying that "the biggest concern right now is the cash flow and the comparison of reported versus real earnings when you consider that they don't write off their R&D expenses like most high-tech companies do." Another analyst observed that if the company "expensed its R&D and bit the bullet as Mitel did recently, that 35 cents profit per share would really be a loss of $1.30 per

---

2 *SFAC 1*, paras. 43-44.

share."[3] Note that to these analysts, reported net income based on allocations of research and development is not "real." The "real earnings" are viewed as those most closely relating to accrual-basis cash flows.

Under the cash flow prediction objective, then, companies will opt for immediate recognition of costs rather than capitalization and amortization. For example, the costs of opening new stores in a retail chain could either be recognized as an expense immediately or could be deferred and amortized. Using a cash flow prediction objective, the costs would be expensed immediately because that treatment reflects the fact that the cash has been spent. Similarly, interest costs incurred on new development activities would be expensed rather than being capitalized as part of the costs of the project.

The third impact of the cash flow prediction objective is that the notes to the financial statements may be used to disclose supplementary information about future cash flows. Some of the disclosures that are currently recommended in the *Handbook* reflect the need for information about future flows. Examples include the detailed information on amounts due for debt repayments and lease payments over the next five years. In addition, however, a company could also disclose information such as major expected changes in cost structure, the size of the order backlog, or the current value of inventories.

Performance Evaluation

Frequently, financial statement readers want to know how well management is running the business. Indeed, managers themselves usually need a report card to see how they are doing. In a small business, the managers may have a good idea of the success of their management, but may need the financial statements in order to show creditors or silent partners how the business is going. On the other hand, managers may think they are doing all right, but need the statements in order to verify their perceptions.

In larger businesses, financial statements are essential for determining how well the company is managed. Investors and creditors are concerned, as well as the directors and the managers themselves. In a diversified corporation, the separate-entity financial statements of the individual operating companies may form the primary basis by which the corporation's top management evaluates the performance of the component companies and their managers.

In the case of a public company, shareholders may want to know how well management is performing. This may seem to be an obvious statement, but most investors are well aware that because so many factors affect the earnings performance of a company, it is very difficult to separate good management from a good economy or simple good luck. Nevertheless, the financial statements can be of some assistance, especially when used in conjunction with the statements of similar businesses and with more general industrial and economic information.

When performance appraisal is the primary objective of the financial statements, the accounting policies should, as much as possible, reflect the way in which decisions are made. For example, suppose that the management of a chain of hotels wants to issue financial statements that show investors how well they are managing. The chain opens new hotels fairly

3 Greg Barr, "Nabu Needs Magic," *Financial Times of Canada* (July 25, 1983), p. 4.

regularly, and has a policy of renovating older hotels. Management decides to build a new hotel based on an analysis of the future market in the area, and on the potential net cash flow and present value of the project. Start-up costs will be substantial, but management believes that these costs will be recovered by future revenues. Since the decision was made by offsetting the start-up costs against revenues in future periods, the performance evaluation objective would call for capitalizing the costs and amortizing them against the future revenues.

The treatment of hotel start-up costs would be different under the cash flow prediction alternative. For cash flow prediction, it would be better to expense the costs immediately because the cash outflow occurred immediately and because start-up costs are a routine part of doing business and opening new hotels.

Another example would be a finance company's recognition of revenue from loans. We are accustomed to think of interest revenue as being simply a function of time. If a loan company lends $10,000 for three years at 18% interest, we might recognize the interest revenue at 18% per annum for whatever period the income statement covers. Total interest revenue for the firm would then be purely a function of the average balance of loans outstanding for the period.

However, the costs of extending the loan are largely incurred at its inception, for checking the credit of the customer and for processing the application. If the business volume of the loan company fluctuates and interest revenue is recognized purely on the basis of time, then expenses will vary in proportion to the volume of new loans, while the revenues will vary in proportion to the loans outstanding. New loans are essential, and yet a period of high new-loan activity will result in poor net income figures. Managers and others may be led to the false impression that the company is better off by not aggressively pursuing new business.

If performance evaluation is an objective, then the accounting policy could be altered in order to achieve a clearer matching of revenues with costs. Instead of recognizing revenue on a straight-line basis over the life of the loan, a larger portion of the revenue could be recognized at the loan's inception. The maximum to be recognized at inception would be the total present value of the spread between the interest charged on the loan and the cost of carrying the loan. If revenue is recognized using this policy, then net income will rise when loan activity is high and will fall when loan activity is down. Of course, loan losses must be estimated and provided for in determining net income.

As it happens, the *CICA Handbook* discourages the recognition of interest revenue under a performance evaluation objective by recommending that interest be recognized "on a time proportion basis" [para. 3400.09]. Historically, banks have not had this problem because they traditionally have charged their business clients a non-refundable administrative fee for negotiating a loan, and this fee has been recognized as income when charged to the client. However, there is now pressure on the banks to defer and amortize these fees over the life of the loan (when the negotiations are successful), an example of conservative accounting policies overriding valid user objectives.

It should be apparent that the performance evaluation objective is quite different from the cash flow prediction objective. Performance evaluation focuses primarily on the current period, while cash flow prediction focuses more on the current period as a basis for predicting future earnings and flows. The performance evaluation objective leads to revenue and expense recognition policies that emphasize matching and consonance with decision-making approaches, while the cash flow prediction objective leads to revenue and expense recognition policies that are related more to accrual-basis cash flows than to the matching of revenue-expense-effort.

One problem with the performance evaluation objective is that it sometimes is indistinguishable from an approach that seeks simply to maximize reported earnings. Statement users who are close to the company, such as managers, directors, owners of private corporations, or controlling shareholders of public companies, are frequently in a position to tell which objective is being followed. But for an external user, it is sometimes hard to tell the two apart. Clues may be gained by closely scrutinizing the accounting policies relating to revenue and expense recognition in the notes to the financial statements.

Originally a **steward** was in charge of a household or an estate. Now we use the term to mean a person who administers finances or property for others. Because a steward is managing for another person or persons, the steward must submit reports to the principals to show what he or she has done with the money and the property under his or her control.

Stewardship and Contract Compliance

In brief, then, **stewardship reporting** is a form of reporting that satisfies the principals that the steward has executed his or her duties in a responsible manner. In the modern corporation with owners who are not actively involved in the management of the business, the managers are the stewards and the shareholders are the principals. Stewardship reporting implies different things to different people. At least three distinct levels of stewardship reporting can be identified:

1. Reporting only on the disposition of assets
2. Reporting on the disposition of assets and on the earnings realized on those assets
3. Reporting on the disposition of assets, the earnings realized on the assets, and the skill of management in administering the assets

The first level is the oldest. The emphasis is on control and disposition, and not on earnings. The first level stresses what the steward has done with the assets, in order to ascertain that they were honestly administered. This level might be satisfied by giving the principals a comparative balance sheet and a funds flow statement to explain the changes. In the history of the corporation, the first level was that demanded by absentee investors in the nineteenth century and the first part of the twentieth. This form of reporting still exists in some forms of organization, such as in certain nonprofit or governmental organizations. Reporting for a fund-raising agency, for example, emphasizes the disposition of the funds raised, either through operating expenses or through grants to the other organizations on whose behalf the funds were solicited.

The second level supplements the first by recognizing that in a profit-oriented business, there is more to administering than simply protecting the assets. Trust fund managers can look very good at the first level of stewardship reporting simply by placing investments in the safest possible places, and not worrying about trying to achieve high earnings. But as principals became aware of the risk-return trade-off, many principals began to demand information on the earnings of the investments, not just on their security. Thus the income statement came to greater prominence in stewardship reporting. The emphasis shifted from simple reporting on the custodianship of the assets to reporting on the profits realized by use of the assets.

The third level of stewardship reporting goes beyond reporting only on realized profits, and attempts to measure the potential of the business and the quality of management. For example, the manager of an investment portfolio may buy an investment at $10,000 in one year and sell it two years later for $15,000. Under the second level of stewardship, a gain of $5,000 would be reported for the second year, reflecting credit on the manager for an astute investment. But suppose that the investment was readily marketable any time and that in the interim, its value had risen to $30,000. The manager then does not appear to have done so well, earning a profit of only $5,000 when there could have been a profit of $20,000. Under the third level of stewardship reporting, the assets might be valued at market values so that the value of the principals' net investment and of the assets controlled by the steward can be discerned.

The third level of stewardship is quite similar to the objective of performance evaluation. However, the fact that stewardship reports are designed to serve users who are at a distance from the corporation suggests that the qualitative criteria of reliability and verifiability may have a strong influence in the development of accounting policies.

Some aspects of stewardship reporting are defined by law. The provincial and federal corporations acts specify the frequency and extent of financial reporting by corporations to their shareholders, and also specify whether the statements need to be audited or not. Requirements vary by province. Additional (and usually more stringent) requirements may be specified for public corporations whose shares are traded on the stock exchanges. There may be additional legislation governing reporting by companies in certain industries. For example, the financial reporting of banks is controlled by the *Bank Act*, and the reporting for mutual funds is controlled by provincial securities acts. Some provinces legislate reporting requirements for condominium associations and for film production companies, among others.

Stewardship reporting can also be defined by contract. A shareholders' agreement or a bond indenture can contain specific provisions as to the content and accounting policies used in financial reporting to the contracting parties. Lenders usually include covenants or maintenance tests in loan agreements. In order to continue to carry a loan, a lender will require that covenants or maintenance tests be met. Failure to meet the requirements of the loan agreement could result in the lender's calling the loan or refusing to renew or extend loans.

Examples of covenants would include the level of the current ratio, the age of receivables, the turnover of inventory, the maximum debt:equity ratio, a minimum times-interest-earned ratio, a maximum dividend payout ratio, and so forth. The lender will use the financial statements of the borrower to determine whether or not the maintenance tests have been met. Since the level of the maintenance tests is determined by the lender after taking into consideration the accounting policies used by the borrower, the lender is concerned not only with the level of the ratios but also whether consistent accounting policies have been used as the basis for their calculation. A major use of financial statements in Canada is lenders testing for compliance with loan agreements and this use tends to be more important than shareholder stewardship as a reporting objective for private corporations.

In most common usage, stewardship reporting for business enterprises is taken to mean the financial disclosure required by statute or by contract. In most instances in Canada, it is the second level of stewardship that is implied by the legal requirements. The statutes or contracts that limit the available accounting alternatives are frequently referred to as the **constraints** on a company's financial reporting. Constraints must be taken into consideration in developing accounting or reporting policies.

In the preceding discussion of user objectives, we have referred both to internal users of the financial statements such as managers and directors, and to external users such as shareholders and creditors. Some users fall into a middle group, such as non-manager owners of private corporations, who are not external like public shareholders but who still may rely primarily on the statements for information about the state of the business. A useful way of distinguishing between internal and external users is to define external users as those who do not have access to financial information beyond that provided by management in its reports. Using this definition, members of the in-between group may be either internal or external, depending on their ability to demand supplementary or other data from management.

Of the three user objectives, stewardship is an objective that relates solely to external users. Stewardship reporting, by definition, is financial reporting to external stakeholders of the company.

The cash flow prediction objective also serves external users primarily; internal users will use budgets and proforma statements to predict or project future cash flows directly rather than attempt to use the current statements. Nevertheless, the current statements can be useful even to internal users in evaluating the reasonableness of cash flow predictions made by middle managers or others within the company.

Performance evaluation relates to both internal and external users. We usually think of reports to management as being a part of managerial accounting, something quite distinct from the preparation of the general purpose financial statements. However, if managers are being judged by external users, then managers also need to evaluate their own performance based on the reports given to outsiders. It does no good for managers to receive special-purpose reports that indicate that they are managing well if the general financial statements being issued to external users indicate something quite different. The awareness of others' evaluation will motivate managers to make decisions that reflect well in the financial statements.

Furthermore, the general financial statements of the company are the only reports that give an overall picture of the financial health and well-being of the enterprise. They serve an important score-card function for managers, whether or not there are external users looking over their shoulders. Therefore, the general financial statements of a company are reports to management as well as to outsiders. Management is able to get additional or more detailed information, but the overall picture as presented in the finan-

User Objectives: Internal vs. External Users

cial statements can be, and frequently is, used by managers as an indication of their success.

Top managers and directors can also use the financial statements of individual subsidiaries or divisions to evaluate the performance of their managers. These strictly internal reports from one level of management to another are obviously management accounting reports. But if they are not prepared using accounting policies that are consistent with those used in the company's external reports, then the consolidated statements will show a picture of the company that is not the sum of its parts. Top management will be evaluated on the basis of the consolidated statements, and they will want the lower-level managers to report results that will contribute to a favourable picture of the overall enterprise.

In summary, financial statements may have both internal and external users. The objectives of stewardship and cash flow prediction are designed primarily or exclusively for the benefit of stakeholders outside the company. Performance appraisals may benefit both external stakeholders and insiders such as managers and directors. Therefore, it should not be assumed that externally released financial statements are read only by external users. Managers are an important user group of financial statements as well.

PREPARER OBJECTIVES

The preceding three objectives all relate to the types of decisions that users will make when using the financial statements of an enterprise. The managers who prepare the statements are likely to have their own set of priorities when they select accounting policies. The policies chosen will have an impact on the reported results and may affect user's perceptions. The policies may also have a more direct impact on the managers themselves, in that compensation levels may be tied to accounting measurements and the managers' future job prospects may be enhanced by reporting the "right" results.

In the following sections, we will discuss four major reporting objectives of the preparers. These are:

1. Income tax deferral
2. Net income maximization or minimization
3. Income smoothing
4. Minimum disclosure and contract compliance

Some accountants would prefer to refer to these preparer reporting objectives as preparer **motivations** rather than as objectives, reserving the term objectives to relate to the legitimate decision needs of the users.

Income Tax Deferral

One of the responsibilities of management is to organize the company's affairs in such a way as to maximize the present value of the enterprise. One way of doing this is to delay the liability for income taxes. There is a time value of money, and a dollar of taxes paid in the future has a smaller present value than a dollar of taxes paid currently. Thus the deferral of tax payments will increase the present value of the company.

The *Income Tax Act* contains specific provisions for the taxation of revenues and the deductibility of expenses. In general, taxation follows the cash flow. However, there are many exceptions to this general rule. Taxes are levied on net taxable income, and Revenue Canada implicitly recognizes the matching concept in measuring income. The costs of inventories and fixed assets are allocated to the periods of use, while other expenses are deductible when paid. For most costs, accounting policy will not affect the tax treatment; companies cannot reduce their taxes by accruing large expenses in advance of their payment.

Where there is some flexibility, however, is in inventory valuation and in revenue recognition. The tax authorities frequently will permit a company to delay the inclusion of revenue in taxable income if there is a good reason for the delay, such as noncompletion of a contract or nonreceipt of cash from the revenue-producing activities. However, delayed taxation will usually be permitted only if the company also uses the same revenue recognition policy in its financial statements. The tax people take a dim view of a company that tells its shareholders and other stakeholders that it has earned revenue, and then tells the tax department that they have not yet earned that same revenue. Therefore, the timing of revenue recognition for tax purposes can be influenced by the accounting policy for revenue recognition used on the income statement.

There is no such thing as "keeping two sets of books," one for financial reporting and one for income tax. A company's financial statements must be reconciled to the computation of taxable income on the tax return, and any differences in accounting will be quite obvious to the government. It is true that some items are treated differently for accounting and for income tax purposes; the obvious example is depreciation versus capital cost allowance. Different schedules must be maintained by the company in order to keep track of the two different measures of capital consumption. But keeping track of a few required differences in treatment does not mean keeping a separate set of books. For the vast majority of items for which the *Income Tax Act* does not require special treatment, the tax treatment is expected to correspond with the accounting treatment. There is only one set of books.

In summary, an objective of tax deferral (sometimes cited as tax minimization) leads to accounting policies that delay revenue recognition and speed up expense recognition. The result reduces net income to a level that is lower than would be reported under alternative acceptable accounting policies. The policies must be long-term in scope; the accounting treatment cannot be changed from year to year.

For some companies, particularly small private corporations, tax deferral may be the dominant (or only) objective of financial reporting. The managers know that net income is on the low side of the permissible range of accounting net income figures, and they can explain the situation to bankers or other major creditors who might be using the statements. Since tax deferral reduces the cash flow drain on the company, bankers may welcome the astute tax management and may evaluate the company's reported performance more favourably.

Tax deferral would seem to be a desirable objective for all companies. But for many enterprises, the low net income that would be reported is incompatible with other objectives of the financial statements. If the company is trying to attract investors, for example, a low reported net income would not help. Bear in mind that the company cannot say in its annual report that the accounting figures should be taken with a grain of salt because they are tax-influenced amounts. The company must live with the results of its accounting policy decisions because they are generally acceptable policies chosen from an array of acceptable alternatives. Therefore, many companies choose not to emphasize tax deferral as an objective of financial reporting, but rather adopt other objectives that are more important to the overall corporate goals.

For other companies, there simply may not be much flexibility for tax purposes. A retail business with a high proportion of cash sales, for instance, has little option in revenue recognition. Expense recognition may offer more flexibility, but not enough to warrant adopting tax deferral as a primary objective of financial reporting.

Finally, it must be recognized that many reporting policies have no impact on income taxes. This is especially true for policies on cost allocations, except as they may affect inventory valuation.

Maximization or Minimization of Earnings

Sometimes management's objective of financial reporting is simply to maximize or minimize the enterprise's reported net income. Management may wish to maximize earnings in order to attract new investors or to allay the fears of present investors. Companies that are having a difficult time have been known to adopt accounting policies that increase earnings by recognizing revenue earlier or expenses later. If bond indentures or loan agreements contain any covenants concerning dividend payout ratios, times-interest-earned ratios, etc., a high level of earnings will make it easier to comply with the restrictions. Other companies may be in satisfactory financial health, but wish to look even better in order to be well perceived in a competitive financial and business market. In addition, management bonuses or salaries may be tied to reported earnings, so that the managers benefit directly by maximizing reported earnings.

On the other hand, management may wish to minimize reported earnings for reasons other than tax deferral. Management may feel that the company's earnings are embarrassingly high and may wish to disguise the fact in order to discourage the entry of new competitors or to avoid attracting public or political attention, or higher wage demands by employees. Management may hope to discourage takeover bids if control is not firmly held by friendly shareholders.

An efficient market would not be fooled by such tactics. Indeed, there is evidence to suggest that the market reacts adversely to changes in accounting policies that would tend to increase earnings, because the change is interpreted as a signal that management expects real earnings to decline.[4]

Similarly, minimization of earnings may not be expected to mislead an efficient market. There is ample empirical evidence that the stock market will adjust for different accounting policies in assigning a value to shares. And understated earnings surely would not lead astray any acquisition-minded

---

4 For example, T. Harrison found evidence that, for firms making accounting changes that tend to increase net income, "on the average, the market has assigned lower relative values to firms that make discretionary accounting changes." Tom Harrison, "Different Market Reactions to Discretionary and Non-discretionary Accounting Changes," *Journal of Accounting Research* (Spring 1977), pp. 84-107.

managers of another company. If anything, reduced reported earnings would only depress the potential price that the acquiree's shareholders would receive.

But managements may not be trying to influence the reactions of the market as a whole. They may be more concerned with the perceptions of individual shareholders or outsiders, and individual users are not necessarily efficient and unbiased processors of information. Indeed, it may be more important to managers to cater to the biases and perceptions of a single large shareholder than to concern themselves about the efficiency of the public securities markets.

Investors and creditors are concerned not only with the level of earnings, but also with the business risk of a company. The level of risk is equated with the volatility of earnings and cash flows. In attempting to influence users' perceptions about the company, managers may wish to select accounting policies that not only increase the apparent level of earnings but also decrease the apparent volatility of earnings. Accounting policies may therefore be chosen that have the effect of smoothing earnings.

Income Smoothing

Smoothing may be accomplished through both revenue and expense recognition policies. Revenue can be smoothed by spreading its recognition over an earnings cycle, such as by using percentage-of-completion rather than completed contract, or by timing the recognition of irregular lumps of revenue to fall into periods of low economic activity. Expenses can be smoothed by amortizing costs over a period of years rather than by recognizing them at inception; such costs would include development costs and start-up costs. Development costs might at first appear to offer little opportunity for income smoothing under the provisions of Section 3450 of the *CICA Handbook*, but since concordance with the criteria in paragraph 3450.21 is largely management-determined, management is able to influence the extent to which development costs are in fact expensed as opposed to deferred and amortized.

The smoothing of expenses is most effective if the expenses can be related to levels of revenue, since smoothing of expenses will not in itself necessarily lead to the smoothing of net income. For example, if net revenue fluctuates substantially, the smoothing of an expense will tend to lower the entire level of earnings over a period of years but will not decrease the fluctuation. Indeed, if the same volatility exists but at a lower overall level of earnings, the relative risk will appear to increase rather than to decrease. If expenditures on development costs are related to the level of revenue in each period, for example, then income smoothing would be better accomplished by expensing development costs rather than by deferring and amortizing them. Therefore, accounting policies that have the effect of matching costs to higher levels of revenue will be most effective in smoothing net income. Inventory valuation policies that allocate substantial amounts of overhead costs to inventory instead of treating them as period costs is another example of an effective smoothing policy.

As with the maximization or minimization of earnings, one might assume that an efficient market would not be fooled by smoothing tendencies. Discerning the impacts of interperiod allocations is easier said than done, however, especially when the effects of the allocations are buried in income statement items such as cost of goods sold. Management is in a position to accomplish income smoothing not only through the selection of accounting policies, but also by the adroit use of accounting estimates. Unlike changes in accounting policies, there is no *Handbook* requirement for the disclosure of changes in accounting estimates,[5] and the cumulative impact of several relatively minor adjustments in accounting estimates can be quite significant when measured in terms of their impact on the bottom line. If the statements are audited, the auditors can challenge the assumptions on which the revised or changed estimates are made, but if the assumptions fall within a reasonable range of feasible alternatives, the auditors are in no position to second-guess management. The statements are, we must remember, management's statements.

Minimum Disclosure or Contract Compliance

Sometimes management wishes to report only the minimum of information to the external stakeholders. This is known as minimum disclosure. In a public company, minimum disclosure takes the form of strict compliance with all of the reporting requirements of the securities and corporations acts without volunteering any additional or supplemental disclosure. Managers may be motivated to use minimum disclosure because they do not wish to reveal what they consider to be confidential information to competitors, labour unions, etc.

When there are explicit accounting-related provisions in contracts, such as maintenance tests in loan agreements or profit-sharing equations in employee contracts, management may choose accounting policies (and influence accounting estimates) with an eye to the impact on the contract provisions. Often, the desire to meet (or, occasionally, to avoid) contract provisions translates to other reporting objectives such as income maximization or smoothing. The real motivation may be the contract provisions, however.

Preparer vs. User Objectives

In any financial reporting situation, there will be a potential conflict between user objectives and preparer objectives or motivations. Since the statements are being prepared by the managers, it would appear that preparer motivations would dominate the selection of objectives. However, users are not without power. Revenue Canada clearly has the power to assess taxes on taxable income determined independently of reported accounting income. Major shareholders can, through the Board of Directors and its Audit Committee, have an influence on reporting objectives. Public shareholders have little direct influence, but security analysts and the financial press can put pressure on corporations to provide financial information that is most useful to outsiders rather than self-serving to managers. Major lenders certainly have more direct power to demand attention to their reporting needs, although this power is tempered by competitive forces; banks sometimes worry that if they are too insistent, the customer will go to another bank. All financial reporting situations therefore involve a trade-off between users and preparers in determining the reporting objectives. The relative strength of the two groups will influence the selection of accounting policies.

5 The *Handbook* does suggest that disclosure may be *desirable* for rare or unusual changes in accounting estimates, but such "desirable" disclosure recommendations are frequently ignored in practice [para. 1506.24].

MATRIX OF OBJECTIVES

The various financial reporting objectives can be classified into three general categories on the basis of a time dimension. The categories are:

1. Retrospective uses, to comprehend and learn from past actions and events of the entity.
2. Contractual uses, to provide for current monitoring and execution of contracts with parties both internal and external to the entity.
3. Predictive uses, to reduce uncertainty for managers and investors.[6]

Among the user objectives, the primary retrospective use is performance evaluation. The current contractual use is stewardship, and the primary predictive use is cash flow prediction.

The time dimension can also be applied to preparer objectives also. There is a subtle distinction between management's retrospective objective on performance evaluation depending on whether they are *using* the financial statements for evaluating their own performance or attempting to *influence other users' perceptions* as to the performance of the company and its management. When management is actually using the statements for evaluation, they are acting as users and the objectives are users' objectives, but when they are trying to affect other users' evaluations (e.g., by maximizing and/or smoothing net income) they then are exercising preparer objectives.

Similarly, management may select accounting policies and make accounting estimates that they hope will influence contractual arrangements; they are then acting as preparers. Income tax deferral is an example of a preparer objective, while assessing income tax is a user (i.e., Revenue Canada) objective. Schedule 2-1 summarizes some of the user and preparer objectives in a matrix, with the time category as the second dimension.

SCHEDULE 2-1		
Some Objectives of Financial Reporting		
TYPE	USERS (uses)	PREPARERS (motivations)
RETROSPECTIVE	Performance evaluation	Optimize performance measures
CONTRACTUAL	Income tax assessment Determine profit sharing/ bonuses Compliance, e.g.: Debt agreements Shareholder agreements	Tax deferral Optimize management compensation Minimum disclosure Optimize contractual measures
PREDICTIVE	Current liquidity/solvency Cash flow prediction	Maximize operating earnings, or minimize "ability to pay"

---

6 These categories are taken from *Conceptual Framework for Financial Reporting*, published by The Accounting Standards Authority of Canada (Vancouver: 1987), section 114, pp.100-104.

HIERARCHY OF OBJECTIVES

In some companies, there may be only one significant reporting objective, be it a user objective or a preparer objective. In most cases, however, there will be several objectives, and the objectives may not be compatible with each other. For example, a corporation's management may (1) need to satisfy covenants in a loan agreement, (2) wish to defer income taxes, and (3) want to maximize reported earnings in order to maximize executive compensation. When choosing from amongst alternative accounting policies, management will not be able to select policies that satisfy all of these objectives simultaneously. Therefore it is necessary to prioritize the objectives by deciding which is the most important, which is the next most important, and so forth.

The prioritizing of reporting objectives is frequently referred to as a **hierarchy** of objectives. A hierarchy of objectives must be tailored to each reporting enterprise; there is no global hierarchy. When there is a conflict in the accounting policies indicated by the various objectives, the objective(s) at the top of the hierarchy will win out over those further down.

QUALITATIVE CRITERIA

For many years, accountants discussed accounting principles in terms of such concepts as historical cost, objectivity, realization, consistency, matching, and freedom from bias. These principles were frequently accorded equal weight in any discussion about possible changes in accounting standards, such as moving away from historical cost to some other measure of value in the primary statements.

The problem with equating concepts such as the six mentioned above is that they really consist of two different types of concepts: (1) measurement methods and (2) qualitative characteristics. Historical cost is a method of representing assets on the balance sheet and expenses on the income statement. One of the reasons for its use is that it displays the qualitative characteristics of objectivity and freedom from bias. A measurement method is a way of representing economic transactions and events in the financial statements. Qualitative characteristics are the criteria by which the suitability of specific measurement methods are judged.

For example, many people have argued that the most useful measure of assets for oil exploration companies is the value of the reserves of oil. However, placing a value on the reserves entails estimating the size of the underground reserves, estimating the rate of production, estimating the cost of production and the market price of the oil, and discounting the net cash flow estimates to find a present value. There is a great deal of subjectivity in making all of those estimates, and different experts could arrive at quite different conclusions as to the asset value. If the oil company's financial statements are to be issued under stewardship reporting requirements, this method of asset measurement may satisfy the qualitative criterion of relevance, but not the criteria of reliability, verifiability, and freedom from bias. Therefore, that measurement technique has been rejected for stewardship reporting in the primary financial statements.

One of the earlier attempts to enumerate and explain the qualitative criteria for accounting measurements was by a committee of the **American Accounting Association**, which issued a report entitled *A Statement of Basic Accounting Theory* in 1966. The committee did not use the term qualitative criteria, but instead recommended four basic "standards for accounting information" and five "guidelines for communicating accounting information."

In the years following, three more sets of qualitative criteria were put forth in the United States, two by the AICPA and one by the FASB. In 1970, the AICPA issued *APB Opinion No. 4, Basic Concepts and Accounting Principles Underlying Financial Statements of Business Enterprises*, which is a massive inventory of U.S. GAAP at that time. Three years later, the report of the AICPA objectives study group (the "Trueblood report") was issued. The Trueblood report recommends seven "qualitative characteristics of reporting."

The most recent set of qualitative criteria in the United States is propounded in the FASB's *Statement of Financial Accounting Concepts No. 2* (1980). *SFAC 2* identifies more than a dozen qualitative criteria and places them in a hierarchical framework, which we will discuss shortly.

In Canada, qualitative characteristics are discussed in Chapter 7 of *Corporate Reporting: Its Future Evolution (CRIFE)*, the report of the CICA study group on corporate reporting issued in 1980. *CRIFE* contains a list of twenty qualitative criteria, arranged in four groups. The first two groups contain potentially conflicting criteria, since the criteria of relevance, comparability, timeliness, clarity, and completeness may possibly conflict with those of objectivity, verifiability, and precision.

The third group contains criteria that are believed to be compatible with those in both of the first two groups: isomorphism, freedom from bias, rationality, nonarbitrariness, and uniformity. The fourth group consists of criteria that may serve as constraints on the criteria in all of the other groups: substance over form, materiality, cost/benefit effectiveness, flexibility, data availability, consistency, and "conservatism (a very minor constraint)." [p. 55] *CRIFE* is useful in both the extensiveness of its list and the identification of conflicting and constraining criteria.

Most recently, the AcSC has added Section 1000 on "financial statement concepts" to the *CICA Handbook*. A major component of Section 1000 is a presentation of qualitative characteristics. Rather than basing the new section on *CRIFE's* thorough listing of qualitative characteristics, the AcSC chose to emulate *SFAC 2*. Section 1000 therefore contains a brief discussion of each of the characteristics identified by the FASB in *SFAC 2*.

Schedule 2-2 is a listing and comparison of the criteria enumerated in the reports and studies mentioned above. Terminology differs somewhat between the various publications, and not all of the criteria in each report or study are necessarily listed. Nevertheless, the schedule gives a summary of the major criteria discussed in each source, and permits comparison of the major characteristics cited.

Schedule 2-2 is partitioned into three sections. The first includes those criteria that relate to the usefulness of reported accounting information. The second section consists of the various criteria that relate to the measurability of the accounting data, while the third section consists of reporting characteristics. The following three sections of the chapter briefly discuss each of these groups of qualitative criteria.

SCHEDULE 2-2

Summary of Qualitative Characteristics

	ASOBAT	APB Statement No. 4	Trueblood report	SFAC 2 and CICA HB	CRIFE
Usefulness:					
Relevance	x	x	x	x	x
Understandability	x	x	x	x	x
Timeliness		x		x	x
Predictive value				x	
Feedback value				x	
Faithfulness				x	x
Measurability:					
Quantifiability	x	x			x
Verifiability	x	x		x	x
Reliability	x		x	x	x
Freedom from bias	x	x	x	x	x
Nonarbitrariness					x
Reporting:					
Comparability	x	x	x	x	x
Consistency	x	x	x	x	x
Completeness	x	x			x
Materiality		x	x	x	x

Sources:
1. American Accounting Association, *A Statement of Basic Accounting Theory* (AAA, 1966), Chapter 2.
2. American Institute of Certified Public Accountants, *APB Statement No. 4: Basic Concepts and Accounting Principles Underlying Financial Statements of Business Enterprises* (AICPA, October 1970), Chapter 4.
3. American Institute of Certified Public Accountants, *Report of the Study Group on Objectives of Financial Statements* (AICPA, 1973), Chapter 10.
4. Financial Accounting Standards Board, *Statement of Financial Accounting Concepts No. 2: Qualitative Characteristics of Accounting Information* (FASB, May 1980).
5. *CICA Handbook*, section 1000.
6. Canadian Institute of Chartered Accountants, *Corporate Reporting: Its Future Evolution* (CICA, 1980), Chapter 7.

Usefulness

Every listing of qualitative criteria starts with **relevance**. There is general agreement that any accounting measurement must be relevant to the needs of the users of the statements, or at least to some of the users. Information that is irrelevant to any perceived need should not be reported. A constraint on relevance, however, is the cost-benefit ratio for the information. Certain information may be quite relevant for some users, but the cost of measuring and reporting the information may well outweigh any possible benefits.

Information is useful only if it is **understandable**. Information that is so obscure or complicated as to be incomprehensible loses any relevance that it may have had. Some accountants argue that the statements should be understandable by a naive investor, that is, by one who has only an imperfect understanding of accounting. Others argue that this argument is itself naive; a naive investor would (or should) consult an expert to interpret the statements. Modern business is too complex to describe simply. The FASB addresses this issue in its objectives statement, *SFAC 1*, and concludes that "cost-benefit considerations may indicate that information understood or used by only a few should not be provided. Conversely, financial reporting should not exclude relevant information merely because it is difficult for some to understand or because some investors or creditors choose not to use it."[7]

The criteria of **predictive value** and **feedback value** are more specific aspects of relevance. Predictive value is defined as the quality of information that helps users to increase the likelihood of correctly forecasting the outcome of past or present events. Thus predictive value relates directly to the primary *SFAC 1* objective of predicting cash flow. Feedback value refers to the feedback loop that we discussed earlier in the chapter. If an item of information helps users to confirm or correct prior expectations, then it has feedback value. The interaction between information useful for predicting and information useful for confirming the predictions enables users to correct deficient decision models. Feedback is important, but is quite elusive in external reporting.

The attribute of **faithfulness** is identified in the major studies under different names. In *SFAC 2*, and in Section 1000 of the *Handbook*, the attribute is called "representational faithfulness." In *CRIFE*, it is "isomorphism." Regardless of what it is called, it means that a measurement should measure what it purports to measure. A lack of faithfulness is most likely to arise when we attempt to measure something that can only be measured indirectly. The process of indirect measurement may be so fraught with peril that we do not succeed in measuring what we want to know.

For example, one way of estimating the current cost of assets is by referring to specific price indices. If there is not an index that tracks the price movements of the asset we are measuring, then we may use a price index for a similar asset. But if we are not sure that the price movements of the two types of assets are really parallel, then we may not end up with a measurement that is representationally faithful.

The concept of faithfulness or measurement validity underlies much of the discussion in the literature, but it has been articulated particularly well in *SFAC 2* and in *CRIFE*.

Measurability: The Many Faces of Objectivity

An interesting aspect of Schedule 2-2 is the absence of the quality of **objectivity** (although the term is used in *CRIFE*). Accountants seem to develop an almost religious fervour over the importance of objectivity, and one would expect that it would be high on everyone's list of desirable characteristics.

The problem is that objectivity means different things to different people. To some, it means "capable of verification." To others, it means "free from bias." Still others interpret objectivity to mean that the same (or very similar) measurements will be obtained by independent professionals.

Because of the difficulty of pinning down a definition of a word with so many connotations, most accounting theoreticians simply avoid using the word altogether. The qualitative characteristics listed in the second section

---

7 *SFAC 1*, para. 36.

of Schedule 2-1 are all aspects of objectivity. Of particular interest are the characteristics of verifiability, reliability, and freedom from bias.

Verifiability is the ability to test the accuracy or correctness of an accounting measurement. For example, the market value of a publicly traded security on the balance sheet date can be confirmed by referring to published security prices on that date; the value is verifiable. On the other hand, the market value of a share investment in a private corporation is difficult to confirm because any valuation placed on the shares by management is bound to be an estimate that is not readily verifiable. Verifiability is an attribute that is quite important when accounting information is communicated to external users who have no way of judging its reasonableness. Therefore, stewardship reporting places considerable emphasis on verifiability, and auditors are concerned with this attribute.

Reliability is a measure of concurrence among equally qualified, independent observers. If five professional accountants, working independently with the same facts and circumstances, arrive at measurements that are identical or similar, the measurement has a high degree of reliability. If, in contrast, the five accountants obtain radically different measurements, then the measurement is not reliable. In statistical terms, reliability is the amount of dispersion around the mean, or the standard error of estimate.

There is an important difference between verifiability and reliability. Suppose that a company uses straight-line depreciation for its fixed assets. Given the company's decision to use that method of depreciation and its assumptions about asset life and salvage value, the depreciation expense can readily be verified. But suppose that instead, five accountants are given the facts about the asset's cost and expected utility and are left to determine a measurement of depreciation expense for the company. The different professionals may well come up with different depreciation methods, useful lives, and estimated salvage values (and perhaps even different measures of the asset's cost), even though they are all starting with the same facts. Depreciation expense, therefore, is not a very reliable measurement.

Unfortunately, different sources use the terms verifiability and reliability in different ways. *SFAC* 2, for example, defines verifiability as we have just defined reliability, and defines reliability as the result of verifiability, freedom from bias, and representational faithfulness. Therefore, it is best to exercise caution when using these terms.

Freedom from bias is achieved when successive or independent measurements are evenly distributed around the "true" value. Statistically, the distribution of an unbiased measurement is not skewed. Bias can arise either from a deficiency in the method of measurement or from the influence of the measurer. To continue with the depreciation example, a company may estimate the salvage values of its assets at the date of acquisition (for the purpose of establishing depreciation) by examining the salvage values of similar assets that are about to be retired. This approach would seem to give an unbiased estimate of salvage value and thus of depreciation expense. However, the approach fails to take inflation into account. When it actually comes time to retire the assets in the future, the estimated salvage values may prove to have been drastically underestimated, or biased. The bias arose as a result of the method used. On the other hand, management may consistently and intentionally underestimate salvage values in order to maximize depreciation expense. This is bias introduced by the measurer.

An additional aspect of measurer bias is that the bias may be introduced either by management or by the accountant. Management bias is difficult to avoid, because so many accounting measures rely on estimates made by management. At best, all the accountant can do is test the reasonableness of the estimates to try to detect any obviously biased estimates. Little can be done about estimates that are on the low or high side of the plausible range of values, as long as they are within the plausible range. Bias by the accountant, however, can be guarded against. The accountant should not introduce her or his personal biases towards conservatism or optimism into the measurements. To do so would constitute an intentional misrepresentation of the financial picture of the company.

To some observers, freedom from bias is the attribute of **neutrality**. To others, neutrality is an attribute pertaining to accounting information that does not have economic consequences. To some people, accounting should be neutral in that reporting standards should not influence managers or investors to act in any certain way. A problem arises, however, because if the information being reported is relevant, then it is used for making decisions and *should* have an effect on users' decisions. Completely neutral information is irrelevant information.

An alternative view of neutrality is "that either in formulating or implementing standards, the primary concern should be the relevance and reliability of the information that results, not the effect... on a particular interest."[8] This view of neutrality is more relevant to standard setters than to individual enterprises. In deciding whether or not to require the capitalization of leases, for example, the FASB and AcSC both considered the substance of the leases and whether the information reported would be useful for users' decisions. They did not make the decision based on possible economic consequences for the leasing industry or for the lessees' perceived financial structures, share values, and debt capacities.

The qualitative characteristics that we have loosely labeled as reporting characteristics in Schedule 2-2 are comparability, consistency, completeness, and materiality. These might also be considered to be measurement attributes, since accounting information will be deficient if it cannot satisfy these criteria. Nevertheless, we often think of these four characteristics as desirable attributes of our accounting policies for reporting purposes.

Reporting Characteristics

Comparability refers to the idea that the accounting measurements among different enterprises should be similar if the economic circumstances are similar. This criterion is highly applicable to standard setting, but may also be applicable in accounting for a single enterprise if an objective is to make the enterprise's reported financial results comparable to others in the same industry. Indeed, companies in specialized industries frequently engage auditors who are experienced in that industry. The use of specialized auditors is desirable because the auditors are familiar with the industry's operations and can perform an audit more efficiently than can auditors who are less experienced in that particular industry. But in addition, the use of specialized auditors will help to achieve comparability in reporting because of their awareness of industry reporting practices.

8 *Statement of Financial Concepts No. 2*, (FASB, 1980), para. 98.

Consistency has two aspects. The first is consistency of measurement approach for similar events in the same company during an accounting period. The other is consistency of measurement method for similar events or transactions in successive accounting periods. Consistency is desirable only as long as the economic circumstances remain the same. If circumstances change, then more relevant information may be provided by changing the accounting policy and introducing an inconsistency. Thus consistency is a virtue only as long as this relevance is not impaired.

The purpose of period-to-period consistency is to improve the usefulness of the accounting information by making the statements of different periods **comparable** to each other. Thus comparability has significance both for comparisons between enterprises and comparisons over time for a single enterprise.

Completeness is sometimes referred to as "full disclosure." Full disclosure is something of a misnomer, since obviously not everything can be disclosed. "Adequate disclosure" might be a better term, since the goal is to disclose sufficient information to avoid misinterpretations of the statements. For example, failure to disclose that an enterprise's assets are fully pledged as security for loans might lead unsecured creditors to believe that they are in a less risky position than they really are. The disclosure of the security arrangement is necessary in order to prevent users from misinterpreting the assets and liabilities of the company, both of which may be reliably measured.

Materiality is a pervasive concept in accounting. Essentially, a piece of information is material if it *may* affect some users' decisions. Cause-and-effect need not be proven, and the information need not be relevant to all users. The potential for affecting decisions is adequate. Quantitative guidelines for materiality have proven to be elusive. The elusiveness is partially due to the variety of possible users and of possible decisions. Materiality could be considered a quantitative characteristic rather than a qualitative characteristic. But since materiality interacts with relevance to determine the usefulness of accounting information, it should be included as being qualitative. In addition, some disclosures may be more important for their potential significance than for their immediate impact. An example would be loans to shareholders that are minor to the company but that may imply a special relationship between the shareholders and the company.

Hierarchy of Qualitative Criteria

Schedule 2-3 reproduces the hierarchy of accounting qualities as described by the FASB in *SFAC 2*. Near the top of the chart are the criteria of understandability and decision usefulness. If information is not useful, then there is no point to reporting it to users. As well, if information is theoretically useful but cannot be understood by the users to whom is directed, then it is not really useful. Thus the FASB places these two criteria at the top of their chart.

Whether information is useful is co-determined by its relevance and its reliability. Information that is highly relevant may not be reliably measurable, and therefore accountants may report data that are less directly relevant but more reliable. There is a trade-off possible between these two criteria. The extent of the trade-off can be affected by the objectives of the particular enterprise's financial statements. If the primary objective is stewardship re-

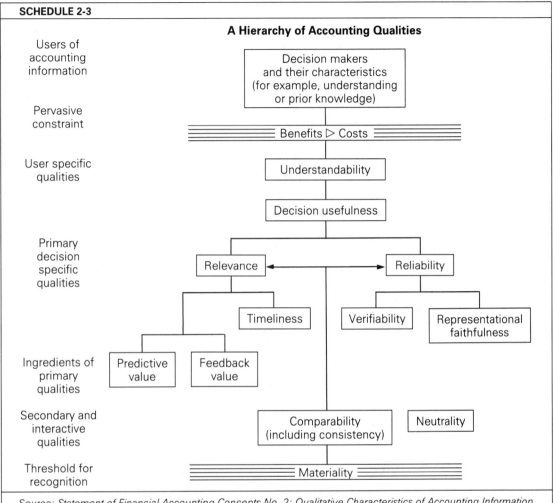

SCHEDULE 2-3

A Hierarchy of Accounting Qualities

Source: *Statement of Financial Accounting Concepts No. 2: Qualitative Characteristics of Accounting Information* (FASB, May 1980), p. 15.

porting, then relevance is apt to be sacrificed for reliability. If instead the primary objective is for performance appraisal and the reports are to be used mainly by managers and directors, then it may be possible to sacrifice some reliability in order to gain in relevance.

In the FASB's view, the components of relevance are predictive value, feedback value, and timeliness. *SFAC 1* establishes the reporting of information to aid the prediction of cash flow as the principal reporting objective. To have relevance under the stated objective, information must either aid in the prediction of cash flow or provide feedback about the accuracy of the predictions. Of course, the information must be timely or it will be received too late to be of any use.

The FASB's definition of reliability is that it is the sum of verifiability, representational faithfulness, and freedom from bias (or neutrality). Our earlier definition of reliability as the relative concurrence of measurements by independent professionals is included by the FASB within the definition of verifiability. Thus the same concepts are there, although the words differ a bit. Under the general heading of reliability, there can be trade-offs among the components. A degree of verifiability can be sacrificed to increase representational faithfulness, for example. Or verifiability and representational faithfulness may both be sacrificed in order to obtain unbiased (or less biased) measurements (neutrality).

Underlying all of the accounting information are the two concepts of materiality and of benefits greater than costs. Immaterial information should not be reported, even though an item may have to be measured before it is seen to be immaterial. We should be reasonably certain that the benefits of information exceed the costs of collecting and reporting. Unfortunately, the benefits are apt to be quite subjective and vague, while the costs will be quite real. Managers sometimes will oppose the reporting of information because the company will have to bear the cost while outsiders reap the possible benefits.

The hierarchy of criteria presented in *SFAC 2* is presented here because it is a helpful way of visualizing the importance of the various criteria and illustrating where the trade-offs between them would occur. Other frameworks could no doubt be developed that would order the criteria somewhat differently and perhaps assign greater or lesser importance to certain ones. A three-dimensional hierarchy would permit a variation in objectives of reporting, for example, and would show how the importance of the individual criteria would be affected by the objectives and by the nature of the users.

The exact framework or hierarchy is unimportant; what matters is that the criteria be digested. It is these criteria that must be applied by the professional accountant in deciding on the appropriate accounting policies to recommend to management, given the reporting objectives of the enterprise.

SUMMARY

This chapter has discussed at some length the various financial reporting objectives that a business enterprise can have and the qualitative criteria by which information is selected or measured in order to satisfy the particular objectives of a specific enterprise. For many readers, this discussion is a review, while for others it is new. In either case, it is essential to recognize that the foregoing material is not just academic doodling. Objectives and qualitative criteria have real impacts on the nature of reported accounting information. Accountants can fulfil their role as professionals only by internalizing the objectives and qualitative criteria discussed in this chapter and applying them to organizations in the real world.

The following chapter demonstrates the impact of objectives and qualitative characteristics in public reporting, and shows how the accounting measurements vary from industry to industry. The variation in reporting for private companies will be even greater. The cases at the end of this and the next chapter offer an opportunity for practice.

REVIEW QUESTIONS

2-1   Define the following terms:

   a. Stakeholder
   b. Objectives of financial reporting
   c. Qualitative characteristics
   d. Measurement rules
   e. Constraints on financial reporting

2-2   What is meant by a **feedback loop** in financial reporting?

2-3   Why is it necessary for the accountant to define the objectives of financial reporting for the enterprise for which he or she is preparing financial statements?

2-4   Since most externally reported financial statements are required to be in accordance with GAAP, how can the existence of specific objectives of financial reporting affect the preparation of the statements?

2-5   If externally reported financial statements are **general purpose** statements, how can specific objectives influence their content?

2-6   How can the accounting policies adopted for financial reporting affect the assessment of income tax?

2-7   Do companies maintain "two sets of books," one for financial reporting and one for income tax purposes? Explain.

2-8   In what general ways would an objective of tax minimization affect the financial statements?

2-9   What is the primary focus of the objectives discussed in the FASB's *Statement of Financial Accounting Concepts No. 1?*

2-10 What is the long-term relationship between cash flow and earnings?

2-11 How does the accrual method of accounting fit into the concept of a cash flow prediction emphasis for financial reporting?

2-12 Explain what is meant by the **quality of earnings**.

2-13 In what general ways would a cash flow prediction objective influence the selection of accounting policies?

2-14 Why is it usually difficult to separate the results of good management from good luck?

2-15 In what general way will the adoption of a performance evaluation objective influence the selection of accounting policies?

2-16 In general, what is meant by **stewardship reporting**?

2-17 Securities acts contain requirements for the reporting of financial information to investors. When financial statements are designed mainly to comply with the requirements of the securities acts, what objective of financial reporting is being applied?

2-18 Why would management adopt an earnings maximization objective?

2-19 Why would management adopt an earnings minimization objective?

2-20 Why would managers be users of their company's general purpose external financial statements?

2-21 What users are served by each of the following objectives of financial reporting:

   a. Stewardship
   b. Cash flow prediction
   c. Performance appraisal

2-22 Explain the difference between user objectives and preparer objectives.

2-23 How can a manager be both a **preparer** and a **user** of financial statements?

2-24 What is the purpose of understanding the qualitative characteristics of accounting information?

2-25 What do all studies of qualitative characteristics consider to be the most important characteristic of accounting information?

2-26 Should reported accounting information be understandable by all users? Explain.

2-27 Explain the concept of representational faithfulness.

2-28 Why do some accounting theoreticians avoid the use of the word **objectivity**?

2-29 Distinguish between these three qualities:

   a. Reliability
   b. Verifiability
   c. Freedom from bias

2-30 What are the possible sources of bias in accounting measurements?

2-31 Distinguish between **comparability** and **consistency**.

2-32 Why might **adequate disclosure** be a more descriptive phrase than **full disclosure**?

2-33 How can a **hierarchy** of qualitative characteristics be useful?

CASE 2-1   Time-Lice Books, Ltd.

Time-Lice Books, Ltd. (TLBL) is a well-established company that publishes a wide variety of general interest nonfiction books. The company is incorporated under the *Canada Business Corporations Act*, and 30% of the shares are held by the heirs of Harold Lice, the founder of the firm. The heirs do not take any active interest in the affairs of the company, but rely on the advice of their professional financial advisor, Mr. Hornblower Weeks, in voting their shares. The remaining 70% of the shares are widely distributed and are traded on the Montreal Exchange.

TLBL distributes some of its books (about 25%) through retail bookstores, but the bulk of the sales (75%) are made directly to customers by direct mail advertising. About half of the direct mail sales are for series of books, and the company has decided to review its accounting policy for this segment of the business.

A book series is a set of books on a particular topic. Rather than publish all of the books at once, the approach is to issue one book at a time, at two-to-four month intervals. Topics of some recently begun series are Great Impressionist Artists, Time-Lice Guides to Home Maintenance, and Lives of Great Accountants (a particularly popular series).

When TLBL decides to begin a new series, the first step is to design an elaborate and expensive full-colour advertising brochure for the series, in which the first book is offered free of charge to those who return a postage-free postal card. This brochure is then mailed to about two million homes in Canada, using TLBL's own mailing list plus purchased mailing lists. While the mail campaign is going on, TLBL contracts writers to prepare the text of the first book in the series, and begins design of the book. However, actual production of the book does not occur until the mail campaign has ended and the number of copies needed has been determined from the returned postal cards.

The second book is produced about two months after the first has been mailed out, and is sent to all those customers who received the first (free) volume. However, customers are then asked either to subscribe to the entire series at a fixed price or to return the second volume without charge. Company experience has been that, on average, 80% of the customers elect to subscribe and about 15% return the second book. The other 5% neither subscribe nor return the book, and TLBL takes no action against these subscribers except to send them a dunning letter and delete their names from their mailing lists. While 80% is the average subscription rate, the rate for specific series may vary anywhere from 70% to 85%.

Customers who do subscribe have a choice of paying for the entire series all at once, or of paying for each book (at a higher price) as it is sent. Roughly half of the customers elect each alternative, although there has been a trend towards advance payment since TLBL began accepting Visa and Mastercard (for advance payments only) two years ago.

The advertising brochure and direct mail campaign is the largest single cost incurred. The writers of the books are under a fixed-fee contract with TLBL and do not receive royalties. The layout and design work on each volume is performed by TLBL's salaried designers. Although printing costs have been escalating sharply, the cost to print and bind each book has been about $2.50 lately. The books are sold to customers at about $20.00 per copy. All customers may cancel their subscriptions at any time. The advance-payment subscribers must send a letter of cancellation, but few do so. The instalment subscribers may cancel simply by returning one of the volumes within fifteen days of receipt, whereupon they are sent no more volumes in the series. At some point before the conclusion of the series, 20 to 30% of instalment subscribers cancel.

Required:
Evaluate the revenue and expense recognition alternatives for TLBL for the book series.

Bay and Eastern Corp.; Harbinger Ltd.   CASE 2-2

Helen Hook is president and chief executive officer of Bay and Eastern Corp. Bay and Eastern is a large, diversified corporation with its head office in Halifax and its executive offices in Toronto. The corporation controls 27 other corporations, mainly in North America, but also in Europe. Bay and Eastern's common shares are traded on both the Toronto Stock Exchange and on the American Stock Exchange in New York. Its preferred shares are held exclusively by a group of life insurance companies that purchased the shares in a private offering several years ago. The same insurance companies hold about half of Bay and Eastern's bonds, while the rest are publicly traded.

Helen's brother, Harvey, is president of Harbinger Ltd., a small chain of employment offices operating in and around Vancouver. The company was founded by Harvey Hook in 1971, when he left the personnel services division of a national consulting firm. Harvey owns 67% of the shares of Harbinger. His father, Henry, owns the other 33%. Henry was an important source of capital for Harvey when he started the business. Henry lent Harbinger $75,000 at its inception, and in 1976 accepted a 33% ownership interest in lieu of repayment of the debt. Harbinger has no other major creditors, although a line of credit has just been negotiated with a branch of the Bank of Nova Scotia.

Required:
Explain how the objectives of financial reporting would differ between Bay and Eastern Corp. and Harbinger Ltd. Be as specific as possible.

Fishbits Inc.   CASE 2-3

Fishbits Inc. is a franchiser of fast-food restaurants that specialize in deep-fried pieces of fish. The restaurants all do business under the name of Fishbits, but all are owned and operated by independent entrepreneurs; the original Fishbits outlets are separately owned by the founding shareholders of Fishbits Inc., and are not owned by the franchiser corporation itself.

Fishbits Inc. sells franchises for $200,000. Of the total amount, $40,000 is due when the franchise agreement is signed, another $40,000 is due when the outlet opens, and the remainder is due eighteen months after the opening. Each payment is non-refundable. Fishbits Inc. also receives a royalty of 3% of the invoice cost of the special supplies which the outlets are required to use, such as the secret coating for the fish, and the paper goods and other supplies, which are imprinted with the Fishbits logo. Fishbits Inc. does not produce any of these goods; special arrangements are made with local suppliers in each region of the country, and the royalties are forwarded to Fishbits directly by the suppliers rather than by the franchisees.

Before the franchise agreement is signed, there is a period of discussion and exploration that can last from one to six months. During this time, the general feasibility of establishing a new outlet is examined. Market surveys are conducted to determine whether the local market could support another fast-food outlet, and the financial strength and backing of the prospective franchisee are examined. The costs incurred during the pre-signing stage are borne by Fishbits Inc.

Once the franchise agreement is signed, Fishbits Inc. actively assists the franchiser in selecting a site, planning the restaurant, gaining building permits, equipping the restaurant, and selecting and training the staff. All of the direct costs of establishing the outlet are paid by the franchisee, but Fishbits Inc. contributes substantial assistance in the form of legal, architectural, planning, and management experts. The experts are retained by Fishbits Inc. as regular staff consultants, and are paid a fixed fee retainer each month, regardless of the amount of service that they provide to Fishbits or its franchisees in that month. A supporting staff is employed directly by the franchiser.

Some of the expert assistance is delivered on site, with Fishbits Inc. paying the travel and other incidental costs. Other assistance, such as drafting of construction blueprints (based on master plans kept at Fishbits Inc. head office) and preparation of supporting documents for city council site-zoning bylaws, is provided by the head office, and Fishbits Inc. absorbs those costs as well. The period of time between the signing of the franchise agreement and the opening of the outlet can vary from six months to two years. On average, though, it takes about one year.

The direct involvement of Fishbits Inc. largely ends when the outlet opens. Some additional management and employee training assistance is sometimes offered, but any significant additional services must be paid for by the franchisee.

Required:

Assume that you are an accounting advisor to Fishbits Inc. Recommend an accounting and reporting policy for revenue and expense recognition for Fishbits Inc. under each of the three following separate cases. Be sure to evaluate all of the alternative policies in light of the objectives of financial reporting in each case, and in light of the qualitative criteria for evaluating accounting measurements.

Case A: Fishbits Inc. is a well-established franchiser that has franchised hundreds of successful outlets throughout North America. The corporation is controlled by the original founders, who own 54% of the outstanding common shares. The remaining shares are publicly traded on the Montreal Exchange. The success rate is very high for the franchisees; only 3% of the licensed franchisees have failed to open during the history of Fishbits Inc., and only 8% have failed before payment of the final instalment of the franchise fee.

Case B: Fishbits Inc. is privately owned by its three founders; each owns one-third of the common shares. There is no long-term debt, and few current liabilities. The company is well established, and has a good record of successful openings, similar to the success rate described in Case A, above.

Case C: Fishbits Inc. is a relatively new company, having been founded only three years previously. Only five franchised restaurants have been opened (in addition to the three owned by Fishbits Inc.'s founders) and all have been successful. Eight more franchise agreements have been signed and good progress is being made towards opening all of the new outlets. Fishbits Inc. is planning to offer shares to the public in the near future. In the meantime, the corporation has been borrowing substantial sums from the bank in order to meet the up-front costs of opening new franchises.

CASE 2-4   Capreol Carpet Corporation

Capreol Carpet Corporation (CCC) is a manufacturer of broadloom carpeting located in Winnipeg, Manitoba. The company enjoys a good reputation for its product, but unfortunately has not been very profitable in recent years, owing to increasing imports of cheaper carpeting. In order to combat this threat, CCC invested substantial sums of money in new equipment to upgrade efficiency. Although efficiency picked up as a result, the improvement seemed only to keep the profit picture from getting any worse, rather than actually increasing net income.

CCC is a public company, but control was held by Bay and Eastern Corporation, a large conglomerate. Three months ago, Bay and Eastern sold its 70% interest in CCC to Upper Lip Enterprises Ltd., a British carpet manufacturer. Upper Lip planned to integrate CCC into its own operations, such that CCC would be the manufacturer of certain carpets sold by all of Upper Lip's distributors, and the North American distributor of Upper Lip's British-made carpets.

Last week, the financial vice-president of Upper Lip sent a letter to David Blase, the controller of CCC, in which he detailed certain changes in accounting policy that CCC should institute in order to make its reporting practices consistent with those of Upper Lip, for purposes of consolidation and divisional performance appraisal. Included in the letter were the following:

1. Inventories, both of raw materials and finished goods, should be valued on the LIFO basis rather than on the average-cost basis previously used by CCC.
2. Carpeting sold to Upper Lip and its other subsidiaries should be billed at standard cost plus 10%, rather than at full list price less 15%, as is now the case. In effect, the gross margin on the intercompany transfers would be reduced from 35% of cost to 10% of cost. Carpet purchased by CCC from the Upper Lip group of companies would also be invoiced to CCC at cost plus 10%.
3. Depreciation on the new equipment should be increased from 8% per year (straight-line) to 12.5% per year. Standard costs would be adjusted to reflect the higher rate.
4. Deferred taxes should not be recorded. The only timing difference is that for CCA/depreciation, and U.K. practice permits nonrecording of tax deferrals if reversal is not likely within the foreseeable future.

The financial vice-president, in his letter to David, has asked for an immediate response to his requests for changes in accounting policy.

Required:
Assume that you are David Blase. Draft a letter in which you respond to Upper Lip's requests.

Neuvo Inc.   CASE 2-5

Neuvo Inc. is incorporated under the *Canada Business Corporations Act*. Neuvo is a computer software company whose business is the custom design of large-scale software packages for large corporations, provincial governments, etc. The company's products are unique and of such a size that copying and unauthorized duplication are not feasible and therefore are not a problem for Neuvo. Neuvo is at the leading edge of software development and while it has a number of competitors, its market position is not threatened.

The company was founded four years ago by Chris Covert and Frances Ferris, two of Canada's most prominent software designers. Two-thirds of the shares of the company are owned indirectly by Frances through a personal holding company and the other third is owned directly by Chris. The two founders brought several major clients with them from their previous employers, so that Neuvo had a significant base of customers right from the beginning. The prominence of Chris and Frances enabled them to attract other highly talented analysts and programmers.

In order to give the professional staff a sense of participation in the company, a profit-sharing plan was put into effect whereby the staff who participated on a project received bonuses that totaled 20% of the gross margin on the project (that is, of the difference between the total revenue and the direct and directly assignable costs). The bonuses on each project are determined only after the project is completed and is accepted by the customer.

The company has seen its revenues grow dramatically in the three years since its founding, from $1,695,000 in the first year to $7,411,000 in the most recent year. These revenues are derived solely from custom software design contracts, and have been reported on a completed contract basis. The contracts have been charged with all direct costs and with all costs that can be directly assigned to the project, such as an internal allocation for computer time and any overhead that can be directly traced to the projects. All indirect overhead and administrative costs have been charged to the income statement as period costs. Using these accounting policies, net income has gone from $11,109 in the first year to $166,046 in the most recent year. Work in process at the end of the past year amounts to $2,776,623.

The company's custom work has resulted in the development of highly sophisticated products, such as a cartography program and a province-wide health care monitoring system. The owners, therefore, have decided to rewrite some of these programs in order to make them generally usable on computer systems other than the one for which they were specifically designed, and to sell them as proprietary products to other large-scale potential customers. For example, the health care system that was designed for one provincial government could be sold to other provinces and perhaps to some states in the United States.

In order to implement this new line of business, Neuvo had to expend considerable time and money to develop the generalized programmes. These costs are being classified as "development costs" in Neuvo's accounting records.

In addition to the head office in Ottawa, the company set up five new offices to act as sales offices for the newly developed proprietary products. New offices were established in Toronto, Quebec City, Calgary, Vancouver, and Halifax. In each location, office space was leased, leasehold improvements were carried out, furniture and equipment was purchased and installed, and professional staff were hired. The equipment consisted mainly of powerful mini-computers that were linked to Neuvo's main computer in Ottawa. All of the costs incurred in setting up these offices, including the personnel costs and interest on the bank loan, have tentatively been classified as "start-up costs" in Neuvo's books.

Financing for the custom design work has been provided by the Queens Bank of Canada through an operating line of credit. The line of credit is limited to the sum of 70% of Neuvo's billed accounts receivable and 50% of contract work in progress (unbilled). The bank has not required audited financial statements from Neuvo. Neuvo has been borrowing against this line of credit to help finance the costs of proprietary product development and of the new offices. The line of credit is almost completely used up, however, and Chris and Frances have undertaken two courses of action to obtain additional funds. One source of financing is a completed sale-and-leaseback arrangement; the other source is a term loan that is currently being negotiated.

The sale-and-leaseback arrangement was for the company's mainframe computer. The computer had been completely written off in the first three years of operation, and the sale therefore generated a gain equal to the proceeds of the sale, almost $1,000,000. The leaseback arrangement took the form of a one-year lease with six-month renewals at the same monthly payment at the option of Neuvo. The computer was expected to be serviceable for at least three more years (with periodic upgrades to be paid for by Neuvo). Neuvo guaranteed the secondary financing that the lessor had obtained to finance the deal.

The term loan is potentially for a five-year period and is being negotiated with the bank to finance the development costs. Chris has been negotiating with the bank but the bank has not yet given an answer either way. The bank has made it clear, however, that if the loan is granted, there will be explicit maintenance tests (i.e., covenants) included as part of the loan agreement. The maintenance tests would include at least a minimum debt:equity ratio, a limit on dividend payout and owners' salary as a proportion of earnings, and a minimum interest coverage ratio. Failure to meet any of these tests would render both the term loan and the operating loan immediately callable by the bank.

In view of the changing nature of Neuvo's operations and the prospective bank financing, the owners have decided to reconsider the company's financial reporting policies. They have engaged Ned Norem as an expert accounting advisor and are looking forward to Ned's recommendations on accounting policies for the future.

Required:
Assume the role of Ned Norem. Prepare a report for Chris Covert and Frances Ferris.
[ICAO]

Printech Ltd.   CASE 2-6

On August 6, 1989, your firm was engaged by Mark Laban, the president of Printech Ltd., to advise the company on its accounting policies. Forty percent of the company's shares had recently changed hands, and the president felt that it was time to reconsider the company's external reporting policies.

Printech is one of over 700 printers located in the Metropolitan Toronto area, the most highly concentrated group of printers in the country. Over 40% of the commercial printing in Canada is done in the Toronto area, and Printech is one of many such companies competing for the local market share.

Printech had annual sales of approximately $6.0 million in 1988, having grown from only $1.5 million in 1979, its first year of operation. The company was founded by Mark Laban and Dan Wolfe, both of whom had worked for another printer. Mark was a master printer and Dan had been a senior salesperson. When they founded Printech, Dan had taken several of his best customers' business with him to the new company. Mark had acquired 60% of the founding shares, and Dan had acquired 40%. A shareholders' agreement allocated the votes for the board of directors equally to the two founders.

Since Dan and Mark had been owner-managers of Printech, they controlled their own salaries, bonuses, and dividends in accordance with their own income needs, and tax deferral was the dominant financial reporting objective.

The company's initial area of expertise was high-quality four-colour printing. The first year's production consisted mainly of advertising flyers and brochures, using Printech's four-colour press. Quality colour printing remained as a principal line of business for Printech, comprising about 55% of the company's current sales volume. However, the capacity of the press was limiting the company's ability to gain business in this area. As well, the profitability of this line of business was being depressed by the necessity to make two press runs if the customer wanted a varnish or coated finish to the product. Competitors were able to offer printing on six-colour presses that could apply varnish or other paper coatings as part of a single run, rather than by using two runs as was necessary on a four-colour press. To protect this line of business, Printech feels that it will be necessary to acquire a new press in the coming year. A new press would cost close to $2.0 million, and it would be necessary to obtain bank financing in order to pay for the press.

Printech also does substantial business in two other areas. One is the printing of custom stationery and forms for small businesses, especially for professional practices such as lawyers and doctors. The other is the printing of covers for paperback books on heavy stock, usually on a two-colour press.

The custom forms business was an innovation of Dan's. Large forms companies didn't seem to be serving that market effectively, while other small companies that were serving the market tended not to be able to offer top quality. Professional service firms generally are very sensitive to the image communicated to their clients by their stationery and forms, and Dan was able to provide an effective service combining quality and low price. The quality was made possible by the expertise of Mark and the production staff, while the low price was made possible by printing in large volumes but delivering to the clients in small quantities. The clients contracted to buy a minimum total volume of output over a two-year period, without committing themselves to delivery or payment at specified times. Printech would then design the forms or stationery, make the printing plates, and print the entire order. Printech would then store the material for the client until needed. Some clients requested delivery only about once a month, while others might call for delivery two or more times a week. Delivery was always made within 24 hours. The custom forms business had grown from zero to 25% of Printech's sales volume in just three years, and was expected to increase substantially in the future.

The bulk of the book cover business (about 60%) was under contract to a single book printer, Owl & Pen, Inc. (OPI). Press runs for the covers varied from 5,000 to 100,000 copies. For larger runs, it was not unusual for Printech to hold most of the covers for OPI until the contents of the book were reprinted by OPI, a period that could run two years or more. OPI typically paid 50% of the contract price at the time of printing and then paid the remainder as the covers were shipped by Printech.

OPI is a Canadian company that is a wholly owned subsidiary of a U.S. broadcasting company that is publicly owned. In June 1989, Dan and Mark completed a transaction with OPI in which each of the founders transferred 20% of the total number of outstanding Printech shares to OPI (a total of 40%) in return for treasury shares in OPI's parent company. This deal permitted the two founders to liquidate part of their investment, if they so desired, without losing control of the company. Dan and Mark would still control Printech jointly, each having 30% of the votes. OPI, of course, would have the other 40% of the votes.

The deal between OPI and Dan and Mark brought no new financing into the company and therefore would not affect the debt:equity ratio. In keeping with normal practice in the industry, Printech was highly leveraged; the debt:equity ratio was 3:1, which was about average. The proposed financing for the new six-colour press would more than double that ratio. Printech's banker had indicated a willingness to finance the new press, but also indicated that he would be required to place a restriction on any new debt thereafter by imposing a limit on Printech's maximum debt:equity ratio.

Now that part of the shares was owned by OPI, the salary arrangements for Dan and Mark were regularized and a formal bonus scheme was put in place, with the managers' bonuses directly tied to the profitability of the company. An OPI nominee on Printech's board of directors would represent OPI when setting the various components of the managers' compensation.

Required:

Draft a letter to the president of Printech Ltd. to advise him on the changes in Printech's financial reporting objectives that you believe will arise as a result of the changed circumstances described above. The letter should include your recommendation of accounting policies for revenue recognition and related matching of costs that would best meet these revised reporting objectives.
[ICAO]

CASE 2-7   Delta Ltd.

Delta Ltd. (Delta) is incorporated under the *Canada Business Corporations Act*. In 1988, the board of directors decided to sell the Printing and Binding Division of the company and concentrate its efforts in its two other divisions: Book Publishing and a new Educational Technology Division. An offer was received for the assets and liabilities of the Printing and Binding Division, and the sale became effective in late January 1989. Delta's financial year ends on December 31.

For the past twenty years Delta had been a public company, with preferred shares listed on a Canadian stock exchange. Its bonds were also publicly traded. On receipt of the offer in 1988 for the assets and liabilities of the Printing and Binding Division, the board began rethinking certain aspects of the status of the company. After several meetings, the board decided that Delta would become a private company, and would therefore call in its bonds for redemption and its preferred shares for cancellation. The necessary legal negotiations were commenced with the provincial securities commissions, the Department of Consumer and Corporate Affairs, the stock exchange and the holders of the bonds and preferred shares.

The board decided to change the company's status from public to private because the company would gain greater privacy and tax benefits, and it would be easier to reach agreement on the company's future direction. During their discussions on the change in status, some board members argued that the financial disclosure required of private companies is less extensive than that required of public companies. In their opinion, not only is the distribution of the financial statements of a private company such as Delta restricted to a relatively small group, but the financial information that must be disclosed is less extensive. While readily acknowledging that the change in status would restrict the distribution of Delta's financial statements, other directors maintained that disclosure requirements will not change significantly.

The bonds were redeemed in January 1989. The preferred shares were bought on the open market in several transactions during January and February and were cancelled in February 1989. On March 7, 1989, Delta became a private company.

During January 1989, the majority shareholder, Mr. Richards, bought out all the minority holders of Delta's common shares.

It is now April 1989. Mr. Richards has engaged you to help Delta adjust efficiently and effectively to being a private company with two divisions. He wants you to prepare a report that includes your recommendations on financial accounting matters. You have assembled the information shown in Exhibit 1.

Required:
Prepare the report requested by Mr. Richards.

EXHIBIT 1
1. Audited financial statements for the year ended December 31, 1988, were made available to interested parties in February 1989. An annual meeting has not yet been scheduled for the calendar year 1989; the previous annual meeting was held in May 1988.
2. The legal costs incurred in dealing with the various governmental and stock exchange officials amounted to $70,000.
3. The bonds had to be redeemed at a 2% premium that amounted to $80,000.
4. Some of the preferred shares were bought on the open market in early January 1989 at a price that was $60,000 less than their recorded book value. But, after discussions with the securities commissions, it is not clear that Delta is entitled to this sum of $60,000; they may have to pay it to sellers of the shares. The remaining preferred shares, also purchased in the open market, were bought at a price that was $75,000 above their book value.

EXHIBIT 1 (continued)

5. The buyer of the Printing and Binding Division agreed to hire most of Delta's production employees, but not the office staff. Thus, Delta had to dismiss some employees, and retire a few early. Severance pay amounted to $200,000.

6. The company's actuary checked into the funding needed for a work force of reduced size. The actuary has estimated that the pension plan is overfunded by about $350,000. This situation has arisen because it had been assumed that 60% of all new employees would stay with the company the necessary six years to qualify for a pension. However, as a result of selling the division, Delta does not have to provide a pension for those who worked for the company for less than six years. Delta has decided to leave the $350,000 in the pension fund. Accordingly, it does not have to make payments to the fund over the next few years.

7. The sale of the Printing and Binding Division has reduced Delta's assets to about $3 million, and annual revenues from $15 million to $6 million.

8. In January 1989, prior to its sale, the Printing and Binding Division's revenue was $820,000, and cost of goods sold was $430,000. The Division incurred other expenses of $170,000.

9. The Educational Technology Division is relatively new to Delta. Its activities involve the coordination of franchise operations for a foreign manufacturer of computer and video equipment. Delta has been granted the entire Canadian territory. The company is required to develop software programs that meet the educational needs of Canadians.

   Franchising is effective as it facilitates the development of specific market segments. Each franchisee is responsible for developing specialized software for its market segment.

   During 1988, six franchisees were signed up, but no cash was received, nor were services performed because the computer equipment from the foreign manufacturer was not scheduled to be delivered until April 1989. During 1988, $120,000 spent on software development was capitalized by Delta. Thus far in 1989, an additional $180,000 has been spent by Delta on software development; the sum is currently in a temporary ledger account awaiting distribution to appropriate accounts.

10. Delta sells franchises for a total price of $200,000 each, with payments due equally over five years. One-half of the sum must be paid to the foreign manufacturer. To date in 1989, Delta has received $240,000, representing payments by the six franchisees at $40,000 each. It also operates four franchises itself.

11. The Book Publishing Division has used the following accounting policies in the years to December 31, 1988:

    a. Revenue is recognized when books are shipped to book stores. Each store is allowed to return up to 20% of purchases made in the past 12 months.
    b. Inventory is valued at the lower of printing and binding cost or net realizable value.
    c. Depreciation is charged in the accounts on a straight-line basis.
    d. Bonuses to employees and royalties to authors are expensed in the year that they are paid, which is normally the year after the period to which they relate. Sales employees receive bonuses for

EXHIBIT 1 (continued)

the net sales in their territory. Editorial staff receive bonuses for successful publications.

e. The Book Publishing Division has signed eight new authors to produce manuscripts in 1989 and 1990.

12. The senior management of Delta was paid a salary plus a bonus of preferred shares in the period to December 31, 1988. The plan was cancelled when the company became private. Senior management of Delta is now seeking a new remuneration and incentive program.

[CICA, adapted]

3

Impact of Industry Characteristics on Financial Reporting

The previous chapter discussed the objectives of reporting for business enterprises and the qualitative criteria by which alternative measurement methods are evaluated. This chapter demonstrates, by the use of two examples, how measurement methods will differ according to the particular characteristics of specific industries. Even within a given industry, however, there will be variation in reporting practices, because the objectives of financial reporting for individual companies will be different.

In the study of accounting, we frequently tend to focus on accounting and reporting for "standard" manufacturing and mercantile companies. In the Canadian economy, however, manufacturing is a less significant activity than it is in many other industrialized countries. The domestic economy has been too small for most manufacturers to be competitive with companies located in the much more broadly based domestic economies of the United States, Japan, and the European Economic Community. The free trade agreement between Canada and the United States may alter that situation by giving Canadian manufacturers direct access to a much larger "home" market, but the North American economy in general is moving away from a manufacturing base.

Instead, the private sector of the Canadian economy is composed mainly of companies in what are sometimes called "specialized industries." We have many mining companies, oil and gas companies, large and efficient real estate developers, extensively developed financial institutions and insurance companies, and highly developed professional service firms, among others. Each of these industries has special characteristics that pose a challenge to professional accountants for financial reporting.

To illustrate the sort of challenges that the specialized industries offer, and the approach necessary to meet those challenges, we have chosen two industries somewhat at random. The first example, in part A, is the extractive industries. We will address issues common to both mining and to oil and gas exploration and development, although we will focus more on mining. In part B of the chapter, we look at the substantially different reporting requirements of open-end investment companies, commonly known as mutual funds.

In some industries, such as banking, insurance, and mutual funds, there are extensive reporting requirements stated in statutes or regulations relating to statutes. It may be thought that reporting in those industries is therefore a product of the legal reporting constraints. In fact, the legal constraints usually evolved from regulators' perceptions of the needs of financial statement users. Thus, the approaches to reporting in an industry are still directly traceable to the objectives of financial reporting and to the qualitative criteria as applied to the possible alternative measurement methods.

This chapter demonstrates how financial reporting is adapted to meet the needs of a particular industry. The intent is to illustrate application of concepts discussed in the previous chapter, rather than to study extractive industries and mutual funds per se.

A. EXTRACTIVE INDUSTRIES

The extractive industries are key components of the Canadian economy. Canada is a major producer of petroleum and natural gas, and one of the major international mining countries. Virtually all of the large international mining companies are active in Canada, mining a vast array of metals and minerals.

Characteristics of the Business

In general, companies in the extractive industries require large amounts of capital invested over long periods of time in order to earn a return. It may take two to fifteen years of exploratory and development work before a mine or an oil field begins to pay off. Enormous costs are incurred during this period of time, and capital must be raised to cover the costs. In the past, large on-going mining companies have relied primarily on internally generated funds to finance exploration and development, supplemented by occasional new stock issues. In recent years, however, mineral deposits have become more difficult and more expensive to find, and the yields have tended to be lower. The industry has had to turn to external debt financing in order to raise the necessary capital. The interest costs arising from debt financing frequently are substantial; moreover, the debt finances exploration and development activities that are not yet producing revenue to cover the costs of servicing the debt.

Much Canadian exploration and development is carried out, not by the large continuing companies, but rather by **junior mining companies**. A junior mining company is one that is engaged in exploration activity in only one or a small number of properties, normally has no operating income because its properties are in the exploration or development stage, and frequently has partners to assist with the development phase. Junior mining companies rely heavily on share capital for financing initial development. Sometimes the share capital is provided by larger companies or by individuals who have extensive interests in other mining companies. More often, however, the shares of such junior mining companies are issued in the public markets to individuals who are willing to invest in highly speculative shares. Once engineering appraisals have established the economic feasibility of the site beyond a reasonable doubt, debt financing will normally be arranged (usually through a bank) to finance further development to the production stage.

Some exploration and development activities will turn out to be completely unproductive. A recent example is the opening of a gold mine in northern Ontario. The actual yield from the ore was only half of the expected yield: twenty-seven tons of ore had to be processed in order to obtain one ounce of gold. At an average production cost of over $1,300 per ounce, the mine proved to be uneconomical and was closed the next year.

The products that are extracted are international commodities. Prices are governed mainly by world-wide supply and demand. The prices tend to be quite volatile, adding another component of risk to the industry. Furthermore, the prices are usually quoted internationally in U.S. dollars, adding the risk of exchange rate change. Mining companies frequently have production and sales contracts with major companies, but the prices in these contracts are usually subject to adjustment if the contract price gets too far out of line with the world price.

What offsets the price risk is the fact that in mining, buyers are usually available; no special marketing is necessary. However, oversupply, in which a mining company cannot sell its output and must suspend operations, sometimes occurs. Operations are also subject to suspension when the price of the commodity falls below the marginal cost of extracting it at a particular site.

In the case of gold mining, the price risk can also be offset by obtaining bank financing through **gold loans**. A gold loan is a loan that is extended in terms of the current monetary equivalent in a fixed amount of gold. When the mine goes into production, the borrower repays the loan by delivering gold to the bank. In addition to protecting the borrower from the risk of a decline in the price of gold, gold loans are also advantageous because they carry a low interest rate; since gold is assumed to be a hedge against inflation, the interest rate does not include the inflation component.

Each extraction site is unique. The costs incurred for development and operation are different for every site, as are both the extent of the underground reserves and the yield of the ore body. Furthermore, there is no relationship between the cost of acquiring and developing a site and the value of its assets. Although costs are incurred in order to generate revenue, there is no direct relationship between the level of costs and the level of revenue generated, as there is in manufacturing.

Eventually, the reserves at every site run out, or become too expensive to extract. When this happens, any remaining unrecovered costs must be accounted for somehow. In addition, there are frequently new costs incurred at the end of a site's life to return it to its original condition. The costs of reclamation can be substantial, and are incurred at a time when there are no offsetting revenues being generated from that site.

Objectives of Financial Reporting

Mining is a risky business. The demand for the commodities is highly cyclical, and the prices are volatile. The costs, however, are large and are incurred well in advance of production. Because of the high level of cyclicality, reporting had tended in the past to be very conservative and to emphasize the liquidity position of the company.

However, the increasing need for external debt and equity financing has tended to shift the focus of financial reporting away from liquidity and stewardship towards performance evaluation and cash flow prediction. Investors and creditors need to be able to predict whether the company will be able to generate sufficient cash flows in order to pay its obligations, finance its continued operation, and return dividends to the shareholders. Thus, public reporting has in recent years emphasized information to aid users in making their predictions.

The nature of the ownership and operations of an individual company will affect the reporting policies adopted to meet users' needs. Policies that are suitable for a large, public company operating several sites in several countries may not be suitable for a small, private company that is developing a single mine.

Taxation of companies in the extractive industries is complex, and there are many regulations and special policies relating to these companies. The income tax is seldom affected by the accounting policies adopted, and therefore tax deferral is seldom a major objective.

Asset Valuation

One of the fundamental problems in accounting for companies in the extractive industries is the valuation of assets. In most industries, there is a relationship between the cost of productive assets and the value of production obtained from their use. No one would buy automatic packaging machines, for example, if their value was not sufficient to recover the cost of the machines. A company would not spend $5,000 to equip a truck with a device that would save one litre of gasoline a month. In the long run, productive equipment must be profitable to use or it will not have a market and will not be produced. Therefore, accountants attempt to match the costs of productive equipment with the revenues generated in order to see whether the company is operating efficiently and profitably.

In mining and in oil and gas exploration, however, there is only a vague relationship between the costs of developing an exploration site and the value of production from that site. The value of the ore body or oil field is the present value of the future net revenue that will result from extraction. Large exploration and development expenditures at one location may yield only a marginal future return, while small expenditures at another location may result in a huge return. Indeed, it is one of the ironies of the industry that the harder it is to develop a site, the lower the prospective returns are likely to be.

The performance of a continuing company is a combination of its ability to operate its existing sites efficiently (and sell the output) and to find new reserves to replace the old. In order to evaluate either the past performance of the company or to predict future cash flows, statement readers need information about the value of reserves, rather than just the cost of developing them. The importance of estimates of future potential is apparent from the strong reaction of the stock market to the shares of a company that announces a major new strike or discovery.

Even for a company that has only a single mine, the value of the asset is possibly the most important single piece of information the statement reader would need. The value of the shareholders' investment (in case they wanted

Specific Accounting and Reporting Issues

to sell their interest) and the future cash flow potential would be implied by the present value of the future output of the mine.

Obviously, however, there are considerable problems with measuring the value of the reserves. The total potential yield of the site, the timing of production, the future selling prices and production costs, and an appropriate interest rate would all have to be estimated. The relevance of the information is indisputable, but there is no way to measure it that adequately satisfies the other qualitative criteria of verifiability, reliability, and freedom from bias.

In a private company, relevance may be permitted to take precedence over objectivity. It may be possible to incorporate estimates of the value of a mine or an oil field directly into the statements, as long as the determinants of that value are disclosed.

An attempt to provide similar information for comparative purposes among public oil companies is the **reserve recognition accounting (RRA)** required by the Securities and Exchange Commission in the United States for publicly traded oil companies. The companies must take their *proven* reserves, project the production level, determine net revenues at *current* selling prices and production costs, and discount the net revenues at 10%. The result is not a real measure of present value, but does provide a means of intercompany comparison that takes into account the level of reserves, the rate of production, and the different revenue-cost structures of individual companies.

Exploration and Development Costs

As noted earlier, there are many up-front costs of exploration and development for new resources. It may take years to get a newly discovered deposit or oil field into production. All of the costs of exploring, developing, and financing the pre-production activities are incurred in anticipation of obtaining a profitable return once production starts. A major accounting issue in the extractive industries is how to account for the pre-production costs.

There are two basic alternatives. One is simply to treat the exploration and development (ED) costs as expenses in the period of expenditure. The second is to accumulate and defer the costs until production begins, and then amortize or expense the expenditures. There are two general approaches under the deferral alternative, popularly known as "successful efforts" versus "full cost." Amortization can be either by units of production or by a time-based method, usually straight-line. The alternative accounting policies for ED costs can be summarized as follows:

1. Immediate expensing
2. Accumulate and defer
   a. Successful efforts
      i. Units-of-production amortization
      ii. Time-based amortization
   b. Full cost
      i. Units-of-production amortization
      ii. Time-based amortization

Immediate expensing is simple and understandable. It yields a net income figure that is much closer to cash flow than any variants of the deferral alternative. It avoids making any assumptions about the future viability of the site. Obviously, management thinks that the expenditures will pay off or they would not be making them, but no asset values are built up as a result. In a company that is continuously developing new locations, cash flow prediction may be aided by a policy of immediate expensing since the expenditures are continuous (although not necessarily at a constant level) and are a normal part of the operating cash flow of the company.

In addition to being relevant, the net income under the first alternative is nonarbitrary because it does not reflect any arbitrary allocations of cost. When a site finally goes into operation, the effects of management's decision to go ahead with production will have a direct impact on the earnings of the company. Production is warranted as long as the selling price of the commodity is high enough to cover the marginal cost of production. The sunk costs of ED are irrelevant to the decision. But if the ED costs have been deferred, amortization of these costs once production has begun will make the operation look less profitable than it really is in terms of its impact on current and future cash flows. If the marginal revenues from operating a mine exceed the marginal cost, the mine should continue to be operated. But if costs are deferred and amortized, a mine could appear to be unprofitable when, in fact, marginal revenues continue to exceed marginal costs.

In a company with a single mining project, however, a policy of immediate expensing will result in a long string of losses and a huge deficit position for the company. The venture will appear to be highly unprofitable, when, in fact, the revenue-generating operations have not even begun. In those circumstances, it would seem to make more sense to attempt to match the pre-production costs with the revenues from operations. Once the site has been developed and is in operation, no more ED costs will be incurred and the past costs can be allocated arbitrarily but unambiguously to the periods of production. Thus what is relevant for a large company with continuing exploration may be irrelevant for a small company with only a single site and a limited life.

The distinction between successful efforts and full cost is relevant only for companies that have mines or oil reserves in different locations. Under the deferral alternative for ED costs, companies can choose to view all of their activities as a single broad undertaking, and allocate all ED costs to production, whether or not the exploration and development activities at specific sites led to productive mines or fields. The reasoning is that some exploration is bound to be fruitless, and going down blind alleys is a part of the cost of finding productive reserves. This is called the full-cost method.

On the other hand, some companies choose to accumulate costs by site or geological area, and write off the accumulated costs if the project is abandoned. This is the successful-efforts approach: only the costs of successful projects are carried as assets and amortized against the revenues generated by those projects. Note that the successful-efforts approach is not applied to specific wells or shafts. A number of dry holes will be drilled by an oil company in the process of defining the limits of an oil field. The costs of drilling these holes are part of the cost of the successful effort, and are not written off as being individual unsuccessful efforts.

Under the successful-efforts approach, there is considerable latitude in defining the geographic areas and in developing amortization methods. There is also flexibility in the timing of the declaration as to when an exploration effort is unsuccessful. This flexibility permits management some latitude to determine the year in which the costs relating to unsuccessful efforts are charged against income. Thus accounting measurements made using the successful-efforts method are apt to be the most arbitrary of the alternatives. In terms of the qualitative criteria, successful efforts is the weakest method.

There is no evidence to indicate that investors find one method of allocation better than any other. As long as the current amount of ED expenditures is disclosed, they can see the cash flow impact of exploration and development and can adjust to a cash flow basis of measuring income if they so desire.

Abandonment

When the marginal cost of production exceeds the current and foreseeable market price of the commodity, production is stopped. This is frequently called an abandonment, although in most cases the mine or field is not really abandoned, but simply shut down. If the market price revives, production may be started up again. The most dramatic instance of mines being re-opened occurred after the United States removed its currency from the gold standard and the price of gold was permitted to rise above $35 U.S. Free market gold prices of several hundred dollars caused the reopening of many gold mines that had been abandoned decades earlier.

Each mine is unique, and the physical structures of a mine cannot be moved. A question arises as to whether the undepreciated cost of the mine structures should be written off, along with any unamortized ED costs (if the full-cost method is not being used). Most frequently, undepreciated and unamortized costs are written off because it has been decided that the mine does not have future benefits, and the cost therefore cannot be carried as an asset.

The impact on the financial statements of closing a mine and writing off the assets may tempt management not to close down operations that are not economically viable. The impact on net income may be less if the mine is continued in operation. If the accounting treatment accorded to mines that are being closed is not consistent with the economic realities of operating the mine, then the accounting measurement is not faithful to the reality that it is attempting to measure. The objectives of performance evaluation, stewardship, and cash flow prediction are not served by unfaithful (or nonisomorphic) measurements. A policy of either expensing all pre-production costs immediately (and thereby avoiding any deferred costs that might still be on the books when the mine is shut down) or deferral of pre-production costs and amortization on a full-cost basis would seem to yield measurements for mine closings that are more consistent with the economics of the situation.

Reclamation Costs

Reclamation costs are incurred at the end of the life cycle of the mine or field. The costs are incurred after no more revenue is being generated, and matching is a problem. In a large company with continuing activities, the costs could be expensed as incurred, as a normal cost of continuing operations on a broad scale. Expensing reclamation costs when incurred is consistent with a policy of expensing ED when incurred.

In a single-site company, however, all of the net revenues could have been distributed as dividends, with nothing left over for the reclamation costs. Therefore, it may seem appropriate to accumulate an estimated liability for these costs, at least in the later years of production, as the mine is winding down and the reserves are being exhausted. Performance evaluation may be impaired, however, if reclamation reserves are being charged to operations as an ordinary expense. The reserves may make the mine look unprofitable and may lead creditors or owners to question management's decision to continue operations. Thus the performance evaluation objective may be better served by simply making a retained earnings appropriation to restrict dividends, and if necessary, setting aside funds to pay for the reclamation.

Inventory Valuation

Most businesses value their inventories at cost, perhaps writing the cost down to "market" when the net realizable value is less than the cost. Cost is the basis of valuation because revenue has not yet been recognized. The sale of the inventory is usually not assured, and other events must occur before revenue can be recognized.

In some businesses, however, the sale of inventory is assured once it has been produced, although the price may be subject to fluctuation. Commodities that are traded on public markets, and thus are always saleable, require no effort greater than a telephone call to sell. Copper, for example, can easily be sold. The value of an inventory of copper can readily be measured, and the measurement is verifiable, reliable, and free from bias. The value may be different on the next day, of course, but at any point in time, the inventory has a measurable net realizable value.

When inventories can be readily sold at any time at a known market price, it is possible to recognize revenue when the inventory is ready for sale rather than when it is actually sold. Management may choose not to sell the inventory at that price, but may hold back the commodity in hope that the price will rise. Such a hold-back strategy is a speculative activity that is related to, but separable from, the production activity. Therefore, the objective of performance appraisal may best be served by recognizing revenue at the time of production, and isolating changes in the value of the inventory after production as unrealized gains or losses. Performance appraisal is enhanced because the results of speculation are disclosed separately from the results of production operations, and because early recognition of revenue helps users to see the economic results (whether fully realized or not) of the current period's production activities.

Some mining companies do report part, or all, of their inventories on a market value or net realizable value basis. The 1983 annual report of Northair Mines Ltd., for example, stated that

> concentrate inventories are recorded at estimated net realizable value which is based on the most current information available with regards to weight, assays, metal prices and foreign exchange. In accordance with the terms of the sales contracts, final settlements are made at prices prevailing at a future date and the amounts eventually received by the company may vary from the amounts shown.

A large company with diversified mining interests would tend to report inventories at cost, more in keeping with a stewardship approach to reporting. A smaller company, or a private company, may place more emphasis on performance appraisal as a reporting objective and may value inventories at market rather than at cost.

Flow-Through Shares

Certain industries frequently spawn unique business practices, practices that have no parallel in general business operations and that therefore have no precedents. As we discussed in Chapter 1, innovative business practices require accountants to apply professional judgment to develop accounting and reporting approaches.

In the extractive industries, one such unique business practice is the issuance of **flow-through shares**. A creation of the *Income Tax Act*, flow-through shares are common shares in a resource company that permit the tax deductibility of exploration and development costs to flow through to the investor who purchases the shares in its initial offering. The company gives up the tax deduction, but the investor gains it. Flow-through shares are very useful for companies that do not have sufficient taxable income to be able to use the tax deduction for their full ED costs. Since they cannot get the benefit, it makes sense to pass the benefit on to someone who can. The purchaser of the shares therefore is buying two things when he or she buys the shares: (1) a tradable common share and (2) a tax deduction. Investors are willing to pay for the tax deduction, and therefore flow-through shares usually sell at a higher price than the shares without the tax deduction. Flow-through shares enable the issuing company to get some benefit from the tax deduction indirectly through an enhanced share price, even though they cannot use the deduction directly.

As the discussion above implies, flow-through shares are of little interest to companies that have a healthy profit flow; they can use the tax deduction themselves. The real intent of flow-through shares is to assist the many junior mining companies that carry out a substantial portion of Canada's mineral exploration. Since these companies have no income from continuing operations, there usually is an active share issue program to provide funds for operations. By creating flow-through shares, the government has improved the attractiveness of the shares of these small companies to high-tax-bracket investors.

Since the issuing company can sell flow-through shares at a higher price than regular shares, an accounting issue has arisen as to how to account for the premium received. One approach is to simply credit the full amount of the proceeds to the capital stock account. The other approach is to separate the basic value of the shares from the tax-deductibility premium; the basic share value would be credited to the capital stock account and the premium would be deducted from the deferred ED costs. The premium is deducted from deferred ED because the company has given up the tax deduction relating to the ED costs, and therefore the value of the ED costs is less than it would be if the tax deductibility remained intact. Not only will the deferred ED costs be overstated relative to ED costs with their tax deductibility intact, but future income will be understated as the higher costs are amortized against revenues when the mining properties become productive.

For larger mining companies that have continuing operations, the allocation of the premium to ED costs has considerable support. The authors of one article, for example, state that this is clearly a more appropriate manner of accounting than the method that credits the full proceeds of the share issue to capital stock.[1] For junior mining companies, however, circumstances may be different. A CICA research study states that

---

[1] M. Barry Dent and John G. Jakolev, "Flow-through Shares, A New Financing Source for the Resource Industry," *CA Magazine*, (April 1985), pp. 22-26.

In the Study Group's opinion, the premium should not be treated separately from share capital. This treatment is proposed because the premium is largely a result of market forces and does not usually correspond directly to the value to the company of the tax benefits given up or the value to the investor of the tax deductions. The premium relates largely to the perceived risk to the investor of fluctuations in price . . .[2]

The study group feels that for junior mining companies, the value of the premium is only vaguely related to the value of the tax deductibility of the deferred ED costs, and therefore there is little point to offsetting one against the other. The Study Group's recommended treatment would have the impact of increasing amortization and reducing net income in the future, however. Although the Study Group is expressing an opinion that is a part of GAAP, it does not rule out other alternatives. GAAP still states that either treatment could be used.

One problem that frequently arises in trying to apply the approach of crediting the premium to deferred ED costs is that of measuring the premium. The premium can be measured only in relation to the value of shares issued or traded without the premium. If the market for the shares is very thin and volatile, then it is difficult or impossible to reliably measure the premium.

Illustrative Statements

An example of the financial statements for a junior mining company is presented at the end of this section of the chapter, in Schedule 3-1. McNellen Resources is a gold mining company incorporated in British Columbia. The company's original property is in the Mount Foley area of British Columbia; in 1987, there was no work done on this property, although "there have been recommendations for a work program," according to the 1987 annual report. There is development work underway on the Magino Joint Venture, an Ontario project in which McNellen Resources is a 50% joint venture partner; the other partner is Muscocho Explorations Ltd., who also functions as Project Operator and as the corporate administrator of McNellen Resources.

As we discussed earlier in this chapter, it is common for mining companies to capitalize all ED costs because these costs will be matched against future revenues, if the properties turn out to be worth developing. In a large mining company, the unsuccessful projects can be offset against the successful ones, so that even though a particular exploration may be unsuccessful, there is reasonable assurance for the company as a whole that the exploration program will recover its costs and therefore the deferred ED costs can be shown as an asset.

In junior mining companies, the activity is much riskier. There is a high rate of failure in exploration, so that the deferral of exploration costs is more an act of faith than for large companies; a certain amount of work has to be done before it becomes apparent whether the site will be economically viable or not. While the exploration is going on, the ED costs will be capitalized until it becomes apparent that it will not be worthwhile to develop the claim. If the claim turns out to be uneconomical, then the deferred ED costs will be written off and, quite often, the company will be liquidated.

Since the sole activity of a junior mining company is the exploration of

2 *Accounting and Financial Reporting by Junior Mining Companies*, a CICA Research Study (CICA, 1988), p. 51.

one or a very few mining claims, it is common practice to defer recognition of *all* operating costs, including interest costs and administrative costs. After all, if the entire activity of the company is directed at developing one site, then it is clear that all of the costs of running the company relate to that future revenue-generating (hopefully) property, and deferral of all costs can be justified. If all costs are deferred, then investment income can be offset against those costs, so that there are neither revenues nor expenses to be reported in the current period. If there are no revenues and expenses, then there is no need for an income statement. Therefore, it is common to find no income statement amongst the financial statements of a junior mining company.

The CICA Study Group surveyed the financial reporting of 115 junior mining companies, and found that 40 did not provide an income statement.[3] The lack of income statements is noteworthy because the *CICA Handbook* explicitly recommends that an income statement be provided [par. 1500.03]. Clearly the companies' managers believe that the activities of a junior mining company are sufficiently distinct that the *Handbook* recommendation is not applicable, and their auditors concur. This is an example of general-purpose GAAP not applying to the particular nature of an industry.

McNellen Resources does, in fact, provide an income statement. The statement reports income from investments less administrative expenses, for a loss of $151,111 in 1987. The company currently defers part of its administrative expenses; $151,207 was charged to deferred development and $190,768 was left on the income statement. Note 2 points out that non-deferral is new; in previous years the administrative expenses were all deferred. The change in accounting policy caused the Retained Earnings to go from a credit of $682,642 to a deficit of $750,718.

On the balance sheet, the dominant asset is the Deferred Exploration and Development Expenditures, which constitutes 83% of total assets. Liabilities are small, only 9% of total assets, and most of those are to the company's joint venture partner. Since deferred ED costs reflect the dominant activities of the company, it is normal for junior mining companies to present a special statement that reflects those activities. McNellen Resources does present a statement of deferred exploration and development expenditures, in which the changes in each of the two properties during the year are shown. The statement does not show the nature of the expenditures, nor does it explain the nature of the "Decreases during year" for the Ontario property; these are not shown as write-downs on the income statement or on the statement of deficit, and so they may have been a transfer of costs to the joint venture partner.

Note 6 shows the activity in the capital stock account. During fiscal year 1987, the company issued shares with an assigned value of over $4.1 million. Some of the shares were issued for services rendered, and some were issued for cash, but the bulk of the new shares (almost 90%) were flow-through shares. About 1.6 million shares were issued with an assigned value of over $3.6 million (the sum of two different lines in Note 6: $1,571,463 + $2,072,905).

McNellen Resources does segregate the premium from the base price and credits the premium to deferred ED costs. Although only $3.6 million was

3 *Accounting and Financial Reporting by Junior Mining Companies*, p.6.

credited to the capital stock account, Note 7 reveals that the total proceeds from the shares were over $4.5 million. About 19% of the proceeds were credited to deferred ED, which represents a premium of 23% over the base price of the shares. This is a fairly large premium for a junior mining company; small mining companies usually experience premiums in the 10-20% range.[4] Note 6(c) discloses that additional flow-through shares were issued for $518,494 subsequent to the balance sheet date.

Summary: Extractive Industries

The extractive industries have been used to illustrate how objectives of financial reporting and the qualitative characteristics of accounting information have an impact on the selection of accounting policies for an entire industry. We have focused mainly on the mining industry, although the oil and gas industry has also been considered.

Given the nature of the mining industry, we have seen that many more costs can be deferred than is normal in manufacturing enterprises. For research and development costs, GAAP leans toward the approach of "when in doubt, expense it," whereas the tendency for exploration and development costs in the extractive industries is quite the opposite; ED costs are deferred unless it is clear that there will be no production on the site, and even then deferral will occur if the accounting policy is one of full cost. Even administrative costs can be deferred, a practice that is rarely followed in other industries.

Certain industries sometimes give rise to unique business methods. The use of flow-through shares is an example in the extractive industries. Unusual business methods require innovation in accounting, and professional judgment must be brought to bear on the problem.

The nature of an industry can even cause a change in the basic set of financial statements. Junior mining companies may have no need for an income statement, but a statement of changes in the deferred ED costs, on a property-by-property basis, is a very useful statement. In part B of this chapter, we look at another example of an industry that requires changes in its basic set of financial statements.

One aspect of financial reporting that has been repeatedly emphasized is the fact that the nature of operations and the nature of the stakeholder group can significantly affect the selection of accounting policies. The policies that are suitable for a large, continuing mining company may be unsuitable for a small, single-project mining company. Similarly, a public company with debt financing will have stakeholders with somewhat different concerns and objectives than will a private company without debt financing.

We could have also discussed many other industries in Canada in this example. Real estate development companies, insurance companies, loan and trust companies, chartered banks, franchisers, high-tech companies, and so forth, all have special characteristics that affect financial reporting. Financial reporting for any industry must take into account the information needs of statement users and all possible qualitative characteristics of the measurements.

4 *Accounting and Financial Reporting by Junior Mining Companies*, p. 51.

SCHEDULE 3-1

McNellan Resources, Inc.
(Incorporated under the laws of British Columbia)
Balance Sheet as at June 30, 1987

	1987	1986
ASSETS		
Current Assets		
Cash	$ 70,837	$ 6,017
Accounts receivable	847	
Deposit with investment dealer	204,869	
Funds held in trust for shares to be issued (note 6(c))	300,000	
	576,553	6,017
Investments, at lower of cost and market value		11,163
Mining claims and properties (notes 3 and 4)	90,142	56,894
Deferred exploration and development expenditures (notes 2, 3 and 4)	5,147,678	1,703,470
Fixed assets (notes 3 and 5)	397,450	79,291
Other assets	2,018	
Incorporation costs		1,014
	$6,213,841	$1,857,849
LIABILITIES		
Current liabilities		
Accounts payable and accrued liabilities	$ 91,915	$ 108,165
Payable to Muscocho Explorations Ltd.	493,804	374,569
	585,719	482,734
SHAREHOLDERS' EQUITY		
Capital Stock (note 6)		
Authorized		
5,000,000 Preferred shares with a par value of $1 per share		
40,000,000 Common shares without nominal or par value		
Issued		
9,735,498 Common shares (6,272,610 shares in 1986)	6,058,840	1,954,722
100,000 shares to be issued (note 6(c))	300,000	
Contributed Surplus	20,000	20,000
Deficit	(750,718)	(599,607)
	5,628,122	1,375,115
	$6,213,841	$1,857,849

SCHEDULE 3-1 (continued)

McNellan Resources, Inc.
Statement of Income
Year Ended June 30, 1987

	1987	1986
Income		
Gain (loss) on sale of investments	$ 32,096	$ (4,499)
Gain on sale of mining claims		14,707
Interest	7,561	
	39,657	10,208
Expenses		
Salaries	135,723	90,444
Office rent	32,348	39,160
Professional and trust company fees	93,539	42,983
Travel	14,177	7,496
Shareholder information	26,969	9,191
Depreciation	2,607	1,402
Licences and taxes	9,379	4,244
Miscellaneous	7,337	3,084
Oil leases written off	19,896	
Mining claims written off		26,048
	341,975	224,052
Deduct amount charged to deferred development	151,207	
	190,768	224,052
Loss for the year	$151,111	$213,844
Loss per share	2¢	4¢

McNellan Resources, Inc.
Statement of Deficit (Retained Earnings)
Year Ended June 30, 1987

	1987	1986
Balance at beginning of year		
Retained earnings, as previously reported	$ (682,642)	$ (698,482)
Adjustment to reflect change in accounting for administrative expenses (note 2)	1,282,249	1,084,245
Deficit, as restated	599,607	385,763
Loss for the year	151,111	213,844
Deficit at end of year	$ 750,718	$ 599,607

SCHEDULE 3-1 (continued)

McNellan Resources, Inc.
Statement of Changes in Financial Position
Year Ended June 30, 1987

	1987	1986
Cash provided by (used for):		
Operations		
Loss for the year	$ 151,111	$213,844
Items not involving cash		
Interest in oil leases written off	(19,896)	
Gain (loss) on sale of investments	32,096	(4,499)
Organization expense written off	(1,014)	
Depreciation	(2,607)	(1,402)
Mining claims written off		(26,048)
Gain on sale of mining claims		14,707
	(159,690)	(196,602)
Change in non-cash working capital	102,138	276,125
	(57,552)	79,523
Financing		
Issue of common shares		
For professional services	10,500	
For cash	399,250	84,209
Issue of flow-through shares	4,508,999	
For acquisition of mining claims		50,250
Shares issued in connection with flow-through share financing	50,000	
Funds received for shares to be issued	300,000	
Repayment of shareholder loans		174,256
Government grants	22,613	
	5,291,362	308,715
Investments		
Exploration and development expenditures net of depreciation expense	(4,316,569)	(357,036)
Acquisition of portfolio investments		(11,162)
Proceeds on sale of portfolio investments	43,260	
Acquisition of mining claims	(33,248)	(71,250)
Acquisition of interest in oil leases	(19,896)	
Proceeds on sale of mining claims		58,705
Investment tax credits recovered		1,398
Acqusition of other assets	(2,018)	
Purchase of fixed assets	(335,650)	
	(4,664,121)	(379,345)
Increase in cash position	569,689	8,893
Cash position at beginning of year	6,017	(2,876)
*Cash position at end of year	$ 575,706	$ 6,017

*Cash position is defined as cash, deposit with investment dealer and funds held in trust.

SCHEDULE 3-1 (continued)

McNellan Resources, Inc.
Statement of Deferred Exploration
and Development Expenditures
Year Ended June 30, 1987

	Balance beginning of year	Increases during year	Decreases during year	Balance end of year
1987				
Ontario	$1,127,442	$3,466,228	$22,613	$4,571,057
British Columbia	576,028	593		576,621
	$1,703,470	$3,466,821	$22,613	$5,147,678
1986				
Ontario	$ 751,718	$ 440,724	$65,000	$1,127,442
British Columbia	575,762	266		576,028
	$1,327,480	$ 440,990	$65,000	$1,703,470

McNellan Resources, Inc.
Notes to Financial Statements
Year Ended June 30, 1987

1. ACCOUNTING POLICIES

(a) Deferred exploration and development expenditures
Deferred exploration and development expenditures incurred in the acquisition and exploration of the company's mining properties net of option payments and government grants received, have been deferred with the intention that the deferred expenditures and the cost of the mining claims and properties be amortized by charges against income from future mining operations. If the mining claims are allowed to lapse or the properties are abandoned, the cost of the mining claims and all associated exploration and development expenditures are written off.

(b) Mining claims
Mining claims are stated at cost or assigned values.

(c) Fixed assets
Fixed assets are recorded at cost. Depreciation is provided on the following basis:
Office furniture and other assets — 20% and 30% declining balance
Magino joint venture assets   — 20% declining balance

(d) Flow-through common shares
Proceeds on flow-through common shares issued or to be issued (which transfer the tax deductibility of exploration expenditures to the investor) that are designated as premiums for such tax deductions are applied to reduce deferred exploration expenditures or general exploration expenditures, depending on the nature of the original expenditure.

SCHEDULE 3-1 (continued)

2. ACCOUNTING CHANGE

The company has changed its method of accounting for administrative expenses. Such expenses formerly charged to deferred expenditures are now being charged against income. As a result of this change, which has been applied retroactively, the loss for 1987 is increased by $163,311, the loss for 1986 is increased by $198,004 and the cumulative effect to July 1, 1986 is reflected as a decrease to retained earnings at that date.

3. RECOVERY OF COSTS

The recovery of the cost of mining claims and properties, deferred exploration and development expenditures and fixed assets is dependent upon obtaining adequate financing and the development of economic mining operations.

4. MINING CLAIMS AND PROPERTIES

(a) Ontario

Magino Property

Exploration and development of the property is being carried out under a joint venture agreement with Muscocho Explorations Limited. Each company has a 50% interest in the property and share equally in the exploration and development expenditures.

(b) Quebec

Pursuant to an agreement dated February 21, 1986 the Company acquired an option to purchase mining claims located in Dieppe Township in the Province of Quebec. In order to complete the acquisition of the claims a further $12,500 is payable in 1987. In addition, $40,000 is payable on or before March 10, 1988 and $50,000 is payable on or before March 10, 1989.

The Company entered into two agreements for the sale of portion of the mining claims referred to above. The option payments required in 1987 were not made.

5. FIXED ASSETS

	1987			1986
	Cost	Accumulated depreciation	Net book value	Net book value
Head office				
Office furniture and other assets	$ 23,322	$13,410	$ 9,912	$ 4,869
Magino joint venture				
Construction in progress	328,000		328,000	
Machinery and equipment	42,788	25,560	17,228	21,535
Power substation	56,204	33,617	22,587	28,234
Trailers	38,446	22,699	15,747	19,683
Automotive	7,766	3,790	3,976	4,970
	$496,526	$99,076	$397,450	$79,291

SCHEDULE 3-1 (continued)

6. CAPITAL STOCK

	Number of shares	Amount
Outstanding as at June 30, 1985	2,224,280	$1,646,007
Issued on repayment of shareholder advances together with accrued interest	697,025	174,256
Issued on acquisition of mining claims (note 4)		
Finan Township, Ontario	35,000	26,250
Dieppe Township, Quebec (option)	20,000	24,000
Issued for cash	150,000	76,709
Issued for cash on exercise of employee and director stock options	10,000	7,500
Outstanding as at June 30, 1986	3,136,305	$1,954,722
Exercise of employee and director stock options	134,000	100,500
Issued for cash	208,333	250,000
Issued for finder's fee in connection with share financing	41,667	50,000
Issue of flow-through shares (note 7)	931,208	1,571,463
Exercise of rights	75,000	48,750
	4,526,513	3,975,435
Subdivision of shares on the basis of 2 for 1	4,526,513	
	9,053,026	3,975,435
Issued for professional services	3,500	10,500
Issue of flow-through shares (note 7)	678,972	2,072,905
Outstanding as at June 30, 1987	9,735,498	$6,058,840

(a) Subdivision of shares

Pursuant to shareholder approval on December 18, 1986 the company's shares were subdivided on the basis of 2 new shares for each old share. Shares outstanding at June 30, 1986 have been restated to reflect the subdivision.

(b) Options to purchase common shares

Under a directors' and employees' incentive options plan to purchase common shares of the company as approved by the shareholders on December 18, 1986, options have been granted to directors and employees to purchase a total of 920,000 common shares of the company's capital stock at a price of $2.85 per share exercisable on or before February 1, 1992.

During the year options to purchase a total of 134,000 shares (1986, 10,000) for $100,500 (1986, $7,500) were exercised under the previous plan. Options on the remaining 39,000 shares outstanding at June 30, 1986 were cancelled.

(c) Subsequent issue of common shares

Subsequent to the date of the balance sheet the company issued 104,154 common shares for $518,494 under a flow-through share agreement and 100,000 shares to Muscocho Explorations Ltd. for the funds held in trust at June 30, 1987.

SCHEDULE 3-1 (continued)

7. FLOW-THROUGH SHARES
    Issues of flow-through shares were accounted for as follows:

Reduction in exploration and development expenditures	$ 864,632
Increase in common stock	3,644,367
Total proceeds	$4,508,999

    The company has entered into exploration agreements with seven mineral partnerships whereby the company is required to incur a maximum of $12.5 million of exploration expenditures on behalf of the partnerships. The partnerships are required to reimburse the company for such expenditures and as consideration the company will issue a maximum of approximately 2.5 million flow-through common shares to the partnerships, subject to regulatory approval. In addition, the company has entered into an exploration agreement for $2 million dollars in 1988.

8. COMMITMENT
    Subsequent to June 30, 1987 the company entered into a contract in conjunction with its joint venture partner, Muscocho Explorations Ltd. to construct a cyanidation test mill. The company's share of the total contract costs amount to $2,650,000.

B. MUTUAL FUNDS

Nature of the Business

An investment company is a company that accepts funds from investors, issues its own shares (if incorporated) or participation units (if unincorporated) in return, and invests the funds in a securities portfolio. Most investment companies stand ready to accept new funds (and issue new shares) at any time, and will also redeem investors' shares at any time on short notice. Such investment companies are known as **open-end** investment companies because participation in the fund is constantly open to investors and the number of shares to be issued is unlimited. The popular term for open-end companies is **mutual fund**, and that is what we will call them in the remainder of this chapter.

Closed-end investment companies, by contrast, have a limited amount of share capital and neither issue nor redeem shares on demand. Like other corporations, a closed-end company issues its shares in discrete offerings. An investor in a publicly traded, closed-end investment company earns a return through dividends and capital gains from market appreciation of the shares. In contrast, mutual fund shares are not traded; share dealings are with the company and not with other traders.

An investor in a mutual fund earns a return through dividends and through increases in the shares' redemption value. The redemption value is determined on the basis of the **net asset value** of the fund. The net asset value is determined by subtracting the fund's liabilities from the market value of its assets, and dividing by the number of fund shares outstanding. The net asset value per share is the price at which new shares may be purchased or outstanding shares redeemed, subject in some funds to a premium on purchase (front-end loading) or, in rare instances, a discount on redemption.

Mutual funds invest mainly in publicly traded securities (stocks or bonds), although investment in private placements and individual loans can be made. The investment policies of mutual funds must be publicly declared. As different investors have different investment objectives, so do mutual funds embody different objectives to serve specific investor communities. A fund may be growth oriented or income oriented, or balanced. A growth-oriented fund strives to achieve a return for its shareholders by investing for capital gains. An income-oriented fund stresses investments that will yield a high level of dividends and interest, which can then be distributed to shareholders as dividends. Some funds are bond funds, focusing on a portfolio of bonds, while others are strictly equity funds. A balanced fund attempts to achieve both income and growth, and invests in both bonds and stocks, as market conditions warrant.

Very few mutual funds borrow money to help finance the investment portfolio. Financial leverage can be obtained by investing in shares of companies with high leverage, rather than by levering the mutual fund's portfolio directly. In addition, individual investors in the fund can lever their own portfolios. Levered mutual funds tend to be very risky, given the amplifying effect of debt on fluctuations in the net asset value per share.

Financial Statement Objectives

The primary users of the financial statements of mutual funds are clearly present and prospective investors. The value of investors' shares in the fund is determined directly as a result of financial information. Evaluation of the performance of the fund and of fund management is essential to investors' participation in the fund and investors' choices as to alternative mutual funds or other investments. Therefore, performance evaluation becomes the major objective of financial reporting for mutual funds.

Performance evaluation is consistent with an objective of stewardship reporting, if stewardship reporting is viewed at the third level cited in Chapter 2 (reporting on the disposition of assets, the earnings realized on the assets, and the skill of management in administering the assets). If viewed as only minimal reporting for legal disclosure, however, then stewardship reporting takes a back seat because the competition for investors' funds leads most mutual funds to more extensive disclosure in order to remain competitive.

Other primary users of performance evaluation are the fund managers and directors. Mutual funds are usually created and managed by securities dealers or professional investment management companies. The individuals who manage the fund do worry about their jobs; they can be fired by the management company. Investment performance is very important to the fund's management company, not only for public credibility of its competence, but also because the management fees are usually based on some measure of financial performance. Therefore, the fund's managers and directors also regard performance evaluation as an objective of financial reporting for mutual funds.

In the investment business, income tax deferral is frequently an important objective of tax planning. However, tax planning is an individual activity. Given the stated investment objectives of a mutual fund, the income tax issues are fairly clear and are not related to financial presentation in the funds' statements. Therefore, income tax deferral is not an objective to consider in financial reporting for mutual funds.

Cash flow prediction is a common objective of financial reporting. As was discussed at some length in Chapter 2, investors and creditors usually need to be able to predict the cash flows of a company in order to predict the likelihood of cash flows to themselves as investors and creditors. In mutual funds, however, the primary cash flow to the investor may be when he or she redeems the mutual fund shares. Redemption is at the option of the investor, and does not depend upon actions of management. As for creditors, since the only debt in most mutual funds' balance sheet is current debt relating to the day-to-day operations of the fund, there are normally no long-term creditors among users of financial statements. Cash flow prediction therefore is not an important objective of financial reporting for mutual funds.

Mutual fund managers are stewards in an almost classical sense. They are entrusted with large sums of money to administer for the benefit of absentee principals. There are many opportunities for abuse in mutual funds. Unscrupulous fund managers can drain substantial amounts of cash out of a fund by charging inordinately high management fees, or the fund can be used to buoy up the shares of companies controlled by the directors of the fund, or money can be invested as loans of doubtful security to other ventures of the directors and managers, and so forth.

The securities laws of each province, as well as the various acts of incorporation, define the minimal reporting requirements and specify the watchdog agency that oversees mutual funds. The securities acts generally provide that the financial details of the mutual fund be disclosed sufficiently for investors and the securities commissions to ascertain that the managers have performed as responsible stewards. For example, the *Ontario Securities Act* regulations specify that the details of the manner of setting the management fee be disclosed in the annual report, so that investors can decide whether management fees are overburdening the fund.

In summary, the primary objective of financial reporting for mutual funds is for performance evaluation, including stewardship. Investors, managers, and regulators have a common interest in the statements, although different motives. Investors are attempting to discern how well the fund is performing relative to other possible investments (including other mutual funds); managers are concerned about the competitiveness of the fund in the financial markets, about their own compensation levels, and about retaining their credibility (and their jobs) as professional investment managers; finally, the regulatory agencies are concerned that fund managers perform their jobs as responsible stewards, and that full information be disclosed to investors.

Financial Reporting Implications

It is clear that a crucial value for mutual fund managers and investors is the net asset value per share. Provincial legislation stipulates the minimum frequency of calculating the net asset value (NAV) per share (often weekly), but most major mutual funds actually calculate it daily. The NAV is directly relevant to investors' decisions, but it is difficult to interpret changes in the net asset value without additional information. An increase in the NAV may be due to accumulated dividends and interest from the portfolio, realized gains on investments and changes in the composition of the portfolio, or unrealized gains on investments. In order for investors to evaluate the performance of the fund, they need to know the factors that had an impact on NAV and changes in NAV during the period. Financial reporting for mutual funds has developed from these needs.

Balance Sheet (or Statement of Net Assets)

The **balance sheet** consists essentially of one large group of assets, the investment portfolio. Small amounts of cash and receivables are normally present, but the investments dominate. Since investors are interested in the asset **value**, the investment portfolio is shown at market value, with cost disclosed parenthetically. The value of the investments is much more relevant to performance appraisal than is the cost, since (1) the value of the funds' own shares is determined therefrom, (2) management cannot disguise poor performance of the investments by holding onto poorly performing securities, and (3) managers cannot manipulate earnings by the timing of transactions that would trigger the recognition of capital gains. It is the value of the portfolio that reflects a fund's performance, not the cost.

Few people would deny that, in general, the value of assets is more useful than their cost. But in accounting for most business enterprises, assets are reported at cost. The dominance of the cost basis of reporting is traceable to several factors. For one thing, most business assets are held for use, not for sale. When cash flow prediction is an important objective, users' needs may be better served by reporting the costs that arose from cash flows, rather than values that will not be reflected in them. For another, problems arise with the measurement of value. Verifiability, reliability, and freedom from bias are frequently difficult to achieve.

The market value of mutual fund investments, in contrast, is directly relevant to the cash flows that can be obtained by the investor. Furthermore, performance appraisal, in the form of management's investment policy, is the primary focus of financial reporting, and performance can be evaluated only if market values are known. Finally, and perhaps most importantly, most of the market values of a mutual fund's investments are readily determinable. For publicly traded securities, the published closing prices of the preceding day can be used. For issues traded less often, the price of recent trades, or the average of bid and asked prices, can be used.

Admittedly, the measurement of market values is not without its problems. Some investments are not publicly traded, and their valuation must be based on the judgment of management. For other issues, the daily quoted price is not necessarily the price that the mutual fund's block of shares would fetch. A large block, dumped unceremoniously on the market, would severely depress the price. A private placement may protect the price, but would take time to arrange, during which time the price would probably change.

Thus the market value of the assets of a mutual fund is not a precise value. It is, however, the contracted value that the investor and the fund have agreed upon in their share transactions. It also is a value that is infinitely more relevant to performance evaluation than cost is. The rather modest deficiencies in the qualitative characteristics are worthwhile trade-offs for far greater relevance.

The balance sheet is frequently titled the **statement of net assets**, as befits its role as the basic summary of the net asset position of the shareholders. An important detailed statement in support of the balance sheet is a **statement**

of investment portfolio, which lists the securities included in the portfolio. A **statement of portfolio transactions** indicates the changes in the composition of the portfolio during the year.

Most companies present their balance sheets in comparative format. The purpose of the comparison is to enable readers to see the financial position of the company the present year in relation to the last year. In mutual funds, however, the balance sheet is not a statement of financial position in the same way as it is for other enterprises. The financial condition of a mutual fund is hardly ever at question, since the current liabilities are minor and there are seldom any long-term liabilities. As stated above, the basic purpose is to support the calculation of the net asset value per share. The value of the net assets per share as compared to the last year may be quite useful to investors; the total net asset value is of doubtful relevance.

A change in the total net asset value can be the result of either increased investment value or increased participation by investors. If there is a net investment in the shares of the mutual fund during the year (that is, if more shares are issued than redeemed) the total net asset value may increase even if the financial performance of the fund caused a decrease in the net asset value per share. As a result, statutory reporting requirements for mutual funds do not require comparative reporting, except for per share amounts. Indeed, some observers have argued that comparative reporting by mutual funds is downright misleading. Nevertheless, many mutual funds do report on a one-year comparative basis. Investors are not assumed to be so naive as to be misled by comparative statements. In addition, the previous year's balance sheet gives the supporting detail for the current year's opening amount of the net asset value.

Income Statement

Generally, asset valuation is linked to revenue recognition. The point at which we choose to recognize revenue is the point at which the net asset value of the enterprise increases. Therefore, one would expect that if market values are used on the balance sheet, changes in those market values would show up on the income statement. For mutual funds, however, that is not the case. The income statement is usually called the **statement of income and expenses**, and reports the income received from dividends and interest, less the expenses of running the fund. Neither unrealized nor realized capital gains are reported on the income statement.

In a mutual fund, net income is a useful concept only insofar as it reflects income earned by the fund on behalf of the investors. The fund does not exist to generate revenues and maximize net income for the enterprise as a whole, but rather to maximize the wealth of the individual shareholders by dividend distributions and increased NAV per share. Net income from dividends and interest is only one part of the operating performance of any mutual fund, and performance as measured by the income statement is not indicative of overall performance. In a growth fund, for example, the strategy is to invest in stocks that promise a high growth rate rather than a high dividend yield. Therefore, the income statement for a growth fund may well show a net loss for the period, even though the fund may have been quite successful in achieving its investment goals.

An important basic measurement method in most financial reporting for businesses is that of matching. The income statement attempts to match the revenues recognized during the period with the costs incurred in earning those revenues. In mutual funds, however, the concept of matching is not so important. The major expenses of a mutual fund are management fees and advising fees. There is no attempt to allocate these costs to the cost of the investments, so that gains can be measured as the difference between market value and full cost of the investments. Brokerage fees and other direct transaction costs may be treated as part of the cost of specific investments, but other costs are charged directly to the statement of income and expense as period costs.

At best, the statement of income and expense only reports the fund income distributable as ordinary dividends, distinct from capital gains dividends. Since different tax treatment is accorded the two types of distributions, capital gains must be kept separate from the dividend and interest income of the fund. More fundamentally, the statement of income and expenses is simply one piece that fits into what is probably the key financial statement for a mutual fund, the **statement of changes in net assets**.

Statement of Changes in Net Assets
We pointed out earlier that a fundamental piece of information for investors is the NAV per share. It is the NAV, plus dividends received from the fund, that determines the income earned by the fund for the individual investor. It follows, therefore, that the factors affecting the NAV are of primary importance to the investor. The statement of changes in net assets summarizes all of those various factors, including the net income from dividends and interest, capital gains or losses realized on portfolio transactions, unrealized gains or losses on investments, dividends paid to investors, and the net increase or decrease in shareholders' investment.

In substance, the statement of changes in net assets is the principal financial statement for mutual funds, although its placement in annual reports would not suggest that fact. The statement of changes tends to be viewed as a supplement to the balance sheet, but in terms of information content, it is really the other way around. The balance sheet details the composition of the net assets at the beginning and end of the year, as shown in the statement of changes. The statement of investment portfolio provides additional detail on the composition of the assets, while the statement of portfolio transactions explains the changes in the investment portfolio during the year. The statement of income and expenses details the net income reported as part of the statement of changes in net assets.

One component of the statement of changes in net assets that is not disclosed in detail is the realized and unrealized gains and losses on the portfolio. Many observers have suggested that an additional statement (or an additional section of the statement of income and expenses) be used to summarize these gains and losses.

Ideally, the statement of changes in net assets should be presented on a per share basis, since the investor wants to know how the various components of the statement affect his or her investment. Per share calculations are not really very practical at that level of detail, however, since there are constant issuances and redemptions of shares that would make it difficult to allocate portfolio gains and losses and income and expenses on a per share basis. Therefore, per share figures are given only for the beginning and ending net assets, and for distributions to shareholders during the year. An investor's net gain or loss for a period is the amount of distributions received from the fund plus the increase in net assets per share during the period (or since the shares were acquired).

Illustrative Statements

Schedule 3-2 presents the 1988 financial statements of Canadian Investment Fund, Ltd. (CIF). The statement of net assets discloses net assets at the beginning of 1988 amounting to $92.6 million and net assets at the end of the year amounting to $88.1 million. The decrease in aggregate net assets during the year amounted to about 5%, but the per share NAV rose slightly, by about 1%, from $6.71 to $6.76. Since the per share amount rose while the aggregate fell, there must have been more shares redeemed than issued during the year. Note that the investment portfolio is almost $87 million at the end of the year; liabilities are minor, amounting to less than $0.4 million.

The statement of changes in net assets confirms our earlier conclusion that the value of share redemptions ($12.9 million) exceeded new issues ($7.8 million). The statement also discloses the realized and unrealized gains and losses on the investments; realized profits were about $2.5 million, and unrealized gains ("increase in unrealized appreciation") amounted to another $2.5 million.

The statement of income reports dividends and interest income, and deducts the expenses. The largest single expense by far is the amount for the management fees. Because of the importance of this amount, the stewardship reporting requirements of the *Ontario Securities Act* provide for detailed disclosure of the method of calculating the management fee. This disclosure can be found in Note 5. Note 4 contains another piece of stewardship reporting information, the total commissions paid. The dealers through which portfolio transactions are effected may be related to the fund management; therefore the amount of commissions is disclosed to discourage unscrupulous charges that may be hidden in the cost of securities in the portfolio.

The statement of income ends with an **earnings-per-share figure**. While it is customary to provide an EPS figure at the end of most income statements, it is a piece of incomplete information in a mutual fund, since it is only one segment of the earnings.

CIF also provides a summary statement of changes in investments. This statement shows the aggregate cost of securities purchased and sold during the year. It only indirectly indicates the profits realized on portfolio transactions by subtracting the profits from the total proceeds in order to obtain the cost of the securities sold.

The per share data can be found in Note 6, reported on a comparative basis for five years. The increase in NAV per share for 1987 was $0.05; distributions totaled $0.49. Thus the total return to an investor who held shares throughout the year was $0.54 on a share value of $6.71 at the beginning of the year.

CIF does not report its portfolio transactions in its annual report; the statement must be specifically requested from the company (notice the box at the end of the Notes). However, a comparison of the portfolio as reported in the statement of investments with the same statement for the previous year will reveal the changes in the composition of the portfolio.

Mutual funds provide an interesting example of how accounting and reporting policies can be drastically affected by the nature of the enterprise and its operations. Since the objective of a mutual fund is to earn a return directly for the individual stakeholders (investors and managers) rather than indirectly through maximizing the return for the enterprise, the objectives of financial reporting change. Income tax minimization and net income maximization or minimization cease to be objectives, and cash flow prediction becomes relatively unimportant. The emphasis in reporting clearly shifts towards performance evaluation and contract compliance or stewardship.

The capital invested in the enterprise is not under the control of management, unlike other businesses. Capital flows in and out of the fund at the discretion of the investors, and management must administer the changing pool of funds as best they can, within the announced investment strategy of the fund. Success is not measured by the amount of net income, either in absolute terms or relative to shareholders' equity. Instead, success is measured by the increase in shareholders' individual wealth resulting from the operations of the fund.

Summary: Mutual Funds

SCHEDULE 3-2

Canadian Investment Fund, Ltd.
(Incorporated under the Canada Business Corporations Act)
Statement of Net Assets

	December 31 1988	1987
ASSETS		
Investments at market value (average cost 1988 — $78,985,545; 1987 — $84,499,769)	$86,851,740	$89,906,289
Cash on deposit, demand	431,515	1,954,411
Interest accrued and dividends receivable	1,160,493	407,581
Receivable in respect of capital stock subscribed	—	646,010
Total assets	88,443,748	92,914,291
LIABILITIES		
Payable in respect of capital stock redeemed	203,111	175,437
Management and directors' compensation payable	99,554	124,035
Accrued expenses and sundry accounts payable	43,032	57,111
United States withholding tax	1,646	1,684
Total liabilities	347,343	358,267
Net assets at market value, representing shareholders' equity	$88,096,405	$92,556,024
Net asset value per share	$6.76	$6.71

SCHEDULE 3-2 (continued)

Canadian Investment Fund, Ltd.
Statement of Income
Year Ended December 31

	1988	1987
Income		
Dividends	$3,524,089	$3,709,078
Interest	588,045	365,822
	4,112,134	4,074,900
Expenses		
Management fees	1,227,820	1,479,765
Transfer and dividend paying agent's fees	117,790	203,827
Shareholder information expenses	61,765	67,102
Custodian's fees	53,175	57,744
General expenses	138,445	115,918
Audit fees	14,350	14,000
Taxes, other than income taxes	14,199	10,061
Legal fees and expenses	21,940	26,265
Directors' compensation	62,750	79,125
	1,712,234	2,053,807
Income before withholding taxes	2,399,900	2,021,093
United States withholding taxes	21,886	26,606
Net income, exclusive of profit or loss from sales of securities	$2,378,014	$1,994,487
Net income per share based on the average number of shares outstanding during the year	$0.17	$0.14

Canadian Investment Fund, Ltd.
Statement of Changes in Investments
Year Ended December 31

	1988	1987
Investments at average cost, beginning of year	$ 84,499,769	$ 88,090,944
Cost of securities purchased	64,962,729	114,777,017
	149,462,498	202,867,961
Proceeds from sales of securities	72,966,780	128,380,077
Less: Profit from sales of securities	2,489,827	10,011,885
Cost of securities sold	70,476,953	118,368,192
Investments at average cost, end of year	$78,985,545	$84,499,769

SCHEDULE 3-2 (continued)

Canadian Investment Fund, Ltd.
Statement of Changes in Net Assets
Year Ended December 31

	1988	1987
Net assets at market value, representing shareholders' equity, beginning of year	$92,556,024	$105,758,288
Add (deduct) changes during year:		
Net income	2,378,014	1,994,487
Realized profits from sales of securities	2,489,827	10,011,885
Increase (decrease) in unrealized appreciation of investments	2,459,675	(9,996,357)
Proceeds from subscriptions to capital stock	7,826,349	16,712,439
Consideration paid on redemption of capital stock	(12,874,123)	(19,424,201)
Dividends declared on capital stock — From net investment income	(1,912,990)	(2,004,691)
From realized profits from sales of securities	(4,826,371)	(10,495,826)
Decrease for the year	(4,459,619)	(13,202,264)
Net assets at market value, representing shareholders' equity, end of year	$88,096,405	$92,556,024

These important differences in operation and objectives have led to a structure of financial statements that is significantly different from other businesses. The key statement becomes the statement of changes in net assets, and the key figures become net assets per share and changes therein.

The qualitative characteristics of financial information play an important part in the selection of measurement methods. Market value of assets is a much more relevant measure for mutual funds than for many other types of enterprises because the earnings of the funds are derived directly from the investments. The fact that mutual funds invest mainly in publicly traded securities makes it feasible to value assets at market value rather than at cost. The measurement of market value is reasonably verifiable, reliable, and free from bias, although there are exceptions in the case of privately placed securities or thinly traded securities. Nevertheless, the nature of operations of mutual funds makes it possible to satisfy the qualitative criteria in a way that is unique to this industry.

SCHEDULE 3-2 (continued)

Canadian Investment Fund, Ltd.
Statement of Investments as at December 31, 1988

	Number of Shares or Par Value	Average Cost	Quoted Market Value	Approximate Percentage
Common Stocks and Convertible Securities				
Communications and Media				
MacLean Hunter Limited "X"	100,000	$ 844,250	$ 1,325,000	1.50 %
Thomson Newspapers Limited "A"	50,000	936,799	1,368,750	1.56
Torstar Corporation "B"	74,000	2,047,537	2,312,500	2.62
		3,828,586	5,006,250	5.68
Consumer Products				
Imasco Limited	50,000	150,662	1,400,00_	
Molson Companies Limited "A"	55,000	1,347,625		
Redpath Industries Limited	50,000	550_		0.43
The Seagram Company Ltd.	20,000			0.53
			588,330	0.67
		_35	522,464	0.59
Financial Services		_214,574	1,013,668	1.15
The Bank of Nova Scotia		661,403	710,015	0.81
Canadian Imperial Bank of Comm_		349,523	487,632	0.55
Power Financial Corporati_		677,887	675,778	0.77
The Royal Bank of _	_,000	706,282	694,385	0.79
The Toro_	17,500	763,558	862,214	0.98
_	10,000	1,067,531	695,130	0.79
		7,249,300	7,097,018	8.06
Total Common Stocks and Convertible Securities		72,799,323	80,844,693	91.77
Preferred Stocks				
Brascade Resources Inc., Floating Rate Cumulative Redeemable Convertible Retractable Voting Preferred Series "A"	100,000	4,104,175	3,925,000	4.46
Short-term Investments				
Caisse Central. Promissory Notes, 11.20% due November 8, 1989	$ 884,000	794,964	794,964	0.90
Government of Canada Treasury Bills, 11.03% due November 10, 1989	$1,375,000	1,238,408	1,238,408	1.41
Government of Canada Treasury Bills, 10.92% due March 31, 1989	$ 50,000	48,675	48,675	0.05
Total short-term investments		2,082,047	2,082,047	2.36
Total investments		$78,985,545	86,851,740	98.59
Cash and other assets, net			1,244,665	1.41
Total net assets			$88,096,405	100.00 %

*Market values in U.S. funds are expressed in Canadian funds at the rate of exchange prevailing at December 31, 1988, 19.08% premium on U.S. funds

SCHEDULE 3-2 (continued)

Canadian Investment Fund, Ltd.
Notes to Financial Statements, December 31, 1988

1. SIGNIFICANT ACCOUNTING POLICIES

   Investments
   Investments are recorded at market values established by the published last sales prices on national securities exchanges at the year-end or, in the absence of recorded sales, at the average of available closing bid and asked prices on such exchanges or over-the-counter.

   Investment transactions are accounted for on the trade date, and realized gains and losses resulting from such transactions are calculated on an average cost basis.

   Income recognition
   Dividend income is recognized on the ex-dividend date and interest income is recognized on the accrual basis.

   Foreign exchange
   The market value of investments and other assets and liabilities expressed in foreign currencies are translated into Canadian dollars at the rate of exchange prevailing at the year-end. Purchases and sales of foreign securities and the related income and expenses are translated at the rate of exchange prevailing on the respective dates of such transactions.

2. INCOME TAXES
   Under the Income Tax Act of Canada, the Corporation is classified as a mutual fund corporation; it also qualifies as an investment corporation and, as such, enjoys the preferential tax treatment afforded such corporations. The Corporation receives dividends from taxable Canadian corporations tax free. Income taxes of $66,749 otherwise payable in respect of capital gains have been eliminated by an available capital gains refund arising from capital gains redemptions during the year.

3. CAPITAL STOCK
   The Corporation's capital stock consists of an unlimited number of shares without nominal or par value which are redeemable on demand by holders at their net asset value.

   The number of shares issued and redeemed is as follows:

	1988	1987
Outstanding at beginning of year	13,794,310	14,094,217
Increase (decrease) during the year—		
Issued	1,229,068	2,234,776
Redeemed	(1,984,994)	(2,534,683)
Outstanding at end of year	13,038,384	13,794,310

4. COMMISSIONS
   The total commission paid to dealers in connection with investment portfolio transactions for the year ended December 31, 1988 amounted to $213,570; (1987 — $667,348).

5. MANAGEMENT FEES
   The management of the investing and reinvesting of the capital of the Corporation is carried out by Calvin Bullock, Ltd., the Manager, in accordance with the terms of an investment supervision agreement. In consideration for such services, the Manager is entitled to receive, on the last day of each month, a fee equal to 1/12 of 1.375% of the value of the average net assets of the Corporation throughout the month not in excess of $100,000,000 and 1/12 of 1% of the value of the average net assets of the Corporation throughout the month in excess of $100,000,000.

SCHEDULE 3-2 (continued)

Management fees and other expenses, excluding taxes, expressed as a percentage of average net assets (determined on the basis of the average of the net assets at the end of each month in the relevant financial year) for each of the last five years are as follows:

	Average net assets	Management fees and other expenses	Management expense ratio
1984	$105,260,035	$1,563,811	1.49%
1985	$112,007,907	$1,656,224	1.48%
1986	$110,448,864	$1,601,302	1.45%
1987	$110,040,860	$2,043,746	1.86%
1988	$ 89,295,976	$1,698,035	1.90%

The management expense ratio may vary from mutual fund to mutual fund.

6. PER SHARE DATA
    The net asset value representing shareholders' equity, and dividends paid for each of the last five years are as follows:

	1988	1987	1986	1985	1984
Net asset value representing shareholders' equity per share —					
At end of year	$6.76	$6.71	$7.50	$7.90	$6.75
At beginning of year	$6.71	$7.50	$7.90	$6.75	$7.26
Dividend per share from —					
Net investment income	$0.14	$0.14	$0.16	$0.23	$0.25
Realized profits from sales of securities —					
"Capital gains dividend"	$0.35	$0.75	$0.44	$0.09	$0.39

A statement of portfolio transactions for the year ended December 31, 1988 will be provided without charge by writing to:

Canadian Investment Fund, Ltd.
630 René-Lévesque Boulevard West
Suite 2690
Montreal, Quebec
H3B 1X1

REVIEW QUESTIONS

3-1 What is generally meant by "specialized industries"?

3-2 What is the purpose of this chapter?

3-3 Briefly describe how the characteristics of the extractive industries give rise to accounting problems that are different from those of most other industries.

3-4 In recent years, mining companies have grown more dependent upon outside financing, rather than financing most of their activities from internally generated funds as they had in earlier years. How has this change in financing affected the objectives of financial reporting for mining companies?

3-5 What major problems of asset valuation are there for mining companies and for oil and gas exploration companies?

3-6 What alternatives are available for reporting the costs of exploration and development in the extractive industries?

3-7 Explain the difference between **full-cost** and **successful-efforts** accounting for exploration and development costs. What is the rationale underlying each approach?

3-8   Which method of accounting for exploration and development costs is apt to yield the highest quality of earnings?

3-9   Is the successful-efforts method applied on a well-by-well basis? Explain.

3-10 Why might the practice of charging reclamation reserves to income impair the performance evaluation objective of reporting?

3-11 Under what circumstances is it appropriate to value inventories of a mining company at market value? What is accomplished by this practice?

3-12 What are **flow-through** shares?

3-13 What are the alternative accounting policies for the premium on flow-through shares?

3-14 What is the difference between an **open-end** and a **closed-end** investment company?

3-15 Is a **mutual fund** open-ended or closed-ended?

3-16 How are the share prices determined in a closed-end fund?

3-17 How are the share prices determined in an open-end fund?

3-18 Who are the primary users of a mutual fund's financial statements?

3-19 What are the dominant objectives of reporting for a mutual fund?

3-20 Why do mutual funds report their investments at market value? What qualitative characteristics affect this reporting practice?

3-21 Very few mutual funds are levered. However, if a mutual fund does use long-term debt as leverage, how would you expect the liability to be valued on the fund's balance sheet?

3-22 Why are neither unrealized nor realized gains on the sale of investments reported as income in the income statement of a mutual fund? What information needs of users are served by this practice?

3-23 Why are comparative statements not considered desirable for mutual funds, as they are for other types of companies?

3-24 What role does the concept of matching play in financial reporting for mutual funds?

3-25 Why do securities acts usually require detailed disclosure of the amount and calculation of management fees for mutual funds?

Azzip Limited   CASE 3-1

Azzip Limited is a medium-sized successful public Canadian company started in 1963 that is engaged in natural resources exploration and production in several of the Canadian provinces. The officer, directors, and one "friendly" financial group control 35% of the company. The remainder of the outstanding shares are widely held in Canada, the United States, and the United Kingdom. Azzip Limited's shares are not listed in the United States nor does the company plan to obtain any financing there in the future.

The company purchases exploration rights and carries out exploration and development activities. On approximately 10% of its successful properties, it undertakes production and sale of the minerals and hydrocarbons that have been discovered. Production rights associated with the remainder of the successful properties are sold.

Since the inception of the company, all costs such as lease acquisition, rentals on undeveloped properties, geological expenses, other exploration costs, and related overheads associated with properties, whether successful or unsuccessful results emerge, have been capitalized and amortized through depletion on a unit of production method based on the company's total mineral reserves. Properties that are abandoned are not written off except through the annual depletion charge. Proceeds from the sale of unproven properties have been credited to the asset account without any recognition of the gain or loss in the income statement of the particular year. Revenues arising from the production undertaken by Azzip on the properties it works itself are recorded when a sale of minerals and hydrocarbons is concluded with a third party. Sales of production rights on the other successful properties are recorded as revenue in the year of sale at the present value of future receipts, or at the lump-sum settlement price for one-time payments.

You have recently been retained as a consultant to the audit committee of the board of directors to help resolve a dispute that has arisen. The president, the two vice-presidents, one of finance and the other of exploration and development, as well as two of the directors on the audit committee, disagree strongly among themselves about the most appropriate approach for reporting the firm's asset values and yearly income. Through discussion with these officers and directors, you realize that a major concern of theirs is that they believe Azzip Limited may be a potential target for a takeover bid within the next two years. In fact, they see signs that some anonymous small-share accumulation may be getting underway right now. This, in their view, is not in the best interests of the company, nor of its other shareholders.

Two of the officers and one director, while understanding the basics of certain technical accounting requirements, believe that the company may be unwittingly contributing to the possibility of its own takeover by refusing to recognize as assets the discovery (exit) values of the firm's undoubtedly successful activities, and by not recognizing the proceeds from the sale of unproven properties through the income account in the year of their sale. This is of major concern, they suggest, because other shareholders may not be fully aware of the firm's success, and might easily be convinced to sell their shares at low prices to individuals or groups seeking control.

The third officer shares the concern about a potential takeover but believes that the firm's assets should be valued on a replacement-cost basis rather than on either the present historical cost or on the suggested discovery-value basis. He also argues that not only should net income be maximized by any legitimate acceptable technique, but that Azzip's good cash flow should be emphasized in the company's financial reports. He suggests that in addition to a successful discovery program in a company such as Azzip Limited, it is actually the cash flow that is of real value to the shareholders. He believes those who may be seeking control are trying to "steal" the unrecognized asset values and the cash flow.

The remaining director also readily acknowledges the possibility of a takeover. He believes, however, that conservative accounting policies and an expansion of the firm through retention and reinvestment of cash are in the best interests of the firm and its shareholders. He argues that the management group should be able to explain the real situation to the shareholders, solicit their proxies, and obtain support for present policies. At an appropriate future time, the entire firm would be sold at prices representing real economic value substantially in excess of the market and what may be offered in a takeover. He thinks, for instance, that costs associated with undeveloped and abandoned properties and costs relating to unsuccessful efforts should be included in the income account in the year of their expenditure. Successful mineral finds should be capitalized at their accumulated cost and amortized on a unit-of-production method for each individual discovery.

Upon returning to the office, you received a telephone call from the president. The president asked you to prepare a position paper that would be discussed at the next audit committee meeting. In the position paper, you are to analyze the subject of the disagreement among the officers and directors, explain the financial impact that may be expected from possible approaches, and recommend a preferred approach for Azzip Limited.

Required:
Prepare the requested position paper.
[CICA, adapted]

CASE 3-2   **Classic Concerts Ltd.**

Classic Concerts (CC) is a private, for-profit corporation that presents classical chamber music concerts in a rented, 483-seat recital hall. CC presents an annual series of twenty concerts by internationally renowned chamber music groups. This series is always completely sold out by advance subscription each year.

The planning of each year's series occurs at least one year in advance. For example, during the 1988-89 concert season, CC invites the participating artists for the 1989-90 series, and all appearances will be firmly contracted (as to date and fee) no later than May 1, 1989. In May 1989, a brochure describing the 1989-90 series will be mailed to all subscribers, who will have until June 30, 1989, to renew their subscriptions. Any unrenewed subscriptions will be offered to the general public after July 1; they are always sold out within a few days because there is a waiting list of people who want to subscribe. The subscribers may pay by cash, money order, cheque, postdated cheque (no later than September 1), or credit card, but they must remit payment when they subscribe.

The concerts themselves will take place between September 15, 1989, and June 30, 1990. On rare occasions, it is necessary to reschedule a concert because of booking conflicts or a performer's ill health. About once every two years, a group will not be able to appear, and CC must then find a substitute group (which may cost somewhat more or less than the original group). Ticket refunds are never made, although Classic Concerts box office will resell tickets for subscribers who cannot attend individual concerts. The proceeds of resale are returned to the subscriber, less a service charge of one dollar per ticket.

The rental of the hall (including ushers, stagehands, and the house manager) is contracted when the concerts are initially planned. CC runs small advertisements in the newspapers for each concert in order to maintain public awareness, even though they are sold out (which fact is clearly indicated in the ads). CC has a small administrative staff throughout the year. Other expenses, such as program printing and hospitality for the artists, are relatively small and can be budgeted fairly accurately.

Required:
The president of Classic Concerts has approached you to ask how to account for the revenue and expenses of the corporation. In particular, he is concerned about when to recognize revenue, and about the balance sheet effects of the different possible methods of revenue recognition. Respond.

Rutherford Systems Limited   CASE 3-3

Rutherford Systems Limited (RSL) was incorporated in 1957 under the *Canada Corporations Act* and was subsequently continued under the *Canada Business Corporations Act*. RSL was formed by five men who wanted to develop a new type of widescreen motion picture projection system that had been devised by A. Wol, one of the founders. The initial capital was provided by the founders, with A. Wol donating his patents on the process to the firm in exchange for shares.

RSL's first successful application of the new system was in the Science pavilion at the 1957 New York World's Fair. With the Fair to showcase the system, the firm obtained several other contracts, mainly from large amusement parks. In succeeding years, RSL continued to place its systems in major exhibition halls, in amusement parks and pavilions, and in some corporate-training centres and public-relations centres. Placements occurred throughout North America and in a few foreign countries. Approximately 40 systems have been installed since 1959.

In the early years, the equipment was sold outright to the purchaser, with no delayed or contingency payments. This practice is still followed when sales are made to nonprofit institutions or to high-risk operators.

However, the "lumpy" cash flow that resulted was unsatisfactory, and therefore the firm decided to alter the payment scheme for most purchasers. Most sales now involve an initial payment at the time of signing the contract to cover the costs of manufacturing and installing the equipment. The purchaser also signs a ten-year lease that obligates him to pay RSL a fixed fee per person admitted to the theatre. This fee is indexed to the Consumer Price Index. At the expiration of the lease, the equipment remains with the acquirer and no further payments are made to RSL. There is normally about a two-year period between signing the initial contract and final acceptance of the installed system by the buyer. The ten-year lease term does not begin until final acceptance.

Three of the five founders are still actively involved in managing the company. A. Wol has sold his shares to the active founders and has retired to Australia. He receives a royalty of 3% of the annual revenue from the projection systems. The fifth founder still holds 20% of the shares, but is engaged in film production in Hollywood.

Rutherford Systems Limited
Statement of Earnings
Year Ended December 31, 1985

Projector sales	$ 836,213
Projector rental	285,004
Royalty revenue	350,598
Maintenance revenue	59,775
Camera rental	119,024
Miscellaneous	52,635
Film distribution	39,208
	1,742,457
Projector cost of sales	247,933
Projector rental expenses	136,631
Royalty costs	37,329
Maintenance costs	41,836
Camera rental expenses	25,581
Film production and distribution expenses	39,621
General expenses	36,767
	565,698
Gross profit	1,176,759
Research and development	56,580
Amortization of deferred costs	40,000
Administrative and marketing expenses	750,233
	846,813
Income (loss) before income taxes	329,946
Income taxes — current	105,150
— deferred (reduction)	59,100
	164,250
Net income (loss) for year (Note 10)	$ 165,696

Attached are the most recent balance sheet and statement of earnings, and selected notes to the financial statements.

Required:
Evaluate the accounting principles used by Rutherford Systems Limited. Recommend alternatives if you think that current practices are inappropriate.

Rutherford Systems Limited
Balance Sheet
December 31, 1985

ASSETS

Cash and term deposit	$ 406,964
Accounts receivable	218,198
Accrued revenue receivable	47,730
Due from shareholders	31,551
Inventory	298,394
Prepaid expenses	39,914
Current assets	1,042,751
Fixed assets (Note 2)	1,594,969
Accrued revenue receivable	160,835
Deferred development costs (Note 3)	261,810
Deferred income taxes	88,537
	$3,148,902

LIABILITIES

Bank advances, against which book debts have been pledged	$ 412,639
Accounts payable and accrued liabilities	498,742
Income taxes payable	—
Mortgages payable (Note 4)	2,296
Current Liabilities	913,677
Mortgages payable (Note 4)	238,131
Deferred revenue	1,359,755
	2,511,563

SHAREHOLDERS' EQUITY

Capital stock	62,702
Contributed surplus	75,087
Retained earnings	499,550
	637,339
	$3,148,902

The explanatory financial notes form an integral part of these financial statements.

Rutherford Systems Limited
Explanatory Financial Notes (excerpts)
Year Ended December 31, 1985

1. SUMMARY OF SIGNIFICANT ACCOUNTING POLICIES
   This summary of accounting policies of the company is presented to assist the reader in evaluating the financial statements contained in this annual report. These policies have been followed consistently in all material respects for the periods covered after giving retroactive effect to the changes referred to in Note 10.

   A. Inventories
      Inventories are represented by lenses and projectors under construction for eventual sale and are valued at the lower of cost and net realizable value.

   B. Depreciation of fixed assets
      The company depreciates fixed assets utilizing annual rates and methods which will fully depreciate the assets over their estimated useful lives. These rates are:

Building	5% Declining-balance
Projection equipment	10% Straight-line
Camera equipment	20% Declining-balance
Production equipment	20% Declining-balance
Office equipment	20% Declining-balance
Truck	30% Declining-balance

   C. Amortization of deferred development costs
      Deferred development costs are amortized over the life of the patents on the Rutherford Motion Picture System.

   D. Income taxes
      Income taxes are recorded on the tax allocation basis whereby the incidence of income taxes on specific transactions is recorded in the period in which the transactions are recognized for accounting purposes.

   E. Recognition of income
      Revenue from the sale of projectors is recognized as income on a straight-line basis from the time of signing the contract to the estimated final acceptance by the customer. Unearned income from these contracts is shown as deferred revenue; income earned but not yet received is shown as an accrued revenue receivable in the balance sheet.

      In addition to the sale of projectors, films and other related equipment, the company enters into front-end loaded leases of projectors, the recognition of income from which is determined as follows:

      (1) The front-end charge on leased projectors is recognized as income on a straight-line basis from the signing date of the lease to the end of the first lease term, not to exceed ten years. Unearned income from this rental charge is shown as deferred revenue in the Statement of Financial Position.

      (2) The company also earns rental revenue from these same projectors based on the customers' paid admissions which is recognized according to the lease period noted in the lease contract.

F. Projection equipment
    The direct costs relating to the lease projectors are capitalized as fixed assets and depreciated as noted in Note 1 (B) above.

2. FIXED ASSETS

	1985
Cost	
Land	$ 75,000
Building	271,505
Projection equipment	1,403,610
Camera equipment	223,103
Production equipment	28,296
Truck	—
Office equipment	46,175
	2,047,689
Accumulated depreciation	
Building	7,012
Projection equiment	267,242
Camera equipment	147,510
Production equipment	16,291
Truck	—
Office equipment	14,665
	452,720
Net book value	$1,594,969

The undepreciated capital cost of fixed assets available to reduce net income for income tax purposes is approximately $1,504,000. Projection equipment includes projectors under construction of $161,146 ($157,276 in 1984).

3. DEFERRED DEVELOPMENT COSTS

	1985	1984
Development costs capitalized	$705,143	$705,143
Accumulated amortization	443,333	403,333
	$261,810	$301,810

The deferred development costs include the costs of developing a new motion picture system utilizing a large-format camera and projector. These costs include an administrative overhead charge.

4. MORTGAGES PAYABLE

12% first mortgage, secured by land and building,
payable in monthly instalments of $1,182 including
principal and interest and maturing March 1, 1989. $123,754

10.75% second mortgage, secured by land and
building, payable in monthly instalments of $1,106
including principal and interest and maturing
March 1, 1989.   116,673

                                                         240,427
Principal portion due within one year   2,296

                                                        $238,131

10. PRIOR PERIOD ADJUSTMENTS

During the year, the company made two changes in the application of accounting principles. These changes are:

A. The front-end rental charge as described in Note 1 (E) is now recognized on a straight-line basis from the date of signing the lease until the end of the first lease term to a maximum of ten years.

    Previously this one-time charge had been recognized from the time of signing the lease to the final installation of the projector and acceptance by the customer.

B. Projection equipment capitalized is depreciated on the 10% straight-line basis.

    Previously, projection equipment had been depreciated on the 20% declining-balance basis.

The application of the above changes has resulted in the loss, (after adjustment for the effect on deferred income taxes) being increased by $13,473, and opening retained earnings being decreased by $372,633 for the year ended December 31, 1984.

The above changes in accounting policies have increased working capital at the beginning of the period by $35,000.

If the company had continued to follow its previous accounting policies, income after taxes would have been $454,647 for the year ended December 31, 1985 and retained earnings at year end would have been $1,174,607.

CASE 3-4   The Outpost Cemeteries Inc.

Douglas Smith is the founder, president, and sole shareholder of The Outpost Cemeteries Inc. (TOCI). Mr. Smith was a real estate broker who had been engaged in speculative land acquisitions for many years. In the early 1950s, Mr. Smith saw an opportunity to develop one of the large tracts of land that he held outside of Vancouver into a privately owned and operated cemetery. He hired a small sales force, obtained the necessary governmental approvals, and opened The Outpost as his first cemetery. In following years, he began to concentrate almost exclusively on acquiring real estate for an expansion of his cemetery business, and by the early

1980s had developed a chain of thirteen cemeteries, operating from Vancouver Island to Quebec.

Only 30% of the sales of cemetery plots and related materials (vaults, caskets, headstones, bronze markers, etc.) by The Outpost cemeteries were sales "at need," that is, sales made to families for the burial of recently deceased relatives. The primary sales focus of The Outpost cemeteries was on "pre-need" sales, wherein individuals and families purchased cemetery plots in advance of their need, so that the acquisition was made calmly and rationally, and the cost need not fall on the relatives or the estate.

Provincial regulations usually provide that a portion of the cost of a cemetery plot be placed in a trust fund with an independent trustee for perpetual care of the burial site. The portion varies by province, but most require 35% to be placed in trust. The capital of the trust fund is permanently retained in trust, but the income is paid by the trustees to the cemetery company to provide care of the site in perpetuity. Payments to the perpetual care fund are required whether the sale is at-need or pre-need. Of the total value of an average sale, only about 25% is allocated for the plot itself; the remainder goes towards the other burial costs.

For pre-need sales, most provinces require that the cemetery company also place a percentage of up to 65% of the total value of each sale in a segregated fund to be managed by the company itself. The capital in fund is restricted for each individual plot, but the interest or other income arising from investing the pre-need funds is not restricted and can be used by the cemetery company as they please.

Upon the death of a pre-need contract holder, the capital relating to that contract reverts to the company, and is intended to cover the costs of providing the contracted burial services. However, TOCI already owns the land, and the company hedges against inflation by acquiring most of the major materials, such as vaults and bronze markers, at the time of making the sale, rather than waiting until the need arises. Thus most of the costs are incurred well in advance of need. On average, eleven years elapse between the sale and the need.

The pre-need sales are made by salespeople who visit the prospective customers in their homes. Most prospects are couples, who may be found in a number of ways. Local television and newspaper advertisements generate about 30% of the eventual sales. The remainder are contacted through referrals of other customers or funeral directors, by telephone solicitation, or by door-to-door sales. Most of TOCI's sales are on the installment basis. The buyer has forty-eight months in which to pay the total cost of the purchase. One of the selling points for pre-need sales is the fact that the pre-need contract can be transferred without charge to any of The Outpost cemeteries. Customers need not feel tied down to living in the same area, nor worry about the cost of transporting their remains back to the site of the contract, should they choose to move to another part of the country.

TOCI was one of only three cemetery chains operating in more than one province. The largest competitor was Memorial Gardens Canada Ltd., which is the operating subsidiary of Arbor Capital Resources Inc. Arbor Capital Resources made a public share offering in the early 1980s that was very successful, and Arbor became one of the few "hot" stocks on the Toronto Stock Exchange during the recession of 1981-82. Mr. Smith felt that TOCI was at a competitive disadvantage because TOCI was not yet truly national as was Memorial Gardens, which had over forty cemeteries across the nation. Therefore, Mr. Smith proposed to make TOCI public by means of offering new shares. The proceeds of the new share issue would finance land acquisition for expansion of the number and geographic dispersion of TOCI's cemeteries.

Because a new share issue would involve publishing financial statements for the first time, the underwriters with whom Mr. Smith was negotiating insisted that TOCI retain an independent professional accountant to review the accounting policies used by the company in reporting its revenues and expenses and related assets and liabilities.

Required:
Assume that you are the independent professional accountant retained by Mr. Smith. Prepare a report to Mr. Smith in which you discuss the feasible alternative accounting policies for The Outpost Cemeteries Inc., and make specific recommendations.

CASE 3-5   ## Collier Custom Jewelry Ltd.

Early in 1989, several independent Ontario jewelry retailers established Collier Custom Jewelry Ltd. (CCJL) as a private corporation under the *Ontario Business Corporations Act*. CCJL was formed primarily in order to provide the participating retail jewelers with an exclusive and reliable source for custom-made jewelry.

Retail jewelers receive requests from customers for the construction of unique pieces of jewelry either from a design that the customer provides or from an original design provided by a designer who is retained by the jeweler. Both the design (if needed) and the construction or fabrication of the piece are normally subcontracted to independent specialists such as designers, goldsmiths, silversmiths, etc.

The intent of forming CCJL was to provide the owner retailers with a readily available and reliable centralized source of design and construction, with profits being returned largely to the retailers. In addition to doing individual custom work for the retailers, CCJL would hold design competitions and select outstanding designs for multiple production. These products would be distributed exclusively through the owner retailers, supported in some instances by regional cooperative advertising by CCJL and the retailers.

Once CCJL was established and operating satisfactorily, additional business would be accepted from retailers who are not owners of CCJL to the extent that capacity permits. This additional outside business would help to even the work load and to maintain full employment of the staff of skilled experts.

The pricing of the outputs of CCJL would differ for each of the three lines of business. For the owner-retailer custom business, the price to the retailer would be equal to the direct cost of the item of jewelry plus a fixed percentage margin to cover overhead and to provide a modest profit margin. The amount of the percentage would be set annually by the board of directors of CCJL.

For the exclusive product lines, production levels would be based on sales estimates of the participating retailers. Production would be maintained to ensure CCJL would have adequate inventory throughout the year. The prices to the retailers would be normal wholesale market prices for comparable products.

Custom work for outside retailers would be charged at normal market rates.

In establishing CCJL, each of eight retailers purchased between one and five shares of CCJL common stock for $50,000 per share. The founders' intent was that the initial investment should be sufficient to maintain the company's productive capacity without additional injections of capital. A shareholders' agreement was drawn up that included the following points:

- the CCJL board of directors was to be comprised of one representative from each of the owner retailers, regardless of the number of shares held;
- new shares would be sold to existing or new shareholders only upon approval of two-thirds of the members of the board of directors;
- existing shareholders who wish to sell part or all of their shares must first offer the shares to CCJL for repurchase, and, if refused, to the remaining shareholders before any offers can be solicited from outside retailers;
- the price of all share transactions will be based on CCJL's net asset value per share at the most recent quarterly reporting date;

The top managers of CCJL had been selected prior to the official incorporation of the company, and many of the leading artisans for the company had been identified as well. Once the company was established, management quickly moved to find suitable quarters to house the company's operations and to equip and adapt the space to CCJL's needs. Loft space in a partially renovated building on Toronto's Duncan Street was obtained at reasonable rental rates, although a substantial one-time signing payment was required at the beginning of the ten-year lease to compensate the lessor for adapting the space to CCJL's needs; the lease also contained renewal options (at the lessee's option). Only about four months would be needed before the company was ready to begin full operation. During that time the managers and artisans would be engaged in a full range of start-up activities, including equipping and stocking the leased space and hiring and training sufficient staff.

The board of directors established a defined contribution pension plan for the company's permanent skilled staff; the plan was based on compulsory contributions from both the company and the employee and was fully vesting from the outset. The board also approved a profit-sharing plan for the managers.

Any additional financing that the company needs beyond the shareholders' investment is to be arranged by the managers through normal bank financing. Interest costs are to be excluded, however, in determining the managers' profit sharing.

As a part of the start-up activity, the managers of CCJL are seeking expert assistance in designing appropriate financial reporting policies for the company. The proposed accounting policies will be submitted to the Board of Directors' newly formed audit committee for approval. It is anticipated that CCJL's fiscal year-end will be January 31, and that quarterly statements will be prepared for submission to the owner retailers and to the bank.

Required:
Assume that you have been retained as the accounting advisor. Prepare a report in which you recommend suitable financial accounting policies, consistent with CCJL's reporting objectives, including the reasons for your specific recommendations.
[ICAO]

Artisan Village   CASE 3-6

Artisan Village (AV) was formed as a partnership in January 1989 after Brown Enterprises Limited (BEL) approached a number of charities and craftsmen with the idea of opening a shopping plaza devoted exclusively to the sale of pottery, hand-made slippers, wall hangings, decorations, and similar items of interest to tourists and others. A plan was developed and a partnership agreement was signed by BEL and the charities and craftsmen. Each partner would like to withdraw an amount equal to a 10% return on investment each year and leave the balance reinvested in AV.

AV's sales have been increasing gradually, and it is becoming known as a good place to shop. However, its board of directors has been devoting its energies primarily to daily operations and has paid little attention to accounting policies, management controls and reporting systems, income taxation, and related matters. The board of directors has engaged you to prepare a report addressing these issues.

It is now September 1989. You have just visited AV's premises and obtained the information presented in Exhibit 1.

Required:
Prepare the report requested by the board of directors.

EXHIBIT 1

Information Gathered by CA

AV is located in an old shopping plaza previously owned by BEL. Over the years the plaza had become run down, and the number of tenants dwindled. Since the neighbourhood was turning into an area frequented by tourists, BEL perceived an opportunity to revive the plaza by converting it into a tourist attraction. With little additional investment, the plaza was given a rustic appearance. The remaining tenants' leases were not renewed, and seven small craft stores owned by AV were opened, selling Canadian-made crafts.

The land and buildings were sold to AV by BEL at what BEL estimated to be fair market value of $150,000 and $350,000 respectively. BEL received an 18%-interest note of $130,000 and a 50% partnership interest in AV in exchange for the land and buildings. The other partners contributed cash and inventory.

The renovation to the plaza required the following expenditures, which were charged to expense:

Store shelving and display counters	$ 75,260
Electrical advertising signs	42,340
Building renovations, primarily to store fronts and windows	102,750
Resurfacing of parking lot	39,000

AV financed the expenditures by taking out a $250,000 mortgage with a trust company on its land and buildings. The mortgage, due in February 1990, bears interest at 13% and has been guaranteed by BEL and by an agency of the federal government.

Most of the goods for sale have been acquired from charities and individual Canadian craftsmen and artists. In order to promote sales and ensure the success of AV, the government agency has agreed to provide a five-year operating subsidy of up to a maximum of $300,000 per year. The subsidy pays 50% of operating expenses excluding depreciation, as long as more than 50% of AV's employees are classified as handicapped. The government agency requires annual financial statements and cost schedules.

Some charities are paying AV to display their merchandise prominently in store windows and on shelves. The payment is calculated by multiplying operating expenses of AV per square foot by the number of square feet used. In order to receive these payments, AV must provide annual financial statements and cost schedules to the charities.

AV has on hand about $625,000 of purchased inventory, valued at cost. The craftsmen, artists, or charities receive on delivery 40% of the suggested retail price of any item sold to AV. The managers of the stores try to sell the items at this suggested retail price. However, they may alter selling prices when an item is moving quickly or slowly. Payments to craftsmen, artists, and charities are adjusted quarterly, based on changes in selling prices.

AV has on hand about $500,000 of consignment inventory, valued at retail. When this inventory is sold, 55% of the selling price is remitted to the consignor. AV's profit margin is lower for consignment sales because AV does not finance the items.

AV has recently begun to sell many of its products to retail stores in other regions of Canada. These stores receive a 20% discount on the suggested retail price and are required to pay within 120 days.

AV sold $200,000 of its $385,000 worth of accounts receivable to a

EXHIBIT 1 (continued)

finance company for $178,000. AV is liable for any shortfall between the $200,000 and what the customers actually pay the finance company.

AV accepts credit cards. The credit card charges are sold to the banks for $0.96 on the dollar.

The store managers are being paid a salary and an annual bonus based on their store's operating income. The seven store managers report to the general manager of AV, who must allocate resources to each store and coordinate all other activities among the stores and with the partners.

AV's accounting records are not complete, and all figures are those as of July 31, 1989. AV has never performed a physical count of its inventories and does not regularly send statements to customers.
[CICA]

4

Financial Reporting for Nonbusiness Organizations

Most study of accounting focuses on business enterprises. This emphasis is quite appropriate in a capitalist economy. However, there are many organizations in Canada that are not businesses. Universities, hospitals, performing arts organizations, museums, trade associations, unions, political parties, and philanthropic foundations are a few examples of the nonbusiness organizations that have an important place in our society. In addition, governments themselves, the entire public sector of the economy, are nonbusiness organizations.

The basic factors that distinguish nonbusiness organizations from business enterprises are that nonbusiness organizations (1) are not owned by any specific individuals and thus have no transferable ownership interest, and (2) do not function in order to earn a profit or yield any direct economic gain for the members or contributors. Any economic gain for the members would be indirect, such as increased wages negotiated by a union for its members.

Nonbusiness organizations can be roughly divided into three groups: (1) governments, (2) governmental units, and (3) nonprofit organizations. Governmental accounting is the body of principles and practices which has been developed for record keeping and reporting by the various levels of government: municipal, regional, provincial, and federal. Governmental accounting is largely regulated by law, although the accounting and reporting principles on which the law is based were developed by governments and by organizations such as the **Municipal Finance Officers Association of the United States and Canada** (which is itself a nonbusiness organization). In Canada, the pronouncements of the CICA's Public Sector Accounting and Auditing Committee influence GAAP for governments.

Governmental units are organizations that are set up by governments in order to carry out some aspect of their policy. Governmental units include organizations such as public housing authorities, parking authorities, public cemeteries, water systems, and electric utilities. Such units may be incorporated, but they are **corporations without share capital** and must be distinguished from **crown corporations**, such as the Canadian National Railway

System, which are business corporations having the government as the only shareholder.

Nonprofit organizations are non-governmental organizations that function as educational, scientific, charitable, artistic, or social agencies. The term "social agency" covers a lot of ground, since a social agency can range anywhere from an amateur baseball club to a hospital, with the Salvation Army, the Liberal Party of Canada, and the Kiwanis in between.

Terms other than "nonprofit organization" (or "not-for-profit organization") are often used to describe the widely diverse types of organizations that are in this sector of the economy. Alternatives sometimes encountered are "third sector" (as distinguished from the other two sectors, public and private) and "volunteer organizations" (arising from the fact that they frequently use the services of volunteers and that the members of the boards of directors of nonprofit organizations are generally prohibited from being paid, and thus are volunteer directors). "Public service sector" is also used. Nevertheless, we will use the traditional term nonprofit organizations in this book.

It is difficult to draw a clear line between governmental units and nonprofit organizations in Canada. Universities, for example, are established as independent corporate entities. But they are dependent on governments for almost all of their funding, and they carry out part of government's educational policy. Similarly, hospitals and public utilities are semi-independent corporations that have some characteristics of governmental units. For accounting purposes, the distinction between nonprofit organizations and governmental units is not crucial. The objectives of both are similar, and there is more variation within the broad group of nonprofit organizations than there is between nonprofit and governmental units.

Governments, on the other hand, have quite different financial statement objectives because of the sources of their funds, and because of their legal reporting obligations. In the main body of this chapter, we focus on nonprofit organizations and governmental units. Our discussion of governmental financial reporting is in the appendix to this chapter, Public Sector Reporting.

CHARACTERISTICS OF NONPROFIT ORGANIZATIONS

Before we look at the financial reporting objectives of nonprofit organizations, we should take note of how nonprofit organizations differ from business organizations. There are four characteristics of nonprofit organizations that directly influence the design of accounting and reporting systems: (1) the composition of the membership and the method of electing the board of directors, (2) the replacement of the profit objective with a service objective, (3) the need for expenditure controls, and (4) the need to segregate funds because of restrictions placed on the use of funds provided by donors or contributors.

Nonprofit organizations have no share capital, and thus have no transferable ownership interest. Since there are no shareholders, there are no share voting rights for electing the board of directors. Instead, the board is elected by

Membership and the Board of Directors

the **members** of the organization at an annual meeting. The constitution of the organization specifies the conditions for membership. Membership may either be **open** or **closed**.

In an open membership, the conditions for membership are clearly specified in the constitution or bylaws of the organization, and membership is available to anyone who chooses to fulfill the membership requirements. The most common form of open membership is that in which any person can join the organization by paying a fee, either as dues or as a donation, and obtains the right to vote at annual meetings as a result. Public art galleries, for example, frequently encourage memberships as a form of fund raising.

A closed membership exists when the members are designated by the board of directors. An organization's constitution frequently gives the board discretion to establish the requirements for membership and to approve new members. Membership is closed because it is not automatically open to all qualified individuals who apply, and because the board has the power to change the requirements for membership at any board meeting. In some nonprofit organizations, the members of the board are the only members of the organization; in effect, the board elects itself.

Since it controls the composition of the membership in a closed membership organization, the board can control the voting for the directors, and thus is essentially self-perpetuating. In contrast, the board of an open-membership organization is vulnerable to direct challenge by the members, if they are dissatisfied with the way in which the board has been carrying out its responsibilities. Opponents of the current management can conduct membership drives to enlist enough new members to support their attempt to oust the current directors. In some cases, part or all of a board may be appointed by other groups that have a vested interest. It is not uncommon for at least some of the directors of organizations that are heavily dependent on government funding to be appointees of government. The government thereby has a direct voice in the management and organizational policies.

The composition of the membership and the method of electing the directors are important, because they affect the relative importance of the users of the organization's financial statements and thus have an impact on the objectives of financial reporting for a specific organization.

Service Rather than a Profit Objective

Another characteristic of nonprofit organizations that is very important for financial reporting is the fact that there is no profit objective. Instead, the emphasis is on some form of service to the membership or the community. While business enterprises certainly cover a wide span of activity, they are similar in that they are all organized in order to earn a return on the investment of the owners. Nonprofit organizations, on the other hand, have neither an equity investment by owners nor any intent to earn profits on the organizations' assets. Therefore, the profit objective that binds together financial reporting for all business enterprises is absent in nonprofit organizations.

The service objective that is common to nonprofit organizations leads to a much different emphasis in financial reporting. The emphasis is on services provided with the resources available rather than on profit and loss (or surplus and deficit). The users of the financial statements are usually concerned with evaluating the performance of the organization. Instead of evaluating that performance by means of profit, return on assets, etc., users evaluate the efficiency and effectiveness of the organization. This can only be done if information is presented in a way that discloses the resources that were devoted to each of the organization's major programs and the outputs of those programs; this is known as **programmatic reporting**. The relationship between the resources or inputs used and the outputs achieved is the measure of **efficiency**; the relationship between the outputs and accomplishment of the goals of the organization is the measure of **effectiveness**. The trend towards programmatic financial reporting and the measurement of efficiency and effectiveness is discussed later in this chapter.

A third characteristic that influences accounting follows from the absence of the profit motive. Since the need for profit cannot act as the overall motivator for maximizing revenues and minimizing costs, it is necessary to have direct expenditure controls in order to keep costs within the available revenues. In governments, expenditure controls are vital because spending is legally limited to the amounts designated by the legislative body. Civil servants are constrained from spending more than has been authorized. In nonprofit organizations, the expenditure controls may not be quite so stringent, since there is not the same legal restriction. Nevertheless, the availability of funds is an important practical constraint, and control in nonprofit organizations is frequently facilitated by building budgetary controls directly into the accounting and reporting system.

Need for Expenditure Controls

The fourth important characteristic is that some of the funds of a nonprofit organization may be restricted for particular uses and must be segregated from the general funds. For example, a school or university will have a large amount of operating funds (grants from government and fees received from students) for operating the school on a day-to-day basis. However, they will also have a capital budget for funds that can be used only for capital projects such as new buildings or substantial renovations. The institution will probably also have scholarship funds that must be used only for student aid.

Need to Segregate Funds

The use of funds can be limited either by the contributor or by the board of directors. Limitations placed on funds by grantors or donors are known as **restricted** funds; the restrictions are legally binding and must be observed by both the board and the managers. Limitations placed on funds by the board are called **designated** or **board-designated** funds and must be observed by the managers, but they can usually be changed by the board.

Not only may specific funds be designated or restricted, they may also be **endowed**. Endowed funds may not be disbursed, but must be held (and invested) by the organization. The interest or other income on the investments may be expended, but the principal amount of the endowment must remain intact. A university scholarship fund may be both endowed and restricted: the capital is endowed, while the income can be expended only for restricted purposes. The accounting and financial reporting system of a nonbusiness organization must be able to distinguish between the various funds and be able to show that the various restrictions and designations have been observed.

OBJECTIVES OF REPORTING FOR NONBUSINESS ORGANIZATIONS

Chapter 2 reviewed the various reporting objectives that a business enterprise may have. The basic objectives of financial reporting for nonprofit organizations are similar to the objectives of reporting for businesses, especially the users' objectives. However, since nonbusiness enterprises have no owners, no profit objective, and frequently no long-term debt, the users and uses of the financial statements of nonbusiness enterprises will be somewhat different from those of businesses.

Preparer Objectives

In business reporting, the preparers have valid economic motivations in the preparation of financial statements, even though their motivations may conflict with users' objectives. The managers have a legitimate concern in deferring income taxes, in supporting share prices through earnings maximization and smoothing, or in reducing the prospect of takeovers or governmental interference by earnings minimization. Management's objectives or motivations may not coincide exactly with the users' needs, but they do ultimately relate to the interests of at least some of the economic stakeholders of the enterprise.

In contrast, nonprofit organizations do not exist in order to yield direct economic benefit to the members, contributors, or managers. The managers will gain economically through salaries and wages, of course, although usually the pay earned in nonprofit organizations is below what the same individuals could earn in the private sector. But maximizing personal compensation is not likely to be an objective of the managers, nor should it be. Since the operating objectives of nonprofit organizations are service oriented rather than economically oriented, preparer objectives take on a different cast. Deferring income taxes is meaningless in an organization that pays no taxes, and profit maximization, minimization, and smoothing are not relevant to an organization that does not operate for profit. What is relevant, however, is financial reporting that helps the organization generate the necessary revenue to maximize the amounts of services that it provides to its constituency group.

Managers frequently want to present the most favourable picture of their organization's financial health to external users in order to enhance the organization's attractiveness to funding agencies and other donors. For example, showing a large deficit may suggest fiscal irresponsibility and scare donors away, while showing a large operating surplus will make it look like the organization does not need additional financial support. Therefore, many managers have a reporting objective of showing annual operating results that are very close to breakeven.

In an organization that obtains revenue from different sources for different programs, revenue may be affected by the way in which certain costs are accounted for and/or allocated to programs. For example, a provincial government ministry may contract to reimburse an organization for the full cost of its visiting nurse service, while the cost of a meals-on-wheels program run by the same organization may be supported out of the organization's general public donations. Since the government will fully reimburse the costs of the nursing program, the organization's overall revenues will increase as the level of costs charged and allocated to that program increase. Accounting policies relating to costs can therefore improve the ability of the organization to generate revenue and thereby to provide services.

Another example relates to the recognition of revenue. A fund-raising drive in the current period may result in a large number of unfulfilled pledges at the end of the fiscal year. If these pledges are recognized as revenue in the current period, the deficit will be smaller (or the surplus larger) than if the revenue is recognized in the following period, when the pledges are actually fulfilled. Organizations that are successful fundraisers often elect to recognize the pledges as revenue in the later period in order to keep from showing a large surplus in the current period. In a successfully managed organization, each year's fund-raising efforts are more successful than the last, and therefore a policy of revenue deferral will serve to create a "reserve" in the form of deferred revenue on the balance sheet and to keep the surplus smaller or nonexistent. (The accounting policy alternatives relating to pledges are discussed more fully in a later section of this chapter.)[1]

We can conclude, therefore, that accounting policies may be chosen by the managers of a nonprofit organization to *enhance the service potential of the organization*. This is the primary preparer objective in nonprofit organizations. It can be carried out through accounting policies relating to the recognition of revenues, recognition and allocation of costs, establishment of separate funds, programmatic reporting, and balance sheet presentation, among others. Revenue enhancement is probably the most frequent intent, and that usually boils down to using accounting policies that make the organization look fiscally responsible and well managed while still needing additional funding; a small annual deficit is often the financial reporting goal.

Because of the innovativeness of many managers in adopting revenue-enhancing accounting policies, funding agencies (especially government ministries) are increasingly requiring the organizations that they fund to use a standard set of accounting policies and accounting classifications. The standardization of reporting is an attempt by the funders to assist themselves with the resource allocation decisions that they must inevitably make. Standardization helps them to compare and evaluate the efficiency and effectiveness of the various organizations that they are supporting, and also to ensure a dominance of user objectives over preparer objectives in those organizations. Nevertheless, the wide range of accounting policy alternatives available in nonprofit accounting (as we will explore throughout this chapter and the next) still leaves quite a broad range of reporting options and results available to the preparers.

User Objectives

In Chapter 2, we discussed the users' business enterprise reporting objectives of performance evaluation, stewardship, and cash flow prediction. These objectives are all valid for nonprofit organizations as well. The primary users of

---

1 A more advanced technique to "manage" the recognition of revenues in operations is to accumulate at least some of the organization's donations in a separate fund and transfer them to the operating fund only as needed to cover expenses or eliminate a deficit.

the financial statements of nonprofit organizations are (1) managers and directors, (2) members, donors, and other financial contributors, (3) creditors, and (4) governments. Secondary users may be employees, recipients of goods and services, and society at large.[2]

We cannot overemphasize the importance of the first group of users: managers and directors. In some larger nonprofit organizations there is an elaborate management reporting system that provides detailed information to the organization's managers. But in most organizations, the managers work with essentially the same financial reports as do the directors and outside users. Additional detail may be available, but the overall perceptions of the managers as to the operating efficiency and effectiveness of the organization is determined on the same basis as for external users.

The heavy reliance placed by managers and directors on the organization's financial statements is directly traceable to two factors. One is the low level of administrative expertise frequently possessed by the managers themselves. This is not to suggest that the managers are in some way incompetent, but rather that the managers' expertise normally lies in program delivery rather than in administration. Therefore the managers, when faced with inadequate financial statements, may not know how to get the information they need even though they may well sense that the information is inadequate. The sense of frustration that such managers feel tends to extend to a broader perception of an inadequacy of accounting and accountants.

The second factor is that nonprofit organizations are often underadministered and understaffed. Available resources are channeled first and foremost into program and service delivery, with only a minimum level of resources devoted to administration. For example, university students undoubtedly will have experienced the effects of low levels of administration, but when university administrators are faced with the question as to whether to hire an additional professor to add depth to an academic program or to hire an additional accountant or other administrator, the choice almost always goes to the professor because that choice serves the basic educational goals of the organization. The relatively low level of accounting expertise that therefore exists in most nonprofit organizations places an extra responsibility on both internal and external accountants to be particularly perceptive and helpful in designing financial statements and related reporting systems that serve the needs of the managers and directors, as well as of the other users of the financial statements.

Performance Evaluation

Performance evaluation is probably the most important reporting objective for most service-oriented nonprofit organizations. The managers, directors, donors, and government overseers are all usually interested in evaluating the extent to which the organization is satisfying its goals efficiently and effectively. Although fiscal performance is important to the well-being of the organization, fiscal performance is not the key to its performance as an organization. The extent to which the organization is fulfilling its social role is determined by performance factors that are not reflected directly in the financial statements.

2 Canadian Institute of Chartered Accountants, *Financial Reporting for Non-Profit Organizations,* (CICA, 1980), Chapter 2.

In a fee-for-service organization, the financial statements can give some indication of the ability of the organization to attract sufficient participants to keep it viable and to permit the organization to recover its costs. There may be some market forces at work in shaping the revenue side of a fee-for-service organization.

Most nonprofit organizations do not operate on a fee-for-service basis, however. The financial statements can be an aid to performance evaluation in that the donors and directors can see whether the organization's management has been able to raise sufficient funds to meet the costs, or has been able to control costs sufficiently not to incur a deficit. But it is not the primary function of a nonprofit organization to raise and spend money. The economic activities are essential to providing whatever service the organization was intended to provide, but the economic activities are the side effects of the primary activities, rather than the focus, as in a business enterprise. The providers of financial support for a nonprofit organization will want supplementary information that describes the nature and extent of the services or activities provided by the organization.

While purely financial reporting cannot serve the performance evaluation objective for nonprofit and governmental organizations as well as it can for business enterprises, financial statements aid both internal and external users in making important resource allocation decisions. Given the scarcity of funds within an organization, managers must be able to ascertain which programs are most efficient and effective in order to guide their budgetary and fund-raising activities. External users such as donors and funding agencies also have limited resources, and they wish to allocate their resources in the most effective manner. The nature of the organization, the types of services it provides, and the sources of its financial support will all affect the way in which the financial results are presented, but performance evaluation is an objective underlying much reporting (both financial and nonfinancial) in the nonprofit sector.

Stewardship

Stewardship reporting in nonprofit organizations consists of (1) reports to donors, members, and other financial supporters, and (2) information returns filed with governmental agencies or ministries. Governments may, of course, be financial supporters. In nonprofit stewardship reporting, the objectives are (1) to report on management's ability to stay within spending constraints or other budget limits, including control over deficits and disposition of surpluses, and (2) to report on the use and segregation of funds in accordance with legal or donor restrictions.

Because of the importance of budgetary control in nonprofit organizations and governmental units, financial statements containing comparative budgeted figures are frequently issued. Budgeted figures are particularly likely to be included in financial reports intended for limited distribution, such as to directors, members, donors, and governmental funding agencies. Financial statements issued for general public reporting are less likely to include budget information.

Statements that are prepared with stewardship as the primary objective will tend to emphasize the acquisition and disposition of resources within the accounting period. They are less likely to contain allocations, both interperiod and intraperiod, than statements that are prepared with performance evaluation as the primary objective. For example, it is normal for nonprofit organizations to treat capital expenditures as expenditures of the current period in stewardship reports. In performance reports, however, the capital expenditures might be capitalized and depreciated if they are expected to contribute to operations for several periods and if operating revenues are expected to recover the cost of the assets.

Cash Flow Prediction

Because of the absence of transferable ownership interests, there is less direct interest in cash flow prediction for nonbusiness enterprises than there is for business enterprises. By definition, the members and directors of the organization do not receive direct economic benefit or gain, although they may receive benefits in other ways. Since there is no benefit derived directly from a cash flow from the organization, the statement users are not so concerned with being able to predict the future cash flows of the organization. They are, of course, keenly interested in the viability of the organization and its ability to live within its means.

For managers, cash flow prediction is vital. They clearly need to manage the cash flow of the organization. Cash budgets are the primary tool in this regard, but historical cash flows should be apparent in the general financial statements through a clearly presented statement of changes in financial position, prepared on a *cash* basis in order to assist managers in predicting cash flows and preparing cash budgets.

One group of external users that is interested in cash flow prediction and liquidity is creditors. Unlike donors, creditors expect to get their money back, with interest. Major creditors would therefore be interested in the liquidity position of the organization and the extent of indebtedness, in relation to current and projected cash inflows and net surpluses or deficits.

As with any cash flow prediction, external factors are of major importance. The prospects for fund raising by the organization, the climate for governmental support, and the perceived effectiveness of the organization in fulfilling its goals are all factors that will affect the creditors' cash flow predictions. The financial statements can be of considerable assistance in these predictions, since they should indicate the sources of financial support, the major classes of expenditure, the resource (asset) position of the organization, and the liabilities. They should also give some indication of the extent to which costs are fixed and are committed to projects or services, as opposed to costs that are more discretionary and could be cut back if funding was less than expected.

Most nonprofit organizations have only the routine current liabilities for supplies and services that any operating enterprise would have. Organizations with large capital investment (e.g., in buildings and equipment) may have substantial long-term debt as well. Governmental units may have authority to issue bonds. Since there is no owners' equity to provide a cushion for the bondholders' risk, bonds of governmental units are usually guaranteed by the government itself. For example, Ontario Hydro has bonds of about $24 billion outstanding, all of which are guaranteed by the Province of Ontario (except for those held directly by the Province).

CICA Research Study

In 1980, the CICA issued a research report by a study group on *Financial Reporting for Non-Profit Organizations* (*FRFNPO*). One of the study group's objectives was to identify the objectives of financial reporting for nonprofit organizations. The conclusions of the study group as they relate to objectives include the following:

- The user groups need information to evaluate the financial position and operations of a non-profit organization to make decisions about some future course of action. The information to satisfy these needs is summarized as follows:
  (a) Nature and objective of the organization;
  (b) Performance;
  (c) Overall financial status;
  (d) Compliance with legal requirements;
  (e) Plans for the future.
- The objective of financial information is to provide users with information to make decisions. While each user will read the same financial statements for an overall view, different choices will be made about what is regarded as important information for decisions . . .[3]

The study group concludes that the overall objective of financial reporting by nonprofit organizations is to provide information that is useful for decision making. The study group also comments on the fact that the basic objectives of reporting for both business and nonprofit organizations are quite similar. Both are concerned with performance evaluation, the proper execution of stewardship responsibilities, and with cash flow prediction. Of course, the exact components of the information given and of the accounting policies used will vary depending on the type of organization or governmental unit.

Summary

Essentially, the three pervasive objectives of financial reporting for nonprofit organizations are (1) performance evaluation, by both internal and external users, (2) stewardship reporting, and (3) cash flow prediction and financial position, mainly for creditors or investors in debt securities.

A general feature of nonbusiness enterprises is the absence of a profit objective and thus the organizations' relative freedom from the financial and performance discipline that is imposed by the open market. Legislative and budgetary constraints are imposed as a partial substitute for the discipline of the marketplace and of the profit motive. This major difference between business and nonbusiness enterprises affects the objectives of financial reporting in two major ways. First, it increases the importance of stewardship reporting in assessing management's execution of its responsibilities. Second, it renders the evaluation of performance and of progress towards organizational goals much more difficult.

Since the primary goal of the organization is not financial, it is difficult for financial reports to communicate information useful for assessing the efficiency and effectiveness of the organization or its management. Both management and external users have a need to assess efficiency and effectiveness, and therefore financial information should be presented in a way that facilitates both performance evaluation and resource allocation decisions. The need to evaluate efficiency and effectiveness has two major impacts on financial reporting for nonprofit organizations: (1) financial reporting must be aligned with programmatic objectives, and (2) a greater vol-

3 *Financial Reporting for Non-Profit Organizations*, pp. 28-29.

ume of nonfinancial data must be reported, usually as supplementary information. The greater volume of nonfinancial data assists the performance evaluation objective. Later sections in the chapter discuss supplementary information and programmatic reporting more fully.

Another way in which the relative importance of specific objectives differs between business and nonbusiness enterprises is in the objective of assisting users to predict future cash flows. The primary financing of most nonbusiness organizations is by donation rather than by investment. There are no shareholders, and thus no need to project future dividend flows. Nonprofit organizations have creditors in the normal process of conducting their affairs, and governmental units may also have long-term creditors, although the obligations are normally guaranteed by governments. Only governments themselves are major direct users of the capital markets, and then only for the debt capital market and not the equity capital market. Therefore, the cash flow prediction objective that is so important for business financial reporting is less important for nonbusiness reporting. Liquidity and resources position is still important, however.

While the users' basic objectives are similar for business and nonbusiness organizations, preparers' objectives are significantly different. In place of the objectives of income tax deferral and of net income maximization, minimization, and smoothing, nonprofit managers have an objective of presenting financial statements that enhance the service potential of the organization. This broad objective usually translates to using accounting policies that enhance the organization's ability to attract revenue, including presenting a financial picture of the organization that instills confidence in the fiscal responsibility of management.

In summary, the most important objective in financial reporting for nonprofit organizations is usually that of performance evaluation. Stewardship is also important, especially for restricted or designated funds. Cash flow prediction remains an important objective for determining the long-run resource needs of the organization and its ability to obtain funds to meet those needs. Financial reporting for nonprofit organizations should reflect these objectives, the relative importance of which will, of course, vary from organization to organization. Later sections of this chapter explore the impacts of those objectives on the financial statements.

QUALITATIVE CRITERIA

If there are differences in the basic characteristics of nonbusiness enterprises as compared to business enterprises, and in the relative importance and thrust of the reporting objectives, it might seem that there may also be differences in the qualitative characteristics of the accounting information.

The FRFNPO study group examined the qualities of useful financial information and concluded that "useful financial information must have the following qualities:

- Relevance
- Materiality
- Understandability

- Reliability and verifiability
- Completeness
- Lack of bias
- Timeliness
- Comparability and consistency
- Emphasis on substance over form"[4]

This list is substantially the same as other lists of qualitative characteristics or criteria relating to financial information provided by business enterprises that were discussed in Chapter 2. The FRFNPO report compares their own list of qualities with the qualities espoused by five other studies, and finds no real difference between them.

The FASB has also considered whether or not the qualitative characteristics are different for nonbusiness organizations. In the July 1983 exposure draft, *Proposed Amendments to FASB Concepts Statements 2 and 3 to Apply Them to Nonbusiness Organizations*, "the Board has concluded that the qualitative characteristics described in Concepts Statement 2 apply to nonbusiness organizations as well as to business enterprises" [p. 1]. "Through their application, however, in certain circumstances the information that is appropriate for business enterprises may differ from the information that is appropriate for nonbusiness organizations" [p. vii]. In December 1985, the Board "reaffirmed the conclusion that the qualitative characteristics of accounting information set forth in Concepts Statement 2 (relevance, reliability, comparability, and related qualities) apply to both not-for-profit organizations and business enterprises."[5]

It is the nature of qualitative criteria that they be universally applicable. The criteria are not ends; they are means to ends. Thus their application in varying circumstances will yield different results. Information that is relevant for the users of business enterprise reports may not be relevant for the readers of nonbusiness financial statements. Similarly, information that is not sufficiently reliable for business statements may be suitable for nonbusiness reports, owing to a higher degree of relevance. Some basic measurement methods that are relevant for measuring business performance, such as revenue-expense matching, may be quite irrelevant for measuring the performance of some nonbusiness enterprises.

In summary, research studies into financial reporting for nonbusiness enterprises have not detected any differences in the qualitative characteristics that are appropriate for business versus nonbusiness organizations. Since the characteristics of the organizations and the objectives of financial reporting are different, the results of applying the criteria will differ, but the criteria themselves are the same.

In the following section, we examine what the information provided by nonbusiness enterprises may look like and how it differs by type of organization. We discuss only the financial reports themselves; the procedural aspects of accounting that are useful in nonbusiness organizations are introduced in Chapter 5.

---

4 *Financial Reporting for Non-Profit Organizations*, pp. 21-22.
5 FASB, Statement of Financial Accounting Concepts No. 6, *Elements of Financial Statements*, a replacement of FASB Concepts Statement No. 3 (incorporating an amendment of FASB Concepts Statement No. 2) (December 1985), p. 93.

TYPES OF FINANCIAL STATEMENTS

We have established that the financial reports of a nonprofit organization should contain information suitable for evaluating performance, assessing financial position, and predicting cash flows. The statements that are necessary to communicate the information will usually consist of the following:

1. Balance sheet
2. Statement of operations
3. Statement of changes in financial position
4. Statement of changes in fund balances

In addition, there should be notes to the financial statements. The statements should be in a comparative format, with comparisons to the previous year, and to the budgeted amounts, or to both.

While this is the normal range of statements, it is quite possible that an organization will present only two statements, a balance sheet and one other statement, which is both a statement of operations and a statement of changes in financial position, explaining the changes in fund balances.

This list of statements looks deceptively simple. The statements do not look much different from those that we are accustomed to seeing for businesses. The differences can be great, however. Let us start with the statement of operations.

In a business enterprise, the statement of operations is the income statement. It is a statement that is common to all business enterprises, because they all are seeking to earn a profit. As we have seen in Chapter 3, the measurement methods may vary considerably from industry to industry, but many of the same basic methods are in use. Virtually all businesses attempt to match their costs with their revenues, for example, even if only for the benefit of the tax authorities. Depreciation is a universal practice, even though methods may vary. Revenue recognition policies seldom rest completely on cash flow; the nature of the earnings process is considered in deciding when to recognize revenues.

In nonbusiness organizations, there is no such underlying similarity because there is no universal need to measure net income. At one extreme are those nonbusiness organizations that charge a fee for their services or outputs and need to match their costs with their revenues in order to report on their performance. These organizations will have a statement of operations that looks very much like an income statement for a business. Schedule 4-1 shows the statement of operations for Ontario Hydro for 1987. The only perceptible difference between Ontario Hydro's statement of operations and any other income statement is the section on the bottom that shows the allocation of the net income. Since the corporation has no shareholders, it does not declare dividends. Instead, it appropriates its net income to retire its debt and to cover contingencies.

For the vast majority of nonbusiness organizations, a statement similar to businesses' income statements is not appropriate. Since there is no profit objective, there is not the same need to allocate costs and revenues between periods. For most nonbusiness organizations, the key to performance is the management of funds, and it is not uncommon to merge the statement of

---

SCHEDULE 4-1

Ontario Hydro
Statement of Operations
For the Year Ended December 31, 1987

	1987	1986
	(in millions of dollars)	
Revenues:		
Primary power and energy		
Municipal utilities	$3,441	$3,116
Rural retail customers	968	885
Direct industrial customers	675	604
	5,084	4,605
Secondary power and energy (note 1)	196	248
	5,280	4,853
Costs:		
Operation, maintenance and administration	1,150	1,014
Fuel used for electric generation	1,124	933
Water rentals (note 2)	90	91
Power purchased	117	128
Nuclear agreement — payback (note 3)	(23)	(63)
Depreciation (note 4)	723	705
	3,181	2,808
Income before financing charges	2,099	2,045
Interest (note 5)	1,702	1,585
Foreign exchange (note 6)	126	213
	1,828	1,798
Net Income	$ 271	$ 247
Appropriation for (withdrawal from):		
Debt retirement	$ 319	$ 292
Stabilization of rates and contingencies	(48)	(45)
	$ 271	$ 247

operations and the statement of changes in financial position into a single report, frequently called a statement of revenues and expenditures.[6] The statement of revenues and expenditures also frequently reconciles the beginning and ending fund balances as well, thereby incorporating the statement of changes in fund balances. Thus we see that many nonprofit organizations

---

6 Where there are substantial current assets and current liabilities that are not "cash equivalents," a separate statement of changes in financial position may still be required. Often, however, non-cash-equivalents are relatively minor, and a separate statement of changes is not provided because the differences between it and the statement of operations would be trivial.

have only two financial statements: a balance sheet, and a statement that combines the statements of operations, changes in financial position, and changes in fund balances.

To illustrate some of the types of statements that may be used by non-profit organizations, we will look at two sets of hypothetical financial statements.

Illustrative Statements

Schedule 4-2 shows an illustrative set of financial statements for a hypothetical club, The Outdoors Club. The statement of revenues and expenditures shows a net excess of revenues over expenses of $230 for 19x3, as compared to a net deficiency of $1,600 for 19x2. The 19x2 balance sheet indicates that the **net asset position** or **fund balance** of the club was $1,300 on December 31,19x2. When the 19x3 excess of revenues over expenditures is added, the 19x3 year-end fund balance is $1,530.

One of the basic reporting issues for nonprofit organizations is whether to report on the cash or accrual basis. The Outdoors Club uses the accrual basis. This is apparent from the fact that the balance sheet shows both current receivables that relate to the revenues (fees and interest) and accounts payable that relate to operating expenses.

A second reporting issue is whether to capitalize the purchase of fixed assets or to treat such purchases as an expenditure of the current period. The Outdoor Club expenditures include $2,000 for the purchase of a photocopier in 19x2. In a business enterprise, a photocopier would be treated as a fixed asset. But since the emphasis in nonbusiness organizations is so frequently on control of resources rather than on matching costs and revenues, expenditures that would be capitalized by businesses are frequently treated as expenditures of the current period by nonbusiness organizations. Purchases of equipment, furniture and fixtures, and even buildings can be charged directly to operations rather than capitalized and depreciated. Indeed, it is the lack of interperiod allocations such as depreciation that makes it feasible to combine the statement of operations and the statement of changes in financial position.

When fixed assets are charged immediately to operations, they do not appear on the balance sheet. Therefore, the balance sheets of many nonbusiness organizations consist only of current assets and liabilities, with a balancing equity amount that represents the accumulated excess (or deficiency) of revenues over expenditures. While parts of this balancing equity amount can be appropriated or restricted, just as retained earnings may be in a business enterprise, *this balancing figure is the only nonliability equity amount in the balance sheet of a nonbusiness organization.* If there is any share capital, then it is not a nonbusiness entity, but is instead a business corporation in which someone has made an investment (usually the government, in the form of a crown corporation).

The financial statements of most nonbusiness entities fall between the simplicity of those of The Outdoor Club and the business-type statements of Ontario Hydro. An example of statements of intermediate complexity is illustrated in Schedule 4-3.

The statement of revenues and expenses for Leggy Dance Company is similar to the statement for The Outdoor Club in format, except that it is divided into two sections: one for operating fund revenues and expenses

SCHEDULE 4-2

The Outdoors Club
Statement of Revenues and Expenditures
Years Ended December 31, 19x3 and 19x2

	19x3	19x2
Revenues:		
Members' dues	$ 9,200	$ 8,800
Nonmembers' participation fees	1,400	1,000
Interest	400	600
	11,000	10,400
Expenditures:		
Office rental	2,520	2,400
Telephone	650	600
Stationery and supplies	1,800	2,200
Newsletter costs	4,000	3,600
Postage	1,800	1,200
Purchase of used photocopier	—	2,000
	10,770	12,000
Excess (deficiency) of revenues over expenditures	230	(1,600)
Fund balance, January 1	1,300	2,900
Fund balance, December 31	$ 1,530	$ 1,300

Balance Sheets
December 31, 19x3 and 19x2

	19x3	19x2
Assets:		
Cash and term deposits	$ 460	$ 2,000
Dues and fees receivable	1,800	700
Accrued interest receivable	70	100
Total assets	2,330	2,800
Liabilities:		
Accounts payable	800	1,500
Fund balance (unrestricted)	$ 1,530	$ 1,300

and a second for the capital fund. Leggy Dance Company (LDC) receives revenue both for operating or performance purposes and for restricted use in commissioning and mounting new choreographic productions. Because the grants are given for two different purposes, LDC must segregate the receipts and expenditures for both. This is the basic thrust of **fund accounting**. For 19x5, LDC experienced a deficit of $5,000 in the operating fund and a surplus of $26,000 in the capital fund.

On the balance sheet, the assets and liabilities of the two funds are consolidated, but they could also have been reported separately. The extent of

SCHEDULE 4-3

Leggy Dance Company
Statement of Operations
Years Ended December 31, 19x5 and 19x4

	19x5	19x4
Operating fund revenues and expenses:		
Revenues:		
Box office receipts, net of commissions and service charges	$150,000	$120,000
Canada Council grant	220,000	210,000
Private contributions to operating fund	50,000	35,000
T-shirts and poster sales	10,000	5,000
	430,000	370,000
Expenses:		
Theatre rental and ancillary expenses	45,000	30,000
Salaries	170,000	150,000
Printing	30,000	20,000
Advertising	94,000	80,000
Wardrobe and set maintenance	60,000	50,000
Rental of sets and lights	14,000	10,000
Office expenses	22,000	20,000
	435,000	360,000
Net performance revenue (expense)	(5,000)	10,000
Operating fund balance (deficit): January 1	(15,000)	(25,000)
December 31	$ (20,000)	$ (15,000)
Capital fund:		
Revenues:		
Arts council choreographic grant	—	$ 20,000
Dewhirst Foundation production grant	$ 80,000	—
Capital-projects fund raising	24,000	17,000
	104,000	37,000
Expenditures:		
Commissioned choreography	18,000	20,000
New productions:		
"Harold in Italy"	—	40,000
"Front Runner"	60,000	—
	78,000	60,000
Net capital revenue (expenditure)	26,000	(23,000)
Capital fund balance: January 1	7,000	30,000
December 31	$ 33,000	$ 7,000

4-3 (continued)

Balance Sheets
December 31, 19x5 and 19x4

	19x5	19x4
Assets:		
Cash	$ 2,000	$ 1,000
Receivable from Canada Council	46,000	41,000
Donor pledges	15,000	10,000
Total assets	$ 63,000	$ 52,000
Liabilities:		
Accounts payable	$ 30,000	$ 40,000
Bank note payable	20,000	20,000
	50,000	60,000
Fund balances:		
Operating fund (deficit)	(20,000)	(15,000)
Capital fund — unrestricted	33,000	7,000
	13,000	(8,000)
Total liabilities and fund balances	$ 63,000	$ 52,000

consolidation of funds for reporting purposes (*not* for recording purposes) is another one of the issues in financial reporting for nonprofit organizations. But even when the assets and liabilities are consolidated, the individual *fund balances* must be shown separately.

As was the case with The Outdoor Club's capital expenditure, LDC charges capital expenditures to the current period. LDC may have spent considerable sums on sets, costumes, and choreography during its history, and these expenditures can be expected to benefit future periods as the company develops its repertoire and continues to present productions developed in prior years. But neither the value nor the cost of these assets appears on the balance sheet.

During 19x5, The Netherlands Dance Theater redesigned its production of "Septet," and donated the old sets and costumes to Leggy Dance Company. Since the production received from the Netherlands Dance Theater cost Leggy nothing, Leggy does not report the value of the donated production on its statements (although it may be disclosed in a note). An alternative treatment would have been to record the estimated value of the production as both a revenue and an expenditure, so that the full value of the resources passing through the organization is measured. Thus the treatment of donated goods and services is another reporting issue for nonprofit organizations. All of the reporting issues mentioned above are discussed more fully in following sections.

Summary: Financial Statements

The financial statements of a nonbusiness organization consist of a balance sheet, a statement of operations, a statement of changes in financial position, a statement of changes in fund balances, and notes to the statements. The statement of operations and the statement of changes are often merged into a single statement because the financial measure of operations is the management of funds rather than the provision of services in return for fees. When an organization does provide goods or services in return for fees, the statement of operations becomes distinct from the statement of changes and resembles more an income statement for a business enterprise.

The balance sheet is a reflection of the accounting policies used in the statement of operations. If all expenditures are treated as period costs and charged to operations in the current period, then no long-term assets will appear on the balance sheet. On the other hand, if expenditures that benefit future periods are capitalized and allocated, then the balance sheet will show the long-term assets and accumulated depreciation or amortization thereon.

The accrual basis is most commonly used in nonprofit organizations, and the balance sheet will show current receivables and payables. As a result, revenues and expenditures will also usually be on the accrual basis. Since expenditure control is an important aspect of the operations of most nonbusiness organizations, liabilities will frequently include amounts **committed** (by purchase order or by contract) rather than only amounts due for executed contracts or for goods or services received. This concept is discussed in Chapter 5.

A major problem with financial statements for nonbusiness organizations is that since the goals of the organization are normally nonfinancial, financial reports cannot give a good picture of how well the organization is achieving its goals. A nonprofit organization or governmental unit should therefore submit an annual report to its members, directors, donors, and others who are attempting to evaluate the performance of the entity. The annual report should contain not only the financial statements and notes thereto, but also nonfinancial information that will facilitate understanding of the organization, its goals and objectives, and its progress towards achieving its goals. A later section discusses the supplementary information that is needed by the users of the financial statements. But first, we will discuss the major financial reporting issues for nonprofit organizations, some of which have been pointed out in the preceding illustrations.

GAAP FOR NONPROFIT ORGANIZATIONS

Until quite recently, there were no generally accepted accounting principles for nonprofit organizations. Accounting policy selection essentially was a free game; management (or the accountant or auditor[7] preparing the statements) could select virtually any accounting policies that they wanted. Nonprofit organizations were explicitly exempted from the recommendations of the *CICA Handbook*. As a result, statements in auditors' opinions that the financial statements were "prepared in accordance with GAAP" had little meaning. The better audit opinions generally used the disclosed basis of ac-

---

7 In theory, auditors should not prepare the financial statements. In practice, auditors often do because of a lack of accounting expertise within the organization.

counting, wherein the opinion referred the reader to the accounting policy note.

In 1987, the Accounting Standards Committee issued an exposure draft to bring financial reporting for nonprofit organizations under the *CICA Handbook* recommendations. With some modifications, the exposure draft was approved in 1988 and the new Section 4230 and related amendments to existing sections became effective for nonprofit organizations for fiscal years commencing on or after January 1, 1989 [para. 4230.25]. The original statement in the *Introduction to Accounting Recommendations* that "Recommendations are intended to apply to all types of profit oriented enterprises" was amended to read

> Recommendations are intended to apply to all types of profit oriented enterprises and to non-profit organizations as defined in paragraph 4230.02, unless a particular Recommendation makes a specific exemption or extension. No Recommendation is intended to override the requirements of a governing statute. [p. 9]

Section 4230 deals largely with disclosure. One of the problems with nonprofit financial reporting has been a lack of adequate disclosure of accounting policies, and Section 4230 attempts to deal with this problem by recommending disclosures relating to a number of measurement and reporting issues. We will refer to these recommendations as we discuss the major reporting issues below.

The new *Handbook* section is an adaptation of some of the recommendations of *FRFNPO. FRFNPO* still remains the primary written discussion of accounting policies for nonprofit organizations in Canada, and we will continue to refer to that research study throughout our discussion.

MAJOR REPORTING ISSUES

Cash vs. Accrual

Some nonprofit organizations use the cash basis of accounting, recording revenues and expenditures only when a cash flow occurs. The cash basis is easier than the accrual basis, and financial reports prepared on the cash basis require no further reconciliation to cash budgets.

The use of the cash basis, however, may result in reported revenues and expenditures that do not properly reflect the commitments made by grantors and donors (on the revenue side) or by the organization (on the expenditure side) during the reporting period. In addition, the balance sheet would not disclose the monetary assets and liabilities of the organization, thereby impairing evaluation of financial position.

In *FRFNPO*, the study group recommended the use of full accrual accounting in preparing financial statements:

> The accrual basis results in a more accurate and complete presentation of an organization's financial activities than the cash basis. In particular, it assures the accurate reporting of the actual cost of providing services in an accounting period .... The accrual basis of accounting is the most relevant basis for reporting both revenues and expenses if the actual financial position and results of operations of a non-profit organization are to be disclosed in general purpose financial statements. [pp. 51-52]

Paragraph 4230.03 of the *CICA Handbook* recommends that "financial statements should be prepared using the accrual basis of accounting." While that would seem to be an unequivocal statement, it is not as clear as it may at first appear. The question is: what should be accrued? It is safe to assume that accrued expenses should be reported, but revenues are another matter. If revenues are received by donations or grants from individuals, charitable foundations, or businesses, the donors' pledges of support are not legally enforceable claims. Recording revenue when pledged may result in an over-statement of revenue, since some pledges may never be paid. On the other hand, it may be possible to make an allowance for uncollectible pledges, thereby permitting current recognition of revenues when pledged. Commit-ments made by governmental ministries or agencies, however, are almost always fulfilled. Therefore a nonprofit organization may choose to recognize governmental revenues when the commitment is made, but to defer recog-nition of pledges by individuals until the cash is received.

The 1987 exposure draft recommended that pledges be recognized as receivables. The *Handbook* recommendation, however, is simply that "The policy followed in accounting for pledges should be disclosed" [para. 4230.12] and that "When pledges are recorded, the amount recorded should be disclosed" [para. 4230.13].

For the stewardship reporting objective, full recognition of pledges as receivables would seem to be the most appropriate accounting policy be-cause users would then be able to see the full amount of resources available to satisfy creditors and other claims on resources. Performance evaluation could also be enhanced by showing readers the results of fund-raising efforts during the period, rather than having the fruits of those efforts show up only in the following year, when collected. The relevancy of the pledges receivable may override the possible measurement error in estimating the amounts uncollectible.

Recognizing pledges as a receivable does not necessarily lead to imme-diate recognition as revenue. Grants and donations should be recorded as revenue in the period for which they were intended by the grantor or donor, or in the same period as the expenditures that they were intended to fund.

For example, if a donor gives or pledges in 19x8 an amount to sponsor a conference in 19x9, the donation should be recognized as revenue only in 19x9. The cash or receivable recorded as an asset in 19x8 should be offset by a deferred or unearned revenue amount until the conference takes place. Proper matching of revenues and expenses is important in nonprofit orga-nizations as well as in business organizations, but the process tends to be one of matching the revenue to the expenditures rather than matching the ex-penses to the revenue, as is more commonly the case in business enterprises.

Expenditure Basis vs. Expense Basis

Nonprofit organizations must decide whether they are going to recognize their costs on the basis of disbursements, expenditures, or expenses. A dis-bursement basis is essentially a cash basis of reporting, and while it may be appropriate (on the basis of materiality) for small organizations with minimal accrued expenses or payables, it is seldom a defensible policy for larger or-ganizations. In the past, some very large organizations have used a disburse-ment basis as they have grown, with the effect that they have lost control of expenditures. Once a disbursement basis is chosen, managers may become reluctant to switch to an expenditure basis as accounts payable grow because the change would put the organization in a substantial deficit position.

The real choice therefore is between recording costs on the basis of expenditures or of expenses. The expenditure basis has little equivalency in the private sector, where we normally think in terms of expenses. But the notion of expenses is related to the concept of profit, which generally does not exist in the nonprofit sector.

The choice rests on two factors: the nature of the revenue and the need for performance evaluation. If the revenue is in the form of a fee-for-service or a reimbursed cost, such as a hospital or a day care centre, then the revenue should be adequate to cover all of the expenses incurred in providing the service. Note that the matching is to the service provided and not to the revenue; the revenue flows from the expenses and not vice versa. Also, if measurement of efficiency is enhanced by recording the expenses of providing services, then an expense basis is appropriate.

The expenditure basis means that costs are recorded in operations when incurred, either by a cash disbursal or by incurring a liability. The purchase of supplies, for example, would be recorded as an operating cost when acquired rather than when used. No supplies inventory would appear on the balance sheet.

An expenditure basis is most appropriate when service and program outputs are difficult to measure and therefore there is no clear basis for allocating expenses or measuring efficiency. Examples would include social clubs and trade unions; some specific activities may be clearly defined but the general operations of the organization cannot be specifically related to programmatic goals with measurable outputs. An expenditure basis is also appropriate when revenues are not directly related to services or when revenues are intended simply to provide the financing for the expenditures.

It is worth pointing out that frequently the choice is immaterial for the organization as a whole. For many nonprofit organizations, salary costs comprise 70-80% of the organizations' total costs, and salary costs are expenditures and expenses at the same time because the benefits of the salary expenditures cannot be deferred to a future period. As a result, there may be little difference in the periodic operating results whether the organization uses an expenditure or an expense basis of reporting. However, the decision as to whether to use an expenditure or an expense basis does not depend only on an overview of the organization as a whole. If, for example, evaluation of the performance of individual programs is improved by using an expense basis, or if program-by-program stewardship reporting requirements point towards an expenditure basis, then the decision on accounting policy should be made by evaluating the appropriateness of the alternative policies for programmatic reporting rather than simply for the organization's overall reporting. Programmatic reporting is discussed and illustrated later in this chapter.

One important but specialized instance where expenditure vs. expense can make a big difference in reported results is in the accounting for fixed assets. The choice of accounting policy for fixed assets is more complex than just expenditure vs. expense, however, as the following section illustrates.

Fixed Assets

There are three principal accounting methods used by nonprofit organizations for fixed assets:

1. Expense immediately.
2. Capitalize and depreciate.
3. Capitalize but do not depreciate.

Other options also exist, such as capitalizing the assets and making periodic appropriations (in lieu of depreciation) to a capital fund to provide for the cost of replacement. An organization may use the same method for all of its fixed assets or different methods for different types of assets.

Expensing immediately is the most common method, which is the expenditure basis as applied to fixed assets. The main reason for the popularity of this approach relates to the nature of the revenue used to acquire the assets.

The operating revenues of many nonprofit organizations are specifically restricted by granting governmental ministries to operating expenditures, *excluding* the acquisition of fixed assets. Separate grants are given as capital grants for the acquisition of fixed assets, and the ministries usually prohibit the inclusion of depreciation in the operating accounts. When a capital grant is given, the revenue from the grant is matched to the cost of acquiring the asset in the period of acquisition, and no capitalization or depreciation occurs. If the organization were to capitalize and depreciate the asset, then recognition of the revenue in the period of acquisition without the offsetting expenditure would make it appear that the organization has a substantial surplus when, in fact, the funds have been fully utilized. In future periods, the depreciation expense would put the organization in an operating deficit position because the operating grant would not be sufficient to offset the cost of depreciation.

It has been argued that depreciation is a cost of providing services and that depreciation should therefore be recorded regardless of the way in which the assets were financed. This argument has reached its zenith in the FASB's *SFAS 93, Recognition of Depreciation by Not-for-Profit Organizations*. The FASB has decided that all nonprofit organizations in the U.S.A. should capitalize and depreciate their fixed assets, regardless of any other factor. The Board argues that "using up assets in providing services ... has a cost whether those assets have been acquired in prior periods or in the current period and whether acquired by paying cash, incurring liabilities, or by contribution" [para. 20].[8] In Canada, however, this view has gained little support.

Sometimes capital grants are given only for major assets such as for buildings, while smaller acquisitions (such as furniture or computers) must be financed through the operating grants. In that case, different accounting policies might be used for the two types of assets due to the differing relationship to revenues.

Even in organizations where revenue comes from general donations rather than from government grants, expenditures for major fixed assets may be financed by means of special capital fund-raising campaigns. There is no intent on the part of either the organization or the donors that part of the cost of assets be charged against operations. If depreciation is taken in periods following the acquisition, then the organization will show a deficit in those periods even if fund-raising activities are sufficient to cover the expenditures for the period (or, conversely, if expenditures are held to the level of the revenue raised).

---

8 In the exposure draft for *SFAS 93*, the Board concluded that "whether an organization's use of an asset results in an expense does not depend on how the asset was acquired and whether and how it will be replaced" [para. 24].

There are two side effects to the policy of expensing fixed assets when acquired: (1) the balance sheet does not disclose the existence of, or investment in, fixed assets, and (2) future operations bear no part of the cost of the fixed assets.

These two problems are separable. The balance sheet problem can be solved rather simply just by debiting a fixed asset account and crediting a designated or appropriated fund balance. For example, suppose The Outdoors Club (Schedule 4-2) wished to treat the expenditure for the copying machine as a period cost in 19x2, but wanted to show the asset on its balance sheet. The entries to accomplish this result would be as follows:

Expenditures — copying machine	$2,000	
Cash		$2,000
Asset — copying machine	$2,000	
Fund balance — designated		$2,000

Since the expenditure was charged to operations completely in 19x2, no cost can be charged to operations in following years. However, the declining usefulness of the machine can be reflected on the balance sheet by depreciating the asset directly to the designated fund balance. Assuming that the machine is depreciated over five years on a straight-line basis, the entry to adjust the carrying value of the machine would appear as follows:

Fund balance — designated	$ 400	
Accumulated depreciation		$ 400

Technically, the establishment of a set of self-balancing accounts for the fixed assets is in itself a type of fund. Since there are no liquid resources in the fixed accounts, however, the set of accounts for fixed assets is usually known as a self-balancing **group** of accounts. In large nonbusiness organizations, the fixed asset group is established partially for control purposes, so that managers can be held accountable for the fixed assets under their control. In a consolidated balance sheet, the fixed asset group can be combined with the operating fund or funds in order to give a better indication of the total resources of the organization.

The second problem cited above for immediate expensing, that future operations bear no share of the cost of the fixed assets, leads to the second method of accounting for fixed assets: capitalize and depreciate. This method is most appropriate under either of two circumstances: (1) the cost of replacing the assets must be borne by, or recovered from, general revenues, or (2) evaluation of efficiency requires that the cost of *all* inputs, including fixed assets, be included in the measurement of inputs. These inputs will then be compared to programmatic outputs in determining the efficiency of the organization.

A third approach to reporting fixed assets is to capitalize the assets and never charge the cost to operations. This approach is particularly appropriate when the assets do not decline in value or in usefulness. The collections of art galleries and museums, for example, do not normally depreciate in value and should not be charged to operations. They may, however, be charged as an expenditure of a special acquisition fund, and would always be shown as a use of funds on a statement of changes in financial position. But charging the cost to the operating fund would be inappropriate.

Unfortunately, some organizations may use the "capitalize but do not depreciate" approach in order to avoid having the cost of the assets affect the operating results at all. When the costs of deteriorating buildings and equipment are reflected only in the balance sheet and never in the statement of operations, then the real needs of the organization for funds to renew the assets may not be apparent. Such an approach tends to defeat all three of the primary users' objectives of financial reporting of performance evaluation, stewardship, and cash flow prediction.

The accounting and reporting for fixed assets is one of the most contentious issues in nonprofit accounting. The FRFNPO study group considered the issue at some length, and concludes in their report that "non-profit organizations should capitalize all material fixed assets" [p. 95] because capitalization gives statement readers a better indication of the resources of the organization. As for depreciating the assets, the study group comes down firmly on all sides of the issue:

(a) The majority of the members of the Study Group believe that depreciation need not always be recorded and:
   • Depreciation based on estimated useful life is significant where fixed assets are purchased (or related debt repaid) from operating funds, but is less significant, and could even be misleading, where fixed assets are purchased from special fund raising or grants.
   • Fixed asset acquisitions written off against current operations should be shown separately on the statement of operations after current activities.
   • Supplementary information on fixed assets, for example, estimated useful lives, should be presented when depreciation is not recorded on the basis of estimated useful life.
   • As noted in Chapter 3, the statement of changes in financial position, which excludes depreciation, should also be provided.
(b) Some members of the Study Group believe that depreciation should always be recorded, as set out in Section 3060 of the *CICA Handbook*.
(c) One Study Group member believes that, in accordance with the cash flow basis of accounting [that is, using accruals but not allocations], depreciation should never be recorded. [p. 95]

The *CICA Handbook* provides only that "the policy followed in accounting for fixed assets should be disclosed." [para. 4230.16] No recommendations are made for valuation or for depreciation, although the issues relating to fixed assets are the subject of a current project of the Accounting Standards Committee.

The foregoing discussion has focused on the reporting of the cost of fixed assets. Another issue is whether nonprofit organizations with appreciating assets should attempt to report the value of their assets. Art galleries and museums are the best examples of organizations having assets that, as a group, increase in value. Estimates of value may be useful to users of the statements, because an apparently large deficit could perhaps be wiped out simply by selling one item of the collection. While it would not speak well for the long-term viability of the organization to have to sell off its collection in order to meet its operating expenses, the existence of very valuable collections certainly improves the financial position of the organization and its ability to repay debts even in periods of severe financial distress.

Although the value of assets may be desirable disclosure, the practice is not generally followed. Estimates of the value of assets inevitably are unreliable, difficult to verify, and may not be free from bias. In addition, there is a cost associated with having independent appraisals made, and most institutions would prefer not to incur that cost. Therefore, reporting the value of assets is more a theory than a practice. Indeed, many galleries and museums do not even capitalize the *cost* of their collections, let alone the *value*.

Donated Goods and Services

Many nonprofit organizations receive donated goods and services. An accounting issue arises from nonmonetary donations: should the donated goods and services be assigned a value and reported in the statements?

In some cases, goods or services are donated as a way of helping the organization to raise money. The goods or services are sold or auctioned off, and the organization ultimately receives cash in exchange for the donated goods or services. In such instances, the inflow of cash determines the value of the donation, and the cash receipts must be recorded as a donation by the nonprofit organization.

More commonly, however, the goods and services are not donated as a way of fund raising, but are donated in order to assist the organization in achieving its objectives. The United Way, for example, receives substantial donations of executive time from businesses to help the appeal manage its campaigns. Should the United Way assign a value to the donated time? As another example, public accounting firms sometimes conduct audits of nonprofit organizations for a fee, which covers the cost of the audit, but which is below the rates that would be charged to a business enterprise. The nonprofit organization could either record the actual amount of the fee as billed, or it could record the fair market value of the services rendered and credit the difference between the actual cost and the full value to donations.

When donated goods or services are assigned a value and recorded by the organization, the credit to revenues offsets the debit to expenditures and there is no impact on the net operating results. However, the absolute values of the revenues and expenses are affected, and it is possible that management's performance could be evaluated differently.

For example, one measure of the efficacy of a fund-raising organization is the proportion of funds raised that are consumed as fund-raising expenses. An organization that spends only 10% of the donations to obtain those donations is perceived as doing a better job than one that spends 40% of the funds it raises. But if the 40% organization is paying for all of the services it receives, while the 10% organization is using enormous amounts of volunteer effort, are the financial results of the two organizations really comparable? If the 10% organization were to record the value of its donated effort, its cost ratio may rise to 60%. Thus the recording of donated goods and services can have an impact on the perceptions of the readers of the statements, at least in terms of performance evaluation.

For stewardship reporting, the advantages of reporting the value of donated goods and services are not so clear. If the primary objective of the statements is to report on how management used the funds at their disposal, then reporting donated services on the statements may only impair the reporting objective, because it will appear that management had more funds at its disposal than was actually the case.

In *Financial Reporting for Non-Profit Organizations*, the study group concludes that:

> donated services, materials and facilities . . . that have a material effect on the

operations of a non-profit organization should be reported in the statement of operations as both current revenue and expenses in the period received. They should be disclosed at fair value at the date donated to the organization when the following conditions exist:

1. They are an essential service, material or facility that is normally purchased and would be paid for if not donated.
2. The organization controls the way they are used.
3. There is a measurable basis for arriving at a dollar value.
4. They are not intended solely for the benefit of the members of the organization.

Services provided by a non-profit organization may depend directly on volunteer efforts and would not be available or would be considerably reduced if there were no volunteer participation. If these services would not be replaced by paid workers, it would not be appropriate to report a dollar amount for them in the general purpose financial statements. Nor should the value of volunteer efforts for fund raising drives, which can be difficult to measure in monetary terms, be included. The nature of the volunteer services can, however, be described in an annual report accompanying the financial statements. [p. 100]

The thrust of the study group's recommendations seems clearly to be in the direction of fulfilling the reporting objective of performance appraisal. The fourth criterion for including the value of donated services excludes those organizations in which stewardship is the main objective, while the third criterion excludes measurements that are unreliable.

Practice has varied considerably. Recording and reporting the value of donated goods and services seems to have been the exception rather than the rule in the past. Recently, however, the Accounting Standards Committee has largely incorporated the FRFNPO recommendations into Section 4230 of the *CICA Handbook*, strengthening them somewhat for donated property, plant, and equipment; "Donated property, plant and equipment should be recorded at fair market value when fair value can be reasonably estimated" [para. 4230.04]. This section goes on to say:

An organization may choose to record the value of donated materials and services, but should do so only when a fair value can be reasonably estimated and when the materials and services are normally purchased by the organization and would be paid for if not donated. When donated materials and services are recorded, fair value should be used as the basis of measurement [para. 4230.06].

The first recommendation would appear to be fairly straightforward, although there is still the issue of whether fair value can be estimated in a particular situation. The second recommendation is much weaker, indicating simply the conditions under which donated materials and services *may* be recorded; the recommendation stops considerably short of saying that such materials and services *should* be recorded. Clearly, there is no point in recording donated materials and services unless the reporting objectives are served thereby.

Other *Handbook* recommendations are for disclosure of the accounting policies used [para. 4230.07] and the nature and amount of any donated goods or services recorded [paras. 4230.05 and .08]. Fair value is defined in the usual sense of "the amount that would be agreed upon by informed parties dealing at arm's length in an open and unrestricted market" [para. 4230.11].

When nonbusiness organizations prepare their financial statements, a question frequently arises as to the extent to which the individual funds should be reported separately. If there is a large number of separate funds under control of management, separate reporting of each would result in quite a voluminous report, even though columnar formats could be used for conciseness. Separate reporting by funds may clarify the status of each individual fund, but may obscure the overall financial position of the organization and the results of its operations. On the other hand, consolidation of the various funds may hide important characteristics of individual funds, and may impede stewardship reporting.

The extent of aggregation or consolidation of funds is, like all reporting issues, an accounting policy that must be decided for each organization; no all-embracing rule can be propounded. There are some guidelines that can be followed, however.

First, the impact of the objectives must be considered. Stewardship reporting may tend to call for minimal consolidation, while performance appraisal would tend to demand more comprehensive reporting, which is achieved by consolidation. Reporting to creditors on financial position would depend on the circumstances of the organization. If the liabilities of the funds are all general obligations of the organization, then consolidated reporting would disclose the overall financial position of the organization. If, instead, some of the liabilities are restricted to the assets for individual funds, then the creditors need to see the financial position of the funds for which they are creditors. If the financial viability of certain funds is reliant upon cash flows generated by the fund (such as in a university bookstore), then the operating statement of the fund should be presented separately.

Another guideline is that similar types of funds or funds with similar objectives can be combined for reporting purposes. All of the ancillary, self-supporting activities of a university, such as the bookstore, food services, parking, and residences could be grouped together because they are similar types of funds. Also, all the student aid funds could be combined for reporting purposes since they serve a similar objective, even though the funds may vary by type: some may be endowment funds that are restricted as to principal, some may be donations that are completely unrestricted, and some may be revolving loan funds in which neither principal nor interest can be disbursed except as a loan.

Finally, the funds do not need to have the same treatment for reporting on all the financial statements. Funds (or groups of funds) can be reported separately on the statement of operations, but combined on the balance sheet. Conversely, the funds may be combined on the statement of operations, but reported separately on the balance sheet and the statement of changes in financial position. The reporting objectives and the operating circumstances of each nonbusiness organization will lead to an accounting policy on consolidation. As with any accounting measurement, it may be necessary to make trade-offs among the qualitative criteria in making a decision on consolidation of funds for reporting purposes.

An issue that is closely related to that of consolidation deals with the relationship between legally distinct but operationally similar organizations under common control. For example, some arts organizations and social service organizations have a **foundation** that serves primarily to raise money for the

Consolidation

Defining the Reporting Entity

main organization. The foundation usually has a board of trustees that is drawn directly from the board of directors of the principal operating arts or social service organization that it controls. Therefore, both the foundation and the operating agency are under common control. Since the foundation is legally a separate organization, however, it usually reports separately from the operating agency. Such a practice makes it difficult to evaluate the operations of the operating agency because a large part of the revenues (and, sometimes, of the expenses) are "hidden" on the foundation's statements. Unless the reader of the operating agency knows that the foundation exists and is able both to obtain the statements and perform an ad hoc consolidation, he or she will have difficulty evaluating the agency's financial position or the results of its operations.

The 1988 Annual Report of the Ontario provincial auditor contains a good example. The Ministry of Health has a practice of providing funds to cover the operating deficits of hospitals. The provincial auditor obtained the financial statements of the foundations for ten of the hospitals that received deficit funding in 1987. Three of the ten had considerable sums available in their respective foundations that were not taken into account by the Ministry in funding their deficits. Two of the examples cited by the provincial auditor are:

- One hospital, which received $2.5 million in deficit funding from the Ministry, had transferred $3.2 million from its operations to the unrestricted capital funds of its Foundation.
- Another hospital, which received approximately $3 million in deficit funding from the Ministry, had approximately $5.4 million of capital funds in its Foundation, not restricted for any specific use. All donations received by this Foundation were classified as capital. Furthermore, this Foundation charged the hospital approximately $3 million in fees, between 1984 and 1987, for managing apartment residences.[9]

Indeed, in reviewing 25 of the 69 hospitals that received deficit funding in 1987, the auditor found that 11 of the 25 "had transferred funds on several occasions from the hospital to a Foundation."[10] As a result, the auditor recommended that the Ministry obtain and review all hospital foundation financial statements before funding the deficits.

The FRFNPO study group discussed the reporting entity issue, which they call **combined** financial statements, and reached the following conclusions; "When a non-profit organization controls other non-profit organizations ... the reporting organization should prepare combined financial statements except when they would be misleading. When organizations are related, but control does not exist, it may be desirable to have combined financial statements."[11]

The study also recommends that where combined statements are not presented, the organization's affiliation with related organizations should be disclosed. The report suggests criteria that would indicate when nonprofit organizations are related and when they should prepare combined statements. Combined statements may be indicated when there are common

9 Office of the Provincial Auditor, *1988 Annual Report* (Queen's Printer for Ontario, 1988), pp. 99-100.
10 *1988 Annual Report*, 99.
11 *Financial Reporting for Non-Profit Organizations*, p. 72.

boards of directors or common memberships, when the money raised by one organization is provided to other organizations for common programs, when the resources of one organization are used substantially for the benefit of another organization, or when the same name is used for more than one organization.[12]

Some organizations do define their reporting entity to include parallel entities. For example, the Gay Community Appeal of Toronto, a fund-raising organization, has regularly presented its members and donors with financial statements that show separate columns for the operating agency and for its related foundation, with a third column showing the combined amounts. Despite such exceptions, however, related organizations under common control frequently are not combined into a single reporting entity at present in Canadian practice.

This last section has discussed at some length six of the major reporting issues that must be resolved when preparing the financial statements of a nonprofit organization: (1) cash vs. accrual, (2) expenditure vs. expense basis, (3) fixed assets, (4) donated goods and services, (5) consolidated reporting, and (6) defining the reporting entity. The first issue, cash vs. accrual, can be resolved in favour of accrual for all of the reporting objectives of performance evaluation, stewardship, and cash flow prediction. Resolution of the other issues, however, depends very much on the nature of the organization and its programs and on the reporting objectives that are most important for the users of its financial statements. The preceding pages have pointed out many of the factors that must be taken into account when accounting policies are being decided upon. Because of the wide variety of nonprofit organizations that exist and the varying nature of their operating revenues, costs, and objectives, there are no easy answers; accounting policies cannot be selected by reference to any "standard" approach to the measurement of revenues or expenses or to the valuation of assets.

A significant influence in the selection of accounting policies is the reporting and budgetary requirements of some fund-granting agencies, especially government ministries. While it is obviously necessary to design an accounting system that will enable an organization to submit funding requests in the ways desired by its major financial contributors, these externally imposed accounting requirements (frequently for specific programs) need not govern the overall financial reporting of the organization. Indeed, many organizations find that they must submit their proposed budgets and statements of operations to different funding organizations in different formats, with different classifications, and using different accounting policies. Even the various local United Way organizations do not use a standard set of reporting requirements (although one has been proposed by the national organization), so that a social service agency that requests funds from several different local United Way organizations may find that it has to submit individually tailored budgets to each.

In any event, the reporting requirements of most major funders relate only to expense (or expenditure) policy, and sometimes to revenue, but very seldom to asset reporting, to the treatment of donated goods and services, to consolidation, or to many of the other facets of accounting policy.

Summary: Major Reporting Issues

12 *Financial Reporting for Non-Profit Organizations*, pp 68-69.

SUPPLEMENTARY INFORMATION

The difficulty of evaluating performance in a nonbusiness organization has led to a demand for a greater volume of nonfinancial data as supplementary information in nonbusiness financial statements. Data on the level of services performed or activities accomplished, membership levels, contributors, etc., can be provided. For example, *FRFNPO* recommends that nonprofit organizations provide the following information along with their annual financial statements:

- The nature and objectives of the organization;
- Plans for the future;
- Significant events during the year and their relationship to or impact on the financial results;
- Any unusual or important items or trends in the financial statements;
- Important non-financial information [pp. 41-42].

Because of the frustrations in trying to appraise program effectiveness from purely financial information, government policy makers and legislators have in some jurisdictions attempted to require program administrators to apply approaches such as **program planning and budgeting systems (PPBS)**. PPBS is a formalized approach in which the goals and objectives of each program are defined and criteria are developed by which progress towards those goals can be measured. The criteria are usually quantitative (at least partially), but frequently are not financial. The costs of the program are then evaluated in light of the level of performance achieved. In the federal government, the Auditor General's development of "value for money" auditing is an example of this approach. Such program evaluation information would be helpful to most users of the financial statements of nonbusiness organizations. Unfortunately, this information, if it exists at all, is usually reported only to internal users. As a minimum, therefore, the types of information listed above from the *FRFNPO* study should be reported in order to aid the important objective of performance evaluation. This information will be most useful if reported in the context of programmatic financial information, which is discussed in the following section.

An example of the type of information that *FRFNPO* recommends is illustrated in Schedule 4-4. This is the chairman's report that accompanied the condensed statement of revenues and expenses sent by the nonprofit radio station CJRT-FM to its donors. The report describes the station's activities (both in general and for the year), the sources of support and the size of the donor list, and unusual events such as the capital grants and the arrangements for satellite and cable transmission. The report is written in an informal style, but it contains much information by which the financial performance of the corporation can be better evaluated.

It would be most useful if quantitative supplementary information were audited. Sometimes the audit opinion does include at least some such information, but normally the supplementary information is outside of the scope of the audit opinion. Auditors find it difficult to verify independently most nonfinancial data unless it is directly tied into the accounting and reporting system. Therefore, financial statement readers have to accept supplementary

SCHEDULE 4-4

Supplementary Information for a Nonprofit Organization
CJRT-FM INC.
Chairman's Report

1986-87 was CJRT-FM INC.'s twelfth successful year as the independent, non-profit corporation that owns and operates CJRT-FM, a listener-supported, non-commercial, educational and cultural radio broadcast service unique in Canada. This year's success involved:

(1) Financial support — we received $836,598 in donations from listeners, corporations and foundations, compared to $769,354 last year. Once again, when we closed the books, CJRT-FM INC. was a non-deficit corporation.

(2) Audience expansion — in December, our full stereo service was extended beyond its former coverage area of a 100-mile radius of the CN Tower, through a co-operative arrangement with TV Ontario via the Anik-C satellite, and through distribution agreements with many local cable companies in Ontario from Dryden in the Northwest (near the Manitoba border) to Kingston in the East.

(3) Programming — we continued to broadcast 19 hours each day and to produce over 90% of the station's programming. CJRT presented: university-level courses, symphony and jazz concerts, operas, music festivals, arts and science features, international public affairs, folk/blues music, big band music, stories and music for children and eight newscasts per weekday plus the BBC News live from London, England.

Our new Open College course this year was the enthusiastically received *History of Science and Technology*. Altogether, CJRT's Open College offered 11 university-level credit courses (compared to 8 last year) through broadcast or cassette study, all accredited by Ryerson Polytechnical Institute and Atkinson College, York University, and 8 university-level credit courses (compared to 7 last year) by correspondence, to be taken as a credit towards Ryerson's Degree and Certificates in Public Administration. Open College also produced several informal series, including *In Sickness and In Health: Issues In Health Care; An Affair With Language*, showing us how poetry can be as accessible to the ear as music: *History of The Opera*; and the ever-popular *Income Tax Phone-In Series*.

In our twelfth Festival Concert Series, five Mozart & Haydn concerts were performed in Ryerson Theatre by the CJRT Orchestra conducted by Paul Robinson and presented with the sponsorship of Imperial Oil Limited and Seagram Distillers Limited. Ted O'Reilly produced nine live concerts at The Ontario Science Centre in our series, the *Benson & Hedges Sound of Toronto Jazz*. With the support of the Ontario Arts Council and the Cultural Affairs Division of Metropolitan Toronto, CJRT recorded over sixty "live performance" concerts for broadcast presentation, providing a showcase for talented Canadian performers.

At the end of CJRT-FM INC's twelfth year, we gave congratulations on a job superby done to Margaret Norquay, retiring as Director of Open College, and to Frank Stone, retiring as Secretary-Treasurer. At the same time, we welcomed their successors, May Maskow and Kerr Gibson.

SCHEDULE 4-4 (continued)

1986-87 was an extraordinary success. The operating grant from the Ministry of Citizenship and Culture was $1,091,816 supplemented with further grants for the capital and operating costs of the satellite distribution of CJRT's signal. Private support amounted to 43% of the year's revenue for station operations. 12,000 individuals and over 400 corporations and foundations contributed $836,598 in donations, of which $353,889 was pledged by 7,432 listeners in two 9-day on-air campaigns to raise money and two 14-hour New Donor Drives to reach listeners who had never given before. The balance was donated in response to written appeals.

In addition, the Capital Renewal Fund grew stronger. A grant of $240,000 was received from the Ministry of Citizenship and Culture in February, 1986, to be held to provide income for CJRT's future capital renewal requirements. The interest earned on this grant, supplemented by foundation and listener donations, enabled us to spend $67,697 this year on desperately needed equipment, including turntables, microphones and control boards that are bringing CJRT into the modern world of broadcast technology.

CJRT's incredibly creative staff produces 7,000 hours a year of stimulating and challenging programming; our volunteer Board and professional management team make sure that expenses never exceed revenues; and the three-way support partnership of the Government of Ontario, the business community, and thousands of caring listeners guarantees that revenues do cover expenses and that CJRT prospers. Our thanks to all who helped CJRT-FM INC.'s twelfth year be the best year of its life!

Mary Alice Stuart
Chairman

---

information largely on trust. Unfortunately, there have been instances of over-enthusiastic managers issuing inflated performance data in order to enhance the apparent efficiency or effectiveness of the organization. For example, one Canadian film festival was alleged a few years ago to have announced attendance figures that were in excess of the combined maximum seating capacities of their theatres! But this type of behaviour is undoubtedly the exception rather than the rule.

PROGRAMMATIC REPORTING

We have pointed out repeatedly that in order for financial statement users (including managers) to be able to evaluate the performance of an organization and its management, they must have information that helps them evaluate efficiency and effectiveness. The previous section discussed the importance of supplementary, nonfinancial information in this regard. If the supplementary information is to be useful, the users must be able to relate the supplementary information to financial information on the related specific programs. If an organization has several different programs, line-item

SCHEDULE 4-5

CJRT-FM INC.
Statement of Revenues and Expenses
For the Year Ended March 31, 1987
(with comparative figures for the previous year)

	1986/87	1985/86(1)
Revenues		
Ontario Government Operating Grant —		
Citizenship and Culture	$1,091,816	$1,004,300
Corporate and listener donations (2)	794,898	718,254
Interest and other income	23,618	18,091
	$1,910,332	$1,740,645
Expenses		
Station Operation and Administration:		
Salaries and related benefits	773,463	773,262
Freelance programming services	90,105	80,482
Operation and maintenance of		
broadcasting facilities	137,346	133,235
Rental of premises	75,921	73,001
Station operation and administrative		
expenses, less share of expenses		
allocated to Open College	317,960	248,419
	$1,394,795	$1,308,399
Open College:		
Salaries and related benefits	561,858	448,211
Operating and office expenses	106,696	105,732
Share of station operation and		
administrative expenses	61,219	51,906
	729,773	605,849
Less fees and cost recoveries	280,670	242,148
	449,103	363,701
Festival Series and other concerts		
recorded for broadcast	172,492	145,548
Less Ontario Arts Council and Metro		
Toronto grants, sponsor grants and		
admission revenues (2)	147,730	130,863
	24,762	14,685
	$1,868,660	$1,686,785
Excess of Revenues over Expenses for		
the year before depreciation	$ 41,672	$ 53,860
Depreciation	(34,775)	(22,593)
Excess of Revenues over Expenses from		
operations	$ 6,897	$ 31,267

SCHEDULE 4-5 (continued)

Notes

(1) The 1985/86 comparative figures have been restated to reflect an additional expense of $5,162 in respect of joint operating costs of the CN Tower FM antenna resulting from a reassessment of such costs received in 1987 relating to three prior years.

(2) In 1986/87 the total of donations was $836,598, four corporate contributions having been designated and shown as "concert" income and three foundation contributions having been specified for the Capital Renewal Fund. The corresponding total in 1985/86 was $769,354.

(3) A copy of the complete audited financial statements of CJRT-FM INC. prepared by Thorne Ernst & Whinney is available on request.

Charitable Organization
Registration Number 0439315-2113

---

reporting by type of expense is not very useful unless the expenses (and revenues, if possible) are broken down by program. While most organizations do not use programmatic reporting of expenses at present, there is a definite trend towards doing so. The following pages show three different approaches to programmatic reporting.

The first example is that of CJRT-FM (Schedule 4-5). The statement of revenues and expenses for 1987, as reported to donors, shows the expenses broken down into the station's three major activities: station operation, open college, and concerts. Some of the grants are received specifically for the concerts, and the station therefore deducts those grants from concert expenses to determine a net amount ($24,762) that must be covered by general revenues. The station's supplementary information (Schedule 4-4) is not specific enough in terms of listenership, open college participation, and concert attendance to permit much evaluation of program efficiency, but Schedule 4-5 nevertheless provides more insight into where the organization is spending its money than would a statement that lumps all of the operating expenses together.

One additional aspect of the CJRT-FM statement that is worth pointing out is the treatment of depreciation. Depreciation expense is not allocated to programs, even though a portion of operation and administrative expense is allocated from the station operation section of the statement to the open college section. Instead, depreciation is deducted at the bottom of the statement, after a net surplus before depreciation is determined. This treatment may help to avoid confusion amongst lay readers of financial statements as to the amount of the accrual-basis cash surplus or deficit.

The second example of programmatic reporting is shown in Schedule 4-6. The second column of this statement contains the same figures as the organization's audited statement of operations, but in this schedule, the actual revenues and expenses are broken into three columns representing the two programs of the organization (home support and home care) with a third column for unallocated administrative revenues and expenses.

A distinguishing aspect of Schedule 4-6 is the inclusion of budgetary information in the first column. One aspect of performance evaluation is ascertaining how well management met its expectations, as reflected in the budget. The *FRFNPO* study recommends that comparative budgetary infor-

SCHEDULE 4-6

Home Support Services for York Region
Supplementary Financial Information by Programme
Year ended March 31, 1987

	Budget	Actual	Home Support	Home Care	Administration
Revenue					
Ministry of Community and Social Services					
Operating subsidy	$165,030	$181,319	$181,319	$ —	$ —
Grant	27,010	24,092	—	—	24,092
Regional Municipality of York — Grant	49,400	47,500	47,500	—	—
Home care fees	352,458	352,194	—	352,194	—
Home support fees	137,752	157,455	157,455	—	—
Meals	9,075	4,426	4,426	—	—
Donations	—	5,599	—	—	5,599
Interest	—	479	—	—	479
	740,725	773,064	390,700	352,194	30,170
Expenses					
Staff					
Homemaker wages	431,635	438,835	188,699	250,136	—
Co-ordinators	83,844	84,594	54,986	29,608	—
Executive director	26,400	27,296	21,837	5,459	—
Bookkeeper	12,990	12,112	4,239	7,873	—
Part-time office wages	39,276	45,222	30,040	15,182	—
Payroll	3,994	4,436	2,174	2,262	—
Employee benefits	20,347	18,323	8,978	9,345	—
Workers' Compensation	15,380	15,585	7,637	7,948	—
Advertising	1,450	1,570	1,021	549	—
Area programmes	—	3,268	—	—	3,268
Audit	2,000	2,000	1,300	700	—
Bank charges and interest	332	405	263	142	—
Furniture and equipment	2,500	28,323	22,380	5,943	—
Insurance	1,790	1,388	902	486	—
Meals	9,900	4,917	4,917	—	—
Office	11,128	10,275	6,678	3,597	—
Printing	3,000	3,629	2,359	1,270	—
Regional meetings	1,720	1,779	1,156	623	—
Rent	16,770	11,845	7,699	4,146	—
Staff training	29,759	25,901	1,176	633	24,092
Telephone	3,582	9,379	6,096	3,283	—
Travel	14,956	13,601	7,831	5,770	—
Volunteer services	2,972	8,332	8,332	—	—
	740,725	773,015	390,700	354,955	27,360
Excess of Revenue over Expense (Expense over Revenue)	$ —	$ 49	$ —	$ (2,761)	$ 2,810

mation be provided along with the actual results for the period [p. 49], but there are few organizations that are currently following that recommendation in external reporting.

Our final example is drawn from the Annual Report of the Metropolitan Toronto Association for Community Living (MTACL). MTACL's annual report is a four-panel, two-sided, 22" x 17" single sheet that folds down to a standard 8-1/2" x 11" size. The report includes summary balance sheets and statements of operations for all funds, notes to financial statements, the auditor's report, the treasurer's report, a report from the board of directors and administration, supplementary statistics, pie charts of revenues and expenditures, and the names of the officers, board members, and committee chairpersons. It is a concise, effective report that gets the maximum amount of information to the reader at the lowest cost, and in an attractive package.

One of the remarkable aspects of the MTACL annual report is the statement of operations of the operating fund, which is reproduced in Schedule 4-7. The major program categories are listed down the left side of the report, and the first column shows the gross operating costs for each category. The next four columns show the sources of revenue, the total of which is then deducted from the gross costs to get the net operating costs, which are then compared to the previous year. Obviously, it is necessary to go to supporting schedules in the full financial statements to get the details underlying the individual amounts on the statement, but the statement does an excellent job of giving the reader an overview of the MTACL's operations on a programmatic basis in a single statement.

The MTACL annual report also includes some statistics on persons served as supplemental information, as shown in Schedule 4-8. The statistics are not comparative with the prior year and do not tie in completely with the programs listed in the operating statement, but the annual report does refer the reader to a companion publication that provides more explanation and detail.

An additional detail on Schedule 4-7 that should be pointed out is that at the end of the statement, a transfer is made to another fund (in this case, the capital fund) to reduce the surplus to zero. It is not unusual for nonprofit organizations to use interfund transfers to reduce an operating surplus or deficit. In most cases the transfer is fairly obvious, as in the MTAMR statements, but sometimes the transfer is hidden. For example, one large community centre organization routinely shows a break-even result for its operating fund, year after year. There are no interfund transfers shown in the statements to explain this result. Only upon inquiry was it determined that a rather innocuous item in the revenue section labeled "Art Affair" is actually a transfer made from a separate fund-raising activity that is not formally a part of the organization and therefore not included in the financial statements. Just enough was transferred from the Art Affair activity each year to make the main organization appear to break even. The overall results of the Art Affair are never included in the statements because the Art Affair is not defined as being part of the reporting entity, even though it clearly is under common control and is operating solely to obtain funds for the operating organization. In this particular organization, the amounts transferred to achieve breakeven were immaterial, less than 0.3% of the total operating expenditures, but such a practice could get out of hand and may also be a disservice to the organization by raising unwarranted suspicions in the minds of financial statement users.

SCHEDULE 4-7

The Metropolitan Association for Community Living
Statement of Operations
Operating Fund
Year Ended March 31, 1988

	Gross operating expenditures	User fees	Provincial Government subsidies	Production and other	Total	Net operating expenditures	Net operating expenditures
			Recoveries			1988	1987
Services for adults							
Residences							
Group homes	$ 7,370,716	$1,590,869	$ 5,582,442	$ 173,168	$ 7,346,479	$ 24,237	$ 28,903
Supported independent living	773,049		773,049		773,049		
Vocational and industrial services (note 3)							
Employment Training Centres	2,395,599	294,203	1,873,292	228,104	2,395,599		
ARC Industries	3,045,618	120,515	2,014,419	910,684	3,045,618		
Sunrise Fine Bone China	902,326		543,000	301,163	844,163	58,163	76,000
Lorimer	248,016		248,016		248,016		
Developmental services for adults							
Gooderham Developmental Centre	613,766		613,766		613,766		
Residential program	1,532,607	230,027	1,302,580		1,532,607		
Adult development programs	1,653,539	100,332	1,545,699	7,508	1,653,539		
Adult support services	416,245		416,245		416,245		
Services for children							
Residences	2,915,834	40,264	2,787,850	5,072	2,833,186	82,648	76,460
Pre-school education	1,287,806	90,180	1,130,118		1,220,298	67,508	66,881
Other support services	788,267		788,267		788,267		
Client services co-ordination							
Adult protective services	303,840		303,840		303,840		
Family support services	91,532		91,532		91,532		
Divisional services	387,020	31,809		19,280	51,089	335,931	322,396
Shadow Lake Centre	307,842	215,557		43,519	259,076	48,766	62,136
Other special projects	1,277,321		754,308	525,524	1,279,832	(2,511)	(1,355)
Administration							
Administrative expenditures after allocations to departments of $2,305,361 (1987, $2,580,139)	33,950					33,950	32,666
Ontario Association for Community Living assessment	68,000					68,000	65,234
	$26,412,893	$2,713,756	$20,768,423	$2,214,022	$25,696,201	716,692	729,321
Less							
Allocation from United Way of Greater Toronto						576,929	553,372
Excess of expenditures over recoveries for the year						139,763	175,949
Recovery from other funds						139,763	175,949
Net assets at the end of the year						Nil	Nil

SCHEDULE 4-8

1987-88: Persons served*

Services for Children

Home Management	93
Preschool Education	206
Children's Living Services	
(including group homes, Lawson, parent relief and	
Individualized Residential Care)	497
Day Respite Care	66
Consultation Services	346
Toy Library	132

Services for Adults

Adult Living Services	
Group Homes	211
Apartments	101
Family Home Program	17
Parent Relief	46
Employment Training Centres	401
Lorimer	22
ARC Industries	733
Sunrise Fine Bone China	14
Sunrise Janitorial Services	12
Job Placements, Competitive Jobs	246
Job Placements, Trial Jobs	217
Developmental Services for Adults	
Group Homes	32
Parent Relief	18
Gooderham Developmental Centre	37
Adult Development Programs	154
Shadow Lake Centre	400

Client Services Co-ordination

Adult Protective Services	252
Crisis Intervention	68
Family Support Services	221
Pilot Parents	54
Home Visit Assessments	117
Legal Liaison Consultation	101
Interpreter Pool Consultation	38
Total	4852*

Community Support Services

Adult socials	435
Bowling leagues	447
Literacy course (three sessions per year)	52
Other leisure programs	330
Parent support	320
Volunteers (general)	280
Volunteers in programs	243

*Some persons may be involved in more than one program.

In summary, programmatic reporting can enhance the ability of financial statement users to evaluate the performance of an organization and its management. Evaluation is further enhanced by the provision of supplementary information that ties in to the financial programmatic breakdown. Performance evaluation may also be improved by presenting the original budget as comparative data. Few organizations have moved very far down the road of programmatic reporting, but there is a clear trend in that direction. The FRFNPO report has had a discernible impact, but perhaps the most effective motivation for better financial reporting is the increasing sophistication of donors (especially governments and foundations) combined with the greater competition for donations amongst an ever-expanding group of nonprofit organizations.

SUMMARY

Nonbusiness organizations are entities (frequently corporations) without owners and without share capital. They are governed by a board of directors or similar group, who are elected by the members. In many instances, the board itself contains all of the voting members, so that it becomes self-perpetuating. The absence of investors removes one of the major user groups of financial statements. However, nonbusiness organizations have to get their money from somewhere, and the sources are members, donors, or governmental granting agencies. Thus investors are replaced by the other suppliers of financial resources as one of the primary groups of financial statement users. Other primary users are managers and directors, creditors, and governmental oversight or regulatory bodies.

A fundamental characteristic of nonbusiness entities is that there is no profit objective for the enterprise. Therefore, the business enterprise objectives of income tax minimization and profit maximization or minimization do not exist for nonbusiness organizations. Indeed, the entire set of preparer objectives should not exist for nonprofit organizations. The preparer objectives are motivated largely by economic self-interest, and nonprofit organizations do not exist for the purpose of providing economic gain to their members or managers.

Instead, preparers are often motivated to adopt accounting policies that are intended to enhance users' perceptions as to the fiscal responsibility of management and as to the organization's need for additional funding. If financial reporting policies can help the organization increase its revenue, then managers will have enhanced the organization's ability to provide services.

The lack of profit motive tends to shift the emphasis of financial reporting away from cash flow prediction and more towards performance evaluation and stewardship reporting. There is little, if any, distinction between financial reporting and managerial accounting in nonprofit organizations, and therefore a very important group of financial statement users is management itself. The generally lower level of financial sophistication of the managers of nonprofit organizations (as compared to business managers) increases the responsibility of accountants and auditors to recommend accounting policies that will enhance the usefulness of the financial statements to the managers for evaluating the efficiency and effectiveness of the organization and its programs. Government ministries and other donors also need to be able to evaluate the performance of an organization, frequently in comparison with other organizations that have similar societal roles.

Stewardship has an enhanced importance in nonprofit organizations because of the responsibility of the organization for observing the restrictions placed by donors and by the board of directors on the uses of certain funds. The objective of cash flow prediction tends to be limited to creditors, who are interested in the sources of funding for the organization and its liquidity and financial status. Thus, while many of the same basic objectives exist for nonbusiness as for business organizations, the emphasis clearly shifts as a result of the basic differences in the nature of the organizations. Thus the implications of the objectives for financial reporting change.

Reporting for business enterprises generally assumes that a basic organizational objective is to earn a return on investment for the owners. This basic objective has no place in reporting for nonprofit organizations. Accounting practices for nonprofit organizations and governmental units consequently seem as varied as the organizations themselves.

The accounting policy choices for nonprofit organizations are much wider than those for business enterprises, including such basic issues as defining the reporting entity, cash versus accrual accounting, and whether or not to capitalize and depreciate fixed assets. In addition, the performance evaluation objective can be fulfilled only if supplementary information on the organization's program outputs and a revenue and expense breakdown by program is provided to the users, whether they be internal or external users.

Fund accounting has been developed in order to assist managers (1) to keep funds for different purposes distinct from one another, (2) to insure that expenditure limits are not exceeded, and (3) to keep track of commitments as well as expenditures. A nonbusiness organization may use fund accounting if any or all of its special characteristics are appropriate for the organization. Some organizations, however, have no need for fund accounting and may use accounting and reporting practices that are virtually indistinguishable from proprietary accounting.

This chapter has discussed the basic issues of financial reporting for nonbusiness organizations. Technical matters have been kept to a minimum. The next chapter presents the techniques of fund accounting in more detail, without repeating the reporting issues that have already been discussed.

Appendix to Chapter 4 Public Sector Financial Reporting

Financial reporting for governments is quite similar to that for nonprofit organizations. Both types of nonbusiness organizations have no investors, have a service rather than a profit objective, use fund accounting, tend to report on an expenditure basis, have a variety of accounting policies for fixed assets, and have trouble defining the reporting entity. Therefore, most of the discussion in the main body of this chapter applies equally to governments as well as to nonprofit organizations.

Nevertheless, there are some differences between the two types of organizations. One of the most basic is the nature of the user group. Nonprofit organizations and business enterprises each have an identifiable group of stakeholders and other interested parties that have specific information needs. Governments, on the other hand, have a far larger potential user group and consequently it is quite difficult to be very specific about who the users really are. One can say that all Canadian citizens are interested in the financial results of the federal government, for example, but such a statement is difficult to translate to reporting objectives.

Another basic difficulty with governmental reporting is that the activities of governments are highly diverse, which makes programmatic reporting for performance evaluation difficult or impossible. A third difficulty is that since much of government activity is one of maintaining the status quo in many service and administrative dimensions, it is difficult to have meaningful supplementary performance measures.

Until the decade of the 1980s, there was not much interest demonstrated by professional accountants in governmental reporting. Since 1980, however, there has been quite a bit of interest in helping to develop governmental reporting, and both the CICA and the Canadian Certified General Accountants' Research Foundation have been active. The developments have followed two separate but parallel tracks, one for senior (i.e., federal, provincial, and territorial) governmental reporting and another for local governmental reporting.

LOCAL GOVERNMENTAL REPORTING

Local government reporting is the subject of a major research study prepared by A. Beedle and published in 1981 by the CGA Research Foundation. Titled *Accounting for Local Government in Canada: The State of the Art*, the study is a massive survey of the then-current financial reporting practices among the thousands of local governments across Canada, and is intended to form a starting point for the development of reporting standards and recommendations for local governments. In 1985, the CICA published another research study, *Local Government Financial Reporting* (*LGFR*), which builds on Beedle's work and makes recommendations on a wide range of issues. Neither study is authoritative, in the sense that the *CICA Handbook* is authoritative, but Beedle tells us where we are and LGFR suggests where we should be heading.

Objectives of Local Government Reporting

Beedle found a lack of focus in the reporting of local governments, which he credits to the lack of guidance and authoritative pronouncements and to an attempt to use the general purpose financial statements as a way of being all things to all people:

> Faced with this paucity of guidance and authoritative pronouncements, present Canadian practice in accounting reports of local governments seems to stab at satisfying an undefined range of users and their needs without (with exceptions) specifically defining those users, their needs, or the objectives of the reports . . . . The result in many cases is a complex, scarcely comprehensible set of reports requiring specialized expert accounting knowledge in the government field. There is a failure to realize that 'general purpose statements are not all purpose statements, and never can be.'[13]

LGFR points out: "Financial reporting must have well-defined objectives, otherwise it becomes the product of an undisciplined set of rules; objectives must relate to the needs of the users of the financial reporting; needs can clearly be thought of only in terms of identified users."[14]

The LGFR study group considers Beedle's findings and the diverse set of potential users of government financial statements, and concludes that the specific objectives of local government reporting are to provide information for:

- Obtaining an understanding of the state of the finances of the local government unit and of its operations.
- Evaluating (a) stewardship and accountability and (b) fiscal, legal and contractual compliance of those entrusted with those responsibilities.
- Making economic and social decisions on the provision and allocation of resources, evaluating expenditure allocations and managing resources.
- Evaluating performance.
- Exercising regulatory functions.
- Developing databases for national accounting and for statistical and other functions of the senior government and their agencies.[15]

Although these are all viable uses of government statements, the study group recognized that it is necessary to make a distinction between general purpose and special purpose financial reporting. While such a distinction is hardly new, it is important in governmental reporting because it makes it clear that the general purpose reports that go to the citizenry at large may

---

13 A. Beedle, *Accounting for Local Government in Canada: The State of the Art* (Vancouver: Canadian Certified General Accountants' Research Foundation, 1981), p. 73.
14 *Local Government Financial Reporting* (Toronto: CICA, 1985), p. 11.
15 *LGFR*, pp. 17-18.

be quite different from special purpose reports that are prepared for making specific operational decisions such as resource allocation or performance evaluation of major programs and activities. Therefore, the study group concludes that the general purpose financial statements that constitute the "official" financial reports "should provide fair presentation of the unit's financial position and its operations and should include, as a minimum, adequate financial information on:

- Financial viability
- Financial condition
- Stewardship and accountability
- Expenditure allocations
- Balancing of inflows and outflows
- Financial compliance with budgets"[16]

The overall thrust of this list of uses is towards the stewardship objective. The study group suggests that other objectives can best be satisfied by special purpose reports or through supplementary information.

After defining the objectives of general financial reporting, the *LGFR* study group considers a wide variety of reporting issues, evaluates pros and cons, and arrives at a number of recommendations. All of the recommendations are not dealt with here, but we will look briefly at a few major issues, particularly those that parallel the issues considered in the main body of this chapter for nonprofit organizations.

> ## Major Local Government Reporting Issues

Given that a strong focus of the local government reports should be to assist users in evaluating the financial position and viability of the government, the study group considers it important that all assets and liabilities be shown in the financial statements. Fixed assets should be shown, regardless of whether or not the initial charge for the asset was to expenditure, and the source of financing of those assets should be shown. Such recording would be accomplished by means of a fixed asset group of accounts that would be consolidated into the general purpose balance sheet. The study group considers the issue of the valuation of the assets, and concludes that depreciation accounting is not appropriate in the general purpose statements. Instead of reporting depreciated amounts, governments should carry their fixed assets "at their initially recorded value until they reach the end of their useful economic lives, when they should be written off."[17]

All liabilities of the government should also be shown. In many cases, when governments issue debt instruments, they credit the proceeds to revenue. Since the credit has been recorded to revenue, there is no credit to a liability account and the liability does not appear in the financial statements. The study group's recommendation therefore means that the debt should be shown as a liability even when the proceeds have been reported as revenue. This is accomplished by means of a debt group of accounts that can be consolidated into the balance sheet when the general purpose financial statements are prepared.

The study group recommends that governments use an expenditure ba-

16 *LGFR*, pp. 15-16.
17 *LGFR*, p. 24.

sis of reporting rather than an expense basis. Given the strong thrust of accountability, expenditure control, and budget compliance in the objectives, the use of an expense basis of reporting would cloud accomplishment of the objectives. Expense basis reporting may be appropriate in special purpose reports, but for the general purpose statements, the stewardship nature of the objectives points to an expenditure basis.

Since one of the major objectives is to permit evaluation of budget compliance, government reports should include budgeted amounts. The study group recognizes, however, that budget figures may not always be meaningful in consolidated statements. "For component parts of a local government entity . . . budget figures of operations would be appropriate."[18]

Definition of the reporting entity is more of a problem in reporting for governments than for nonprofit organizations. The *LGFR* study group recommends that "the general-purpose financial statements should contain information about the entire local government entity, irrespective of legal or organizational structures under which activities are carried on."[19] On the other hand, separate governmental entities should be reported separately. For example, school boards are a part of local government, but they are frequently administered by a separately elected board of trustees that has its own financial responsibility. Consolidation of the school board's financial results with those of the municipality would only decrease the usefulness of the financial statements, because it would be impossible to tell whether excessive expenditure, for example, was the responsibility of the school board or of the city council. The study group proposes a series of criteria that could be used to decide whether a government unit is independent or not; the criteria include the dimensions of legislation, independence of management, and independence in financial matters.

Fund reporting is one issue that the study group feels strongly about. Fund *accounting* is ubiquitous in municipal accounting, but fund accounting need not lead to fund-basis *reporting*. Reporting on the basis of funds causes a multiplicity of statements and an inability to get an overview of the financial condition and operations of the government. While fund-basis reporting is inappropriate, financial statements can and should group together the various activities of the government into those activities and programs of similar nature, so that statement users can get some idea as to the resource flows associated with the major activities of the government. This is similar to programmatic reporting in nonprofit organizations, except that the activity groupings may be larger.

The *LGFR* study comments on quite a few other issues as well, but the major issues have been outlined above. The study group's recommendations for these major issues are not authoritative, but they do provide a guide to making some sense out of the diverse and almost random practice that exists at present. Some provinces have attempted to influence local government reporting and to achieve a degree of standardization,[20] but like nonprofit

---

18 *LGFR*, p. 31.

19 *LGFR*, p. 37.

20 An example is *Financial Disclosure to the Public: A Code for Municipalities in Ontario, 1984.* This document prescribes minimum disclosure requirements and presents a series of examples of financial reports for different levels of government.

organizations, the diversity of types of local governments inhibits attempts toward prescribing a uniform set of standards of financial reporting.[21]

SENIOR GOVERNMENT FINANCIAL REPORTING

In 1980, the CICA issued a research study on *Financial Reporting by Governments (FRG)* that focuses on financial reporting by the federal, provincial, and territorial governments. The report analyzes the financial reporting of these senior governments, the users and uses of financial statements, and a number of important issues in governmental financial reporting. The issues include the ways in which the senior governments report on financial condition, financial results, and changes in financial condition.

Objectives of Senior Government Reporting

The users of the financial reports of governments fit into five categories: (1) policy makers, (2) legislators, (3) program administrators, (4) investors, and (5) the general public.[22] Each of these five groups will have advisors, and the advisors or analysts for each group can be viewed as being a part of that group rather than a separate user group.

Governmental policy making is an exercise in resource rationing and allocation. There are never enough funds available to undertake all of the programs that are deemed to be desirable in the public sector. Therefore, policy makers must have information that assists them in making the necessary choices. Financial statements, to the extent possible within the limitations of financial reporting, can provide some of the information that is needed by policy makers in making their resource allocation decisions.

Legislators, too, are concerned with making the correct decisions in approving budgets and programs. In addition, legislators are concerned with how the government has spent the funds appropriated in the past. Thus stewardship reporting is also an important objective of governmental financial statements.

Administrators have the responsibility for seeing that the programs under their control are managed efficiently and effectively. Financial statements can provide information that assists them in evaluating the performance of the programs. Policy makers, of course, are also interested in data that helps them to evaluate the performance of continuing programs.

Unlike most nonprofit organizations and governmental units, governments can, and usually do, issue substantial amounts of notes and bonds. Indeed, governments dominate the bond markets in North America. The risks associated with buying government bonds are quite different from those associated with buying corporate bonds, because the credit worthiness of the bonds is a function of the taxing ability of the government instead of a function of the ability to attract revenue in an open market.

---

21 For example, Beedle presents a table of "Forms of Local Government in Canada" (p. 9) that lists over 20 forms of government and the number in each group in 1980. The list identifies 1425 rural municipalities, 1117 villages, 805 towns, 311 local improvement or service districts, 181 cities, 129 counties, 38 local commissions, and so forth.

22 CICA, *Financial Reporting by Governments* (CICA, 1980), pp. 24-27.

Although default by a government (especially by the federal govern-ment) is unlikely, it nevertheless is a real possibility. Recent years have seen defaults by a few cities in the United States, and certain state obligations have become rather risky. Municipal bonds are riskier than those of higher levels of government because of the more limited taxing authority of the cities, which tend to live somewhat at the mercy of their provincial governments. Thus, investors need information to assist them in measuring liquidity and predicting cash flows.

The general public is interested in how government is raising its reve-nues and spending its tax dollars. The public will be interested in both per-formance appraisal (judging the effectiveness of governmental programs) and stewardship. Very few members of the general public will directly ex-amine the financial reports of a government, which tend to be voluminous and complex because of the broad scope of government's activities and pro-grams. However, the reports may be analyzed and the results presented to the public by analysts in citizens' public interest groups or in the news media. The force of public scrutiny can be quite strong.

The financial reporting objectives for senior governments have been stated by the *FRG* study as follows:

1. To facilitate evaluation of economic impact.
2. To facilitate evaluation of program delivery choices and their management.
3. To demonstrate stewardship and compliance with legislative authority.
4. To display the state of the government's finances.[23]

The first two objectives in the *FRG* list are performance evaluation objectives; the third and fourth are stewardship and cash flow prediction, respectively. Policy makers, legislators, and the general public are seen to be concerned with all four objectives, while program administrators would be interested only in the second and third. Investors are seen to be concerned only with the state-of-finances objective, or the prediction of cash flow.

The study group conducted interviews with a sample of representatives from various categories of users of governmental financial reports. Not sur-prisingly, the users expressed a wide diversity of needs. However, the users tended to stress similar qualitative characteristics of good financial reports. The report cites four qualities that were stressed by the interviewees. These four qualities are (1) comparability among governments, (2) consistency be-tween years, (3) completeness, and (4) timeliness. The users were particularly emphatic about comparability:

> Almost above everything else, users wanted to compare the reports of various governments. This meant they wanted consistency among governments in the basis for:
> *   defining the reporting entity to make clear what kinds of Crown corpora-tions were included and excluded;
> *   classifying and reporting revenues, expenditures, assets and liabilities; and
> *   reporting government debt including contingent debt.
> They also wanted consistency, to the extent possible, between the Public Ac-counts and various statistical compilations of government figures (e.g., the Na-tional Accounts) and the ability to reconcile two sets of figures where differences in basis are justified by the different purposes served by the two sets of figures.[24]

23 *Financial Reporting by Governments*, pp. 27-29.
24 *Financial Reporting by Governments*, p. 31.

One of the recommendations of the FRG study group is that the CICA consider creating "a standing committee comparable to the two committees that already exist, the Accounting Standards Committee and the Auditing Standards Committee."[25] In March 1981, the CICA did set up a Public Sector Accounting and Auditing Committee to issue statements on financial reporting and auditing in the public sector. The Committee issues recommendations in the form of accounting statements and auditing statements on its own authority, that is, without going through the other two standards committees. The intent of establishing the Committee is to influence the development of financial reporting in the public sector, even though the statements of the Committee cannot have as strong an impact as those of the AcSC because there is not the force of statute behind them. The legislation of public sector reporting standards lies with the senior governments themselves, and not with an outside body such as the CICA.

The mandate of the public sector committee is to deal with reporting and auditing for all governmental levels, senior and local. Of the first five accounting statements issued, however, four are specifically applicable to senior governments. Only Accounting Statement 1, *Disclosure of Accounting Policies* (September 1983), is intended to apply to all governments. Nevertheless, the recommendations contained in all of the statements can also be applied to local governments.

The specific recommendations of AcS 1 are as follows:

.03 A clear and concise description of all significant accounting policies of a reporting entity should be included as an integral part of its financial statements.

.10 As a minimum, disclosure of information on accounting policies should identify and describe:
  (i) the reporting entity and, where applicable, the method of consolidation or combination;
  (ii) the basis of accounting used in the financial statements; and
  (iii) the specific accounting policies selected and applied to significant assets, liabilities, revenues and expenditures.

.12 All significant accounting policies of a reporting entity should be disclosed in one place.

.15 Whenever there is a change in an accounting policy that has a material effect in the current period or may have a material effect in subsequent periods, the nature of the change, the reason for it and its effect on the financial statements of the current period should be disclosed in a separate note.

Whenever financial statements are prepared, the preparers should state *what* organizations or parts of organizations are included, *how* the measurements are made, and whether there have been any *changes* in the entity or measurements. In addition, these basic facts should be reported together in one place, and not scattered around. These recommendations may not seem earth-shattering, but the fact that they need to be recommended at all suggests that many governments have not been observing even these most basic disclosure principles.

Accounting Statement 2 is *Objectives of Government Financial Statements* (November 1984). AcS 2 defines qualitative criteria and reporting objectives

Standard Setting in the Public Sector

---

25 *Financial Reporting by Governments*, p. 190.

for senior governments. Five objectives are stated. The first objective relates to the qualitative characteristics [para. 23], and the second defines the reporting entity to include the "full nature and extent of the financial affairs and resources for which the government is responsible including those related to the activities of government agencies and enterprises." [para. 29] Objectives 3, 4, and 5 state the objectives of reporting and they relate strongly to the stewardship objective of financial reporting, much as do those recommended for local governments, described earlier in this appendix:

.34 Financial statements should demonstrate the accountability of a government for the financial affairs and resources entrusted to it.

(i) Financial statements should provide information useful in evaluating the government's performance in the management of financial affairs and resources.

(ii) Financial statements should provide information useful in assessing whether financial resources were administered by the government in accordance with the limits established by the appropriate legislative authorities.

.39 Financial statements should account for the sources, allocation and use of the financial resources required by the government in the period.

(i) Financial statements should account for all government expenditures by nature and purpose, all revenues by source and type and the extent to which revenues were sufficient to meet expenditures.

(ii) Financial statements should show how government financed its activities in the period and how it met its cash requirements.

.48 Financial statements should present information to display the state of government's finances.

(i) Financial statements should present information to describe the government's financial condition at the end of the accounting period.

(ii) Financial statements should provide information that is useful in evaluating the government's ability to finance its activities and to meet its liabilities and commitments.

While the word "evaluate" appears in these objectives, it does not refer to performance evaluation in the same sense as we have used it in Chapters 2 and 4, but rather in a stewardship sense of evaluating whether the government lived up to its responsibilities in terms of expenditure control and financial condition.

Accounting Statement 3, *General Standards of Financial Statement Presentation for Governments*, was issued in November 1986. Like AcS 2, this statement is intended to apply only to senior governments. The statement begins with ten recommendations on general reporting principles, which basically are qualitative characteristics.

The first recommendation is that the statements "should include or be accompanied by an acknowledgement of the government's responsibility for their preparation" [para. 05]. Users should be made aware of whose statements they are, and not be left with the possible impression that the statements are somehow the result of an objective process that is remote from the government and its managers.

The last recommendation is that "notes and supporting schedules . . . should not be used as a substitute for proper accounting treatment" [para. 28]. In other words: *measure,* don't just *disclose.* Note disclosure is a useful way of communicating information that cannot be measured, but when measurement is possible, then the amounts should be included in the statements proper. "Inappropriate treatment of financial statement items is not rectified either by disclosure of accounting policies used or by notes or explanatory schedules" [para. 29].

AcS 3 then goes on to recommend 22 standards of disclosure. These include standards of measurement and presentation for assets, liabilities, revenues, and expenditures. The statement recommends that physical assets be reported, a practice generally not currently used because "most governments do not now maintain systems which enable them to report fully on acquired physical assets" [para. 66]. The statement also recommends use of the expenditure basis (using accrual accounting), and recommends that expenditures be reported both by function or major program and by object of expenditure. These recommendations fit in with our emphasis on programmatic reporting in the main body of the chapter.

The final section of AcS 3 focuses on legislative control and financial accountability. There are three recommendations made, all of which merit direct quotation:

.98 Financial statements should present a comparison of the actual results with those originally forecast by the fiscal plan.

.100 Planned results should be presented on a basis consistent with that used for actual results.

.103 Financial statements should present information to show where a government has exceeded its borrowing, investing or expenditure authority limits.

To evaluate effectively the results of government's stewardship, statement users must know what the initial plan of operations was. Therefore, budget information, presented on a basis consistent with the actual results, should be shown. When a government has exceeded its legislated limits, users should be able to discern that fact from the financial statements.

In the main body of this chapter, we discussed the problem of defining the reporting entity for nonprofit organizations. This problem not only exists for governments as well, but is actually much more severe. Accounting Statement 4, issued in November 1988, addresses the issue in its title, *Defining the Government Reporting Entity.*

Government activities are carried out through a very complex set of ministries, agencies, crown corporations, quasi-business enterprises, and nonprofit organizations formed by government for the purpose of carrying out parts of government's policies. When financial statements are prepared for a government, which of the many bodies that are directly or indirectly related to the government are to be included in the statements? AcS 4 recommends that the government reporting entity include all agencies and organizations that are owned or controlled by government and that are directly accountable for their financial affairs (either through a minister or directly to the legislature) [para.13]. The definition of the reporting entity excludes those organizations that are instruments of government or that are dependent on government but that are not directly accountable to government. As a result, hospitals and universities would be excluded from the reporting entity.

AcS 4 also addresses the question as to how organizations that constitute parts of the reporting entity should be reported in the financial statements. In general, the conclusions of the statement are that (1) investments in entities that are not controlled by the government should be reported on the cost basis [para. 26], (2) investments in business or quasi-business enterprises, such as public utilities or transportation companies, should be reported on a modified equity basis,[26] and (3) the financial statements of all other organizations or agencies that are part of the reporting entity should be consolidated with the government's own financial statements [para. 23].

The first four public sector accounting statements all deal with broad aspects of financial reporting for governments, particularly for senior governments. Accounting Statement 5 is the first statement to deal with a specific accounting topic, pension accounting. Titled *Accounting for Employee Pension Obligations in Government Financial Statements*, AcS 5 recommends accounting measurements and disclosures that are essentially parallel to those recommended by the AcSC in section 3460 of the *CICA Handbook* for reporting enterprises in the private sector. For example, AcS 5 recommends that, when a defined benefit pension plan is in effect, pension cost and liability should be determined in accordance with an accrued benefit method based on employee service to date, that projected benefits should be prorated on services, that best estimates should be used, and that actuarial assumptions should be internally consistent. By recommending pension accounting approaches that are consistent with those used by public companies in the private sector, users of the government's financial statements will be better able to evaluate government's pension costs in comparison with those in the private sector.

The Public Sector Accounting and Auditing Committee issued five accounting and four auditing statements from 1983 through 1988, a quite respectable record in dealing with such a poorly defined area of financial reporting. While the accounting recommendations are directed mainly towards the federal, provincial, and territorial governments, many of the recommendations are also applicable to local governments. The Public Sector Committee's recommendations are not authoritative in the same sense as are those of the Accounting Standards Committee for the private sector, but nevertheless, the PSAcS recommendations help greatly to delineate GAAP for the public sector.

SUMMARY

In this appendix, we have examined the financial reporting by governments, both local and senior. While the attention of professional accounting bodies has been split between the two levels of government, there is actually not very much difference between them at the level of objectives and general principles. At both levels, there is an increased emphasis on stewardship reporting in the general purpose financial statements. Accrual basis expenditure reporting should be used, with full reporting of physical assets (undepreciated). Liabilities should also be fully reported, a practice that is frequently not followed with the current emphasis on fund-basis reporting. Instead of using fund reporting, governments should report their activities on a consolidated basis, with a breakdown for major groups of activities and

26 Under the modified equity basis, the net profit or loss of each enterprise is included in the government's statement of operations and is added (net of dividends or distributions) to the investment account relating to that enterprise. The equity method of reporting will be discussed in Part 2 of this text.

programs. Budget information should be reported, so that users can see how the actual results compared to the budget.

While the Public Sector Accounting and Auditing Committee's Accounting Statements 2 through 5 are explicitly restricted to senior governments, the recommendations contained therein can also be applied to local governments. Provincial governments can pressure local governments for improved and consistent reporting, although few at present do so.

Interest in governmental reporting has increased quite markedly in the past dozen years, and progress is beginning to be made. The next dozen years should show considerable further progress. Professional accounting bodies cannot press for improved financial reporting for governments as effectively as they can for business organizations or for nonprofit organizations, where a wide-spread expectation of audit reporting in accordance with GAAP leads users to expect a certain standard of reporting quality. Nevertheless, bodies such as the Public Sector Committee can provide guidance for governments who are motivated to improve their reporting. Much of the motivation comes from auditors general in the federal and provincial governments, who have been quite effective in some instances at pressuring governments to improve their reporting practices. Recommendations of the Public Sector Committee can give the provincial auditors additional clout in pressing for improved reporting standards in government.

REVIEW QUESTIONS

4-1 Who owns nonprofit organizations?

4-2 Why are nonprofit organizations sometimes called "voluntary organizations?"

4-3 What distinguishes nonbusiness organizations from business organizations?

4-4 Explain the difference between **nonbusiness** organizations and **nonprofit** organizations.

4-5 What distinguishes nonprofit organizations from governmental units?

4-6 What is the difference between governmental units and crown corporations?

4-7 Who elects the directors of a nonprofit organization?

4-8 Distinguish between an open membership nonprofit organization and a closed membership organization.

4-9 Explain what is meant by a "self-perpetuating board."

4-10 How does the basic organizational objective of nonbusiness organizations differ from that of business enterprises?

4-11 Why do nonbusiness organizations need to be more concerned about expenditure controls than do businesses?

4-12 Why do nonbusiness organizations frequently need a formal mechanism for segregating funds?

4-13 What objectives of financial reporting for businesses do not exist for nonbusiness organizations?

4-14 Who are the primary users of the financial statements of nonprofit organizations?

4-15 Who are the users of the financial statements of governments?

4-16 What three objectives of financial reporting are common to businesses, nonprofit organizations, and governments?

4-17 How can the financial statements of a nonprofit organization be used to evaluate performance?

4-18 How similar are the qualitative criteria applied to the accounting measurements of nonprofit organizations to those that are applied to the accounting measurements of businesses? Explain the similarity or difference.

4-19 What types of financial statements will a nonbusiness enterprise normally issue?

4-20 How standardized are the statements of nonprofit organizations, as compared to business organizations?

4-21 Why might it be possible for a nonprofit organization to combine the statement of operations with the statements of changes in financial position?

4-22 Under what circumstances are the financial statements of a nonbusiness entity likely to look most similar in form and content to the financial statements of a business?

4-23 Why is information that is supplementary to the financial statements of a nonbusiness organization so important?

4-24 If the emphasis in accounting for many nonprofit organizations is on the control of cash flows, why is the accrual basis recommended?

4-25 Why might an organization accrue its expenses and yet record its revenue on the cash basis?

4-26 For businesses, consolidated financial statements are normally required. Why is there no such requirement for nonbusiness organizations?

4-27 Why might a nonbusiness organization consolidate its balance sheet but not its statements of operations?

4-28 Why would an organization want to report the value of donated services in its statement of operations?

4-29 Why do most nonbusiness organizations not capitalize their fixed assets?

4-30 What is a **fixed asset group** of accounts? What is the purpose of such a group?

4-31 When is a nonbusiness organization most likely to charge depreciation to operations?

4-32 Why is nonfinancial supplementary information often needed for performance evaluation?

4-33 Define programmatic reporting.

4-34 Why are many nonprofit organizations moving towards programmatic reporting?

CASE 4-1   Reporting Objectives

You have recently been appointed auditor of three different organizations. The first organization is a mining company that was formed a year ago to develop a gold mining site in northern Ontario. The largest single part of the initial investment was provided by a major, publicly held mining company in exchange for 36% of the common shares. The remaining shares were issued publicly in the over-the-counter market, where they are very thinly traded. The company is still in the development stage and does not expect to commence production for at least another year.

The second organization is a nonprofit secondary school that provides courses for students who intend to pursue a career in one of the performing arts. The school is fully recognized by the provincial ministry of education, which provides about 50% of the school's operating budget. Another 20% of the operating funds are provided by the ministry of culture and recreation, while the remainder are derived from student fees and by fund raising in the private sector. The school occupies an old public high school building that was no longer being used by the city; the school acquired the building on a twenty-year lease from the city's board of education.

The third organization is a labour union for the graduate students at a major university. The union receives its funding from dues that are mandatorily deducted by the university from the earnings of all members of the bargaining unit, whether they are members of the union or not. A portion of the funds is sent to the union's parent national organization, and another part is set aside for the strike fund, which is held and invested by a trustee until such time as it is needed to pay striking union members.

Required:
Explain how the objectives of financial reporting would likely differ for these three organizations.

Rosen Hall (Part A)

Rosen Hall is a 2,700-seat concert hall located in the centre of a large Canadian city. The hall was completed three years ago as a replacement for an aging and deteriorating concert hall. The older hall remains in use at a sharply reduced activity level, pending accumulation of sufficient funds to renovate it extensively.

The new hall cost approximately $30 million to build. Of that amount, two-thirds were provided by the various levels of government. The remaining one-third was paid for privately, although fund raising is still going on in order to retire the $8 million loan that is still outstanding. The largest single private contribution was provided by the Rosen family, in memory of S. L. Rosen, a famous publisher of accounting textbooks; the hall was named after Rosen in appreciation of the donation.

Both the new and old halls are governed by an independent board of governors. A sizeable full-time professional staff operates both halls, although the old hall requires very little of their time. The professional staff is augmented by a substantial operating crew of ushers, bartenders, and cleaning and maintenance personnel. Both halls are expected to be self-supporting, although "manageable" deficits on the new hall were anticipated by the board in the first couple of years. Any profits derived from the operation of the new hall will be put towards renovations of the old hall, which Rosen Hall replaced.

The primary tenant of the new hall is the City Symphony Orchestra, which gives about 120 concerts per year in the hall. The hall is also rented to other performing groups for both afternoon and evening performances. The board of governors of the hall has established its own series of concerts, bringing in performing artists and orchestras from around the world. The board's own concert series is an important part of the hall's total activities, and helps to ensure that it is in use most of the time, a necessary condition to enable the hall to meet its costs.

Required:
What are the issues that arise for reporting the financial results of the activities under control of the halls' board of governors? Outline the objectives of reporting in this situation, and how the issues and characteristics of reporting for nonprofit organizations apply.

The New Canadian Counselling Centre

The New Canadian Counselling Centre (NCCC) is a nonprofit organization dedicated to professional counseling of individuals who have recently moved into the urban Canadian environment and who are having difficulty in adjusting to their new lifestyle and surroundings. NCCC also offers peer counseling for people who do not need the services of a professional psychologist, psychiatrist, or social worker.

The professional counselors who work for NCCC do not rely on NCCC for their primary income. Almost without exception, the counselors have primary employment with a hospital or other social agency, or have private practices. The reason is that since NCCC is not government supported, the counselors provide their services at substantially below their market rates.

Originally, NCCC operated out of rented offices. Two years ago, however, the organization was able to buy a downtown town house, with the aid of a substantial bequest that was restricted to providing funds for permanent quarters. The bequest not only permitted NCCC to purchase the house, but also to establish an endowment fund to help maintain the premises. The earnings of the fund are not sufficient to provide for all of the maintenance costs, but do contribute significantly to the cost.

NCCC does not qualify for participation in the province's health care program because it does not limit its patients to those referred by other health practitioners. About half of its operating funds are obtained from fees charged to patients on a scale that is tied to each individual's ability to pay. Another 25% of the budget is provided by social fund-raising organizations, and the remainder is raised through private donations.

The organization does not have any accumulated surplus, and thus has no way to support a deficit except by further financial sacrifices by its counselors. The peer counselors are not paid, and there is no charge for their services. There is a two-person, full-time administrative staff.

Required:
Outline the objectives of financial reporting as they pertain specifically to NCCC. What accounting policies seem appropriate for this organization?

CASE 4-4   Comparison of Objectives

William Witherspoon III is executive vice-president of Marble Industries Ltd., a publicly held industrial company. Mr. Witherspoon III has just been elected to the city council of Turnwater, a major industrial city. Prior to assuming office as a city councillor, he asks you, as his accountant, to explain the major differences that exist in accounting and financial reporting for a large city when compared to a large industrial corporation.

Required:
a. Describe the major differences that exist in the purpose of accounting and financial reporting and in the types of reports of a large city when compared to a large industrial corporation.
b. Why are inventories often ignored in accounting for governmental units? Explain.
c. Under what circumstances should depreciation be recognized in accounting for governmental units? Explain.
[CGA-Canada]

CASE 4-5   Minicom Youth Training Association

The executive director of Minicom Youth Training Association has approached you to advise the Association on the appropriate financial reporting policies for its first year of operations.

Minicom Youth Training Association is a charitable organization incorporated without share capital under the Ontario Corporations Act in 1988. The mandate of the organization is to assist youth who face severe employment barriers to gain the skills, experience, and confidence required to find stability in employment. The program consists of four basic components: (1) general office training, including business computer applications; (2) work experience in a data processing service run by Minicom; (3) a six-week work placement with an outside employer; and (4) permanent job search and placement assistance.

Minicom completed its first year of operations on June 30, 1989, and is in the process of drafting its financial statements. One of the areas of concern is the recognition of revenue. The primary source of revenue is grants from the Canada Employment and Immigration Commission (CEIC). The grants received from that source in fiscal 1989 were as follows:

Job Corps	$263,050
Skills Growth Fund	32,619
Total CEIC	$295,669

All of the grant from the Skills Growth Fund and $32,349 of the grant from the Job Corps were specifically designated for the purchase of computer equipment. In accordance with a request by the funders, the computers were recorded as fixed assets on the books of Minicom. The remainder of the Job Corps grant was intended for operating expenses for fiscal 1989.

In late 1988, Minicom received confirmation of a $30,000 grant from the City of Toronto. The City gave the grant to cover the cost of computer software that Minicom acquired in fiscal 1989. Payment by the City of two-thirds of the grant was delayed until fiscal year 1990, however.

A fund-raising committee of Minicom's Board of Directors solicited donations from businesses and individuals. Pledges totaling $27,933 were received during fiscal 1989; $13,433 of this amount had not been received by the fiscal year-end.

In common with most charitable organizations, Minicom receives donations of goods and services. One such donation was by the Toronto Planet and Courier, which gave Minicom free advertising space for the job placement aspect of the program. Had the space not been donated, Minicom would have had to purchase this space at a cost of $2,460.

Required:
Write a report to the Executive Director of Minicom in which you recommend appropriate revenue recognition policies for the revenue sources described above. Also include any related expense recognition policies that are appropriate.
[ICAO]

Red River Rehabilitation Centre

CASE 4-6

It is May 1989. You have just returned from your first meeting with Barry Wells, the executive director of Red River Rehabilitation Centre (the Centre). You are an accountant working in industry and have recently been elected to the board of directors of the Centre. Barry Wells assumed the post of executive director only one month before your meeting with him; the previous executive director left the Centre for a position with an educational institution.

At the meeting, Barry told you that he is not satisfied with the information provided in the annual financial statements. He does not see how he, as executive director, and the board of directors can make useful decisions on the basis of the information presented in the financial statements. Indeed, he cannot even be certain from the current financial statements that the Centre has been meeting its 80% disbursement quota. (The *Income Tax Act* requires a registered charity to spend at least 80% of its preceding year's receipted donations on charitable activities.)

The Centre is a nonprofit organization incorporated under the provincial corporations act as a corporation without share capital. It is a registered charity under the provisions of the *Income Tax Act*. The Centre's corporate objective is to aid in the care and rehabilitation of children and young adults suffering from physical or mental disabilities. The Centre has a wide range of programs for various age groups and for people with various disabilities. The principal programs are the children's residence program, the adolescent program, the pre-school program, the home-care program, and the summer day camp. The Centre also sponsors research activities and conducts educational activities for affected persons, their relatives, and the general public.

Revenues for the Centre's activities are obtained from a wide variety of sources. About 30% of the total revenue is obtained from the provincial Ministry of Social Services. Another 10% is obtained from the Ministry of Education for the children's residence program, which includes an academic component. Most of the remainder is obtained from bequests and from donations by foundations, corporations, and individuals. Some funds have been obtained from lottery grants, although these are generally used to cover the costs of special projects rather than the costs of operations.

The grants from the Ministries of Social Services and Education are provided based on annual budgets prepared for each program. Many of the public donations are also designated for specific programs or purposes such as research or education. The bequests are frequently given under the condition that the principal amount cannot be expended; only the income from investing the bequest can be used. Unrestricted donations, bequests, and other revenue (such as from special fund-raising events) can be allocated by the board of directors at its discretion.

About 80% of the staff of the Centre are paid employees; the remainder are volunteers. Most of the patient-care staff are assigned to specific programs. A program director is in charge of each program, except for the summer day camp program, which is directed by the children's residence program director. About 25% of the paid staff are administrative or service staff. They cannot be identified with a single program. Maintenance staff and kitchen staff are examples of employees who serve more than one program.

Most of the Centre's activities take place at a 100-acre farm located close to the provincial capital city. The Centre has constructed several buildings over the years to house the various programs. All the buildings were paid for by a combination of specific capital grants from the municipal and provincial governments and funds raised for capital projects by public campaigns. The repair and replacement of furniture and equipment, as well as general maintenance of the buildings, are paid for out of operating funds as needed.

The Centre, like most nonprofit organizations, is thinly administered because the board prefers to devote as much of the Centre's resources as possible to its charitable objectives rather than to administration. There is no professional accountant on staff, and the annual financial statements prepared by the bookkeeper are the primary financial document used by the board and the executive director.

After the meeting with Barry Wells, you sit in your office at home organizing your thoughts about the appropriate reporting framework for the Centre. You examine your notes on the accounting system and practices used by the Centre (Exhibit 1) and extracts from its most recent financial statements (Exhibit 2) and prepare to write a report to the board of directors. The report will discuss the adequacy of the accounting information the board is receiving and the adequacy of the internal control system. You want to include in your report any other pertinent financial accounting and reporting issues, together with your recommendations for improvements.

Required:
Prepare the report.
[CICA]

EXHIBIT 1

Notes on Accounting System and Practices

The Centre uses a manual accounting system (except for some of the processing of certain donations, discussed below) that is maintained by one bookkeeper, who also is the secretary to the board of directors. Cheques are prepared by the bookkeeper and signed by the executive director. Expenditures are charged to accounts on the basis of the type of expenditure; for example, all salaries are charged to a single account, all furniture replacements and repairs are charged to a single account, and so forth.

The Centre has a microcomputer with a hard disc. This computer is used to maintain the file of individual, corporate, and foundation donors who have given as a result of mail solicitation or in response to a direct approach by a member of the board. The computer file contains a record of all such individual donors who have given within the past five years and all such corporate and foundation donors who have given within the past ten years. The file is used to generate "personalized" letters each year requesting donations, to record pledges and donations as they are received throughout the year, to generate charitable tax receipts, and to serve as a mailing list for the condensed financial statements that are sent to all donors after the end of the fiscal year. The computer file currently contains data on approximately 50,000 donors. Volunteers are used to input the current data, but output is controlled by the bookkeeper. A monthly report summarizing pledges and donations (many of which are in the form of postdated cheques or credit card donations) is produced by the computer.

Official tax receipts are issued in two ways. For the donations received from donors who are recorded in the computerized data base, receipts are generated by the computer shortly after the end of the calendar year. The receipts are printed on continuous-feed, serially numbered tax-receipt forms by the computer's printer. For donations made in the door-to-door canvassing, the volunteers issue handwritten receipts when requested by the donor. The receipt forms are the same as those used by the computer system. Each volunteer picks up a supply of forms from a box in the Centre's administration offices before going canvassing. The forms are signed in advance by an authorized person.

Grants from governments, foundations, and corporations are recorded as revenue when pledges or grants are announced. Donations from individuals are recorded as revenue when the cash, cheque, or credit card voucher is received, regardless of whether the cheque or voucher is currentdated or postdated. The proceeds from door-to-door canvassing are recorded when each canvasser turns in the contributions he or she has collected. Pledges are recorded in the computer file for subsequent follow-up, but are not recognized as revenue.

Since the fund-raising activities are carried on throughout the year, revenues for the year are very difficult to predict. The uncertainty about revenues introduces a considerable degree of uncertainty into the annual budgeting exercise. In order to reduce the uncertainty in budgeting, the Centre bases its estimates for the forthcoming year's budget on the revenues actually received in the current year, together with an estimate for the remaining months of the current year. The budgeted amounts include any grants that the Centre knows it will receive or that it can reasonably expect to receive.

The budget is prepared annually by the treasurer of the board, in

EXHIBIT 1 (continued)

cooperation with the executive director. A monthly comparison of the year-to-date actual expenditures with the total budgeted amounts, on a line-by-line basis, is prepared by the bookkeeper and forwarded to the executive director and the treasurer. The treasurer presents the budget comparison to the board at its monthly meetings. The budgetary amounts are not formally recorded in the accounts.

The historical cost of the buildings and land is carried on the balance sheet. Depreciation is not taken. The cost of furniture and equipment is charged to operations when the expenditure is made. Similarly, there is no inventory of supplies; all purchases are charged as expenditures.

EXHIBIT 2

Red River Rehabilitation Centre
Extracts from Statement of Revenues and Expenditures
and Unappropriated Surplus
For the Year Ended March 31

	1989	1988
Revenues		
Donations and bequests	$ 996,628	$ 935,826
Government grants	828,452	852,997
Lottery grants	—	130,660
Camp fees	88,420	78,292
Interest	8,663	1,843
	1,922,163	1,999,618
Expenditures		
Salaries and benefits	1,494,038	1,404,396
Purchased services	71,685	65,781
Supplies	34,197	33,244
Research support	64,110	50,970
New furniture and equipment	29,429	180,759
Food costs	60,799	60,160
Health costs	8,897	9,758
Travel	24,966	27,422
Staff training	32,215	38,195
Vehicle maintenance	8,865	7,555
Other maintenace	13,228	18,782
Communications	15,107	17,607
Utilities and taxes	16,618	17,760
Insurance	8,897	8,635
Advertising	3,293	8,597
Other	18,193	21,006
	1,904,537	1,970,627
Excess of revenues over expenditures	17,626	28,991
Unappropriated surplus at the beginning of the year	178,230	149,239
Unappropriated surplus at the end of the year	$ 195,856	$ 178,230

EXHIBIT 2 (continued)

Red River Rehabilitation Centre
Extracts from Balance Sheet
As at March 31

	1989	1988
ASSETS		
Current		
Cash	$ 17,016	$ 1,011
Term deposits	—	90,000
Post-dated donations	139,538	129,387
Government grants receivable	75,815	80,588
	232,369	300,986
Fixed assets		
Land	9,000	9,000
Land improvements	12,236	12,236
Buildings	306,326	306,326
Roadways	7,494	7,494
Swimming pool	19,620	19,620
	354,676	354,676
	$587,045	$655,662
LIABILITIES		
Current		
Bank indebtedness	$ —	$ 42,158
Accounts payable and accrued liabilities	31,815	66,037
Accrued wages payable	4,476	1,026
Payroll deductions payable	222	13,535
	36,513	122,756
SURPLUS		
Investment in property	354,676	354,676
Unappropriated surplus	195,856	178,230
	550,532	532,906
	$587,045	$655,662

5

Fund Accounting

Chapter 4 discussed in general terms the financial reporting for nonbusiness organizations, including nonprofit organizations, governmental units, and governments. In most cases, the nature of the organization and its operations necessitates the use of **fund accounting**. Fund accounting has three attributes, any or all of which may be useful in accounting for specific nonbusiness organizations. The three attributes are (1) the segregation of funds by purpose or restriction, (2) the ability to account for commitments, and (3) the capacity to incorporate budgetary controls directly into the accounts. In this chapter, we explore these three characteristics of fund accounting more fully.

SEGREGATION OF FUNDS

Fund accounting has been defined as: "Accounting procedures in which a self-balancing group of accounts is provided for each accounting entity established by legal, contractual or voluntary action, especially in governmental units and non-profit organizations."[1]

The focus of fund accounting is to keep track of resources that are designated for specific purposes, in order to avoid mixing up resources that are intended for diverse purposes and to assure that management fulfills its stewardship responsibility for proper disposition of the resources. A single nonbusiness organization can have several (or many) such accounting entities.

As the definition suggests, the entities can be created as the result of legal or regulatory requirements, by contract with donors or grantors, or voluntarily by the directorate of the organization. If the primary financial reporting objective is stewardship, then the accounting emphasis is on inflows and

---

1 Canadian Institue of Chartered Accountants, *Terminology for Accountants*, 3rd ed. (CICA, 1983), p. 69.

outflows for the individual funds, and interperiod allocations of cost are seldom made. On the other hand, interperiod allocations (to improve matching) can still be used if performance evaluation or program evaluation is an important objective. The use of fund accounting need not impair the accomplishment of objectives other than stewardship, but the use of fund accounting can enhance stewardship reporting.

The extent to which funds need to be segregated in an organization is largely a matter of common sense. When a donor gives a contribution that is earmarked for a specific purpose, there must be some way of assuring that the contribution is used only as designated. If an organization operates an ancillary enterprise in order to perform a service or to raise money, it makes sense to segregate all the revenues and costs of that enterprise in order to measure the net cost of providing the service or the net revenue raised. Thus there are no hard and fast rules as to the types of funds that an organization may have.

Fund-basis *recording* does not necessarily imply fund-basis *reporting*. As discussed in the previous chapter, it is common to consolidate several or all funds when preparing the financial statements, especially the statement of operations. The balance sheets can also be consolidated, although the amounts of restricted, designated, and appropriated fund balances should still be segregated in the fund balance section of the balance sheet. At the minimum, similar types of funds should be combined in the financial statements. Fund accounting should not be used as an excuse for fractionated reporting; the reporting for some municipalities has in the past been broken down into so many little funds that it was virtually impossible for a citizen to get an overall view of the municipality's finances. Fund accounting should not be used as an excuse to avoid programmatic and/or consolidated reporting.

Types of Funds

There are several different types of funds. Distinctions between types of funds generally relate to either the nature of the activity being carried out by the fund or to restrictions on the uses of monies, or both. Nomenclature varies somewhat, but we can distinguish between six basic types of funds.

Operating or general funds

Nonprofit organizations tend to use the term **operating** fund; governments tend to call them **general** funds. As the name implies, this is the central fund of the organization that bears the costs of conducting the organization's primary functions, and into which unrestricted funds flow. An organization could have more than one operating fund if it conducted more than one primary function, and if it were desirable for managerial purposes to keep the assets, and liabilities and the revenues and expenses of the primary functions separate. But if the revenues, expenses, assets, and liabilities are not directly assignable to the various functions, then segregation is not really feasible and only a single operating fund would be maintained.

The maintaining of separate funds should not be confused with maintaining separate *accounts* within the operating fund for different activities. As the previous chapter emphasizes, it is important to use an account classification system that permits programmatic reporting, but programmatic reporting does not imply separate funds for each program.

Self-sustaining funds

This type of fund accounts for those activities that generate their own revenues to recover their costs, and thus are segregated from the other funds both for control purposes and for performance appraisal. Self-sustaining funds are also known as **enterprise** funds or **revolving** funds. Self-sustaining funds may be created by money advanced from the general fund. In such instances, the amount advanced is a receivable in the general fund accounts and a liability in the self-sustaining fund accounts; the interfund obligation is eliminated if consolidated statements are prepared.

Special funds

A special fund is a fund created to record the resource flows associated with a special project or event. Special funds could be created, for example, to carry out a specific research project, to conduct a special event such as a benefit concert, or to institute a new program using a special grant from a donor or a government grantor. Special funds may generate their own revenue (as for a concert), may be carried out with funds voluntarily segregated by the directorate of the organization and transferred from the operating fund, or may be financed by restricted grants from outside the organization.

Trust funds

An organization may hold funds in trust for other organizations or groups, and not be entitled to any of the benefits of the funds. For example, a church or university may hold cash and provide accounting services for clubs or subgroups within the organization but the funds are those of the clubs and not those of the church or university that is functioning as trustee. Similarly, employee pension funds are sometimes administered by a government or a nonprofit organization for the benefit of its employees. Trust funds can also be called **agency**, **fiduciary**, or **custodial** funds.

Endowed funds

The capital in an endowed fund is not only restricted, but also cannot be disbursed at all. Endowment funds, scholarship funds, and loan funds are examples. The income arising from the investment of the fund capital may or may not be disbursed. If the income can be disbursed, it may be restricted (i.e., as to purpose), depending on the conditions of the donor. Sometimes, a fund is endowed only for a designated period of time, after which the capital becomes available for use as directed by the donor.

The distinction must be clear between a fund that is legally restricted by the donor and one that is voluntarily restricted by the organization's directors. Voluntary restrictions can be reversed at a later date by the directors. Only funds in which the capital is non-expendable by order of the donor should be called endowed funds. *Financial Reporting for NonProfit Organizations (FRFNPO)* recommends that voluntarily restricted funds be called **board designated funds**.

Capital funds

A capital fund (or **plant** fund) is one in which the resources are intended for use for capital improvements or new fixed assets. The fund may be a restricted fund if it contains moneys given specifically for capital purposes only, as with a capital grant by a province to a hospital. Capital funds may also be board-designated funds, if the capital was appropriated by the board of directors for capital improvements rather than being specifically restricted by the donor. If a capital fund contains both restricted amounts and designated amounts, then the fund balance should segregate the net resources within each category. Note that a capital fund differs from an endowed fund in that the resources within a capital fund will be expended, but only for restricted purposes, while the donated fund balance in an endowed fund can only be invested, not expended, as long as the donor's restriction is in effect.

ACCOUNTING FOR FUNDS

In theory, each fund is a separate group of accounts. In practice, however, it is not always necessary to be so formal about the individual funds. For example, suppose that an organization receives a special grant to produce its literature in French translation. Technically, this is a donation that is restricted to a specific use and would call for the establishment of a special fund. More likely, however, the organization will create a single control account in its operating fund and credit the grant to that account. All expenditures relating to the translation and production of the French materials will be charged to that account, so that the account balance corresponds to what would be the fund balance if a separate set of accounts had been established. A subsidiary set of accounts could be maintained in support of the control account, if desired.

When the financial position of a nonbusiness organization is reported on the balance sheet, the fund balances must be segregated into restricted, appropriated, and available resources. **Restricted** balances can only be expended for designated purposes (or cannot be expended at all, as with endowed funds) due to legal or contractual requirements, as we have already discussed. **Appropriated** amounts are those balances that are not legally restricted, but have been voluntarily designated for specific purposes by the directors. For example, the board of directors may designate part of the operating fund balance for future fixed asset acquisitions. These amounts are appropriated and should also be shown as such in the fund balance section of the balance sheet. However, the appropriation is reversible, and that fact should be made apparent by not combining legally restricted balances with voluntarily appropriated balances. Note that as in business enterprise accounting, an appropriation of part of the fund balance (or of retained earnings, in a business) is only a segregation of that fund balance, a "paper entry." There may or may not be a concomitant segregation of monetary resources.

Another form of appropriation is a provision in the accounts to make clear that not all of the unrestricted fund balances are available for future expenditures. For example, an organization may need a fairly substantial inventory of supplies in order to function. If the supplies are inventoried on the balance sheet rather than charged to expense when purchased, then the net assets (and the balance) of the fund will be larger. In order to warn readers that the total fund balance is not available for future expenditure or to cover future deficits, the directors may appropriate or designate an amount of the fund balance that is equivalent to the inventory of supplies as shown on the balance sheet.

The amount of the fund balance that is left over after restrictions and appropriations is the amount that is available for future operations. The organization may intentionally budget a deficit in the following year in order to use up the unrestricted and unappropriated fund balance. This amount is sometimes called the **unappropriated surplus**.

Transfers between funds create a potential problem area for financial reporting. The problem arises from the difficulty of making the distinction between three types of transfers (1) interfund loans, (2) redesignations of fund balances by the board of directors, and (3) expenditures by one fund that are revenues to the other. The first type of transfer results in a receivable in the lending fund and a payable in the borrowing fund; the expectation is that the loan will be repaid sometime in the foreseeable future. Interfund loans will show on the balance sheets and on the statements of changes in financial position, but will not affect the statement of operations or the fund balances.

Redesignation of fund balances by the board represent a permanent shift of resources from one fund to another. These transfers should be reflected in the statement of changes in fund balance for both the paying and the receiving funds, but should not result in an offsetting receivable and payable or have any impact on the statement of operations. If, on the other hand, the transfer is recognition that one fund is using the services of another fund and is paying for the services rendered, then the transaction should flow through the statement of operations of *both* funds.

The problem that often exists in practice is that the accounting treatment of the transaction is often determined more by management's desire to influence the reported operating results rather than by the real nature of the transaction. If the operating fund has a substantial surplus, for example, management may redesignate part of the fund balance and transfer the surplus to another fund (e.g., the capital fund). Rather than report the transfer simply as a fund balance transfer, management may list it as an expenditure in the operating fund in order to bring down the apparent surplus so that potential donors won't think that the organization doesn't really need more money.

A similar ploy is not to transfer the surplus to another fund but simply to make an appropriation within the operating fund, separating the fund balance into appropriated and unappropriated amounts, and to charge the appropriation against operations as though it were an expenditure instead of simply debiting the fund balance. Unfortunately, both ploys are common in practice, making the "bottom line" of the statement of operations even less meaningful than it already is (due to the multiplicity of alternative accounting policy choices, almost all of which affect the bottom line).

Types of Account Groups

In addition to the types of funds explained above, nonbusiness organizations can also have either or both of two **groups** of accounts. Groups differ from funds in that there are no liquid assets within the group; the group is simply a self-balancing set of accounts that is intended to keep track of assets and liabilities that may otherwise not be included within the control systems of the organization.

The first type of group is the **fixed asset group**. Acquisitions of new fixed assets are often treated as current expenditures of the fund making the acquisition, such as the operating fund. In order to include the cost of the fixed assets on the organization's balance sheet, the assets may be recorded as a debit to an asset account within a group of fixed asset accounts, with an offsetting credit to a fund or group balance account. This more general group of accounts is frequently used by governments instead of capitalizing the fixed assets in the accounts of the individual funds that made the purchases, so that all of the accounts relating to the fixed assets of the organization are grouped together to improve control. The group really represents a collection of memorandum entries; there are no resources or transactions relating to the group itself. Fixed asset groups are used more frequently in governments than in nonprofit organizations.

Similarly, governments (and large governmental units) frequently have **bonded debt groups** as well. These are self-balancing groups of accounts that are used to keep track of long-term debt (usually in the form of bonds) that has been incurred by the organization. When bonds are issued, the issuing fund (e.g., the general fund) debits cash and credits revenue. Simultaneously, an entry is made in the bonded debt group in which the face amount of the bonds is credited to a bonds payable account, with an offsetting debit to an "account" that simply indicates the fund that issued the debt. When (or if) consolidated statements are prepared, the bonds payable can then be brought into the consolidated balance sheet; the debit side of the group is eliminated against the fund balance of the fund that originally issued the debt, since the issuing fund has treated the bonds as revenue when issued.

Fixed asset and bonded debt groups are used mainly by governments, and largely for control purposes. If fixed assets are capitalized by a nonprofit organization, the more common practice is to capitalize the asset within the capital fund, the operating fund, or whichever other fund has expended the resources to acquire the fixed assets. Few nonprofit organizations have bonded debt, and therefore a bonded debt group is even more rare outside of government. Nonprofit organizations will normally treat any long-term debt as an obligation of the fund for which management arranged the borrowing.

THE ENCUMBRANCE SYSTEM

In the preceding chapter, we explained some of the major characteristics of nonbusiness organizations, as compared to business enterprises. The most important of those distinguishing characteristics is the absence of profit as an operating objective and the resultant discipline that that objective imposes on the operations of an organization. Because they cannot rely on the profit objective to motivate their managers to control costs, nonbusiness organizations have developed an accounting procedure to aid in cost control, and that procedure is known as the **encumbrance system**. Unique to nonbusiness organizations, the encumbrance system records the estimated cost of commitments in the formal accounting system when the commitments are made rather than when a legal liability has arisen. For example, purchase orders for supplies are recorded as an **encumbrance** at the estimated cost of the supplies when the purchase order is issued, even though no liability (in a legal and an accounting sense) exists until the supplier delivers the supplies.

The objective of using such a system is that it keeps track of the commitments that an organization's managers have made for the acquisition of goods and services. If there is a budgetary or legislative limit on the total amount of expenditure that a manager can make during the year, then use of the encumbrance system keeps the manager from overcommitting the organization and running up a large deficit. Even in the absence of fixed budgetary limits, encumbrances can be used simply as an aid to planning and control. This is particularly true when commitments on the same budget amount can be made by several people within the organization. When control is decentralized, an encumbrance system improves control and communicates to managers and to the people making the expenditures just what the actual level of commitment is.

The encumbrance system is widely used in governmental accounting; budget amounts are legislated maxima that must not be exceeded. In other nonbusiness organizations, however, whether or not an encumbrance system is used depends on the nature of the organization and its operations. In fact, encumbrance accounting can be used in some parts of an organization and not in others, and for some types of expenditure (such as for supplies) and not others (such as salaries). The system is most appropriate when the following conditions are present:

1. The organization, fund, or activity is a cost centre *or* has no relationship between costs and revenues.
2. Goods and services acquired discretionally are a significant part of the total budget.
3. There is a significant lag between the commitment e.g., purchase order) and the receipt of the purchased items.
4. Levels of activity (and expenditure) within the organizational unit are not affected in the short run by an autonomous demand, either external to the organization or from other parts of the organization.
5. Reporting is on an expenditure basis rather than an expense basis.
6. Responsibility for making commitments and expenditures is decentralized throughout a large organization.

If, in contrast, a small organizational unit must vary its level of activity in response to market demand for its services, if it is able to match revenues with expenses, and if externally acquired goods and services are either of little consequence or are received very shortly after ordering, then there is little reason to use an encumbrance system. Encumbrance systems are used to control costs when expenditure limits are basically fixed and are not tied to revenue or activity levels. If these conditions do not exist, then encumbrances are of limited usefulness. Also, if only a very small part of expenditures is discretionary rather than being tied to longer-term employment or supply contracts, then there is little point to using encumbrances.

A later section of this chapter discusses and demonstrates the use of budgetary accounts within the accounting system. When the budget is formally incorporated into the accounts, an encumbrance system is almost always used as well. But encumbrances can readily be used without budgetary accounts.

Assume that the Viable Foundation is a private eleemosynary institution funded by contributions from the family of U.N. Viable, an eminent industrialist. The contributions are restricted as to capital; only the income from investments of the capital can be disbursed either as charitable donations or for operating expenses. On January 1, 19x7, the balance sheet of the foundation appeared as follows:

Illustration of Encumbrance Accounting

Cash	$ 10,000	Accounts payable	$ 20,000
Investments (at cost)	500,000	Fund balance:	
Accrued interest	40,000	Restricted	480,000
Other receivables	20,000	Unrestricted	70,000
Total assets	$570,000	Total equities	$570,000

The balance sheet indicates that of the net assets, $70,000 is unrestricted and thus is available for grants or operating expenses. Since the principal of $480,000 is restricted, the foundation uses the encumbrance system in order to ensure that the total of expenditures, liabilities, and commitments does not exceed the unrestricted amount available.

During the month of January, the foundation issued purchase orders for books and supplies. The estimated cost of the purchases as indicated on the purchase orders amounts to $10,000. In addition, the foundation engaged a consultant for four weeks, beginning on January 24, to advise the foundation on a number of requests for contributions received from several small theatre companies. The consultant was to be paid $20,000 in early March, and the grants to the theatres were to be made in February.

To record the issuance of the purchase orders, the following entry would be made:

Encumbrances — books and supplies (S/O)	$10,000	
Estimated commitments (B/S)		$10,000

Similarly, the commitment for the consultant's fee would be recorded:

Encumbrances — consultant's fees (S/O)	$20,000	
Estimated commitments (B/S)		$20,000

The Encumbrances account is like an expenditure (or expense) account; it can appear on an interim statement of operations as a use of resources, even though it represents only a commitment at this stage. The offsetting credit is to a liability account, **Estimated commitments**. The traditional title of this credit is **reserve for encumbrances,** but we have used a more descriptive title to more clearly indicate the nature of the account as an estimated liability. Estimated commitments is a balance sheet account. To help the reader, the nature of each account is indicated either as a **Statement of Operations (S/O)** or a **Balance Sheet (B/S)**.

During the month of January, some of the ordered books and supplies were received by Viable and were invoiced for $7,000. The estimated cost of these goods had been $6,000, part of the total of $10,000 recorded as an encumbrance above. Two entries are required when the goods are received, one to reverse the encumbrance *for the same amount as it was originally set up,* and a second to record the actual expenditure and liability:

Estimated commitments (B/S)	$6,000	
Encumbrances — books and supplies (S/O)		$6,000

Expenditures — books and supplies (S/O)	$7,000	
Accounts payable (B/S)		$7,000

We have assumed that Viable charges its purchases directly to operations, and does not record an inventory for books and supplies.

Of course, these two entries can be simplified by means of a special journal. A purchases journal may be used, which contains columns for both the invoice amount and the estimated amount as shown on the purchase order, thereby permitting a single compound entry.

By the end of January, the consultant will have worked with the foundation for one week, and will have earned one-fourth of the $20,000 fee. Since the foundation is now liable for payment for one week's consulting, a liability will be accrued for $5,000. The related encumbrance will be reversed:

Estimated commitments (B/S)	$5,000	
Encumbrances — consultant's fees (S/O)		$5,000
Expenditures — consultant's fees (S/O)	$5,000	
Accrued liabilities (B/S)		$5,000

Notice, however, that the offsetting account for Encumbrances is the Estimated commitments account, and vice versa. This will almost always be the case; entries will be self-contained within the encumbrance system, and no entries will normally be made that involve both encumbrance system and non-encumbrance accounts. The only exception is for end-of-period balances, when the outstanding commitments may be incorporated into the fund balance.

For example, suppose that we prepare a trial balance for the Viable Foundation after the above entries have been recorded. The trial balance would appear as shown in Schedule 5-1, ignoring any other transactions or accruals that would have occurred during the month. If we prepare financial state-

---

SCHEDULE 5-1

Viable Foundation
Trial Balance
January 31, 19x7

	Dr.	Cr.
Cash	$ 10,000	
Investments	500,000	
Accrued interest	40,000	
Other receivables	20,000	
Accounts payable		$ 27,000
Accrued liabilities		5,000
Fund balance, restricted		480,000
Fund balance, unrestricted		70,000
Estimated commitments		19,000
Expenditures — books and supplies	7,000	
Expenditures — consultant's fees	5,000	
Encumbrances — books and supplies	4,000	
Encumbrances — consultant's fees	15,000	
	$601,000	$601,000

ments from the trial balance,the expenditure for books and supplies and the accrued expenditure for one week of the consultant's fee would be charged to operations, thereby reducing the unrestricted fund balance to $58,000. An issue arises, however, in how to treat the encumbrances and the estimated commitments in the financial statements. Two basic approaches are possible.

The first basic approach is to maintain the separate nature of the encumbrance system accounts so that there is no impact of the outstanding $19,000 (in encumbrances and estimated commitments) on the fund balance. Under this approach, there are three ways that the $19,000 balances can be reported on the balance sheet. The first (1a) is to view the outstanding commitments as executory contracts that should not be reflected in the financial statements. Under this approach, the encumbrance accounts and the estimated commitments are offset and do not appear on the balance sheet at all. The second variation (1b) is to show the estimated commitments in the liabilities section but to deduct the encumbrances therefrom, leaving a zero balance. The third (1c) is to include the estimated commitments with the liabilities and to include the encumbrances with the assets, as a deferred charge. Under any of these three variations, the encumbrances would not be reflected on the statement of operations.

The second basic approach is to charge the encumbrances to January's operations, thereby reducing the unrestricted fund balance to $39,000 ($70,000 beginning balance, less $12,000 expenditures, less $19,000 encumbrances). The estimated commitments would then be included as a liability on the balance sheet. Schedule 5-2 shows the balance sheet as it would appear under each of these alternatives.

Ordinarily, the encumbrance system is used in order to control expenditures by controlling commitments for expenditure. If there are expenditure constraints in the organization, then management's compliance with those constraints can be most easily seen by charging the encumbrances to the period in which the commitment was made. Therefore, most nonbusiness organizations that record encumbrances will also use the second basic method of reporting the encumbrances and commitments, as shown in the last column of Schedule 5-2.

In the case of Viable Foundation, however, management probably has some control over the timing of its charitable grants. Since managers can delay the giving of grants from one period to another, the encumbrance system may be more useful simply as a way of keeping track of the commitments as an aid to planning, rather than as a means of strict control over expenditures. Thus it would be possible to use one of the alternatives under the first basic approach; the first alternative is the least attractive, since it does not disclose the level of commitments on the face of the statements, although the information could be disclosed in a note. In most cases, however, encumbrances are charged to operations in the period of the commitment rather than in the period of the receipt of the goods and services.

When end-of-period encumbrances are not closed out to the fund balance (i.e., if the first basic approach is used), then the recording of goods and services received in the following period will not differ from the transactions illustrated above; the original encumbrance will be reversed for the amount of the estimate, and the real liability and expenditure will be recorded for the invoice amount. On the other hand, if end-of-period encumbrances are closed to the fund balance, then the receipt of goods ordered in one period

SCHEDULE 5-2

Viable Foundation
Balance Sheet
January 31, 19x7

	Alternative 1: not charging encumbrances to operations			Alternative 2: charging encumbrances to operations
	1a	1b	1c	
Assets:				
Cash	$ 10,000	$ 10,000	$ 10,000	$ 10,000
Investments	500,000	500,000	500,000	500,000
Accrued interest	40,000	40,000	40,000	40,000
Other receivables	20,000	20,000	20,000	20,000
Encumbrances	—	—	19,000	—
Total assets	$570,000	$570,000	$589,000	$570,000
Liabilities:				
Accounts payable	$ 27,000	$ 27,000	$ 27,000	$ 27,000
Accrued liabilities	5,000	5,000	5,000	5,000
Estimated commitments	—	19,000	19,000	19,000
Less encumbrances	—	(19,000)	—	—
Total liabilities	32,000	32,000	51,000	51,000
Fund balance:				
Restricted	480,000	480,000	480,000	480,000
Unrestricted	58,000	58,000	58,000	39,000
Total fund balance	538,000	538,000	538,000	519,000
Total equities	$570,000	$570,000	$589,000	$570,000

but received in the next will require an entry that offsets the estimated commitments against the actual expenditure.

For example, assume that Viable charges the January 31 outstanding encumbrance to operations, as shown in the last column of Schedule 5-2. The $19,000 of estimated commitments includes $4,000 for books and supplies and $15,000 for consultant's fees. Assume that in February, the remaining ordered books and supplies are received, together with an invoice for $4,500. Since the encumbrances account for January has been closed, the estimated commitment must be cancelled as follows:

Estimated commitments (B/S)	$4,000	
Expenditures — books and supplies (O/S)		$4,000

The actual expenditure can then be recorded as usual:

Expenditures — books and supplies (O/S)	$4,500	
Accounts payable (B/S)		$4,500

The net effect is that February's operations will bear only $500 of the cost of books and supplies received in that period, the difference between the estimate and the actual. If the actual cost is less than the estimate, then a net **credit** will flow through to February's statement of operations.

BUDGETARY ACCOUNTS

So far in this chapter, we have discussed the concept of funds and illustrated the use of encumbrance accounts, two of the three major characteristics of fund accounting. In this section we illustrate the third characteristic, the use of budgetary accounts that are formally incorporated into the accounting system.

The purpose of incorporating budgetary accounts directly into the accounting system is to permit the ready comparison of budgeted with actual amounts (of revenue and expenditure) and, as with encumbrance accounting, monitor the level of expenditure. It is quite possible to accomplish the same result without formally including the budget in the accounting system; many businesses routinely have budget-vs.-actual comparisons on their internal statements. The difference in nonbusiness organizations, and especially in governments, is that when strict expenditure limits are in effect, a formalized system acts as an internal control, so that managers are not permitted to issue purchase orders that will push the expenditure total above the budgeted limit. The comparison between the budget and the combined total of expenditures and encumbrances is constant and routine, rather than being occasional and special.

In the illustration that follows shortly, we show the use of budgetary accounts in a manual system, using the traditional double entry system. In practice, the systems that use budgetary accounts are now almost always computerized. In a computerized accounting system, the organization of the account structure is most efficiently accomplished by the use of a data base that permits multiple classification of single amounts; debits and credits are a bit of an anachronism in such systems. Computerized systems routinely churn out monthly statements that show each manager the budget limit for each type of expenditure under her or his control, the expenditures to date, the outstanding encumbrances, and the uncommitted balance. An example of such a report is shown in Schedule 5-3.

Schedule 5-3 shows only the summary budget and expenditure report for a particular program, and as such, it shows only the major categories of expenditure on the left side of the report. There are two columns for the budgeted amounts, both original and revised, which are the same in this particular example. The next two columns show the expenditures for the current month and for the year-to-date (i.e., "fiscal year"). Additional pages of the full report, not reproduced here, show the current expenditures in complete detail. The fifth column is the amount of the encumbrances, or "open commitments;" these are detailed at the bottom of the page. The open commitments are for account 4030, Travel — General — Full-time Students. The budget for that category of expenditure is $4,800. There were no expenditures in the current month, but so far during the year, expenditures have

SCHEDULE 5-3

York University
Financial Records System
Statement in whole dollars for 31/10/87
Faculty of Administrative Studies — PhD Program

Sub code	Description	Budgets Original	Revised	Actual Current Month	Fiscal Year	Open Commitments	Balance Available	Perc. Used
3222	Print — ext — other	5,000	5,000				5,000	0
3260	Photocopying — general	2,000	2,000		236		1,764	12
3320	L.D. Telegrams etc.	200	200		29		171	14
3330	Books — periodicals			35	35		35 −	0
	Operational expenses	7,200	7,200	35	300		6,900	4
4010	Travel gen'l faculty	500	500				500	0
4030	Travel gen f-t stud	4,800	4,800		2,082	1,800	918	81
4050	Travel vis' speakers	4,800	4,800	444	444		4,356	9
4060	Functions — campus			308	308		308 −	0
4063	Hospitality — ext	1,000	1,000		465		535	47
4026	Equip comp + w.p. ned	200	200				200	0
	General expenses	11,300	11,300	752	3,299	1,800	6,201	45
6320	Course materials	600	600				600	0
	Total expenses	19,100	19,100	787	3,599	1,800	13,701	28
	Account total	19,100	19,100	787	3,599	1,800	13,701	28

This is a summary of your account's current month transactions.
Please review details on FOM091.

Open Commitments Status

Account	Ref. No.	Date	Description	Original Amount	Liquidating Expenditures	Adjustments	Current Amount
2-14620-4030	G000232	28/07	K. MacDonald	600.00			600.00
2-14620-4030	G000233	28/07	K. Mcbey	600.00			600.00
2-14620-4030	G000234	15/09	C. Hammah	600.00			600.00
			Account Total	1,800.00			1,800.00

To identify entries you cannot validate please refer to York Handbook
"Where to Direct More Enquiries"

totaled $2,082. If the report stopped there, it would appear that there is $2,718 (i.e., $4,800 — $2,082) available for spending. However, $600 has been promised to each of three students to support their travel expenses to present papers at professional conferences (open commitments), and deducting the total open commitments of $1,800 leaves only $918 to be spent. The last column indicates that 81% of the budgeted amount has been either expended or committed.

Notice that two of the account lines show negative balances available. This indicates that the budgeted amounts for each expense category are not absolute limits. In fact, the program can exceed its budget in individual expenses as long as the total budget of $19,100 is not exceeded. This demonstrates that budgetary and encumbrance accounting can be applied even when the budget amounts are not binding, or when only certain total amounts are binding.

To make the illustration of how debits and credits actually work as simple as possible, let's assume that on January 1, 19x4, the Adolescent Training Centre (ATC) had the following balance sheet:

Cash	$20,000
Fund balance, unrestricted	$20,000

ATC is a social service agency that works with troubled teenagers. The agency receives approximately 70% of its funding from the provincial ministry of health, 20% from the United Way, and the remaining 10% from its own fund-raising efforts.

For 19x4, its budget called for total revenues of $400,000 and expenditures of $410,000, a projected operating deficit of $10,000. To record this information in the accounts, the following entry would be made at the beginning of the fiscal year:

Estimated revenues (control)	$400,000	
Fund balance — budget deficit	10,000	
Budgeted expenditures (control)		$410,000

The accounts for the revenues and expenditures are shown above as control accounts, in order to emphasize that they would usually be entered in some greater detail. The budgeted expenditures account can also be called **appropriations**.

Since the objective of using budgetary accounts is to control expenditures, the control is best exercised at the same level of detail as was approved by the board of directors in the budget. Note that the estimated revenues are recorded as *debits*, while the budgeted expenditures are recorded as *credits*. This apparent reversal is due to the fact that the budgetary accounts will be *offsets* to the actual revenues and expenditures during the period. The difference between the debit balance of actual expenditures and the credit balance of budgeted expenditures will indicate the unexpended balance that is available for the remainder of the year.

The balancing amount for the budgetary entry, the budget deficit or surplus, indicates what will happen to the fund balance if the budgeted revenues and expenditures are achieved. In this example, the deficit would cause the fund balance to decrease by $10,000.

During the year, ATC received $270,000 from the Ministry of Health and $80,000 from the United Way. These amounts would be recorded in the usual manner:

Cash	$350,000	
Revenues		$350,000

In order to raise its own supplemental funds, ATC arranged a benefit concert by a country-rap band, Scrunge. The net proceeds from the concert amounted to $55,000. The concert could have been accounted for by setting up a separate fund, with the net revenue being transferred to the operating fund after all the expenses were paid. Alternatively, the concert could be accounted for by using a control account in the operating fund itself. In either case, there would most likely be no budgetary accounts relating to the expenses of the concert. Since the concert was a separate enterprise with a profit motive, little would be served by limiting expenditures through a budgetary account system. In general, it is not necessary to use the formal budgetary account system for *all* funds or for all aspects of an organization's operations. Budgetary accounts may be useful for some funds and not for others.

Assuming that the concert was accounted for in a separate fund and the net proceeds transferred to the operating fund, the entry would appear as follows:

Cash	$55,000	
Revenues		$55,000

Actual expenditures for the year amounted to $417,000. The summary entry to record the expenditures would be:

Expenditures (control)	$417,000	
Cash		$417,000

In this example, we assume expenditures that were in excess of the budgeted amounts. In some circumstances, managers are not permitted to exceed their budgeted amounts. In governments, expenditures cannot legally exceed the appropriated amounts. If ATC had tight budget controls, then budgeted expenditures would have to be increased before the managers could spend more than $410,000. For example, a budget supplement of $8,000 would be recorded as follows:

Fund balance — budget deficit	$8,000	
Budgeted expenditures (control)		$8,000

The supplemental budgetary entry could also have included revised revenue estimates, based on the actual receipts described above.

After all the above entries have been recorded, the trial balance of ATC's operating fund will appear as shown in Schedule 5-4. The trial balance shows both the budgetary amounts (indicated by B/A) and the actual amounts. At the end of the period, the budgetary accounts are closed:

Budgeted expenditures (control)	$418,000	
Estimated revenues (control)		$400,000
Fund balance — budget deficit		18,000

The budgetary accounts are a self-contained group of accounts; at no time is there ever an entry that involves both a budgetary account and a real or a nominal account. Therefore, the closing entry is also completely self-contained and affects no accounts other than the budgetary accounts.

Once the budgetary accounts have been closed, the operating statement and the balance sheet for ATC can be prepared. In condensed form, the statements for 19x4 will appear as illustrated in Schedule 5-5. The actual deficit for the year was $12,000, thereby reducing the fund balance to $8,000.

SCHEDULE 5-4

Adolescent Training Centre
Operating Fund Trial Balance
December 31, 19x4

	Dr.	Cr.
Cash	$ 8,000	
Fund balance, unrestricted		$ 20,000
Fund balance — budget deficit (B/A)	18,000	
Estimated revenues (B/A)	400,000	
Budgeted expenditures (B/A)		418,000
Revenues		405,000
Expenditures	417,000	
	$843,000	$843,000

SCHEDULE 5-5

Adolescent Training Center
Statement of Operations
Year Ended December 31, 19x4

Revenues	$405,000
Expenditures	417,000
Deficit	(12,000)
Fund balance, unrestricted, January 1, 19x4	20,000
Fund balance, unrestricted, December 31, 19x4	$ 8,000

Adolescent Training Center
Balance Sheet
December 31, 19x4

Assets:	
Cash	$ 8,000
Equities	
Fund balance, unrestricted	$ 8,000

COMPREHENSIVE ILLUSTRATION

Having discussed and illustrated each of the major characteristics of fund accounting, we now combine them all into a single, comprehensive example.

Our illustration is for a year's summary transactions for the Social Services Agency (SSA). The balance sheets for SSA's operating, capital, and fixed asset funds are shown in Schedule 5-6. SSA uses budgetary accounts to control expenditures and to monitor revenues, and uses the encumbrance system for its operating fund only. The operating fund uses the accrual basis for revenues and expenditures, and charges outstanding encumbrances to operations at year-end. The capital fund accrues expenditures and interest revenue, but not grant revenue.

The fixed asset group or fund includes assets purchased both from the capital fund and the operating fund. In some nonbusiness organizations, the balance of the fixed asset group is broken down by source of funds. For example, the fund balance could appear as follows, assuming the management has elected to record depreciation in the fixed asset group:

Fund balance:		
Provided by operating funds	$ 70,000	
Less accumulated depreciation	(25,000)	$ 45,000
Provided by capital funds	170,000	
Less accumulated depreciation	(60,000)	110,000
		$155,000

In this example, however, we will assume that SSA does not make a distinction by source.

Summary of Transactions and Events for 19x2:

1. The SSA board of directors approved the budget for the operating fund as follows:

Estimated revenues:	
Fees for services	$100,000
Grants from community organizations	300,000
Other contributions	60,000
Fund-raising events	80,000
	540,000
Budgeted expenditures:	
Salaries, wages, and related costs	380,000
Supplies and materials	70,000
Other administrative costs	80,000
	530,000
Budgeted surplus	$ 10,000

2. During the year, SSA issued purchase orders for goods and services for the operating fund totaling $140,000.
3. Invoices were received for goods and services totaling $155,000. Of this amount, $13,000 was for purchase orders issued in 19x1 and included in the balance sheet as estimated commitments of $11,000. The remainder was for costs initially estimated at $130,000.
4. Accounts payable of $152,000 were paid.
5. Salaries and wages of $377,000 were paid.
6. SSA charged fees totaling $115,000 to users during the year, and collected $103,000. Fees of $6,000 were judged to be uncollectible, but were not yet written off.

SCHEDULE 5-6

Social Services Agency
Fund Balance Sheets
January 1, 19x2

OPERATING FUND

ASSETS		EQUITIES	
Cash	$ 10,000	Accounts payable	$ 7,000
Temporary investments	20,000	Accrued salaries and wages	5,000
Interest receivable	1,000	Estimated commitments	11,000
Fees receivable	1,500	Fund balance, unrestricted	9,500
	$ 32,500		$ 32,500

CAPITAL FUND

ASSETS		EQUITIES	
Cash	$ 1,000		
Term deposits	30,000	Fund balance	$ 31,000
	$ 31,000		$ 31,000

FIXED ASSET GROUP

ASSETS		EQUITIES	
Furniture	$ 60,000	Fund balance	$155,000
Fixtures	80,000		
Leasehold improvements	100,000		
	240,000		
Accumulated depreciation and amortization	(85,000)		
	$155,000		$155,000

7. Community organizations pledged operating support totaling $320,000. Of that amount, $25,000 had not been received by year-end.
8. SSA received private contributions for operations from businesses and individuals totaling $50,000. Of this amount, $5,000 was in the form of cheques dated after December 31, 19x2.
9. SSA received a commitment from the provincial government to contribute $300,000 towards the acquisition and conversion of an old downtown house for the exclusive use of SSA. One-third of the grant was received in 19x2, and the remainder was to be paid in 19x3.
10. SSA paid expenses of $50,000 towards acquiring a suitable house, including a deposit, lawyer's and architect's fees, and the costs of obtaining zoning changes to permit the conversion of the house. Estimated additional costs incurred but not yet invoiced at year-end were $8,000.
11. Forty thousand dollars of the government grant was invested in term deposits. The deposits were renewed every 30 days, with accumulated interest reinvested along with the principal. By year-end, total accumulated interest in the capital fund (including $1,000 accumulated at the beginning of the year) amounted to $6,000.

12. The temporary investments of the operating fund were sold for $24,000. In addition, interest of $3,000 was collected, including the January 1 accrual.
13. Year-end accrued salaries and wages were $7,000.
14. The board of directors authorized a $100-a-plate benefit dinner to be held in the ballroom of the Forest Seasonings Hotel on December 13, 19x2. To cover the organizing and production costs of the dinner, $20,000 was advanced from the operating fund to set up a special dinner fund.
15. The dinner fund incurred costs totaling $35,000 and generated revenues of $95,000. By December 31, all of the revenues had been received but invoices for $5,000 in costs had not yet been received and were unpaid. Seventy-five thousand dollars cash had been paid to the operating fund: $20,000 as repayment of the initial loan and $55,000 as a loan to the operating fund.
16. SSA records depreciation in the fixed asset group, but does not charge the depreciation to the operating fund. The depreciation and amortization for 19x2 totals $30,000.

Entries

The entries to record the preceding transactions are presented below, in general journal form, with explanations only when the entry is not clear from the illustrations presented earlier in this chapter. The abbreviations OF, CF, DF, and FAG will be used to indicate entries in the operating fund, capital fund, dinner fund, and fixed asset group, respectively.

1. OF:		
Estimated revenues (control)	$540,000	
Budgeted expenditures (control)		$530,000
Fund balance — budget surplus		10,000
2. OF:		
Encumbrances (control)	$140,000	
Estimated commitments		$140,000
3a. OF:		
Estimated commitments (19x1)	$11,000	
Expenditures — goods and services		$11,000
Estimated commitments (19x2)	$130,000	
Encumbrances (control)		$130,000
3b. OF:		
Expenditures — goods and services	$155,000	
Accounts payable		$155,000

In entry 3a, the amount of estimated commitments that had been charged to operations for 19x1 and included as a liability in the opening balance sheet is *credited* to expenditures in order to remove it from the 19x2 expenditures, as we described in the previous section. There are several other ways of handling the opening balance of estimated commitments, all of which yield the same result. Perhaps the easiest is simply to make a **reversing entry** at the beginning of the year for the 19x1 charge to operations:

Encumbrances	$11,000	
Expenditures — goods and service		$11,000

The entry to record the receipt of invoices and the reversal of the related encumbrance would then be quite routine:

Estimated commitments	$141,000	
Encumbrances		$141,000
Expenditures	$155,000	
Accounts payable		$155,000

Another alternative is not to make an opening reversing entry, but to wait until year-end to make an adjusting entry.

4. OF:

Accounts payable	$152,000	
Cash		$152,000

5. OF:

Expenditures — salaries and wages	$377,000	
Cash		$377,000

6. OF:

Fees receivable	$115,000	
Revenue from fees		$115,000
Revenue from fees — estimated uncollectible	$6,000	
Allowance for uncollectible fees		$6,000
Cash	$103,000	
Fees receivable		$103,000

7. OF:

Pledges receivable	$320,000	
Revenue from community organizations		$320,000
Cash	$295,000	
Pledges receivable		$295,000

This entry and the next one raise the issue as to whether pledges made but not received should be recognized as revenue in 19x2, or only when received, as we discussed in Chapter 4. In this example, we are assuming that the organization does accrue its pledges and also recognizes them as revenue in the period pledged. Remember that these are two different accounting policy issues: (1) the accrual of pledges and (2) the timing of revenue recognition.

8. OF:

Cash	$45,000	
Postdated cheques receivable	5,000	
Revenue from contributions		$50,000

In this case, we are assuming that the cheques are likely to be honoured when due. An allowance for estimated dishonoured cheques could be set up. In essence, the postdated cheques account is a receivable.

9. CF:

Cash	$100,000	
Revenue from government		$100,000

In the capital fund, grant revenue is not accrued. This is common, because the grants are frequently intended to match payments for capital expenditures. The government prefers not to give out the money any earlier than necessary. Nevertheless, alternatives are possible. Some organizations would accrue the $200,000 commitment by the government.

10. CF:

Expenditures — building project	$58,000	
Cash		$50,000
Accrued expenses payable		8,000

FAG:

Building	$58,000	
Fund balance		$58,000

11. CF:

Term deposits	$40,000	
Cash		$40,000
Term deposits	$5,000	
Interest revenue		$5,000

The capital fund does not accrue revenue. The interest recorded above is not an accrual, but is accumulated and reinvested. SSA could have taken the interest in cash, had they wanted to. The amount of $5,000 is the total accumulation of $6,000 less the $1,000 accumulated at the beginning of the year and already included in term deposits at that date.

12. OF:

Cash	$24,000	
Temporary investments		$20,000
Gain on sale of investments		4,000
Cash	$3,000	
Interest receivable		$1,000
Interest revenue		2,000

13. OF:

Expenditures — salaries and wages	$2,000	
Accrued salaries and wages payable		$2,000

The entry provides the amount necessary to adjust the beginning balance of $5,000 upwards to the ending balance of $7,000. Alternatively, $5,000 of the salaries and wages paid in Item 5 could have been debited to accrued salaries and wages; then the above entry would be for $7,000.

14. OF:

Receivable from dinner fund	$20,000	
Cash		$20,000

DF:

Cash	$20,000	
Payable to operating fund		$20,000

15. DF:

Cash	$95,000	
Revenue		$95,000
Expenditures	$35,000	
Cash		$30,000
Accrued expenses payable		5,000
Payable to operating fund	$20,000	
Receivable from operating fund	55,000	
Cash		$75,000

OF:

Cash	$75,000	
Receivable from dinner fund		$20,000
Payable to dinner fund		55,000

The net proceeds of the dinner fund will ultimately be transferred to the operating fund, and the dinner fund will be closed out. We have assumed that this has not yet happened.

16. FAG:

Fund balance	$30,000	
Accumulated depreciation		$30,000

17. Adjustments to OF:

Expenditures — goods and services	$10,000	
Encumbrances (control)		$10,000

This entry charges 19x2 operations with the estimated cost of the outstanding purchase orders at year-end.

Budgeted expenditures (control)	$530,000	
Fund balance-budget surplus	10,000	
Estimated revenues (control)		$540,000

This entry closes the budgetary accounts.

The trial balances of the three funds and the fixed asset group are shown in Schedule 5-7, after recording all of the above entries.

Schedule 5-8 shows the statement of operations and the balance sheet for each of the three funds and for the fixed asset group. Since the proceeds of the benefit dinner have not yet been transferred to the operating fund, the operating statement for this fund shows a deficit of $52,000 for the year. This deficit is misleading, however, since the dinner fund exists only in order to generate revenue for the operating fund. Therefore, either the net profit from the dinner should be recognized by the operating fund, or the statements of the operating and dinner funds should be combined.

If the net profit from the dinner is recognized as revenue by the operating fund, the entries to record the recognition at year end would be:

OF:

Receivable from dinner fund	$ 5,000	
Payable to dinner fund	55,000	
Revenue from special events		$60,000

DF:

Fund balance	$60,000	
Receivable from operating fund		$55,000
Payable to operating fund		5,000

These entries eliminate the existing interfund liability and establish a new interfund liability for the amount not yet remitted by the dinner fund to the operating fund, $5,000.

If instead, the statements of the dinner fund are consolidated with those of the operating fund, then the statement of operations would include $60,000 net revenue from the dinner, and the operating fund would show a net surplus (or excess of revenues over expenditures) of $8,000.

The example of a dinner fund in this illustration was quite simple. Many nonprofit organizations engage in ancillary or supplemental activities in order to provide special services or to generate additional revenue. In general, the financial statements are likely to be more useful if the operations of these special funds are combined or consolidated with those of the general or op-

Financial Statements

SCHEDULE 5-7

Social Services Agency
Trial Balance
December 31, 19x2
Dr./(Cr.)

	Operating fund	Capital fund	Dinner fund	Fixed asset group
Cash	$ 6,000	$ 11,000	$ 10,000	
Term deposits		75,000		
Fees receivable	13,500			
Allowance for uncollectible fees	(6,000)			
Pledges receivable	25,000			
Postdated cheques receivable	5,000			
Receivable from operating fund			55,000	
Accounts payable	(10,000)			
Payable to dinner fund	(55,000)			
Accrued expenses		(8,000)	(5,000)	
Accrued salaries and wages	(7,000)			
Estimated commitments	(10,000)			
Fund balance	(9,500)	(31,000)		$(183,000)
Revenue from community organizations	(320,000)			
Revenue from government		(100,000)		
Revenue from contributions	(50,000)			
Revenue from fees	(115,000)			
Gain on sale of investments	(4,000)			
Estimated uncollectible fees	6,000			
Interest revenue	(2,000)	(5,000)		
Other revenue			(95,000)	
Expenditures — goods and services	154,000			
Expenditures — salaries and wages	379,000			
Other expenditures		58,000	35,000	
Furniture				60,000
Fixtures				80,000
Leasehold improvements				100,000
Building				58,000
Accumulated depreciation				(115,000)
	$ 0	$ 0	$ 0	$ 0

erating fund, in order to give an overall view of the operations of the organization.

Frequently, the results of special aspects of the organization's activities are disclosed in the operating fund's operating statement as separate activities, rather than consolidated on a line-by-line basis. For example, one would subtract the expenses of SSA's dinner directly from the dinner revenues, instead of adding the gross revenue of the dinner to revenues and adding the expenses of the dinner to the expenditures — goods and services account. That way, the results of the individual activities can still be discerned.

SCHEDULE 5-8

Separate Fund Financial Statements
December 31, 19x2

Operating Fund
Statement of Operations

Revenue:		
Fees	$115,000	
Less estimated uncollectible	6,000	$109,000
Community organizations		320,000
Contributions		50,000
Gain on sale of investments		4,000
Interest		2,000
		485,000
Expenditures:		
Goods and services		154,000
Salaries and wages		379,000
		533,000
Excess of expenditures over revenue		(48,000)
Fund balance, January 1, 19x2		9,500
Fund balance, December 31, 19x2 (deficit)		$ (38,500)

Balance Sheet

ASSETS		EQUITIES	
Cash	$ 6,000	Accounts payable	$10,000
Fees receivable (net)	7,500	Payable to dinner fund	55,000
Pledges receivable	25,000	Accrued salaries and wages	7,000
Postdated cheques receivable	5,000	Estimated commitments	10,000
		Fund balance	(38,500)
	$43,500		$43,500

Schedule 5-9 shows fully consolidated financial statements for SSA. Not only have the results of the benefit dinner been consolidated with the operating fund, but also the operating fund and fixed asset group have been brought into the primary statements. The balance sheet then shows the total resources of the organization, with the fund balance section showing the breakdown of net assets by fund (although with the dinner fund combined with the operating fund).

On the statement of operations, the operating activities are clearly separated from the capital activities, and the opening and closing fund balances are disclosed by fund. Alternatively, the statement of operations could have been divided into two completely distinct sections for the operating fund and the capital fund, as was illustrated in Schedule 4-3 for the Leggy Dance Company.

It must be emphasized that the form and content of financial statements for nonbusiness organizations are quite varied because the nature of these organizations is varied. The samples of statements that have been illustrated in these two chapters are only examples, and must not be taken as models. Financial statements are communications devices, and their form and content must be adaptable to the operating characteristics of the individual organization.

SCHEDULE 5-9

Social Services Agency
Consolidated Statement of Operations
Year Ended December 31, 19x2

Revenues:		
Community organizations	$320,000	
Fees (net)	109,000	
Contributions	50,000	
Benefit dinner (net of expenses of $35,000)	60,000	
Gain on sale of investments	4,000	
Interest	2,000	
		$545,000
Expenditures:		
Goods and services	154,000	
Salaries and wages	379,000	533,000
Operating surplus		12,000
Capital transactions:		
Revenue to capital fund:		
Government grant	100,000	
Interest	5,000	
	105,000	
Expenditures to acquire building	58,000	
Net addition to capital fund		47,000
Total excess of revenues over expenditures		59,000
Fund balances, January 1, 19x2:		
Operating fund	9,500	
Capital fund	31,000	40,500
Fund balances, December 31, 19x2:		
Operating fund	21,500	
Capital fund	78,000	$ 99,500

SCHEDULE 5-9 (continued)				
Consolidated Balance Sheet				
December 31, 19x2				
ASSETS		EQUITIES		
Cash	$ 27,000	Accounts payable		$ 10,000
Term deposits	75,000	Accrued expenses		20,000
Fees receivable (net)	7,500	Estimated commitments		10,000
Pledges receivable	25,000			
Postdated cheques receivable	5,000	Total current liabilities		40,000
Total current assets	139,500	Fund balances:		
		Operating fund		21,500
Furniture	60,000	Capital fund		78,000
Fixtures	80,000			
Leasehold improvements	100,000	Total current		99,500
Building acquisition costs	58,000	Invested in long-lived assets		183,000
Accumulated depreciation				
and amortization	(115,000)			
Total long-lived assets	183,000	Net assets		282,500
Total assets	$322,500	Total equities		$322,500

SUMMARY

In this chapter, we have briefly discussed six different types of funds that nonbusiness organizations can have (plus two types of account groups). Although it is possible to attach names to the various types of funds (e.g., restricted, operating, endowed, capital, etc.), it is not necessary to categorize a fund in order to establish it. The nature of, and limitations on, each fund is what really determines the appropriate accounting treatment, rather than the label attached to it. Fund accounting is substantially a matter of common sense.

We also have illustrated three of the distinctive aspects of fund accounting. The first aspect related to the frequent need of nonbusiness organizations to segregate funds that are restricted or designated for specific purposes. While the maintenance of separate groups of accounts can be a useful way of protecting the integrity of restricted amounts, control accounts or subsets of accounts within the general account structure can often accomplish the same purpose. Even when individual funds are used for bookkeeping purposes, financial reporting need not follow the same pattern. Similar types of funds should be grouped together, and functionally related funds (such as special funds that serve part of the functions of another fund) should be reported on a consolidated basis. Fund *recording* need not lead to fund *reporting*.

The second special aspect of fund accounting is the capability of recording executory contracts as commitments, a process known as encumbrance accounting. Encumbrance accounting is useful in a variety of circumstances, especially when the responsibility for expenditure is decentralized and it is important to control the level of financial commitment by the organization (or a part thereof). Encumbrance accounting is an important component of fund accounting, but it should not be used when it will not enhance financial control.

The third aspect of fund accounting, the inclusion of budgetary accounts in the formal accounting system, is the most difficult to understand within the context of a manual, debit/credit accounting system. Understanding is impaired by the fact that estimated revenues are debits and estimated expenditures are credits, the reverse of accountants' normal expectation for revenues and expenses. The key to the budgetary accounts is that they are *offset* accounts; the difference between the budget accounts and the actual revenues and expenditures represents the deviation from budget (or the available resources remaining).

In a manual system, especially in a small organization, it is easier and less confusing to maintain the budget amounts as memorandum amounts, which may or may not be noted in the general ledger accounts. The real power of budgetary accounts shows up in computerized accounting systems, however, where control can be considerably improved by automatic reporting of budget-vs.-actual results and by controlling against commitments that will cause budget limits to be exceeded.

Like encumbrance accounting, budgetary accounts should not be used unless control is enhanced thereby. Encumbrance accounting and budgetary accounts are available aspects of fund accounting, but not necessary aspects.

REVIEW QUESTIONS

5-1 What are the major characteristics that distinguish fund accounting from proprietary accounting (as used in business enterprises)?

5-2 Why is it important to segregate funds in a nonbusiness organization?

5-3 Explain each of the following:

   a. General fund
   b. Trust fund
   c. Endowment fund
   d. Special fund
   e. Bonded debt group
   f. Self-sustaining fund
   g. Fixed asset group
   h. Capital fund

5-4 How does the fixed asset **group** differ from a **fund**?

5-5 What is the difference between **restricted** balances and **appropriated** balances?

5-6 Define **unappropriated surplus**.

5-7 Why do interfund transfers represent a potential reporting problem?

5-8 What is an **encumbrance**?

5-9 What is the **reserve for encumbrances**?

5-10 What is the purpose of the encumbrance system?

5-11 When would it *not* be appropriate to use an encumbrance system?

5-12 What is the accounting disposition of outstanding encumbrances at the fiscal year-end?

5-13 Is the encumbrance system likely to be used in all funds?

5-14 Explain the purpose of recording budgetary amounts in the accounts.

5-15 When budgetary accounts are used, why is the amount for estimated revenues a debit instead of a credit?

5-16 Why would a nonbusiness organization allocate its administrative costs to several funds, rather than simply report the costs as expenditures of the general fund?

5-17 To what extent have the financial statements of nonbusiness organizations been standardized?

Rosen Hall (Part B)   CASE 5-1

The primary purpose and activity of Rosen Hall (see Case 4-2) is the rental of the hall for concerts (and occasional large meetings). The hall is rented for approximately 400 events during the year, at rates that vary depending on the day of the week, the time of day, the support staff (ushers, etc.) needed, and whether the bars are in operation. The rental is less if the bars are operational because the profits from the bars go to the hall and not to the renting organization.

In addition to renting the main hall, however, Rosen Hall also rents several other spaces in the building. The lobby area is available for rental, either when the main hall is not in use or in conjunction with rental of the main hall, such as for a reception preceding or following a concert. A rehearsal hall also exists underneath the main stage, which is available for rental. Banquet rooms are also below the auditorium and are rented out.

The hall administration also engages in certain ancillary services (in addition to operation of the bars). There is an outside dining area around a reflecting pool that is operated in the summer months. The food is catered by a nearby restaurant, as the hall has no kitchen facilities. A shop in the main lobby is open during the daytime and during concerts, and offers a wide variety of records, books, posters,and other items relating to music or to the hall. The record business has, in fact, been very successful and has expanded rapidly. A 500-car underground garage is situated beneath the hall. The garage's operation, including routine cleaning and maintenance, is contracted to City Park Inc., a city-wide operator of parking facilities.

General maintenance of the hall is programmed and budgeted in advance, but unexpected maintenance requirements arise from time to time, especially as the hall is relatively new and some aspects of its mechanical and architectural systems are innovative. Because of the nature of the materials used in the hall (i.e., the light-coloured carpets, the wall coverings, and the glass and mirrors), regular cleaning is essential. Cleaning expenditures are closely controlled, but the extent of cleaning is somewhat dependent on the frequency of use of the hall's spaces and on the weather (especially for the carpets).

The staff for the box office is separate from the staff for the operation of the hall itself. The box office has its own computerized ticketing operation and sells the tickets for virtually all of the attractions that appear in the hall, except for those of its major user, the City Symphony Orchestra, which sells its tickets through Ticketron. Events that are not sponsored by the hall's board of governors are assessed a flat fee for box office service plus 50 cents per ticket sold.

Overall, the hall is expected at least to break even on its operations. The board of governors for the hall has no other sources of revenue, although deficits can be financed temporarily through borrowings. Ideally, the board would like to see the hall become a net generator of funds, so that the funds can be used to renovate the older concert hall, which the board also operates.

Required:
Discuss the form that the accounting and reporting system for Rosen Hall should take. Be as specific as possible.

The Community Appeal   CASE 5-2

The Community Appeal is a tax-exempt, nonprofit organization incorporated under the *Ontario Corporations Act*. The Appeal was founded in 1979, and received its incorporation papers in January 1980. The purpose of the organization is to raise funds from individuals in certain minority communities, and then to distribute those funds (less fund-raising expenses) to other organizations, groups, and individuals for projects or activities of service to those same communities. The Appeal is intended to provide a stronger base of financial support for services not funded by the government or by the United Way.

In 1981, the Appeal launched its first fund-raising campaign, using a sophisticated slide and tape presentation designed to be shown informally in people's homes. The show was prepared on a volunteer basis by professional writers, photographers, and producers, and was presented by volunteers; there was no paid staff. Many of the supplies and materials used in preparing the show were donated. The 1981 campaign raised a total of $60,000 over a period of about seven months.

Towards the end of 1981, the Appeal formed a separate organization, called The Community Appeal Foundation, and application was made to Revenue Canada for charitable tax status. The purpose of the Foundation was to attract donations from individuals who wanted a tax receipt for their donation. Since many of the organizations and projects that were supported by the Appeal did not qualify as charitable activities under the regulations of Revenue Canada, those non-qualifying activities would continue to be supported by the general funds of the Appeal, while qualifying activities were to be funded by the Foundation. The Foundation was not incorporated, but was a legal subgroup within the Appeal. The trustees for the Foundation were the officers of the Appeal. Contributions were accepted into the Foundation beginning in late 1981, pending approval of the charitable tax application. After several exchanges of correspondence between Revenue Canada and the Appeal, charitable tax status was granted retroactively in late 1982.

In 1982, the style of the audio-visual presentation was altered, but the production was still a volunteer effort. The 1982 campaign raised $90,000 in four months.

Fund raising in 1983 proved to be much more difficult than anticipated, owing largely to the severe recession then underway. A goal of $120,000 had been set, but after six months of effort, less money had been raised than in 1982. The 1983 campaign dragged into 1984, and it became clear that the goal would not be achieved through its traditional fund-raising method.

Fortunately, a professional theatrical producer and a director came forward with a suggestion that the Appeal underwrite a major, original musical review that would use mainly amateur talent, reinforced by selected professional actors who would donate their services, Actors' Equity permitting. The show would be written, casted, directed, staged, and produced by theatre professionals. After much deliberation, the board of directors of the Appeal approved the venture. The show turned out to be a complete success, selling out a local 1,400-seat theatre for four performances and grossing over $100,000. After expenses, the show netted $40,000 and enabled the Appeal belatedly to reach its goal for 1983.

At the end of each campaign, the Appeal held a reception and dance in a local "castle" that was popular for dances, dinners, etc. At this function, known as the "Casa Loma Boogie," awards were made to those projects and groups that the Appeal (and the Foundation) were supporting with the funds raised in that year's campaign. The Boogie was always budgeted to break even, but actually it made modest profits each year, thanks to high liquor consumption by the attendees. The profits from each year's Boogie were designated as a loan fund, available to groups within the community that needed advance money for their own fund-raising activities. The loans were interest-free, repayable on terms negotiated on a loan-by-loan basis. Defaults by borrowers were rare and represented less than 5% of the loans granted.

In 1984, some changes were made to the operation of the Appeal. The official fund raising period was limited to ten weeks in the fall, and the production of the audio-visual show for 1984 was assigned to a commercial production company, rather than to volunteers. In addition, the show was to be transferred to videotape (both half-inch and three-quarter-inch formats) commercially, so that presentations could be made using TV rather than the more cumbersome slide and tape equipment. More emphasis was to be placed on special events as a fund-raising device, the first of which was to be an elegant reception in the lobby of Rosen Hall, the city's new concert hall, with the chairperson of the Canadian Civil Rights Commission as the guest of honour. The Appeal also hoped to be able to hire a half-time executive director within a year, as coordination of volunteers was becoming too difficult for the board to manage.

A special mail campaign was also conducted in the summer of 1984 to raise funds for an AIDS awareness project. The campaign raised $25,000, considerably less than expected. Expenses of the special campaign totaled 10% of the amount raised, without considering any allocations of the general costs of the Appeal.

The board of the Appeal typically budgeted the fund-raising expenses at not more than 20% of the total funds raised in each year's general campaign (including donations to the Foundation). In the first year, actual expenses were 23%, but in each following year, the expenses were less than 20%. There was some concern, however, that the cost of the 1984 campaign would exceed 20% because of the cost of the commercially produced audio-visual show. The expense ratios quoted above do not include the cost of the audio-visual equipment, including four commercial-quality slide projectors, zoom lenses, tape recorders, and a dissolve unit (a computerized unit that automatically controls and synchronizes the audio and visual portions of the show). The Appeal sends a copy of its annual statement of operations to all of its donors. Information returns for the Foundation, most of the contents of which are open to public scrutiny, are sent annually to Revenue Canada.

Because of the increasing volume and activity of the Appeal, the board of directors engaged an accountant to advise them on the organization of the accounting system and on the most suitable financial reporting policies. The board wants a system that is effective, but not too cumbersome or expensive to operate easily with volunteer effort.

Required:
Assume the role of the accounting advisor. Write a report to the board of directors.

Province of Ottawa   CASE 5-3

You are an investigative reporter for the leading financial newspaper in Canada, *The Bay Street Journal*. Your editor suspects that the premier of the province of Ottawa made exceptional efforts to report a surplus in the general fund of the province for the fiscal year that has just ended. Such efforts would be consistent with a plan to call a provincial election in the near future. You have managed to obtain copies of the financial statements of the province and of the budgets for the present and the following year.

Required:
Explain carefully the short-term actions that a provincial government could take that would increase a general fund surplus (or reduce a deficit). For each action, indicate how the financial statements might provide a clue as to whether or not that particular form of action had been used by the present government.
[CGA–Canada]

CASE 5-4   Joton City

The following comments were made to you by a newly elected member on City Council.

"I am amazed at Joton City's treatment of fixed assets. It seems that some are recorded but not in the funds. Some are not recorded at all, and those that are recorded generally have no depreciation taken on them. I realize that each manager has an inventory of assets for control purposes, but we do not put that on the city's financial statements. How would a creditor or taxpayer know what the city's assets are? Also, I know that bridges and streets, etc., last a long time, but we do replace them or conduct major repairs; there appears to be no depreciation on these assets. This is really very different from a large profit-oriented organization."

Required:
Draft a detailed reply to the above comments. Point form is acceptable but you must be *precise* and respond to each of the concerns.
[CGA-Canada]

CASE 5-5   The Valentine Society

The Valentine Society is a nonprofit, charitable organization whose primary role is to ensure the provision of services required by physically handicapped children, young adults, and their families in Quebec. For over 60 years, the Society has promoted a high level of awareness and acceptance of the handicapped through public education and advocacy in support of their rights. The Society works to reduce disabling conditions in children through prevention programs and the support of research. The Society collaborates with handicapped children and young adults, their families, government, other nonprofit organizations, and volunteers in the attainment of its objectives. Through these combined resources, the Society seeks to assist physically handicapped children and young adults to function in the community at the highest level of their ability.

To help children and families achieve independence and integration into the community, the Society offers the following range of programs and services:

- Twenty-two district offices are maintained, where 36 district nurses with public health and rehabilitation nursing training offer direct and consultative services to children and families in the community.
- Community support services are provided, such as transportation service, equipment and financial support to families.
- Two preschool developmental centres are administered.
- Camping and recreational experiences for children and their families are provided at the Society's five camps in the summer, and through the Track Three ski program in the winter.
- A Central Case Registry is maintained, a computer-based information system on the caseload of children served by the Society.
- A Resource Centre provides information of interest to families and staff working with handicapped children.

The latest annual report of the Society contains the following additional descriptions of programs and services:

Joining our first major public awareness campaign "Safe Passage," the Society launched "Head First," a campaign aimed at reducing brain damage from head injuries. More than 100,000 poster/brochures have been produced and distributed. Radio, television, and printed inserts in hydro and gas bills have been used effectively to tell this important story. As a result, a considerable amount of public interest has been generated as well as wide press coverage. In all, approximately half a million dollars' worth of advertising value was produced by this program. We are particularly indebted to the Consumers' Gas System for its assistance with continued funding of this campaign.

Approximately 2,500 children were transported from their homes to treatment facilities, schools, children's nursery programs, and other special events. The cost of this service was $100,000. Another major expenditure for the Society was equipment and special services. In the Montreal area alone, more than $35,000 was spent on purchasing equipment, repairs, and subsidizing of therapy and day nursery programs. Home renovations to permit greater accessibility for disabled children is another area that called for considerable investment.

The Society operates a "Loan Cupboard," which annually provides assistance to about 300 persons. Parents awaiting equipment (such as wheelchairs) may borrow from the Loan Cupboard free of charge.

"Horizons," our quarterly newspaper, had three major achievements. First, its circulation reached 135,000 with readership mostly in Quebec. This is roughly 35% greater than magazines such as "Canadian Business." Second, we have begun to accept limited advertising to offset the cost of production and mailing. And third, a second colour has been added to make "Horizons" a more visually impactful publication.

In addition to its direct services and programs, the Society provides financial support and assistance to the Conn Smythe Research Foundation, the Blissymbolics Communications Institute, and the Augmentative Communication Service.

The major sources of revenue are the Valentine Seal campaign (27% of revenues), bequests (26%), lotteries (12%), special events (9%), telethons (8%), investment income (6%), and camp fees (5%). Government grants are very minor, amounting to less than 1% of revenue.

The major classes of expenditure are for nurses (21%), direct support for children (17%), fund raising (13%), research support (10%), general administration (9%), and camping and recreation (9%).

In 1987, the Society acquired major new computer facilities to assist both in administration and in program support. The cost of the computer facilities and of their development and integration into the Society was provided by a special grant from Digital Equipment Corporation. As a part of the computer systems development, the Society has engaged an advisor to make recommendations on the format and dimensions of the accounting system. The Society's management is dedicated to using the capabilities of the computer to design a financial and managerial reporting system that will enable the Society to measure the efficiency and effectiveness of its activities and to exercise control over the responsibility centres within the Society.

As part of the computer development, the Society wishes to review its existing financial accounting framework and policies, including the appropriateness or application of fund accounting and the applicability of an encumbrance system for part or all of its operations.

Required:
Assume the role of accounting advisor to the Society. Prepare a report in which you recommend, in as much detail as possible from the foregoing information, the reporting framework and accounting policies that should be used by the Society.

CASE 5-6   Cornish House

The Cornish House is a home for adolescent boys that is located in Kamloops, British Columbia. The boys in the home are there at the request of law enforcement agencies; if Cornish House did not exist, most of the boys placed there would probably end up in jail.

Cornish House operates in three neighbouring houses, of which one is owned by Cornish House and the other two are leased. The home has residence facilities for 29 boys. There is a total staff of 24. Cornish House changed auditors in 1989. The national firm of Touche Riddell and Co. assumed the audit responsibilities in June of that year, replacing the sole practitioner who had been Cornish House's auditor since its founding in 1973. At a board of directors' meeting in June, 1990, the directors are reviewing the draft financial statements for the fiscal year ended March 31, 1990. The new auditors have proposed several changes in accounting policy and have incorporated these changes into the draft statements.

You have recently been appointed to the Board of Directors of Cornish House, largely because of your expertise in accounting and other financial matters. The other members of the board therefore are expecting you to provide leadership in responding to the auditors' draft statements.

Required:
Evaluate the draft statements that are attached, including the notes thereto.

Cornish House
Statement of Revenue, Expenditure and Appropriations
Year Ended March 31, 1990

	1990	1989
Revenue		
Room and board — full-pay residents	$276,289	$270,395
— part-pay residents	11,248	7,607
Operating subsidy — Province of British Columbia	142,602	89,878
Donations	22,412	15,566
Interest on term deposits	6,003	5,594
Gain on sale of land	46,517	
	505,071	389,040
Expenditure and appropriations		
Food	37,850	31,502
Boys' physical needs	13,969	11,190
Recreation program	7,928	8,091
Salaries, wages, and benefits	320,520	263,496
Psychiatrist	1,145	1,245
Accommodation	25,946	26,540
Administration	32,778	34,112
Replacements — Furnishings, equipment and motor vehicles	8,539	12,515
Depreciation and write-offs (Note 5)	3,638	7,702
Appropriation for capital purposes	53,500	4,220
	505,813	400,613
Excess of expenditure and appropriations over revenue	$ (742)	$ (11,573)

Cornish House
Balance Sheet as at March 31, 1990

	1990	1989
ASSETS		
Current assets:		
Cash	$ 7,822	$ 6,793
Short-term deposits	57,011	26,850
Accounts receivable — land sale	55,000	
Accounts receivable — general	24,382	28,381
Interest receivable	548	
	144,763	62,024
Memorial and bequest funds:		
Cash	657	229
Short-term deposits	2,686	2,650
	3,343	2,879
Leasehold improvements:		
217 Seaton Street	1	1
219 Seaton Street	1	1
	2	2
Fixed assets:		
Land	16,966	25,449
Building — 221 Seaton Street	116,893	116,893
Furnishings and equipment	1	3,639
Motor vehicles	4	4
	133,864	145,985
	$281,972	$210,890
LIABILITIES		
Current liabilities:		
Accounts payable	$ 24,669	$ 6,809
Memorial and bequest funds	3,343	2,879
	28,012	9,688
CAPITAL		
Accumulated excess of revenue over expenditure and appropriations	196,240	196,982
Appropriations for capital purposes	57,720	4,220
	253,960	201,202
	$281,972	$210,890

Cornish House
Statement of Accumulated Excess of Revenue
over Expenditure and Appropriations
Year Ended March 31, 1990

	1990	1989
Balance at beginning of year	$196,982	$208,555
Excess of expenditure and appropriations over revenue	(742)	(11,573)
Balance at end of year	$196,240	$196,982

Statement of Appropriations for Capital Purposes
Year Ended March 31, 1990

	1990	1989
Balance at beginning of year	$ 4,220	
Add appropriations for the year	53,500	$ 4,220
Balance at end of year	$ 57,720	$ 4,220

Cornish House
Notes to Financial Statements
Year Ended March 31, 1990

1. ACCOUNTING POLICIES

   (a) Capital expenditures
   Replacements of existing capital items are expensed when made. Furnishings and equipment, motor vehicles and leasehold improvements are recorded at nominal value. Land and building are recorded at cost.
   (b) Depreciation
   No depreciation for fixed assets has been charged in the accounts.

2. MEMORIAL AND BEQUEST FUNDS
   The funds collected for memorial and bequest funds totalling $3,343 are held in a separate bank account and short-term deposits as indicated on the balance sheet.

3. LEASE 217 SEATON STREET
   The lease of the property at 217 Seaton Street expired December 31, 1988. Tenancy is presently on a month-to-month basis and negotiations are proceeding for a new lease.

4. OPERATING STUDY
   An agreement between the Province of British Columbia and Cornish House provides that any full-pay revenue collected in excess of a predetermined amount for the year ($304,779 for 1990) will be shared by the parties on a specified basis. If such sharing is necessary, following past practice, the province's share will be deducted from the following year's operating subsidy. No such sharing was required for the year ended March 31, 1990.

5. DEPRECIATION AND WRITE-OFFS

For the year ended March 31, 1989, Cornish House changed its accounting practice and commenced expensing replacements of existing capital items in the year that the replacing expenditure was made. Existing values for motor vehicles and leasehold improvements were written down to a nominal value in the year. In 1990 a further write-down was made to record furniture and equipment at a nominal value.

Rivervale Community Centre   CASE 5-7

Rivervale Community Centre (RCC) is a registered charitable organization located in the City of Saskapeg. RCC has a record of public service dating back to 1926, but recent changes in the board of directors and in the officers and some managers have breathed new life into the organization.

A number of years ago, RCC suffered from a declining public image. The organization was perceived as not meeting current social needs and of being rather poorly managed. Four years ago, a dynamic government official was hired as Executive Director of RCC, and she, in turn, was instrumental in changing the complexion of the board of directors. The new board and executive director completely revamped RCC's programs, hiring new or replacement staff as needed, and moved to put RCC on a stronger financial footing.

The executive director and the finance committee of the board feel that the current financial reporting systems of RCC are neither adequate for proper management nor for external reporting. The finance committee has asked you to recommend improved financial reporting systems that will assist decision-making by managers at all levels, by the board of directors and by outside funding agencies.

Facilities and Programs

RCC is actually not just one community centre. RCC owns and operates five community centre buildings located in five different areas of Saskapeg. In addition, RCC leases a summer camp facility from the YMCA and operates the camp each summer from mid-June through Labour Day.

Two of the community centre buildings are new, having been opened within the past two years. The other three buildings have been extensively refurbished and re-equipped. All of the buildings offer state-of-the-art fitness and exercise facilities, aerobic facilities, a gymnasium, swimming pool, meeting and conference rooms, offices for staff, and large "general purpose" spaces that can be used for anything from charity balls to overnight sleeping facilities.

The new buildings and the extensive renovations of the older buildings were financed by means of major capital grants from the provincial and municipal governments and by a major fund-raising campaign in the private sector. A remaining shortfall in funds was financed by a bank loan (secured by mortgages on the properties) that is being paid down as additional funds are raised.

RCC offers a variety of programs. One of the most publicly visible programs is the health and fitness program, which is offered in a variety of "packages" to all members of the public. The fitness program is priced at or slightly higher than the prices charged by private exercise clubs for similar programs. Initial membership also requires a $100 to $500 one-time donation to RCC's building fund, to help pay the cost of the renovations and of the new buildings and equipment, as described above. As well, an annual membership is charged; the size of the fee depends on the package of benefits that the member is subscribing to. The fitness program is intended to make a profit; the profits are used to help cover the general administrative costs of RCC and to subsidize RCC's nonprofit social programs.

A second major program is day care. Offered at all of RCC's facilities, the day care program is for children under the age of 13 and a fee is charged. The fee is competitive with other day care centres in the area, since RCC cannot charge more than the market rate charged by other public and private day care centres. Not all parents pay the full fee. When a parent qualifies for income assistance, part or all of the fee is paid by the provincial government's Ministry of Social Services. Each year, the Ministry sets a maximum upper rate that it will pay. The maximum rate is set by reference to the fees charged by private sector (i.e., for profit) day care centres.

A third program is a series of teen youth programs. The components of the programs vary from facility to facility, depending on the local needs of the community. The programs include organized athletic programs, vocational training, self help, group counseling, and crisis centres. There are no fees of any sort, and funding is obtained from a variety of sources, including the City of Saskapeg, the Ministry of Social Services, several private foundations, and the general funds of RCC.

Two of the inner city facilities offer hostel facilities to homeless people. The hostels are set up each evening in the general purpose spaces; sleeping accommodations are available every night from 10:00 pm to 7:00 am. RCC operates only one of the hostels year-round; reduced demand in the summer months enables RCC to operate the other hostel only from November through April. The hostels' main financial support comes from the City of Saskapeg. The City pays the full direct cost of operating the hostels, plus an overhead charge for the facilities. So far, the City has not questioned the costs of the hostels, but the City auditors do have the right to examine RCC records if the costs seem too high.

As noted above, RCC operates a summer residence camp on a site leased from the YMCA. The camp is for disadvantaged children from 6 to 16; different age groups are at the camp at different times. The campers are referred to RCC by other social agencies in the city; RCC accepts as many of the referrals as it is possible to accommodate. Each child stays at the camp for 10 days, and campers can return for up to three years in a row. The emphasis in selection is on children with poor or hostile home environments.

In addition to the usual camp activities, group counseling sessions are conducted by professional counselors retained by RCC for the summer. Individual counseling is also available, but the camp is not adequately staffed to deal with intensive psychological counseling. The camp program is financed by RCC's general funds.

RCC also operates a day camp in the summer months. The camp is for inner city youth and operates out of a public school building that is provided free of charge by the Saskapeg Board of Education. The day camp has two paid counselors, but the rest of the staff is composed of volunteers, mainly university students with experience in youth work or in supervising athletic or other activity programs. Most of the supplies and equipment used by the day camp are donated, although they would have to be purchased if they were not donated. There is no explicit funding source for this program; funds are provided as needed from RCC's general funds.

Management Structure
The senior management of RCC consists of the paid executive director, the volunteer treasurer, and the volunteer president (both of whom are members of the board of directors). There is a small support staff for the senior management group.

The second tier of management consists of the managers of each of the five physical facilities plus the camp program manager (who is responsible for both the residence camp and the day camp). There also are four program directors, one each for the fitness program, the day care program, the hostels, and the teen programs.

The six facility managers currently have the direct budget authority within RCC. The facility managers are primary participants in the budgeting process (together with senior management and the board) and have the sole spending authority for activities within their facilities once the budget is finalized. The budget is prepared annually, approved by the board, and then divided by four to prorate to quarters. The managers are not permitted to exceed the total budget for their facility for the year without board approval, but they may shift their budget allocations, as between types of expenses.

The program directors have supervisory authority over the programs in the different facilities but no direct budget authority. The role of the program directors is to aid personnel in the individual facilities to design and present the programs and to assure consistency of approach amongst the several facilities. The program directors are also the primary representatives of the programs in RCC's dealings with funding agencies and with other social agencies, since they have the most intimate knowledge of the programs.

Financial Reporting

At present, costs are accumulated on a line-item basis (i.e., by type of expense: salaries, supplies, etc.) by physical facility. The managers of each of the six facilities receives a quarterly statement of expenses, with a comparison to their quarterly budget. There is no breakdown of expenses by program in either the budget or the cost accumulation system.

Each quarter, all senior and facility managers and all program directors receive a year-to-date statement of revenues and expenses for RCC as a whole. All of the facilities' expense statements are combined for the main report, but the individual operating results are presented in columnar format as an explanatory schedule. These statements are also distributed to the board of directors.

A balance sheet and a statement of changes in financial position are prepared only annually, as part of the annual financial statements. Aside from the treasurer, no member of the board sees these statements until they are presented at the board meeting immediately preceding the Annual General Meeting. At that board meeting, the statements must be approved so that they can be presented at the annual meeting.

Once approved, the financial statements are available to all interested parties and a summary of the statement of revenues and expenses is included in RCC's printed annual report. The annual report contains the reports of the president, the executive director, and each of the program directors (plus the camp manager). Statistics on levels of service are sometimes included in the various reports, but no nonfinancial information is included in or provided as supplementary information to the financial statements themselves.

RCC has found that negotiating with the funding agencies, particularly with the Ministry of Social Services, has become increasingly difficult because of the reporting approach used. The Ministry would like to be able to see more clearly the actual operating costs of the programs that it helps to fund.

To help improve the financial reporting and control, RCC has recently acquired a VAX minicomputer that can support up to 25 separate work stations, and has acquired a powerful and flexible accounting software package that can readily accommodate virtually any accounting and reporting structure that you recommend. RCC senior managers expect to be able to receive much more timely and useful information once a new accounting system has been designed and installed.

Required:
Prepare a report to the Finance Committee in which you recommend a suitable framework for an accounting and control system and for external financial reporting.
[Touche Ross]

P5-1

There has been much discussion in accounting literature over the past several years as to how nonprofit organizations should account for fixed assets. For example, Robert Sterling asserts that "the most difficult problem in university accounting is that of deciding on an appropriate policy for accounting for capital expenditures." Emerson Henke states that "the question of depreciation for nonprofit organizations has been debated strenuously in accounting literature." The American Accounting Association's Committee on Accounting Practice of Not-For-Profit Organizations devotes 29 pages of its report to discussing the issues in accounting for fixed assets.

Required:
Discuss clearly and concisely the major arguments for and against recording depreciation, as they would apply specifically to your college or university. Explain how fixed assets would be recorded, how depreciation would be determined, how this information would appear on financial statements, and how it might be helpful to users of the statements. Your answer should be specific to your university or college rather than general.

P5-2

The Michael Township Water Works (MTWW) is a governmental unit that purifies and distributes water to homes, businesses, and industry in and around Michael Township. MTWW charges a flat fee to users, based on the estimated water consumption of each user. The fees are the only source of operating revenue. Funds for capital improvements are provided by the township from real estate taxes.

MTWW uses the encumbrance system for supplies in the operating fund; outstanding encumbrances at the end of each year are carried as an asset, Supplies on order. Estimated commitments are carried forward as a liability. Budgetary accounts are not used in the formal accounting system. At December 31, 19x7, the balance sheet of MTWW appeared as follows:

	Operating fund	Plant fund
Cash	$ 90,000	$ 50,000
Receivable from customers	60,000	—
Supplies inventory: on hand	50,000	—
on order	20,000	—
Inventory of parts and tools	30,000	80,000
Plant, equipment, and mains	—	3,400,000
Accumulated depreciation		(1,100,000)
Total assets	$250,000	$ 2,430,000
Accounts payable	$ 50,000	—
Estimated commitments	20,000	
Fund balance	180,000	2,430,000
Total equities	$250,000	$ 2,430,000

During 19x8, the following transactions and events occurred:

1. Water bills totaling $250,000 were mailed to users.
2. The township approved an expenditure of $500,000 to extend the water mains into previously unserviced areas.
3. MTWW issued purchase orders for water treatment chemicals and other operating supplies. The estimated cost of the supplies was $140,000.
4. After competitive bidding, MTWW accepted a bid of $470,000 for construction of the new mains. Completion is expected in early 19x9.
5. Cash of $270,000 was received from customers.
6. Wages and salaries totaling $100,000 were paid for operating personnel.
7. Supplies were received, with invoices for $150,000. Of the amount received, material costing $25,000 was in fulfillment of the purchase orders outstanding at the beginning of the year. The remaining $125,000 had originally been estimated to cost $115,000.
8. $250,000 was received from the township as part of the funds for the extension of the water mains.
9. Progress billings of $350,000 were received from the contractor.
10. MTWW paid $320,000 of the contractor's billings, after borrowing $40,000 from the operating fund.
11. Accounts payable of $180,000 were paid.
12. Depreciation of $60,000 was charged in the plant fund; the operating fund is required to transfer funds equivalent to depreciation to the plant fund. The $40,000 interfund loan was cancelled, and $20,000 was transferred.
13. An inventory of supplies at year-end revealed that supplies costing $80,000 had been used during the year.
14. An inventory of parts and tools revealed that inventory of $10,000 remained for operations; $60,000 remained for plant.

Required:
a. In general journal form, prepare journal entries to record the above information. Keep the two funds separate.
b. Prepare a complete set of nonconsolidated financial statements for the Michael Township Water Works.

P5-3

The Campus Connection (CC) is a peer counseling group that serves a major Canadian university. CC has a staff of 24 volunteer counselors and one paid half-time coordinator. All of the counselors (as well as the coordinator) are students at the university. They offer counseling to students and staff on whatever types of problems that a client may have, including alcohol and drug abuse, loneliness, broken relationships, family problems, stress, birth control, sexual orientation, and sexually transmitted diseases. The counselors frequently refer clients to other agencies and organizations that are better able to help, including both on-campus and off-campus organizations.

The board of directors of The Campus Connection is comprised of five members of the university's faculty and administrative staff, a representative of the university's central student government, and two representatives chosen from among the volunteer counselors. The paid coordinator attends all meetings of the board but is not a member of the board and does not have a vote.

CC is not an official organization within the university and receives no funding from the university administration, although the board has on several occasions requested some form of support from the officers of the university. However, the university does provide a "courtesy account" against which CC can charge expenditures incurred on the campus. The university also charges the cost of telephone service to the courtesy account. In view of the reluctance of the university to directly fund The Campus Connection, the board had decided in the past not to pay the telephone charges that appear on the courtesy account, but to pay all other charges. The current board reaffirmed that decision. Thus far, the university has not demanded payment of the telephone charges.

On July 1, 1988, the balance owing to the university in the courtesy account was $3,161, of which $2,940 represented telephone charges and $221 was for other expenses charged by CC, such as duplicating and supplies. At June 30, 1989, the balance owing in the account was $5,238, of which $3,983 was for telephone and the remainder ($1,255) was for other charges.

Funding for the operations of CC is solicited from the governing student councils of the colleges that comprise the university and from the Central Student Council (CSC). Grants are also solicited from other major student groups and from the executive committees of the Faculty Association and the Staff Association. In the fiscal year ended June 30, 1989, CC received a total of $8,150 cash in grants from these sources. Included in the cash received was $300 from one college council that had pledged that amount in the 1987-88 fiscal year but did not fulfill the pledge until July 13, 1988. Not included in the $8,150 was $800 that had been pledged by another college council but that had not been received by June 30, 1989 (it was received on July 25, 1989).

Of the total received, $4,800 was paid by the Central Student Council. CSC also assisted CC by devoting one-eighth of a page of its regular space in the campus newspaper to an advertisement or announcement for CC in each weekly issue. Without this donated space, CC would have had to buy advertising space on its own, although probably not on a weekly basis. The value of the space donated by CSC in 1988-89 was $2,000 at the special bulk rate that CSC received from the newspaper, or $2,900 at the regular rates that CC would have had to pay.

The coordinator was paid a salary of $600 per month for 9.5 months. This salary is the major cost of operating The Campus Connection. Vacation pay, CPP, and UIC added another $485 to the cost of the coordinator. An analysis of the chequebook for the organization revealed the following additional disbursements during the 1988-89 fiscal year:

● typesetting for posters and handbills — $107
● miscellaneous supplies — $167
● costs of training the volunteers — $588
● temporary transfer of cash to the savings account — $3,000

During the year, the bank deducted $5 in service charges from the chequing account and added $247 in interest to the savings account. The bank pays interest on the savings account on March 31 and September 30; the current rate of interest is 6% per annum. CC owed $13 to the campus newspaper at June 30, 1989, for typesetting services. No payments were made to the university for the courtesy account during the year.

Following is the balance sheet at June 30, 1988 (the end of the previous fiscal year).

Required:
Prepare a balance sheet at June 30, 1989, and a statement of operations for the year then ended. Identify any reporting issues that you see, and explain the reasons for your choice of alternatives.

Campus Connection
Balance Sheet
June 30, 1988

ASSETS:
Cash in chequing account	$3,231
Cash in savings account	2,460
Grant receivable	300
Total assets	$5,991

LIABILITIES:
University courtesy account	$3,161
Other	—
	3,161
FUND BALANCE	2,830
Total liabilities and fund balance	$5,991

P5-4

Poohbear Township has recently decided to establish a municipal art gallery. The gallery will specialize in collecting both contemporary and earlier works by local artists, with an emphasis on living artists. No non-Canadian works will be collected.

By an act of the Township Council, a by-law was passed that established Poohbear Art Gallery as an independent, nonprofit organization governed by a board of governors, of which half of the members would be appointed by the Mayor of Poohbear and the other half would be elected by the public members of the Gallery. During the gallery's first year, the following events occurred:

1. The Township Council gave the gallery a grant of $100,000 for start-up costs and other first-year operating expenses.
2. At the beginning of the year, a director and a business manager were hired for $30,000 and $20,000 per year, respectively.
3. The Township Council leased surplus space in the town hall to the gallery for five years at a cost of $1,000 per year. If it were used for offices, the space could probably be rented for $3,000 per month.
4. The provincial arts council gave the gallery a grant of $500,000 to be used for the acquisition of art works. Neither the amount of the grant nor any investment earnings thereon can be used for other types of expenditure. The gallery's business manager intends to maintain independent accounts for these monies.
5. In mid-year, a campaign to recruit public members was conducted. Two thousand citizens pledged their support as members, and the first annual membership fee of $40 was received from 80% of them. Campaign costs totaled $15,000, including $3,000 allocable to membership brochures that had not been used at year-end. Campaign costs were included in the additional operating expenses (see 10.).
6. The gallery made acquisitions of art works for a total of $260,000. Unused acquisition funds had been invested in term deposits and had yielded a total interest revenue of $40,000. At year-end, $8,000 of the interest revenue had not been received and $250,000 was invested in term deposits.
7. The gallery contracted for installation of a track lighting system for $60,000.

The work was substantially completed during the year and the contractor was paid, except for a 15% hold-back pending final acceptance of the system.

8. A security system worth $40,000 was installed by a friendly contractor for only $25,000 cash.

9. Volunteers contributed approximately 6,000 hours of their time to staffing the gallery and to performing administrative tasks.

10. Additional operating expenses amounted to $40,000. Year-end accounts payable were $7,000.

11. A single bank account is maintained for both acquisition funds and operating funds.

Required:
Prepare a year-end balance sheet and a statement of operations for Poohbear Art Gallery. Where alternative accounting and reporting choices are possible, indicate what the alternatives are and the reason for your choice.

P5-5

(a) Fair City makes the following journal entries:

	DR	CR
Estimated revenues	$1,463,000	
Fund balance	47,000	
Appropriations		$1,510,000
Taxes receivable — current	$ 950,000	
Revenues		$ 910,000
Estimated uncollectible taxes — current		40,000

Required:
Explain these journal entries to a new employee who is familiar with "traditional" or profit-oriented accounting. Be precise and cover all aspects of the entries, including sources of numbers and implications for the accounting system.

(b) Nice City had the following transactions during the fiscal year 1985:

1. Received goods and an invoice for the goods amounting to $42,000, for which a purchase order had been issued for $43,800.

2. On January 15, 1985, $88,000 of cash was received for taxes in advance of their due date, which is July 2, 1985.

3. At the beginning of the year, the city had $225,000 of bonds that came due during the year. These bonds had $26,000 of accrued interest attached to them at their due date. The city uses a debt service fund and transfers the cash from the general fund to the debt service fund as required. (The city does not use a general long-term debt fund.)

4. The road maintenance fund sent $3,000 of materials to the general fund. No cash was exchanged.

5. A piece of property that had been seized in 1984 for unpaid taxes of $45,000 was sold for $56,000. The city had put a lien against the property and had spent $3,200 in costs exercising the lien, taking possession and selling the property.

Required:
Prepare journal entries to record the above information. Be careful to identify clearly which account and which fund you are using.
[CGA-Canada]

P5-6

The following transactions are independent of each other but represent typical transactions of municipal governments:

1. On October 12, 19x2, the general fund of Thereville repaid to the utility fund a loan of $2,000 plus $40 interest. The loan had been made earlier in the fiscal year.
2. A prominent citizen, L. Black, died and left ten acres of undeveloped land to Overville City for a future football stadium. The donor's cost of the land was $55,000. The fair value of the land was $85,000.
3a. On March 6, 19x2, Underville City issued 14% special assessment bonds payable March 6, 19x7, at face value of $90,000. Interest is payable annually. Underville City, which operates on a calendar year, will use the proceeds to finance a tree planting project.
  b. On October 29, 19x2, the full $84,000 cost of the complete project was accrued. Also, appropriate closing entries were made with regard to this project.
4a. On February 23, 19x2, the town of Bottomville, which operates on a calendar year, issued 14% general obligation bonds with a face value of $300,000 payable February 23, 19x12, to finance the construction of an addition to the city hall. Total proceeds were $308,000.
  b. On December 31, 19x2, the addition to the city hall was officially approved, the full cost of $297,000 was paid to the contractor, and appropriate closing entries were made.

Required:
For each transaction, prepare the necessary journal entries for all of the pertinent funds and groups of accounts. (No explanations are required.) Use the following headings:

Transaction number	Journal entries	Dr.	Cr.	Fund or group of accounts

[CGA-Canada]

P5-7

The trial balance for the general fund of the city of Applesack Junction on January 1, 19x2, was as follows:

	Dr.	Cr.
Cash	$25,000	
Taxes receivable	25,000	
Allowance for uncollectible taxes		$ 3,000
Interest and penalties receivable	1,000	
Allowance for uncollectible interest and penalties		75
Vouchers payable		11,500
Estimated commitments		4,000
Unappropriated surplus		32,425
	$51,000	$51,000

The following took place in 19x2:

1. The budget was approved as follows:

Revenues	$190,000
Expenditures	193,500

√ 2. The taxes receivable at the beginning of the year became delinquent and were reclassified as Taxes receivable — delinquent.

√3. Current taxes were levied amounting to $150,000; an allowance of 4% was made for possible losses.

√4. Cash was received as follows:

Current taxes	$135,000
Licenses	22,000
Delinquent taxes	20,000
Interest and penalties	200

√ 5. Purchase orders were issued, the aggregate estimated amount of the purchases being $121,800.

√ 6. Tax penalties of $700 were levied.

7. Liabilities were incurred as follows (credit vouchers payable):

Purchases of materials and supplies (encumbered for $118,400)	$123,000
Payment of bond interest	4,000
Payment of matured bonds	20,000
Payment of land for municipal parking lot	15,000
Payrolls	35,000

√8. Vouchers payable of $195,000 were paid.

√9. The budget was amended to provide for an additional appropriation of $3,500 to cover the excess expenditures for 19x2, plus the amount that was still encumbered at the end of the year.

√10. The materials that were encumbered at the end of 19x1 were received and the invoice for $3,700 was paid.

√ 11. The bond fund gave $17,000 to the general fund to pay for part of the land that was purchased.

√12. The remaining delinquent taxes were written off.

Required:

√a. Prepare general journal entries as required by the information above, including budgetary accounts.

b. Prepare closing entries at December 31, 19x2.

c. Prepare financial statements for 19x2.

P5-8

The general fund of the City of Crowston had the following trial balance at January 1, 19x6.

	Debits	Credits
Cash	$25,000	
Supplies	13,000	
Taxes receivable — 19x5	20,000	
Allowance for uncollectible taxes receivable — 19x5		$12,000
Reserve for supplies		13,000
Estimated commitments		3,000
Accounts payable		10,000
Unappropriated surplus		20,000
	$58,000	$58,000

The budget for 19x6 was passed by city council, as follows:

Estimated revenues	$170,000
Appropriations	184,000

During 19x6, the following transactions took place:

1. The 19x6 property taxes were levied in the amount of $100,000. Two percent of this amount was estimated to be uncollectible.
2. Purchase orders were issued for goods estimated to cost $160,000.
3. Sales tax revenue of $40,000 and parking meter revenue of $35,000 was collected.
4. Goods were received as a result of purchase orders issued in (2), above, which had been estimated at $140,000. The actual cost of the goods was $137,000. Accounts payable were set up.
5. An invoice for $4,000 was received for goods ordered in 19x5 and encumbered for $3,000. The goods were received in 19x6.
6. A $10,000,000 bond issue was successfully placed through an underwriter. The net proceeds of the issue were $9,785,000. The proceeds are to be used to construct a curling rink in downtown Crowston and will be transferred to a special fund set up for that purpose. The bonds are not a liability of the general fund.
7. Property taxes of $98,000 were collected. Of this amount, $5,000 was from the 19x5 levy.
8. Accounts payable amounting to $145,000 were paid.
9. Land was purchased for $25,000 to be used for a parking space for Mayor Wallace.
10. A physical inventory of supplies showed that supplies costing $16,000 were on hand at the end of 19x6.

The city follows the practice of recording the budget amounts in its accounts.

Required:
In general journal form, prepare entries to record the foregoing information as it would appear in the general fund, including any adjusting and closing entries for the end of 19x6. Prepare a post-closing trial balance.

P5-9

You have been engaged by the city of Whereville to examine its balance sheet, at June 30, 19x2. You are the first professional accountant to be engaged by the town, and find the methods used by the previous clerk somewhat dubious. The books have not been closed and you are presented with the following pre-closing trial balance of the general fund as at June 30, 19x2.

	Debit	Credit
Cash	$150,000	
Taxes receivable — 19x2	59,200	
Estimated losses — 19x2		$ 18,000
Taxes receivable — 19x1	8,000	
Estimated losses — 19x1		10,200
Estimated revenues	310,000	
Appropriations		348,000
Donated land	27,000	
Expenditures — building addition	50,000	
Expenditures — serial bonds paid	16,000	
Other expenditures	280,000	
Special assessment bonds payable		100,000
Revenues		354,000
Accounts payable		26,000
Fund balance		44,000
	$900,200	$900,200

Additional Information:

The estimated losses of $18,000 for current year taxes receivable were determined to be a reasonable estimate.

Included in the revenues account is a credit of $27,000 representing the value of land donated by the state as a grant-in-aid for construction of a municipal park.

The expenditures — building addition account balance is the cost of an addition to the town hall building. This addition was constructed and completed in June 19x2. The general fund recorded the payments as authorized.

The serial bonds paid account reflects the annual retirement of general obligation bonds issued to finance the construction of the town hall. Interest payments of $7,000 for this bond issue are included in other expenditures.

Operating supplies ordered in the prior fiscal years and chargeable to that year were received, recorded, and consumed in July 19x1. The outstanding purchase orders for these supplies, which were not recorded in the accounts at June 30, 19x1, amounted to $8,800. The vendors' invoices for these supplies totaled $9,400. Appropriations lapse one year after the end of the fiscal year for which they are made.

Outstanding purchase orders at June 30, 19x2, for operating supplies totaled $2,100. These purchase orders were not recorded on the books.

The special assessment bonds were sold in June 19x2 to finance a street paving project. No contracts have been signed for this project and no expenditures have been made.

The balance in the revenues account includes credits for $20,000 for a note issued to a bank to obtain cash in anticipation of tax collections and for $1,000 for the sale of scrap iron from the town's water plant. The note was still outstanding at June 30, 19x2. The operations of the water plant are accounted for in the water fund.

Required:

Prepare the required adjusting and closing journal entries for the general fund for the fiscal year ended June 30, 19x2.

[CGA-Canada]

P5-10

The following accounts are contained in the partial pre-closing trial balance of the operating fund of Central Community Centre at the 19x6 fiscal year-end.

	DR	CR
Fund balance		$ 555,000
Estimated revenues	$1,357,000	
Revenues		1,468,000
Appropriations		1,135,000
Expenditures	975,000	
Encumbrances	311,000	
Reserve for encumbrances		311,000

Required:

a. Prepare the appropriate closing entries for the above accounts.
b. Assuming that the opening balance of the fund balance account was $333,000 credit, prepare, in good form, the statement of changes in the fund balance.
c. At the beginning of 19x6, an entry was made to the operating fund recording the budget into the accounts. From the data given above, recreate the budget entry.

[CGA-Canada]

P5-11

Big City had the following post-closing account balances in the general fund at December 31, 19x5:

		Debits
Cash		$141,000
Taxes receivable — current	$111,000	
Less: Estimated uncollectible	17,000	94,000
Taxes receivable — delinquent	43,000	
Less: Estimated uncollectible	9,000	34,000
Due from other funds		6,000
		$275,000
		Credits
Liabilities		
Vouchers payable	$137,000	
Due to other funds	19,000	$156,000
Reserve for encumbrances — 19x5		42,000
Fund balance		77,000
		$275,000

The following information was obtained from the records of Big City:

1. On December 27, 19x5, the City Council approved a budget for 19x6 with expenditures anticipated to be $917,000 and revenues estimated to be $1,012,000. The total of the tax bills that will be sent out is $837,000, of which 7% is estimated to be uncollectible. An additional $92,000 will be received from the provincial government.
2. In 19x6, the City borrowed $43,000 from a bank and issued purchase orders for $832,000. They also purchased $39,000 of spare parts inventory that had been ordered in 19x5 and received in 19x6. (No additional purchases were to be made related to the 19x5 budget.)
3. Various expenditures were made related to the 19x6 budget:

Inventory items (to be used in 19x6, 19x7, 19x8)	$192,000
Materials (to be used in 19x6)	213,000
Trucks and vehicles	297,000
Payroll	87,000

All items, except payroll, had been journalized through the purchase orders at the following amounts:

Inventory	$199,000
Materials	196,000
Trucks and vehicles	272,000

4. The City must repay bonds with a value of $150,000 and accrued interest of $17,000. An order was issued authorizing these expenditures.
5. Taxes of $43,000 were collected before they were due.
6. Revenues of $89,000 (which were not previously recognized even though they were anticipated) were received.
7. The $43,000 liability to the bank was repaid with $4,000 of accrued interest.
8. The cash for the bonds of $150,000 and the accrued interest of $17,000 was forwarded to the debt service fund.

9. The amounts due to and from the other funds were paid.
10. An amount of $96,000 was received from the provincial government.
11. Of the taxes that were delinquent in 19x6, cash of $93,000 was collected and penalties of $12,000, not previously recorded, were received. The remainder of the delinquent taxes was deemed to be uncollectible and was written off.

Required:

Prepare the journal entries to record the above information in the *general fund*. Do not prepare closing entries. Explanations are not necessary.
[CGA-Canada]

PART

6

Intercorporate Investments: An Introduction

The Canadian economy has frequently been called a "branch plant" economy. This sobriquet is frequently used in a somewhat negative sense to suggest that much of our economic activity is controlled by foreign-based corporations. But the fact is that much of our economic activity is indeed carried out by corporations that are subsidiaries of other corporations, both foreign and domestic. The political, legal, and tax structures of the country make it particularly convenient to carry out operations not just through one corporate entity, but through several. Differing provincial income taxes, for example, render it most practical to have business conducted by a separate corporation in each province.

Even relatively small businesses frequently use more than one corporate entity to conduct business. A small chain of restaurants, for example, may incorporate each restaurant individually in an attempt to isolate the business risk of each restaurant; the failure of one will not bring down the whole group.

Each of the various corporate entitites that comprise an operating group will prepare its own financial statements. To the user of the statements, however, such a fragmented view of the overall economic entity would be of limited usefulness. In fact, the high level of intercorporate (and non-arms-length) transactions that take place between related companies may well make it almost impossible to get a clear view of the complete entity's overall operations solely by looking at the financial statements of the individual companies. Therefore, a broad set of reporting principles has developed over time, requiring related enterprises to report in ways that enable financial statement users to understand more clearly the overall financial position and operating results of a family of related companies. This set of principles is known simply as reporting for intercorporate investments, and is a good practical example of reporting economic substance over legal form, one of the qualitative characteristics that we discussed in Chapter 2.

Part 2 of this book, Chapters 6 through 13, consists of an analysis of accounting and reporting for intercorporate investments and business combinations. In this chapter, we review the types of intercorporate investments, the concepts of control and of significant influence, and the basic approach to the preparation of consolidated financial statements. Chapter 7 discusses business combinations and the alternative approaches to achieving and reporting business combinations. Chapters 8 through 13 then discuss and illustrate various facets of preparing consolidated financial statements.

BRANCH ACCOUNTING

Before plunging into our discussion of intercorporate investments, we should point out that while subsidiaries may be branches of the parent corporation in a substantive sense, they are not really branches in an accounting sense. Branch accounting is an application of control account procedures for keeping track of operating results of individual branches that are *not* separate corporations. In traditional practice, branches have their own set of operating accounts and these are supporting accounts to a general ledger control account at head office. The extent of the branch account structure depends on whether the branch is a cost centre, revenue centre, profit centre, or investment centre. When the head office prepares financial statements for the company as a whole, the control accounts for the branches must be disaggregated, so that the revenues and expenses for the branches are included in the company's overall revenues and expenses rather than being reported as a single, net amount. The process of aggregation has much in common with the process of preparing consolidated financial statements, which is the focus of these eight chapters, but without the completeness and much of the complexity of consolidation.

In modern, computerized accounting systems, branch accounts are usually integrated into the head office reporting structure rather than being tied into a control account. The account numbering system classifies each account by both branch and type (and perhaps by other dimensions, such as by product line), thereby permitting a matrix approach to reporting; the operating results of each branch can easily be drawn from the system, and the combined results can equally easily be reported. Since the branch and head office account systems are integrated, there is no need for control accounts and there is no need for quasi-consolidation procedures to disaggregate the control accounts.

In contrast, "branches" that are separate subsidiary corporations *must* have separate accounts and separate financial statements for legal and tax reasons, and the parent keeps track of the subsidiaries through a single investment account for each subsidiary. In modern practice, therefore, there is a fundamental procedural difference between accounting for a branch (as a responsibility centre) and accounting for a corporate subsidiary. Management accounting systems are designed to report on responsibility centres, including branches. In this book, our focus is on financial reporting, whether internal or external, of corporate entities.

DEFINITION OF INTERCORPORATE INVESTMENTS

An intercorporate investment is any purchase by one corporation of the securities of another corporation. Broadly speaking, the investment may be in bonds, preferred shares, or common shares.

Many intercorporate investments are made simply as temporary uses of excess cash or as investments to yield interest, dividend income, or capital gains. These investments do not give the investor any ability to control or influence the operations of the investee corporation, and are accounted for as portfolio investments.

A substantively different type of intercorporate investment is an investor corporation's purchase of enough of the voting shares of an investee corporation to give the investor the ability to control or significantly influence the affairs of the investee corporation. The reporting practices used for portfolio investments are not adequate for share investments that give the investor the ability to affect the investee's operations. Entirely different reporting procedures are usually necessary. The reporting and accounting practices for intercorporate investments will be surveyed in following sections.

ACCOUNTING FOR PORTFOLIO INVESTMENTS

Portfolio investments are reported on the **cost basis**, wherein the investments are carried on the balance sheet at their historical cost. Dividends are reported as revenue when received, and interest is recognized as revenue as it accrues. The only departure from the cost basis for portfolio investments occurs when the market value drops below the historical cost and the decline is judged to be "other than temporary," that is, that the decline in value is more long lived than simply a routine fluctuation in market price. If such a decline occurs, then the carrying value of the investment is written down. The reader should note, however, that the decision to write down an investment is highly judgmental; accounting history is littered with disputes between managements and auditors as to whether specific investments should be written down.[1]

A reduction of carrying value may also be called for when dividends received are in excess of the investor's proportionate share of the investee's net earnings. When dividends are in excess of earnings, the excess amount can be viewed as a liquidating dividend and credited to the investment account as a return of capital. For some types of investments, a liquidating dividend approach is quite appropriate, such as in investment companies, mining companies with an expiring resource base, and companies that are intentionally down-sizing their operations. In other situations, however, the dividend-paying company may simply be maintaining a constant dividend policy through a period of temporarily depressed earnings. In these cases, it

---

1 For a good discussion of the basis for writing down portfolio investments, see Ross M. Skinner, *Accounting Standards in Evolution* (Toronto: Holt, Rinehart and Winston of Canada, 1987), pp. 271-272.

is more common practice to recognize the dividends fully as revenue instead of treating the excess portion as a liquidating dividend; the excess is viewed essentially as an advance against future earnings.

Accounting for bonds purchased as portfolio investments normally entails amortization of the discount or premium. The discount or premium is not the amount thereof on the original issue of the bonds, unless the investor purchased the original issue. Instead, the relevant amount is the spread between the price paid by the investor and the face value of the bonds. Original issue discount/premium is usually quite small, but subsequent discount/premium can be substantial; the market value of bonds can fluctuate widely, in response to fluctuations in the market rates of interest. When an investor buys a bond on the market at a discount or premium, that discount/premium should be amortized over the remaining life of the bond; if the investment is long term, the amortization is credited/charged to interest revenue. Amortization can be either straight-line or "scientific" (i.e., on an effective yield basis); the choice is essentially arbitrary, and thus the method is selected that is most consistent with the investor's reporting objectives.

When bonds are purchased as a temporary investment, however, there is no point to amortizing discount or premium because long-term interest yield is not the objective of the investment.

Accounting for portfolio investments is a topic that is discussed extensively in intermediate accounting textbooks and is not discussed further here. A brief review of portfolio investment accounting was presented as a refresher and to clarify the distinction between portfolio investments and those investments that are intended to control or significantly influence the investee corporation. The remainder of this chapter discusses non-portfolio investments, beginning with a discussion of the meaning of control.

THE MEANING OF CONTROL

In a legal and reporting sense, **control** exists when one corporation has the ability to elect a majority of the board of directors of another corporation. Ordinarily, control is obtained by owning a majority of the voting shares of the controlled corporation. The controlled corporation is a **subsidiary** of the investor or **parent** corporation.

In rare cases, one corporation may control another without owning a majority of the voting shares. This situation can arise if the parent corporation holds convertible securities or stock options that, if converted or exercised, would assure voting control of the board of directors. Another situation that sometimes arises in private corporations is that a **shareholders' agreement** may give voting control to a shareholder who owns 50% or less of the shares. In any event, control can exist only if there is an exercisable legal right to elect a majority of the board of directors.

Control need not be direct. **Indirect control** exists when a subsidiary is controlled by another subsidiary rather than by the parent company. Schedule 6-1 shows three examples of indirect control.

In Case 1, the parent (P) controls subsidiary A by owning 70% of A's voting shares, and A controls C by owning 60% of C's voting shares. Since P controls A, P can control A's votes for C's board of directors. Therefore, P has

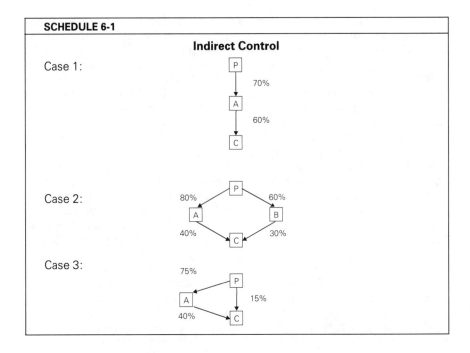

SCHEDULE 6-1

Indirect Control

Case 1:

Case 2:

Case 3:

indirect control of C. C is a subsidiary of A, and both C and A are subsidiaries of P.

Note that the voting control is not multiplicative, but is a yes-no affair. P controls A, and A controls C; therefore P controls C. The sum of one corporation's direct and indirect interest in another corporation is known as the **beneficial interest**. P has a 60% beneficial interest in C; as a result of its indirect control of A's 60% interest, P can control 60% of the votes for C's board of directors, not just 42% (70% x 60%).

In Case 2, control of P over C is achieved indirectly through two direct subsidiaries of P: A and B. Neither A nor B has control of C because each has less than a majority of C's voting shares. However, P can control C because P controls 70% of the votes in C through its control of A and B (40% + 30%). In this example, A, B, and C are all subsidiaries of P, but C is *not* a subsidiary of either A or B.

In Case 3, P has both direct and indirect ownership interests in C. Control is achieved only by virtue of the shares of C that are owned by both P and A, and thus P's control of C is still indirect, despite P's direct ownership of 15% of C's voting shares. P has a 55% beneficial interest in C. A and C are subsidiaries of P; C is *not* a subsidiary of A.

Other types of ownership arrangements can exist; these three examples are merely illustrative. Some intercorporate ownerships are very complex, and require careful analysis in order to determine who controls whom.

In everyday language, one often hears of one corporation having control or "effective control" over another corporation by owning considerably less than a majority of the controlled corporation's shares. Argus Corporation controlled the destiny of Massey-Ferguson (the former name of Varity Corporation) for many years while holding only about 17% of Massey-Ferguson's voting shares. Brascan had a substantial impact on the operations of Royal Trust while owning only about 18% of Royal Trust's shares. Brascan was not even the largest shareholder; Olympia and York held about 24% (which they subsequently sold to Brascan).

Apparent control such as this can be achieved if the investee corporation's shares are widely distributed and there is no effective opposition to the minority investor's active involvement. Legally, however, control does not exist in such situations. It is possible for another investor or group of investors to acquire control over a majority of the shares of the investee, and then to wrest control from the hands of the minority investee. When such a change in control takes place against the wishes of the previously controlling shareholder (and, usually, against the wishes of the board of directors), the change is known as a **hostile takeover**. Hostile takeovers have been rather common in the 1980s; the financial press has usually been reporting on at least one hostile takeover battle at any point in time.

When operations are being substantively controlled by means of a minority share ownership, there is no control in a legal or an accounting sense. To report one corporation as being controlled by another in the financial statements, the investor corporation must be able to control a majority of the votes either directly, indirectly through other subsidiaries or convertible securities, or by means of voting agreements with the other shareholders. The ability to affect an investee corporation's operations or corporate policies substantively while owning a minority of the voting shares is called **significant influence** in accounting terminology. Accounting and reporting for significantly influenced corporations will be discussed in a later section.

Limitations on Control

The ownership of a majority of votes of another corporation gives the parent effective control over the policies of the subsidiary, but not **absolute** control. Legislation generally requires that **special resolutions** be approved by at least two-thirds of the votes of the shareholders. Special resolutions include proposals to change a corporation's charter or bylaws, including any changes to the structure of the share ownership. Thus a parent cannot be assured of the ability to restructure a subsidiary, to amalgamate it, or to change its business purposes unless the parent owns at least two-thirds of the voting shares.

While two-thirds ownership can guarantee the approval of special resolutions, it still does not give absolute control. As long as there are outside ("minority") shareholders, the parent corporation cannot require the subsidiary to follow any policies that are detrimental to the interests of the minority shareholders.

For example, assume that ParentCorp owns controlling interest in SubLtd, and that SubLtd is the major source of supply for the primary raw material that is used by ParentCorp. The board of directors of ParentCorp may want SubLtd to sell the raw material to ParentCorp at less than market value. If ParentCorp owns 100% of SubLtd, then SubLtd can do so without harming any shareholders. The reduced profit in SubLtd is offset by increased profit in ParentCorp. But if ParentCorp owns only 70% of SubLtd, then the shifting of profits from SubLtd to ParentCorp will harm the 30% minority shareholders in SubLtd. Their equity, their potential dividends, and the market value of their shares will all be reduced.

Therefore, many corporations prefer to own 100% of their subsidiaries. One hundred percent ownership is particularly common when there is a close working relationship between the parent and the subsidiary, or among the various subsidiaries.

Because of the relatively unfettered ability of a parent to control the affairs of a wholly owned subsidiary, creditors of such a subsidiary frequently take steps to protect their own interests. Creditors may insist that the parent guarantee the subsidiary's debts, may require fairly liquid collateral (such as assignment of accounts receivable), or may include restrictive covenants in bond indentures.

A parent corporation can acquire a subsidiary in either of two ways: (1) by forming a new corporation, or (2) by buying a controlling interest in an existing corporation.

Founding a Subsidiary

Most subsidiaries are founded by the parent corporation in order to carry out some segment of the parent's business. Subsidiaries are formed for a variety of legal, regulatory, and tax reasons. For example, if a corporation is subject to taxation in several countries or provinces, it usually simplifies matters if there is a separate legal entity in each taxation jurisdiction.

Similarly, lines of business that are subject to regulation are usually carried out in separate legal entities. The corporate reorganization of Bell Canada and its subsidiaries in 1982 is an example of a regulatory inspired intercorporate organization.

Financing arrangements may also be facilitated by having subsidiaries rather than a single legal entity conduct all the corporation's business. A separate corporation is frequently established to conduct customer financing activities because the financial structure of this separate finance company is quite different from that of the parent industrial corporation; it may be easier to arrange the secondary financing of customers' installment debt or leases if the receivables from customers are assets of a distinct corporate entity.

The vast majority of parent-founded subsidiaries are wholly owned by the parent. Sometimes the parent will reduce its ownership below 100% once the subsidiary is established. There are two ways by which the parent can dilute its ownership interest. One is by selling part of its holding of the subsidiary shares to the public or to a private buyer. The other is by having the subsidiary issue new shares to public or private buyers. Both approaches reduce the parent's ownership share, but the first approach also reduces the parent's investment in the subsidiary. The second approach maintains the parent's share investment and raises new capital for the subsidiary.[2] The sale of Air Canada shares to the public illustrates both approaches. The initial public share offer, in 1988, was an issuance of new shares by the corporation while the second share offer in 1989 was a sale of the government's shares. The 1988 proceeds went to Air Canada, while the 1989 proceeds went to the federal government.

A reduction in the parent's ownership of a parent-founded subsidiary sometimes occurs when a parent establishes a subsidiary in a foreign country. The host country may encourage or require local participation in the

---

2 The accounting and reporting implications of changes in the parent's ownership share are discussed in Chapter 13.

ownership of subsidiaries of foreign-owned parents in order to improve the subsidiary's responsiveness to economic conditions in the host country and in order to establish a basis for accountability to the host country's citizens or government.

Instead of founding a subsidiary, a corporation can purchase a controlling interest in an existing corporation as a going concern. One corporation may buy another for one of several reasons. The acquired subsidiary may fit into the parent's existing business organization in a variety of ways. The new subsidiary may have been a supplier, a customer, or a competitor of the acquiring corporation. Either vertical or horizontal integration of the parent may be improved by the new acquisition.

Purchasing a Subsidiary

Alternatively, the new subsidiary may represent a venture by the parent into a new line of business. The new business may be complementary to the parent's existing activities in either a business or a financial sense. For example, a meat packing company may acquire a dairy in an attempt to achieve synergy by utilizing similar distribution channels; this would be complementary in a business sense.

Even if the new business has no obvious line-of-business relationship to the parent's other activities, the new subsidiary may give the parent some financial benefits. The subsidiary's business may be counter-cyclical to the parent's, thereby increasing the parent's overall stability and reducing investors' and creditors' perceptions of the financial risk of the total entity. Or, the subsidiary may generate a large cash flow that is needed by the parent. Conversely, the parent may be generating a substantial continuing cash flow that can be invested in a cash-hungry development-stage enterprise, such as computer software development or oil exploration.

Finally, it is possible that the newly acquired subsidiary may simply be an investment in a completely unrelated activity in either a business or financial sense. Either the parent is a conglomerate, buying various businesses when the price is right, or else the parent is using the new subsidiary as a means of entry into an industry in which the parent hopes its future will lie. It is quite difficult to enter new lines of business from scratch. A newspaper chain may have substantial capital to invest in the retail business, for instance, but would lack the management expertise, the store locations, the sources of supply, the customer base, etc., which are necessary for success. Therefore, it is much more feasible for the newspaper chain simply to buy an existing retailer, as Thompson Newspapers did when they purchased a controlling interest in the Hudson's Bay Company.

Whenever one corporation buys a controlling interest in another, and thereby obtains control over the net assets of the acquired company, a **business combination** has occurred. A business combination can be accomplished in a variety of ways, and the accounting problem is to report the substance of the combination regardless of the legal form of the transaction. This topic is discussed in Chapter 7.

Frequently, one corporation will purchase only a minority of the voting shares of another corporation. As we have discussed above, ownership of less than 50% does not give the investor control over the investee in either a

Significant Influence

legal or accounting sense. However, the investor may nevertheless be able to have a substantial impact on the operations of the investee. The ability to affect substantively the operating and financial policies of another corporation is called **significant influence** in accounting terminology. Since control does not exist, the significantly influenced company is not a subsidiary, but is an **affiliate** of the investor corporation.

It is usually clear when control exists. The investor either can legally elect a majority of the board of directors or it cannot. In contrast, the presence of significant influence is not so clearly determinable. The general numerical guideline according to the *CICA Handbook* [para. 3050.21] is that significant influence is presumed to exist if the investor corporation owns between 20% and 50% of the voting shares of the investee. But the percentage of ownership is only a guideline; it is the substance of the relationship between the two companies that must be examined.

The issue is important because investments in significantly influenced companies are reported on a different basis than are portfolio investments. Portfolio investments are reported on the cost basis, and income from portfolio investments is recorded only when dividends are declared by the investee. If the investor has the ability to influence significantly the financial policies of the investee, then reporting the investment as a portfolio investment would give the investor the ability to manipulate its own income by influencing the affiliate's dividend policy. If the investor wanted to smooth its reported net income, the affiliate could be "influenced" to declare small dividends in years in which the investor had high operating income, and to declare large dividends in years of low investor operating income.

There are a number of factors that must be examined in order to determine whether significant influence exists. The composition of the board of directors is one important factor. If the board contains representatives of the investor, these representatives may be able to influence corporate policies significantly in the boardroom. This is particularly true when the investor's minority shareholding is the largest single block of shares. In that case, a majority of the investee's board may be representatives of the investor.

Significant influence may also be indicated by the extent of intercorporate transactions. If the investor is a major supplier or major customer of the investee, significant influence can be exercised not only by the ownership of shares but also by means of the supplier-customer relationship.

Other indications of significant influence include substantial debt financing provided by the investor, the investor's ownership of patents, trademarks or processes upon which the affiliate's business depends, and the provision of technical assistance to the affiliate.

Clearly, the determination of whether significant influence exists is based on more than the extent of share ownership. A voting interest of less than 20% can carry significant influence if there are other important relationships between the two companies, or if the affiliate's shares are widely held and all other owners are passive, or if the investor corporation has the active support of other shareholders. Conversely, a voting interest of up to 50% can be impotent if the management and controlling shareholders of the investee corporation are hostile to the investor corporation, and will not accede to the investor's demands or permit the investor's nominees to sit on the investee's board.

Obviously, there is a larger grey area for the existence of significant influence than there is for the existence of control. Nevertheless, it is reasonably clear in most real situations whether or not significant influence does exist. If there is doubt, then significant influence probably does not exist. But the doubt must arise as a result of examining the substance of the operating situation, and not merely by looking at the percentage of ownership of the voting shares.

REPORTING INVESTMENTS IN AFFILIATES AND SUBSIDIARIES

When an investor corporation prepares its financial statements, there are three basic ways in which investments in the voting shares of other corporations can be reported: (1) the **cost method**, (2) the **equity method**, and (3) **consolidation**.

The cost method or cost basis is the approach that is used for portfolio investments; that is, for investments in the shares of companies over which the investor does not have significant influence. The investment is shown in the balance sheet at cost, and dividends are reported in the investor's income when declared by the investee.

The equity method or equity basis is the method that is used for reporting investments in the voting shares of significantly influenced investee corporations. Because the investor has the ability to significantly influence the operations of the investee, the investee's economic performance is closely bound to that of the investor. To give the investor's stakeholders a fair presentation of the corporation's overall economic performance, it is necessary to include in the investor's earnings its proportionate share of (or equity in) the investee's earnings, rather than just the dividends declared. The financial reporting objective of performance evaluation is thereby better served. The cash flow prediction objective is also better served; since the investor can control the dividend policy of the investee, the equity method requires that the full amount of earnings available as dividends (and thus hypothetically transferrable in cash) be reported in the investor's income statement.

Historically, the manipulative possibilities inherent in reporting income on a dividend-only basis from controlled or significantly influenced investee corporations led to accounting standards that recommend the equity method. Section 3050, "Long-Term Investments," of the *CICA Handbook* is a good example of an accounting standard that gives precedence to user objectives over preparer objectives; it removes the ability of the investor to manipulate its own net income by regulating the dividend flow from the affiliate.

On the balance sheet, the investment account is reported at cost, plus the investor's share of the affiliate's net income, less dividends received.[3] The net result is that at any point in time, the investment account reflects the historical cost of the shares to the investor plus the investor's proportionate share

---

3 In many situations, it is necessary to make adjustments to the reported earnings of the affiliate before the investor's share is reported on the investor's income statement. These adjustments and the reasons for them will be explained in Chapter 8.

of the increase in the investee's net asset value since the date of the initial investment.

Consolidation is the process of reporting the full amount of assets and liabilities under the control of a parent corporation. It is accomplished by combining the financial statements of subsidiaries with those of the parent corporation. On the balance sheet, there will be no investment account for the consolidated subsidiaries. Instead, the assets and liabilities of the subsidiaries will be added to those of the parent in order to show the economic resources of the entire economic entity comprising the parent and its controlled subsidiaries. On the income statement, the revenues and expenses will be the totals for each item for the parent and the subsidiaries. The effects of any intercompany transactions will be eliminated in order to avoid double-counting.

In certain circumstances, some subsidiaries may be excluded from consolidation. Unconsolidated subsidiaries are usually reported on the equity basis. The next section gives an introductory illustration of consolidation. The pros and cons of consolidated statements are discussed following the illustration.

Before turning our attention to the preparation of consolidated statements, however, it is important to point out that the *reporting* of intercorporate investments is usually not the same as the *recording* of the investments in the books of the investor. Investments in significantly influenced affiliates are normally reported in the investor's financial statements on the equity basis, but the investment account on the books of the investor corporation may be carried on the cost basis. The necessary adjustments to convert from the cost to the equity basis for reporting purposes are then made on working papers and are not necessarily recorded on the books of the investor.

Consolidated statements are prepared by means of a series of adjustments and eliminations that are always only made on working papers and are *never* recorded on the books of the parent company. An investor corporation's recording procedures for investments in affiliates and subsidiaries is frequently based on ease of record keeping; the reported amounts on financial statements are derived from schedules and worksheets that are prepared expressly for reporting purposes.

Example of an Intercorporate Structure

A good example of a Canadian corporation that has an extensive network of subsidiaries is Ivaco Inc. In its 1988 annual report, the company lists ten operating divisions of Ivaco Inc., the parent company. These divisions are engaged in different operations such as producing wire (Sivaco Ontario Division), hot rolled wire rods (Ivaco Rolling Mills Division), and fasteners (Infasco Division and Infasco Nut Division). Divisions are not separate legal entities, but are part of a single corporation.

Ivaco also discloses the company's direct ownership of eighteen subsidiaries and indirect control of 26 others. These 44 subsidiaries are listed in Schedule 6-2, together with their line of business (where disclosed) and the percentage of ownership by the subsidiary's immediate parent. All but three of the direct subsidiaries are wholly owned, through which sixteen indirect subsidiaries are wholly owned. Canron Inc. is 79% owned by Ivaco, and Canron has seven wholly owned subsidiaries, which gives Ivaco 79% bene-

SCHEDULE 6-2

Ivaco Inc. Subsidiaries, 1988

Subsidiary	Nature of business	% of ownership		
Arrowhead Metals Ltd.	copper, copper alloy	100		
Atlantic Steel Company	steel construction products	100		
16th Street Corp.			100	
Allstate Wholesale Fence Supply Company			100	
Authority Land Company			100	
Fourteenth Land Corporation			100	
Mecaslin Street Corp.			100	
Patterson Wire Company	fencing, wire		100	
Bakermet Inc.	scrap metal processing	50		
Bel-Air Fence Ltd.	fencing products distribution	100		
Canron Holdings Inc.		100		
Canron Inc.	pipe products, steel/iron	79		
Canron Europe B.V.	financial and trade services		100	
Canron Industries Inc.			100	
Canron Construction Corporation	construction products			100
Canron Pipe Corp.				100
Tamper Corporation	railway maintenance equipment			100
Tamper (Australia) Pty. Ltd.	railway maintenance equipment		100	
Tamper Canada	railway maintenance equipment		100	
Docap (1985) Corporation	dist. to mill supply outlets	66.6		
I.F.C. (Fasteners) Inc.	bolts and nuts	100		
Infasco Division	bolts, nuts, fasteners	100		
Infasco Nut Division	bolts, nuts, fasteners	100		
Ingersoll Machine and Tool Company Limited	precision components	100		
I.F.C. (Bolt) Inc.	bolts and nuts		100	
Infatool Limited	dies, specialty tooling		100	
P.C. Drop Forgings Ltd.	steel forgings		100	
Ivaco Equities Inc.		100		
Ivaco Holdings Inc.		100		
Ivaco Steel Mills Ltd.		100		
Laclede Steel Company	specialty wire, bars, rods	51		
Laclede Chain Mftg. Company	chain manufacturing		100	
Laclede Mid America Inc.	oil-tempered wire		100	
Presidents Island Steel and Wire Inc.	wire		100	
National Wire Products Industries, Inc.	wire, wire fabric	100		
Capitol Wire & Fence Company	wire and chain link fencing		100	
Florida Wire and Cable Company	specialty wire		100	
Amercord Inc.	steel tire cord			41
Flo-Lube	wire drawing lubricants			100
Flo-mach Inc.	wire processing equipment			100
Wiremil Inc.	high carbon wire			100
Niagara Lockport Industries Inc.	paper machine clothing		100	
Niagara Lockport Quebec Industries Inc.	paper machine clothing	100		
Ayers Felt Inc.	wet felts, dryer fabrics		100	
Pacific Press & Shear Corp.	CAD/CAM programming systems	100		
Wrights Canadian Ropes Ltd.	wire, ropes, cables	100		

ficial interest in Canron's subsidiaries. Ivaco owns 51% of Laclede Steel Company, which has three wholly owned subsidiaries. In Ivaco's annual report, all of the assets and liabilities of all 45 companies (including the parent entity and its divisions) are consolidated.

In addition to its divisions and subsidiaries, Ivaco Inc. also has a 50% interest in Bakermet Inc., a processor of scrap metal, and a smaller share of Amercord Inc. (owned through a subsidiary of the subsidiary, National Wire Products Industries, Inc.). The Bakermet and Amercord investments are reported on the equity basis.

Example of Accounting for Intercorporate Investments

To illustrate the process of consolidation (and, thereafter, the equity method of accounting), assume that Parco established a subsidiary in 19x3 by creating a new corporation named Subco. Subco issued 100 common shares to Parco in return for $80,000 cash paid by Parco for the shares. Parco has remained the sole shareholder of Subco in succeeding years.

On December 31, 19x8, several years after the incorporation of Subco, the trial balances of the two companies appear as shown in Schedule 6-3. Parco's investment in Subco is carried on Parco's books at cost, and dividends re-

---

SCHEDULE 6-3

Trial Balances
December 31, 19x8
Dr. (Cr.)

	Parco	Subco
Cash	$ 70,000	$ 40,000
Accounts receivable	200,000	110,000
Receivable from Subco	60,000	—
Inventories	150,000	120,000
Land	100,000	
Buildings and equipment	1,000,000	450,000
Accumulated depreciation	(300,000)	(100,000)
Investment in Subco (at cost)	80,000	—
Accounts payable	(120,000)	(80,000)
Due to Parco	—	(60,000)
Long-term notes payable	—	(300,000)
Future income taxes	(140,000)	(30,000)
Common shares	(300,000)	(80,000)
Retained earnings (December 31, 19x7)	(762,000)	(60,000)
Dividends declared	30,000	20,000
Sales	(800,000)	(400,000)
Dividend income (from Subco)	(20,000)	—
Cost of goods sold	480,000	280,000
Depreciation expenses	130,000	30,000
Income tax expense	32,000	20,000
Other expenses	110,000	40,000
	$ 0	$ 0

ceived from Subco during the year are shown as dividend income on Parco's trial balance. The sales of Parco include $100,000 of merchandise sold to Subco, all of which was sold by Subco to outside customers during the year. The trial balance also includes an amount of $60,000 that is owed by Subco to Parco. The amount is a current asset for Parco and a current liability for Subco.

We have already pointed out that the recording and the reporting for a subsidiary may be quite different. While a subsidiary should normally be consolidated or reported on the equity basis, the investment is most commonly recorded on the books of the investor on the cost basis for simplicity of recording. While the recording method does not affect the reporting method, it does affect the way in which we make worksheet adjustments to achieve consolidated statements. We will begin our illustration by preparing consolidated statements under the assumption that the cost method of recording is used on the parent's books. We will then use the same example to illustrate the use of the equity basis of reporting in unconsolidated statements. Finally, we will prepare consolidated statements assuming that the equity method of recording is used on the parent's books.

Consolidation When the Cost Method is Used

To prepare its consolidated financial statements, Parco will add together the amounts in the two trial balance columns of Schedule 6-3. In the process of doing so, however, a few adjustments must be made. First of all, it must be borne in mind that the consolidated statements are being prepared by Parco for submission to its shareholders. The net assets and shareholders' equity that will be shown in Parco's consolidated balance sheet will be the net assets from the point of view of the Parco shareholders. The common shares that are outstanding for Parco are the $300,000 shown in Parco's trial balance, not the total of $300,000 + $80,000 that would be obtained by adding the two trial balance amounts together. Therefore, the $80,000 common share amount for Subco must be eliminated in preparing the consolidated balance sheet.

Since a credit balance of $80,000 is being eliminated, there must be an offsetting elimination in order to preserve the equality of debits and credits on the balance sheet. The offset is the $80,000 debit shown as investment in Subco on the Parco trial balance. When a subsidiary is consolidated with the parent on the financial statements, the parent and the subsidiary are viewed as a single economic entity. The investment account is really just an aggregate that represents the net assets of the subsidiary; instead of showing the *net* investment in the subsidiary as an asset, the consolidated statements show all of the assets and liabilities of the subsidiary that underlie the investment. Thus neither the $80,000 debit for the investment nor the $80,000 credit for the common shares of Subco will appear on the consolidated balance sheet; both amounts are eliminated.

A second elimination must be made to offset the dividends paid by Subco against the dividend income recorded by Parco. The consolidated statements must only reflect the results of transactions between the consolidated entity and outsiders. Since the payment of dividends by a subsidiary to its parent is an intercompany transaction, the dividend flow must not be reported on the consolidated statements.

Third, the amount owed by Subco to Parco must also be eliminated. The current assets of Parco are reduced by $60,000 and the current liabilities of Subco are reduced by an equal amount.

Similarly, the intercompany sales of $100,000 have to be eliminated. The sales account is reduced by $100,000 to eliminate the amount from consolidated sales. The cost of the merchandise purchased from Parco was recorded as $100,000 on Subco's books. When Subco subsequently sold the merchandise to outsiders, the cost of goods sold would be recorded as $100,000. Therefore, the offsetting account for elimination of the sales amount is the cost of goods sold.

When these eliminations have all been taken into account, the consolidated balance sheet and income statement will appear as shown in Schedule 6-4.

When the statements to be consolidated are fairly simple, it is possible to compile the consolidated statements as we have in this example, by adding the relevant amounts together and making any necessary adjustments. When we prepare consolidated statements in this manner, we are using the **direct approach**. The direct approach is perfectly legitimate and is preferred by many people because the approach focuses constantly on the financial statements themselves. In more complex situations, however, (such as those that we encounter in later chapters), it may become difficult to keep track of the many adjustments, with the frustrating result that the financial statements won't balance! In complex situations, therefore, it may be clearer and easier to use a worksheet to summarize the necessary eliminations and adjustments.

Schedule 6-5 illustrates a worksheet approach in condensed form. The trial balances of the parent and the subsidiary or subsidiaries are listed in the first columns of the worksheet, and the eliminations and adjustments are inserted in the next column. Cross-adding the rows yields the consolidated trial balance, the amounts that will be used to prepare the consolidated statements.

The eliminations that were made in preparing Parco's consolidated statements can be summarized as follows, in general journal format. The company on whose trial balance the accounts being adjusted appear is indicated in parentheses:

(a) Common shares (of Subco)	$80,000	
Investment in Subco (by Parco)		$80,000
(b) Dividend income (Parco)	$20,000	
Dividends declared (Subco)		$20,000
(c) Due to Parco (Subco)	$60,000	
Receivable from Subco (Parco)		$60,000
(d) Sales (Parco)	$100,000	
Cost of goods sold (Subco)		$100,000

In each of the preceding eliminations, one side adjusts an amount on Subco's trial balance while the other side of the entry adjusts an amount on Parco's trial balance. It therefore should be obvious that there is no way that these entries can or should be recorded on either company's books. Consolidation elimination "entries" are entered only on working papers in order to prepare the consolidated statements, and are never entered on the formal books of account of either the parent or the subsidiary.

SCHEDULE 6-4

Parco
Consolidated Balance Sheet
December 31, 19x8

ASSETS

Current assets:

Cash	$ 110,000	
Accounts receivable	310,000	
Inventories	270,000	
Property, plant and equipment		$ 690,000
Land	100,000	
Buildings and equipment	1,450,000	
Accumulated depreciation	(400,000)	
		1,150,000
Total assets		$1,840,000

EQUITIES

Current liabilities:

Accounts payable		$ 200,000
Long-term notes payable		300,000
Total liabilities		500,000
Future income taxes		170,000
Shareholders' equity:		
Common shares	$ 300,000	
Retained earnings	870,000	
		1,170,000
Total equities		$1,840,000

Parco
Consolidated Statement of Income and Retained Earnings
Year Ended December 31, 19x8

Sales revenue ($800,000 + $400,000 − $100,000)	$1,100,000
Operating expenses:	
Cost of goods sold ($480,000 + $280,000 − $100,000)	660,000
Depreciation expense	160,000
Income tax expense	52,000
Other expenses	150,000
	1,022,000
Net income	78,000
Retained earnings, December 31, 19x7	822,000
Dividends declared	(30,000)
Retained earings, December 31, 19x8	$ 870,000

SCHEDULE 6-5

Consolidation Based on Cost-Method Accounting by the Parent
Dr. (Cr.)
December 31, 19x8

| | Trial Balances | | | Consolidated |
	Parco	Subco	Eliminations	trial balance
Current assets	$ 480,000	$ 270,000	$ (60,000)c	$ 690,000
Property plant and equipment (net)	800,000	350,000		1,150,000
Investment in Subco (at cost)	80,000	–	(80,000)a	–
Current and long-term liabilities	(120,000)	(440,000)	60,000 c	(500,000)
Future income taxes	(140,000)	(30,000)		(170,000)
Common shares	(300,000)	(80,000)	80,000 a	(300,000)
Retained earnings (December 31, 19x7)	(762,000)	(60,000)		(822,000)
Dividends declared	30,000	20,000	(20,000)b	30,000
Sales	(800,000)	(400,000)	100,000 d	(1,100,000)
Dividend income	(20,000)	–	20,000 b	–
Operating expenses	752,000	370,000	(100,000)d	1,022,000
	$ 0	$ 0	$ 0	$ 0

Separate-Entity Financial Statements: The Equity Method

The preparation of consolidated financial statements does not eliminate the need for each separate legal entity to prepare its own financial statements. Each corporation is taxed individually, and unconsolidated statements are necessary for income tax reporting if for no other purpose. Frequently, consolidated statements are not adequate for the needs of creditors or other users of financial statements. Creditors have claims on the resources of specific corporations, not on the resources of other corporations within a consolidated group of companies. Therefore it may be of little benefit to a creditor to see the consolidated assets and liabilities when the credit risk is associated with the financial position of a single company.

The preparation of financial statements for the subsidiary as a separate entity poses no particular problems. The trial balance for Subco as shown in Schedule 6-3 can be used to prepare financial statements without further adjustment.

When separate-entity statements are prepared for the parent corporation, the investment in the unconsolidated subsidiaries should be reported on the equity basis, as discussed earlier. On Parco's books, the investment in Subco is being carried at cost. Therefore, preparation of Parco's unconsolidated financial statements requires the conversion of the accounts relating to Subco to the equity basis for reporting purposes.

We explained earlier that under the equity method, the parent's share of the earnings of the subsidiary or affiliate is reported on the parent's income statement. On Parco's 19x8 unconsolidated income statement, the dividend income is eliminated and is replaced by a line for equity in earnings of subsidiary. Since Parco is the sole owner of Subco, 100% of Subco's 19x8 earnings will be reported on Parco's income statement. The increase of $10,000 in Parco's earnings that results from deleting the $20,000 dividend income and replacing it with Subco's $30,000 net income is treated as an increase in Parco's investment in Subco. The debit/credit effect of the adjustment is as follows:

Investment in Subco	$10,000	
Dividend income	20,000	
Equity in earnings of subsidiary		$30,000

In addition to the unremitted earnings (i.e., net income less dividends) of Subco for 19x8, the investment account should also include the unremitted earnings for the years between the creation of Subco by Parco and the beginning of the 19x8 fiscal year. The amount of unremitted earnings from prior years is equal to the amount of the retained earnings of Subco at the beginning of 19x8, $60,000. Therefore, the investment account and Parco's prior years' earnings must be adjusted before the unconsolidated statements for Parco are prepared:

Investment in Subco	$60,000	
Retained earnings		$60,000

These two adjustments increase the balance of the investment account from $80,000 under the cost method to $150,000 under the equity method of reporting. The offsetting credits are a net increase of $10,000 in 19x8 income and an increase of $60,000 in retained earnings for prior years' income.

The adjustments to the equity basis can be recorded in Parco's books, but do not need to be. Indeed, it is most likely that Parco would not record the adjustments, but would continue to carry the investment account on the cost basis for ease of bookkeeping. In that case, the adjustments would appear only on the working papers used to prepare the unconsolidated financial statements for Parco as a separate entity.

The separate-entity financial statements for Parco and Subco are shown in Schedule 6-6. Note that even though the statements shown in Schedule 6-6 for Parco are unconsolidated, both the net income for 19x8 and the re-

---

SCHEDULE 6-6

Separate-Entity Financial Statements
Statements of Income and Retained Earnings
Year Ended December 31, 19x8

	Parco	Subco
Sales	$800,000	$400,000
Operating expenses:		
Cost of goods sold	480,000	280,000
Depreciation expense	130,000	30,000
Income tax expense	32,000	20,000
Other expenses	110,000	40,000
	752,000	370,000
Net income from operations	48,000	30,000
Equity in earnings of subsidiary	30,000	—
Net income	78,000	30,000
Retained earnings, December 31, 19x7	822,000	60,000
Dividends declared	(30,000)	(20,000)
Retained earnings, December 31, 19x8	$870,000	$ 70,000

SCHEDULE 6-6 (continued)

Balance Sheets
December 31, 19x8

	Parco	Subco
ASSETS		
Current assets:		
Cash	$ 70,000	$ 40,000
Accounts receivable	200,000	110,000
Receivable from Subco	60,000	—
Inventories	150,000	120,000
	480,000	270,000
Property, plant, and equipment		
Land	100,000	—
Buildings and equipment	1,000,000	450,000
Accumulated depreciation	(300,000)	(100,000)
	800,000	350,000
Other assets:		
Investment in Subco (at equity)	150,000	—
Total assets	$1,430,000	$ 620,000
EQUITIES		
Current liabilities:		
Accounts payable	$ 120,000	$ 80,000
Due to Parco	—	60,000
	120,000	140,000
Long-term notes payable	—	300,000
Future income taxes	140,000	30,000
Shareholders' equity:		
Common shares	300,000	80,000
Retained earnings	870,000	70,000
	1,170,000	150,000
Total equities	$1,430,000	$ 620,000

tained earnings at the end of 19x8 are identical to the amounts reported on the consolidated statements in Schedule 6-4. A basic and important attribute of the equity method is that the parent's reported net income and net assets (shareholders' equity) will be the same whether or not the subsidiaries are consolidated. The effect of consolidation is to disaggregate the net investment in the subsidiary into the component assets and liabilities, and to disaggregate the parent's equity in the earnings of the subsidiary into its components of revenue and expense. Because the equity method achieves the same net impact on the parent's earnings and shareholders' equity as does consolidation, the equity method is frequently referred to as **one-line consolidation**. There is one line on the balance sheet that shows the net asset value of the subsidiary, and one line on the income statement that shows the net earnings derived from the subsidiary (except for the investor's share of any extraordinary items of the investee, which would normally retain their extraordinary classification on the investor's income statement).

Consolidation When the Equity Method is Used

In our earlier illustration of consolidation and of the consolidation worksheet, we assumed that the parent company carried the investment in Subco at cost. While the cost method is most commonly used for internal record keeping, the equity method may also be used. If Parco had been using the equity method, then the investment account would be $150,000 at the end of 19x8, Parco's opening retained earnings would be $822,000 instead of $762,000, and the income statement accounts would include the $30,000 equity in the earnings of Subco rather than dividend income of $20,000. All of these amounts are explained in the immediately preceding section.

The first column of Schedule 6-7 shows the trial balance for Parco, assuming that the investment has been recorded by use of the equity method. The accounts and amounts that are affected by using the equity method rather than the cost method are highlighted by boldfaced type. When the eliminating entries are prepared, the two entries to eliminate the balance of the investment account differ from those shown in Schedule 6-5 because the composition of the balance in the investment account is different. Under the cost method, only the original cost of the investment is included in the in-

---

SCHEDULE 6-7

Consolidation Based on Equity-Method Accounting
Dr. (Cr.)
December 31, 19x8

| | Trial Balances | | | Consolidated |
	Parco	Subco	Eliminations	trial balance
Current assets	$ 480,000	$ 270,000	$ (60,000)c	$ 690,000
Property, plant, and equipment (net)	800,000	350,000		1,150,000
Investment in Subco (at equity)	**150,000**	—	$\left\{\begin{array}{l}\textbf{(140,000)}a \\ \textbf{(10,000)}b\end{array}\right\}$	—
Current and long-term liabilities	(120,000)	(440,000)	60,000 c	(500,000)
Future income taxes	(140,000)	(30,000)		(170,000)
Common shares	(300,000)	(80,000)	80,000 a	(300,000)
Retained earnings (December 31, 19x7)	**(822,000)**	(60,000)	**60,000** a	(822,000)
Dividends declared	30,000	20,000	(20,000)b	30,000
Sales	(800,000)	(400,000)	100,000 d	(1,100,000)
Equity in earnings of subsidiary	**(30,000)**	—	**30,000** b	—
Operating expenses	752,000	370,000	(100,000)d	1,022,000
	$ 0	$ 0	$ 0	$ 0

vestment account, and the only elimination necessary is one to offset the cost of the investment against the common share account of the subsidiary.

Under the equity method, however, the investment account includes both the original cost of the investment and the unremitted earnings of the subsidiary. Both of these amounts must be eliminated. The parent's retained earnings also include the earnings of the subsidiary, since the subsidiary's earnings are taken into the parent's income each year. If the retained earnings of Subco were added to the retained earnings of Parco, as we did in deriving the consolidated retained earnings under the cost method, we would be double-counting Subco's retained earnings. Therefore, the entries to eliminate the investment account are shown as follows when the equity method of recording the investment has been used:

(a) Common shares (Subco)	$80,000	
Retained earnings (Subco)	60,000	
Investment in Subco (Parco)		$140,000
(b) Equity in earnings of subsidiary (Parco)	$30,000	
Dividends declared (Subco)		$20,000
Investment in Subco (Parco)		10,000

The first adjustment eliminates the original investment and the accumulated retained (and unremitted) earnings of Subco of prior years. The second adjustment eliminates the dividends and the double-counting of Subco's earnings for the current year. In effect, the two adjustments reverse the entries that were originally made by Parco to record its interest in the earnings of Subco and to record the original investment. That is one of the reasons companies use the cost method to record their investment in subsidiaries that will be consolidated; since the process of consolidation cancels out entries made for the equity pick-up of the subsidiaries' earnings, it is simpler not to use the equity method for *recording* the investment.

The remaining two eliminations, for the intercompany debt and the intercompany sales, are unaffected by the method of recording the investment.

EXCLUSION OF SUBSIDIARIES FROM CONSOLIDATION

Canadian practice generally requires that the financial statements of subsidiaries be consolidated with those of the parent company. Nevertheless, there are circumstances when the statements of the parent company may exclude certain subsidiaries from consolidation. The specific situations in which the *Handbook* [paras. 3050.07-3050.12] provides for nonconsolidation are (1) when control over the subsidiary's assets or operations is seriously impaired, (2) when control is temporary because a formal plan of divesture exists, or (3) when the subsidiary is a bank whose statements do not conform to generally accepted accounting principles. In addition, the *Handbook* gives a more general basis for exclusion in the concept of compatibility of reporting practices: "When the financial statement components of a subsidiary are such that consolidation would not provide the more informative presentation to the shareholders of the parent company, the investment in the subsidiary should be accounted for by the equity method" [para. 3050.14].

The rationale for excluding a subsidiary from consolidation rests on two basic concepts. The first is that consolidation implies control; if control does not really exist, then consolidation is inappropriate because the parent is not able to direct the operations or to gain access to the resources of the subsidiary. Control could also be restricted if the parent cannot exercise voting control, as would be the case if the subsidiary is in receivership. Or, control over the assets could be impaired if, for example, the subsidiary is in a foreign country that has exchange restrictions preventing the transfer of funds out of the country.

The second basic concept underlying nonconsolidation is that the financial reporting practices for some industries are substantially different from the usual form of GAAP presentation. In Chapter 3, for example, we examined the financial reporting for investment companies and saw that the asset valuation and revenue recognition policies for these companies are quite specialized. If the statements for two companies in industries with radically different reporting practices are consolidated, the resultant consolidated statements are likely to be impossible to interpret. Therefore, a reasonable degree of compatibility in financial reporting must exist before consolidation can occur.

The expectation of a lack of compatability in reporting practices is quite specific in the *Handbook* as regards banks (and, until 1989, life insurance companies). The reporting practices in these industries are strongly affected by legislation, and the legislative requirements (e.g., for various types of reserves) are not acceptable for reporting in other industries. Therefore, the *Handbook* recommends that banking subsidiaries be reported on the equity basis, except that the subsidiary's earnings would not be adjusted to conform to GAAP.

In recent years, the AcSC has been working to move the financial reporting for banks and life insurance companies towards GAAP (and has succeeded in doing so with life insurance), with an ultimate goal of eliminating the general *Handbook* exclusion of these regulated industries and thereby permitting their consolidation with other companies. Part of the motivation for removing the bank and insurance company exclusions is the changing nature of the financial industry. Banks and life insurance companies no longer are stand-alone companies with a single business purpose. In particular, life insurance companies are increasingly becoming parts of broader financial services groups of companies. The prior lack of GAAP conformity for life insurance companies inhibited consolidated, economic-entity reporting by financial conglomerates. For example, Crownx Inc. owns 93% of Crown Life Insurance Co., and Trilon owns 98% of London Life Insurance Co. Both parent companies attempted to consolidate their life insurance subsidiaries as early as 1984, but, as public companies, were blocked from doing so by the Ontario Securities Commission (OSC). The OSC did, however, strongly recommend that the AcSC address the issue of nonconsolidation of life insurance subsidiaries. Thus the specific exclusion for life insurance companies has now been eliminated, and it is quite likely that we will shortly see the exclusion relating to banks also removed from the *Handbook*, thereby permitting full consolidated reporting in the financial industry.

The more general provision for nonconsolidation of paragraph 3050.14, as quoted above, would still permit nonfinancial companies that own life insurance subsidiaries to not consolidate. Indeed, this provision is currently used by many companies to justify not consolidating their finance subsidiaries. These companies don't want to consolidate because they feel that the large volume of monetary assets and liabilities in a finance subsidiary is so substantively different from the assets and liabilities of an industrial company that consolidation "would provide a form of presentation which may be difficult to interpret" [para. 3050.13]. When the finance subsidiary is an autonomous company that offers its services outside of the family of companies controlled by the parent, then nonconsolidation makes sense. Often, however, the unconsolidated finance subsidiary is serving the parent's own customers, and the finance company is simply a facilitating mechanism for obtaining secondary financing. In such cases, the receivables and liabilities on the subsidiary's statements are, in substance, receivables and liabilities of the parent, especially when the liabilities of the subsidiary are guaranteed by the parent, as is usually the case.

One possible motivation for not consolidating finance subsidiaries may be that removal of the customers' receivables and the corresponding debt financing from the consolidated balance sheet will have the effect of increasing the apparent return on assets and decreasing the debt:equity ratio. A study of 87 U.S. public companies found that if they had consolidated their finance subsidiaries, their debt:equity ratios would have increased by an average of 38%, from 1.77 to 2.45.[4] If an "average" company had a debt covenant that restricted the debt:equity ratio to 2.0 (a common covenant), the company would be in violation of the covenant if the finance subsidiary were consolidated.

More broadly speaking, the mere fact that a subsidiary operates in a completely different industry from that of the parent is not an adequate reason for nonconsolidation under the provisions of the *Handbook*. A coal mining company may own a toy store subsidiary; the industries are much different, but the basic reporting practices are compatible, and therefore consolidation is deemed appropriate. Many individuals disagree with this view, and argue that more meaningful information would be provided by supplying separate financial statements for subsidiaries, or groups of subsidiaries that are in different industries. This view may be particularly appropriate for foreign subsidiaries, where significant exchange rate movements and possible restrictions on currency flows reduce the meaningfulness of consolidated data for the statement users. The AcSC approach, however, is to require consolidation, and then to rely on disclosure by industry and geographic segments (for public companies) to provide additional information. Segmented reporting will be discussed in Chapter 14.

When one or more subsidiaries are excluded from consolidation, the notes to the parent's financial statements should include the separate financial statements of the unconsolidated subsidiaries, perhaps in condensed form. The reason for exclusion from consolidation should also be given.

Summary of Accounting Approaches for Intercorporate Investments

Schedule 6-8 broadly summarizes the appropriate accounting approaches for investments by one corporation in the voting shares of another. Some minor points about nonconsolidated subsidiaries have been omitted for clarity. In general, the equity method of reporting is used for investments in significantly influenced affiliates and for unconsolidated subsidiaries. Most subsi-

---

4 Rosanne M. Mohr, "Unconsolidated Finance Subsidiaries: Characteristics and Debt/Equity Effects," *Accounting Horizons* (March 1988) pp. 27-34.

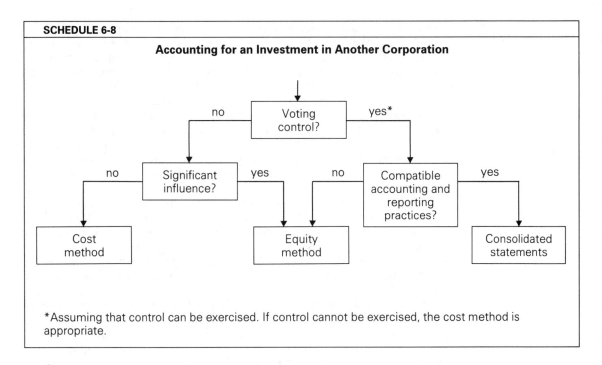

SCHEDULE 6-8

Accounting for an Investment in Another Corporation

*Assuming that control can be exercised. If control cannot be exercised, the cost method is appropriate.

diaries are consolidated, however, and the parent's consolidated financial statements disclose the aggregated assets, liabilities, revenues, and expenses of the parent plus those of the consolidated subsidiaries.

The appropriate reporting approach for a particular investment may vary over time. An investment may start out as a portfolio investment, reported on the cost basis, and then become a significant influence (reported on the equity basis) as more shares are purchased or as other investors drop out. If over 50% ownership is eventually acquired, then consolidation will normally be appropriate.

Similarly, an investment may move from right to left on Schedule 6-8, starting out as a subsidiary but shifting to equity-basis reporting and eventually to the cost basis as ownership is reduced. Ownership can be reduced either by selling part of the investment or by not participating in new issues of common shares of the subsidiary. The reporting effects of changes in ownership interest are considered in Chapter 13.

USEFULNESS OF CONSOLIDATED STATEMENTS

We have stated earlier that the theory underlying consolidated financial statements is that financial statements should disclose the resources and obligations of the economic entity. This is a straightforward application of the entity concept in accounting. When one corporation can control the resources of another, the economic entity includes the combined assets of both companies over which the directors of the parent corporation have control.

Thus, a consolidated balance sheet shows the parent company's shareholders all of the assets and liabilities over which the parent company has command, either directly or indirectly. Since the parent is assumed to be able to control the resources of the subsidiary, unconsolidated statements are frequently viewed as potentially misleading because they do not reflect the total economic resources that are at the disposal of the parent.

For example, a parent company may have little cash available within its own accounts, but a subsidiary may have surplus cash balances. The parent can obtain access to the subsidiary's cash, such as by instructing the subsidiary to declare dividends, by charging management fees to the subsidiary, or by borrowing. Since the parent controls the subsidiary, a loan need not be repaid at any specific date, if ever.

Similarly, a parent corporation has the ability to control the operations of a subsidiary, particularly if there are substantial intercompany transactions. For example, the parent could improve its apparent sales level by requiring the subsidiary to purchase unneeded quantities of goods from the parent, or it could generate other revenue by charging high management fees or royalties to the subsidiary. Consolidated statements eliminate the potential benefit of such intercompany activities.

The recommendations of the *CICA Handbook* are firmly in favour of consolidated statements. In the view of the AcSC, consolidated statements "with few exceptions ... [are] ... more informative to the shareholders of the parent company than separate financial statements of the parent company and of its subsidiaries." [para. 3050.05] The *Handbook* also states that "in almost all circumstances, consolidated financial statements provide the most informative presentation to the shareholders of the parent company." [para. 3050.13]

Canada and the United States are the most enthusiastic consolidators in the world. All other industrialized countries require *both* consolidated and unconsolidated statements for public reporting. Only in North America (among developed countries) do consolidated statements *replace* unconsolidated statements.

The shortcoming of relying only on consolidated statements is that while it is true that the parent and its subsidiaries are an economic entity, they are still separate legal entities. The title to assets and the obligation for liabilities attaches to the legal entity and not to the economic entity. A parent can go bankrupt while the subsidiaries remain healthy. Consolidated statements may hide the precarious financial position of a parent corporation because the stronger net asset position of the subsidiaries cloaks the shaky structure of the parent. Creditors of the parent have no claim on the assets of the subsidiaries, unless the parent has deliberately been transferring assets to the subsidiaries in order to get them out of reach of the creditors in anticipation of bankruptcy. The share investment in the subsidiaries is, of course, an asset of the parent that can be sold in order to satisfy creditors' claims. But the assets of the subsidiaries are beyond the reach of the parent's creditors. For example, in 1987, Texaco Inc. declared bankruptcy as the result of an $11 billion legal judgment against the company. The lawsuit and the bankruptcy affected only the parent company (plus two small capital subsidiaries), however; the major operating subsidiaries were not affected, and the unaffected operating subsidiaries accounted for about 96% of the Texaco's consolidated revenues and assets.[5]

5 "U.S. Oil Giant Texaco Files for Bankruptcy," *The Toronto Star* (April 13, 1987), p. A5.

As a result of this shortcoming, many observers recommend that consolidated statements be supplemented or replaced by unconsolidated statements. Equity-method reporting for the subsidiaries on unconsolidated statements still shows the total economic earnings of the combined entity and eliminates income manipulation, and the amount of the investment accounts may give creditors and others a better idea of the value of the assets held by the parent, even though book value of an investment is not a good indicator of market value.

The case for consolidation is strongest for domestic subsidiaries that are wholly owned by the parent, are an integral part of the parent's operations, and are directly controlled by the parent company's management. Consolidation is most debatable for subsidiaries that are located in a foreign country, are not wholly owned, and that operate autonomously. Between these two extremes are domestic subsidiaries that are not wholly owned, are in a different line of business than the parent, and operate fairly independently of the parent.

This discussion has focused entirely on the financial statements of the parent, and the decision to consolidate or not to consolidate. When subsidiaries are not wholly owned by the parent, there are minority shareholders of the subsidiary. These minority shareholders will receive separate-entity financial statements for the subsidiary, not the parent's consolidated statements.

For example, BCE Inc. owns 52.5% of Northern Telecom Limited. Since BCE controls Northern Telecom, the BCE consolidated statements include Northern Telecom. The owners of the other 47.5% of Northern Telecom's shares receive financial statements for Northern Telecom, not for BCE. Of course, Northern Telecom has its own subsidiaries, and thus would consolidate them.

SUMMARY

This chapter has examined the accounting and reporting approaches that are taken for investments by one corporation in the voting shares of another. Subsidiaries may be defined as those corporations in which the investor corporation has the ability to elect a majority of the board of directors. It is the power of control that defines a subsidiary, not the fact of control. A parent corporation may choose not to exercise its control, and may not intervene in the subsidiary's operations or put its nominees on the board. In such cases, the parent is content with the way the subsidiary is being managed, and is passive. But the parent has the ability to exercise its control should it become displeased, and thus a subsidiary is defined by the *ability* of the parent to control it.

When a parent corporation prepares its financial statements, normal procedure in Canada calls for the consolidation of the subsidiaries' accounts with those of the parent. While the nearly universal application of consolidation in Canada can be criticized, it is a logical reporting requirement for the substantial numbers of subsidiaries that are wholly owned and are an integral part of the parent's business activities.

An investor corporation may own enough shares of another corporation to enable it actively to control the investee, without actually having the legal ability to elect a majority of the board of directors. When an investor has apparent control of an investee with a minority of the voting shares, the investee is called an affiliate, and the investor is said to have significant influence rather than control. Significantly influenced corporations are reported by the investor corporation on the equity basis in order to show shareholders and others the full earnings of the investor corporation and its share of the earnings of its affiliated companies. Any subsidiaries that are not consolidated are also reported on the equity basis.

Subsidiaries can be acquired either by creation as a new corporation by the parent, or by purchase as a going concern. Most subsidiaries are established by the parent for legal, tax, or operating reasons, but many other subsidiaries are the result of a purchase. This chapter has illustrated a simple consolidation of a parent-founded subsidiary. When a subsidiary is acquired by purchasing all or a part of a going concern, the transaction is called a business combination. The accounting and reporting principles for a subsidiary acquired in a business combination are usually more complicated than they are for a parent-founded subsidiary. The following chapter examines the nature of business combinations, and discusses the various possible approaches for consolidating purchased subsidiaries.

SELF-STUDY PROBLEM 6-1[6]

Archie Corp. is a wholly owned subsidiary of Bunker Ltd. Archie was formed by Bunker with an initial investment of $1,000,000 in order to produce some of the merchandise sold by Bunker in its retail stores. Archie also sells some of its output to other, unrelated companies.

During 19x3, Archie sold goods that cost $2,600,000 to produce to Bunker for $4,000,000. Bunker subsequently sold the goods to its customers for $7,000,000.

At December 31, 19x3, the condensed trial balances for Archie and for Bunker appeared as follows on the books of the two companies:

	Bunker	Archie
Cash and current receivables	$ 200,000	$ 400,000
Inventories	900,000	500,000
Furniture, fixtures, and equipment	2,000,000	1,700,000
Buildings under capital leases, net of related amortization	6,000,000	3,000,000
Investment in Bunker Ltd. (at cost)	1,000,000	
Current liabilities	(1,500,000)	(400,000)
Long-term liabilities	(4,000,000)	(2,000,000)
Common shares	(1,500,000)	(1,000,000)
Retained earnings	(2,100,000)	(1,600,000)
Dividends declared	2,000,000	500,000
Sales	(13,000,000)	(5,000,000)
Dividend income	(500,000)	—
Cost of sales	7,000,000	3,200,000
Other operating expenses	3,500,000	700,000
	$ 0	$ 0

6 The solutions to the self-study problems are at the end of the book, following Chapter 18.

Included in Bunker's current receivables is $80,000 in dividends receivable from Archie. Included in Archie's current receivables is $200,000 due from Bunker for merchandise purchases.

Required:
Prepare a consolidated income statement and a consolidated balance sheet for Bunker Ltd. for the year ended December 31, 19x3.

REVIEW QUESTIONS

6-1 Define the following terms:

    a. Intercompany investment
    b. Subsidiary
    c. Significant influence
    d. Indirect control
    e. Beneficial interest
    f. Business combination
    g. Consolidated statements
    h. Equity method
    i. Portfolio investment

6-2 P Corporation owns 75% of S Corporation, and S Corporation owns 55% of T Corporation. Is T a subsidiary of P?

6-3 P Corporation owns 55% of Q Corp.and 58% of R Corp. Q and R each own 30% of W Ltd. Is W a subsidiary of one or more of the other three companies? If so, which one(s)?

6-4 In questions 6-2 and 6-3, what is P Corporation's beneficial interest in T Corporation and W Ltd.?

6-5 Why do many parent corporations prefer to own 100% of the shares of their subsidiaries, rather than smaller proportions?

6-6 What advantages are there to a parent in owning *less* than 100% of its subsidiaries?

6-7 Why do corporations frequently establish subsidiaries?

6-8 Why would a company purchase a subsidiary rather than simply establish a new subsidiary of its own?

6-9 Why would a corporation want to continue a purchased subsidiary as a separate legal entity?

6-10 When should an investor corporation report its investment in the shares of another corporation on the equity basis?

6-11 "The extent of share ownership does not necessarily coincide with the extent of control exercised." Explain.

6-12 Invor owns 12% of Invee's common shares. Is the cost method of reporting the investment necessarily appropriate?

6-13 What factors should be examined to determine whether significant influence exists?

6-14 Distinguish between the **recording** and the **reporting** of intercorporate investments.

6-15 Why might a corporation use the cost method of recording while using the equity method or consolidation for reporting?

6-16 How are dividends received from an investee corporation reported by an investor corporation if the investor is using the equity method?

6-17 What is the objective of preparing consolidated financial statements?

6-18 Explain the purpose of consolidation eliminating entries.

6-19 When intercompany sales are eliminated, why is cost of sales reduced by the amount of intercompany sales?

6-20 Are consolidation eliminating entries entered on the books of the parent or of the subsidiary?

6-21 Why might it be necessary for a parent company to prepare **unconsolidated** financial statements as well as consolidated statements?

6-22 How does the process of consolidation differ when the parent company has used the equity method of recording its investment in a subsidiary, as compared to consolidation when the cost method of recording has been used?

6-23 What are the general criteria for excluding a subsidiary from consolidation?

6-24 What is the essential or necessary condition for consolidating a subsidiary in Canada?

6-25 P Ltd. is a public company that operates a nation-wide chain of fast-food outlets. One of P's subsidiaries is S Ltd., a shipbuilder in Halifax. Would it be appropriate for P to report its investment in S on the equity basis instead of consolidating, owing to the radically different businesses of the two companies?

6-26 When might consolidated statements be misleading?

6-27 When might consolidated statements be less informative than equity reporting for subsidiaries?

CASE 6-1	Contrasting Views on Consolidated Statements

Three public accountants, A, B, and C, were discussing various problems they encountered in their practices. The subject of the requirements in the *CICA Handbook* for consolidated financial statements arose, and the following conversation took place:

A: One of the things that causes me a lot of problems is the requirement that any company having subsidiaries must consolidate. That means even small private companies. I don't think that's reasonable. Some of my clients don't want them, don't need them, don't understand them, and sure don't want to pay for them.

B: I agree. Several of our small clients refuse to present consolidated statements at all, claiming that they just don't need them. For our larger clients, we often report on a dual set of statements, one consolidated and the other prepared on a nonconsolidated basis for corporation purposes. We approach both problems by qualifying whenever statements are not consolidated. Many of the clients don't really care if we qualify on a technical point like that and it saves a lot of trouble.

C: Well, I'm inclined to agree with the *Handbook*. We'll generally give an adverse opinion, where the statements are not consolidated, in accordance with Section 3050. What we do for clients issuing a dual set of statements is address our report on the nonconsolidated statements to the directors. Then our report to the directors contains a clean opinion. After the opinion paragraph, we have a final paragraph saying that because the statements are not prepared for issuance to the shareholders, they are prepared on a nonconsolidated basis and that the statements differ materially from the consolidated statements on which we reported to shareholders.

A: Whenever we are reporting on nonconsolidated financial statements, we change our opinion paragraph to say "in accordance with the basis of accounting outlined in Note X" instead of "in accordance with generally accepted accounting principles." Note X then outlines the basis of accounting (nonconsolidated) and the client's reasons for not consolidating the statements. This overcomes problems where a dual set of statements is issued or where the client simply refuses to consolidate.

Required:
Discuss each of the viewpoints of A, B, and C.
[CICA]

CASE 6-2	Holding Corp.

Holding Corp. (HC) is an Ontario corporation that is 53% owned by Mr. Able Body. The rest of the shares are owned by other wealthy individuals, many of whom were schoolmates of Mr. Body. HC does not engage in direct operations, but holds investments in a number of other companies. Part of the financing for these investments has been provided by the Winnipeg Dominion Bank.

One of HC's principal investments is its 71% voting interest in Operating Corporation (OC). A smaller investment is that in United States, Inc. (USI), in which HC has a 15% interest. USI is the U.S. producer and distributor of OC's principal product; this product accounts for 80% of USI's total revenue. USI operates autonomously, but makes substantial per-unit royalty payments to OC, as well as payment of annual license fees to OC. OC can cancel the licensing arrangements upon six months' notice to USI.

OC owns 40% of the common shares of Associated Corporation (AC), which, like OC, is incorporated under the *Canada Business Corporations Act*. Another 20% of the shares of AC is owned by Able Body.

Required:
a. What accounting and reporting policies should be followed by HC and OC for the various share holdings? How will the direct and indirect ownerships be reflected in the various companies' financial statements?
b. Assume that AC acquires 36% of USI's common shares. Has a business combination occurred? Explain.

Salieri Ltd.   CASE 6-3

Salieri Ltd. is a manufacturer of musical instruments that is controlled by Tony Antonio. Salieri Ltd. was originally a private company, but it became public in 1954 when a substantial public share issue occurred. The Antonio family now holds 68% of the shares of Salieri; the remaining 32% are widely distributed throughout Canada.

Although Salieri is an operating company, it also has substantial investments in a number of other Canadian corporations. One such investment is its ownership of 80% of the shares of Bach Burgers, Inc., a chain of fast-food outlets. Salieri acquired its shares in Bach from the original founder of the company, John Sebastian, in 1962. Bach Burgers is run completely independently; Teresa Antonio (Tony's wife) is one of the members of Bach Burgers' twelve-person board of directors, but otherwise Salieri exercises no direction over the operations of Bach Burgers.

Another investment of Salieri Ltd. is its 45% interest in Pits Mining Corporation. This investment was the outcome of a takeover attempt by Salieri two years ago. Salieri was frustrated in its attempt by a coalition of other companies in the extraction industry, which effectively blocked Salieri's bid for control. Salieri was left with the 45% interest that it had managed to acquire. Although Salieri's block of Pits shares is by far the largest single block, Salieri has not been able to gain representation on the Pits board of directors. Salieri Ltd. has instituted court action against Pits Mining in order to force the other shareholders to admit Salieri nominees to the board.

Mozart Piano Corporation is a piano manufacturer that is 20% owned by Salieri Ltd. Although Salieri does manufacture musical instruments, it does not produce pianos, and Salieri and Mozart frequently conduct joint marketing efforts since their products are complementary and not competitive. Mozart is a private company; all of the other shares are held by the Amadeus family. Mozart has an 80% owned subsidiary, Leopold Klaviers, Inc., which manufactures harpsichords and clavichords to be sold domestically through Mozart and internationally through other agents.

Salieri Ltd. also owns 15% of Frix Flutes, Ltd. The 15% share was acquired several years ago to provide Frix with some new financing at a time when the company was experiencing financial difficulties. Salieri also assisted Frix by licensing to Frix the rights to use patents owned by Salieri. The licensing agreement can be cancelled by Salieri upon six months' written notice.

The only other corporate share investment held by Salieri is its 100% ownership of Salieri Acceptance Corporation (SAC). SAC was formed by Salieri to aid its customers in purchasing Salieri instruments on an installment basis. Six of the nine SAC directors are also directors of Salieri Ltd. The other three are representatives of the financial institutions that finance SAC's operations.

Required:
Discuss the manner in which Salieri should account for its various investments when issuing its annual financial statements. Specify what additional information you would like to have, if any. Recommend an accounting approach for each investment, stating any assumptions that you make in arriving at your recommendations.

CASE 6-4   ## Latins Health Spas, Inc.

Latins Health Spas, Inc. is a publicly owned company that operates a chain of 28 health spas across the country. Total operating assets (exclusive of investments in other companies) amount to $400,000,000. In addition to the operating assets, Latins' unconsolidated balance sheet shows approximately $500,000,000 in investments in subsidiaries. In recent years, the company has obtained about 30% of its financing from debt; the other 70% has come from operations and from issuance of common shares. The equities side of Latins' balance sheet now shows about 20% long-term debt.

One of Latins' subsidiaries is Eastcoast Transmission Company, a natural gas pipeline company that distributes gas at retail outlets throughout Labrador. The company is under the jurisdiction of the Newfoundland Public Utilities Commission, which regulates the rates charged by Eastcoast, and which requires specific accounting procedures somewhat at variance with practices in nonregulated enterprises such as Latins. Like most public utilities, Eastcoast is highly leveraged; almost 70% of its financing has been obtained from long-term bond issues. Latins owns 60% of Eastcoast; the other 40% is held by the New England Light and Power Co., a U.S. corporation.

About three years ago, Latins started a plan whereby the members of its health clubs could buy a life membership for only $2,000 per person. In order to improve the attractiveness of this offer, Latins also offered a 50-month installment plan for paying for the life membership. To aid in selling the installment life memberships, Latins formed a new subsidiary called Latins II, Inc. Latins II is, in essence, a finance company. Latins II sells the life memberships, receives promissory notes for the monthly payments of $40, sells the notes to a financial institution at the market rate of discount, and remits 95% of the net proceeds to the parent company. The other 5% is retained and invested as a reserve against defaulted notes. Since the notes are all sold with recourse, Latins II carries the full amount of the notes receivable as an asset and shows the financing provided by other financial institutions as debt. The debt:equity ratio for Latins II is 96:4; 95% of the assets are financial assets. Latins has been considering the possibility of letting Latins II operate as a general consumer finance company.

A third subsidiary is a smaller chain of health clubs, Vic Tawny Ltd. Tawny is headquartered in Port Hardy, B.C., and runs ten clubs in British Columbia. Owing to a decline in memberships, Tawny had difficulty in meeting its obligations and entered receivership six months ago. Tawny is still operating, and the receivers hope to be able to have a financial reorganization in place within the next year. Controlling interest in Tawny was purchased from its founder about nine years ago. Twenty-three percent of the Tawny shares are held by the public, but are not actively traded.

The audit committee of the board of directors of Latins Health Spas, Inc. has begun to review Latins' accounting policies. At their next meeting, they wish to review consolidation policy, and they have asked you to prepare recommendations on whether the three subsidiaries should be consolidated in Latins' financial statements.

Required:
Prepare the report requested by the board. Include an analysis of the relevant factors relating to each subsidiary, stating alternatives where appropriate.

P6-1

On April 30, 19x1, Super Inc. established a subsidiary known as Blue Inc. Super invested $100,000 in the shares of Blue. Blue has no other shares outstanding. Since its establishment, Blue has had the following earnings and paid the following dividends.

Year	Net income (loss)	Dividends
19x1	$(10,000)	–
19x2	15,000	$ 6,000
19x3	12,000	15,000
19x4	25,000	18,000

Required:
a. Determine the amount of Blue's earnings that will be reported as investment income by Super Inc. in 19x4, under the equity method.
b. Calculate the balance of the investment in the Blue Inc. account on Super Inc.'s books at December 31, 19x4, assuming that Super Inc. maintains the investment account on the equity basis.

P6-2

Caldwell Corporation has a wholly owned subsidiary, Wren Ltd., that was formed several years ago. Wren's initial capital was provided by Caldwell, which purchased all of Wren's shares for $400,000. At December 31, 19x7, the balance sheet accounts of Caldwell and Wren appeared as follows:

	Caldwell	Wren
Cash	$ 80,000	$ 10,000
Accounts receivable	150,000	90,000
Receivable from Wren	120,000	–
Property, plant and equipment	2,000,000	1,100,000
Accumulated depreciation	(650,000)	(310,000)
Investment in Wren	400,000	–
Total assets	$2,100,000	$ 890,000
Accounts payable	$ 200,000	$ 70,000
Payable to Caldwell	–	120,000
Bonds payable	900,000	–
Future income taxes	100,000	50,000
Common shares	200,000	400,000
Retained earnings	700,000	250,000
Total equities	$2,100,000	$ 890,000

During 19x7, Wren paid dividends of $50,000 to Caldwell, and purchased goods from Caldwell at a total price of $1,000,000. All of the purchases from Caldwell were subsequently sold to third parties during the year.

Required:
Prepare a consolidated balance sheet for Caldwell Corporation at December 31, 19x7.

P6-3

Hook Corp. is a wholly owned, parent-founded subsidiary of Chappell Inc. The unconsolidated statements of income and retained earnings for the two companies for the year ended December 31, 19x8, are as follows:

	Chappell	Hook
Revenues:		
Sales	$5,000,000	$2,000,000
Interest	100,000	20,000
Dividends	90,000	—
	5,190,000	2,020,000
Expenses:		
Cost of goods sold	2,600,000	1,200,000
Depreciation expense	400,000	150,000
Administrative expense	700,000	250,000
Income tax expense	550,000	160,000
Other expenses	300,000	100,000
	4,550,000	1,860,000
Net income	640,000	160,000
Dividends declared	260,000	90,000
Increase in retained earnings	380,000	70,000
Retained earnings, January 1, 19x8	1,710,000	410,000
Retained earnings, December 31, 19x8	$2,090,000	$480,000

Additional Information:
1. During the year, Hook acquired merchandise from Chappell at a total sale price of $700,000. None of the merchandise was in Hook's inventory at year-end.
2. At the beginning of the year, Hook borrowed $600,000 from Chappell at 10% interest per annum. The loan (and accrued interest) was still outstanding at the end of the year.
3. Chappell carries its investment in Hook at the cost basis in its accounts.

Required:
Prepare a consolidated statement of income and retained earnings for Chappell Inc., for the year ended December 31, 19x8.

P6-4

Patrick Corporation owns 100% of Sally Ltd. During 19x2, Patrick sold $3 million of goods to Sally at cost. At the end of 19x2, Sally still had $400,000 of these goods in inventory. The total inventory of Sally at year-end was $1 million, and the total inventory of Patrick was $1.5 million. Partial income statements (unconsolidated) for the two companies were as follows:

	Patrick	Sally
Sales	$10,000,000	$6,000,000
Cost of goods sold	7,000,000	4,000,000
Gross margin	$ 3,000,000	$2,000,000

Required:

Compute the amounts that would be shown on Patrick's consolidated financial statements for 19x2 for:

a. Inventory
b. Sales
c. Cost of goods sold
d. Gross margin

P6-5

Lacey Ltd. is a wholly owned subsidiary of Cagney Corporation. The balance sheets and statements of retained earnings for each company are shown below. Additional information is as follows:

1. Lacey sells most of its output to Cagney. During 19x8, intercompany sales amounted to $3,000,000. Cagney has accounts payable to Lacey for $100,000.
2. Cagney owns the land on which Lacey's building is situated. Cagney leases the land to Lacey for $25,000 per month.
3. The long-term note payable on Lacey's books represents a loan from Cagney. The note bears interest at 12% per annum.
4. Both companies declare dividends quarterly. The last quarter's dividends were declared on December 31, 19x8, payable on January 10, 19x9.

Required:

Prepare a consolidated balance sheet and a consolidated statement of income and retained earnings for Cagney Corporation.

Separate-Entity Financial Statements
Statements of Income and Retained Earnings

	Cagney	Lacey
Sales revenue	$5,500,000	$4,500,000
Interest, dividend and lease income	600,000	10,000
Equity in earnings of Lacey	200,000	—
Total revenue	6,300,000	4,510,000
Cost of sales	4,300,000	2,400,000
Interest expense	—	84,000
Other expenses	1,500,000	1,826,000
Total expenses	5,800,000	4,310,000
Net income	500,000	200,000
Retained earnings, January 1	1,530,000	170,000
Dividends declared	(400,000)	(120,000)
Retained earnings, December 31	$1,630,000	$ 250,000

Balance Sheets
December 31, 19x8

	Cagney	Lacey
ASSETS		
Current assets:		
Cash	$ 150,000	$ 30,000
Accounts receivable	600,000	120,000
Temporary investments and accrued		
investment income	350,000	70,000
Inventories	—	300,000
	1,100,000	520,000
Property, plant and equipment:		
Land	800,000	—
Buildings and equipment	—	1,400,000
Accumulated depreciation	—	(400,000)
		1,000,000
Long-term note receivable	700,000	—
Investment in Lacey	750,000	—
Total assets	$3,350,000	$1,520,000
EQUITIES		
Current liabilities:		
Accounts payable and accrued liabilities	$ 220,000	$ 40,000
Dividends payable	100,000	30,000
		70,000
Long-term note payable	—	700,000
Total liabilities	320,000	770,000
Shareholder's equity:		
Common shares	1,400,000	500,000
Retained earnings	1,630,000	250,000
	3,030,000	750,000
Total equities	$3,350,000	$1,520,000

Empire Optical Co., Ltd. is a chain of eyeglass outlets. Empire owns 100% of Class Glass Ltd., a competing chain that Empire established in order to serve a different market segment. To obtain the best deal from suppliers, Empire buys most of the materials and frames for both chains, and resells to Class whatever that chain needs.

During 19x6, Empire sold materials costing $3,000,000 to Class at cost. At the end of the year, Class still owed Empire $150,000 for purchases of the materials.

Empire records its investment in Class on the equity basis. During 19x6, Class declared and paid dividends totaling $300,000. Empire has not yet recorded its equity in the earnings of Class for 19x6. The pre-consolidation trial balances for the two companies are as shown below.

Required:
Prepare a consolidated balance sheet and income statement for Empire Optical Co., Ltd. for 19x6.

	Trial balances Dr. (Cr.)	
	Empire	Class
Cash	$ 300,000	$ 100,000
Accounts receivable	200,000	100,000
Inventory	1,000,000	500,000
Fixtures and equipment (net)	5,000,000	2,000,000
Investment in Class Glass Ltd.	1,900,000	
Other investments	800,000	—
Accounts payable	(600,000)	(400,000)
Common shares	(1,500,000)	(1,000,000)
Retained earnings	(6,600,000)	(1,200,000)
Dividends paid	600,000	300,000
Sales	(15,000,000)	(7,000,000)
Cost of goods sold	10,000,000	4,000,000
Other operating expenses	4,000,000	2,600,000
Dividend and interest income	(100,000)	—
	$ 0	$ 0

P6-7

The Selby Hotel Corporation of Vancouver held 100% of the shares of Lotus Hotel, Inc. of Toronto. Lotus was established by Selby in 19x2 with an investment of $2,000,000. Selby provides management services to Lotus for a fee, and also provides financing when needed. During 19x9, relations between the two hotels included the following:

1. Selby charged Lotus $180,000 for management services. At year-end, $40,000 of this amount had not yet been paid by Lotus.
2. Lotus was engaged in extensive room renovations. During the year, the amount of financing provided by Selby increased from $2,000,000 to $3,200,000. Interest of $300,000 accrued during the year, and was recorded by both companies, but none of the interest had yet been paid at year-end.
3. Lotus declared dividends of $200,000. One-fourth of the dividends (for the final quarter) were not paid until January 6, 1910. Selby recorded the dividends as dividend income.

The unconsolidated trial balances of the two companies are shown below.

Required:
a. Prepare a consolidated balance sheet and a consolidated income statement for 19x9 for Selby.
b. Determine Selby's 19x9 net income and the balance of Selby's retained earnings at December 31, 19x9, assuming that Selby did not consolidate Lotus but instead reported Lotus on the equity basis.

	Trial balances December 31, 19x9 Dr. (Cr.)	
	Selby	Lotus
Cash	$ 400,000	$ 150,000
Accounts receivable	1,300,000	400,000
Accrued revenue	500,000	150,000
Advances to Lotus	3,500,000	—
Investment in Lotus	2,000,000	—
Building	20,000,000	10,000,000
Furnishings	8,000,000	5,000,000
Accumulated depreciation	(9,750,000)	(2,600,000)
Accounts payable	(250,000)	(200,000)
Accrued liabilities	(200,000)	(400,000)
Dividends payable	—	(50,000)
Mortgage note payable	(10,000,000)	(6,000,000)
Due to Selby		(3,200,000)
Common shares	(8,000,000)	(2,000,000)
Retained earnings	(7,300,000)	(1,200,000)
Dividends declared	700,000	200,000
Hotel revenue	(5,600,000)	(3,000,000)
Other revenues	(700,000)	(400,000)
Investment income and interest	(500,000)	—
Salaries and wages expense	2,400,000	900,000
Depreciation expense	600,000	400,000
Maintenance and repairs	700,000	300,000
Supplies	200,000	100,000
Income taxes	600,000	200,000
Interest expense	1,100,000	900,000
Other expenses	300,000	350,000
	$ 0	$ 0

7

Business Combinations

When one corporation obtains control of the assets of another as a going concern, a **business combination** is said to have occurred. The transaction requires the acquisition of control over an operating business or division of another corporation; a purchase of a group of idle assets, therefore, is not a business combination.

There are two basic ways in which a business combination can be accomplished: (1) by a direct purchase of the assets or net assets (assets and liabilities) of one company (or a division of one company) by another, or (2) by an acquisition of at least a majority of the outstanding voting shares of one company by another company. The assets or shares acquired can be paid for by cash, by other assets, or by an issuance of the buying company's shares in exchange for the assets or shares acquired. Business combinations can be very complex, and the financial statements should report the economic substance of the transaction, rather than the legal form.

This chapter discusses and illustrates various forms of business combinations and their accounting and reporting implications. First, we will discuss the accounting for a direct purchase of another company's net assets. Then, business combinations that are accomplished by means of an acquisition of shares will be illustrated.

Finally, we will discuss the alternative approaches to the preparation of consolidated financial statements for business combinations that are accomplished by acquiring shares; we will illustrate the preparation of consolidated statements at the date of acquisition of the shares of another company. In this chapter and the next, we will limit our discussion to purchases of 100% of the acquired company's shares. In later chapters we will remove this simplifying assumption.

PURCHASE OF NET ASSETS

General Approach

The most direct way to obtain control over another company's net assets is simply to buy them outright. The purchasing company (the acquiror) takes title to the assets and may also assume the liabilities of the selling company. The purchase may be for a division or other operating unit of the selling company, rather than for the net assets of the whole company.

The acquiror may pay for the assets in cash or other assets or by issuing its own shares as consideration for the net assets acquired. When the purchase is by cash, it is not difficult to determine the total cost of the net assets acquired. When the purchase is paid for with other assets, such as shares in a third company that have been held as an investment, then the cost is measured by the fair value of the assets surrendered in exchange, if ascertainable.

One of the most common methods of acquiring the net assets of another company is for the acquiror to issue its own shares in payment for the net assets acquired. When shares are issued as consideration for the purchase, the cost of the purchase is the value of the shares issued. If the acquiror is a public company, then the valuation of the shares issued is based on the market value of the existing shares. Valuation of shares in a private company is more difficult. If it is not feasible to place a reliable value on the shares issued, it may instead be necessary to rely upon the fair value of the net assets acquired in order to measure the cost of the purchase. We will consider the valuation of shares in a private company later in this chapter.

Once the cost of the purchase has been determined, that total cost must be apportioned or allocated to the various assets and liabilities that have been acquired. Allocation is necessary so that, for example, depreciation (on fixed assets acquired) and cost of sales (from inventories acquired) can be measured in subsequent periods, and also so that the assets and liabilities can be properly presented on the post-acquisition balance sheet of the acquiror.

It is a generally accepted principle of accounting that when an accounting entity acquires a group of assets for a single price, the total cost of the assets acquired is allocated to the individual assets on the basis of their fair market values. If a company buys land and a building for a lump sum, for example, the land and building are recorded at their proportionate cost, as determined by estimates of their fair values.

The same general principle applies to assets and liabilities acquired as a going concern. The total cost of the purchase is allocated on the basis of the fair market values of the assets and liabilities acquired. It might appear that an alternative basis of allocation would be the book values of the assets, the values listed on the selling company's books. But the carrying values to the selling company are irrelevant to the buying company. The cost of the net assets to the acquiror is the amount that was paid for them by the acquiror, and that cost is determined at least partially by the fair values of the assets at the time of acquisition and not by the unamortized historical cost of the seller.

Fair value is a somewhat nebulous concept. In general, however, fair value is interpreted to mean the current replacement cost for productive assets and net realizable value for assets held to be sold. The concept of fair value will be discussed more fully in a later section of this chapter.

In a business combination, the acquiror buys control over the assets and liabilities of another company as a going concern. The net assets acquired make up an operating business unit. As such, the price paid for the operating unit will be determined in part by its earnings ability. The acquiror may or may not choose to continue to operate the unit in the same manner, but regardless of the acquiror's plans, the price to be paid will take into account the acquired unit's estimated future net revenue stream. If the unit has been successful and has demonstrated an ability to generate above-average earnings, then the acquiror will have to pay a price that is higher than the aggregate fair value of the net assets. On the other hand, if the unit has not been successful, the price may be less than the fair value of the net assets (but not less than the liquidating value of the net assets including tax effects).

The difference between the fair value of the net assets (assets less liabilities assumed) and the purchase price is the **purchase price discrepancy**. The purchase price discrepancy is more commonly known as **goodwill** when the price is higher than the fair value of the net assets, and as **negative goodwill** when the price is less.

Goodwill acquired in a purchase of net assets is a purchased asset, and is recorded along with the fair values of the other assets and liabilities acquired. Negative goodwill, however, is not recorded as such (although it was once the practice to do so). Instead, the costs assigned to the **nonmonetary** assets on the basis of their fair values are reduced until the total of the costs allocated to the individual assets and liabilities is equal to the total purchase price of the acquired net assets.

Illustration of a Purchase of Net Assets

To illustrate the accounting for a direct purchase of net assets, assume that on January 1, 19x1, Investor Ltd. (IOR) acquires all of the assets and liabilities of Investee Ltd. (IEE) by issuing 40,000 no-par IOR common shares to IEE. Before the transaction, IOR had 160,000 common shares outstanding. After the transaction, 200,000 IOR shares are outstanding, of which IEE owns 20%. The pre-transaction balance sheets of both companies are shown in Schedule 7-1. The estimated fair values of IEE's assets and liabilities are shown at the bottom of Schedule 7-1. The aggregate fair value is $1,100,000. If we assume that the market value of IOR's shares is $30 each, then the total cost of the acquisition is $1,200,000. The transaction would be recorded *on the books of IOR* as follows:

Cash and receivables	$200,000	
Inventory	50,000	
Land	400,000	
Buildings and equipment	550,000	
Goodwill	100,000	
Accounts payable		$ 100,000
Common shares		1,200,000

The selling company, IEE, will record the transaction by writing off all of its assets and liabilities and entering the new asset of IOR's shares, recognizing a gain of $400,000 on the transaction.

The post-transaction balance sheets for the two companies will appear as shown in Schedule 7-2. IOR's assets and liabilities increase by the amount of the fair values of the acquired assets and by the purchased goodwill, while

SCHEDULE 7-1		

Pre-Transaction Balance Sheets

January 1, 19x1

	Investor Ltd.	Investee Ltd.
Cash	$ 1,000,000	$ 50,000
Accounts receivable	2,000,000	150,000
Inventory	200,000	50,000
Land	1,000,000	300,000
Buildings and equipment	3,000,000	500,000
Accumulated depreciation	(1,200,000)	(150,000)
Total assets	$ 6,000,000	$ 900,000
Accounts payable	$ 1,000,000	$ 100,000
Future income taxes	400,000	–
Common shares (no par)	2,600,000*	200,000
Retained earnings	2,000,000	600,000
Total equities	$ 6,000,000	$ 900,000

*160,000 shares

Fair values of Investee Ltd.'s net assets:

Cash	$ 50,000
Accounts receivable	150,000
Inventory	50,000
Land	400,000
Buildings and equipment	550,000
Accounts payable	(100,000)
Total	$1,100,000

IEE's previous net assets have been replaced by its sole remaining asset, the shares in IOR. If the transaction had been for cash instead of IOR shares, IEE's sole remaining asset would have been the cash received. Note that while the purchase of IEE's net assets by IOR is a business combination, it is not an intercorporate investment by IOR because IOR is not investing in the shares of IEE. Since IOR is acquiring the assets and liabilities directly instead of indirectly through the purchase of IEE shares, IOR records the assets and liabilities directly on its books and there is no need for consolidated statements; IEE is not a subsidiary of IOR.

SCHEDULE 7-2

Post-Transaction Balance Sheets

	January 1, 19x1	
	Investor Ltd.	Investee Ltd.
Cash	$ 1,050,000	
Accounts receivable	2,150,000	
Inventory	250,000	
Land	1,400,000	
Buildings and equipment	3,550,000	
Accumulated depreciation	(1,200,000)	
Goodwill	100,000	
Investment in IOR shares		$1,200,000
Total assets	$ 7,300,000	$1,200,000
Accounts payable	$ 1,100,000	
Future income taxes	400,000	
Common shares (no par)	3,800,000*	$ 200,000
Retained earnings	2,000,000	1,000,000
Total equities	$ 7,300,000	$1,200,000

*200,000 shares

PURCHASE OF SHARES

Instead of buying the assets or net assets of another company directly, a much more common method of acquiring control over the assets of another company is to buy the common shares of the other business. If one company buys a majority of the voting shares of another company, then control over the assets has been achieved, and the acquiror has a new subsidiary.

An acquiror can obtain a controlling share interest by (1) buying sufficient shares on the open market, (2) entering into private sale agreements with major shareholders, or (3) issuing a public tender offer to buy the shares, or some combination of the three methods. In all cases, the acquiror purchases shares already outstanding, and the acquisition can be achieved without any participation by the acquired company. Unlike a direct purchase of assets, a business combination that is achieved by an acquisition of shares does not have any impact on the asset and equity structure of the acquired company.[1]

Indeed, an acquisition of control through share purchases may be accomplished whether the management of the acquired company likes it or not. As long as the existing owners of a majority of the shares can be convinced to sell to the acquiror, a business combination can be accomplished even if the managers of the acquired company are hostile to the combination. Thus, business combinations that are accomplished by means of share purchases are usually known as **takeovers**, and offers to buy a majority of the shares are called **takeover bids**. If the directors of the acquired company are opposed to the takeover, it then is called a **hostile takeover**.

Reasons for Purchasing Shares

1 An exception is when "push-down" accounting is used. We will discuss this concept towards the end of the chapter.

Takeover bids are regulated by the corporations acts of the provinces and the federal government, as well as by the various securities acts. Such legislation limits the ability of the acquiror to make special private deals with selected shareholders of a target company. For example, the *Canada Business Corporations Act* provides that if an offer to purchase shares will give the offeror 10% or more of the shares of any class of stock of the offeree corporation, the same offer must be made to all shareholders, if they number more than fifteen. The purpose of such legislation is to protect shareholders and to ensure that all shareholders are treated equally.

If an offer is made to all existing shareholders to purchase the shares of a target company, the offering company can limit the proportion of shares that it will accept. For example, in 1988, Kinburn Technology Corp. wanted to increase its ownership of SHL Systemhouse Inc. from 32% to 50.5%. Kinburn made a public offer to acquire 4.75 million Systemhouse shares, and in response, the public shareholders offered (or **tendered**) 12.4 million shares. Kinburn consequently accepted only about 38% of the shares tendered by each offering shareholder.[2]

The offering company can also make the offer conditional on a specified minimum number of shares being tendered. For example, a company may offer to buy 70% of the outstanding shares of another corporation, conditional upon at least 51% of the shares being tendered. By making the offer conditional, the acquiror can avoid buying any of the shares if control cannot be achieved as a result.

Purchase of shares rather than assets has the obvious advantage that control can be obtained by buying considerably less than 100% of the shares. Thus control can be obtained at substantially less cost than would be the case if the acquiror purchased the assets directly.

There are several other advantages as well. One advantage is that the shares may be selling at a price on the market that is less than the fair value per share (or even book value per share) of the net assets. The acquiror can therefore obtain control over the assets at a lower price than could be negotiated for the assets themselves. In 1982, for example, Norcen Energy Resources offered to buy 51% of the shares of Hanna Mining Co. at $45 per share, a price that was 50% higher than the market price of about $30 per share. Yet the book value of Hanna's shares was even higher, at an estimated $50 per share, and estimates of the fair value of Hanna's net assets per share were as high as $70.[3] Thus Norcen was offering a substantial premium over market price to the existing shareholders, while still paying a bargain price relative to the fair value of the assets.

Second, by buying shares rather than assets, the acquiror ends up with an asset that is more easily saleable than the assets themselves, in case the acquiror later decides to divest itself of the acquired business.

Third, the acquiror may prefer to retain the newly acquired business as a separate entity for legal, tax, and business reasons. The acquired business's liabilities need not be assumed, and there is no interruption of the business relationships built up by the acquired corporation.

Finally, income tax impacts can be a major factor in the choice between purchasing assets and purchasing shares. A purchase of shares may benefit

2 "Company News," *Globe and Mail* (February 20, 1988).
3 Spence, Richard, "The Last Shuffle at Argus," *Financial Times of Canada* (July 26, 1982), p. 1.

the seller because the sale of shares will be taxed as a capital gain, while the sale of assets may be subject to tax at full rates as CCA recapture, as a sale of inventory, and as a sale of intangibles that were fully deducted for tax purposes when paid for initially.

For the buyer, however, a purchase of assets may be more desirable than a purchase of shares from a tax viewpoint. When the assets are purchased directly, their cost to the acquiring company becomes the basis for their tax treatment. For example, depreciable assets are recorded on the acquiring company's books at fair values, and CCA will be based on those fair values. Similarly, goodwill purchased is treated as **eligible capital property** for tax purposes and 75% of the goodwill is subject to CCA at a 7% rate (the other 25% is not deductible). If control over the assets is obtained via a share purchase, on the other hand, there is no change in the tax basis for the assets because there is no change in ownership. Thus the buyer cannot take advantage of any increased tax shields if fair-value increments are paid for indirectly through the purchase of shares.

The decision as to the method of acquisition, obviously, is subject to many variables. In a friendly takeover of control, the method of purchase and the purchase price are subject to negotiation, taking into account the various factors affecting both parties, including income tax. If the takeover is unfriendly, then a purchase of shares is the only alternative.

The acquisition of shares can be accomplished by paying cash or other assets, or by issuing new shares of the acquiror, or by some combination thereof. When the acquiror issues new shares as consideration for the shares of an acquired business, the transaction is frequently called an **exchange of shares**. When there is an exchange of shares, it is important to keep track of who owns which shares, in order to determine who exercises control over whom.

Types of Share Exchanges

There are many different ways in which shares can be exchanged in order to accomplish a business combination. Some of the more common and straightforward methods include the following:

1. The acquiror issues new shares to the shareholders of the acquired company in exchange for the shares of the acquired company (the acquiree).
2. Subsidiaries of the acquiror issue shares in exchange for the acquiree's shares.
3. A new corporation is formed; the new corporation issues shares to the shareholders of both the acquiror and the acquiree in exchange for the outstanding shares of both companies.
4. The shareholders of the two corporations agree to a statutory amalgamation.
5. The acquiree issues new shares to the shareholders of the acquiror in exchange for the acquiror's outstanding shares.

The first method listed above is the most common approach. The acquiror ends up having more shares outstanding in the hands of shareholders, while the acquiree's shares that were previously held by external shareholders are now held by the acquiror. Both corporations continue to exist as separate legal entities, but the acquiror's shareholder base has been expanded to include shareholders who had previously been shareholders of the acquiree. The acquiree does not hold any shares in the acquiror; it is the former *shareholders* of the acquiree who hold the newly issued acquiror shares.

The second approach is similar to the first, except that the acquiror does not issue its own shares to acquire the company directly. Instead, the acquiror obtains indirect control by having its subsidiaries issue new shares to acquire the company. This approach is useful when the acquiror does not want to alter the ownership percentages of the existing shareholders by issuance of additional shares. For example, if the controlling shareholder of the acquiror owns 51% of the acquiror's shares, the issuance of additional shares would decrease the controlling shareholder's interest to below 50%, and control would be lost. But if the acquiror has a subsidiary that is, say, 70% owned by the acquiror, quite a number of additional shares could be issued by the subsidiary without jeopardizing the parent's control.

Under the third method, a new company is created that will hold the shares of both the other combining companies. The holding company issues its new shares in exchange for the shares of both the acquiree and the acquiror. After the exchange, the shares of both operating companies are held by the holding company, while the shares of the holding company are held by the former shareholders of both the acquiree and the acquiror.

In a statutory amalgamation, the shareholders of the two corporations approve the combination or amalgamation of the two companies into a single surviving corporation. Statutory amalgamations are governed by the provincial or federal corporations acts under which the companies are incorporated. For two corporations to amalgamate, they must be incorporated under the same act. The shareholders of the combined company are the former shareholders of the two combining companies.

Statutory amalgamation is the only method of combination wherein the combining companies cease to exist as separate legal entities. It is also the only method of share exchange in which the assets of both companies end up being recorded on the books of one company, similar to the recording of assets in a direct purchase of net assets. In all other forms of share exchange, there is no transfer of assets and thus no recording of the acquiree's assets on the acquiror's books; the results of the combination are reported by means of consolidated financial statements, as we discussed in the previous chapter. After a statutory amalgamation, in contrast, consolidated statements are not needed for the combined companies because only one company survives. Of course, if either amalgamating company had subsidiaries, it would still be necessary to prepare consolidated statements that include those subsidiaries.

The foregoing four methods of combination all specify one corporation as the acquiror. The acquiror is identified as the corporation whose pre-combination shareholders have a majority of the votes in the combined corporation, and thus have control of the combined operation.

It is possible to arrange the combination in such a way that the company that legally appears to be the acquiror is, in substance, the acquiree (the fifth method). For example, suppose that InvesteeCorp has 100,000 shares outstanding before the combination, and issues 200,000 new shares to acquire all of InvestorCorp's shares. InvesteeCorp will own all of the shares of InvestorCorp and thus will legally control InvestorCorp. However, two-thirds of the shares of InvesteeCorp will be owned by the former shareholders of InvestorCorp, and the former shareholders of InvestorCorp will have voting control of InvesteeCorp after the combination. The substance of the combination is that control resides with InvestorCorp's shareholders even though the legal form of the combination is that InvesteeCorp acquired InvestorCorp. This form of business combination is called a **reverse take-over**.

Reverse takeovers used to be relatively rare, but in the late 1980s, quite a number of reverse takeovers took place. For example, the *Globe and Mail* reported the following:

> In a reverse takeover pact, Cartier Resources Inc., a mining, oil and gas company, has agreed to acquire all of the shares outstanding of Savage Shoes Ltd. for $5.3 million, to be met with the issuance of 200 million Cartier shares.
>
> As a result of the transaction, the Ng family of Toronto, which acquired Savage in 1987, will own about 91 percent of Cartier.
>
> Trading in Cartier shares, halted on the Toronto Stock Exchange on Friday morning, had not resumed by yesterday's close of trading. At the halt, the stock was at 4 cents a share.
>
> "Savage was looking for a public company already listed on an exchange," said France Crawford, secretary-treasurer of Cartier . . .[4]

This quotation reveals the main reason for reverse takeovers: to acquire a stock exchange listing. Cartier had a TSE listing and Savage wanted one, so rather than go to the trouble and expense of applying to the Ontario Securities Commission (OSC) for a listing, a reverse takeover was arranged. Although Cartier is the legal acquiror, the fact that the shareholders of Savage ended up with 91% of Cartier's shares after the share exchange clearly indicates that Savage was, in substance, the actual acquiror. Savage's owners can now use Cartier's TSE listing for better access to equity financing for Savage's operations.

In the Cartier-Savage example, both companies were operating companies. In some instances, the legal acquiror (and in-substance acquiree) is just a shell company that has an exchange listing but no other assets. The consolidated assets of the economic entity after the business combination would then consist entirely of those of the legal acquiree (and in-substance acquiror).

The accounting problem in any business combination is to report for the substance of the combination, and not to be misled by the legal form that it takes. Accountants must be sensitive to the objectives of managers and owners in arranging business combinations, and must examine the end result in order to determine who purchased what and for how much.

Illustration of a Purchase of Shares

To illustrate the acquiror's accounting for a purchase of shares, assume that on January 1, 19x1, Investor Ltd. (IOR) acquires all of the outstanding shares of Investee Ltd. (IEE) by issuing 40,000 no par IOR shares with a market value of $30, or $1,200,000 total, in exchange. (This transaction is similar to the illustration that was used earlier in the chapter for a direct purchase of net assets.) After the exchange of shares, all of the IEE shares will be held by the corporate entity of IOR, while the newly issued shares of IOR will be held by the former shareholders of IEE and *not* by IEE as a corporate entity.

4 "Savage Shoes and Cartier Resources join forces through reverse takeover," *Globe and Mail* (January 24, 1989), p. B9.

IEE will have no shareholders who are external to the combined entity, while the shareholder base and the number of shares outstanding for IOR have increased.

When IOR acquires the shares, the entry to record the purchase on the books of IOR will be as follows:

Investment in IEE	$1,200,000	
Common shares		$1,200,000

There will be no entry on IEE's books, because IEE is not a party to the transaction; the transaction is with the shareholders of IEE and not with the company itself. After the original purchase is recorded, the investment is accounted for on IOR's books by either the cost or equity method, as discussed in Chapter 6.

IEE is now a subsidiary of IOR, and therefore IOR will prepare consolidated financial statements for public reporting purposes. The preparation of consolidated statements for a purchased subsidiary is somewhat more complex than for parent-founded subsidiaries, and involves choices from among several optional approaches. Consolidation of a purchased subsidiary at the date of acquisition will be illustrated shortly.

Tax Implications of an Issuance of Shares

We have seen that a business combination takes place when an acquiring company either buys the acquiree's assets directly or buys control over the assets (and liabilities) by acquiring a majority of the shares of the acquiree. We have also pointed out the major income tax implications of the two alternative forms of purchase.

There also are tax implications to the form of consideration given by the acquiror in exchange for the acquiree's assets or shares. If the acquiror pays for the assets or shares in cash (or notes payable), the value of the transaction is determined by the amount of cash surrendered or promised. The sellers of the assets or shares will be taxed on any gains arising from the sale. Similarly, when consideration is paid in the form of other types of assets, the sale will be taxed based on the fair market value of the assets given in consideration.

When the acquiror issues shares in exchange for either assets or shares, however, quite a different tax situation may arise. Under the provisions of Section 85 of the *Income Tax Act*, a taxpayer may not have a taxable gain if the taxpayer transfers most kinds of capital property (including shares) to a corporation and receives the corporation's shares in exchange. In such a transaction, known as a **rollover**, the tax basis of the property given up is carried forward as the tax basis of the newly acquired shares. The seller then is taxed only when the newly acquired shares are sold, rather than being taxed on the original exchange of shares.

For business combinations, the rollover provisions of the *Act* most frequently come into effect in a share exchange. The shareholders of the acquired company exchange their shares for shares in the acquiror. The cost of their acquiree shares becomes the cost of the acquiror's shares received in exchange, for tax purposes. If and when the acquiror's shares are sold, the taxable gain is the difference between the proceeds from selling the acquiror's shares and the original cost of buying the acquiree's shares.

A share exchange may include some amount of cash consideration. That is, one acquiree share may be exchanged for one acquiror share plus $5 cash. The existence of partial cash consideration need not affect the status of an exchange as a rollover. Any cash received by the seller will cause an adjustment in the tax basis rather than result in a taxable gain.

The *Income Tax Act* contains many exclusions, limitations, and qualifications in the rollover provisions. Not all business combinations in which the consideration is shares of the acquiror will qualify as rollovers. Nevertheless, the possibility of deferring taxation of the exchange is an important factor in the form of a business combination.

CONSOLIDATION AT DATE OF ACQUISITION

Alternative Approaches

Schedule 7-3 shows the balance sheets of IOR and IEE on January 1, 19x1, both before and after the purchase of IEE's shares by IOR. The pre-transaction amounts are the same as were shown in Schedule 7-1, when IOR purchased the net assets of IEE.

In Chapter 6, we demonstrated the preparation of consolidated statements for Parco. To obtain the Parco consolidated balance sheet, we essentially just added the balances of Subco's assets and liabilities to those of Parco, after eliminating the intercompany balances. It might seem logical to use the same procedure to prepare IOR's consolidated balance sheet, adding the book values of the two companies' assets and liabilities together to get the consolidated amounts.

SCHEDULE 7-3

Balance Sheets, January 1, 19x1

	Before the exchange of shares		After the exchange of shares	
	Investor Ltd.	Investee Ltd.	Investor Ltd.	Investee Ltd.
Cash	$ 1,000,000	$ 50,000	$ 1,000,000	$ 50,000
Accounts receivable	2,000,000	150,000	2,000,000	150,000
Inventory	200,000	50,000	200,000	50,000
Land	1,000,000	300,000	1,000,000	300,000
Buildings and equipment	3,000,000	500,000	3,000,000	500,000
Accumulated depreciation	(1,200,000)	(150,000)	(1,200,000)	(150,000)
Investment in IEE			1,200,000	
Total assets	$ 6,000,000	$ 900,000	$ 7,200,000	$ 900,000
Accounts payable	$ 1,000,000	$ 100,000	$ 1,000,000	$ 100,000
Future income taxes	400,000	—	400,000	—
Common shares (no par)	2,600,000*	200,000	3,800,000*	200,000
Retained earnings	2,000,000	600,000	2,000,000	600,000
Total equities	$ 6,000,000	$ 900,000	$ 7,200,000	$ 900,000

*160,000 shares before the exchange; 200,000 shares after the exchange.

A difference arises, however, from the fact that in Chapter 6 we were demonstrating consolidation of a parent-founded subsidiary, in which case the carrying values of the subsidiary's assets represent the unamortized cost of the assets to the economic entity. When a subsidiary is purchased, however, the cost of the net assets to the reporting enterprise (i.e., to the parent) is likely to be different from the carrying value of the net assets on the subsidiary's books. In the case of IOR and IEE, IOR issued shares worth $1,200,000 to acquire net assets with a carrying value of only $800,000, as shown by the IEE balance sheet in Schedule 7-3. Any method of combining the balance sheets of the two companies must find a way of disposing of the $400,000 difference.

Three general alternative approaches are available for combining the balance sheets of IOR and IEE in order to obtain a consolidated balance sheet for IOR. These alternatives are:

1. Add together the book values of the assets and liabilities of the two companies (the **pooling-of-interests** method).
2. Add the fair values of IEE's assets and liabilities at the date of acquisition to the book values of IOR's assets and liabilities (the **purchase** method).
3. Add the fair values of IEE's assets and liabilities to the fair values of IOR's assets and liabilities (the **new-entity** method).

The two variables that determine the results are (1) the valuation of the parent's net assets and (2) the valuation of the subsidiary's net assets. The alternatives can be summarized as follows:

Method	Consolidated value of parent company	Net assets of subsidiary
Pooling of interests	Book value	Book value
Purchase	Book value	Fair value
New entity	Fair value	Fair value

The results that would be obtained under each of these three methods are shown in Schedule 7-4. The rationale for each method will be discussed in the following sections.

Pooling of Interests

Under the pooling-of-interests method of consolidation, the carrying or book values of both the parent and the subsidiary are combined and carried forward to the consolidated balance sheet. The assumption underlying the use of the pooling method is that the combined economic entity is simply a continuation under common ownership of two previously separate going concerns, and that the operations of both companies will continue without substantial change. If the companies continue to function as separate entities, although now under common ownership, then it is presumed that there should be no change in the basis of accountability for the assets and liabilities as a result of the combination.

If the net assets of the two companies are consolidated at book values, then it is necessary to find an appropriate treatment for the $400,000 differential between the $800,000 net asset book value of IEE and the $1,200,000 worth of IOR shares that were issued in order to purchase IEE's shares. The theoretically correct approach in a pooling of interests is to carry forward the pre-acquisition combined shareholders' equity of the two companies. The

SCHEDULE 7-4

Alternative Approaches to Consolidated Statements

Investor Ltd.
Consolidated Balance Sheet
January 1, 19x1
(in thousands of dollars)

	Pooling	Purchase*	New entity
Cash	$ 1,050	$ 1,050	$ 1,050
Accounts receivable	2,150	2,150	2,150
Inventory	250	250	250
Land	1,300	1,400	2,400
Buildings and equipment (net)	3,500	3,550	2,850
Accumulated depreciation	(1,350)	(1,200)	—
Goodwill	—	100	100
Total assets	$ 6,900	$ 7,300	$ 8,800
Accounts payable	$ 1,100	$ 1,100	$ 1,100
Future income taxes	400	400	400
Common shares	2,800	3,800	3,800
Reappraisal surplus	—	—	1,500
Retained earnings	2,600	2,000	2,000
Total equities	$ 6,900	$ 7,300	$ 8,800

*Fair values assumed:

	Investor Ltd.	Investee Ltd.
Cash	$ 1,000	$ 50
Accounts receivable	2,000	150
Inventory	200	50
Land	2,000	400
Buildings and equipment	2,300	550
Accounts payable	(1,000)	(100)
Future income tax	(400)	—
Net asset value	$ 6,100	$1,100

common shares and retained earnings of IEE are simply added to those of IOR prior to the purchase (as shown in the first two columns of Schedule 7-3) to obtain the consolidated figures, as shown in the first column of Schedule 7-4. The consolidated (pooled) shareholders' equity is $5,400,000, as compared to IOR's unconsolidated shareholders' equity of $5,800,000 after the combination. The $400,000 difference is offset against the investment account upon consolidation, thereby completely eliminating the $1,200,000 investment account.

The difficulty with this approach is that corporations acts in Canada generally provide that corporations must record and report issued shares at the current cash equivalent at the date of issue. For example, Article 25 of the *Canada Business Corporations Act* provides that "a share shall not be issued until the consideration for the share is fully paid in money or in property or past service that is *not less in value than the fair equivalent of the money that the corporation would have received if the share had been issued for money"* (emphasis added). Article 26 states that "a corporation shall add to the appropriate stated capital account the full amount of any consideration it receives for any shares it issues." If the IOR shares were worth $1,200,000 at the date of their issue, then it would be in contravention of the *Act* to report the shares at only $800,000 on the consolidated financial statements. Therefore, the IOR shareholders' equity cannot legally be reduced to $5,400,000 for consolidated reporting; the full $5,800,000 must be reported.

While there is a legal impediment to application of the pooling-of-interests approach in many instances of corporate combination, there can be combinations that would satisfy the legal requirements, as when shares are issued whose market value approximates the book value of the shares acquired. Also, there are ways to accomplish pooling for the assets and liabilities without violating the corporations acts. We will address these alternatives in Chapter 11.

Nevertheless, the pooling approach is not often used in Canada. The reason is that in the vast majority of business combinations, one corporation is clearly taking control of another. After IOR buys the shares of IEE, IEE shareholders hold only 20% of IOR's outstanding shares; control of the combined enterprise will quite assuredly rest with the former shareholders of IOR rather than there being any sort of equal partnership. Therefore, most business combinations in Canada are not reported as poolings, but rather as purchases of one corporation by another.

Purchase Method

The point of IOR's purchase of IEE's common shares was to obtain control over the net assets and the operations of IEE. The control thereby obtained was essentially the same as would have been acquired if IOR had purchased the net assets of IEE as a going operation. If IOR had purchased the net assets, there would be no question but that the assets acquired would be recorded by IOR at their fair values. If the price paid exceeded the total fair value, the excess would be assigned to goodwill.

Since the purchase of shares achieves the same result as does the direct purchase of assets, the objective of the purchase method of consolidation is to report the results of the purchase of shares as though the assets had been acquired directly. The fair values of the subsidiary's assets and liabilities are added to those of the parent (at book value), because the fair value is considered to be the cost of the assets and liabilities to the acquiror. Any excess of the purchase price over the aggregate fair value is assigned to goodwill. The purchase-method consolidated balance sheet in the second column of Schedule 7-4 is therefore exactly the same as the post-transaction balance sheet for direct purchase of the assets as shown in Schedule 7-2.

But note that when there is a direct purchase of assets, the newly acquired assets are recorded directly on the acquiror's books. When there is a purchase of shares, on the other hand, the assets are not recorded on the books of the acquiror because they do not belong to the acquiror. Instead, the assets and liabilities of the acquiree are shown on the acquiror's balance sheet only through the process of preparing consolidated financial statements.

The New-Entity Method

The purchase method has been criticized because the consolidated balance sheet contains a mixture of old book values (for IOR's assets) and current fair values (for IEE's assets). It can be argued that when a business combination occurs, a new economic entity is formed, and that a new basis of accountability should be established for all of the assets. Under the new-entity approach, the assets and liabilities of IOR would be revalued to fair value, so that the consolidated balance sheet would disclose the current fair values (on the date of the combination) of all of the assets for the combined entity. The third column of Schedule 7-4 shows IOR's consolidated balance sheet under the new-entity method.

Under certain circumstances, there is merit in the arguments for the new-entity method. If the combining enterprises are of roughly comparable size, and if the operations of the newly combined enterprises are going to be substantially different from the predecessor operations, then a case can be made for establishing a new basis of accountability. However, there are significant practical problems in implementing the method. Obtaining fair values for all of the assets is likely to be an expensive and time-consuming project, unless the acquiring company already uses current values for internal reporting purposes. In addition, a substantial degree of subjectivity would inevitably exist in the fair-value determination.

While subjective estimates are required to assign the purchase price of a subsidiary to the subsidiary's specific assets and liabilities, the total of the fair values assigned is limited by the total purchase price paid by the parent. But in revaluing the parent's assets for application of the new-entity method, there is no verifiable upper limit for the fair values because no transaction has occurred. In addition, the measurement of goodwill for the parent corporation would be highly subjective. Since it is not clear how the new-entity method would improve the decisions of users of the consolidated financial statements, the method does not seem to be justifiable on the basis of the qualitative criteria for accounting information, and thus has not been accepted in practice.

Other Approaches

In the past, approaches to consolidation other than the three discussed above have been used in practice. One of the more common was to value the transaction at the fair value of the consideration given, as in a purchase, but to consolidate the subsidiary's assets and liabilities at their book values, as under pooling. The difference between the book value and the purchase price would be assigned to goodwill on the consolidated statements.

This approach, sometimes called the carrying-value purchase method, does have the same net impact on the acquiror's net assets as does the fair-value purchase method. However, the assignment of the entire excess of the purchase price over net book value to goodwill can have a significant impact on consolidated earnings subsequent to the acquisition, because amortization of goodwill will most likely be different in impact than would subsequent reporting of the fair values of specific assets and liabilities.

Approaches other than fair value and pooling are no longer acceptable in Canada. Section 1580 of the *CICA Handbook*, which applies to business combinations after March 31, 1974, eliminated the use of the carrying-value purchase method and other variations.

However, there was no requirement that the provisions of Section 1580 be applied retroactively. Acquisitions made prior to March 31, 1974, continue to be reported by the method originally used by the acquiring company. These methods frequently assigned a much larger portion of the purchase price to goodwill. Substantial variation then existed in the post-acquisition reporting of goodwill. In many instances, goodwill was considered to be of indefinite or perpetual life in the absence of direct evidence to the contrary, and was not amortized. In other cases, pre-1974 goodwill was charged directly to retained earnings.

Consequently, some annual reports still contain explicit reference to pre-1974 goodwill. Note 1 of the annual report of Thomson Newspapers Ltd., for example, states that "Goodwill acquired before April 1, 1974 is not being amortized but will be written down if there should be a diminution in its value."

Purchase vs. Pooling

Before leaving our discussion of the alternative methods of consolidation, we should consider further the use of the purchase method as opposed to the pooling-of-interests method. Both methods are currently acceptable in Canada, although the use of pooling is sharply constrained by the *CICA Handbook*.

In most business combinations, one company clearly is acquiring the other. The acquiror is the company whose pre-combination shareholders have a majority of the voting shares in the combined enterprise, regardless of which company is legally acquiring the shares of the other. If one company can be identified as the acquiror, then it is appropriate to consolidate the financial statements by the purchase method, as outlined above. An acquiror can always be identified when the purchase of shares is for cash, notes, or other assets of the acquiror. In such an acquisition, the former shareholders of the acquiree have no stake in the combined venture, and clearly they are not pooling their interests with those of the acquiror's shareholders. An exchange of shares must occur for the possibility of pooling even to arise.

Even in an exchange of shares, an acquiror can usually be identified on the basis of the shareholder group that dominates the combined company. In some instances, however, it may not be possible to identify an acquiror, and a business combination is sometimes viewed as the combining of two essentially equal partners. The *Handbook* [paras. 1580.19-1580.24] does permit the use of the pooling method when an acquiror cannot be identified.

The most well-known use of pooling in Canada in recent years was for the 1980 merger of Hiram Walker with Consumers Home (formerly Consumers Gas). Former Walker shareholders ended up with 58% of the voting shares, but the auditors of both companies concurred in the use of the pooling method. There were some major cash-flow, financing, and risk-sharing advantages to the merger, but Walker's management clearly was in no position actively to control the very different business operations of Consumers Home.

The financial picture presented by consolidated financial statements can be drastically affected by the use of pooling as contrasted with purchase accounting. The consolidated asset values could be much different under pooling versus purchase, especially for intangible assets. Goodwill that would be reported under the purchase method would not be shown under pooling. The difference in the asset values would have a consequent impact on earnings measurement because the amounts of amortization would be different.

Another important difference between purchase and pooling is that pooling is applied retroactively, while the purchase method is applied only from the date of the purchase. Under pooling, the two enterprises are reported as though they had always been combined. The comparative financial statements and other financial information (such as earnings per share, total assets, total sales, and so forth) are restated for the periods prior to the combination in order to reflect the operations of both companies. Under the purchase method, however, there is no restatement of prior years' results. The business combination is viewed as any other investment by the acquiring company, and the acquired company's operating results are reflected in the acquiror's operating results only from the date of acquisition.

The difference in reporting can cause impacts not only on the size of earnings, but also on the comparative direction over time. Pooling could cause post-combination earnings per share (EPS) to increase, relative to pre-combination earnings, while purchase accounting could cause EPS to decrease. The reverse situation could also occur.

In view of the difference in results of the two methods, it is not surprising that managements have sometimes been accused of first deciding which accounting method they wanted to use, and then shaping the form of the transaction to justify the accounting method.[5] For example, it was sometimes argued that if one company issued its shares to acquire the shares of another company, the transaction was a purchase, but if a new corporation was formed to acquire the shares of both existing corporations, then the combination was a pooling.

The use of the pooling method was particularly common in the United States in the 1960s, when the conglomerate movement led to repeated charges of "dirty pooling." As a result, the Accounting Principles Board in the United States issued *APB Opinion No. 16* in 1970, which limited the use of the pooling-of-interests method, but still left appreciable flexibility for managements to shape a transaction in order to meet the criteria for pooling. In the United States, there is still no basic requirement that the purchase method be used if one corporation is clearly obtaining control of another. Pooling can be used even if the pooled company's shareholders own only a very small portion of the shares of the combined corporation.

Pooling was never as popular a method in Canada as it was in the United States. A CICA research study tabulated 998 Canadian business combinations from 1960 through 1968, and found that only 52 (5%) were reported on a pooling basis. A more detailed analysis of 507 of these combinations revealed that 37 of the 507 (7%) were pooled. The low percentage is a little misleading, since an exchange of shares is essential for pooling, and only a third of the combinations involved an issue of shares by the acquiror.[6] Nevertheless,

5 See, for example, Abraham J. Briloff, "Of Pools and Fools," Chapter 8 of *More Debits than Credits* (New York: Harper and Row, 1976).
6 Samuel A. Martin, Stanley N. Laiken, and Douglas F. Haslam, *Business Combinations in the '60s: A Canadian Profile* (CICA, 1970), pp. 16-19.

pooling clearly was much less commonly used than some form of the purchase method, at least amongst public companies. Pooling may be more commonly used when private corporations combine.

Perhaps because of less interest in pooling in Canada, the Accounting Standards Committee was able to issue a stronger recommendation on accounting for business combinations than was the APB. Section 1580 of the *CICA Handbook* became effective in 1974 and sharply restricted the use of the pooling method to "those rare business combinations in which it is not possible to identify one of the parties as the acquirer" [para. 1580.21]. As a result of Section 1580, the use of pooling by public companies almost disappeared in Canada after March 31, 1974. The biennial editions of *Financial Reporting in Canada* reported that from March 31, 1974, through 1986, only five of the 886 business combinations entered into by the surveyed companies were accounted for as a pooling of interests. All of the rest were reported by use of the purchase method.

Owing to the dominance of the purchase method in Canada, we devote most of our discussion in this textbook to its application. The purchase method yields the same results for consolidated financial statements as does the direct purchase of assets for the financial statements of the buying company, and is a good example of accounting following the economic substance of the transaction rather than the legal form. The pooling-of-interests method will be discussed in greater detail in Chapter 11, including an analysis of the difference in reported results that arises from using pooling rather than the purchase method.

Consolidation Procedures

There are two general approaches to the preparation of consolidated statements. One is simply to sit down with the separate entity financial statements of the two companies and combine them, line by line, adding in fair-value increments and making eliminations as we go. The advantage of this approach is that it is relatively easy to understand the financial statement impacts that our combinations and adjustments make, and we can always see the end result.

The disadvantage of such a direct approach, however, is that it also is easy to lose track of the offsets for some of the adjustments, especially in years subsequent to the combination. In practice, a direct approach is usually impractical because of the size and complexity of the account structure.

The alternative to the direct approach is to use a worksheet. A worksheet can be somewhat confusing because we do not see the form of the financial statements on the worksheet and it is easier to lose sight of our final goal. On the other hand, the systemization forced on us by a worksheet sharply reduces the chances of our making only half of an adjustment; we can readily see that our debits equal our credits!

In Chapter 6, we illustrated both approaches. We will touch on the direct method again in Chapter 9, and then in Chapter 10 we will use both approaches in a summary example. In the intervening chapters, we will use only the worksheet approach, because we feel that the worksheet approach is more likely to be encountered in practice and aspiring professional accountants should become comfortable with using worksheets. But the approach used is really a matter of indifference. What matters is the results: the consolidated statements. The route taken to get there is irrelevant. Therefore, the reader should not hesitate to use whichever approach (or variant thereof) that he or she feels most comfortable with.

Consolidation Worksheet

Schedule 7-5 illustrates the worksheet to prepare the IOR consolidated balance sheet, using the purchase method. The trial balance columns for the individual companies correspond to the post-transaction trial balances shown in the last two columns of Schedule 7-3.

The eliminations and adjustments that are necessary in order to prepare the consolidated trial balance are composed of three elements. First, it is necessary to eliminate the shareholders' equity accounts of the acquired company, IEE, by offsetting the balances of these accounts against the investment account:

(a) Common shares (IEE)	$200,000	
Retained earnings (IEE)	600,000	
Investment in IEE (IOR)		$800,000

The second entry adjusts the asset accounts of the subsidiary from their carrying values on the subsidiary's books to the fair values at the date of acquisition:

(b) Land (IEE)	$100,000	
Buildings and equipment (IEE)	200,000	
Goodwill	100,000	
Investment in IEE (IOR)		$400,000

The net result of these two adjustments is to eliminate the investment ac-

---

SCHEDULE 7-5

Consolidation Worksheet
Dr. (Cr.)

	Trial balances, January 1, 19x1		Adjustments and eliminations	IOR consolidated trial balance
	IOR	IEE		
Cash	$ 1,000,000	$ 50,000		$ 1,050,000
Accounts receivable	2,000,000	150,000		2,150,000
Inventory	200,000	50,000		250,000
Land	1,000,000	300,000	$ 100,000 b	1,400,000
Buildings and equipment	3,000,000	500,000	$\left\{\begin{array}{l}200,000 \text{ b}\\(150,000)\text{c}\end{array}\right.$	3,550,000
Accumulated depreciation	(1,200,000)	(150,000)	150,000 c	(1,200,000)
Investment in IEE	1,200,000		$\left\{\begin{array}{l}(800,000)\text{a}\\(400,000)\text{b}\end{array}\right.$	—
Goodwill			100,000 b	100,000
Accounts payable	(1,000,000)	(100,000)		(1,100,000)
Future income taxes	(400,000)			(400,000)
Common shares	(3,800,000)	(200,000)	200,000 a	(3,800,000)
Retained earnings	(2,000,000)	(600,000)	600,000 a	(2,000,000)
	$ 0	$ 0	$ 0	$ 0

count, eliminate the subsidiary's share equity accounts at the date of acquisition, and establish the fair values of the assets and liabilities acquired by IOR through purchase of IEE's shares.

One further necessary adjustment offsets the subsidiary's accumulated depreciation at the date of acquisition against the fixed asset account to which it applies:

(c) Accumulated depreciation (IEE)	$150,000	
Buildings and equipment (IEE)		$150,000

The purpose of this adjustment is to report the entire fair value of IEE's buildings and equipment as an increase in the buildings and equipment asset account on IOR's consolidated balance sheets. If this adjustment were not made, the reported balance of IOR's accumulated depreciation would increase as a result of the combination, contrary to the expected results when additional assets are purchased.[7]

These three adjustments will be made in every subsequent period when the consolidated statements are prepared. While it is important to understand the reason for each adjustment, we will combine the three entries in later chapters into a single summary adjustment to eliminate the investment account, as follows:

Land	$100,000	
Buildings and equipment	50,000	
Accumulated depreciation	150,000	
Goodwill	100,000	
Common shares	200,000	
Retained earnings	600,000	
Investment in IEE		$1,200,000

The debit to buildings and equipment for $50,000 is the net effect of the $200,000 debit for the increase to fair value and the $150,000 credit to eliminate IEE's accumulated depreciation. The net reported value of IEE's buildings and equipment is thereby increased by $200,000: a direct adjustment of buildings and equipment by $50,000, plus the elimination of the accumulated depreciation deduction of $150,000 relating to IEE's fixed assets. The net result is to increase the consolidated buildings and equipment by $200,000, exactly as when IOR purchased the assets directly. After the investment account has been fully eliminated, the consolidated trial balance can be prepared, and the consolidated financial statements can be prepared from the trial balance.

ACQUISITIONS BY PRIVATE CORPORATIONS

Most corporations in Canada are private companies. Statistics Canada, for example, reported that in 1983, almost 98% of the 448,409 Canadian corporations were private. This percentage undoubtedly includes a large number of very small companies, nonoperating shell companies, personal professional service corporations, and wholly owned operating subsidiaries of pub-

---

7 Para. 1580.45 of the *CICA Handbook* recommends that "the accumulated depreciation of the acquired company should not be carried forward by the acquiring company."

lic companies and of foreign corporations; therefore, the percentage may be somewhat overstated in substantive terms. Nevertheless, it is still quite clear that the vast majority of Canadian corporations are private, not public, as we pointed out in Chapter 1.

When the acquiror is a private company, shares will not be issued to acquire a public company because that would result in the acquiror becoming a public company, in contravention of the securities acts. Even when the acquiree is also a private company, the acquiror may be reluctant to issue shares in the purchase because the ownership of the acquiror would be diluted.

There are acquisitions by private companies that are accomplished by an exchange of shares, however. When this happens, two issues arise. One is the determination of fair value of the shares issued in exchange; the second is the use of pooling of interests accounting.

When shares are issued by an acquiror in a business combination, the cost that is assigned to the acquisition should be the fair value of the shares issued. When the acquiror is a public company, a market value is available for the shares. There will be some flexibility in assigning an exact value, since market prices fluctuate and there are a number of options available for selecting a value, such as the spot rate on the date of the agreement, and average price over the preceding period of time (e.g., 60 days), or a discounted price based on the price at which an underwriter would accept the shares. Nevertheless, there is an objective value upon which to base the fair value of an acquisition. When the acquiror is a private company, on the other hand, there is obviously no market value that can be used to determine the value of the exchange.

Business valuation theory generally holds that the value of shares in a private corporation should be the discounted earnings or operating cash flow stream, with the fair value of the company's net assets as a lower bound. In practice, however, it seems that the valuation of unlisted shares is tied more closely to historical earnings and book values. In an extensive empirical study of unlisted share valuations, professional business valuators agreed (in a questionnaire) with the hypothesis that future earnings prospects and fair market value of net assets were considered the most important variables. In an analysis of 290 actual valuations, however, the researcher found that the most important factors actually seemed to be "historical earnings and book value of net assets."[8]

The association between assigned values and book values may relate to the prevalence of **shareholders' agreements**. In private companies, it is normal for the shareholders to sign a contract that outlines the rights and responsibilities of the various shareholders, including voting rights. One of the most important components of a shareholders' agreement is the provision that governs the sale of shares by a shareholder. There is usually a provision that requires a selling shareholder to offer shares first to the other shareholders or to the corporation itself. The formula for determining the price of the shares in a buyout arrangement is usually specified in the agreement in order to avoid disagreements and potential lawsuits. Typically, the formula is tied to book values and historical earnings because those are relatively objec-

---

8 Jeffrey Kantor, *Valuation of Unlisted Shares* (Don Mills, Ontario: CCH Canadian Limited, 1988), p. 224.

tive amounts. It is not surprising, therefore, that the same type of formula carries over into independent valuations of unlisted shares. The result is that when unlisted shares are issued in a business combination, the value placed on the shares is often heavily influenced by the book value of the acquiror.[9]

When unlisted shares are issued by an acquiror, it is normal for a new shareholders' agreement to be arranged that includes the interests of the new shareholder(s) (i.e., the previous owner(s) of the acquiree). Voting rights, sellout rights, buyout rights, estate matters, and the extent of management control will all be specified. Such an agreement may well have the effect of indicating that, in substance, a pooling of interests has occurred even if the resulting share ownerships are not equal. Control and participation are governed by the shareholders' agreement, not by (or not only by) the relative numbers of voting shares held. Therefore, pooling of interests accounting is much more likely to be encountered among private corporations than is the case among public corporations.

In summary, the issuance of shares of a private company in a business combination raises two issues, (1) valuation of the shares and (2) method of consolidated reporting. Valuation "should" be based on fair values and future earnings, but is more likely to be tied rather closely to book values and historical earnings. Relative share ownerships after the combination may indicate that a purchase has occurred because the shareholder(s) of one corporation have a majority of the post-combination shares, but the shareholders' agreement may contain provisions that make the application of pooling of interests reporting quite appropriate.

ESTIMATION OF FAIR VALUES

The general guidelines for the estimation of the fair values of individual assets and liabilities of purchased subsidiaries in Canada are described in paragraph 1580.45 of the *CICA Handbook*. In general, monetary assets and liabilities are valued on the basis of the expected cash flows in the normal course of business. Nonmonetary assets are valued at net realizable value if they are designated to be sold (such as marketable securities and inventories) or at replacement cost of the available capacity of productive assets (such as plant and equipment). Plant and equipment that is to be sold rather than used would be valued at net realizable value.

Long-term monetary receivables and payables should be discounted at market rates of interest for comparable maturities and risk at the date of acquisition. The *Handbook* does not require discounting, however, but only suggests that "discounting may be considered to be an aid in valuation where an asset would not be realized or an obligation would not be discharged in the current operating cycle" [para. 1580.45]. Thus the carrying values for long-term receivables and payables are sometimes used in practice when consolidated statements are prepared. Consolidating a long-term receivable or payable at face value instead of at a discounted amount would

---

9 For a broader discussion of shareholders' agreements, see Jack Bernstein, *Shareholder Agreements: A Tax and Legal Guide* (Don Mills, Ontario: CCH Canadian Limited, 1988), especially Chapter 1, "General Contents of Shareholder Agreements."

affect the amount of the purchase price allocated to goodwill, and would also affect subsequent amortization of the goodwill amount (discussed in the next chapter).

The replacement cost of productive assets can be estimated by means of (1) appraisals, (2) estimated market values to replace the assets, if a secondary market exists, or (3) price indices for specific types of assets. Fair values that are estimated by reference to prices or price indices for new assets must be adjusted for depreciation to reflect only the remaining productive capacity of the assets. The methods of estimation are essentially the same as would be used to obtain estimates of current cost for compliance with the current cost reporting recommendations of Section 4510 of the *CICA Handbook*.

Intangible assets that can be specifically identified should also be assigned their fair values, whether or not the specific assets are currently recognized on the books of the acquired company. Patents, franchises, uncompleted contracts, and subscription lists are examples of intangible assets that may contribute significantly to the value of the enterprise. If no attempt is made to determine their fair values, then an important component of the acquired assets may be overlooked, and too much of the purchase price may be allocated to goodwill. Measurement of the fair values of intangible assets, however, is easier said than done. Estimates are usually based on the revenue-generating potential of the asset, but it is very difficult to distinguish between the value of individual intangible assets and the value of goodwill. Skinner suggests that "valuation of specific intangible factors acquired in a business combination should be restricted to those assets whose utility can be transferred to other parties independent of the business and therefore have some hope of a value in exchange. Even for these, hard evidence should be available to justify the basis of valuation."[10]

Future income tax balances raise another problem when the business combination is effected by a purchase of shares.[11] As we noted earlier, when control of assets is obtained by acquiring control of the company's shares rather than by a direct purchase of the assets, there is no change in the tax status of the assets. The acquired company continues to be taxed as a separate entity, and timing differences between accounting and taxable income will be carried forward into the future until reversed, unaffected by the change in control of the acquired company.

Many accountants argue that the balance of future income taxes is the result of an accounting allocation, and does not represent a current obligation to sacrifice assets in the future. In their view, the fair value of future income taxes is zero because it is not a liability, but is only a deferred credit. Other accountants argue that the future income tax balance represents a future cash flow for taxes deferred in previous years and therefore should be assigned a fair value (although perhaps discounted).

---

10 Ross M. Skinner, *Accounting Standards in Evolution* (Toronto: Holt, Rinehart and Winston of Canada, 1987) p. 333.

11 As this text is being written, the November 1988 AcSC exposure draft on corporate income taxes is outstanding, and is scheduled for re-exposure. While it is impossible to predict the final results of the AcSC's due process, we have assumed that the liability approach will replace the deferral approach, and accordingly we have adopted the account title "future income taxes" to replace "deferred income taxes" in our discussion and illustrations (except for the examples of actual disclosures at the end of chapters 7 and 9; the terminology used by the companies has been retained).

However, it is important to bear in mind that the value of depreciable assets arises partially from their productive capacity and partially from their tax deductibility. The future income tax balance represents accumulated tax deductibility that has been used up in the past and that is not available in the future. If the tax deductibility has been used up, then the fair value of the assets is less than would otherwise be the case, and the future income tax credits reduce the fair value of the asset.

In Canada, treatment of future income taxes in determining fair values is not standardized. The *CICA Handbook* suggests that future income taxes should "be taken into account in the amounts assigned to assets and liabilities" [para. 1580.48], which implies that the future income taxes should be deducted from the assets and liabilities to which they relate. In other words, the fair values of the assets and liabilities could be determined as net-of-tax amounts.

On the other hand, the same paragraph of the *Handbook* also suggests that "it is, in the opinion of the Committee, appropriate for the acquiring company to reflect, in its consolidated financial statements, future income taxes previously recorded by the acquired company, since the acquired company has experienced a deferral of income taxes . . . which continues and is not affected by the acquisition." In other words, it is appropriate for the future income tax balance not to be offset against the specific asset and liability accounts, but to be recognized as a credit on the consolidated balance sheet. This approach is consistent with the method of tax allocation used in Canada, where future income taxes are not offset against the specific assets and liabilities to which they relate as they would be if the net-of-tax method of tax allocation were used.

The practice of carrying forward the aggregate future income tax balance of the acquired company also has the advantage of simplifying post-acquisition consolidation. Since there will be no difference between the book value and the assigned fair value of the future income taxes, there is no need to make any consolidation adjustments when the timing differences reverse on the books of the acquired company.

Whether the future income taxes are netted against specific assets and liabilities or not, the important point is that the fact of having previously received the tax benefits of asset ownership does reduce the fair value of the net assets acquired, and therefore the lower tax shield of the assets should be taken into account when assigning fair values. The future income taxes balance should not simply be ignored.

If the acquired company has tax-loss carry-forwards, these carry-forwards may be an asset if the benefits can be realized. The likelihood of realizing the benefits of tax-loss carry-forwards may be greater after the combination than before, even though the acquired company continues to be taxed as a separate entity, because the acquiring company may be able to take a number of actions that improve the profitability of the acquired company. Such actions may include replacing the management, discontinuing unprofitable segments, injecting new capital to improve inefficient or obsolete facilities, or increasing profitability by directing a larger volume of business to the new subsidiary, changing the price on intercompany sales, or by lowering royalty or management fees charged to the subsidiary.

When a company acquires another company that has tax-loss carry-forwards, the acquiror usually has evaluated the likelihood of utilizing the carry-forwards. If the carry-forwards are likely to be utilized, then the acquiror will have considered their value in determining the price for the acquired company. Therefore, the likely realizable present value of the tax-loss carry-forwards should be recognized when assigning fair values in a business combination.

Tax-loss carry-forwards may be recognized in a business combination even though they have not been recognized on the acquiree's books. Canadian practice discourages recognition of an asset for a tax-loss carry-forward on the taxpayer's books (in this case, the acquiree). A taxpayer corporation can recognize a tax-loss carry-forward only when there is *virtual certainty* that the benefit will be realized.[12] In reporting a business combination in the acquiror's consolidated financial statements, however, the *CICA Handbook* states that a tax-loss carry-forward can be recognized if there is *reasonable assurance* that the benefits will be realized [para. 1580.50].

The difference is that on the acquiree's books, no asset has been acquired; recognition is of an asset that is anticipated (i.e., a future tax reduction) and is recognized only in order to improve the measurement of current net income (loss) by matching the future benefit against the current loss giving rise to that benefit. Virtual certainty is required in order to avoid setting up an asset that was not paid for and may not really exist.

In a business combination, on the other hand, the acquiror is actually paying for a collection of future benefits, one of which is a tax-loss carry-forward. The accounting problem is one of allocating the cost of a basket purchase of future benefits, very few of which are virtually certain of realization. Therefore, the general guideline for allocating the total cost of the purchase is the likelihood or reasonable assurance of realization, not virtual certainty of realization.

Finally, we should consider briefly the impact of preferred shares on the allocation of the purchase price. Obviously, preferred shares are a part of shareholders' equity and are not normally considered to be a liability. However, when an acquiror purchases the common shares but not the preferred shares of an acquiree, a question arises as to how to treat the preferred shares in the purchase equation and in consolidated statements. Chapter 12 contains a full discussion of this issue, but basically the approach is to treat preferred shares as though they were a liability. When the purchase price is assigned to the assets and liabilities, the call or redemption price of the shares is included as a liability (plus any dividend arrearages). The value assigned to the acquiree's preferred shares is included as **minority interest** on the acquiror's consolidated balance sheet, rather than as shareholders' equity, since the shares are held by people outside of the acquiror's shareholder group.

Clearly, there is much room for the exercise of professional judgment in assigning fair values. Different managers and accountants can easily come to different conclusions in assigning fair values to the various assets and liabilities of an acquired company. However, the apportionment of the purchase price in a business combination in Canada must be defensible under the general guidelines set forth in the *Handbook*.

---

12 The AcSC has proposed to eliminate even this highly constrained recognition and is suggesting that tax-loss carry-forwards should never be reported as an asset. CICA Accounting Standards Committee, *Exposure Draft: Corporate Income Taxes*, (November, 1988).

Although the estimation of fair values involves a certain amount of subjectivity, the dangers inherent in not using a fair-value approach are even greater. The use of book values for the acquired assets and liabilities, although superficially more objective, would violate the important accounting principle of substance over form. Business combinations would be engineered with a view towards the illusory impact on the financial statements of the acquiror, rather than towards the substantive effect on the acquiror's economic performance. Therefore, fair values are required in Canada in reporting the results of business combinations that are, in substance, purchases of assets or of control over assets.

NEGATIVE GOODWILL

In the example of a business combination used earlier in this chapter, control over net assets with a total fair value of $1,100,000 were assumed to have been acquired for $1,200,000. A positive purchase price discrepancy of $100,000 thus existed, and the discrepancy was treated as goodwill in accordance with Canadian practice.

It is not unusual, however, for the total fair value of the assets and liabilities to be greater than the purchase price, thereby resulting in a negative purchase price discrepancy. This excess of fair values over the purchase price is commonly known as **negative goodwill**, although the title is not particularly indicative of the accounting treatment of the amount.

Negative goodwill is, in essence, an indication that the acquiror achieved a bargain purchase. A bargain purchase is possible for a variety of reasons. If the acquisition is by a purchase of shares, then the market price of the acquiree's shares may be well below the net asset value per share. Or if the acquiree is a private company, a bargain purchase may be possible if the present owners are anxious to sell because of the death of the founder-manager, divorce, changed family financial position, or simply an inability to manage effectively.

Regardless of the reason, negative goodwill should be viewed as a discount on the purchase and not as a special credit to be created and amortized. When any company buys an asset at a bargain price, the asset is recorded at its cost to the purchaser, and not at any list price or other fair value. For example, suppose that a company buys a minicomputer from a financially troubled distributor for only $80,000. The price of the computer from any other source would be $120,000. On the buyer's books, the computer obviously would be recorded at $80,000, not at $120,000 with an offsetting credit for $40,000.

The same general principle applies to bargain purchases in business combinations. The purchase price is allocated to the acquired assets and liabilities on the basis of fair values, but not necessarily *at* fair values if the total fair value exceeds the purchase price. A problem does arise, however, in deciding to which assets and liabilities the bargain prices or negative goodwill should be assigned.

A business combination involves the assets and liabilities of a going concern. The net assets acquired usually comprise a mixture of monetary and nonmonetary, current and long-term assets and liabilities. Because the various assets and liabilities have varying impacts on reported earnings, the allocation of negative goodwill will affect the amount of future revenues and expenses.

For example, suppose that IOR acquired all of the shares of IEE, as above, but at a cost of only $1,050,000. Since the fair value of IEE's net assets is $1,100,000, a negative purchase price discrepancy of $50,000 exists. IEE's assets and liabilities will be reported on IOR's consolidated balance sheet at a total amount of $1,050,000, $50,000 less than their fair values. At least one of the IEE assets must be reported at an amount that is less than its fair value.

If the negative goodwill is assigned to inventory, IEE's inventory would be consolidated at zero value, since the fair value of IEE's inventory was assumed to be $50,000 (Schedule 7-4). Reduction in the cost assigned to inventory will flow through to the income statement in the following year as a reduction in cost of goods sold and an increase in net income. If, on the other hand, the negative goodwill were assigned to buildings and equipment, then the effect of the bargain purchase would be recognized over several years in the form of reduced depreciation. Allocation of the negative goodwill to land would result in no impact on earnings until the land were sold; allocation to monetary receivables would result in a gain when the receivables were collected.

The choice of assets to report at less than fair values is essentially arbitrary. In Canada, the choice has been made by the AcSc to allocate the negative goodwill to identifiable *nonmonetary* assets, both current and noncurrent [para. 1580.44]. Within that guideline, there is much flexibility. The allocation need not be proportional. Common practice is to allocate more of the negative purchase price discrepancy to those assets with the "softest" fair values, or those most difficult to determine. Intangible assets seem to be particularly prone to absorbing the negative goodwill, followed by fixed tangible assets, and then by current nonmonetary assets.

It is quite possible for the total nonmonetary assets to be less than the amount of negative goodwill. In that case, the identifiable nonmonetary assets cannot fully absorb the negative purchase price discrepancy. There then is little option but to report a deferred credit for the unabsorbed excess, and to amortize the credit over an arbitrary period of years.

RECORDING FAIR VALUES: PUSH-DOWN ACCOUNTING

We have emphasized that the fair values of the net assets of the acquiree are never recorded in the books of the acquiror; the full purchase price is simply recorded in an investment account on the acquiror's books. We have also stated that when a business combination is accomplished by a purchase of shares (rather than by a direct purchase of assets), the acquiree continues to exist as a separate legal and reporting entity, and that the carrying values of the acquiree's net assets are not affected by the acquisition or by the fair values attributed to the assets by the acquiror.

An exception to the general rule that the acquiree's carrying values are unaffected by the purchase may arise when substantially all of the acquiree's shares are purchased by the acquiror. In that case, the acquiror may direct the acquiree to revalue its assets in accordance with the fair values attributed thereto by the acquiror. This practice is known as **push-down accounting,** because the fair values are "pushed down" to the acquiree's books. The net effect is the same as if the acquiror had formed a new subsidiary, which then purchased all of the assets and liabilities of the acquiree.

There are two advantages to push-down accounting. The first is that the financial position and results of operations of the acquiree will be reported on the same economic basis in both the consolidated statements and its own separate-entity statements. Without push-down accounting, for example, it would be possible for the subsidiary to report a profit on its own and yet contribute an operating loss to the parent's consolidated results, if the fair-value amortizations are sufficient to tip the balance between profit and loss. The second advantage is that the process of consolidation will be greatly simplified for the parent. Since the carrying values will be the same as the acquisition fair values, there will be no need for recurring adjustments for fair-value increments and amortization each time consolidated statements are prepared.

Push-down accounting is not yet widely used in Canada, although there are indications that its application is growing.[13] The practice is more prevalent in the United States, where the Securities and Exchange Commission requires its registrants to use the practice when an acquired subsidiary is "substantially" wholly owned and there is no publicly held debt or senior shares. In response to the SEC requirement, the Steering Committee of the AcSC issued an Accounting Guideline in October 1987 which suggested that push-down accounting be applied only when "(a) virtually all of [the acquiree's] voting common shares have been acquired; and (b) no significant outstanding public interest remains in its debt securities, preferred shares, non-voting common shares or other securities."[14]

While application of push-down accounting has been largely limited to companies that have few external shareholders or major debtholders after they have been acquired, there is no inherent reason that the process could not be applied to other companies when control changes hands in a business combination. The *Handbook* does not effectively constrain the revaluation of fixed assets, and a takeover could certainly be considered to be one of those "instances where it is appropriate to reflect fixed assets at values which are different from historical costs" [para. 3060.01]. Instead, the reason that push-down accounting is less commonly applied where significant shares or debt remain in the hands of the public is that the basis for stewardship reporting, in the form of contract compliance, is disturbed by an asset revaluation. Reported results (e.g., earnings per share) will be discontinuous, and debt covenants may be violated or rendered less suitable if the reporting basis is changed. Indeed, debt agreements with banks may be based on accounting principles in effect on the date of the agreement and thereby effectively constrain the application of push-down accounting.

A special case of push-down accounting arises in a reverse takeover. In a reverse takeover, it is the legal acquiror that is really the acquiree, so that the

---

13 For a discussion of the issues in push-down accounting, see James M. Sylph, "Push-Down Accounting: Is the US Lead Worth Following?" *CA Magazine* (October, 1985), pp. 52-55, and Paula B. Thomas and J. Larry Hagler, "Push Down Accounting: A Descriptive Assessment," *Accounting Horizons* (September, 1988), pp. 26-31.
14 CICA Accounting Guideline, *Push-Down Accounting* (October, 1987), para. 7.

fair values reported on the consolidated statements will be those of the company issuing the statements. In that case, it makes little sense for the in-substance acquiree to be carrying its assets and liabilities at book values that will never be reported in its own financial statements. Therefore it is logical simply to put the fair values on the books of the acquiree.

LEVERAGED BUYOUTS

When one company takes over another by the purchase of shares, it is not unusual for the acquiror to borrow money to finance the purchase. The purchase is thereby **leveraged**; the acquisition has to yield a return that is higher than the cost of borrowing in order for the acquiror to benefit. If the yield is substantially less than the cost of borrowing, then the borrower may get into financial difficulty because there is not sufficient cash flow to service the debt. In the early 1980s, there were some spectacular failures of large businesses in the petroleum industry due to the combined impact of falling oil prices and rising interest rates on high debt loads incurred to acquire other companies.

While heavy borrowing to finance a takeover would seem to qualify as a leveraged buyout, that is not what the term has come to mean in the financial lexicon. In the type of situation described above, the debt is assumed by the acquiror, and it is the acquiror who is responsible for meeting debt service requirements and who is therefore bearing the risk. In the modern **leveraged buyout** (or **LBO**), the risk is assumed not by the acquiror but by the acquiree. This result is accomplished by using the acquiree's own assets and potential cash flow as the source of both security and debt service (i.e., interest and principal repayment). If the post-acquisition cash flow of the acquiree is insufficient to service the debt, then it is the acquiree that falls into receivership rather than the acquiror.

LBOs began life largely as a way for managers to buy control of their own companies when the existing owners indicated an interest in divesting themselves of their shares. The managers could seldom afford to buy the shares outright, but they could put their own managerial ability on the line by borrowing against the company's assets and managing the company sufficiently well that the debt could be serviced. If the managers failed in their endeavour, then they lost their company and their jobs. Such an LBO is not a business combination because it is not another corporation that is buying the shares, but rather the individual managers themselves.[15]

As the use of LBOs expanded throughout the 1980s, it increasingly became outsiders rather than managers who used the technique to gain control without assuming any significant risk themselves; the debt was generally without recourse to the acquirors. Since the current operating cash flow of the target company is frequently insufficient to service the debt, the gamble is that the new owners can sell off "surplus" assets to get cash to pay down

15 See Edward K. Crawford, *A Management Guide to Leveraged Buyouts* (New York: John Wiley and Sons, 1987), for a discussion of LBOs aimed at their traditional participants, the managers themselves. The book includes case descriptions of 16 LBOs (in the United States) in the mid-1980s.

the loan and slash costs to increase cash flow. These strategies frequently lead to a down-sizing of the target company as both its assets and its scale of operations are reduced. Sometimes, the acquiror can generate enough short-term cash flow to pay off the debt and issue enough dividends to recover whatever small initial investment was made, plus a healthy profit. If the gamble doesn't pay off, it is the target company that suffers; the acquiror is not seriously scathed.

Even when an ethical acquiror is in for the long haul and is not trying to turn a quick profit, an LBO can create potentially severe problems for the acquiree simply as a result of the high debt load that results. The high leverage leaves little room for normal business risk; if the company's fortunes turn down, even temporarily, receivership could follow rather quickly. For example, Mother's Restaurants Ltd., which had 10% of all pizza customers in Canada in 1986, was the subject of a leveraged buyout in that year. Subsequently, overheads increased, sales decreased, and funds for renovation were not available. Despite the efforts of management to turn the chain's operations around, "the darn thing was bowed by the weight of the debt."[16] On December 30, 1988, Citibank (the major lender in the LBO) announced that it was placing Mother's into receivership.

When the acquiror in an LBO is a corporation, then a business combination occurs. The reporting principles for a company that acquires another via an LBO are no different than in any other purchase of shares. The fair values of the assets and liabilities (including the concurrently incurred debt) must be determined and allocated, and goodwill recognized when necessary. Since more than usual of the acquired assets may be sold after the buyout, net realizable values may play an important part in the assignment of the purchase price. Indeed, it may be difficult to account for the purchase in the short run:

> In view of the occasionally severe difficulties in valuation, it may take several months to a year before a cost can be allocated on the basis of reasonably satisfactory evidence. Initial allocations, therefore, must be regarded as tentative and subject to adjustment when all the necessary information is obtained.[17]

SUMMARY

A fairly common transaction in our economy is the purchase of control over the net assets of one going concern by another. Control over the assets can be obtained directly by purchasing the assets of another business (or an operating segment or division of another business), or indirectly by purchasing its voting shares. Either type of purchase can be made for cash or by an exchange of shares. Such a transaction is called a business combination.

When assets or net assets (assets less the liabilities) are purchased directly, the total cost of the purchase is measured by the fair value of the cash, other assets, or securities issued as consideration for the purchase. The assets and

---

16 Jennifer Wells, "Dough Play," *Financial Times of Canada* (January 16, 1989), p. 16.
17 Skinner, *Accounting Standards*, p. 333. Skinner is referring here to the general problems of allocating fair value in a business combination, not specifically to leveraged buyouts.

liabilities acquired are recorded on the books of the purchaser at the fair market values of the assets acquired. If the transaction price is for more than the total fair value of the net assets, the surplus is viewed as goodwill. If the transaction price is less than the fair value of the net assets acquired, then the values assigned to the nonmonetary assets are reduced until the discrepancy disappears.

Instead of purchasing the assets or net assets directly, the acquiror may buy the shares of the acquiree company. The purchase of shares is simpler to accomplish than is a purchase of assets, and is likely to be more desirable for the seller for tax purposes. In addition, a purchase of shares makes it possible for the acquiror to control the net assets of the acquiree by buying less than 100% interest, thereby reducing the amount of capital needed for the transaction. Further advantages to a share purchase are that a share purchase can be accomplished without the support of the acquired company's management, and that the price of the shares may be cheaper than the value of the net assets acquired, including goodwill.

Disadvantages of obtaining control via share purchase are that there is no tax benefit to the acquiror as the result of the higher fair values of depreciable assets, that goodwill acquired by means of a purchase of shares is not tax deductible, and that control over the assets may be hampered by the existence of minority interests if not all of the acquiree's shares are purchased.

A purchase of shares may be accomplished by issuing shares of the acquiror in exchange for the acquiree's shares. The former shareholders of the acquiree then become shareholders of the acquiror. There are various ways of designing an exchange of shares, but regardless of the legal form of the transaction, the acquiror is that company whose pre-combination shareholders own a majority of the shares of the controlling corporation after the combination. An important advantage of buying shares with shares is that under the right circumstances, the exchange may be nontaxable to the selling shareholders until they sell the shares that they received in exchange.

Regardless of the way in which an acquisition of shares is accomplished, the accounting problem is to report the substance of the combination. Since control over net assets is obtained, the acquiror corporation prepares consolidated financial statements that include the acquiree's assets, liabilities, revenues, and expenses.

There are three basic methods by which consolidated statements can be prepared. The two variables are (1) the valuation of the parent's net assets on the consolidated statements and (2) the valuation of the subsidiary's net assets. If the assets and liabilities of both companies are reported at book values, then the pooling-of-interests method is being used. Since the pooling-of-interests method ignores the substance of most business combinations (i.e., that one company is buying control over another's net assets), the pooling-of-interests method is used in Canada only for those rare business combinations in which it is not possible to identify an acquiror.

If the assets and liabilities of both companies are reported at fair values, then the new-entity method is being used. The new-entity method has not been accepted in practice because of the practical problems associated with determining the parent's fair values, and because the added cost and subjectivity of the measurements have not been shown to yield any significant increase in the usefulness of the resultant consolidated financial statements.

The purchase method is the third method. Since the purchase of control through share acquisition accomplishes substantially the same result as does direct purchase of assets, Canadian practice calls for reporting the assets and liabilities of the acquired company at their fair values on the parent's consolidated statements, with recognition of purchased identifiable intangibles and goodwill. Thus the book values of the parent's net assets are combined with the fair values at the date of acquisition for the subsidiary's net assets. The result is similar to that obtained when the purchase of assets is direct. By requiring the use of the purchase method of reporting business combinations, Canadian practice avoids the spectre of having substantively similar purchase transactions reported in significantly different ways, depending on the legal form of the transaction.

Normally, the recorded carrying values of the acquired company's assets and liabilities are unaffected by the fair values assigned to those assets by the acquiror. Sometimes, however, the acquired company will record the fair values of its assets and liabilities directly on its books. This practice is generally restricted to those instances when substantially all of the acquiree's voting shares have been acquired by the acquiror and the acquiree has no other securities in the hands of the public. Push-down accounting creates a consistency of reporting between the consolidated statements and the separate-entity statements, and also simplifies the preparation of consolidated statements in subsequent reporting periods.

This chapter has illustrated the alternative approaches to consolidation of a purchased subsidiary on the date of acquisition. The method of reporting the acquired company's assets and liabilities on the parent's consolidated financial statements has important implications for consolidated reporting in subsequent periods. Chapter 8 discusses these reporting issues.

Both this chapter and the next look only at business combinations wherein the acquiror has obtained control over 100% of the voting shares of the acquiree. Other issues arise when the purchase is for more than 50% but less than 100%. These issues are discussed and illustrated in Chapters 9 and 10.

SELF-STUDY PROBLEM 7-1[18]

Ace Corporation acquired Blue Corporation on August 31, 19x4. Both corporations had fiscal years ending on August 31. Exhibit 1 contains a balance sheet for each corporation as of August 31, 19x4, immediately prior to the merger, and net income figures for each corporation for the fiscal year ended August 31, 19x4. You have obtained the following additional information as of the date of the merger:

1. The fair values of the assets and liabilities on August 31, 19x4, of Ace Corporation and Blue Corporation were as follows:

18 The solutions to the self-study problems are at the end of the book, following Chapter 18.

	Ace	Blue
Current assets	$ 4,950,000	$ 3,400,000
Plant and equipment (net)	22,000,000	14,000,000
Patents	570,000	360,000
Market research	150,000	40,000
Total assets	27,670,000	17,800,000
Liabilities	(2,650,000)	(2,100,000)
Net assets	$25,020,000	$15,700,000

2. Ace Corporation capitalized its fiscal year 19x4 market research costs and has always amortized them over five years beginning with the year of expenditure. All market research costs of Ace have been appropriately capitalized and amortized for the current and preceding years. Blue Corporation incurred $50,000 of market research costs that were expensed during the fiscal year ending August 31, 19x4. Blue will adopt Ace's method of accounting for market research costs.
3. Internally generated general expenses incurred because of the merger were $25,000 and are included in the current assets of Ace as a prepaid expense.
4. There were no intercompany transactions during the year.
5. Before the merger, Ace had 3,000,000 shares of common stock authorized, 1,200,000 shares issued, and 1,100,000 shares outstanding. Blue had 750,000 shares of common stock authorized, issued, and outstanding.

EXHIBIT 1		
Ace Corporation and Blue Corporation **August 31, 19x4**		
	Ace Corporation	Blue Corporation
Current assets	$ 4,350,000	$ 3,000,000
Plant and equipment (net)	18,500,000	11,300,000
Patents	450,000	200,000
Market research	150,000	—
Total assets	$23,450,000	$14,500,000
Liabilities	$ 2,650,000	$ 2,100,000
Common shares	16,200,000	6,950,000
Retained earnings	5,850,000	5,450,000
	24,700,000	14,500,000
Less treasury shares, at cost, 100,000 shares	1,250,000	—
Total liabilities and share equity	$23,450,000	$14,500,000
Net income (no extraordinary items) for fiscal year ended August 31, 19x4	$ 2,450,000	$ 1,300,000

Required:
Prepare the Ace Corporation balance sheet and determine the amount of net income under each of the following independent situations. Include explanations of adjustments.

a. Ace Corporation exchanged 400,000 shares of previously unissued common stock and 100,000 shares of treasury stock for all the outstanding common stock of Blue Corporation. The market value of Ace's shares was $40 per share.

b. Ace Corporation purchased the assets and assumed the liabilities of Blue Corporation by paying $3,100,000 cash and issuing debentures of $16,900,000 at face value.

(AICPA, adapted)

REVIEW QUESTIONS

7-1 Define the following terms:
   a. Business combination
   b. Purchase price discrepancy
   c. Negative goodwill
   d. Takeover
   e. Takeover bid
   f. Tender offer
   g. Exchange of shares
   h. Reverse takeover

7-2 Describe the two basic types of acquisition that can result in a business combination.

7-3 What are the forms of consideration that can be used in a business combination?

7-4 When one corporation buys the assets or assets and liabilities of another company, at what values are the acquired assets recorded on the buyer's books?

7-5 Does a direct purchase of assets constitute an intercorporate investment by the buying company?

7-6 P Ltd. has just purchased all of the assets of S Corp.'s automobile parts division. S Corp. had shut down the division the year before. Has a business combination occurred? Explain.

7-7 When an acquiror buys the net assets of another company by issuing shares, what is the relationship between the two companies after the transaction has taken place?

7-8 On what basis is the cost of a purchase of assets allocated?

7-9 What are the advantages for the acquiror of obtaining control over assets by a purchase of shares rather than by a direct purchase of assets?

7-10 What are the disadvantages for the acquiror of obtaining control by a purchase of shares?

7-11 For the acquiror, what is the difference in income tax treatment of goodwill acquired in a direct purchase of assets as compared to goodwill acquired in a purchase of shares?

7-12 How can an acquiror obtain control if the management of the acquiree is hostile to the business combination?

7-13 If an acquiror issues a tender offer, is it necessary for the offering company to buy all of the shares tendered?

7-14 From an income tax standpoint, what may be the disadvantages for an acquiror in obtaining control through a purchase of shares rather than by a direct purchase of net assets?

7-15 Company P issues its shares in exchange for the shares of Company S. After the exchange, who owns the newly issued shares of P?

7-16 In an exchange of shares, how can the acquiror be identified?

7-17 What is a statutory amalgamation?

7-18 In what form(s) of business combination do the combining companies cease to exist as separate legal entities?

7-19 When a business combination is executed via a purchase of shares, at what values are the assets and liabilities of the acquiree recorded on the books of the acquiror?

7-20 What may be the income tax advantages of

an exchange of shares to the shareholders who surrender their shares in exchange?

7-21 Briefly explain the difference between these three approaches to preparing consolidated financial statements:

a. Pooling-of-interests method
b. New-entity method
c. Purchase method

7-22 What is the logic underlying the use of pooling-of-interests reporting for a business combination?

7-23 How prevalent is pooling-of-interests reporting in Canada?

7-24 What is the essential characteristic that must be present in a business combination in order for it to be reported as a pooling of interests in Canada?

7-25 How does the treatment of pre-combination financial data differ under pooling-of-interests reporting as compared to purchase reporting for a business combination?

7-26 Why has the new-entity method not found acceptance in practice?

7-27 In general, how would fair values be determined for productive fixed assets?

7-28 What alternatives are there for measuring the fair values of long-term monetary assets and liabilities?

7-29 Income tax balances frequently arise on the balance sheet as a result of the difference between CCA for tax purposes and depreciation for reporting purposes. What impact should these income tax balances have on the fair valuation of the assets to which the balances relate?

7-30 To what extent must tax-loss carry-forwards be potentially realizable in order to assign a value to them as an asset acquired in a business combination?

7-31 Company P has 800,000 common shares outstanding. The shares are traded on the Montreal Exchange. The founders and managers of Company P hold 200,000 shares, and another 250,000 are held by institutional investors as long-term investments. P's board of directors has approved issuance of an additional 300,000 shares to acquire the net assets of Company S. What difficulties may arise in attempting to set a value on the newly issued shares in order to determine the cost of the acquisition?

7-32 Under what circumstances would a corporation be able to obtain control over the net assets of another corporation for less than the fair value of those net assets?

7-33 Define **push-down accounting**.

7-34 Under what circumstances is push-down accounting most likely to be used?

7-35 What is a **leveraged buyout**?

7-36 What are the risks associated with the modern form of a **leveraged buyout?**

Mark Corp.

CASE 7-1

On December 12, 1989, Mark Corp. owned 30% of the shares of Randy Ltd. Mark was by far the largest shareholder of Randy and most of Randy's directors were nominees of Mark. Randy Ltd. had a 70% owned subsidiary, Eric Inc., which in turn owned 50.1% of the voting shares of Jamie Ltd. Jamie Ltd. had an investment in 15% of the shares of Randy Ltd.

On December 13, 1989, Mark Corp. purchased another 19% of the shares of Randy Ltd., bringing Mark's total share of Randy's voting shares up to 49%.

Required:

Has a business combination occurred as a result of Mark Corp.'s acquisition of additional shares of Randy Ltd.? Explain.

Ames Brothers Ltd.

CASE 7-2

Ames Brothers, Ltd. (ABL) is a relatively small producer of petrochemicals located in Sarnia. The common shares of the firm are publicly traded on the Brampton stock exchange, while the nonvoting preferred shares are traded on the over-the-counter market. Because of the strategic competitive position of the firm, there was considerable recent interest in the shares of the company. During 19x9, much active trading occurred, pushing the price of the common shares from less than eight dollars to more than twenty dollars by the end of the year. Similarly, the trading interest in the preferred shares pushed the dividend yield from 12% to only 9%.

Shortly after the end of 19x9, three other firms made public announcements about the extent of their holdings in ABL shares. Silverman Mines announced that they had acquired, on the open market, 32% of the common shares of ABL; Hislop Industries announced that they had acquired 24% of ABL's common shares in a private transaction with an individual who had previously been ABL's major shareholder; and Render Resources announced that they had accumulated a total of 58% of ABL's preferred shares.

However, Silverman Mines and Hislop Industries are not unrelated. The Patterson Power Corporation owns 72% of the voting shares of Hislop Mines and 38% of the voting shares of Silverman Mines. There are no other large holdings of stock of either Silverman or Hislop. Render Resources is not related to either Silverman, Hislop, or Patterson.

Required:
a. Has a business combination occurred in 19x9, with respect to ABL, as the term "business combination" is used in the context of the *CICA Handbook* recommendations? Explain fully.
b. What implications do the various accumulations of ABL shares have for the financial reporting (for 19x9 and following years) for:

   1. Silverman Mines
   2. Hislop Industries
   3. Render Resources
   4. Patterson Power Corporation

CASE 7-3   Baar Inc. and Spencer Ltd.

Baar Inc. and Spencer Ltd. are both public companies incorporated under the *Canada Business Corporations Act*. The common shares of Baar have been selling in a range of $30 to $43 per share over the past year, with recent prices in the area of $33. Spencer's common shares have been selling at between $18 and $23; recently the price has been hovering around $20.

The two companies are in related lines of business. In view of the increasing exposure of the companies to world competition arising from the reduction in tariff barriers, the boards of directors have approved an agreement in principle to combine the two businesses. The boards have also agreed that the combination should take the form of a share exchange, with one share of Baar equivalent to two shares of Spencer in the exchange.

The manner of executing the combination has not yet been decided. Three possibilities are under consideration:

1. Baar could issue one new share in exchange for two of Spencer's shares.
2. Spencer could issue two new shares in exchange for each of Baar's shares.
3. A new corporation could be formed, BS Enterprise Inc., which would issue one share in exchange for each share of Spencer and two shares in exchange for each share of Baar.

The directors are uncertain as to the accounting implications of the three alternatives. They believe that the fair values of the assets and liabilities of both companies are approximately equal to their book values, but are uncertain about the treatment of future income taxes. They have asked you to prepare a report in which you explain how the accounting results would differ under the three share exchange alternatives, and how the results would be affected by the inclusion or exclusion of the future income taxes in the fair value determination. They have provided you with the condensed balance sheets of both companies. Baar Inc. presently has 1,600,000 common shares outstanding, and Spencer Ltd. has 1,200,000 shares outstanding.

Required:
Prepare the report requested by the boards of directors.

Condensed Balance Sheets

	Baar Inc.	Spencer Ltd.
Current assets	$ 7,000,000	$ 4,500,000
Fixed assets	63,000,000	22,500,000
	$70,000,000	$27,000,000
Current liabilities	$ 6,000,000	$ 1,500,000
Long-term debt	11,000,000	3,000,000
Future income taxes	3,000,000	2,500,000
Common shares	17,000,000	16,000,000
Retained earnings	33,000,000	4,000,000
	$70,000,000	$27,000,000

Asgar Inc.   CASE 7-4

Asgar Inc. has just acquired control of Casao Ltd. by buying 100% of the Casao outstanding shares for $6,500,000 cash. The condensed balance sheet for Casao on the date of acquisition is shown below.

In order to account for the acquisition, Asgar's management has had all of Casao's major productive assets appraised by two separate, independent engineering consultants. One consultant appraised the productive assets at $7,800,000 in their present state. The other consultant arrived at a lower figure of $7,100,000, based on the assumption that technological changes were imminent that would soon decrease the value-in-use of Casao's productive assets by about 10%.

The asset for leased building is the discounted present value of the remaining lease payments on a warehouse that Casao leased to Asgar Inc. five years ago. The lease is noncancellable and title to the building will transfer to Asgar at the end of the lease term. The lease has fifteen years yet to run, and the annual lease payments are $500,000 per year. The interest rate implicit in the lease was 9%.

Casao's debentures are thinly traded on the open market. Recent sales have indicated that the bonds are currently yielding about 14%. The bonds mature ten years hence.

The future income tax balance is the accumulated balance of CCA/depreciation timing differences. The management of Casao sees no likelihood of the balance being reduced in the foreseeable future, because projected capital expenditures will enter the CCA classes in amounts that will more than offset the timing difference reversals for the older assets.

The book value of Casao's inventory appears to approximate replacement cost. However, an overstock of some items of finished goods may require temporary price reductions of about 10% in order to reduce inventory to more manageable levels.

Required:

How should Asgar Inc. value the net assets acquired for purposes of preparing consolidated financial statements? Discuss any alternative valuations that are feasible.

Casao Ltd.
Condensed Balance Sheet

Cash	$ 200,000
Accounts receivable	770,000
Inventories	1,000,000
Productive assets (net)	5,000,000
Leased building	4,030,000
	$11,000,000
Accounts payable	$ 300,000
8% Debentures payable	7,000,000
Future income taxes	700,000
Common shares	1,000,000
Retained earnings	2,000,000
	$11,000,000

CASE 7-5   **Greymac Credit Corp.**

In October, 1982, Greymac Credit Corporation purchased 54% of the shares of Crown Trust Co. from Canwest Capital Corporation at $62 per share. Greymac Credit was a private investment company controlled by Leonard Rosenberg, a Toronto mortgage broker. Greymac also negotiated a purchase of another 32% of Crown Trust shares from BNA Realty Ltd. at a somewhat lower price. BNA Realty had purchased its block of Crown Trust shares only a few weeks earlier, but BNA's ownership was being challenged by the Ontario Securities Commission because "the regulators had alleged that Mr. Burnett [who controlled BNA Realty] was unfit to hold what amounted to veto control over the affairs of Crown."[19] The two purchases of blocks of Crown Trust shares, in addition to other shares already held by Greymac, gave Greymac 97% of the shares of Crown Trust. Greymac was expected to make an offer for the remaining minority shares.

A little earlier in 1982, Greymac Credit Corporation had arranged a deal to purchase most of Cadillac Fairview Corporation's Toronto-area apartment buildings. The purchase involved some 10,931 apartments in 68 buildings, and was in line with Cadillac-Fairview's intention of leaving the residential housing market.

Required:
a. Had business combinations occurred with respect to Greymac's purchase of (1) the Crown Trust shares and (2) the Cadillac-Fairview apartments?
b. How could the OSC view a 32% minority interest as having "veto control?"

CASE 7-6   **Sudair Ltd.**

On February 7, 1989, Sudair Ltd. and Albertair Ltd. jointly announced a merger of the two regional airlines. Sudair had assets totaling $500 million and had one mil-

19 Jack Willoughby, "Rosenberg Gets 97% Control of Crown Trust," *Globe and Mail* (October 9, 1982), p. B15.

lion common shares outstanding. Albertair had assets amounting to $400 million and 600,000 shares outstanding. Under the terms of the merger, Sudair will issue two new Sudair shares in exchange for each share of Alberair outstanding. The two companies will then merge their administrative and operating structures and will coordinate their routes and schedules to improve interchange between the two lines and to enable the combined fleet of nine jet aircraft to be more efficiently used. Both companies are publicly owned.

Required:
How should the merger of Sudair and Albertair be reported?

P7-1

Company P and Company S have reached agreement in principle to combine their operations. However, the boards of directors are undecided as to the best way to accomplish the combination. Several alternatives are under consideration:

1. P acquires the net assets of S (including the liabilities) for $1,000,000 cash.
2. P acquires all of the assets of S (but not the liabilities) for $1,400,000 cash.
3. P acquires the net assets of S by issuing 60,000 shares in P, valued at $1,000,000.
4. P acquires all of the shares of S by exchanging them for 60,000 newly issued shares in P, valued at $1,000,000.

The current, condensed balance sheets of P and of S are attached. Prior to the combination, P has 240,000 shares outstanding and S has 30,000 shares outstanding.

Required:
a. In a comparative, columnar format, show how the consolidated balance sheet of P would appear immediately after the combination under each of the four alternatives using the purchase method.
b. For each of the four alternatives, briefly state who owns the shares of each corporation and whether P and S are related companies.

Condensed Balance Sheets, P Co. and S Co.
(in thousands of dollars)

	P Co.		S Co.	
	Balance sheet	Fair values	Balance sheet	Fair values
Current assets	$ 2,000	$ 2,000	$ 300	$300
Fixed assets	8,000	10,000	400	700
Investments	—	—	300	200
	$10,000		$1,000	
Current liabilities	$ 1,000	1,000	100	100
Long-term liabilities	4,000	4,000	400	300
Future income taxes	1,000	1,000	100	—
Common shares	1,000	10,000	200	900
Retained earnings	3,000		200	
	$10,000		$1,000	

P7-2

North Ltd. acquired 100% of the voting shares of South Ltd. In exchange, North Ltd. issued 50,000 common shares, with a market value of $10 per share to the common shareholders of South Ltd. Both companies have a December 31 year-end, and this transaction occurred on December 31, 19x4. The outstanding preferred shares of South Ltd. did not change hands. The call price of the South Ltd. preferred shares is equal to their book value.

Following are the balance sheets of the two companies at December 31, 19x4, before the transactions took place:

Balance Sheets
December 31, 19x4

	North Ltd.		South Ltd.	
	Book Value	Fair Market Value	Book Value	Fair Market Value
Current assets	$ 250,000	$300,000	$210,000	$260,000
Fixed assets, net	850,000	720,000	780,000	860,000
Goodwill	110,000		—	
Total assets	$1,210,000		$990,000	
Current liabilities	$ 200,000	$190,000	$165,000	$185,000
Long-term liabilities	400,000	420,000	200,000	230,000
Preferred shares	—		270,000	270,000
Common shares	300,000		100,000	
Retained earnings	310,000		255,000	
Total liabilities	$1,210,000		$990,000	

Required:

Prepare the consolidated balance sheet for the date of acquisition, December 31, 19x4, under each of the following methods:

(a) Pooling of interests
(b) Purchase
(c) New entity

[CGA-Canada, adapted]

P7-3

On December 31, 19x1, the balance sheets of the Dee Company and the Sor Company are as follows:

	Dee Company	Sor Company
Cash	$ 500,000	$ 800,000
Accounts receivable	1,500,000	1,700,000
Inventories	2,000,000	1,500,000
Plant and equipment (net)	2,500,000	4,000,000
Total assets	$6,500,000	$8,000,000

Current liabilities	$ 700,000	$ 400,000
Long-term liabilities	800,000	500,000
Common shares	2,500,000	1,000,000
Contributed surplus	800,000	1,500,000
Retained earnings	1,700,000	4,600,000
Total equities	$6,500,000	$8,000,000

Dee Company has 100,000 shares of common stock outstanding, and the Sor Company has 45,000 shares outstanding. On January 1, 19x2, the Dee Company issues an additional 90,000 shares of its common stock to the Sor Company in return for all of the assets and liabilities of that company. The Sor Company distributes the Dee Company common stock to its shareholders in return for their outstanding common stock, and ceases to exist as a separate legal entity. At the time of this transaction the cash, accounts receivable, inventories, and current liabilities of both companies have fair values equal to their carrying values. The plant and equipment and long-term liabilities have fair values as follows:

	Dee Company	Sor Company
Plant and equipment (net)	$2,900,000	$4,300,000
Long-term liabilities	1,500,000	400,000

The plant and equipment of both companies has a remaining useful life of nine years on December 31, 19x1, and the long-term liabilities of both companies mature on December 31, 19x9. Goodwill, if any, is to be amortized over 30 years.

For the year ending December 31, 19x1, the Dee Company, as a separate company, has a net income of $980,000. The corresponding figure for the Sor Company is $720,000. On December 31, 19x1, the shares of the Dee Company are trading at $90 per share. Prior to the dissolution of the company, the shares of the Sor Company are trading at $202.50 per share.

Required:

Assume that this business combination is to be accounted for by the fair-value purchase method of accounting for business combinations. Prepare the balance sheet at January 1, 19x2, for each company, after the purchase but before the dissolution of Sor Company.
[SMA, adapted]

P7-4

On December 31, 19x5, Retail Ltd. purchased 100% of the outstanding shares of Supply Corporation by issuing Retail Ltd. shares worth $760,000 at current market prices. Supply Corporation was a supplier of merchandise to Retail Ltd.; Retail had purchased over 80% of Supply's total output in 19x5. Supply had experienced declining profitability for many years, and in 19x3 began experiencing losses. By December 31, 19x5, Supply had accumulated tax-loss carry-forwards amounting to $280,000. In contrast, Retail Ltd. was quite profitable, and analysts predicted that Retail's positioning in the retail market was well suited to weather economic downturns without undue deterioration in profit levels.

The balance sheet for Supply Corporation at the date of acquisition is shown below, together with estimates of the fair values of Supply's recorded assets and liabilities. In addition, Supply held exclusive Canadian rights to certain Swedish production processes; the fair value of these rights was estimated to be $200,000.

Required:
Explain what values should be assigned to Supply Corporation's assets and liabilities when Retail Ltd. prepares its consolidated financial statements (including goodwill, if any).

Supply Corporation

	Balance sheet December 31, 19x5		Fair values
Current assets:			
Cash	$ 10,000		$ 10,000
Accounts receivable (net)	30,000		30,000
Inventories	110,000		100,000
		$150,000	
Plant, property, and equipment:			
Buildings	500,000		400,000
Machinery and equipment	400,000		270,000
Accumulated depreciation	(350,000)		
	550,000		
Land	100,000		260,000
	650,000		
Investments in shares	100,000		110,000
Total assets		$900,000	
Current liabilities:			
Accounts payable	$ 50,000		50,000
Unearned revenue	160,000		140,000
Current portion of long-term debt	90,000		90,000
		$300,000	
Bonds payable		200,000	180,000
Shareholders' equity:			
Common shares	150,000		
Retained earnings	250,000		
		400,000	
Total liabilities and shareholders' equity		$900,000	

P7-5

Askill Corporation (Askill), a corporation continued under the *Canada Business Corporations Act*, has concluded negotiations with the Basket Corporation (Basket) for the purchase of all of Basket's assets at fair market value, effective January 1, 19x3. An examination at that date by independent experts disclosed that the fair market value of Basket's inventories was $150,000; the fair market valve of its machinery and equipment was $160,000. The original cost of the machinery and equipment was $140,000 and its unclaimed capital cost at December 31, 19x2, was $110,000. It was determined that accounts receivable were fairly valued at book value.

Basket held 1,000 common shares of Askill and the fair market value of these shares was $62,000. This value corresponds with the value of Askill's common shares in the open market and is deemed to hold for transactions involving a substantially large number of shares.

The purchase agreement provides that the total purchase price of all assets will be $490,000, payable as follows:

1. The current liabilities of Basket would be assumed at their book value.
2. The Basket debenture debt would be settled at its current value in a form acceptable to Basket debenture holders.
3. Askill shares held by Basket and acquired by Askill as a result of the transaction would be subsequently returned to Basket at fair market value as part of the consideration.
4. Askill holds 1,000 shares of Basket and these would be returned to Basket. The value to be ascribed to these shares is 1/10 of the total purchase price of all assets stated above ($490,000) less the current value of its liabilities.
5. The balance of the purchase consideration is to be entirely in Askill common shares, except for a possible fractional share element that would be paid in cash.

The Basket debenture holders, who are neither shareholders of Askill nor Basket, have agreed to accept face value of newly issued Askill bonds equal to the current value of the Basket bonds. The Basket debentures are currently yielding 10%. The Askill bonds carry a 10% coupon and trade at par.

Basket, upon conclusion of the agreement, would be wound up. The balance sheets of both corporations, as at date of implementation of the purchase agreement (January 1, 19x3), are as follows:

	Askill Corp.	Basket Corp.
Cash	$ 100,000	$ —
Accounts receivable	288,000	112,000
Inventories at cost	250,000	124,000
Investment in Basket (1,000 shares)	20,000	—
Investment in Askill (1,000 shares)	—	40,000
Machinery and equipment — net	412,000	100,000
Total assets	$1,070,000	$376,000
Current liabilities	$ 60,000	$ 35,000
7% debentures due Dec. 31, 19x7 (Note 1)	—	100,000
10% bonds due Dec. 31, 19x7 (Note 1)	500,000	—
Premium on bonds	20,000	—
Capital — common shares (Note 2)	200,000	100,000
Retained earnings	290,000	141,000
Total liabilities and shareholders' equity	$1,070,000	$376,000

Note 1 — Interest is paid annually.
Note 2 — Each company has issued 10,000 shares.
Both corporations have fiscal years that are identical to the calendar year.

Required:

a. Prepare Askill's pro-forma balance sheet at January 1, 19x3.
b. Draft a note to the 19x3 Askill financial statements disclosing the purchase of Basket's net assets.
c. Prepare Basket's pro-forma balance sheet at January 1, 19x3, following the exchange but before winding up.

[CICA, adapted]

P7-6

Par Ltd. purchased 100% of the voting shares of Sub Ltd. for $1,100,000 on October 1, 19x7. The balance sheet of Sub Ltd. at that date was:

Sub Ltd.
October 1, 19x7

	Net Book Value	Fair Market Value
Cash	$ 200,000	$ 200,000
Receivables	310,000	270,000
Inventory	560,000	650,000
Fixed assets, net	1,320,000	1,020,000
	$2,390,000	
Current liabilities	$ 240,000	$ 270,000
Preferred shares (Note 1)	800,000	
Common shares	300,000	
Retained earnings	1,050,000	
	$2,390,000	

Notes to Financial Statements:

Note 1:
The preferred shares are cumulative, pay dividends of $4 per year (or $1 per quarter at the end of quarter) and have a call (redemption) premium of $1 per share. There are 100,000 preferred shares outstanding and they are nonparticipating.

Required:
Prepare the eliminating entry(ies) required *at the date of acquisition.*
[CGA-Canada, adapted]

P7-7

On December 31, 19x7, Prager Limited acquired 100% of the outstanding voting shares of Sabre Limited for $2 million in cash; 75% of the cash was obtained by issuing a five-year note payable. The balance sheets of Prager and Sabre and the fair values of Sabre's identifiable assets and liabilities immediately before the acquisition transaction were as follows:

	Prager Limited	Sabre Limited BV	Sabre Limited FV
Assets:			
Cash	$ 800,000	$ 100,000	$ 100,000
Accounts receivable	500,000	300,000	300,000
Inventory	600,000	600,000	662,500
Land	900,000	800,000	900,000
Buildings and equipment	6,000,000	1,400,000	1,200,000
Accumulated depreciation	(2,950,000)	(400,000)	
Patents	—	200,000	150,000
	$ 5,850,000	$3,000,000	

Liabilities and shareholders' equity:			
Accounts payable	$ 1,000,000	$ 500,000	$ 500,000
Long-term debt	2,000,000	1,000,000	900,000
Common shares	1,500,000	950,000	
Retained earnings	1,350,000	550,000	
	$ 5,850,000	$3,000,000	

Required:
Prepare the consolidated balance sheet for Prager Limited immediately following the acquisition of Sabre Limited.
[SMA, adapted]

8

Wholly Owned Subsidiaries: Reporting Subsequent to Acquisition

In the last chapter, we introduced the principal alternative approaches to the preparation of consolidated financial statements for an acquired subsidiary. We focused on consolidation at the date of acquisition in order to illustrate the essential characteristics of the different approaches.

The date of acquisition is the easiest date upon which to perform a consolidation, since only the balance sheet needs to be dealt with. However, the date of acquisition occurs only once, and consolidated statements are seldom prepared on that date for external reporting although they may be prepared on a pro-forma basis. Consolidated financial statements must thenceforth be prepared subsequent to the date of acquisition, and after revenues have been generated and expenses incurred. This chapter focuses on the preparation of financial statements for periods subsequent to the parent's acquisition of the shares of the subsidiary, or after the formation of a parent-founded subsidiary. In this chapter, as in the illustration given in Chapters 6 and 7, we deal only with subsidiaries that are wholly owned by the parent.

A. CONSOLIDATION ONE YEAR AFTER ACQUISITION

In order to illustrate the process of consolidation one year after the parent has bought control of a subsidiary, assume that on January 1, 19x1, Investor Ltd. (IOR) purchased all of the outstanding shares of Investee Ltd. (IEE) by issuing 40,000 new shares of IOR in exchange for the shares of IEE. The newly issued IOR shares had a market value of $30 per share, resulting in a total cost of the purchase of $1,200,000. The total cost was apportioned to the fair values of IEE's assets and liabilities and to goodwill *at the date of acquisition* as shown in Schedule 8-1. These fair values and goodwill are the same amounts as were used in the illustration in the previous chapter.

The unconsolidated trial balances for IOR and IEE are shown in Schedule

8-2. We have assumed that IOR *records* its investment in IEE on the cost basis in its accounts, as is usually the case. When preparing unconsolidated financial statements, however, IOR would *report* its investment on the equity basis; adjustment to the equity basis for reporting purposes will be discussed

---

SCHEDULE 8-1

Acquisition of IEE's Shares by IOR
January 1, 19x1

	Book Value	Fair Value	Fair-value increment
Cash	$ 50,000	$ 50,000	—
Accounts receivable	150,000	150,000	—
Inventory	50,000	50,000	—
Land	300,000	400,000	$100,000
Buildings and equipment	500,000 ⎱	550,000	200,000
Accumulated depreciation	(150,000) ⎰		
Accounts payable	(100,000)	(100,000)	—
Total	$ 800,000	1,100,000	300,000
Purchase price		1,200,000	
Goodwill		$ 100,000	100,000
Excess of cost over net book value of net assets acquired			$400,000

SCHEDULE 8-2

Trial Balances, December 31, 19x1
Dr. (Cr.)

	IOR	IEE
Cash	$ 980,000	$ 97,500
Accounts receivable	2,200,000	250,000
Inventory	250,000	70,000
Land	1,000,000	300,000
Buildings and equipment	3,000,000	500,000
Accumulated depreciation	(1,300,000)	(167,500)
Investment in IEE (at cost)	1,200,000	—
Accounts payable	(800,000)	(200,000)
Future income taxes	(400,000)	—
Common shares	(3,800,000)	(200,000)
Retained earnings (January 1, 19x1)	(2,000,000)	(600,000)
Dividends paid	—	30,000
Sales	(2,400,000)	(300,000)
Cost of goods sold	1,750,000	180,000
Depreciation expense	100,000	17,500
Income tax expense	200,000	20,000
Other expenses	50,000	2,500
Dividend income (from IEE)	(30,000)	—
	$ 0	$ 0

in a later section of this chapter. Additional information relevant to the preparation of consolidated statements is as follows:

1. IEE's buildings and equipment have an estimated remaining useful life from the date of acquisition of IEE by IOR of twenty years, and will be depreciated on the straight-line basis.
2. IOR will amortize goodwill over a 40-year period (the maximum permitted), on the straight-line basis.
3. During 19x1, IEE had sales totaling $55,000 to IOR. The cost of goods sold by IEE to IOR was $33,000, for a gross margin of 40% on sales.
4. On December 31, 19x1, $20,000 of the goods purchased by IOR from IEE were still in IOR's inventory.
5. During 19x1, IEE declared and paid dividends totaling $30,000. As IOR was the sole shareholder of IEE after January 1, 19x1, all of the dividends were received by IOR and were recorded (in keeping with the cost method) as dividend income by IOR.

Adjustments and Eliminations

Acquisition Adjustment

The first adjustment that must be made towards the preparation of consolidated statements for IOR is the adjustment for the initial acquisition of IEE's shares by IOR. This adjustment is the same as is made in the last chapter in preparing the date-of-acquisition consolidated balance sheet:

(1)	Land	$100,000	
	Buildings and equipment	50,000	
	Accumulated depreciation	150,000	
	Goodwill	100,000	
	Common shares	200,000	
	Retained earnings	600,000	
	Investment in IEE		$1,200,000

The acquisition adjustment does three things. First, it adjusts the carrying values of IEE's net assets to their fair values at the date of acquisition, and establishes the amount of goodwill. These amounts are derived from Schedule 8-1. Second, the adjustment eliminates IEE's common shares and retained earnings at the date of acquisition, since these are not a part of the shareholders' equity of IOR, and should not appear on a balance sheet that is reporting to IOR's shareholders. And third, the entry eliminates the investment account on IOR's trial balance. The investment account, as we discuss earlier, is being replaced on consolidated statements by the detailed asset and liability accounts of the subsidiary.

When IOR's consolidated balance sheet was prepared on the date of acquisition, only the above adjustment was necessary. But now that some time has elapsed since the acquisition, additional adjustments are necessary for amortization and for intercompany transactions and balances. These adjustments are described in the following two sections.

Amortization of Fair-Value Increments and Goodwill

If IOR had purchased the assets and liabilities of IEE directly, the assets would have been recorded on IOR's books at their fair values, and the goodwill would also have been recorded. Subsequent accounting for the assets acquired would have been in accordance with IOR's accounting policies for the depreciation of fixed assets and the amortization of goodwill. Since the buildings and equipment acquired had a fair value of $550,000 and an estimated remaining useful life of twenty years, these newly acquired assets would have been depreciated at the rate of $27,500 per year over the twenty years following acquisition.

In fact, however, the assets and liabilities were not acquired directly and thus were not recorded on IOR's books. Instead, the buildings and equipment of IEE remain on IEE's books at a net carrying value of $350,000 at the date of acquisition of IEE's shares by IOR. As a result, IEE has taken depreciation of only $17,500 on its books, as can be verified by looking at IEE's trial balance on Schedule 8-2. The difference of $200,000 between the net book value and the fair value of buildings and equipment is recognized only upon consolidation. Since the purpose of the purchase method of preparing consolidated financial statements is to recognize the **substance** of the transaction as a purchase of control over assets and liabilities, the consolidated statements should reflect the same information as would be obtained had the assets been purchased directly. Therefore, it is necessary to amortize or depreciate the $200,000 fair-value increment for the buildings and equipment to recognize the using up of the assets acquired. Assuming a twenty-year remaining useful life, the adjustment for amortization would be one-twentieth of the $200,000 fair-value increment, or $10,000 per year. For December 31, 19x1, the adjustment would be as follows:

(2a) Depreciation expense $10,000
           Accumulated depreciation $10,000

Similarly, the goodwill must be amortized. In theory, goodwill should be amortized over the expected period of above-average returns from the investment. In practice, goodwill is amortized over a period not exceeding 40 years in accordance with the *CICA Handbook* [para. 1580.58]. If IOR's policy is to use the forty-year period, then the annual amortization would be $2,500:

(2b) Amortization expense $ 2,500
           Goodwill $ 2,500

Each year, the unamortized amount of goodwill shown on the consolidated balance sheet will decline by $2,500.

Intercompany Transactions and Balances

During the year, IEE sold goods to IOR. Sales by a subsidiary to its parent are known as **upstream** sales, while sales by a parent to its subsidiary are called **downstream** sales. When consolidated financial statements are prepared, all such intercompany sales must be eliminated in order to avoid double-counting. To illustrate this point, assume for the moment that all of the $55,000 of upstream sales in 19x1 were sold by IOR to third parties outside the consolidated enterprise for $80,000. The books of IEE and IOR would show the following (recall that IEE sold the goods to IOR at a 40% gross margin on sales):

	IEE	IOR
Sales	$55,000	$80,000
Cost of sales	33,000	55,000
Gross margin	$22,000	$25,000

For the consolidated entity as a whole, the sales amounted to the $80,000 sold by IOR to outsiders, and the cost of sales was the $33,000 cost to IEE. Consolidated gross margin is the difference between these two amounts, $80,000 minus $33,000, or $47,000. To avoid showing sales as $135,000 and cost of sales as $88,000 on the consolidated income statement, the intercompany sales must be eliminated as follows:

Sales	$55,000	
Cost of sales		$55,000

However, if IOR has not sold all of the inventory acquired from IEE, then an additional adjustment is necessary because the ending inventory of IOR includes goods that are carried at the price sold to IOR by IEE rather than at the cost to the consolidated entity. In this example, we are assuming that $20,000 of the goods remain in IOR's ending inventory. Goods sold by IEE to IOR for $20,000 would include a gross profit to IEE of 40% of that amount, or $8,000. Therefore, IOR's ending inventory includes goods that cost $20,000 to IOR as a separate entity, but that cost only $12,000 to the consolidated entity; unrealized profit of $8,000 must be eliminated from the consolidated ending inventory.

Since the ending inventory is subtracted from purchases plus beginning inventory to determine the cost of goods sold, the inclusion of $8,000 of unrealized profit in the ending inventory causes the cost of goods sold to be understated by $8,000. Therefore, the adjustment to eliminate the unrealized profit from the ending inventory also adjusts the cost of sales on the consolidated working papers:

Cost of sales	$ 8,000	
Inventory		$ 8,000

The two preceding adjustments, to eliminate the intercompany sales and to eliminate the unrealized profit, can be combined into a single entry on the consolidation working papers:

(2c)	Sales	$55,000	
	Cost of sales		$47,000
	Inventory		8,000

The final adjustment that must be made before the consolidated financial statements are prepared eliminates the intercompany payment of dividends:

(2d)	Dividend income	$30,000	
	Dividends paid		$30,000

This adjustment is based on the fact that in our example, IOR is recording its investment in IEE on the cost basis; the dividends received by IOR have been credited to dividend income and must be eliminated. Similarly, the credit to dividends paid is based on a scrutiny of the IEE balance sheet in Schedule 8-2, which reveals that IEE debits that account when dividends are declared. If IEE's debit had been directly to retained earnings, then the credit in the elimination entry would be to retained earnings.

If there had been any other intercompany transactions during the period, they would also have to be eliminated. For example, intercompany interest payments or accruals, lease payments, management fees, or royalty fees would be eliminated, along with any outstanding intercompany receivables and payables.

One final note: each corporation is taxed as a separate entity. As a result, IEE will be taxed on its earnings, including the profit on the sales to IOR that are still unrealized by the consolidated entity at year-end. The elimination of the unrealized profit will therefore have implications for the consolidated income tax expense. For simplicity, we will ignore this tax effect for the time being. We will, however, introduce the tax implications of unrealized profit (in a slightly different context) in part B of this chapter.

Schedule 8-3 illustrates the consolidation worksheet for IOR for 19x1. For greater clarity, we have provided separate adjustments columns for (1) the acquisition adjustment and (2) the adjustments and eliminations relating to the transactions and adjustments for 19x1 (operations). Different worksheet layouts are feasible, as is a direct approach; the form is irrelevant, as long as it enables you to keep track of what you are doing! The consolidated financial statements for IOR will be prepared from the final column of Schedule 8-3. We will illustrate the statements themselves after the next section, on equity-basis reporting.

SCHEDULE 8-3

IOR Consolidation Worksheets
December 31, 19x1
Dr. (Cr.)

	Trial balances		Adjustments		IOR consolidated trial balance
	IOR	IEE	(1) Acquisition	(2) Operations	
Cash	$ 980,000	$ 97,500			$ 1,077,500
Accounts receivable	2,200,000	250,000			2,450,000
Inventory	250,000	70,000		$ (8,000)c	312,000
Land	1,000,000	300,000	$ 100,000		1,400,000
Buildings and equipment	3,000,000	500,000	50,000		3,550,000
Accumulated depreciation	(1,300,000)	(167,500)	150,000	(10,000)a	(1,327,500)
Investment in IEE (at cost)	1,200,000		(1,200,000)		—
Goodwill			100,000	(2,500)b	97,500
Accounts payable	(800,000)	(200,000)			(1,000,000)
Future income taxes	(400,000)				(400,000)
Common shares	(3,800,000)	(200,000)	200,000		(3,800,000)
Retained earnings (1-1-19x1)	(2,000,000)	(600,000)	600,000		(2,000,000)
Dividends paid	—	30,000		(30,000)d	—
Sales	(2,400,000)	(300,000)		55,000 c	(2,645,000)
Cost of sales	1,750,000	180,000		(47,000)c	1,883,000
Depreciation expense	100,000	17,500		10,000 a	127,500
Income tax expense	200,000	20,000			220,000
Other expenses	500,000	2,500			52,500
Dividend income	(30,000)			30,000 d	—
Amortization expense				2,500 b	2,500
	$ 0	$ 0	$ 0	$ 0	$ 0

Equity-Basis Reporting of Unconsolidated Subsidiaries

In Chapter 6, we discussed the reporting of subsidiaries and emphasized that in the vast majority of cases, a parent company will consolidate its subsidiaries when preparing its financial statements. In some instances, however, a subsidiary will not be consolidated but will be reported by application of the equity method of accounting. In addition, the parent may prepare unconsolidated statements as well as consolidated statements. We have already emphasized that the information content of consolidated statements may not be adequate for the needs of some of the parent's stakeholders, such as creditors. If IOR prepares unconsolidated financial statements as well as consolidated statements, then the investment in IEE must be reported on the equity basis.

When the equity method of reporting is used, the parent corporation includes in its net income the parent's share of the subsidiary's earnings. The 19x1 net income after taxes of IEE can be determined from Schedule 8-2 as being $80,000: sales revenue of $300,000 less expenses totaling $220,000.

Using the equity method, the $80,000 net income will be reported (after adjustment) in the income statement of IOR as a single amount, rather than by combining the individual revenue and expense amounts of IEE with those of IOR, as is the result of consolidation.

The IEE net income cannot be reported by IOR simply at $80,000, because to do so would ignore the substance of the purchase transaction. Since IOR has purchased control over the assets and liabilities of IEE, the earnings of IEE must be reported in IOR's statements *as though the net assets of IEE had been purchased directly by IOR*. If the assets and liabilities had been purchased directly, then they would have been recorded at their fair values, and goodwill of $100,000 would have been recorded. The fair values and the goodwill would have been depreciated or amortized, and any transactions between the IEE division and the rest of the company would not appear on the financial statements of IOR. In other words, it is necessary to adjust the earnings of IEE to reflect *all of the same adjustments that would have been made had IEE been consolidated.*

Schedule 8-4 shows the computation of the adjusted earnings of IEE. Starting with the IEE reported net income of $80,000, deductions are made for (a) depreciation of the fair-value increment on buildings and equipment, (b) amortization of goodwill, and (c) elimination of the unrealized profit on intercompany sales. The adjusted IEE earnings then amount to $59,500. Since IOR owns 100% of the shares of IEE, IOR will report this entire amount on IOR's income statement as equity in the earnings of Investee Ltd. Since the IEE earnings are after-tax earnings, the equity in earnings would be shown as an addition to IOR's separate-entity after-tax net income.

Part B of Schedule 8-4 summarizes the impact of the equity method on the investment account. The year-end balance of $1,229,500 will be reported on IOR's unconsolidated balance sheet. The investment account reflects (1) the cost of the investment plus (2) the cumulative amount of unremitted adjusted earnings since the date of acquisition.

The adjustments made to IEE's net income are made only for reporting on *IOR's* statements. IEE would still report net income of $80,000 on its own separate-entity financial statements. IOR may choose to record the equity-basis earnings of IEE in its accounts, in which case the adjustment would appear as follows:

SCHEDULE 8-4

Equity Basis of Reporting IOR's Investment in IEE Year Ended December 31, 19x1	
A. EQUITY IN EARNINGS OF IEE:	
IEE earnings as reported by IEE	$ 80,000
Adjustments:	
(a) Depreciation of fair-value increment on buildings and equipment: 5% per year	− 10,000
(b) Amortization of goodwill: 2.5% per year	− 2,500
(c) Elimination of unrealized profit on upstream sales on goods still in IOR inventory	− 8,000
Adjusted IEE earnings, equity basis	$ 59,500
B. INVESTMENT IN IEE:	
Cost of investment in IEE, January 1, 19x1	$1,200,000
IOR's share of 19x1 earnings of IEE, equity basis	59,500
Dividends received from IEE	− 30,000
Balance, investment in IEE, December 31, 19x1	$1,229,500

Investment in IEE	$59,500	
Equity in earnings of IEE		$59,500

The credit to the income statement account is offset by a debit to increase the investment account. When IEE declares dividends, the declaration would then be recorded as follows:

Dividends receivable	$30,000	
Investment in IEE		$30,000

When the dividends are paid, the entry would debit cash and credit the dividends receivable account.

However, it is not necessary for IOR to *record* its investment in IEE on the equity basis, even though it would *report* the investment on the equity basis. As we have emphasized previously, the reporting for intercorporate investments involves adjustments that are either not, or may not be, recorded on the investor's books: consolidation adjustments are never recorded on the books, and equity-basis adjustments may or may not be recorded on the investor's books. As a bookkeeping convenience, it is most common for the investment account to be maintained by the investor on the cost basis, even though reporting is by consolidation or is on the equity basis.

Now that we have illustrated the adjustments that are necessary in order for IOR to report its investment in IEE, we can examine the resulting financial statements for IOR. Schedule 8-5 shows the balance sheet and income statement for IOR for the year ended December 31, 19x1. The first column shows the results of reporting IEE on the equity basis, while the second column

Consolidation vs. Equity Reporting

shows the results of consolidating IEE. The consolidated statements were prepared from the final column of Schedule 8-3, and the unconsolidated statements were prepared from the IOR trial balance shown in Schedule 8-2, as adjusted by the information in Schedule 8-4.

In the unconsolidated statements, the assets and liabilities are those only of IOR, and the revenues and expenses are also only those generated or incurred by IOR. One of the assets of IOR is the investment in IEE, which appears as a noncurrent asset on the balance sheet. Similarly, the income statement shows IOR's earnings from that investment as investment income. On Schedule 8-5, the income statement is a three-step statement, to illustrate the point that the investment earnings are after-tax earnings. In a single-step format, the investment income would simply be included as one of the revenues of IOR.

When we consolidate IOR and IEE, however, we eliminate the investment in the IEE account on the balance sheet and instead show all of the individual assets and liabilities of IEE that that investment represents. The shareholders' equity accounts are exactly the same in both columns. The total

---

SCHEDULE 8-5

Investor Ltd.
Balance Sheet at December 31, 19x1

	Unconsolidated	Consolidated
Current assets:		
Cash	$ 980,000	$1,077,500
Accounts receivable	2,200,000	2,450,000
Inventories	250,000	312,000
	3,430,000	3,839,500
Property, plant, and equipment:		
Land	1,000,000	1,400,000
Buildings and equipment (net)	1,700,000	2,222,500
	2,700,000	3,622,500
Investment in Investee, Ltd.	1,229,500	—
Goodwill	—	97,500
Total assets	$7,359,500	$7,559,500
Current liabilities:		
Accounts and other payables	$ 800,000	$1,000,000
Future income taxes	400,000	400,000
Shareholders' equity:		
Common shares (200,000 issued and outstanding)	3,800,000	3,800,000
Retained earnings	2,359,500	2,359,500
	6,159,500	6,159,500
Total liabilities and shareholders' equity	$7,359,500	$7,559,500

SCHEDULE 8-5 (continued)

Investor Ltd.
Income Statement
Year Ended December 31, 19x1

	Unconsolidated	Consolidated
Sales revenue	$2,400,000	$2,645,000
Operating expenses:		
Cost of goods sold	1,750,000	1,883,000
Depreciation expense	100,000	127,500
Amortization expense	—	2,500
Other operating expense	50,000	52,500
	1,900,000	2,065,500
Net income before taxes	—	579,500
and earnings of subsidiary	500,000	—
Income taxes	200,000	220,000
Net income before earnings of		
subsidiary	300,000	
Equity in earnings of subsidiary,		
Investee, Ltd.	59,500	
Net income	$ 359,500	$ 359,500
Earnings per share	$1.80	$1.80

---

net asset value of IOR is not altered by the process of consolidation; all that happens is that the investment account is disaggregated so that the readers of IOR's financial statements can see the total resources (of both IOR and IEE) that are under the control of the management of IOR.

The unconsolidated income statement includes the net earnings of IEE in a single line. Upon consolidation, the line for IOR's equity in IEE's earnings disappears and the net amount thereof ($59,500) is disaggregated by including the revenues and expenses of IEE in the main body of the statement, along with those of IOR. The consolidated net income is exactly the same as the unconsolidated net income of IOR, since the investment in IEE has been reported on the equity basis.

Because the equity-basis investment account and equity-in-earnings account summarize the investor's interest in the net assets and earnings from operations of the investee corporation in a single line on the financial statements of the investor, the equity method is sometimes referred to as **one-line consolidation**. The net income and the shareholders' equity on the equity-basis unconsolidated statements are the same as they are on the consolidated statements.

If an unconsolidated subsidiary has extraordinary items, then the parent will normally report its proportionate share of the extraordinary items on the equity-basis income statement as extraordinary items, rather than by including the extraordinary items in the one-line equity pick-up of the subsidiary's earnings. The distinction between operating income and extraordinary gains and losses is preserved, even in equity-basis unconsolidated statements. Similarly, prior-period adjustments and capital transactions of an equity-reported investee are reported in keeping with the nature of the transaction, rather than in combination with the operating earnings in accordance with the *CICA Handbook* [para. 1600.80]. The treatment of extraordinary items will be discussed more fully in Chapter 12.

Because the investor's equity in the earnings of the investee is computed by making the same adjustments as would be made for consolidation, this approach to equity-basis accounting is sometimes called the **consolidation method** of equity reporting.

B.   CONSOLIDATION IN SECOND SUBSEQUENT YEAR

In order to be able to generalize the approach to preparing consolidated financial statements for wholly owned subsidiaries, the example is extended for one more year. Assume that during 19x2, the following events occurred:

1. IEE reported operating income of $90,000, and paid dividends of $20,000.
2. IOR reported net income of $360,000, excluding dividends received from IEE; IOR paid dividends of $135,000.
3. IEE had sales of $60,000 to IOR; IEE's 19x2 gross margin was 45%; $10,000 of the goods are in IOR's inventory on December 31, 19x2.
4. IOR had sales of $20,000 to IEE; IOR's 19x2 gross margin was 30%; $6,000 of the goods sold to IEE are in IEE's 19x2 ending inventory.
5. IOR borrowed $500,000 from IEE on December 29, 19x2.
6. IEE sold its land to IOR for $540,000; the gain on disposal is not included in operating income, but is an extraordinary item for IEE.

The first two columns of Schedule 8-6 present the trial balances at December 31, 19x2, for IOR and IEE.

When we consolidated financial statements at the date of acquisition, only one adjustment was necessary: disaggregating the purchase price (in the investment account) to reflect the fair values of the individual assets and liabilities that had been acquired. When we consolidated the statements one year after acquisition, an additional group of adjustments was necessary in order to adjust the current year's operations for (1) amortization of the fair-value increments and (2) intercompany transactions and balances. When we prepare consolidated financial statements more than one year after the acquisition, one more type of adjustment is necessary—adjusting the balance sheet accounts for earnings and fair-value amortizations that occurred between the date of acquisition and the *beginning* of the year for which we are preparing consolidated financial statements.

For example, if we prepare consolidated statements for IOR for 19x6, we will provide for $10,000 amortization of the fair-value increment of the buildings and equipment for 19x6, just as we did in Schedule 8-3 for 19x1. However, the net amount of the fair-value increment that is included on the *balance sheet* on December 31, 19x6, will only be $140,000: $200,000 original increment reduced by six years of amortization at $10,000 per year. Therefore, we would first need to make an adjustment for the amortization in the

---

SCHEDULE 8-6

IOR Consolidation Worksheets
December 31, 19x2
Dr. (Cr.)

	Trial balances		Adjustments and eliminations			IOR consolidated trial balance
				Operations		
	IOR	IEE	1: Acquisition	2: Cumulative	3: Current	
Cash	$ 400,000	$ 70,000				$ 470,000
Accounts receivable	1,900,000	775,000			$(500,000)e	2,175,000
Inventory	300,000	60,000			(4,500)c / (1,800)d	353,700
Land	1,540,000	—	$ 100,000		(240,000)f	1,400,000
Buildings and equipment	3,800,000	500,000	50,000			4,350,000
Accumulated depreciation	(1,400,000)	(185,000)	150,000	$(10,000)	(10,000)a	(1,455,000)
Investment in IEE (at cost)	1,200,000		(1,200,000)			—
Goodwill			100,000	(2,500)	(2,500)b	95,000
Accounts payable	(865,000)	(150,000)			500,000 e	(515,000)
Future income taxes	(500,000)	—			90,000 f	(410,000)
Common shares	(3,800,000)	(200,000)	200,000			(3,800,000)
Retained earnings	(2,330,000)	(650,000)	600,000	20,500		(2,359,500)
Dividends paid	135,000	20,000			(20,000)g	135,000
Sales	(3,000,000)	(400,000)			60,000 c / 20,000 d	(3,320,000)
Cost of sales	2,100,000	220,000		(8,000)	(55,500)c / (18,200)d	2,238,300
Depreciation expense	100,000	17,500			10,000 a	127,500
Amortization expense					2,500 b	2,500
Other operating expenses	200,000	12,500				212,500
Income tax expense	240,000	60,000				300,000
Dividend income	(20,000)				20,000 g	—
Gain on sale of land (net tax)		(150,000)			150,000 f	—
	$ 0	$ 0	$ 0	$ 0	$ 0	$ 0

---

five years prior to 19x6, and then we can make the adjustment for the 19x6 amortization to expense.

On Schedule 8-6, the three different types of adjustments are shown in three separate columns for clarity. The first adjustment column ("Acquisition") contains exactly the same adjustment as was shown in Schedule 7-5 and Schedule 8-3.

The second adjustment column ("Cumulative") shows the adjustment that is necessary in order to restate the balances at January 1, 19x2, correctly:

(2) Retained earnings	$20,500	
Cost of sales (opening inventory)		$ 8,000
Accumulated depreciation		10,000
Goodwill		2,500

This entry (1) adjusts the balance sheet accounts for amortization for the period from the date of acquisition to the beginning of the current year, and (2) adjusts the *beginning* inventory for the amount of unrealized profit at the beginning of the year. Since the opening inventory has already been transferred to the cost of sales, we adjust the cost of sales instead of inventory.

The beginning of year unrealized profit has now been realized in 19x2, but since the opening inventory on IOR's books has been overstated by the amount of the unrealized profit, the adjustment has the effect of decreasing the cost of sales, thereby increasing the income to reflect the fact that the previously unrealized profit has now been realized.

The debit to retained earnings is the cumulative effect of the adjustments to IEE's earnings that have been made in prior years to amortize the fair-value increments and to eliminate unrealized profits. IEE's unadjusted retained earnings is $650,000, consisting of the $600,000 balance at the date of acquisition plus the $50,000 earnings retained in 19x1. The adjustment reduces the IEE 19x1 retained earnings from the nominal $50,000 to $29,500, the same amount as we calculated earlier as the equity-basis earnings of IEE.

The third column of adjustments contains all the figures necessary to adjust the balance sheet at the end of the year and the income statement accounts for intercompany transactions during the year.

The first and second figures adjust for the 19x2 depreciation on the fair-value increment for buildings and equipment and for the amortization of goodwill for 19x2:

(3a)	Depreciation expense	$10,000	
	Accumulated depreciation		$10,000
(3b)	Amortization expense	$ 2,500	
	Goodwill		$ 2,500

The third adjustment is for the intercompany sales during 19x2 and the unrealized profit, which is included in IOR's ending inventory at year-end. Total sales to IOR were $60,000; of that amount, $10,000 is still in the IOR inventory. Since IEE had a gross margin of 45%, unrealized gross profit is $4,500. Therefore, we need to adjust sales and cost of sales to eliminate the intercompany sale, and we need to reduce the ending inventory by the amount of the unrealized profit:

(3c)	Sales	$60,000	
	Cost of sales		$55,500
	Inventory (ending)		4,500

During 19x2, there also were downstream sales. IOR sold $20,000 to IEE, of which $6,000 is still in IEE's year-end inventory. IOR's gross margin is 30%, and therefore IEE's ending inventory includes $1,800 of unrealized profit:

(3d)	Sales	$20,000	
	Cost of sales		$18,200
	Inventory (ending)		1,800

Adjustments (3c) and (3d) could have been combined into a single adjustment, which would have appeared as follows:

Sales	$80,000	
Cost of sales		$73,700
Inventory (ending)		6,300

At the end of 19x2, IOR borrowed $500,000 from IEE. On the books of IEE, this amount will appear as a receivable, while on IOR's books there will be an offsetting liability. This offsetting receivable and payable must be eliminated before preparing the consolidated financial statements, because they are the result of a transaction within the consolidated entity and not with outsiders:

| (3e) | Accounts payable | $500,000 | |
| | Accounts receivable | | $500,000 |

The next adjustment that we must make concerns the sale of land by IEE to IOR. The cost of the land to IEE was $300,000 and it was sold to IOR for $540,000. IOR would record the land at its cost to IOR of $540,000. However, the $540,000 includes unrealized profit of $240,000, which must be eliminated before the consolidated balance sheet is prepared. The IEE trial balance shows gain on sale of land of $150,000 net of tax; the $90,000 difference ($240,000 — $150,000) is the income tax payable on the capital gain. To eliminate the unrealized profit, we must debit the gain by $150,000 and credit the land by $240,000. What do we do with the tax?

Bear in mind that as a separate legal and taxpaying entity, IEE will have actually paid (or be currently liable for) the tax on the sale. The fact of tax payment is not altered by the process of preparing consolidated statements. However, the net income of the consolidated entity as reported on the consolidated financial statements excludes the gain on the land, and thus there is a difference between taxable income and reported accounting income. For reporting purposes, the gain will only be recognized when it is realized by sale of the land to a third party. Therefore, elimination of the gain upon consolidation creates a *timing difference* between taxable and accounting income, and the tax effect must be *debited* to future income taxes:

(3f)	Gain on sale of land	$150,000	
	Future income taxes	90,000	
	Land		$240,000

Note that as is the case with all adjustments that we make when preparing consolidated statements, adjustment (3f) does not appear on the books of either IOR or IEE. The future income tax debit arises solely from the process of consolidation.

The sale of the land is introduced at this point in the text in order to make the reader aware that there are impacts on consolidated tax expense that occur as a result of consolidation. Indeed, if we were being fastidious, we would have adjusted for the tax effect on all intercorporate profit eliminations in this chapter. However, we have avoided doing so until now in order not to cloud the basic concept of unrealized profit elimination. Chapter 12 discusses the tax factors relating to consolidation in more detail.

The final adjustment that is made on Schedule 8-6 is the elimination of the intercompany dividend payment:

| (3g) | Dividend income | $20,000 | |
| | Dividends paid | | $20,000 |

Completed Consolidated Financial Statements

Schedule 8-7 presents the complete consolidated financial statements for Investor, Ltd. as of December 31, 19x2. Since financial statements should be comparative statements, the 19x2 statements also include 19x1.

The preparation of a consolidated statement of changes in financial position (SCFP) involves no particular difficulties. The statement can be prepared by combining the statement of changes of the separate entities and eliminating intercompany transactions. Alternatively, the statement can be prepared directly from the consolidated income statement, balance sheet,

SCHEDULE 8-7

Investor Ltd.
Consolidated Statement of Income
Years Ended December 31

	19x2	19x1
Sales revenue	$3,320,000	$2,645,000
Less operating expenses:		
Cost of goods sold	2,238,300	1,883,000
Depreciation expense	127,500	127,500
Amortization expense	2,500	2,500
Other operating expenses	212,500	52,500
	2,580,800	2,065,500
Net income before taxes	739,200	579,500
Income taxes	300,000	220,000
Net income after taxes	$ 439,200	$ 359,500
Earnings per share	$2.20	$1.80

Investor Ltd.
Consolidated Balance Sheet

	December 31	
	19x2	19x1
ASSETS		
Current assets:		
Cash	$ 470,000	$1,077,500
Accounts receivable	2,175,000	2,450,000
Inventories	353,700	312,000
	2,998,700	3,839,500
Property, plant, and equipment		
Land	1,400,000	1,400,000
Buildings and equipment (net)	2,895,000	2,222,500
	4,295,000	3,622,500
Goodwill	95,000	97,500
Total assets	$7,388,700	$7,559,500
LIABILITIES AND SHAREHOLDERS' EQUITY		
Current liabilities:		
Accounts and other payables	$ 515,000	$1,000,000
Future income taxes	410,000	400,000
Shareholders' equity:		
Common shares (200,000 issued and		
outstanding)	3,800,000	3,800,000
Retained earnings	2,663,700	2,359,500
	6,463,700	6,159,500
Total liabilities and shareholders' equity	$7,388,700	$7,559,500

SCHEDULE 8-7 (continued)

Investor Ltd.
Consolidated Statement of Retained Earnings
Years Ended December 31

	19x2	19x1
Balance, January 1	$2,359,500	$2,000,000
Net income for year	439,200	359,500
Dividends declared	(135,000)	—
Balance, December 31	$2,663,700	$2,359,500

Investor Ltd.
Consolidated Statement of Changes in Financial Position
Years Ended December 31

	19x2	19x1
Operations:		
Consolidated net income	$ 439,200	$ 359,500
Add expenses not requiring funds:		
Depreciation	127,500	127,500
Amortization	2,500	2,500
Future income taxes	10,000	—
Changes in working capital items:		
Accounts receivable	275,000	(300,000)
Inventory	(41,700)	(62,000)
Accounts payable	(485,000)	(100,000)
Net cash from (used in) operations	327,500	27,500
Issuance of 40,000 common shares to acquire Investee Ltd. (see below)	—	1,200,000
Payment of dividends	(135,000)	—
Investing activities:		
Purchase of buildings and equipment	(800,000)	—
Purchase of Investee Ltd., consisting of:		
Working capital, excluding cash	—	(100,000)
Land	—	(400,000)
Buildings and equipment	—	(550,000)
Goodwill	—	(100,000)
Net increase (decrease) in cash	$(607,500)	$ 77,500

and statement of retained earnings in exactly the same manner as from any other set of financial statements.

The *CICA Handbook* provides that in the year in which a business combination occurs, the acquisition appears both as an *financing* activity (e.g., the issuance of shares) and as an *investing* activity (the acquisition of assets) [para. 1540.22]. The amount of the investment is the total purchase price less any cash or cash equivalents acquired in the transaction. The investment can be shown in detail, as illustrated in the SCFP in Schedule 8-7, or as a lump sum with the detail shown in a note. The latter treatment is more common in practice.

The difference between the full purchase price (shown as a financing activity) and the non-cash assets acquired (shown as an investing activity) is, of course, the cash acquired in the deal, and that amount flows through the SCFP to affect the net change in cash. The net change, therefore, is the difference between the acquiror's previous year cash balance *without* including the acquiree's cash and the current year-end consolidated cash balance *including* the new subsidiary.

The changes in current assets and liabilities that are shown as adjustments in the operations section of the SCFP are a little tricky in the year of acquisition. The ending balances are those shown on the year-end consolidated balance sheet, which is no problem. The "beginning" balances, however, are the sum of the acquiror's beginning-of-year amounts plus the balances acquired in the combination, at the date of acquisition. When a business combination occurs in the middle of a year, it is impossible for an external reader to reconcile the amounts shown in the SCFP with the beginning and ending balance sheets, unless he or she also has the acquiree's balance sheet at the date of acquisition.

For example, in 1984, Cineplex Corporation acquired Canadian Odeon Theatres, a transaction that quadrupled the assets of Cineplex. Cineplex's current liabilities *rose* from $8.5 million to $15.9 million in 1984, according to the comparative balance sheet, and yet the SCFP showed a *reduction* of current liabilities of $17.2 million. In order for this to have happened, Cineplex must have acquired current liabilities of $24.6 million in the Odeon takeover:

($8.5 + $24.6) − $15.9 = $17.2 net change during the year.

Note Disclosure

While Schedule 8-7 does present the complete set of statements, it does not present the notes thereto. In accordance with the *Handbook*, the notes should contain additional disclosure of the IEE purchase, including the date of acquisition, the method of accounting for the acquisition (i.e., the purchase method), the assets and liabilities acquired, goodwill, the consideration given, the nature of the business acquired, and the percentage of ownership acquired [paras. 1580.77-.80]. To the extent that any of the required information is disclosed on the face of the statements (in this example, on the statement of changes in financial position), it need not be repeated in the note. The accounting policy for amortizing the goodwill should also be disclosed.

The 1987 edition of *Financial Reporting in Canada* reported on the disclosure of business combinations by its surveyed companies from 1983 through 1986. Out of 251 instances of business combinations, 61% provided all of the information recommended by the *Handbook*; another 30% provided some of the information, and the remaining 9% provided no supplementary disclosure.[1] The report does not speculate on the reasons for non-compliance with the disclosure recommendations, but a lack of materiality may have been a factor in at least some instances.

---

1 *Financial Reporting in Canada* 1987 edition (Toronto: CICA, 1988), p. 21. All further references will be to this edition.

Because the results of operations of an acquired company are consolidated only from the date of acquisition, a financial statement reader can only surmise what impact the newly acquired company will have on the consolidated results for a full year. It therefore could be deemed desirable for companies to report the results of operations on a pro-forma basis for a full year, as though the newly acquired company had been acquired at the beginning of the fiscal year rather than during the year. Such pro-forma reporting is similar in purpose to reporting adjusted and/or pro-forma earnings per share, which is to give shareholders a basis for comparison of management's earnings projections. For example, if an increase in EPS is forecasted, is the increase the result of improved operating performance or simply a reflection of the full impact of the acquisition? In the United States, pro-forma reported results are mandatory for public companies. In Canada, however, the disclosure of pro-forma results is voluntary and is rarely done. The *Handbook* contains a suggestion that "it is desirable to provide supplemental information, on a pro-forma basis..." [para. 1580.80], but *Financial Reporting in Canada* found only 13 instances of pro-forma reporting between 1983 and 1986 [p.22].

Schedules 8-8 through 8-11 contain illustrations of business combinations reported by Canadian public companies in their annual reports. The first example (Schedule 8-8) is of the well-known acquisition of CP Air by Pacific Western Airlines (or, to be exact, by its parent company, PWA Corporation) in January 1987. The purchase was of 100% of the shares of CP for cash consideration of $300 million. Added to that amount is acquisition cost of $1,504,000, bringing the total cost to $301,504,000. No goodwill was recognized in the allocation of the purchase price. Indeed, it would have been difficult to justify allocating any amount to goodwill, since goodwill arises essentially from future anticipated excess earnings and cash flow, but the earnings record of CP Air was hardly distinguished.

Since goodwill is not likely to have been present, the excess of the purchase price over the net book values acquired must have been due either to higher fair values of the physical assets or to specific intangible assets. In fact, PWA allocated the purchase price to both tangible and intangible assets, with almost $50 million going to "route acquisition costs," an intangible asset. The CP Air route structure had considerable value to an acquiror, even if the company had not been particularly successful in generating high earnings therefrom.

The total fair values of the assets were judged to be about $1.4 billion, offset by liabilities of $1.1 billion. Note that the CP Air *preference shares* are listed as a liability; while preferred shares are not technically a liability, they do represent an external obligation and are normally treated as such in the acquisition equation or calculation. The subject of preferred shares will be explored more fully in Chapter 12.

While the total cost of the acquisition was $301,504,000, the PWA consolidated statement of changes in financial position shows the following line under "Investing Activities":

Acquisition of subsidiary, including cash deficiency of
$107,656,000 (note 1) $(409,160,000)

As we pointed out earlier, the cost of an acquisition is shown on the SCFP net of any cash acquired in the combination. In the case of CP Air, there was

---

SCHEDULE 8-8

1. Acquisition

   On January 30, 1987 the Corporation acquired all the issued and outstanding common shares of Canadian Pacific Air Lines, Limited (CPAL), a domestic and international air carrier, for cash of $301,504,000 including costs of acquisition of $1,504,000. This acquisition has been accounted for as a purchase and accordingly the results of operations of CPAL have been included in these consolidated financial statements from the date of acquisition. The excess of the purchase price over the net book value of the assets acquired has been allocated to property and equipment and route acquisition costs and is being amortized on the same basis as the related assets.

   The acquisition is summarized as follows:

Current assets		$ 173,997
Investments		11,250
Property and equipment		1,178,336
Route acquisition costs		49,712
Other assets		6,300
		1,419,595
Current liabilities	$488,689	
Long term debt	437,662	
Obligations under capital leases	141,740	
Preference shares	50,000	1,118,091
		$ 301,504

   Source: PWA Corporation annual report, year ended December 31, 1987.

---

a cash overdraft of over $100 million, and this amount must be added to the cost of the acquisition, given the definition of funds that is used in the SCFP of cash plus cash equivalents, net of current borrowings or overdrafts.

The second example is drawn from the 1987 annual report of Erskine Resources Corporation (Schedule 8-9). Note 2 of the annual report describes two acquisitions. The first acquisition described was the creation of a new corporation, Erskine Resources Corporation, to issue shares in exchange for the shares of Erskine Resources Limited (ERL) and Canadian Bashaw Leduc Oil and Gas Limited (Bashaw). After the exchange, the former shareholders of ERL held 84.4% of the shares of the new company, making ERL the clear acquiror in the transaction. Subsequently, the new parent corporation and ERL were amalgamated, eliminating ERL as a separate corporation but leaving its former shareholders in firm control of the amalgamated company. Bashaw apparently continues to exist as a separate, wholly owned subsidiary of Erskine. The shares issued by Erskine Resources Corporation were valued at approximately $4.53 per share.

One important aspect of the Erskine amalgamation is that it did not in itself constitute a business combination, but only a reorganization of already existing ownership interests. Therefore, the amalgamation did not trigger

---

SCHEDULE 8-9

2. Acquisition of Subsidiaries

 (i) Effective May 1, 1987, Erskine Resources Limited ("ERL") merged with Canadian Bashaw Leduc Oil and Gas Limited ("Bashaw") to form Erskine Resources Corporation ("Erskine"). As a result of the merger, the former shareholders of Bashaw (other than ERL) hold 15.6% of the shares of the merged company, and the former shareholders of ERL hold 84.4% of the shares of the merged company. This transaction has been accounted for as a purchase by ERL of Bashaw and accordingly, the consolidated statement of earnings includes earnings of Bashaw from the date of acquisition. In prior years ERL had acquired shares of Bashaw representing an interest of 21% which had been carried in ERL's accounts at $800,000. The additional 1987 investment in Bashaw of $3,583,000 was acquired in exchange for 790,701 shares.

   On June 30, 1987, Erskine, ERL and another wholly-owned Canadian subsidiary of Erskine were amalgamated under section 178 of the Business Corporations Act (Alberta).

   Pursuant to the terms of the merger described above, options to purchase common shares of ERL that had not been exercised prior to the merger were exchanged for options to purchase the equivalent number of common shares of the Company.

 (ii) Effective June 1, 1987, the Company acquired 100% of the outstanding shares of Brown Energy Ltd. ("Brown") valued at $1,892,081 in exchange for cash of $616,081 and 282,301 shares of the Company. This transaction has been accounted for using the purchase method and accordingly, the consolidated statement of earnings includes earnings of Brown from the date of acquisition.

 (iii) The net assets of subsidiaries acquired are summarized below:

Fixed assets	$12,222,720
Working capital (including bank indebtedness of $6,907)	259,361
Deferred income taxes	(4,467,331)
Long term debt	(1,710,000)
Deferred revenue	(29,669)
	6,275,081
Less previous investment, at cost	800,000
	$ 5,475,081

Source: Erskine Resources Corporation annual report, year ended December 31, 1987.

Section 1580 of the *CICA Handbook* and did not result in fair valuing the net assets. A business combination is seldom accomplished by a statutory amalgamation, although it could be. Instead, a combination is usually accomplished by a cash purchase or an exchange of shares; an amalgamation may come later, in which case the fair values established in the business combination are simply carried forward and recorded on the surviving company's books. Amalgamations that are business reorganizations will be discussed more extensively in Chapter 11.

A second Erskine acquisition was Brown Energy Ltd., for just under $1.9 million. That acquisition was accomplished by the issuance of shares (valued at about $4.52 per share) for two-thirds of the consideration and one-third for cash.

The note disclosure combines the two acquisitions into a single list of net assets acquired. As was the case in the CP Air acquisition described above, none of the purchase price was allocated to goodwill. Instead, almost all of the value was assigned to fixed assets ($12.2 million), with a substantial offset by deferred income taxes ($4.5 million).

Our third example is of a business combination made by The Peter Miller Apparel Group Inc. (Schedule 8-10). This combination was a 100% share purchase made by cash and a long-term promissory note. The total cost of the purchase was $1,585,419, most of which was for working capital ($1,057,080). The remainder was allocated almost entirely to goodwill; goodwill accounts for 30% of the total purchase price.

The purchase was effective on March 31, 1987, but the closing did not

---

SCHEDULE 8-10

The company acquired a 100% interest in Hudson Sportswear Manufacturing Company Limited ("Hudson"), with effect from March 31, 1987, however, no sales, expenses, nor earnings were included from March 31, 1987 to April 30, 1987 since they were not material.

A summary of the acquisition is as follows:

Working capital	$1,057,080
Fixed assets	60,039
Goodwill	468,300
	$1,585,419

The acquisition is reflected in the financial statements as being financed by:

Amounts due on purchase of subsidiary	$1,235,419
Long term debt, promissory note (note 6)	350,000
	$1,585,419

The final closing occurred on June 25, 1987 at which time the former shareholders of Hudson were paid cash totaling $1,235,419. These cash payments were financed by the private placement after year end (note 12). In connection with this acquisition, a former shareholder of Hudson has been granted an option to acquire 7-1/2% of Hudson for approximately $127,000.

Source: Peter Miller Apparel Group Inc. annual report, year ended April 30, 1987.

occur until June 25, 1987, subsequent to the fiscal year-end of April 30, 1987. There are normally three dates in a business combination: (1) the date of the agreement, (2) the effective date, and (3) the closing date. The date of the agreement is just what it sounds like: the date on which the parties sign the agreement to combine. The effective date is the date on which operating control passes to the acquiror, and the closing date is the date on which the final documents are signed and the shares and consideration change hands. In private deals, the sequence of dates is normally that cited above. When a public company is being acquired, the closing date may come before the effective date, especially when the takeover is hostile.

Most commonly, the date on which consolidated reporting begins is the

---

SCHEDULE 8-11

11. Acquisitions

The company acquired all of the outstanding shares of Bowmaker (Plant) Limited and Caledonian Tractor Holdings Limited effective July 1, 1983 and October 1, 1983 respectively. Both companies, which operate in the United Kingdom, distribute and service Caterpillar products.

The results of these operations have been included in the consolidated financial statements from the dates the acquisitions were made. The value of the net assets acquired exceeded the purchase price by $14,139,918. This difference, or purchase discount, is being credited to consolidated income over two years from the respective acquisition dates.

Net assets acquired at assigned values include:

	Bowmaker	Caledonian	Combined
Accounts receivable	$17,015,509	$ 7,896,597	$24,912,106
Inventories:			
Equipment	9,892,051	5,319,484	15,211,535
Parts and supplies	5,959,108	2,249,812	8,208,920
Equipment leased to			
customers	—	1,655,659	1,655,659
Land, buildings and			
equipment	8,114,580	5,009,453	13,124,033
	$40,981,248	$22,131,005	$63,112,253
Bank indebtedness	$ 7,437,536	$ 6,407,152	$13,844,688
Accounts payable and			
accruals	11,223,117	7,896,917	19,120,034
Income taxes payable	3,222,971	370,936	3,593,907
	$21,883,624	$14,675,005	$36,558,629
Cash consideration	$19,097,624	$ 7,456,000	$26,553,624

Source: Finning Tractor & Equipment Company Limited annual report, year ended December 31, 1983.

effective date. Under the provisions of the *Handbook*, however, any of the three dates could be designated as the date of acquisition for reporting purposes [para. 1580.39]. In the Peter Miller example, consolidation did not begin on the effective date, although the reason given is one of immateriality: "No sales, expenses, nor earnings were included from March 31, 1987 to April 30, 1987 since they were not material."

The final example is of negative goodwill as shown in Schedule 8-11. Since negative goodwill is absorbed into the fair values allocated to the net assets, the existence of negative goodwill is seldom reported in published financial statements. Schedule 8-11 shows one instance when negative goodwill was explicitly reported in the 1983 acquisitions by Finning Tractor & Equipment Company Limited. The fair value of the net assets acquired was about $41 million, but the purchase price was only $27 million, resulting in negative goodwill of $14 million.

A curious aspect of Finning reporting of this acquisition is that the negative goodwill, "or purchase discount, is being credited to consolidated income over two years from the respective acquisition dates." It is not clear how the company is accomplishing the amortization, since the values assigned to the net assets are equal to the purchase price. As there is no balance sheet credit for the negative goodwill (to create such a credit would contravene the *Handbook* [para. 1580.44], and Finning is listed on the Toronto, Montreal, and Vancouver stock exchanges), the debit to offset the credit to income must be to the long-lived assets, thereby increasing their reported values to fair value. The amount of the credit to income was substantial; in 1984, the credit was $7.0 million on total net income of $16.9 million. The amount of the credit was disclosed only in the SCFP; the credit was not given "unusual item" treatment on the income statement.

Parent-Founded Subsidiaries

The example used throughout this chapter is that of a business combination. IOR purchased control over the net assets of IEE at a price that included both fair-value increments and goodwill. By using a business combination as the basis for the example, we can fairly comprehensively illustrate the major types of adjustments that may be required when consolidated statements are prepared.

However, we pointed out in Chapter 6 that most subsidiaries are not the result of one corporation's acquiring another in a business combination. Instead, most subsidiaries are formed by their parent to conduct or facilitate some component of the parent's business. The process of consolidation for a subsidiary that was founded and wholly owned by its parent is considerably easier than for a subsidiary that was acquired as a going concern.

Since the investment by the parent was directly in the subsidiary (rather than by buying the subsidiary's shares from another shareholder), the paid-in capital accounts of the subsidiary directly offset the original investment in the investment account of the parent. There are no fair-value increments or goodwill to worry about. The lack of fair-value increments and goodwill means that there is no periodic amortization of those amounts to adjust for. Consolidating a wholly owned, parent-founded subsidiary simply requires adjusting for intercompany transactions and the related unrealized profits, losses, and balances.

In chapters 6 and 7, we pointed out that a parent company may control a subsidiary indirectly through other subsidiaries, rather than by direct ownership. When the parent prepares its consolidated financial statements, not only the direct subsidiaries are consolidated, but also the indirect subsidiaries. Procedurally, indirect subsidiaries can be consolidated in either of two ways. The first is to consolidate by steps, from the bottom up. If P controls A who controls B and C, then consolidated statements for A can be prepared that include its direct subsidiaries, B and C. A's *consolidated* statements will then include all of the assets and liabilities of B and C just as if A owned them directly, and the investment accounts will have been eliminated. The next step is then to consolidate A's *consolidated* statements with P's statements. If the consolidation is being performed by the direct approach rather than via a worksheet, then the step method is almost certainly the best one to use.

The second procedural approach is to perform the consolidation of all subsidiaries, direct and indirect, on a single worksheet. The elimination and adjustment procedure is no different from that illustrated in this chapter for directly owned subsidiaries.

Indirect Holdings

SUMMARY

In this chapter, we have explored the major considerations involved in preparing consolidated financial statements subsequent to the acquisition (or establishment) of a wholly owned subsidiary. Consolidation subsequent to acquisition requires not only that the fair-value increments and goodwill be reported as part of the assets and liabilities of the consolidated entity, but also that the income statement amounts be adjusted. Adjustments are necessary in order to depreciate or amortize the fair-value increments and goodwill, as though the assets and liabilities had been acquired directly by the parent instead of through the acquisition of shares. In addition, the effects of all intercompany transactions must be eliminated from the reported amounts. Unrealized profits must be eliminated, and the tax effects must be recognized if tax allocation policies are being followed.

In certain circumstances, unconsolidated financial statements may be prepared for the parent corporation. When unconsolidated statements are prepared, the subsidiaries will be reported on the equity basis. The equity basis yields the same shareholders' equity and the same net income for the parent corporation as would consolidation. The detail of the asset, liability, revenue, and expense accounts differs, however. The consolidated statements have the effect of disaggregating the investment account and the investment earnings and including instead, the subsidiary's individual assets, liabilities, revenues, and expenses along with those of the parent.

Chapters 9 and 10 cover much of the same ground as do Chapters 7 and 8, but do so for subsidiaries in which the parent owns less than 100% of the shares. Equity-basis reporting for non-wholly owned subsidiaries and for significantly influenced companies are also be covered.

SELF-STUDY PROBLEM 8-1[2]

On January 1, 19x3, Par Ltd. bought 100% of Sub Ltd. for $761,000. Sub Ltd. depreciates its assets over ten years on a straight-line basis, and any goodwill is to be amortized over twenty years on a straight-line basis. The following is the balance sheet of Sub Ltd. at January 1, 19x3:

	Historical Cost	Fair Market Value
Cash	$ 80,000	$ 80,000
Accounts receivable	99,000	95,000
Inventory	178,000	195,000
Fixed assets, net	579,000	642,000
	$936,000	
Current liabilities	$ 70,000	70,000
Long-term liabilities	201,000	201,000
Common shares	250,000	—
Retained earnings	415,000	—
	$936,000	

The accounts receivable are expected to be collected within one year. The inventory has a turnover of six times per year, and the company uses the FIFO method.

During 19x5, the following intercompany transactions took place:

a. Par Ltd. sold goods with a cost of $300,000 to Sub Ltd. for $390,000. Twenty percent of these goods remain in Sub's inventory at the end of the year.

b. Sub Ltd. sold goods with a cost of $100,000 to Par Ltd. for $150,000. Forty percent of these goods remain in Par's inventory at the end of the year.

c. Par Ltd. sold land to Sub Ltd. on January 1, 19x5, for $700,000. The original cost of the land was $500,000 to Par Ltd. The gain was netted out to "other expenses."

At the beginning of 19x5, Par Ltd. had inventory on hand that it had bought from Sub Ltd., at a cost of $45,000. An amount of $12,000 of intercompany profit was included in that price.

Financial statements are as follows:

Balance Sheets
December 31, 19x5

	Par Ltd.	Sub Ltd.
Cash	$ 120,000	$ 110,000
Accounts receivable	150,000	135,000
Inventory	240,000	195,000
Fixed assets, net	890,000	706,000
Goodwill	75,000	—
Investment in Sub Ltd.	761,000	—
	$2,236,000	$1,146,000

---

2 The solutions to the self-study problems are at the end of the book, following Chapter 18.

Current liabilities	$ 142,000	$ 60,000
Long-term liabilities	600,000	201,000
Common shares	500,000	250,000
Retained earnings	994,000	635,000
	$2,236,000	$1,146,000

Income Statements
Year ended December 31, 19x5

	Par Ltd.	Sub Ltd.
Sales	$1,200,000	$987,000
Cost of goods sold	800,000	650,000
Gross profit	400,000	337,000
Other expenses	234,000	146,000
Net income before income tax	166,000	191,000
Income Tax	66,000	76,000
Net income	$ 100,000	$115,000

Required:
Prepare the consolidated financial statements at the fiscal year-end, i.e., both the balance sheet and income statement for December 31, 19x5. Ignore income tax impacts. (Hint: Note the dates carefully.)
[CGA-Canada, adapted]

REVIEW QUESTIONS

8-1 Define the following terms:

   a. Unrealized profits
   b. Upstream sales
   c. Downstream sales
   d. One-line consolidation
   e. Equity pick-up of earnings

8-2 What is accomplished by the acquisition adjustment when consolidated statements are prepared?

8-3 How would the acquisition adjustment for an acquired subsidiary differ from that for a parent-founded subsidiary?

8-4 What limitations are there on the amortization of goodwill arising from a business combination?

8-5 Why are the fair-value increments and decrements on depreciable fixed assets amortized? What is the basis for determining the amount of amortization?

8-6 When is it necessary to eliminate the profit on intercompany transactions?

8-7 Explain why the adjustment for unrealized profit in ending inventories appears to *increase* cost of goods sold.

8-8 Why is the equity method of reporting, which is prescribed in Canada, sometimes called the consolidation method of equity reporting?

8-9 How does a parent company's total net assets differ under consolidated reporting as compared to equity reporting for a subsidiary?

8-10 Under equity reporting, how does an extraordinary item of an investee corporation affect the income statement of the investor corporation?

8-11 How does unrealized profit in the beginning inventories affect the consolidated net income, if the inventories have been sold during the year?

8-12 Briefly explain the implications of unrealized profits on consolidated income tax expense.

8-13 What disclosure should be made in the financial statements of an acquiror as to the details of a business combination?

8-14 In what general ways will consolidation of a

parent-founded subsidiary differ from con-solidation of a purchased subsidiary?

8-15 Are consolidated statements required after one corporation directly acquires the net as-sets of another corporation?

CASE 8-1   McIntosh Investments Ltd.

McIntosh Investments, Ltd. (MIL), is a diversified closed-end investment company that is traded on the Toronto Stock Exchange. Forty percent of the common shares of MIL are owned by Loraine McIntosh, the president. Another 30% are owned jointly by Loraine's brother, Blair, and his friend, Douglas. The 70% ownership by Loraine and her associates gives her control of the company. The remaining 30% of the shares are widely distributed.

On April 1, 1988, the first day of MIL's fiscal year, Loraine succeeded in nego-tiating the acquisition by MIL of 30% of the outstanding common shares of Efrim Auto Parts, Inc. (EAPI). EAPI was an important supplier of parts to Candide Cars Corporation (CCC), a maker of specialty automobiles ("the best of all possible cars"), which was 40% owned by MIL. Loraine was particularly pleased at being able to arrange the purchase of the shares of EAPI because she was certain that great efficiency could be obtained by having the operations of EAPI and CCC more closely coordinated.

The EAPI shares were purchased from a descendent of the founder of EAPI, Jeffrey Efrim. The shares were purchased for a consideration of $600,000 cash and the issuance of 10,000 shares of MIL common stock. MIL shares were currently being traded on the TSE at $40 per share. In order to help finance the cash part of the deal, Loraine arranged a loan from the Royal Bank of Nova Scotia for $350,000. Exhibit 1 presents the balance sheet of EAPI as of March 31, 1988, the end of EAPI's fiscal year.

During the following year, Loraine and her fellow managers took an active interest in the affairs of both CCC and EAPI. CCC became EAPI's major customer, and purchased $2,000,000 of parts from EAPI during fiscal 1989. At the end of fiscal 1989, CCC had parts in inventory that were purchased from EAPI at a cost (to CCC) of $300,000, as compared to only $100,000 of such parts in inventory a year earlier. The attentions of MIL management had increased EAPI's efficiency so that average gross profit on sales rose to 35% in fiscal 1989. EAPI's net income after tax in fiscal 1989 reached a record high of $300,000 after tax, enabling EAPI to declare a dividend of $1.50 per common share on March 31, 1989.

Required:
Determine what impact MIL's investment in EAPI shares and EAPI's fiscal 1989 activities will have on the financial statements of MIL. Where alternatives are pos-sible, state them and briefly explain the alternatives you choose. State any assump-tions which you find it necessary to make.

EXHIBIT 1		

EAPI Balance Sheet
March 31, 1988

	Book value	Fair value
Cash	$ 200,000	$ 200,000
Accounts receivable	300,000	300,000
Inventories	400,000	440,000
Equipment (net)	2,100,000	2,400,000
Long-term investments (at cost)	300,000	360,000
	$3,300,000	
Accounts payable	$ 100,000	100,000
Debentures outstanding (12%, due		
March 31, 1986)	600,000	500,000
Deferred income taxes	200,000	
10% preferred shares		
(4,000 shares cumulative, nonvoting)	400,000	300,000
Common shares		
(60,000 shares, no par)	500,000	
Retained earnings	1,500,000	
	$3,300,000	

Fish Crates Limited

CASE 8-2

You are the new auditor of Fish Crates Limited (FCL). The requirement for an audit is specified in FCL's debt covenant with the bank.

FCL continued its plant expansion program in 1987, adding two new sizes to its line of fish-crate products. The president of FCL is pleased with the continuing expansion program. Annual sales are $800,000, the highest level in FCL's history and a real achievement for a firm of this size. The president attributes the increase in sales to the exacting standards of quality incorporated in its new products.

"We have never amortized goodwill and don't plan to this year either," the president of FCL stated. Last year I wrote a note at the bottom of the audit report sent to the bank, stating that amortization of goodwill is unnecessary since goodwill is being built up, not used up. I do not agree with the audit report qualification that we have received in recent years.

"We also wrote off the deferred tax balance this year because it doesn't mean anything. In fact, our banker adds the accumulated deferred tax balance to retained earnings when he reviews our annual financing proposals. I just couldn't think of any reason why we should pay you to calculate deferred taxes when no one uses them."

Required:
Discuss the president's comments.
[CICA]

CASE 8-3   M Aluminum Products

M Aluminum Products (MAP) is a manufacturer of doors, windows, greenhouses, and sunrooms.

In February 1988, MAP's common shareholders arranged for a receiver/manager to take over the management of MAP. The common shares had been owned in equal percentages by Mr. and Mrs. Mansfield since MAP's federal incorporation. In the year ended December 31, 1987, sales of MAP, according to the audited financial statements, had been over $6 million. However, as a result of Mr. Mansfield's illness, and due to uncollected receivables, profits were negligible and the cash and liquid assets position had deteriorated.

In August 1988, the receiver/manager was able to sign an agreement with Eric Cooper, who agreed to buy the common shares of MAP for $90,000 and to have MAP make various other payments to settle with creditors and preferred shareholders, effective September 1, 1988. The agreement was approved by all parties and the court, and Mr. Cooper assumed responsibility for MAP on September 1, 1988. A tax ruling confirmed that for tax purposes, no change in control has occurred, since Mr. Cooper is Mrs. Mansfield's brother.

Mr. Cooper has engaged your firm Hansen & Boyd. You visit MAP's offices and learn the following:

As at August 31, 1988, the condensed balance sheet of MAP showed the following (in thousands of dollars):

ASSETS

Receivables		$1,175
Inventory		530
Land		800
Building, net	(Note 1)	895
Equipment, net	(Note 1)	1,240
Goodwill, net	(Note 2)	610
Franchise	(Note 3)	470
Deficit	(Note 8)	1,120
		$6,840

LIABILITIES AND SHAREHOLDERS' EQUITY

Accounts payable	(Note 4)	$1,060
Notes payable	(Note 4)	800
Mortgage payable	(Note 5)	1,320
Preferred shares	(Note 6)	2,000
Common shares		1,000
Appraisal increase	(Note 7)	660
		$6,840

Notes:
1. The building and the equipment are shown at cost to MAP less accumulated depreciation.
2. Goodwill is shown at cost to MAP less accumulated amortization.
3. MAP has local rights to manufacture and distribute some types of aluminum products. The franchise cost of these rights is being amortized over ten years, which is an estimate of their useful life.
4. The notes payable and accounts payable creditors agreed to accept $0.60 on the dollar, and MAP made payments to them of $1,116,000 on September 1, 1988. Mr. Cooper was owed $100,000 by MAP and therefore received $60,000 on settlement of the debt.

5. The mortgage payable liability was restructured on September 1, 1988, to lower the interest rate to 9% and lengthen the period for repayment of principal from fifteen to twenty years. As at August 31, 1988, the interest rate of 14% on the mortgage was equal to current market rates. MAP paid $400,000 to the mortgage holders for the restructuring.
6. The preferred shareholders had the option under the agreement to:
   a. have their shares redeemed for $0.30 on the dollar on September 1, 1988; or
   b. have their shares redeemed for $1.00 on the dollar in ten years, if they waived their 10% dividend.

   All the preferred shareholders are friends of the former owners of MAP. Not surprisingly, therefore, 95% of the preferred shareholders agreed to option a.
7. MAP's land holdings were appraised years ago at $660,000 higher than their cost.
8. The non-capital loss carry-forward for income tax purposes is $3,180,000. Before the company got into difficulties, a normal annual taxable income for MAP was $950,000.

In addition to the above-noted items, MAP paid $120,000 in September 1988 to the receiver/manager and the court for their fees.

Mr. Cooper advanced to MAP the monies required to make all payments.

During the negotiations with the receiver/manager of MAP, Mr. Cooper estimated that the assets of the company had the following worth to him as of September 1, 1988:

Receivables	$ 200,000
Inventory	500,000
Land	1,400,000
Building	750,000
Equipment	950,000
	$3,800,000

In order to continue its operations, MAP requires financing. The bank has requested financial statements prepared in accordance with generally accepted accounting principles.

Mr. Cooper is wondering whether he can eliminate the deficit from the balance sheet. He wants you to prepare a balance sheet as at September 2, 1988, so that he can visualize what the assets, liabilities, and shareholders' equity would look like (a) "as is" and (b) after the possible reduction or elimination of the deficit. He wants to know your reasons for whatever you prepare.

Mr. Cooper has to spend most of his time at another business he owns and will therefore have to hire a competent general manager for MAP. The person whom he is considering hiring wants an incentive of either 10% of income after income tax and before bonus, or 5% of income before income tax and bonus.

Mr. Cooper believes that MAP's main assembly line has to be re-aligned in order to attain better economies of production. The cost of this will be $350,000 and will involve a plant shutdown of three days, plus a weekend or two. The realignment is scheduled for late September 1988.

Most of the employees of MAP will be retained. However, some were dismissed by the receiver/manager before they attained the ten years of employment necessary for admission to the pension plan. As a result, MAP's actuary believes that a surplus of $390,000 exists in the pension fund.

You have been engaged by Mr. Cooper to assist in all financial accounting, income tax, and related matters that concern his takeover of MAP. Mr. Cooper does not expect to hire a controller for MAP for at least a year. Therefore, he wants a thorough report from you, giving supported recommendations.

Required:
Prepare the report for Eric Cooper.
[CICA]

P8-1

Archibald Corporation is a retailer of office supplies and equipment in Halifax. On March 5, 19x3, Archibald formed a new corporation in New Brunswick in order to operate the same type of business in St. John. Archibald invested $100,000 cash in exchange for 10,000 common shares in the new subsidiary, to be known as Ross Limited.

During 19x3, Ross Limited commenced operations. Most of Ross's initial inventory came from Archibald. In total, goods that had cost Archibald $200,000 were sold to Ross at an assigned value of $250,000. These goods were repriced by Ross to sell for $500,000 at retail. At year-end, 20% of the merchandise acquired from Archibald was still in Ross's inventory.

Archibald also extended a loan to Ross to finance the start-up costs. A total of $150,000 was lent during the year, of which $75,000 was still owing at year-end. Interest of $10,000 on the loan had been accrued by both companies, of which only $6,000 had actually been paid during 19x3.

The pre-closing trial balances of both companies are presented below, as of December 31, 19x3.

Required:
Prepare a consolidated balance sheet and income statement for Archibald Corporation at December 31, 19x3.

	Trial balances: Dr. (Cr.) December 31, 19x3	
	Archibald	Ross
Cash	$ 85,000	$ 15,000
Accounts and other receivables	275,000	125,000
Inventories	440,000	60,000
Fixed assets	600,000	300,000
Accumulated depreciation	(200,000)	(30,000)
Investment in Ross (at cost)	100,000	—
Accounts and other payables	(300,000)	(150,000)
Long-term liabilities	(370,000)	(200,000)
Common shares	(50,000)	(100,000)
Retained earnings	(410,000)	—
Dividends paid	200,000	40,000
Sales	(2,000,000)	(600,000)
Expenses	1,700,000	540,000
Other income	(70,000)	—
	$ 0	$ 0

P8-2

At the end of 19x4, the trial balances of Archibald Corporation and Ross Limited were as they appear below. Intercompany activites during 19x4 were as follows:

1. Ross sold all of its opening (i.e., December 31, 19x3) inventory, including that acquired from Archibald (see P8-1).
2. Ross purchased merchandise from Archibald for $400,000. This price included a 25% markup over the cost to Archibald. At year-end, 40% of these goods was still in Ross's inventory.
3. Ross sold to Archibald some merchandise that Ross had acquired for $120,000. The sale to Archibald was at a price of $100,000. The merchandise was all in Archibald's inventory at year-end, but is expected to sell for $150,000 in 19x5.
4. Ross fully repaid Archibald the $75,000 loan that had been outstanding at the beginning of the year, plus $9,000 in interest ($4,000 of the interest pertained to 19x3).
5. Archibald purchased a plot of land in St. John for $80,000 and resold it to Ross for $120,000.

Required:
Prepare a consolidated income statement, balance sheet, and statement of changes in financial position for Archibald Corporation for 19x4.

	Trial balances: Dr. (Cr.) December 31, 19x4	
	Archibald	Ross
Cash	$ 50,000	$ 10,000
Accounts and other receivables	240,000	60,000
Inventories	470,000	195,000
Fixed assets	650,000	420,000
Accumulated depreciation	(230,000)	(60,000)
Investment in Ross (at cost)	100,000	—
Other investments	140,000	—
Accounts and other payables	(360,000)	(250,000)
Long-term liabilities	(350,000)	(230,000)
Common shares	(50,000)	(100,000)
Retained earnings	(580,000)	(20,000)
Dividends paid	220,000	45,000
Sales	(2,300,000)	(720,000)
Expenses	2,100,000	650,000
Other income	(100,000)	—
	$ 0	$ 0

P8-3

On January 1, 19x1, Paternal Inc. acquired 100% of the outstanding shares of Subservient Corp. for $5,000,000 cash. On this date, Subservient had shareholders' equity of $4,000,000, including $2,000,000 in retained earnings. Subservient had buildings and equipment that had a fair value of $600,000 less than book value, inventory that had a fair value of $150,000 greater than book value, and investments that had a fair value of $900,000 greater than book value.

On December 31, 19x1, the balance sheets of the two companies were as follows:

	Balance sheets December 31, 19x1	
	Paternal	Subservient
Cash	$ 1,000,000	$ 300,000
Accounts receivable	1,600,000	400,000
Inventories	2,400,000	700,000
Plant and equipment	21,000,000	7,000,000
Accumulated depreciation	(6,000,000)	(2,500,000)
Goodwill	—	400,000
Long-term investments (at cost)	5,000,000	1,600,000
Total assets	$25,000,000	$7,900,000
Accounts payable	$ 3,000,000	$ 500,000
Bonds payable	5,000,000	3,000,000
Common shares (no par)	7,000,000	2,000,000
Retained earnings	10,000,000	2,400,000
Total equities	$25,000,000	$7,900,000

Additional Information:

1. The goodwill on Subservient's books arose from the purchase of another company several years ago, a company that has since been amalgamated into Subservient. The goodwill is being amortized at the rate of $50,000 per year. It was assumed to have a fair value of zero on January 1, 19x1.
2. Subservient's plant and equipment has an estimated average remaining life of ten years from January 1, 19x1. The net book value of the plant and equipment was $5,000,000 on that date, after deducting $2,000,000 of accumulated depreciation.
3. On January 1, 19x1, Paternal held inventory of $400,000 that had been acquired from Subservient. Subservient had sold the merchandise to Paternal at a 100% mark-up over cost.
4. On December 31, 19x1, Paternal held inventory of $500,000 that had been purchased from Subservient during 19x1 at 100% above Subservient's cost.
5. At the end of 19x1, Paternal owed Subservient $200,000 for merchandise purchased on account.
6. During 19x1, Subservient sold an investment for $400,000. The investment had cost Subservient $180,000, and had a fair value of $300,000 on January 1, 19x1.
7. Paternal's retained earnings on December 31, 19x1, include dividend income received from Subservient. Subservient declared dividends of $200,000 in 19x1.

Required:
Prepare a consolidated balance sheet for Paternal Inc. at December 31, 19x1.

P8-4

On January 1, 19x3, Parent Ltd. purchased 100% of the outstanding voting common shares of Sub Ltd. for $2,800,000. Any revaluation arising from the purchase of depreciable assets is to be amortized over ten years and any goodwill created on consolidation is to be amortized over 25 years, straight-line.

During 19x3, the following events occurred:

1. No dividends were paid on the shares by either company.

2. Sub Ltd. sold inventory costing $494,000 to Parent Ltd. for $682,000, 30% of which was not sold at year-end.
3. During 19x3, all of the current assets that had a fair market value greater than book value were sold to outside parties or were collected.
4. On July 1, 19x3, Parent Ltd. purchased 60% of the outstanding 10% bonds payable of Sub Ltd. for $129,000. These bonds have a twenty-year total life with fifteen years remaining at January 1, 19x3.
5. Parent Ltd. has made no entries in the Investment in Sub Ltd. account following the acquisition.

Sub Ltd.

	Post-closing Trial Balance January 1, 19x3	Fair Market Value January 1, 19x3	Pre-closing Trial Balance December 31, 19x3
Cash	$ 185,000	$185,000	$ 135,000
Accounts receivable, net	432,000	450,000	385,000
Inventory	680,000	730,000	730,000
Land	510,000	570,000	510,000
Buildings and equipment, net	974,000	850,000	963,000
Goodwill	120,000	—	110,000
	$2,901,000		$2,833,000
Current liabilities	$ 320,000	$320,000	$ 310,000
Bonds payable, 10%	215,000	215,000	215,000
Common shares	400,000	—	400,000
Retained earnings	1,966,000	—	1,966,000
Sales	—	—	1,430,000
Cost of goods sold	—	—	(867,000)
Depreciation	—	—	(11,000)
Other expenses	—	—	(588,500)
Bond interest expense	—	—	(21,500)
	$2,901,000	—	$2,833,000

Parent Ltd.
Pre-closing Trial Balance
December 31, 19x3

Cash	$ 275,000
Accounts receivable, net	384,000
Marketable securities**	129,000
Inventory	860,000
Land	730,000
Buildings and equipment, net	862,000
Goodwill*	140,000
Investment in Sub Ltd.	2,800,000
	$6,180,000

Current liabilities	$ 395,000
Bonds payable	685,000
Common shares	1,100,000
Retained earnings	3,757,000
Sales	1,930,000
Cost of goods sold	(1,463,000)
Depreciation	(27,000)
Other expenses	(203,450)
Bond interest income	6,450
	$6,180,000

  *Not related to Sub Ltd.
**Bonds of Sub Ltd.

Required:
Prepare a consolidated statement of income and retained earnings and a consolidated balance sheet for Parent Ltd. for the year ended December 31, 19x3.
[CGA-Canada, adapted]

P8-5

Parent Ltd. acquired 100% of the voting shares of Sub Ltd. on January 1, 19x3, for $1,255,000. The balance sheet of Sub Ltd. is as follows:

Sub Ltd.
Balance Sheet
January 1, 19x3

	Book Value	Fair Market Value
Cash	$ 40,000	$ 40,000
Accounts receivable	110,000	130,000
Inventory	280,000	320,000
Land	310,000	400,000
Depreciable fixed assets, net	460,000	495,000
Total assets	$1,200,000	
Current liabilities	$ 250,000	$250,000
Common shares	400,000	—
Retained earnings	550,000	—
Total liabilities	$1,200,000	

The inventory will be sold and the accounts receivable collected within six months, and the depreciable fixed assets will be depreciated over ten years, straight-line, with no salvage value. Any goodwill arising on consolidation will be amortized over twenty years, straight-line.

During 19x3, Sub Ltd. sold inventory to Parent Ltd. for $150,000 with a 20% markup on retail. At the end of 19x3, $30,000 (at retail) of these goods were still in the inventory. Parent Ltd. sold $200,000 of goods to Sub Ltd. during 19x3, with a

25% markup on retail, and $40,000 (at retail) of these were still in inventory at the end of 19x3. All of these goods remaining in inventory were sold during 19x4.

During 19x4, Parent Ltd. sold $180,000 of goods to Sub Ltd. with a 25% markup on retail and $50,000 (at retail) of these goods were in inventory at the end of 19x4. In addition, Sub Ltd. sold goods to Parent Ltd. for $220,000 with a 20% markup on retail and $60,000 (at retail) of these were still in inventory at the end of 19x4. All of these remaining goods were sold during 19x5.

The following are the financial statements of the two companies at December 31, 19x4:

Balance Sheets
December 31, 19x4

	Parent Ltd.	Sub Ltd.
Cash	55,000	$ 40,000
Accounts receivable	140,000	110,000
Inventory	400,000	320,000
Land	670,000	385,000
Depreciable fixed assets, net	864,000	520,000
Investment in Sub Ltd.	1,255,000	—
Total assets	$3,384,000	$1,375,000
Current liabilities	$ 98,000	$ 175,000
Common shares	1,136,000	400,000
Retained earnings	2,150,000	800,000
Total liabilities	$3,384,000	$1,375,000

Income Statements
for the year ended December 31, 19x4

		Parent Ltd.	Sub Ltd.
Sales		$852,000	$789,000
Less:	Cost of goods sold	542,000	479,000
	Depreciation	120,000	110,000
	Other expenses	80,000	70,000
	Net income	$110,000	$130,000

Neither company paid any dividends during 19x3 or 19x4.

Required:
Calculate the following, considering all dates carefully:

a. Consolidated goodwill at December 31, 19x4.
b. Investment income, under the equity method, for 19x3.
c. Consolidated net income for 19x4.
d. Consolidated balance of accounts receivable at December 31, 19x4.
e. Consolidated balance of depreciable fixed assets at December 31, 19x4.
f. Consolidated balance of inventory at December 31, 19x4.
[CGA-Canada, adapted]

P8-6

Pancho Ltd. and Cisco Inc. have pooled to form a consolidated entity. Pancho Ltd. owns 100% of the shares of Cisco Inc., but the former shareholders of Cisco Inc. own one-half of Pancho Ltd. Your subordinate has brought you the following problems in preparing the consolidated financial statements:

a. Both companies have goodwill on the books. Pancho Ltd. has $200,000 that is being amortized at $20,000 per year. Cisco Inc. has $100,000 and is amortizing it at $10,000 per year.

b. There was an intercompany transfer of inventory that had cost $80,000 from Pancho Ltd. to Cisco Inc. for $140,000. One-third of the amount transferred was left in Cisco Inc.'s inventory at the end of the year.

c. Dividends paid were as follows:
   - By Pancho: $50,000
   - By Cisco: $40,000

Required:
For each of items a, b, and c, briefly discuss how the item would affect the consolidated financial statements. Remember that consolidated financial statements are composed of the income statement, balance sheet, and statement of changes in financial position.
[CGA-Canada]

P8-7

On January 4, 19x1, Practical Corp. acquired 100% of the outstanding common shares of Silly Inc. by a share-for-share exchange of its own shares valued at $1,000,000. The balance sheets of both companies just prior to the share exchange are shown below. Silly has patents that are not shown on the balance sheet, but that have an estimated fair value of $200,000 and an estimated remaining productive life of four years. Silly's buildings and equipment have an estimated fair value that is $300,000 in excess of book value, and the deferred charges are assumed to have a fair value of zero. Silly's building and equipment are being depreciated on the straight-line basis and have a remaining useful life of ten years. The deferred charges are being amortized over the following three years.

	Balance sheets December 31, 19x0	
	Practical	Silly
Cash	$ 50,000	$ 45,000
Accounts and other receivables	140,000	80,000
Inventories	110,000	55,000
Buildings and equipment	1,500,000	800,000
Accumulated depreciation	(700,000)	(400,000)
Deferred charges	—	120,000
	$1,100,000	$700,000
Accounts and other payables	$ 200,000	$100,000
Bonds payable	—	200,000
Common shares*	600,000	150,000
Retained earnings	300,000	250,000
	$1,100,000	$700,000

*Practical = 300,000 shares; Silly = 150,000 shares.

Required:
Prepare a consolidated balance sheet for Practical Corp. immediately after the share exchange.

P8-8

Refer to P8-7. The trial balances of Practical and Silly at December 31, 19x1, are shown below, **before** Practical has made any adjustment for its equity in the earnings of Silly. Dividends received from Silly during the year have been credited to the investment in Silly account.

During the year, Silly borrowed $100,000 from Practical; $40,000 was repaid and $60,000 is still outstanding at year-end. No interest is being charged on the loan. Through the course of the year, Silly sold goods to Practical totaling $400,000. Silly's gross margin is 40% of selling price. All of these goods were resold by Practical to its customers for $600,000. There were no intercompany transactions other than those described above.

Required:
a. Prepare a statement of income and retained earnings and a balance sheet for Practical Corp. for 19x1, assuming that Practical does not consolidate Silly but instead reports its investment on the equity basis.
b. Prepare a complete set of consolidated financial statements for Practical Corp., including a statement of changes in financial position and a statement of changes in consolidated retained earnings.
c. Assume that Practical Corp. maintained its investment in Silly account on the cost basis. The investment account would then have a balance of $1,000,000 at year-end, and the dividends received from Silly would be shown in a dividend income account (for $50,000) on the Practical trial balance. How would this change in accounting affect your consolidating adjustments and eliminations? What would be the impact on Practical's consolidated statements?

	Trial balances: Dr. (Cr.) December 31, 19x1	
	Practical	Silly
Cash	$ 20,000	$ 15,000
Accounts and other receivables	210,000	80,000
Inventories	120,000	55,000
Buildings and equipment	1,300,000	900,000
Accumulated depreciation	(570,000)	(445,000)
Land	—	60,000
Investment in Silly	950,000	—
Other investments	70,000	30,000
Deferred charges	—	80,000
Accounts and other payables	(150,000)	(180,000)
Bonds payable	—	(170,000)
Common shares	(1,600,000)	(150,000)
Retained earnings (net of dividends)	(220,000)	(200,000)
Sales	(1,500,000)	(900,000)
Cost of sales	1,000,000	540,000
Depreciation expense	70,000	45,000
Amortization expense	—	40,000
Other expenses	300,000	200,000
	$ 0	$ 0

P8-9

Refer to P8-8. During 19x2, Silly Inc. had sales of $800,000 to Practical Corp. Silly's gross margin was still 40% of selling price. During the year, Practical sold $680,000 of these goods to its customers for $1,000,000. On October 1, 19x2, Silly sold its land to Practical for $150,000. Practical paid Silly $50,000, and gave a promissory note for $100,000 that was due in three years at 10% interest per year, simple interest to be paid at maturity. The $60,000 that Silly owed to Practical at the beginning of the year was repaid during 19x2. The trial balances of the two companies are shown below. Practical paid dividends of $100,000 during the year. Silly paid dividends of $70,000.

Required:

a. Determine Practical Corp.'s equity in the earnings of Silly Inc. for 19x2. Determine the balance of the investment in Silly account on Practical's books at December 31, 19x2, assuming that Practical records its investment on the equity basis.

b. Prepare a comparative consolidated balance sheet, income statement and statement of changes in financial position for Practical Corp. for 19x2, assuming that Practical's investment in Silly is first adjusted for its equity in the 19x2 earnings of Silly.

c. How would the consolidation eliminations and adjustments differ if:
   1. Practical had *not* first recorded its equity in Silly's 19x2 earnings?
   2. Practical had maintained its investment account on the cost basis? (On the cost basis, the investment in Silly account would have been $1,000,000 instead of $909,500 on Practical's December 31, 19x2, trial balance; retained earnings would have been $400,000 instead of $379,500, and dividend income would have been $700,000.)

	Trial balances: Dr. (Cr.) December 31, 19x2	
	Practical	Silly
Cash	$ 27,000	$ 35,000
Accounts and other receivables	160,000	100,000
Inventories	140,000	75,000
Buildings and equipment	1,700,000	900,000
Accumulated depreciation	(655,000)	(495,000)
Land	150,000	—
Investment in Silly	909,500	—
Due from Practical	—	102,500
Other investments	100,000	50,000
Deferred charges	—	40,000
Accounts and other payables	(225,000)	(215,000)
Payable to Silly	(102,500)	—
Common shares	(1,800,000)	(150,000)
Retained earnings	(379,500)	(275,000)
Dividends paid	100,000	70,000
Sales	(1,680,000)	(1,200,000)
Cost of sales	1,120,000	720,000
Depreciation expense	85,000	50,000
Amortization expense	—	40,000
Other expenses	350,500	245,000
Other income	—	(2,500)
Gain on sale of land	—	(90,000)
	$ 0	$ 0

9

Consolidation of Non-Wholly Owned Subsidiaries

The previous two chapters dealt with some of the major issues in and approaches to the preparation of consolidated statements when the subsidiaries are wholly owned. Most subsidiaries are wholly owned because they were initially formed by the parent corporation in order to facilitate the conduct of some aspect of the parent's business. As well, subsidiaries acquired in a business combination are more often 100% acquired than not.

Nevertheless, a parent's initial ownership interest may well be less than 100%. When subsidiaries are not wholly owned, the reason is usually that the subsidiary was acquired in a business combination and not all of the subsidiary's shares were acquired. A second reason for less than 100% ownership is that a parent may form a new subsidiary with the involvement of a minority partner who is providing specialized expertise, management ability, market access, governmental support, etc. The formation of a subsidiary with outside equity participation presumes that the parent controls the new subsidiary.

Sometimes a corporation will form a new venture with outside partners and contribute a majority of the investment and receive a majority of the shares, but still not actually control the new venture because of the terms of the shareholders' agreement. When a shareholders' agreement removes the investor's ability to control the venture (or requires control to be exercised only with the concurrence of the other equity participants), then the new venture is not a subsidiary; it is a **joint venture**. We will discuss joint ventures in Chapter 10; our primary concern at present is for subsidiaries that are not wholly owned.

Some parent corporations prefer to control their subsidiaries with appreciably less than full ownership. This permits the parent to control the subsidiary without investing the full value of the subsidiary's net assets. Liquid resources may be conserved by the smaller investment or, if the investment is a business combination that is accomplished by an exchange of shares, the parent's own share distribution is affected less by an under-100% acquisition.

In addition, the maintenance of a significant minority interest in the subsidiary will help to spread the ownership risk, may provide valuable links with other corporate shareholders, and may maintain a market for the subsidiary's shares.

Minority interests may also exist if the parent initially establishes the subsidiary, but subsequently sells subsidiary shares to others. The sale may be of shares originally owned by the parent (i.e., a secondary offering by the parent) or may be of new shares (i.e., a direct or primary offering by the subsidiary). In either case, the parent ends up holding less than 100% of the subsidiary.

This chapter deals with the problems that arise in preparing consolidated financial statements when the parent's ownership interest is greater than 50% but less than 100% and is the result of a business combination. Somewhat different problems arise when the minority interest is the result of a parent's reduction in its ownership interest of a subsidiary. Reporting the results of a change in ownership interest are considered in Chapter 13.

A.   ALTERNATIVE APPROACHES

Conceptual Alternatives

As is also the case with most other aspects of accounting, there is no single approach to accounting for subsidiaries when a minority interest exists, although there is a currently recommended approach in the *CICA Handbook*. At issue is the treatment of the minority shareholders' share of the subsidiary's net assets. Two questions arise:

1. Should the minority interest's share of net assets be included in the consolidated balance sheet?
2. If included, should they be shown at their book value on the subsidiary's books or at their fair value as of the date of acquisition?

The answers to these two questions are, to some extent, dependent upon the theory of consolidation used, described in Chapter 7. For example, the pooling-of-interests approach assumes that two previously independent businesses combine on equal terms and both carry on jointly and equally. It would be mechanically possible to exclude the minority interest's share of assets from the consolidated balance sheet, but to do so would be inconsistent with the underlying philosophy of the pooling approach. Similarly, the new-entity approach to consolidations would seem to call for inclusion of the minority interest at fair value; to exclude the minority interest or to include it at book value is inconsistent with the underlying conceptual basis of the new-entity method.

The widest choice of approaches to minority interest exists under the fair-value purchase method. Three alternatives exist:

1. Include only the parent's share of the fair value of the subsidiary's assets and liabilities, and revenues and expenses (excluding entirely minority interest). This is known as the **proportionate consolidation approach**.
2. Include the parent's share of the fair values of the subsidiary's assets and liabilities, plus the book value of the minority interest's share. This approach is most commonly called the **parent-company** approach. The

consolidated income statement would include 100% of the subsidiary's revenues and expenses.

3. Include 100% of the fair value of the subsidiary's assets and liabilities, and 100% of all revenues and expenses. This is usually called the **entity** method, but should not be confused with the new-entity approach to consolidations, which was discussed in the previous chapter.

If we include all of the subsidiary's net assets in the parent company's consolidated balance sheet (using either the entity or the parent-company approaches), we must offset the minority shares of assets and liabilities by including an amount for minority interest in or near the shareholders' equity section of the parent company's consolidated balance sheet. Similarly, when we include 100% of the subsidiary's revenues and expenses in the consolidated income statement, then we must subtract the minority interest's share of the earnings of the subsidiary, so that net income on the parent's consolidated income statement will reflect only the share of the subsidiary's net income that is attributable to the parent company's interest in the subsidiary.

Schedule 9-1 summarizes the alternative approaches to the treatment of the minority interest's share of net assets under each of the three methods of consolidation. As described above, exclusion of the minority interest is known as *proportionate consolidation*, inclusion at book value is known as the *parent-company approach*, and inclusion at fair value is known as the *entity approach*. An exception to this terminology is that under the pooling-of-interests approach, the treatment of minority interest net assets is part of the overall concept and approach to pooling, and the "parent company" label is not appropriate under pooling. Pooling-of-interests will be discussed and illustrated in Chapter 11.

In order to clarify the conceptual issues underlying the three different approaches to minority interest, we will apply the three alternatives to a simple example. Our example uses the fair-value purchase method of consolidation because this is the only method that conceptually permits the use of all three alternatives. The example uses the same facts as the illustration in Chapter 7, except that less than 100% of the shares are purchased.

Illustration of the Alternative Approaches

SCHEDULE 9-1			
Alternative Approaches to Minority Interest (MI)			
Consolidation method	Include MI net assets?	At book value or fair value?	Name of alternative
1. Pooling of interests	yes	book value	[pooling]
2. Fair-value purchase a. no		—	proportionate consolidation
b. yes		book value	parent company
c. yes		fair value	entity
3. New entity	yes	fair value	entity

Let us assume that instead of buying 100%, IOR buys only 70% of the outstanding shares of IEE on January 1, 19x1, giving 28,000 IOR shares in exchange. If we assume that the market value of IOR's shares is $30 per share, then the total cost of the purchase is $840,000. The post-acquisition balance sheets of IOR and IEE, and the fair values of IEE's assets and liabilities, are shown in Part 1 of Schedule 9-2.

Part 2 of Schedule 9-2 shows the allocation of the purchase price and derivation of the goodwill. Note that in this case, the goodwill is 70% of the

---

SCHEDULE 9-2

IOR Acquires 70% of IEE, January 1, 19x1

1. NET ASSET POSITIONS, SUBSEQUENT TO ACQUISITION:

| | Balance sheets, January 1, 19x1 | | IEE fair values |
	IOR	IEE	January 1, 19x1
Cash	$1,000,000	$ 50,000	$ 50,000
Accounts receivable	2,000,000	150,000	150,000
Inventory	200,000	50,000	50,000
Land	1,000,000	300,000	400,000
Buildings and equipment	3,000,000	500,000	550,000
Accumulated depreciation	(1,200,000)	(150,000)	
Investment in IEE	840,000		
Total assets	$6,840,000	$900,000	
Accounts payable	$1,000,000	$100,000	100,000
Future income taxes	400,000		
Common shares	3,440,000	200,000	
Retained earnings	2,000,000	600,000	
Total equities	$6,840,000	$900,000	

2. ASSIGNMENT OF PURCHASE PRICE:

| | 70% Share of IEE | | |
	Book value	Fair value	Fair-value increment
Cash	$ 35,000	$ 35,000	—
Accounts receivable	105,000	105,000	
Inventory	35,000	35,000	—
Land	210,000	280,000	$ 70,000
Buildings and equipment (net)	245,000	385,000	140,000
Accounts payable	(70,000)	(70,000)	—
	$560,000	$770,000	$210,000
Purchase price		840,000	
Goodwill		$ 70,000	70,000
Excess of purchase price over net book value acquired			$280,000

goodwill of $100,000 that resulted from IOR's 100% purchase of IEE in Chapter 7. Note also that the nature of the calculations in Schedule 9-2 is exactly the same as was used in Chapters 7 and 8 (Schedule 8-1), except that only 70% of IEE's assets and liabilities are included in the analysis instead of 100%.

Schedule 9-3 shows the IOR consolidated balance sheet immediately after the business combination, prepared (by the direct approach) under each of the three alternatives, each of which will be discussed in turn.

Proportionate Consolidation

The first column of Schedule 9-3 shows the IOR consolidated balance sheet as it would appear using the proportionate consolidation approach. Under this approach, the IOR balance sheet includes only IOR's share of IEE's assets and liabilities. Since IOR does not own 30% of the IEE shares, the assets and liabilities that are represented by the non-owned shares are excluded from IOR's consolidated statements. The net result is to disaggregate the investment account balance of $840,000 that is shown on the unconsolidated IOR balance sheet (Schedule 9-2), and to distribute the purchased portion of the fair values to the appropriate assets and liabilities and to goodwill.

The proportionate consolidation approach takes the point of view that the only subsidiary assets and liabilities that should be shown on the parent's

---

SCHEDULE 9-3

Alternative Accounting for Minority Interest
IOR Consolidated Balance Sheets
January 1, 19x1

	(1) Proportionate consolidation	(2) Parent company	(3) Entity
Cash	$1,035,000	$1,050,000	$1,050,000
Accounts receivable	2,105,000	2,150,000	2,150,000
Inventory	235,000	250,000	250,000
Land	1,280,000	1,370,000	1,400,000
Buildings and equipment	3,385,000	3,490,000	3,550,000
Accumulated depreciation	(1,200,000)	(1,200,000)	(1,200,000)
Goodwill	70,000	70,000	100,000
Total assets	$6,910,000	$7,180,000	$7,300,000
Accounts payable	$1,070,000	$1,100,000	$1,100,000
Future income taxes	400,000	400,000	400,000
Minority interest	—	240,000	360,000
Common shares	3,440,000	3,440,000	3,440,000
Retained earnings	2,000,000	2,000,000	2,000,000
Total equities	$6,910,000	$7,180,000	$7,300,000

Derivation of assets and liabilities:
(1) Book value of IOR + 70% of fair value of IEE.
(2) Book value of IOR + 70% of fair value of IEE + 30% of book value of IEE.
(3) Book value of IOR + 100% of fair value of IEE.

balance sheet are those in which the shareholders of the parent have an ownership interest. Because of the strict identification of consolidated assets and liabilities as only those owned by parent shareholders, this approach is also called the **proprietary** method. However, in this text we prefer to avoid using that label because of possible confusion with the proprietary theory of accounting, in which the accounting is performed from the point of view of the residual common shareholders. The proprietary theory of accounting underlies virtually all private enterprise accounting in North America, including the alternative methods of accounting for minority interest, and thus we prefer not to use the term to describe a particular method of consolidation.

The problem with the proportionate consolidation approach for subsidiaries is that it focuses on ownership interest rather than on control. When a parent controls a subsidiary, the parent controls all of the net assets of the subsidiary, not just the proportion represented by the parent's ownership interest. Users of the statements would not be given a complete picture of the resources, obligations, and revenue-generating activities of the combined entity. They would have no way of compensating for the deficiency, unless they could also obtain financial statements for the subsidiary, thus filling in the missing information. Therefore, proportionate consolidation has not been accepted in practice for accounting for controlled subsidiaries.

However, proportionate consolidation has gained acceptance in Canada for accounting for **joint ventures**. Joint ventures will be discussed in Chapter 10.

Parent-Company Approach

The second column of Schedule 9-3 shows the IOR consolidated balance sheet as it would appear under the parent-company approach. In this approach, all of IEE's assets and liabilities are reflected in IOR's consolidated statements in recognition of the fact that IOR controls all of the IEE assets.

The parent-company approach is a strict application of the historical cost basis of accounting. The IOR consolidated assets show (1) the historical cost of IOR's separate entity assets, (2) the historical cost to IOR of IOR's share of IEE assets (i.e., the purchase price of IEE shares acquired) and (3) the historical cost to IEE of the 30% portion of the net assets not purchased by IOR. Since the minority share of net assets has been included, it is necessary to offset these net assets with the amount of IEE shareholders' equity that relates to the minority interest. The consolidated balance sheet includes the 30% of the book value of the IEE net assets that relates to minority interest, and therefore the offset is 30% of the IEE unconsolidated shareholders' equity (or net assets), which is $240,000.

The parent-company approach can be criticized because it results in the anomaly that the same assets (of IEE) are reported on two different bases: fair value for part of each asset and book value for the remainder of each asset. If one of the purposes of consolidated statements is to give the user a view of the total resources controlled by the parent, then it is difficult to rationalize the parent-company approach; the parent company controls the fair value of all of the subsidiary's assets, not just part of the fair value. Nevertheless, the parent-company approach is the basis of the approach currently recommended in the *CICA Handbook* [para. 1600.15].

Entity Approach

The third column of Schedule 9-3 shows the IOR consolidated balance sheet as it would appear if the entity approach to minority interest were used. The entity approach includes the full fair value of IEE's assets and liabilities in the IOR consolidated balance sheet, rather than just the fair-value increments that relate to IOR's 70% share.

The total fair value of IEE's identifiable net assets is $1,100,000, as is shown in Schedule 9-2. Thus the total amount of IOR's identifiable net assets is increased by that amount upon consolidation. In addition, IOR paid $70,000 for goodwill; therefore the total IEE goodwill, based on the price which IOR paid for its 70% interest, could be calculated at $100,000. Since 30% of the goodwill pertains to the IEE minority shareholders, minority interest is shown as $360,000 ([30% x $1,100,000] + [30% x $100,000]) (as shown in Schedule 9-3).

The assignment of goodwill to the minority shareholders' interest can be defended since if 70% of IEE is worth $840,000, then 30% must be worth 3/7 of that amount, or $360,000. Securities laws give some support to this approach because when there has been a block purchase of shares in certain publicly traded companies,[1] an offer to buy minority shareholders' shares must be at least as attractive as the price paid for the majority shares.

However, an acquiring company may be willing to pay a bonus in order to gain control, and it may be *control* of the assets that gives rise to goodwill, not just a share interest in the assets. That control gives rise to goodwill is evidenced by the fact that many tender offers or takeover bids propose a high price, but offer to buy only enough of the outstanding shares (i.e., 51%) to gain control. Other evidence of the value of a controlling block of shares is suggested by testimony in a court case involving Crown Trust Co. shares. In a 1979 transaction involving 43.65% of Crown Trust's shares, the seller was alleged to have received a high price only because the seller had the cooperation of another holder of 10% of shares, thereby "ensuring that the buyer could obtain more than 50 per cent of the firm's shares."[2]

A very public battle over control of Canadian Tire in 1986 and 1987 gave dramatic support to the idea that a buyer is willing to pay a considerable premium for a control block, but not for non-controlling (or nonvoting) common shares. Canadian Tire has two classes of shares that share equally in all respects except that one class ("common") has voting rights while the other class ("Class A") does not. The two classes generally sold at about the same price since their dividend expectations were identical. In an attempted takeover, however, the price of the voting shares shot up to about ten times that of the nonvoting shares, clearly indicating that control was worth a lot and non-controlling shares were worth less.

Therefore, a modification of the entity approach provides that only the goodwill actually purchased by the parent is shown on the consolidated balance sheet; no goodwill would be assigned to the minority interest. In that case, the last column of Schedule 9-3 would differ in two respects: (1) the amount shown for goodwill would be $70,000, and (2) the amount for

---

1 For example, those covered by the *Ontario Securities Act* (Section 91).
2 Allan Robinson, "Black Was Aiding Widows in Crown Trust Deal," *The Globe and Mail* (October 29, 1983), p. B7.

minority interest would be only \$330,000, or 30% of the fair value of IEE's identifiable net assets. Some authors refer to this approach as the **parent-company extension** approach.

It should be noted that the *entity* approach to minority interests is consistent with, but not the same as, the *new-entity* approach to consolidated financial statements discussed in Chapter 7. The two should not be mixed up: *new entity* is an approach to consolidation that involves the reporting of fair values for the parent's assets and liabilities; *entity* is an approach to accounting for the minority interest of non-wholly owned subsidiaries at fair values.

Since the currently recommended approach for accounting for minority interests in Canada is essentially the parent-company approach to the fair-value purchase method, the following illustrations of consolidations use that approach. Consolidation under the entity approach would essentially be identical; the only difference would be that the consolidated assets and liabilities and the minority interest would include the minority interest's share of the subsidiary's fair-value increments. Amortization of the minority interest's fair-value increments would be charged against minority interest on the consolidated balance sheet.

Summary of Consolidation Approaches

When a business combination occurs, there are two main variables to the consolidation approach: (1) the valuation of the *acquired* company's net assets, and (2) the valuation of the *acquiring* company's net assets. The existence of a minority interest introduces a third variable, the valuation of the minority interest's share of the net assets. We can summarize the variables as follows:

1. Valuation of the acquiring company's net assets:
   a. Book value
   b. Fair value

2. Valuation of the acquired (majority) share in the subsidiary's net assets:
   a. Book value
   b. Fair value

3. Valuation of the minority interest's share of the subsidiary's net assets:
   a. Book value
   b. Fair value
   c. Exclude

Mathematically, there are twelve possible combinations of these alternatives. But as we have already seen, only five are viable, as shown in the last column of Schedule 9-1.

If there is no minority interest, then the third variable disappears, leaving four possible but three practical alternatives. These are the three alternatives in the first column of Schedule 9-1.

If a non-wholly owned subsidiary was founded by the parent corporation rather than acquired by purchase (or business combination), then matters are simplified even further. There is no valuation variable for either the parent or the majority share of the subsidiary. The only variable is whether to include or exclude the book value of the minority interest's share of net assets.

B. CONSOLIDATION AT DATE OF ACQUISITION

The IOR consolidated balance sheet at date of acquisition (January 1, 19x1) is illustrated in the second column of Schedule 9-3. In order to clarify the procedure, the process of consolidation is presented in Schedule 9-4, using two different direct approaches.

SCHEDULE 9-4

Consolidation at Date of Acquisition, January 1, 19x1

Direct Approaches
(in thousands of dollars)
Dr. (Cr.)

APPROACH A:

	IOR unconsolidated net assets		IEE net assets 70% of fair value		30% of book value		IOR consolidated net assets
Cash	$1,000	+	$ 35	+	$ 15	=	$1,050
Accounts receivable	2,000		105		45		2,150
Inventory	200		35		15		250
Land	1,000		280		90		1,370
Buildings and equipment	3,000		385		105		3,490
Accumulated depreciation	(1,200)		—		—		(1,200)
Goodwill			70				70
Accounts payable	(1,000)		(70)		(30)		(1,100)
Future income taxes	(400)		—				(400)
Minority interest					$240		(240)
IOR net assets	$4,600		$840				$5,440

APPROACH B:

	IOR unconsolidated net assets		IEE net assets 100% of book value		Cost of fair-value increments		IOR consolidated net assets
Cash	$1,000	+	$ 50	+		=	$1,050
Accounts receivable	2,000		150		—		2,150
Inventory	200		50		—		250
Land	1,000		300		$ 70		1,370
Buildings and equipment	3,000		350		140		3,490
Accumulated depreciation	(1,200)		—		—		(1,200)
Goodwill					70		70
Accounts payable	(1,000)		(100)		—		(1,100)
Future income taxes	(400)		—		—		(400)
Minority interest			(240)				(240)
IOR net assets	$4,600		$560		$280		$5,440

In Approach A, we can directly obtain the consolidated amount for the assets and liabilities by starting with IOR's book values and adding 70% of the fair values and 30% of the book values for IEE's assets and liabilities. The sum of the amounts in the 30% book value column represents the minority interest, which is extended into the consolidated column. The resultant consolidated net asset balance of $5,440,000 is balanced by IOR's shareholders equity: $3,440,000 in common shares and $2,000,000 in retained earnings. Thus the consolidated balance sheet can be prepared from the figures in the last column, plus IOR's shareholders' equity account balances. When calculating the consolidated amount of buildings and equipment in Schedule 9-4, IOR's accumulated depreciation is carried forward. The accumulated depreciation for IEE, however, is netted against the asset account and only the net book value is carried forward. Therefore, the consolidated accumulated depreciation at the date of acquisition is only the amount relating to IOR's own assets. In future periods, the consolidated accumulated depreciation will include both depreciation on IOR's own assets plus depreciation on IEE's assets *since the date of acquisition* only, including amortization of the fair-value increments.

Approach A is a literal representation of the derivation of the consolidated assets and liabilities at the date of acquisition. IEE's assets and liabilities are consolidated at 70% of their fair values plus 30% of their book values. A somewhat different approach that yields the same result is presented as Approach B in Schedule 9-4. In this approach, the IEE assets are consolidated at 100% of book value plus the fair-value increment relating to the 70% of the net assets purchased. Since the net assets' fair value is equivalent to the book value plus the fair-value increment, the two approaches are mathematically equivalent:

70% (fair value) + 30% (book value)
= 70% [book value + (fair value − book value)] + 30% (book value)
= (70% + 30%) (book value) + 70% (fair value − book value)

The minority interest, calculated at 30% of IEE's net book value, is included in the second column of Approach B as a credit. The sum of the second and third columns is $840,000, which is the purchase price paid by IOR for 70% of IEE's shares. The sums of each of these two columns can be reconciled directly with the analysis of the purchase as was shown in Schedule 9-2, Part 2.

Since both approaches give the same result, it is immaterial which one is used. Approach B, however, is a more useful way of looking at consolidation subsequent to the date of acquisition, because we can take the total book value of the assets existing at the balance sheet date without trying to separate them into those existing at the date of acquisition (for fair values) and those acquired thereafter.

Schedule 9-4 illustrates the direct approach to preparing the balance sheet at the date of acquisition. A worksheet approach is illustrated in Schedule 9-5. The adjustment shown can be broken down into two components: (1) elimination of IEE's shareholders' equity, and (2) adjustment of IEE's net assets by the amount of the fair-value increment for which IOR has paid.

(1) Common shares	$200,000	
Retained earnings	600,000	
Investment in IEE		$560,000
Minority interest		240,000

SCHEDULE 9-5

IOR Consolidation Worksheet
January 1, 19x1
Dr. (Cr.)

	Trial balances		Eliminations and adjustments	IOR consolidated trial balance
	IOR	IEE		
Cash	$ 1,000,000	$ 50,000		$ 1,050,000
Accounts receivable	2,000,000	150,000		2,150,000
Inventory	200,000	50,000		250,000
Land	1,000,000	300,000	$ 70,000	1,370,000
Buildings and equipment	3,000,000	500,000	(10,000)	3,490,000
Accumulated depreciation	(1,200,000)	(150,000)	150,000	(1,200,000)
Investment in IEE	840,000	—	(840,000)	—
Goodwill	—	—	70,000	70,000
Accounts payable	(1,000,000)	(100,000)		(1,100,000)
Future taxes	(400,000)	—		(400,000)
Minority interest			(240,000)	(240,000)
Common shares	(3,400,000)	(200,000)	200,000	(3,440,000)
Retained earnings	(2,000,000)	(600,000)	600,000	(2,000,000)
	$ 0	$ 0	$ 0	$ 0

---

(2) Land	$ 70,000	
Accumulated depreciation	150,000	
Goodwill	70,000	
Building and equipment		$ 10,000
Investment in IEE		280,000

Entry 1 distributes the IEE net asset book value of $800,000 to the minority interest (for 30%) and IOR's controlling interest (to eliminate the investment account). The recording of minority interest is the only substantive difference between the eliminations for wholly owned subsidiaries and for non-wholly owned subsidiaries when we consolidate on the date of acquisition. On the worksheet shown in Schedule 9-5, these two entries have been combined into one in the eliminations and adjustments column:

Land	$ 70,000	
Accumulated depreciation	150,000	
Goodwill	70,000	
Common shares	200,000	
Retained earnings	600,000	
Buildings and equipment		$ 10,000
Investment in IEE		840,000
Minority interest		240,000

The credit to buildings and equipment for $10,000 is the net result of eliminating IEE's accumulated depreciation of $150,000 at the date of acquisition and recording the fair-value increment of $140,000. The total impact of the adjustment on the net of buildings and equipment less accumulated depreciation is to increase net buildings and equipment on the balance sheet by $140,000.

Acquisition Disclosure

Schedules 9-6 through 9-8 illustrate disclosures of business combinations when less than 100% of the shares are acquired. The first note (Schedule 9-6) is for the acquisition by Indal Limited of 80% of the shares of Season-All Industries. The minority interest is shown as a deduction from the net assets acquired in the amount of $2.8 million. Since the 20% minority interest of Season-All's net book value is $2.8 million, we can infer that the total net book value of Season-All's share equity is $14 million, and 80% is $11.2 million. The purchase price of $30 million (for 80%) must therefore have been about $18.8 million above book value, and the full excess apparently was allocated to goodwill.

The second example (Schedule 9-7) shows the acquisition of *100%* of the shares of Pafcon Limited by National Sea Products Limited. Acquisition of 100% may not seem to be a partial purchase, but in reality the purchase was of Pafcon's 64.6% interest in Pacific Aqua Foods Ltd. The assets over which control was purchased were those of Pacific Aqua Foods, and control over assets of $8.5 million was obtained by paying cash of $2.1 million and issuing non-voting shares valued at $3.1 million. Note that as is the case in the acquisition illustrated in Schedule 8-10, no operating results for the acquired company were included in National Sea Product's statements even though the subsidiary was owned for about six weeks of 1987.

The final example is that of First Toronto Capital Corporation's acquisition of control over Walhalla Mining Company (Schedule 9-8). The acquisition was of only 37% of the Walhalla shares, but the 37% was added to 20% already owned by First Toronto to bring First Toronto's total share up to 57%. The change in ownership interest triggered a change in reporting

---

SCHEDULE 9-6

1. Acquisition of business

   On December 31, 1987, the Company acquired 80% of the issued share capital of Season-All Industries, Inc., a company manufacturing vinyl and aluminum replacement windows in the United States. This acquisition has been accounted for by the purchase method.

   The consideration for this acquisition was $30.0 million in cash, allocated based on the fair values of the assets and liabilities at the date of acquisition, as follows:

   (in millions of dollars)

Current assets	$ 22.3
Fixed assets	11.0
Goodwill	19.0
Deferred charges	0.2
Current liabilities	(9.7)
Long-term liabilities	(10.0)
Minority shareholders' interests	(2.8)
	$ 30.0

   Source: Indal Limited annual report, year ended December 31, 1987.

SCHEDULE 9-7

2. Business acquisition

On November 20, 1987 and December 31, 1987, the Company purchased 100% of the outstanding common shares of Pafcon Limited. Pafcon Limited's only investment is a 64.6% interest in Pacific Aqua Foods Ltd., a company operating in the salmon aquaculture business on the west coast of Canada.

This transaction has been accounted for by the purchase method. Operating results will be included in these financial statements effective January 3, 1988. The net assets acquired with consideration given are as follows:

(in thousands of dollars)

Assets acquired:	
Current assets, net of cash of $2,375	$2,264
Fixed assets	4,197
Investments	974
Total assets	7,435
Less liabilities	(689)
Net tangible assets acquired	6,746
Goodwill	1,730
Total net assets acquired	$8,476
Consideration given:	
Cash, net of cash acquired of $2,375	$2,119
National Sea Products Limited's Non-Voting Equity Shares	3,147
	5,266
Minority interest	3,210
	$8,476

Source: National Sea Products Limited annual report, fifty-two weeks ended January 2, 1988.

method, from cost or equity reporting to consolidation.[3] There are three unusual aspects to this acquisition. One is that the amount allocated to goodwill was "subsequently expensed" or written off in the year of acquisition, probably on the basis of immateriality. The second is that the consideration was neither cash nor the acquiror's shares, but shares of another company (Giant Resources Limited) held by the acquiror. The third is that the shares acquired by the acquiror were not purchased from shareholders of Walhalla but from the company itself; this is apparent only from the fact that the Giant Resources Limited shares that were given as consideration appear in the list of

3 Accounting for changes in ownership interests presents special problems in consolidation; these problems will be addressed in Chapter 13.

SCHEDULE 9-8

2. Acquisition of Walhalla Mining Company N.L.:

Effective August 31, 1987, the corporation acquired control of Walhalla Mining Company N.L. by the sale to Walhalla of 18,600,000 shares of Giant Resources Limited in exchange for shares of Walhalla valued at $55,264,000. Walhalla is an Australian based publicly-listed merchant bank which operates primarily in the natural resources sector, and was previously owned as to 20% by the corporation. As a result of this transaction, the corporation's interest in Walhalla was increased to approximately 57%, from which time the results of Walhalla have been consolidated.

Details of the transaction are as follows (000's):

Net assets acquired:	
Cash	$ 28,609
Shares in Giant Resources Limited referred to above	55,264
Other, principally marketable securities	56,654
	140,527
Less:	
Bank indebtedness	19,944
Other liabilities	5,362
Minority interest	49,092
Net assets previously acquired by the corporation	11,931
	54,198
Goodwill (subsequently expensed)	1,066
	$55,264

Source: First Toronto Capital Corporation annual report, year ended December 31, 1987.

---

net assets acquired, and must therefore have been received in the exchange by Walhalla and not by any of its shareholders. Walhalla must have issued new shares or treasury shares to First Toronto.

C. CONSOLIDATION ONE YEAR AFTER ACQUISITION

For the year ended December 31, 19x1 (i.e., the year following the business combination), the following occurred:

1. IOR reported earnings of $300,000, excluding dividends received from IEE; IOR declared no dividends.
2. IEE reported earnings of $80,000; IEE declared and paid dividends totaling $30,000.
3. IEE sold merchandise to IOR for $55,000; the gross margin was 40% of sales. At year-end, $20,000 of these goods were still in IOR's inventory.

Schedule 9-9 shows the separate-entity pre-closing trial balances for IOR and IEE in the first two columns. The trial balances are almost identical to those shown in Schedule 8-3 for 100% ownership. The differences are:

1. The investment account is for the cost of 70% of the shares, or $840,000, instead of $1,200,000.
2. The IOR common shares are $3,440,000 instead of $3,800,000, reflecting the fact that 28,000 shares were issued to accomplish the business combination instead of 40,000 shares.
3. The dividend income received by IOR is only 70% of the $30,000 paid by IEE, or $21,000.
4. The cash is less by $9,000 owing to the smaller amount of dividends received by IOR from IEE: 70% of $30,000 instead of 100%.

The elimination and adjusting entry in the third column eliminates IEE's shareholders' equity accounts and the investment account, and adds the fair-value increments. This entry (or pair of entries, if broken down) is exactly

---

SCHEDULE 9-9

IOR Consolidation Worksheet, December 31, 19x1
(70% ownership of IEE)
Dr. (Cr.)

	Trial balances		Eliminations and adjustments		IOR consolidated trial balance
	IOR	IEE	1: Acquisition	2: Operations	
Cash	$ 971,000	$ 97,500			$ 1,068,500
Accounts receivable	2,200,000	250,000			2,450,000
Inventory	250,000	70,000		$ (8,000)c	312,000
Land	1,000,000	300,000	$ 70,000		1,370,000
Buildings and equipment	3,000,000	500,000	(10,000)		3,490,000
Accumulated depreciation	(1,300,000)	(167,500)	150,000	(7,000)a	(1,324,500)
Investment in IEE (at cost)	840,000		(840,000)	–	
Goodwill			70,000	(1,750)b	68,250
Accounts payable	(800,000)	(200,000)			(1,000,000)
Future income taxes	(400,000)				(400,000)
Minority interest			(240,000)	$\left\{\begin{array}{l}9,000\ f\\(24,000)d\\2,400\ e\end{array}\right.$	(252,600)
Common shares	(3,440,000)	(200,000)	200,000		(3,440,000)
Retained earnings (January 1, 19x1)	(2,000,000)	(600,000)	600,000		(2,000,000)
Dividends paid	–	30,000		(30,000)f	–
Sales	(2,400,000)	(300,000)		55,000 c	(2,645,000)
Cost of sales	1,750,000	180,000		(47,000)c	1,883,000
Depreciation expense	100,000	17,500		7,000 a	124,500
Other operating expenses	50,000	2,500			52,500
Income tax expense	200,000	20,000			220,000
Dividend income	(21,000)			21,000 f	–
Amortization expense				1,750 b	1,750
Minority interest in earnings of IEE				$\left\{\begin{array}{l}24,000\ d\\(2,400)e\end{array}\right.$	21,600
	$ 0	$ 0	$ 0	$ 0	$ 0

the same as the elimination entry that was used for consolidating at the date of acquisition in the previous section (Schedule 9-5).

The fourth column shows the adjustments that are necessary as a result of operations for 19x1. These adjustments are similar to those illustrated in Chapter 8 (Schedule 8-3), except that they are complicated somewhat by the fact that in this chapter we are assuming that IOR owns 70% of IEE rather than 100%. Therefore the minority interest must be accounted for.

The first two adjustments amortize the fair-value increments relating to buildings and equipment and to goodwill:

(2a)	Depreciation expense	$7,000	
	Accumulated depreciation		$7,000
(2b)	Amortization expense	$1,750	
	Goodwill		$1,750

The amortization is only for the fair-value increments relating to the 70% share purchased by IOR. Since the minority interest's share of assets and liabilities is being reported at book value, there is no additional amortization relating to the other 30%.

The third adjustment eliminates the intercompany sales in order to avoid double-counting, and reduces the inventory by the total amount of unrealized intercompany profit:

(2c)	Sales	$55,000	
	Cost of sales		$47,000
	Inventory		8,000

Adjustment (2c) is exactly the same adjustment as was made in Chapter 8 when we were assuming that IEE was 100% owned by IOR. The existence of minority interest does not affect this adjustment; since the entire inventory will be included in the consolidated balance sheet, the entire unrealized profit must be removed. However, the elimination of the unrealized profit does have another effect on consolidated earnings when there is a minority interest; we will discuss this effect shortly.

The IOR consolidated income statement will show the total revenues and the total expenses for IOR and IEE added together. The resultant income from operations will be the entire income for both companies. However, the shareholders of IOR will benefit from only 70% of the IEE earnings. The 30% share of IEE's earnings that increases the equity of IEE's minority shareholders must be subtracted from the total earnings of the two companies in order to determine consolidated net income from the point of view of IOR's shareholders. This is accomplished by adjustment (2d):

(2d)	Minority interest in earnings of IEE (I/S)	$24,000	
	Minority interest (B/S)		$24,000
	(30% of IEE reported net income of $80,000)		

The account debited in adjustment (2d) will be shown in the IOR consolidated income statement as a subtraction from earnings from operations; the account credited is the balance sheet minority interest account.

The intercompany sales were upstream sales, and thus the profit is included in IEE's reported net income of $80,000. Elimination of the unrealized profit of $8,000 reduces the IEE net income that will be included in the consolidated results to $72,000.

This reduction has two implications. First, it reduces the consolidated earnings from operations by $8,000, but IOR's share of the reduction is only $5,600. Second, it reduces the consolidated net asset value of IEE by $8,000. If the IEE net assets are reduced by $8,000, then minority interest must be reduced by 30% of that amount because minority interest on the consolidated balance sheet must always be the minority interest percentage times the value of the subsidiary net assets included on the consolidated balance sheet. Both of these effects are achieved by means of adjustment (2e):

(2e)	Minority interest (B/S)	$2,400	
	Minority interest in earnings of IEE (I/S)		$2,400
	(30% of unrealized profit in inventory of $8,000)		

The credit in adjustment (2e) is to the income statement account. Sales and cost of sales have both been decreased by adjustment (2c), but in such a way as to reduce consolidated earnings from operations by the full amount of the unrealized profit, $8,000. By crediting minority interest in earnings of IEE, we are *reducing* the deduction from consolidated earnings by $2,400, so that although the consolidated gross margin is reduced by $8,000, the consolidated net income will be reduced by only $5,600.

Adjustments (2d) and (2e) could have been combined. Instead of basing the minority interest's share of earnings on IEE's book net income, as in entry (2d), we could have based it on the IEE net income after adjustment for unrealized profits. The consolidation entry would then be a single entry for $21,600: ($80,000 — $8,000) x 30%:

Minority interest in earnings of IEE (I/S)	$21,600	
Minority interest (B/S)		$21,600

One final point must be made about the reduction of minority interest's share in the consolidated financial statements. Adjustment (2e) is made only on the working papers to prepare *IOR's* consolidated statements. The financial statements of IEE as a separate legal entity are in no way affected by the adjustments made in Schedule 9-9. IEE will still report to the minority shareholders a net income of $80,000 for 19x1, and net assets of $850,000 at year-end. Adjustment (2e) is a necessary part of the consolidation process for IOR, but it does not affect the income or financial position of IEE itself or the rights of minority shareholders in the earnings of IEE.

The final adjustment eliminates the dividends paid by IEE. Since 30% of the dividends were paid to IEE's minority shareholders, the entry reduces the minority interest to reflect the fact that IEE's net assets have been reduced by the payment of dividends:

(2f)	Dividend income	$21,000	
	Minority interest	9,000	
	Dividends paid		$30,000

The consolidated statements are reports to the parent company's shareholders, and therefore all of the subsidiary's dividend payments must be eliminated when consolidated statements are being prepared.

After the foregoing adjustments have been made, the balance sheet minority interest will total $252,600. This amount is 30% of the book value of the net assets of IEE that will be included in IOR's consolidated financial statements on December 31, 19x1. The amount of minority interest can be verified as follows:

	100%	30%
IEE net assets, January 1	$800,000	$240,000
IEE net income, as reported	80,000	24,000
IEE dividends	−30,000	−9,000
Unrealized profit	−8,000	−2,400
IEE net assets, December 31	$842,000	$252,600

All of IEE's net assets of $842,000 will be included in the consolidated balance sheet, but the minority interest reduces the interest of the IOR shareholders to the 70% ownership of IEE by IOR.

Equity-Basis Reporting

If IOR prepares unconsolidated financial statements, its investment in IEE will be reported on the equity basis. When the investor corporation owns less than 100% of the investee, the investor will report only its share of the investee's adjusted earnings. IEE's reported net income is $80,000, and thus IOR's share is $56,000, or 70%. To this amount, adjustments must be made for (a) amortization of the fair-value increment on buildings and equipment, (b) amortization of goodwill, and (c) unrealized profit on intercompany sales.

SCHEDULE 9-10

IOR's Investment in IEE, December 31, 19x1

	IOR equity (70%)
IEE net income, as reported: 70% of $80,000	$ 56,000
Amortization of fair-value increments:	
Buildings and equipment (20 years)	−7,000
Goodwill (40 years)	−1,750
Unrealized profit on upstream sales:	
$20,000 inventory @ 40% gross margin × 70% share	−5,600
IOR equity in IEE earnings, 19x1	$ 41,650
IOR dividends received: $30,000 × 70% share	−21,000
Investment in IEE, January 1, 19x1 balance	840,000
Investment in IEE, December 31, 19x1	$860,650

Schedule 9-10 summarizes the determination of IOR's equity in the earnings of IEE. After adjustments, the equity pick-up of earnings amounts to $41,650. The investment account at year-end will reflect the addition of the earnings of $41,650 less dividends received of $21,000. The year-end balance of $860,650 can be reconciled as follows:

	100%	70%
IEE net assets, December 31, 19x1	$850,000	$595,000
Less unrealized profit	−8,000	−5,600
Adjusted net asset book value	$842,000	$589,400

Plus *unamortized* FVI on:

Buildings and equipment	$133,000
Land	70,000
Goodwill	68,250
	$860,650

The investment account consists of the investor's share of the investee corporation's net assets adjusted for unrealized profits, plus the unamortized amount of fair-value increments on the investee's assets and liabilities and goodwill.

SCHEDULE 9-11

Investor, Ltd.
Balance Sheet
December 31, 19x1

	Unconsolidated	Consolidated
Current assets:		
Cash	$ 971,000	$1,068,500
Accounts receivable	2,200,000	2,450,000
Inventories	250,000	312,000
	3,421,000	3,830,500
Property, plant, and equipment:		
Land	1,000,000	1,370,000
Buildings and equipment (net)	1,700,000	2,165,500
	2,700,000	3,535,500
Investment in Investee, Ltd.	860,650	—
Goodwill	—	68,250
Total assets	$6,981,650	$7,434,250
Current liabilities:		
Accounts and other payables	$ 800,000	$1,000,000
Future income taxes	400,000	400,000
Minority interest	—	252,600
Shareholders' equity:		
Common shares (188,000 issued and outstanding)	3,440,000	3,440,000
Retained earnings	2,341,650	2,341,650
	5,781,650	5,781,650
Total liabilities and shareholders' equity	$6,981,650	$7,434,250

SCHEDULE 9-11 (continued)		
Investor, Ltd. **Income Statement** Year Ended December 31, 19x1		
	Unconsolidated	Consolidated
Sales revenue	$2,400,000	$2,645,000
Operating expenses:		
Cost of goods sold	1,750,000	1,883,000
Depreciation expense	100,000	124,500
Amortization expense	—	1,750
Other operating expenses	50,000	52,500
	1,900,000	2,061,750
Net income before income tax and earnings of subsidiary or minority interest	500,000 —	— 583,250
Income tax expense	200,000	220,000
	300,000	363,250
Plus equity in earnings of Investee, Ltd.	41,650	—
Less minority interest in earnings of Investee, Ltd.	—	21,600
Net income	$ 341,650	$ 341,650
Earnings per share	$1.82	$1.82

Comparison of Equity Reporting and Consolidation

We have already seen in the previous two chapters that if IOR prepared unconsolidated financial statements, the IOR earnings and retained earnings would be the same as they are on a consolidated basis, as long as IOR uses the equity basis of reporting its investment in IEE. Schedule 9-11 shows both the unconsolidated and consolidated balance sheet and income statement. In both cases, IOR's net income is $341,650, and the net assets (i.e., shareholders' equity) are $5,781,650.

However, the consolidated financial statements disaggregate the investment in Investee account and the equity in earnings of investee. The consolidated statements show all of the assets, liabilities, revenues, and expenses for the total economic entity.

Schedule 9-11 is directly comparable to Schedule 8-5, which also compared the unconsolidated with the consolidated financial statements. The only substantive difference between the two schedules is the percentage of ownership.

In Schedule 8-5, IOR owns 100% of IEE, whereas in Schedule 9-11, IOR owns only 70% of IEE. The real assets of the consolidated entity are no different, except that with the smaller share of ownership, IOR would have $9,000 less cash because 30% of the IEE dividends was paid to outsiders. But even though the assets of IOR and IEE are not otherwise affected by the degree of ownership, the consolidated balance sheets show different asset amounts.

Schedule 9-12 compares the balance sheet asset amounts; the 100% column is from Schedule 8-5 and the 70% column is from Schedule 9-11. Although the only real difference in the resources of the consolidated entity is the $9,000 in cash as noted above, the total assets differ by $125,250: the consolidated book value of land differs by $30,000, buildings and equipment differs by $57,000, and goodwill differs by $29,250.

These differences are the result of using the parent company approach to reporting the acquisition. The two columns in Schedule 9-12 differ by 30% of the fair-value increment of the subsidiary's assets at the date of acquisition. If the entity approach to the business combination had been used, then the asset values would have been the same regardless of the percentage of ownership, and the minority interest would have been based on the fair values rather than on the book values.

Effect of Ownership Percentage on Consolidated Assets

SCHEDULE 9-12

Comparison of Consolidated Assets for Investor, Ltd.
December 31, 19x1

	Ownership of Investee, Ltd.	
	100%*	70%**
Cash	$1,077,500	$1,068,500
Accounts receivable	2,450,000	2,450,000
Inventories	312,000	312,000
Land	1,400,000	1,370,000
Buildings and equipment	2,222,500	2,165,500
Goodwill	97,500	68,250
Total assets	$7,559,500	$7,434,250

*From Schedule 8-5
**From Schedule 9-11

CONSOLIDATION WHEN THE EQUITY METHOD IS USED

Throughout our discussion of consolidation, we have generally assumed that the parent company maintains the investment account on the cost basis. However, the parent may use the equity method of recording its investment. In that case, as we have seen, the parent would record its share of the subsidiary's earnings in the investment account and in a special income statement account. Dividends received from the subsidiary would reduce the investment account balance. Dividend income (from the subsidiary) would not appear on the parent's trial balance.

If IOR has recorded its investment in IEE on the equity basis, the trial balance of IOR on December 31, 19x1, would differ from that shown in Schedule 9-9 under the cost basis as follows:

Account	Cost basis (Schedule 9-6)	Equity basis
Investment in IEE	$840,000 Dr.	$860,650 Dr.
Dividend income	21,000 Cr.	—
Equity in earnings of IEE	—	41,650 Cr.

All other account balances would be the same as in Schedule 9-9.

The acquisition elimination entry would be unaffected by the method of maintaining the investment account; the initial cost of the investment of $840,000 would be eliminated. An additional worksheet entry would then be required in order to eliminate the $20,650 in unremitted earnings in the investment account. This amount can easily be eliminated by making a worksheet adjustment that reverses the original recording of the equity-basis earnings:

Equity in earnings of IEE	$41,650	
Investment in IEE		$41,650

The worksheet entry to eliminate IEE's dividends (adjustment 2f) would then debit the investment account instead of dividend income:

(2f)	Investment in IEE	$21,000	
	Minority interest	9,000	
	Dividends paid		$30,000

These two eliminating entries can be combined into a single entry. In that case, adjustment (2f) would be:

(2f)	Equity in earnings of IEE	$41,650	
	Minority interest	9,000	
	Investment in IEE		$20,650
	Dividends paid		30,000

In summary, maintenance of the investment account on the equity basis requires only minor modifications to the worksheet elimination entries. The entries that were recorded *on the parent's books* to recognize the subsidiary's earnings and dividends must be reversed *on the consolidation worksheet*. It is because of the necessity to reverse the recording under the equity basis that most companies use the cost basis of recording when consolidated statements are to be prepared. There is little point in recording amounts that must be undone when the consolidated financial statements are prepared.

SUMMARY

Frequently, a subsidiary is not wholly owned by its parent. The consolidation of non-wholly owned subsidiaries introduces another variable into the consolidation process: the valuation of the minority interest's share of the subsidiary's net assets.

Proportionate consolidation excludes the minority interest's share of the net assets from the consolidated balance sheet, and also includes only the parent's share of the subsidiary's revenues and expenses on the consolidated income statement. Proportionate consolidation is not considered appropriate for subsidiaries, because the parent controls all of the subsidiary's net assets and not just the proportion represented by ownership percentage. Proportionate consolidation is considered appropriate for joint ventures, however, when joint ventures make up a significant portion of the venturer's activities.

When 100% of the subsidiary's net assets are consolidated, there is no question but that the parent's share of those assets must be consolidated at their cost to the parent, as reflected by the fair value of the proportionate part of the assets and liabilities acquired, plus goodwill. A question does arise, however, as to whether the minority share of the net assets should also be consolidated at fair value, or carried forward at book values.

Current Canadian practice is to use book values, even though this results in the subsidiary's net assets being valued on two different bases. The use of book values is consistent with the historical cost concept of reporting. The use of fair values for the minority interest would depart from historical cost, would complicate consolidation in subsequent years, and does not seem to provide more useful information to users despite its apparent internal consistency.

Consolidation of a non-wholly owned subsidiary is somewhat more complex than for a wholly owned subsidiary, because the minority interest must be a portion of the net assets, and earnings must be recognized as a minority interest. The minority interest's share is reduced by the proportionate share of unrealized profits in upstream sales, but is not affected by amortization of fair-value increments.

This chapter has discussed and illustrated the major factors in consolidating non-wholly owned subsidiaries. The next chapter illustrates consolidation in more complex situations, and also demonstrates consolidation several years subsequent to acquisition.

SELF-STUDY PROBLEM 9-1[4]

On January 1, 19x9, Regina Ltd. acquired 60% of the shares of Dakota Ltd. by issuing common shares valued at $150,000. The balance sheet of Dakota Ltd. as of the date of acquisition was as follows:

---

4 The solutions to the self-study problems are at the end of the book, following Chapter 18.

Dakota Ltd.
Balance Sheet
January 1, 19x9

	Book value	Fair value
Current assets:		
Cash	$ 10,000	$ 10,000
Accounts and other receivables	20,000	20,000
Inventory	30,000	30,000
	60,000	
Fixed assets:		
Land	45,000	80,000
Building	150,000	130,000
Accumulated depreciation	(50,000)	
Equipment	130,000	10,000
Accumulated depreciation	(80,000)	
	195,000	
Total assets	$255,000	
Accounts payable	$ 40,000	40,000
Bonds payable, due January 1, 19x19	50,000	60,000
Total liabilities	90,000	
Common shares	100,000	
Retained earnings	65,000	
Total shareholders' equity	165,000	
Total liabilities and share equity	$255,000	

Prior to the acquisition of Dakota, Regina's balance sheet appeared as follows:

Regina Ltd.
Balance Sheet
December 31, 19x8

Current assets:	
Cash	$ 50,000
Accounts and other receivables	70,000
Inventory	80,000
	200,000
Fixed assets:	
Land	—
Building	260,000
Accumulated depreciation	(40,000)
Equipment	175,000
Accumulated depreciation	(70,000)
	325,000
	$525,000

Accounts payable and accrued liabilities	$ 80,000
Bonds payable, long term	—
Total liabilities	80,000
Common shares	220,000
Retained earnings	225,000
Total shareholders' equity	445,000
Total liabilities and share equity	$525,000

Required:
Prepare a consolidated balance sheet for Regina Ltd., as it would appear immediately following the acquisition of Dakota.

SELF-STUDY PROBLEM 9-2

During 19x9, the following transactions occurred between Regina Ltd. and Dakota Ltd. (see SSP9-1):

a. Regina lent $50,000 at 10% interest to Dakota Ltd. on July 1, 19x9, for one year. The interest was unpaid at December 31, 19x9.
b. During 19x9, Regina purchased inventory from Dakota at a cost of $400,000; $100,000 of that amount was still in Regina's inventory at year end.
c. During 19x9, Dakota purchased inventory of $200,000 from Regina; $40,000 of that amount was still in Dakota's inventory at the end of 19x9.

Other Information:
d. Dakota's building and equipment were estimated to have remaining useful lives from January 1, 19x9, of 10 and 5 years, respectively. Straight-line depreciation is being used.
e. Goodwill, if any, is to be amortized over 20 years.
f. Dakota's bonds were originally issued at par.
g. No fixed assets were sold or written off during 19x9.

The trial balances for both companies appear below, as of December 31, 19x9.

Required:
For the year ended December 31, 19x9, prepare consolidated financial statements for Regina Ltd., consisting of:

1. Income statement
2. Statement of changes in retained earnings
3. Comparative balance sheet
4. Statement of changes in financial position (cash basis)

Trial Balances
December 31, 19x9
Dr. (Cr.)

	Regina	Dakota
Cash	$ 30,000	$ 10,000
Accounts and other receivables	110,000	30,000
Inventory	160,000	60,000
Land	–	135,000
Building	300,000	150,000
Accumulated depreciation – building	(45,000)	(60,000)
Equipment	200,000	130,000
Accumulated depreciation – equipment	(80,000)	(90,000)
Investment in Dakota Ltd.	150,000	–
Accounts payable and accrued liabilities	(40,000)	(80,000)
Bonds payable, long term	(65,000)	(50,000)
Common shares	(370,000)	(100,000)
Retained earnings	(225,000)	(65,000)
Dividends paid	20,000	40,000
Sales	(2,000,000)	(1,000,000)
Cost of sales	1,000,000	600,000
Operating expenses	839,000	170,000
Dividend income	(24,000)	–
Other income	(7,000)	–
Interest expense	2,000	10,000
Income tax expense	45,000	110,000
	$ 0	$ 0

REVIEW QUESTIONS

9-1 Define the following terms:

a. Minority interest
b. Entity method
c. Proportionate consolidation
d. Parent-company approach

9-2 Why do some corporations prefer to control their subsidiaries with less than full ownership?

9-3 How can the inclusion of 100% of a subsidiary's assets on the consolidated balance sheet be justified when the parent owns less than 100% of the subsidiary's shares?

9-4 When all of a non-wholly owned subsidiary's revenues and expenses are consolidated, what recognition is given to the fact that the parent's share of the subsidiary's earnings is less than 100%?

9-5 Under a pure application of the entity method of reporting minority interest, what value is assigned to goodwill?

9-6 How does the parent-company extension approach modify the entity approach? What is the rationale for this modification?

9-7 Using generally accepted accounting principles, explain why a subsidiary's assets and liabilities are consolidated using two different valuations under the parent-company approach.

9-8 At the date of acquisition, how is the amount of minority interest measured?

9-9 One year after the date of acquisition, how is the amount of minority interest on the balance sheet measured?

9-10 How do unrealized profits on upstream sales affect the minority interest's share of a subsidiary's earnings?

9-11 How do unrealized profits on downstream sales affect the minority interest's share of a subsidiary's earnings?

9-12 How are minority shareholders likely to react to the reduction of their share of the subsidiary's earnings as a result of unrealized profits?

9-13 Why are a non-wholly owned subsidiary's dividend payments completely eliminated even though the parent does not receive all of the dividends?

9-14 What does the equity-basis balance of the investment account for a subsidiary represent (e.g., cost of the investment, market value of the investment, etc.)?

9-15 In Canada, all of a subsidiary's assets and liabilities are consolidated regardless of the ownership percentage of the parent. Nevertheless, the ownership percentage may affect the amount of the reported (consolidated) assets. Explain.

9-16 Explain briefly how the process of consolidation differs when the equity method is used by the parent for recording the investment account as compared to the cost method.

ITT & GTE   CASE 9-1

On March 31, 19x0, at the end of its fiscal year, I.T. Trace Co. (ITT) acquired 80% of the outstanding shares of G.T. Ellis, Ltd. (GTE), at a price in excess of the fair values of GTE's net assets. At the subsequent annual meeting of GTE, ITT voted its shares in GTE in favour of a motion dissolving GTE and distributing the net assets of the company to the shareholders. An amount equal to 20% of the fair value of the net assets would be distributed in cash to the minority shareholders; all remaining assets and liabilities would be distributed to the majority shareholder (ITT). This plan of dissolution received the required two-thirds majority of the shareholders and was implemented later in 19x0.

Required:
Explain how the financial statements of ITT after the dissolution of GTE would differ from or be similar to the consolidated financial statements of ITT had the dissolution not occurred.

Simpson Ltd.   CASE 9-2

Simpson Ltd. is a private Ontario corporation controlled by Ted Simpson. The company owns a series of chocolate chip cookie stores throughout Ontario, and also has a wholly owned Quebec subsidiary that operates stores in Montreal and Quebec City. Because of its lack of stores in Western Canada and its managers' lack of knowledge about that part of the country, Simpson Ltd. has just acquired 70% of the outstanding class A voting shares of Ong Inc. for $5,000,000 cash. Ong Inc. is another cookie store chain that is headquartered in Vancouver and has stores throughout Vancouver and Victoria, as well as in Edmonton, Saskatoon, and Winnipeg.

Ted expects that the acquisition will greatly help the Simpson Ltd. "bottom line," which in turn will help Simpson Ltd. to obtain expanded debt financing because of the greater net income and cash flow. The management of Ong Inc. will not change as a result of the purchase; the former sole owner, John Ong, retains the remaining 30% of the Ong Inc. shares and has agreed to continue as CEO of Ong Inc. for at least five years after the change in control. The president and chief operating officer, Travis Hubner, will also stay on, and thus there is no reason that the acquired company should not continue to be highly profitable. The condensed balance sheet of Ong Inc. at the date of acquisition is shown in Exhibit 1.

The acquisition was financed mainly by debt; $3,500,000 was borrowed by Simpson Ltd. from the Hong Kong Bank of British Columbia, secured by the assets of both Simpson Ltd. and Ong Inc. The bank has requested audited financial statements of both companies on an annual basis, supplemented by unaudited quarterly statements.

Ong Inc. owns the buildings in which some of its stores are located, but most are leased. None of the land is owned. The buildings are being depreciated over 30 years. John has obtained two separate appraisals of the owned buildings; one appraisal firm has placed the aggregate current value at $8,000,000, while the second firm arrived at a value of $7,400,000. Ong Inc. owns all of the equipment in its stores; the equipment is being depreciated over ten years, and is, on average, 40% depreciated. It would cost $3,300,000 to replace the existing equipment with new equipment of similar capacity. Inventories are generally worth their book values, except that the replacement cost of the stock of imported Belgian chocolate in the Vancouver warehouse is $20,000 less than book value because of the strengthening Canadian dollar. On the other hand, the accounts payable shown in Exhibit 1 include an unrealized gain of $10,000 because much of the liability is denominated in Belgian francs.

Required:

Determine, on a line-by-line basis, the impact on Simpson Ltd.'s consolidated assets and liabilities as a result of the acquisition, in accordance with Ted Simpson's objectives in acquiring Ong. Where alternative values could be used, explain the reasons for your selection.

EXHIBIT 1		
Ong Inc. **Condensed Balance Sheet** **May 8, 1989**		
Cash		$ 200,000
Accounts receivable		100,000
Inventories — raw materials and supplies		1,200,000
Buildings	$7,000,000	
Accumulated depreciation	1,400,000	5,600,000
Equipment	3,000,000	
Accumulated depreciation	1,200,000	1,800,000
Total assets		$8,900,000
Accounts payable		$ 350,000
Accrued expenses		50,000
Bank loan payable, due May 3, 1991		2,700,000
Future income taxes		1,100,000
Shareholders' equity:		
Common shares-Class A voting	$1,000,000	
Retained earnings	3,700,000	4,700,000
Total liabilities and shareholders' equity		$8,900,000

[ICAO]

CASE 9-3   Craig Ltd.

Craig Ltd. is a large Canadian manufacturer of construction and manufacturing equipment, the shares of which are widely held and actively traded on the Alberta Stock Exchange. In recent years, operating results have been poor due to general economic conditions. The financial community has become anxious about the future earnings capability of the company.

In January, 19x5, Craig Ltd. acquired 19% of the outstanding common stock of Teller Ltd. on the open market. The purchase price was $3.4 million. At that time, the book value of Teller Ltd. was $12 million, which, in the opinion of Craig Ltd.'s executive committee, reflected the fair market value of Teller's tangible assets. The executive committee felt the $3.4 million purchase price was justified in light of Teller's expertise and experience in computer-assisted design (CAD) systems, an area Craig's strategic planning group had identified as a growth area in the next decade.

Teller Ltd. represents Craig's first investment in another company's common shares. Craig's executive committee hopes for a long-term relationship between the companies, including some sharing of technology.

The purchase makes Craig Ltd. Teller's second largest shareholder. The largest shareholder holds 22% of Teller's common shares. When exercised as a voting block, Craig's holdings will entitle it to place two members on Teller's ten-person board of directors. In addition, Craig has just lent Teller $5 million in the form of a ten-year debenture, and this entitles Craig to a third member on that ten-person board, for the term of the loan.

In the current year, Craig expects to earn $200,000 in dividends on Teller's forecast total earnings of $2.5 million. Teller normally reinvests a significant portion of earnings in capital expansion and research and development.

Required:
Identify and evaluate the methods that might be used to account for Craig's investment in Teller Ltd. Your answer should include:

1. arguments based on the facts given in the case to justify the use of each method;
2. the impact each method will have on Craig's financial statements; and
3. your recommendation, with reasons, as to which method of accounting for Craig's investment should be used, in accordance with generally accepted accounting principles.

[SMA]

D. Ltd.   CASE 9-4

In early September, 19x0, your firm's audit client, D. Ltd. (D), acquired in separate transactions an 80% interest in N Ltd. (N) and a 40% interest in K Ltd. (K). Prior to the acquisitions, both N and K were audited by other public accounting firms. D's bank and shareholders have requested that the audited consolidated financial statements of D for the year ended August 31, 19x1, be available by the end of October. Your firm has been appointed the auditor of N but not of K.

All three companies are federally incorporated Canadian companies and have August 31 year-ends. They all manufacture small appliances but they do not compete with each other.

You are the senior on the audits of D and N. The partner has just received the preliminary consolidated financial statements attached (Exhibits 1 and 2) from the controller of D. He has given you the statements and requested that you provide him with a memorandum discussing the important financial accounting issues of D and its subsidiary and investee companies. The partner has requested that the memorandum also deal with any other issues that should also be brought to the attention of D's management.

D acquired the 80% interest in N for $4,000,000 paid as follows:

(1) $2,000,000 in cash
(2) 160,000 common shares of D recorded in the books of D at $2,000,000.

D acquired its 40% interest in K at a cost of $2,100,000 paid as follows:

(1) $100,000 in cash
(2) 160,000 common shares of D recorded in the books of D at $2,000,000.

During the course of the audits of D and N the following information was obtained:

1. The book value of 80% of N's net assets at the date of acquisition was $2,280,000. D's management provided the following acquisition data:

Price paid in excess of the book value of the shares, at the
date of acquisition $1,720,000

Including:

Excess of the current value of land over the book value	$ 800,000
Excess of the current value of plant and equipment over the book value	700,000
Adjustment for the 20% minority interest's share of the excess of the current value of land, plant, and equipment over the book value	(300,000)
Goodwill of N written off	(48,000)
Deferred research and development expenditures written off	(72,000)
Pension liability not recorded (unfunded past service cost)	(200,000)
Unallocated costs	840,000
	$1,720,000

2. The price paid by D for its investment in K was 10% lower than 40% of the fair market value of K's net assets.

3. Five years ago, D purchased 100,000 shares of X Ltd. (X), being an 18% interest, at a cost of $780,000 and 50,000 shares of Y Ltd. (Y), being a 20% interest, at a cost of $200,000. On February 19, 19x1, X declared a common stock dividend. At that date, the additional shares to be received by D had a market value of $56,000. By the date of receipt of the shares in June 19x1, the market value had dropped to $42,000.

4. The 20% minority shareholder in N owns a retail store that makes 30% of its purchases from N. On August 1, 19x1, this shareholder leased equipment to N on a ten-year lease at $3,000 per month, with an option to renew for five years at $1,000 per month. At the end of the ten years, N can purchase the asset for $40,000, or, at the end of the fifteen years N can purchase the asset for $1.

5. During August 19x1, K sold goods to D as follows:

Cost to K	$100,000
Normal selling price	125,000
Price paid by D	120,000

D had not sold these goods as of August 31, 19x1. N also sold goods to D in August 19x1, and D had not sold them by August 31, 19x1:

Cost to N	$60,000
Normal selling price	75,000
Price paid by D	85,000

6. For the year ended August 31, 19x1, D's sales were $8,423,300 and N's sales were $6,144,500.

Required:
Prepare the memorandum requested by the partner.
[CICA, adapted]

EXHIBIT 1

D Ltd.
Preliminary Consolidated Income Statement
For the Year Ended August 31, 19x1

Revenue	$14,567,800
Cost of goods sold	14,324,800
Gross profit	243,000
Selling and administrative expenses	1,345,000
	(1,102,000)
Income of K Ltd.	200,000
Loss before income taxes	(902,000)
Income tax recovery on loss	450,000
Loss before extraordinary item	(452,000)
Extraordinary gain on disposal of investments, less income taxes of $300,000 thereon	900,000
Net income	$ 448,000

D Ltd.
Preliminary Consolidated Balance Sheet
August 31, 19x1

ASSETS			LIABILITIES AND SHAREHOLDERS' EQUITY		
Current assets:			Current liabilities:		
Cash	$ 17,600		Bank loan payable		$ 3,000,000
Receivables	2,211,400		Accounts payable and		
Inventories:			accrued liabilities		4,475,500
Finished goods at standard			Provision for warranties		505,500
cost	3,487,700				7,981,000
Raw materials at FIFO	1,062,300				
Work in process	480,000		Deferred income taxes		285,000
Prepaid expenses	16,000		Long-term debt of N Ltd.		
	7,275,000		in U.S. dollars		1,000,000
Investment in K Ltd., at equity	2,155,000		Minority interest in N Ltd.		568,000
Investment in other companies,			Shareholders' equity:		
at cost	980,000		Capital		
			– 1,320,000 common shares	5,000,000	
Plant and equipment	14,988,500		– 10,000 preferred;		
Less accumulated			10%, convertible to eight		
depreciation	9,373,500		common shares per		
	5,615,000		$100 stated value		1,000,000
Land	675,000		Retained earnings		866,000
	6,290,000				
	$16,700,000				$16,700,000

EXHIBIT 1 (continued)

D Ltd.
Preliminary Consolidated Retained Earnings
For the Year Ended August 31, 19x1

Balance, September 1, 19x0	$ 618,000
Add net income	448,000
	1,066,000
Deduct dividends on preferred shares	200,000
Balance, August 31, 19x1	$ 866,000

D Ltd.
Preliminary Consolidated Statement of Changes in Financial Position
For the Year Ended August 31, 19x1

Sources:	
From operations	
Net income	$ 448,000
Add (deduct):	
Extraordinary item	(900,000)
Depreciation	1,317,300
Income of K Ltd.	(200,000)
	665,300
Dividend from K Ltd.	80,000
Issues of shares	4,000,000
Sale of investments	1,900,000
Other, net	165,000
Total sources of funds	$6,810,300
Uses:	
Acquisition of common shares of K Ltd. plus advance to K Ltd.	$2,450,000
Purchase of N Ltd.	4,000,000
Purchase of building and equipment	420,000
Increase in receivables	355,300
Decrease in working capital, excluding receivables	(415,000)
Total uses of funds	$6,810,300

EXHIBIT 2

N Ltd.
Preliminary Balance Sheet
August 31, 19x1

ASSETS		LIABILITIES AND SHAREHOLDERS' EQUITY	
Current assets:		Current liabilities:	
Cash	$ 10,000	Accounts payable and	
Receivables	900,000	accrued liabilities	$1,220,000
Inventory, at standard cost:		Income taxes recoverable	(18,500)
Finished goods	360,000	Provision for warranty	5,500
Prepaid expenses	5,000		1,207,000
	1,275,000		
		Deferred income taxes	125,000
Fixed assets at cost:			
Building, machinery and		Long-term debt of $1,000,000	
equipment	7,638,000	U.S. due in 10 equal	
Less accumulated		yearly installments of	
depreciation	4,331,000	$100,000 U.S. commencing	
	3,307,000	February 19x2	1,000,000
Land	450,000	Shareholders' equity:	
	3,757,000	Common shares	1,000,000
		Retained earnings	1,840,000
Goodwill	60,000		2,840,000
Deferred research and			
development: $150,000			
less $10,000 annual			
amortization to date	80,000		
	$5,172,000		$5,172,000

N Ltd.
Preliminary Retained Earnings Statement
For the Year Ended August 31, 19x1

Balance, September 1, 19x0	$1,850,000
Add net income	36,500
	1,886,500
Less dividends	46,500
Balance, August 31, 19x1	$1,840,000

P9-1

On December 30, 19x9, the balance sheets of the Perk Company and the Scent Company are as follows:

	Perk	Scent
Cash	$ 7,000,000	$ 200,000
Accounts receivable	1,000,000	600,000
Inventories	1,300,000	800,000
Plant and equipment (net)	6,700,000	3,400,000
Total assets	$16,000,000	$5,000,000
Current liabilities	$ 3,000,000	$ 200,000
Long-term liabilities	4,000,000	800,000
No-par common shares	5,000,000	–
Common shares — par $100	–	1,000,000
Contributed surplus	–	1,000,000
Retained earnings	4,000,000	2,000,000
Total equities	$16,000,000	$5,000,000

For both companies, the fair values of their indentifiable assets and liabilities are equal to their carrying values except for the following fair values:

	Perk	Scent
Inventories	$ 1,000,000	$ 600,000
Plant and equipment (net)	7,000,000	5,000,000
Long-term liabilities	3,800,000	1,100,000

The following cases are *independent*:
1. On December 31, 19x9, the Perk Company purchases the net assets of the Scent Company for $5.5 million in cash. The Scent Company distributes the proceeds to its shareholders in return for their shares, cancels the shares, and ceases to exist as a separate legal entity.
2. On December 31, 19x9, the Perk Company purchases 75% of the outstanding voting shares of the Scent Company for $4.5 million in cash. The Scent Company continues to operate as a separate legal entity.

Required:
For each of the two independent cases, prepare a consolidated balance sheet for Perk Company at December 31, 19x9, subsequent to the business combination. For the second case, prepare a consolidated balance sheet using *each* of the following four approaches:

a. Fair-value purchase:
    1. Proportionate consolidation
    2. Parent company
    3. Entity
b. New entity

[SMA, adapted]

P9-2

Zoe Ltd. has the following balance sheet at December 31, 19x9:

Zoe Ltd.
Balance Sheet
December 31, 19x9

Current assets		$ 70,000
Fixed assets		
Land	$ 30,000	
Building, net	100,000	
Equipment, net	50,000	180,000
Goodwill, net		20,000
		$270,000
Current liabilities		$ 45,000
Bonds payable		80,000
Common shares		100,000
Retained earnings at January 1, 19x9		60,000
Net loss for 19x9		(15,000)
		$270,000

On December 31, 19x9, Halifax Ltd. bought 70% of the outstanding shares of Zoe Ltd. and paid $190,000. The current fair values of the net assets of Zoe Ltd. on December 31, 19x9, are:

Current assets	$ 70,000	Current liabilities	$45,000
Land	180,000	Bonds payable	70,000
Building	160,000		
Equipment	20,000		

Halifax Ltd. is an investment company that has assets composed only of cash and short-term marketable investments.

Required:
Calculate the following items, as they would appear on the Halifax Ltd. consolidated balance sheet at December 31, 19x9:
a. Land
b. Goodwill
c. Minority interest
[CGA-Canada]

P9-3

Calgary Ltd. acquired a subsidiary, Ottawa Ltd., on July 1, 19x9, by paying $200,000 for 70% of the outstanding shares. The fiscal year for both companies is December 31. The balance sheets of Ottawa Ltd. and Calgary Ltd. are:

Ottawa Ltd.
Balance Sheet
July 1, 19x9

	Book values	Fair values
Current assets	$130,000	$130,000
Fixed assets		
Land	80,000	140,000
Building, net	115,000	100,000
Equipment, net	60,000	90,000
	$385,000	
Current liabilities	$ 60,000	60,000
Bonds payable	100,000	115,000
Common shares	100,000	—
Retained earnings at January 1, 19x9	70,000	—
Net income (January 1 to July 1)	55,000	—
	$385,000	

Calgary Ltd.
Balance Sheet
July 1, 19x9

		Book values	Fair market values
Current assets		$ 150,000	$100,000
Fixed assets			
Land	$400,000		800,000
Building, net	550,000		400,000
Equipment, net	360,000	1,310,000	200,000
Investment in Ottawa Ltd.		200,000	
Goodwill		400,000	
		$2,060,000	
Current liabilities		$ 60,000	60,000
Bonds payable		200,000	170,000
Common shares		1,000,000	—
Retained earnings at July 1, 19x9		800,000	—
		$2,060,000	

Required:
Prepare the consolidated balance sheet as at July 1, 19x9, for Calgary Ltd., following *CICA Handbook* recommendations.
[CGA-Canada]

Qorp Ltd. has the following balance sheet at December 31, 19x1.

Qorp Ltd.
Balance Sheet
December 31, 19x1

Current assets		$ 75,000
Fixed assets		
Land	$ 40,000	
Building, net	110,000	
Equipment, net	60,000	210,000
Goodwill, net		50,000
		$335,000
Current liabilities		$ 55,000
Bonds payable, due 19x19		80,000
Common shares		120,000
Retained earnings January 1, 19x1		140,000
Net loss for 19x1		(60,000)
		$335,000

On January 1, 19x2, Zip Ltd., whose assets are composed entirely of share invest-ments and cash, paid $185,000 for 70% of the outstanding shares of Qorp Ltd. The current fair values of the net assets of Qorp Ltd. on January 1, 19x2, were:

Current assets	$ 75,000	Current liabilaities	$55,000
Land	85,000	Bonds payable	80,000
Building	190,000		
Equipment	20,000		

Zip Ltd. had the following shareholders' equity on January 1, 19x2.

Common shares	$ 480,000
Retained earnings	710,000
	$1,190,000

Required:
a. Assume a consolidated balance sheet is prepared on January 1, 19x2. Calculate the dollar amounts for the following items as they would appear on that con-solidated balance sheet:
1. Goodwill
2. Land
3. Equipment
4. Common shares
5. Retained earnings
6. Minority interest

b. Explain precisely the term "minority interest" (as you would to a shareholder).
[CGA-Canada]

P9-5

On January 1, 19x6, Big Ltd. purchased 80% of the shares of Small Ltd. for $1,400,000 and, on the same day, Small Ltd. purchased 60% of the shares of Smaller Ltd. for $930,000. Any excess of the purchase price was allocated to goodwill and amortized over ten years.

At January 1, 19x6

	Big Ltd.	Small Ltd.	Smaller Ltd.
Shares	$ 950,000	$ 600,000	$ 400,000
Retained Earnings	1,300,000	910,000	830,000
	$2,250,000	$1,510,000	$1,230,000

During 19x6

	Big Ltd.	Small Ltd.	Smaller Ltd.
Net income (cost basis)	$ 400,000	$ 300,000	$ 200,000
Dividends paid	80,000	70,000	50,000

Ignore income taxes. There were no intercompany transactions.

Required:

Calculate the balance of minority interest as it would be shown on the consolidated balance sheet of Big Ltd., as at December 31, 19x6.
[CGA-Canada]

P9-6

On January 1, 19x9, Regina Ltd. acquired 60% of the common shares of its new subsidiary, Dakota Ltd. for $150,000. The balance sheet of Dakota Ltd. as of the date of purchase was:

Dakota Ltd.
Balance Sheet
January 1, 19x9

	Book values	Fair market values
Current assets	$ 60,000	$ 60,000
Fixed assets		
Land	45,000	80,000
Building (net of $50,000 accum. deprec.)	100,000	130,000
Equipment (net of $80,000 accum. deprec.)	50,000	10,000
	$255,000	$280,000
Current liabilites	$ 40,000	$ 40,000
Bonds payable, due 19x19	50,000	60,000
Common shares	100,000	
Retained earnings, January 1, 19x9	65,000	
	$255,000	

Additional Information:

1. As of January 1, 19x9, the building and equipment are estimated to have remaining useful lives of ten years and five years, respectively. Straight-line depreciation is being used. Goodwill, if any, is to be amortized over twenty years.
2. Dakota's bonds were originally issued at par.
3. Regina Ltd. lent $50,000 at 10% interest to Dakota Ltd. on July 1, 19x9, for one year. (The interest was unpaid at December 31, 19x9.)
4. During 19x9, Dakota Ltd. earned $110,000 and paid $40,000 in dividends.

Required:

Prepare the journal entries to record the above events on the books of Regina Ltd. for the year 19x9, using the equity method.
[CGA-Canada]

P9-7

Parent Ltd. pays $450,000 cash for 70% of the outstanding voting shares of Sub Ltd. on January 1, 19x8. The following information was available:

Sub Ltd.
Trial Balance
January 1, 19x8

	Book value	Fair value
Cash	$ 20,000	$ 20,000
Inventory	40,000	30,000
Equipment, net	120,000	100,000
Building, net	200,000	260,000
Land	70,000	180,000
	$450,000	$590,000
Liabilities	10,000	6,000
Common shares	150,000	—
Retained earnings	290,000	—
	$450,000	—

During 19x8, Sub Ltd. earns $130,000 and pays no dividends. The inventory on hand at January 1, 19x8, was sold during 19x8. The equipment will be depreciated over ten years straight-line, the building will be depreciated over twenty years straight-line, and any goodwill will be amortized over forty years straight-line. The liabilities were paid during 19x8. Parent company uses the cost method of accounting for its investment.

Required:

Prepare the eliminating entries that would appear on the consolidated working papers at December 31, 19x8, based on the above information.
[CGA-Canada]

P9-8

On June 30, 19x1, Paul Ltd., acquired for cash of $19 per share 80% of the outstanding voting common shares of Sand Ltd. Both companies continued to operate as separate entities and both have calendar year-ends. On June 30, 19x1, after closing the nominal accounts, Sand's condensed balance sheet was as follows:

ASSETS:	
Cash	$ 700,000
Accounts receivable, net	600,000
Inventories	1,400,000
Property, plant, and equipment, net	3,300,000
Other assets	500,000
Total assets	$6,500,000

LIABILITIES AND SHAREHOLDERS' EQUITY:	
Accounts payable	$ 700,000
Long-term debt	2,600,000
Other liabilities	200,000
Common shares, par value $1.00 per share	1,000,000
Contributed surplus	400,000
Retained earnings	1,600,000
Total liabilities and shareholders' equity	$6,500,000

On June 30, 19x1, Sand's assets and liabilities having fair values different from the book values were as follows:

	Fair value
Property, plant, and equipment net	$16,400,000
Other assets	200,000
Long-term debt	2,200,000

The difference between the fair values and book values resulted in a gross charge or credit to income for the consolidated statements for the six-month period ending December 31, 19x1, as follows:

Property, plant, and equipment, net	$500,000 charge
Other assets	10,000 credit
Long-term debt	5,000 charge

The amount paid by Paul in excess of the fair value of the net assets of Sand is attributable to expected future earnings of Sand and will be amortized over the maximum period allowable.

On June 30, 19x1, there were no intercompany receivables or payables. During the six-month period ending December 31, 19x1, Sand acquired merchandise from Paul at an invoice price of $500,000. The cost of the merchandise to Paul was $300,000. At December 31, 19x1, one-half of the merchandise was not sold and Sand had not yet paid for any of the merchandise. The 19x1 net income (loss) for both companies was as follows:

	Paul	Sand
January 1 to June 30	$350,000	$ (750,000)
July 1 to December 31	600,000	1,250,000

On July 1, 19x1, Paul sold Sand an acre of land (historical cost $200,000) for $80,000 and a building (historical cost $260,000, accumulated depreciation $169,000, i.e., six and a half years of depreciation) for $455,000. Sand will depreciate the asset on the same basis as Paul since the building is expected to be of zero value in three and a half years.

On December 31, 19x1, after closing the nominal accounts, the condensed balance sheets for both companies were as follows:

	Paul	Sand
ASSETS:		
Cash	$ 3,500,000	$ 600,000
Accounts receivable, net	1,400,000	1,500,000
Inventories	1,000,000	2,500,000
Property, plant, and equipment, net	2,000,000	3,800,000
Investment in subsidiary, cost	15,200,000	—
Other assets	100,000	500,000
Total assets	$23,200,000	$8,900,000
LIABILITIES AND SHAREHOLDERS' EQUITY:		
Accounts payable	$ 1,500,000	$1,800,000
Long-term debt	4,000,000	2,600,000
Other liabilities	500,000	250,000
Common shares, par value $1.00 per share	10,000,000	1,000,000
Contributed surplus	5,000,000	400,000
Retained earnings	2,200,000	2,850,000
Total liabilities and shareholders' equity	$23,200,000	$8,900,000

Required:
Prepare a condensed consolidated balance sheet (in good form) of Paul Ltd. as of December 31, 19x1. Show supporting computations in good form. Ignore income tax and deferred tax considerations in your answer.
[CGA-Canada]

P9-9

Consult the data in P8-3. Assume that instead of buying 100% of the shares for $5,000,000 cash, Paternal buys 70% of Subservient's common shares for $3,500,000 cash. The other information in P8-3 is the same, except that on Paternal's December 31, 19x1, balance sheet, cash will be $2,500,000 and investments will be $3,500,000.

Required:
a. Prepare a consolidated balance sheet for Paternal Inc. at December 31, 19x1, following the parent-company approach.
b. If P8-3 has been solved, explain the differences in the consolidated asset values for Paternal Inc. shown under 70% ownership of Subservient as compared to those shown when Paternal owns 100% of Subservient.

P9-10

On January 1, 19x6, Par Ltd. purchased 80% of the voting shares of Sub Ltd. for $906,400. The balance sheet of Sub Ltd. on that date was as follows:

Sub Ltd.
Balance Sheet
January 1, 19x6

	Net Book Value	Fair Market Value
Cash	$ 160,000	$160,000
Accounts receivable	200,000	240,000
Inventory	300,000	380,000
Net fixed assets	900,000	750,000
Total	$1,560,000	
Current liabilities	$ 150,000	$110,000
Bonds payable	400,000	*
Discount on bonds	(38,000)	*
Common shares	200,000	—
Retained earnings	848,000	—
Total	$1,560,000	

*Assumed to be equal to book value.

The accounts receivable, inventory, and current liabilities have "turned over" by December 31, 19x6, and the net fixed assets will be amortized over ten years, on a straight-line basis. Any goodwill created by the purchase will be amortized over twenty years on a straight-line basis.

Additional Information:
1. During 19x6, Par Ltd. sold goods costing $100,000 to Sub Ltd. for $140,000. At December 31, 19x6, 20% of these goods were still in the inventory of Sub Ltd.
2. In 19x6, Sub Ltd. sold goods costing $200,000 to Par Ltd. for $250,000. At December 31, 19x6, 30% of these goods were still in the inventory of Par Ltd.
3. In 19x6, Sub Ltd. sold land to Par Ltd. for $300,000. The land had cost Sub $240,000.

The financial statements for Par Ltd. and Sub Ltd. at December 31, 19x6 are presented below.

	Par Ltd.	Sub Ltd.
Cash	$ 200,000	$ 140,000
Accounts receivable	300,000	190,000
Inventory	500,000	460,000
Net fixed assets	1,200,000	900,000
Investment in Sub Ltd.	906,400	—
Other investments	417,600	—
Total	$3,524,000	$1,690,000

Current liabilities	300,000	200,000
Bonds payable	600,000	400,000
Discount on bonds	(87,000)	(32,000)
Common shares	500,000	200,000
Retained earnings at January 1, 19x6	2,211,000	922,000
Total	$3,524,000	$1,690,000
Sales	$2,000,000	$2,000,000
Cost of goods sold	1,400,000	1,700,000
Gross profit	600,000	300,000
Depreciation	100,000	90,000
Interest expense	63,000	44,000
Other expenses	264,000	152,000
Investment income	(37,000)	(60,000)
Net income	$ 210,000	$ 74,000

There are no dividends, and income taxes may be ignored.

Required:
a. Prepare the consolidated income statement for the year ended December 31, 19x6.
b. Present the following as they would appear on the consolidated balance sheet at December 31, 19x6:
   (1) Net fixed assets
   (2) Goodwill
   (3) Retained earnings
[CGA-Canada]

P9-11

Refer to P8-7. Assume instead that Practical Corp. acquires 90,000 shares (60%) of Silly Inc. by issuing 40,000 of its own shares, which are worth $600,000. Other facts are as stated in P8-7.

Required:
Using a consolidation worksheet, prepare consolidated balance sheets for Practical Corp. immediately following the share exchange, assuming alternatively that:
a. The parent-company approach is used.
b. The entity approach is used.

P9-12

Refer to P9-11, P8-7, and P8-8. The trial balances of Practical Corp. and Silly Inc. are shown below. On July 16, 19x1, Silly borrowed $100,000 from Practical; $40,000 was repaid before year-end. The loan was non-interest-bearing. Through the course of the year, Silly sold goods to Practical for $400,000. Silly's gross margin is 40% of selling price. All of these goods were resold by Practical to its customers for $600,000. There were no other intercompany transactions.

(Note: This problem is parallel to P8-8 but supposes 60% ownership instead of 100%.)

Required:

a. Determine Practical's equity in the income of Silly and the year-end balance of the investment, assuming that Practical reports its investment in Silly on the equity basis.

b. Prepare a complete set of consolidated financial statements for Practical Corp., including a statement of changes in financial position and a statement of changes in consolidated retained earnings. Use the parent-company approach, consistent with the current *CICA Handbook* recommendations.

Trial balances
Dr. (Cr.)
December 31, 19x1

	Practical	Silly
Cash	—	$ 15,000
Accounts and other receivables	$ 210,000	80,000
Inventory	120,000	55,000
Buildings and equipment	1,300,000	900,000
Accumulated depreciation	(570,000)	(445,000)
Land	—	60,000
Investment in Silly Inc. (at cost)	600,000	—
Other investments	70,000	30,000
Deferred charges	—	80,000
Accounts and other payables	(150,000)	(180,000)
Bonds payable	—	(170,000)
Common shares	(1,200,000)	(150,000)
Retained earnings (net of dividends)	(220,000)	(200,000)
Sales	(1,500,000)	(900,000)
Dividend income	(30,000)	—
Cost of sales	1,000,000	540,000
Depreciation expense	70,000	45,000
Amortization expense	—	40,000
Other expenses	300,000	200,000
	$ 0	$ 0

9-13

Refer to P9-12. Assume the same facts as given therein.

Required:

Prepare a complete set of consolidated financial statements for Practical Corp., using the entity method for reporting Practical's investment in Silly.

10

Reporting Intercorporate Investments in Later Years

The previous chapters have discussed the basic concepts underlying the reporting of intercorporate investments, including equity-basis reporting, consolidated financial statements, and the reporting of minority interests. In this chapter, we round out the discussion of intercorporate investments by exploring in a more general way the reporting of intercorporate investments subsequent to the date of acquisition. Part A continues the example begun in Chapter 9 by extending the illustration of consolidation of non-wholly owned subsidiaries to the second year subsequent to acquisition. Part B discusses equity-method reporting for significantly influenced investee corporations and for unconsolidated subsidiaries. Part C then illustrates the general approach to consolidation several years after acquisition of a subsidiary, using a new example (i.e., different from our continuing IOR/IEE example). Both the direct approach and the worksheet approach are illustrated. In Part D, we look at consolidated reporting for joint ventures.

A. CONSOLIDATION IN SECOND SUBSEQUENT YEAR

So far in our discussion of non-wholly owned subsidiaries, we have dealt only with consolidation at the date of acquisition and one year thereafter. In order to generalize the approach to consolidated financial statements for non-wholly owned subsidiaries, we will carry the example in Chapter 9 forward one additional year.

Assume that during 19x2, the following occurred:

1. IEE reported operating income of $90,000 and paid dividends of $20,000.
2. IOR reported net income of $360,000, excluding IOR's equity in the earnings of IEE; IOR paid dividends of $135,000.

3. IEE had sales of $60,000 to IOR; IEE's 19x2 gross margin was 45%; $10,000 of the sales are in IOR's inventory on December 31, 19x2.
4. IOR had sales of $20,000 to IEE; IOR's 19x2 gross margin was 30%; $6,000 of the goods sold to IEE are in IEE's 19x2 ending inventory.
5. IOR borrowed $500,000 from IEE on December 29, 19x2.
6. IEE sold its land to IOR for $540,000; the gain on disposal is not included in operating income, but is viewed by IEE as an extraordinary gain.

These facts are exactly the same as those used in Part B of Chapter 8; they are repeated here for convenience. The trial balances for IOR and IEE are shown in the first and second columns of Schedule 10-1.

To derive the consolidated financial statements at December 31, 19x2, we must make the same three types of worksheet adjustments and eliminations as we did in Part B of Chapter 8:

SCHEDULE 10-1

Preparation of IOR Consolidated Financial Statements
December 31, 19x2
(70% ownership of IEE)
Dr. (Cr.)

| | Trial balances | | Adjustments and eliminations | | | IOR consolidated trial balance |
	IOR	IEE	1: Acquisition	2: Cumulative	3: Current	
Cash	$ 385,000	$ 70,000				$ 455,000
Accounts receivable	1,900,000	775,000			$(500,000)g	2,175,000
Inventory	300,000	60,000			{ (4,500)c (1,800)d }	353,700
Land	1,540,000	—	$ 70,000		(240,000)e	1,370,000
Buildings and equipment (net)	3,800,000	500,000	(10,000)			4,290,000
Accumulated depreciation	(1,400,000)	(185,000)	150,000	$ (7,000)	(7,000)a	(1,449,000)
Investment in IEE (at cost)	840,000		(840,000)			—
Goodwill			70,000	(1,750)	(1,750)b	66,500
Accounts payable	(865,000)	(150,000)			500,000 g	(515,000)
Future income taxes	(500,000)	—			90,000 e	(410,000)
Minority interest			(240,000)	(12,600)	{ (28,050)f 6,000 h }	(274,650)
Common shares	(3,440,000)	(200,000)	200,000			(3,440,000)
Retained earnings (Jan. 1, 19x2)	(2,321,000)	(650,000)	600,000	29,350		(2,341,650)
Dividends paid	135,000	20,000			(20,000)h	135,000
Sales	(3,000,000)	(400,000)			{ 60,000 c 20,000 d }	(3,320,000)
Cost of sales	2,100,000	220,000		(8,000)	{ (55,500)c (18,200)d }	2,238,300
Depreciation expense	100,000	17,500			7,000 a	124,500
Amortization expense					1,750 b	1,750
Other operating expenses	200,000	12,500				212,500
Income tax expense	240,000	60,000				300,000
Dividend income	(14,000)				14,000 h	—
Minority interest in earnings of IEE					28,050 f	28,050
Gain on sale of land (net of tax)		(150,000)			150,000 e	—
	$ 0	$ 0	$ 0	$ 0	$ 0	$ 0

1. The adjustment for the acquisition, including
   a. establishment of the fair values of IEE's net assets,
   b. elimination of IEE shareholders' equity at the date of acquisition,
   c. establishment of minority interest at the date of acquisition, and
   d. elimination of the investment account.
2. The adjustment for the amortization of fair-value increments and goodwill and for IEE's earnings between the date of acquisition and the beginning of the current year.
3. The adjustments and eliminations for the current year's operations.

The only difference between the adjustments that need to be made at December 31, 19x2, in this chapter and those that were made in Chapter 8 is that here, we must recognize the existence of a minority interest when we make the worksheet adjustments and eliminations. The first adjusting entry (in the third column of Schedule 10-1) is to recognize the substance of the original acquisition. This entry is exactly as shown in Schedules 9-5 and 9-9.

The second adjustment ("cumulative") is for the balance sheet changes that have occurred since acquisition, but prior to the current year. These include (a) cumulative fair-value amortizations to the beginning of the current year, (b) unrealized profits in the asset balances at the beginning of the year, and (c) minority interest's share of the subsidiary's retained earnings since the date of acquisition. Also included in this worksheet entry would be adjustments for gains and losses on sales of fair-valued assets to third parties that occurred in prior years. We will illustrate the sale of fair-valued assets in Part C of this chapter.

On Schedule 10-1, the cumulative adjustment appears as follows:

(2) Retained earnings	$29,350	
Accumulated depreciation		$7,000
Goodwill		1,750
Cost of sales (beginning inventory)		8,000
Minority interest		12,600

The credit of $12,600 to minority interest consists of 30% of the change in the subsidiary's retained earnings since the date of acquisition, less the minority interest's portion of the unrealized profit on the upstream sales that is in the beginning inventory for the current year. The $12,600 can be derived as follows:

Change in IEE retained earnings from acquisition to the beginning of the current year	$50,000	
Minority interest portion (30%)		$15,000
Unrealized profit in IOR's inventory at the beginning of the current year	$ 8,000	
Minority interest portion (30%)		2,400
Net adjustment to minority interest for operations from acquisition to the beginning of the current year		$12,600

The debit to retained earnings in adjustment (2) reduces the IEE earnings retained since the date of acquisition for amortization ($7,000 + $1,750), unrealized profit ($8,000), and the minority interest's share of retained earnings ($12,600, as explained above). The remaining amount of IEE's retained earnings, $21,650 ($50,000 — $29,350), represents IOR's share of the IEE retained earnings, and flows through to the IOR consolidated retained earnings.

The third set of adjustments is shown in the current operations column of Schedule 10-1. This set of adjustments (a) eliminates the effects of intercompany transactions during the year and (b) adjusts the consolidated balance sheet amounts to the end of the current year.

Adjustments (a) and (b) record the amortization of the fair-value increments for 19x2:

(3a)	Depreciation expense	$7,000	
	Accumulated depreciation		$7,000
(3b)	Amortization expense	$1,750	
	Goodwill		$1,750

The third adjustment is for the upstream sales, which totaled $60,000 during the year. Of the upstream sales, $10,000 still remained in IOR's inventory at the end of 19x2. Since IEE's gross margin was 45%, the unrealized profit on these sales is $4,500, which must be credited to inventory:

(3c)	Sales	$60,000	
	Cost of sales		$55,500
	Inventory		4,500

The fourth adjustment eliminates the downstream sales, along with the unrealized profit thereon ($6,000 remaining in inventory at 30% gross margin):

(3d)	Sales	$20,000	
	Cost of sales		$18,200
	Inventory		1,800

Next, the intercompany sale of the land from IEE to IOR must be eliminated. This adjustment is exactly the same as when we assumed that IEE was wholly owned by IOR (Schedule 8-6):

(3e)	Gain on sale of land	$150,000	
	Future income taxes	90,000	
	Land		$240,000

Once all of the unrealized profits have been eliminated, the minority interest's share of the earnings of IEE for 19x2 can be calculated. The IEE net income as reported on the pre-consolidation trial balance is $90,000 after taxes, but before extraordinary items. This amount will be included in the consolidated earnings, reduced by those earnings that are included in the $90,000 but that have not yet been realized by the consolidated entity. There has been one adjustment for IEE unrealized earnings in 19x2 (exclusive of the extraordinary item), for the $4,500 profit as yet unrealized from upstream sales, reducing the amount of IEE profit included in IOR's consolidated earnings to $85,500. But in addition, we must recognize that the *beginning* inventory included unrealized profits that have now been realized in 19x2. Consolidated earnings were increased by $8,000 in adjustment (2) by decreasing cost of sales by the amount of the unrealized IEE profit in IOR's beginning inventory. Therefore, the total amount of IEE earnings included in IOR's 19x2 income statement will be $93,500: $90,000 - $4,500 + $8,000. Of this amount, 30% accrues to the minority interest:

(3f)	Minority interest in earnings of IEE (I/S)	$28,050	
	Minority interest (B/S)		$28,050

Note that the amount of unrealized profit relating to the *downstream* sales does not affect the minority interest. Any unrealized profit from downstream transactions is in the accounts of the parent corporation and 100% of this amount must be eliminated; there can be no minority interest share of the parent's earnings, only of the subsidiary's.

In this example, the extraordinary gain of $150,000 in the accounts of the subsidiary was completely eliminated because the gain arose from an inter-company transaction. If instead the land had been sold to a buyer outside of the consolidated entity, the extraordinary gain would have remained on the consolidation worksheet. In that event, 30% of the gain would also have been credited to the minority interest on the balance sheet, but the debit would have been to the extraordinary gain itself, and not to the minority interest on the income statement. The distinction between operating earnings and extraordinary items extends to the treatment of minority interests on the income statement. The treatment of extraordinary items will be discussed more fully in Chapter 12.

The penultimate adjustment eliminates the intercompany receivable and payable:

(3g)	Accounts payable	$500,000	
	Accounts receivable		$500,000

And finally, the dividends paid by IEE must be eliminated:

(3h)	Dividend income	$14,000	
	Minority interest (B/S)	6,000	
	Dividends paid		$20,000

SCHEDULE 10-2

Investor Ltd.
Consolidated Statement of Income
Years Ended December 31

	19x2	19x1
Sales revenue	$3,320,000	$2,645,000
Expenses:		
Cost of goods sold	2,238,300	1,883,000
Depreciation expense	124,500	124,500
Amortization expense	1,750	1,750
Other operating expenses	212,500	52,500
	2,577,050	2,061,750
Income before taxes and minority interest	742,950	583,250
Income taxes	300,000	220,000
	442,950	363,250
Minority shareholders' interest in earnings of Investee, Ltd.	28,050	21,600
Net income	$ 414,900	$ 341,650
Earnings per share	$2.21	$1.82

SCHEDULE 10-2 (continued)

Investor Ltd.
Consolidated Statement of Changes in Retained Earnings
Years Ended December 31

	19x2	19x1
Balance, January 1	$2,341,650	$2,000,000
Net income for year	414,900	341,650
Dividends declared	(135,000)	—
Balance, December 31	$2,621,550	$2,341,650

Investor Ltd.
Consolidated Balance Sheet

	December 31	
	19x2	19x1
ASSETS		
Current assets:		
Cash	$ 455,000	$1,068,500
Accounts receivable	2,175,000	2,450,000
Inventories	353,700	312,000
	2,983,700	3,830,500
Property, plant, and equipment:		
Land	1,370,000	1,370,000
Buildings and equipment (net)	2,841,000	2,165,500
	4,211,000	3,535,500
Goodwill	66,500	68,250
Total assets	7,261,200	7,434,250
LIABILITIES AND SHAREHOLDERS' EQUITY		
Current liabilities:		
Accounts and other payables	515,000	1,000,000
Future income taxes	410,000	400,000
Minority interest in Investee Ltd.	274,650	252,600
Shareholders' equity:		
Common shares (188,000 no-par shares issued and outstanding)	3,440,000	3,440,000
Retained earnings	2,621,550	2,341,650
	6,061,550	5,781,650
Total liabilities and shareholders' equity	$7,261,200	$7,434,250

SCHEDULE 10-2 (continued)

Investor Ltd.
Consolidated Statement of Changes in Financial Position
Years Ended December 31

	19x2	19x1
Operations:		
Consolidated net income	$ 414,900	$ 341,650
Add expenses not requiring cash:		
Depreciation	124,500	124,500
Amortization	1,750	1,750
Future income taxes	10,000	—
Minority interest in earnings of Investee, Ltd.	28,050	21,600
Changes in working capital items:		
Accounts receivable	275,000	(300,000)
Inventory	(41,700)	(62,000)
Accounts payable	(485,000)	(100,000)
Net cash from (used in) operations	327,500	27,500
Issuance of 28,000 common shares to acquire 70% of Investee Ltd. (see below)	—	840,000
Payment of dividends	(135,000)	—
Dividends paid to minority shareholders of Investee Ltd.	(6,000)	(9,000)
Investing activities:		
Purchase of buildings and equipment	(800,000)	—
Net assets of Investee Ltd. (Note 1), financed by shares (see above)	—	(790,000)
Net increase (decrease) in cash	$(613,500)	$ 68,500

Note 1: Acquisition of Investee Ltd.

Net assets acquired:		
Working capital, net of cash		$ 100,000
Land		370,000
Building and equipment		490,000
Goodwill		70,000
Minority interest (30%)		(240,000)
		$ 790,000

Schedule 10-2 presents the final comparative consolidated financial statements for Investor Ltd. for 19x2. The statements have been prepared from the final columns of Schedule 9-9 (for 19x1) and 10-1 (for 19x2). If the 19x2 consolidated balance sheet in Schedule 10-2 is compared to the 19x2 balance sheet in Schedule 8-7, it is apparent that the asset values for land and for buildings and equipment are different in the two balance sheets, even

Completed Consolidated Financial Statements

though the assets are actually identical. The reason, as noted previously for 19x1 (Schedule 9-12), is that the parent-company approach does not include the fair-value increments for the minority interest's share of the assets.

The consolidated statement of changes in financial position for 19x2 is essentially the same in Schedule 10-2 as it is in Schedule 8-7, except for the dividend payments to IEE's minority shareholders.[1] The net cash from operations is the same regardless of the percentage of ownership because the operational funds flows are not affected by the existence of minority shareholders; the income statement deduction for minority interest earnings is added back as an expense that does not require the use of funds. Of course, the investment in IEE (in 19x1) is for a different amount in Schedule 10-2 than in Schedule 8-7, due to the lower percentage of ownership. The IEE net assets acquired in Schedule 10-2 represent 70% of the fair values (net of cash), plus the goodwill.

B. REPORTING ON THE EQUITY BASIS

In Chapter 9, we showed how IOR's investment in IEE would be reported for 19x1 if IOR was reporting on the equity basis rather than by consolidating IEE. In this section, we illustrate equity reporting by IOR for 19x2. Equity reporting for significantly influenced companies is exactly the same as that illustrated herein. Only the percentage of ownership varies; a parent's ownership interest in unconsolidated subsidiaries is greater than 50%, while the investor's ownership interest in significantly influenced companies is 50% or less.

The relevant information regarding the operations of IOR and its 70% owned subsidiary, IEE, were summarized at the beginning of Part A of the chapter. When the investment in IEE is to be reported on the equity basis, then 70% of IEE's earnings is picked up by the investor corporation, adjusted for unrealized profits and for amortization of the fair-value increments and goodwill.

IEE's separate-entity net operating income after taxes was $90,000 for 19x2. IOR's unadjusted share of that amount is 70%, or $63,000. From this amount, we must deduct amortization of the fair-value increment on the buildings and equipment of $7,000, and amortization of goodwill of $1,750. The unrealized profit in IEE's reported net income must be deducted, and the unrealized profit in the opening inventory that has now been realized in 19x2 must be added.

The 19x2 upstream sales were $60,000, of which $10,000 remains in IOR's inventory at year-end. Since IEE's gross profit margin was 45% in 19x2, the unrealized profit in IOR's ending inventory is $4,500. The entire $4,500 is included in IEE's reported net income of $90,000, but IOR's share of the unrealized profit is only 70%, or $3,150. Therefore, IOR's share of IEE's net income must be reduced by that amount.

---

1 The dividends paid to minority shareholders could have been shown as a reduction of cash from operations, instead of as a financing activity.

The procedure for adjusting the equity-method earnings may appear to be different from that used to adjust when consolidating. In consolidation, the entire $4,500 of unrealized profit is removed from the consolidated net income, rather than just the ownership proportion. However, the minority interest in earnings is then deducted from the consolidated earnings, and the minority interest in earnings has also been adjusted for 30% of the unrealized profits. Therefore, the result is the same under either approach. Consolidation eliminates 100% of the profit, but then reduces the minority interest deduction by 30% of the unrealized profit. The net effect is to adjust earnings for only 70% of the unrealized earnings, just as is done somewhat more directly in equity reporting.

Similarly, the unrealized profit at the beginning of the year that has now been realized must be added to IOR's share of IEE's net income. IOR's opening inventory included $20,000 of goods that had been purchased from IEE. IEE's gross margin in the year of the sale (19x1) had been 40%. Thus the total unrealized profit in the beginning inventory was $8,000. Seventy percent of that amount is $5,600, which is added to IOR's 70% share of IEE's net income.

So far, the adjustments reduce IOR's share of IEE's earnings to $56,700, as follows:

70% of IEE's reported earnings	$63,000
Amortization of FVI on buildings and equipment	(7,000)
Amortization of goodwill	(1,750)
70% of unrealized profit in ending inventory	(3,150)
70% of unrealized profit in beginning inventory	5,600
	$56,700

The share of adjusted earnings that IOR would report as its earnings from its investment in IEE would therefore appear to be $56,700. However, one more adjustment remains.

In addition to the upstream sales, there were also downstream sales from IOR to IEE during the period. Of these sales, $6,000 remains in IEE's ending inventory at the end of 19x2. At a gross margin of 30%, the unrealized profit from the downstream sales is $1,800, all of which was eliminated when we performed the 19x2 consolidation in Part A.

Since the unrealized profit from the downstream sales is in IOR's accounts and is not reflected in IEE's reported net income, it would seem logical to make an adjustment to IOR's accounts by reversing that portion of the sale entry relating to the unsold goods. We could debit sales for $6,000 and credit cost of sales for $4,200. That would reduce IOR's reported earnings by $1,800, as desired. But then we have to do something with the remaining $1,800 credit in the adjustment.

When we consolidate, the credit goes to inventory, in order to reduce the asset to its cost to the consolidated entity. Under equity reporting, however, the inventory is not reported on IOR's balance sheet because it is IEE's inventory, not IOR's. Instead, the asset on IOR's books that relates to IEE is the investment account. Therefore, the unrealized profit must be credited to the investment account. Since the investment account under the equity method is the investor's equity in the net assets of the investee, including unremitted earnings, a credit to the investment account to reflect a reduction in IEE's net asset value for unrealized profits should be shown in the investor's equity in earnings in the investee on the income statement.

As a result, the adjustment for IOR's unrealized profit from downstream sales is deducted from IOR's share of IEE's earnings. This additional adjustment reduces IOR's equity pick-up of IEE's earnings from the $56,700 shown above to $54,900. Schedule 10-3 summarizes the calculation of IOR's share of IEE's earnings, and the effect on the investment account.

Note that the profit on the downstream sales is deducted in full; the percentage of ownership is irrelevant because the profit is in the investor, not the investee. One problem with the practice of deducting the unrealized profit on downstream sales from the earnings of the investee is that if the volume of unsold inventory is large, then the investment could look poorer than it really is. In extreme cases, a profitable investee corporation could be made to look unprofitable, while the investor's own operations could be made to look more profitable than they really are. The final net income of the investor corporation will not be affected by the placement of the deduction for unrealized downstream profits, but analyses based on the components of the income statement can be affected.

For example, bankers frequently watch the gross margin percentage of their customers in order to monitor their ability to maintain margins and ultimately to service the debt. If margins are declining, managers may be motivated to ship large quantities of inventory to a subsidiary. On the parent's separate-entity (i.e., unconsolidated) statements, profitability of the subsidiaries may seem to suffer, but the parent company will appear to be stronger than it really is.

SCHEDULE 10-3

IOR's Investment in Investee Ltd.
to December 31, 19x2

IEE 19x2 net income before extraordinary item, as reported:	
70% of $90,000	$ 63,000
Amortization of fair-value increments:	
Buildings and equipment (20 yrs.)	−7,000
Goodwill (40 yrs.)	−1,750
Unrealized profit on upstream sales:	
Add unrealized profit in beginning inventory:	
$20,000 inventory @ 40% gross margin × 70% share	+5,600
Subtract unrealized profit in ending inventory:	
$10,000 inventory @ 45% gross margin × 70% share	−3,150
Unrealized profit on downstream sales:	
Subtract unrealized profit in ending inventory:	
$6,000 inventory @ 30% gross margin	−1,800
IOR equity in IEE earnings, 19x2	54,900
IEE dividends received: $20,000 × 70% share	−14,000
Investment in IEE, balance, January 1, 19x2 (from	
Schedule 9-10)	860,650
Investment in IEE, balance, December 31, 19x2	$901,550

C. SUBSEQUENT-YEAR CONSOLIDATIONS: GENERAL APPROACH

So far, we have discussed the process of preparing consolidated financial statements (1) at the date of acquisition, (2) one year subsequent to acquisition, and (3) two years subsequent to acquisition. In the course of our discussion, we have explored the basic concepts underlying consolidation and the treatment of minority interest. The major procedural aspects of consolidation have also been presented. In the remainder of this chapter, we break the reliance on a specific date of consolidation, and instead discuss the general approach to preparing consolidated financial statements, regardless of the time elapsed since a subsidiary was founded or purchased.

Both this chapter and the previous chapter have emphasized that consolidated financial statements must reflect adjustments for three types of events: (1) the acquisition transaction, (2) the cumulative effects of amortization and transactions in previous periods, and (3) the effects of amortization and transactions in the current period. It is immaterial whether these adjustments and eliminations are made directly to the draft financial statements or on a worksheet, and it is irrelevant whether the three types are kept separate or combined.

Basic Conceptual Approach

The general nature of these adjustments is portrayed in Schedule 10-4 by reference to a time line. The first point of interest on the time line is point A, the date of acquisition of the parent's controlling interest in the subsidiary. The consolidation worksheet entry for this event is a constant, and has been thoroughly discussed.

Point C on the time line is that most recent point, which is the current balance sheet date. The worksheet adjustments for point C and for the year then ended (the time between point B and point C) have been reviewed four times in these chapters and should be reasonably clear.

The more problematic adjustment is apt to be that for the time between acquisition (point A) and the beginning of the current year (point B). We have pointed out that the consolidation adjustments for the intervening period (points A to B) are essentially *cumulative* adjustments. We can simply accumulate the effects of each year's current operations adjustments, bearing in mind that the net effect of all adjustments to income statement accounts and to previous years' current nonmonetary accounts (e.g., inventories) will usually be reflected in retained earnings. The result will then be the point A-to-B adjustment when we prepare the consolidated statements for the next accounting period (points B to C).

The cumulative effect is illustrated in Schedule 10-5 for IOR, assuming 70% ownership of IEE. When we add together the current operations adjustments from the worksheets for 19x1 and 19x2, the result is the cumulative adjustment that we would make in preparing the 19x3 consolidated financial statements:

Accounts payable	$500,000	
Future income taxes	60,000	
Retained earnings	238,450	
Accounts receivable		$500,000
Cost of sales (beginning inventory)		6,300
Land		240,000
Accumulated depreciation		14,000
Goodwill		3,500
Minority interest		34,650

SCHEDULE 10-4

1. Acquisition adjustments

   a. Record fair-value increments (and/or decrements) and goodwill.
   b. Eliminate purchase price in investment account and subsidiary's common equity accounts; establish minority interest.

2. Cumulative adjustments to *start* of current year (affecting current year's *beginning* balance sheet amounts):

   a. Accumulated amortization of fair-value increments (decrements) and goodwill.
   b. Establish minority interest's share of subsidiary retained earnings from date of acquisition to start of current year.
   c. Eliminate the *cumulative* impact of intercompany transactions, including
      i. unrealized gains and losses, and
      ii. sale of previously fair-valued assets or liabilities.

3. Adjustments for current year:

   a. Amortize fair-value increments (decrements) and goodwill.
   b. Eliminate intercompany transactions for current year.
   c. Eliminate current subsidiary earnings (equity basis, if used) and dividends.
   d. Provide for realization of previously unrealized profits (losses), if realized in current period.
   e. Eliminate unrealized profits (losses) from intercompany transactions in current year.
   f. Establish minority interest in subsidiary's earnings.
   g. Eliminate intercompany balances at year-end.

t ———————————————————————————————————— t

A. Date   B. Start   C. End
   of   of   of
acquisition   current   current
                   year   year

SCHEDULE 10-5

Cumulative Adjustment for 19x3
Dr. (Cr.)

	19x1[a]	19x2[b]	Cumulative
Accounts receivable		(500,000)	(500,000)
Inventories (beginning)		(6,300)	(6,300)
Land		(240,000)	(240,000)
Accumulated depreciation	(7,000)	(7,000)	(14,000)
Goodwill	(1,750)	(1,750)	(3,500)
Accounts payable		500,000	500,000
Future income taxes		90,000	90,000
Minority interest	(12,600)	(22,050)	(34,605)
Retained earnings[c]	21,350	187,100	208,450

Notes:

a. From Schedule 9-9, "Operations" column.
b. From Schedule 10-1, "Operations: Current" column.
c. Includes all adjustments to income statement accounts and dividends paid.

This may seem to be a very mechanistic approach, and indeed it is an approach commonly used for just that reason. For example, in a computerized accounting system, succeeding years' operations adjustments can be routinely accumulated and stored for use in the next period's consolidation. However, what the cumulative entry really accomplishes is the adjustment of the beginning balances for the current year to reflect changes in the assets and liabilities since acquisition.

Rather than mechanically accumulate the consolidation adjustments in succeeding years, accountants should be able to derive the necessary adjustments in any year directly from the information given about the purchase transaction and about the intercompany transactions. In order to illustrate the preparation of consolidated financial statements in any year, we will use an example different from the one used up to now. First we will demonstrate consolidation of an income statement and balance sheet directly, without use of a worksheet. Then the same consolidation will be performed by using a worksheet.

Example

On January 1, 19x1, Pepper Corp. acquired 80% of the outstanding common shares of Salt Ltd. by issuing Pepper shares worth $800,000. At the date of acquisition, Salt's shareholders' equity totaled $855,000, consisting of $300,000 in the common share account and $555,000 in retained earnings. The fair values of Salt's assets and liabilities differed from the book values at the date of acquisition as follows:

	Excess of fair value over book value: dr./(cr.)	
	100%	80%
Inventories	$ 10,000	$ 8,000
Machinery	75,000	60,000
Investments	30,000	24,000
Bonds payable	(20,000)	(16,000)
Total		$ 76,000

The fair-value increment for the bonds is a credit, indicating that the current value of the bonds is higher than the carrying value. This difference would most likely be caused by the fact that the nominal interest rate for the bonds was higher than the market rate for the appropriate term and risk.

Once the fair-value increments have been determined, the purchase transaction can be analyzed as follows:

Purchase price		$800,000
Book value of net assets acquired ($855,000 x 80%)	$684,000	
Fair-value increments (above)	76,000	760,000
Goodwill		$40,000

Schedule 10-6 shows the trial balances for Pepper and Salt at December 31, 19x6, six years after Pepper's acquisition of its 80% interest in Salt. Other relevant information is as follows:

1. Salt's machinery had an estimated remaining useful life of ten years from January 1, 19x1; the bonds had a remaining term of eight years; Pepper's policy is to amortize goodwill over 40 years. All depreciation and amortization is on the straight-line basis.
2. In 19x3, Salt sold its investments for a profit of $45,000 over book value.
3. During 19x6, intercompany sales were as follows:
    a. Pepper had sales totaling $100,000 to Salt at a gross margin of 40% of selling price; on December 31, 19x6, $40,000 of the amount sold was still in Salt's inventory.
    b. Salt had sales of $700,000 to Pepper at a gross margin of 40% of sales; at year-end, $70,000 was still in Pepper's inventory.
4. The inventories on January 1, 19x6, contained intercompany purchases as follows:
    a. Salt held goods purchased from Pepper for $20,000.
    b. Pepper held goods purchased from Salt for $100,000. The gross margin on intercompany sales held in the beginning inventories was 40% of selling price for both companies. All of the beginning inventories were sold to third parties during 19x6.
5. Pepper collects royalties from Salt (as well as from other companies); between January 1, 19x1, and January 1, 19x6, Salt had paid a total of $500,000 in royalties to Pepper; during 19x6, Salt paid $90,000 to Pepper for royalties.
6. At December 31, 19x6, Pepper owed Salt $50,000 on current account.

For simplicity, the effect of income taxes will be ignored in the following analysis.

SCHEDULE 10-6

Pepper Corp. and Salt Ltd.
Condensed Trial Balances
December 31, 19x6

	Pepper Corp.	Salt Ltd.
Cash	$ 50,000	$ 20,000
Accounts receivable	150,000	160,000
Inventory	180,000	100,000
Machinery	5,000,000	2,700,000
Accumulated depreciation	(1,769,000)	(1,240,000)
Investment in Salt Ltd. (at cost)	800,000	—
Other investments	100,000	—
Current payables	(450,000)	(100,000)
Bonds payable	—	(500,000)
Common shares	(1,200,000)	(300,000)
Retained earnings (January 1, 19x6)	(2,446,000)	(770,000)
Dividends declared	300,000	90,000
Sales revenue	(2,000,000)	(1,400,000)
Royalty revenue	(140,000)	—
Dividend income	(75,000)	—
Cost of sales	1,200,000	840,000
Other expenses	300,000	400,000
	$ 0	$ 0

Income Statement

Direct Approach

The consolidated income statement for Pepper Corp. is shown in Schedule 10-7. For each item of revenue and expense, the calculation of the amount is shown in parentheses. The amounts from the Pepper and Salt trial balances (Schedule 10-6) are shown first, followed by the additions and subtractions for the consolidation adjustments. The calculation of each amount is discussed below.

Sales
The consolidated sales is simply the total sales for the two companies less the intercompany sales during 19x6 of $100,000 (downstream) and $700,000 (upstream).

Royalties
These are reduced by the intercompany royalties of $90,000 paid by Salt to Pepper.

Dividends
Salt paid dividends of $90,000 during 19x6. Of this amount, 80% was received by Pepper. Therefore the dividend income of Pepper is reduced by the amount of the intercompany dividends of $72,000.

SCHEDULE 10-7	
Pepper Corp. **Condensed Consolidated Statement of Income** **and Retained Earnings** Year Ended December 31, 19x6	
Revenues:	
Sales ($2,000,000 + $1,400,000 − $100,000 − $700,000)	$2,600,000
Royalties ($140,000 − $90,000)	50,000
Dividends ($75,000 − $72,000)	3,000
	2,653,000
Expenses:	
Cost of sales ($1,200,000 + $840,000 − $100,000 − $700,000 + $16,000 + $28,000 − $8,000 − $40,000)	1,236,000
Other expenses ($300,000 + $400,000 + $6,000 − $2,000 + $1,000 − $90,000)	615,000
Minority interest in earnings of Salt Ltd. ($32,000 − $5,600 + $8,000)	34,400
	1,885,400
Net income	767,600
Retained earnings, January 1, 19x6 ($2,446,000 + $770,000 − $555,000 − $43,000) − $24,000 − $30,000 + $10,000 − $5,000 − $8,000 − $40,000	2,521,000
Dividends declared	(300,000)
Retained earnings, December 31, 19x6	$2,988,600

Cost of sales

The cost of sales of the two companies is adjusted for (1) the intercompany sales, (2) the unrealized profits in the ending inventories, and (3) the realization of the previously unrealized profits in the beginning inventories. The intercompany sales are $100,000 and $700,000, which are deducted from cost of sales as the offset to the deduction from sales, above. The unrealized profits in the ending inventories are $16,000 for the downstream sales ($40,000 x 40%) and $28,000 for the upstream sales ($70,000 x 40%). All of the unrealized profit is eliminated from the consolidated gross margin by this adjustment; the minority interest's share of the unrealized profits on the upstream sales will be recognized below. The now-realized profits from the beginning inventory are $8,000 ($20,000 x 40%) for downstream sales (Salt's inventory) and are $40,000 ($100,000 x 40%) for upstream sales (Pepper's inventory).

Other expenses

Operating expenses are adjusted for the amortization of the fair-value increments, the goodwill, and for the intercompany royalties. On a straight-line basis, the $60,000 fair-value increment on the machinery is amortized over ten years at $6,000 per year. The increased value of the bonds of $16,000 is amortized over eight years at $2,000 per year; this amortization is similar to the amortization of any bond premium and is treated as a reduction of interest expense.[2] The goodwill of $40,000 is amortized over 40 years at $1,000 per year. The royalty expense of $90,000 contained in Salt's 19x6 expenses is eliminated, as was the royalty income of Pepper, above.

Minority interest in earnings of Salt Ltd

From the trial balance given in Schedule 10-6, Salt's separate-entity net income can be calculated at $160,000. Pepper has an equity in only 80% of this amount. The remaining 20% is equity of the minority interest. Therefore, the minority interest starts out at $32,000 ($160,000 x 20%). This amount must be adjusted for the unrealized profits from upstream sales. Pepper's ending inventory contains unrealized profit of $28,000, 20% of which ($5,600) pertains to the minority interest and is subtracted from the minority interest's earnings. Added to the minority interest's earnings is its share of the unrealized profit in Pepper's beginning inventory that has now been realized: $40,000 x 20% = $8,000.

After these adjustments have all been made to the revenues and expenses, Pepper Corp.'s consolidated net income is $767,600 for 19x6. None of the adjustments explained above is new; they are no different in nature for 19x6 than they were for IOR for 19x2 in Part A of this chapter.

Retained Earnings

Once the net income for the year has been determined, the ending retained earnings can be calculated. First, however, it is necessary to determine the consolidated retained earnings at the beginning of the current year, January 1, 19x6. The opening balance of retained earnings will include Pepper's separate-entity retained earnings, plus Pepper's share of Salt's retained earnings *since the date of acquisition*, plus and minus adjustments for amortization, unrealized profits, and sale of fair-valued assets.

Salt's retained earnings at the date of Pepper's acquisition of its 80% interest was $555,000. By the beginning of 19x6, Salt's retained earnings had grown to $770,000. Of the increase of $215,000, Salt's equity is 80%, or $172,000. This amount can then be added to Pepper's own retained earnings. In Schedule 10-7, the same result is obtained by subtracting the 20% minority interest in the retained earnings increase for Salt since the date of acquisition, $43,000 ($215,000 x 20%).

Included in Salt's retained earnings is a gain of $45,000 from selling its investments in 19x3. These investments had a fair value in excess of book value of $30,000 on January 1, 19x1. When Pepper purchased its share of Salt, Pepper in effect purchased 80% of Salt's investments at market value, which was $24,000 above cost. When Salt subsequently sold these investments, the gain to Pepper as a consolidated entity was not the difference between the book value of the investments and the proceeds from the sale; instead, the gain to Pepper is the difference between the proceeds from the sale and the price paid for the investments by Pepper. In other words, the gain on the

---

2 The effective yield method of amortization could be used instead. The choice between the two amortization methods is an accounting policy choice that will be made in a particular circumstance on the basis of the objectives of financial reporting for that company.

sale must be adjusted by the amount of the fair-value increment on the investments. Therefore, the gain on the sale from the point of view of the consolidated entity was not $45,000 as stated in the introductory information, but rather was $45,000 less the $24,000 fair-value increment, or $21,000. Since the gain is now in retained earnings, an adjustment to retained earnings is made by subtracting the $24,000. Had the sale occurred in the current year, the adjustment would have been to the gain on the sale.

Five years have elapsed from the date of Pepper's acquisition to the *beginning* of the current fiscal year, 19x6. During that time, the fair-value increment on the machinery has been amortized at the rate of $6,000 per year, for a total amortization of $30,000. Similarly, the fair-value increment (premium) on the bonds has been amortized at $2,000 per year ($10,000 total) and the goodwill has been amortized at $1,000 per year ($5,000 total). The consolidated retained earnings at book value must be adjusted by these cumulative amortization amounts in order to recognize the cumulative impact of the fair-value purchase method of reporting.

The final adjustments are for the amounts of unrealized inventory profits at the *beginning* of the year. The opening unrealized profits are subtracted because the beginning retained earnings include those amounts as having been earned by the individual entities, but for the consolidated entity they are not earned until 19x6.

There is no need to adjust for the royalties paid by Salt to Pepper prior to the beginning of 19x6. These $500,000 in royalties have reduced Salt's retained earnings, but have increased Pepper's retained earnings by the same amount. On consolidation, the effects are directly offsetting. No adjustment needs to be made for intercompany expenses in prior years.

Once the opening balance of consolidated retained earnings has been established, all that remains is to subtract the dividends declared by Pepper during the year. Salt's dividends are completely eliminated; 80% were deducted from Pepper's dividend income and the other 20% will be deducted from the minority interest on the balance sheet.

Balance Sheet

Schedule 10-8 shows the consolidated balance sheet for Pepper Corp. at December 31, 19x6. The calculation of the individual amounts is summarized below.

Accounts receivable
The combined amounts are reduced by the $50,000 intercompany receivable.

Inventories
The inventories are reduced by the full amount of the unrealized earnings in the ending inventories, both downstream ($16,000) and upstream ($28,000).

Machinery
Adjustments are necessary to eliminate Salt's accumulated depreciation at the date of acquisition ($460,000) and to add the fair-value increment of $60,000. This adjustment assumes that all of the machinery to which the fair-value increment applies is still held by Salt.

SCHEDULE 10-8

Pepper Corp.
Condensed Consolidated Balance Sheet
December 31, 19x6

ASSETS

Current assets:

Cash ($50,000 + $20,000)		$ 70,000
Accounts receivable ($150,000 + $160,000 − $50,000)		260,000
Inventories ($180,000 + $100,000 − $16,000		
− $28,000)		236,000
		566,000

Property, plant, and equipment:

Machinery ($5,000,000 + $2,700,000 − $460,000		
+ $60,000)		7,300,000
Accumulated depreciation ($1,769,000 + $1,240,000		
− $460,000 + $36,000)		2,585,000
		4,715,000

Other assets:

Investments		100,000
Goodwill ($40,000 − $6,000)		34,000
		134,000
Total assets		$5,415,000

LIABILITIES AND SHAREHOLDERS' EQUITY

Current liabilities:

Current payables ($450,000 + $100,000 − $50,000)		$ 500,000
Bonds payable ($500,000 + $16,000 − $12,000)		504,000
		1,004,000
Minority interest in Salt Ltd. ($228,000 − $5,600)		222,400

Shareholders' equity:

Common shares		1,200,000
Retained earnings (from Schedule 10-7)		2,988,600
		4,188,600
Total liabilities and shareholders' equity		$5,415,000

Accumulated depreciation
Salt's accumulated depreciation at the date of Pepper's acquisition is eliminated, and the amortization of the fair-value increment over the six years is added ($6,000 x 6 = $36,000).

Goodwill
Goodwill is reduced by six years' amortization at $1,000 per year.

Current payables
The intercompany payable is eliminated.

Bonds payable
The fair-value increment is added to the book value of the bonds, less the amortization of the increment at $2,000 per year for six years. An implicit assumption is that all of the bonds outstanding at January 1, 19x1, are still outstanding. If any had been retired, then the related amount of fair-value increment would have been offset against any gain or loss on retirement, as explained above for the sale of Salt's investments.

Minority interest
The minority interest starts out as 20% of Salt's net assets (i.e., shareholders' equity) at the balance sheet date. On December 31, 19x6, Salt's net assets amount to $1,140,000: common shares and retained earnings totaling $1,070,000 at the beginning of the year, plus net income of $160,000 for 19x6, less dividends of $90,000. The minority interest's share of the net asset value is 20%, or $228,000. From that amount must be subtracted the minority interest's share of the unrealized profit from the upstream sales at the end of the year, or $5,600.

Shareholders' equity
The common shares are those only of Pepper. The retained earnings are Pepper's consolidated retained earnings as shown on Schedule 10-7 and explained above.

Worksheet Approach

Cost Method of Recording

Schedule 10-9 illustrates the preparation of consolidated financial statements for Pepper Corp. by use of a consolidation worksheet, assuming that Salt carries its investment in Pepper on the cost basis. For greater clarity, the adjustments and eliminations have again been shown in three columns, although the use of three columns is certainly not necessary.

The entry to record the initial acquisition of Pepper's 80% interest is, as usual, an entry to establish the fair-value increments and goodwill, to establish the minority interest, to eliminate the investment account, and to eliminate Salt's shareholders' equity accounts at the date of acquisition. The fair-value increment for inventory ($8,000) is charged directly to retained earnings, however, because the inventory has been sold and the retained earnings must be adjusted to reflect the cost of goods sold to Pepper rather than just the cost to Salt. Similarly, the fair-value increment relating to Salt's investments is charged to retained earnings because the investments have since been sold, as explained in the previous section. Otherwise, the entry is straightforward.

The cumulative operations column contains those adjustments that are necessary to adjust the balance sheet accounts at the beginning of the year:

a. Increases the minority interest by 20% of the increase in Salt's retained earnings between January 1, 19x1, and January 1, 19x6: ($700,000 − $555,000) x 20% = $43,000.

b. Adjusts for the amortization of the fair-value increments on machinery and bonds and of goodwill for the five years between January 1, 19x1, and January 1, 19x6.

c. Adjusts for unrealized earnings in the opening inventories, both downstream ($8,000) and upstream ($40,000). Of the $40,000 unrealized earnings in Pepper's inventory at the beginning of the year, 20% or $8,000 is credited to the minority interest's earnings for 19x6, since that amount has now been realized.

The current operations column contains all of the eliminations and adjustments that pertain to the current year:

d. Adjusts for the amortization of fair-value increments and goodwill for 19x6.
e. Eliminates the intercompany sales, both downstream and upstream.
f. Eliminates the unrealized profit from upstream sales.

SCHEDULE 10-9

Consolidation Worksheet for Pepper Corp., Cost Method
December 31, 19x6
Dr. (Cr.)

| | Trial balances | | Eliminations and adjustments | | | Consolidated trial balance |
	Pepper	Salt	1: Acquisition	2: Cumulative	3: Current	
Cash	$ 50,000	$ 20,000				$ 70,000
Accounts receivable	150,000	160,000			$ (50,000)k	260,000
Inventories	180,000	100,000			{(28,000)f (16,000)g}	236,000
Machinery	5,000,000	2,700,000	{$ 60,000) (460,000}			7,300,000
Accumulated depreciation	(1,769,000)	(1,240,000)	460,000	$(30,000)b	(6,000)d	(2,585,000)
Investment in Salt Ltd. (at cost)	800,000	—	(800,000)			—
Other investments	100,000	—				100,000
Goodwill	—	—	40,000	(5,000)b	(1,000)d	34,000
Current payables	(450,000)	(100,000)			50,000 k	(500,000)
Bonds payable	—	(500,000)	(16,000)	10,000 b	2,000 d	(504,000)
Minority interest	—	—	(171,000)	(43,000)a	{(26,400)h 18,000 j}	(222,400)
Common shares	(1,200,000)	(300,000)	300,000			(1,200,000)
Retained earnings	(2,446,000)	(770,000)	{555,000 24,000 8,000}	{43,000 a 25,000 b 40,000 c}		(2,521,000)
Dividends declared	300,000	90,000			(90,000)j	300,000
Sales revenue	(2,000,000)	(1,400,000)			800,000 e	(2,600,000)
Royalty revenue	(140,000)	—			90,000 i	(50,000)
Dividend income	(75,000)	—			72,000 j	(3,000)
Cost of sales	1,200,000	840,000		(48,000)c	{(800,000)e 28,000 f 16,000 g}	1,236,300
Other expenses	300,000	400,000			{5,000 d (90,000)i}	615,000
Minority interest in earnings of Salt Ltd.	—	—		8,000 c	26,400 h	34,400
	$ 0	$ 0	$ 0	$ 0	$ 0	$ 0

g. Eliminates the unrealized profit from downstream sales.

h. Establishes the minority interest's share of Salt's 19x6 net income, after adjustment for unrealized profits: ($160,000 - $28,000) x 20% = $26,400. Note that the profits realized from the opening inventory are already included in adjustment (c).

i. Eliminates the intercompany royalty payments for 19x6. There is no need to adjust for the payments in the preceding five years because the results are offsetting; the amounts paid by Salt have decreased Salt's retained earnings but have increased Pepper's retained earnings by the same amount.

j. Eliminates Salt's dividend payments.

k. Eliminates the intercompany receivable and payable.

A balance sheet and income statement prepared from the last column of Schedule 10-9 would be the same as those illustrated in Schedules 10-7 and 10-8.

Equity Method of Recording

If Pepper Corp. records its investment in Salt Ltd. on the equity basis, then the investment account will include Pepper's 80% share of Salt's undistributed earnings. At the beginning of 19x6 (December 31, 19x5), the balance of the investment account would be $875,000, as indicated by amount A on Schedule 10-10. The increase of $75,000 since the date of acquisition is 80% of the change in Salt's retained earnings, adjusted for (a) five years' amortization of fair-value increments and goodwill, (b) unrealized earnings in the inventories of December 31, 19x5, and (c) fair-value increments on assets sold since acquisition.

The $75,000 increase can be confirmed by reference to Schedule 10-9, the cost basis worksheet. On that schedule, the Salt retained earnings balance at December 31, 19x5 (on the December 31, 19x6 trial balance) is $770,000. There are six eliminations relating to retained earnings. When the $770,000 is adjusted for these eliminations, a net amount of $75,000 Salt retained earnings flows through to the consolidated retained earnings. Under the equity method, the $75,000 in undistributed earnings will already be in Pepper's opening retained earnings for 19x6, increasing the retained earnings from $2,446,000 under the cost basis (Schedule 10-9) to $2,521,000 under the equity method.

For 19x6, Pepper's share of Salt's earnings is $124,600 after adjustment, amount B on Schedule 10-10. This amount will appear as equity in the earnings of Salt Ltd. on Pepper's 19x6 trial balance. The earnings will also have been debited to the investment account, and the $72,000 dividends received by Pepper from Salt will have been credited to the investment account. As a result, the balance of the investment account at year-end will be $927,600, amount C on Schedule 10-10.

Thus, under the equity method, the balances of Pepper's accounts differ from those under the cost method as follows:

	Cost method	Equity method
Investment in Salt Ltd.	$ 800,000 Dr.	$ 927,600 Dr.
Retained earnings	2,446,000 Cr.	2,521,000 Cr.
Dividend income	75,000 Cr.	3,000 Cr.
Equity in earnings of Salt Ltd.	—	124,600 Cr.

SCHEDULE 10-10

Pepper Corp.'s Investment in Salt Ltd.
Equity Basis

Cost of investment, January 1, 19x1		$800,000

Pepper's equity in Salt retained earnings,
  January 1, 19x1 to December 31, 19x5:
  Increase in Salt retained earnings, Pepper share:
  ($770,000 − $555,000) × 80%
		172,000

Cumulative amortization:		
Machinery: $6,000 × 5	$30,000	
Goodwill: $1,000 × 5	5,000	
Bonds payable: $(2,000) × 10	(10,000)	(25,000)
Unrealized profits in inventory, December 31, 19x5:		
Downstream	8,000	
Upstream: $40,000 × 80%	$32,000	(40,000)
Fair-value increments on assets disposed of:		
Inventory	8,000	
Investments	24,000	(32,000)
Cumulative earnings less dividends of Salt accruing to Pepper		75,000
Investment account balance, December 31, 19x5		**$875,000** A
Pepper's equity in Salt's 19x6 earnings:		
Salt net income, as reported: $160,000 × 80%		128,000
Amortizations for 19x6: $6,000 + $1,000 − $2,000		(5,000)
Unrealized profits in inventory:		
Beginning: Downstream	(8,000)	
Upstream: $40,000 × 80%	(32,000)	
Ending: Downstream	16,000	
Upstream: $28,000 × 80%	22,400	1,600
		$124,600 B
Dividends received from Salt in 19x6		72,000
Investment account balance, December 31, 19x6		**$927,600** C

Schedule 10-11 contains the equity-method trial balances for Pepper and Salt. The accounts and amounts that are affected by the equity method are shown in boldfaced type.

The use of the equity method in Pepper's accounts requires only three changes to the cost-basis consolidation process. First, the $75,000 of accumulated earnings of Salt that are reflected in Pepper's retained earnings (and in the investment account) must be eliminated. Since these earnings are included in the retained earnings of both companies, failure to eliminate them would result in double-counting Salt's earnings. The elimination is entry x in the cumulative operations column of Schedule 10-11. Second, the 19x6 equity pick-up of Salt's earnings must be reversed. This reversal is entry z in the current operations column. And finally, Pepper's share of Salt's 19x6 dividends is debited to the investment account (instead of to dividend income)

SCHEDULE 10-11

Consolidation Worksheet for Pepper Corp., Equity Method
December 31, 19x6
Dr. (Cr.)

| | Trial balances | | Eliminations and adjustments | | | Consolidated |
	Pepper	Salt	1: Acquisition	2: Cumulative	3: Current	trial balance
Cash	$ 50,000	$ 20,000				$ 70,000
Accounts receivable	150,000	160,000			$ (50,000)k	260,000
Inventories	180,000	100,000			$\begin{cases}(28,000)f \\ (16,000)g\end{cases}$	236,000
Machinery	5,000,000	2,700,000	$\begin{cases}\$ \ 60,000 \\ (460,000)\end{cases}$			7,300,000
Accumulated depreciation	(1,769,000)	(1,240,000)	460,000	$(30,000)b	$\begin{cases}(6,000)d \\ (124,600)z\end{cases}$	(2,585,000)
Investment in Salt Ltd. (at equity)	**927,600**	–	(800,000)	**(75,000)**x	$\begin{cases}72,000 \ j\end{cases}$	–
Other investments	100,000	–				100,000
Goodwill	–		40,000	(5,000)b	(1,000)d	34,000
Current payables	(450,000)	(100,000)			50,000 k	(500,000)
Bonds payable	–	(500,000)	(16,000)	10,000 b	2,000 d	(504,000)
Minority interest	–	–	(171,000)	(43,000)a	$\begin{cases}(26,400)h \\ 18,000 \ j\end{cases}$	(222,400)
Common shares	(1,200,000)	(300,000)	300,000			(1,200,000)
Retained earnings	**(2,521,000)**	(770,000)	$\begin{cases}555,000 \\ 24,000 \\ 8,000\end{cases}$	$\begin{cases}\textbf{75,000} \ x \\ 43,000 \ a \\ 25,000 \ b \\ 40,000 \ c\end{cases}$		(2,521,000)
Dividends declared	300,000	90,000			(90,000)j	300,000
Sales revenue	(2,000,000)	(1,400,000)			800,000 e	(2,600,000)
Royalty revenue	(140,000)	–			90,000 i	(50,000)
Dividend income	**(3,000)**	–			0 j	(3,000)
Equity in earnings of Salt Ltd.	**(124,600)**	–			124,600 z	–
Cost of sales	1,200,000	840,000		(48,000)c	$\begin{cases}(800,000)e \\ 28,000 \ f \\ 16,000 \ g\end{cases}$	1,236,300
Other expenses	300,000	400,000			$\begin{cases}5,000 \ d \\ (90,000)i\end{cases}$	615,000
Minority interest in earnings of Salt Ltd.	–	–		8,000 c	26,400 h	34,400
	$ 0	$ 0	$ 0	$ 0	$ 0	$ 0

in order to reverse the credit entry made by Pepper when the dividends were received (entry j).

In summary, consolidation when the equity method is used differs from consolidation under the cost method only by the necessity to eliminate the equity-method entries made by the parent. The investment account must be completely eliminated, as must all subsidiary earnings credited to the parent's retained earnings. After these additional eliminations are made, the rest of the consolidation process can continue, unaffected by the method of maintaining the investment account on the parent's books.

D. CONSOLIDATION OF JOINT VENTURES

In a joint venture, two or more corporations agree to an arrangement that is rather like a partnership for forming and operating a new, separate entity (either incorporated or unincorporated), usually for accomplishing a single major business objective. Joint ventures are formed for a variety of reasons. They are a way for corporations to pool their resources, whether technical, managerial, or financial, as well as a way to share business risk. In Canada, they are sometimes formed in order to share productive resources or facilities when the domestic market is not large enough to support separate facilities; an example is the partnership formed by Molson's and Carling O'Keefe to combine their brewing capacities and eliminate inefficient duplication. Joint ventures are also very useful in foreign countries, where a Canadian company may form a joint venture with a company that is based in the foreign country. Such foreign joint ventures can provide advantages to the Canadian company such as providing local management, access to markets, reduced concerns by the foreign government and access to local resources.

It is an essential attribute of a joint venture that no one investor (or **co-venturer**) has voting control. The rights and responsibilities of each of the investors are defined in the joint venture agreement, which is essentially a shareholders' agreement. The agreement describes each co-venturer's equity contribution, voting rights, management participation, equity (or dividend) withdrawal rights, and so forth. One of the investors may provide over half of the equity, but that investor will not be given more than half of the votes or board of directors nominees.

Since, by definition, the individual participating co-venturers do not have control over the joint venture's net assets, the venture is not a subsidiary and since the investor corporations do not have control over the assets of the venture, it would be misleading to consolidate 100% of the venture's net assets. The co-venturers do have significant influence over a joint venture, however, and equity reporting is therefore a viable reporting approach

Another approach that *may* be used in Canada, as an alternative to equity reporting, is that of **proportionate consolidation**. The *CICA Handbook* recommends that proportionate consolidation is appropriate "when a significant portion of the venturer's activities is carried out through joint ventures" [para. 3055.11]; what constitutes "a significant portion" is a matter for the exercise of professional judgment. Only the investor's proportionate share of the joint venture's assets and liabilities is consolidated; the share held by other co-venturers is not included, and thus there is no minority interest shown on the consolidated balance sheet. Proportionate consolidation is an approach that reflects the co-venturer's active participation in the joint venture, and yet does not imply that one co-venturer has access to the full resources of the joint venture.

To illustrate the preparation of proportionately consolidated statements, let us assume the following:

1. Pacific Coast Limited (PCL) invested $400,000 in 19x1 for a 40% interest in Jumble Veneer Corporation (JVC), a new company.
2. In 19x2, PCL extended a long-term loan to JVC amounting to $500,000; the note bears interest of 10% per annum.

3. In 19x4, PCL sold goods to JVC for $1,000,000; of that amount, $200,000 is still in JVC's inventory at the end of 19x4. PCL's gross margin is 30% of sales.

4. Also in 19x4, JVC sold goods to PCL for $400,000; all of these goods are still in PCL's inventory at year-end; JVC's gross margin is 25% of sales.

The year-end 19x4 trial balance for JVC is shown in Schedule 10-12.

To prepare a consolidated balance sheet for PCL that includes JVC, we could prepare a worksheet that starts with the full trial balances of both PCL and JVC, and then eliminate the 60% of all JVC's accounts that do not pertain to PCL. Alternatively, and more simply, we could enter only 40% of the JVC balances on the consolidation worksheet at the outset. We will use the second approach, and the trial balances of PCL and 40% of the balances of JVC are presented in the first two columns of Schedule 10-13.

As with any consolidation, we must eliminate (1) the investment account against the venture's share equity, (2) intercompany balances, (3) unrealized profits on intercompany sales, and (4) intercompany revenues and expenses.

The first elimination is straightforward enough, and that is for the investment account:

| (a) Common shares | $400,000 | |
| Investment in JVC | | $400,000 |

The second elimination is for the intercompany loan of $500,000. However, we immediately run into a problem if we try to eliminate the full $500,000, because the liability on JVC's proportionate trial balance is for only $200,000. Therefore, we can eliminate only PCL's proportionate share of the loan:

SCHEDULE 10-12

Jumble Veneer Corporation
Trial Balance
December 31, 19x4

	Dr.	Cr.
Cash	$ 100,000	
Accounts receivable	500,000	
Inventories	600,000	
Plant and equipment (net)	1,700,000	
Accounts payable		$ 400,000
Long-term debt		500,000
Future income tax		200,000
Common shares		1,000,000
Retained earnings		600,000
Sales revenue		5,000,000
Cost of sales	3,500,000	
Operating expenses	1,100,000	
Income tax expense	150,000	
Interest expense	50,000	
	$7,700,000	$7,700,000

(b) Long-term debt	$200,000	
Long-term advance to JVC		$200,000

The remaining 60% of the loan will appear on PCL's consolidated balance sheet, representing the amount loaned to the joint venture that relates to the proportion not owned (and certainly not controlled) by PCL.

A similar situation prevails for the unrealized intercompany profits. Only the investor's proportion of the intercompany sales and unrealized profits is eliminated, for both downstream and upstream sales. For the downstream sales, 40% of the $1,000,000 sales and 40% of the total unrealized gross profit of $60,000 ($200,000 x 30%) are eliminated:

(c) Sales	$400,000	
Inventories		$ 24,000
Cost of sales		376,000

The remaining sales are considered to be arm's-length transactions because PCL does not control JVC. PCL's portion must be eliminated, however, to avoid double-counting.

SCHEDULE 10-13

Proportionate Consolidation of a Joint Venture
December 31, 19x4
Dr. (Cr.)
(in thousands of dollars)

	Trial balances			Consolidated
	PCL	40% of JVC	Eliminations	trial balance
Cash	$ 200	$ 40		$ 240
Accounts receivable	700	200		900
Inventories	1,400	240	$ (24)c / (40)d	1,576
Long-term advance to JVC	500		(200)b	300
Plant and equipment (net)	2,500	680		3,180
Investment in JVC (at cost)	400	—	(400)a	—
Accounts payable	(600)	(160)		(760)
Long-term debt	(1,000)	(200)	200 b	(1,000)
Future income taxes	(700)	(80)		(780)
Common shares	(1,200)	(400)	400 a	(1,200)
Retained earnings	(1,800)	(240)		(2,040)
Sales revenue	(11,200)	(2,000)	400 c / 160 d	(12,640)
Interest revenue	(50)	—	20 e	(30)
Cost of sales	8,400	1,400	(376)c / (120)d	9,304
Operating expenses	2,000	440		2,440
Income tax expense	350	60		410
Interest expense	100	20	(20)e	100
	$ 0	$ 0	$ 0	$ 0

For the upstream sales, 40% of the $400,000 sales and 40% of the $100,000 unrealized profit is eliminated:

(d) Sales	$160,000	
Inventories		$ 40,000
Cost of sales		120,000

Finally, the intercompany payment of interest must be eliminated. As was the case for the intercompany sales, only 40% is eliminated:

(e) Interest revenue	$20,000	
Interest expense		$20,000

We have assumed throughout this example that PCL was an original co-venturer in JVC; therefore, the investment account equalled PCL's proportionate share in JVC's common share account, as is the case with parent-founded subsidiaries. While this is the most common situation, it is quite possible for a venturer to buy its share of a joint venture after the venture has been established. The share can be acquired either from another venturer or by direct purchase of shares from the venture itself. In either case, the acquisition would be reported on a fair-value purchase basis, and any fair-value increments and/or goodwill will have to amortized. The procedure is no different than for the business combinations that have been amply demonstrated in the foregoing chapters; since only the investor's share of fair-value increments is reported, no problems arise from the fact that only the proportionate share of the net assets is consolidated.

SUMMARY

When consolidated financial statements are prepared subsequent to acquisition, it is necessary to make three types of adjustments. First, the substance of the purchase transaction must be recognized by establishing the fair-value increments on the subsidiary's assets and liabilities and by establishing goodwill. To the extent that the parent does not own all of the subsidiary's shares, minority interest in the subsidiary's net book value must be recognized.

Second, the balance sheet must be updated to the beginning of the current period. Such updating involves recognition of the cumulative effect of amortization of fair-value increments and goodwill, the effect of prior years' sales of fair-valued assets, and allocation of part of the increase in the subsidiary's retained earnings to minority interest.

Third, the effects of the current year's transactions, amortizations, and balances must be recognized. All balance sheet accounts, including minority interest, must be updated to reflect consolidated amounts at the end of the year.

These adjustments and eliminations can be carried out either directly when preparing consolidated statements, or with the aid of a worksheet. Regardless of the method used, the consolidation process is most difficult when the subsidiary is not wholly owned by the parent and was acquired rather than founded by the parent. Ownership of 100% of the shares of the subsidiary eliminates the need to adjust for the minority interest, while founding of a subsidiary by the parent eliminates the need to adjust for fair-value increments and goodwill.

Part C of this chapter has demonstrated consolidation of a non-wholly owned, purchased subsidiary. Not all of the possible transactions and situations have been illustrated, but a good grasp of the principles and procedures contained in this chapter will arm the reader with a reasonable understanding of the reporting implications for parent-founded subsidiaries and for subsidiaries acquired in a business combination, as well as for significantly influenced corporations. Some of the additional issues and complications that can arise in consolidated and purchase-method reporting are presented in Chapters 12 and 13, for those readers who wish to go further into the topic.

When joint ventures are consolidated, proportionate consolidation is used. Only the investor's share of the venture's assets, liabilities, revenues, and expenses are included in the investor's consolidated financial statements.

Since an individual investor does not control a joint venture, transactions between a joint venture and the investor are viewed as arm's-length transactions. Only the investor's proportionate share of intercompany transactions, balances, and unrealized profits are eliminated, regardless of whether the transactions are upstream or downstream.

Now it is time to explore in more detail the alternative approach to reporting business combinations, *pooling of interests*. We discussed the basic theory and ramifications in Chapter 7; Chapter 11 will take a closer look at this sometimes controversial approach.

SELF-STUDY PROBLEM 10-1[3]

Regina Ltd. owns 60% of the common shares of Dakota Ltd., acquired on January 1, 19x9. The details of the purchase are given in SSP 9-1, and the trial balances for December 31, 19x9, and selected transactions for 19x9 are shown in SSP 9-2. The trial balances of both companies (unconsolidated) at December 31, 19x10 are shown below.

Additional Information:
1. On November 15, 19x10, Dakota sold land to Regina for $105,000. The land originally cost Dakota $45,000 and had a fair value of $80,000 on January 1, 19x9. The gain on the transaction as reported by Dakota is net of income tax.
2. During 19x10, Dakota sold inventory to Regina for $160,000 at the normal markup. One-half of that amount is still in Regina's inventory at year-end.
3. Late in 19x10, Regina sold inventory to Dakota at cost, amounting to $40,000, all of which is still in Dakota's inventory on December 31, 19x10.
4. The one-year, $50,000 loan that Regina extended to Dakota on July 1, 19x9, was extended for two more years (to July 1, 19x12). Simple interest

---

3 The solutions to the self-study problems are at the end of the book, following Chapter 18.

(at 10%) has been accrued by both companies, but no interest will be paid until the loan is repaid.

5. On April 15, 19x10, Regina sold some equipment to an unrelated company for $30,000. The equipment cost $50,000 and had a book value of $20,000 on the date of sale.

6. During the year, Dakota purchased new equipment for $100,000 and wrote off old, fully depreciated equipment that had originally cost $60,000.

7. Regina issued $80,000 face-value, ten-year bonds on April 1, 19x10, at a net price of 105.

Required:

Prepare a complete set of consolidated financial statements for Regina Ltd. for the year ended December 31, 19x10, including a consolidated statement of changes in financial position.

Trial Balances
December 31, 19x10
Dr. (Cr.)

	Regina	Dakota
Cash	$ 9,800	$ 2,500
Accounts and other receivables	120,000	27,000
Inventory	130,000	55,000
Land	105,000	90,000
Building	380,000	150,000
Accumulated depreciation — building	(56,200)	(70,000)
Equipment	230,000	170,000
Accumulated depreciation — equipment	(68,000)	(47,000)
Investment in Dakota Ltd. (at cost)	150,000	—
Accounts payable and accrued liabilities	(82,900)	(77,500)
Bonds payable, long term	(145,000)	(50,000)
Premium on bonds payable	(3,700)	—
Common shares	(370,000)	(100,000)
Retained earnings	(350,000)	(135,000)
Dividends paid	25,000	60,000
Sales	(2,200,000)	(1,100,000)
Cost of sales	1,300,000	660,000
Operating expenses	826,000	362,000
Dividend income	(36,000)	—
Gain on sale of fixed assets	(10,000)	(45,000)
Other income	(12,000)	—
Interest and bond retirement expense	20,000	18,000
Income tax expense	38,000	30,000
	$ 0	$ 0

SELF-STUDY PROBLEM 10-2

(Continuation of text example.)

The status of IOR's 70% investment in IEE at the end of 19x2 is shown in Schedule 10-3. The investment account balance was $901,550 on December 31, 19x2.

During 19x3, the following occurred:

1. IEE reported net income of $80,000.
2. IEE declared dividends amounting to $24,000 and paid $18,000. The remaining $6,000 was to be paid on January 10, 19x4, to holders of record on December 31, 19x3.
3. IEE had sales to IOR that amounted to $50,000. IEE's gross margin in 19x3 was 30%. Of the goods purchased by IOR from IEE, $12,000 is still in IOR's inventory on December 31, 19x3.
4. IOR had sales to IEE which totaled $30,000. IOR's 19x3 gross margin was 35%. All of the merchandise acquired by IEE from IOR has been sold.
5. Both companies sold all of their opening inventories during the year.
6. IEE's net income includes $20,000 profit from the sale of a small parcel of land to IOR. IOR is using the land as a parking lot. The land originally cost IEE $50,000 and was valued at $80,000 on January 1, 19x1, the date on which IOR acquired its 70% interest in IEE.

Required:
a. Prepare a schedule in which you compute the amount of IOR's equity in the earnings of IEE for the year ended December 31, 19x3.
b. In general journal form, make the entries that affect IOR's investment in IEE account during 19x3. Compute the post-closing balance of the investment account on December 31, 19x3.

REVIEW QUESTIONS

10-1 What is the impact on minority interest of unrealized profits in beginning inventories?

10-2 Why is the minority interest in earnings normally deducted from consolidated earnings *after* taxes?

10-3 Explain the composition of consolidated retained earnings in terms of the parent's and subsidiary's separate-entity retained earnings.

10-4 What is the effect of the minority interest in earnings on the consolidated statement of changes in financial position?

10-5 Since all of the subsidiary's dividend payments are eliminated on consolidation, why are dividends paid to the minority shareholders shown in the consolidated statement of changes in financial position?

10-6 Under equity reporting, why are unrealized profits from **downstream** sales deducted from the investor's equity in the earnings of the investee, instead of from the parent's own earnings?

10-7 In what way do consolidation adjustments for the amortization of fair-value increments and goodwill for prior years differ from those for the current year?

10-8 When a fair-valued asset is sold by a subsidiary to its parent, how does the amount of the fair-value increment affect the unrealized profit elimination?

10-9 When a fair-valued asset is sold to outsiders, what is the disposition of the fair-value increment when the statements are consolidated in the year of the sale? What is the disposition of the increment in years following the sale?

10-10 What is a **joint venture**?

10-11 What alternatives are available to the venturers under Canadian GAAP for reporting their investment in a joint venture?

10-12 When is it appropriate to use **proportionate consolidation**?

10-13 In normal consolidated reporting, the full amount of intercompany balances is eliminated, regardless of the ownership proportion of the parent. Why is that not the case under proportionate consolidation?

10-14 How do the adjustments for intercompany unrealized profits differ under proportionate consolidation compared to full consolidation?

CASE 10-1   Canadian Carpets, Ltd.

Canadian Carpets, Ltd. (CC) has been a producer of carpets since 1937. Headquartered in Montreal, the company is federally chartered and was continued under the *Canada Business Corporations Act* in 1979. The company is effectively controlled by its founder Arjen van der Schaaf, who learned the business as a young man in Amsterdam and who started CC shortly after emigrating to Canada. In 1957, the company offered its shares to the public for the first time. In 1962, CC was listed on the Montreal Exchange.

CC deals mainly with retailers, and the retailers' inventory of carpets is usually rather slow-moving. In order to assist the retailers in carrying their inventories, CC had always offered generous credit terms. In 1958, the management of CC decided to create a separate legal entity to perform the financing function, and therefore established the Canadian Carpets Acceptance Corporation (CCAC). CCAC now arranges the financing (on an installment note basis) of the purchases of those CC customers who require financing. The customer arranges a purchase of carpets from CC and gives notes for the total amount of the purchase plus interest to CCAC. CCAC then pays to CC the discounted present value of the notes, which is the same as the original amount of the purchase. CCAC, in turn, uses the installment notes receivable as collateral for obtaining financing from the Bank of Montreal. In general, the term of the debt financing is intended to match the terms of the notes receivable, so that CCAC is not exposed to the risk of having the current rate chargeable on customers' notes fall below the cost of the debt financing. CCAC has usually been able to maintain about a 1% spread between the interest rates charged to customers and the interest rate paid to the bank, mainly because CC guarantees the debt of its subsidiary, CCAC.

In 1978, CC decided to enter the retail business directly. Since CC had no experience as a retailer, it entered into a joint venture with Harbinger, Inc., a U.S. operator of a chain of home improvement stores. The joint venture was incorporated under the *CBCA* in 1979 as Decorator's Paradise, Inc. (DP), and the share interest was divided equally between CC and Harbinger. DP opened its first store in Montreal in 1981, and since then has expanded to twelve stores in the Montreal and Toronto metropolitan areas. Decorator's Paradise stores sell a wide range of floor and wall coverings, including paint. Most of the carpet is supplied by CC, but other suppliers are used as well in order to broaden the variety of products offered.

In 1986, Canadian Carpets acquired 100% of the shares of a small manufacturer of carpet tiles, Cartil, Inc. The purchase price of $600,000 was $100,000 in excess of the fair values of the net assets acquired. In 1988, Cartil Inc. was amalgamated into Canadian Carpets and ceased to exist as a separate legal entity.

One of the principal suppliers to Decorator's Paradise was Canada Tile, Ltd., an old and well-established manufacturer of non-carpet floor coverings: vinyl, asbestos, and cork tiles, linoleum, and ceramic tiles. Incorporated in Ontario, Canada Tile (CT) was a private company.

In the early 1980s, CT began to experience a series of losses because of (1) increased competition from imported ceramic tile, (2) a decline in demand for cork tiles and linoleum, and (3) rapidly escalating prices for the petroleum products used in vinyl and asbestos tile. By the beginning of 1990, CT had accumulated unused (and unrecognized) tax loss carry-forwards amounting to $500,000.

As a result of the deteriorating financial condition of CT, the board of directors of CC agreed to purchase 60% of the shares of CT from its owner; the remaining 40% would rest in the hands of the original owner, who would continue as president of the company. The 60% purchase was intended to keep CC's interest below the two-thirds necessary to approve certain measures, so that CC could not act unilaterally on major financial reorganization or on amalgamation.

The purchase took effect on January 2, 1990. The purchase price was $990,000. The fair values of CT's net assets generally approximated their carrying values on CT's books, except for the tax loss carry-forwards and the value of CT's ceramics plant, which was estimated to have a fair value of $100,000 less than its carrying value.

In order to improve the profitability of CT, the gross margin on sales to DP was increased from 30% to 50% (of sales), effective on the date of the sale. DP also, with Harbinger's agreement, increased its inventory level of products from Canada Tile. At the end of 1990, DP held inventory from CT amounting to $320,000, or 40% of the total sales from CT to DP during 1990. In return for the potential dividend income from his remaining 40% share of CT, the CT president agreed to reduce his salary by 50%.

Because the increased cost of DP purchases from CT reduced DP's net income and Harbinger's share thereof, CC reduced its margin on sales to DP to 30% from 40%. During 1990, CC sold $1,500,000 to DP; DP's 1990 ending inventory contained $240,000 of these sales, as compared to $200,000 from CC at the beginning of the year.

The trial balances of CC, CCAC, CT, and DP at December 31, 1990, are shown below. The amount due from CT is a $1,000,000 loan made by CC to CT on July 1, 1990, which bears interest at 6% per year. CC's receivables include $500,000 due from CCAC for recent CC sales that were financed by CCAC.

Required:
a. Discuss the alternatives that Canadian Carpets could use in its annual financial statements in accounting for CCAC, CT, and DP. Evaluate the alternatives in view of the operating relationships between the companies. How useful will the resulting information be to readers of CC's statements?
b. What constraints are placed upon the management of Canadian Carpets in the exercise of control of, or influence on, the three related companies?
c. Prepare a consolidated balance sheet for Canadian Carpets, Ltd., at December 31, 1990, and a consolidated income statement for the year then ended.

Trial Balances
December 31, 1990
Dr. (Cr.)

	CC, Ltd.	CCAC	CT, Ltd.	DP, Inc.
Cash	$ 50,000	$ 500,000	$ (20,000)	$ 150,000
Accounts and notes receivable	590,000	9,000,000	200,000	850,000
Due from CT	1,030,000			
Inventories	620,000		600,000	1,000,000
PPE (net)	4,760,000		2,400,000	4,000,000
Investment in CCAC (100%)	500,000			
Investment in CT (60%)	990,000			
Investment in DP (50%)	1,480,000			
Goodwill	80,000			
Accounts and notes payable	(900,000)	(3,075,000)	(570,000)	(700,000)
Due to CC		(500,000)	(1,030,000)	
Long-term debt	(1,800,000)	(5,400,000)		(1,200,000)
Deferred taxes	(900,000)			(600,000)
Common shares	(600,000)	(200,000)	(1,000,000)	(1,000,000)
Retained earnings	(5,400,000)	(300,000)	(500,000)	(2,000,000)
Dividends paid	800,000	100,000		800,000
Sales	(8,000,000)		(1,800,000)	(16,000,000)
Finance income	(30,000)	(1,200,000)		
Dividend income	(500,000)			
Cost of sales	5,000,000		1,100,000	7,400,000
Operating expenses	1,430,000	950,000	620,000	6,000,000
Income tax expense	800,000	125,000	40,000	1,300,000
Income tax benefit (extra-ord.)			(40,000)	
	$ 0	$ 0	$ 0	$ 0

CASE 10-2   Syntax Inc.

Syntax Inc. (Syntax), a public company, has undertaken to purchase Tubular Ltd. (Tubular), a manufacturer of home heating units and industrial heating systems. Your firm, Cox & Williams, Chartered Accountants, is the current auditor of Syntax and is advising the company on the acquisition of Tubular.

Tubular is a Canadian-controlled private corporation that was founded in 1921 by Jason Kent and continues to be wholly owned by the Kent family. The company's original business was casting and assembling wood stoves. Subsequently, Tubular improved its line to cast new energy-efficient wood and coal stoves. In the past decade, under the management of the eldest son, Allen, the company expanded its plant for the fabrication of industrial heating systems for installation in large industrial and commercial complexes. Because of recent high interest charges and rigorous competition, cash flow has been poor, and the company is about to report the first large loss in its history, amounting to $500,000. Small losses in previous years were created mainly by depreciation.

To become more competitive, Tubular will have to purchase new machinery and equipment and obtain additional financing. The Kent family considered the financing requirement too great and therefore decided to sell its common shares to Syntax. Syntax has sufficient cash to purchase the common shares and if so desired, to extinguish the outstanding debt of Tubular.

Extracts from the share-purchase agreement that Syntax and Tubular negotiated are provided below.

1. Tubular is to provide financial statements for the year ending June 30, 1986. These financial statements are to be audited by the current auditors of Tubular, Robert & Rosberg, Chartered Accountants.

2. The closing date of the agreement is to be July 31, 1986, and a balance sheet at that date is to be prepared by Cox & Williams. The communication covering the balance sheet will be in the form of accountant's comments. This closing balance sheet will be used to determine the final purchase price.
3. The preliminary purchase price is $7 million, based on the audited financial statements of June 30, 1985. The price is to be adjusted upwards or downwards, dollar for dollar, based on the change in equity during the thirteen-month period between June 30, 1985, as shown in the audited financial statements of that date, and July 31, 1986, as shown on the balance sheet prepared for the closing of the agreement on July 31, 1986.
4. The settlement date for the transaction is August 15, 1986.
5. The closing balance sheet will be prepared in accordance with generally accepted accounting principles applied on a basis consistent with the preceding period.
6. Syntax and its representatives are permitted to review the auditors' working papers on the audited financial statements, and they are entitled to perform any additional audit work required.

Although the current audit of Tubular is being carried out by Robert & Rosberg, the partner in charge of your firm is enthusiastic about the review engagement and the prospects of obtaining the audit of Tubular for the year ending June 30, 1987.

The partner informed you that Robert & Rosberg had completed their field work on the June 30, 1986, audit of Tubular but had not yet issued their report. Because of the time constraint, the partner asked you to conduct a preliminary review of the audit working papers. Your notes are presented in Exhibit 1, and extracts from Tubular's balance sheet are given in Exhibit 2.

It is August 10, 1986. Having examined your notes, the partner calls you into his office and instructs you to prepare a report analyzing the significant issues and recommending a strategy for the work to be performed on the closing balance sheet.

Required:
Prepare the report to the partner.
[CICA]

EXHIBIT 1

CA's Notes on Tubular's Audit File
June 30, 1986

1. Tubular started a pension plan for its employees in 1970. The last valuation report from the actuary, dated September 30, 1985, shows a surplus amounting to $97,000. This surplus occurred due to a better return on investments than anticipated. On June 30, 1986, Tubular recognized the surplus by a journal entry offsetting the amount against current year service costs.

   Management adopted this treatment because the surplus relates to the business prior to the date of sale. Furthermore, management said that, according to the *CICA Handbook*, an adjustment in accrued pension calculations brought about by an actuarial revaluation can be included in the pension costs of the current period.

2. The prepaid expenses include legal fees of $10,000 related to the negotiation of a loan. They were capitalized and are to be amortized over the term of the loan. The loan was made on August 1, 1985, and is due July 31, 1995. Management has not made the adjustment of $1,000 because the amount is immaterial.

EXHIBIT 1 (continued)

3. Because of the decline in value of the Canadian dollar, Tubular decided to explore the opportunities in the United States market by displaying their products at a trade show in New York City. There were some enquiries during the show, and management is hopeful that some sales will result. The cost for the show, which took place in April 1986, was $30,000. Management decided to amortize this cost, which was included in prepaid expenses, over 30 months commencing April 1, 1986.

4. Tubular owns and maintains an airplane which is used mainly by Allen Kent. According to Allen Kent, he uses the plane extensively for business. Over the years, the company has accrued $5,000 per month as a provision for major maintenance work on the aircraft. In April 1986, a new, technologically improved engine costing $153,000 was installed in the aircraft. The balance of the unapplied provision of $17,000 was reversed at the end of April, as no major maintenance was expected in the future following the installation of the new engine.

5. In May 1985, the company paid a $60,000 deposit on a tube-bending machine costing $200,000. The machine was delivered in July 1985. The balance of the purchase price was to be paid by September 1985; however, before the final payment was made, the manufacturer of the tube-bending machine went into bankruptcy. The trustees of the bankrupt company have not made any claim.

   Management feels that no additional liability should be set up since the manufacturer has breached the contract, which warranted that the manufacturer would service the machine for two years. Up to June 30, 1986, the company incurred and expensed $20,000 of service costs which should have been covered under the warranty. Management has determined that the machine has four years of service remaining as at June 30, 1986.

6. From discussions with the controller it has been determined that the "Construction in Progress" account, consisting of costs of $600,000 and budgeted gross profit to date, is related to a $1-million contract to fabricate and install a vent system in a commercial building. The vent system was shipped to the site at the very end of last year, and management estimates that the job will cost an additional $50,000 in labour to complete. The customer has not been invoiced because information from the site manager is still outstanding. The gross profit has been calculated according to the budgeted percentage of 25%.

7. The deferred income taxes have resulted primarily from timing differences in the recognition of capital cost allowance (CCA) claimed for income tax purposes in excess of depreciation recorded. Even though the realization of the tax benefit from the loss carry-forward is not virtually certain, management is reasonably certain that the tax benefit can be realized by claiming less CCA than depreciation. It has therefore reduced the current year's losses by recognizing the future tax benefit. The average tax rate of the company is 30%.

   When filing its income tax return for the last five years, the company reported no taxable income as a result of claiming enough CCA to offset its net income. This year no CCA has been claimed because of the loss. Depreciation is calculated at 20% on a declining-balance basis.

   The deferred income taxes balance is made up of the following amounts:

EXHIBIT 1 (continued)

	1986	1985
	(unaudited)	(audited)
Capital cost allowance	$72,000	$ 96,000
Maintenance provision	—	(36,000)
Trade show	8,100	—
Loan negotiation cost	3,000	—
	$83,100	$60,000

EXHIBIT 2

Tubular Ltd.
Extracts from Balance Sheet
June 30
(thousands of dollars)

	1986	1985
	(unaudited)	(audited)
ASSETS		
Current		
Accounts receivable, net	$11,350	$10,000
Income tax recoverable	233	—
Inventories	7,500	4,750
Prepaid expenses	940	440
Deposit on purchase of equipment	60	60
Construction in progress	800	350
	20,883	15,600
Fixed assets, net	320	400
	$21,203	$16,000
LIABILITIES		
Current		
Bank indebtedness	$ 8,000	$ 7,000
Accounts payable and accrued liabilities	6,170	3,580
Maintenance reserve	—	120
Deferred income taxes — construction contracts	60	—
	14,230	10,700
Long-term debt	2,000	—
Deferred income taxes	83	60
	2,083	60
SHAREHOLDERS' EQUITY		
Capital stock	1,000	1,000
Retained earnings	3,890	4,240
	4,890	5,240
	$21,203	$16,000

CASE 10-3   ## Cineplex Corporation

A regular client for whom you provide accounting advice on both his own financial affairs and on the financial statements of his prospective investees has come to you with the 1984 annual report of Cineplex Corporation. He is intrigued by the note to the financial statements on "Acquisitions," and he asks you to provide enlightenment on the transactions described in the note and the probable impact of these transactions on Cineplex's subsequent financial statements. In particular, he is curious as to how (1) Cineplex could acquire all of the shares of Canadian Odeon Theatres Ltd. for only $1, and (2) how goodwill in the amount of $273,868 could be assigned to the acquisition of Citadel Film Distributors Ltd., when the total purchase price was only $77,233.

Required:
Prepare a memo to your client.

NOTE A — ACQUISITIONS
(a) On June 28, 1984, the Corporation acquired all the issued and outstanding shares of Canadian Odeon Theatres Ltd. (Canadian Odeon) for $1. Prior to closing, dividends in kind totaling approximately $4,215,000 were paid and cash dividends totaling approximately $17,389,230 were declared of which $5,389,230 was paid by Canadian Odeon to its shareholders. Subsequently, the Corporation acquired for cash $12,000,000 of Canadian Odeon common shares from treasury. Canadian Odeon used these funds to pay an equivalent portion of such cash dividends. Upon receipt of the dividends, the shareholders lent the sum of $5,000,000 to Canadian Odeon.

As part of an auxillary agreement, the Corporation issued 510,597 common shares to acquire the joint venture interest of an outside party in six theatre locations operated by Canadian Odeon. In addition, as part of the consideration to acquire the joint venture interest, the Corporation entered into a management contract with the joint venturer for a period of eight years.

These transactions have been accounted for using the purchase method. The results of operations of Canadian Odeon and the joint venture interest have been included in the consolidated statement of operations of the Corporation since June 29, 1984. The net assets acquired and the amount of the consideration given, at fair market value, are as follows:

Net Assets Acquired	
Assets	$ 80,581,111
Liabilities	(76,885,340)
	3,695,771
Minority interest in net assets	(142,637)
	$ 3,553,134
Consideration	
Cash	$ 1
Common shares	1,429,670
Debt	782,689
Costs of acquisition	1,340,774
	$ 3,553,134

Effective August 31, 1984, Cineplex Corporation amalgamated with its wholly owned subsidiary, Canadian Odeon Theatres Ltd. The name of the new corporation is Cineplex Corporation.

b. On April 27, 1984, the Corporation acquired all the issued and outstanding shares of Kernels Gourmet Popcorn Limited. The purchase price consisted of 175,000 treasury shares of the Corporation. The corporate name of Kernels Gourmet Popcorn Limited was subsequently changed to Kernels Popcorn Limited. This transaction has been accounted for using the purchase method. Goodwill arose as a result of this acquisition, in the amount of $578,315.

c. On August 30, 1984, the Corporation acquired all the issued and outstanding shares of Citadel Film Distributors Ltd. for $77,233. This transaction has been accounted for using the purchase method. Goodwill arose as a result of this acquisition, in the amount of $273,868.

Computer Corporation

CASE 10-4

Computer Corporation (CC) and Technographics Ltd. (TL), two unrelated companies, agreed to share the latest technology in manufacturing of personal computers that respond to the human voice. On January 1, 1986, CC and TL incorporated a new company, Executive Computers Ltd. (ECL). Two classes of ECL common shares were issued. Each share in both classes participates equally in the company's earnings. Class A shares are nonvoting, whereas Class B shares are voting. In return for 59 Class A shares and 1 Class B share, CC contributed land with a fair market value of $1,200,000 (CC's book value was $600,000). In return for 39 Class A shares and 1 Class B share, TL contributed cash of $800,000. Of the five-member board of directors of ECL, three are nominees of CC and two are nominees of TL. Initially, it was decided that ECL would conserve its cash by paying no dividends. Under a written agreement, any change in the dividend policy of ECL, and any transactions between ECL and either CC or TL, must be approved in advance by both CC and TL. CC has retained the right to select ECL's chief executive officer. The primary activities of CC consist of the manufacturer of personal computers.

Extracts from the income statements and balance sheets for CC and ECL are as follows (income taxes ignored):

Income Statements
For the Year Ended December 31, 1986

	CC	ECL
Sales	$3,100,000	$1,000,000
Cost of goods sold	1,500,000	500,000
	1,600,000	500,000
Depreciation	600,000	200,000
Other operating expenses	600,000	200,000
	1,200,000	400,000
Income before undernoted item	400,000	100,000
Gain on sale of land	600,000	150,000
Net income	$1,000,000	$ 250,000

Balance Sheets
December 31, 1986

	CC	ECL
Cash	$2,000,000	$ 450,000
Accounts receivable	400,000	300,000
Inventory	1,500,000	500,000
Investment in ECL, at cost	1,200,000	—
Building and equipment — net	1,800,000	600,000
Land	800,000	600,000
	$7,700,000	$2,450,000
Accounts payable	$ 200,000	$ 200,000
Common shares	5,000,000	2,000,000
Retained earnings	2,500,000	250,000
	$7,700,000	$2,450,000

Additional Information:
1. During 1986, ECL sold one-half of the land transferred from CC for proceeds of $750,000, and recorded a gain of $150,000.
2. A management fee of $100,000, paid to CC by ECL during 1986, is included in other operating expenses of ECL and sales of CC in the above 1986 income statements.
3. ECL's ending inventory includes goods purchased from CC for $400,000. CC's cost for these goods was $275,000. CC's ending inventory includes goods purchased from ECL for $250,000. ECL's cost for these goods was $150,000.

Required: (Ignore income taxes)
The following are four possible alternatives for accounting for CC's investment in ECL:

(1) cost
(2) equity
(3) proportionate consolidation
(4) full consolidation

a. Discuss the appropriateness of using **each** of these alternatives.
b. Calculate CC's net income for 1986 under **each** alternative. Explain any assumptions used.
[SMA]

P10-1

On January 1, 19x7, P acquired 90% of the voting shares of S for $170,000. At that date, the following additional information was available.

Company S

	Book value	Fair value
Nondepreciable assets	$ 50,000	$ 70,000
Depreciable assets (net)*	100,000	120,000
	$150,000	
Liabilities	$ 10,000	10,000
Owners' equity	140,000	
	$150,000	

*Estimated remaining life five years. Straight-line depreciation.

Required:
a. Calculate the amount of goodwill purchased at acquisition date.
b. Assume that you are preparing a consolidated balance sheet for the year ended December 31, 19x9. At that date, the following balances are reported:

	P	S
Depreciable assets (net)	$200,000	$180,000

Calculate the consolidated balance of depreciable assets.
[CGA-Canada]

P10-2

On January 1, 19x1, Company P purchased 70% of the outstanding voting common shares of Company S at a cost of $137,200. At acquisition date, the book value of Company S was $159,000, inventory was undervalued by $1,250, and depreciable fixed assets were undervalued by $6,250. Relevant information for 19x4 is shown below:

Required:
a. Calculate minority interest in net income for 19x4 assuming consolidation is appropriate.
b. Calculate minority interest in the consolidated balance sheet as of the end of 19x4.
c. Calculate goodwill remaining at the end of 19x4, assuming a twenty-year amortization period.
d. Calculate consolidated net income for 19x4, assuming a ten-year remaining life at acquisition date for depreciable assets and sum-of-the-years' digits depreciation. Note that Company P uses the cost method and that Company S paid dividends during the year.

| | Reported at end of 19x4 | |
	P	S
Net income	$ 44,000	$ 11,000
Dividends paid	4,000	1,000
Current assets	170,800	40,000
Investment in S (at cost)	137,200	
Fixed assets (net)	330,000	160,000
	$638,000	$200,000
Liabilities	$138,000	$ 30,000
Common stock	400,000	150,000
Retained earnings (end)	100,000	20,000
	$638,000	$200,000

[CGA-Canada]

P10-3

Alpha Company owns a controlling interest in Beta Company and Gamma Company. Alpha purchased a 75% interest in Beta at a time when Beta reported retained earnings of $450,000. Alpha purchased a 70% interest in Gamma at a time when Gamma reported retained earnings of $100,000. In each acquisition, the purchase price was equal to the proportionate net book value of the acquired company's shares, and the fair values of the assets and liabilities approximated their book values.

An analysis of the changes in retained earnings of the three companies during the year 19x5 gives the following results:

	Alpha Company	Beta Company	Gamma Company
Retained earnings on January 1, 19x5	$ 726,000	$ 682,000	$ 457,000
Net income for the year	450,000	248,000	210,000
Dividends paid	(200,000)	(150,000)	(100,000)
Retained earnings on December 31, 19x5	$ 976,000	$ 780,000	$ 567,000

Gamma sells some raw materials to Alpha. After further processing and assembly, these parts are sold by Alpha to Beta where they become a part of the finished products sold by Beta. Intercompany profits included in inventories at the beginning and end of the current year are estimated as follows:

	January 1, 19x5 Inventory	December 31, 19x5 Inventory
Intercompany profit included		
on sales from Gamma to Alpha	$60,000	$40,000
on sales from Alpha to Beta	50,000	70,000

Beta also rents a building to Gamma. Gamma is paying $3,000 per month according to the lease contract. Alpha carries its investments on a cost basis.

Required:
a. Compute the consolidated net income for 19x5.
b. Prepare a statement of consolidated retained earnings for 19x5.
c. What change would there be in consolidated net income if the three companies had engaged in the same transactions, but all purchases and sales had been with firms outside the affiliated group? Give the amount of the difference and explain how it is derived.
[SMA]

P10-4

Parent Ltd. prepares consolidated financial statements and owns 60% of a subsidiary that had net income of $300,000 and paid dividends of $100,000. During 19x6, the subsidiary sold a piece of land, which cost the subsidiary $310,000, to the parent for $378,000. The minority interest was $986,000 on January 1, 19x6.

Required:
Demonstrate how this information would be reflected in the statement of changes in financial position prepared by Parent Ltd. from its consolidated financial statements. Ignore income taxes.
[CGA-Canada]

P10-5

The following financial statements at December 31, 19x5, reflect the ownership by Parco of Subco.

Parco and Subco Ltd.
Individual and Consolidated Balance Sheets
December 31, 19x5

	Parco	Subco	Consolidated
ASSETS			
Current	$ 270,000	$180,000	$ 450,000
Investment in Subco — at cost	310,000		
Fixed assets (net)	880,000	210,000	1,090,000
Goodwill			37,000
	$1,460,000	$390,000	$1,577,000
LIABILITIES AND EQUITIES			
Current	$ 80,000	$ 60,000	$ 140,000
Long term	180,000		180,000
Shareholders' equity			
Capital stock	800,000	200,000	800,000
Retained earnings	400,000	130,000	424,000
Minority interest			33,000
	$1,460,000	$390,000	$1,577,000

Additional Information:
1. Parco purchased its interest in Subco on January 1, 19x3.
2. There have been no intercompany transactions.
3. Goodwill at acquisition was $40,000.

Required:
Based on the financial statements presented above:
a. What percentage of ownership does Parco have in Subco?
b. What was the balance in Subco's retained earnings account at the date of acquisition?
c. How is the consolidated retained earnings figure of $424,000 calculated?
(Support your answers with calculations.)
[SMA, adapted]

P10-6

On December 31, 19x5, the Joyce Company purchased 80% of the outstanding voting shares of the Blume Company for $5 million in cash. On that date, the carrying value of the net identifiable assets of the Blume Company totaled $6 million. Both companies use the straight-line method to calculate all depreciation and amortization charges. Goodwill, if any arises as a result of this business combination, is to be amortized over ten years.

For the year ending December 31, 19x9, the income statements for Joyce and Blume are as follows:

	Joyce Company	Blume Company
Sales and other revenue	$12,500,000	$ 5,600,000
Cost of goods sold	8,000,000	4,000,000
Depreciation expense	1,500,000	1,000,000
Other expenses	1,800,000	1,200,000
Total expenses	11,300,000	6,200,000
Income (loss) before extraordinary items	1,200,000	(600,000)
Extraordinary loss		(1,400,000)
Net income (loss)	$ 1,200,000	$(2,000,000)

Additional Information:
1. On December 31, 19x5, Blume had a building with a fair value that was $220,000 greater than its carrying value. The building had an estimated remaining useful life of twenty years.
2. On December 31, 19x5, Blume had inventory with a fair value that was $100,000 less than its carrying value. This inventory was sold during 19x6.
3. On January 1, 19x7, Blume sold Joyce a machine for $30,000. When Blume had purchased the machine on January 1, 19x2, for $80,000, it was estimated that its service life would be ten years to January 1, 19x12. There is no change in this estimate at the time of the intercompany sale.
4. During 19x9, Joyce sold merchandise to Blume for $200,000, a price that includes a gross profit of $80,000. During 19x9, one-half of this merchandise was resold by Blume and the other half remains in its December 31, 19x9 inventories. On December 31, 19x8, the inventories of Blume contain merchandise pur-

chased from Joyce on which Joyce had recognized a gross profit in the amount of $25,000.
5. On December 31, 19x9, Blume owed Joyce $100,000 on open account.
6. During 19x9, Blume sold merchandise to Joyce for $400,000. All of these sales were priced to provide a gross profit to Blume equal to 50% of the sale price. On December 31, 19x9, $60,000 of this merchandise remained in the inventories of Joyce. On December 31, 19x8, the inventories of Joyce contained merchandise purchased from Blume at a sale price of $150,000. The 19x8 gross profit percentage on intercompany sales was the same as for 19x9.
7. Blume's extraordinary loss resulted from the sale of the company's unprofitable manufacturing division.
8. During 19x9, Joyce declared and paid dividends of $300,000 while Blume declared and paid dividends of $100,000.
9. Joyce carries its investment in Blume by the cost method.
10. Between December 31, 19x5 and December 31, 19x8, Blume earned $4 million and declared dividends of $400,000.

Required:
Using the recommendations of the *CICA Handbook*:
a. Prepare the consolidated income statement for the Joyce Company and its subsidiary, the Blume Company, for the year ending December 31, 19x9.
b. Calculate the amount of the minority interest that would be shown in the consolidated balance sheet on December 31, 19x9.
[SMA]

P10-7

On January 1, 19x1, the Brown Company acquires 65% of the outstanding shares of the Moran Company in return for cash in the amount of $5,825,000. On this date, the book values and the fair values for the Moran Company's balance sheet accounts were as follows:

	Book values	Fair values
Cash and current receivables	$ 325,000	$ 325,000
Temporary investments	1,560,000	1,000,000
Inventories	3,450,000	1,275,000
Land	2,960,000	3,400,000
Plant and equipment (net)	3,470,000	5,000,000
Total assets	$11,765,000	
Current liabilities	$ 950,000	950,000
Long-term liabilities	2,980,000	2,550,000
No-par common stock	5,350,000	
Retained earnings	2,485,000	
Total equities	$11,765,000	

On the acquisition date, the remaining useful life of the Moran Company's plant and equipment was ten years. The long-term liabilities mature on June 30, 19x3. The temporary investments disclosed in the preceding balance sheet were sold during 19x1 for $1,200,000, and the inventories were sold during 19x1, at normal sales prices. The land is still on the company's books at December 31, 19x2. Any goodwill arising from this business combination is to be amortized over twenty years.

The income statements of the Brown Company and its subsidiary the Moran Company for the year ending December 31, 19x2, are as follows:

	Brown Company	Moran Company
Revenues	$12,540,000	$2,535,000
Cost of goods sold	8,970,000	1,460,000
Depreciation expense	2,350,000	375,000
Other expenses	790,000	465,000
Total expenses	12,110,000	2,300,000
Income before extraordinary items	430,000	235,000
Extraordinary gain	0	115,000
Net income	$ 430,000	$ 350,000

Additional Information:

1. The Brown Company carries its investment in the Moran Company using the cost method.
2. Both companies calculate all depreciation and amortization charges using the straight-line method.
3. Moran's extraordinary gain resulted from the sale of a group of common shares of the Landry Company. These shares had been purchased during 19x1 for $200,000 with the intention of holding them as a long-term investment; however, the Moran Company decided to sell the shares during 19x2. Half of the shares were sold to the Brown Company for $170,000, while the remaining half were sold in the open market for $145,000. The difference in price reflects the fact that the two sales took place at different times during 19x2. Moran uses the cost method to account for its investment in the Landry Company.
4. During 19x2, Moran sold merchandise to Brown at sales prices of $500,000. Of this amount, $200,000 is in the December 31, 19x2, inventories of the Brown Company. On January 1, 19x2, the inventories of Brown contained merchandise purchased from Moran at sales prices of $150,000. Also during 19x2, Brown sold merchandise to Moran for $600,000. One-sixth of this merchandise remains in the December 31, 19x2, inventories of Moran. All intercompany merchandise sales are priced to provide the selling company with a gross profit of 25% on sales prices. Both companies use the first-in, first-out cost flow assumption for inventory valuation.
5. During 19x2, Moran declared and paid dividends of $125,000, while Brown declared and paid dividends of $210,000.
6. The December 31, 19x1, retained earnings balance of Brown was $8,940,000, while the December 31, 19x1, retained earnings balance of Moran was $3,235,000.
7. In preparing consolidated financial statements, the Brown Company follows the current recommendations of the CICA Handbook.
8. Income taxes are to be ignored in all of the required parts of this problem.

Required:

a. Prepare a consolidated income statement for the Brown Company and its subsidiary, the Moran Company, for the year ending December 31, 19x2.
b. Calculate the retained earnings balance that would be disclosed in the consol-

idated balance sheet of Brown, and its subsidiary Moran, as at December 31, 19x2.

c. Calculate the minority interest that would be disclosed in the consolidated balance sheet of Brown and Moran at December 31, 19x2.

P10-8

On June 30, 19x1, Putnam Corporation acquired 80% of the outstanding common stock of Simons Ltd. for $4,326,000 in cash plus Putnam Corporation common stock estimated to have a fair market value of $1,200,000. On the date of acquisition, the fair market value and book value of each of Simons Ltd.'s assets were generally equal, except for inventory, which was undervalued by $225,000, and plant and equipment (net), which was overvalued by $1,000,000. The shareholders' equity of Simons at that time was $4,440,000, consisting of:

Common stock	$2,900,000
Retained earnings	1,540,000
	$4,440,000

Balance Sheets at June 30, 19x6, are as follows:

	Putnam Corp.	Simons Ltd.
ASSETS		
Cash and marketable securities	$ 4,432,000	$ 321,000
Accounts and other receivables	2,153,000	950,000
Inventory	2,940,000	1,206,000
Plant and equipment (net)	17,064,000	7,161,000
Other long-term investments	2,038,000	3,240,000
Investment in Simons Ltd.	5,526,000	—
Total assets	$34,153,000	$12,878,000
LIABILITIES		
Current liabilities	$ 3,025,000	$ 2,090,000
Mortgage note payable	12,135,000	4,000,000
Total liabilities	15,160,000	6,090,000
SHAREHOLDERS' EQUITY		
Common shares	10,000,000	2,900,000
Retained earnings	8,993,000	3,888,000
Total shareholders' equity	18,993,000	6,788,000
Total liabilities and shareholders' equity	$34,153,000	$12,878,000

Additional Information:

1. Simons Ltd. had income of $1,460,000 for the year ended June 30, 19x6. Dividends of $480,000 were declared during the fiscal year but were not paid until August 12, 19x6.
2. Simons Ltd. has had an average inventory turnover of four times per year over the last decade.
3. The plant and equipment that was overvalued on the date of acquisition had a remaining useful life of twenty years at that date.

4. Simons sold goods to Putnam during the year ended June 30, 19x5, at a gross profit margin of 25%. The opening inventory of Putnam at July 1, 19x5, included items purchased from Simons in the amount of $160,000. There were no sales from Simons to Putnam during the year ended June 30, 19x6.
5. Putnam sold goods to Simons Ltd. during the current fiscal year at a gross profit margin of 30%. Of the $750,000 of sales, goods worth $200,000 were in Simons' closing inventory at June 30, 19x6. None of these intercompany sales still in inventory had been paid for at the fiscal year-end.
6. Both companies follow the straight-line method for depreciating plant and equipment.
7. The controller of Putnam has informed you that the company has adopted the policy of goodwill amortization that results in the highest net income in accordance with generally accepted accounting principles.

Required:
a. Prepare the consolidated balance sheet for Putnam Corporation and its subsidiary, Simons Ltd., at June 30, 19x6.
b. Calculate the amount for goodwill that would appear on a consolidated balance sheet for Putnam Corporation and its subsidairy, Simons Ltd., as at June 30, 19x6, had the *entity* approach to consolidation been used. Explain the difference between this amount and the amount calculated under generally accepted accounting principles.
[SMA]

P10-9

Selected items from the adjusted general ledger trial balances at December 31, 19x4, of Penn Ltd. and its 80% owned subsidiary, Suny Inc., are given below.

	Penn	Suny
Inventory (FIFO cost) at December 31,19x3	$ 70,000	$ 50,000
Other long-term assets — net	200,000	150,000
Capital stock	(300,000)	(100,000)
Retained earnings at December 31, 19x3	(88,400)	(60,000)
Cash dividends declared in 19x4	15,000	10,000
Sales	(190,000)	(180,000)
Purchases	120,000	100,000
Depreciation and amortization expenses	15,000	10,000
Other expenses, including interest	30,000	20,000
Other income, including investment and interest income	(44,800)	—

Additional Information:
1. Penn Ltd. acquired an 80% interest in Suny Inc. on January 1, 19x1; on that date, Suny's shareholders' equity was comprised of capital stock, $100,000, and retained earnings, $10,000. On January 1, 19x1, the acquisition cost in excess of acquired net assets was assigned:
   • $12,000 to equipment to be amortized over five years on a straight-line basis;
   • $40,000 to goodwill to be amortized over ten years.
2. The inventory (FIFO Cost) balances at December 31, 19x4, were $60,000 for Penn and $40,000 for Suny.
3. During 19x4, Suny sold merchandise to Penn for $20,000 at a gross profit of

$4,000. Fifty percent of this merchandise remained in Penn's inventory at December 31, 19x4. Penn's December 31, 19x3, inventory included unrealized profit of $5,000 on merchandise purchased from Suny.
4. Suny did not acquire any merchandise from Penn in 19x4. However, Suny's December 31, 19x3, inventory included an unrealized profit of $6,000 on goods acquired from Penn. Suny sold all of these goods during 19x4.

Required:
a. Calculate the account balance of Penn's investment in Suny at December 31, 19x4, by the equity method.
b. Prepare a consolidated statement of income for 19x4.
c. Prepare a consolidated balance sheet as at December 31, 19x4, which is as complete as possible, using the information provided.
[SMA, adapted]

P10-10

On January 1, 19x1, Porter Inc. purchased 85% of the outstanding voting shares of Sloan Ltd. for $3,025,000 in cash. On this date, Sloan had no-par common stock outstanding in the amount of $2,200,000 and retained earnings of $1,100,000. The identifiable assets and liabilities of Sloan had fair values that were equal to their carrying values except for the following:

 i) Plant and equipment (net) had a fair value $200,000 greater than its carrying value. The remaining useful life on January 1, 19x1, was twenty years with no anticipated salvage value.
 ii) Accounts receivable had a fair value $75,000 less than carrying value.
iii) Long-term liabilities had a fair value $62,500 less than carrying value. These liabilities mature on June 30, 19x9.

It is the policy of Porter to amortize all goodwill balances over five years. Both Porter and Sloan use the straight-line method for amortization and depreciation. Porter Inc. is a public company and, therefore, is required to follow generally accepted accounting principles.

Other Information:
1. Between January 1, 19x1, and December 31, 19x3, Sloan earned $345,000 and paid dividends of $115,000.
2. On January 1, 19x2, Sloan sold a patent to Porter for $165,000. On this date, the patent had a carrying value on the books of Sloan of $185,000, and a remaining useful life of five years.
3. On September 1, 19x3, Porter sold land to Sloan for $93,000. The land had a carrying value on the books of Porter of $72,000. Sloan still owned this land on December 31, 19x4.
4. For the year ending December 31, 19x4, the statements of income revealed the following:

	Porter	Sloan
Total revenues	$2,576,000	$973,000
Cost of goods sold	1,373,000	467,000
Depreciation expense	483,000	176,000
Other expenses	352,000	153,000
Total expenses	2,208,000	796,000
Net income	$ 368,000	$177,000

Porter records its investment in Sloan using the cost method and includes dividend income from Sloan in its total revenues.

5. Porter and Sloan paid dividends of $125,000 and $98,000 respectively in 19x4.
6. Sloan issued no common stock subsequent to January 1, 19x1. Selected balance sheet accounts for the two companies at December 31, 19x4, were:

	Porter	Sloan
Accounts receivable (net)	$ 987,000	$ 133,000
Inventories	1,436,000	787,000
Plant and equipment (net)	3,467,000	1,234,000
Patents (net)	263,000	–
Land	872,000	342,000
Long-term liabilities	1,876,000	745,000
Retained earnings	4,833,000	1,409,000

7. During 19x4, Porter's merchandise sales to Sloan were $150,000. The unrealized profits in Sloan's inventory on January 1, and December 31, 19x4, were $14,000 and $10,000 respectively. At December 31, 19x4, Sloan still owed Porter $5,000 for merchandise purchases.
8. During 19x4, Sloan's merchandise sales to Porter were $55,000. The unrealized profits in Porter's inventory on January 1, and December 31, 19x4, were $1,500 and $2,500 respectively. At December 31, 19x4, Porter still owed Sloan $2,000 for merchandise purchases.

Required:
a. Compute the balances that would appear in the consolidated balance sheet of Porter and Sloan as at December 31, 19x4, for the following:

(1) Patent (net)
(2) Goodwill
(3) Minority interest
(4) Retained earnings

b. Porter has decided not to prepare consolidated financial statements and will report its investment in Sloan by the equity method. Calculate the investment income that would be disclosed in the income statement of Porter for the year ended December 31, 19x4.
[SMA]

P10-11

(Note: This problem is parallel to P8-9 but supposes 60% ownership instead of 100%.)

Refer to P9-12. During 19x2, Silly Inc. had sales of $800,000 to Practical Corp. Silly's gross margin continued to be 40% of selling price. During the year, Practical sold $680,000 of these goods to its customers for $1,000,000. On October 1, 19x2, Silly sold its land to Practical for $150,000. Practical paid Silly $50,000 and gave a promissory note for $100,000 due in three years at 10% interest; simple interest is all to be paid on October 1, 19x5. The $60,000 that Silly owed to Practical at the beginning of 19x2 was repaid during the year. The trial balances of the two companies at December 31, 19x2, are shown below.

Required:
Prepare a complete set of consolidated financial statements for Practical Corp. for 19x2, including a statement of changes in financial position. If P9-12 has been solved, prepare the 19x2 statements as comparative statements.

| | Trial balances, December 31, 19x2 | |
	Practical	Silly
Cash (overdraft)	$ (21,000)	$ 35,000
Accounts and other receivables	160,000	100,000
Inventory	140,000	75,000
Buildings and equipment	1,700,000	900,000
Accumulated depreciation	(655,000)	(495,000)
Land	150,000	—
Investment at Silly (at cost)	600,000	—
Due from Practical	—	100,000
Other investments	100,000	50,000
Deferred charges	—	40,000
Accounts and other payables	(225,000)	(215,000)
Payable to Silly	(102,500)	—
Common shares	(1,400,000)	(150,000)
Retained earnings	(380,000)	(275,000)
Dividends paid	100,000	70,000
Sales	(1,680,000)	(1,200,000)
Dividend income	(42,000)	—
Cost of sales	1,120,000	720,000
Depreciation expense	85,000	50,000
Amortization expense	—	40,000
Other expenses	350,500	245,000
Gain on sale of land	—	(90,000)
	$ 0	$ 0

P10-12

Parent Inc. paid $438,000 cash for 60% of the outstanding shares of Sub Inc. on January 1, 19x4. The following information was available.

| | Sub Inc., January 1, 19x4 | |
	Book value	Fair value
Cash	$ 15,000	$ 15,000
Inventory	55,000	60,000
Equipment (net)	150,000	110,000
Building (net)	260,000	320,000
Land	80,000	160,000
	$560,000	$665,000
Liabilities	$ 30,000	$ 35,000
Common shares	150,000	
Retained earnings	380,000	
	$560,000	

During 19x4, Sub Inc. earned $80,000 and paid no dividends. The inventory on hand at the beginning of the year was sold during 19x4. The equpment will be depreciated over ten years, straight-line; the building over twenty years, straight-line; and any goodwill over forty years, straight-line. The liabilities were all paid during 19x4.

Required:
Determine the amount of Parent Inc.'s investment income for Sub Inc. for 19x4, under the equity method.
[CGA-Canada, adapted]

P10-13

On April 1, 19x8, McBurney Ltd. purchased 25% of the outstanding common shares of Kangsepp Corp. for $3,000,000. The book value of Kangsepp's net assets was $10,000,000, an amount that also approximated their fair value. For the year ended December 31, 19x8, Kangsepp reported net income of $1,400,000 and Mc-Burney reported net income of $9,600,000. Kangsepp paid dividends of $80,000 in each of the first two quarters of 19x8, and $100,000 in each of the last two quarters. There were no intercompany transactions during the year. Both companies generate their incomes fairly evenly throughout the year.

Required:
Compute the amounts that would appear on McBurney's 19x8 income statement as income from investment in Kangsepp, and the balance of the investment account on the December 31, 19x8 balance sheet, assuming that McBurney uses:
a. The cost method.
b. The equity method.

P10-14

On April 2, 19x3, Coriander Ltd. acquired 40% of the outstanding common shares of Turmeric Ltd. by issuing one share of Coriander plus $5 cash for each of Turmeric's shares acquired. At the time of the purchase, Coriander's shares were trading at $25 per share and Turmeric's shares were trading at $28. Turmeric had a total of one million shares outstanding.

At the date of acquisition, the shareholders' equity of Turmeric totaled $18,000,000. The fair values of Turmeric's assets and liabilities were the same as their net book values except for the following fixed assets:

	Book value	Fair value
Land	$3,000,000	$6,000,000
Building	7,000,000	6,000,000
Equipment	6,000,000	8,000,000

The building and equipment have estimated remaining useful lives of ten years and five years, respectively. Turmeric uses straight-line depreciation.

For the year ended March 31, 19x4, Turmeric reported net income of $1,500,000. Turmeric's dividend-payout ratio was 60% for fiscal 19x4.

Required:
For the year ended March 31, 19x4, compute (1) Coriander's equity in the earnings of Turmeric and (2) the balance of the investment account at the fiscal year-end, using the equity method. Provide supporting schedules for your calculations. Assume that Coriander follows a policy of amortizing intangible assets over twenty years (straight-line).

P10-15

(Continuation from P10-14)

At the 19x4 annual meeting of Turmeric's shareholders, Coriander nominated seven directors for Turmeric's twelve-person board of directors. After some negotiation, five of Coriander's nominees were accepted onto the board. During fiscal year 19x5, the following occurred:

1. Coriander shifted a substantial amount of business to Turmeric. Turmeric became the major supplier of one of Coriander's raw materials and had sales totaling $7,000,000 to Coriander. Of that total, $1,000,000 was in Coriander's raw materials inventory at year-end. The other $6,000,000 had been utilized in finished goods, of which one-third was still in inventory on March 31, 19x5.
2. Coriander began selling some product to Curry Corp., a wholly owned subsidiary of Turmeric. Fiscal 19x5 sales totaled $2,500,000, all within the last two months of the year. Sixty percent of the sales were still in Curry's inventories at year-end.
3. Operating results for fiscal 19x5 were reported as follows:

	Coriander	Turmeric
Sales	$ 80,000,000	$ 20,000,000
Cost of sales	(56,000,000)	(12,000,000)
	24,000,000	(8,000,000)
Operating expenses	(6,000,000)	(4,000,000)
Income tax expense	(7,200,000)	(1,600,00)
Net income	$ 10,800,000	$ 2,400,000

Required:

Utilizing the information above and in P10-14, prepare a schedule(s) in which you:

a. compute the amount of investment income that Coriander should recognize in fiscal 19x5 from its investment in Turmeric.
b. compute the balance of Coriander's investment account for its investment in Turmeric at March 31, 19x5.

P10-16

King Oil Company, to maintain closer ties with associated companies in the oil business, decided to purchase holdings of common stock in several companies. The following is a list of activities associated with these acquisitions during 19x5.

February 15   Acquired 75,000 shares of Lub Oil Co. at $8 per share representing 70% of the outstanding shares. At date of acquisition book value of the Lub Oil Co.'s net assets was $800,000. Assets were considered to be valued at market.

April 13   Acquired 130,000 shares of Richman Refineries at $11 per share representing 65% of the outstanding shares. The purchase price corresponds to the underlying book value.

May 17   Acquired 50,000 shares of Discovery Co. Ltd. at $6 per share representing 2% of the outstanding shares.

June 30	Lub Oil Co. announced a loss of $40,000 for the first six months of 19x5. Richman Refineries announced earnings of $110,000 for the first six months of 19x5 and declared a dividend of 15¢ per share.
August 15	Dividend received from Richman Refineries.
October 11	Dividend of 5¢ per share received from Discovery Co. Ltd. with a statement of earnings for the six months ending September 30 indicating net earnings of $50,000.
December 31	Lub Oil Co. announced a loss of $35,000 for the year. Richman Refineries announced earnings of $190,000 for the year, including an extraordinary gain of $30,000. Discovery Co. Ltd. announced earnings of $80,000 for the nine months ending December 31.

Additional Information:
The King Oil Company's policy is to amortize goodwill over 40 years.

Required:
a. Investments in stocks could be recorded and/or reported using either the equity method or cost method. Distinguish between the two methods, indicating under what circumstances each method should be used.
b. Prepare journal entries to record the above transactions in the books of King Oil Company, assuming the use of the equity method of accounting where appropriate for reporting purposes.
[SMA]

P10-17

The North Salem Company has supplied you with information regarding two investments that were made during 19x5 as follows:

1. On January 1, 19x5, North Salem purchased for cash 40% of the 500,000 shares of voting common stock of the Yorktown Company for $2,400,000, representing 40% of the net worth of Yorktown. The book value of Yorktown's net assets was $5,000,000 on January 1, 19x5, which amount approximated the fair value of the net assets. Yorktown's net income for the year ended December 31, 19x5, was $750,000. Yorktown paid dividends of $0.50 per share in 19x5. The market value of Yorktown's common stock was $14 per share on December 31, 19x5. North Salem exercised significant influence over the operating and financial policies of Yorktown.
2. On July 1, 19x5, North Salem purchased for cash 15,000 shares representing 5% of the voting common stock of the Mahopac Company for $450,000. Mahopac's net income for the six months ended December 31, 19x5, was $350,000 and for the year ended December 31, 19x5, was $600,000. Mahopac paid dividends of $0.30 per share each quarter during 19x5 to stockholders of record on the last day of each quarter. The market value of Mahopac's common stock was $32 per share on January 1, 19x5, and $34 per share on December 31, 19x5.

Required:
As a result of these two investments, determine the following:

a. What should be the balance in the investment account for North Salem at December 31, 19x5?

b. What should be the investment income reported by North Salem for the year ended December 31, 19x5?

Show supporting computations in good form. Ignore income taxes and deferred tax considerations in your answer. North Salem's management wishes to report the highest net income permissible under Canadian GAAP. The equity method of recording investments is used when appropriate for reporting purposes.
[AICPA, adapted]

P10-18

On January 1, 19x1, Parkade Company purchased for $89,000, 35% of the outstanding voting shares of Summit Company. The following is Summit's balance sheet at that date:

	Book value
Cash	$ 20,000
Accounts receivable	30,000
Equipment (net)	80,000
	$130,000
Accounts payable	$ 10,000
Common shares	20,000
Retained earnings	100,000
	$130,000

Book values were equal to fair values except for equipment, which had a net fair value of $100,000. Summit is depreciating the equipment on a straight-line basis and the remaining life is seven years. The original salvage value was $10,000. Parkade's policy on purchased goodwill is to amortize it over the maximum period on a straight-line basis. The estimated life of this goodwill is 50 years. Summit reported profits and paid dividends as follows:

Year	Profits	Dividends
19x1	$10,000	$ 5,000
19x2	15,000	15,000
19x3	20,000	30,000

Required:
a. Prepare a schedule that calculates the amount of goodwill purchased at date of acquisition of the investment
b. Calculate the balance in Parkade Company's investment account at the end of 19x3 if the equity method were used.
c. Calculate the balance in this account if the cost method were used.
[CGA–Canada]

P10-19

On January 1, 19x1, Company P purchased 90% of the outstanding common shares of Company S for $150,000. At that date, Company S's condensed balance sheet and fair values were:

	Book value	Fair value
Cash	$10,000	$10,000
Land	20,000	30,000
Building (net)	20,000	25,000
	$50,000	
Liabilities	$10,000	10,000
Common shares	10,000	
Retained earnings	30,000	
	$50,000	

Assume a ten-year amortization period for any depreciable assets excess and a twenty-year period for any goodwill.

Required:

a. Assume the following information regarding net income and dividends of Company S:

Year	Net income	Dividends
19x1	$ 10,000	$ 2,000
19x2	12,000	2,000
19x3	9,000	2,000
19x4	(10,000)	2,000*
19x5	10,000	26,000

*The 19x4 dividend was a 20% stock dividend.

Calculate the balance in the investment account in Company P's books at the end of 19x5, assuming that Company P uses the equity method in its books.

b. Assume that Company P uses the cost method of accounting for its investment. Prepare journal entry or entries to reflect the information given previously for 19x4 and 19x5.

[CGA-Canada]

P10-20

The Fostor Company purchased 30% of the outstanding voting shares of the Festee Company for $1,400,000 in cash on January 1, 19x7. On that date, the Festee Company's shareholders' equity was made up of common stock of $2 million, other contributed capital of $500,000, and retained earnings of $1.5 million. There were no differences between the carrying values and the fair values of any of its net identifiable assets or liabialities. The net income and dividends declared and paid by the Festee Company for the two years subsequent to its acquisition were as follows:

	19x7	19x8
Net income (loss)	$(100,000)	$160,000
Dividends	40,000	50,000

The income statements for the year ending December 31, 19x9, prior to the recognition of any investment income, for the Fostor and Festee Companies are as follows:

	Fostor	Festee
Sales	$2,000,000	$550,000
Other revenues	100,000	—
Total revenues	2,100,000	550,000
Cost of goods sold	1,000,000	300,000
Other expenses	200,000	50,000
Total expenses	1,200,000	350,000
Income before extraordinary items	900,000	200,000
Extraordinary loss	—	30,000
Net income	$ 900,000	$170,000

During 19x9, Foster Company declared and paid dividends of $100,000 while Festee Company declared and paid dividends of $70,000. The Festee Company declares and pays its dividends on December 31 of each year.

Required:
a. Assume that Fostor can exercise significant influence over the affairs of Festee. Provide the following:

1. The income statement of the Fostor Company, including recognition of any investment income or loss, for the year ending December 31, 19x9.
2. The balance in the investment in Festee Company accouant as it would appear on the December 31, 19x9, balance sheet of the Fostor Company.
   Goodwill, if any, is to be amortized over 40 years.

b. Assume that Fostor cannot exercise significant influence over the affairs of Festee. Provide the journal entry of the Fostor Company related to its investment in the Festee Company for 19x9.
[SMA]

P10-21

Gladeau Industries is an unincorporated joint venture that was formed in 19x2 by four corporations. Cousineau Corporation invested $2,000,000 cash as its share of the start-up capital. Cousineau provided 20% of the total initial Gladeau capital and under the joint venture agreement enjoys 20% of Gladeau's profits and losses.

The preliminary balance sheet accounts for Cousineau and Gladeau at December 31, 19x6, are shown below

Additional Information:
1. Cousineau's advances to Gladeau are callable only with one year advance notice; the advances bear interest at 12% per annum, and the interest is paid each December 31.
2. Most of Gladeau's output is sold through the co-venturers. In 19x6, Cousineau purchased $6 million of Gladeau's output, of which 10% remained in Cousineau's inventory at the end of 19x6. Gladeau's gross margin in 19x6 was 40% of sales.
3. In December 19x6, Cousineau sold some of its specialty product to Gladeau for $2 million, all of which remains in Gladeau's inventory. Cousineau's gross margin was 30% of selling price.
4. At the end of 19x5, Cousineau's inventory included $400,000 that had been purchased from Gladeau, at a gross profit of $120,000.

	Cousineau	Gladeau
Cash	$ 1,000,000	$ 1,500,000
Accounts receivable	3,000,000	8,000,000
Inventories	4,000,000	10,000,000
Plant and equipment (net)	10,000,000	15,000,000
Investment in Gladeau	2,000,000	—
Advances to Gladeau	1,500,000	—
	$21,500,000	$34,500,000
Accounts payable	$ 2,000,000	$ 3,000,000
Loans payable (long-term)	3,000,000	5,000,000
Equity interest of venturers, Dec. 31, 19x5	—	10,000,000
Common shares	6,000,000	—
Retained earnings, Dec. 31, 19x5	9,500,000	14,000,000
Net income for 19x6	3,000,000	5,500,000
Dividends and distributions	(2,000,000)	(3,000,000)
	$21,500,000	$34,500,000

Required:
Prepare Cousineau's consolidated balance sheet at December 31, 19x6; Cousineau reports Gladeau by proportionate consolidation.

P10-22

On July 1, 19x1, Grace Ltd. joined in a 50/50 joint venture to form Golden Glades Corporation (GGC). Grace contributed cash of $1,000,000 and intangible assets (i.e., patents and trademarks) valued at $3,000,000 to the joint venture. The book value of the contributed intangible assets was $1,200,000 on January 1, 19x1; Grace had been amortizing them at a rate of $400,000 per year. In accordance with GAAP, Grace recorded its investment in GGC at $4,000,000 with a gain on disposal of the intangible assets of $2,000,000. GGC plans to amortize the cost of the intangibles over five years, beginning in 19x2. Grace and its co-venturer will share equally in GGC's profits and losses. Grace will report its share of GGC by using proportionate consolidation.

Required:
Explain the impact that the contributed intangibles will have on Grace's net income and balance sheet for 19x1 and for 19x2. Be specific as to accounts and amounts.

11

Pooling of Interests

Previous chapters have explained the preparation of consolidated financial statements when one company owns a controlling interest in another company. If the control was obtained by buying the majority of the voting shares, a business combination took place. In the large majority of cases, a business combination involves one company acquiring another (or a functioning part thereof) as a going concern; when an acquiror can be identified, the purchase method of reporting for the combination is normally used in Canada.

But there are situations in which two (or more) companies combine wherein an acquiring company cannot be identified. This is particularly apt to be the case for combinations involving private companies, wherein a shareholders' agreement may indicate that post-combination control is to be shared, even when share ownership is uneven. In such instances, the purchase method may not be appropriate and the pooling-of-interests method should be used. This chapter examines the application of the pooling-of-interests method.

Note that the purchase-versus-pooling choice is only relevant for business combinations, not for parent-founded subsidiaries or for reporting an investment in significantly influenced affiliates. The major variable that distinguishes the two methods is valuation of one company's assets and liabilities at fair values versus book values. When a parent's investment in a subsidiary represents the initial investment in a parent-founded subsidiary, the book value *is* the fair value at the time of the investment. Thus nothing in this chapter affects the previously described reporting for parent-founded subsidiaries.

APPLICABILITY OF POOLING

In their 1970 CICA research study, Martin, Laiken, and Haslam trace the origin of pooling-of-interests accounting back to the 1946 merger of Celanese Corporation and Tubize Rayon Corporation. These were corporations of comparable size in similar industries, and the equity and management interests of both companies would continue after the combination. After analyzing the Celanese-Tubize Rayon merger and the history of poolings since then, the authors derived a set of four criteria that had developed in practice to decide whether a specific business combination would qualify for pooling-of-interests accounting treatment:[1]

1. Continuity of equity interests
2. Continuity of management influence
3. Comparability of size
4. Similarity of industry

While this list of criteria is intuitively appealing, the authors found that only the first criterion was consistently applied in practice. The second criterion is particularly ephemeral; management can be continued today and gone tomorrow, once the statements are issued and the combination has been reported therein on a pooled basis.

Nevertheless, there are certain conditions that are logically prerequisite to accounting for a business combination as a pooling of interests (hereinafter referred to simply as **pooling**). First, it is clear that the combination must be executed primarily via an exchange of shares. Only a share exchange can result in the former shareholders of both combining companies having a voting interest in the combined company. If the combination was executed by having one company pay cash or other assets for the shares of the second company, then the operations and assets of the combined companies would be firmly under the control of the shareholders of the company paying cash. In any cash purchase, one company is clearly the acquiror, and pooling is not appropriate.

This is not to say that cash cannot be involved in the deal at all. A small cash component may be necessary in order to equalize the values of the shares exchanged. Nevertheless, there must be an exchange of shares before pooling can be considered as an alternative.

Second, the combining companies must be of comparable size in terms of voting power.[2] If one is much larger than the other, then an exchange of shares will reflect that fact and the shareholders of the larger company will have voting control over the combined enterprise. It is difficult to rationalize a combination as a pooling if the former shareholders of the combining companies do not have approximately equal voting shares in the combined enterprise. Otherwise, the larger company would appear to be the acquiror of the smaller.

In this context, "size" does not refer to asset value or not necessarily to common share equity value. For example, the common shares of one combining company could be in two classes, one voting and one nonvoting. If the voting shares comprise only half of the total shares, then the company could combine with another company that has only half the size (in asset or earnings value) and still be of equal size in post-combination voting power.

1 Samuel A. Martin, Stanley N. Laiken, and Douglas F. Haslam, *Business Combinations in the '60s: A Canadian Profile* (CICA, 1970), p. 39.
2 *CICA Handbook*, para. 1580.14. It should be noted, however, that while the equal-size condition seems logical, it is not a requirement for using the pooling method in some jurisdictions, such as in the United States.

The rule of comparable size should not be taken too literally. A 50-50 split in post-combination ownership is not necessary. In fact, the 1980 merger of Hiram Walker with Consumers Home resulted in a 58-42 division of ownership, but the merger was reported as a pooling. One important factor is the distribution of shares in the combining companies. The more widely the shares of both companies are distributed, then the greater the imbalance in resulting share ownership might be without jeopardizing the use of pooling. The diffusion of voting rights effectively prevents the domination of one shareholder group by the other. On the other hand, if at least one of the companies is closely controlled (or solely owned), then a combination that results in the shareholder(s) of the closely controlled company holding even a bare majority of the shares of the combined company could give the previous shareholder(s) of that company the ability to elect a majority of the board of directors. When *private* companies combine, it is not uncommon for the shareholders of the two combining companies to sign a shareholders' agreement that controls voting rights, among other things, and that thereby prevents one party from dominating the other, even if more shares are owned.

A third condition for pooling is that a substantial minority interest should not exist. The concept of pooling suggests that two companies are coming together to operate jointly as one. But if there are large minority interests that do not participate in the combination, then it does not seem that the two companies are really coming together. Instead, the existence of a substantial minority interest after the combination suggests simply that the ownership of one of the companies has been altered, the majority interest having been purchased by the acquiring company.

It is not clear what constitutes a substantial minority interest. Obviously, 49% is large and 1% is small, but where should the line be drawn? In the United States, *APB Opinion No. 16* restricts pooling to those instances in which the minority interest is no more than 10%. In Canada, no explicit guideline is given, but some guidance can be drawn from legislation. Any minority interest that is large enough to block special resolutions of the shareholders would impede control by the majority shareholders. In corporations acts, special resolutions generally require approval by two-thirds of the votes cast. Therefore any minority interest of one-third or larger of any class of shares would rule out pooling, since joint control of the two companies would be restricted. If the minority interest is 10% or less, some corporations acts (including the *Canada Business Corporations Act*) empower the majority shareholder to acquire the minority shares, even if the minority shareholders are unwilling to sell. Thus we can see that a 10% minority interest is no serious impediment to control and thus to pooling, while a 34% minority interest is a significant potential impediment; 11% to 33% is the grey area.

One of the criteria for pooling that was suggested at the beginning of this section is that the combining companies should be in the same or similar industries. The idea is that operations can be pooled to form a single, continuing entity only if they are compatible; the combination would increase either vertical or horizontal integration or would reduce competition within an industry. A contrary view would be that a business combination can be viewed as a pooling if the combining companies are in totaly different industries and *no* integration of operations will occur; the combining companies will conduct their operations after the combination much as they had before. The purpose of the combination would then probably be for financial stability and the reduction of risk by industry portfolio diversification. Once again, the Hiram Walker-Consumers Home merger provides an example; that merger was a combination of oil and water (i.e., 80-proof), and there was never any intention to try to combine the operations of the distiller with the oil company.

As we pointed out in Chapter 7, the use of pooling as a reporting method for business combinations by public companies in Canada is quite rare. *Financial Reporting in Canada* has found only two such combinations between 1981 and 1986 amongst its 300 sample companies. One of those was a 1986 pooling, in which Rayrock Resources Limited issued 4,501,791 shares on a one-for-one basis to acquire 100% of the shares of Yellowknife Bear Resources Inc. After the combination, Rayrock had 9,902,791 shares outstanding, 45% held by the former shareholders of Yellowknife. Yellowknife thereby became a wholly owned subsidiary of Rayrock. In its annual report for 1986, Rayrock's management justified the use of pooling by pointing out that the two companies had equal representation on the post-combination board of Rayrock and that the combined company management included managers from both predecessor companies. Since the companies were also in the same industry, post-combination share ownership was close to equal, and there was no minority interest outstanding, all of the criteria that have been suggested for pooling seemed to be satisfied.[3]

Pooling is more common among private companies than public companies. Shareholders' agreements can be used to assure equality of interests and voting power even when the share ownerships are unbalanced.

Pooling-of-interests accounting is also used when the shareholdings of already affiliated companies are reorganized, and this is a common occurance among both public and private companies. In such instances, the pooling is the result of a non-arms-length transaction rather than of a business combination. We will address the reorganization of intercorporate ownership near the end of this chapter, but the accounting approach for an ownership reorganization is the same as for pooling.

FINANCIAL REPORTING FOR A POOLING OF INTERESTS

When a business combination is reported as a pooling, the normal expectation is that external reporting would be in the form of consolidated financial statements. The form of a pooling combination may be that one company issues new shares in exchange for the shares of the second company. The first company would therefore legally own the second, as was the case in the Rayrock example cited above. The second company may legally be a subsidiary of the first, but in substance the two companies (or their former owners) are equal partners in the new, combined economic entity. Under these cir-

3 In 1987, the two companies amalgamated under the name Rayrock Yellowknife Resources Inc. The shares are traded on the Toronto Stock Exchange.

cumstances, it would violate the economic substance of the combination to report on an unconsolidated basis, with the first company simply reporting the second company as an equity-basis investment.

Of course, separate-entity financial statements may still be needed for creditors, managers, and tax authorities. Since the two companies are still separate legal entities, creditors and owners may need to be able to appraise the credit risk, earning power, etc., of each entity. Separate statements are needed to test compliance with restrictive covenants in bond indentures. Top management may need separate-entity statements in order to appraise the performance of the managers of each legal or operating entity, or to help devise financial strategies. And since each corporation is still taxed separately, separate statements are needed for the income tax return.

While public companies would normally be expected to report a pooling-accounted business combination on a consolidated basis, the expectation of consolidation does not extend to other subsidiaries of the pooled companies that have been accounted for by the purchase method. Corporations A and B may combine in a pooling of interest, and each may have subsidiaries that were acquired by purchase. Consolidated statements must be prepared for A and B, but the purchased subsidiaries of A and B may be consolidated or may be reported on the equity basis, in accordance with the criteria discussed in Chapters 6 and 7.

A pooling of interests is intended to carry forward the pre-combination book values of the combining companies rather than revaluing one company's assets and liabilities at fair value. As a result, the process of preparing consolidated financial statements is somewhat different for pooled companies than for purchased companies. On average, consolidation under pooling is easier than purchase-method consolidation because there are no fair-value increments or goodwill to recognize or to amortize. On the other hand, a legal requirement to value shares issued in exchange at fair market value may complicate the process. Intercompany transactions and unrealized profits thereon that occur after the combination takes place are eliminated in essentially the same manner under pooling as they are under purchase accounting.

Differences in Approach to Consolidation

A major difference between consolidations under pooling versus purchase is that under pooling, the two companies are viewed as though they had always been combined. Since no new basis of accountability is established under pooling, financial performance evaluation must be carried out by use of comparisons with pre-combination performance measures.

For example, consolidated earnings per share (EPS) after the combination will include the results of both companies, computed on essentially the same accounting basis as before the combination. Historical comparisons must therefore be made to pre-combination EPS for both companies together, not for just one of them.

Thus pooling requires that all prior years' comparative statements, financial statistics, and performance measures be restated on a combined basis. If any changes in accounting policy are made in either or both of the companies at or after the date of combination, the pre-combination accounting results must be retroactively adjusted.

The retroactive restatement for pooling is different from the treatment under the purchase method, where no restatement occurs. Purchase accounting recognizes that an investment has been made by the acquiror, and future operating results are an indication of the return on that investment. Pooling, on the other hand, recognizes no investment as having taken place; resources have simply been pooled, as the *CICA Handbook* points out [para. 1580.64].

The fact that pooled companies should be accounted for as though they had always been combined means that prior years' financial results must be adjusted for any arm's-length intercompany transactions prior to the date of the combination. Under purchase accounting, pre-combination transactions are normally viewed as irrelevant to accounting for the combination. But under the pooling method, such intercompany transactions and unrealized profits must be eliminated from prior years' figures. The work of restating historical results need be done only once, of course. Once restated, no further restatement is needed in subsequent years.

The remainder of this chapter will illustrate consolidations using pooling. Primary attention will be focused on 100% combinations, with discussion of the treatment of minority interests later in the chapter.

Consolidation at Date of Combination

The boards of directors and the shareholders of PoolInc and PondCorp have agreed to combine the two companies effective January 1, 19x4. The form of the combination is that PoolInc will issue two PoolInc shares in exchange for each share of PondCorp. Prior to the combination, there are 100,000 shares of PoolInc and 50,000 shares of PondCorp issued and outstanding.

Before the combination was announced publicly by the boards of the two companies, PoolInc's shares had been trading at $60 per share and PondCorp's shares had been trading at $100 per share. After the announcement, the price of PoolInc's shares dropped to $55 while the price of PondCorp's shares rose to $110 per share.

The condensed balance sheets of both companies prior to the combination are shown in Schedule 11-1. The book value of PoolInc's net assets is $4.6 million, and the book value of PondCorp's net assets is $3.4 million.

To effect the combination, PoolInc will issue 100,000 new shares in exchange for all of the PondCorp shares. PoolInc will then have 200,000 shares outstanding, of which 50% will be held by the pre-combination shareholders of PoolInc and the other 50% will be held by the former shareholders of PondCorp. All of PondCorp's shares will be held by PoolInc, making PondCorp a wholly owned subsidiary of PoolInc in legal form. In substance, however, a pooling of interests has occurred, since control of PoolInc is equally divided between the two pre-combination shareholder groups.

The market value of the shares issued by PoolInc in the exchange is $5.5 million if valued at the time of the exchange, or $6.0 million if valued at the time of the announcement of the combination. These amounts are $2.1 million to $2.6 million in excess of PondCorp's net asset book value. Under purchase accounting, we would need to allocate the excess to the fair values of the net assets and to goodwill. But under pooling, we ignore the market value (and the net asset fair values) altogether.

When the share exchange takes place, PoolInc must record the issuance of its new shares. Ideally, under the theory of pooling, the market value of the shares should be irrelevant because the goal is to record the newly issued

SCHEDULE 11-1

Pre-Combination Balance Sheet
January 1, 19x4

	PoolInc	PondCorp
Cash and receivables	$3,000,000	$1,000,000
Inventory	200,000	250,000
Land	1,000,000	1,500,000
Building and equipment	3,000,000	2,500,000
Accumulated depreciation	(1,200,000)	(750,000)
Total assets	$6,000,000	$4,500,000
Accounts payable	$1,000,000	$ 900,000
Future income taxes	400,000	200,000
Common shares (no par)	2,600,000	1,000,000
Retained earnings	2,000,000	2,400,000
Total equities	$6,000,000	$4,500,000

shares at the book value of the net assets acquired. In practice, this may not be feasible for public companies, owing to the requirements of the federal and provincial corporations acts. In order to illustrate the "pure" application of pooling, however, we shall first assume that the newly issued shares can be recorded by the issuer at the net book value of the shares acquired, as they usually would be in a pooling that involves only private companies.

In theory, PoolInc should record the issuance of shares by crediting the PoolInc shareholders' equity accounts for exactly the same amounts as are shown in PondCorp's shareholders' equity accounts. The entry *on PoolInc's books* would appear as follows:

Investment in PondCorp	$3,400,000	
Common shares		$1,000,000
Retained earnings		2,400,000

After the combination, the trial balances of the two companies will appear as shown in the first two columns of Schedule 11-2. PondCorp's balances are unchanged from Schedule 11-1, while PoolInc's accounts are changed only by the issuance of shares and the recording of the investments, as presented by the entry above.

When the statements are consolidated, the investment account must be eliminated. For pooling, the entry is simply to reverse the entry that was recorded on PoolInc's books for the share issuance. The *worksheet* elimination entry would be:

(a) Common shares	$1,000,000	
Retained earnings	2,400,000	
Investment in PondCorp		$3,400,000

This adjustment eliminates the shareholders' equity accounts of Pond-Corp. But since the PoolInc shareholders' equity accounts now include the balances from PondCorp as a result of the entry for the issuance of shares,

SCHEDULE 11-2

Consolidation at Date of Acquisition
January 1, 19x4
Dr. (Cr.)

	Trial balances		Eliminations	PoolInc consolidated trial balance
	PoolInc	PondCorp		
Cash and receivables	$3,000,000	$1,000,000		$4,000,000
Inventory	200,000	250,000		450,000
Land	1,000,000	1,500,000	$ (200,000)b	2,300,000
Buildings and equipment	3,000,000	2,500,000		5,500,000
Accumulated depreciation	(1,200,000)	(750,000)		(1,950,000)
Investment in PondCorp	3,400,000		(3,400,000)a	—
Accounts payable	(1,000,000)	(900,000)		(1,900,000)
Future income taxes	(400,000)	(200,000)	50,000 b	(550,000)
Common shares	(3,600,000)	(1,000,000)	1,000,000 a	(3,600,000)
Retained earnings	(4,400,000)	(2,400,000)	{ 2,400,000 a⎱ 150,000 b⎰	(4,250,000)
	$ 0	$ 0	$ 0	$ 0

the net result of the elimination is that the two companies' shareholders' equity accounts are effectively combined on the consolidated balance sheet.

As noted earlier, there may be legal impediments to crediting retained earnings for the issuance of new shares. For now, however, we will continue to assume that PoolInc does record retained earnings that are equal to those of PondCorp.

We have already pointed out that consolidation under pooling must eliminate pre-combination intercompany transactions. Assume that in 19x2, two years before the combination, PondCorp has sold land costing $500,000 to PoolInc for its fair market value of $700,000, and had paid income tax of $50,000 on the gain. The $200,000 unrealized profit on the sale must be eliminated from the land account, the PondCorp retained earnings must be adjusted for the after-tax gain of $150,000, and the tax must be transferred to future (or deferred) income taxes:

(b) Retained earnings	$150,000	
Future income taxes	50,000	
Land		$200,000

In addition, the comparative net income and earnings per share for PondCorp must be adjusted in the year of sale, and PoolInc's assets for each year since the sale must be adjusted for the unrealized profit. The retroactive adjustments are made only for the comparative statistics and the consolidated financial statements, and are *not* recorded on the companies' books.

The combined (consolidated) trial balance after these two adjustments is shown in the last column of Schedule 11-2. There are two aspects of this trial balance which should be noted. The first is that in effect, the retained earnings of *both* companies are carried forward to the consolidated balance sheet as a result of our having recorded the share issuance as we have. The other is that the accumulated depreciations of both companies are also combined.

Recall that in purchase accounting, the accumulated depreciation of the acquired company is not carried onto the consolidated balance sheet; instead, the fair value at the date of acquisition is incorporated entirely into the asset account just as if the acquiror had bought the assets directly. Pooling is substantially different in that all of the book values of *both* companies are carried onto the consolidated balance sheet.

Alternative Form of Combination

In the preceding example, PoolInc issued shares in exchange for PondCorp's shares and thus PoolInc ended up owning PondCorp. A common alternative to this arrangement would be to form a new corporation that would issue its shares in exchange for the shares of both PoolInc and PondCorp. For example, assume that the directors of PoolInc and PondCorp agree to form LakeLtd. LakeLtd will issue one share in exchange for each share of PoolInc and will issue two shares for each share of PondCorp. In theory, the exchange will be recorded on LakeLtd's books at the net book value of the shares acquired, with the issuance credited to common shares and retained earnings in accordance with the amounts shown on the trial balances (Schedule 11-3) for the two acquired companies:

Investment in PoolInc	$4,600,000	
Investment in PondCorp	3,400,000	
Common shares (no par)		$3,600,000
Retained earnings		4,400,000

SCHEDULE 11-3

Consolidation at Date of Acquisition
January 1, 19x4
Dr. (Cr.)

		Trial balances			LateLtd consolidated trial balance
	LakeLtd	PoolInc	PondCorp	Eliminations	
Cash and receivables		$3,000,000	$1,000,000		$4,000,000
Inventory		200,000	250,000		450,000
Land		1,000,000	1,500,000	$ (200,000)b	2,300,000
Buildings and equipment		3,000,000	2,500,000		5,500,000
Accumulated depreciation		(1,200,000)	(750,000)		(1,950,000)
Investment in PoolInc	$4,600,000			(4,600,000)a	—
Investment in PondCorp	3,400,000			(3,400,000)a	
Accounts payable		(1,000,000)	(900,000)		(1,900,000)
Future income taxes		(400,000)	(200,000)	50,000 b	(550,000)
Common shares	(3,600,000)	(2,600,000)	(1,000,000)	3,600,000 a	(3,600,000)
Retained earnings	(4,400,000)	(2,000,000)	(2,400,000)	{ 4,400,000 a 150,000 b }	(4,250,000)
	$ 0	$ 0	$ 0	$ 0	$ 0

The trial balances of the three companies after the exchange of shares are shown in the first three columns of Schedule 11-3. LakeLtd is a pure holding company; its only assets are the shares of the other two companies.

The elimination entry for the intercorporate investment, adjustment (a), completely eliminates all of the balances in LakeLtd's accounts. What is left are the accounts of PoolInc and PondCorp, which merely need to be adjusted to eliminate the unrealized gain on the land, alternative (b).

The resultant consolidated trial balance for LakeLtd, shown in the last column of Schedule 11-3, is the same as that shown for PoolInc in the last column of Schedule 11-2.

Consolidation Subsequent to the Date of Combination

We have seen that consolidation at the date of combination is easier for pooling than for purchase accounting because there is no need under pooling to ascertain the purchase price or the fair values of the assets, and thus no need to allocate a purchase price to individual assets and to goodwill. Subsequent consolidations are similarly eased, because there also is no need to amortize fair-value increments or goodwill.

To demonstrate consolidation subsequent to combination, let us return to the first example in which PoolInc issued shares in exchange for PondCorp's shares. Assume that PondCorp earns $500,000 after taxes in 19x4 and pays $200,000 in dividends. If PoolInc uses the cost method, then PoolInc's accounts would include the dividend income received from PondCorp. The December 31, 19x4, trial balances for PoolInc and PondCorp are shown in the first two columns of Schedule 11-4.

To prepare the consolidated statements, only three adjustments are necessary (assuming that there were no intercompany transactions other than the payment of dividends). Adjustments (a) and (b) are the combination adjustments. Adjustment (a) eliminates the share exchange that effected the combination, while (b) adjusts the land account to remove the unrealized profit. Adjustment (a) will be made each year, while (b) will be made each year until the land is sold to a third party. These adjustments are exactly the same as those shown in Schedule 11-2. Adjustment (c) eliminates the intercompany dividends for 19x4. Schedule 11-5 illustrates consolidation four years after the combination took place, December 31, 19x7, using the cost method. The only worksheet eliminations are as follows:

(a)	Common shares	$1,000,000	
	Retained earnings	2,400,000	
	Investment in PondCorp		$3,400,000
	(to eliminate the initial investment)		
(b)	Dividend income	$ 300,000	
	Dividends paid		$ 300,000
	(to eliminate intercompany dividends)		

Since there are no fair-value increments or goodwill to amortize, consolidated earnings are the sum of the separate entities' earnings, subject only to the elimination of unrealized profits.

SCHEDULE 11-4

Consolidated Financial Statements
December 31, 19x4
Dr. (Cr.)

	Trial balances		Eliminations & adjustments	PoolInc consolidated trial balance
	PoolInc	PondCorp		
Cash and receivables	$3,620,000	$1,550,000		$5,170,000
Inventory	200,000	250,000		450,000
Land	1,000,000	1,500,000	$ (200,000)b	$2,300,000
Buildings and equipment	3,000,000	2,500,000		5,500,000
Accumulated depreciation	(1,400,000)	(1,000,000)		(2,400,000)
Investment in PondCorp	3,400,000		(3,400,000)a	
Accounts payable	(1,000,000)	(900,000)		(1,900,000)
Future income tax	(400,000)	(200,000)	50,000 b	(550,000)
Common shares	(3,600,000)	(1,000,000)	1,000,000 a	(3,600,000)
Retained earnings (January 1, 19x4)	(4,400,000)	(2,400,000)	{ 2,400,000 a } { 150,000 b }	(4,250,000)
Dividends paid	—	200,000	(200,000)c	
Sales	(2,400,000)	(3,000,000)		(5,400,000)
Cost of sales	1,440,000	1,600,000		3,040,000
Operating expenses	560,000	500,000		1,060,000
Income tax expense	180,000	400,000		580,000
Dividend income	(200,000)		200,000 c	
	$ 0	$ 0	$ 0	$ 0

SCHEDULE 11-5

Consolidated Financial Statements
December 31, 19x7
Dr. (Cr.)

	Trial balances		Eliminations	Consolidated trial balance
	PoolInc	PondCorp		
Investment in PondCorp	$3,400,000		$(3,400,000)a	—
Other assets	9,400,000	$7,000,000		$16,400,000
Liabilities and deferred tax	(2,000,000)	(1,250,000)		(3,250,000)
Common shares	(3,600,000)	(1,000,000)	1,000,000 a	(3,600,000)
Retained earnings (beginning of year)	(6,300,000)	(4,400,000)	2,400,000 a	(8,300,000)
Dividends paid	—	300,000	(300,000)b	—
Revenue	(4,000,000)	(4,500,000)		(8,500,000)
Expenses	3,300,000	3,950,000		7,250,000
Dividend income	(300,000)		300,000 b	—
	$ 0	$ 0	$ 0	$ 0

Shares Issued at Fair Market Value

Federal and provincial corporations acts include specific requirements as to the valuation of issued shares and the maintenance of a stated capital account for each class of shares. The purpose of such requirements is to avoid "hidden reserves" (in the case of undervaluation) or "watered stock" (in the case of overvaluation).

Generally speaking, the stated capital account should include the full fair value of the shares issued in an arm's-length exchange. Thus, when pooling is applied to a business combination (that is, a share exchange between previously unrelated companies), there is no legal provision for either (1) recording the transaction at book value or (2) crediting part of the value to retained earnings.

If the fair value of the shares issued is less than the total shareholders' equity of the pooled company, no major problem arises. If, for example, the value of the newly issued PoolInc shares was $3.0 million, then the entry *on PoolInc's books* to record the share issuance on the date of combination would be:

Investment in PondCorp	$3,000,000	
Common shares		$3,000,000

When the consolidated statements are prepared, the investment account is eliminated, first by crediting common shares for the full amount of PondCorp's common share account in order to eliminate PondCorp's shares from PoolInc's consolidated balance sheet. The remainder of the balance of the investment account is debited to other contributed capital accounts, to the extent that they can absorb the remainder. If the contributed capital accounts cannot absorb the full remainder, then the balance is charged to retained earnings. Since neither PondCorp nor PoolInc have any contributed capital accounts other than common shares, the *worksheet* elimination entry would be as follows:

Common shares	$1,000,000	
Retained earnings	2,000,000	
Investment in PondCorp		$3,000,000

If a consolidated balance sheet is prepared on the date of combination, the shareholder's equity section would appear as follows (after adjusting for the unrealized profit of $150,000):

Common shares	$5,600,000
Retained earnings	2,250,000
Total	$7,850,000

The total shareholders' equity is the same as it would be if we had recorded the share issuance at book values, as in the previous section (Schedule 11-3), but the detail is different. Recording the full value in the common share account reduces the consolidated retained earnings, and thereby violates the pooling concept of carrying forward the pooled retained earnings as though the companies had always been combined. But the more important concept of pooling is that the assets and liabilities are consolidated at book values, and this concept is not violated by recording the issuance at fair value.[4]

If the fair value of the issued shares is in excess of the net book value of the pooled company, the impact on consolidated shareholders' equity is greater. In the case of PoolInc and PondCorp in the previous section, the fair market value of the PoolInc shares issued in exchange was $5.5 million. The share issuance would therefore be recorded as follows *on PoolInc's books*:

Investment in PondCorp	$5,500,000	
Common shares		$5,500,000

The consolidation *worksheet* elimination entry would be:

Common shares	$1,000,000	
Retained earnings	4,500,000	
Investment in PondCorp		$5,500,000

The resultant consolidated shareholders' equity on the date of combination would be:

Common shares	$8,100,000
Retained earnings (deficit)	(250,000)
Total	$7,850,000

The fair value is so high that the retained earnings that PoolInc carried into the combination are completely offset and a deficit is created on the consolidated statements. Of course, the retained earnings of the separate legal entities are not affected by the preparation of consolidated statements, and therefore the dividend paying capacity of the pooled companies is not affected by the appearance of the consolidated deficit.

Minority Interest

The accounting treatment of a minority interest in a pooled company raises no special problems. The pooled company's assets are consolidated at book values, and therefore the minority interest is valued at book values, just as under purchase accounting. Since the majority interest is also accounted for at book values under pooling, there is no discrepancy in valuation between the majority and minority interests.

If PoolInc had issued 90,000 shares in exchange for 90% of PondCorp's common shares (rather than 100,000 shares to acquire 100%), the transaction would have been recorded *on PoolInc's books* as follows, assuming the book value method is used:

Investment in PondCorp	$3,060,000	
Common shares		$ 900,000
Retained earnings		2,160,000

Upon consolidation, PondCorp's shareholders' equity accounts are eliminated and the minority interest is established by means of the following *worksheet* entry:

---

4 The *CICA Handbook* recommendations accommodate the problem of mandatory fair-value recording by specifying only that the *total* shareholders' equity be pooled, not necessarily the individual components [para. 1580.67].

Common shares	$1,000,000	
Retained earnings	2,400,000	
Investment in PondCorp		$3,060,000
Minority interest		340,000

The minority interest is 10% of PondCorp's common share equity at book value: $3,400,000 x 10% = $340,000.

If the PoolInc share issuance was recorded at fair value in accordance with statutory requirements, the transaction would appear as follows *on PoolInc's books*, assuming a value of $55 per share:

Investment in Pond Corp	$4,950,000	
Common shares		$4,950,000

The consolidation elimination entry would then appear as follows on the *worksheet*:

Common shares	$1,000,000	
Retained earnings	4,290,000	
Investment in PondCorp		$4,950,000
Minority interest		340,000

The debit of $4,290,000 to retained earnings can be verified as follows:

Elimination of PondCorp's retained earnings:		
90% eliminated against investment account		$2,160,000
10% allocated to minority interest		240,000
Capitalization of PoolInc retained earnings by issuance of		
shares in exchange; excess of fair value over book value		
acquired per share: ($55 − $34) x 90,000 shares		1,890,000
		$4,290,000

PondCorp's retained earnings include $150,000 in unrealized profit on the intercompany sale of land. When this profit is eliminated, 10% must be charged to minority interest on the consolidation *worksheet*:

Retained earnings	$135,000	
Future income taxes	50,000	
Minority interest	15,000	
Land		$200,000

When consolidated statements are prepared at dates subsequent to the combination, 10% of PondCorp's retained earnings accumulated since the combination and 10% of PondCorp's current earnings must be assigned to the minority interest. This adjustment process is no different than it is under the purchase method.

Impact of Pooling vs. Purchase

Since pooling is not often used in Canada for business combinations involving *public* companies, we have not devoted much space to it in this book. However, the reorganization of ownership interests among companies under common control (which *is* a common occurence in Canada) has reporting impacts that are exactly the same as pooling. In addition, Canadians may frequently have occasion to read or analyze financial information of U.S.-based companies, and pooling is much more prevalent in the United States.

Therefore, we should be aware of the impact of pooling and the resultant differences in reported financial information.

There are three major ways in which financial reports prepared under the pooling approach differ from those prepared under purchase accounting. Under pooling:

1. The historical information is restated as though the companies had always been combined, including the elimination of intercompany arm's-length transactions and unrealized profits.
2. The assets and liabilities assets of the "acquired" company are consolidated at book values rather than at fair values.
3. There is no periodic amortization of fair-value increments or goodwill, since fair values and goodwill are not recognized under pooling.

These three differences can have a major impact on performance measures such as earnings per share or return on investment.

Schedule 11-6 presents four years of data for PoolInc and PondCorp. The 19x4 data correspond to the amounts in Schedule 11-4, and 19x3 year-end data (total assets and net assets) are taken from Schedule 11-1. The rest of the data are new.

When the companies are pooled, the historical earnings are added together and adjusted for unrealized profits. In 19x1, the combined net income is $530,000, the sum of the separate-entity net incomes. In 19x2, the combined net income is the sum of the separate-entity net incomes minus the unrealized profit on the intercompany sale of land ($300,000 + $350,000 − $150,000 = $500,000). The first line of Schedule 11-7 shows these combined net income figures, just as they will be reported by PoolInc after the combination takes place. Earnings per share are then calculated by dividing the combined net income by the number of shares outstanding *after* the combination, i.e., 200,000 shares.

SCHEDULE 11-6

Selected Financial Data, 19x1–19x4

Years ended December 31

	19x1	19x2	19x3	19x4
SEPARATE-ENTITY DATA				
Net income:				
PoolInc	$ 280,000	$ 300,000	$ 200,000	$ 220,000*
PondCorp	250,000	350,000	400,000	500,000
Total assets:				
PoolInc	5,400,000	5,700,000	6,000,000	6,220,000*
PondCorp	4,600,000	4,500,000	4,500,000	4,800,000
Net assets:				
PoolInc	4,220,000	4,400,000	4,600,000	4,820,000*
PondCorp	3,040,000	3,200,000	3,400,000	3,700,000

*Excluding any investment in or earnings from PondCorp.

SCHEDULE 11-7

PoolInc
Comparative Performance Measures
Pooling vs. Purchase

	19x1	19x2	19x3	19x4
POOLING-OF-INTERESTS METHOD:				
Consolidated net income	$530,000	$500,000	$600,000	$720,000
Earnings per share	$2.65	$2.50	$3.00	$3.60
Total assets	$10,000,000	$10,000,000	$10,300,000	$10,820,000
Shareholders' equity	$ 7,260,000	$ 7,450,000	$ 7,850,000	$ 8,370,000
Return on assets	5.3%	5.0%	5.8%	6.7%
Return on shareholders' equity	7.3%	6.7%	7.6%	8.6%
Growth in earnings per share		−6%	+20%	+20%
PURCHASE METHOD:				
Consolidated net income	$280,000	$300,000	$200,000	$570,000
Earnings per share	$2.80	$3.00	$2.00	$2.85
Total assets	$ 5,400,000	$ 5,700,000	$ 6,000,000	$13,170,000
Shareholders' equity	$ 4,220,000	$ 4,400,000	$ 4,600,000	$10,670,000
Return on assets	5.2%	5.3%	3.3%	4.3%
Return on shareholders' equity	6.6%	6.8%	4.3%	5.3%
Growth in earnings per share		+7%	−33%	+43%

Similarly, the historical summary of total assets and net assets, as well as all other historical data, will be combined retroactively for the two companies and adjusted for unrealized profits. The PoolInc annual report for the year ended December 31, 19x4, will include the figures shown in the first four lines of Schedule 11-7 in PoolInc's financial summary.

Under purchase accounting, the historical data for PoolInc is not changed. The lower section of Schedule 11-7 shows the historical information for PoolInc as it would be reported in PoolInc's 19x4 annual report if the acquisition of PondCorp's shares had been accounted for as a purchase. The data for 19x1 through 19x3 are the same as those shown in Schedule 11-6. The 19x4 data are derived by applying purchase accounting to the combination.

The fair value of the shares issued on January 1, 19x4, was $5.5 million. If the fair value of the PondCorp liabilities is assumed to be equal to their book values ($1.1 million), then the fair value of the assets and goodwill can be assumed to be $6.6 million. The assets' book value is $4.5 million, and therefore there was a total of $2.1 million paid in excess of book values. Assume that the average amortization period of the fair-value increments and goodwill is fourteen years. Then one-fourteenth of the excess of purchase price over book value must be amortized in 19x4, an amount of $150,000. PoolInc's consolidated net income for 19x4 will be the combined net incomes minus the amortization, or $570,000 ($220,000 + $500,000 − $150,000), significantly less than under pooling.

The PoolInc consolidated assets and shareholders' equity at December 31, 19x4, under the purchase method, would amount to $13,170,000 and $10,670,000, respectively. These amounts can be verified as follows:

	Total assets	Shareholders' equity
Totals at date of acquisition:		
Poollnc before acquisition	$ 6,000,000	$ 4,600,000
Plus PondCorp acquisition	6,600,000	5,500,000
	12,600,000	10,100,000
19x4 earnings:		
Poollnc	220,000	220,000
PondCorp	500,000	500,000
Less amortization	− 150,000	− 150,000
Totals at December 31, 19x4	$13,170,000	$10,670,000

The December 31, 19x4 liabilities are $1.4 million for Poollnc and $1.1 million for PondCorp, which accounts for the $2.5 million difference between the total assets and shareholders' equity.

Having calculated the impact of purchase accounting on Poollnc's reported results, it is interesting to compare the upper and lower portions of Schedule 11-7. Under pooling, earnings per share (EPS) show a 36% increase over the four-year period. Aside from a modest dip in EPS in 19x2, earnings growth appears to have been steady. The return on shareholders' equity has also improved over the period, from 7.3% in 19x1 to 8.6% in 19x4.

Under purchase accounting, however, quite a different picture appears. 19x4 EPS, while much better than 19x3's depressed earnings, are just barely above the 19x1 figure of $2.80. The recording of fair values causes lower earnings (because of amortization) and higher asset values under purchase than under pooling. As a result, the return on both assets and shareholders' equity has declined over the four-year period. In addition, Poollnc's earnings look much more volatile under purchase accounting. The factors that affect the comparative performance of Poollnc under the two accounting approaches are complex. Important variables include the relationship between net asset book values and fair values and between the book values and fair values of the shares issued, the number of shares issued, and the relative historical earnings levels of the two firms.

If given a choice, managers would presumably prefer to use whichever reporting method shows the results of a combination in the most favourable light. Therefore it is tempting for managers to shape the combination transaction in such a way as to qualify for the desired accounting treatment. In Canada, little latitude exists for such maneuvering, at least in situations where the requirements of the CICA Handbook are relevant. But in the United States, considerable flexibility does still exist in designing a combination in order to qualify for one accounting treatment or the other. Since the annual reports of U.S. companies are not exactly rare in Canada, we will briefly discuss the U.S. requirements for pooling in the next section.

Pooling in the USA

Earlier in this chapter, we cited three conditions that must be present in order for pooling to be used in reporting a business combination in Canada: (1) the combination must take the form of an exchange of shares, (2) the resulting voting interests must be of comparable size, and (3) substantial minority interests should not exist. In addition, we pointed out two other conditions that some accountants believe should exist, a continuity of management influence and a similarity of industry, although other accountants would argue that these are not necessary conditions.

In the United States, a different and much more complex set of criteria exists, and certain business combinations that would be reported as a purchase in Canada would be reported as a pooling in the U.S. Similarly, those few combinations that qualify for pooling in Canada could possibly be viewed as a purchase in the U.S. While there is an overlap between the two countries' requirements on the criteria of share exchange and low minority interest, the Canadian criterion of comparable voting interest is not present in the U.S. Therefore, an exchange of shares that results in a large company taking over a much smaller company could be reported in the U.S. as a pooling, whereas in Canada the transaction would most likely be viewed as a purchase.

For example, Pegasus Gold Inc. was formed in 1984 by the amalgamation of Pegasus Gold Ltd. and Montoro Gold Inc. After the combination, the former shareholders of Pegasus owned 83% of the voting shares of the combined company, while the former shareholders of Montoro held only 17%. Under Canadian GAAP, Pegasus would clearly be identified as the acquiror and purchase reporting would have been required. In fact, the amalgamation was reported as a pooling of interests. The notes to the financial statements explained that the company's operations are conducted entirely in the United States through wholly owned subsidiaries, and "the company, a British Columbia Corporation, presents all financial statements in United States dollars and under generally accepted accounting principles as practiced in the United States."[5]

The U.S. reporting of business combinations is governed by *Accounting Principles Board Opinion No. 16: Business Combinations (APB 16)*, issued in August 1970. *APB 16* sets forth twelve specific conditions for pooling. If all of the criteria are satisfied, pooling *must* be used; if any one of the criteria is not satisfied, then the combination must be reported by the purchase method.

The criteria are subdivided into three sets, which specify certain required attributes of (1) the combining companies, (2) the manner in which the combination is accomplished, and (3) planned post-combination actions. In essence, the first set of attributes ensures that the combining companies are unrelated and have not been a subsidiary or division of any other company within two years. The second set focuses on the combination transaction itself: it must be a single transaction involving common shares only, with an exchange of substantially all of one corporation's shares for those of another.

The third set of attributes are prohibitions against certain types of planned, post-combination transactions that would reveal that a pooling was not really taking place. There cannot be an agreement to retire or reacquire the shares issued in exchange or to enter into other financial arrangements that would negate the pooling in substance, nor can there be an expressed intent to dispose of a significant portion of the assets within two years of the

---

5 Pegasus Gold Inc. annual report for the year ended December 31, 1986, Note 1(c). The use of U.S. dollars for reporting by Canadian companies is not unusual when the majority of the company's operations are conducted in U.S. dollars; gold is traded in U.S. dollars worldwide.

combination. Note that the prohibition is of *planned* transactions, those that are a part of the combination agreement, either directly or indirectly. These prohibited transactions can actually occur, but cannot be a condition or intention at the time of the combination.[6]

The intent of the requirements of *APB 16* was to restrict the application of pooling, which in the United States had been applied even to transactions in which the acquiree's shares had been purchased for cash by the acquiror, with absolutely no continuity of ownership interest. The need to satisfy twelve requirements might appear on the surface to sharply restrict the use of pooling, but the greater impact is to affect the ways in which business combinations are effected. In the previous section, we saw that the reported results can differ quite remarkably depending on whether pooling or purchase treatment is used. The managers of an acquiror will not enter into a takeover deal without knowing the impact of the combination on their company's financial statements. If they conclude that the "best" results are obtained by pooling, then there will be strong motivation to structure the deal in such a way as to satisfy all twelve criteria, if possible within the actual circumstances of the combination. If, on the other hand, the managers would prefer to use the purchase method, then they only need to structure the deal so that at least one of the *APB 16* conditions for pooling is not satisfied. Given the great flexibility of U.S. practice and the motivation of managers to issue statements that reflect favourably on the results of their decisions, readers of U.S. consolidated financial statements should exercise caution in analyzing the performance of companies that have pooled major acquisitions.

The FASB added "Consolidations and Related Matters" to its agenda in January 1982. This project is intended to address a number of issues of consolidation policy and consolidation techniques, but it does not appear to be addressing the issue of business combinations. There seems to be little likelihood that U.S. accounting standards on pooling vs. purchase will be modified in the foreseeable future.[7]

Reorganization of Intercorporate Ownerships

On occasion, a parent company will reorganize the ownership of its subsidiaries. Such reorganization would include instances in which (1) a parent creates a new, wholly owned holding company to hold the shares of its subsidiaries; (2) the shares of a subsidiary of a subsidiary (i.e, indirect holdings) are transferred to the parent to become direct holdings or vice versa; or (3) two or more subsidiaries are amalgamated into a single company or into the parent, etc. The reorganization of intercorporate ownerships may be motivated by financial, tax, legal, or operating reasons.

When reorganizations take place, there is an exchange of shares among the companies that sometimes involves outside shareholders as well. These are non-arm's-length transactions, and therefore do not qualify as business combinations. Despite the fact that legal control of one or more companies within the affiliated group is changed, there is no decision to be made re-

---

6 For greater detail on the U.S. criteria for pooling, refer to *APB Opinion No. 16*, paragraphs 45-48.

7 The only result so far of the Board's deliberations on consolidations has been the release of *SFAS No. 94* in October 1987, which requires parent companies to consolidate virtually *all* of their majority-owned subsidiaries.

garding pooling versus purchases. Since the transactions are not at arm's length, the carrying values of assets and liabilities are not adjusted to fair values.

For example, on June 15, 1987, Central Capital Corporation (CCC) acquired control of Traders Group Limited; another company, Central Trust Co., was already controlled by CCC. Traders owned 77% of yet another company, Guaranty Trust Co. In November 1987, Guaranty acquired 98.6% of Central Trust from CCC (and others), by issuing its own shares in exchange. As a result of the exchange, Central Trust went from being a subsidiary of CCC to being a subsidiary of Guaranty. In addition, the dilution of ownership caused by Guaranty's issuance of shares caused Traders' interest in Guaranty to fall from 77% to 45%; Guaranty ceased to be a subsidiary of Traders' but continued to be an indirect subsidiary of CCC, through CCC's direct ownership interest in Guaranty plus its indirect interest through Traders. The change in ownership arrangements is diagrammed in Schedule 11-8.

While there was a reshuffling of shares among the affiliated companies, there was no substantive change in the ownership of any of the companies as a result of the November 1987 reorganization. There was an impact on Traders' reporting, because the drop in its Guaranty Trust ownership from 77% to 45% meant that it was no longer appropriate to consolidate Guaranty Trust. But there was no impact on the economic entity comprising CCC,

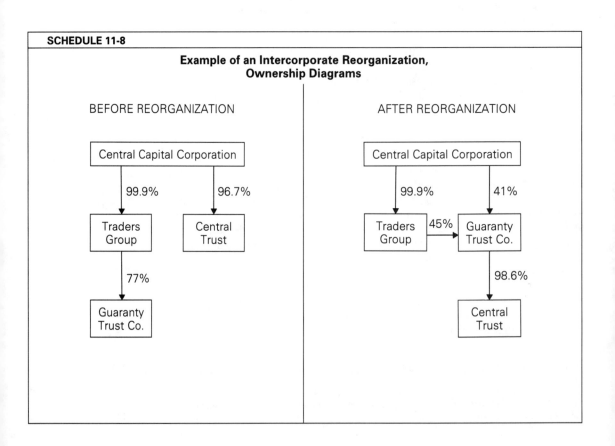

SCHEDULE 11-8

Example of an Intercorporate Reorganization, Ownership Diagrams

BEFORE REORGANIZATION

AFTER REORGANIZATION

Traders, Guaranty, and Central Trust; no additional outside ownership interest had been created, and CCC continued to be the controlling company of the group.

Because the transaction was a non-arms-length transaction between related companies, there was no business combination. Because there was no business combination, purchase reporting is not appropriate; the carrying values and reported values of the assets and liabilities of the various companies are not affected. The financial statement impact of the change in ownership therefore is reported *as if* it were a pooling of interests. The distinction is subtle, but important: pooling is a way of reporting business combinations, but since no business combination has occurred, pooling is not used. Instead, the results are reported "in a manner *similar* to the pooling of interests method," to use the wording of Traders' note in Schedule 11-9.

It is also important to recognize that CCC's acquisition of control over Traders is an event quite distinct from the reorganization that occurred later in the year. The acquisition of control is a change in ownership and therefore is a business combination. The subsequent reorganization results in no change in beneficial ownership and therefore is not a business combination. That the reorganization may have been envisioned by CCC when Traders was acquired is irrelevant.

Another type of legal reorganization is a statutory amalgamation of two

---

SCHEDULE 11-9

Traders Group Limited
Notes to Consolidated Financial Statements
December 31, 1987

Corporate Reorganization

On November 4, 1987 Traders participated in a corporate reorganization with its parent company, Central Capital Corporation. Under the plan of reorganization, Guaranty Trustco Limited, then a Subsidiary of the Corporation, acquired from Central Capital and others 98.6% of the outstanding common shares of Central Trust Company, an associated company, in exchange for common shares of Guaranty Trust Co. The reorganization followed Central Capital's acquisition on June 15, 1987 of a Controlling interest in Traders.

This share exchange reduced Traders' ownership interest in Guaranty Trustco from 77% to 45% and, as a result, the consolidation method of accounting ceased to be appropriate. Accordingly, the corporation has adopted the equity method to account for this investment and given retroactive effect to this change by restating the prior year's financial statements. This change in accounting has no effect on reported net income or retained earnings for the current or prior year.

The reorganization has been accounted for in the financial statements of Guaranty Trustco in a manner similar to the pooling of interests method since it resulted in no significant change in ownership and control and, accordingly, no adjustment was made to the carrying value of Traders' investment in Guaranty Trustco at the time of the reorganization.

related companies. A parent corporation may buy 90% or more of the shares of another company and report the acquisition by use of the purchase method. After a period of operation as two separate legal entities, a decision may be made to amalgamate the two companies, provided that the two companies are incorporated under the same legislation. One of the companies (usually the subsidiary) will cease to exist as a separate legal entity, and the surviving corporation will take over the other's assets and liabilities. A business combination occurred when the subsidiary's shares were first purchased, and that is when the purchase method was appropriate. The amalgamation is not a business combination in a substantive sense, but only in a legal sense. Therefore the parent records *on its books* the book values of the subsidiary's assets and liabilities, plus any unamortized fair-value increments and decrements and goodwill that remain from the initial business combination.

Occasionally, one corporation will acquire control of another and immediately amalgamate. Even when this happens, the accounting *for the combination* is based on the substance of the combination, which is usually a purchase. The *CICA Handbook* states that the fact of statutory amalgamation cannot be used to justify pooling when the combination was substantively a purchase [para. 1580.22].

SUMMARY

Pooling-of-interests accounting for a business combination is a relatively rare occurrence in Canada, at least among public companies. Under GAAP in Canada, pooling is restricted to business combinations in which an acquiror cannot be identified. In general, an acquiror cannot be identified when the shareholder group that previously controlled one of the combining companies does not have the ability to elect a majority of the board of directors. When ownership of both combining companies is widely distributed and the companies are of similar size, then the absence of a clear controlling block of shares will tend to favour pooling.

In addition, pooling presumes that no substantial minority interest is outstanding in either combining company. The definition of "substantial" is not precise, but presumably a minority interest would be substantial if it was large enough to block special resolutions presented to the shareholders, such as for changes in the corporate by-laws, corporate reorganizations, or special share issues. In most corporations acts, a two-thirds vote of the shareholders is required to pass special resolutions, and therefore a one-third or larger minority interest would intefere with the exercise of control by the majority shareholders and would mitigate against the use of pooling.

Other suggested criteria for pooling are that the combining companies be in the same or similar industries and that the managements of both combinors continue in the operations of the combined company. These criteria are not binding, however, and are often not applied in practice.

Under pooling, the combining companies are reported as though they had always been combined as a single economic entity. Historical financial data are restated, and arm's-length intercompany transactions and unrealized profits prior to the combination are eliminated. The assets and liabilities of both combining companies are carried forward at book values, as is the total shareholders' equity.

Legal requirements may impair the "pure" application of pooling in Canada. The common share accounts of the corporation that is issuing new shares in the exchange should normally be credited with the current cash equivalent value of the shares issued. Therefore, other consolidated shareholders' equity accounts, including retained earnings, will be affected by the difference between the fair value of the shares issued and the carrying value of the shares received in exchange.

Accounting and reporting procedures similar to pooling are used in intercorporate reorganizations, including statutory amalgamations, but care must be taken not to confuse these procedures with pooling in arm's-length business combinations. When a statutory amalgamation occurs, one company ceases to exist as a separate legal entity and its assets, liabilities, and shareholders' equity accounts are transferred to the surviving company's books at book values. Amalgamation may occur as a part of a combination. Substantively, however, the amalgamation is accounted for as an event separate from, and subsequent to, the combination. Amalgamation cannot be used as a rationale for reporting the combination by the pooling method, if the combination is, in substance, a purchase.

Although Canadian business combinations seldom meet the necessary condition for pooling under Canadian GAAP, the requirements of U.S. GAAP are more flexible, at least in substance if not in form. Thus readers of U.S. financial statements must be aware of the impact of pooling on financial reporting, as described in this chapter.

REVIEW QUESTIONS

11-1 Corporation A acquired 100% of the shares of Corporation B for cash. Both corporations are of equivalent size and will continue to operate individually. Might the combination be a pooling of interests? Explain.

11-2 Why is the presence of a substantial minority interest after execution of a business combination an indication that a pooling of interests has not occurred?

11-3 Explain the basic difference in reporting a business combination as a pooling rather than as a purchase.

11-4 When a business combination is reported as a pooling of interests, why are prior years' financial results restated?

11-5 Under pooling, what recognition is given to intercompany transactions that occurred *prior* to the combination?

11-6 Theoretically, how should the consolidated retained earnings be reported when a pooling of interests has occurred?

11-7 What practical impediment exists in Canada

to the theoretically "correct" approach to pooled retained earnings?

11-8 Subsequent to a combination that is reported as a pooling of interests, how is consolidated net income determined?

11-9 Under what circumstances could a pooling of interests result in a deficit in consolidated retained earnings, even though both of the pooled companies had a credit balance in retained earnings?

11-10 Explain briefly how consolidated net income would differ under pooling of interests as compared to purchase accounting.

11-11 Why might managers be tempted to design a business combination in such a way as to qualify for pooling-of-interests accounting rather than purchase accounting?

11-12 Corporations A and B are both subsidiaries of Company P. Company P sells its shares of A to Corporation B. Has a business combination taken place? Explain.

11-13 When a corporate reorganization occurs in

which an exchange of shares takes place, why are fair values not considered when reporting the results of the share exchange?

11-14 Corporations D and E, previously unrelated, combine by means of a statutory amalgamation. Does the fact that the combination was an amalgamation indicate that the pooling-of-interest method of reporting the combination should be used?

11-15 After two companies combine by means of a statutory amalgamation, are consolidated financial statements necessary?

11-16 A statutory amalgamation takes place between Companies G and H, with G the surviving company. Prior to the amalgamation, H had been a subsidiary of G. When the amalgamation is recorded on the books of G, at what values will the assets and liabilities of H be recorded?

CASE 11-1   Camco Inc.

In 1977, Canadian General Electric Ltd. (CGE) and GSW Inc. formed a new corporation, Camco Inc., to produce major household appliances for Canada and for export. Sixty percent of the Camco shares were acquired by CGE and 40% by GSW. CGE, GSW, and Camco are all Canadian corporations, but CGE is 92% owned by General Electric, a U.S. corporation. In order to avoid having Camco dominated by a foreign-controlled corporation, CGE agreed to share voting control with GSW on a 50-50 basis. Therefore, half of Camco's board of directors were nominees of CGE and half were nominees of GSW. However, CGE retained the right to select Camco's chief executive officer.

Required:
How should each of the investor corporations (CGE and GSW) show its investment in Camco in its financial statements? For example, should Camco be treated as a subsidiary and be consolidated, should the investment be treated as a joint venture, or should the Camco investment simply be shown as an equity-accounted investment?

CASE 11-2   Boatsman Boats Limited

Boatsman Boats Limited (BBL) is a dealer in pleasure boats located in Kingston, Ontario. The company is incorporated under the *Ontario Business Corporations Act* and is wholly owned by its founder and president, James Boatsman. In 19x2, BBL had revenues of $2,500,000 with total assets of about $1,000,000 at year-end.

Late in 19x3, Jim Boatsman reached an agreement with Clyde Stickney for the combination of BBL and Stickney Skate Corporation (SSC). SSC is a manufacturer of ice skates and is located in Ottawa, Ontario. SSC's 19x2 revenue totaled $2,000,000 and year-end assets totaled $1,500,000. Clyde Stickney is president and general manager of SSC, and he owns 65% of the SSC shares. The other 35% is owned by Clyde's former partner who left the business several years previously due to a policy disagreement with Clyde.

Clyde and Jim decided to combine the two businesses because their seasonal business cycles were complementary. Common ownership would permit working capital to be shifted from one company to the other, and the larger asset base and more stable financial performance of the combined company would probably increase the total debt capacity.

Under the terms of the agreement, BBL would issue common shares to Clyde Stickney in exchange for Clyde's shares in SSC. As a result of the exchange, Jim's share of BBL would drop to 60% of the outstanding BBL shares, and Clyde would hold the remaining 40%. Clyde and Jim signed a shareholders' agreement that gave each of them equal representation on the BBL board of directors.

As the end of 19x3 approached, Jim, Clyde, and CA (the BBL auditor), were discussing the appropriate treatment of the business combination on BBL's 19x3 financial statements. Clyde was of the opinion that CA should simply add together the assets and liabilities of the two companies at their book values (after eliminating intercompany balances and transactions, of course). Jim, on the other hand, thought that the combination had resulted in a new, stronger entity, and that the financial statements should reflect that fact by revaluing the net assets of both BBL and SSC to reflect fair values at the date of the combination. CA, however, insisted that only SSC's net assets should be revalued, and then only to the extent of the 65% of the assets that were represented by BBL's shareholdings in SSC.

While Jim and Clyde disagreed with each other on the appropriate valuation of the assets, both disagreed with CA's proposal. Jim and Clyde clearly controlled SSC through BBL, they argued; that was the whole point of the combination. In their opinion it would be inappropriate to value the same assets on two different bases, 65% current value and 35% book value. If only SSC's assets were to be revalued, then they reasoned that the assets at least should be valued consistently, at 100% of fair value.

In an effort to resolve the impasse that was developing, Jim and Clyde hired an independent consultant to advise them. The consultant was asked (1) to prepare pro-forma consolidated balance sheets under each of the four alternatives that were being debated, (2) to advise the shareholders on the pros and cons of each alternative in BBL's specific case, and (3) to make a recommendation on a preferred approach. The consultant was supplied with the condensed balance sheets of BBL and SSC as shown in Exhibit 1, and with CA's estimate of fair values (Exhibit 2).

Required:
Prepare the consultant's report. Assume that the business combination took place on December 31, 19x3.

EXHIBIT 1

Condensed Balance Sheets
December 31, 19x3

	Boatsman Boats Ltd.	Stickney Skate Corp.
Current assets	$ 600,000	$ 350,000
Land	—	250,000
Buildings and equipment	—	2,500,000
Accumulated depreciation	—	(1,500,000)
Furniture and fixtures	800,000	300,000
Accumulated depreciation	(330,000)	(100,000)
Investment in Stickney Skate Corp.	1,300,000	—
Total assets	$2,370,000	$1,800,000
Current liabilities	$ 340,000	$ 250,000
Long-term liabilities	300,000	900,000
Deferred income taxes*	30,000	150,000
Common shares	1,500,000	200,000
Retained earnings	200,000	300,000
Total equities	$2,370,000	$1,800,000

*Accumulated CCA/depreciation timing differences only.

EXHIBIT 2		
Net Asset Fair Values December 31, 19x3		
	Boatsman Boats Ltd.	Stickney Skate Corp.
Current assets	$ 600,000	$ 350,000
Land	—	700,000
Buildings and equipment:		
estimated replacement cost new	—	5,000,000
less depreciation	—	(3,000,000)
less present value of deferred taxes*	—	(120,000)
Furniture and fixtures:		
estimated replacement cost new	1,300,000	500,000
less depreciation	(520,000)	(240,000)
less present value of deferred taxes*	(20,000)	(10,000)
Current liabilities	(340,000)	(250,000)
Long-term liabilities*	(270,000)	(930,000)
Net asset fair value	$ 750,000	$2,000,000
*Discounted at current long-term interest rates.		

[ICAO]

P11-1

On January 1, 19x2, the following data are available:

	Pet Ltd.		Sat Ltd.
Common shares; 50,000 issued and outstanding	$ 500,000	50,000 shares	$150,000
Retained earnings	600,000		800,000
	$1,100,000		$950,000

On January 2, 19x2, Pet Ltd. issues 50,000 shares (market value $40 per share) to the shareholders of Sat Ltd. in exchange for all of the shares of Sat Ltd. Any excess of fair market value over book value is attributable to land.

	Pet Ltd.	Sat Ltd.
Land, book value	$ 90,000	$ 40,000

Required:
a. Is this a purchase or pooling? Why?
b. Prepare any and all journal entries that would be required for either Pet Ltd. or Sat Ltd. to record the above information.
c. Prepare the consolidated shareholders' equity at January 2, 19x2 (after the issue of shares).
d. Calculate the balance, on the consolidation balance sheet, of the land account.
[CGA-Canada]

P11-2

The shareholders' equities of Black Ltd. and Bart Ltd. are as follows:

December 31, 19x9

	Black Ltd.	Bart Ltd.
Shares $10 par	$100,000	$ 80,000
Contributed surplus		
Premium on issues of shares	20,000	30,000
Retained earnings	200,000	300,000
	$320,000	$410,000

Black Ltd. issues 10,000 shares to the shareholders of Bart Ltd. The shares have a market value of $180,000 and Black Ltd. records the issue at market value.

Required:
a. Show how the consolidated shareholders' equity would appear after the issuance of the new shares.
b. Demonstrate how (1) would change if Black Ltd. recorded the shares issued at par value of $10 per share.
c. Is it possible for Black Ltd. to acquire the shares of Bart Ltd. by issuing shares, and for the situation to be treated as a purchase? If so, describe the circumstances. If not, explain why.
[CGA-Canada]

P11-3

Consult P7-3. Assume that the Dee Company issues 90,000 shares to the shareholders of Sor Company in exchange for 100% of the Sor Company shares, and that the business combination described therein is to be reported as a pooling of interests.

Required:
For the combined company, prepare the balance sheet at December 31, 19x1, and calculate the 19x1 net income and the 19x1 earnings per share.
[SMA, adapted]

P11-4

On December 31, 19x7, the Acquisition Company issues 400,000 shares with a total market value of $20,000,000 in exchange for 100% of the common shares of the Acquiree Company. The $4,000,000 excess of cost over book value resulted from the fact that the Acquiree Company's nonmonetary assets were undervalued by $2,000,000 and the fact that the Acquiree Company had $2,000,000 in unrecorded goodwill.

On that date, the condensed balance sheets of the Acquisition Company and Acquiree Company are as follows:

	Balance Sheets December 31, 19x7	
	Acquisition	Acquiree
Monetary assets	$13,000,000	$ 5,000,000
Nonmonetary assets	27,000,000	15,000,000
Total assets	$40,000,000	$20,000,000
Monetary liabilities	$10,000,000	$ 4,000,000
Common shares — par $20	18,000,000	2,000,000
Contributed surplus	4,000,000	2,000,000
Retained earnings	8,000,000	12,000,000
Total equities	$40,000,000	$20,000,000

Required:
Prepare a December 31, 19x7, balance sheet for the combined company under each of the following two assumptions:
a. The business combination qualifies for the application of the purchase method of accounting.
b. The business combination qualifies for the application of the pooling-of-interests method of accounting.
[SMA]

P11-5

At December 31, 19x7, the following data are available:

	Pet Ltd.
Shares, common 5,000 × $10 par	$ 50,000
Retained earnings	250,000
	$300,000

	Clark Ltd.
Shares, common 2,000 × $2 par	$ 4,000
Retained earnings	80,000
	$ 84,000

The fair market value of the net assets of Clark Ltd. is $120,000 and any excess is attributable to land. On January 1, 19x8, Pet Ltd. issues 5,000 shares to the shareholders of Clark Ltd. in exchange for their shares.
The market value of the 5,000 shares of Pet Ltd. is $150,000.

Required:
(Note: Parts a. and b. are independent of each other.)

a. Assuming this is a pooling of interests, show:
   1. The journal entry (with explanation) on Pet Ltd.'s books to record the issue of shares.
   2. The shareholders' equity as it would appear on the consolidated financial statements at January 1, 19x8.

b. Assuming this is a purchase, show:
   1. The journal entry on Pet Ltd.'s books to record the issue of shares.
   2. The shareholders' equity as it would appear on the consolidated financial statements at January 1, 19x8.

c. Briefly and specifically describe any differences between the consolidated financial statements at January 1, 19x8, prepared under assumptions (a) and (b) (other than shareholders' equity).

[CGA-Canada]

P11-6

On October 1, 19x6, Jack Ltd. issued 200,000 shares to the shareholders of Jill Ltd. in exchange for all of their shares. The fair market value of the shares issued by Jack Ltd. was $1,420,000. The balance sheet of Jill Ltd. at the date of the transaction was:

Jill Ltd.
Balance Sheet
October 1, 19x6

	Net Book Value	Fair Market Value
Cash	$ 100,000	$100,000
Accounts receivable	200,000	175,000
Inventory	300,000	390,000
Net fixed assets	700,000	850,000
Goodwill	40,000 *	—
	$1,340,000	

*Amortized at $4,000 per year

Current liabilities	$ 150,000	190,000
Common shares	500,000	—
Retained earnings at January 1, 19x6	600,000	—
Net income, January 1, 19x6 to October 1, 19x6	90,000	—
	$1,340,000	

There were no intercompany transactions during the remaining part of 19x6. The financial statement data for the two companies at December 31, 19x6 are:

	Jack Ltd.	Jill Ltd.
Cash	$ 133,000	$ 65,000
Accounts receivable	200,000	240,000
Inventory	610,000	320,000
Net fixed assets	2,160,000	710,000
Goodwill	47,000	39,000
Investment in Jill Ltd.	1,420,000	—
	$4,570,000	$1,374,000
Current liabilities	$ 210,000	$ 180,000
Common shares	2,220,000*	500,000
Retained earnings at January 1, 19x6	2,000,000	600,000
Net income, 19x6	140,000	94,000
	$4,570,000	$1,374,000

*Represents 400,000 shares

Required:
Prepare a consolidated balance sheet at December 31, 19x6.
[CGA-Canada]

P11-7

Both West Ltd. and East Ltd. have December 31 year-ends. On December 1, 19x4, both companies decided to pool. West Ltd. issued 25,000 new voting shares to the shareholders of East Ltd. in exchange for all the voting shares of East Ltd. The December 1, 19x4 financial statements of the two companies are presented below:

	December 1, 19x4 West Ltd.		December 1, 19x4 East Ltd.	
	Book Value	FMV*	Book Value	FMV*
Current assets	$ 130,000	$147,000	$190,000	$230,000
Fixed assets, net	878,000	989,000	686,000	949,000
Goodwill	54,000		88,000	
Total	$1,062,000		$964,000	
Current liabilities	$ 80,000	94,000	$ 85,000	90,000
Long-term liabilities	300,000	350,000	400,000	460,000
Common shares**	250,000		25,000	
Retained earnings	432,000		454,000	
	$1,062,000		$964,000	

*fair market value
**There are 25,000 shares of West Ltd. and 1,000 shares of East Ltd. issued and outstanding.

Income Statements
For the 11 months ended December 1, 19x4

	West Ltd.	East Ltd.
Sales	$565,000	$462,000
Less: Cost of goods sold	450,000	380,000
Depreciation	35,000	40,000
Other expenses	30,000	18,000
Net income	$ 50,000	$ 24,000

Neither company is certain how to value the investment account on the books of West Ltd. The market value of the shares was $17 per share before the pooling was announced, but since such a large number was issued, the companies are uncertain about using the market value.

If any consolidated goodwill exists, it is to be amortized over ten years straight-line.

Required:
a. Discuss briefly how the investment account should be valued. Be precise and explain your reasoning.
b. Prepare the consolidated income statement and balance sheet at December 1, 19x4.
[CGA-Canada]

P11-8

On December 31, 19x8, the balance sheets and the identifiable fair values of the Pascal Company and the Sherwood Company are as follows:

	December 31, 19x8	
PASCAL COMPANY	Balance sheet	Fair values
Cash and receivables	$2,500,000	$2,500,000
Inventories	1,200,000	1,400,000
Property, plant, and equipment (net)	6,000,000	6,500,000
Total assets	$9,700,000	
Current liabilities	$ 700,000	700,000
Long-term liabilities	2,500,000	2,400,000
Common stock — no par	3,000,000	
Retained earnings	3,500,000	
Total equities	$9,700,000	

	December 31, 19x8	
SHERWOOD COMPANY	Balance sheet	Fair values
Cash and receivables	$1,000,000	$1,000,000
Inventories	2,000,000	2,300,000
Property, plant, and equipment (net)	5,900,000	4,000,000
Total assets	$8,900,000	
Current liabilities	$1,200,000	1,200,000
Long-term liabilities	4,000,000	4,200,000
Common stock — no par	2,000,000	
Retained earnings	1,700,000	
Total equities	$8,900,000	

The Pascal Company has 300,000 common shares outstanding with a market price of $20 per share. The Sherwood Company has 100,000 common shares outstanding with a market price of $23 per share. On September 1, 19x8, the Sherwood Company sold a tract of land that had cost $50,000 to Pascal for $80,000. The purchase price will be paid on January 30, 19x9.

Required:

Assume that on December 31, 19x8, subsequent to the preparation of the preceding single entity balance sheets, the Pascal and Sherwood Companies enter into a business combination. The following list describes three *independent* cases based on differing assumptions with respect to how the combination was effected. In each case, prepare the appropriate consolidated balance sheet as at December 31, 19x8, subsequent to the business combination.

a. The Pascal Company issues 300,000 common shares to the shareholders of Sherwood Company in exchange for all of the Sherwood Company's outstanding shares. No acquirer can be identified in this transaction.
b. The Pascal Company purchases 60% of the outstanding shares of the Sherwood Company for $1,500,000 in cash. The consolidated balance sheet will be prepared using the *entity* approach to consolidated financial statements.
c. The Pascal Company issues 75,000 of its shares and uses them to acquire 60% of the Sherwood Company shares. The consolidated balance sheet will be prepared using the *parent-company* approach to consolidated financial statements.
[SMA]

12

Consolidated Financial Statements: Additional Aspects

The previous chapters have discussed the alternative approaches to accounting for intercorporate investments and have examined in some detail the accounting approaches generally used in Canada. In the process, most of the major problems have been explored and many common types of intercorporate transactions have been dealt with. However, several topics have been avoided so far in order not to confuse the reader, and some types of transactions have only been touched upon. The purpose of this chapter is to fill in some of the major gaps.

First, we will examine in greater detail the general issue of intercompany sales of assets, paying particular attention to depreciable assets. Second, we will consider the treatment of subsidiaries' extraordinary items in the consolidated statements. The third topic is a broader discussion of the impact upon consolidated income tax expense of unrealized intercompany profits and losses. And finally, we will examine the accounting for intercompany bond holdings.

One additional category of problems not considered in this chapter is the family of issues that arise from the presence of senior or restricted shares in a subsidiary and from changes in ownership interests. These problems are addressed in Chapter 13.

A. INTERCOMPANY SALE OF ASSETS

General Concept

The previous chapters have firmly established the concept that when items are sold from one company to a related company, the profit on the sale must be removed from the consolidated net income or from the investor's equity in the earnings of the investee until such time as it is realized on sale to a third party. Chapter 8 extended the concept from inventory to fixed assets, using land as the example.

The concept of eliminating unrealized intercorporate profits or gains is applicable to any sale between members of a group of controlled or significantly influenced companies. The sale need not involve the parent or investor corporation; sales from one subsidiary to another or from one significantly influenced investee corporation to another require elimination of unrealized profit.

Losses on intercompany sales may or may not be eliminated according to the *CICA Handbook* [para. 1600.27]. The key question is whether or not the loss is a recognition of a decline in value of the asset sold. If there is no evidence of impairment of value of the asset sold, then the intercompany loss on the sale should be eliminated. But if the sale price reflects a new, lower value-in-use for the asset, then the asset should have been written down even without the sale, because the loss on the sale simply reflects a decline in the value of the asset that should have been reflected by a reduction in the carrying value of the asset anyway. Thus, the crucial question in deciding whether or not to eliminate a loss is whether the item that was sold should have been written down had it *not* been sold.

For fixed assets, market or resale value may not be relevant for answering this question. An intercompany sale may occur at a fair market price that results in a loss. But a decline in market value (or net realizable value) of productive assets is not normally recognized, as long as the productive usefulness of the asset is not impaired. Book value of a productive fixed asset represents its unrecovered cost, not its realizable value. Therefore, a loss on an intercompany sale of a productive asset would normally be eliminated unless the loss reflects a decline in the recoverable cost of the asset.

The discussion in previous chapters has focused on intercompany sales of inventory. However, any type of asset may be sold, current or long-term, tangible or intangible. Common types of noninventory sales include sales of customer receivables from an operating to a finance subsidiary, sales of investments from one subsidiary to another, sales of existing fixed assets, and construction of new buildings or equipment by one subsidiary for the use of the parent or another subsidiary. Sales of tangible fixed assets may take the form of capital leases, either direct-financing or sales-type leases.

Intercompany sales of inventory result in an unrealized profit in one period that is usually realized in the next period. Inventory eliminations generally affect only two periods. When the assets sold are long-term assets, the eliminations must continue as long as the asset is in the group of companies. In the case of assets whose carrying value does not change (e.g., land), the same elimination is made year after year.

When the assets sold have changing carrying values, then the elimination will change each year because the amount of unrealized profit will change each year. Examples of assets with changing carrying values include any depreciable or amortizable asset and any installment-basis financial asset such as customer notes or capital leases. We will illustrate the approach to unrealized profit adjustments by using an example of a sale of a depreciable fixed asset.

Adjustments for Depreciable Assets

To illustrate the adjustments for unrealized profits on the intercompany sale of depreciable assets, let us assume that Company S buys a piece of equipment and sells it to its parent company, Company P. The cost to S of the asset is $20,000, and S sells it to P for $25,000 at the end of Year 1. P will depreciate the asset over ten years on a straight-line basis, beginning in Year 2 (and assuming zero salvage value).

Equity-Basis Reporting

In Year 1, S will include $5,000 of unrealized profit in its net income. When P reports its equity in S's earnings for Year 1, it will be necessary to reduce P's share of S's earnings by the unrealized profit. For example, if S is wholly owned by P and reported $60,000 net income for Year 1, P's equity pick-up of S's earnings would be $55,000: 100% of the $60,000 net income less 100% of the unrealized profit of $5,000. If P owns 80% of S, then the equity pick-up would be $44,000: 80% of $60,000 less 80% of the unrealized profit.

In Year 2, S's revenue and expense accounts will reflect no aspect of the sale. However, P will be depreciating the asset on its own books at $2,500 per year. The cost of the asset to the combined entity was only $20,000, which should call for depreciation of only $2,000 per year. Thus P is deducting an extra $500 of depreciation as a result of having the $5,000 unrealized profit in its equipment account. To reflect the real cost of the asset to the combined entity, depreciation expense must be decreased (and net income increased). When P is reporting its investment in S on the equity basis, the adjustment is made by *increasing* P's share of S's earnings by the proportionate amount of the "excess" depreciation. If S is 100% owned by P, the adjustment would be to increase the equity pick-up by $500.

The $500 increase in P's equity in earnings of S can be viewed as an offset to the $500 depreciation expense that arises from depreciating the unrealized profit in P's equipment account. However, a different interpretation is to view the $500 adjustment as the portion of the previously unrealized profit on the sale that has now been realized in Year 2. On intercompany inventory sales, the profit is realized when the inventory is eventually sold to an outside party. On depreciable assets, the profit is realized not by direct sale to outsiders, but rather by using the asset to produce goods or services to be sold to outsiders. Therefore, it is quite appropriate to view the $500 adjustment to S's earnings in Year 2 as recognition of the realization of one-tenth of the Year 1 unrealized profit on the equipment sale.

If S is 80% owned by P, then the Year 2 adjustment will be for P's share of the profit realized in Year 2, or $400.

Consolidation

When consolidated statements are prepared, the adjustments are necessarily more complex because both the balance sheet and the income statement accounts must be adjusted. Schedule 12-1 shows the required worksheet adjustments, assuming that P owns 100% of S.

In Year 1, the consolidation adjustment eliminates the intercompany sale, thereby removing the unrealized profit from consolidated net income. In this example, the elimination is very similar to the customary adjustment for intercompany sales of inventory because Company S is assumed to be a distributor of equipment.

If instead, Company S had sold a piece of its productive equipment (i.e., one of its own fixed assets), the sale entry by S would have been to credit the asset account, debit the accumulated depreciation, and debit or credit a gain or loss account for the difference. Upon consolidation, the sale entry

SCHEDULE 12-1

Consolidation Worksheet Adjustments for Upstream Equipment Sale*
P Owns 100% of S

Operations adjustments

Year	Cumulative			Current		
1				Sales	25,000	
				Cost of sales		20,000
				Equipment		5,000
2 Retained earnings	5,000			Accum. deprec. — equipment	500	
Equipment		5,000		Depreciation expense		500
3 Retained earnings	4,500			Accum. deprec. — equipment	500	
Accum. deprec. — equipment	500			Depreciation expense		500
Equipment		5,000				
4 Retained earnings	4,000			Accum. deprec. — equipment	500	
Accum. deprec. — equipment	1,000			Depreciation expense		500
Equipment		5,000				
11 Retained earnings	500			Accum. deprec. — equipment	500	
Accum. deprec. — equipment	4,500			Depreciation expense		500
Equipment		5,000				

*Excludes income tax effects

would be reversed and the gain (or loss) eliminated, just as was done in Chapter 8 for the sale of land from IEE to IOR.

In either case, the important point is that the unrealized profit or gain on the sale is eliminated in the year of the transaction, and it is that total amount of unrealized profit that is gradually realized and recognized over future years, as the asset is depreciated.

In each year from Year 2 to Year 11, one-tenth of the total profit is realized through productive use. The recognition of the $500 annual realized profit is accomplished upon consolidation by reducing each year's depreciation by $500. Therefore, the consolidation adjustment for the remaining unrealized profit decreases by $500 each year. The unrealized profit at the beginning of each year is the debit to retained earnings in the beginning-of-year adjustment, shown in the cumulative column of Schedule 12-1.

In Year 11, the depreciable cost of the asset is exhausted, and there will be no depreciation expense in subsequent years if the equipment continues in productive use. The only consolidation adjustment that will be made in Year 12 and thereafter (until the asset is retired) will be a cumulative adjustment that has no impact on consolidated net income or on consolidated retained earnings:

Accumulated depreciation — equipment	$5,000	
Equipment		$5,000

If Company P were to dispose of the equipment at the beginning of Year 5 by selling it for $22,000, the entry *on the books of P* would be:

Cash	$22,000	
Accumulated depreciation — equipment	7,500	
Equipment		$25,000
Gain on sale of equipment		4,500

Upon consolidation, the entire unrealized balance or profit on S's sale of the equipment to P would be recognized. The adjustment *on the consolidation worksheet* would be:

Retained earnings	$3,500	
Gain on sale of equipment		$3,500

Thus the gain on P's sale would be increased by the remaining unrealized profit on S's sale, reflecting the fact that for the consolidated entity as a whole, a profit of $8,000 was realized on the sale of the equipment to an unrelated party:

Sales price		$22,000
Consolidated carrying value		
Cost to S	$20,000	
Depreciation (3 years @ $2,000)	6,000	14,000
Gain to consolidated entity		$8,000

If there is a minority interest in S, the consolidation adjustments are slightly more complex, because the minority interest's share of the unrealized profit must be accounted for. Schedule 12-2 summarizes the adjustments necessary for the same transaction, but assumes instead that P owns 80% of S.

In Year 1, the reduction of consolidated gross income by the full amount of S's profit makes it necessary also to reduce the minority interest's deduction from consolidated income. The result will be to reduce the consolidated net income by $4,000, reflecting P's 80% interest in S, exactly as was illustrated in Chapter 9 for upstream sales of inventory.

In each succeeding year, the reduction of depreciation expense (and accumulated depreciation) by $500 must be accompanied by an *increase* in the minority interest in order to reflect the minority interest's 20% share in the annual realized profit and in order to cause only 80% or $400 of the realized profit to flow through to consolidated net income.

If the asset were sold at the beginning of Year 5 for $22,000, the entry on P's books would be the same as illustrated above, but the consolidation adjustment would be changed slightly by the presence of the minority interest:

Retained earnings	$2,800	
Minority interest in earnings of S	700	
Gain on sale of equipment		$3,500

The entire unrealized profit is added to P's gain to recognize that the consolidated entity has realized a total profit of $8,000 on the sale as above. But 20% of the previously unrealized profit (of $3,500) belongs to the minority interest. Thus consolidated net income, from the point of view of the shareholders of P, is increased by $7,300:

SCHEDULE 12-2

Consolidation Worksheet Adjustments for Upstream Equipment Sale*
P Owns 80% of S

Operations adjustments

Year	Cumulative			Current		
1				Sales	25,000	
				Cost of sales		20,000
				Equipment		5,000
				Minority interest (B/S)	1,000	
				Minority interest in earnings of S (I/S)		1,000
2	Retained earnings	4,000		Accum. deprec. — equipment	500	
	Minority interest	1,000		Depreciation expense		500
	Equipment		5,000			
				Minority interest in earnings of S(I/S)	100	
				Minority interest (B/S)		100
3	Retained earnings	3,600		Accum. deprec. — equipment	500	
	Minority interest	900		Depreciation expense		500
	Accum. deprec. — equipment	500				
	Equipment		5,000	Minority interest in earnings of S(I/S)	100	
				Minority interest (B/S)		100
4	Retained earnings	3,200		Accum. deprec. — equipment	500	
	Minority interest	800		Depreciation expense		500
	Accum. deprec. — equipment	1,000				
	Equipment		5,000	Minority interest in earnings of S(I/S)	100	
				Minority interest (B/S)		100
11	Retained earnings	400		Accum. deprec. — equipment	500	
	Minority interest	100		Depreciation expense		500
	Accum. deprec. — equipment	4,500				
	Equipment		5,000	Minority interest in earnings of S(I/S)	100	
				Minority interest (B/S)		100

*Excludes income tax effects

80% of unrealized profit on sale of S to P	$2,800
100% of gain on sale of P to outsider	4,500
	$7,300

The preceding example has focused on an upstream sale. When a sale of a depreciable asset is from the parent to a subsidiary, all of the unrealized profit belongs to the parent, and therefore 100% of the unrealized profit would be eliminated regardless of the ownership percentage of the parent in the subsidiary. If the sale is horizontal, between two subsidiaries, then the transaction is accounted for as would be an upstream sale; the impact of minority interest is determined by the ownership percentage of the parent in the *selling* subsidiary, since the profit resides in the seller's accounts.

Intercompany Sale of Fair-Valued Assets

On occasion, a subsidiary (or significantly influenced investee) will sell to its parent depreciable assets that the subsidiary had owned at the time that the parent acquired its interest in the subsidiary, and that had been assigned a fair-value increment. Any unrealized gain or loss on the intercompany sale must be eliminated upon consolidation or equity-basis reporting, just as for non-fair-valued assets discussed so far in this chapter.

An intercompany sale of a noncurrent asset is illustrated in Part B of Chapter 8 by a sale of land from IEE to IOR. Land costing $300,000 was sold to IOR for $540,000. The fair-value increment that had been assigned to the land was $100,000. On the consolidated balance sheet after the sale, the carrying value of the land now on IOR's books ($540,000) is increased by the fair-value increment of $100,000 by means of the acquisition adjustment, and then reduced by the unrealized profit of $240,000. The net result is to return the land on the consolidated balance sheet to its fair value at the date of IOR's acquisition of IEE, or $400,000: $300,000 (IEE's cost) + $100,000 (fair-value increment) = $540,000 (IOR's carrying value) + $100,000 (fair-value increment) − $240,000 (unrealized profit) = $400,000. In subsequent years, as long as the land remains within the possession of the consolidated entity, the unrealized gain will be eliminated from IEE's retained earnings and from the carrying value of the land (ignoring income tax effects):

Retained earnings	$240,000	
Land		$240,000

If the subsidiary is not wholly owned, then minority interest on the balance sheet would be charged for its percentage of the unrealized gain, and consolidated retained earnings would be charged only for the majority ownership share.

Suppose that eventually, IOR sold the land to a third party for $600,000. The realized gain to the consolidated entity is $200,000: $600,000 − $400,000. *On IOR's books*, however, the sale would be recorded as a gain of $60,000 (ignoring income tax effects):

Cash	$600,000	
Land		$540,000
Gain on sale of land		60,000

Two approaches can be taken to adjusting the consolidated statements to reflect the $200,000 actual gain in the year of the sale. Under the first approach, the acquisition adjustment would continue to debit the land account for the fair-value increment of $100,000. Since the land has now been sold, however, the adjustment to restate the gain on the land would credit land for the $100,000 in order to eliminate the fair-value increment:

Retained earnings	$240,000	
Land		$100,000
Gain on sale of land		140,000

The alternative approach is to charge the fair-value increment relating to the asset to retained earnings as part of the acquisition adjustment. Then the adjustment for the gain on sale will be as follows:

Retained earnings	$140,000	
Gain on sale of land		$140,000

Under both approaches, the retained earnings are debited for a total of $240,000, the previously unrealized gain that is included in IEE's retained earnings, and the gain is increased to $200,000 ($60,000 on IOR's books plus $140,000 from the consolidation worksheet adjustment).

In the years following the sale of the land by IOR to a third party, the book retained earnings of IEE will include $240,000 profit from the intercompany sale, and the book retained earnings of IOR will include the gain of $60,000 from the sale to a third party. The total book gain of $300,000 ($240,000 + $60,000) is reduced to the consolidated gain of $200,000 simply by debiting the $100,000 fair-value increment relating to the land to retained earnings when the acquisition adjustment is made. This adjustment was illustrated in Part B of Chapter 10, for a sale of fair-valued investments. The example in Chapter 10 did not involve an intercompany sale, but *the fact of an intervening intercompany sale does not affect the adjustment once a fair-valued asset has been sold to a buyer outside of the consolidated entity.* The fair-value increment is charged to retained earnings; minority interest is not affected because the fair-value increment relates only to the investor corporation's proportionate share of the asset.

Summary: Sale of Assets

Sale of an asset from one company to an affiliated company requires elimination of the unrealized profit. The profit on an intercompany sale is recognized in the consolidated or equity-basis financial statements of the investor corporation only when realized. When the sale is of a current asset such as inventory or a current note receivable, the profit is normally realized in the next period. Consolidation or equity-basis adjustments must therefore transfer the gain from retained earnings in the period of the intercompany sale to consolidated or equity earnings in the period of the sale or other realization (e.g., collection of a note receivable) in a transaction with a third party.

For nondepreciable or nonamortizable long-term assets, gains on intercompany sales of assets must similarly be delayed until the period of realization by sale or transaction with an unrelated party.

When the asset involved in an intercompany sale is subject to depreciation or amortization, then the gain is realized gradually through time as the asset is put to productive use and thus is depreciated or amortized. If the asset is subsequently sold to a third party, any remaining unrealized gain will be recognized at that time.

Intercompany sales of fair-valued assets involve no significant complications as long as the asset is not sold to an outsider. The unrealized gain on the books of the selling company must be eliminated, just as for non-fair-valued assets. When a fair-valued asset is subsequently sold to a third party, any previously unrealized gain is recognized in the period of the sale, reduced by the amount of the unamortized fair-value increment. In years following the external sale of a fair-valued asset, the unamortized fair-value increment at the time of the sale is charged to consolidated retained earnings in order to adjust retained earnings to reflect the gain from the sale from the viewpoint of the parent company's shareholders.

The foregoing discussion has ignored the impact of intercompany transactions on reported income taxes. The tax effect was introduced in Chapter 8 in order to make the reader aware of its existence. Part C of this chapter discusses the income tax implications of consolidation.

B.   EXTRAORDINARY ITEMS

Classification

As a general rule, an extraordinary gain or loss that is shown on the income statement of an individual company retains its status as an extraordinary item when that company's financial statements are consolidated with those of one or more other companies. One objective of equity-basis reporting is to achieve a net income figure for the investor corporation that is identical to consolidated net income. Therefore, the same general rule is applied in Canada to companies that are reported on an equity basis (*CICA Handbook* [para. 1600.80]). If A owns 40% of B, and if A accounts for its investment in B on the equity basis, then A would normally show as an extraordinary item 40% of any extraordinary item reported by B.

An example of equity reporting of an investee's extraordinary item is an extraordinary loss reported by United Keno Hill Mines Limited. United Keno wrote off $10,577,000 of previously deferred costs for a major project. Falconbridge Nickel Mines Limited owned 48.4% of United Keno's shares and reported its investment on the equity basis. Therefore, Falconbridge reported an extraordinary loss of $5,122,000 as its share of the United Keno extraordinary loss. Another company, McIntyre Mines, owned 37.1% of Falconbridge's shares reported on the equity basis. Thus the McIntyre income statement showed an extraordinary loss of $1,901,000, representing 37.1% of the 48.4% of the United Keno loss reported by Falconbridge.

However, the general rule may be subject to modification in certain circumstances. Recall that the *CICA Handbook* states three conditions that a gain or loss must satisfy in order to be classified as extraordinary rather than as an operating gain or loss [para. 3480.05]:

1. It must be material in amount.
2. It must be nonrecurring in nature.
3. It must not be related to the normal business activities of the enterprise.

A transaction in a subsidiary or a significantly influenced company may meet these criteria and be properly classified as extraordinary. But when the transaction is considered from the viewpoint of the parent or investor corporation, it may fail to meet one or more of the criteria. The most obvious potential failing is on the dimension of materiality; what is material to a subsidiary may not be material to a much larger consolidated entity.

An extraordinary item may fail to satisfy one of the other two criteria instead of, or in addition to, the materiality criterion. Transactions that are nonrecurring in an individual company may actually be recurring in the consolidated entity. Similarly, gains and losses may arise from nonoperating sources in a subsidiary and yet may be a part of normal operations in the parent.

For example, a subsidiary may recognize a substantial gain from sale of a major investment. If the subsidiary is a manufacturer, the gain may be properly treated as an extraordinary item. But suppose that the parent company is a large investment company. Gains and losses from the sale of investments are a normal part of the parent's business. To treat the subsidiary's investment gain as an extraordinary item would be inconsistent with the notion that the consolidated entity should be reported as a single economic entity: a primary business activity of the consolidated entity is to buy and sell investments, and thus the subsidiary's gain is an operating gain from the point of view of the larger entity. In addition, the gain would be recurring for the consolidated entity. Finally, it may not even be material for the entity, thereby possibly failing all three tests for an extraordinary item.

Thus the general rule of maintaining the status of an extraordinary item is, like many other recommendations in accounting, one that must be applied with professional judgment.

When consolidated statements report an extraordinary item that arose in a non-wholly owned subsidiary, provision must be made for the minority interest's share of the extraordinary gain or loss. The deduction for minority interest that appears as a reduction of operating income should include only the minority interest's share of *operating* income. If the minority interest's share of extraordinary gains or losses were included in that deduction, consolidated operating income would not reflect solely the parent company's shareholders' interest in the results of consolidated operations; net income (and earnings per share) before extraordinary items would be distorted by inclusion of a portion of extraordinary items.

Minority Interest

Therefore, the minority interest's share of extraordinary items is deducted directly from those items; the subsidiary extraordinary items are shown net of minority interest on the parent's income statement.

In preparing the consolidated statements, the worksheet adjustment is quite simple. Minority interest is credited (debited) for its share of the extraordinary gain (loss), and the extraordinary gain is debited (credited). Thus, extraordinary items are shown both net of income tax and net of minority interest. The minority interest share is, of course, calculated net of tax.

C. CONSOLIDATION TAX EFFECTS

In the United States, corporations have the option of filing income tax returns on a consolidated basis. In Canada, no such option exists. With certain exceptions, Revenue Canada assesses each individual corporation as a separate taxation entity. When two or more separately taxed corporations are consolidated into a single reporting entity, the basis of accountability for financial reporting to shareholders differs from that for taxation. For tax purposes, income is taxed when realized by the individual company; for financial reporting, income is recognized only when it arises from transactions with outsiders.

Since Canadian practice calls for the application of comprehensive tax

The Basic Concept

allocation, the income tax expense shown on a consolidated income statement must include the tax effects of only those items of revenue and expense that are included in consolidated net income before taxes. If revenues or expenses are eliminated upon consolidation, then the related tax expense must be eliminated from consolidated income tax expense.

The elimination of income tax expense will cause a change in the future income tax account on the balance sheet in one of three ways:

1. If the item of revenue or expense that has been eliminated upon consolidation has been subject to tax in the current year, then the tax effect is transferred from tax expense to future taxes.
2. If the item of unrealized revenue or expense has *not* been subject to tax in the current year but will be taxed in a future period, then a future tax liability or asset would have been set up for the item; elimination of the item requires elimination of both the tax expense and the related amount in the future tax balance.
3. If the item of unrealized revenue or expense has not been taxed in the current period but was taxed in a previous period, then the future tax balance must be reinstated upon consolidation in each period until the revenue or expense is realized.

Although these are three different types of impact, the net effect is the same for all three and is simple: the offsetting account to any consolidation adjustment of tax expense is the future income tax account on the balance sheet.[1]

Intercompany Sales

Extraordinary Items

Chapter 8 illustrated an intercompany sale of land from IEE to IOR that was treated as an extraordinary item on IEE's income statement. The original transaction was recorded *on IEE's books* as follows:

Cash	$540,000	
Land		$300,000
Gain on sale of land		150,000
Income taxes payable		90,000

Extraordinary items are reported net of tax, and therefore the tax expense relating to this sale is included in the computation of the gain. The sale could have been recorded as follows:

Cash	$540,000	
Income tax expense — extraordinary gain	90,000	
Land		$300,000
Gain on sale of land		240,000
Income taxes payable		90,000

For greater clarity, let us assume that the second method of recording was used.

1 At the time of writing, the appropriate account would actually be *deferred* income taxes. We have adopted the terminology of the AcSC's exposure draft on *Corporate Income Taxes* (November 1988) under the (possibly rash) assumption that Canadian tax allocation will change from the deferral to the liabilitiy approach. We have ignored the possibility of discounting, however.

When the subsidiaries are consolidated, the gain must be eliminated and the carrying value of the land must be reduced to the original cost. The *worksheet* adjustment would be:

Gain on sale of land	$240,000	
Land		$240,000

Now that the gain has been eliminated, the related income tax expense must also be eliminated. IEE is currently liable for income tax on a transaction that is not yet being recognized for reporting purposes, and therefore the taxes are the result of a timing difference. The timing difference is for a revenue item that is taxed before it is recognized, and therefore the impact is to create a future tax *debit* upon consolidation:

Future income taxes	$90,000	
Income tax expense — extraordinary gain		$90,000

Note that both this and the preceding entry are *worksheet* entries; they do not appear on the books of either IEE or IOR.

Now let us change the example a bit. Suppose that instead of receiving cash, IEE received a note from IOR that promised payment in the following tax year. Assume also that tax will not be due on the transaction until IEE actually receives the cash. In that case, IEE would have recorded the sale as follows:

Note receivable	$540,000	
Income tax expense — extraordinary gain	90,000	
Land		$300,000
Gain on sale of land		240,000
Future income taxes		90,000

A timing difference now exists on IEE's books; the gain has been recognized but will not be taxed until next year. This timing difference has caused a deferred tax *credit* balance of $90,000.

When the gain is eliminated upon consolidation, the income tax expense must also be eliminated, as before:

Future income taxes	$90,000	
Income tax expense — extraordinary gain		$90,000

In this case, the adjustment to future income taxes has the effect of eliminating the future taxes that IEE set up in order to recognize the timing difference. Since the transaction has not been taxed, and the accounting recognition of the gain has now been eliminated, no timing difference exists on a consolidated basis. The balance of future taxes (relating to the land sale) is zero on the consolidated statements.

The worksheet adjustment that will be necessary in the following year will be the continuing adjustment to eliminate the gain:

Retained earnings	$150,000	
Future income taxes	90,000	
Land		$240,000

This entry will be unaffected by the fact that IOR will honour the note and IEE will become liable for the taxes. IEE will credit taxes payable and debit future income taxes. But since no tax *expense* is recorded, no consolidation adjustment is necessary for the tax liability. IEE's payment of the taxes will have the effect of changing the consolidated balance of deferred taxes (relating to the land sale) to a *debit* balance of $90,000.

Operating Items

When intercompany transactions involve operating revenues and expenses, essentially the same tax elimination process is required. Any *unrealized* profits must be eliminated, as must any income tax effects related thereto. Only unrealized profits are of concern. If IEE sells $55,000 of goods to IOR and IOR sells them all during the same year, then there is no unrealized profit and no tax adjustment.

However, if $20,000 worth of intercompany purchases remains in IOR's inventory at year-end, then the unrealized profit must be eliminated. If IEE's gross margin was 40% of sales, then inventory and cost of sales must be reduced by $8,000. Since the unrealized profit is being removed from the consolidated income statement, so must the income taxes relating thereto. Assuming a 45% tax rate, the *worksheet* adjustment would appear as follows:

Future income taxes	$3,600	
Income tax expense		$3,600

When the goods are sold in the following period, the previously unrealized profit must be recognized upon consolidation, and the related income tax expense must also be recognized by reversing the prior year's tax adjustment *on the consolidation worksheet*:

Income tax expense	$3,600	
Future income taxes		$3,600

It is quite possible that IOR and IEE may be subject to different tax rates if they are in different provinces. For example, IEE may be taxed at a rate of 45% while IOR may be taxed at a rate of 42%. Total taxes on a sale of goods manufactured by IEE and sold through IOR would be $7,800, assuming IEE and IOR have gross margins of 40% and 33% respectively:

Tax on IEE:		
Sales (to IOR)	$20,000	
Cost of sales	12,000	
Gross margin	$8,000	
Tax @ 45%		$3,600
Tax on IOR:		
Sales	$30,000	
Cost of sales (from IEE)	20,000	
Gross margin	$10,000	
Tax @ 42%		$4,200
Total taxes		$7,800

A difference in tax rates causes no particular problem. The only caution is to remember that the tax expense elimination for unrealized profit must be based on the tax rate for the company that is taxed on the profit. If IEE sells to IOR in one year, and IOR sells to outsiders in a later year, then expense recognition of IEE's tax ($3,600 in this example) must be deferred until the year of IOR's sale, so that the entire tax expense can be matched to the revenue generated by the sale to outsiders.

When an intercompany sale is of a depreciable asset, the tax expense is not recognized all at once, but year by year as the asset is depreciated on the acquiring company's books. In the first part of this chapter, we pointed out that depreciation expense would be adjusted downward each year as the intercompany profit is realized. The increased profit must be matched by increased tax expense. The increased tax expense is the proportionate recognition of the total tax on the initial sale that was deferred on the consolidated statements.

If an intercompany sale is an upstream (or horizontal) sale and there is a minority interest in the subsidiary, the minority interest will be affected by any elimination of unrealized profit. The deduction for the minority interest in the earnings of the subsidiary must be computed on the subsidiary's net income *after* taxes. Therefore, the minority interest on the consolidated statements will absorb its share of the tax effect of any unrealized profit eliminations.

Intercompany Dividends

Dividends received by a Canadian corporation from another taxable Canadian corporation are generally not taxed to the receiving company. When there is no tax effect of intercompany dividends, elimination of the dividends upon consolidation does not require any adjustments to income tax expense or future taxes.

However, some intercompany dividends are subject to income tax, such as dividends received by a Canadian parent from certain foreign subsidiaries. The income from such a subsidiary is included in consolidated net income (or equity-basis net income), and thus the tax expense incurred in transferring those earnings to the parent in the form of dividends is a business expense that would be included in the determination of the parent's net income. In other words, no adjustment is necessary for taxes paid on dividends; in substance, the tax is on the earnings that are *included* in net income rather than on the dividends that are *eliminated* from net income.

The possibility of an adjustment for income taxes arises from taxable dividends that have *not* been paid. Since the tax arises from a transfer of earnings in the form of dividends, proper matching would seem to call for recognizing the tax expense in the period in which the earnings are recognized, rather than in the period in which the dividends are paid.

Suppose, for example, that a subsidiary earns net income of $100,000 in 19x1 and nothing in 19x2. Suppose also that the subsidiary transfers the 19x1 income to the parent in 19x2 by paying $100,000 in dividends. If the dividends are taxed at a 40% rate, consolidated net income will be increased by the $100,000 profit in 19x1 and be decreased by the tax expense of $40,000 in 19x2. But the $40,000 19x2 reduction in consolidated net income was really caused by the 19x1 profit. The matching concept suggests that the two amounts should both be recognized in 19x1. This could easily be accomplished by making a consolidation *worksheet* adjustment in 19x1 to provide for future income taxes on the unremitted earnings:

Income tax expense	$40,000	
Future income taxes		$40,000

In 19x2, the dividends are paid and tax is incurred by the parent company. Upon consolidation, the tax expense on the parent's books would be eliminated by offsetting it against the future taxes that were set up in the previous year (and carried forward on the 19x2 consolidation worksheet as part of the cumulative operations adjustment):

Future income taxes	$40,000	
Income tax expense		$40,000

Both of these adjustments are *worksheet* adjustments; no entry would be made for the future taxes on either company's books.

The provision for future taxes on unremitted earnings seems logical when applied to a simple situation, as above. But the fact is that many, if not most, companies do not transfer all of their earnings to the parent. Indeed, some parents leave all of the subsidiary's earnings in the subsidiary, especially when the subsidiary's dividends are taxable to the parent. Provision for future taxes in such instances would result in a continuous buildup of future taxes on the consolidated balance sheet with no prospect of reversal. Therefore, provision for future taxes on unremitted earnings is seldom encountered in practice.

Reporting on the Equity Basis

An investor corporation should report its investment in a significantly influenced company on the equity basis. In addition, unconsolidated subsidiaries and joint ventures are usually reported on the equity basis. As we have already seen, equity-basis accounting calls for the same types of adjustments to earnings as are required for consolidated statements. These adjustments include those for tax effects. Thus any adjustment to eliminate unrealized profit must take into account the income tax effect, as outlined above.

In Chapter 8, IOR's equity in the earnings of IEE (assuming 100% ownership) was calculated as $59,500 for 19x1. The calculation is shown in Schedule 8-4, and can be summarized as follows:

IEE reported earnings	$80,000
Amortization of fair-value increments	– 10,000
Amortization of goodwill	– 2,500
Unrealized upstream profit	– 8,000
	$59,500

The starting point of the preceding calculation ($80,000) is the earnings *after tax* of IEE. All of the adjustments to the after-tax earnings should also be net of tax. In this example, the only adjustment having a tax impact is the elimination of the unrealized profit. The amortization of the fair-value increment on buildings and equipment is a permanent difference between taxable income and accounting income, since CCA will never be deducted for the fair-value increments.

As well, the amortization of the goodwill is a deduction for accounting (i.e., reporting) that is not deductible for tax purposes. If IOR had directly purchased the assets and liabilities of IEE, then any goodwill actually purchased would have been recorded on IOR's books, and 75% of the purchased goodwill would have been considered to be *eligible capital property* for tax purposes. Eligible capital property is subject to capital cost allowance at a rate of 7% on a declining-balance basis. When an investor corporation purchases the *shares* of another company rather than its net assets directly, however, no tax deduction results. In this example, therefore, the amortization of goodwill by IOR on the consolidated financial statements is a permanent difference, not a timing difference. There is no tax effect upon consolidation that relates to goodwill or its amortization.

We have already seen that the elimination of unrealized profit will reduce tax *expense*. The reduction in tax expense will partially offset the reduction in pre-tax earnings, so that the after-tax adjustment to IOR's equity in IEE's earnings will be reduced by the amount of the tax rate. If we assume that IEE's tax rate is 20%, then $8,000 of pre-tax unrealized profit is equivalent to $6,400 in after-tax profit. Therefore, the correct, after-tax adjustment to IEE's reported earnings is $6,400, not $8,000 as was shown on Schedule 8-4.

The net impact of income taxes on the equity-basis adjustments for the 19x1 earnings of IEE is $1,600. The correct after-tax equity of IOR in the earnings of IEE is $61,100: $59,500 from Schedule 8-4 plus the $1,600 reduction of the unrealized earnings in inventory to an after-tax basis. If IOR reports its investment in IEE on the equity basis (that is, without consolidating financial statements of IEE into those of IOR), then there is no need to worry about an impact on future taxes or on any other balance sheet account (except for the investment in IEE account). The $61,100 will be shown on IOR's income statement as IOR's equity in the earnings of IEE.

Common practice in Canada is to show the equity pick-up of an unconsolidated subsidiary or of a significantly influenced investee corporation as an after-tax amount. An alternative is to show it as a pre-tax amount. IEE's pre-tax net income for 19x1 was $100,000. Income tax expense was $20,000. IOR could choose to include IEE's income as a pre-tax return on an investment, and to include the IEE income tax expense as a part of IOR's income tax expense. If this alternative were chosen, then IOR would report its equity in IEE's earnings at $79,500 and would increase its tax expense by $18,400. The amounts can be summarized as follows:

	Pre-tax earnings	Tax effect
IEE reported earnings	$100,000	$20,000
Amortization of fair-value increments	−10,000	—
Amortization of goodwill	−2,500	—
Unrealized upstream profit	−8,000	−1,600
	$ 79,500	$18,400

The $79,500 would be included in IOR's pre-tax earnings on the income statements, and IOR's 19x1 income tax expense would be increased from $200,000 to $218,400. Schedule 12-3 shows how the lower part of IOR's income statement would appear under both the after-tax and pre-tax approaches.

Schedule 12-3 also shows, in the last column, how the IOR income statement would appear if IOR consolidated IEE. The pre-tax approach to equity-basis accounting yields the same results as does consolidation. Obviously, the before-tax alternative is a departure from the concept of a one-line consolidation. But since equity-basis accounting is intended to yield the same net income as would consolidation, it can be argued that this congruence should apply to net income both before and after taxes.

SCHEDULE 12-3			
Equity-Basis Income Tax Accounting Approaches **Investor, Ltd.** **Partial Income Statements** Year Ended December 31, 19x1			
	Equity-basis accounting: IOR's share of IEE's earnings reported:		
	After taxes	Before taxes	Consolidated
IOR net operating income, before income taxes	$500,000	$500,000	
Equity in earnings of IEE (*before* income taxes)		79,500	
Net income before income taxes	500,000	579,500	$579,500
Income tax expense	200,000	218,400	218,400
	300,000		
Equity in earnings of IEE (*after* income taxes)	61,100		
Net income	$361,100	$361,100	$361,100

Summary: Tax Effects

Adjustments for unrealized profits or losses usually have a related income tax effect. Since each corporation in an affiliated group of companies is taxed individually, transferring the accounting recognition of gains and losses on intercompany transactions from one period to another upon consolidation requires the transfer of the related tax expense as well. It is necessary to recognize that the tax effect of unrealized gains and losses applies equally to operating items and to extraordinary items.

The adjustment for the tax effect upon consolidation is always straightforward; the offsetting account for any adjustment to income tax expense is the future income taxes account on the balance sheet. The most common situation is the deferral of recognition of unrealized earnings; eliminating unrealized profits requires elimination of related income tax expense, thereby causing a debit to the future taxes balance. If there is no existing credit balance of future taxes, then a future tax debit balance is created by the profit elimination. The income tax effect must be recognized for equity-basis reporting of earnings as well as for consolidated statements. Intercompany dividends do not generally call for any income tax adjustments, even when the intercompany dividends are taxable. Unremitted earnings of a subsidiary also do not require any tax provision. There is no certainty that the earnings will ever be remitted to the parent as dividends, and thus no tax may ever be levied.

D.   INTERCOMPANY BOND HOLDINGS

On occasion, one company in an affiliated group of companies will buy bonds issued by another company of the group. When the purchase is directly from the issuing company, the transaction is clearly an intercompany transaction. If consolidated financial statements are prepared, the intercompany transaction must be eliminated in order to prevent the intercompany receivable and payable from appearing on the consolidated balance sheet. Only bonds that are held by bondholders who are outside the affiliated group can be shown as a liability of the consolidated entity. As long as the bonds are held within the group, intercompany interest expense (to the issuer) and interest revenue (to the holder) must be eliminated, as well as any amortization of related discount or premium.

When the bonds are retired, the indebtedness and the investment will both be removed from the books. However, if the retirement occurs prior to the maturity date of the bonds, a gain or loss may result on the separate company books. Any such gain or loss must also be eliminated upon consolidation.

In general, intercompany transactions in bonds pose no particular reporting problems for consolidation or for the equity method. Adjustments and eliminations for bond transactions are similar to those that are required for asset transactions. Both offsetting transactions and offsetting balances must be eliminated when consolidated statements are prepared.

Intercompany Bond Transactions

Somewhat different problems arise when one company buys bonds in an affiliated company not directly from the issuer, but rather from an outside holder of the bonds. In this case, the buying company still ends up holding bonds that are an indebtedness of an affiliated company and that must be eliminated upon consolidation, but the buying price and the issuer's carrying value are likely not to be the same.

For example, suppose that SubCorp has a bond issue outstanding that has a face value of $1,000,000, an unamortized premium of $50,000, a nominal interest rate of 12%, and five years remaining to maturity. All of the bonds are held by nonaffiliated investors. Market rates of interest have risen above the nominal rate on the bonds, and have caused the market price of SubCorp's bonds to fall. SubCorp's parent, ParCorp, then buys $100,000 face value of the SubCorp bonds on the open market for $90,000.

When consolidated statements are prepared, the intercompany interest must be eliminated, and the amount of the bonds held by ParCorp must be eliminated against the proportionate part of the indebtedness of SubCorp. On ParCorp's books, the bond investment is carried at $90,000, while on SubCorp's books, the bond indebtedness is carried at $105,000 (10% of the $1,000,000 face value and of the $50,000 premium). The problem is how to dispose of the $15,000 difference in carrying values.

To solve this problem, we must look at the substance of the transaction. SubCorp could have used its own cash to purchase the bonds itself. If SubCorp had done so, it would have recognized a gain on the retirement of

Indirect Acquisitions of Bonds

debt of $15,000. Alternatively, SubCorp could have borrowed $90,000 from ParCorp and used that cash to buy the bonds. A gain of $15,000 would still have been recognized by SubCorp, and an intercompany payable (and receivable) for $90,000 would exist, which payable (and receivable) would be eliminated upon consolidation.

However, instead of lending SubCorp the money, ParCorp simply bought the bonds directly. SubCorp still has a legal liability (to ParCorp) for the bonds, but the substance is that for the consolidated entity, the indebtedness no longer exists. From the viewpoint of the readers of the consolidated statements, the bonds have been retired. Therefore, the $15,000 difference between SubCorp's carrying value and ParCorp's acquisition cost must be treated as a gain when the statements are consolidated and the intercompany bond holdings are eliminated. The Year 1 worksheet elimination would appear as follows, assuming that the bonds were acquired at the end of Year 1 ex-interest, and that *Subcorp is wholly owned by ParCorp*:

Bonds payable	$100,000	
Premium on bonds payable	5,000	
Bond investment		$90,000
Gain on retirement of bonds		15,000

If the bonds were truly being retired, the gain on redemption would be taxable. Since the gain in the above entry is only the result of a consolidation adjustment, a timing difference arises, which calls for a tax allocation entry. Assuming a potential tax impact of 20%, the worksheet adjustment would be:

Income tax expense	$3,000	
Future income taxes		$3,000

In subsequent years, the carrying value of the bonds on SubCorp's books will decrease due to the continuing amortization of the premium. If we assume straight-line amortization, then the carrying value to SubCorp will decline by $1,000 per year. This decline is offset by a decrease in SubCorp's interest expense (assuming that the premium amortization is credited directly thereto). Therefore, the Year 2 elimination, including the intercorporate payment of interest, would appear as follows (ignoring income tax effects):

Bonds payable	$100,000	
Premium on bonds payable	4,000	
Interest income (to ParCorp)	12,000	
Bond investment		$90,000
Interest expense (to SubCorp)		11,000
Retained earnings		15,000

Each year that ParCorp holds the bonds, the above entry will change only by the decreasing balance of the premium; the decrease in the premium will be offset by a decrease in the credit to retained earnings, reflecting the continuing amortization of the premium. The Year 3 elimination would be:

Bonds payable	$100,000	
Premium on bonds payable	3,000	
Interest income	12,000	
Bond investment		$90,000
Interest expense		11,000
Retained earnings		14,000

The consolidation adjustment for future income taxes would be reduced each year as the amount of the unrealized gain (i.e., the credit to retained earnings) declines.

The above example assumes that ParCorp is accounting for its investment in SubCorp's bonds as a "temporary" investment, that is, without amortizing the purchase discount on the bonds. If, instead, ParCorp accounts for the bonds as an investment to maturity, then each year ParCorp will amortize one fifth of its $10,000 purchase discount by charging $2,000 to the bond investment account and crediting it to interest income. In that case, the elimination entry in years subsequent to acquisition would have to reflect the difference in both the investment and the interest income account, as follows:

YEAR 2

Bonds payable	$100,000	
Premium on bonds payable	4,000	
Interest income	14,000	
Bond investment		$92,000
Interest expense		11,000
Retained earnings		15,000

YEAR 3

Bonds payable	$100,000	
Premium on bonds payable	3,000	
Interest income	14,000	
Bond investment		$94,000
Interest expense		11,000
Retained earnings		12,000

In each of Years 4 and 5, the balance in SubCorp's premium account will decline by $1,000 while the balance of ParCorp's bond investment will rise by $2,000. The combined effect is to reduce the credit to retained earnings in the elimination entry by $3,000 per year, which represents the gradual recognition (through amortization) on both companies' books of the issue premium and purchase discount.

At the end of Year 6, SubCorp will officially retire the bonds, transferring $100,000 to ParCorp for its amount held. The bonds payable and bond investment accounts will disappear from both companies' books, and the only remnant of the bonds that will remain on the pre-consolidation trial balances will be the interest income and expense accounts. These would be eliminated in Year 6 as follows:

Interest income	$14,000	
Interest expense		$11,000
Retained earnings		3,000

Non-Wholly Owned Subsidiaries

If SubCorp is not a wholly owned subsidiary, then a question arises as to whether the gain on elimination of the intercompany bond holdings is a gain to SubCorp, to ParCorp, or partially to each. The significance of this question lies in the fact that if all or part of the gain is attributable to SubCorp, then the minority interest will be assigned its proportionate share of the gain.

There are two views of the gain. One is that it is attributable to each corporation based on the difference between the bond's carrying value on

the books of the company and the face value of the bonds. This is known as
the **par-value approach**. Under this approach, the $15,000 total gain would
be attributed as $5,000 to SubCorp and $10,000 to ParCorp. The result is what
would have happened if SubCorp had redeemed the bonds at face value.
Indeed, if ParCorp holds the bonds until maturity, SubCorp will in fact amortize the $5,000 premium and ParCorp will amortize the purchase discount
as a credit to income over the five years. Thus the first approach attributes
the gain to the two parties in relation to their respective roles as debtor and
creditor, as though they were unaffiliated companies. If SubCorp is 80%
owned by ParCorp, then 20% of the $5,000 gain attributed to SubCorp under
the par-value approach would be allocated to the minority interest. The Year
1 worksheet elimination entry would be as follows, assuming the gain is not
an extraordinary item:

Bonds payable	$100,000	
Premium on bonds payable	5,000	
Minority interest in earnings of SubCorp (I/S)	1,000	
Bond investment		$90,000
Gain on retirement of bonds		15,000
Minority interest (B/S)		1,000

If the gain is an extraordinary item, then the net amount of $14,000 (net of
minority interest) would appear on the consolidated income statement.

However, SubCorp could easily have borrowed $90,000 from ParCorp
and retired the bonds itself. In that case, the par-value method would have
assigned the entire $15,000 gain to SubCorp. Since there is no difference in
substance between ParCorp buying the bonds or lending SubCorp the
money to buy the bonds, the second approach to allocating the $15,000 total
gain is to attribute it entirely to the issuing corporation, SubCorp in this
example. Since this approach views ParCorp as acting as agent for SubCorp
in buying the bonds, this method is called the **agency approach**. The Year 1
elimination entry would appear as follows, assuming that the gain was not
an extraordinary item (and ignoring income taxes):

Bonds payable	$100,000	
Premium on bonds payable	5,000	
Minority interest in earnings of SubCorp (I/S)	3,000	
Bond investment		$90,000
Gain on retirement of bonds		15,000
Minority interest (B/S)		3,000

The minority interest is increased by 20% of the full $15,000 gain. Unlike the
par-value method, the agency method yields the same results regardless of
the way in which the bond repurchase transaction was structured. Since the
agency method stresses substance over form, many accountants prefer it.
Both approaches are encountered in practice, however. In many cases, the
difference between the two is immaterial.

In years following ParCorp's purchase of SubCorp's bonds, the eliminating entries will differ from those shown above for Year 1 as a result of the
amortization of the issue premium and the purchase discount. Assuming
that both are amortized on a straight-line basis over the five years to maturity, SubCorp's premium account will decrease by $1,000 per year and
ParCorp's carrying value of the bond investment will increase by $2,000 per
year. The resultant combined recognition of $3,000 per year of the spread

between the issue and repurchase prices causes the *unrecognized* portion of the spread (i.e., gain) to decline by $3,000 per year, exactly as described in the previous section. If SubCorp were wholly owned by ParCorp, the $3,000 decline would be reflected in the year-by-year worksheet eliminations as a reduction in the amount credited to retained earnings. When SubCorp is not wholly owned, then the change in the unrecognized gain is allocated to retained earnings and minority interest; the relative proportions depend on whether the par-value or the agency approach is being used.

The annual worksheet entry to eliminate intercompany interest income and expense (assuming that *both* the premium and the discount are being amortized) will be as follows if SubCorp is wholly owned:

Interest income	$14,000	
Interest expense		$11,000
Retained earnings		3,000

Since the full amount of the gain was recognized on the consolidated statements in Year 1, the separate-entity recognition of the gain through amortization must not be permitted to flow through to the consolidated income statement again. Therefore, the balancing credit is to retained earnings rather than to a gain account.

When SubCorp is only 80% owned, then part of the balancing credit of $3,000 must be allocated to minority interest. The portion allocated depends on the approach used. Under the par-value approach:

Interest income	$14,000	
Interest expense		$11,000
Minority interest		200
Retained earnings		2,800

The $200 represents 20% of the SubCorp $1,000 discount amortization for each year.

Using the agency approach:

Interest income	$14,000	
Interest expense		$11,000
Minority interest		600
Retained earnings		2,400

The $600 represents 20% of the combined amortizations of $3,000 per year.

The worksheet elimination entries for the principal amount (and the related issue premium and purchase discount) are shown in Schedule 12-4. Under both methods, the combined credits to minority interest and retained earnings are $12,000 at the end of Year 2, down from $15,000 at the bond acquisition in Year 1. The combined credit declines by $3,000 each year as the carrying values of the bonds on both companies' books merge towards the maturity value of $100,000. In Year 6, the bonds mature and are retired; therefore, the only consolidation adjustment relating to the bonds in Year 6 will be for the intercompany interest.

Subsidiary Purchase of Parent's Bonds

The foregoing example dealt solely with the purchase of a subsidiary's bonds by the parent. When the situation is reversed, how do the consolidation adjustments differ?

If the par-value method is used, then the adjustment approach does not

SCHEDULE 12-4

	Year 2		Year 3		Year 4		Year 5	
Bond Elimination Entries Subsequent to Acquisition (in thousands)								
PAR-VALUE APPROACH								
Bonds payable	100.0		100.0		100.0		100.0	
Premium	4.0		3.0		2.0		1.0	
Bond investment		92.0		94.0		96.0		98.0
Minority interest (B/S)		0.8		0.6		0.4		0.2
Retained earnings		11.2		8.4		5.6		2.8
AGENCY APPROACH								
Bonds payable	100.0		100.0		100.0		100.0	
Premium	4.0		3.0		2.0		1.0	
Bond investment		92.0		94.0		96.0		98.0
Minority interest (B/S)		2.4		1.8		1.2		0.6
Retained earnings		9.6		7.2		4.8		2.4

depend at all on which company is the issuer and which is the buyer. The redemption gain or loss for each company is determined, and the minority interest is allocated its proportion of the gain or loss attributed to the subsidiary.

If the agency approach is used, the full gain or loss is attributed to the issuing company. When the issuing company is the parent, there obviously would be no minority interest effects; the consolidation eliminations would be exactly the same as those illustrated in the section for wholly owned subsidiaries.

Summary: Bond Holdings

Direct intercompany bond transactions are treated no differently from other intercompany indebtedness when consolidated statements are prepared. The offsetting liability and investment must be eliminated, as well as all intercompany interest payments and any premiums and discount amortizations.

When bonds of an affiliated company are purchased from an unaffiliated holder subsequent to their original issuance, the carrying value of the bonds on the books of the issuer is likely to be different from the cost to the acquirer. The difference in carrying values can be assigned wholly to the issuer of the bonds (the agency approach) or allocated to both the issuer and the buyer on the basis of the face value of the bonds (the par-value approach). The method of allocation will affect the minority interest and the consolidated net income.

The essence of consolidated reporting is to show the assets *and liabilities* that are under the control of the parent company. Since the parent can structure the liability position of the affiliated companies in a number of ways with the same substantive result, the reporting of an in-substance debt retirement should not be affected by the technical manner by which it is accomplished. Only the agency approach achieves substance over form; the par-value approach will yield different consolidated net income depending on the technical structure of the repurchase.

Indeed, the par-value approach can lead to some odd results. For example, if the parent has bonds outstanding that were issued at a premium, then the parent can trigger recognition of a gain in its consolidated income statement by having a non-wholly owned subsidiary buy the bonds, regardless of the price paid by the subsidiary. The subsidiary could pay a price that is even higher than the carrying value of the bonds on the parent's books, and an overall loss to the combined entity would clearly result. But the par-value approach would still attribute a gain to the parent and a loss to the subsidiary, with part of the loss allocated to minority shareholders. Thus the agency approach seems more consistent with the overall objectives of consolidated reporting, as well as being easier to apply. Nevertheless, both methods can be found in practice.

When part of a bond issue is retired at a gain, GAAP permits the gain to be recognized either in a lump sum or amortized over the remaining life of the bond issue. In this chapter, we have assumed for the sake of simplicity that the gain is recognized in the year of the repurchase.

SELF-STUDY PROBLEM 12-1[2]

Barrows Inc. is an 80% owned subsidiary of Parks Corp., a manufacturer of industrial equipment. During 19x3, Barrows purchased a grummling machine from Parks for $100,000. The machine has been produced by Parks at a cost of $60,000. Barrows uses straight-line depreciation over a ten-year period for its grummling machine, and follows the practice of depreciating its assets by one-half year in both the year of acquisition and the year of disposal. No salvage value is assumed. Single asset accounting (i.e., not group depreciation) is used. Barrows used the machine in its productive operations from 19x3 to 19x16, in which year it was sold for scrap for $1,000.

Required:
a. Prepare the consolidation adjustments that would be necessary in each of 19x3, 19x4, 19x8, 19x15, and 19x16 for the grummling machine in Parks Corp.'s consolidated statements. Ignore tax effects.
b. Prepare the appropriate adjustments to recognize the tax effects of the preceding adjustments. Assume that both companies are taxed at a rate of 40%.

SELF-STUDY PROBLEM 12-2

Sweetness Corporation is 70% owned by Passion Limited. At the beginning of 19x1, Sweetness issued $1,000,000 in 12%, ten-year bonds for $958,000. On December 31, 19x4, Passion purchased 50% of the bonds from their original buyer for $479,000. Passion reports the bond investment as a long-term investment. Both companies calculate amortization on a straight-line basis.

2 The solutions to the self-study problems are at the end of the book, following Chapter 18.

Required:
Construct the eliminating entry for the bonds (including interest) at the following dates, first using the agency approach and then using the par-value method. Ignore income tax impacts.

a. December 31, 19x4
b. December 31, 19x6
c. December 31, 19x10

SELF-STUDY PROBLEM 12-3

On January 1, 19x5, the Power Company purchased 80% of the outstanding voting shares of the Spencer Company for $2,500,000 in cash. On that date, the Spencer Company had no-par common stock of $2,000,000 and retained earnings of $1,000,000. On January 1, 19x5, all of the identifiable assets and liabilities of Spencer had fair values that were equal to their carrying values except for:

1. A building that had a fair value of $600,000 less than its carrying value and a remaining useful life of ten years.
2. Long-term liabilities that have fair values of $500,000 less than their carrying values and that mature on December 31, 19x12.

Any goodwill that arises from the acquisition should be amortized over 40 years.

The income statements of the Power Company and the Spencer Company for the year ending December 31, 19x9, were as follows:

	Power	Spencer
Sales	$2,000,000	$ 900,000
Investment income	1,000,000	100,000
Total revenues	3,000,000	1,000,000
Cost of goods sold	1,300,000	500,000
Other operating expenses	500,000	200,000
Income tax expense	460,000	120,000
Total expenses	2,260,000	820,000
Net income before extraordinary items	740,000	180,000
Extraordinary gain (net of tax)	—	68,000
Net income	$ 740,000	$ 248,000

Additional Information:
1. On January 1, 19x6, the Spencer Company sold the Power Company a machine for $210,000 that it had purchased for $400,000 on December 31, 19x0. At the date of purchase, the machine had an estimated life of twenty years and no estimated salvage value. There is no change in these estimates on January 1, 19x6.
2. Both companies use the straight-line method to calculate all depreciation and amortization.

3. During 19x8, Power sold $500,000 of merchandise to Spencer, of which $100,000 remained in Spencer's December 31, 19x8, inventories. Also during 19x8, Spencer sold to Power $300,000 of merchandise, of which $70,000 remains in Power's December 31, 19x8, inventories.

4. During 19x9, Power had sales of $400,000 to Spencer of which $90,000 was not resold to parties outside the consolidated entity in 19x9, while Spencer sold Power $250,000 of merchandise, of which $60,000 was not resold in 19x9.

5. Intercompany inventory transactions are priced to provide Power with a gross profit of 30% of the sales price and Spencer with a gross profit of 40% of the sales price. Both companies use the first-in, first-out inventory flow assumption.

6. On September 1, 19x9, Spencer Company sold a parcel of land to Power Company for $150,000 that it had originally purchased for $65,000. The gain on the sale is considered an extraordinary item for reporting purposes.

7. During 19x9, Power declared and paid $250,000 in dividends, while Spencer Company declared and paid $40,000 in dividends and amounted to $68,000 net of tax.

8. The Power Company accounts for its investment in Spencer Company by the cost method.

9. Both companies pay income taxes at a rate of 40%.

Required:
Prepare a consolidated income statement for the Power Company and its subsidiary, the Spencer Company, for the year ending December 31, 19x9. Show supporting calculations for each figure in the consolidated income statement.
[SMA, adapted]

REVIEW QUESTIONS

12-1 Under what conditions is a profit on an intercompany sale considered to be **unrealized**?

12-2 Under what circumstances would an unrealized loss on an intercompany sale of inventory *not* be eliminated?

12-3 A fixed asset is sold by a subsidiary to its parent company at the asset's fair market value, which is less than the asset's carrying value on the subsidiary's books. Would the unrealized loss on the sale be eliminated upon consolidation? Explain.

12-4 Company P owns 60% of Company S1 and 90% of Company S2. S1 sells inventory to S2 at a profit of $10,000. All the goods are still in S2's inventory at year-end. By what amount should consolidated net income be adjusted to eliminate the unrealized profit?

12-5 Company IR owns 30% of Company IE1 and 40% of Company IE2. IE1 sells inventory to IE2 at a profit of $10,000. All the goods are still in IE2's inventory at year-end. By what amount should IR's equity-basis investment income be adjusted to eliminate the unrealized profit?

12-6 In what way is the profit on intercompany sales of depreciable assets **realized**?

12-7 Company IR owns 40% of Company IE. IE reported an extraordinary gain on its income statement. How should the extraordinary gain of IE affect IR's financial reporting for the year, under equity-method accounting?

12-8 Company P owns 70% of Company S. S reported an extraordinary loss on its income statement. How should S's extraordinary loss normally be reflected in P's consolidated financial statements?

12-9 Under what circumstances might an extraordinary item of a subsidiary *not* be shown as an extraordinary item on the consolidated income statement?

12-10 On consolidated income statements, the amount shown as a deduction from consolidated earnings for minority interest in earnings of subsidiaries is computed on the basis of the subsidiaries' net income before extraordinary items. Explain why the computation is based on income **before** rather than **after** extraordinary items.

12-11 When unrealized profits are eliminated upon consolidation, why is an adjustment normally made to income tax expense as well?

12-12 What is the offsetting account for adjustments to income tax expense that arise from the elimination of unrealized profit?

12-13 Under what conditions would an adjustment to income tax expense *not* be necessary when intercompany unrealized profits are eliminated?

12-14 Companies S1 and S2 are both subsidiaries of Company P. S2's income statement includes $10,000 of unrealized profit on sales to S1. S1 is taxed at a combined federal and provincial rate of 40%, while S2 is taxed at a combined rate of 50%. By how much should consolidated income tax expense be adjusted when P's consolidated statements are prepared?

12-15 Intercompany dividends are eliminated upon consolidation. Why is there no adjustment to income tax expense as a result of the dividend elimination?

12-16 Under what circumstances should provision be made in the consolidated statements for income taxes on the unremitted earnings of a subsidiary?

12-17 Parent Company holds debentures of Sub Company that were purchased by Parent as a part of the original issuance by Sub. What eliminations are necessary in preparing Parent's consolidated financial statements?

12-18 Parent Company holds bonds of its subsidiary, Sub Company, that were purchased on the open market at a substantial discount. Upon consolidation of Parent's financial statements, how should the difference in carrying values of the bonds on the two companies' books be reported?

12-19 Explain the difference in concept between the par-value and the agency approaches to eliminating intercorporate bond holdings.

12-20 "Substance over form" is an important qualitative criterion for external financial reporting. Which method of intercompany bond elimination better satisfies this criterion? Explain why.

CASE 12-1   Alkalyn Beverages Ltd.

Alkalyn Beverages Ltd. (AB) was federally incorporated in 1972. In the initial years, the company produced an orange drink for sale at sporting and entertainment events in western Canada. In 1979, operations were expanded to include sales to bars, restaurants, and fast-food outlets. To penetrate additional markets, AB started manufacturing a wide variety of soft drinks and acquired the distributorship of another company's cola syrup. Sold under the brand name, "Sun Brite," the soft drink sales were only moderately successful.

In 1982, a management review indicated that while sales of the new soft drink line had increased, AB's cost to manufacture was also greater than that of its competitors. Much of the profit was being made on the distribution of cola syrup.

In an attempt to improve profitability, the company entered the retail market in 1983. To finance the expansion, AB obtained funds from two sources, bank loans and its first public issue of shares. The funds were used to purchase a bottling plant in Vancouver and to provide working capital during the first year of operation. The retail operation was administered by a newly incorporated, wholly owned subsidiary, Sunbrite Flavours Ltd. (SF). In the first year, the company incurred a loss on its retail operations but subsequent years were profitable.

SF continued to expand until it had a nationwide bottling and distribution network. In major cities, the bottlers were wholly owned subsidiaries of SF; in smaller cities, the bottlers were independents who bottled other products as well. In all cases, AB sold its syrups to the bottlers.

In 1986, AB acquired 70% of the shares of Concentrated Vending Ltd. (CV), a manufacturer of soft drink vending machines, located in Windsor, Ontario. AB purchased CV at a price well below its proportionate book value, since CV had encountered financial difficulties. AB lent CV funds to finance a plant modernization program. AB contracted with the founders to continue as senior management since AB had no experience in the equipment manufacturing industry. The management contract stipulated that a bonus would be paid, amounting to 20% of income before taxes of CV, in each of the next five consecutive years. Although the plant modernization was successful, CV had difficulty selling enough machines to achieve a breakeven point.

Sales of soft drinks through vending machines were increasing rapidly. This was a segment of the market in which the AB group did not participate. Therefore, early in 1988, AB created a wholly owned subsidiary, VendSell Ltd. (VS). VS buys the machines from CV at regular retail price and then sells them to local operators with the condition that only AB products be sold in the machines. The intent was to place machines in as many locations as possible.

VS sells the majority of machines under conditional sales contracts, in which the buyer agrees to make an initial payment of $350 and payments of $75 per month for the next 48 months, for a total of $3,950. Machine maintenance is the responsibility of the operator. The payment plan was devised with three objectives in mind:

1. To place the maximum number of machines by the use of an easy payment plan
2. To defer payment of income tax by deducting the full cost of the machines when sold and deferring recognition of the revenue until the cash was collected
3. To assure that only AB products were used during the payment period, since title to the machine would not transfer until all payments have been made

The syrup and paper cups for the machines are purchased by the local operators from the bottler in the particular area, who in turn had purchased the syrup from AB. The operator is charged an amount equal to the cost to the bottler plus 20%.

During 1988, VS expects to buy 7,000 machines from CV at a price of $2,500 each. The machine currently cost CV $1,500 to manufacture. This cost to CV is significantly lower than in previous years. In order to supply VS, the volume of production in 1989 is expected to be twice that of 1987. As a result, CV expects to show a profit in 1988.

By the end of 1988, VS expects to sell 5,800 machines. The revenue from initial payments will amount of $2,030,000 and VS expects to receive total revenues of $3,117,500 from initial payments and installments in 1988.

In its annual report for 1987, AB reported after-tax earnings of $2,275,000 on consolidated revenue of $72,770,000. Since CV accounted for less than 10% of AB's consolidated assets, revenues, and income, no segmented information was presented in the 1988 annual report.

Within the management of AB there is disagreement over the proper accounting treatment for the activities of AB, VS, SF, and CV for 1988 and the effect on consolidation and reporting.

Required:
In August, 1988, you were engaged as an independent advisor. Prepare a report that:

a. outlines the major accounting and reporting issues faced by the company and its subsidiaries.
b. identifies alternative policies to deal with the issues outlined.
c. provides recommendations on the preferred policies.
[CICA, adapted]

CASE 12-2   Empire Investments Limited

Empire Investments Limited is a large Canadian public company that holds investments in four subsidiaries. The company and its subsidiaries all pay combined federal and provincial income taxes at the rate of 50%.

Three subsidiaries, A Sub Limited, B Sub Limited, and C Sub Limited, are all 100% owned; D Sub Limited is 60% owned.

A Sub Limited is in the publishing business. It publishes several trade magazines, a monthly family magazine, and some books, usually of a technical nature.

B Sub Limited prints and sells greeting cards. It also prints calendars, business cards, etc., on a contract basis. In addition, it prints the books published by A Sub Limited.

C Sub Limited has large forestry holdings in Canada. Most of the forests are used for pulp and paper production. The company manufactures many grades of paper and virtually all of the production is sold to A Sub Limited and B Sub Limited. C Sub Limited also produces lumber, much of which is sold to builders near its manufacturing plants, but about 20% of which is sold to D Sub Limited.

D Sub Limited is a real estate development company. It operates around two large cities and owns substantial tracts of land near those cities. Zoning by-laws require that the land be fully serviced before buildings are put up. Several years ago, the company started building houses, but because the zoning restrictions had led to a shortage of serviced land, it expanded its operations into the servicing of land. It then began servicing industrial lots and building industrial plants and buildings.

For the year ended June 30, 1988, consolidated financial statements had been presented to the shareholders accompanied by an audit report, which was unqualified. Reported consolidated net income was $500,000. Shortly after that year-end, CA was appointed auditor of Empire Investments Limited.

During the course of the audit of D Sub Limited for the year ended June 30, 1989, CA found that one of the company's major building contracts was construction of an office building for A Sub Limited. By June 30, 1989, $8,000,000 had been incurred by D Sub Limited in construction of the building, estimated to cost $10,000,000 on completion.

CA had known that A Sub Limited was planning a major expansion. Largely, the expansion consisted of converting A Sub Limited's monthly family magazine into a weekly news magazine, to make A Sub Limited more able to compete with certain large periodicals. It meant, however, that the company had to expand its facilities considerably. CA had been under the impression that no progress billings had yet been received with respect to the new building.

On checking into the matter further, CA found that part of the reason for this was that the building qualified for a government grant and that grants of the type involved are paid by the government on behalf of the owner of the building to the builder. On the strength of certain commitments made by A Sub Limited as to the ultimate cost of the building and the number of jobs that would be created, D Sub Limited had, in May, 1988, received $3,000,000 towards the grant, which was equal to 50% of the $6,000,000 cost incurred on the building to that date and 25% of the total contract price of $12,000,000. The building was 60% complete at that date.

Also, prior to June, 1988, D Sub Limited required more money to finance the construction. Instead of sending a progress billing to A Sub Limited, however, it was decided to obtain lumber from C Sub Limited for the houses under construction, but not to pay for it. The price charged to D Sub Limited was $4,500,000, which is the cost of the lumber to C Sub Limited plus a markup of 12.5%. The lumber shipments were received in the accounts of D Sub Limited by a charge to inventory and the credit was treated as a revenue item.

C Sub Limited then obtained an advance payment of $4,500,000 from A Sub Limited for the large quantities of paper that would be required when the news magazine went into production. This payment was recorded by A Sub Limited as prepaid expense.

D Sub Limited's accounting practice, unlike many development companies, was to present a balance sheet that segregated working capital items from non-working capital items. D Sub Limited used the percentage-of-completion basis of accounting.

No consolidation adjustments had been made in respect to the building for the year ended June 30, 1988, or the $4,500,000 shipment of lumber.

Required:
Outline the financial accounting and reporting issues that must be resolved in presenting consolidated financial statements for the year ended June 30, 1989, with comparative figures. State how these issues should be resolved and give the additional consolidating journal entries that should have been made at June 30, 1988. [CICA, adapted]

P12-1

In September, 19x6, Quest Ltd. issued a public tender offer for up to 70% of the outstanding common shares of Dudes Outfitters, Ltd. The offer was successful, and on January 2, 19x7, an exchange of shares took place by which Quest acquired 70% of Dudes' shares.

On December 31, 19x6, Quest's inventory included $80,000 in merchandise that had been acquired from Dudes. Dudes' gross margin was 40% of sales. During the year ending December 31, 19x7, Quest acquired another $220,000 in merchandise from Dudes, of which $100,000 was still in inventory at year-end. The 19x7 year-end inventory also still included $20,000 of the merchandise that had been acquired from Dudes in 19x6.

On January 10, 19x7, Dudes sold some display cases to Quest for $180,000. The display cases were carried on Dudes' books at a depreciated cost of $100,000, which also approximated fair value at the date of the business combination. Quest intends to depreciate the cases over five years on a straight-line basis, starting in 19x7.

Required:
Prepare the adjustments and eliminations for the intercompany transactions described above that would be required to prepare Quest Ltd's. consolidated financial statements on December 31, 19x7. Ignore income tax effects.

P12-2

Quest Ltd. and Dudes Outfitters, Ltd. (P12-1, above) are both taxed at a rate of 40%. The sale by Dudes of the display cases resulted in a current tax liability of $20,000 on the transaction. On its own income statement, Dudes reported the net-of-tax gain as an extraordinary item.

Required:
Prepare the adjustments called for in P12-1, *including* income tax effects.

P12-3

Dudes Outfitters, Ltd., is a 70% owned subsidiary of Quest Ltd. On January 10, 19x7, Dudes sold some display cases to Quest Ltd. for $180,000, recognizing a gain of $80,000 before tax and $60,000 after tax on the transaction. On its own income statement, Dudes reported the net-of-tax gain as an extraordinary item. Quest Ltd. depreciated the cases on a straight-line basis over five years, taking a full year's depreciation in 19x7.

On February 12, 19x10, Quest sold the display cases to an unaffiliated company for $100,000, incurring a tax liability of $8,000 on the sale.

Required:
a. Prepare the appropriate consolidated adjustments relating to the display cases for each year ending December 31, 19x7 through 19x10, ignoring income tax effects.
b. Prepare the appropriate consolidation adjustments to recognize the tax effect of the adjustments in requirement (a) for each year.

P12-4

On January 1, 19x3, Sub Ltd., 80% owned by Par Ltd., sold a building to Par Ltd. for $750,000. The building cost Sub $300,000 and was 60% depreciated (at 5% per year). Par will continue to depreciate the building on a straight-line basis over the 8 year remaining life.

Required:
Give the consolidation eliminating entries relating to this transaction for the years ended:
a. 19x3
b. 19x5
[CGA-Canada, adapted]

P12-5

On January 1, 19x1, the Partial Company acquires 70% of the outstanding voting shares of the Sum Company for $3,500,000 in cash. On this date, the Sum Company has $2,000,000 in no-par common stock outstanding and $2,000,000 in retained earnings. Any excess of cost over book value is to be recorded in the consolidated financial statements as goodwill and will be amortized over fourteen years. On December 31, 19x8, the balance sheets of the two companies are as follows:

	Balance Sheets — December 31, 19x8	
	Partial Company	Sum Company
Cash	$ 4,000,000	$ 1,000,000
Accounts receivable	6,000,000	2,000,000
Inventories	4,500,000	3,000,000
Investment in Sum	3,500,000	—
Plant and equipment (net)	7,000,000	5,000,000
Total assets	$25,000,000	$11,000,000

Liabilities	$ 5,000,000	$ 3,000,000
Common stock — no par	7,000,000	2,000,000
Retained earnings	13,000,000	6,000,000
Total equities	$25,000,000	$11,000,000

Additional Information:

1. Sum Company sells merchandise to the Partial Company at a price that provides Sum with a gross margin of 50% of the sales price. During 19x8, these sales amounted to $1,000,000. The December 31, 19x8, inventories of the Partial Company contain $200,000 of these purchases while the December 31, 19x7, inventories of Partial contained $100,000 in merchandise purchased from Sum.
2. At the end of 19x8, Partial owes Sum $50,000 for merchandise purchased on account. The account is non-interest-bearing.
3. On December 31, 19x5, the Partial Company sold equipment to the Sum Company for $500,000. At the time of the sale, the equipment had a net book value in Partial's records of $400,000. The remaining useful life of the asset on this date was ten years.

Required:

Prepare a consolidated balance sheet for the Partial Company and its subsidiary Sum Company at December 31, 19x8.

[SMA]

P12-6

On January 1, 19x5, the Perkins Company purchased 70% of the outstanding voting shares of the Staton Company for $850,000 in cash. On that date, the Staton Company had retained earnings of $400,000 and no-par common stock of $500,000. On the acquisition date, the identifiable assets and liabilities of the Staton Company had fair values that were equal to their carrying values except for equipment, which had a fair value $200,000 greater than its carrying value, and long-term liabilities, which had fair values that were $100,000 greater than their carrying values. The equipment had a remaining useful life of ten years on January 1, 19x5, and the long-term liabilities mature on December 31, 19x14. Both companies use the straight-line method to calculate all depreciation and amortization.

The trial balance of the Perkins Company and the Staton Company on December 31, 19x9, were as follows:

	Perkins	Staton
Cash	$ 50,000	$ 10,000
Current receivables	250,000	100,000
Inventories	3,000,000	520,000
Equipment (net)	6,150,000	2,500,000
Buildings (net)	2,600,000	500,000
Investment in Staton (at cost)	850,000	—
Cost of goods sold	2,000,000	400,000
Depreciation expense	300,000	100,000
Other expenses	200,000	150,000
Dividends declared	200,000	20,000
Total debits	$15,600,000	$4,300,000

Current liabilities	$ 300,000	$ 170,000
Long-term liabilities	4,000,000	1,100,000
No-par common stock	3,000,000	500,000
Retained earnings	4,500,000	1,600,000
Sales revenue	3,500,000	900,000
Other revenues	300,000	30,000
Total credits	$15,600,000	$4,300,000

Additional Information:

1. Perkins carries its investment in Staton on its books by the cost method.
2. During 19x8, Perkins sold Staton $100,000 worth of merchandise, of which $60,000 was resold by Staton in the year. During 19x9, Perkins had sales of $200,000 to Staton, of which 40% was resold by Staton. Intercompany sales are priced to provide Perkins with a gross margin of 30% of the sales price. Both companies use the first-in, first-out cost-flow assumption.
3. On December 31, 19x8, Perkins had in its inventories $150,000 of merchandise purchased from Staton during 19x8. On December 31, 19x9, Perkins had in its ending inventories $100,000 of merchandise that had resulted from purchases of $250,000 from Staton during 19x9. Intercompany sales are priced to provide Staton with a gross margin of 60% of the sale price.
4. Liabilities resulting from intercompany inventory purchases were as follows on December 31, 19x9:

    Staton owes Perkins $50,000
    Perkins owes Staton $25,000

5. On January 1, 19x8, Staton sold a building to Perkins for $730,000. The building had the following history on Staton's records:

    Purchase date: December 31, 19x5
    Purchase price: $480,000
    Estimated life at acqusition: 30 years
    Estimated salvage at acquisition: $30,000

    The estimates are still applicable on January 1, 19x8.

6. Any goodwill arising from the business combination is to be amortized over 30 years.

Required:

Prepare, for the Perkins Company and its subsidiary, the Staton Company, the following:
a. The consolidated income statement for the year ending December 31, 19x9.
b. The consolidated balance sheet at December 31, 19x9.
c. A verification or independent calculation of the consolidated retained earnings balance at December 31, 19x9.
d. A verification or independent calculation of the minority interest as shown on the consolidated balance sheet at December 31, 19x9.
[SMA]

P12-7

On January 1, 19x3, the Harris Company purchased 70,000 of the Smith Company's outstanding voting shares at a price of $330 per share. On that date, the

Smith Company had common stock (par $100) of $10 million, paid in capital in excess of par of $6 million, and retained earnings of $14 million. At the time of this acquisition, the fair values of the Smith Company's identifiable assets and liabilities were equal to their carrying values; however, the Smith Company had developed a valuable patent that had not been recorded on the company's books. On January 1, 19x3, it was estimated that this patent had a fair value of $2 million and a remaining useful life of ten years. If any goodwill arises on this business combination, it is to be amortized over the maximum permissible period of 40 years.

On January 1, 19x6, the Smith Company sold a depreciable asset to the Harris Company for $880,000. The Smith Company had purchased the asset on January 1, 19x1, at a cost of $900,000, and had subsequently depreciated the asset using the straight-line method over an estimated life of 30 years. There was no change in the estimated life on January 1, 19x6.

Between January 1, 19x3, and January 1, 19x9, the Smith Company had earnings of $6 million and paid dividends of $3 million. The Harris Company uses the cost method to carry its investment in the Smith Company. On January 1, 19x9, the retained earnings of the Harris Company amounted to $40 million.

The income statements for the year ended December 31, 19x9, of the two companies are as follows:

	Harris	Smith
Revenues	$10,000,000	$2,000,000
Cost of goods sold	6,000,000	1,000,000
Other expenses	2,000,000	600,000
Total expenses	8,000,000	1,600,000
Net income	$ 2,000,000	$ 400,000

During 19x9, the Harris Company paid dividends of $1,000,000 while the Smith Company paid dividends of $200,000. The revenues of the Harris Company contain the dividends received from the Smith Company. Also during 19x9, 40% of Smith's revenues resulted from sales to the Harris Company. Half of this merchandise remains in the ending inventories of the Harris Company. On January 1, 19x9, the inventories of Harris contained purchases from Smith that were sold during 19x9 for $150,000. All intercompany sales are priced to provide the selling company with a gross margin of 50% of the sales price. The Harris Company pays income tax at a rate of 30%; the rate for the Smith Company is 40%.

Required:

a. Compute the following balances for inclusion in the consolidated balance sheet at December 31, 19x9:
   1. The net book value of the patent that was owned by Smith Company when the Smith shares were acquired by the Harris Company
   2. The net book value of the depreciable asset that Smith sold to Harris
   3. Goodwill
b. Prepare a consolidated income statement for the year ended December 31, 19x9, for the Harris Company and its subsidiary, the Smith Company.
c. Prepare a consolidated statement of retained earnings for the year ended December 31, 19x9, for the Harris Company and its subsidiary, the Smith Company.
d. Compute the minority interest in the consolidated net assets of the Smith Company at December 31, 19x9.

[SMA, adapted]

P12-8

Parent Ltd. owns 70% of the voting shares of Sub Ltd. During 19x8, Sub Ltd. sold inventory costing $320,000 to Parent Ltd. for $400,000. At December 31, 19x8, Parent Ltd. still had $150,000 of these goods in its inventory, and had not yet paid for $240,000 of the goods. All of the remaining goods were sold in 19x9.

Sub Ltd. also sold a piece of land (cost of $94,000) to Parent Ltd. on July 1, 19x8, for $130,000, for which Parent Ltd. had issued Sub Ltd. a five-year, 10% per annum note. The interest will be paid on July 1, 19x13.

Sub Ltd. pays income tax at a 40% rate; Parent Ltd.'s current tax rate is 45%. Both companies account for income tax in accordance with the *CICA Handbook*.

Required:
a. Prepare the eliminating entries as they would appear on the consolidated worksheet for 19x8 and 19x9, as related to the foregoing information. Assume that Sub Ltd. was taxed in 19x8 on its gain on the sale of land.
b. Assuming that Sub Ltd. earned $340,000 after taxes during 19x8 and $440,000 after taxes during 19x9, calculate the minority interest in the earnings of Sub Ltd.
c. Assume instead that Sub Ltd. will not be taxed on the sale of the land until 19x13. How will this change in assumption affect your answers to the two preceding requirements?

[CGA-Canada, adapted]

12-9

A Ltd. owns 80% of the outstanding shares of B Ltd. A Ltd. also owns 70% of the shares of X Ltd. During the year, 19x9, A sold $400,000 (cost) of goods (widgets) to B at a 30% markup. X sold $300,000 (cost) of goods to A at a 25% markup.

A sold a piece of land (cost $90,000) to B for $30,000.

On October 1, 19x9, X sold land (cost $70,000) and a building (cost $100,000) to A for $300,000; 40% of the price was allocated to land and 60% of the price was allocated to building. The building had five years of expected life at October 1, 19x9, and was 30% depreciated at that time.

The $300,000 was unpaid at year-end and A had agreed to pay $8,000 interest on the unpaid amount.

An inventory count showed that 20% of the widgets that B had purchased from A were unsold at December 31, 19x9. Seventy percent of the gadgets that A had purchased from X were also unsold.

Required:
Assume that A Ltd. uses the cost method of keeping its accounts.
a. Prepare the eliminating entries on the working papers that would be required at December 31, 19x9, to prepare the consolidated financial statements.
b. Calculate the effect on the minority interest; by how much would the income to each minority interest be changed? Keep the two subsidiaries separate.

[CGA-Canada]

P12-10

Beluga Ltd. is a wholly owned subsidiary of Orcas Ltd. On January 1, 19x1, Beluga issued $200,000 of 5%, ten-year bonds payable for $240,000. The interest is paid annually, on December 31. On January 1, 19x8, Orcas Ltd. purchased $50,000 face value of the Beluga bonds for $41,000.

Required:

a. Give the eliminating entries relating to the bonds as they would appear on the consolidated worksheet at December 31, 19x8.

b. Assume instead that Beluga is 75% owned by Orcas. Give the eliminating entries for the bonds at December 31, 19x8, using:
1. agency method
2. par-value method

[CGA-Canada, adapted]

P12-11

Poseidon Ltd. (P Ltd.) bought 80% of the voting shares of Submarine Ltd. (S Ltd.) for $470,000 at January 1, 19x2. S Ltd. had the following balance sheet at that date:

Submarine Ltd.
Balance Sheet
January 1, 19x2

Cash	$ 10,000
Accounts receivable	30,000
Inventory	50,000
Land	150,000
Plant and equipment, net	200,000
	$440,000
Current liabilities	$ 20,000
Bonds — 20-year, 15% interest	100,000
Common shares	100,000
Retained earnings	220,000
	$440,000

The fair values on January 1, 19x2, of S Ltd.'s assets were:

Inventory	$ 90,000
Land	$220,000
Plant and equipment, net	$170,000

The bonds on S Ltd.'s balance sheet were issued on January 1, 19x2, at face value; interest is paid July 1 and December 31.

All inventory on the books of S at January 1, 19x2, was sold during the year. P sold $400,000 (cost of goods) to S for $500,000 during 19x2, and 20% of the inventory was on hand at the end of the year. P sold land to S (cost $30,000) for $90,000. P purchased $60,000 face value of S's bonds on July 2, 19x2, for $64,000. The premium will be amortized straight-line over the remaining life of the bonds. Any goodwill will be amortized over the maximum period allowable. S's plant and equipment have ten years (straight-line) remaining.

S had a net income of $100,000 for 19x2 and paid no dividends.

The balance sheets for the two companies at December 31, 19x2 are:

	P Ltd.	S Ltd.
Cash	$ 70,000	$ 15,000
Accounts receivable	100,000	45,000
Inventory	240,000	80,000
Land	600,000	240,000
Plant and equipment, net	800,000	250,000
Investment in subsidiary equity*	550,000	—
Investment in bonds of subsidiary	63,898	—
	$2,423,898	$630,000
Current liabilities	$ 80,000	$110,000
Bonds	—	100,000
Common shares	1,000,000	100,000
Retained earnings	1,343,898	320,000
	$2,423,898	$630,000

*Includes only the parent's share of subsidiary net income.

Required:
Calculate the balances of the following selected accounts, at December 31, 19x2, which would appear on the consolidated balance sheet.
a. Inventory
b. Land
c. Plant and equipment
d. Bonds payable
e. Retained earnings
[CGA-Canada]

P12-12

On January 1, 19x14, the Pentil Company purchased 90% of the outstanding voting shares of the Sun Company for $300,000. Sun's assets and liabilities all had fair values that were equal to their carrying values. The $60,000 excess of purchase price over 90% of the book values of the Sun Company's net assets was allocated to goodwill and is being amortized over twenty years. Between January 1, 19x14 and January 1, 19x20, the Sun Company earned $100,000 and paid dividends of $20,000. Both companies use the straight-line method to calculate depreciation and amortization.

Additional Information:
1. On January 1, 19x10, the Sun Company purchased a machine for $100,000 that had an estimated useful life of twenty years. On January 1, 19x15, the Sun Company sold the machine to the Pentil Company for $60,000. The estimated useful life of the machine remains unchanged at a total of twenty years (fifteen years from January 1, 19x15).
2. During 19x20, the Sun Company had sales of merchandise in the amount of $200,000 to the Pentil Company of which $50,000 remains in the December 31, 19x20 inventories of the Pentil Company. The Pentil Company had no sales to the Sun Company during 19x20, but had sales of $100,000 to the Sun Company in 19x19. Of these sales, $30,000 remained in the December 31, 19x19 inventories of the Sun Company. Intercompany sales are priced to provide the selling company with a 40% gross profit on sales prices.
3. On September 1, 19x20, the Sun Company sold a piece of land to the Pentil

Company for $40,000. The land had been purchased for $25,000. The gain on this land is not considered extraordinary for reporting purposes.

4. During 19x20, the Sun Company declared dividends of $3,000 and the Pentil Company declared dividends of $25,000.

5. During 19x20, the Sun Company paid the Pentil Company $7,000 in management fees.

6. On July 1, 19x20, the Pentil Company lent the Sun Company $80,000 for five years at an annual interest rate of 10%. Interest is paid on July 1 of each year for which the loan is outstanding.

The Pentil Company carries its investment in the Sun Company by the cost method. On this date, the income statements of the Pentil Company and the Sun company for the year ending December 31, 19x20, are as follows:

	Pentil	Sun
Merchandise sales	$2,000,000	$1,000,000
Investment income	50,000	
Other revenue	40,000	60,000
Total revenues	2,090,000	1,060,000
Cost of goods sold	1,200,000	700,000
Depreciation expense	300,000	200,000
Selling and administrative	400,000	150,000
Total expenses	1,900,000	1,050,000
Income before extraordinary items	190,000	10,000
Loss on sales of investments		(26,000)
Net income (loss)	$ 190,000	$ (16,000)

Required:

a. Prepare the consolidated income statement for the Pentil Company and its subsidiary, the Sun Company, for the year ending December 31, 19x20.

b. Assume that the Pentil Company does not consolidate its investment in the Sun Company and that the reason for the exclusion from consolidation is such that the equity method of accounting is appropriate. Provide a detailed calculation of the Pentil Company's ordinary and extraordinary investment income for the year ending December 31, 19x20.

[SMA]

P12-13

Your assistant is preparing consolidated financial statements at December 31, 19x6, for your company and has come to you with the following problems:

1. Subone Ltd., a 70% owned subsidiary, sold land and buildings to Parent Ltd. for $1,180,000 ($300,000 was allocated to the land). The land cost Subone Ltd. $200,000; the building cost $1,400,000 and was 45% (i.e., nine years) depreciated at the date of sale. Parent Ltd. took a full year's depreciation on the building and will depreciate it over the original remaining life. Subone Ltd. took no depreciation on the building in 19x6.

2. Subtwo Ltd., a 90% owned subsidiary, purchased $600,000 of Parent Ltd.'s bonds on July 1, 19x6, in the open market for $680,000. The bonds have a 12% interest rate, which will be paid on January 5, 19x7, and will be due on January 1, 19x10. All consolidated income statement adjustments arising from intercompany bond transactions are to be allocated between the two parties.

3. On December 1, 19x6, Subthree Ltd. split their stock three to one. Prior to the split, Parent Ltd. owned 90% of the shares (90,000 shares) of Subthree Ltd. and had the account "Investment in Subthree Ltd." on the books at $2,400,000 cost basis.

Ignore income taxes.

Additional Information:

	At December 31, 19x5		At December 31, 19x6	
	Subone Ltd.	Parent Ltd.	Subone Ltd.	Parent Ltd.
Land	$4,000,000	$8,100,000	$4,200,000	$8,400,000
Buildings, net	5,200,000	9,320,000	4,982,000	9,178,000
Depreciation expense	460,000	530,000	420,000	570,000

	At December 31, 19x5		At December 31, 19x6	
	Subtwo Ltd.	Parent Ltd.	Subtwo Ltd.	Parent Ltd.
Investment in bonds	—	—	$ 668,571	—
Interest income (total from all sources)	—	—	111,000	—
Bonds payable	—	$2,000,000	—	$2,000,000
Discount on bonds	—	(130,000)	—	(97,500)
Interest expense (total on all debt)	—	368,070	—	392,462

	During 19x6	
	Subone Ltd.	Subtwo Ltd.
Net income	($421,000)	$400,000
Dividends	—	20,000

Required:
a. For each item in parts (1) and (2), calculate the amounts that would appear on the consolidated financial statements for 19x6.
b. For problem (3), calculate the amounts that would be in the investment in subsidiary account and the journal entries that would appear *on the books of Parent Ltd.* If no journal entries are needed, *explain why*.
c. Calculate for Subone Ltd. and Subtwo Ltd. the amount for minority interest that would appear on the consolidated income statement for 19x6.

[CGA-Canada]

P12-14

On April 14, 19x3, Gerhard, Inc. (GI) purchased 60% of the shares of Hans, Ltd. (HL). The acquisition was accomplished by means of a public tender offer of one preferred share of GI plus $10 cash for each share of HL. Immediately before the tender offer, GI preferred shares were trading for $25 and HL common shares were trading at $32. As a result of the offer, GI acquired 120,000 of HL's 200,000 outstanding common shares.

Subsequent to the acquisition, HL (at GI's request) had its land holdings appraised and also estimated the current replacement cost of its depreciable fixed assets by using various specific price indices. The land was appraised at $1,000,000 in excess of its carrying value on HL's books, and the depreciable assets were estimated to have a replacement cost (depreciated) that was $600,000 higher than their book values. The average remaining life of the depreciable assets was twenty years from January 1, 19x3. GI's policy is to take a full year's depreciation in the year of acquisition of a depreciable asset. The book value of HL's common share equity at the date of GI's share acquisition was $5 million. GI amortizes goodwill over 40 years.

Intercompany sales occurred routinely in each year. The intercompany sales since 19x2 were as follows:

	GI to HL		HL to GI	
	Total	End. inventory	Total	End. inventory
19x2	$300,000	$ 50,000	$ 90,000	—
19x3, before April 14	90,000	—	9,000	—
19x3, after April 14	330,000	30,000	42,000	$10,000
19x4	450,000	60,000	90,000	20,000
19x5	510,000	100,000	210,000	40,000
19x6	600,000	20,000	300,000	30,000
19x7	810,000	160,000	270,000	40,000

Both GI and HL set their prices at 100% above cost.

In 19x7, HL sold a parcel of land for a pre-tax gain of $500,000. The cost of the land to HL was $100,000, and it had been appraised at $250,000 in 19x3 during the general valuation of HL's assets. The gain, net of $100,000 in capital gains tax, is considered to be an extraordinary gain for HL. The purchaser of the land was a real estate development corporation not related to GI or HL in any way.

Required:
Prepare the consolidated income statement and balance sheet for Gerhard, Inc. at December 31, 19x7. Adjust for any income tax effects that arise upon consolidation. The tax rate for both companies is 40%.

Trial Balances
December 31, 19x7
Dr. (Cr.)

	Gerhard, Inc.	Hans, Ltd.
Cash	$ 100,000	$ 500,000
Accounts receivable	700,000	1,200,000
Inventories	400,000	300,000
Land	—	5,000,000
Depreciable fixed assets (net)	700,000	3,000,000
Investment in Hans, Ltd. (at cost)	4,200,000	—
Other investments	1,200,000	450,000
Accounts payable	(320,000)	(200,000)
Bonds payable	(1,500,000)	—
Future income taxes	(300,000)	(700,000)
Preferred shares (10% dividend, cumulative)	(3,000,000)	(1,000,000)
Common shares	(1,000,000)	(3,000,000)
Retained earnings	(1,000,000)	(4,500,000)
Dividends paid	700,000	300,000
Sales	(4,800,000)	(6,000,000)
Cost of sales	3,200,000	4,000,000
Other operating expenses	600,000	500,000
Income tax expense	400,000	600,000
Gain on sale of land (net)	—	(400,000)
Dividend income	(280,000)	(50,000)
	$ 0	$ 0

P12-15

Cebeuq Ltd. has a 70% owned subsidiary, Awatto Ltd., with whom it conducted the following transactions during 19x9:

1. Purchased $70,000 of merchandise from Awatto Ltd. (cost Awatto Ltd. $40,000).
2. Sold merchandise to Awatto Ltd. for $150,000 at 20% markup on cost.
3. Sold land to Awatto Ltd. (cost $80,000) for $1.
4. Purchased equipment on July 1, 19x9, from Awatto Ltd. for $150,000, (cost $150,000, 30% depreciated to date of sale, 10% per year straight-line). Cebeuq Ltd. recorded no depreciation.
5. Cebeuq Ltd. purchased $100,000 face value of ten-year bonds (four years left to redemption) for $96,000. The bonds were on the books of Awatto Ltd. at par. The interest rate is 10% but was not paid during the year. (Assume the bonds were held by Cebeuq Ltd. for the entire fiscal period.)
6. At the end of the year, Cebeuq Ltd. had 30% of the intercompany merchandise on hand and Awatto Ltd. had 10% of the intercompany merchandise on hand.
7. Awatto Ltd. earned $340,000 during the year and paid $50,000 in dividends.

Required:
Prepare the eliminating entries that would be required on the working papers leading to consolidated financial statements at the fiscal year-end, December 31, 19x9.
[CGA-Canada]

P12-16

On January 1, 19x5, Paco Ltd. purchased 70% of the common shares of Sco Ltd. for $506,100.

Financial data for Sco Ltd. are as follows:

Sco Ltd.
Balance Sheet
January 1, 19x5

	Book Value	Fair Market Value
Cash	$ 56,000	$ 56,000
Accounts receivable	102,000	108,000
Inventory	197,000	180,000
Fixed assets, net	750,000	700,000
	$1,105,000	
Current liabilities	$ 140,000	$140,000
Long-term liabilities		
Bonds payable at 12% interest	300,000	300,000
Bond discount	(60,000)	(60,000)
Preferred shares	100,000	
Contributed surplus on preferred		
shares	75,000	
Common shares	200,000	
Retained earnings	350,000	
	$1,105,000	

Additional Information:
1. Accounts receivable will be collected within the year.
2. Inventory is on the FIFO method and has a turnover of two times per year.
3. The fixed assets are being written off over ten years on a straight-line basis.
4. Any goodwill on the purchase will be amortized over twenty years on a straight-line basis.
5. The bond discount is being amortized over the remaining ten years on a straight-line basis. Interest is payable semi-annually.
6. The preferred shares are non-cumulative, non-participating and redeemable at par ($100) plus a $2 premium.

During the year the consolidated entity had the following intercompany transactions:

1. Sco Ltd. sold a building that had a cost of $300,000, and had accumulated depreciation of $180,000 at the date of sale, to Paco Ltd. for $195,000 cash. (This building was being depreciated over ten years straight-line with no residual value, but no depreciation had been recorded for the year 19x5 to the date of sale.) It is company policy that assets receive a full year's depreciation in the year of acquisition and none in the year of disposal. It is also company policy that the acquiring company amortize the asset over the remaining life of the asset.
2. On *July 1, 19x5*, Paco Ltd. purchased *one-half* of the bonds payable of Sco Ltd. for $107,250. It is company policy that the *purchaser* be allocated any gain or loss on an intercompany transaction of this nature.

3. On September 1, 19x5, Paco Ltd. sold land costing $135,000 to Sco Ltd. for $175,000.

Financial statements of Paco Ltd. and Sco Ltd. as at December 31, 19x5 are:

Balance Sheets
December 31, 19x5

	Paco Ltd.	Sco Ltd.
Cash	$ 145,500	$ 85,000
Accounts receivable	300,000	200,000
Inventory	500,000	400,000
Bond investment	109,500	–
Fixed assets, net	1,000,000	800,000
Investment in subsidiary (on cost basis)	506,100	–
	$2,561,100	$1,485,000
Current liabilities	$ 100,000	$ 331,000
Long-term liabilities		
Bonds payable at 12% interest	–	300,000
Bond discount	–	(54,000)
Preferred shares	–	100,000
Contributed surplus on preferred shares	–	75,000
Common shares	400,000	200,000
Retained earnings	2,061,100	533,000
	$2,561,100	$1,485,000

Income Statements
Year Ended December 31, 19x5

	Paco Ltd.	Sco Ltd.
Sales	$900,000	$800,000
Cost of goods sold	500,000	500,000
	400,000	300,000
Less:		
Depreciation	(80,000)	(70,000)
Interest expense	–	(42,000)
Other expenses	(100,000)	(80,000)
Plus:		
Interest income on bonds	11,250	–
Gain on sale of land	40,000	–
Gain on sale of building	–	75,000
Net income	$271,250	$183,000

Required:

a. Calculate the consolidated goodwill that would appear on the consolidated balance sheet at December 31, 19x5.

b. Prepare the consolidated income statement for the year 19x5.

c. Calculate the following as they would appear on the consolidated balance sheet at December 31, 19x5:

1. Inventory
2. Fixed assets, net
3. Bond discount
4. Minority interest (Be precise.)

[CGA-Canada]

P12-17

On January 1, 19x3, the Portly Company purchased 75% of the Slim Company at a cost of $4,500,000. On that date, the net identifiable assets of the Slim Company had carrying values of $5,500,000. All the assets and liabilities of the Slim Company had carrying values that were equal to their fair values, except from plant and equipment that had a fair value $200,000 greater than its carrying value, and long-term liabilities that had a fair value $100,000 less than their carrying value. The plant and equipment had a remaining useful life of fifteen years and is being depreciated by the straight-line method. The long-term liabilities mature on January 1, 19x9. Goodwill, if any, is to be amortized over a period of 40 years.

On December 31, 19x4, the Slim Company issued 8% coupon bonds payable with a par value of $500,000. The bonds are sold at 105% and mature on December 31, 19x14. On January 1, 19x7, the Portly Company purchased one-half of these bonds in the open market for $230,000 in cash.

On January 1, 19x5, the Slim Company sold a patent to the Portly Company for $300,000. The carrying value of this patent on the books of the Slim Company on this date is $400,000 and its remaining useful life is five years.

The income statements of the two companies for the year ending December 31, 19x7, are as follows:

	Portly	Slim
Total revenues	$3,200,000	$1,400,000
Cost of goods sold	2,000,000	700,000
Other expenses	500,000	300,000
Total expenses	2,500,000	1,000,000
Net income	$ 700,000	$ 400,000

Additional Information:
1. During 19x7, the Slim Company sold merchandise to the Portly Company for $200,000. Of this merchandise, $100,000 was still in the inventories of the Portly Company on December 31, 19x7. On December 31, 19x6, the inventories of the Portly Company contained merchandise purchased from the Slim Company for $75,000. All of the Slim Company's sales to the Portly Company were priced to provide a gross margin on sales prices of 20%.
2. During 19x7, the Portly Company sold merchandise to the Slim Company for $500,000. All of this merchandise has been resold by the Slim Company to individuals outside the consolidated entity. This merchandise was priced to provide the Portly Company with a gross margin on sales prices of 25%.
3. The Portly Company carries its investment in the Slim Company at cost.
4. During 19x7, the Slim Company declared and paid dividends of $120,000 while the Portly Company declared and paid dividends of $200,000.
5. Both Portly and Slim are merchandising companies. As a result, cost of goods sold consists entirely of merchandise that has been purchased and resold.

All of their other types of expenses have been aggregated under the heading of other expenses.

Required:
The consolidated income statement for the year ending December 31, 19x7, for the Portly Company and its subsidiary, the Slim Company, is being prepared to facilitate this process. You are to provide detailed calculations for each of the following:

a. Consolidated total revenue. (Any gain on the intercompany bond purchase would be included here.)
b. Consolidated cost of goods sold.
c. Consolidated other expenses. (Any loss on the intercompany bond purchase would be included here.)
d. The minority interest to be disclosed in the consolidated income statement for the year ending December 31, 19x7.
e. Consolidated net income for the year ending December 31, 19x7. This calculation should be independent of the expenses and revenues calculated in the preceding parts of this question.

[SMA, adapted]

P12-18

On January 1, 19x1, Green Inc. purchased 80% of the shares of Red Corp. for $3,000,000. On that date, Red Corp.'s assets had fair values that were the same as their book values except for inventory, which was worth $100,000 less than book value, temporary investments that were worth $700,000 more than book value, and bonds payable that had a fair value $200,000 greater than their book value. The January 1, 19x1, shareholders' equity of Red Corp. totaled $3,000,000, consisting of $1,000,000 in common shares and $2,000,000 of retained earnings.

On December 31, 19x5, the post-closing trial balances of the two companies were as follows:

	Green Inc.	Red Corp.
Cash and current receivables	$ 900,000	$ 400,000
Inventories	400,000	200,000
Temporary investments	—	1,100,000
Property, plant, and equipment (net)	2,100,000	3,500,000
Investment in Red Corp. (at cost)	3,000,000	—
	$6,400,000	$5,200,000
Accounts payable	$ 600,000	$ 100,000
Bonds payable	1,200,000	800,000
Future income taxes	500,000	300,000
Common shares	1,500,000	1,000,000
Retained earnings	2,600,000	3,000,000
	$6,400,000	$5,200,000

In 19x3, Red Corp. sold part of its temporary investments. The investments sold included some that had had a fair value in excess of cost of $400,000 on January 1, 19x1. The proceeds from the sale were $1,000,000. Tax of $120,000 was paid on the sale.

At the beginning of 19x4, Red Corp. sold to Green Inc. a machine that Red Corp. had purchased in 19x1 for $700,000 and that had a book value at the time of the sale to Green Inc. of $490,000. The machine had an estimated remaining useful life of seven years from the date of the intercorporate sale. The machine was sold to Green Inc. for $700,000, its estimated fair value at the time of the sale.

At December 31, 19x4, Green Inc. had merchandise in its inventory that had been purchased from Red Corp. at $60,000 above the cost to Red Corp. Red Corp. had goods in its inventory that had been purchased from Green Inc. at $80,000 above the cost of the goods to Green Inc.

During 19x5, sales to Green Inc. from Red Corp. totaled $2,000,000, of which 30% was in Green Inc.'s ending inventory. Sales to Red Corp. from Green Inc. were $1,400,000, all of which had been resold by Red Corp. during the year. Intercompany sales were priced to yield a gross margin of 100% of cost.

During 19x5, Red Corp. declared and paid $120,000 in dividends. Green Inc. credited the dividends received from Red Corp. to dividend income. Both companies use the straight-line method for all depreciation and amortization. Inventories are accounted for on the FIFO basis. The tax rate is 40%. Green Inc. amortizes goodwill over 40 years. The Red Corp. bonds mature on December 31, 19x8.

Required:
Prepare a consolidated balance sheet for Green Inc. at December 31, 19x5, with supporting schedules for all calculations.

P12-19

The following are extracts from the consolidated working papers of Pinch Inc. for the year ended December 31, 19x6, prior to income tax adjustments.

	Pinch Inc.	Steele Inc.	Consolidated
Cash	$ 10,000	$ 3,850	$ 13,850
Accounts receivable	248,007	169,800	342,807
Inventories (at cost)	109,600	46,900	142,500
Land	18,900	11,500	30,400
Building (net)	46,980	32,000	90,230
Machinery (net)	43,320	12,100	56,935
Investment in 12% bonds	100,000	—	100,000
Investment in Steele	118,193	—	—
Goodwill	—	—	4,375
	$659,000	$276,150	$ 781,097
Current liabilities	$219,500	$ 51,700	$ 196,200
Notes payable	50,000	—	50,000
Customer advances	48,000	3,800	51,800
Minority interest	—	—	20,665
Common stock	150,000	100,000	150,000
Retained earnings	227,500	120,650	312,432
	$695,000	$276,150	$ 781,097

Sales	$969,900	$414,300	$1,259,200
Cost of goods sold	824,415	331,440	1,019,855
Gross profit	145,485	82,860	239,345
Operating expenses:			
Selling	67,890	29,400	98,035
General & administrative	39,620	15,500	55,120
Total operating expenses	107,510	44,900	153,155
Operating income	37,975	37,960	86,190
Interest income	12,000	—	12,000
Investment income	37,800	—	—
Income before income taxes	87,775	37,960	98,190
Income taxes	36,860	9,460	46,320
Net income before minority interest	50,915	28,500	51,870
Less minority interest	—	—	3,950
Net income	$ 50,915	$ 28,500	$ 47,920
Opening retained earnings	$221,585	$134,150	$ 309,512
Net income	50,915	28,500	47,920
Dividends	(45,000)	(42,000)	(45,000)
Closing retained earnings	$227,500	$120,650	$ 312,432

Additional Information:
1. Pinch Inc. acquired 90% of the voting shares of Steele Inc. on the open market on January 1, 19x2. At that time, all the assets and liabilities of Steele Inc. were recorded at fair market value, except for its building. Both Pinch Inc. and Steele Inc. depreciate their buildings on a straight-line basis over twenty years. The buildings of both Pinch Inc. and Steele Inc. each had an estimated remaining useful life of fifteen years on January 1, 19x2. Pinch Inc. decided to amortize goodwill over the maximum allowable period. No acquisitions or disposals of buildings have occurred since 19x2 in either company.
2. On December 31, 19x5, Pinch Inc. sold a machine to Steele Inc. The machine had a remaining useful life of four years at that date. Both Pinch Inc. and Steele Inc. depreciate machinery on a straight-line basis over five years.
3. In 19x6, as in prior years, Steele Inc. sold merchandise to Pinch Inc. Even though Steele Inc. was a subsidiary of Pinch Inc., Steele Inc. still earned its normal gross profit on these sales. On December 31, 19x6, Pinch Inc. owed Steele Inc. a balance on these sales.

Required:
a. Is Pinch's investment in Steele Inc. accounted for under the cost or the equity method? Support your answer.
b. Determine the following amounts, showing all calculations:
   1. the goodwill at the acquisition date
   2. the fair market value of Steele Inc.'s building at the acquisition date
   3. Steele Inc.'s retained earnings at the acquisition date
   4. the intercompany gain or loss on the sale of machinery
   5. the intercompany sales
   6. the profit in the ending inventory
   7. the profit in opening inventory
   8. the intercompany debt

c. Provide an independent calculation for (ignoring tax effects):
   1. consolidated net income of $47,920
   2. minority interest of $20,665
[SMA]

P12-20

On January 2, 19x3, Prague Limited acquired 80% of the outstanding voting shares of Sofia Limited for $1,600,000 in cash. The balance sheet of Sofia Limited and the fair values of its identifiable assets and liabilities were as follows:

	Book Value	Fair Value
ASSETS:		
Cash	$ 100,000	$ 100,000
Accounts receivable	300,000	300,000
Inventory	600,000	662,500
Land	800,000	900,000
Building (net)	1,000,000	1,200,000
Patents (net)	200,000	150,000
Total assets	$3,000,000	
LIABILITIES AND SHAREHOLDERS' EQUITY:		
Accounts payable	$ 500,000	500,000
14% bonds payable, due December 31, 19x12	1,000,000	900,000
Common stock	950,000	
Retained earnings	550,000	
Total liabilities and shareholders' equity	$3,000,000	

At acquisition date, the building had a remaining useful life of ten years with zero net salvage value, while the patent had a remaining economic life of eight years. With respect to any recorded amounts of goodwill, it is corporate policy to amortize such amounts over 40 years.

Both companies use the FIFO method to cost their inventories and the straight-line method to calculate all depreciation and amortization. Prague Limited uses the cost method to account for its long-term investment in Sofia Limited.

The net incomes for the two companies for the year ended December 31, 19x8, were determined as follows:

	Prague	Sofia
Sales	$4,000,000	$2,000,000
Gain on sale of land	—	100,000
Dividend revenue	40,000	—
Rental revenue	—	70,000
Total revenue	4,040,000	2,170,000
Cost of goods sold	2,000,000	800,000
Selling and administrative expense	855,000	680,000
Interest expense	250,000	140,000
Depreciation: building	300,000	100,000
Depreciation: equipment	150,000	125,000
Patent amortization	—	25,000
Rental expense	35,000	—
Total expenses	3,590,000	1,870,000
Net income	$ 450,000	$ 300,000

The amount of retained earnings for the two companies for the year ended December 31, 19x8, was determined as follows:

	Prague	Sofia
Retained earnings, January 1	$2,000,000	$ 900,000
Add: Net income	450,000	300,000
	2,450,000	1,200,000
Less: Dividends	100,000	50,000
Retained earnings, December 31	$2,350,000	$1,150,000

The balance sheets for the two companies at December 31, 19x8, were as follows:

	Prague	Sofia
ASSETS:		
Cash	$ 300,000	$ 150,000
Accounts receivable	800,000	500,000
Inventory	800,000	400,000
Investment in Sofia		
Ltd. (cost)	1,600,000	—
Land	900,000	800,000
Building (net)	1,200,000	400,000
Equipment	3,000,000	1,500,000
Less: Accumulated		
depreciation	1,750,000	300,000
Patents (net)	—	50,000
Total assets	$6,850,000	$3,500,000
LIABILITIES AND SHAREHOLDERS' EQUITY:		
Accounts payable	$1,000,000	$ 400,000
14% bonds payable, due December		
31, 19x12	—	1,000,000
Notes payable	2,000,000	—
Common stock	1,500,000	950,000
Retained earnings	2,350,000	1,150,000
Total liabilities and shareholders'		
equity	$6,850,000	$3,500,000

Additional Information:

1. In 19x4, Prague sold a parcel of land, costing $200,000, to Sofia for $300,000. In 19x8, Sofia sold the land to an unrelated company for $400,000.
2. Sofia regularly sells merchandise to Prague at the same terms it sells to other customers. Intercompany sales totaled $500,000 in 19x7 and $600,000 in 19x8. At December 31, 19x7, Prague's inventory contained $200,000 of merchandise purchased from Sofia. At December 31, 19x8, Prague's inventory contained $150,000 of merchandise purchased from Sofia.
3. On January 2, 19x5, Sofia acquired a piece of equipment for $140,000. The equipment had an estimated useful life of seven years and no salvage value. On January 2, 19x7, Sofia sold the equipment to Prague Limited for $80,000. There were no changes in the asset's estimated useful life.
4. Prague Limited's entire rental expense relates to equipment rented from Sofia Limited.

Required:

a. Schedules of calculation and allocation of the purchase price discrepancy.
b. Consolidated *income statement* calculations for:
   1. Cost of goods sold
   2. Minority interest
   3. Interest expense
c. Consolidated *balance sheet* December 31, 19x8, amounts for:
   1. Net book value of equipment
   2. Goodwill
   3. Bonds payable
   4. Minority interest

[SMA]

13

Intercorporate Investments: Factors Affecting Ownership Interests

So far in our discussion of intercorporate investments and consolidated statements, we have treated one very important variable as though it were a constant. That variable is the percentage of ownership interest held by an investor corporation. This simplification has permitted us to focus more directly on the substantive issues of accounting for intercorporate investments. In this chapter, we will remove that simplification. An investor corporation may either increase or decrease its ownership interest. When that happens, we must alter the amounts of fair-value increments, goodwill, and investee earnings that we recognize. Parts B and C deal with increases and decreases, respectively, in an investor's ownership percentage. But first, Part A examines the effect that the existence of preferred shares and restricted shares has on an investor corporation's ownership share.

A. PREFERRED AND RESTRICTED SHARES IN INVESTEE CORPORATIONS

Throughout our discussion of intercorporate investments, we have dealt almost entirely with voting common shares. We only briefly touched on preferred shares, and that was in Chapter 7 in the context of allocating the purchase price to the fair values of assets, liabilities, and preferred shares. In the examples in the intervening five chapters, none of the investments was in senior or preferred shares, and none of the investee corporations (either subsidiaries or significantly influenced companies) had preferred shares in their capital structure. This section discusses these issues. First, we will examine the effect that investee preferred shares have on the investor's ownership interest. Then we will briefly look at the accounting for an investment in preferred shares. After discussing preferred shares, we will then look at the impact of restricted common shares that have reduced (or nonexistent) voting rights.

It is not unusual for a subsidiary or a significantly influenced investee corporation to have preferred shares outstanding. The parent or investor corporation may not own all or even any of the preferred shares. For example, one company may acquire 100% of the common shares of another, while outsiders continue to own the subsidiary's preferred shares. How does the existence of the subsidiary's preferred shares affect the parent company's ownership interest? Can the parent be said to own 100% of the subsidiary even though the parent does not own the preferred shares?

A simple example will help to demonstrate the issue. Suppose that SubInc has net assets of $1,000,000 and shareholders' equity consisting of $400,000 par-value preferred shares and $600,000 in common share equity. Assume further that ParInc buys all of SubInc's common shares for $1,200,000. What is ParInc's ownership interest in SubInc? Two alternatives seem to exist. First, ParInc can be said to own 100% of SubInc because ParInc owns 100% of the voting shares and can elect 100% of the board of directors. Alternatively, it can be argued that ParInc owns less than 100% because there is an outstanding ownership interest of $400,000 in SubInc. ParInc's ownership interest may be viewed as 60% (based on book value) or 75% (based on fair values: $1,200,000 paid for the common shares plus $400,000 par or redemption value of the preferred shares).

The level of ownership interest is important for several reasons. If the financial statements of SubInc are consolidated with those of ParInc, the percentage of ownership will affect (1) the proportion of the fair-value increments of SubInc's assets that are included on ParInc's balance sheet, (2) the amount assigned to minority interest, (3) the amount of the purchase price to be assigned to goodwill, and (4) amount of consolidated net income.

Consolidated net income is affected because the allocation of the purchase price between fair-value increments and goodwill will result in different annual amortization expense. If ParInc reports its investment in SubInc on the equity basis (rather than by consolidating), the equity pick-up of SubInc's earnings will be similarly affected.

To resolve the issue, we can first approach the problem from the standpoint of measuring earnings. If ParInc owns 100% of the common shares of SubInc, then ParInc has an interest in all of the residual earnings of SubInc. SubInc must pay (or provide for) the preferred dividends out of net income; all of the remaining earnings accrue to the benefit of the common shareholders. Therefore, ParInc must report 100% of SubInc's residual earnings. If consolidated statements are prepared, then all of SubInc's revenues and expenses are included, and the deduction for minority interest in earnings of SubInc would consist solely of the dividend entitlement of SubInc's preferred shareholders. On the equity basis, ParInc would pick up 100% of SubInc's earnings after provision for the preferred dividends. Therefore, from the standpoint of an income statement, it appears that ParInc should view its investment as 100% ownership, subject to the prior dividend claim

Effect of Preferred Shares on Investor's Ownership Interest

SCHEDULE 13-1			
Assignment of Purchase Price: **ParInc Buys 100% of SubInc Common Shares**			
	SubInc		Fair-value increment
	Book value	Fair value	
Net assets	$1,000,000	$1,350,000	$350,000
Preferred share equity	400,000	400,000	—
Common equity acquired	600,000	950,000	
Purchase price	1,200,000	1,200,000	
Goodwill		$250,000	250,000
Excess of purchase price over net book value acquired	$ 600,000		$600,000

of the preferred shareholders. Clearly, ParInc would not report less than 100% of the residual earnings of SubInc, whether SubInc is consolidated or is reported on the equity basis.

A similar conclusion may be reached by considering the issue from the viewpoint of the balance sheet. If ParInc is viewed as owning only 60% (or 75%) of SubInc, then only 60% (or 75%) of the fair-value increments for SubInc's net assets will be included on ParInc's consolidated balance sheet. By implication, the remainder of the fair-value increments would benefit the minority shareholders.

However, the minority interest in preferred shares is not a residual interest. Instead, it is a fixed amount determined by call or redemption value of the preferred shares, plus any dividend arrearages. Increases in the value of SubInc's assets increase only the common share equity; preferred shareholders do not benefit, except perhaps by the reduced risk of dividend nonpayment. Therefore, ParInc's purchase of 100% of the SubInc common shares should be viewed as an acquisition of 100% of the SubInc net assets, less the claim on those assets represented by the preferred shares.

Schedule 13-1 shows the assignment of the purchase price, assuming that the fair value of SubInc's net assets is $1,350,000. The preferred share equity is subtracted in order to find the net asset value for common equity. The remainder of the schedule is similar to previous analyses, such as that shown in Schedule 8-1.

In Schedule 13-1, the preferred share equity is shown to be identical for book value and fair value. Such is not usually the case. The fair value of the preferred equity should reflect the preferred shareholders' claim on assets. This claim would be measured by the shares' call price or redemption value, if any, plus any dividends in arrears. Call prices are frequently higher than par values or issue prices, and thus fair value may be higher than book value.

Investment in Preferred Shares

In the preceding section, we assumed that the preferred shares were all owned by outsiders. However, the parent may own some of the subsidiary's preferred shares, as well as its common shares.

On the books of the parent, the cost of the shares will be debited to an investment account. When consolidated statements are prepared, the parent's investment account for the preferred shares must be eliminated, as must the portion of the subsidiary preferred share equity that is owned by the parent.

Similarly, preferred dividends paid by a subsidiary to its parent are intercompany transfers and would be eliminated on consolidation. Consolidated earnings (or the equity-basis earnings) must include the parent's share of the subsidiary's net income after provision only for the portion of preferred dividends paid or payable to outside shareholders.

The cost of the preferred shares to the parent will most likely be different from the carrying value of the preferred shares on the subsidiary's balance sheet. If the parent purchased the preferred shares on the open market, it is obvious that the cost of the shares would be different from the par or other carrying value. It is less obvious that a difference may exist even when the preferred shares were purchased directly from the subsidiary. Any premium on the shares that was paid by the parent would be included in the investment account, but that premium would not be a part of preferred shareholders' equity in the subsidiary because the preferred shareholders have an equity in the subsidiary only to the extent of their redemption value.

From the viewpoint of the consolidated entity, subsidiary preferred shares owned by the parent do not exist; they have the same general status as do intercompany receivables and payables, and must be eliminated. When there is a difference in the preferred share carrying value, the worksheet elimination entry must be balanced by a debit or credit for the difference. This difference is charged or credited to the shareholders' equity on the consolidated balance sheet, generally to a contributed surplus account if one exists; otherwise to retained earnings. In effect, the shares are treated as having been retired.

Pooling of Interests

The preceding discussion is oriented towards intercorporate investments that are reported on the purchase basis. If, instead, a business combination is reported as a pooling, there would be little or no difference in the way preferred shares were treated. The existence of preferred shares in either or both of the combining companies would not affect the proportionate ownership interests of the voting shareholders. Preferred shares outstanding would represent a minority interest and would be reported as such on the consolidated balance sheet at their book or stated value on the issuing company's books, *not* at their redemption value if that differed from the book value.

If one of the pooled companies owns preferred shares in the other, then the investment account must be eliminated. The elimination procedure is exactly the same as that described in the preceding section.

Restricted Shares

Much of Canadian enterprise is conducted by family-controlled corporations. As these corporations grow, it frequently becomes impossible to finance them adequately without going to the public equity markets. If shares are sold to the public, however, the controlling shareholders risk losing control of "their" companies, which the shareholders are loathe to do. The answer to the need to raise equity capital without losing control is to issue

restricted shares rather than regular common shares. A restricted share is usually just like a regular common share, except that its voting rights are sharply reduced or nonexistent. Restricted shares normally share equally with regular shares in dividends and in assets upon dissolution (although they can be subordinated in those regards as well).

At the time of writing, there are approximately 200 listings of restricted shares on the Toronto Stock Exchange alone. A prime example is Canadian Tire, whose restricted shares provide 96% of the common share equity but have 10% of the votes; there are over 84 million nonvoting shares in Canadian Tire.

As we described above, a prime motivation for issuing restricted shares (which may be designated as "Class A" shares, or a similar appellation) is to raise equity capital while maintaining control in the hands of the original group of shareholders. While earnings accrue to all shareholders equally, the voting power resides wholly or mainly in the hands of a few. This situation then raises the question as to how to treat restricted shares in consolidated financial statements when a parent controls the voting shares but does not own the restricted shares.

There are two different issues. The first is that of control. Control exists when the investor has sufficient votes to elect a majority of the board of directors. If an investee has restricted shares, control exists when the investor has more than half the votes, regardless of the proportion of shares owned. For example, suppose that Gordon Inc. has 1,000 shares of regular common shares outstanding and 10,000 restricted shares. The regular shares have one vote each, while the restricted shares have 0.1 votes each. A takeover could occur when a buyer acquires 1,001 of the available 2,000 votes (i.e., 1,000 for the regular shares plus 1,000 for the restricted shares). It doesn't matter whether the buyer acquires all of the regular shares plus one restricted share, or 10,000 restricted shares plus one regular share, or any linear combination in between.

Restricted shares sometimes have a **coattail provision**, which is a provision that comes into effect when a buyer attempts to buy control of a company. If a control block is about to change hands, then the restricted shares may become fully voting shares for limited purposes. The nature of coattail provisions differs significantly between companies, and they do not exist at all for many (if not most) companies. But when coattail provisions exist, the number of shares that must be *held* in order to maintain control is quite different from the number of shares that must be *purchased* in order to acquire control.

The second issue that relates to restricted shares in an investee corporation's equity structure is how to treat the percentage of ownership for consolidation or equity reporting purposes. It is important not to confuse the proportion of votes with the proportion of common equity investment. The crucial question is how much of the investee's earnings are available to the investor. If the restricted shares participate equally with the regular shares in dividends, then the investor's ownership percentage is simply the proportion of shares owned relative to the total number of shares outstanding, regular and restricted. For example, if Gordon Inc.'s common shares are equal in dividend participation and an acquiror obtains 1,000 regular shares plus one restricted share, then the ownership percentage for consolidation purposes is 1,001/11,000 or about 9%. If, on the other hand, control was obtained by buying all 10,000 restricted shares plus one regular share, then the ownership percentage is 10,001/11,000, or about 91%. It is obvious, therefore, that it is quite possible to have control of a subsidiary while still having a minority interest of over 90%!

In summary, the key points to remember are that (1) when determining control, count votes, but (2) when determining minority interest, look at participation in earnings and dividends. The two measures are not the same when restricted shares exist in an investee corporation.

B.   INCREASES IN OWNERSHIP INTEREST

Throughout the preceding chapters, we have implicitly assumed that an investor corporation acquires its ownership interest in another company at a single point in time. Frequently, however, an investor corporation may acquire its shares in an investee corporation in several steps or by gradual accumulation over a period of time, sometimes over several years. Sequential purchases are known as **step purchases** or **step acquisitions**. Schedule 9-8 shows an example of a step purchase in which First Toronto Capital Corporation increased its ownership interest in Walhalla Mining Company from 20% to 57%, thereby giving First Toronto control over Walhalla.

We have seen that when a significant portion of the shares of an investee corporation is acquired by an investor corporation, fair values and goodwill must be measured and amortized in future years, when appropriate. When a subsidiary is consolidated, consolidated assets include the subsidiary's assets at book values plus the fair-value increments and goodwill for the majority interest's share only. The valuation of assets and the measurement of income are affected when the investor or parent increases its proportion of ownership.

There are three situations involving increases in ownership interest. The first arises when an investor holds shares in another corporation as a portfolio investment, and then acquires sufficient additional shares to give the investor significant influence over the investee. The investor's reporting would shift from the cost basis to the equity basis when significant influence was achieved.

The second situation arises when an investor has significant influence in the investee and then acquires enough additional shares to give the investor control over the investee. The investor's reporting would then change from equity-basis reporting to consolidation.

The third situation arises when an investor buys additional shares without affecting the nature of the reporting for the investment. The investor may have significant influence and may increase the size of its minority position. Similarly, the investor may control the investee and prepare consolidated statements, and additional share purchases simply increase the parent's controlling interest. In these cases, the method of reporting does not change, but the increase in ownership interest nevertheless does have an impact on the financial reporting of the investor corporation.

In the next section, we will focus on increases in the ownership percentage of controlled investees, i.e., subsidiaries. In the later sections, increases in minority interests will be discussed, including those situations that call for a change in reporting practice.

Increases in Controlling Interest

Assume that on December 31, 19x2, Parent Corporation (PC) acquires 60% of the shares of Subsidiary Corporation (SC) for $600,000. The condensed balance sheets for PC and SC are shown in Part 1 of Schedule 13-2, together with the fair values for SC.

Part 2 of Schedule 13-2 shows the allocation of the purchase price. PC paid a price that was $270,000 above the book value of the 60% share of net assets acquired; of this amount, $180,000 is assigned to the fixed assets and the remainder ($90,000) to goodwill.

If a consolidated balance sheet were prepared for PC on the date of the acquisition, it would appear as shown in the first column of Schedule 13-3. PC's consolidated assets would include 100% of the book values plus 60% of the fair-value increments of SC's assets. Minority interest would be included as an offset for the 40% book-value share of SC's net assets.

Now let us assume that during 19x3, SC reported net income of $70,000 and paid dividends totaling $20,000. The remaining useful life of SC's fixed

---

SCHEDULE 13-2

1. Net Asset Positions, Subsequent to Acquisition

	Condensed balance sheets December 31, 19x2		SC fair values, Dec. 31, 19x2
	PC	SC	
Current assets	$1,000,000	$ 400,000	$ 400,000
Fixed assets (net)	1,900,000	1,100,000	1,400,000
Investment in SC	600,000		
Total assets	$3,500,000	$1,500,000	1,800,000
Liabilities	$1,500,000	$ 950,000	950,000
Shareholders' equity	2,000,000	550,000	
Total equities	$3,500,000	$1,500,000	
Net asset fair value			$ 850,000

2. Assignment of Purchase Price

	60% of SC		Fair-value increment
	Book value	Fair value	
Current assets	$240,000	$240,000	—
Fixed assets (net)	660,000	840,000	$180,000
Liabilities	(570,000)	(570,000)	—
	$330,000	510,000	180,000
Purchase price		600,000	
Goodwill		$ 90,000	90,000
Excess of purchase price over net book value acquired			$270,000

assets is ten years from December 31, 19x2; PC's management has decided to amortize goodwill over 30 years. There are no intercompany transactions. The separate-entity balance sheets for PC and SC at December 31, 19x3, are shown in Part 1 of Schedule 13-4. As calculated in Part 2 of Schedule 13-4,

---

SCHEDULE 13-3

Parent Corporation
Consolidated Balance Sheets
December 31

	19x2	19x3
Current assets	$1,400,000	$1,500,000
Fixed assets (net)	3,180,000	3,062,000
Goodwill	90,000	87,000
Total assets	$4,670,000	$4,649,000
Liabilities	$2,450,000	$2,200,000
Minority interest	220,000	240,000
Shareholders' equity	2,000,000	2,209,000
Total equities	$4,670,000	$4,649,000

SCHEDULE 13-4

1. Condensed Balance Sheets, December 31, 19x3

	PC	SC
Current assets	$1,000,000	$ 500,000
Fixed assets (net)	1,900,000	1,000,000
Investment in SC (equity basis)	609,000	
Total assets	$3,509,000	$1,500,000
Liabilities	$1,300,000	$ 900,000
Shareholders' equity	2,209,000	600,000
Total equities	$3,509,000	$1,500,000

2. PC's Equity in Earnings of SC, 19x3

60% of SC's reported net income of $70,000	$ 42,000
Amortization of fair-value increments:	
Fixed assets ($180,000 ÷ 10 years)	−18,000
Goodwill ($90,000 ÷ 30 years)	−3,000
Increase in consolidated net income due to earnings of SC	$ 21,000

3. Investment Account

Cost of purchase of 60% share of SC	$600,000
Plus equity in net income of SC for 19x3	21,000
Less dividends received from SC in 19x3 (60% of $20,000)	−12,000
Balance, December 31, 19x3	$609,000

consolidated retained earnings include PC's share of SC earnings, $21,000. Part 3 shows the changes in the investment account for the year. The consolidated balance sheet for Parent Corporation for 19x3 is shown in the second column of Schedule 13-3.

So far, there has been nothing new in this analysis. The December 31, 19x3, consolidated balance sheet includes SC's net assets at their book values plus 60% of the amortized December 31, 19x2, fair-value increments. But assume that on January 2, 19x4, PC buys an additional 10% of the shares of SC for $140,000 cash, thereby increasing PC's ownership interest in SC to 70%. If we prepare a pro-forma balance sheet using the new percentage of ownership, we may appear to have two choices of valuation for SC's net assets:

1. 100% of book value on January 2, 19x4, plus 70% of the fair-value increments at January 2, 19x4, or
2. 100% of book value on January 2, 19x4, plus 60% of the fair-value increments at December 31, 19x2, plus 10% of the fair-value increments at January 2, 19x4.

Under the first alternative, the second purchase of (10%) would cause a general revaluation of the assigned costs from the first purchase. The purchase price would be viewed as a total cost of $749,000 for a 70% share interest, and goodwill would be recalculated based on the difference between 70% of the net asset fair values and the total purchase price.

Part 1 of Schedule 13-5 shows the result of the first alternative, assuming that the fair value of SC's fixed assets is $1,500,000 on January 2, 19x4. When viewed as a total purchase of 70% of SC, the goodwill previously recorded for the 60% purchase disappears and negative goodwill appears instead; 70% of the fair values of SC's net assets at January 2, 19x4, exceeds the total cost of the investment of $749,000 (including the $9,000 unremitted earnings from 19x3) by $21,000. The shift from positive goodwill to negative goodwill is caused by the relative movement of the book and fair values of SC's fixed assets between the two acquisition dates. From December 31, 19x2 to January 2, 19x4, the book value went down by $100,000, while the fair value went up by $100,000. Thus, the greater spread between the fair value and the book value at the later date has created a much larger fair-value increment. As a result, the full amount of the excess of the purchase price over the net book value is allocated to the fair-value increment, with nothing allocated to goodwill.

Under the second alternative, the assigned valuations for the first purchase are left untouched by the second purchase. The cost of the second purchase ($140,000 for 10%) is allocated to fair-value increments and goodwill at the date of the purchase as a separate investment. This allocation is shown in Part 2 of Schedule 13-5.

Under the second alternative, $50,000 is the amount allocated to fixed assets as the fair-value increment on the 10% share acquired. The remaining $30,000 purchase price discrepancy is goodwill. Therefore, the total amount of goodwill on the pro-forma consolidated balance sheet under the second alternative is $117,000 at January 2, 19x4: $90,000 from the first purchase less the $3,000 amortization for 19x3, plus $30,000 from the second purchase. In 19x4 and following years, the two goodwill amounts will be amortized separately, as will the two fair-value increments assigned to the fixed assets.

SCHEDULE 13-5

Assignment of Asset Values
January 2, 19x4

1. Based on 70% of fair values at January 2, 19×4

	SC book value (100%)	70% share of SC		Fair-value increment
		Book value	Fair value	
Current assets	$ 500,000	$350,000	$ 350,000	—
Fixed assets (net)	1,000,000	700,000	1,050,000	$350,000
Liabilities	(900,000)	(630,000)	(630,000)	—
	$ 600,000	$420,000	770,000	350,000
Purchase price*			749,000	
Negative goodwill			$ 21,000	(21,000)
Excess of purchase price over net book value acquired; all assigned to fixed assets				$329,000

*Cost of 60% purchase, December 31, 19x2	$600,000	
Unremitted earnings (equity basis) for 19x3	9,000	
Cost of 10% purchase, January 2, 19x4	140,000	
	$749,000	

2. Based on 10% of fair values at January 2, 19×4

	10% share of SC		Fair-value increment
	Book value	Fair value	
Current assets	$ 50,000	$ 50,000	—
Fixed assets (net)	100,000	150,000	$50,000
Liabilities	(90,000)	(90,000)	—
Net assets	$ 60,000	110,000	50,000
Purchase price		140,000	
Goodwill		$ 30,000	30,000
Excess of purchase price over net book value acquired			$80,000

The pro-forma consolidated balance sheets for the two alternatives are shown in Schedule 13-6. The only differences in this example are in the values shown for fixed assets and goodwill because we assumed that the other assets and liabilities all had fair values that equalled their book values. The derivation of the values for the fixed assets is explained in the lower portion of the schedule. The differences may seem relatively immaterial in this example, amounting to only about 2.5% of total assets and 3.5% of fixed assets. However, other situations could cause more substantial differences in consolidated balances. Furthermore, the impact of the amortization of good-

SCHEDULE 13-6		
Parent Corporation **Pro-Forma Consolidated Balance Sheet** January 2, 19x4		
	Alternative 1 (70%)	Alternative 2 (60% + 10%)
Current assets	$1,360,000	$1,360,000
Fixed assets (net) (see below)	3,229,000	3,112,000
Goodwill	—	117,000
Total assets	$4,589,000	$4,589,000
Liabilities	$2,200,000	$2,200,000
Minority interest	180,000	180,000
Shareholders' equity	2,209,000	2,209,000
Total equities	$4,589,000	$4,589,000
FIXED ASSETS		
PC: 100% of Dec. 31, 19x3, book value	$1,900,000	$1,900,000
SC: 100% of Dec. 31, 19x3, book value	1,000,000	1,000,000
70% of Jan. 2, 19x4, fair-value increment	329,000	
60% of Dec. 31, 19x2, fair-value increment		180,000
less 19x3 amortization		(18,000)
10% of Jan. 2, 19x4, fair-value increment		50,000
Consolidated fixed assets, Jan. 2, 19x4	$3,229,000	$3,112,000

will and of the fair-value increments on fixed assets could cause a significant impact on net income even in this example.

Proponents of the first alternative would argue that a general reallocation based on fair values at the date of the latest purchase is desirable because it recognizes the fair value of the subsidiary's assets at a single point in time. The second alternative, it is argued, includes pieces of fair values of the same assets at different points in time, resulting in a hodgepodge of valuations that are meaningless when added together.

The first alternative does adhere to the historical cost concept because the total amount allocated is the aggregate cost of the purchased share interests. The change in the net book value of the subsidiary's net assets between purchases is taken into account because the investment account includes the parent's share of the change in the subsidiary's retained earnings (i.e., the excess of net income over dividends paid, otherwise known as the unremitted earnings). Therefore, the first alternative allocates the total cost of the purchases (including unremitted earnings) on the basis of the fair values at the time of the most recent substantive change in ownership position. The first alternative is consistent both with the parent company approach to consolidated financial statements and with the historical cost approach.

Advocates of the second alternative would argue that it correctly views each purchase as a separate transaction and allocates the cost of each purchase individually. If the acquiror purchased one division of another company by buying the assets directly (rather than by buying shares), the accounting for those assets would not be affected by a later purchase of another division of the same company. Each asset or group of assets must be accounted for as of the date of purchase, subject to adjustment only for contingent consideration for that particular purchase. In Chapter 7, we observed that the general principle in accounting for business combinations is to end up with essentially the same results whether the assets are purchased directly or indirectly through shares acquisition. Following this principle, only the second alternative to step-by-step purchases is appropriate.

A related criticism of the first approach is that it results in reallocating costs based on values that were not in effect at the time of purchase. When Parent Corporation bought its initial 60% interest in Subsidiary Corporation, the fair value of the fixed assets was $1,400,000. The purchase price of $600,000 implicitly recognizes that fair value, not the fair value of $1,500,000 that existed one year later. If the fair value of $1,500,000 had existed at the time of the initial purchase, then the cost of the 60% share interest may well have been higher than the $600,000 paid. The first method is flawed, therefore, because it reallocates the cost on the basis of values that did not underlie the initial purchase price.

We noted above that some people would object that the second alternative includes asset values in the consolidated balance sheet at a mixture of valuations for the same assets. Others counter by pointing out that the balance sheet is (in most industrial and mercantile operations) a collection of costs, not values. The costs of assets acquired are stored on the balance sheet for assignment or allocation as expenses in future periods in order to estimate periodic net income. There is no intent in general accounting practice to show assets at their estimated fair values in the primary financial statements. Only the second alternative achieves the objective of showing assets at their historical costs.

Finally, the question of usefulness arises. The allocation of cost in a share acquisition clearly is somewhat arbitrary. Little is to be gained by reallocating the cost at a later point in time. Such a reallocation process would reduce the comparability of successive years' statements since both the basis of valuation and the amortization would change whenever a significant change in ownership occurred. Since it would probably not be feasible to provide detailed information on the impact of such a reallocation, we cannot fall back on the efficient markets hypothesis (EMH) to rationalize the changes in accounting; to be effective, the EMH requires adequate disclosure.

Also, the stewardship objective would seem not to be well served by the first alternative. In this example, application of the first alternative results in negative goodwill, thereby suggesting that management of PC obtained a bargain purchase. But the facts are that in each purchase, PC paid more than the proportionate fair value of the net assets acquired. Management's use of resources and the resultant return on investment appear to be obscured by application of the first method.

For reasons discussed above, current Canadian recommendations in the *CICA Handbook* [para. 1600.13] call for use of the second alternative for reporting the effect of step purchases in consolidated financial statements.

The foregoing discussion relates to situations in which the purchase method of reporting intercorporate investments is appropriate. If one corporation obtains most of the shares of another through a series of acquisitions over time, a takeover has occurred and, by definition, there has not been a pooling. When an *initial* exchange of shares does result in a business combination that meets the criteria for a pooling of interests, then subsequent additional share exchanges that reduce the minority shareholdings will be reported on the consolidated balance sheet simply by reducing the minority interest. Since fair values are not involved, there is no allocation problem.

Increases in Equity-Basis Investments

Equity-method accounting is intended to yield the same net income and investor-corporation retained earnings as would consolidation. Therefore, it will come as little surprise that when an investment is being reported on the equity basis, the same principles apply for step acquisitions as were discussed above in accounting for consolidated subsidiaries. In general, each significant purchase of shares is accounted for separately, with separate estimates of fair values and goodwill at each date of purchase. For practical purposes, numerous small purchases can be grouped together and treated as a single purchase [*CICA Handbook*, para. 1600.11].

For example, suppose that Investor Corporation (IRC) buys 20% of the shares of Investee Corporation (IEC) for $200,000 on December 31, 19x2; the share acquisition gives IRC significant influence over IEC. The book values and fair values of IEC on the date of acquisition are the same as were shown in the first part of Schedule 13-2 (for PC and SC). Part 1 of Schedule 13-7 shows the allocation of the purchase price and the determination of goodwill. The $90,000 excess of the purchase price over the book value of the net assets acquired is allocated $60,000 to the fair-value increments on the nonmonetary assets and $30,000 to goodwill.

During 19x3, IEC reported net income of $70,000 and paid dividends totaling $20,000. The remaining useful life of IEC's nonmonetary assets is estimated to be ten years. IRC's management has decided to amortize goodwill over 30 years. IRC's share of IEC's net income, adjusted for amortization of the fair-value increments and goodwill, amounts to $7,000; the calculation is shown in Part 2 of Schedule 13-7. The investment account (on IRC's books) will be increased by the $7,000 share of IEC income and reduced by the dividends received by IRC (20% of $20,000, or $4,000). Therefore, at the end of 19x3, the investment account will amount to $203,000, as summarized in Part 3 of Schedule 13-7.

Now, suppose that on January 2, 19x4, IRC buys an additional 10% of the shares of IEC for $140,000. The total interest of IRC in IEC is now 30%, and the total cost of that investment is $340,000. The condensed balance sheet of IEC on December 31, 19x3, (immediately before the additional purchase by IRC) is shown in Schedule 13-8, together with estimated fair values on that date. The fair value of the net assets of IEC is now $1,100,000.

The January 2, 19x4, purchase is exactly the same as the situation cited in the previous section. As is shown in Part 2 of Schedule 13-5, $110,000 of the purchase price is allocated to net assets (10% of $1,100,000 total net asset fair value) and the remaining $30,000 is allocated to goodwill. Of the $110,000 allocated to net assets, $60,000 reflects 10% of the book value of IEC's net assets and $50,000 is the fair-value increment.

SCHEDULE 13-7

IRC Acquires 20% of IEC
December 31, 19x2

1. Assignment of Purchase Price

	IEL, total		20% share		Fair-value increment
	Book value	Fair value	Book value	Fair value	
Current assets	$ 400,000	$ 400,000	$ 80,000	$ 80,000	—
Fixed assets	1,100,000	1,400,000	220,000	280,000	$60,000
Liabilities	(950,000)	(950,000)	(190,000)	(190,000)	—
Net assets	$ 550,000	$ 850,000	$110,000	170,000	
Purchase price				200,000	
Goodwill				$ 30,000	30,000
					$90,000

2. IRC's Equity in Earnings of IEC, 19x3

	IRC equity
20% of IEC's reported net income of $70,000	$14,000
Amortization of fair-value increments:	
Fixed assets ($60,000 ÷ 10 years)	−6,000
Goodwill ($30,000 ÷ 30 years)	−1,000
IRC equity in IEC earnings for 19x3	$ 7,000

3. Investment Account

Purchase of 20% interest in IEC, December 31, 19x2	$200,000
Equity in IEC earnings for 19x3	7,000
Dividends received from IEC during 19x3	−4,000
Balance, December 31, 19x3	$203,000

During 19x4, IEC reports net income of $100,000 and pays dividends of $40,000. IRC's 30% share of IEC's net income is $16,410, assuming that the *remaining* useful life (from January 2, 19x4) of IEC's fixed assets is nine years and goodwill is being amortized over 29 years from January 2, 19x4. The calculation of IRC's equity in the 19x4 earnings of IEC is shown in Part 1 of Schedule 13-9.

These amortization assumptions are based on the presumption that the amortization of the fair-value increments on fixed assets and goodwill of both purchases should expire on the same date. For fixed assets, such a presumption is reasonable if the fixed assets of IEC were the same on both December 31, 19x2, and January 2, 19x4. For goodwill, such a presumption is not necessary, since the allocation is largely arbitrary anyway.

Dividends received by IRC from IEC amount to $12,000 (30% of $40,000) during 19x4. The balance of the investment account on IRC's balance sheet

---

SCHEDULE 13-8

Investee Corporation
Condensed Balance Sheet
December 31, 19x3

	Book value	Fair value
Current assets	$ 500,000	$ 500,000
Fixed assets	1,000,000	1,500,000
	$1,500,000	2,000,000
Liabilities	$ 900,000	900,000
Shareholders' equity	600,000	
	$1,500,000	
Net assets		$1,100,000

SCHEDULE 13-9

1. IRC's Equity in Earnings of ICE, 19x4

30% of IEC's reported net income of $100,000	$ 30,000
Amortization of fair-value increments:	
Fixed assets:	
20% purchase ($60,000 ÷ 10 years)	−6,000
10% purchase ($50,000 ÷ 9 years)	−5,556
Goodwill:	
20% purchase ($30,000 ÷ 30 years)	−1,000
10% purchase ($30,000 ÷ 29 years)	−1,034
IRC equity in IEC earnings for 19x4	$ 16,410

2. Investment Account

Purchase of 20% interest, December 31, 19x2	$200,000
Equity in IEC earnings, 19x3	7,000
Dividends received from IEC, 19x3	−4,000
Balance, December 31, 19x3	$203,000
Purchase of 10% interest, January 2, 19x4	140,000
Equity in IEC earnings, 19x4	16,410
Dividends received from IEC, 19x4	−12,000
Balance, December 31, 19x4	$347,410

---

at the end of 19x4 will be $347,410, as shown in Part 2 of Schedule 13-9. The year-end balance includes the new 10% purchase, as well as the 19x4 equity-basis income and dividends.

An investor corporation may increase its ownership in a significantly influenced company to the point where the investor becomes the majority shareholder and consequently controls the investee. Once control is achieved, consolidation becomes appropriate, rather than equity-basis reporting. Since the equity method is completely consistent with the parent-company approach to consolidation, shifting from equity reporting to consolidation poses no additional problems.

So far, we have examined increases in ownership of consolidated subsidiaries and of equity-method investments. One further situation that should be considered is where the initial purchase (or purchases) is reported on the cost basis because significant influence does not exist, but an additional purchase does give significant influence to the investor corporation.

Acquisition of Significant Influence

To illustrate this type of situation, let us assume exactly the same facts as in the previous section, except that significant influence does not exist until the second purchase of IEC shares (10%) in 19x4. The initial purchase of 20% for $200,000 would therefore be reported on the cost basis, and IRC would report as income in 19x3 only the $6,000 dividends received.

When the purchase of the additional 10% is made on January 2, 19x4, and equity-method accounting becomes appropriate, three alternative approaches to accounting for the acquisition are possible:

1. Treat the total cost ($340,000) of both the 20% and the 10% acquisition as an acquisition of 30% of the fair value of IEC's net assets on January 2, 19x4.
2. Treat the two purchases independently by (a) allocating the cost of the 10% purchase to 10% of IEC's fair values on January 2, 19x4, and (b) retroactively allocating the cost of the earlier 20% purchase on the basis of the fair values of IEC's net assets on December 31, 19x2.
3. Continue to report the first purchase on the cost basis, but account for the second purchase on the equity basis.

The first two of these three alternatives are the same as the two alternative reporting practices discussed earlier in the section on accounting for step purchases of consolidated subsidiaries. In that section, we saw that the second alternative is recommended because it treats each purchase as a separate transaction and yields results that are most similar to direct purchase of assets.

The discussion in the previous sections was based on the premise that all of the purchases of shares had been reported on the equity basis. Subsequent purchases would not affect the accounting for previous purchases. However, a different situation exists when the earlier purchases were reported on the cost basis, as we are assuming in this section. The subsequent acquisition of significant influence calls for a change in accounting policy for the investment, and thus we must re-examine the alternatives.

The third alternative, that of leaving the first purchase on the cost basis, is clearly unsound. This alternative results in different reporting practices for two transactions that meld together in substance. The 20% interest and the 10% interest are not wielded individually by IRC; it is the combination of 30% that is exercised and that gives rise to significant influence.

In addition, reporting 20% on the cost basis and 10% on the equity basis would mean that IRC would report on its income statement investment income from IEC composed of 20% of IEC's dividends (cost basis) and 10% of IEC's adjusted net income (equity basis), a nonsensical result. Thus, it should be clear that the equity basis of reporting must be adopted for the full 30% interest once significant influence is deemed to exist.

Changing to the equity method is a change of accounting policy. Changes in policy generally require retroactive application of the new policy [*CICA Handbook*, para. 1506.11]. However, the equity method would not have been appropriate prior to January 2, 19x4, because significant influence did not exist. Instead, the fact of changing the method of accounting for the initial 20% purchase implies only that the $200,000 cost of the original purchase should be allocated on the basis of fair values *at the time of purchase* in order to determine the amounts of goodwill and fair-value increments to be amortized against future investment income. In theory, therefore, the second alternative should be used when equity-basis accounting is adopted. Each purchase should be accounted for independently, exactly as outlined in the previous section.

A practical problem arises, however. It is likely to be difficult, if not impossible, to obtain fair-value estimates retroactively to the time of the first purchase. In addition, since the first purchase is likely to be relatively small, the refinement obtained by retroactive restatement may be immaterial to the investor corporation's financial reporting and thus not worth the effort. As a result, the first alternative is usually applied in practice. The *CICA Handbook* states that the total cost of all purchases is allocated to net assets and goodwill on the basis of fair values at the date on which the equity method is first deemed appropriate [para. 1600.11].

While use of the first alternative is accepted for practical purposes, it does not necessarily yield the same results as would the second alternative. Schedule 13-10 summarizes the allocation of the $340,000 total cost under each of the two methods. Goodwill, for example, is valued at only $10,000 under the first alternative but is $60,000 under the second alternative. The difference may not be material to the investor corporation and thus to the user of IRC's financial statements, but in some situations a significant impact could arise.

Similarly, a purchase that, in conjunction with an earlier portfolio investment, gives an investor *control* of another corporation will be reported as a business combination that occurred on the date when control was obtained. If IRC owned a 20% interest in IEC (reported on the cost basis) and then had purchased an additional 45%, IRC would have acquired control over IEC

SCHEDULE 13-10

Allocation of Purchase Cost

	Alternative 1	Alternative 2			
	30% Jan. 2, 19x4	20% Dec. 31, 19x2	+ 10% Jan. 2, 19x4	= Total
Book value acquired	$180,000	$110,000	$ 60,000	$170,000
Fair-value increment on fixed assets	150,000	60,000	50,000	110,000
Goodwill	10,000	30,000	30,000	60,000
Total cost	$340,000	$200,000	$140,000	$340,000

and would prepare consolidated statements. IRC would consolidate IEC by including 65% of the fair-value increments for IEC's assets and liabilities at the date of the second purchase.

C. DECREASES IN OWNERSHIP INTEREST

On occasion, an investor corporation may reduce its share of ownership of a subsidiary or of a significantly influenced affiliate. A reduction may be accomplished by selling part of the investor's holdings, thereby directly reducing its ownership percentage. For example, Campbell Soup Co., a U.S. company, sold 30% of its previous 100% interest in its Canadian subsidiary (Campbell Soup Co. Ltd.) to the public in 1982. Alternatively, the investor's ownership interest may indirectly be reduced if the investee issues new shares and the investor does not buy a proportionate part of the new offering.

In this part of the chapter, we examine the reporting implications of a reduction in ownership interest by a parent or an investor corporation. First, we will look at reductions that arise from an investor corporation's direct sale of a part of its shares in the investee. Second, we will consider indirect reductions in ownership that are caused by new share offerings. Since the accounting aspects are similar whether applied to parent-subsidiary relationships or to equity-basis investments, we will explicitly discuss only reductions in interest experienced by a parent corporation. The same principles apply to equity-basis minority investments.

When a parent corporation sells part of its investment in a subsidiary, the accounting *on the parent's books* is quite straightforward. The investment account must be reduced by the proportionate part of the carrying value of the investment, and the difference between the carrying value of the investment and the proceeds from the sale is a gain or loss on the sale.

Sale of Part of an Investment

For example, assume that on December 31, 19x2, Parent Corporation (PC) acquired 30,000 of the 50,000 outstanding shares of Subsidiary Corporation (SC) for $20 per share, or $600,000 total. During 19x3, PC reported its equity in the earnings of SC as $21,000, and received dividends from SC of $12,000. At the end of 19x3, the investment in SC account has a balance of $609,000 ($600,000 cost + $21,000 income − $12,000 dividends).

On January 1, 19x4, PC decides to reduce its share of SC to the minimum of 51% needed to retain control. Therefore, PC sells 4,500 of its SC shares, which is 15% of its 60% ownership interest (or a 9% interest in SC) for $30 per share, or $135,000. The carrying value assigned to the portion sold is 15% of the total carrying value of $609,000, or $91,350. The entry to record the sale on *PC's books* will be as follows, assuming that PC carries its investment in SC at cost on its books:

Cash	$135,000	
Investment in SC		$90,000
Gain on sale of investment		43,650
Retained earnings		1,350

The credit to retained earnings simply records 15% of the unremitted earnings of SC that PC has already recognized in its financial statements for 19x3 but that have not been recorded on PC's books ($9,000 x 15% = $1,350). If PC carries its investment in SC on the equity basis, then the $9,000 equity in 19x3 unremitted earnings will already have been recorded, and the entry for the sale would be:

Cash	$135,000	
Investment in SC		$91,350
Gain on sale of investment		43,650

These entries are no different in substance from any entry to record the sale of part of an investment. However, the sale of part of PC's interest in SC has implications that a sale of a portfolio investment does not have. The sale will affect consolidated net assets, minority interest (which has now risen to 49%), and PC's equity in the earnings of SC. In order to evaluate the impact of the sale, we must disaggregate the equity-basis carrying value of $609,000.

The original purchase of 60% of SC is the same example used in the first section of Part B of this chapter. Schedule 13-2 shows the date-of-acquisition balance sheet, and the allocation of the purchase price. Schedule 13-4 shows the balance sheets for PC and SC at December 31, 19x3, as well as the computation of equity-basis earnings and the balance of the investment account.[1] The $600,000 purchase price was allocated as follows:

Book value of net assets acquired (60%)	$330,000
Fair-value increment on fixed assets (60%)	180,000
Goodwill	90,000
	$600,000

By selling 15% of its interest, PC was effectively selling 15% of each of the components of the carrying value, plus 15% of the earnings retained for 19x3. The $91,350 carrying value of the investment sold ($609,000 x 15%) can be broken down as follows:

15% of the book value of PC's share of SC's net assets at December 31, 19x3 (15% x 60% x $600,000)	$54,000
15% of the unamortized fair-value increment at December 31, 19x3 (15% x $162,000)	24,300
15% of the unamortized goodwill at December 31, 19x3 (15% x $87,000)	13,050
	$91,350

An alternative reconciliation can be based on the allocation of the purchase price at acquisition (per Schedule 13-2), plus the unremitted earnings for 19x3:

15% of December 31, 19x2 book values acquired (15% x $330,000)	$49,500
15% of the fair-value increment at acquisition (15% x $180,000)	27,000
15% of goodwill at acquisition (15% x $90,000)	13,500
15% of equity in IEC earnings in excess of dividends received (15% x $9,000)	1,350
	$91,350

[1] It is not necessary to have studied Part B to understand Schedules 13-2 and 13-4 and the discussion in this section.

The adjustment for the unremitted earnings includes the amortization of the fair-value increments and goodwill as well as the change in net asset value of SC that is reflected in SC's retained earnings.

On PC's consolidated balance sheet, the consolidated net asset values are changed by the amounts shown above. All of SC's assets continue to be included on the consolidated balance sheet because PC still controls SC. But after the sale, PC can include the fair-value increments on only 51% of PC's assets and liabilities rather than on 60% before the sale. Consolidated fixed assets therefore will decline by $24,300 as a result of the sale, even though no fixed assets have been sold. Goodwill will be reduced by $13,050. Minority interest will increase by $54,000, which is the result of increasing the minority interest from 40% to 49% of SC's net book value of $600,000.

Schedule 13-11 illustrates PC's consolidated balance sheet before and after the sale. Retained earnings have been increased by the $43,650 profit on the sale, and current assets include the $135,000 proceeds from the sale.

The change in PC's net assets as a result of the sale amounts to $43,650, the amount of the profit. This is the net change using the parent-company approach, and it would also be the net change under the entity approach to preparing consolidated financial statements. However, some people find the decline in fair-valued assets under the parent-company approach to be disturbing. As noted above, consolidated fixed assets decline as a result of the sale even though PC has *control* over exactly the same fixed assets after the sale as it did before the sale. It can be argued that the assets should remain unaffected by the sale (except for an increase due to the proceeds); *net* assets should be reduced simply by an increase in the minority interest.

Under the entity approach, such would be the result. Since the entity approach includes 100% of the fair-value increments on the subsidiary's assets, sale of part of the majority interest would not affect the asset carrying values on the consolidated balance sheet; the net asset values relating to the portion sold would simply be transferred to minority interest.

The decline in fair-value increment under the parent-company approach is a valid result of that method, however. The parent-company approach views the subsidiary's net assets from the point of view of their *cost* to the

SCHEDULE 13-11		
Parent Corporation **Consolidated Balance Sheet**		
	December 31, 19x3 PC owns 60% of SC	January 1, 19x4 PC owns 51% of SC
Current assets	$1,500,000	$1,635,000
Fixed assets	3,062,000	3,037,000
Goodwill	87,000	73,950
Total assets	$4,649,000	$4,746,650
Liabilities	$2,200,000	$2,200,000
Minority interest	240,000	294,000
Shareholders' equity	2,209,000	2,252,650
Total equities	$4,649,000	$4,746,650

parent. When the parent sells a portion of its investment, that portion of the cost is recovered and the appropriate assets are reduced accordingly. The amount of fair-value increment to be allocated to future earnings is reduced by the sale, and the change in asset values reflects the reduction.

Issuance of Shares by Subsidiary

At first glance, it may appear that issuance of new shares by the subsidiary to outside parties should not affect the parent. The parent corporation still holds the same number of shares, and the cost of acquiring those shares is not directly affected by the new issue of the subsidiary.

However, it is not quite so simple. While it is true that the number of shares held by the parent is not changed, the percentage of ownership *is* changed. After the issuance, the parent owns a smaller percentage of the subsidiary and the minority interest is larger. Under the purchase method of accounting for business combinations, the parent is considered to have purchased a proportionate share of the fair value of the subsidiary's net assets. If a subsidiary issues additional shares to outsiders, then new capital is brought into the subsidiary, thereby increasing its net asset value. But the parent's proportionate interest in the increased net asset value is decreased. The parent's equity in the subsidiary is affected by both factors, the increase in the subsidiary's net assets and the decrease in the parent's proportionate interest.

To illustrate the impact of a new issue, assume that on January 1, 19x4, Subsidiary Corporation issues 8,824 new shares to outside interests for net proceeds of $264,706 (about $30 per share). The new issue will increase SC's total outstanding shares to 58,824, and will thereby reduce Parent Corporation's holdings of 30,000 shares to 51% of the total, the same level of ownership that we used in the example in the previous section. Before the new issue, SC had total shareholders' equity of $600,000. The new issue has increased that amount to $864,706. PC formerly owned 60% of $600,000 book value; now PC owns 51% of the $864,706 book value.

The change in the net assets of SC and PC's share thereof is illustrated in Schedule 13-12. PC's equity in the book value of SC's net assets has increased from $360,000 to $441,000 as a result of SC's new issue of shares. But the change in book value is not the only impact that SC's new issue has on PC's equity in SC. PC now has an interest in only 51% of the date-of-acquisition fair-value increment on SC's net assets and only 51% of the goodwill. PC will include in consolidated net income only 51% of SC's future net income. If PC continues to amortize 60% of the fair-value increment and goodwill, PC will be understating its share of SC's earnings.

Therefore, the fair-value increment and the goodwill must be adjusted to reflect PC's lessened interest. PC's ownership interest has declined from 60% to 51%, a decline of nine percentage points, or 15% of the original 60% interest. The fair-value increment attributable to PC's equity declines by 15%, from $162,000 to $137,700 ($162,000 x 85%), and goodwill declines from $87,000 to $73,950 ($87,000 x 85%). These decreases in PC's equity partially offset the increase in PC's share of the net book value, with the result that the equity underlying PC's investment in SC increases from $609,000 to $652,650, a change of $43,650, as shown on the bottom of Schedule 13-12.

The net change in PC's equity in SC amounts to $43,650. This amount is exactly the same as the profit that was recognized in the previous section

SCHEDULE 13-12

	January 1, 19x4			
	Before new issue		After new issue	
	SC total book value	PC share (60%)	SC total book value	PC share (51%)
Current assets	$ 500,000	$300,000	$ 764,706	$390,000
Fixed assets (net)	1,000,000	600,000	1,000,000	510,000
	$1,500,000	900,000	$1,764,706	900,000
Liabilities	$ 900,000	540,000	$ 900,000	459,000
Shareholders' equity	600,000		864,706	
	$1,500,000		$1,764,706	
PC equity in book value of SC net assets		360,000		441,000
PC share of fair-value increment on fixed assets (originally $180,000, amortized for one year)		162,000		137,700
Goodwill on PC share (originally $90,000, amortized for one year)		87,000		73,950
Total equity of PC in SC net assets		$609,000		$652,650

when PC sold part of its holdings. Thus the general impact of a reduction in the parent's proportionate interest in the subsidiary is the same regardless of whether the reduction is the result of a sale by the parent or a new issue by the subsidiary.

When PC prepares consolidated statements just after the new share issue, the consolidated net assets will include the full amount of the book value of SC's net assets plus the reduced amount of fair-value increments and goodwill. The minority interest will be calculated as 49% of SC's new shareholders' equity of $864,706, or $423,706.

Consolidated shareholders' equity will consist of PC's share equity of $2,200,000, plus PC's $9,000 share of SC's unremitted 19x3 earnings ($21,000-$12,000, from Schedule 13-4), plus the gain to PC of $43,650 resulting from the new issue of SC shares. Since SC's shareholders' equity is $864,706, the consolidation worksheet adjustment must eliminate all but $9,000 of that amount, or $855,706. The worksheet entry that accomplishes the foregoing would appear as follows, assuming that the investment account is carried on the cost basis:

Shareholders' equity (of SC)	$855,706	
Fixed assets	137,700	
Goodwill	73,950	
Minority interest		$423,706
Investment in SC		600,000
Shareholders' equity (of PC)		43,650

The credit of $43,650 reflecting the gain to PC can be viewed in two ways: (1) as a gain, to be reflected in consolidated income, or (2) as a capital transaction, to be credited directly to contributed capital.

Under the parent-company approach to consolidations, the consolidated financial statements are prepared from the viewpoint of the shareholders of the parent corporation. A reduction in ownership interest in a subsidiary is deemed to be a voluntary disposal of part of an investment. When a subsidiary issues new shares, the parent's decision not to purchase all or part of the new issue is voluntary, and thus the reduction in interest is voluntary. Also, since the parent controls the subsidiary, the parent must have agreed to the new issue in the first place. Gains on the voluntary disposal of investments are normally treated as income.

Furthermore, it would be inconsistent to treat gains on sales of the parent's shareholdings as income while treating gains from new issues as a capital transaction. Thus the recommended Canadian practice is to treat the credit as a gain to be reported in consolidated net income.[2]

In the example used above, the new issue resulted in a gain to PC and an equivalent increase in PC's equity in SC. However, assume instead that the 8,824 new shares had been issued at $15 per share rather than at $30 per share. The proceeds to SC would have been $132,360, thereby increasing SC's net assets from $600,000 to $732,360. The impact on PC's investment would have been as follows:

Change in net asset book value:	
New share: 51% of $732,360	$373,504
Old share: 60% of $600,000	360,000
Increase in net asset book value	13,504
Decrease in fair-value increment	
(15% x $162,000)	(24,300)
Decrease in goodwill	
(15% x $87,000)	(13,050)
Net decrease in PC's equity in SC	$ 23,846

In this case, PC would have to report a *loss* of $23,846.

If the investment account is carried on the cost basis, the consolidation *worksheet* entry to eliminate the investment account, establish the minority interest, and establish the fair-value increments would appear as follows:

Shareholders' equity (of SC)	$723,360	
Loss on issuance of new shares by subsidiary	23,846	
Fixed assets	137,700	
Goodwill	73,950	
Minority interest		$358,856
Investment in SC		600,000

The debit to eliminate SC's shareholders' equity is for the entire amount after the new issue of $732,360 less PC's $9,000 equity in SC's unremitted 19x3 earnings. The credit for minority interest is 49% of SC's new net asset book value of $732,360.

Finally, assume that the 8,824 shares are sold at a price to net $179,127 total, or $20.30 per share. The impact on PC's equity in SC will be:

---

2 *CICA Handbook*, para. 1600.45. U.S. practice, in contrast, tends to favour treating the gain as a capital transaction.

Change in net book value:

New share: 51% of $779,127	$397,355
Old share: 60% of $600,000	360,000
Increase in book value	37,355
Decrease in fair-value increment	(24,300)
Decrease in goodwill	(13,050)
Net increase in PC's equity in SC	$ 5

Sale at $20.30 per share results in no *net* change for PC and thus no gain or loss.[3] Any new issue at proceeds above $20.30 will result in a gain to PC; any new issue below $20.30 per share will result in a loss to PC. The breakeven point of $20.30 is simple to determine: it is the new carrying value per share of PC's investment. Before the net issue, PC's equity in SC was $609,000. Dividing this amount by the 30,000 shares held by PC yields $20.30, the breakeven proceeds per share.

While issuance at $20.30 will not cause a gain or loss to PC, the new issue still alters the composition of the total investment equity of $609,000, and affects the consolidated balance sheet accordingly. Schedule 13-13 shows the PC consolidated balance sheet both before and after the new issue, assuming the new shares were issued at $20.30. Fixed assets are reduced by the $24,300 decline in the fair-value increment, and goodwill is reduced by the $13,050 that represented a 9% share of SC. These adjustments to consolidated adjustments will be the same regardless of the price at which the new shares are issued. The issue price will affect only the current assets (for the proceeds), consolidated retained earnings (for the gain or loss), and the minority interest.

SCHEDULE 13-13

PC Consolidated Balance Sheet
January 1, 19x4

	Before new issue*	After new issue**
Current assets	$1,500,000	$1,679,127
Fixed assets (net)	3,062,000	3,037,700
Goodwill	87,000	73,950
Total assets	$4,649,000	$4,790,777
Liabilities	$2,200,000	$2,200,00
Minority interest	240,000	382,772
Shareholders' equity	2,209,000	2,209,005
Total equities	$4,649,000	$4,790,777

*From Schedule 13-3 second column.
**8,824 shares issued at $20.30; net proceeds = $179,127.

---

3 The $5 gain in this example is the result of rounding. The issuance of 8,824 new shares will reduce PC's ownership interest to 50.9995% rather than 51% exactly.

SUMMARY

In this chapter, we have discussed the principal impacts on consolidated statements arising from changes in ownership interest. The existence of subsidiary preferred shares does not affect the parent's ownership share of the subsidiary. However, the parent's ownership interest applies to the common share equity rather than to total net assets, because the preferred shares represent a prior claim on the resources of the subsidiary. Similarly, consolidated net income (or the parent's equity in the earnings of the subsidiary) is reduced by the prior claim of the preferred dividends before the parent's share of earnings is determined.

A subsidiary or investee corporation may have restricted shares outstanding. Restricted shares are common shares that have less voting power than regular common shares; frequently, restricted shares are nonvoting. The existence of control or of significant influence is determined by the percentage of votes held by the investor. However, the percentages of fair-value increments, equity pick-up of earnings, and minority interest are determined by the investor's share of earnings available to common shares (both regular and restricted).

When an investor corporation increases its percentage of ownership by acquiring additional shares, the cost of the added portion of ownership is allocated separately. There is a separate and independent determination of fair-value increments and goodwill for each share purchase or for the aggregate purchase in a year, if there were many small purchases.

If an investor sells part of its shares in a subsidiary or significantly influenced company, a gain or loss is recognized on the sale. The amounts of fair-value increments and goodwill decline proportionately, and the minority interest increases.

The issuance of new shares to third parties by the subsidiary or affiliate would not, on the surface, appear to affect the investor's investment. But since a new issue does decrease the investor corporation's ownership share, a new issue is deemed to be a voluntary disposal of a portion of the investor's ownership interest. A gain or loss will be recognized by the investor corporation, similar to the gain or loss recognized when the investor sells a portion of its own interest. A gain will result if the new shares are issued at a price higher than the investor's equity in the investee per share of investment; a loss will arise if the new issue proceeds are less than the investor's per-share equity in the investee.

Many possible changes in ownership interest have not been explored in this chapter. Changes resulting from the conversion of the subsidiary's convertible securities by either the investor or outside interests have not been addressed, for example. The problems of reporting the effects of changes in ownership interests can be quite complex; many of these complexities are beyond the scope of this text.

This chapter concludes our discussion of the reporting of investments by Canadian corporations in other Canadian companies. We have not yet touched on the reporting implications of corporate investments in *foreign* companies, however. Therefore, we will return to intercorporate investments in Part 3 of this text, particularly in Chapters 17 and 18.

SELF-STUDY PROBLEM 13-1[4]

Subco Ltd. has the following balance sheet at July 1, 19x3. On that date, Parco Ltd. purchased 6,000 of the common shares of Subco Ltd. for $312,500 and achieved "significant influence" over the affairs of Subco Ltd.

Subco Ltd.
Balance Sheet
July 1, 19x3

	Historical Cost	FMV (1)
Cash	$ 75,000	$ 75,000
Inventory	200,000	250,000
Fixed assets, net	800,000	750,000
	$1,075,000	
Current liabilities	$ 50,000	50,000
Long-term liabilities	150,000	150,000
Common shares (2)	200,000	
Retained earnings at January 1, 19x3	575,000	
Net income, 19x3 to date	100,000	
	$1,075,000	

(1) Fair Market Value
(2) There are 20,000 shares issued and outstanding.

Subco Ltd. amortizes its fixed assets over ten years straight-line and its intangible assets over twenty years. The inventory is expected to turn over six times per year and is on a FIFO cost system.

Consolidated goodwill is to be amortized over a period of twenty years. On September 1, 19x4, Parco purchased 3,000 more shares of Subco Ltd. for $183,500. The balance sheet of Subco Ltd. at that time was:

Subco Ltd.
Balance Sheet
September 1, 19x4

	Historical Cost	FMV
Cash	$ 80,000	$ 80,000
Inventory	190,000	200,000
Fixed assets, net	1,020,000	1,200,000
	$1,290,000	
Current liabilities	$ 40,000	40,000
Long-term liabilities	150,000	150,000
Common shares	200,000	
Retained earnings at January 1, 19x4	775,000	
Net income, 19x4 to date	125,000	
	$1,290,000	

4 The solutions to the self-study problems are at the end of the book, following Chapter 18.

Subco Ltd. did not pay any dividends and earned $30,000 from September 1, to December 31, 19x4.

On January 1, 19x5, Parco Ltd. sold 4,000 of its shares of Subco Ltd. for $300,000.

Required:

Calculate the gain or loss on the disposal of the shares at January 1, 19x5. Ignore income tax considerations.

[CGA-Canada]

REVIEW QUESTIONS

13-1 Corporation S has 100,000 shares of common stock and 100,000 shares of nonvoting preferred stock outstanding. Corporation P owns 60,000 of S's common shares and 45,000 of S's preferred shares. When P prepares its financial statements, what proportion of S's earnings will be reflected in P's net income?

13-2 S Corporation has 10,000 shares of common stock and 10,000 shares of nonvoting preferred stock outstanding. The preferred stock carries a cumulative dividend of $10 per share per year. S reported net income of $600,000 for the year just ended. If P Corporation owns 7,000 of S's common shares and 2,000 of S's preferred shares, how much of S's net income will be included in P's net income for the year just ended?

13-3 When a subsidiary has both common and preferred shares outstanding, how is the parent's proportionate ownership interest determined?

13-4 If a parent company has purchased some of its subsidiary's preferred shares at a price higher than the carrying value of the shares on the subsidiary's books, how is the difference treated when the parent prepares consolidated financial statements?

13-5 What is meant by a **step purchase**?

13-6 What is a **restricted share**?

13-7 Irene Ltd. has 500,000 common shares outstanding, consisting of 100,000 regular shares with ten votes each and 400,000 restricted shares with one vote each. The shares participate equally in dividends on a share-for-share basis. Gordon Inc. owns 165,000 of the 500,000 shares, 65,000 regular plus 100,000 restricted.
 a. Does Gordon control Irene?
 b. What proportion of Irene's earnings would be included in Gordon's equity-basis earnings?

13-8 What is a **coattail provision**?

13-9 P Ltd. acquired 51% of S Inc. by means of a tender offer on April 1, 19x4. On February 14, 19x6, P increased its ownership of S by an additional 19% through additional purchases. How would P determine the total goodwill pertaining to its 70% interest in S?

13-10 When a step acquisition has occurred, why are the fair-value increments of the subsidiary's net assets not measured entirely at the date of the last purchase?

13-11 P Corp. owned 40% of the voting shares of S Ltd. and exercised significant influence over the affairs of S. Subsequently, P acquired an additional 20% of S's shares. How would the additional acquisition affect the nature of P's reporting of its investment in S?

13-12 P Inc. owned 22% of S Corp. and reported the investment on the cost basis. Subsequently, P acquired an additional 20% interest; the additional shares gave P the ability to significantly influence the affairs of S. How would the fair-value increments and goodwill be determined for the 42% total interest?

13-13 When an investor corporation holds a cost-basis investment in an investee corporation, and then acquires sufficient shares to have significant influence, why is the equity method *not* applied retroactively to the date of the first purchase?

13-14 What are two basic ways in which a parent company can decrease its ownership interest in a subsidiary?

13-15 Why would a parent company want to decrease its share of a subsidiary?

13-16 When a parent company sells part of its investment in a subsidiary, how is the gain or loss on the sale determined?

13-17 When a parent sells part of its investment in a subsidiary, how is the consolidated balance sheet affected?

13-18 When a parent's ownership interest in a subsidiary declines, why would consolidated assets change even though the parent still has control over the same assets?

13-19 Why does the issuance by the subsidiary of new shares to outsiders affect the parent's consolidated assets?

13-20 Why does the parent corporation recognize a gain or loss when the subsidiary issues new shares to third parties?

13-21 How can one determine whether the issuance by a subsidiary of new shares to outsiders will result in a gain or a loss to the parent company?

Dominion Drug Limited
CASE 13-1

In the course of the audit of Dominion Drug Limited (DDL), CA, while reviewing the draft financial statements for the year ended August 31, 1987, noticed that DDL's investment in Canada Pharmaceuticals Limited (CPL) was valued on the cost basis. In 1986, it had been valued on the equity basis. Representing a 22% interest in CPL, this investment had been made ten years ago to infuse fresh equity, with a view to protecting DDL's source of supply for drugs.

DDL's controller informed CA that CPL had suffered a large loss in 1987, as shown by the May interim financial statements. DDL's representative on CPL's board of directors had resigned because DDL's purchases from CPL now constitute less than 5% of its total purchases. In addition, CPL had been uncooperative in providing profit data in time to make the year-end equity adjustment. Consequently, DDL's controller had revised the method of accounting for the investment in CPL.

CA then found out that DDL's managers are planning a share issue in 1988 and do not want their earnings impaired by CPL's poor performance. However, they are reluctant to divest themselves of CPL in case the rumoured development by CPL of a vaccine for a serious viral disease materializes.

When CA approached CPL's managers, they refused to disclose any information on CPL's operations. CA then learned from a stockbroker friend that CPL's poor results were due to its market being undercut by generic drug manufacturers. The loss had been increased when CPL's management wrote off most of CPL's intangible assets. CA summarized the relevant information on the treatment of the investment for his audit file (Exhibit I).

Required:
Discuss the matters raised above.
[CICA]

EXHIBIT I

CA's Notes on Investment in CPL's Shares

Extracts from DDL's draft financial statements for the year ended August 31, 1987, in thousands of dollars, follow:

	1987		1986	
	(Draft)			
Investment in CPL (Note 3)	$25,000	(Note 1)	$27,400	(Note 2)
Retained Earnings:				
Opening balance	$ 6,500		$ 2,350	
plus: net earnings	4,500		7,300	
	11,000		9,650	
less: prior period				
adjustment (Note 1)	2,400		—	
dividends	2,250		3,150	
Closing balance	$ 6,350		$ 6,500	

Note 1:
Represents original cost. The 1986 balance has been reduced by the amount of previously recorded equity interest of $2.4 million. In the nine months ended May 31, 1987, CPL reported a net loss of $140 million after writing off development and patent costs as extraordinary items.

Note 2:
Valued on equity basis. Equity adjustment for 1986 involved the elimination of $5 million unrealized profit included in ending inventory, on sales from CPL to DDL.

The unrealized profit in DDL's ending inventory for 1987 amounts to $1 million.

Note 3:
Stock-market trading in CPL's common shares has been heavy in 1987. Prices for the year are as follows:

August 31, 1986:	$20.00
February 28, 1987:	$ 5.00
August 31, 1987:	$13.00

DDL owns 2,000,000 common shares of CPL; in neither 1986 nor 1987 did CPL declare or pay any dividends.

CASE 13-2   Computo Ltd.

Every Friday afternoon, the audit staff of the firm of Tidua & Co. Chartered Accountants meets to discuss various technical and professional client matters. These meetings are used for training, planning audits, or discussing the results of audit work.

Computo Ltd. (CL), a new client, was the subject of discussion at one of these meetings. Roy Gray, an audit manager with Tidua & Co., had made several visits to CL. During these visits, Jeff Jax, the president, had explained the operations of his company at some length. He had also described some of CL's accounting practices, including its revenue recognition policies. At this Friday afternoon meeting, Gray relayed portions of his conversations with Jax and provided background information on the company.

CL, a favourite of the investment community, is a public company with shares listed on Canadian stock exchanges. Its shares, originally issued at $4.50 five years ago, have recently been trading in the $25-to-$30 range. Jeff Jax owns 65% of the voting shares of CL.

Five months ago, Jax approached the senior partner of Tidua & Co., stating that he had heard of the firm's excellent reputation and wanted it as auditor. Jax indicated that CL was growing quickly, and that he wanted Tidua & Co. to handle all financial affairs for both CL and himself personally.

Jax indicated that owing to the significance of debt financing, maintaining good relations with CL's various lenders was important. He did not want any difficulties with them resulting from disputes over the financial statements. Also, Jax made it clear that he wanted to maintain the company's rising profit picture. He said it correctly portrayed the growth and innovation of the company and facilitated further expansion.

CL manufactures the hardware and develops the software for Computo, a full line of microcomputers for home and small office applications. Even though CL is faced with strong competition from the well-known products of Tandy, Apple, IBM, and others, Jax expects great expansion ahead through franchising and special contracts.

CL operates five company stores in three major cities. In order to expand into more cities and increase its share of the market, CL sells store franchises. The number of franchise stores dealing exclusively in the Computo line is growing quickly. The franchisee is granted the exclusive right to the Computo name and products for a store in a specific area. CL is required to supply advice on store location, and to provide technical training, advertising, and other specified franchise-support activities. Each store handles only the Computo line of microcomputer products, but noncompeting lines of electronic merchandise can also be carried.

New, advanced products with good consumer acceptance are continually emerging as a result of the major expenditures on research and development during the past few years. CL's revenues were growing as the following financial statement excerpts indicate:

	Year ended December 31, 1989	Year ended December 31, 1988
	(in thousands of dollars)	
Sales of franchises	$4,520	$2,459
Sales of equipment	2,896	2,270
Continuing fees	898	549
Software and other sales	3,066	1,781

Franchises are sold for a franchise price ranging from $80,000 to $150,000, depending on store location. Terms of payment include a downpayment and a series of notes payable to CL with terms ranging from five to ten years. The notes bear interest at rates significantly below the market rate at the time the agreement is signed. The financial arrangements are intended to help the new franchisees become established. CL recognizes the franchise price as revenue when contracts with franchisees are signed. Jax stated that the notes receivable are recorded by CL at face value to conform to generally accepted accounting principles.

Continuing fees are charged as a percentage of each franchisee's monthly sales of the Computo line. These fees are recorded on an accrual basis each month when reports are received from the franchisees. Revenue from both equipment and software sales is recognized when shipments are made from CL's plant.

In common with other growing firms, CL is highly leveraged and owes slightly over $10 million at an average interest rate of nearly 17%. A substantial part of the proceeds from this debt was used to finance research and development. A second major portion was used to finance two special projects. The remainder was used to finance the manufacturing assets for the Computo line.

In 1989, research costs and development costs other than interest were close to $2 million each. CL had capitalized nearly 90% of the total $4 million to match these costs with the applicable future revenues. In addition, CL capitalized the interest on the debt applicable to the research and development expenditures. In Jax's opinion, all these costs would have a highly beneficial effect on CL in the future.

Jax was uncertain about what accounting policy he should use for the interest charges on debt relating to CL's two new special projects. He thought these interest charges should probably be capitalized because the benefits and revenues would flow in a future period.

One project is the design and construction by CL's engineers of a manufacturing facility for a line of video games. This project has been underway for nine months and will be completed in the next fiscal year. Production and marketing of the video games will commence immediately upon completion of the facility. The other project is the manufacturing of a large number of special-design, computerized components for Canadian Armed Forces equipment. All of the design costs and about 30% of the production costs will be incurred in this fiscal year. Delivery of the components will be made next year.

The interest on the debt related to the manufacturing assets for the Computo line was expensed because Jax said that it would not benefit future periods.

Jax has also discussed CL's subsidiary companies with Gray. CL has both active and dormant subsidiaries. The eight active subsidiaries consist of the five company stores and three franchise stores. These three franchise stores were acquired when their principals became ill or encountered other problems. All eight stores are currently operated by the company. The dormant subsidiaries consist of companies that had been acquired by CL from franchisees who wanted out of the business and had closed the stores.

When CL acquired the franchise companies, it bought the shares by issuing notes payable. The interest rate on these notes is at half the market rate at the settlement date. After acquisition, any outstanding notes receivable relating to the original sale of the franchise were treated by CL as increments to the investment in subsidiaries account.

Jax noted with satisfaction that he adhered to a strict policy of amortizing, over forty years, the excess of the cost of shares of subsidiary companies acquired over their book value at the date of acquisition. Goodwill in the balance sheet was $1,552,000 in 1989 and $1,514,000 in 1988. Jax explained that a large part of these amounts arose on the acquisition of the problem stores.

When CL sells the franchise companies, gains are recorded after contracts are signed, consideration has passed, and initial support conditions have been met. The downpayment is received in cash while the remainder of the consideration is recorded as notes receivable. Gains on sales of these companies are included in the income statement under software and other sales.

CL's accounting policy for intercorporate investments is to consolidate all of the companies in which it owns more than a 50% interest. It uses the equity basis for those companies where it holds 50% or less and is able to exercise significant influence.

Considerable discussion of CL's financial and accounting affairs took place during the Friday afternoon meeting. Gray closed the meeting by summarizing the issues raised and requesting you to prepare a written report on the accounting issues. He asked you to recommend and justify the accounting policies that should be followed.

Required:
Prepare the report for Roy Gray.
[CICA]

P13-1

On July 1, 19x1, Super Corp. purchased 80% of the common shares and 40% of the preferred shares of Paltry Corp. by issuing Super Corp. shares that had a total market value of $3,700,000. On that date, Paltry's shareholders' equity accounts appear as follows:

Common shares, no par (200,000 shares)	$2,000,000
Preferred shares, no par (10,000 shares)	1,100,000
Other contributed capital	400,000
Retained earnings	1,500,000
	$5,000,000

Paltry's preferred shares are cumulative and nonparticipating and carry a dividend rate of $12 per year per share. The dividends are paid at the end of each calendar quarter. The redemption price of the preferred shares is $100 per share. At the time of Super's purchase, the Paltry preferred shares were selling on the market at $85.

The fair values of Paltry's net assets were identical to their book values on July 1, 19x1. Super Corp.'s policy is to amortize goodwill (if any) over twenty years.

During 19x1 and 19x2, Paltry's net income and dividends declared (common and preferred) were as follows:

Years ended December 31	Net income	Dividends
19x1	$300,000	$200,000
19x2	$400,000	$250,000

All preferred dividends were declared and paid quarterly, as due. Paltry earns its income ratably throughout the year.

Required:
a. Determine the amounts at which each of Super's investments in the common and preferred shares of Paltry should appear in Super's balance sheet on December 31, 19x1, and on December 31, 19x2, assuming that Super does not consolidate Paltry. Show all calculations clearly.
b. Assume that on January 2, 19x3, Super Corp sells 1,000 of its Paltry preferred shares. Determine the balance remaining in the investment account for the preferred shares after the sale.

P13-2

Consult P13-1. Assume that on January 2, 19x3, Super Corp. sells 1,000 of its preferred shares and 40,000 of its common shares in Paltry. The sales net $96 per preferred share and $20 per common share.

During 19x3, Paltry earns net income of $100,000, pays the preferred dividends for only the first three quarters, and pays no common dividends.

Required:

a. Determine the gain or loss to be reported by Super that arose from the sale of the preferred and common shares of Paltry.

b. Determine the balances of the investment accounts to be reported by Super on December 31, 19x3, assuming that Super does not consolidate Paltry.

P13-3

On January 2, 19x2, Playful Inc. purchased 60% of the outstanding common shares of Serious Ltd. for $6,000,000.

Serious's condensed balance sheet at that time was as follows:

Current assets		$ 8,000,000
Fixed assets		17,000,000
		$25,000,000
Current liabilities		$ 5,000,000
Long-term liabilities		10,000,000
Shareholders' equity:		
Common shares (100,000, no par)	$2,500,000	
Preferred shares (100,000, no par, $4 dividend, callable at $40; cumulative and nonvoting)	4,200,000	
Retained earnings	3,300,000	
		10,000,000
		$25,000,000

The fair value of Serious's assets was the same as their book value except for fixed assets, which had a fair value of $20,000,000. The fixed assets have a remaining useful life of fifteen years. Goodwill on the purchase, if any, will be amortized over twenty years.

On October 1, 19x2, Playful purchased 20,000 of Serious's preferred shares at $32 per share. There were no dividend arrearages. Serious declared the fourth-quarter preferred dividend on December 15, 19x2, payable on January 15, 9x3, to holders of record on December 30, 19x2.

The condensed balance sheets for both Playful and Serious were as follows on December 31, 19x2:

	Playful Inc.	Serious Ltd.
Current assets	$12,000,000	$ 7,000,000
Fixed assets	20,000,000	20,000,000
Investments (at cost)	6,640,000	—
	$38,640,000	$27,000,000
Current liabilities	$10,000,000	$ 6,000,000
Long-term liabilities	5,000,000	10,000,000
Shareholders equity:		
Common shares	8,000,000	2,500,000
Preferred shares	—	4,200,000
Retained earnings	15,640,000	4,300,000
	$38,640,000	$27,000,000

Required:

Prepare a consolidated balance sheet for Playful Inc. at December 31, 19x2.

Pike Ltd. is a producer of plastics that uses oil in the manufacturing process. To ensure a reliable supply of oil at current prices, on January 1, 19x3, the company purchased 80% of the common shares and 25% of the preferred shares of Spike Ltd. for $205,000. The preferred shares were purchased at their stated value of $5 each. On the date of acquisition, Spike Ltd.'s shareholders' equity was as follows:

Preferred 6% cumulative, 20,000 shares outstanding	$100,000
Common, no par value, 200,000 shares outstanding	200,000
Retained earnings	100,000
	$400,000

On January 1, 19x3, the fair values of net identifiable assets of Spike Ltd. equalled their book values except for oil-related fixed assets, which were worth $200,000 less than their recorded values. All allocations of the excess of purchase price over book value are to be amortized over ten years.

Additional Information:
1. Spike Ltd. has incurred minor losses in the two years prior to acquisition, and was expected to operate at a breakeven level after acquisition. On January 1, 19x3, $5,000 of accumulated potential tax benefits in respect of non-capital losses were unrecorded by Spike Ltd.
2. During 19x7, Spike sold oil to Pike at a price of $500,000, which included a markup of 5% on cost. The price at which Spike was selling to Pike was well below fair market value for oil, and the policy of 5% markup on cost had been followed since acquisition. On December 31, 19x7, Pike's ending inventories included $42,000 in oil (some of which was in manufactured products and work-in-progress) purchased from Spike. This closing inventory represented a 20% reduction over 19x6's closing inventory of oil purchased from Spike. Pike's oil inventory turns over twice per year.
3. On January 1, 19x7, Spike sold fixed assets to Pike for proceeds of $20,000. These assets had a net book value of $40,000 and a remaining useful life of four years.
4. During 19x7, as a result of a terrorist act, Pike's uninsured warehouse, which had a net book value of $100,000, was blown up and destroyed. The land on which the warehouse was situated was then sold to Spike at a gain of $2,000.
5. On January 1, 19x7, Spike's preferred dividends were one year in arrears. During 19x7, Spike paid $20,000 in dividends to common shareholders.
6. During 19x7, Pike's capital stock consisted of 100,000 common shares. Pike's long-term debt consisted of 10% debentures that are convertible into 100,000 common shares.
7. Summarized adjusted trial balances as at December 31, 19x7, are as follows:

	Pike	Spike
Cash	$ 35,000	$ 34,000
Accounts receivable	112,000	53,000
Inventories	210,000	40,000
Land	27,000	35,000
Fixed assets (net)	905,000	429,000
Investment in Spike	205,000	—
Accounts payable	(281,000)	(74,000)
Long-term debt	(500,000)	(190,000)
Preferred shares	—	(100,000)
Common shares	(250,000)	(200,000)
Retained earnings	(388,000)	(62,000)
Dividends paid	—	32,000
Revenues	(1,794,000)	(1,190,000)
Dividend income	(19,000)	—
Cost of sales	1,148,000	840,000
Other expenses	492,000	333,000
Loss on disposal of fixed assets	98,000	20,000
	$ 0	$ 0

Required:

In accordance with generally accepted accounting principles, calculate the following. (Show all calculations and supporting analysis. Ignore income taxes.)

a. Consolidated earnings per share, basic and fully diluted, for 19x7.
b. The following consolidated balance sheet accounts at December 31, 19x7:
   1. Inventory
   2. Land
   3. Fixed assets
   4. Goodwill
   5. Minority interest
   6. Retained earnings

[SMA]

P13-5

On January 1, 19x6, Jeffries, Inc. paid $700,000 for 10,000 shares of Wolf Company's voting common stock, which was a 10% interest in Wolf. At that date, the net assets of Wolf totaled $6,000,000. The fair values of all of Wolf's identifiable assets and liabilities were equal to their book values. Jeffries does not have the ability to exercise significant influence over the operating and financial policies of Wolf. Jeffries received dividends of $0.90 per share from Wolf on October 1, 19x6. Wolf reported net income of $400,000 for the year ended December 31, 19x6.

On July 1, 19x7, Jeffries paid $2,300,000 for 30,000 additional shares of Wolf Company's voting common stock, which represents a 30% investment in Wolf. The fair values of all of Wolf's identifiable assets net of liabilities were equal to their book values of $6,500,000. As a result of this transaction, Jeffries has the ability to exercise significant influence over the operating and financial policies of Wolf. Jeffries received dividends of $1.10 per share from Wolf on April 1, 19x7, and $1.35 per share on October 1, 19x7. Wolf reported net income before taxes of $500,000 for the year ended December 31, 19x7, and $200,000 for the six months ended December 31, 19x7. Jeffries amortizes goodwill over a 40-year period.

Required:

a. Prepare a schedule showing the income or loss before income taxes for the

year ended December 31, 19x6, which Jeffries should report from its investment in Wolf in its income statement issued in March 19x7.

b. During March 19x8, Jeffries issues comparative financial statements for 19x6
and 19x7. Prepare schedules showing the income or loss before income taxes
for the years ended December 31, 19x6 and 19x7 that Jeffries should report
from its investment in Wolf. Show supporting computations in good form.
[AICPA, adapted]

P13-6

The December 31, 19x9, balance sheets of Encanto Corporation and its subsidiary,
Norris Corporation, are presented below:

	Encanto Corporation	Norris Corporation
ASSETS		
Cash	$ 167,250	$101,000
Accounts receivable	178,450	72,000
Notes receivable	87,500	28,000
Dividends receivable	36,000	
Inventories	122,000	68,000
Property, plant, and equipment	487,000	252,000
Accumulated depreciation	(117,000)	(64,000)
Investment in Norris Corporation	240,800	
	$1,202,000	$457,000
LIABILITIES AND SHAREHOLDERS' EQUITY		
Accounts payable	$ 222,000	$ 76,000
Notes payable	79,000	89,000
Dividend payable		40,000
Common shares	400,000	100,000
Retained earnings	501,000	152,000
	$1,202,000	$457,000

Additional Information:
1. Encanto initially acquired 60% of the outstanding common shares of Norris in
19x7. This purchase resulted in no difference between cost and net assets acquired. As of December 31, 19x9, the percentage owned is 90%. An analysis of
the investment in Norris account is as follows:

Date	Description	Amount
Dec. 31, 19x7	Acquired 6,000 shares	$ 70,800
Dec. 31, 19x8	60% of 19x8 net income of $78,000	46,800
Sept. 1, 19x9	Acquired 3,000 shares	92,000
Dec. 31, 19x9	Subsidiary income for 19x9:	67,200*
Dec. 31, 19x9	90% of dividends declared	(36,000)
		$240,800

*Subsidiary income for 19x9:

60% of $96,000	$57,600
30% of $96,000 × 33⅓%	9,600
	$67,200

Norris's net income is earned evenly over the year. The excess of cost over the
net assets acquired is to be amortized over 60 months.

2. On December 13, 19x9, Norris declared a cash dividend of $4 per share of common, payable to shareholders on January 7, 19x10.

3. During 19x9, Encanto sold merchandise to Norris. Encanto's cost for this merchandise was $68,000, and the sale was made at 125% of cost. Norris's inventory at December 31, 19x9, included merchandise purchased from Encanto at a cost to Norris of $35,000.

4. In December 19x8, Norris sold merchandise to Encanto for $67,000, which was at a markup of 35% over Norris's cost. On January 1, 19x9, $54,000 of this merchandise remained in Encanto's inventory. This merchandise was subsequently sold by Encanto at a profit of $11,000 during 19x9.

5. On October 1, 19x9, Encanto sold excess equipment to Norris for $42,000. Data related to this equipment is as follows:

Book value on Encanto's records	$36,000
Method of depreciation	Straight-line
Estimated remaining life on October 1, 19x9	10 years

6. Near the end of 19x9, Norris reduced the balance of its intercompany account payable to Encanto to zero by transferring $8,000 to Encanto. This payment was still in transit on December 31, 19x9.

Required:

Prepare the consolidated balance sheet for Encanto Corporation as of December 31, 19x9. Supporting computations should be in good form.
[AICPA, adapted]

P13-7

On December 31, 19x2, the Brown Company acquired 20% of the outstanding voting shares of the Best Company for $2 million in cash. On that date, the shareholders' equity of the Best Company was as follows:

Common shares	$5,000,000
Retained earnings	3,000,000
Total	$8,000,000

Also on this date, all of the identifiable assets and liabilities of the Best Company had fair values equal to their carrying values except for plant and equipment, which had a fair value that was $150,000 greater than its carrying value. This plant and equipment had a remaining useful life of twelve years and was being depreciated by the straight-line method.

On December 31, 19x4, the Brown Company acquired an additional 40% of the Best Company's outstanding voting shares in return for cash in the amount of $6 million. At this date, the shareholders' equity of the Best Company was as follows:

Common shares	$ 5,000,000
Retained earnings	7,500,000
Total	$12,500,000

At the time of this second purchase, all of the identifiable assets and liabilities of the Best Company had fair values equal to their carrying values except for plant and equipment, which had a fair value that was $600,000 greater than its carrying value. The remaining useful life of the plant and equipment is ten years and it is being depreciated by the straight-line method.

Any goodwill arising on either of the preceding purchases should be amortized over a period of twenty years from the date of the purchase.

There were no intercompany transactions in any of the years 19x2 through 19x6.

On December 31, 19x6, the balance sheets of the two companies were as follows:

	Brown	Best
Net monetary assets	$ 7,000,000	$ 3,000,000
Investment in Best (cost)	8,000,000	
Plant and equipment (net)	15,000,000	11,000,000
Total	$30,000,000	$14,000,000
Common shares	$10,000,000	$ 5,000,000
Retained earnings	20,000,000	9,000,000
Total	$30,000,000	$14,000,000

Required:
Prepare, for the Brown Company and its subsidiary, the Best Company, a consolidated balance sheet at December 31, 19x6. All calculations should be shown. Assume that the initial purchase had given Brown Company significant influence in Best Company.
[SMA]

P13-8

Pinto Ltd. had the following transactions in the shares of Saddle Ltd.:

Year	Date	%*	Cost	Equity Jan. 1	Equity Dec. 31	Goodwill
19x1	January 1	30%	$ 80,000	$150,000	$220,000	$35,000
19x2	January 1	35%	100,000	220,000	300,000	23,000
19x3	July 1	6.5%	—	300,000	410,000	—

*Of Saddle Ltd.'s shares.

The income of Saddle Ltd. is earned evenly over the year.

Any excess of purchase price over book value is attributable solely to goodwill, which will be amortized over the maximum allowable period.

Saddle Ltd. has 100,000 shares outstanding.

The July 1 transaction is a sale of shares by Pinto Ltd. The proceeds were $40,000.

Pinto uses the equity method of recording investments where appropriate.

Required:
Prepare the journal entries for Pinto Ltd. for 19x1, 19x2, and 19x3, up to July 2, 19x3, assuming no dividends.
[CGA-Canada]

P13-9

On October 1, 19x6, Par Ltd. sold its 80% interest in the subsidiary, Sub Ltd., for $1,950,000. Prior to the date of sale, Par Ltd. had recorded the investment in a subsidiary account on the *cost* basis, which showed $1,100,000. At the date of sale, the consolidated entity had a residual unamortized revaluation of the fixed assets (from the original purchase price discrepancy) of $250,000 and unamortized goodwill arising from the acquisition of the subsidiary of $152,500. The goodwill was being amortized at the rate of $10,000 per year. There were no intercompany transactions between the parent and the subsidiary.

At the date of the sale, October 1, 19x6, the balance sheet of Sub Ltd. was:

Sub Ltd.
October 1, 19x6

	Net Book Value	Fair Market Value
Cash	$ 130,000	$130,000
Receivables	160,000	160,000
Inventory	520,000	580,000
Fixed assets, net	940,000	890,000
	$1,750,000	
Current liabilities	$ 124,000	124,000
Common shares	300,000	
Retained earnings	1,006,000	
Income — January 1 to October 31, 19x6	320,000	
	$1,750,000	

Par Ltd.'s 19x5 and 19x6 consolidated balance sheets were as follows:

Par Ltd.
Consolidated Balance Sheet

	December 31, 19x5	December 31, 19x6
Cash	$ 256,000	$1,420,000
Receivables	368,000	246,000
Inventory	742,000	538,000
Fixed assets, net	1,720,000	845,000
Goodwill	160,000	—
	$3,246,000	$3,049,000
Current liabilities	$ 422,000	$ 115,000
Minority interest	261,200	—
Common shares	500,000	500,000
Retained earnings	2,062,800	2,434,000
	$3,246,000	$3,049,000

The net income for the year for the consolidated entity was $371,200, but this was after the extraordinary item for the gain on the sale of the subsidiary. No dividends were paid. The consolidated depreciation expense was $104,000, which included the depreciation of the fixed asset revaluation. Ignore income taxes on the sale.

Required:
Calculate the gain on the sale of the subsidiary.
[CGA-Canada]

P13-10

Par Limited has three subsidiaries, all 80% owned, and, at December 31, 19x7, they have the following balance sheets:

	Sub 1 Limited	Sub 2 Limited	Sub 3 Limited
Cash	$ 100,000	$ 120,000	$ 140,000
Receivables	200,000	230,000	250,000
Inventory	520,000	590,000	610,000
Fixed assets, net	660,000	890,000	920,000
	$1,480,000	$1,830,000	$1,920,000
Current liabilities	$ 130,000	$ 140,000	$ 150,000
Common shares	300,000	400,000	500,000
Retained earnings	1,050,000	1,290,000	1,270,000
	$1,480,000	$1,830,000	$1,920,000

Note: The retained earnings include 19x7 net income.

Selected balance sheet information of *Par Limited* as at December 31, 19x7, with respect to each subsidiary is as follows:

	Sub 1 Limited	Sub 2 Limited	Sub 3 Limited
Investment in Sub	$1,370,000	$1,252,000	$1,536,000
Fixed asset, unamortized revaluation	150,000	(100,000)	—
Goodwill	140,000	—	120,000
Number of shares outstanding	50,000	100,000	10,000

The "Investment in Sub" account for each subsidiary is kept on the equity basis and includes all entries for 19x7, with the exception of the following:

On the last day of the year, after all the accounts had been brought up to date but before the closing entries had been made, the subsidiaries had the following transactions:

- Sub 1 Limited issued a 100% stock dividend to all common shareholders.
- Sub 2 Limited issued shares equal to 10% or 10,000 shares of the present outstanding amount, to the minority interest shareholders for $38 per share.
- Sub 3 Limited purchases and retires 10% or 1,000 shares of the outstanding shares from the minority interest for a price of $150 per share.

Par Limited will consolidate the subsidiaries but has kept the investment in subsidiary accounts on the equity basis.

Required:
Considering that the parent company is using the equity method for its investment in subsidiary accounts, prepare a separate journal entry(ies) to record the above events for each subsidiary on the parent company's books. (If no journal entry on the parent's books is needed, then *explain why*.) Indicate any gain or loss that would appear on the consolidated financial statements. If no gain or loss is present, *explain why*. (Be precise.)
[CGA-Canada]

P13-11

Presented in Exhibit 1 are the trial balances (unconsolidated) for the year ended December 31, 19x5, of Royal Company and its subsidiary, Butler Company.

Additional Information:

1. On January 3, 19x3, Royal acquired from John Roth, the sole shareholder of Butler Company, for $440,000 cash, both a patent valued at $40,000 and 80% of the outstanding shares of Butler. The net book value of Butler's shares on the date of acquisition was $500,000, and the book values of the individual assets and liabilities were equal to their fair market values. Royal charged the entire $440,000 to the account designated, "investment in stock of Butler Company." The patent, for which no amortization had been charged, had a remaining legal life of four years as of January 3, 19x3.

2. On July 1, 19x5, Royal reduced its investment in Butler to 75% of Butler's outstanding common shares, by selling shares for $70,000 to an unaffiliated company at a profit of $16,000. Royal recorded the proceeds as a credit to its investment account.

3. For the six months ended June 30, 19x5, Butler had net income of $140,000. Royal recorded 80% of this amount on its books of account prior to the time of sale.

4. During 19x4, Butler sold merchandise to Royal for $130,000, which was at a markup of 30% over Butler's cost. On January 1, 19x5, $52,000 of this merchandise remained in Royal's inventory. This merchandise was subsequently sold by Royal in February 19x5, at a profit of $8,000.

5. In November 19x5, Royal sold merchandise to Butler for the first time. Royal's cost of this merchandise was $80,000, and the sale was made at 120% of cost. Butler's inventory at December 31, 19x5, contained merchandise that was purchased from Royal at a cost to Butler of $24,000.

6. On December 31, 19x5, there was a $45,000 payment-in-transit from Butler Company to Royal Company. Accounts receivable and accounts payable include intercompany receivables and payables.

7. In December 19x5, Butler declared and paid cash dividends of $100,000 to its stockholders.

8. On December 31, 19x5, Royal purchased 50% of the outstanding bonds issued by Butler for $58,000. The bonds mature on December 31, 19x9, and were originally issued at a discount. On December 31, 19x5, the balance in Butler's account for unamortized discount on bonds payable was $2,400. It is the intention of the management of Royal to hold these bonds until their maturity.

Required:

Prepare a consolidated balance sheet and statement of income and retained earnings for Royal Company as of December 31, 19x5.
[AICPA, adapted]

EXHIBIT 1		

Royal Company and Subsidiary Trial Balances
December 31, 19x5
Dr. (Cr.)

	Royal Company	Butler Company
ASSETS		
Cash	$ 486,000	$ 249,600
Accounts receivable	235,000	185,000
Inventories	475,000	355,000
Machinery and equipment	2,231,000	530,000
Investment in shares of Butler Company	954,000	—
Investment in bonds of Butler Company	58,000	—
	$ 4,439,000	$ 1,319,600
LIABILITIES AND OWNERS' EQUITY		
Accounts payable	$ (384,000)	$ (62,000)
Bonds payable	—	(120,000)
Unamortized discount on bonds payable	—	2,400
Common shares		
Royal Company	(1,200,000)	—
Butler Company	—	(250,000)
Contributed capital	—	(50,000)
Retained earnings January 1, 19x5	(2,100,000)	(640,000)
Dividends paid	170,000	100,000
Sales	(4,000,000)	(1,700,000)
Cost of sales	2,982,000	1,015,000
Operating expenses	400,000	377,200
Dividend income	(75,000)	—
Subsidiary income	(232,000)	—
Interest expense	—	7,800
	$(4,439,000)	$(1,319,600)

P13-12

On January 1, 19x1, Princess Ltd. became the largest shareholder of Sun Ltd. by acquiring 30% of the outstanding voting shares of Sun Ltd. for $242,000. On January 1, 19x4, Princess Ltd. purchased an additional 50% of Sun Ltd.'s shares for $558,000. Sun Ltd.'s shareholders' equity section at each date of acquisition was as follows:

	January 1, 19x1	January 1, 19x4
Common shares	$700,000	$700,000
Retained earnings	20,000	112,000
	$720,000	$812,000

On January 1, 19x1, the fair value of Sun Ltd.'s inventory was $20,000 greater than its carrying value. On January 1, 19x4, the fair value of Sun Ltd.'s inventory was

$10,000 greater than its carrying value. Also on January 1, 19x4, Sun Ltd. had a favourable operating lease contract on one of its buildings, with rental payments well below market rent. The fair value of the difference between the remaining contractual payments and market rent of an equivalent property was estimated to be $150,000. As of January 1, 19x4, there were three years remaining in the lease contract. Princess Ltd. amortizes any recorded amount of goodwill over 40 years.

The net incomes for the two companies for the year ended December 31, 19x5, were determined as follows:

	Princess Ltd.	Sun Ltd.
Sales	$2,100,000	$735,000
Dividend revenue	50,400	—
	2,150,400	735,000
Cost of goods sold	1,058,050	469,000
Selling and administrative expense (including income taxes)	910,350	175,000
	1,968,400	644,000
Net income	$ 182,000	$ 91,000

The amount of retained earnings for the two companies at December 31, 19x5, was determined as follows:

	Princess Ltd.	Sun Ltd.
Retained earnings, January 1	$787,500	$130,000
Add: Net income	182,000	91,000
	969,500	221,000
Less: Dividends	87,500	63,000
Retained earnings, December 31	$882,000	$158,000

The condensed balance sheets for the two companies at December 31, 19x5, were as follows:

	Princess Ltd.	Sun Ltd.
ASSETS		
Current assets	$ 490,000	$385,000
Investment in Sun Ltd. (at cost)	800,000	
Other assets	1,510,000	536,000
Total assets	$2,800,000	$921,000
LIABILITIES AND SHAREHOLDERS' EQUITY:		
Current liabilities	$ 100,000	$ 63,000
Bonds payable	300,000	—
Common shares	1,518,000	700,000
Retained earnings	882,000	158,000
Total liabilities and shareholders' equity	$2,800,000	$921,000

Additional Information:

1. On average, the inventory of Sun Ltd. turns over four times a year.
2. During 19x4, Sun Ltd. sold inventory costing $140,000 to Princess Ltd. for $175,000. One-quarter of these goods was in Princess Ltd.'s inventory on De-

cember 31, 19x4. During 19x5, Sun Ltd. sold inventory costing $168,000 to Princess Ltd. for $210,000. One-third of these goods was in Princess Ltd.'s inventory on December 31, 19x5.

3. Equipment with a remaining useful life of three years was sold to Sun Ltd. from Princess Ltd. on January 2, 19x4, for $270,000. The equipment, which originally cost $400,000 and had accumulated depreciation of $100,000 at the date of transfer, was being depreciated on a straight-line basis over four years by Princess Ltd. Annual depreciation of $90,000 was recorded by Sun Ltd. for the equipment during 19x4 and 19x5.

Required:

Prepare the following in accordance with generally accepted accounting principles:

a. Fully labeled schedules of calculation and allocation of the excess of the purchase price over book value at each date of acquisition.
b. A consolidated statement of income for 19x5.
c. A consolidated statement of retained earnings for 19x5.

Show all supporting calculations.
[SMA]

14

Segmented and Interim Reporting

A. SEGMENTED REPORTING

In the past eight chapters, we discussed the preparation of consolidated financial statements. In our discussion, we pointed out that consolidated statements may be of limited usefulness to some readers, because they may hide more than they reveal. The intent of consolidated statements is to portray the entire span of economic resources over which the reporting enterprise has control, and the equities in those resources.

Despite the substance of control over subsidiaries' assets, the form of the enterprise is still that of separate legal entities, and readers of the statements such as creditors may in fact have access only to those assets directly owned by the reporting enterprise in the event of bankruptcy or other financial difficulties. One of the assets of a parent company would be its shares in its subsidiaries, and these *shares* would be available to satisfy creditors; however, the *assets* of the subsidiary would be beyond the reach of the parent's creditors.

Thus consolidated statements can give a misleading picture of the financial health of the legal entity that constitutes the reporting enterprise and could cloak a high-risk situation. It is for this reason that the vast majority of the industrialized countries, excepting only Canada and the United States, require reporting of both consolidated and unconsolidated statements. Other countries seem to feel that stewardship reporting is better served if stakeholders can see the unconsolidated as well as the consolidated statements.

Consolidated statements can also mask poor investments. Managers sometimes go into ventures that turn out not to perform as anticipated. A common modern example is that of corporations establishing subsidiaries to develop computer peripheral equipment or software. In many cases, the subsidiaries turned out not to have the necessary expertise either technically or in marketing to make the ventures successful. While bad investments will certainly adversely affect the parent's operating performance, the true dimensions of a fiasco are hidden when the unsuccessful ventures are consolidated with the successful parts of the business. Performance evaluation by external users can be made more difficult by consolidated statements.

A third problem with consolidated statements is that when a company is engaged in several lines of business, it is difficult for an investor or creditor to appraise the future earnings and cash flow prospects for the firm and to evaluate the riskiness of the company's business. Each type of business will be affected by different factors relating to markets, supply, competition, etc. An analyst can make reasonable predictions of cash flow and earnings only on the basis of information not included in the consolidated financial statements.

The difficulty of trying to analyze a corporation based only on the consolidated statements was heightened by the conglomerate movement in the 1960s, particularly in the United States. Companies were combining with other companies in totally different lines of business, such as a manufacturer of trucks merging with a supermarket chain. The conglomerate movement led to widely diversified companies such as Gulf and Western and ITT. The consolidated financial statements of corporations engaged in highly disparate lines of business were of limited use to analysts.

The problems of using consolidated statements led to the requirement by the Securities and Exchange Commission in the United States for "line of business" reporting. Beginning in 1969, SEC registrants were required to disclose revenues and pre-tax profits from each line of business that constituted 10% or more of the corporation's total activity. Thus began a trend to the reporting of segmented information in order to overcome some of the problems of consolidated reporting.

Segmented reporting helps analysts to predict the prospects of the business by disaggregating much of the data that the consolidated statements have aggregated. Reporting by segments also prevents the hiding of poorly performing lines of business, or at least makes their obfuscation more difficult.

Segment reporting is not the same as business-entity reporting. Reporting by line of business or by industry or geographic segment does not necessarily result in reporting the results of individual corporate entities. Thus the first criticism of consolidated reporting cited above is still not appeased. Only if there is a correspondence between segments and corporate entities is the shareholder or creditor able to gain some insight into the viability of the individual corporation in which she or he has a stake.

In Canada, the conglomerate movement was not so pronounced as it was in the United States, and the need for explicit reporting requirements for segments did not evolve as quickly. Some of the corporations acts began to include requirements for reporting classes of business, such as Section 47 of the *Canada Business Corporations Act*, which provides that "the financial statements of a corporation shall disclose separately or in a schedule thereto a summary of the financial information for each class of business the revenue from which is 10 per cent or more of the corporation's total revenues for the period."

In 1979, the AcSC issued Section 1700 (*Segmented Information*) of the *CICA Handbook*. This section lays out guidelines for reporting on classes of business, both by industry and by geographic area. The recommendations are quite broad, and permit substantial flexibility in reporting. In the following pages, we will focus mainly on the recommendations of Section 1700.

Unlike almost all other sections of the *Handbook*, Section 1700 applies only to *public* companies, i.e., those that have either shares or bonds traded in the public capital markets, either on an exchange or over the counter. This section of the *Handbook* therefore does not apply to most companies in Canada, although the recommendations could be used as a guideline for those private companies whose managers wish to voluntarily disclose segmented information. Banks or other holders of privately placed debt could also require the borrower to provide segmented results. More commonly, however, banks require borrowers to supply separate-entity statements rather than segmented breakdowns of consolidated results.

In formulating the recommendations in Section 1700, the AcSC was cognizant of the cost-benefit relationship in presenting segmented information. In general, the AcSC preferred to recommend disclosure only of information that was already readily available within the reporting enterprise, mainly from management accounting information. Thus some of the variability that exists in practice is the result of differing management accounting systems.

There are three components to segment reporting as recommended by Section 1700: reporting for (1) industry segments, (2) geographic segments, and (3) export sales. We will discuss each of these in turn.

Industry Segments

Quantitative Guidelines

The general guidelines for reporting an industry segment are that a segment is considered reportable if it comprises 10% or more of the consolidated enterprise's (1) revenues, (2) pre-tax operating profits, *or* (3) identifiable assets. Only one of the 10% tests needs to be met. If an industry segment does not meet any of these criteria, it can be combined with another related segment or lumped into an "other" category. In general, at least 75% of the enterprise's revenues should be disclosed by industry segment.

Since similar or related segments should be grouped together, it is difficult to evade the segment reporting recommendations by breaking the business up into so many segments that each is less than 10%. On the other hand, segments need not be reported if one industry segment accounts for 90% of the company's revenues, assets, and operating profits; such a segment is called a **dominant industry segment**.

Unconsolidated subsidiaries should be included in the segment data, although the data can be included in the note that provides the supplementary information on the subsidiary rather than being included in the segmentation of the consolidated results [para. 1700.08].

In applying the 10% guideline for operating profits, a problem arises when some of the identifiable segments operate at a loss while others are profitable. The offsetting effect of profits and losses reduces the size of the company's total profit (or loss), and thereby would reduce the level of segment profit or loss that would satisfy the 10% criterion. The approach taken by the AcSC to dealing with the offset effect is that the 10% guideline is based on the larger of two sums: (1) the sum of the profits of the profitable segments, or (2) the sum of the losses of the unprofitable segments [para. 1700.23].

For example, suppose that a company has four identifiable segments:

Segment	Operating profit (loss)
A	$ 35,000
B	(5,000)
C	55,000
D	(45,000)
Total	$ 40,000

The 10% guideline would be based, in this example, on the sum of the profitable segments, $90,000, which is larger in absolute amount than the sum of the losing segments, $50,000. Therefore, segments A, C and D would be reportable because the absolute amount of their operating profit/loss is greater than $9,000. Segment B would not be reportable under this guideline.

While the various percentage guidelines seem unambiguous, professional judgment must still be applied. It is quite possible for an identifiable segment to satisfy one of the 10% criteria in one year and not the next, or vice versa. Therefore, the determination of reportable segments must be based on more than a one-year view. If a segment is likely to exceed a 10% guideline more often than not, then it probably should be reported *each* year even if it may not meet the guideline every year.

The qualitative criterion of *consistency* suggests that the same segment breakdown should be reported each year until a significant shift in relative importance of lines of business causes a segment to drop below the 10% guidelines more or less permanently. The guidelines should also be used to identify emerging segments, those that are increasing in importance in the consolidated enterprise.

Identifying Industry Segments

There is a difference between an *identifiable* segment and a *reportable* segment. To be reportable, a segment must be separately identifiable, and then must satisfy at least one of the 10% criteria. In some instances, identifying industry segments is no problem. If a telephone company buys a gas pipeline company, it is clear that those are two distinct segments; they share no resources, market, management expertise, or common costs, except at the top corporate level. Operationally, there is no similarity.

In determining industry segments, one of the tests that can be applied is whether the revenues, cost, and operating assets are separately identifiable. If the revenues, costs, *or* assets of apparently different lines of business are intermingled in the enterprise's operations, then it would seem that the businesses are not really separable and are not different segments. However, if the assets, revenues, and operating profits are easily determinable separately, then they *may* be two different segments. In other words, separability is a necessary, but not a sufficient, condition for segment reporting.

Another criterion for identifying segments is whether the businesses serve the same general market (although not necessarily the same customers). If the products are complementary, or are substitutes for each other, then the enterprise may simply be horizontally integrated in the same market rather than being in two different segments. For example, Canada's major wineries are owned by beer companies. Beer and wine could be considered to be two different segments. But since both beer and wine serve the same general market only one alcoholic beverages segment could be reported rather than two segments, despite the fact that the two businesses are quite distinct in operations and therefore easily separable.

The degree of vertical integration can also be used as a criterion for segmentation. A company may produce a raw material, refine it, convert it into manufactured products, and sell the products through its own chain of stores. Is the company in three segments (resources, manufacturing, and retailing) or in one vertically integrated segment? The answer depends on the relative independence of the various levels of the business and the degree of reliance by each on the others. If substantially all of the raw material goes into the enterprise's own manufacturing plants, and the output of the plants is sold mainly through the company's stores, then the high level of interdivisional product flows suggests that there is only one integrated segment.

On the other hand, if the three levels of business operate fairly autonomously, buying materials from external suppliers and selling intermediate outputs on the open market, then the enterprise would seem to be in separate segments rather than in just one.

Different companies with seemingly comparable operations could quite legitimately segment their results differently. One company may report several related industry segments while another company with seemingly similar segments may choose to report the segments together as a single, dominant, integrated segment. The second company's lack of segmented reporting may suggest that the sales between divisions account for the bulk of each division's revenues, and that sales to third parties may not be sufficiently important to justify segmentation.

One of the problems with defining a line of business as a segment when there are substantial intersegment sales is that the segmented operating profits are strongly influenced by the transfer price. If the transfer price is the open market price, then distortion may be minimal. But suppose that the transfer price is set by some internal mechanism. If intersegment sales account for 50% of a segment's revenues, and the operating profit is 8% of sales, then a 2% variation in the transfer price will result in a 12.5% change in operating profit for that segment.

Data to be Reported

Once the industry segments have been identified and the 10% guidelines have been applied to determine the reportable segments, the information to be reported for each of those segments must be determined. The *Handbook* recommends five pieces of annual data for each segment; presented on a comparative basis with the preceding year [para. 1700.33]:

1. Revenue, broken down between sales to outsiders and intersegment sales
2. Operating profit, including disclosure of any unusual items
3. Identifiable assets at the end of the year
4. Depreciation, amortization, and depletion expense
5. Capital expenditures

In addition, there should be a general description of the products and services from which each segment derives its revenue. A reconciliation of the segmented sales, profits, and assets to the amounts in the consolidated financial statements is recommended [para. 1700.33].

Segment operating profit is determined by subtracting attributable or assignable expenses from the segment revenue. Any expenses that are allocated among segments will introduce an element of arbitrariness into the measurement of operating profit. Thus the segment operating profit is subject to the vagaries of both revenue allocation (transfer pricing) and cost allocation. If a major portion of costs must be allocated (for instance, because products serving different segments are produced with shared facilities or from a common raw material), then the segments to which the allocations must be made probably are not separate segments at all.

For example, coal tar is a residual from the process of making steel. There are companies (such as Domtar) that buy the coal tar from the steel companies and convert it into pitch for the aluminum industry. A major joint product of producing pitch is distillates, which are sold to entirely different customers in different industries. It might appear that the converter is in two product segments, pitch and distillates. However, the fact that the raw material is common to the two types of product means that there is no nonarbitrary way of allocating the cost of the coal tar. A pitch producer must therefore be in a single segment, defined by the raw material input and the commonality of costs rather than by the markets served by the output.

Segment operating profit does not include income tax, although many companies do allocate the income tax as well. Nor does segment profit include general corporate expenses or extraordinary items.

Since intersegment revenue and cost allocations may have a significant impact on the reported data, there should be disclosure of the basis of allocating costs and of measuring intersegment sales revenue, if the impact is material [para. 1700.31].

Determining Geographic Segments

In addition to industry segments, a company may report segments on a geographic basis. Geographic segments are those areas outside of Canada that contribute significantly to the operations of the consolidated enterprise. The guidelines provided in Section 1700 suggest that a foreign segment is significant either if 10% of the sales to customers outside of the consolidated enterprise is attributable to that segment, or if 10% of the corporation's identifiable assets are in that geographic area.

The company's domestic operation is considered to be a reportable geographic segment in itself. Canada and the United States cannot, for example, be combined into a single geographic segment [para. 1700.37].

A geographic segment is not necessarily a single country. The objective of reporting geographic segments is to disclose the extent to which the enterprise's earnings and assets are at risk in a foreign environment. Therefore, a segment may be defined as an area with similar economic and political conditions. A good example of a geographic area in which segmentation by country would be inappropriate is Europe. Since the European Economic Community (EEC) functions in a common economic environment and with similar (although certainly not identical) political systems, the countries of the EEC can be viewed as a single geographic segment.

The earnings of a foreign geographic segment may not be independently calculable. The segment may be a major mine in Argentina, for example, transferring most of its product to other divisions of the company. If the mine represents a substantial investment and a significant part of the cor-

Geographic Segments

poration's assets, it should be reported as a segment because of the exposure to risk if the Argentinian environment should become hostile, either economically or politically.

Even when a foreign operation is a profit centre, the apparent results of its operations can be significantly affected by the transfer pricing mechanisms used in international operations. As we will discuss in Chapter 15, international transfer prices are usually set with objectives other than performance appraisal in mind. Furthermore, the translation method used in converting the results of operations of a foreign subsidiary to Canadian dollars will affect the measurement of segment profit.

For these reasons, therefore, the criteria as to whether a geographic segment should be reported do not include the operating profit criterion as do the criteria for industry segments.

Data to be Reported

In general, Section 1700 recommends three pieces of data for each reportable geographic segment, including the Canadian segment (which must be reported separately):

1. Revenue, broken down between sales to outsiders and intersegment sales
2. Identifiable assets at the end of the fiscal year
3. Operating profit or some other measure of profitability

Measurement of segment revenue in Canadian dollars usually poses no severe problems. However, measurement of segment assets can vary considerably, depending on the inflation rate in the foreign country and the translation method used. If the identifiable assets are primarily fixed assets and are located in a country with high inflation, converting the carrying value of the assets at the historical rate of exchange will yield a high dollar-equivalent value, while translating at the current exchange rate will yield a low value. Thus, the measures of assets and of profitability must both be interpreted with a great deal of caution.

Export Sales

A third type of disclosure that falls under the general classification of segmented reporting is the disclosure of export sales. A domestic company may be dependent on exports for a significant volume of its sales. If exchange rates change unfavourably, or if the country or countries to which the goods are exported impose new tariffs or enforce "buy local" regulations, the export sales may be jeopardized. Therefore, Section 1700 recommends that domestic corporations disclose the volume of their export sales if they are a significant portion of total revenue. The guideline for significance is the 10% rule generally applied throughout the section [para. 1700.45].

The measurement of export sales does not include sales made by a foreign geographic segment. Export sales refer exclusively to sales made by the domestic segment to foreign customers. A company may report both foreign geographic segments and export sales. Export sales could perhaps have been routed through a foreign subsidiary, rendering export sales and foreign segment revenues somewhat interchangeable, but there is no double-counting.

SCHEDULE 14-1

Note 16: Segmented Information

The Corporation operates in two business segments:

Natural resources, comprising: exploration, development, production, transportation and marketing activities for crude oil, natural gas, field liquids, sulphur and oil sands; and extraction of liquids from natural gas.

Refined oil products, comprising: purchase and sale of crude oil; refining crude oil into oil products; and distribution and marketing of these and other purchased products.

Financial information by business segment is presented in the following table as though each segment were a separate business entity. Inter-segment transfers of products, which are accounted for at market value, are eliminated on consolidation. Corporate and other includes investment income, interest expense and unallocated general corporate revenues and expenditures. Corporate and other assets are principally cash and short-term deposits, investments in other companies and general corporate assets.

	Natural Resources		Refined Oil Products		Corporate and Other		Consolidated	
	1987	1986	1987	1986	1987	1986	1987	1986
Revenue								
Sales to customers and other revenues	$ 571	$ 546	$4,461	$4,588	$ 47	$ 38	$5,079	$5,172
Inter-segment sales	567	534	—	—	—	—		
Segment Revenue	$1,138	$1,080	$4,461	$4,588	$ 47	$ 38		
Earnings								
Operating earnings before depreciation, depletion and amortization	$ 623	$ 470	$ 327	$ 365	$ (25)	$ 57	$ 925	$ 892
Depreciation, depletion and amortization	(266)	(245)	(139)	(141)	(7)	(8)	(412)	(394)
Interest	—	—	—	—	(73)	(67)	(73)	(67)
Provision for income taxes	(195)	(168)	(93)	(109)	61	28	(227)	(249)
Net Earnings (Loss) Before Dividends on Redeemable Preferred Shares	$ 162	$ 57	$ 95	$ 115	$ (44)	$ 10	$ 213	$ 182
Capital Expenditures								
Capital expenditures on property, plant and equipment, deferred charges and investments	$ 328	$ 319	$ 118	$ 118	$ 180	$ 92	$ 626	$ 529
Acquisitions including minority interest	—	—	—	301	—	—	—	301
	$ 328	$ 319	$ 118	$ 419	$ 180	$ 92	$ 626	$ 830
Total Assets	$4,431	$4,392	$3,436	$3,222	$ 586	$ 525	$8,453	$8,139
Capital Employed	$4,207	$4,102	$2,815	$2,695	$ 567	$ 318	$7,589	$7,118

Source: Petro-Canada 1987 annual report.

Examples of Segmented Reporting

There is no specific format prescribed by the *Handbook* for the reporting of information by segments. Section 1700 does recommend that the segment data be reconciled to consolidated amounts, but the method of presentation is left entirely up to the preparers.

Schedules 14-1 through 14-3 show how three Canadian companies present segment data in their annual reports. The first, Petro-Canada (Schedule 14-1), is an example of a company that has industry segments but no geographic segments. Petro-Canada reports two explicit segments, (1) Natural Resources and (2) Refined Oil Products, plus an "other," miscellaneous segment. Half of the sales of the natural resources segment is to the refined oil products segment; the inter-segment sales are "accounted for at market value." The earnings information is given before and after depreciation, interest, and income taxes. This extra disclosure permits computation of EBIT (earnings before interest and taxes) as well as of operating income before taxes. The 1986 business combination (the acquisition of the assets of Gulf Canada Limited) is reported separately from other capital expenditures.

An example of geographic segment reporting is that of National Sea Products Limited (Schedule 14-2). The company effectively declares itself to be in a single (or dominant) industry at the beginning of its note, and then presents its two geographic segments of Canada and the United States. The reconciliation of segment data to consolidated data is done vertically rather than horizontally as Petro-Canada did it.

Note that the company discloses the general basis for valuing inter-segment sales. This type of disclosure is recommended in the *Handbook* [para. 1700.44(b)], but many companies do not follow the recommendation. The 1987 edition of *Financial Reporting in Canada* reports that only about half of the companies that report inter-segment sales also disclose the basis of accounting therefore [p.58].

The Molson Companies Limited (Schedule 14-3) reports both industry and geographic segments. The Molson note starts with an explanation of the nature of the different industry segments, as is recommended in para. 1700.33. The segment data is presented for industry segments first, followed by the geographic segments. Reconciliation to consolidated amounts is performed horizontally. Molson does not comment on the basis for valuing inter-segment sales.

Summary: Segmented Reporting

Consolidated financial statements give a broad view of the complete economic entity and of the aggregate resources under control of the parent corporation. However, the process of aggregation also hides information that may be useful to the readers of financial statements, particularly in predicting future earnings and cash flows, in evaluating management's performance, and in assessing the business risk exposure of the enterprise.

As a partial remedy for the lack of detail in consolidated statements, companies may provide segmented data to supplement the consolidated figures. The segmented data disclose detail on lines of business and on exposure to foreign risks that otherwise would not be available to the readers of the statements. Some companies have provided information on business or industry segments on a voluntary basis. Added motivation, however, has come

SCHEDULE 14-2

12. Segmented information

The Company is primarily engaged in the seafood industry, which involves purchasing or harvesting, processing and marketing of seafood. Operations and identifiable assets by geographic region for the periods indicated are as follows:

	Fiscal 1987	Fiscal 1986
	(in thousands of dollars)	
Net Sales		
Canadian operations:		
To Canadian markets	$167,395	$154,573
To International markets	59,173	50,953
To United States markets	80,909	69,522
Inter-segment to United States operations	117,834	111,421
United States operations:		
To United States markets	242,057	241,367
Inter-segment to Canadian operations	11,501	7,344
	678,870	635,180
Less inter-segment	129,335	118,765
Consolidated net sales	$549,535	$516,415
Segment contribution to income		
Canadian operations	$ 51,398	$ 51,960
United States operations	4,480	7,351
	55,878	59,311
Add (deduct) inter-segment	204	(5,261)
	56,082	54,050
Unallocatable expenses		
Share of affiliated companies' net earnings	776	347
Dividends on preference shares of subsidiary companies	(673)	(4,977)
Profit sharing contribution	(5,619)	(4,942)
Income tax expense	(23,000)	(22,714)
Extraordinary items	(2,747)	14,360
Net income	$ 24,819	$ 36,124
Assets		
Canadian operations	$210,229	$199,870
United States operations	91,465	88,541
	$301,694	$288,411

Inter-segment sales are valued at market prices reduced by selling costs.

Source: National Sea Products Limited 1987 annual report.

SCHEDULE 14-3

13. Segmented Financial Information

The Corporation's operations consist of the following major business segments:

BREWING GROUP
Molson Breweries produces and markets 19 brands of beer in Canada from nine breweries in seven provinces. In addition, Molson is the leading exporter of Canadian beer to the United States, and also exports to the United Kingdom, the Caribbean, and Japan.

CHEMICAL SPECIALTIES GROUP
The Chemical Specialties business is conducted by Diversey Corporation, which markets specialty chemical products and dispensing systems to industrial, institutional and commercial users in over 100 countries. Its products include cleaning and sanitizing compounds, bactericides, lubricants, laundry detergents, metal finishing products and water treatment chemicals.

RETAIL MERCHANDISING GROUP
Retail Merchandising's principal operations are carried on by Beaver Lumber Company, the major Canadian retailer of lumber, building materials and related hard goods to the consumer and commercial building trade. The Group also includes specialty retailers of lighting fixtures (Lighting Unlimited), fabrics and wallcoverings (B.B. Bargoon's), and housewares (Wares & Wares).

OTHER
Other industry segment includes corporate items, venture capital operations, oil and gas ventures, and Molstar Communications, a communications enterprise specializing in the production of sports and entertainment programming.

---

from explicit provisions in the corporations acts and more recently from recommendations included in the *CICA Handbook* that apply specifically to public companies.

Segmentation is performed both in terms of lines of business (industry segments) and international places of business (geographic segments). The general criterion for disclosure as a segment is 10% of the enterprise's total activity. The measures of activity to which the 10% criterion applies are revenue, investment (assets), and operating profits, in the case of industry segments; the operating profits criterion is not used in determining reportable geographic segments.

At least 75% of the company's activities must be explained by means of segments. A company cannot avoid segmented reporting simply by not consolidating its subsidiaries; the subsidiaries are included in the overall measure of operating activity of the enterprise, whether they are consolidated or not. Minority-owned affiliates are not included in the segmented reporting, even if they are significantly influenced and are reported on the equity basis on the consolidated statements.

The information that should be reported for a geographic segment is (1) segment revenue, (2) identifiable assets, and (3) operating profit (if feasible). Those data should also be reported for industry segments, with the addition of (4) capital expenditures and (5) depreciation, depletion, and amortization expense.

SCHEDULE 14-3 (continued)

13. Segmented Financial Information
(in millions of dollars)
INDUSTRY SEGMENTS

	Consolidated		Brewing		Chemical Specialties		Retail Merchandising		Other	
	1988	1987	1988	1987	1988	1987	1988	1987	1988	1987
Sales and other revenues	2,434.9	2,250.4	1,383.4	1,275.0	685.4	630.7	362.5	343.6	3.6	1.1
Inter-segment sales	—	—	—	—	3.7	3.3	—	—	—	—
			1,383.4	1,275.0	689.1	634.0	362.5	343.6	3.6	1.1
Segment operating profit	145.5	104.5	77.8	50.1	44.0	42.0	25.4	23.1	(1.7)	(10.7)
Net interest expense	(12.6)	(17.6)								
Earnings before income taxes	132.9	86.9								
Total assets	1,365.4	1,236.8	525.2	489.8	396.5	355.7	277.6	227.7	166.1	163.6
Capital expenditures	103.4	78.6	53.3	36.3	30.4	26.7	18.8	15.2	0.9	0.4
Depreciation	58.8	51.2	32.6	29.0	20.9	18.4	4.9	3.4	0.4	0.4

GEOGRAPHIC SEGMENTS

	Consolidated		Canada		U.S.A.[1]		Europe		Other	
	1988	1987	1988	1987	1988	1987	1988	1987	1988	1987
Sales and other revenues	2,434.9	2,250.4	1,708.3	1,575.4	356.4	370.9	289.2	233.3	81.0	70.8
Inter-segment sales			85.5	87.0	3.7	2.9	0.8	0.9	—	—
			1,793.8	1,662.4	360.1	373.8	290.0	234.2	81.0	70.8
Segment operating profit	145.5	104.5	116.3	74.2	0.4	10.3	23.9	17.5	4.9	2.5
Total assets	1,365.4	1,236.8	1,012.4	912.5	128.8	133.0	174.1	146.3	50.1	45.0

[1]U.S.A. segment operating profit is after charging a markup on beer Imported from Canada.

Source: The Molson Companies Limited annual report, year ended March 31, 1988.

If 90% of a corporation's assets, revenues, and operating profits are derived from a single segment, then the company is operating in a dominant industry segment and need not report any segmented data. There is considerable leeway in defining an industry segment, however, so that outwardly similar operations could be judged by the management of one company to be in a single segment, but judged by the management of a similar company to be in several segments. Many variables affect the designation of segments, including the separability of operations, the extent of inter-segment transfers, and the commonality of operations or costs. Thus a wide divergence of practice should be expected.

B. INTERIM REPORTING

Interim reporting is the issuance of financial statements for any period of time of less than one year. Interim statements may be prepared for external use or for management's internal use only. Public companies are generally required to submit quarterly reports to their shareholders. For example, the *Ontario Securities Act* (Section 76) requires comparative quarterly statements consisting of an income statement and a statement of changes in financial position (Regulations, Section 7). The interim reports need not be audited.

Section 1750 of the *CICA Handbook* contains explicit recommendations for the preparation of interim statements. Section 1750 applies only to *public* companies; private companies need not follow the recommendations of this section.

The more common use of interim statements is for internal management use. Internal reporting may be monthly rather than quarterly, and may be more detailed than those prepared for external release. It may at first appear that the preparation of internal interim statements is a function of management accounting and is irrelevant in a text on financial accounting. However, as was discussed in Chapter 2, managements are frequently major users of the financial statements. Although interim reports may be prepared in less detail than the annual statements and may include more estimates, it would be a rude shock to managers and shareholders alike if the annual statements were not consonant with the operations as described by the interim statements. Thus interim statements should be prepared in a manner that is consistent with the annual statements. The same accounting policies should be used, including consolidation policy, so that the successive interim statements accumulate to the final annual results.

In general, interim statements can either be for individual interim periods or for the year to date, or both. If quarterly statements are prepared, for example, the statements for the third quarter could include only the operating results for the third quarter, or they could be the cumulative amounts for the first three quarters. Public reporting is generally for the year-to-date, while internal reporting is frequently for individual periods, perhaps with year-to-date and budget figures as well.

Since financial statements need to have a basis for comparison, interim reports produced for external users are normally prepared on a comparative basis, the comparison being with the same period of the preceding year. For internal reports, budgeted figures for the period may provide a more relevant comparison.

The General Problem

At first glance, it may appear that the preparation of interim statements poses no special problems. Since the same accounting principles are to be used as for the annual reports, the interim period would seem to require only the same application of accounting, but for a shorter period.

Unfortunately, the situation is not so simple. Accounting for an annual period poses major problems of estimation. Revenue recognition can pose significant difficulties, the costs of tangible and intangible fixed assets must be allocated, and future costs must be estimated in order to achieve matching. When these accounting problems are confronted for a period shorter than a year, their significance increases proportionately.

Estimation errors will have a much larger impact on the operating income for a month or a quarter than they will on the operating income for a year. Cutoff procedures are not likely to be as stringent for the unaudited interim statements, and interim inventories are most likely to be estimated or to be taken from perpetual inventory records whose accuracy has not been verified by a physical count.

In addition, a whole new host of estimation and allocation problems arise as the result of the shorter accounting period. Some costs and revenues are seasonal or annual in nature, and interim statements require allocations where none would be required for annual statements.

For example, annual insurance costs pose no problems if the accounting period is a year, but how should the cost be allocated if the period is a month? An easy answer would be to allocate one-twelfth of the cost to each month. However, suppose that the insurance is an expensive public liability policy for an amusement park that is open all year, but that does the bulk of its business in the summer months. How then should cost be allocated, by time or by volume of activity, in order to match the cost with the revenue?

Another example would be a factory that shuts down in the month of August for a vacation for all production employees. The fixed costs of the factory during August could be viewed as a cost to be allocated to all of the interim periods, or as a cost of the individual period in which August falls. Similarly, annual costs such as retooling costs or once-a-year major maintenance costs could either be allocated, or could be allowed to fall into the interim period in which they occur.

Some costs are determined not only on an annual basis, but also after the end of the year. Customer rebates, sales bonuses, and income taxes are examples of these costs. Should an attempt be made to estimate and allocate these costs, or should they be allowed to fall into the last interim period?

As the preceding examples suggest, there are two basic approaches to the preparation of interim statements. The interim period can be viewed either as a distinct and separate accounting period of its own, or as a part of a year.

Separate-Period Approach

Under the separate-period approach, each interim period is accounted for by using the company's normal accounting policies applied to the interim period as though it were a year. A company's policy may be to expense immediately all costs that may have future benefits that are difficult to measure, such as development costs or factory retooling costs. Under this accounting policy, deferred charges and credits are normally not carried on the balance sheet. A company that follows such a policy will also apply it to the interim periods under the separate-period approach. Costs will generally be permitted to fall into the period in which they are incurred, even though they may be annual costs that benefit other interim periods.

This approach implicitly recognizes that since revenues and expenses are likely to be "lumpy," the interim earnings are also going to be lumpy, and not just a proportionate part of the annual earnings. A company following this approach would tend to treat the insurance costs, vacation costs, or retooling and maintenance costs as period costs rather than allocate them to the other periods.

On the other hand, a company could follow a general accounting policy of capitalization and amortization of costs that benefit future periods. If this policy is followed, then there could be an attempt to allocate costs that are incurred in early periods to later periods, and to accrue costs in early periods that will not be incurred until later periods. There still would be no attempt to normalize costs and revenues, however, by spreading out seasonal costs such as heating, seasonal maintenance, annual bonuses, etc., or by spreading out seasonal revenues.

Under the separate-period approach, income taxes would be viewed as cumulative. Income taxes would be accrued for the first period based on the net operating income for the period. Income taxes for the second period would be based on the *additional* taxes payable as a result of the operations for the second period, and so forth. If a loss occurred in the first period, no benefit would be recognized. Deferred taxes would be provided for all timing differences arising during the interim period, even if the timing difference is expected to reverse within the taxation year.

Part-of-a-Year Approach

Under this approach, the interim period is viewed simply as a part of the longer period of a year. Expenses would be allocated across the interim periods in such a way as to portray the company's likely annualized operating results. Theoretically, if a company is heading for a year in which the operating margin (net income divided by sales) is 10%, then the interim statements should reflect that fact. Under this view, the interim statements should be the best predictor available of the company's operating results for the year.

For the examples cited above, the part-of-a-year approach would allocate the insurance costs proportionately to the volume of business, and would allocate the costs of the plant closing, the annual retooling and maintenance costs, and the estimated bonuses and rebates to all of the interim periods. In an extreme application of the approach, revenues could be annualized using statistical techniques similar to those used for macroeconomic, seasonally adjusted statistics; however, it is doubtful that revenue would ever be statistically smoothed in practice.

Income taxes would be viewed as an annual expense to be allocated to interim periods in proportion to the pre-tax interim net income. There would be no separate computation of income taxes for the interim period as though it were a separate taxation period, and timing differences would be determined on an annual basis and allocated to the interim periods. A first-quarter loss would be accorded an income tax benefit if the company expected to earn a profit for the tax year as a whole.

Application in Practice

For internal interim reports, the separate-period approach is most likely to be used. The comparative amounts for internal users are likely to be budgeted figures for the period (perhaps supplemented by the previous year's figures), and budgets generally include major costs as expenses of the period in which they occur. Controllability is a concern in budgeting, and costs allocated from previous periods are not controllable in the later periods to which they are allocated. Also, internal reports frequently do not include any estimates of income tax, thereby removing one major estimation problem.

For public interim statements, reporting is guided by Section 1750 of the *CICA Handbook*. Section 1750 generally favours the separate-period approach: Interim financial reports should present information with respect to the results of operations of a company for a specified period rather than a proration of expected results for the annual period [para. 1750.13].

The section does recognize that certain annual costs may need to be allocated, and that "where necessary, appropriate estimates and assumptions should be made to match costs and revenues" [para. 1750.14]. Specific reference is made to those costs that are based on levels of income or sales, such as bonuses, volume discounts, and sales commissions [para. 1750.25]. Extraordinary items are *not* allocable, but should be reported in the period in which they arise. Nevertheless, considerable latitude seems to be present within the recommendations for deciding how costs should be allocated.

The one area in which rather specific guidance is given is in the estimation of income tax expense for the interim periods. The basic approach taken in the *Handbook* recommendations is that the taxes payable should be based on the interim period's earnings and not be a proration of the estimated annual taxes. An exception pertains to situations in which a two-rate tax system is applicable. In that case, the recommendations permit allocation of the benefits of the lower rate over the interim period, either by direct allocation or by using a lower estimated effective tax rate for the tax computation.

In accordance with the separate-period view, the tax benefits of interim losses are accorded essentially the same treatment as is recommended in Section 3470 for the tax benefits of annual losses. If taxes paid in previous years are available for tax loss carry-backs, then a tax benefit may be recorded for the interim loss to the extent that previously paid taxes are recoverable. If the taxes recoverable are not sufficient to use up the entire interim loss, then the tax benefit of the excess loss that will be realizable in future periods (*including future interim periods in the same tax year*) can be recognized in the current period only if virtual certainty exists.[1] Previously unrecognized benefits of loss carry-forwards from earlier years can be recognized in the current year's interim reports either as a final period benefit or proportionately throughout the year.

Since the income tax is estimated for each period, the future tax impact of timing differences should also be estimated each period.

Schedule 14-4 shows the third quarter interim financial statements for Air Canada for 1988. Air Canada reports its operating results both for the current quarter ("3 months") and for the year-to-date ("9 months"). Note that the income statement is very highly condensed, as is normal in public interim statements. A balance sheet is also provided, which is required neither by the *CICA Handbook* recommendations nor by the securities acts. The interim statements were distributed to shareholders in a Third Quarter Report that also included some commentary by management and highlights of operating changes during the quarter.

---

1 The exposure draft on Corporate Income Taxes (November 1988), which is being considered at the time this is being written, would eliminate the application of virtual certainty; future benefits of current losses could be recognized only to the extent that timing differences will reverse (or be forced to reverse) within the carry-forward period.

SCHEDULE 14-4

Interim Statements of Air Canada
Third Quarter, 1988

Consolidated Statement of Income (unaudited)
Periods ended September 30
(in millions of dollars)

	3 Months		9 Months	
	1988	1987	1988	1987
Operating revenues	$962.3	$945.0	$2,621.2	$2,502.2
Operating expenses				
Depreciation, amortization and obsolescence	42.5	46.8	127.3	144.2
Other	825.9	781.9	2,391.0	2,139.0
	868.4	828.7	2,518.3	2,283.2
Operating income	93.9	116.3	102.9	219.0
Non-operating expenses (income)				
Interest on long-term debt and capital lease obligations	28.4	31.0	84.4	91.1
Investment income	(9.5)	(11.8)	(30.4)	(33.6)
Other	1.4	(13.5)	(25.6)	(36.5)
	20.3	5.7	28.4	21.0
Income before income taxes and minority interest	73.6	110.6	74.5	198.0
Provision for income taxes	(28.7)	(44.2)	(22.1)	(78.6)
Minority interest	0.3	0.0	0.8	(0.2)
Net income	$ 45.2	$ 66.4	$ 53.2	$ 119.2
Earnings per share expressed in dollars (Note 2)	$1.10	$1.61	$1.29	$2.90

Summary: Interim Reporting

Most publicly traded corporations issue quarterly financial reports to their shareholders. The interim reports need not be complete sets of statements, but rather can consist only of an income statement (including earnings per share) and a statement of changes in financial position, both presented on a comparative basis. Nevertheless, some companies do present a condensed balance sheet as well. The interim reports usually are cumulative, showing year-to-date figures.

Other corporations prepare interim statements for strictly internal use. Internal statements may be monthly, bimonthly, or quarterly, and usually include the period's budgeted amounts as comparative figures so that management can judge operating performance to date.

Interim statements do not need to be audited, but the *CICA Handbook*

SCHEDULE 14-4 (continued)

Consolidated Changes in Financial Position (unaudited)
(in millions of dollars)

	9 Months	
	1988	1987
Cash provided by (used for)		
Operations		
Net income	$ 53.2	$119.2
Non-cash items included in net income	61.6	133.6
Income results	114.8	252.8
Change in net trade balances	(116.1)	(115.0)
Increase in advance ticket sales	2.8	(6.1)
Decrease (Increase) in spare parts, materials and supplies	(2.0)	(12.8)
Other	(30.7)	(22.5)
	(31.2)	96.4
Financing		
Repayment of long-term debt and capital lease obligations	(57.9)	(98.6)
Long-term borrowings	68.9	43.1
Other	(20.1)	(22.5)
	(9.1)	(78.0)
Investments		
Additions to fixed assets	(428.0)	(145.2)
Proceeds from disposal of assets	132.7	120.6
Dividends received	6.7	1.8
Investment in subsidiaries and other companies	(20.1)	(229.7)
	(308.7)	(252.5)
Decrease in cash position	(349.0)	(234.1)
Cash position at beginning of period	223.1	382.4
Cash position at end of period	($125.9)	$148.3

Cash position consists of cash, short-term investments, and bank indebtedness.

does contain recommendations for the preparation of interim statements that are to be issued publicly. The *Handbook* recommendations follow the separate-period approach to the preparation of interim statements, although the recommendations do recognize the need to accrue or allocate some costs in order to achieve matching that is consistent with the revenue-cost relationships in the annual statements.

Whether for external or internal reporting, interim statements should follow the same accounting policies that are used in the annual statements.

SCHEDULE 14-4 (continued)

Consolidated Balance Sheet (unaudited)
(in millions of dollars)

	September 30	
	1988	1987
Assets		
Cash and short-term investments	$ 0.0	$ 148.3
Other current assets	716.0	683.4
Property and equipment	1,908.6	1,816.8
Investment in other companies	188.1	145.0
Deferred charges	335.1	269.1
Goodwill	102.3	95.6
	$3,250.1	$3,158.2
Liabilities, Minority interest, Subordinated		
Perpetual Bonds and Shareholders' Equity:		
Bank indebtedness	$ 125.9	$ 0.0
Other current liabilities	678.0	700.1
Long-term debt and capital lease obligations	1,033.6	1,030.9
Other long-term liabilities	29.9	23.1
Deferred credits	384.0	385.9
Minority interest	10.3	9.6
Subordinated perpetual bonds	336.0	336.0
Share capital	329.0	329.0
Retained earnings	323.4	343.6
	$3,250.1	$3,158.2

Notes to Consolidated Financial Statements

Note 1.
Effective January 1, 1988, the Corporation increased the estimated residual values of substantially all of its aircraft and the estimated service lives of B-767 aircraft in the determination of 1988 depreciation expense. This change increased net income in the third quarter and year-to-date by $2.3 million and $7.1 million, respectively, after deducting deferred income taxes of $1.7 million and $5.2 million.

Note 2.
Earnings per share reflect a September 26 stock split whereby 125 common shares were issued to replace each common share outstanding. 41,126,125 common shares were issued to replace 329,009 common shares.

On October 13, 1988, a further 30,769,469 common shares were issued through a Public Share Offering. Proceeds net of underwriters' fees and other expenses are estimated to be $233.8 million. In addition, 2,874,709 common shares have been reserved for further issuance to employees on terms described in the Prospectus. This issue has not been reflected in earnings per share.

Note 3.
Certain 1987 figures have been restated.

Otherwise, neither managers nor shareholders may fully realize the impact of the interim results on the annual statements. The preparation of interim statements does require a considerable amount of estimation and allocation of annual or seasonal costs, as well as allocation over shorter periods of costs that are also amortized on an annual basis. Therefore, interim statements must always be viewed as approximations, even more so than annual statements. In statistical terms, the standard error of measurement of interim earnings is significantly higher than it is for annual earnings.

REVIEW QUESTIONS

14-1 In a diversified corporation, why is prediction of future earnings and cash flow difficult when only consolidated statements are presented?

14-2 What are the objectives of segmented reporting?

14-3 When a corporation reports financial information by segments, do the segments correspond to specific subsidiaries?

14-4 How can a segment be **identified**?

14-5 What are the guidelines for determining whether an industry segment is **reportable**?

14-6 Companies L and D both operate food processing plants, and both operate a chain of retail food stores. Company L transfers all of the output from its processing plants to its stores, while Company D's processing plants produce private-label products for other retailers. How might the segment reporting of the two companies differ?

14-7 Define a **dominant industry segment**.

14-8 How much of the consolidated enterprise's business activity must be reported in industry segments in order to satisfy the requirements of the *CICA Handbook*?

14-9 How can horizontal integration influence the reporting of industry segments?

14-10 What data are to be reported for industry segments?

14-11 What criteria are applied in determining reportable geographic segments?

14-12 What is the reason for requiring companies to report geographic segments?

14-13 Must a geographic segment be a single country, or can several countries be combined into a single segment? Explain.

14-14 Seapounds Ltd. wishes to report Canada and the United States as a single North American geographic segment, owing to the common economic and political environment in the two countries. Is this in accordance with the recommendations of Section 1700 of the *CICA Handbook*? Explain.

14-15 What data must be reported for each geographic segment? How do these data differ from the data reported for industry segments?

14-16 In determining the volume of export sales, are sales made by a foreign geographic segment included?

14-17 Does segment reporting include the business activities of significantly influenced affiliates?

14-18 Explain briefly why interim reporting poses problems different from those of annual reporting.

14-19 What are the two basic approaches to the preparation of interim statements?

14-20 Which approach to interim statements is recommended by the *CICA Handbook*?

14-21 Under the separate-period approach to interim statements, how would an annual, onetime expenditure such as retooling cost be reported? How would the reporting differ under the part-of-a-year approach?

14-22 How does the measurement of income tax expense differ between the two approaches to interim reporting?

14-23 When the quarterly statements of a public Canadian company are reported, are the same financial statements prepared as for annual reporting?

14-24 "If extraordinary items are permitted to fall exclusively into a single quarter, the operating results for that quarter are distorted. Extraordinary items should be allocated across the remaining quarters of the year so as to normalize reported earnings." Comment on this quotation.

CASE 14-1   Ermine Oil Limited

Ermine Oil Limited (Ermine) is a fully integrated Canadian oil company. Ermine commenced as a petroleum exploration company and was very successful in its oil field discoveries. In order to attain market security and improve profits, Ermine was forced to embark on a program of vertical integration. It first acquired a refining division and then marketing and transportation divisions. From the beginning, management appreciated the integrated nature of the business, and production was transferred between divisions at standard cost. The management control system recognized the exploration, refining, and transportation divisions as cost centres and the marketing division as a revenue centre. While the exploration, refining, and transportation divisions did make external sales, historically, none of these divisions' external sales accounted for 10% of Ermine's total sales. However, in the last fiscal year, due to unusual world market conditions, the transportation division's sales accounted for 11% of Ermine's total sales. Over 90% of Ermine's sales were within Canada, with the balance spread over many countries worldwide. Ermine did not feel it was necessary to disclose segmented information in its annual financial statements.

Beluga Petroleum Limited (Beluga) was similar to Ermine in size and also in scope of operations except that, in addition, it had a chemical division. However, Beluga was a subsidiary of a foreign oil company and its divisions were each organized as profit centres with products transferred between divisions at world market prices. Each division purchased and sold products extensively to outside companies. In addition, about 15% of Beluga's sales were export, almost exclusively to the U.S. In its annual financial statements, Beluga showed segmented information by the five divisions (exploration, refining, transportation, chemical, and marketing) and sales were divided between domestic and export operations.

Required:
Discuss how both Ermine and Beluga could report differently with respect to disclosure of segmented information, and yet be in accordance with generally accepted accounting principles.
[SMA]

CASE 14-2   Wardair International Ltd.

The 1981 annual report of Wardair International Ltd. listed the following corporations as 100% owned subsidiaries:

> International Vacations Ltd.
> Wardair Holidays GmbH (Germany)
> Wardair (U.K.) Ltd.
> Wardair Canada (1975) Ltd.
> Wardair Jamaica Ltd. (inactive)
> Wardair Equipment Ltd.
> Wardair Hawaii, Ltd.

In addition, Redrock Reinsurance Limited is listed as a wholly owned subsidiary of Wardair Canada (1975) Ltd.

Wardair Canada (1975) Ltd. is the primary operating company of the group. This company owns directly two Wardair aircraft and operates seven planes. The other five aircraft are owned by Wardair Equipment Ltd. and are leased to Wardair Canada (1975) Ltd.

International Vacations (InterVac), and the German and U.K. subsidiaries engage in the wholesaling and retailing of vacation packages, and sell at retail the seats on the aircraft that they charter from Wardair Canada (1975) Ltd.

Two other subsidiaries are described in the annual report as follows:

Redrock Reinsurance Limited
Redrock Reinsurance Limited, a Bermuda Company, is wholly owned by Wardair Canada (1975) Ltd. and is managed by Insurance Managers Ltd. of Hamilton, Bermuda. Redrock reinsures certain lines of travel-related insurance, issued by primary underwriters, such as passenger cancellation, baggage liability, medical and accident coverage. Redrock's loss ratios remain favourable, premium volume has increased and 1981 was a profitable year for this company.

The board of directors of Redrock has recently approved a study to determine if it should participate more actively in underwriting property and casualty loss insurance in the general reinsurance market. A decision as to possible expansion of underwriting activities will be made in 1982.

Wardair Hawaii, Limited
Wardair Hawaii, Limited of Honolulu, a wholly owned subsidiary of Wardair International, owns 33 condominium units and manages approximately 200 other rental units on a fee basis at the Waikiki Banyan in Honolulu.

This operation incurred a small loss in 1981. Fees based on rental revenues will increase in 1982 due to growth in volume. The long-term outlook for this operation remains favourable.

Required:
a. What consolidation policy would seem to be appropriate for Wardair International? What criteria should be used to decide whether any of the individual subsidiaries should *not* be consolidated? Relate your discussion explicitly to the specific Wardair subsidiaries.
b. What segment reporting would seem appropriate for Wardair International, given the above information *only*?
c. The Wardair annual report also includes the following note:

  Segmented Information
  The company considers its international airline operations to be the dominant segment of its business.

  Revenue from sales originating in foreign countries approximated $72,000,000 in 1981 (1980 — $64,000,000).

  Assuming that Wardair is complying with *CICA Handbook* guidelines for segment reporting, what assumptions about Wardair's operations can be derived from this note?

P Manufacturing Limited

CASE 14-3

P Manufacturing Limited is a Canadian-controlled public company that issued shares to the public for the first time in 19x5. The shares are listed on both Canadian and U.S. stock exchanges. Mr. X, the president of the company, approaches CA, who is currently performing the interim audit of the company. The company has decided to issue interim financial statements for the first time, and the president presents to CA the following interim consolidated income statement prepared by the company accountant:

Consolidated Statement of Earnings
for the three months ended December 31, 19x6
(with comparative figures for 19x5)
(reviewed by CA & Co.)

	19x6	19x5
Sales	$19,000,000	$20,000,000
Cost of operating and administrative		
expenses	23,000,000	20,000,000
Interest on short term debt	700,000	500,000
Depreciation	300,000	400,000
Net income (loss) before extraordinary items		
and provision for income taxes	(5,000,000)	(900,000)
Extraordinary item:		
Gain on sale of fixed assets	–	3,000,000
Net income (loss) before provision for		
income taxes	(5,000,000)	2,100,000
Provision for income taxes	(2,500,000)	200,000
Net income (loss) for the period	$ (2,500,000)	$ 1,900,000
Income (loss) per share	$ (5.00)	$ 3.80

Mr. X would like to publish these results following CA's review, and has asked CA to suggest whatever changes are necessary to present this interim statement in accordance with generally accepted accounting principles.

From discussion with the company's accountant, CA is able to determine the following:

1. As of December 31, 19x5, and December 31, 19x6, there were 500,000 common shares outstanding, and warrants outstanding to purchase a further 225,000 common shares at $7.00 each. No preferred dividends were paid in 19x6, and, as a result, dividends in arrears amounted to $300,000 at December 31, 19x6 (19x5 – $250,000). The company can invest its surplus funds to earn 10% after tax.

2. In the first quarter of 19x6, the company changed its accounting policy for depreciation, from the straight-line to the declining-balance method. As a result, depreciation for the three months ended December 31, 19x6, is $100,000 lower than it otherwise would have been. Had the company always used the declining-balance method, the depreciation expense would have been decreased by $50,000; the income tax provision would have been increased by $25,000 for the three months ended December 31, 19x5, and the retained earnings at September 30, 19x6, would have been decreased by $200,000.

3. After the longest depression in the history of its industry, current company projections indicate an encouraging outlook for the remaining three quarters of the year ending September 30, 19x7 and an overall breakeven position from operations for the entire year, as was the case for the operations of the year ended September 30, 19x6. For this reason, the company accountant has recorded a full provision for the tax benefits resulting from the loss suffered during the three months ended December 31, 19x6.

The prior year's annual financial statements show an extraordinary gain *before* tax, on the sale of a division's fixed assets, of $3,000,000. This resulted in an income tax provision (recaptured CCA) of $650,000, being the only income tax paid in respect of the year ended September 30, 19x6.

Required:
Prepare in good form, to comply with Canadian reporting requirements, a revised consolidated statement of earnings for the three months ended December 31, 19x6, together with comparative figures for 19x5. Include any necessary notes to the statement.
[CICA]

P14-1

The Tripartite Corporation has internal reporting for four divisions. The following data have been gathered for the year just ended.

	Div. A	Div. B	Div. C	Div. D
Interdivisional sales	$100,000	$ 20,000	—	—
External sales	10,000	200,000	$150,000	$400,000
Direct divisional expenses	50,000	120,000	30,000	100,000
Allocated joint costs	—	—	60,000	120,000
Depreciation	30,000	35,000	20,000	40,000
Capital expenditures	20,000	60,000	80,000	160,000
Identifiable assets	180,000	210,000	120,000	240,000

Additional Information:
1. Division A sells over 90% of its output to Division B on a cost-plus basis.
2. Divisions C and D share production facilities. Joint product costs, depreciation, capital expenditures, and much of the identifiable assets are allocated one-third to Division C and the remainder to Division D.
3. Unallocated corporate expenses not included above amount to $115,000 including $50,000 in income tax expense.

Required:
a. From the preceding information, what are the industry segments that should be reported by Tripartite? Explain.
b. Prepare a schedule of supplementary financial information by segments, in accordance with the *Handbook* recommendations, together with a condensed consolidated income statement.

P14-2

The following information is available for Westward Home Corporation's operating subsidiaries throughout the world, in thousands of Canadian dollars:

	External sales	Sales to other operating regions	Identifiable assets	After-tax profit
Canada	$ 40,000	$200.000	$ 20,000	$ 5,000
United States	190,000	40.000	80,000	4,500
Europe	150,000	20.000	70,000	9,000
Asia	30,000	—	15,000	3,500
South America	40,000	—	20,000	5,000
General Corporate			30,000	3,000*
Consolidated	$450,000	—	$235,000	$30,000

*Investment income, less general corporate expenses.

Required:
Determine which regions are reportable geographic segments, as defined by the *CICA Handbook*, and which ones can be reported as "rest of the world." Identify the characteristics that led to your choices.

P14-3

This year, for the first time, the Argyle Corporation must report supplementary information by industry segment. The controller has prepared the following note for inclusion in the annual report.

SEGMENTED DATA

Your company operates in several different industries. Selected financial data by division is provided below, in thousands of Canadian dollars.

	Men's Wear	Tires	Other	Consolidated
Sales to outsiders	$400	$200	$300	$ 900
Sales between divisions	50	10	60	120
Total sales	$450	$210	$360	$1,020
Operating profit	$ 15	$ 40	$ 20	$ 62
Capital expenditures	$ 5	$ 25	$ 30	$ 70
Assets	$ 65	$240	$ 90	$ 455

During the year, your company had export sales that resulted in gross profit of $50,000.

Required:
Criticize the note as prepared by the controller. Identify any missing information, either numerical or verbal, and indicate errors in presentation.

P14-4

The Shaw Navigational Company is a public Canadian corporation that operates a fleet of ships on the Great Lakes. In common with other Great Lakes shipping companies, rates are quoted and revenues are collected in U.S. dollars, regardless of the location or nationality of the shipper. Over 90% of Shaw's consolidated gross revenues, operating profits, and identifiable fixed assets relate to the shipping business, and thus Shaw's management claims exemption from segmented reporting requirements on the grounds that shipping represents a dominant industry segment. In 19x4, Shaw's consolidated net income was $1,200,000.

Shaw does have two subsidiaries that are not in the shipping business. One is a bus company that operates on intercity routes in Manitoba, and that is consolidated with the shipping operation. The bus fleet has recently been modernized, and the new buses have been acquired by means of leases rather than by outright purchase.

The other subsidiary, which is reported on the equity basis, is a casualty insurance company located in Michigan. About 20% of the insurance company's business involves Great Lakes shipping, although mainly for shipping companies other than Shaw. Shaw's equity in the earnings of the insurance company amounted to $180,000 in 19x4.

Required:
Comment on management's assertion that Shaw is exempt from segment reporting because of the existence of a dominant industry.

P14-5

The Georgian Bay Company is a retail department store chain. The company's fiscal year ends on the Saturday closest to January 31 of each year. The company is publicly held, and submits quarterly financial statements to the shareholders.

Like most retail establishments, Georgian Bay operates at a loss for most of the year, but generally recovers the losses in the fourth quarter to finish the year with a profit. In fiscal year 19x3, the company reported pre-tax net income of $2,000,000, and paid taxes at a rate of 46%.

In the first quarter of 19x4, the company suffered a loss of $1,800,000 before taxes. In the second quarter, economic conditions improved slightly, but the cumulative six-month loss was $2,900,000, the worst in the company's history. Nevertheless, management predicted that the losses would be recovered as the economy pulled out of the recession, and forecast a breakeven performance for the year as a whole.

The loss did decline in the third quarter, to a cumulative loss of $1,600,000; the fourth quarter almost completely wiped out the loss, ending the year with a fiscal pre-tax loss of only $200,000.

Required:
Assume that tax losses can be carried back for only one year. Determine the provision for income taxes that should be reported on Georgian Bay's interim income statements for fiscal year 19x4, assuming:

a. That each quarter is reported separately, not cumulatively.
b. That each quarter is reported cumulatively.

P14-6

In 19x1, Roly Ltd. reported net income before taxes of $1,000,000 and had taxable income of $850,000. The difference was due to an excess of CCA over depreciation. At December 31, 19x1, the CCA/depreciation timing difference had accumulated to $600,000. Depreciation is straight-line, at $200,000 per year. For 19x2, quarterly earnings (before tax) were as follows:

Quarter 1	$ 200,000	profit
2	$1,400,000	loss
3	$ 300,000	loss
4	$ 500,000	profit
19x2, year	$1,000,000	loss

Maximum CCA deductible in 19x2 is $320,000. There are no other timing differences between accounting and taxable income. Roly pays taxes at a rate of 40% of taxable income. Roly reports in accordance with the *CICA Handbook* recommendations.

Required:
Compute the provision for income taxes that would appear on the income statement for:

a. Each of the first three quarters, reported separately.
b. Each of the first three quarters, reported cumulatively.
c. The year.

P14-7

Duncan-Dean Ltd. experienced the following events during the first quarter 19x2:

1. The annual sales catalogue was produced and printed, at a cost of $1,000,000.
2. Owing to a strike at the principal supplier's factory, Duncan-Dean's inventory fell to the lowest level in fourteen years. Duncan-Dean used the LIFO method for financial reporting.
3. A notice of assessed value for property taxes was received. The tax assessment will be received and be due in the second quarter. Taxes for 19x7 are estimated at $400,000.
4. Duncan-Dean uses sum-of-digits depreciation. The total depreciation for 19x7 on assets held at the start of the year will be $600,000.
5. The company's top management receives annual bonuses based on annual net income after taxes.
6. Duncan-Dean bought new equipment during the first quarter that entitles the company to an investment tax credit of $50,000. The company uses the flow-through method of reporting investment tax credits.
7. The company sold a long-term investment at a profit of $1,200,000, net of taxes. The profit qualifies as an extraordinary item.

Required:

For each event reported above, indicate what impact it would have on the first quarter interim report under each approach to interim statements:

a. The part-of-year approach.
b. The separate-period approach.

PART

15

Accounting for International Activities

Many companies engage in some form of international activity. The range of possible activities is vast. At one extreme is the company that has only an occasional transaction in a foreign currency. For example, a Canadian corporation may borrow money from a New York bank. If the loan is extended in U.S. dollars, then the liability of the borrowing corporation is a debt that is **denominated** in a foreign currency. Assuming that the reporting currency of the Canadian company is the Canadian dollar, the presence of the U.S. dollar liability creates a reporting problem (which we will explore in Chapter 16). At the opposite extreme is the corporation with a network of foreign subsidiaries that operate on a global basis. A good example of a Canadian-based international corporation is Varity Corporation (formerly Massey-Ferguson Limited). Varity has manufacturing subsidiaries in Canada, France, Italy, the United Kingdom, the United States, and West Germany. In addition, the company has significantly influenced associate companies (with ownership interests ranging from 19% to 49%) in countries such as India, Libya, Mexico, Morocco, Saudi Arabia, and South Africa. Only about 5% of Varity's consolidated sales are in Canada; the company sells its products throughout the world, including Europe, Latin America, Africa, the Near East, Asia, and Australia.

While there are many Canadian corporations that have international operations, there also are many foreign corporations that have subsidiaries in Canada. Thus the Canadian accountants must be concerned about the accounting problems of international business from two perspectives: (1) the problems faced by a domestic parent with foreign subsidiaries, and (2) the problems faced by domestic Canadian subsidiaries of foreign parents.

Corporations that engage in international activities inevitably experience accounting problems that are not shared by their domestic counterparts. The fact of doing business in more than one currency raises both measurement and interpretative difficulties. Naturally, the more extensive the international activities, the more important these difficulties become.

This chapter will provide an introduction to the major accounting problems faced by the international company. Subsequent chapters will elaborate on some of these problems. An extensive analysis of all of the problems is beyond the scope of this book, however.

TYPES OF INTERNATIONAL ACTIVITY

Before we look at the various types of problems that arise in accounting for international activities, it may be helpful to draw some distinctions among the various types of international involvement. The various types of activity give rise to different sets of accounting problems, and thus it may be easier to understand the nature of the problems if we first understand the context within which the problems arise.

The volume of international activity varies considerably from company to company. Schedule 15-1 shows the proportion of revenues derived from Canada, the United States, and other countries by fifteen internationally active Canadian corporations. The relative revenues shown in Schedule 15-1 are generated by the companies' identifiable business *operations* in foreign countries, not by direct *exports* from the domestic operation.

The number of countries in which a company operates can also vary considerably, from only one foreign country to world-wide. Of the fifteen companies in Schedule 15-1, eight report foreign operations only in the United States, while the other seven operate in two or more foreign countries.

Both the level of foreign activity and the number of countries involved

---

SCHEDULE 15-1

Examples of Some Canadian Companies with Foreign Operations

	Percentage of revenues derived from		
	Canada	U.S.	Europe and Other
Alcan Aluminium Ltd.	13	32	55
Bell Canada Enterprises Ltd.	69	28	3
Bramalea Ltd.	72	28	
Chief Development Co.	76	24	
Coscan Development Corporation	59	41	
Denison Mines Ltd.	66		34
Derlan Industries Ltd.	72	28	
Develcon Electronics Ltd.	39	61	
Dominion Textile Inc.	63	24	12
Falconbridge Ltd.	25	38	37
Inco Limited	18	30	51
Indahl Limited	45	55	
Ivaco Inc.	51	49	
Moore Corporation	10	62	28
Provigo Inc.	89	11	

Sources: 1987 corporate annual reports.

affect the severity of the accounting problems associated with international activities. However, neither the relative size nor the geographic distribution of nondomestic activity affects, in itself, the nature of the accounting problems. A more useful way of classifying internationally active corporations is by the nature of those activities, rather than by their volume or geographic dispersion. In recent years, observers of international corporations have defined four general types of international business:

1. Corporations that directly engage in transactions in foreign currencies in one or more foreign countries
2. Corporations that have one or more "branch" operations in a foreign country or countries
3. Corporations that have autonomous or semi-autonomous, decentralized operations in one or more foreign countries
4. Multinational corporations that operate on a global basis, with world mandates given to individual subsidiaries

The simplest type of activity to account for is the first type. Corporations frequently transact business in another country directly, without establishing a foreign office or subsidiary. Business that is transacted in a foreign country is usually transacted in the foreign country's currency rather than in the Canadian dollar. Sometimes, the transactions are denominated in a third currency, frequently the U.S. dollar. When the corporation records these foreign-currency-denominated foreign transactions on its books, the transactions must be translated into their equivalent in Canadian dollars. Most Canadian companies that engage in such **foreign currency transactions** do so in the United States. Raw materials may be purchased from U.S. sources at prices that are quoted in U.S. dollars; goods may be sold to U.S. customers at prices quoted in U.S. dollars; or money may be borrowed (and thus must be repaid) in U.S. dollars. Of course, the transactions may be in any country or in several countries; the United States is simply the most common site for the international operations of Canadian companies.

If a company does a substantial amount of business in a certain foreign country, then the company may create a separate entity in that foreign country to carry out business in its name. A **foreign operation** is usually an incorporated subsidiary. If the primary activity of the foreign operation is to act as an extension of the parent, e.g., as a sales office, then the foreign subsidiary is acting as a branch of the parent and usually has no real autonomy or independence. A branch-type operation could also be a production-oriented subsidiary, with substantially all of the product being transferred to the parent. A mining company may have such branch operations, for example, by operating mines in foreign countries and exporting all of the output back home for processing or distribution.

One characteristic of a branch operation is that there is a high degree of interdependence between the parent and the branch. Substantial cash flows usually occur between the two, and the branch may be performing functions little more complex than the parent could perform itself through extensive direct foreign currency transactions or by operating through an agent.

Another characteristic of a branch-type foreign operation is that in terms of objectives and management style, the branch operates as an extension of the parent company. The branch does not take on many (if any) of the foreign country's characteristics in the way in which it operates. Therefore, such branch-style foreign operations are dubbed "home-country oriented" or **ethnocentric**.[1]

A corporation may operate foreign subsidiaries that are less one-directional than those examples cited above. The subsidiary may not be simply a sales or a production branch, but may engage in a broader range of activities. The subsidiary may manufacture products locally and sell them locally, and thus may appear to be an independent business. But if the operations of the foreign subsidiary are tightly controlled by the parent, and if the parent's management methods, evaluation methods, performance appraisal techniques, and other norms and standards of operation are required to be used by the foreign subsidiary, then the operation is still ethnocentric and may still be viewed as a branch-type operation.

Most companies that are engaged in international operations recognize that a foreign subsidiary cannot best be run as a foreign version of the parent corporation. A foreign subsidiary, to be most effective, must function in harmony with the economic, legal, and cultural environment of the foreign country in which it is located. Many American firms learned rather unpleasantly that management techniques that work in the United States may not work in other countries. Other cultures have different norms of behaviour and different attitudes towards the workplace, and an international corporation ignores this fact only at its peril.

Therefore, foreign subsidiaries have frequently been permitted (or encouraged) to adapt to local conditions and markets. Management is recruited from and trained in the local environment, and the foreign subsidiary is usually permitted to function largely autonomously, with little direct intervention from the parent corporation. Frequently, the foreign subsidiary is not wholly owned by the parent but has minority ownership by citizens of the foreign country (and sometimes by the foreign government itself). This type of foreign operation is the third type of international activity listed above, the internationally decentralized corporation. Such foreign operations are termed "host-country oriented" or **polycentric**.

Polycentric organizations frequently rely on divisional performance appraisal techniques such as return-on-investment or residual income in order to evaluate the foreign operations to see if the overall objectives of the corporation are being served by the individual foreign subsidiaries. But since the foreign subsidiaries are encouraged to adapt to conditions in the host countries, and since non-wholly owned subsidiaries will have to report to their minority shareholders within the reporting framework of the host country, there may be problems with comparability of reported results between the various foreign operations. The difficulties are compounded if the parent company management insists on translating the foreign operations' financial statements to the domestic (e.g. Canadian) currency before evaluating the results of the subsidiaries' operations. And if there are interpretive problems for management use of the information, then there will probably also be compatibility and interpretative problems when the results of foreign operations are consolidated into the parent's financial statements.

Polycentric organizations are apt to be more successful in the interna-

1 This terminology is based on the classification system suggested by Howard V. Perlmutter in "The Tortuous Evolution of the Multinational Corporation," *Columbia Journal of World Business* (January-February 1969), which seems to have gained widespread acceptance.

tional marketplace than are ethnocentric corporations. But a problem with the host-country orientation is that it is not truly international. Rather than having an international operation, the polycentric corporation tends to have a series of more-or-less successful national operations that operate independently in various host countries. The decentralized nature of a polycentric operation prevents the international rationalization of a corporation's resources. Therefore, the most advanced stage of development (at present) in international business is the evolution of the "globally oriented" or **geocentric** corporation.

A global corporation does not permit its subsidiaries to operate fully autonomously. Intersubsidiary competition is discouraged, if not prohibited (except perhaps in new-product development stages). Instead, each foreign operation is given fairly specific mandates as to what markets it is selling in and what products it will produce. By limiting product production, the parent concentrates production of each item in the subsidiary or subsidiaries that can produce it most economically for the world market. Subsidiaries have "world mandates" for individual products, and the resultant allocation of resources on a global basis helps to achieve economies of scale.

Because of its ability to capitalize on distinctive competencies and competitive advantages and to use world-wide resources most effectively, the global corporation may be challenged only by other geocentric multinational corporations. Thus the geocentric corporation may be the only major international player in the future in those markets that are truly international in scope. Where markets are only national or regional (e.g., food products, where tastes vary from country to country), the polycentric corporation will compete with local corporations. But the nature of operation of a geocentric corporation brings with it many accounting problems. Reporting the results of operations of such corporations is no simple matter. Indeed, some people wonder whether it can be done at all.

Before examining the nature of the accounting problems of the international corporation, we should mention one other type of international activity that is becoming increasingly widespread, the **foreign joint venture** approach to business. In high-cost, high-risk lines of business, we are increasingly seeing corporations from several different countries jointly undertaking large-scale projects. This is particularly apparent in Europe, where several corporations have jointly undertaken airframe (airplane) development and production, and another group has undertaken joint development of computer technology in competition with U.S. and Japanese companies operating individually.

Foreign joint ventures are also a way to obtain access to markets and better access to management and technical expertise in the host country. Furthermore, some host country governments insist on domestic participation as a price for international companies' access to their markets; sometimes, the co-venturer is the host country government itself.

PROBLEMS OF ACCOUNTING FOR INTERNATIONAL ACTIVITIES

As might be expected, the tremendous range of possible levels of international activity leads to radically varying circumstances in different corporations. Therefore, corporations engaged in each of the four levels of activity described above will experience somewhat different accounting problems, and will also experience some of the same problems but with differing degrees of complexity and different reporting implications.

In 1980, two researchers published a study in which they reported eighty-eight problems in international accounting.[2] The problems were identified by surveying international accounting experts from numerous countries. The top twelve of these issues are listed in Schedule 15-2, arranged so as to list together problems relating to basically similar issues. Six problem areas emerge that were considered to be either "extremely important" or "moderately important" by the respondents. In summary, these problem areas are:

1. The lack of adequately trained accounting educators
2. The problems of translating host country currencies into the home country currency
3. Accounting for the impact of varying rates of inflation in different countries
4. The lack of comparability of accounting and reporting standards in host countries as compared with the home country
5. The influence of tax law on financial reporting in various countries
6. The lack of uniformity in auditing standards and audit reports among countries

The study reveals other problems in accounting for international activity in addition to the six major problem areas listed above. Other observers have also pointed out major areas of difficulty. These additional problem areas include the following:

1. The practice of consolidating foreign operations
2. Reporting of geographic segments
3. International transfer pricing
4. Performance evaluation of foreign subsidiaries and of foreign managers

Many of these problem areas are interrelated. Currency exchange rates do not change willy-nilly; one important determinant of relative movements in exchange rates is the relative rates of inflation in the various countries. Thus, the problems of accounting for exchange rate fluctuations and of adjusting for inflation are related. Similarly, the problems of performance evaluation are compounded by the existence of differing accounting standards, by transfer prices that are designed for other purposes, and by some managements' desire to translate the results of foreign operations before evaluating the performance of foreign subsidiaries.

The lack of accounting educators was seen as the most important problem in international accounting. While this is clearly a serious problem in Canada and the United States as well as in the rest of the world, it is not directly a problem in reporting the results of a corporation's international activities, and therefore we will not discuss it further. The issue of segmented reporting has already been discussed in Chapter 14.

In the remainder of this chapter, we will briefly discuss the other major problem areas and attempt to identify what the specific problems are. Solu-

2 George M. Scott and Pontus Troberg, *Eighty-eight International Problems in Rank Order of Importance — A DELPHI Evaluation* (American Accounting Association, 1980).

SCHEDULE 15-2

Six Important Problems in International Accounting

A. ACCOUNTING EDUCATION:

  1. There is a lack in many countries of adequately trained accounting educators.
  2. There is no extensive program to promote the development of accounting education in those countries where this education is lagging.
  3. There is a lack in many countries of adequately trained indigenous accountants.

B. CURRENCY EXCHANGE RATES:

  1. In a world of shifting exchange rates, it is difficult to measure the economic effect of exchange rate changes on a particular company having dealings with foreign affiliates or other foreign operations, or the net effect of these rate changes on a system of interrelated companies in different countries; in some circumstances the swings in the parities of currencies are largely unrelated to the operations of affiliated companies in that country.
  2. Translation gains and losses other than on currency conversion transactions-in-process often do not reflect economic reality.
  3. Too many translation approaches are now in existence around the world.

C. INFLATION:

  1. Different rates and structural characteristics of inflation in different countries make it difficult to achieve comparability of financial status and results among companies in different countries for external financial reporting.
  2. The lack of uniformity in approaches of inflation accounting as indicated by the emergence of different inflation accounting systems in different countries (such as different versions of current-value accounting) further hampers comparability among unrelated companies as well as among affiliated companies in different countries.

D. ACCOUNTING AND REPORTING STANDARDS:

  1. The lack of international accounting standards greatly diminishes the usefulness of financial statements to users in countries other than the country on whose accounting standards the statements are based.

E. TAX IMPACTS:

  1. The necessity in many countries to conform the financial accounting and reporting to tax law impedes the development of sound accounting standards and affects the international comparability of the published financial statements.

F. AUDITING STANDARDS:

  1. An auditor's report may not be easily or properly interpreted by readers in another country because it is prepared on the basis of

---

SCHEDULE 15-2 (continued)

the auditing standards and using accounting terminology of another country, or because different types of attestations are used in varous countries which have different meanings.

2. Basic principles of independence and ethics differ among countries' auditors.

Source: George M. Scott and Pontus Troberg, *Eighty-eight International Problems in Rank Order of Importance — a DELPHI Evaluation* (American Accounting Association, 1980).

---

tions to these problems are elusive, owing partially to the fact that only recently has international business emerged on a large scale and partially to the problems of performing research and gaining agreement in a multicultural and multilingual environment. The cases at the end of this chapter will help to highlight the problems. In the following three chapters, we will then explore the problems and procedures of foreign currency translation and of reporting the results of foreign operations.

Foreign Currency Translation

Life would be much simpler for accountants if the relative values of different currencies were constant. Indeed, exchange rates were constant for many years following World War II, as the result of an international conference that set the values of all major currencies in terms of the U.S. dollar. These **pegged** rates of exchange were intended to encourage international business by removing a major source of risk from the international marketplace. Fixed rates of exchange were beneficial to business, but changing balances of trade and payments among countries placed a considerable strain on the system. Consequently, fixed rates were eventually abandoned in 1971 and exchange rates were generally allowed to **float**.

Schedule 15-3 illustrates the movement of exchange rates between 1970 and 1988. The U.S. dollar had been quite stable (in terms of the Canadian dollar) for many years, increasing only about 12% over the first ten years. In the early 1980s, however, the U.S. dollar rose sharply, peaking in 1986 and then falling back in 1987 and 1988. The Swiss franc, however, has increased in value quite dramatically and almost continuously; over the seventeen-year period, the Swiss franc rose by 268%. The British pound declined steadily for several years, then recovered to earlier levels by 1980, only to fall 27% between 1981 and 1984; it again recovered somewhat after 1984.

Floating exchange rates reintroduced an element of risk into international business: the risk of losing value in terms of domestic currency as the result of doing business in a foreign currency. If a Canadian company borrows money in Swiss francs and the value of the Swiss franc rises, then the company will have to expend a larger quantity of Canadian dollars to pay off the loan, thereby losing money on the exchange.

In order to offset the risk inherent in conducting business in foreign currencies, a company engaged in foreign currency transactions or operations can arrange forward exchange contracts with a bank or foreign currency dealer to offset the company's exposure to gain or loss from exchange rate

SCHEDULE 15-3				

Foreign Currency Exchange Rates
Annual Averages
(in Canadian dollars per unit)

Year	U.S. dollar	British pound	German mark	Swiss franc	Japanese yen
1970	1.0440	2.5016	0.2863	0.2422	.002916
1971	1.0098	2.4687	0.2900	0.2456	.002912
1972	0.9905	2.4797	0.3108	0.2594	.003270
1973	1.0001	2.4533	0.3782	0.3175	.003696
1974	0.9780	2.2884	0.3785	0.3295	.003354
1975	1.0173	2.2594	0.4144	0.3942	.003430
1976	0.9861	1.7811	0.3920	0.3947	.003327
1977	1.0635	1.8571	0.4586	0.4444	.003980
1978	1.1402	2.1890	0.5691	0.6432	.005480
1979	1.1715	2.4855	0.6394	0.7046	.005375
1980	1.1690	2.7196	0.6444	0.6986	.005183
1981	1.1990	2.4287	0.5318	0.6122	.005450
1982	1.2341	2.1579	0.5086	0.6091	.004966
1983	1.2324	1.8683	0.4834	0.5837	.005190
1984	1.2948	1.7300	0.4564	0.5527	.005457
1985	1.3652	1.7701	0.4677	0.5615	.005767
1986	1.3894	2.0388	0.6425	0.7769	.008296
1987	1.3260	2.1725	0.7384	0.8905	.009188
1988	1.2309	2.1929	0.7028	0.8443	.009614

Source: *Bank of Canada Review*.

fluctuations. If a company has a debt that is payable in Swiss francs, the risk of loss from changes in the exchange rate can be offset by buying a similar quantity of Swiss francs in a forward contract. The details and accounting mechanics of forward contracts will be explored in Chapter 16.

As long as a company is conducting business in a foreign currency, it will be faced with the problem of reporting the transactions and any balances arising therefrom in its Canadian-dollar financial statements. The general problem of *translation of foreign currencies* is applicable regardless of the type of international activity in which the company engages. However, the specific problems and the approaches to solving these problems do depend upon whether the company is geocentric, polycentric, ethnocentric, or simply has a few direct foreign transactions.

One author has identified six general needs for the translation of foreign currency amounts.[3] They are:

1. To record transactions that are measured or denominated in a foreign currency
2. To prepare financial statements that report on the economic entity as a whole

3 Elwood L. Miller, *Accounting Problems of Multinational Enterprises* (Toronto: Lexington Books, 1979), pp. 144-148.

3. To evaluate the operations of a foreign business segment
4. To evaluate the performance of foreign management
5. To direct and control foreign operations
6. For the convenience of users

The first need applies to virtually all companies that are engaged in international business. However, the approach to translating foreign currency transactions may be affected by the type of operation. The approach taken in ethnocentric corporations will tend to be affected by the view of the foreign subsidiary as an extension of the parent, while the approach taken in a polycentric corporation may be different owing to the more autonomous nature of foreign subsidiaries in a polycentric operation. We will explore these different approaches in Chapter 17.

The second need applies to all those companies that operate through foreign subsidiaries or through significantly influenced foreign affiliates. If it is desirable to report the financial position and results of operations of the combined economic entity in domestic currency, then the accounts of foreign investee corporations must be translated into the home-country currency. But once again, the method of translation will be affected by the nature of the relationship between the foreign subsidiary or investee and the home-country parent or investor.

Needs 3 and 4 arise mainly with polycentric corporations. If foreign subsidiaries are permitted to operate fairly autonomously, then the parent company needs to be able to evaluate the results of the foreign operation. Evaluating the foreign business segment and evaluating the foreign segment management are not quite the same thing. Management must be judged on the basis of factors under their control, while the business segment must be evaluated on a broader basis, including all of the business and financial risks inherent in the business, whether controllable by management or not.

Both ethnocentric and geocentric corporations will experience need 5, to direct and control foreign operations, but for different reasons. Ethnocentric corporations treat the foreign subsidiaries as extensions of the parent's operations. They are controlled centrally, specifically in order to further the parent's domestic business interests. In geocentric operations, the motive for control is quite different in that the parent is attempting to manage a group of international companies to the best global effect. Since the nature of the operations is different, the method of translation may be quite different.

The sixth need, for the convenience of users, simply refers to the fact that the users of financial statements generally prefer to see the statements in their home-country currency. There are two aspects to this need. One is the need to translate all operations to the domestic currency even if most of the business is conducted in a foreign currency. If shares are traded on the Toronto Stock Exchange, then investors presumably would find it most convenient to read statements in Canadian dollars. If the statements were in another currency, then the investor would have to translate the results him- or herself in order to relate the results of operations to the share price (in Canadian dollars), and in order to evaluate the dividend and earnings potential of the company. Nevertheless, some Canadian companies with large U.S. operations have chosen to report their results in U.S. dollars. Examples include Inco, Varity, Alcan Aluminium, Moore Corporation, and the Seagram Company. While reporting in U.S. dollars is inconvenient for investors trading on the Canadian stock exchanges, it is very convenient for U.S. investors when the corporation's shares are also traded on a U.S. stock exchange.

The other aspect of convenience relates to the international financial markets. If a corporation is competing internationally for investment funds, it must make its statements available to users in various countries. This implies that the statements may be translated to the various user groups' currencies. For example, a Japanese company that reports domestically in Japanese and in yen may also issue English-language statements in U.S. dollars.

But the translation into other currencies raises another issue: should the translated statements also be adjusted to suit the accounting and reporting principles and practices that are used in each country in which investment funds are sought? Thus, the problem of translating statements interacts with the problem of incompatible accounting standards among countries.

The translation of foreign currencies is the major focus of the remaining chapters of this book. Chapter 16 examines the translation of foreign transactions, while Chapter 17 focuses on the problems inherent in translating the results of foreign operations. Chapter 18 addresses the problems of reporting the results of foreign subsidiaries and affiliates in the parent company's financial statements, either by consolidation or by equity reporting.

Inflation

Inflation has been a persistent problem in most countries. North Americans have been concerned about "double-digit" inflation from time to time, but on a world-wide basis, North American inflation has been rather less than in most other countries. In some countries, triple-digit inflation is a fact of life. In contrast, the inflation rate in some developed countries such as Switzerland and West Germany has been very low. The presence of varying levels of inflation causes three problems for the internationally active corporation:

1. Exchange rates are directly affected by differential inflation rates.
2. A few countries have altered their accounting standards in order to take inflation into account directly in the primary financial statements, while most have not.
3. Requirements for supplemental disclosures of inflation-adjusted information differ among countries.

The first problem is that inflation rates and exchange rates are inextricably interrelated. Between 1971 and 1981, the general level of prices in Canada rose 245% (as measured by the GNP deflator), while prices in the United States rose by 201%.[4] Inflation was 22% greater in Canada than in the United States (245-201). During the same period, the price of the U.S. dollar rose from $1.01 to $1.20 Canadian, an increase of 19%. Thus the difference in inflation rates was almost fully reflected in the change in the exchange rate.

Of course, exchange rate changes do not always reflect differential inflation rates so closely, especially over the short run. After 1981, the U.S. dollar rose dramatically against the Canadian dollar, soaring from $1.1990 to an all-time high of $1.4465 in 1986. The U.S. dollar then dropped even more sharply than it rose, to a low of $1.1843 in late 1988 and closing 1988 at $1.1925. Clearly, these fluctuations were not the result of inflation differentials be-

---

4 Donald J. Daly and Donald C. MacCharles, "Corporate Responses to Exchange Rate Depreciation," Administrative Sciences Association of Canada annual conference, June 1983.

tween the two countries, but in the long run, the relative values of the two currencies did return to a spread that was closely related to the inflation differential.

Currencies are seldom freely floating, but instead are usually managed by each country's government or central bank to delay or suppress the effects of inflation and of interest rate differentials. Over the long run, differential inflation has been found to be the greatest single factor affecting exchange rates; this effect is known to economists as the **purchasing-power parity** concept of exchange rates. An alternative concept for explaining changes in exchange rates is that changes in rates are a reflection of differences in interest rates between countries; this concept is known as the **Fisher Effect**, after the eminent economist who developed the theory. Interest rates, however, respond to inflation, and differential interest rates are largely traceable to differential inflation expectations.[5]

When a corporation has a foreign subsidiary, translation of the subsidiary's financial statements to the parent's home currency may result in combining monetary units of different purchasing powers. The over-100% per year inflation rate of Argentina has caused the Argentian currency to decline precipitously in value. Translating the statements of an Argentinian subsidiary for consolidation with a Canadian parent may impound that inflation in the consolidated statements. Thus, it is important to recognize the effects of inflation when deciding on a translation method for a foreign operation.

The second problem is obviously related to the first and arises because a few countries have explicitly recognized the impact of inflation in the accounts. Brazil, for example, requires that a company's permanent assets (net fixed assets and equity investments) and its shareholders' equity be adjusted each year by means of a general price index prepared by the government. When the index rises, the net gain (if the assets subject to adjustment exceed the shareholders' equity) or net loss (if the assets are less than shareholders' equity) is credited or charged to income for the period. Thus any translation of a Brazilian subsidiary's accounts must take into account the fact that they have been inflation-adjusted.

One issue is whether the Brazilian accounts should be adjusted to conform to Canadian standards (that is, restated to nominal dollars) and then translated to Canadian dollars, or whether the accounts should be translated without adjustment, but by using a translation method that recognizes the interaction of the inflation rate and the exchange rate.

The Brazilian price-level adjustment is a general price-level adjustment applied to historical-cost accounts. In the Netherlands, however, a company may use the replacement-cost basis rather than historical cost in its primary statements. Thus, a subsidiary that is not wholly owned by its Canadian parent could choose to report to its Dutch shareholders by using a current-cost basis of reporting. In this case, the basis of reporting is completely different from Canadian practice, and the subsidiary's accounts cannot be adjusted to remove the inflation adjustments by using different exchange rates

---

5 One empirical test, for example, found that purchasing-power parity (PPP) is the central tendency for exchange rate movements, although "there are significant deviations from PPP theory for some years. The theory's validity increases as the length of the period is increased." Robert Z. Aliber and Clyde P. Stickney, "Accounting Measures of Foreign Exchange Exposure: The Long and Short of It," *The Accounting Review* (January, 1975), pp. 44-57.

for translation. Instead, a substantially different accounting system would have to be maintained in order to be able to produce the required historical-cost statements for consolidation. However, any apparent success of the Dutch operation may be quite different when reported on the historical-cost basis than it is when reported on a current-cost basis. Therefore, the performance appraisals by the two shareholder groups may not be in accord, raising both interpretive problems for the users and motivational problems for the Dutch managers.

The third problem applies to subsidiaries in those countries that have recognized the impact of inflation only by supplemental disclosure. The AcSC has attempted to cope with the accounting implications of inflation by issuing Section 4510 of the *CICA Handbook*. In the United States, the FASB issued *SFAS No. 33*, while the U.K. standard-setters issued *SSAP 16*. In all three countries, the accounting standard-setters have recognized that historical-cost accounting information is of limited usefulness in the presence of inflation. However, the approaches taken to adjusting for inflation are quite different, and several sets of data will have to be accumulated by subsidiaries in each country. For example, a U.K. subsidiary of a Canadian company, if both are subject to public reporting requirements, will have to maintain adequate data to produce four sets of statements:

1. Historical-cost statements for reporting in the United Kingdom (using U.K. GAAP)
2. Historical-cost statements for consolidation by the Canadian parent (using Canadian GAAP)
3. Supplementary current-cost statements to comply with SSAP 16
4. Supplementary current-cost statements to comply with Section 4510, consolidated with the parent's current cost data

As one author puts it:

Managers can become confused when they are faced with historical cost statements prepared in local currency, those same statements translated into dollars, the local currency statements adjusted for inflation according to local requirements, and additional inflation-adjusted information required for [parent-company] reporting. . . . Managers will want to know which statements to pay attention to while planning the management of corporate assets. As can be seen, the decision is a difficult one in the international context.[6]

The decline in general inflation in the mid-1980s has led to a marked decline in price-adjusted reporting in both the United States and Canada. The FASB has made *SFAS 33* compliance voluntary, while the percentage of Canadian companies complying with Section 4510 (which was always voluntary) has approached zero. Nevertheless, inflation is still rampant in many parts of the world (and threatens to return to North America), and the concerns expressed above are still relevant.

Comparability of Accounting and Reporting Standards

Different countries have different GAAPs, a fact that we observed in the intercorporate investments section of this text and that we also referred to in the preceding section on inflation accounting. The reasons for the differing accounting standards are complex, and include cultural differences, educa-

6 J. S. Arpon and L. H. Radebaugh, *International Accounting and Multinational Enterprises* (John Wiley and Sons, 1981), p.191.

tional differences, varying levels of development of the accounting profession, the influence of alternative political systems, national economic objectives, and linguistic differences.[7]

The lack of comparability of accounting standards is a serious problem for the international financial and economic community. It is difficult enough to compare two corporations that are reporting within the same accounting framework; evaluation of relative performance when the corporations are reporting under different accounting standards is much more difficult.

Several international accountancy groups have been formed over the years to attempt to increase the comparability of accounting standards. The most viable of these groups for financial accounting is the International Accounting Standards Committee (IASC), which was formed in 1973. The founding member countries were Australia, Canada, France, Germany, Ireland, Japan, Mexico, the Netherlands, the United Kingdom, and the United States. Over 30 associate members have since joined.

The objective of IASC is "to formulate and publish in the public interest, standards to be observed in the presentation of audited financial statements and to promote their worldwide acceptance and observance." By early 1989, IASC had issued 29 standards, which are listed on the inside back cover of this book. While the hope was that each member country would comply with the IASC standards, not all countries have been willing to surrender their own standard-setting autonomy. Neither Canada nor the United States has given full authority to IASC recommendations. The CICA recognizes the IASC standards and the Accounting Standards Committee reviews new IASC standards as they are issued with a view to possibly revising appropriate *CICA Handbook* sections, but the *Handbook* does state, "until such time as the Accounting Standards Committee issues new or revised Handbook Recommendations the existing Canadian practice will prevail" [para. 1501.03].

To aid companies that must report in an international environment, the CICA has issued a publication that compares each of the International Accounting Standards (IAS) to Canadian practice as reflected both in *Handbook* recommendations and in general practice.[8] This publication is not authoritative, but is only descriptive.

Despite the reluctance of some developed countries to adopt the IASC standards, IASC has been a force towards more comparable accounting standards. While the lack of international comparability has been a problem in the international financial community, the immediate problem for a multinational corporation is that foreign subsidiaries must conform to local reporting standards, as well as provide information to the parent that is compatible with accounting standards in the home country. Even if a foreign subsidiary is wholly owned, the subsidiary cannot usually ignore host-country accounting practices. The governments of host countries frequently require all resident corporations, whether private or public, to file annual financial statements with the government. These filings must conform to local requirements. If the subsidiary is partially owned by host-country citizens, then the reports may be released publicly.

---

7 For a good, brief summary of these causes, see John N. Turner, "The Need for International Harmony in Accounting Standards," *CA Magazine*, (January 1983), pp. 40-44.
8 *Financial Reporting in an International Environment: A Comparison of International Accounting Standards with Canadian Practice* (CICA, 1984); updated in 1985, 1986, and 1988.

The difference in accounting standards then creates two problems for the manager. One is the necessity to maintain an information or accounting system that can produce two different sets of financial statements. The other is the conflict that arises when the subsidiary is evaluated by two groups of owners using different financial statements. As well, the host-country government may be evaluating the subsidiary in light of the economic and political goals of the government. Harmonization of accounting standards would go a long way towards eliminating much of this conflict.

Tax Impacts

The goal of harmonizing international accounting standards is further complicated by the influence of tax law. Many countries require public reporting to conform to income tax reporting. Other countries have a more modest tie between tax and financial accounting. Canada is no exception; for example, Revenue Canada frequently will accept a revenue recognition policy only if it is also used in the corporation's financial statements.

Tax law is formulated with the objectives of generating revenue for the government and of influencing investment and expenditures by businesses. These are quite different objectives from those generally perceived for accounting standards. Corporations are obviously unwilling to change their financial reporting if doing so would require them to pay more tax, and governments are unwilling to change their tax laws simply in order to facilitate corporations' financial reporting.

In some countries, tax avoidance is common. When taxes are being avoided by understating revenue or overstating expenses, the taxpayer will not reveal the true financial affairs of the company in filings with the government. Even statements sent to an overseas parent corporation are likely to disguise the real state of affairs. The parent corporation then faces the ticklish business of getting the information needed to adjust the subsidiary's statements for consolidation or equity reporting without jeopardizing the tax status of the subsidiary.

Transfer Pricing

Taxation has another important impact on accounting for the international enterprise — **transfer pricing**. Transfer prices are the values assigned to goods or services that are transferred between subdivisions of an organization. In an international context, we are interested in the transfer of goods and services between subsidiaries located in different countries.

Traditionally, transfer prices have been used by domestic corporations as a way of assigning revenue to a department or division that is being evaluated as a profit or investment centre. Transfer pricing systems are used as part of a control system to enable top management to evaluate the performance of segment managers and to help motivate the managers to make decisions that are in the best interests of the firm overall.

In international business, however, transfer prices take on a somewhat different set of functions. One author has suggested that "at least a dozen different considerations impact international pricing decisions. These factors can be grouped under four objectives: to control or coordinate operations, to minimize taxes, to circumvent controls, and to reduce risks."[9]

9 Miller, *Accounting Problems of Multinational Enterprises*, p.174.

Suppose that Intercorp Ltd. is a Canadian corporation that has an operating subsidiary in the country of Brigham. Intercorp manufactures a product in Canada and sells it both in Canada and in Brigham. The subsidiary is subject to income taxes in Brigham, and the corporate tax rate in that country is 60%. When Intercorp ships its product to Brigham, the price that is charged to the subsidiary in Brigham is the transfer price. The transfer price is revenue to the parent but is an expense (cost of goods sold) to the subsidiary. When the subsidiary files its tax return in Brigham, it will show revenue in the amount of its sales to its customers and will include in expenses the amount "paid" to the parent. Thus, the higher the transfer price is, the lower the subsidiary's taxable income will be. If the Canadian corporate income tax rate is 40%, then the overall corporate taxes will be reduced if net income is reported in Canada by the parent corporation rather than in Brigham by the subsidiary. Intercorp will be highly motivated to set the transfer price quite high in order to increase taxable income in Canada, where the tax rate is lower, and to decrease taxable income in Brigham, where the tax rate is higher.

Naturally, taxation authorities are aware of this temptation and in most countries will not permit a resident corporation to claim excessively high transfer prices from a foreign affiliate for tax purposes. The transfer price cannot be purely arbitrary and cannot be set with tax avoidance as the sole basis for determining the price. But a wide range of possible transfer prices still exists, such as pricing at variable cost, marginal cost, full cost, full cost plus a profit margin, or market price. There may be several methods of computation for each of those alternatives, so that the international corporation may still have considerable latitude in setting its transfer prices in such a way as to shift a significant amount of the consolidated corporate net income into those countries where tax rates are lower.

Transfer pricing for goods is only one aspect of the use of transfer prices to minimize taxes. It is not unusual for a parent corporation to charge its foreign subsidiaries a management fee for services performed by the parent. Licence fees and royalties are additional devices for shifting income from one jurisdiction to another. Interest rates charged on intercorporate loans can also be set and altered as conditions warrant.

Income taxes are not the only taxes affected by transfer prices. Since the transfer price establishes the value of the goods transferred, ad valorem taxes such as import duties and property taxes are also affected.

The range of possible avenues that exist for the minimization of taxes can also serve to circumvent controls. Many countries have attempted to impose currency restrictions at one time or another, but the judicious use of transfer prices for goods and services has frequently enabled companies to transfer considerable sums out of the restricting country without violating restrictions on dividend and investment flows. Similarly, exchange restrictions (such as those that limit the monetary volume of imports) can be circumvented to some extent by placing a low transfer price on the goods transferred into the country, thereby increasing the physical volume of imports within the monetary limits.

The reduction of risk is another objective that can be served by transfer prices. If an investment in a foreign country seems to be in jeopardy, the parent can use high transfer prices as a device for gaining a payback as quickly as possible. On the other hand, if a corporation wishes to appear as a good corporate citizen in a foreign country, or wishes to attract investors and creditors in the host country, then transfer prices can be set low; this may increase the apparent profitability of the subsidiary (thereby attracting investors) and win government approval (for contributing to the tax base and reinvesting earnings in the host country). The presence of host-country investors in the subsidiary may also make dividend declaration more politically acceptable, since part of the dividends will go to host-country citizens (while the remainder will go out of the country to the parent).

It should be apparent that the three objectives of decreasing taxes, circumventing controls, and reducing risk may be in conflict in a particular situation. For example, charging a subsidiary maximum transfer prices will serve all three objectives if the host country has a high tax rate, has restrictions on trans-border dividend payments, and is not politically stable. But if instead of having a high tax rate, the host country is a tax haven, then the tax minimization objective would call for a low transfer price, while the dividend restrictions would call for a high transfer price. Obviously, multinational corporations have quite a juggling act to perform if they attempt to maximize their overall corporate well-being.

In the foregoing discussion, we have devoted no attention at all to the more traditional objectives of transfer prices as control devices for motivation and performance appraisal. When a multinational corporation uses transfer prices to allocate resources, it is out of the question to use the transfer prices for the evaluation of either the individual business units or of their managements. Other means of control and performance appraisal must be used. One alternative would be to use a dual-price system: one price for public and governmental reporting and a different transfer price for internal evaluation. While outwardly appealing, dual-price systems are difficult to administer in a complex situation and are apt to backfire if host governments get wind of their existence.

Very few Canadian corporations operate subsidiaries in a large number of foreign countries. Most international Canadian companies actually operate only in two countries, Canada and the United States, while quite a few others also operate in the European Economic Community (common market). There are very few world-wide corporations, such as Moore Corporation or Inco, which are headquartered in Canada. As a practical matter, therefore, the complexities of international transfer pricing for Canadian corporations are not so great as they might be. Nevertheless, the objectives served by transfer pricing in even a two-country operation are not the same as those served by transfer pricing in a strictly domestic context, and international management and control is complicated by the difference.

Consolidated Financial Reporting

In Chapters 6 and 14, we examined the objectives of consolidated financial statements and their shortcomings. Consolidated statements are intended to provide the user with an overall view of the resources that are under the direct or indirect control of the parent company. However, many people argue that consolidated statements hide more than they show. Creditors of an individual corporation within the intercorporate network do not have access to the assets outside of the one corporation. Weak corporations are combined with strong ones. Accounting classifications are muddled. Apparent control of a subsidiary may not imply accessibility to the assets by the parent.

If these criticisms of consolidated reporting can be made of strictly domestic corporations, the criticisms are even more applicable in multinational business. Consolidated reports commingle different currencies, which in turn reflect various exchange rates, inflation rates, and interest rates. It can be argued that there is no way in which the various legal, economic, cultural, political, and monetary factors that shape business activity and financial reports in each country can be distilled into a single set of financial statements having any real economic meaning or practical benefit.

Current Canadian practice generally calls for the consolidation of all controlled foreign subsidiaries, and equity reporting of significantly influenced foreign investee corporations. But since changing the method of translation of foreign operations can drastically affect the apparent financial performance of the parent, some observers call for discontinuing the practice of consolidating foreign subsidiaries.

The United States and Canada are the most enthusiastic pro-consolidation countries in the world. Japan has resisted consolidation until very recently, even of domestic subsidiaries, while other countries follow some intermediate practice. But most countries outside of North America require that unconsolidated statements be provided as well as consolidated, so that the shareholders and creditors of the parent corporation can see just what shape their corporation is really in.

Alternatives to consolidation of foreign subsidiaries include:

1. Reporting foreign subsidiaries on the equity basis. This alternative avoids the problem of combining translated foreign accounts with those of the parent but still leaves the problem of computing the domestic-currency equivalent of foreign-currency earnings.
2. Reporting foreign subsidiaries on the cost basis, perhaps modified to provide for the elimination of unrealized profits from intercompany sales on the parent's books. This approach treats as income only the earnings realized from the subsidiary's dividends and eliminates the problem of translating balances and disposing of translation gains and losses.
3. Continuing to consolidate foreign operations, but supplementing the total consolidation with additional statements that consolidate only the domestic subsidiaries. The unconsolidated subsidiaries would presumably be reported on the cost basis.

If the foreign subsidiaries are not consolidated, then condensed financial statements for the major foreign subsidiaries could be presented as supplementary information. These supplementary statements could be stated in either their individual currencies or translated to Canadian dollars at the exchange rate in effect at the balance sheet date. For most internationally active Canadian companies, such supplementary disclosure would be only for U.S. operations.

SUMMARY

Many Canadian corporations engage in some form of international business activity. The international activities may range from an occasional loan in a foreign currency to a highly developed network of subsidiaries in other countries that operate in consort on a global basis. Few Canadian corporations have achieved a global basis of operation, but quite a few do have foreign subsidiaries. The most common site for foreign subsidiaries is the United States, with the United Kingdom as the second most common.

Even corporations that do not have foreign subsidiaries still frequently engage in transactions in one or more foreign countries. Such transactions most commonly consist of sales at prices quoted in foreign currencies, purchases of raw materials from foreign suppliers, or financing obtained by loans or by bonds issued in a foreign country. Again, the most common site for these transactions by a Canadian corporation is in the United States.

Scholars in the field of international business have identified four major classes of international activity by a domestic corporation:

1. Foreign transactions entered into directly by a domestic corporation, as described in the immediately preceding paragraph
2. Foreign subsidiaries that operate under direct control of the parent corporation (ethnocentric)
3. Foreign subsidiaries that operate more or less autonomously in their host countries, and that are responsive to the local environment in which they operate (polycentric)
4. A network of foreign subsidiaries that operate on a global basis, under objectives and guidelines mandated by the parent (geocentric)

Accounting for international business activities involves several difficulties that are not encountered in accounting for purely domestic operations. Among the problems of international accounting are the following:

1. Foreign currency translation
2. Inflation
3. Differing accounting standards
4. Impact of taxes on accounting
5. Transfer pricing
6. Performance appraisal
7. Consolidation and equity-basis reporting

The severity of the accounting problems varies with the level of sophistication of the international activities. A company that is engaged only in foreign currency transactions will have to deal solely with the problem of foreign currency translation. At the other extreme, a geocentric corporation will have to cope with all of the above problems, plus a few more as well. Those ethnocentric or polycentric Canadian corporations that have foreign operations only in the United States will not be significantly affected by the problems of inflation and differing accounting standards, since inflation rates and accounting standards are similar between the United States and Canada, but they will be affected to a varying extent by the other problems on the list.

The severity of the above problems is intensified by the fact that they interact. Exchange rates are affected by inflation rate differentials between countries. Transfer pricing is affected largely by income tax considerations. Performance appraisal is made more difficult because of varying reporting requirements in different countries, different tax laws, transfer prices set to satisfy nonevaluative criteria, and inflation.

These accounting difficulties are further intensified if the foreign operations are partially owned by host country citizens. Management will then have to serve at least three powerful constituencies: the parent corporation, the host-country shareholders, and the host-country government, each of which may well place conflicting demands on the subsidiary's management.

In view of the great difficulties that are inherent in accounting for foreign operations, many observers have questioned the efficacy of consolidated financial statements. Nevertheless, consolidation of foreign subsidiaries (with a few exceptions) is the standard practice in North America at present.

In the chapters that follow, we will examine those problems that are of the most immediate practical concern in accounting for the international activities of a domestic corporation. Chapters 16 and 17 deal with the issue of translating foreign currencies. Chapter 16 discusses translation of foreign currency *transactions*, while Chapter 17 explores the problems of translating the results of foreign *operations*. The process of equity reporting and consolidation for foreign affiliates and subsidiaries is presented in Chapter 18.

REVIEW QUESTIONS

15-1 Distinguish between **foreign currency transactions** and **foreign operations**.

15-2 What country is the most common site for international transactions by Canadian corporations?

15-3 How could one determine whether a foreign operation is a branch-type operation or is an autonomous operation?

15-4 How does the relationship of an **ethnocentric** foreign operation to its host-country environment differ from that of a **polycentric** foreign operation?

15-5 Why are polycentric organizations apt to be more successful in the international marketplace than their ethnocentric counterparts?

15-6 Why do globally oriented multinational corporations frequently place restrictions on their subsidiaries' operations and freedom to compete?

15-7 Why are geocentric corporations likely to be more effective in international markets than polycentric corporations?

15-8 Distinguish between **pegged** rates of exchange and **floating** rates of exchange.

15-9 Explain why floating exchange rates are risky for a company that conducts part of its business in a foreign currency.

15-10 What is the primary cause of changes in exchange rates over the long run?

15-11 How do the adjustments for price changes that are used in Brazilian accounts differ from the current cost accounting that may be used by companies in some countries, such as the Netherlands?

15-12 Why don't all countries use the same accounting principles?

15-13 Why is the existence of differing accounting and reporting standards in different countries a problem for the international financial community?

15-14 Forco is the 60% owned subsidiary of Domco and is located in the country of Foreign. The remaining 40% of the shares are owned by Foreign citizens. What problems will arise for the management of Forco if Foreign requires accounting practices that differ significantly from those used by Domco?

15-15 Explain how the motivation for setting transfer prices for foreign operations is likely to differ from the primary purpose of transfer pricing in domestic operations.

15-16 How can transfer prices affect the total income taxes paid by the consolidated enterprise?

15-17 How can transfer prices be used to circumvent restrictions on expatriating profits from a foreign subsidiary to the parent?

15-18 If a foreign subsidiary is in an unstable country, how can the parent reduce its exposure to the risk of expropriation by the use of transfer prices and management fees?

15-19 Why do some observers question the usefulness of parent company consolidated financial statements when a significant proportion of the consolidated activities are carried out in foreign operations?

15-20 What are the suggested alternatives to consolidation of foreign subsidiaries?

CASE 15-1	C Ltd.

CA's firm has recently acquired the statutory audit of C Ltd., a company incorporated under the *Canada Business Corporations Act*. C Ltd. is 55% owned by a U.S. company, X Inc., and 45% owned by many shareholders across Canada. A firm of certified public accountants, unrelated to CA's firm, audits X Inc.

During the course of the midyear interim audit, CA, who was in charge of the engagement, learned the following about C Ltd.:

1. Management has received a request from the parent company, X Inc., to prepare its annual report to the shareholders for the current year in U.S. dollars, using accounting principles generally accepted in the United States. X Inc. files the consolidated statements with the Securities and Exchange Commission (SEC).
2. C Ltd.'s business consists of manufacturing electronic components. By written agreement signed four years ago, X Inc. buys 60% of normal plant capacity production of C Ltd. at a discount of 15% from the currently prevailing market value. C Ltd. receives payment in U.S. dollars for X Inc. C Ltd. has always had orders on hand for the remaining output because of the exceedingly high demand for these intricate, patented components. Most of these sales are to federal and provincial governments.
3. Management of C Ltd. is well along the process of planning a doubling of plant capacity to service growth in sales to the Canadian industrial market segment. Acquisition cost of plant and machinery for the expansion is likely to be three times that of the cost of the original plant. The expansion is to be financed by a Canadian bond issue.
4. For eight years, senior management (five people) has received a bonus based on the excess of actual net income over annual budgeted net income. This plan was approved three months before X Inc. sold 45% of its shares to the Canadian public. Management of C Ltd. is pleased with their bonus plan because it results in "good bonuses."
5. As all of the current output is readily saleable, the company recognizes revenue in its accounts at the completion of the manufacturing process, even though packaging in cardboard containers is still necessary and shipment could occur any time from one to three months thereafter.
6. Terms of sale are net 90 days for government accounts and net 180 days for others. A warranty extends for one year from the date of shipment.
7. In lieu of dividends, a $300,000 management fee is paid to the parent company. Also, a cheque (usually between $375,000 and $400,000) is sent to X Inc. annually to pay the gross amount of royalties payable for designing some of the components.

The terms of engagement appointing CA's firm request, in addition to the annual audit, that helpful advice on all accounting (including management accounting) matters be given to the management, and communicated to the audit committee of C Ltd.

C Ltd.
Income Statement
For year ended December 31, 1988
(in thousands of Canadian dollars)

	Audited Actual (12,000 components sold)		Budgeted (100,000 components sold)	
Revenue		$22,675		$20,200
Cost of goods sold:				
Direct material	$6,580		$6,000	
Direct labour	4,388		4,000	
Manufacturing cost:				
Fixed	1,690		2,000	
Variable	3,242	15,900	3,200	15,200
Gross profit		6,775		5,000
Selling, administrative and interest expense (fixed costs)		3,840		3,500
Income before income tax		2,935		1,500
Income tax (all currently payable)		1,470		750
Net income		$1,465		$ 750

Actual depreciation charged to
income $1,200,000

C Ltd.
Balance Sheet
December 31, 1988

	Audited actual (in thousands of Canadian dollars)	
Working capital		$ 14,820
Land, building and equipment		26,540
Accumulated depreciation		(19,640)
		21,720
Bonds payable in U.S. dollars — 10% — due December 31, 1991 (Note 1)	$ 5,000	
Deferred credits	300	
Due to parent — 12%	14,000	(19,300)
Shareholders' equity		$ 2,420

Note 1
The bonds were issued at face value on January 1, 1987, and are carried at that amount at December 31, 1988. They are translated at the historical exchange rate.

CA gathered the following information on exchange rates:

December 31, 1986	$1 U.S. = $1.36 Cdn.
December 31, 1987	$1 U.S. = $1.28 Cdn.
December 31, 1988	$1 U.S. = $1.20 Cdn.
December 31, 1989 (estimated)	$1 U.S. = $1.18 Cdn.

Required:
Identify and discuss the accounting issues that must be resolved before the 1989 financial statements for C Ltd. are prepared and issued.
[CICA, adapted]

CASE 15-2   Tustian Enterprises, Ltd.

Tustian Enterprises is a Canadian-based multinational company. Within the past year, Tustian has purchased controlling interests in a company in each of two other countries, Brazil and Sweden. The stock market responded favourably to the purchases, pushing Tustian's shares to a new high. Tustian has been very successful in the past in getting the best out of its far-flung foreign operations (in terms of impact on Tustian's consolidated statements), without imposing the parent company's operating style on the subsidiaries.

Both of the newly acquired subsidiaries are prominent companies in their countries and are publicly traded. Thus both must abide by reporting requirements in their own countries when preparing their financial statements. For Tustian's purposes, however, the subsidiaries' statements must be recast to conform to Canadian GAAP and to Canadian dollars before they can be consolidated with Tustian's other subsidiaries. The prospect of needing to report financial results that will be favourable both in the subsidiaries' own statements and when consolidated with Tustian's has caused concern among the senior executives of the two new subsidiaries.

In the Brazilian company, management is concerned about the revision of the Brazilian statements for inflation. The general price level in Brazil has increased by 752.5% in the last five years, a compounded rate of 50% per year, according to the government's general price index. Inflation in the most recent year was 98%. Long-term debt is indexed, so that interest and principal payments are automatically adjusted to reflect the rapidly shrinking value of the currency. These inflated interest costs are reported in income. On the other hand, long-term investment (and shareholders' equity) are also adjusted on the primary statements, and any price-level gains on net investment are also taken into income, thus offsetting the increasing interest costs. Interest costs in current cruzeiros are thereby matched to holding gains in current cruzeiros. The balance sheet at the end of each period reflects the long-term investment and long-term financing in terms of current purchasing power.

The concern of the Brazilian management is that the statements of their company will be drastically restated for consolidation purposes, and will no longer reflect the true performance of the subsidiary in its own environment. Since Canadian reporting requirements do not permit restatement for inflation, Brazilian management fears that the Canadian accountants will remove the price-level restatements from the balance sheet and the holding gains from the income statement, and then translate the statements into Canadian dollars at historical exchange rates. This process will, it is feared, be to the apparent disadvantage of the Brazilian company. The price-indexed interest payments will continue to be reflected as an expense in the income statement because the payments represent real transactions, but the offsetting gains will be gone. Since Tustian's management will want the subsidiaries to contribute favourably to the consolidated results, the Brazilian management is greatly concerned about the need to serve two masters, the minority Brazilian shareholders and Tustian's shareholders.

Inflation in Sweden has not been so severe, having amounted to 64.3% over five years, almost exactly the same as the 63.4% inflation in Canada for the same period. Therefore, the concern of the Swedish management is quite different from that of their Brazilian counterparts.

In Sweden, the law requires that companies report on their income statements the same items that they report as revenues and expenses on their tax returns. Since tax minimization is always the goal of tax management, the publicly released income statements reflect the same goal. Investors in Sweden are accustomed to this fact of life, and are prepared to interpret the statements accordingly. The Swedish management is concerned, however, that Tustian's management will not exhibit the same understanding when evaluating their performance.

The concern of the Swedes has been intensified recently because of a change in the operations of the Swedish company that was mandated from Canada. The Swedish subsidiary produces a product that is distributed throughout northern Europe. A few months ago, Tustian asked that the product not be processed by the Swedish firm through its final production stage, except for that quantity to be sold directly in Sweden. The rest of the (unfinished) product is to be delivered to another Tustian subsidiary in the Netherlands for completion and subsequent distribution. The transfer is to occur at the cost of production plus a 20% markup.

Tustian requested the change because income taxes are lower in the Netherlands than in Sweden. The 20% markup permits a reasonable return to the Swedish company, and does not appear to violate OECD guidelines or Swedish tax regulations on trans-border transfer pricing for products without a fair market value. But for the Swedish company, the overall return will be less than if the product were completed in Sweden and then transferred at fair market price.

The senior managers of both the Swedish and the Brazilian companies have therefore flown to Tustian's executive offices in Vancouver to consult with the chief executive officer about their concerns.

Required:

Assume the role of the chief executive officer of Tustian. Respond to the concerns of the subsidiaries' managers, bearing in mind the need of Tustian to present favourable financial results to its own shareholders.

(The inflation rates used in this case were derived from statistics reported by the International Monetary Fund, and are for the five-year period from 1978 to 1982.)

16

Foreign Currency Transactions

The previous chapter discussed the fact that many companies conduct at least some of their business activities in countries other than that in which they are based. Whenever a Canadian corporation has transactions with principals in foreign countries, the corporation is engaged in **foreign transactions**. The transactions may be conducted in Canadian dollars. For example, Bombardier Inc. could sell a train set to Amtrak in the United States at a price stated in Canadian dollars. If the foreign transactions are denominated in Canadian dollars, then no unusual accounting problems arise from the fact that the customer is in a foreign country.

However, it is quite common for a Canadian company to engage in foreign transactions that are denominated in a foreign currency. For example, a Canadian electronics manufacturer would probably buy all of its semiconductor chips from the United States at prices quoted in U.S. dollars. Or a carpet manufacturer who regularly sells its carpets in the United Kingdom would quote prices in pounds. When a Canadian company has transactions that are denominated in a foreign currency, the company is engaged in **foreign currency transactions**.

Whenever a Canadian company carries on business in a foreign currency, a problem arises from the fact that the company's accounting records and financial statements are in Canadian dollars (normally), while some of the transactions are effected in foreign currency. In order to report the results of the transactions that were denominated in foreign currencies, it is necessary to translate these transactions or the results thereof into Canadian dollars.

Foreign currency transactions include only those transactions to which the Canadian company is a party. Instead of directly conducting business in the foreign country, the company may establish a subsidiary in the foreign country. The subsidiary then carries out the transactions, the net results of which are reflected in the subsidiary's own financial statements, expressed in the host country's currency. The accounting problem then becomes one of **translating foreign operations** rather than recording the effects of foreign currency transactions. The accounting approaches to translating foreign operations will be discussed in Chapter 17, and the problems of consolidating or equity-reporting foreign subsidiaries will be presented in Chapter 18.

In this chapter, we are concerned exclusively with direct foreign currency transactions, not with foreign operations. Our discussion will be in three parts: (a) accounting for current transactions and balances, (b) accounting for long-term balances, and (c) hedging transactions.

A. TRANSACTIONS AND CURRENT BALANCES

Suppose that on March 5, 19x1, Domestic Corporation sells 100 units of its product in Germany for 100 thousand deutsche marks, or DM100,000. Domestic Corporation must record this sale on its books, but it would be nonsensical to record it at 100,000 because the deutsche mark cannot simply be added to the Canadian dollar. It is necessary to translate the sale into the equivalent amount in Canadian dollars. If we assume that the exchange rate on the date of sale was DM1 = Can. $ 0.50 (that is, that each deutsche mark is worth $0.50, or that one dollar is worth two deutsche marks), then the Canadian equivalent is $50,000. The sale can be recorded as follows, assuming that it was a sale on account:

Transactions

Accounts receivable	$50,000	
Sales		$50,000

The amount of the sale in its Canadian equivalent will then be aggregated with the other domestic and foreign sales without further difficulties.

If the German customer pays the amount owing on March 21, DM100,000 will be received by Domestic Corporation. If the exchange rate is DM1 = $0.51, Domestic will receive $51,000 when the marks are converted to Canadian dollars. Domestic will debit cash for $51,000 and credit accounts receivable for $50,000. The $1,000 difference represents a gain that has been realized by Domestic because the value of the mark went up while Domestic was holding a receivable that was denominated in marks. If the exchange rate had gone down instead of up, Domestic would have realized a loss instead of a gain.

The gain on the exchange rate change could be treated either of two ways: (1) by increasing the amount of revenue recognized by $1,000, or (2) by crediting a separate gain account. The difference may seem to be minor, since both treatments will result in an increase in net income in the same period. The alternative treatments can have a substantive impact, however, when a company *buys* inventory or fixed assets in a foreign currency and the exchange rate changes between the date of purchase and the date of payment. Any exchange gain or loss realized by holding the liability could either be added to the cost of the assets acquired or be treated as a gain or loss of the period.

The first approach, to attach exchange gains and losses to the asset or the revenue that results from the initial transaction, is known as the **one transaction theory** because the accrual and the cash settlement are viewed as a single economic event. The second approach, in contrast, views the accrual (i.e., the sale or purchase) as one economic event and the eventual cash settlement (collection of the receivable or payment of the liability) as a separate financing activity; this is known as the **two transaction theory**. Under the two transaction theory, exchange gains and losses normally flow through directly to the income statement in the period that they occur.

The two transaction theory has been more widely adopted and is the one reflected in the recommendations of the *CICA Handbook*. The financing component of a foreign currency transaction is separated from the purchase or sale itself because the cash flow is controlled by the domestic company, and the results of such essentially speculative activity should not be hidden in gross revenue or in the cost of assets. The financing component can be controlled because the company has options: purchases can be paid for by bank drafts at the time of the transaction; receivables can be sold to banks or finance companies, or can be financed by the sale of credit "paper" denominated in the same currency; the foreign currency denominated payable or receivable can be hedged (which is the subject of part C of this chapter); and so forth.

Under the two transaction approach, the collection by Domestic of the DM100,000 receivable would be recorded as follows:

Cash (DM100,000)	$51,000	
Accounts receivable		$50,000
Foreign currency exchange gain		1,000

Current Monetary Balances

Now assume instead that the fiscal year of Domestic Corporation ends on March 31, and that on that date, the account receivable from the German sale is still outstanding. The receivable is recorded on Domestic's books at $50,000, but actually the receivable is for DM100,000. If the deutsche mark is worth $0.52 on March 31, then the value of the DM100,000 receivable is $52,000, a $2,000 gain over the original recorded amount of the transaction. The accounting problem then becomes whether or not to recognize the change in value of the foreign-currency-denominated monetary balance on the balance sheet and, if it is recognized on the balance sheet, then whether or not the gain should be taken into income.

The recognition issue arises whenever foreign transactions result in current *monetary* balances at the balance sheet date. Monetary balances are those that are fixed in a given amount of currency, such as receivables and payables. The alternatives are as follows:

1. Report the current monetary balance at the historical rate, possibly with note disclosure of the effect of the changed exchange rate.
2. Report the current monetary balance at the current rate; capitalize the gain or loss on the balance sheet to defer recognition of the gain or loss on the income statement until the amount is **settled** (that is, until the receivable or payable is paid).
3. Report the current monetary balance at the current rate, and include the gain or loss in income for the period.

In our example, the DM100,000 sale resulted in an account receivable at the balance sheet date of $52,000 when translated at the current rate (that is, at the rate in effect at the balance sheet date). The impacts of applying each of the three alternatives listed above are illustrated in Schedule 16-1, assuming that the receivable is settled in April, 19x1, when the mark is worth $0.527.

SCHEDULE 16-1

	Years ended March 31		
	19x1		19x2
Alternative	Income statement	Balance sheet	Income statement
1. Historical rate:			
Receivable balance		$50,000 Dr.	
Foreign currency gain	—		$2,700 Cr.
2. Current rate; deferred gain:			
Receivable balance		$52,000 Dr.	
Deferred foreign currency gain		$ 2,000 Cr.	
Foreign currency gain	—		$2,700 Cr.
3. Current rate; current recognition:			
Receivable balance		$52,000 Dr.	
Foreign currency gain	$2,000 Cr.		$ 700 Cr.

The first approach, that of simply leaving the receivable balance at the historical amount of $50,000, is certainly the easiest of the three alternatives. Proponents of this approach argue that since the amount has not yet been settled, it is premature to recognize any gain or loss. A gain recognized in the current year may well be offset in the following year if the exchange rate declines before the balance is paid. Since any gains or losses on current balances can be viewed as temporary, the balance should best be left at the exchange rate that was in effect at the date of the transaction, consistent with the historical cost concept. Of course, parenthetical or note disclosure could be made of the current rate equivalent at the balance sheet date. A lower-of-cost-or-market approach could also be taken, wherein gains would be deferred but losses would be recognized.

Under the second alternative, the change in the Canadian dollar equivalent of the DM100,000 balance is recognized by reporting the balance on the balance sheet as $52,000 rather than as $50,000. The $2,000 gain, however, is not recognized as a component of income in fiscal 19x1, but is carried on the balance sheet as a deferred credit until the account is settled. The adjustment of the account would be:

| Accounts receivable | $2,000 | |
| Deferred foreign currency gain | | $2,000 |

If the balance is subsequently paid in April when the exchange rate is DM1 = $0.527, the entry to record the receipt of the DM100,000 would be as follows, assuming that the preceding entry had been recorded on Domestic's books and not just on the financial statement working papers:

Cash	$52,700	
Deferred foreign currency gain	2,000	
Accounts receivable		$52,000
Foreign currency gain		2,700

Under this approach, the entire gain on the transaction is reflected in net income in the period in which the account is paid. Alternatively, a lower-of-cost-or-market-rule could be applied, with gains deferred but losses recognized when they occur, rather than deferred until settlement.

The third approach recognizes the change in the balance owing, but also recognizes the gain in the income statement. The adjusting entry would be:

Accounts receivable	$2,000	
Foreign currency gain		$2,000

If the account is subsequently settled when the mark is worth $0.527, the entry to record the payment would be:

Cash	$52,700	
Accounts receivable		$52,000
Foreign currency gain		700

Under this approach, the change in the current equivalent of the foreign currency balance is recognized in income in the period in which it occurs. Since $2,000 of the gain occurred in March, that portion of the gain is recognized in income in the income statement for the year ended March 31, 19x1. The remaining $700 gain occurred in April and will be included in income for that period.

The proponents of the third alternative argue that it has two advantages over the other approaches:

1. It shows the account balances at the current Canadian dollar equivalent of amounts legally owing (e.g., DM100,000) at the balance sheet date.
2. It reflects in net income the impact of the economic events of the period; specifically, the impact on the reporting enterprise of changes in the exchange rates.

The third alternative is generally used in practice and is recommended in Section 1650 of the *CICA Handbook* [para. 1650.20]. However, the first approach, wherein the current balances are reported at their historical exchange rates, may occasionally be used, especially by private companies. If a company engages in foreign currency sales quite often, perhaps in several different currencies, gains and losses may fluctuate from year to year. Reporting exactly how much gain or loss is attributable to currency fluctuations in each year may not significantly improve the determination of periodic net income.

Nonmonetary Balances

In the foregoing discussion, we have focused on the translation of current *monetary* balances. If the foreign currency transaction was not a sale but was, for example, a purchase of inventory, then the transaction would result in two balance sheet amounts: an account payable and inventory. The account payable is a monetary balance and would be treated exactly as would the account receivable discussed above, assuming that the two transaction approach is used. The inventory, however, is a nonmonetary balance; how should it be treated? Since a nonmonetary balance is, by definition, *not* an amount that is fixed in terms of a currency and does not represent a claim against monetary resources, it is not affected by changes in the exchange rate. If inventory is carried at historical cost, then the historical cost of inventory that was purchased with a foreign currency is simply the domestic currency equivalent of the foreign currency at the date of the purchase. In other words, nonmonetary balances are carried at historical exchange rates because that is the historical cost.

An exception arises when a nonmonetary asset is reported on the balance sheet at current value rather than at historical cost. For example, suppose that Domestic Corporation purchased a security in Germany as a temporary investment, and that Domestic reports such investments at their current market value. If the current market value is quoted in deutsche marks, then it would make little sense to take a current value and translate it at a historical rate. In order to report the current value of the investment in Canadian dollars, the current value in deutsche marks must be converted into dollars at the current exchange rate.

Summary: Transactions and Current Balances

Foreign currency transactions are translated into the equivalent amount in domestic currency at the exchange rate at the time of the transaction. Current monetary balances that are denominated in a foreign currency are normally reported in the equivalent amount in domestic currency at the balance sheet date. When current monetary balances are reported at the current exchange rate, the gain or loss arising from any change in the exchange rate between the transaction date and the balance sheet date is recognized currently in income.

Nonmonetary balances that arise from foreign currency transactions are ordinarily reported at historical cost, which is the foreign currency amount translated at the exchange rate in effect at the time of the transaction. However, nonmonetary balances that are reported at current values in foreign currency on the balance sheet should be reported in the domestic currency equivalent at the balance sheet date in accordance with the *CICA Handbook* [para. 1650.18].

As a practical matter, companies that engage in a large volume of foreign currency transactions may not actually use the current rate for translating each transaction. If, for example, a company has thousands of sales transactions in U.S. dollars during a year, it is impractical to check on the current exchange rate (the "spot" rate) every time a sale occurs. Instead, the sales may be accumulated for a period of time and a single rate applied to the aggregate. Alternatively, a company might use the rate at the beginning of each month for that month's transactions. Each of these approaches is an expedient for accounting for a large volume of transactions. Minor differences between the actual spot rate and the rate used for translation of the transactions will be adjusted for when the accounts are settled, or when the monetary account balances are adjusted to the current rate on the balance sheet date.

Some companies use a standard rate for translating foreign currency transactions. If a company uses a profit-centre approach to appraising its managers, it may be desirable to remove the effects of uncontrollable currency fluctuations from the profit centre's operating results before attempting to appraise the performance of the managers. The total balance of current monetary balances would then be adjusted to the current rate for external reporting.

B.   LONG-TERM BALANCES

The foregoing discussion dealt exclusively with current transactions and with current asset and current liability balances that arise from foreign currency transactions. Similar problems and alternatives also arise when foreign currency transactions give rise to long-term balances. If the long-term balances are nonmonetary assets carried at historical cost, then the carrying value is not adjusted for changes in the exchange rate. This treatment is exactly the same as that discussed above for historical-cost inventories. But if the balances are long-term monetary balances, then the accounting treatment might be different than that for short-term monetary balances.

The most common type of long-term foreign currency balance in Canada is undoubtedly long-term debt that has been raised outside of Canada, usually in the United States. Schedule 16-2 shows the total volume of foreign financing by Canadian corporations. In the ten years from 1978 through 1987, 67% of corporations' net new bond issues were placed outside of Canada. Financial corporations placed 82% of their debt outside of Canada, but nonfinancial corporations also raised a majority of their debt abroad, 55%.

Schedule 16-3 shows some specific examples of domestic versus foreign long-term obligations for companies that have heavy capital requirements. These five companies have over $14.5 billion in foreign debt; most is in U.S. dollars, with the remainder in Swiss francs and deutsche marks. Note that all five of these companies are domestic Canadian corporations. The substantial amounts of foreign debt have all been incurred to finance a domestic asset structure, not foreign subsidiaries.

Long-term monetary balances may also arise from activities such as long-

SCHEDULE 16-2						
Net New Bond Issues (in millions of Canadian dollars)						
	Financial corporations		Nonfinancial corporations		Total	
	placed in:		placed in:		placed in:	
Year	Canada	Abroad	Canada	Abroad	Canada	Abroad
1978	$ 933	$ 480	$ 2,260	$ 1,014	$ 3,193	$ 1,494
1979	806	808	466	691	1,272	1,499
1980	445	1,093	1,147	1,100	1,592	2,193
1981	708	1,341	1,071	2,914	1,779	4,255
1982	(493)	1,308	604	3,096	111	4,404
1983	(271)	977	838	909	567	1,886
1984	(3)	610	722	819	719	1,429
1985	305	2,853	1,162	1,230	1,467	4,083
1986	1,430	6,578	2,324	2,129	3,754	8,707
1987	356	2,992	2,778	2,421	3,134	5,413
10-year totals	$4,216	$19,040	$13,372	$16,323	$17,588	$35,363

Source: *Bank of Canada Review*

SCHEDULE 16-3

**Examples of Foreign Currency Debt,
Long-term Notes and Bonds**
(in millions of Canadian dollars)

	Denominated in:		
	Canadian dollars	Other currencies	Proportion in foreign currencies
Air Canada	$ 279	$1,082	79%
Bell Canada	2,504	1,930	44
Imperial Oil Limited	461	294	39
Ontario Hydro	15,406	9,504	38
TransCanada Pipelines	1,453	1,702	54

Source: Corporate annual reports for 1987.

---

term leasing, mortgage financing, or other long-term financing provided to a customer or client. When long-term monetary balances are denominated in a foreign currency, the question again arises as to whether or not the balances should be shown on the balance sheet at the current exchange rate. And if the current rate is used, then what should be done with the gains or losses due to changes in the exchange rate?

The basic range of alternative treatments includes all of those cited above for short-term monetary balances, plus one additional possible treatment for the gain or loss. The added alternative is to defer the translation gain or loss and amortize it over the remaining life of the balance.

For example, assume that Domestic Corporation issues bonds in England on January 1, 19x2, for one million pounds sterling (£1,000,000). On that date, the exchange rate was £1 = $1.80. Domestic Corporation therefore received $1,800,000 from the bond issue. The bonds will mature in five years, on January 1, 19x7. At the fiscal year-end of December 31, 19x2, the value of the British pound has fallen to $1.75. The alternative valuations of the bonds payable are (1) at the historical rate of $1.80, or $1,800,000, or (2) at the current rate of $1.75, or $1,750,000 total. If the current rate is used, then there are three alternative treatments of the $50,000 gain:

1. Defer the gain until the bonds are retired and the gain is realized.
2. Recognize the gain immediately in income.
3. Defer the gain and amortize it over the five years until maturity (at $10,000 per year, if straight-line amortization is used).

Defer until Realized

Prior to the effective date of the current version of Section 1650 of the *CICA Handbook* (July 1983), the most common method of valuing long-term bonds in Canada was to leave the bonds at the historical rate, with note disclosure of either the amount at the current rate or the currency in which the debt must be paid, or both. Such disclosure then enabled users to make their own adjustments if they wished to do so.

Financial Reporting in Canada reported that in 1977, 74% of the 121 companies (out of 325) that had foreign-denominated long-term debt carried that debt at historical rates. By 1980, the proportion had declined to 54% (of 152 companies), owing to the impact of U.S. and Canadian pronouncements that recommended current-rate valuation of long-term monetary balances. Thus, in 1980, nearly half of the surveyed companies had foreign debt and over half of those were still using the historical-rate method, thereby implicitly deferring all gains or losses until realized at maturity.

The then common treatment for bonds seems on the surface to be in conflict with the common treatment for short-term balances, which was to report them at current rates. The conflict is not so illogical as it may at first appear, however. Short-term monetary balances represent assets that will be realized or liabilities that will require payment in liquid assets within the next year. There is little doubt that settlement of the balances will directly affect the reporting company's financial position in the near future, and that exchange rate fluctuations are the real economic events that trigger the realization of gains and losses on short-term balances.

Exchange rate fluctuations that affect long-term balances, however, have a much more tenuous impact on the financial position of the company. Exchange gains or losses on long-term debt will not be realized for many years in the future, if at all. Since the amount of debt that is denominated in foreign currencies may be quite large, gains or losses arising from this debt can have a substantial impact on reported earnings. Domestic Corporation may recognize the $50,000 gain on its income statement in 19x2, but if the pound strengthens in 19x3, Domestic will then recognize a loss in 19x3. Neither the gain in 19x2 nor the loss in l9x3 is realized, and neither may suggest what the value of the pound will be in 19x7 when the bond issue matures.

Another reason for the popularity of the historical rate for long-term debt is that the debt may effectively never be repaid. If the corporate policy is to refinance the debt when it comes due, then it can be argued that no gain or loss is realized even at maturity because it is refinanced in replacement debt in the same foreign currency.

Finally, a third justification offered for the use of the historical rate is that, in some instances, the debt is used to finance assets in the foreign country in which the bonds are issued. For example, a Canadian company could buy a small building in Chicago to use as a U.S. sales headquarters and finance the building largely by means of a mortgage from a Chicago bank. The mortgage will be denominated in U.S. dollars. When the company prepares its financial statements (in Canadian dollars), it will include the Chicago building at its historical cost, computed at the historical exchange rate. If the mortgage on that building is translated at the current exchange rate, then the company will be recognizing a gain or loss on the debt without recognizing any change in the value of the building. Thus it is argued that the related asset and liability should be reported in a similar manner: at the historical exchange rate. In such a case, the asset (the building) may be viewed as an **implicit hedge** of the liability (the mortgage) because it generates sufficient revenue in U.S. dollars to service the U.S. debt.

If no gain or loss is to be recognized currently, then there are only two alternatives for reporting the bonds: (1) either the liability balance must be carried at the historical exchange rate, or else (2) the liability can be reported at the current exchange rate with the exchange gain or loss capitalized and deferred. Many companies (and many financial statement users) prefer not to have large deferred debits or credits on the balance sheet, and thus the only remaining alternative is to leave the balance at the historical rate with note disclosure as to the nature of the debt.

Immediate Recognition

The second alternative is to restate the long-term balances at the current exchange rate at the balance sheet date, and to report the change in the dollar-equivalent as a gain or loss for the period. This approach will result in a balance sheet that fully reflects the current value of long-term monetary balances in terms of the Canadian dollar.

Any gains or losses arising from translating the balances at the current rate are reported in the income statement because the change in the exchange rate is an economic event of the period. This year's change in rates is not related to future periods; the movement of the exchange rates in the future is dependent upon economic conditions in future periods. Therefore, it is viewed as inappropriate for both income measurement and balance sheet valuation to defer all or part of the gains or losses to future periods.

Furthermore, it is frequently within management's ability to realize any gains or losses by refinancing the balances or by buying in or calling outstanding bonds. Whether management exercises its options or not is irrelevant, it is argued; the gains or losses should be reported in either case.

A counterargument is that gains or losses on the market value of long-term monetary balances are not ordinarily reported, even for domestic balances. If a company's bonds decline in price on the bond market, no gain is reported on the income statement unless the company actually buys back the bonds at a discount. If a change in exchange rates is viewed simply as an added component of market value, then consistency of treatment with domestic bonds would suggest that no gain or loss should be reported on foreign-currency-denominated bonds unless the company actually extinguishes or refinances the debt.

Defer and Amortize

In the United States, the FASB recommends in *SFAS No. 52* that gains and losses from translating long-term balances be reported in income, with no deferrals. In Canada, however, immediate recognition of the exchange gains or losses was deemed by the AcSC to have too great a potential impact on the income statement because of the extent to which Canadian companies engage in foreign-currency financing. Since exchange gains or losses on long-term monetary balances would be realized only at maturity, the AcSC recommended in Section 1650 that the exchange gains and losses on long-term foreign-denominated balances be deferred and amortized over the remaining time until maturity, including the current year.

Thus the current *Handbook* position is the last one in our list of alternatives above. The $50,000 gain on the bonds would be amortized over five years if the *Handbook* recommendations are followed [para. 1650.23]. For 19x2, Domestic Corporation would report $10,000 of the gain in its income statement and the remaining $40,000 would appear as a deferred credit on the balance sheet.

Suppose that in 19x3, the value of the pound increased to $1.84 at year-end. If the bonds are being carried at current exchange rates, then the reported balance on the balance sheet at December 31, 19x3, would be

$1,840,000. Compared to the reported balance of $1,750,000 at the beginning of the year (December 31, 19x2), Domestic Corporation has experienced a loss of $90,000 during the year 19x3. Following the *Handbook* recommendations, the $90,000 would be amortized over the then remaining *four* years until maturity, at $22,500 per year. The amortization that would be reported on the income statement for 19x3 would be the net of the amortization of $10,000 credit from the 19x2 gain and the amortization of $22,500 debit from the 19x3 loss, or a net debit of $12,500 ($22,500 debit minus $10,000 credit). On the balance sheet, the deferred gain (credit) would be debited $10,000 for the current amortization of the amount deferred from 19x2, and debited for the $67,500 deferred from 19x3. Thus the balance of the deferred gains and losses would be a debit of $37,500:

Gain in 19x2	$50,000 cr.
Amortized in 19x2	10,000 dr.
Balance, December 31, 19x2	$40,000 cr.
Loss in 19x3	90,000 dr.
Amortized in 19x3:	
from 19x2 gain	10,000 dr.
from 19x3 loss	22,500 cr.
Balance, December 31, 19x3	$37,500 dr.

In each succeeding year, the period of amortization of the exchange gain or loss for that year is shorter. The gain or loss for 19x4 will be amortized over three years; the gain or loss for 19x5 will be amortized over two years; and the gain or loss for 19x6 will all be recognized in 19x6.

If the exchange rate for the pound sterling fluctuates from year to year, then there will be a gain in some years and a loss in others. In that case, the process of amortization will tend to result in the amortization of the successive years' gains and losses offsetting each other. Part A of Schedule 16-4 illustrates this effect. If we assume that the bonds were issued when the exchange rate was $1.80, and that the exchange rate then fluctuates up and down to end up at $1.80 at maturity (December 31, 19x6), then there will be no net gain or loss realized when the bonds are retired. The exchange rate is the same at retirement as it was at the date of issue. If gains and losses were recognized immediately in each year, then the annual debit or credit to income would be the amounts indicated in the third column of Schedule 16-4 (Part A). Over the five-year period, the gains and losses would offset each other, but in the meantime there would be substantial impacts on annual net income.

Similarly, a practice of deferring all gains and losses *without* amortizing them would result in a net deferral of zero at maturity because the gains and losses would offset each other.

When the gains and losses are deferred and amortized on a straight-line basis, the resultant charges and credits to net income are shown in the last column of Schedule 16-4, Part A. The amortizations of the successive gains and losses tend to offset each other so that the amounts recognized in net income for each year are relatively small. Note, however, that the direction and magnitude of the impact has little direct relationship to the economic event of the exchange rate change during that period. In 19x4, for example, the exchange rate went down, causing a $30,000 decrease in the balance

---

SCHEDULE 16-4

A. Fluctuating Exchange Rates

Year	Pound sterling exchange rate December 31	Gain or loss for year on £1 million	Amortization period (years)	Annual amortization amount	Total amortization for year
19x1	$1.80				
19x2	1.75	$50,000 gain	5	$10,000 cr.	$10,000 cr.
19x3	1.84	90,000 loss	4	22,500 dr.	12,500 dr.
19x4	1.81	30,000 gain	3	10,000 cr.	2,500 dr.
19x5	1.77	40,000 gain	2	20,000 cr.	17,500 cr.
19x6	1.80	30,000 loss	1	30,000 dr.	12,500 dr.
		$ 0			$ 0

B. Continuous Trend in Exchange Rates

Year	Pound sterling exchange rate December 31	Gain or loss for year on £1 million	Amortization period (years)	Annual amortization amount	Total amortization for year
19x1	$1.80				
19x2	1.83	$ 30,000 loss	5	$ 6,000 dr.	$ 6,000
19x3	1.86	30,000 loss	4	7,500 dr.	13,500
19x4	1.89	30,000 loss	3	10,000 dr.	23,500
19x5	1.92	30,000 loss	2	15,000 dr.	38,500
19x6	1.95	30,000 loss	1	30,000 dr.	68,500
		$150,000			$150,000

---

sheet value of the bonds, a gain for the period. In the income statement, however, the impact will be a *debit* or loss of $2,500 due to amortization of the loss from the preceding year.

Part B of Schedule 16-4 illustrates the impact of an exchange rate that moves in a constant direction. We have assumed that the rate moves up by $0.03 each year, and that the bonds mature when the rate for the pound is $1.95. Over the entire five-year life of the bonds, the total loss due to changes in the exchange rate amounts to $150,000. If a policy of immediate recognition is followed, then a loss of $30,000 would be recognized in income each year. If, instead, the policy is to defer recognition of all exchange gains and losses until retirement, then the entire $150,000 loss would be recognized in income at maturity.

Under a policy of deferral and amortization, each year's loss of $30,000 would be amortized over successively shorter periods. The result would be the charges to income that are shown in the last column of Schedule 16-4. The charge to income would rise from only $6,000 in the first year to a high of $68,500 in the final year. When the rates are tending to move in a single direction, either up or down, the defer-and-amortize approach causes small charges or credits to income in the early years of the life of the bond, but causes quite large charges or credits in the later years.

The *CICA Handbook* recommends that the net unamortized balance of deferred exchange gains and losses "should be recorded in the balance sheet as a deferred charge or as a deferred credit" [para. 1650.24]. The reason for showing the deferred amounts apart from the liability balances to which they relate is that if the deferred amounts are added to or subtracted from the liability balance, the effect would be to restate the balance back to historical cost.

For example, if a long-term bond is issued for U.S. $1 million when the exchange rate is $1.20, the historical carrying value of the bond would be C$1.2 million. If, on the balance sheet date, the exchange rate is $1.30, then the bond would be restated to a carrying value of C$1.3 million and a loss of $0.1 million would be recorded, but deferred. If the deferred loss of $0.1 million is then deducted from the current-rate value of the bond of $1.3 million on the balance sheet, the net amount of the liability shown on the balance sheet will be $1.2 million, which was the historical-rate value in the first place. Of course, amortization of deferred gains and losses will prevent the net amount from exactly equalling the historical-rate value, but clearly the effect will be in that direction.

Despite the *Handbook* recommendation, some companies nevertheless do include the deferred gains and losses with long-term debt. The 1987 edition of *Financial Reporting in Canada* reported that about 12% of the companies that disclosed deferred exchange gains or losses on long-term debt included the deferred amounts with long-term debt. Most of these companies, however, "stated that the long-term debt was considered to be hedged by a future revenue stream and the deferred amount was not being amortized" [p. 41]. We will discuss revenue stream hedges in the next section.

Implicit Hedges

An exception to the defer-and-amortize approach recommended in Section 1650 arises when a long-term monetary balance is *hedged*. Explicit hedges, wherein an offsetting monetary balance is deliberately entered into, are discussed in Part C of this chapter. Implicit hedges, however, often arise when foreign currency monetary balances (usually liabilities) are incurred to finance assets or sales activities in a foreign country.

Earlier in this chapter, we cited an example of a company's borrowing in U.S. dollars to finance acquisition of a building in the U.S. to serve as a U.S. sales office. Another example would be the incurrence of debt in U.S. dollars as secondary financing for receivables that are denominated in U.S. dollars. In both cases, an *implicit* hedge arises because an offsetting asset/liability position is created as the result of business transactions rather than for the sole (or *explicit*) purpose of creating a hedge. In the first example, the implicit hedge is a nonmonetary asset that effectively hedges a monetary liability exposure. In the second example, a monetary liability arises that effectively hedges a monetary asset position. The exposure is always the existence of a monetary balance, but the implicit hedge could be either a monetary or nonmonetary balance.

When the implicit hedge is by a monetary balance, then the periodic foreign exchange gains and losses for both the asset and liability balances are offset against each other and are deferred until settlement, regardless of whether the balances are short term or long term [para. 1650.54].

When a liability balance is implicitly hedged by a nonmonetary asset, it is usually not the asset itself that provides the hedge; the hedge is the net revenue stream generated by the asset. Under such circumstances, exchange gains/losses on the liability are deferred until maturity of the debt (which may be in installments, as with a term loan or mortgage). Any exchange losses or gains arising from the foreign currency revenue stream would also be deferred and offset against the deferred gains/losses on the liability balance [para. 1650.53].

While the concept of designating a nonmonetary asset (or the revenue stream therefrom) as an implicit hedge is intuitively appealing, it gives rise to unresolved difficulties in execution. It is unlikely that a nonmonetary asset would be sold at the same time that a long-term liability balance is paid, and therefore there would be no gain/loss on the nonmonetary asset to offset the deferred exchange rate losses/gains on the liability. The accumulated deferral will therefore have to be written off somehow when the debt is settled, either to income or to the carrying value of the asset. The *Handbook* provides no guidance.

When the designated hedge is a revenue stream, the *Handbook* recommends that each year's revenue (but apparently not the expenses) be "translated at the exchange rate in effect when the revenue stream is identified as a hedge" [para. 1650.53]. The difference between the historical rate at which revenues are translated and the current rate at which the concommitant cash and receivables are translated would be offset against the exchange gains/losses on the balance being hedged. The side effect of such a procedure is to distort current revenues; the effect is at least as great and certainly more obscure than simply crediting or charging the annual gain or loss on the foreign currency balance directly to income each year. In addition, the *Handbook* recommendation implies that long-term debt is serviced by a revenue stream, rather than by *net* revenue or by net cash flow from operations.

These difficulties in actually accounting for implicit hedges in a logical manner have led one emminent accountant to conclude that "a nonmonetary asset can never be shown to be an effective hedge of a foreign exchange risk."[1] He further suggests that "there is no need to engage in the fantasy of revenue-stream hedges."[2]

These difficulties have not prevented companies from designating either nonmonetary assets or revenue streams as implicit hedges. What companies appear to be doing is simply deferring exchange gains and losses on implicitly hedged liabilities until settlement and then rolling the accumulated deferral into a gain or loss on retirement.

The whole problem of accounting for designated hedges arose because Section 1650 now recommends that long-term monetary balances be reported at current exchange rates. The problem didn't arise when companies were permitted to report long-term liabilities at historical exchange rates. The irony in the present situation is that many companies, by (1) designating a hedge, (2) deferring the exchange gains/losses on the liability, (3) adding/subtracting the deferred amounts to/from the liability balance, and (4) recognizing the deferred amounts at settlement, are accomplishing a reporting result that is exactly the same as if the liability were reported at the historical exchange rate in the first place!

---

1 Ross M. Skinner, *Accounting Standards in Evolution* (Toronto: Holt, Rinehart and Winston of Canada, Limited, 1987), p. 382. Chapter 20 of this book contains an excellent discussion of the alternatives in accounting for foreign currencies and hedges.

2 *Ibid*, p. 385.

Debt Without Fixed Maturity

In the preceding discussion, we have assumed that the long-term debt had a specified maturity date. Therefore, it is possible to amortize gains or losses over the period remaining to maturity.

Sometimes, long-term debt has no fixed maturity. The debt may be repayable at the option of the debtor or the creditor (with notice), or may be contingent upon some event or events that are written into the debt contract and that trigger a repayment clause. Note that we are referring here to debt that is classifiable as long term; a long-outstanding loan that is callable by the lender on short notice (e.g., operating loans extended by a bank that depend on the borrower's adherence to covenants) would be classified as a current liability and therefore not be included in our current discussion.

When debt that is properly classifiable as long-term debt has no fixed maturity, then there is no definite period over which to amortize the annual exchange gains and losses. These gains and losses therefore are recognized in income, just as are gains and losses on short-term monetary balances [para. 1650.22], assuming that eventual repayment will be required.

Of course, if any monetary balance is hedged, then gains and losses are deferred until settlement. Hedging and its impact on recognition of foreign currency gains and losses will be discussed in Part C, below.

One final observation relates to bonds that need never be repaid. Such debt is referred to as **perpetual bonds**; the option to call or retire lies exclusively with the borrower. An example of perpetual bonds is the $500,000,000 Swiss franc bonds issued by Air Canada. In substance, these bonds are the equivalent of preferred shares; they carry a fixed rate of interest but are not redeemable by the holder. When Air Canada issued these bonds, the company was still a crown corporation that had no access to equity financing in the private sector. The perpetual bonds provided a source of capital without requiring repayment. By issuing them in Swiss francs, the company was able to obtain a significantly lower interest rate (about 6%, due to the inflation-free Swiss economy) than could have been obtained domestically, and unlike preferred share dividends, the interest is tax deductible.

Since perpetual bonds have no maturity date at all, the effects of exchange rate changes will never be realized. Therefore, Air Canada carries the bonds at a historical book value of $336 million, even though the value at the end of 1988 was about $363 million at the current exchange rate. The annual report contains the following explanation:

> The maturity of these bonds is only upon the liquidation, if ever, of the Corporation. Principal and interest payments on these bonds are subordinated to the prior payment in full of all indebtedness for borrowed money. Since it is not probable that circumstances will arise requiring redemption of the bonds, they are valued at the historical exchange rate, and no provision is made for foreign exchange fluctuations.

On the balance sheet, the perpetual bonds are reported separately from long-term debt; they appear after Minority Interest and just before Shareholders' Equity.

Summary: Long-Term Balances

The range of possible accounting treatments for long-term monetary balances denominated in a foreign currency is not much different from that for current or short-term balances. One additional alternative exists, that being the possibility of amortizing the effects of each year's exchange gain or loss over the remaining life of the balance (assuming that there is a fixed maturity date).

Despite the apparent similarity between short-term and long-term balances, however, there are reasons for treating long-term balances differently from short-term balances. The gains and losses that arise from translating long-term balances at current exchange rates are much less certain of realization than they are for short-term balances. In addition, long-term debt may be refinanced in the same foreign currency, thereby postponing any substantive realization of changes in exchange rates even beyond the life of the debt presently outstanding. A further complication is that long-term monetary balances may effectively be hedged by offsetting long-term nonmonetary balances.

As a result of these factors, it is not uncommon for short-term monetary balances to be converted at current exchange rates while long-term balances are converted at historical rates. Many reporting enterprises, of course, must follow the recommendations of the *CICA Handbook*, including the recommendations to defer and amortize gains and losses on long-term monetary balances of fixed maturity that cannot be designated as hedges of specific monetary or nonmonetary items. Gains and losses on long-term debt without fixed maturity are normally recognized in the income statement when they occur, except for perpetual debt for which gains and losses may be perpetually deferred.

C.   HEDGING TRANSACTIONS

When a company holds a receivable denominated in a foreign currency, there will be a loss if the foreign currency falls in value relative to the Canadian dollar. Conversely, a loss on a foreign currency denominated liability will occur if the foreign currency strengthens or increases in value relative to the Canadian dollar. To protect against foreign currency losses, companies frequently *hedge* their monetary foreign currency balances.

Nature of Hedging

Hedging is accomplished by creating an offsetting balance in the same foreign currency. If a company is holding a receivable of one million French francs, the risk of gain or loss can be neutralized by incurring a liability of FF1,000,000 for an equal term.

There are several ways of hedging. The most common is to enter into a forward exchange contract with a bank or currency dealer. If a receivable is being hedged, then the company would contract to pay a bank an equivalent amount of foreign currency in exchange for Canadian dollars at a specified rate at a specified time in the future.

Some major currencies are also traded in a futures market. Futures markets for agricultural products are well known. Wheat, oats, and corn are traded on the commodities exchanges, as well as cattle, cotton, copper, coffee, orange juice, plywood, and heating oil. The commodity that is of immediate concern here is money. On the Chicago Mercantile Exchange, for example, one can buy a futures contract for Canadian dollars, U.S. dollars, West German marks, British pounds, or Japanese yen, among others. Thus the purchase or sale of foreign currency futures is another way of hedging foreign-currency-denominated receivables and payables.

In this chapter, we focus on forward exchange contracts rather than on futures contracts, since forward contracts are the most common form of hedge. Forward contracts are individually negotiated and thus can be tailored to suit the needs of the hedger. Futures contracts, by contrast, are for standard terms (e.g., 30, 60, 90, and 180 days) and for limited denominations and currencies.

Hedging a Monetary Position

To illustrate the use of hedging, suppose that on April 15, Domestic Corporation sells some of its product in Germany for DM100,000. At the date of the sale, the mark is selling at a current or **spot rate** of $0.5062 in Canadian funds. As a result of the sale, Domestic has acquired a foreign currency monetary balance (account receivable) of $50,620. If Domestic wishes to protect itself against a possible exchange loss caused by a fall in the value of the mark, Domestic can buy a forward contract for an equivalent amount of marks. Assuming that the receivable will be collected in one month (on May 15), Domestic can buy a contract for the *payment* of DM100,000 one month hence. The commitment to pay DM100,000 will offset the commitment to receive DM100,000 from the German customer.

Assume that a one-month forward contract for German marks is available for $0.5079. Since the mark is viewed as a strong currency, the future price can be higher than the current price. Domestic would then contract to deliver or pay DM100,000 in one month, and the contract would be for $50,790. In effect, Domestic is selling the marks that it will receive from the German customer. But since Domestic will not receive the marks until the following month, the contract to deliver the marks will not be executed until the following month. As a result, Domestic will have a receivable (from the customer) that is denominated in marks, but will also have a payable that is denominated in marks. Both will be due at the same time. Thus any loss that occurs on the receivable *due to a fall in the exchange rate* will be offset by an equal gain on the liability.

The entries to record the sale of the merchandise and the sale of the marks for delivery in the future would be as follows:

APRIL 15:		
Account receivable (DM100,000)	$50,620	
Sales		$50,620
Exchange contract receivable	$50,790	
Exchange contract payable (DM100,000)		$50,790

In the second entry, it appears that the receivable and the payable for the forward exchange contract (the second entry) are offsetting. However, such is not the case. The receivable represents the amount to be received by Domestic in Canadian dollars when Domestic delivers the marks. The payable, on the other hand, is the current Canadian equivalent of a balance that is denominated in German marks. Thus the receivable from the customer and the payable to the purchaser of the forward contract are both denominated in a foreign currency, German marks.

One month later, the customer settles his debt and Domestic delivers the marks in execution of the forward contract. Let us assume that on the settlement date, the spot rate for the mark is $0.4800. The receipt of the DM100,000 from the customer would be recorded as follows:

```
MAY 15:
Cash (DM100,000)                            $48,000
Exchange gains and losses                     2,620
     Account receivable                                  $50,620
```

To execute the forward contract that is now due, Domestic would deliver DM100,000, and would receive the contracted amount of $50,790 in return. The entries to record this transaction would appear as follows:

```
MAY 15:
Cash                                        $50,790
     Exchange contract receivable                        $50,790

Exchange contract payable                   $50,790
     Cash (DM100,000)                                    $48,000
     Exchange gains and losses                            2,790
```

Domestic would recognize a loss of $2,620 on the receivable from the sale, but would recognize a gain of $2,790 on the forward contract. The net amount is a gain of $170. The existence of this net gain may suggest that the forward contract was not completely successful at eliminating risk, but that is not quite the case. The $170 gain is the difference between the spot rate on the date of the original sale and the forward rate, multiplied by the amount of the foreign currency balance being hedged: DM100,000 x ($0.5062 — $0.5079). What the hedge actually does is limit any possible gain or loss to a known amount, the spread between the spot rate and the forward rate. The same net gain would have resulted in our example regardless of the actual exchange rate at the settlement date.

For example, suppose that instead of a rate of $0.4800, the actual rate on the settlement date was $0.5300. The three entries to record the receipt from the customer and the settlement of the forward contract would then be as follows:

```
MAY 15:
Cash                                        $53,000
     Account receivable                                  $50,620
     Exchange gains and losses                            2,380

Cash                                        $50,790
     Exchange contract receivable                        $50,790

Exchange contract payable                   $50,790
Exchange gains and losses                     2,210
     Cash (DM100,000)                                    $53,000
```

Settlement of the customer receivable and of the forward contract causes a gain of $2,380 and a loss of $2,210 respectively, leaving a net gain of $170, exactly as in the first example.

In the example that we have used above, the forward rate happened to be higher than the spot rate, resulting in a net gain. Forward rates may be either higher or lower than the spot rate. The spread between the spot rates depends (1) on the interest rate differential between the two countries and (2) on how the market predicts the rate will move. At noon on March 29, 1989, the rates for three major currencies were as shown in Schedule 16-5. The forward rates for the U.S. dollar and the West German mark were both higher than the spot

SCHEDULE 16-5

Foreign Currency Rates
March 29, 1989
(in Canadian Dollar Equivalents)

	U.S. dollar	British pound	West German mark
Spot rate	$1.1949	$2.0182	$0.6317
1 month forward	1.1966	2.0172	0.6347
3 months forward	1.2005	2.0152	0.6409
6 months forward	1.2061	2.0166	0.6499
12 months forward	1.2150	2.0235	0.6671

Source: *The Globe and Mail*, March 30, 1989, p. B17. The reported data were prepared by the Bank of Montreal Treasury Group.

rates and rose as the term rose. The forward rate for the pound sterling, in contrast, was less than the spot rate through at least six months, and then rose above the spot rate for a twelve-month forward contract.

A three-month hedge of a receivable denominated in pounds at the above rates would lock the hedger into a loss, since the forward rate for the pound is less than the spot rate. But the loss would be quite minor in comparison to the potential loss from an unprotected position. The day-to-day change in the spot rate can easily be larger than the spread between the spot and forward rates quoted above. Thus the small assured loss can be viewed as the cost of insurance against a possibly substantial loss. Of course, hedging also eliminates the possibility of realizing a gain as well.

When the forward rate is higher than the spot rate, the contract has a **premium**. When the forward rate is less, then a **discount** exists. If the hedge is of a foreign currency receivable, as above, a premium results in a gain while a discount results in a loss.

Conversely, if the hedge is of a foreign currency liability, a premium results in a loss while a discount causes a gain. The following table summarizes this relationship:

	Net result if forward contract is priced at a:	
Item being hedged	Premium	Discount
Monetary asset	gain	loss
Monetary liability	loss	gain

Alternative Recording Methods

In the example in the preceding section, the forward contract was recorded by means of a journal entry that assigned equal values to the receivable and the payable. There are two alternative methods of recording the hedge that yield the same result. The first is to record the deutsche mark liability at its current equivalent (that is, at the current spot rate) of $50,620. The difference between the receivable of $50,790 and the payable of $50,620 is the premium on the forward contract. Since the premium will not be realized until the settlement date, it should be treated as a deferred gain. Under this approach, the initial entry to record the purchase of the forward contract would be as follows:

APRIL 15:

Exchange contract receivable	$50,790	
Exchange contract payable (DM100,000)		$50,620
Deferred premium		170

When the account receivable is collected and the forward contract is settled, the entries would appear as follows (assuming a spot rate at settlement date of $0.4800):

MAY 15:

Cash (DM100,000)	$48,000	
Exchange gains and losses	2,620	
Account receivable		$50,620
Cash	$50,790	
Exchange contract receivable		$50,790
Exchange contract payable	$50,620	
Deferred exchange premium	170	
Cash (DM100,000)		$48,000
Exchange gains and losses		2,790

The net result will be the same as in the earlier example.

While the practice of recording the premium or discount on the forward contract at the date of entering into it may seem to complicate the recording of the transaction, the purpose is to identify the gain or loss in order to facilitate its appropriate treatment between the contract date and the settlement date. As is discussed in the next section, the premium or discount is not always recognized solely at the settlement date; sometimes, part of the premium or discount is recognized in the income statement or as part of the cost of an asset prior to the settlement date.

The second alternative method of handling the forward contract on the books is not to record it formally at all until the settlement date. A forward contract is, by its very nature, an **executory contract**. An executory contract is a contract that represents an agreement by two parties to perform in the future. For accounting purposes, no liability or receivable is normally deemed to exist for an executory contract until one of the parties has actually performed, or **executed** the contract. Under a forward foreign exchange contract, neither party will perform until the settlement date, and thus no accounting recognition needs to be given to the contract. The liability and the receivable relating to the contract will not be recorded, and on settlement date, the net gain or loss will flow out of the cash transactions:

MAY 15:

Cash (DM100,000)	$48,000	
Exchange gains and losses	2,620	
Accounts receivable		$50,620
Cash	$50,790	
Exchange gains and losses		$ 2,790
Cash (DM100,000)		48,000

The three approaches to recording the forward contract are shown in a comparative format in Schedule 16-6. Note that the two entries for the sale and the collection of the receivable from the customer are not affected by the accounting for the forward contract.

SCHEDULE 16-6

Alternative Recording Methods for Hedging Contracts

	1			2			3	

ENTRIES AT DATE OF SALE: (APRIL 15)

	1			2			3	
Account rec.	50,620		Account rec.	50,620		Account rec.	50,620	
Sales		50,620	Sales		50,620	Sales		50,620
Contract rec.	50,790		Contract rec.	50,790				
Contract pay.		50,790	Contract pay.		50,620			
			Deferred premium		170			

ENTRIES AT DATE OF PAYMENT AND SETTLEMENT: (MAY 15)

	1			2			3	
Cash	48,000		Cash	48,000		Cash	48,000	
Exchange G & L	2,620		Exchange G & L	2,620		Exchange G & L	2,620	
Acct. rec.		50,620	Acct. rec.		50,620	Acct. rec.		50,620
Cash	50,790		Cash	50,790		Cash	50,790	
Contract rec.		50,790	Contract rec.		50,790	Exchange G & L		2,790
						Cash		48,000
Contract pay.	50,790		Contract pay.	50,620				
Cash		48,000	Deferred premium	170				
Exchange G & L		2,790	Cash		48,000			
			Exchange G & L		2,790			

Since a forward contract is an executory contract, the exchange contract receivable and payable will not be shown on the balance sheet. If the end of an accounting period occurs between the time that the contract is entered into and the settlement date, the receivable and the payable (and the related premium or discount) would be offset against each other, and any remaining balance would be treated as a deferred debit or credit on the balance sheet.

The third method, of treating the forward contract as an executory contract and thus not formally recording it, is the most common in practice. Therefore, we will restrict our subsequent discussion to this method alone.

The previous paragraphs described the accounting for an asset **exposure**. In that case, the hedge is of a monetary asset that already exists. Similar treatment would be accorded to a monetary liability, such as an account payable that is denominated in a foreign currency, except that the corporation would then be buying a contract to *receive* a foreign currency instead of to deliver a foreign currency. A forward contract to receive creates a foreign-currency-denominated receivable to offset the risk inherent in the foreign-currency-denominated liability.

Intervening Year-End

The foregoing illustration dealt with the simplest situation, in which all of the related events occurred within the same accounting period. A slight complication arises when financial statements must be prepared after the forward contract is entered into but before the settlement date. The complication involves the disposition of the premium or discount.

The premium or discount represents the only gain or loss that arises on a hedged monetary position. In the previous example, recognition of the gain of $170 was deferred until the settlement date. However, if the contract is outstanding for more than one accounting period, the question arises as to in which period the gain or loss should be recognized. Since the premium or discount is the benefit or cost of limiting the risk exposure of the company over the period of time in which the monetary asset or liability being hedged is outstanding, it is common to allocate the premium or discount over all the periods affected. In addition, it is necessary to recognize the change in the exchange rate as it affects the account receivable from the customer.

To illustrate, we can amend the previous example by assuming that Domestic's fiscal year-ends on April 30. Assume also that the spot rate for the deutsche mark on April 30 is $0.50.

If the receivable were *not* hedged, the entries relating to (a) the sale, (b) the year-end adjustment to current rate, and (c) the settlement would be as follows:

(a) APRIL 15:

Account receivable	$50,620	
Sales		$50,620

(b) APRIL 30:

Exchange gains and losses	$620	
Account receivable		$620

(c) MAY 15:

Cash (DM100,000)	$48,000	
Exchange gains and losses	2,000	
Account receivable		$50,000

In the absence of a hedge, the exchange loss would be recognized in the period in which each part of it occurred. If the receivable is hedged, however, no part of the loss should be recognized because the loss will be offset by a gain on the settlement date. Since it is necessary to adjust the receivable balance to the current rate on the balance sheet date (April 30), any gain or loss on exchange rate changes must be deferred. When the receivable is hedged, the year-end adjustment to the customer receivable would be as follows:

APRIL 30:

Deferred exchange loss	$620	
Account receivable		$620

In addition, one-half the premium would be recognized as a benefit to the year ended March 31:

APRIL 30:

Unrealized forward premium	$85	
Exchange gains or losses		$85

When the customer's account is settled, the entry to record the receipt of DM100,000 (at the May 15 spot rate of $0.4800) would be:

MAY 15:

Cash (DM100,000)	$48,000	
Exchange gains or losses	2,620	
Deferred exchange loss		$ 620
Account receivable		50,000

The settlement of the forward contract would be recorded as follows:

MAY 15:

Cash	$50,790	
Unrealized forward premium		$ 85
Exchange gains and losses		2,705
Cash (DM100,000)		48,000

The exchange loss of $2,620 recognized from settlement of the customer's account is offset against the $2,705 exchange gain from settlement of the forward contract. The net result is a gain of $85, the remaining half of the premium that is allocable to the second fiscal year. Instead of using an unrealized forward premium account, the premium amortization could simply be charged or credited to the deferred exchange loss account.

The premium or discount on a forward contract is allocated to the periods during which the contract is outstanding, because the cost of the contract is thereby assigned to the periods that receive the benefit of the protection. Another reason for allocating the premium or discount is that a major determinant of the spread between the current spot rate and the forward rate is the interest rate differential between the domestic country and the foreign country. If interest rates are higher in Germany than in Canada, then an investor could make money on an arbitrage-type operation. The investor could convert dollars into marks, invest the marks in Germany, and then reconvert the marks back into dollars when the investment matures.

Of course, the investor would be exposed to risk of changes in the exchange rate while the investment was in effect. If the forward rate on marks was the same as the spot rate, then the investor could protect himself by hedging the investment. However, the market recognizes this possibility, and the mark is traded (relative to the dollar) by taking the interest differential into effect. The demand for forward contracts to deliver marks will create a surplus of marks being offered for the future and thus will drive the price down. The resulting discount on the forward contract will then offset any advantage that an investor might hope to achieve by investing overseas.

Since the forward premium or discount is partially related to interest rate differentials, the premium or discount can be allocated to periods on the rationale that the spread really represents an incremental interest cost (or cost reduction) to the company.

Hedging a Commitment

So far, we have discussed the accounting and reporting only for hedges of monetary assets and liabilities. These are receivables or payables that appear on the books of the company as the result of transactions that have already occurred. Companies frequently have **commitments** to buy or to sell goods, however, and these commitments do not immediately result in any receivables or liabilities being recorded on the company's books because the commitments are executory contracts that have not yet been executed by either party. Nevertheless, the risk exposure to foreign currency exchange rate fluctuations begins with the commitment and not with the formal recording of a transaction in the accounts.

For example, assume that Domestic Corp. issues a purchase order to Francais Ltee. on October 31, 19x1, to purchase a machine for 500,000 French francs. The machine is delivered on November 30, and payment is made on January 31, 19x2. Domestic Corp. made the decision to purchase the machine on or before October 31, based on the Canadian-dollar equivalent cost of the machine at that time. If the French franc appreciates significantly in value between October 31 and the payment date, Domestic Corp. will incur substantial additional cost for the machine. Therefore, it is common to enter into a hedge as soon as commitment is made, even though no actual liability is established until the machine is delivered.

Suppose that on October 31, 19x1, the spot rate for the French franc is FF1 = Can. $0.1746. The FF500,000 commitment is then worth $87,300 in Canadian funds. Domestic Corp. decides to hedge its French franc commitment by entering into a forward contract to receive FF500,000 on January 31, 19x2. The three-month forward rate for the French franc is $0.1600 on October 31. The initial discount on the forward contract therefore is $0.0146 per franc or $7,300 in total.

By November 30, 19x1, the spot rate has declined to $0.1700 per franc. On that date, the machine is delivered and the monetary liability is recorded at $85,000 (FF500,000 x $0.1700). The initial discount on the hedge therefore has been reduced to $5,000 by the movement of the spot rate during the commitment period.

The basic accounting question when a commitment is being hedged is how to treat the discount or premium. If the commitment will result in the acquisition of an asset, one alternative is to treat the entire discount or premium as part of the cost of the asset. Since the company knows the cost of entering into a hedge at the time that the commitment is made, the net cost of the hedge should be considered as part of the decision to buy the asset. This is the position taken by the AcSC in the *CICA Handbook*, which recommends that "when a purchase or sale of goods or services in a foreign currency is hedged before the transaction, the Canadian dollar price of such goods or services is established by the terms of the hedge" [para. 1650.52].

Following the capitalization approach, the entries to record the purchase of the machine would appear as shown in Schedule 16-7, assuming that the forward contract is not formally recorded on the books (that is, by following the executory contract approach, the third alternative recording practice illustrated in Schedule 16-6).

On November 30, when the machine is delivered, an account payable is established at the spot rate on that date ($0.1700). The machinery account, however, is debited for the forward rate of $0.1600. At the settlement date, whatever gain or loss arises *since the date of the commitment* on the liability to Francais Ltee. will be offset by an equal loss or gain on the forward contract. Therefore, *the value of the forward contract establishes the cost of the machine.*

All of the remaining entries (after November 30, 19x1) on Schedule 16-7 have no impact on the cost assigned to the new machine. The entries simply adjust the value of the recorded liability and defer all exchange gains and losses and the forward discount until the settlement date so that everything will cancel out at that time.

The entry on December 31, 19x1, is an adjustment of the FF500,000 liability to the spot rate at that date, for balance sheet purposes. Since the loss arising from the increase in the exchange rate from $0.1700 to $0.1800 will be offset against a corresponding gain on the forward contract, recognition of the loss is deferred until the settlement date by debiting the amount of the adjustment to a deferred exchange gains and losses account.

On the settlement date, January 31, 19x2, Domestic Corp. pays FF500,000 to Francais Ltee. at the spot rate of $0.1780, or $89,000. The debit to account payable is for the balance in that account as adjusted to the spot rate on the last balance sheet date, December 31. A gain of $1,000 arises from the change in the spot rate between December 31 and January 31; this gain, plus the debit balance in the deferred exchange gains and losses account of $5,000, results in a net exchange loss of $4,000 since November 30.

SCHEDULE 16-7

Entries for a Hedge of a Commitment

EXCHANGE RATE ASSUMPTIONS:	FF spot rate	3-month forward rate
October 31, 19x1	$0.1746	$0.1600
November 30, 19x1	0.1700	
December 31, 19x1	0.1800	
January 31, 19x1	0.1780	

OCTOBER 31, 19x1: no entries necessary

NOVEMBER 30, 19x1:

Machinery (FF500,000 @ $0.1600)	$80,000	
Deferred forward discount	5,000	
Account payable (FF500,000 @ $0.1700)		$85,000

DECEMBER 31, 19x1: year-end adjustment

Deferred exchange gains and losses	$ 5,000	
Account payable		
[FF500,000 × ($0.1800 − 0.1700)]		$ 5,000

JANUARY 31, 19x2:

Account payable (@ $0.1800, per Dec. 31, 19x1 balance)	$90,000	
Exchange gains and losses [FF500,000 × ($0.1780 − 0.1700)]	4,000	
Cash (FF500,000 @ $0.1780)		$89,000
Deferred exchange gains and losses		5,000

Cash (receipt of FF500,000 @ $0.1780)	$89,000	
Cash (payment of Canadian dollar liability)		$80,000
Deferred forward discount		5,000
Exchange gains and losses		4,000

The settlement of the forward contract results in a cash outflow of $80,000 (the contract price) and an inflow of FF500,000 worth $89,000. The $9,000 net gain on the settlement is offset (in the last entry) against the $5,000 deferred forward discount and the $4,000 exchange loss realized by settling the account payable.

The above treatment for the commitment and the assignment of the cost of the hedge to the asset acquired is common in practice, and is consistent with the recommendations of the *Handbook*.

However, an alternative view is that the treatment described above is inconsistent with the common treatment of the discount or premium on a hedge of a monetary balance. As we discussed in the preceding section of this chapter, the premium or discount is usually allocated as an expense or benefit of the periods over which the hedge is outstanding. Under this approach, the cost of the machine is determined at the spot rate at the time of the commitment, plus the portion of the premium or discount allocable to the period between the commitment date and the transaction date. The remainder of the premium or discount is then allocated to the periods during which the monetary liability is outstanding.

Under this alternative, the forward premium or discount is treated as an additional expense (or reduction of expense), in accordance with the fact that a major determinant of the spread between the spot rate and the forward rate is the difference in interest rates between Canada and the foreign country (France, in this example). In substance, the allocation of the discount related to the period between recording the liability and paying the liability recognizes the spread as an adjustment of interest expense for a foreign liability, even though it is not labeled as interest on the statements.

In the preceding discussions, we have made some implicit simplifying assumptions. In all examples, we have assumed that a perfect hedge is possible; that is, a hedge of the exact amount of exposure for the exact period of exposure in the currency of exposure. In practice, hedges do not always work out so neatly.

Complicating Factors

A practical problem for companies that engage in a large volume of foreign transactions (usually sales or purchases of inventory) is that to attempt to hedge each individual transaction is too cumbersome. Instead, such a company may attempt to hedge the net *balance* of its exposure by hedging the balance monthly. Since the hedges are not related to specific transactions, the gains and losses arising from the forward contracts cannot be directly matched to, and offset against, gains and losses arising from the settlement of foreign currency receivables and payables. Instead, all gains and losses tend to be recognized in income when they occur, with only approximate matching.

It is beyond the scope of this text to explore all of these problems (and others that have not even been mentioned). Instead, the intent is to introduce the reader to the basic concepts and alternatives in accounting for foreign-currency-denominated transactions, including hedging. Canada is a major world trader, and foreign currency transactions are an important part of doing business in Canada. Accountants should be aware of the basic issues in reporting these transactions.

SUMMARY

This chapter has dealt exclusively with transactions that are denominated in foreign currencies and the balances that arise from such transactions. The transactions are entered into directly by a domestic Canadian corporation, and not by a foreign subsidiary. Transactions by a foreign *subsidiary* are known as foreign *operations*, and will be discussed in the following chapter.

There are no particularly severe accounting problems involved in accounting for foreign currency transactions themselves. The transactions must be recorded on the corporation's books at their equivalent in Canadian dollars at the time of the transaction. The problems arise in accounting for the *balances* that are the result of those transactions. There are three distinct types of balances that merit attention: (1) nonmonetary balances, (2) current monetary balances, and (3) long-term monetary balances.

Nonmonetary balances are the easiest to account for. Assets such as inventories or fixed assets that are acquired in foreign currency transactions are valued at their equivalent cost in Canadian dollars at the time of the transaction to acquire them. In the event that a commitment is made to acquire nonmonetary assets and the commitment is hedged, then the historical cost of the asset is affected by the terms of the hedge. All of the premium or discount on the hedge may be assigned as part of the cost of the asset, or only the portion of the premium or discount that is allocable to the time between the commitment (and hedge) and the actual acquisition of the asset may be allocated to the asset. The remaining premium or discount would be considered a cost of funds for the period between incurring the liability for the asset and the payment of the liability.

Current monetary balances are usually reported at their Canadian dollar equivalent at the balance sheet date. If there has been a change in the exchange rate during the period of time between the creation of the balance (by a transaction) and the balance sheet date, the exchange gain or loss can either be deferred until the balance is paid in the following period or be recognized in income immediately. If the balance has not been hedged, then the exchange gain or loss is usually recognized immediately in the income statement.

If the balance has been hedged, then the gain or loss must be deferred until settlement of the hedge, since any gain/loss from the outstanding balance will be offset by a corresponding loss/gain from the hedge. The premium or discount on the hedge is allocated to the periods during which the hedge is in effect, since the premium or discount can be viewed as either additional interest cost or as the cost of insurance against a possibly substantial risk exposure.

Long-term monetary balances can be hedged only by means of a series of successive forward contracts. The gains and losses on these contracts, along with the gains and losses on the monetary balances, should be deferred until either termination of the hedge or payment of the balance. The premium or discount on the forward contract will be allocated to the accounting periods during which the hedge is outstanding.

Long-term monetary liabilities may also be hedged by nonmonetary foreign assets or income flows. Such hedges are termed implicit hedges because there is no explicit contract providing for a hedge. When there is an implicit hedge, it is possible to defer recognition of any exchange gains and losses on the monetary balance until realization because the nonmonetary asset is assumed to generate the foreign currency cash flows that will be used to retire the debt. Gains and losses on the cash flows will offset losses and gains on the debt.

When forward contracts are used for hedging monetary balances, there are at least three different ways in which the transactions involving the forward contracts can be recorded. In essence, however, a forward contract is an executory contract, and unsettled receivables and payables relating to a forward contract are offset for reporting purposes.

SELF-STUDY PROBLEM 16-1[3]

On December 2, 19x2, Domestic Corporation sold merchandise to a German customer for DM100,000; the mark was worth $0.50 on that date. On the next day, Domestic entered into a forward contract to deliver DM100,000 in 60 days at a rate of $0.52.

At Domestic's year-end, December 31, 19x2, the mark was worth $0.51. On February 1, 19x3, the customer paid the balance owing, and Domestic also settled the forward contract. The exchange rate on the settlement date was $0.525.

Required:
a. In general journal form, record the entries in 19x2 and 19x3 relating to the account receivable and to the forward contract, assuming the hedge is recorded as an executory contract.
b. How would the entries relating to the account receivable have differed if Domestic had not hedged the receivable?

SELF-STUDY PROBLEM 16-2

On October 14, 19x7, Buycorp signed a contract with Sellco, a U.S. company, to purchase a piece of equipment for U.S. $200,000. The equipment was to be delivered on December 1, 19x7, with payment to be made (in U.S. dollars) no later than January 30, 19x8.

Having signed the contract, Buycorp immediately arranged a forward contract for U.S. $200,000 with its bank as a hedge against the commitment. The spot rate for the U.S. dollar was $1.20 on October 14; the forward rate was $1.22.

Sellco delivered the equipment to Buycorp on December 7, 19x7, slightly late owing to customs delays. The spot rate on that date was $1.18, as compared to $1.19 on December 1. On December 31, 19x7, the spot rate was $1.19. Despite the late delivery, Buycorp paid the amount due on January 30, 19x8, per the contract. The spot rate was $1.24 on January 30.

Required:
Prepare journal entries to record the acquisition of the equipment and the related hedge, through January 30, 19x8. Buycorp's fiscal year coincides with the calendar year.

REVIEW QUESTIONS

16-1 Distinguish between **foreign transactions** and **foreign currency transactions**.

16-2 A Canadian corporation has a subsidiary in the United States. The subsidiary has numer-

---

3 The solutions to the self-study problems are at the end of the book, following Chapter 18.

ous transactions denominated in U.S. dollars. Is the Canadian corporation thereby engaged in foreign currency transactions? Explain.

16-3 CarpCorp, a Canadian company, bought a machine from the United States for U.S. $100,000 when the exchange rate was Cdn. $1.20. The liability for the machine was paid when the exchange rate was Cdn. $1.25. At what cost should the machine be recorded in the accounts, assuming (1) the one transaction theory and (2) the two transaction theory?

16-4 CarpCorp bought inventory from the United Kingdom when the pound was worth Cdn. $1.80. When the year-end balance sheet was prepared, the pound was worth Cdn. $1.70. If the account payable for the inventory was unpaid at year-end, and the amount of the purchase was £5,000, how should the liability be reported on the balance sheet? How should the change in the value of the pound be reported (if at all)?

16-5 What is the argument for recognizing exchange gains or losses on current monetary balances in income in the year of the gain or loss rather than in the year of settlement?

16-6 A mutual fund has investments in shares in U.S. companies that are traded on the American Stock Exchange. The mutual fund reports its investments at current value. What exchange rate should the fund use in translating the investments when the balance sheet is prepared?

16-7 Why have many companies followed a practice of reporting their foreign-currency-denominated long-term debt at the historical exchange rate on the balance sheet?

16-8 When might a nonmonetary asset be considered a hedge of a long-term monetary balance?

16-9 What practical difficulties arise in financial reporting when a foreign currency revenue stream is designated as an implicit hedge of a long-term monetary liability?

16-10 Why is the issue of accounting for long-term foreign-currency-denominated balances more important in Canada than in the United States?

16-11 If the foreign currency in which a bond is denominated fluctuates in value relative to the Canadian dollar, what will be the effect of the defer-and-amortize procedure that is recommended in the *Handbook*?

16-12 If the foreign currency in which a bond is denominated continuously rises in value relative to the Canadian dollar, what will be the impact of the changes in the exchange rate on net income from year to year, assuming that each year's exchange gain or loss is deferred and amortized?

16-13 What is the purpose of **hedging**?

16-14 CarpCorp has a liability of FF400,000. If CarpCorp wants to hedge the liability, should the company enter into a forward contract to *buy* francs or to *sell* francs?

16-15 Does hedging eliminate all gains and losses arising from a foreign currency exposure? Explain.

16-16 Why is a forward exchange contract viewed as an executory contract?

16-17 Why is the discount or premium on a forward contract allocated to the periods during which the monetary balance and the hedge are outstanding, rather than being recognized in the period of settlement?

16-18 How does hedging a **commitment** differ from hedging a liability?

16-19 CharCo signs a contract to buy a special-order machine from a Swiss manufacturer. Charco then hedges the commitment. How will the Canadian dollar cost of the machine be determined?

CASE 16-1   Beaver Enterprise Limited

Beaver Enterprises Limited (Beaver) has just negotiated the purchase of an office building for £10 million in London, England, which is to be used as the head office of its newly incorporated wholly owned European operating subsidiary, Beaver Overseas Limited (BOL). Transfer of ownership to BOL is to be made on January 1, 19x5. Beaver has arranged a loan for £10 million to finance the purchase through its bankers. The loan, to be dated January 1, 19x5, is at 12% and is repayable in twenty equal annual installments commencing January 1, 19x6. The loan would be made to BOL, which would make all interest and principal payments in pounds sterling.

The building will be depreciated on a straight-line basis over twenty years. Assume the following exchange rates: January 1, 19x5, £1 = $2.50; December 31, 19x5, £1 = $2.00.

Required:
Discuss fully the options available to Beaver in structuring its relationship to BOL, and evaluate the impact of each alternative on the consolidated financial statements. Show all supporting calculations.
[SMA]

Video Displays, Inc. (Part A)   CASE 16-2

Video Displays, Inc. (VDI) is a privately held corporation chartered under the *Canadian Business Corporations Act*. The corporation was formed in 1978 by four engineers who found themselves jobless after their previous employer (Argo Corporation) discontinued the production of television sets in Canada.

One of the sidelines of Argo had been the assembly of video display units (VDUs). A VDU is the basic chassis containing the cathode ray tube and related components that are used in video-display computer terminals, in computer game sets, and in word processors. When Argo discontinued production, the four engineers purchased some of Argo's assembly and testing equipment and formed VDI.

VDI has been fairly successful because it is the only Canadian producer of VDUs. Some computer terminal manufacturers have a policy of obtaining their components in the country in which they manufacture the terminals, and thus VDI has enjoyed the benefits of local-sourcing policies since it is the only Canadian producer.

In 1980, VDI needed additional debt financing. After being refused by several Canadian banks, the executives of VDI went to New York, where on March 1, they quickly obtained a five-year, 12% term loan of $3,000,000 (U.S.) from Citibank, interest payable annually on the anniversary date of the loan. The U.S. dollar was worth $1.20 Canadian on March 1, 1980. By the end of 1980, the exchange rate had slipped to $1.18.

In 1981, VDI extended its operations into the United States by contracting with an electronics component distributor in Cambridge, Massachusetts. The U.S. distributor supplies component assemblies to small manufacturers, and saw an opportunity to sell VDI's VDUs to independent manufacturers of computer terminals and word processors. The December 31, 1981, VDI unadjusted trial balance showed a balance due from the U.S. distributor of $500,000. The 1981 shipments to and payments from the distributor are shown in Exhibit 1. VDI gave the distributor $60,000 U.S. on April 4 as an accountable advance for financing promotional expenses. By December 31, 1981, the distributor had spent and accounted for $40,000 of this advance. At the end of 1981, the exchange rate was $1.25 Canadian to $1.00 U.S.

Required:
Explain the impact of the transactions described above on VDI's financial statements on December 31, 1981. Where alternatives are possible, state them and explain your choice of approach. Be as specific as possible. Assume that all amounts are material.

EXHIBIT 1			
Current Account with U.S. Distributor 1981*			
	Dr.	Cr.	Balance
Feb. 1: Shipment ($100,000 U.S.)	$115,000		$115,000
April 1: Shipment ($180,000 U.S.)	207,000		322,000
May 1: Payment ($100,000 U.S.)		$118,000	204,000
July 1: Shipment ($200,000 U.S.)	240,000		444,000
Aug. 30: Payment ($150,000 U.S.)		186,000	258,000
Nov. 15: Shipment ($200,000 U.S.)	242,000		500,000
*In Canadian dollars.			

CASE 16-3   Canadian Inferior Oil Co.

Canadian Inferior Oil Co. (CIO) is a federally chartered Canadian corporation that is 69.6% owned by Intercontinental Petroleum Corp., a U.S.-based multinational oil company. CIO's common shares are publicly traded on both the Toronto and New York Stock Exchanges. The CIO fiscal year ends on June 30.

On July 1, 1976, CIO raised $1,000,000 U.S. by issuing ten-year bonds through a U.S. investment banker. At the time of the bond issue, the dollar exchange rate was $1 U.S. = $0.9861 Canadian. The actual exchange rate for each year thereafter, until maturity of the bonds in 1986, is shown below.

Required:
a. Determine the amount that would be shown on CIO's income statement for foreign currency exchange gains or losses relating to the bonds for each year from 1977 to 1986, under each of the following assumptions:
   1. The bonds are carried on the balance sheet at the historical exchange rate until redemption.
   2. The bonds are valued at the current exchange rate on each balance sheet date, and each year's exchange gain or loss is:
      (a) recognized currently,
      (b) deferred until realized, and
      (c) amortized over the remaining period until maturity of the bonds.

b. Evaluate each of the preceding alternatives from the viewpoint of:
   1. The president of CIO.
   2. The controller of Intercontinental Petroleum Corp.
   3. A securities analyst.

c. How would your answers to Part b (above) differ if:
   1. The bonds were highly likely to be refinanced in U.S. dollars at maturity.
   2. The bonds had a sinking fund provision which required payments of $150,000 U.S. in each year beginning in 1975.

U.S.-Canadian dollar exchange rates, 1976-1986
(Canadian dollar equivalent to one U.S. dollar)

1976	$0.9861	1981	$1.1990
1977	1.0635	1982	1.2341
1978	1.1402	1983	1.2324
1979	1.1715	1984	1.2948
1980	1.1690	1985	1.3652
		1986	1.3894

Source: Bank of Canada

P16-1

Domestic Corp., a Canadian company, sells its products to customers in the United Kingdom at prices quoted in pounds sterling. On November 14, 19x1, Domestic sold and shipped goods that had cost $80,000 to produce to an English company for £100,000. On December 20, Domestic received an international draft for part of the amount due, £40,000. At year-end (December 31), the remaining £60,000 balance was unpaid.

On February 12, 19x2, Domestic received payment of the remaining £60,000.

Required:
In general journal form, prepare journal entries to record the above events, and any adjustments necessary at year-end. Exchange rates (Canadian dollar equivalent to £1) are as follows:

November 14	1.80
December 20	1.85
December 31	1.87
February 12	1.84

P16-2

At the end of the fiscal year, December 31, 19x4, Export Ltd. finds itself with two accounts receivable in pesos:

1. from a sale on July 1, 19x4, and due to be collected on December 1, 19x5, for 1,500,000 pesos.
2. from a sale on September 1, 19x4, and due to be collected on December 1, 19x7, for 3,000,000 pesos.

Exchange rates (spot):

$1 = 160 pesos	July 1, 19x4
$1 = 174 pesos	September 1, 19x4
$1 = 180 pesos	December 31, 19x4
$1 = 110 pesos	December 1, 19x5
$1 = 90 pesos	December 31, 19x5

Required:
Prepare the journal entries for December 31, 19x4, and December 1 and December 31, 19x5, assuming that the foreign exchange risk is *not* hedged.
[CGA–Canada]

P16-3

On December 31, 1984, Freidlan Corporation (a Canadian corporation) obtained a four-year term loan from a bank in Switzerland for SF1,000,000. Interest of 10% was payable annually. On December 31, 1988, Freidlan Corp. repaid the loan in full.

Required:
a. Using the exchange rates quoted in Schedule 15-3 for the Swiss franc as the year-end rate, determine the gain or loss to be credited or charged to Freidlan's net income for each year, assuming straight-line amortization of unrealized gains or losses.
b. Determine the interest expense relating to the loan for each year, in dollars.

P16-4

On December 31, 1984, Jackil Ltd. borrowed SF1,000,000 for four years at 10% per year. The money was invested in a limited-life joint venture. Over the next four years, Jackil's share of the joint-venture earnings was SF200,000 per year, all of which was paid in dividends at each year-end. On December 31, 1988, the investment was liquidated; the SF1,000,000 initial investment was recovered and the loan repaid.

Required:
Using the exchange rates in Schedule 15-3 as if they were year-end rates, compute the net effect of these transactions on Jackil's net income for each year, including interest paid, dividends received, and exchange gains and losses, under each of the following alternatives for treatment of the exchange gains or losses on the debt. Assume that the investment is a nonmonetary asset.
a. Immediate recognition
b. Capitalization and amortization
c. Deferral until repayment

P16-5

At the beginning of 19x1, Domo Industries Ltd. obtained a four-year loan of U.S. $100,000 from a bank in New York City. At the time of the loan, the U.S. dollar was worth $1.20 Canadian. At the end of 19x1, the exchange rate had changed to U.S. $1.00 = Can. $1.24. By the end of 19x2, the U.S. dollar was worth $1.30 Canadian.

During 19x2, Domo Industries Ltd. sold goods to a German customer for 200,000 marks. At the time of the sale, the mark was worth $0.50. The customer paid one-fourth of the amount due later in the year, when the mark was worth $0.47. By the end of 19x2, the mark had declined in value to $0.45.

Required:
Determine the impact of the transactions described above on Domo Industries' financial statements for the year ended December 31, 19x2 (including the statement of changes in financial position), assuming that the recommendations of Section 1650 of the *CICA Handbook* are followed.

P16-6

Zimmerman, Ltd. is a private Ontario corporation. On March 30, 19x3, the company negotiated a five-year loan from Chase Manhattan bank for $1,000,000 in U.S. funds. At the inception of the loan, the U.S. dollar was worth $1.20 in Canadian funds.

Zimmerman's fiscal year-ends on September 30. At fiscal year-end, 19x3, the exchange rate was U.S. $1.00 = Can. $1.26. Zimmerman prepares its financial statements in Canadian dollars.

Required:
List the alternative reporting treatments for the loan and any related gain or loss in Zimmerman's 19x3 financial statements. For each alternative:
a. Determine the amounts and the financial statement presentation.
b. Briefly state the arguments in *favour* of each alternative.
c. State whether the alternative is acceptable within the recommendations of the *CICA Handbook*.

Zip Ltd. purchased a fixed asset from France, which arrived on November 1, 19x6, priced at 1,450,000 French francs. The company hedged the debt with a foreign currency contract at the time the machine arrived in Vancouver, since the final price was not known prior to that time. The debt is due February 1, 19x7. Relevant exchange rates are:

Spot rate
| November 1, 19x6 | $1 = 5 French francs |
| December 31, 19x6 | $1 = 4 French francs |

Hedge rate at November 1, 19x6
$1 = 4.4 French francs

Required:
a. Prepare the journal entries for 19x6 to record the above information.
b. Assuming instead that the debt was due February 1, 19x8, and there was no hedge, prepare for 19x6 the journal entries to record the above information.
[CGA-Canada]

On May 5, 19x5, Khalil Corp. purchased inventory from a Japanese supplier, and gave the supplier a 90-day note for yen10,000,000. On the same date, Khalil entered a forward contract with its bank to receive yen10,000,000 in 90 days. The spot rate for the yen was $0.0050. The forward rate was $0.0055.

Required:
Prepare general journal entries to record the purchase, the hedge, and final settlement of both the note and the hedge, assuming each of the following spot rates at the settlement date:
a. $0.0050
b. $0.0055
c. $0.0048
d. $0.0057

On October 15, 19x6, Zap Limited sold merchandise to two companies in Portugal. In the first transaction, the price was 1,500,000 escudos and was to be paid in 90 days. Worried about the exposure to the exchange risk, the company hedged the receivable for a 90-day period with a forward exchange contract.

In the second transaction, the price was 1,800,000 escudos and the date of payment was November 15, 19x9. Due to the difficulty of getting a forward contract to match the date payment is due, the company decided to remain in an "unhedged" position on this receivable.

Exchange rates:

October 15, 19x6, spot rate	$1 = 800 escudos
December 31, 19x6, spot rate	$1 = 910 escudos
January 13, 19x7, spot rate	$1 = 945 escudos
October 15, 19x6, forward rate 90 day rate	$1 = 926 escudos
December 31, 19x7, spot rate	$1 = 775 escudos

Required:
Ignoring closing entries:
a. Prepare all the related journal entries required for the first sale for 19x6 *and* 19x7;
b. Assume instead that the company had not hedged the receivable from the first sale in any way, prepare the appropriate journal entries for 19x6 *and* 19x7 to record this situation;
c. Prepare all the related journal entries for the *second* sale for 19x6 *and* 19x7.
[CGA-Canada]

P16-10

Following are transactions of Import Ltd., a company engaged in importing products into Canada.

September 1, 19x4
Incurred a liability for 500,000 pesos, due February 1, 19x5, for purchasing inventory.

October 1, 19x4
Incurred a liability for 3,000,000 yen, due November 1, 19x5, for purchasing inventory.

November 1, 19x4
Incurred a liability for 11,000 Russian rubles, due March 1, 19x6, for purchasing inventory.

Exchange Rates:

September 1, 19x4
$1 = 150 pesos   Spot rate
$1 = 120 pesos   Forward exchange contract rate

October 1, 19x4
$1 = 800 yen   Spot rate
$1 = 950 yen   Forward exchange contract rate

November 1, 19x4
$1 = 1.80 rubles   Spot rate
$1 = 1.60 rubles   Forward exchange contract rate

December 31, 19x4
$1 = 100 pesos
$1 = 1,000 yen
$1 = 1.50 rubles

Required:
Parts a. and b., below, are based on different policies regarding hedging. Answer each part as an independent problem.
a. Import Ltd. did not hedge or cover its exchange risk position. Prepare the journal entries for 19x4. The company has a December 31 year-end.
b. At the time of each transaction, Import Ltd. paid $100 for a forward exchange contract, which was a perfect and complete hedge against the foreign exchange risk. Prepare the journal entries for 19x4. The company has a December 31 year-end.
[CGA-Canada]

P16-11

Harley Ltd., a manufacturer of motorcycles located in Burnaby, B.C., successfully negotiated a contract to sell 100 small motorcycles to the police department of Fairbanks, Alaska. The contract price for the cycles was U.S. $5,000 each. The contract was signed on May 12, 19x3, with payment to be made by October 1. Harley then entered into a forward contract to hedge against changes in the U.S. dollar exchange rate.

Delivery of the motorcycles began on June 11 and continued in twenty cycle lots at two-week intervals until the last delivery on August 30, 19x3. The buyer then paid the U.S. $500,000 contract price when due, and Harley settled with the bank.

The exchange rates were as follows:

	Canadian equivalent of U.S. $1.00	
	Spot rate	Forward rate
May 12, 19x3	$1.15	$1.18
June 11 — August 30, 19x3	1.10	1.08
October 1, 19x3	1.12	1.14

Required:
a. What amounts relating to the sale and the hedge would appear on Harley's income statement and balance sheet for the year ended December 31, 19x3?
b. Assume instead that Harley's year-end was August 30. What amounts would appear on Harley's financial statements at August 30, 19x3?

P16-12

Chan Can Corporation (CCC), a Canadian corporation, engaged in the following transactions in late 19x1 and early 19x2:

December 2	Purchased sheet aluminum from a U.S. subsidiary of a Canadian aluminum company for U.S. $80,000, payable in 60 days.
December 2	Acquired a forward contract to receive U.S. $80,000 in 60 days, as a hedge of the account payable. The forward contract rate was Can. $1.10.
December 20	Sold large cans to a Buffalo canner for U.S. $100,000, due in 60 days.
January 31	Received U.S. $80,000 on the forward contract; paid U.S. $80,000 to the aluminum company.
February 18	Received U.S. $100,000 from the Buffalo canner.

Spot rates for the U.S. dollar were as follows:

December 2	$1.07
December 20	1.12
December 31	1.14
January 31	1.20
February 18	1.17

Required:
Prepare journal entries for these transactions, including any adjusting entries needed at the December 31, 19x1, year-end.

17

Translating Foreign Operations

The previous chapter explored the problems and alternatives that arise when a Canadian company transacts some of its business in a foreign currency. When a company carries out a substantial volume of business in a foreign country, it is common for the company to establish a separate operation in that country. Usually the foreign operation is incorporated, although incorporation is not essential; the foreign operation could be a branch, an unincorporated joint venture, or a partnership.

Ordinarily, the foreign operation maintains its own bank accounts in the currency of the host country and conducts its business in that currency. It may sell its product or service in the host-country currency, may pay its employees, and may buy its supplies and assets in that currency. Periodically, the foreign operation will summarize its activities in financial statements and will send this report of activities to the parent company. The statement or statements of the foreign operation will be presented in the currency in which it is transacting its business. When the parent company incorporates the results of the foreign operation or subsidiary into its own financial statements, the statements of the foreign operation must be translated into the currency of the parent company. Thus, the problem of *translating foreign operations* arises.

TRANSLATION METHODS

Introductory Example

To illustrate the nature of the problem, let us assume that Domestic Corporation decides to establish a sales subsidiary in the country of Pantania. Domestic's legal representatives in Pantania draw up the papers for a corporation in that country, to be named Forsub Ltd. The founding board of directors of Forsub is nominated (by Domestic) and Forsub begins operating. One hundred common shares of Forsub are issued to Domestic Corporation for 500 pants per share, the pant being the local currency of Pantania. Forsub will record the investment *in Pantanian pants* as follows:

Cash	P50,000	
Common shares		P50,000

If the pant is worth two dollars Canadian at the time of the transaction, then P50,000 will be worth $100,000 and Domestic will record the investment on its books at cost as it would any initial investment:

Investment in Forsub Ltd.	$100,000	
Cash		$100,000

Now, suppose that after receiving the cash, Forsub begins organizing itself for operations by acquiring some inventory for P20,000 (partially on account) and a piece of land for P40,000. To finance this purchase, Forsub issues five-year bonds amounting to P25,000. The transactions would be recorded as follows on Forsub's books:

Cash	P25,000	
Bonds payable		P25,000
Inventory	P20,000	
Cash		P15,000
Accounts payable		5,000
Land	P40,000	
Cash		P40,000

At the time of these transactions, the exchange rate is still P1 = $2. The balance sheet of Forsub will then appear as follows:

Cash	P20,000
Inventory	20,000
Land	40,000
Total assets	P80,000
Accounts payable	P 5,000
Bonds payable	25,000
Common shares	50,000
Total equities	P80,000

A short while later, Domestic Corporation's fiscal year-end occurs. Since Forsub is a subsidiary of Domestic, Domestic will be expected to consolidate Forsub. As with any subsidiary that is consolidated, the investment account is eliminated and Forsub's assets and liabilities are added to those of the parent company in Domestic's balance sheet. However, Forsub's assets and liabilities are expressed in pants, not dollars. It is necessary to convert Forsub's assets and liabilities to Canadian dollars before consolidation is possible. The process of translating the account balances from pants to dollars is the process of *translating foreign operations*; we must translate the *results* of Forsub's transactions for the period, as reflected in the Forsub balance sheet, rather than the individual transactions as we discussed in the preceding chapter. As might be expected, there are several ways in which the results of foreign operations can be translated.

Temporal Method

One approach to translating Forsub's balance sheet is the **temporal method**. We can begin by translating all of the accounts that represent cash or claims payable in cash at the exchange rate that exists at the balance sheet date. Forsub has P20,000 in cash, and Domestic could instruct Forsub to remit the cash to the parent company, such as by declaring a dividend. If the cash were remitted to Domestic, it would be convertible directly into Canadian dollars at the exchange rate then prevailing. If the rate was P1 = $2.30, then P20,000 would be equivalent to $46,000. Other assets that represent cash claims, such as notes receivable and accounts receivable, would also be translated at the exchange rate in effect at the balance sheet date. The rate at the balance sheet date is known as the **current** rate.

Since cash and cash-equivalent assets are translated at the current rate, claims against cash are also translated at the current rate. All accounts payable, notes payable, bonds payable, and similar liabilities would be translated at the current rate because they are all payable in cash. In addition, nonmonetary assets that are reported in the financial statements at their current value (such as certain types of inventory or investments) are translated at the current rate because their value represents an amount that can be converted to cash.

Nonmonetary items that are reported at historical cost are translated at the exchange rate in effect at the date of the transaction that created the nonmonetary items. The rate on the date of the transaction is known as the **historical** rate. In essence, the temporal approach uses the same translation rules as we described in the previous chapter for monetary and nonmonetary balances arising from foreign currency transactions.

For Forsub Ltd., the nonmonetary items are inventory and land, both purchased when the rate was P1 = $2.00. Thus, these two assets would be translated at the $2.00 historical rate, while the cash and bonds would be translated at the $2.30 current rate. Note that the historical rate is $2.00 because that was the rate existing at the time that the inventory and land were purchased. The fact that the rate was also $2.00 when the original investment in Forsub was made by Domestic is coincidental. If the land had been purchased when the rate was $2.10 and the inventory was bought when the rate was $2.15, then those would be the historical rates used for translating each account balance.

The only account on the Forsub balance sheet that we have not yet discussed is the common shares. Since this is a nonmonetary item, it is logical that it should be translated at the historical rate of $2.00. An additional consideration, however, is the fact that this account will be eliminated when Forsub is consolidated. Since the offsetting account in Domestic's balance sheet is the investment in Forsub account, the subsidiary's common share account should be translated at the historical rate in order to facilitate the elimination on consolidation.

In summary, the accounts on Forsub's balance sheet would be translated as follows under the temporal method:

- Cash @ current rate
- Inventory @ historical rate
- Land @ historical rate
- Bonds payable @ current rate
- Common shares @ historical rate

Since the accounts are being translated at two different rates, the translated balance sheet will not balance until we allow for a **translation gain or loss**. The total gain or loss will be the amount needed to balance the translated balance sheet, and is a loss of $3,000 in this example. With this addition to the balance sheet, the translated balance sheet of Forsub Ltd. will appear as shown in the last column of Schedule 17-1.

SCHEDULE 17-1

Forsub Ltd.
Translation of Year-end Balance Sheet:
Temporal Method*
(current rate: P1 = $2.30)

	Balance on Forsub's books	Exchange rate	Translated amount
Cash	P20,000	$2.30	$ 46,000
Inventory	20,000	2.00	40,000
Land	40,000	2.00	80,000
Total assets	P80,000		$166,000
Accounts payable	P 5,000	$2.30	$ 11,500
Bonds payable	25,000	2.30	57,500
Common shares	50,000	2.00	100,000
Translation loss			(3,000)
Total equities	P80,000		$166,000

CALCULATION OF NET TRANSLATION LOSS:

Cash:	P20,000 asset	× ($2.30 − $2.00) = $6,000 gain
Accounts payable:	P 5,000 liability	× ($2.30 − $2.00) = 1,500 loss
Bonds payable:	P25,000 liability	× ($2.30 − $2.00) = 7,500 loss
Net:	P10,000 liability	× ($2.30 − $2.00) = $3,000 loss

*The Monetary/Nonmonetary Method yields the same results in this example.

The $3,000 loss can be derived directly from the information given about Forsub's transactions. There are three components to the loss. The first is a gain of $6,000 on the balance of cash. Forsub originally received P50,000 in cash when the exchange rate was $2.00, and obtained another P25,000 from the issuance of bonds.

While the rate was still $2.00, the company purchased land and inventory, thereby reducing the cash balance to P20,000. The company then held this balance of cash while the exchange rate rose to $2.30. The increase in the exchange rate meant that the P20,000 balance was worth $46,000 at the end of the fiscal year (P20,000 @ $2.30) as compared to only $40,000 (P20,000 @ $2.00) when the cash was received. Thus, holding a cash balance when the exchange rate rose resulted in an increase in the equivalent amount in Canadian dollars: a gain of $6,000 ($46,000 − $40,000).

The second component of the $3,000 translation loss is a loss of $1,500 on the accounts payable. Forsub still owes P5,000 to its trade creditors, but the dollar equivalent of this amount has changed from $10,000 (P5,000 @ $2.00) to $11,500 (P5,000 @ $2.30). In Canadian dollar terms, the value of the debt has risen, thereby resulting in a loss.

The final component of the overall translation loss arises from the bonds payable. The P25,000 in bonds were issued when the exchange rate was

$2.00, or a Canadian equivalent of $50,000. At year-end, the Canadian equivalent of the bond indebtedness is $57,500, at the year-end exchange rate of $2.30. Therefore, a loss of $7,500 ($50,000 − $57,500) has arisen as a result of holding a liability that is denominated in pants as the Canadian equivalent increased because of changes in the exchange rate.

By breaking the translation loss down into its component amounts, we can see that the loss of $3,000 is really a net amount arising from a loss of $9,000 ($1,500 + $7,500) on monetary liabilities less a gain of $6,000 on holding cash. This information is summarized at the bottom of Schedule 17-1. We will examine the nature of this loss and its accounting implications more extensively later in the chapter.

For the moment, however, note that the only items that give rise to translation gains or losses are those account balances that are translated at the *current* rate. The net amount of balances that are translated at the current rate is the measure of the foreign operation's **accounting exposure** to currency rate fluctuations. In Schedule 17-1, the accounting exposure is a net monetary liability balance of P10,000 (P20,000 − P5,000 − P25,000). We will discuss the concept of accounting exposure later in the chapter.

Balances that are translated at historical rates do not give rise to translation gains or losses because the rate at which they are translated does not change. Thus the net amount of the exchange gain or loss can be calculated by looking only at the net changes in those balances that are translated at the current rate.

Relationship of Temporal Method to Transaction Accounting

In Schedule 17-1, we translated Forsub's year-end balances by using the temporal method, and we calculated a gain on the balance of cash and a loss on the balance of bonds and accounts payable. An important characteristic to note about the temporal method is that *it yields exactly the same results in terms of the translated amounts as would have resulted from translating each transaction separately*, assuming that all monetary and current value balances are reported at the current rate, as recommended by paragraphs 1650.16 and 1650.18 of the *CICA Handbook*. In substance, the temporal method views the operations of the foreign company as though the transactions had been carried out directly by Domestic Corporation from Canada.

Schedule 17-2 illustrates the individual transactions as they would have been recorded by Domestic if they had been direct transactions. The first transaction shows the depositing of $100,000 in the Bank of Pantania, which amount is translated to P50,000 by the bank. The remaining transactions record the issuance of the bonds and the purchase of the inventory and land, recorded in the equivalent amount of Canadian dollars. At year-end, it is necessary to record the monetary foreign-currency-denominated balances at their current equivalents. These adjustments (for cash, accounts payable, and bonds payable) result in a net foreign currency loss of $3,000. The impact of these individual transactions on Domestic Corporation's balance sheet would be exactly the same as translating Forsub's balance sheet and consolidating.

Monetary/ Nonmonetary Method

A second method of translating the results of foreign operations is known as the **monetary/nonmonetary method**. Monetary items are translated at the current rate, while *all* nonmonetary items are translated at historical rates.

SCHEDULE 17-2

Transactions in Pantania*

RECORDED ON DOMESTIC'S BOOKS:

Cash (in Bank of Pantania)	$100,000	
Cash (in Canadian bank)		$100,000
[to record transfer of cash to Pantanian bank account]		
Cash (in Pantania)	$ 50,000	
Bonds payable (P25,000)		$ 50,000
[to record issuance of bonds in Pantania]		
Inventory (cost = P20,000)	$ 40,000	
Cash (in Pantania)		$ 30,000
Accounts payable (P5,000)		10,000
[to record purchase of inventory in Pantania, in pants]		
Land (cost = P40,000)	$ 80,000	
Cash (in Pantania: P40,000)		$ 80,000
[to record purchase of land in Pantania, in pants]		
Cash (P20,000)($2.30 − $2.00)	$ 6,000	
Foreign currency gains and losses		$ 6,000
[to adjust the year-end balance of cash to the current rate]		
Foreign currency gains and losses	$ 1,500	
Accounts payable (P5,000)($2.30 − $2.00)		$ 1,500
[to adjust the year-end balance of accounts payable to the current rate]		
Foreign currency gains and losses	$ 7,500	
Bonds payable (P25,000)($2.30 − $2.00)		$ 7,500
[to adjust the year-end balance of bonds payable to the current rate]		

*Assuming that Domestic does not establish Forsub Ltd. to conduct Domestic's business in that country.

The only difference in theory between this approach and the temporal method is in the treatment of nonmonetary amounts that are reported at current value; the temporal method translates these items at the current rate while the monetary/nonmonetary method translates them at historical rates.

The difference between these two methods is more apparent than real. Most companies carry all of their nonmonetary balances at historical cost. For these companies, there will be no difference in results, whether the monetary/nonmonetary method or the temporal method is used. Both methods will result in the translation of monetary assets and liabilities at the current rate, and translation gains and losses will arise therefrom to the extent that the exchange rate has changed during the period. Nonmonetary items, all of which are carried at historical cost, will be translated at their individual historical rates, and no translation gains or losses will arise therefrom. A difference in translation results between the two methods will arise only for those few companies carrying one or more of their nonmonetary items at market value, current value, or current replacement cost.

Because of the consistency in treatment of current value balances (whether monetary or nonmonetary) in the temporal method, this method is frequently considered to be preferable to the monetary/nonmonetary method. But since the two methods yield identical results in practice in most cases, the choice between the two methods is usually a matter of indifference. In the remainder of this chapter, we will drop any explicit reference to the monetary/nonmonetary method and will refer to this related pair of methods simply as the temporal method.

Current-Rate Method

A third approach to the translation of the results of foreign operations, the **current-rate method**, is to translate *all* of the asset and liability balances at the current rate. This calculation is shown in Schedule 17-3. Under this method, the total assets of Forsub translate to $184,000 as compared to $166,000 under the temporal method. The much larger amount is due to the fact that under the temporal method, the large nonmonetary assets were translated at the lower historical rate. Conversely, if the exchange rate had declined during the period, the total assets would be less under the current-rate method than under the temporal method.

When the current-rate method is used, the net balance of those balance sheet accounts that are translated at the current rate will always be a net *asset* balance (assuming that the subsidiary's share equity is positive). Since all of the assets and all of the liabilities are translated at the current rate, the total assets will exceed the total liabilities, and the balance that is exposed to gains and losses from fluctuations in the exchange rate will be the excess of the assets over the liabilities. This net balance is obviously equal to the shareholders' equity in the foreign operation, or its net asset value. Thus, under the current-rate method, the accounting exposure to currency fluctuations is always measurable as the net investment in the foreign subsidiary. Under the temporal method, in contrast, the exposure could be either a net asset or net liability balance, depending on whether monetary assets exceed monetary liabilities, or vice versa.

SCHEDULE 17-3

Forsub Ltd.
Translation of Balance Sheet
(Current-rate method)

	Balance on Forsub's books	Exchange rate	Translated amount
Cash	P20,000	$2.30	$ 46,000
Inventory	20,000	2.30	46,000
Land	40,000	2.30	92,000
Total assets	P80,000		$184,000
Accounts payable	P 5,000	$2.30	$ 11,500
Bonds payable	25,000	2.30	57,500
Common shares	50,000	2.00	100,000
Translation gain*			15,000
Total equities	P80,000		$184,000

*Translation gain = net asset position times change in exchange rate:
$50,000 × ($2.30 − $2.00) = $15,000 credit or gain.

A distinct characteristic of the current-rate method is that the proportionate amounts of the various asset and liability accounts do not change when the balance sheet is translated. For example, bonds are 31% of Forsub's total assets in pants (P25,000/P80,000), and they continue to be 31% of total assets in dollars ($57,500/$184,000). Under the temporal method, however, the proportion changes from 31% to 35% ($57,500/$166,000). Many individuals feel that this characteristic is an advantage of the current-rate method: the "true" financial position of Forsub is that shown by the balance sheet in pants, and the process of currency translation should not change this picture of the foreign operation. As one eminent author puts it: "It is analogous to painting a stone wall; the colour may change, but the bumps remain; the wall is the same as before, just a different colour."[1]

Current/Noncurrent Method

The fourth (and final) approach to translating foreign operations is the **current/noncurrent method**. As its name implies, the current/noncurrent method distinguishes between assets and liabilities on the basis of whether they are current or noncurrent assets or liabilities. Current items are translated at the current exchange rate and noncurrent items are translated at their historical rate. The results of translating Forsub's balance sheet by this method are shown in Schedule 17-4. The net balance of items that are translated at the current rate is equal to the net working capital, or current assets minus the current liabilities. For Forsub, the net working capital is P35,000, and thus the accounting exposure is also P35,000. Since the exposure is a net

---

SCHEDULE 17-4

Forsub Ltd.
Translation of Balance Sheet
(Current/Noncurrent Method)

	Balance on Forsub's books	Exchange rate	Translated amount
Cash	P20,000	$2.30	$ 46,000
Inventory	20,000	2.30	46,000
Land	40,000	2.00	80,000
Total assets	P80,000		$172,000
Accounts payable	P 5,000	$2.30	$ 11,500
Bonds payable	25,000	2.00	50,000
Common shares	50,000	2.00	100,000
Translation gain*			10,500
Total equities	P80,000		$172,000

*Translation gain = net working capital × change in exchange rate.
(P40,000 current assets − P5,000 current liabilities) × ($2.30 − $2.00)
= P35,000 × ($0.30) = $10,500 credit or gain.

---

1 Dr. Pierre Vézina, *Foreign Currency Translation: An Analysis of Section 1650 of the CICA Handbook* (Toronto: CICA, 1985), p. 6.

asset position and the exchange rate rose by $0.30 during the period, there is a translation gain of $10,500 (P35,000 x $0.30).

Historically, the current/noncurrent method was the most commonly used method in Canada, at least among public companies. The 1981 edition of *Financial Reporting in Canada* reported that of the 142 companies (from among the 350 surveyed) that reported an accounting policy for translating foreign operations, 65% used the current/noncurrent method. By comparison, only 18% used the current-rate method, and 17% used either the temporal (11%) or monetary/nonmonetary (6%) methods. This percentage using the current/noncurrent method had been rather constant since 1978, but was a decline from the 76% who used it in 1977. The decline was accompanied by an increase in the use of the temporal method, presumably in response to the FASB's short-lived requirement to use this method in *SFAS No. 8* (since withdrawn and replaced by *SFAS No. 52*).

The popularity of the current/noncurrent method in Canada can be traced to two factors. The first factor is that under the current/noncurrent method, the accounting exposure to exchange rate fluctuations (and the concomitant accounting gain or loss) can be managed. If the net working capital is maintained at zero, that is, with current assets equalling current liabilities, then there will be no net balance translated at the current rate, and thus no translation gain or loss. If the size of the foreign operation or operations is significant in comparison to the domestic operation, then the avoidance of recognizing an unrealized translation gain or loss can be perceived by management as a significant advantage.

The second factor embraces the concept of an implicit hedge, as we discussed in the previous chapter. The current assets, much of which may be composed of nonmonetary assets such as inventory, are viewed as a hedge against the current liabilities, many of which are likely to be monetary. Both the current assets and the current liabilities will be realized within the next year, and the gains from one will tend to offset the losses from the other. Thus, it is logical to translate both the current assets and current liabilities at the current exchange rate.

Similarly, the long-term assets (most likely fixed assets) are viewed as being financed by the long-term monetary liabilities, and constitute an implicit hedge against them. Since the gains or losses from the long-term items will be realized only over the long run, the noncurrent items are translated at the historical rate, and any foreign currency gains or losses will be recognized only when they are realized. None of the alternate methods of translation can achieve a similar result. The temporal method translates the monetary liabilities at the current exchange rate but leaves the related fixed assets at the historical rate, thereby forcing recognition of a possibly substantial unrealized gain or loss. The current-rate method translates both the noncurrent assets and the noncurrent liabilities at the current exchange rate, thereby permitting the long-term assets and liabilities to offset each other and reducing the potential gain or loss, but then the balance of the fixed assets goes up and down in response to unrealized currency rate changes. An exposure to unrealized translation gains and losses is still present under the current/noncurrent method to the extent that there is a net balance of long-term items.

Empirical research has suggested that the validity of purchasing power parity and the Fisher Effect indicates that most assets and liabilities are not really exposed to exchange gains and losses over longer periods of time but that for shorter periods they are. "Over relatively short horizons (two or three years), all assets and liabilities tend to be exposed."[2] These findings suggest that while the current/noncurrent method is not ideal, it may come closer to reflecting the realities of exchange rate risk than the other methods presently available. Unfortunately, the current/noncurrent method has no place in the authoritative pronouncements of either Canada or the United States at present.

The translation methods that we have discussed so far can be summarized as follows (ignoring the monetary/nonmonetary method):

Summary of Translation Methods

1. Temporal method
   a. Translates all monetary and current value items at the current exchange rate; translates all nonmonetary historical cost items at their individual historical rates.
   b. Yields an accounting exposure to exchange rate fluctuations of the net balance of monetary and current value assets and liabilities, depending on the financial structure of the company.
   c. Does not give effect to implicit hedges of monetary items by offsetting nonmonetary items.

2. Current-rate method
   a. Translates all assets and liabilities at the current rate, whether current or noncurrent and whether monetary or nonmonetary.
   b. Yields an exposure to exchange rate changes that is always a net asset position, equivalent to the owners' equity in the foreign operation.
   c. Preserves the proportionate relationships between the various balance sheet items; does not "distort" the statement compared to the way it would appear in local currency.

3. Current/noncurrent method
   a. Translates current assets and current liabilities at the current exchange rate; translates long-term assets and liabilities at their individual historical rates.
   b. Yields an exposure to exchange rate changes that is equal to the net working capital position of the foreign operation.
   c. Permits "managing" of the current rate exposure through working capital management.
   d. Implicitly treats nonmonetary items as hedges against offsetting monetary balances within each of the current and noncurrent groups of accounts.

   While the temporal method does not in itself treat nonmonetary assets (or the revenue stream therefrom) as hedges of monetary liabilities, such hedges may be identified and recognized under the temporal method, as we discussed in the "Implicit Hedges" section of the previous chapter on foreign currency transactions.
   So far, we have been treating the net translation gain or loss under

2 Robert Z. Aliber and Clyde P. Stickney, "Accounting Measures of Foreign Exchange Exposure: The Long and Short of It," *The Accounting Review* (January, 1975), p. 52.

each of the methods as a balance sheet item. However, there actually are various treatments possible *under each method* of translation. Before we consider these alternative treatments of the translation gain or loss, however, we should further address the issue of *exposure*.

ACCOUNTING EXPOSURE VS. ECONOMIC EXPOSURE

Throughout the foregoing discussion, we have pointed out that under each translation method, we can anticipate the nature of the translation gain or loss. We know which items will be translated at the current exchange rate, and only those amounts will give rise to a translation gain or loss. If we know which way the exchange rate is moving, then we can predict whether the translation will result in a gain or a loss for the current period.

We have also observed that since the different methods translate different accounts at the current exchange rate, a given movement in the exchange rate may cause a gain under one method but may cause a loss under another method. In the case of Forsub, above, we calculated a loss of $3,000 under the temporal method, a gain of $15,000 under the current-rate method, and a gain of $10,500 under the current/noncurrent method.

The net balance of those balance sheet amounts that we translated at the current exchange rate has been referred to as the *accounting exposure* to fluctuations in the foreign exchange rate. This exposure arises as the result of the accounting method of translation that we are using at the time. If a translation gain or loss is to be reported on the financial statements of the parent corporation, then the qualitative characteristic of "representational faithfulness" (in the FASB and *CICA Handbook* sets of criteria) or "isomorphism" (in the CICA Study Group set) should be present. In other words, is there really an *economic* gain to the parent when an accounting gain is reported?

It can be argued that when a Canadian company holds an asset that is denominated in a foreign currency and the currency rises in value against the Canadian dollar, the company experiences an economic gain because the asset increases in value as measured in dollars. Since a Canadian company's equity in a foreign operation is necessarily a net asset position, then one could argue that an increase in the exchange rate will result in a gain to the parent because that net investment will be worth more as a result of the change in the rate.

Such an argument, however, fails to appraise the impact of changes in the relative values of the currencies on the earnings ability of the foreign subsidiary. In most instances, the foreign operation exists as a going concern that is expected to contribute favourably to the profits of the parent. Therefore, it makes sense to evaluate the impact of currency realignments on the earnings ability of the foreign operation. This impact is known as the **economic exposure** of the foreign operation. The economic exposure is much more complicated than the accounting exposure because many more factors are involved than simply the mechanical aspects of the translation method and the direction of change in the exchange rates.

Suppose, for example, that the business of Forsub Ltd. is to import a product from Canada and to sell it in Pantania. The cost to produce the product is $10.00, and it is sold in Pantania at P6. When the exchange rate is

P1 = $2.00, the value of the sale is $12.00 (P6 X $2), resulting in a gross profit of $2.00 ($12 - $10) to Domestic Corporation. But if the exchange rate goes up to P1 = $2.30, the value of each sale will then be $13.80, for an increased gross profit of $3.80. In such a situation, the increase in the value of the pant is a real gain in economic terms. Forsub will either have a larger profit on its sales (if it maintains the same selling price in pants), or it may decrease its price and increase its volume of sales in Pantania (owing to the price elasticity of demand). Either way, Domestic may be better off as a result of the increase in the value of the pant.

Now, suppose instead that the business of Forsub is to produce a product from materials in Pantania and then to transfer the product to Domestic Corporation for sale in Canada. The product costs P10 to produce in Pantania, and sells for $25 in Canada. When the exchange rate is P1 = $2.00, the cost of production is the equivalent of $20, yielding a gross margin of $5. An increase in the value of the pant to $2.30 will cause the production cost to rise to $23 in Canadian dollars, thereby lowering the gross margin to $2.00. In this situation, an increase in the value of the pant can be disadvantageous to Forsub and Domestic Corporation. Instead of being a gain, a rise in the value of the pant is actually a loss in earnings ability.

Of course, things are not really all that simple. Exchange rates do not change autonomously, but are the result of other economic factors, such as relative rates of inflation and interest rate differentials in the various countries. If the value of the pant increased because of high inflation in Canada, then Domestic may be able to charge a higher price for the product and maintain or possibly even increase the relative gross margin on it.

The point is that the economic impact of changes in exchange rates is quite complex and will vary from company to company and situation to situation. The economic exposure is a result of the economic characteristics of the foreign operation, such as the sources of its raw materials, the sources of its debt financing, the market in which its products are sold, the price elasticity of demand for its products, and much more. Furthermore, the economic exposure is forward-looking. Economic exposure is the impact on the present value of future cash flows.

Accounting exposure, in contrast, is historically oriented. It measures the mechanical impact of translating the results of past transactions. The economic exposure is not determinable from the accounting exposure, which is mechanical in origin and is not necessarily indicative of the earnings impact of a change in exchange rates.

However, application of the concept of representational faithfulness leads to the conclusion that in any situation, the preferred accounting translation method is the one that yields an accounting exposure that best reflects the economic exposure. If an increase in the exchange rate is likely to have a beneficial economic impact on the foreign operation and the consolidated subsidiary, then the accounting translation method should yield a translation gain when the exchange rate goes up, rather than a loss.

REPORTING OF TRANSLATION GAINS AND LOSSES

So far in this chapter, we have treated the gain or loss arising from the translation of the balance sheet of a foreign operation simply as a balancing figure on the balance sheet. However, several alternatives are available for the disposition of these gains or losses. All but one of the alternatives have already been discussed in Chapter 16. The broad alternatives are:

1. Recognize the net gain or loss immediately in the consolidated income statement.
2. Disaggregate the net gain or loss and recognize each component in accordance with the treatment of similar types of *transaction* gains or losses.
3. Treat as a balancing amount in the consolidated balance sheet (e.g., as a separate component of shareholders' equity).

Each of these alternatives can be applied under any one of the three methods of translation described in the earlier sections of this chapter. However, some of the alternatives are more logical under certain of the methods, as we shall see later.

The first alternative was the one which the FASB adopted in 1975, *SFAS No. 8*, which caused a considerable furor. The FASB considered the various alternatives and found them all lacking. The Board concluded, however, that current recognition was the least misleading or artificial treatment: "... Rate changes are historical facts, and the Board believes that users of financial statements are best served by accounting for the changes as they occur. It is the deferring or spreading of those effects, not their recognition and disclosure, that is the artificial process" [para. 198].

Since the Board works on the premise that the users of financial statements are not unsophisticated, it felt that users would recognize that the translation gains and losses were unrealized, and would not be misled by recognizing the net gains or losses in income.

While the Board was probably correct in assessing the reaction of an efficient market, they failed to anticipate the reactions of managers to the prospect of showing possibly substantial unrealized gains or losses on their companies' income statements. The market as a whole could no doubt properly evaluate the translation gains and losses, but managers were concerned about individuals' reactions to reported amounts, especially losses. The losses would affect net income from operations and therefore would affect earnings per share, dividend payout ratios, and profit-sharing and bonus calculations, as well as certain debt-covenant calculations such as times-interest-earned.

Furthermore, the translation gains and losses were a product of the accounting exposure and were not necessarily an indication of the economic exposure of the company. Particularly in reporting segmented data, the results of operations from a geographic segment could look quite unfavourable if translation losses were taken into account, when in fact the impact of a change in exchange rates could have been quite beneficial to the reporting entity.

Empirical research following the implementation of *SFAS No. 8* indicated that many managers were taking actions to minimize the accounting exposure of their companies, even though those actions might be dysfunctional or represent a misallocation of resources. Some managers were engaging in massive hedging operations in order to offset possible losses from an accounting exposure in a foreign operation. The point of hedging, however, is to offset one economic exposure with another economic exposure in the opposite direction. If hedging is used to offset a potential paper translation loss, then a real economic exposure is created by the hedge in order to offset a paper translation loss.

Other managers were reorganizing the financial affairs of their foreign subsidiaries in order to reduce the accounting exposure. If we assume that the managers made the best decisions in the financial structure of the subsidiaries in the first place, then changes in those decisions as the result of an accounting exposure must be changes that are less than optimal in economic terms.

An additional problem that was perceived by researchers was that the actions of managers to cover their accounting exposures was placing considerable pressure on the U.S. dollar. Ironically, the foreign currency fluctuations that were causing managers to take possibly dysfunctional actions were themselves causing greater fluctuations in the value of the U.S. dollar.

In response to the objections of many people and to the research findings, the FASB reconsidered its position on the disposition of translation gains and losses and issued *SFAS No. 52* in 1981. The FASB concluded that, in certain circumstances, the translation gains and losses should not be recognized in income, but should instead be reported on a cumulative basis as a separate component of shareholders' equity.

The experience in the United States with *SFAS No. 8* clearly indicated the inadvisability of mandating the current recognition of translation gains and losses in all cases. Those instances in which current recognition seems particularly inappropriate are when the foreign operation is substantially autonomous in its activities, as in polycentric corporations. If a foreign operation functions as a separate business unit, either as a profit center or as an investment center, then recognition of a translation gain or loss is apt to be misleading because the accounting exposure is not necessarily indicative of the economic exposure. The FASB concluded that current recognition "produces results that are not compatible with the expected economic effects of changes in exchange rates" [*SFAS No. 52*, para. 88].

The second of the broad approaches to the disposition of translation gains and losses is that of disaggregating the net gain or loss and treating each component individually. Under this alternative, gains and losses arising from current assets and liabilities would be viewed separately from gains and losses issuing from long-term amounts. If the company's approach to foreign currency *transactions* is to recognize gains and losses from current items immediately and to defer and amortize any gains and losses from long-term items, then this same approach would be applied to the components of any gain or loss from translating the results of foreign operations. The translation effects of current items would be recognized in income, while the effects arising from long-term items would be deferred (on the consolidated balance sheet) and amortized.

When applied to relatively autonomous or polycentric operations, the disaggregation alternative seems inappropriate. Disaggregation implies that the parent has direct involvement with the subsidiary, and that the assets and liabilities of the subsidiary should be viewed as direct assets and obligations of the parent. But if the foreign operation is engaged in its own day-to-day activities with little direct interaction from the parent, perhaps arranging its own financing and using the foreign profits to retire the debt, then the parent does not have direct control of the subsidiary's assets and liabilities. The AcSC has dubbed such autonomous foreign operations as **self-sustaining** operations in Section 1650 of the *CICA Handbook*.

However, there are ethnocentric foreign operations that are merely extensions of the parent's domestic business. Examples would include those foreign operations that are simply foreign sales offices or foreign production centres, without any real economic autonomy. Such operations would usually be treated as revenue centres or cost centres from a management accounting standpoint. These operations are largely or entirely dependent on the parent, either as a source of product or for disposition of production. Dependent foreign operations are a direct arm of the parent and the parent controls the assets and liabilities of the subsidiary. Section 1650 refers to dependent foreign operations as **integrated** operations, meaning that the operations of the foreign subsidiary are integrated with those of the parent, rather than being self-sustaining.

For integrated operations, the approach of disaggregating the translation gains and losses is more logical than it is for self-sustaining operations. Since the parent is directly involved in the foreign operation, the parent is, in effect, using the subsidiary as a facilitating mechanism for a series of foreign currency transactions. Using the disaggregation approach yields the same results as would accounting for the foreign operation as a series of transactions, provided that the accounting policy that the parent uses for foreign *operations* is the same as the policy used for foreign *transactions*. Thus the disaggregation alternative seems best suited for those operations that are not autonomous, self-sustaining, or polycentric, but rather are highly dependent upon the parent. The definition of integrated operations in the *Handbook* is that an integrated operation is "a foreign operation which is financially or operationally interdependent with the reporting enterprise such that the exposure to exchange rate changes is similar to the exposure which would exist had the transactions and activities of the foreign operation been undertaken by the reporting enterprise" [para. 1650.03].

The third alternative for the disposition of the translation gain or loss is to treat it as a balance sheet item. This approach can be justified by arguing either (1) that the gain or loss is the result of a mechanical process of translating from a foreign currency into the reporting currency, and thus has no real economic impact on the reporting entity, or (2) that the gain or loss is real, but that it has not been realized and is not likely to be realized by the parent corporation.

Either justification seems to be applicable only when the foreign operation is self-sustaining. If the foreign operation is integrated with, and serves as an extension of, the parent, then the translation gains and losses cannot be viewed as either purely mechanical or unrealizable; the nature of an integrated operation suggests that there are frequent monetary flows between the parent and the foreign subsidiary, causing real economic gains and losses that are likely to be realized. Treatment of the cumulative gain or loss as a deferred credit or charge would imply that the translation gain or loss is a liability or an asset. Since there is no logic to support this view, the FASB decided to view the cumulative foreign currency adjustment as a separate component of consolidated shareholders' equity, and the AcSC followed suit.

Having discussed in general terms the alternatives both for the method of translation and for the disposition of the translation gains and losses, we can now look at the current recommendations of the *CICA Handbook*, Section 1650.

As noted in the previous section, the AcSC has distinguished between integrated and self-sustaining foreign operations. Since integrated operations are by definition those operating as extensions of the parent company in a foreign country, their operations are viewed simply as a series of foreign currency *transactions*, in substance. Under this view, the results obtained by translating the financial statements of the foreign operation should be the same as though the parent had engaged in the foreign currency transactions directly, rather than through a foreign subsidiary. Thus the method used for translating *integrated* operations should be compatible with that used for reporting the results of foreign currency transactions. The method that accomplishes this objective is the *temporal method*. Therefore, the *Handbook* recommends the temporal method for translating integrated foreign operations [para. 1650.29].

Since the objective of translating integrated operations is to achieve the same results as for foreign currency transactions, the disposition of the translation gains and losses that arise from translating integrated foreign operations is treated in the same manner as for transactions [para. 1650.31]. That is, the net gain or loss is disaggregated and reported as follows:

1. In the current year's net income, to the extent that the gain or loss relates to current items or to the current amortization of long-term items
2. As a deferred charge or deferred credit, to the extent that the gain or loss relates to monetary items of fixed maturity and represents the portion being deferred to future years
3. As a part of retained earnings, to the extent that the gain or loss has been recognized in previous years' income

We will demonstrate the application of this disaggregation in the following sections.

The *Handbook* does provide for hedges of specific foreign-currency-denominated items. Thus specific assets or liabilities in an integrated foreign operation could be hedged by the parent. In that case, any gain or loss arising from the hedge would be offset against the exchange loss or gain on the hedged balance [para. 1650.54]. The *Handbook's* provisions for designating a monetary or nonmonetary balance (or the revenue stream therefrom) as an implicit hedge, as was discussed in Chapter 16, also are applicable to integrated foreign operations.

A self-sustaining foreign operation is viewed as being an individual, semi-autonomous foreign business entity. The parent company's accounting exposure to exchange rate changes is limited to the net investment of the parent in the foreign subsidiary. Therefore, the AcSC recommends the use of the *current-rate method* for translating the financial statements of self-sustaining operations [para. 1650.33]. But since the accounting exposure may not be indicative of the economic exposure, and since this exchange gain or loss has no direct effect on the activities of the reporting enterprise, the net gain or loss that arises from translating self-sustaining operations is not recognized on the income statement, but is reported as a separate component of shareholders' equity [para. 1650.34].

The translation gains or losses from self-sustaining foreign operations will continue to accumulate in the shareholders' equity account. Section 1650 recommends that companies disclose "the significant elements which give rise to changes" in the accumulated amount in the shareholders' equity account [para. 1650.39], but most companies do not follow this recommendation.[3] The reason for wide-spread noncompliance may be due to a lack of clarity as to what constitutes "significant elements;" the nature of the current rate method is such that individual components of the overall exchange gain or loss are not identified.

If the parent's net investment in the subsidiary is decreased, a proportionate part of the accumulated amount will be transferred from shareholders' equity to net income [para. 1650.38]. Thus, as long as dividends declared by a self-sustaining subsidiary do not exceed current earnings, and as long as the parent does not sell part of its investment in the subsidiary, none of the translation gain will be recognized in income.

The parent may choose to hedge its net investment in a self-sustaining subsidiary. Any gains or losses from the hedge would be offset against the cumulative translation loss or gain in the separate component of shareholders' equity [para. 1650.55].

An exception to the general recommendation to translate self-sustaining operations by using the current-rate method is when the self-sustaining operation is in a country that has a high inflation rate. There are many countries that have very high rates of inflation, sometimes well over 100% per year. Historical-cost financial statements will show long-term nonmonetary assets at a cost that is expressed in currency of a far different purchasing power than the current exchange rate would suggest. One solution would be to adjust the foreign operation's financial statements for changes in the price level in the foreign country, and then to translate the adjusted statements. But since price level adjustments are not normally included in primary financial statements in Canada, the AcSC has rejected this approach.

Instead, the alternative that is recommended is to use the temporal method for translating the statements of operations in highly inflationary economies [para. 1650.33]. In substance, the effects of inflation are removed from the foreign accounts by restating the accounts using the historical exchange rates for nonmonetary items. Of course, the effects of Canadian inflation are still present in the accounts, but the relative difference in inflation rates between Canada and the foreign country is adjusted for by using the temporal method. The AcSC does not provide guidelines as to what constitutes a "highly inflationary" economy, but the similar recommendations in the FASB's *SFAS No. 52* suggest that an inflation rate of 100% over a three-year period (that is, averaging 26% per year, compounded) would be highly inflationary. However, the FASB guideline is absolute, whereas the *Handbook* criterion is relative to the Canadian inflation rate.

Section 1650 [para. 1650.10] provides a set of six suggestions to aid preparers in deciding whether a foreign operation is self-sustaining. They are as follows:

---

3 According to *Financial Reporting in Canada, 1987*, 33 companies out of 112 (30%) made the recommended disclosure (p. 42).

a. Are the cash flows of the operation independent of the parent?
b. Are prices responsive to local market conditions?
c. Are the sales made primarily in foreign markets?
d. Are operating costs, products, and services obtained primarily in the foreign country?
e. Are the day-to-day operations financed from its own operations?
f. Does the foreign operation function without day-to-day transactions with the parent?

It must be emphasized that these are only guidelines, not rules. Applying the guidelines is not a matter of score-keeping (e.g., four "yes" versus two "no") but is an exercise of professional judgment in determining the substance of the relationship between the domestic parent and its foreign operation(s).

An implicit assumption underlying Section 1650 is that foreign operations can be categorized as integrated or self-sustaining with little ambiguity. It may be, however, that many foreign operations fall into a grey area, with some aspects of each type of operation. In particular, the operations of geocentric corporations tend to be neither integrated nor self-sustaining, but to display aspects of both. The selection of translation method from among the limited alternatives currently offered in the *Handbook* therefore becomes a matter of professional judgment.

Application of the *Handbook* Recommendations

Let us return to the introductory example of Domestic Corporation and its Pantanian subsidiary, Forsub Ltd. We determined earlier in the chapter that under the temporal method of translation, there was a net translation loss of $3,000 in the first year. If Forsub is considered an integrated subsidiary, application of the *Handbook* recommendations would call for the temporal method, and for disaggregating the net translation loss *on Domestic Corporation's statements*.

Schedule 17-1 shows that the $3,000 loss is composed of three components: a $6,000 gain from holding cash, a $1,500 loss from the accounts payable, and a $7,500 loss from the bonds payable. The current items account for a net gain of $4,500 ($6,000 gain less $1,500 loss), and if the *Handbook* recommendations are followed, then this entire gain would be recognized currently in net income. The loss arising from the bonds, however, would be amortized over the life of the bonds. Since the bonds have a five-year life, one-fifth of the $7,500 loss, or $1,500, would be recognized in income in the current year. The remaining $6,000 would be capitalized and carried as a deferred debit, to be charged to expense at the rate of $1,500 per year over the remaining four years.

In summary, then, application of the *Handbook* recommendations to Forsub Ltd. as an integrated foreign operation would result in a net translation gain of $3,000 being reported on Domestic's 19x1 income statement: the $4,500 net gain from the current accounts (cash and accounts payable), less the $1,500 current year amortization of the loss from the bonds. Domestic's December 31, 19x1, balance sheet would show a deferred debit of $6,000 for the unamortized portion of the loss on the bonds payable.

Instead, suppose that Forsub Ltd. was viewed as a self-sustaining foreign operation. Then the current-rate method would be recommended by the

Handbook, and the entire translation gain or loss would be reported as a separate component of Domestic Corporation's shareholders' equity. Schedule 17-3 shows that the current-rate method would yield a net translation gain of $15,000, none of which would be included in net income.

Obviously, a key facet of applying the AcSC recommendations is the determination of whether a foreign operation is integrated or is self-sufficient. Bear in mind, however, that if the foreign operations are relatively minor or if the parent is not otherwise constrained to follow the *Handbook* recommendations, it may be simpler and no less informative to apply the current-rate method across the board to all foreign subsidiaries and to report the translation gains or losses either in the parent's consolidated shareholders' equity or in income.

A FURTHER EXAMPLE

Earlier in this chapter, we described the initial transactions for the establishment of Forsub Ltd. by Domestic Corporation. After Forsub was established, the subsidiary purchased land and inventory and issued bonds. Schedules 17-1, 17-3, and 17-4 illustrate translation of Forsub's balance sheet accounts under three different translation methods. For simplicity, we assumed that Forsub had no operating revenues or expenses for the first year, 19x1 (even though, strictly speaking, there should have been some bond interest accrued). While we did point out that some of the translation gain or loss may be taken into income in 19x1, it is taken into income by the *parent* company and reported on the consolidated income statement.

Now let us make the example more realistic by looking at Forsub's financial statements for the next year, 19x2. Forsub Ltd.'s separate-entity balance sheet and income statement are shown in Schedule 17-5. Additional information is as follows:

1. At the beginning of 19x2, Forsub purchased some equipment for P30,000; the equipment has an expected useful life of six years.
2. Total sales for 19x2 were P60,000, and purchases of inventory amounted to P30,000.
3. The ending inventory was purchased in the last quarter of the year, when the exchange rate was $2.45.
4. The exchange rate at December 31, 19x2, was $2.50; the average rate during the year was $2.40.

Current-Rate Method

The translation of Forsub's account balances by using the current-rate method is shown in Schedule 17-6. All of the assets and liabilities are translated at the year-end exchange rate of $2.50. The shareholders' equity accounts are translated at the historical rates: common shares at the rate that existed at the time of the initial investment, and retained earnings at the rate that existed at the time the earnings were recognized. In this example, the only amount in retained earnings is the current earnings for 19x2, and thus the translated amount is the same as that shown on the translated income

SCHEDULE 17-5

Forsub Ltd.
Financial Statements
December 31, 19x2

Balance Sheet

ASSETS		EQUITIES	
Cash	P 15,000	Accounts payable	P 22,000
Accounts receivable	15,000		
Inventory	10,000	Bonds payable	25,000
Land	40,000	Common shares	50,000
Equipment	30,000	Retained earnings*	8,000
Accumulated depreciation	(5,000)		
Total assets	P105,000	Total equities	P105,000

*Assumes no revenues or expenses were recognized in the previous year, 19x1.

Income Statement

Sales revenue		P60,000
Cost of sales:		
Beginning inventory	P20,000	
Purchases	30,000	
	50,000	
Ending inventory	10,000	
		40,000
Gross margin		20,000
Operating expenses:		
Depreciation	5,000	
Interest	3,000	
Other	4,000	
		12,000
Net income		P 8,000

statement. The balancing figure for the balance sheet is the cumulative translation gain of $25,800.

Under a pure application of the current-rate method, the income statement would also be translated at the year-end rate. However, Schedule 17-6 shows the income statement being translated at the average rate for the year rather than at the year-end rate. This is known as the **average-rate approach** to the current-rate method, and is used primarily in order to ensure additivity of the interim earnings figures of the parent company. Both Section 1650 and *SFAS No. 52* recommend the use of the average rate for income statement amounts.

On the income statement, all items are translated at the current (average) rate, regardless of the type of revenue or expense, assuming that the revenue

SCHEDULE 17-6

Forsub Ltd.
Current-Rate Method Translation
December 31, 19x2

		Exchange rate	Translated amounts
BALANCE SHEET:			
Cash	P 15,000	$2.50	$ 37,500
Accounts receivable	15,000	2.50	37,500
Inventory	10,000	2.50	25,000
Land	40,000	2.50	100,000
Equipment	30,000	2.50	75,000
Accumulated depreciation	(5,000)	2.50	(12,500)
	P105,000		$262,500
Accounts payable	P 22,000	2.50	$ 55,000
Bonds payable	25,000	2.50	62,500
Common shares	50,000	2.00	100,000
Retained earnings	8,000		19,200
Cumulative translation gain*			25,800
	P105,000		$262,500
INCOME STATEMENT:			
Sales	P 60,000	$2.40	$144,000
Cost of sales:			
Beginning inventory	20,000		
Purchases	30,000		
	50,000		
Ending inventory	10,000		
	40,000	2.40	96,000
Gross margin	20,000		48,000
Operating expenses:			
Depreciation	5,000	2.40	12,000
Interest	3,000	2.40	7,200
Other	4,000	2.40	9,600
	12,000		28,800
Net income	P 8,000		$ 19,200

*Cumulative translation gain:
From 19x1, gain on P50,000 net investment
   P50,000 × ($2.30 − $2.00) = $15,000

From 19x2, gain on P50,000 net investment
   P50,000 × ($2.50 − $2.30) =   10,000

Gain on retained earnings
   P8,000 × ($2.50 − $2.40) =   800

                               $25,800

and expense accrued evenly through the year. Allocations of past costs, such as depreciation, are translated the same as are current costs, such as interest expense. As a result, the translated amount of net income is also equal to the current (average) rate times the net income as expressed in pants.

The cumulative translation gain of $25,800 that arises under the current-rate method can be broken down into three components: (1) the $15,000 gain arising from the first year's change in the exchange rate from $2.00 to $2.30 (Schedule 17-3), (2) an additional $10,000 gain in the current year, 19x2, caused by a further increase in the exchange rate from $2.30 to $2.50, and (3) an $800 gain on the retained earnings from the period of their generation (mid-19x2) to the end of 19x2, during which period the exchange rate changed from $2.40 to $2.50. These components of the cumulative gain are summarized at the bottom of Schedule 17-6.

Temporal Method

If, instead, the accounts of Forsub Ltd. are translated by using the temporal method, then the procedure is somewhat more complicated. Schedule 17-7 illustrates the application of the temporal method for 19x2. The monetary assets and liabilities are translated by using the current rate. The nonmonetary assets are translated at their historical rates. It is assumed that the ending inventory was purchased when the exchange rate was $2.45, and thus that is the historical rate for inventory. The specific historical rate for land is $2.00 and for the equipment is $2.30. The accumulated depreciation must be translated at the same rate as was used for the gross asset cost.

On the income statement, the revenues and expenses are translated at the rates that were in effect at the time that the revenues were realized or the costs incurred. For many revenue and expense items, realization coincides with recognition, so that the historical rate is essentially the same as the average rate for the period as was used in the current-rate method. Although the result is the same for some income statement items, the concept is quite different.

Under the current-rate method, cost of sales could be translated simply by taking the cost of sales in pants and multiplying it by the average exchange rate for the period. Under the temporal method, however, the cost of sales amount must be derived by multiplying the beginning inventory by its historical rate of $2.00, adding the purchases at the historical/average rate of $2.40, and subtracting the ending inventory at its historical rate of $2.45. The resultant figure for cost of sales, $87,500, cannot be derived directly by multiplying any exchange rate by the cost of sales in pants, P40,000.

Similarly, any depreciation or amortization expense must be translated at the exchange rates that existed at the time the original costs were incurred. In this example, the only such expense is the depreciation of the equipment. Since the equipment was purchased when the rate was $2.30, the depreciation expense must be translated at $2.30. Other expenses are translated at the rate that existed when they were accrued. It does not matter whether they have been paid in cash or not. Thus interest expense and other expenses have been translated at the average rate for the year.

The net income that results from using the temporal method amounts to $28,200 before considering any components of the translation loss. This amount cannot be derived directly from the original net income of P8,000; it must be obtained by working through the income statement and translating

SCHEDULE 17-7

Forsub Ltd.
Temporal Method Translation
December 31, 19x2

		Exchange rate		Translated amounts
		type	amount	
BALANCE SHEET:				
Cash	P 15,000	C	$2.50	$ 37,500
Accounts receivable	15,000	C	2.50	37,500
Inventory	10,000	H	2.45	24,500
Land	40,000	H	2.00	80,000
Equipment	30,000	H	2.30	69,000
Accumulated depreciation	(5,000)	H	2.30	(11,500)
	P105,000			$237,000
Accounts payable	P 22,000	C	2.50	$ 55,000
Bonds payable	25,000	C	2.50	62,500
Common shares	50,000	H	2.00	100,000
Retained earnings	8,000			28,200
	P105,000			245,700
Cumulative translation loss				$ 8,700
INCOME STATEMENT:				
Sales	P 60,000	H/A	$2.40	$144,000
Cost of sales:				
Beginning inventory	20,000	H	2.00	40,000
Purchases	30,000	H/A	2.40	72,000
	50,000			112,000
Ending inventory	10,000	H	2.45	24,500
	40,000			87,500
Gross margin	20,000			56,500
Operating expenses:				
Depreciation	5,000	H	2.30	11,500
Interest	3,000	A	2.40	7,200
Other	4,000	H/A	2.40	9,600
	12,000			28,300
Net income, before				
translation gains or losses	P 8,000			$ 28,200

Exchange rates:
  C   = current, year-end rate
  A   = average rate for the year
  H   = historical rate for the particular item
  H/A = historical rate, assumed to be the average rate for the year

all of its individual components by the appropriate historical rates. Note that the temporal method net income of $28,200 is quite different from the current-rate method net income of $19,200. This difference is due to the lags in expense recognition of two types of costs: inventory and depreciable fixed assets.

Translation of Forsub Ltd.'s accounts to dollars results in total assets of $237,500, as compared to total equities of $245,700. The cumulative translation loss therefore is $8,700. In Schedule 17-7, the cumulative translation loss is shown as a single amount pending disposition, rather than being distributed to the income statement, the balance sheet, or both. The reason is that when the foreign operation's statements are translated, the translation gain or loss is not part of the statements of the subsidiary, but is an amount that must be allocated or assigned *on the parent's consolidated statements*.

We know from Schedule 17-1 that $3,000 of the $8,700 cumulative translation loss arose in 19x1, and therefore that the loss arising in 19x2 must be the remainder, or $5,700. The $5,700 loss for 19x2 has two components: (1) a loss arising from the long-term liability of the bonds payable, and (2) a loss from the net current items. The loss on the bonds payable is the P25,000 balance times the exchange rate change during the period, $2.30 to $2.50. Thus the loss on the bonds is $5,000 for 19x2. The remainder of $700 is attributable to the current items.

The gain or loss from holding current monetary assets and liabilities can be computed by analyzing the flow of these items. Unlike the bonds payable in this example, the current assets and liabilities are not constant throughout the year. The impact of the exchange gains and losses must be measured only for the period of time that the current monetary items are in the enterprise. For example, sales revenue increased current monetary assets, either as cash or as accounts receivable, by P60,000. Assuming that the sales were even throughout the year, we can measure the gain from holding monetary assets resulting from the sales by multiplying the P60,000 by the change in the exchange rate from the average for the year ($2.40) to the end of the year ($2.50). Similarly, the current expenses (or expenditures) that caused either a decline in monetary assets or an increase in monetary liabilities must be taken into account.

The easiest way to measure the net gain or loss from the current monetary assets and liabilities is to construct a funds-flow statement, with funds defined as net current monetary assets. Starting with the beginning-of-year balance of these net assets, we can add the inflows and subtract the outflows, to arrive at the year-end balance of net current monetary assets expressed in pants. We then need only to convert each balance or flow at the exchange rate in effect at the time of the balance or flow, and find the difference at year-end between the balance in foreign currency and the derived amount in domestic currency.

Such a funds-flow statement is shown at the top of Schedule 17-8. The ending balance in pants is P8,000, as can be verified by referring to Schedule 17-5. The year-end balance is equivalent to $20,000 at the balance sheet date. The sum of the inflows and outflows, however, when translated at the rates in effect during the year, amounts to $20,700. In effect, the $20,700 shows what the ending balance of the net current monetary assets would have been if Domestic Corporation had maintained all of its Pantanian balances

SCHEDULE 17-8

Forsub Ltd.
Temporal Method: Analysis of
Cumulative Translation Loss, 19x2
Dr. (Cr.)

		Exchange rate	Translated amounts
AMOUNTS ARISING IN 19X2:			
Current monetary items:			
Balance, January 1, 19x2	P15,000	$2.30	$ 34,500
Changes during 19x2:			
Sales revenue	60,000	2.40	144,000
Purchases of inventory	(30,000)	2.40	(72,000)
Interest expense	(3,000)	2.40	(7,200)
Other expenses	(4,000)	2.40	(9,600)
Purchase of equipment	(30,000)	2.30	(69,000)
Derived balance, Dec. 31, 19x2			20,700
Actual balance, Dec. 31, 19x2	P 8,000	2.50	20,000
Net exchange loss from current monetary items, 19x2			700
Long-term debt:			
19x2 loss arising from change in exchange rate during 19x2:			
(P25,000) × [$2.50 − 2.30] =			5,000
Total for 19x2			5,700
AMOUNTS RELATING TO PREVIOUS PERIODS (SCHEDULE 17-1):			
Current monetary items (gain)	$ (4,500)		
Long-term debt	7,500		
Total loss for previous years			3,000
Cumulative translation loss, December 31, 19x2			$ 8,700

in dollars rather than in pants, and had converted to and from dollars only on the transaction dates. Since the actual dollar-equivalent balance of the accounts in pants is only $20,000, Domestic Corporation has suffered a loss of $700 by having Forsub Ltd. hold balances in pants.

The remainder of Schedule 17-8 summarizes the remaining amounts included in the $8,700 cumulative translation loss at December 31, 19x2. As we stated above, a total of $3,000 of the loss pertains to 19x1, while the remaining loss of $5,700 pertains to 19x2.

Disposition of this cumulative loss may cause additional complications. When Domestic consolidates Forsub's translated statements, the loss may be (1) capitalized as a separate component of shareholders' equity, (2) split between retained earnings (for the 19x1 loss) and current income (for the 19x2 loss), or (3) disaggregated and reported as though the individual gains and losses arose from foreign currency transactions. The first two alternatives pose no serious difficulties. The disaggregation alternative, however, requires careful analysis.

Schedule 17-9 shows the disaggregation of the losses for 19x1 and 19x2 in separate columns in accordance with the *Handbook* recommendations. The loss for each year is distributed between (1) prior years' income, as reflected in retained earnings, (2) current income, and (3) future years' income, via deferred charges or credits. When Domestic Corporation prepares its consolidated financial statements at December 31, 19x2, consolidated retained earnings would be decreased by the $3,000 relating to 19x1 income; the 19x2 income statement would be charged with a translation loss of $3,450; and the balance sheet would show a deferred charge of $8,250.

The results shown in Schedule 17-9 are in accordance with the *CICA Handbook* recommendations for consolidating an integrated foreign subsidiary. The results are also consistent with the view that the temporal method should yield the same results as would have been obtained if the subsidiary's transactions had actually been foreign currency transactions of the parent.

SCHEDULE 17-9

**Distribution of Temporal Method
Translation Losses (Gains)**

	Amounts arising in:		
	19x1	19x2	Cumulative
TO PREVIOUS YEAR'S INCOME (RETAINED EARNINGS):			
Current items	$(4,500)	n/a	$(4,500)
Long-term debt:			
Amortization of 19x1 loss	1,500	n/a	1,500
Total			$(3,000)
TO CURRENT YEAR'S INCOME:			
Current items	—	700	700
Long-term debt:			
Amortization of 19x1 loss	1,500	n/a	1,500
Amortization of 19x2 loss	n/a	1,250	1,250
Total			3,450
TO FUTURE YEARS' INCOME:			
Long-term debt:			
Unamortized 19x1 loss	4,500	n/a	4,500
Unamortized 19x2 loss	n/a	3,750	3,750
Total			8,250
Total translation loss	$3,000	$5,700	$8,700
n/a = not applicable			

SUMMARY

When a Canadian corporation conducts part of its business in a foreign country through a foreign subsidiary, a number of problems arise that are not present when we account only for domestic subsidiaries. Chapter 15 discussed many of these problems, of which the most pressing and most pervasive is the problem of translating the results of the foreign subsidiary's operations into Canadian dollars.

In an era of floating exchange rates, there are constant fluctuations in the relative values of the various currencies. When a parent corporation reports the results of its foreign operations in its domestic financial statements, the changing exchange rates create translation gains and/or losses. These translation gains and losses are not the result of transactions between the parent and the foreign subsidiary, but rather are unrealized amounts relating entirely to the subsidiary's host-country activities.

Several methods of translating the statements of the foreign operation have evolved, none of them fully satisfactory in reflecting the parent corporation's interest in its foreign operations. All methods yield some form of translation gain or loss, but the accounting exposure that arises as the result of any particular translation method has little, if any, correspondence to the real economic exposure of the subsidiary or the parent to the effects of changes in the exchange rate.

Prior to the effective date of the current Section 1650 (fiscal periods beginning on or after July 1, 1983), the current/noncurrent method of translation had been the most popular in Canada. This method recognizes the fact that current assets and liabilities will be realized in the short term, and takes the gains and losses arising from current balances into income. But it also recognizes that noncurrent assets (usually nonmonetary in nature) are implicit hedges for noncurrent liabilities (usually monetary). The cash flows generated by the noncurrent assets will be used to extinguish the noncurrent liabilities, and thus the current/noncurrent method translates all noncurrent balances at historical rates, recognizing no translation gains or losses on long-term assets or liabilities. The current/noncurrent method has the additional advantage that the accounting exposure is generally quite small, so that there is usually only a small translation gain or loss to account for.

The current-rate method of translation has received increasing attention, and is the method recommended by the *CICA Handbook* for self-sustaining or relatively autonomous foreign subsidiaries. The current-rate method accepts the fact that the subsidiary's transactions occurred in a foreign currency, and maintains the foreign currency as the unit of measure for the subsidiary's operations. Upon translation, the relationships among the subsidiary's account balances are preserved, and the translated amounts are consolidated with the parent company's accounts in preparing the consolidated financial statements. Since all of the accounts are translated at the current rate, the accounting exposure is always equal to the net investment of the parent in the subsidiary.

In general, the translation gain or loss under the current-rate method can be accounted for either by including it in income on the parent's consolidated income statement, or by deferring it and reporting it on the balance sheet either as a deferred charge/credit or as a separate component of shareholders' equity. The alternative of disaggregating the gain or loss does not seem to be logical under the current-rate method, since the method does not distinguish between the various types of transactions and balances that the subsidiary has. The disposition of the gain or loss recommended in the *Handbook* is to treat it as a separate component of the parent's consolidated shareholders' equity.

The temporal method reflects the view that a foreign subsidiary is simply an extension of the parent that happens to be in a foreign country. In the terminology of Chapter 15, the temporal method is consistent with the operations of a home-country-oriented or ethnocentric international corporation. The temporal method translates the accounts of the foreign subsidiary into the amounts that would have existed if the subsidiary's transactions had actually occurred in Canadian dollars. Thus the unit of measure for the foreign operation is not really the host-country currency, but rather is deemed to be the Canadian dollar.

The *CICA Handbook* recommendations adopt the temporal method for reporting the results of operations for an integrated foreign subsidiary. The concept of an integrated subsidiary is somewhat similar to that of a home-country-oriented foreign operation, in that the parent is presumed to have direct and significant influence in the operations of the subsidiary. Therefore, it is logical to view the operations of the subsidiary as though they had been conducted directly by the parent.

In accordance with the view of the subsidiary's operations as being substantively a series of foreign currency transactions of the parent, the *Handbook* recommends that the translation gains and losses arising from application of the temporal method be disaggregated and accounted for the same as for foreign currency transactions. An alternative approach, which is logical but which is not envisaged by the *Handbook*, is simply to report each year's translation gain or loss in the parent company's income statement. This alternative is certainly easier and may be more suitable in certain circumstances, depending upon the nature of the translation gains and losses, and the users of the statements.

The primary purpose of translating the results of a foreign operation is to enable the parent corporation to report the results of the foreign segment on its own financial statements. The translated amounts and the translation gains or losses do not affect the foreign subsidiary's separate-entity statements at all.

In this chapter, we have examined the alternatives available for translating foreign operations and for the disposition of the translation gains and losses on the parent's statements. We have not, however, looked at the problems of actually preparing the consolidated statements, or of reporting on the equity basis any unconsolidated subsidiaries or significantly influenced foreign affiliates. These problems are examined in Chapter 18.

SELF-STUDY PROBLEM 17-1[4]

In early 19x1, Var Corporation established a subsidiary in Simonia. The subsidiary was named McDonald Ltd., and Var's investment was $1,250,000.

---

4 The solutions to the self-study problems are at the end of the book, following Chapter 18.

When this investment was translated into Simonion Frasers (the currency of Simonia), the initial capitalization amounted to SF500,000.

McDonald negotiated a three-year loan of SF200,000 from a Simonian bank (when the exchange rate was $2.40) and subsequently purchased depreciable assets for SF600,000 (the exchange rate was $2.30). McDonald then began operations, and at the end of 19x2, its comparative balance sheet and income statement appeared as shown below.

McDonald paid most of its net income to Var as dividends at the end of each year, but owing to currency restrictions, cash accumulated in McDonald's coffers. Thus in 19x2 (when the exchange rate was $1.90), McDonald invested SF200,000 in nonmonetary temporary investments.

Exchange rates for the Simonion Fraser were as follows:

19x1 average	$2.20
19x1 year-end	$2.00
19x2 average	$1.70
19x2 year-end	$1.50

Required:
Assume that McDonald is a self-sustaining subsidiary. Determine how the financial statement amounts shown in McDonald's financial statements would affect Var Corporation's consolidated statements for 19x1 and for 19x2, including disposition of the cumulative translation gain or loss.

McDonald Ltd.
Income Statement
Years ending December 31

	19x2	19x1
Revenue	SF300,000	SF220,000
Depreciation	SF 60,000	SF 60,000
Interest expense	40,000	40,000
Other expenses	120,000	80,000
	SF220,000	SF180,000
Net income	SF 80,000	SF 40,000

McDonald Ltd.
Balance Sheets
December 31

	19x2	19x1
Cash	SF 30,000	SF160,000
Accounts receivable	40,000	30,000
Temporary investments (at cost)	200,000	—
Fixed assets	600,000	600,000
Accumulated depreciation	(120,000)	(60,000)
Total assets	SF750,000	SF730,000
Accounts payable	SF 10,000	SF 20,000
Notes payable (due January 1, 19x4)	200,000	200,000
Common shares	500,000	500,000
Retained earnings	40,000	10,000
Total equities	SF750,000	SF730,000

SELF-STUDY PROBLEM 17-2

Refer to the information in SSP17-1. Assume instead that McDonald Ltd. is an integrated foreign operation, under Section 1650 of the *CICA Handbook*.

Required:
a. Translate McDonald's 19x1 financial statements.
b. Disaggregate the 19x1 translation loss or gain. Prove the amount of gain or loss relating to current monetary items. Indicate how the translation gains or losses would appear on Var Corporation's consolidated statements.
c. Translate McDonald's 19x2 financial statements.
d. Determine the amount of translation gain or loss on the current monetary items for 19x2.
e. Show the disaggregated amounts of the cumulative translation gain or loss and how they would be reported on Var's 19x2 consolidated statements.

REVIEW QUESTIONS

17-1 Distinguish between foreign currency **transactions** and foreign currency **operations**.

17-2 Explain the differences between these four translation methods:
a. Monetary/nonmonetary
b. Temporal
c. Current rate
d. Current/noncurrent

17-3 Which assets and liabilities of a foreign operation are translated at the same rate under all of the translation methods?

17-4 Why is the common share account of a foreign subsidiary translated at the historical rate under all translation methods?

17-5 Under what circumstances will the monetary/nonmonetary method yield the same results as the temporal method?

17-6 Which translation method views the foreign subsidiary's operations as though they were foreign currency transactions of the parent?

17-7 What is meant by the **accounting exposure** of a foreign operation? How is the accounting exposure measured?

17-8 How does the accounting exposure under the temporal method differ from the accounting exposure under the current-rate method?

17-9 For a given foreign operation for a given accounting period, is it possible for the accounting exposure under the temporal method to result in a translation loss, while the accounting exposure under the current-rate method results in a translation gain? Explain.

17-10 Some people consider a translation method to be desirable when it results in the same *relative* values for the translated assets and liabilities as for the untranslated amounts. Which method or methods achieve this result?

17-11 Prior to 1983, what was the most common translation method used by Canadian companies for their foreign operations?

17-12 Explain how the current/noncurrent method assumes the existence of a hedge.

17-13 Define **economic exposure**. Distinguish between economic exposure and accounting exposure.

17-14 What is the basic criterion by which the appropriateness of a translation method should be judged in a specific situation?

17-15 In the case of many foreign operations, gains and losses arising from translation will not be realized by the parent corporation. What then is the argument in favour of immediate recognition of translation gains and losses in the parent's consolidated income statement?

17-16 Forop Ltd. is a foreign subsidiary of Domop Inc. Domop's accounting exposure to exchange rate changes when translating the accounts of Forop is a substantial net liability exposure. Domop's management expects the foreign currency in which Forop operates to increase in value relative to the Canadian dollar; such an increase will result in a large translation loss. The management of Domop proposes to enter into a forward contract to receive an equivalent amount of foreign currency in order to hedge against the potential translation loss. Would you recommend that Domop's management follow their proposed course of action? Explain.

17-17 Distinguish between **self-sustaining** foreign operations and **integrated** foreign operations.

17-18 What translation method is recommended by the *CICA Handbook* for **integrated** foreign operations? Why is this method recommended?

17-19 What recommendation does the *Handbook* make regarding the financial statement disposition of translation gains or losses for integrated foreign operations? Why?

17-20 How can management decide whether a foreign operation is integrated or self-sustaining?

17-21 Mammoth Corporation has subsidiaries in thirteen different countries, operating in ten different currencies. Do all thirteen have to be viewed the same way, or can some be considered integrated operations while others are considered self-sustaining?

17-22 What translation method is recommended in the *Handbook* for self-sustaining foreign operations?

17-23 Why does the *Handbook* (and *SFAS No. 52*) recommend that the cumulative translation gain or loss from self-sustaining foreign operations be shown as a separate component of consolidated shareholders' equity?

17-24 Under the current-rate method, why are the revenue and expense accounts translated at exchange rates that existed during the year, rather than at the current rate at the balance sheet date?

17-25 How does the translation of cost of goods sold differ between the current-rate method and the temporal method?

17-26 How does the translation of depreciation and amortization differ under the current-rate method as opposed to the temporal method?

17-27 Explain how the translation gain or loss on current monetary items can be computed. Is the amount of gain or loss affected by the translation method used?

CASE 17-1   Champion Distributors Limited

Champion Distributors Limited is a Canadian public company that has been undergoing rapid expansion. The company is based in a major Canadian port, and several years ago found it necessary to open a sales office in the United States, in order to transact business directly in that country.

Champion also has a wholly owned subsidiary, located in Singapore, which manufactures one of the main products that Champion sells in Canada. Substantially all of the Singapore subsidiary's sales are to Champion. There is a second (80% owned) subsidiary, located in the Republic of Ireland, which was acquired in an attempt to diversify. This company sells exclusively through its own sales offices throughout Northern Europe, and has very few transactions with Champion, except for the regular payment of dividends.

Required:
Recommend the appropriate accounting policies for Champion to follow with respect to each of these foreign operations. Support your recommendations.
[SMA]

CASE 17-2   Marten Manufacturing Limited

Marten Manufacturing Limited (Marten) is a Canadian manufacturer of automatic blood testing equipment. United Kingdom Imports Limited (Imports) was one of Marten's foreign customers. In December of 1986, the owner of Imports advised Richard Biggs, the president of Marten, that, as a consequence of a heart attack he had suffered earlier in the year, he wished to sell Imports. Biggs and other managers at Marten judged that the purchase of Imports would be desirable. The negotiations that ensued were amicable and brief, and Marten purchased Imports for 1.2 million U.K. pounds in cash on January 1, 1987. Marten paid the full price on that date.

Marten's comptroller, Elizabeth Collins, knew that Biggs wished to be able to show a high return on equity from Imports — a point he could use as part of the justification of the purchase of Imports to Marten's shareholders. She also knew that Biggs initially planned to operate Imports as a sales branch for Marten's products. However, the choice of an advantageous method of currency translation might call for another way of organizing Imports. If this turned out to be the case, Collins wished to present this alternative to Biggs. Finally, she wanted to minimize any exchange losses as Marten was planning a public offering of its own shares in 1988. She had reasons to believe that the Canadian dollar would likely strengthen against the United Kingdom pound during 1987.

Collins began her analysis by preparing, according to Canadian generally accepted accounting principles, the balance sheet of Imports for the date of acquisition, January 1, 1987, and her best estimates of the forecast balance sheet as at December 31, 1987 (see Exhibit 1), and forecast statement of earnings and retained earnings for 1987 (see Exhibit 3). She then obtained the relevant historical Canadian dollar equivalents of one United Kingdom pound, and the relevant estimates of forecast exchange rates (see Exhibit 2).

Required:
a. Which generally accepted method of foreign currency translation would show the higher earnings for Marten? Why?
b. Which method should Collins recommend and how should Imports be organized in order to use this method?
[SMA]

EXHIBIT 1

United Kingdom Imports Limited
Balance Sheet
(in thousands)

	Actual 1/1/87 U.K. pound	Forecast 31/12/87 U.K. pound
Net monetary assets	£ 200	£ 360
Inventory	500	650
Fixed assets:		
Buildings and equipment	2,500	2,800
Less accumulated depreciation	(1,000)	(1,560)
	£2,200	£2,250
Long-term debt (Note 1)	£1,000	£1,000
Shareholders' equity:		
Common shares	1,100	1,100
Retained earnings	100	150
	£2,200	£2,250

Note 1: The 10%, £1 million long-term debt was issued at face value on January 1, 1985, and is due on December 31, 1991.

EXHIBIT 2

Canadian Dollar Equivalents of One United Kingdom Pound

HISTORICAL RATES

January 1, 1985, date of purchase of buildings and equipment by Imports	$5.00
November 15, 1986, date of purchase of 1/1/87 inventory balance by Imports	$2.10
January 1, 1987	$2.00

FORECAST RATES

1987 Average rate	$1.80
July 1, 1987, scheduled date of purchase of additional fixed assets	$1.75
December 31, 1987	$1.50
Average rate for December 31, 1987, closing inventory assuming FIFO accounting flow of goods	$1.70

EXHIBIT 3

United Kingdom Imports Limited
Forecast Statement of Earnings and Retained Earnings
For the year ending December 31, 1987
(in thousands)

	U.K. pound
Sales	£10,000
Cost of sales: Opening inventory	500
Purchases	8,000
	8,500
Closing inventory	650
	7,850
Gross profit	2,150
Selling and administration	1,140
Depreciation (Note 1)	560
Interest	100
	1,800
Income before income taxes	350
Income taxes	140
Net Income	210
Retained earnings (1/1/87)	100
	310
Dividends (Note 2)	160
Retained Earnings (31/12/87)	£ 150

Notes:
(1) Depreciation is calculated straight-line over five years. A full year's depreciation is taken in the year of acquisition. No disposals are anticipated for 1987.
(2) To be declared and paid December 31, 1987.

Video Displays, Inc. (Part B)

In early 1982, Video Displays, Inc. (VDI) became dissatisfied with the performance of the U.S. distributor of its video display units (see Case 16-2) and decided to establish its own sales subsidiary in the United States. Consequently, in February 1982, VDI formed Vidisplay Corp. (VC) under the laws of California. Vidisplay Corp. would sell the VDI video display units (made in Canada) directly to the U.S. computer terminal and word processing manufacturers. The units would be imported into the United States from Canada, and the price to VC would be the manufacturing cost to VDI plus 10%. Since VC is a subsidiary of VDI, VC would be far better suited to deal with manufacturers than was the independent U.S. distributor. VC would be able to speak directly to VDI and would be able to negotiate design changes in order to make VDI's units meet the manufacturer's needs and specifications.

VDI had a reputation for high quality and excellent quality control, which are vital factors from the viewpoint of the computer terminal manufacturers. Therefore, VC was able to generate significant sales rather quickly. In the first four months of operation, VC obtained orders for over 6,000 units at an average price of about $250.

VDI's primary competition was from the Far East, particularly from Taiwan. Most of the cost of a video display unit can be attributed to the cost of parts, which makes up about 70%-80% of the total cost. Since the labour component of cost is small, there is little direct labour cost advantage in Taiwanese production. However, most of the cathode ray tubes (the single most costly component) are produced in Taiwan, and the CRT producers had simply integrated forward into the production of video display units.

In mid-1982, the U.S. dollar strengthened considerably against all major foreign currencies. However, owing to the strong dependence of the Canadian dollar on the U.S. economy, and high interest rates in Canada (which were competitive with U.S. interest rates), the Canadian dollar fell less against the U.S. dollar than did most other currencies. Thus, while the prices of Canadian goods fell in terms of the U.S. dollar, the fall was less than that of goods from other countries.

By the end of 1982, VC had delivered 4,800 units to its U.S. customers and had on hand 1,400 additional units, which were acquired from VDI in December, and were being held by VC pending final acceptance by the customers. VC's furniture and equipment were acquired in February and March, and were financed by VDI's capital investment and a $1 million four-year loan from the Bank of America.

Required:

a. Translate the income statement and balance sheet for Vidisplay Corp., the U.S. subsidiary, into Canadian dollars under each of the following translation methods:

1. Current/noncurrent
2. Temporal
3. Current rate

   Assume that the average exchange rate for VC's 1982 operating period was $1 U.S. = $1.30 Canadian, and that the amount payable by VC to VDI is a liability of $260,000 Canadian.

b. Evaluate the results of the three alternative translation methods in light of the economic risk exposure of Vidisplay Corp. Which method is most likely to reflect in VDI's statements the impact of foreign currency fluctuations on Vidisplay's operations? Which method seems most appropriate for VDI to use, given the nature of Vidisplay's operations and its relationship with the parent, VDI?

Vidisplay Corp.
Trial Balance
December 31, 1982
(in U.S. dollars)

	Dr.	Cr.
Cash	$ 50,000	
Accounts receivable	800,000	
Inventory	300,000	
Furniture and equipment	350,000	
Accumulated depreciation		$ 50,000
Accounts payable		75,000
Due to Canadian parent co.		200,000
Note payable (due March 1, 1986)		1,000,000
Common shares		100,000
Sales		1,200,000
Cost of sales	1,000,000	
Operating expenses	100,000	
Income tax expense	25,000	
	$2,625,000	$2,625,000

Assumed exchange rate for $1.00 U.S.:

December 31, 1981		$1.15 Canadian	
1982: January	1.16	July	1.30
February	1.20	August	1.25
March	1.20	September	1.30
April	1.24	October	1.28
May	1.25	November	1.32
June	1.30	December	1.36
December 31, 1982			1.40

CASE 17-4   Hi-Tech Industries Ltd.

Hi-Tech Industries Ltd. is a corporation formed under the provisions of the *Canada Business Corporations Act*. Its shares are held by a small group of private investors. Hi-Tech is a company that is engaged primarily in various facets of computer applications and computer software development. It carries out its business mainly through a series of wholly owned subsidiaries.

In 1985, Hi-Tech acquired 100% of the shares of Houston Dataserve, Inc., a computer service bureau located in Houston, Texas. The purchase was for cash, and was financed by borrowing 80% of the necessary funds from a Houston bank on a five-year renewable term loan. The remaining 20% was financed by liquidating some of Hi-Tech's temporary investments.

Houston Dataserve (HDI) owned a large main-frame computer and sold computing time to business clients in the Houston area. The company specialized in the processing of oil industry exploration data, using special programs that had been developed by HDI. However, the company would rent computer time, either in-house or time-sharing, for any purpose. The range of services went from straight time rental, with no provisions of programs or processing expertise, to full-service computer applications, operating essentially as though HDI were the data-processing department of the client company.

By 1985, the computer service bureau industry was in a depression, owing to a sharp decline in processing costs that enabled clients to acquire their own in-house micro- and minicomputers. HDI had fallen into a state of profit decline in the early 1980s; the profits turned to losses in 1984 and 1985. The declining fortunes of HDI made it possible for Hi-Tech to acquire the company at a price significantly below the fair market value of HDI's facilities and the estimated value of its customer base.

In order to turn HDI back into a profitable business, Hi-Tech undertook a series of moves. The first was to lend HDI the money to reorganize its operations and to update much of the peripheral equipment, especially the terminals and printers located in clients' premises.

The second was to supply HDI with the advanced videotext and graphics software that had been developed by Hi-Tech's other subsidiaries. HDI paid a royalty for the use of the software. But the software gave HDI an important technological edge in its market through providing clients with a capability that could not be matched by direct competitors or duplicated on the small computers that had seriously eroded the computer-service-bureau market.

Third, Hi-Tech organized a software development division in HDI to extend many of Hi-Tech's other products and services into the lucrative corporate market in the southwest United States. Most, but not all, of this new division's activities were directed from the Canadian operations; it was expected that the division would become more self-sufficient sometime in the future, and would perhaps then be spun off from HDI as a separate company.

The most recent move was the acquisition in 1988 of HDI's major service bureau competitor in Houston, McClean Service Corp. Hi-Tech purchased all of the outstanding shares of McClean by using funds obtained primarily by having HDI declare a substantial dividend. Hi-Tech then had McClean sell all of its assets to HDI for $1 and liquidated McClean. HDI sold most of the McClean assets and transferred the McClean customers and applications to the HDI equipment. This last move was expected to complete the earnings turnaround for HDI; HDI was expected to make a positive contribution to Hi-Tech's consolidated earnings for the first time in 1988.

In 1985, 1986, and 1987, Hi-Tech had used the current-rate method of translation for HDI because it seemed the easiest method to use. However, the company was considering broadening its equity base through the sale of additional shares to new investors, and the management of Hi-Tech was considering engaging an auditor and striving for a "clean" audit opinion. Management therefore retained an accounting advisor to advise Hi-Tech on the reporting implications for 1988 of the investments in HDI and McClean, as well as on any other matters relating to their U.S. activities.

Required:
Assume the role of the accounting advisor. Write the requested report to the managers of Hi-Tech.

Vulcan Manufacturing Limited   CASE 17-5

Vulcan Manufacturing Limited (VML) is a Canadian-based multinational plastics firm, with subsidiaries in several foreign countries and worldwide consolidated total assets of $500 million. VML's shares are listed on a Canadian stock exchange. Since 1983, the company has included supplementary current cost information in its annual report.

VML is attracted by the growing demand for its products in developing countries. In recognition of trade barriers designed to encourage domestic production in those countries and in order to service local demand, VML incorporated a foreign subsidiary in a South American country on September 1, 1984. The subsidiary, South American Plastics Inc. (SAPI), manufactures patented sheet-plastic and sells virtually all of its output locally. Also, almost all labour and raw materials are provided locally. SAPI finances its day-to-day activities from its own operations and local borrowing.

During 1984 and 1985, the South American country suffered an inflation rate of more than 100%, accompanied by substantial devaluation of the local currency and a drastic increase in interest rates. The government is expected to impose wage and price controls in 1986. The inflation rate is expected to stabilize at more moderate levels sometime in 1986 or 1987.

The chief financial officer (CFO) of VML has recently received SAPI's draft financial statements for the year ended August 31, 1985, together with some comments prepared by SAPI's controller. (Extracts from the draft financial statements and controller's comments are provided in Exhibits I and II.) He is somewhat surprised by the return on investment of nearly 12%. This figure is well above the target rate agreed upon for bonus purposes, which was set at 3% in recognition of start-up costs associated with the first year of operations. The apparently favourable performance will result in large bonuses having to be paid to SAPI's management.

Increases in SAPI's domestic selling price have kept pace with the general rate of inflation and with increases in input prices and borrowing costs in the South American country. The CFO is satisfied that the inflation and devaluation the country has experienced has not seriously affected SAPI's cash flows from operations.

VML assesses its exposure to exchange rate changes on a worldwide basis. Each subsidiary is required to submit to head office a report on its projected foreign currencies position for the upcoming quarter. The report lists receivables and payables and other committed cash flows to be settled in various currencies during the upcoming quarter. The CFO makes decisions on appropriate hedging strategies once such reports are received. SAPI's report for the first quarter of the 1985-86 fiscal year has just been received (Exhibit III).

In the annual report to Canadian shareholders for the year ended August 31, 1985, the CFO wants to communicate to shareholders the economic impact that inflation and devaluation in the South American country have had on VML's investment in SAPI. He is concerned that gains or losses arising from translation of the statements in accordance with Section 1650 of the *CICA Handbook* will mislead shareholders. The CFO believes that the exchange gains and losses will obscure the true impact of foreign inflation and devaluation on SAPI's economic value in Canadian dollar terms. He has called the audit partner and you, the CA in charge of the audit, into his office. The following conversation ensues:

CFO: "We have to issue our financial statements soon, and we have to apply Section 1650 to our South American subsidiary. I must confess that I don't know Section 1650 as well as you two do. My staff tells me that we must use the temporal method this year, due to the local hyperinflation, although I confess that I don't see why. Apparently we will have a choice between the temporal method and the current-rate method once the inflation rate stabilizes, which I expect to happen in 1986 or 1987. I am very reluctant to use the temporal method on this year's statements. It forces me to include fictitious gains and losses in our consolidated income statement."

Partner: "Your staff is correct in stating that the *Handbook* requires the use of the temporal method for the year just ended. However, shareholders should not be misled by exchange gains or losses in consolidated income provided that they are fully disclosed as such."

EXHIBIT 1

South American Plastics Inc.
Extracts from Draft Financial Statements
Balance Sheet
August 31, 1985
Foreign Currency Units* (in thousands)

	1985
ASSETS	
Current	
Cash	FCU 10,020
Marketable securities, at cost	3,120
Accounts receivable	93,000
Inventory, at cost	67,200
Prepaid expenses	8,040
	181,380
Fixed	
Cost	143,111
Less accumulated depreciation	14,311
	128,800
	FCU310,180
LIABILITIES AND SHAREHOLDERS' EQUITY	
Current	
Revenue received in advance from customer	FCU 10,000
Accounts payable	38,400
Taxes payable	4,920
Other payables	11,820
	65,140
Non-current	
Long-term debt	157,200
Shareholders' Equity	
Capital stock	51,000
Retained earnings	36,840
	87,840
	FCU310,180

*A Foreign Currency Unit (FCU) is a unit of the currency used in the South
American country in which SAPI is located.

CFO: "I guess I just do not understand Section 1650. For example, how might
the adoption of the current-rate method in 1986 or 1987 improve matters? It seems to me that an overall exchange loss will arise, if the rate
keeps on going down. What does the loss mean? As long as our subsidiary's cash flows keep pace with local inflation, it will be able to maintain

EXHIBIT 2

South American Plastics Inc.
Controller's Comments on Financial Statements

1. OPENING BALANCES
   SAPI's balance sheet on September 1, 1984, consisted of cash of FCU 208,200,000, long-term debt of FCU 157,200,000 and common stock of FCU 51,000,000.

2. MARKETABLE SECURITIES
   The marketable securities, portfolio equity investments in a number of local companies, were purchased when one FCU = $0.30. The investments are considered temporary and can be sold easily on short notice. The aggregate market value for the securities at August 31, 1985, is FCU 3,000,000.

3. INVENTORIES
   Inventories were purchased when one FCU = $0.30. The Canadian parent company, Vulcan Manufacturing Limited, values inventory at the lower of cost and replacement cost. The aggregate replacement cost of the inventory is FCU 100,000,000.

4. PREPAID EXPENSES
   The amounts, representing prepaid rent and property taxes, were paid when one FCU = $0.25.

5. FIXED ASSETS
   Fixed assets were purchased shortly after the date of SAPI's formation, at a time when one FCU = $0.40. The current replacement cost of the fixed assets (in their current condition) is FCU 200,000,000.

6. CURRENT LIABILITIES
   All current liabilities were incurred at a time when one FCU = $0.25.

7. LONG-TERM DEBT
   The debt represents a floating interest rate loan which will be repaid in foreign currency units on August 31, 1988.

8. RETAINED EARNINGS
   No dividends were paid during the 1984-85 fiscal year.

9. EXCHANGE RATES

September 1, 1984	1 FCU = $0.40
August 31, 1985	1 FCU = $0.20
Average rate for the period September 1984 to August 1985	1 FCU = $0.30

its expected rate of profitability and therefore its ability to pay dividends to us. Yet shareholders will see an exchange loss!"

Partner: "I will have CA prepare a report that explains to you how the exchange gains or losses under either translation method tie in with the notion of risk underlying Section 1650. We will also explain how this notion alleviates your concern about communicating the true economic risk to shareholders. CA will recommend ways to tell the whole story to shareholders."

EXHIBIT 3

South American Plastics Inc.
Projected Foreign Currencies Position Report
Prepared by the Controller
First Quarter of the Fiscal Year Beginning September 1, 1985
(in thousands)

	Foreign Currency Units (FCU)	Deutsche Marks
Amounts to be received during first quarter of the fiscal year beginning September 1, 1985:		
Accounts receivable at August 31, 1985	FCU 20,000	
Foreign currency purchase contract at August 31, 1985	—	DM 5,000 (Note 1)
Signed sales commitments from customers at August 31, 1985	7,500	7,000 (Note 2)
	27,500	12,000
Amounts to be paid during first quarter of the fiscal year beginning September 1, 1985:		
Accounts, taxes, other payables at August 31,1985	50,000	—
Signed purchase commitments to suppliers at August 31, 1985	8,500	5,000 (Note 3)
	58,500	5,000
Net exposed position in various currencies for first quarter of the fiscal year beginning September 1, 1985	FCU (31,000)	DM 7,000

Note 1:
Represents a Deutsche mark forward contract to receive 5,000 Deutsche marks, maturing on November 1, 1985.

Note 2:
Represents a one-time sales order from a customer in West Germany, to be delivered and settled during October 1985.

Note 3:
Represents an amount owing to a West German supplier to be paid on November 15, 1985, for equipment to be delivered in October 1985.

CFO: "Sounds great. I would also like CA to provide advice on any other important issues related to SAPI. For starters, I have some concerns about the way our bonus plan for SAPI's management is working. One possibility I am considering is to evaluate SAPI's performance in Canadian dollar terms."

That afternoon, CA and the partner meet in his office to discuss the report requested by the CFO. SAPI has just appointed its auditors for the year ended August 31, 1985. In addition to the report for the CFO, the partner asks you to prepare a draft letter to SAPI's auditors specifying areas of suspected audit risk as well as other pertinent guidelines.

Required:
Prepare the report to the CFO and the draft letter to SAPI's auditors.
[CICA]

CASE 17-6   Willard Co. Ltd.

Willard Co. Ltd. is a medium-sized Canadian company, incorporated in 1954, the shares of which are traded on the Toronto Stock Exchange. It began its operations as a processor and distributor of frozen fiddleheads, but quickly branched out until it provided a full line of Canadian specialty foods. Some of these products were processed by Willard itself, while some were processed for Willard under contract with other Canadian companies.

The company's strategic plan calls for steady growth in sales and earnings. Accordingly, expansion into the lucrative United States market in 1980 is under serious consideration. A major concern is changes in the exchange rate of the Canadian and American dollars as the company has received very different predictions from various analysts with respect to the exchange rate.

Willard is considering the following proposals. One would involve setting up sales offices in the United States with orders filled from Willard's Canadian warehouses. The sales offices would be responsible for sales, billings, and collections. All transactions would be in U.S. dollars.

Alternatively, Willard is considering establishing a wholly owned subsidiary in the United States to process and distribute a full line of specialty foods. It has not yet been decided how to finance the purchase of plant and equipment for this subsidiary.

The president has asked you, the controller, to prepare a report for possible use at a meeting of the board of directors. Specifically, he wants you to recommend which of the above proposals is preferable with respect to the impact of each on current and future reported income. He wants you to support your recommendation and to limit your discussion to foreign currency translation issues, ignoring hedging and income tax considerations.

Required:
Prepare the report to the president.
[SMA]

P17-1

On January 1, 19x6, Wilson Ltd. formed a foreign subsidiary that issued all of its currently outstanding common shares on that date. Selected captions from the balance sheets, all of which are shown in local currency units (LCU), are as follows:

	19x7	19x6
Accounts receivable, net of allowance for uncollectable accounts of 2,200 LCU at December 31, 19x7 and 2,000 LCU at December 31, 19x6	40,000	35,000
Inventories, at cost	80,000	75,000
Property, plant, and equipment, net of accumulated depreciation of 31,000 LCU at December 31, 19x7 and 14,000 LCU at December 31, 19x6	163,000	150,000
Long-term debt	100,000	120,000
Common stock, authorized shares par value 10 LCU per share, issued and outstanding 5,000 shares at December 31, 19x7 and December 31, 19x6	50,000	50,000

Additional Information:

EXCHANGE RATES

January 1, 19x6 to July 31, 19x6	2.0 LCU to $1
August 1, 19x6 to October 31, 19x6	1.8 LCU to $1
November 1, 19x6 to June 30, 19x7	1.7 LCU to $1
July 1, 19x7 to December 31, 19x7	1.5 LCU to $1
Average rate for 19x6	1.9 LCU to $1
Average rate for 19x7	1.6 LCU to $1

ACCOUNTS RECEIVABLE — ANALYSIS

	19x7	19x6
	(in LCU's)	
Balance beginning of year	37,000	—
Sales (36,000 LCU per month in 19x7 and 31,000 per month in 19x6)	432,000	372,000
Collections	423,600	334,000
Write-offs (May 19x7 and December 19x6)	3,200	1,000
	42,200	37,000

ALLOWANCE FOR UNCOLLECTABLE ACCOUNTS

	19x7	19x6
	(in LCU's)	
Balance beginning of year	2,000	—
Provision for uncollectables	3,400	3,000
Write-offs	3,200	1,000
	2,200	2,000

INVENTORY, FIFO BASIS

	19x7	19x6
	(in LCU's)	
Balance beginning of year	75,000	—
Purchases (June 19x7 and June 19x6)	335,000	375,000
Less: Inventory at year-end	80,000	75,000
Cost of goods sold	330,000	300,000

On January 1, 19x6, Wilson's foreign subsidiary purchased land for 24,000 LCU and plant and equipment for 140,000 LCU. On July 1, 19x7, additional equipment was purchased for 30,000 LCU. Plant and equipment are being depreciated on a straight-line basis over a ten-year period with no salvage value. A full year's depreciation is taken in the year of purchase.

On January 15, 19x6, 7% bonds with a face value of 120,000 LCU were sold. These bonds mature on July 15 and January 15. The first payment was made on July 15, 19x6.

Required:
Prepare a schedule translating the selected captions above into Canadian dollars at December 31, 19x6, and December 31, 19x7, using the temporal method. Show supporting computations in good form.
[CGA-Canada]

P17-2

Efren Ltd. is a foreign subsidiary of a Canadian parent located in the country of Matos. The balance sheet accounts of Efren are as follows, stated in mats (M):

Cash	M 20,000
Accounts receivable	10,000
Inventory (at market)	60,000
Plant and equipment	200,000
Accumulated depreciation	(80,000)
Long-term note receivable	50,000
Total assets	M260,000
Accounts and notes payable	M 40,000
Bonds payable	150,000
Common shares	70,000
Total equities	M260,000

Additional Information:
1. Efren Ltd. is wholly owned by Hialea Corp. Hialea established Efren when the mat was worth $2.00.
2. The fixed assets were purchased when the mat was worth $2.40.
3. The bonds payable were issued when the exchange rate for the mat was $2.30.
4. The long-term note receivable arose when the mat was worth $2.60.
5. The inventory was purchased when the mat was worth $2.80.
6. The current exchange rate for the mat is $3.00.

Required:

a. Translate the balance sheet accounts of Efren Ltd. into Canadian dollars, using each of the following methods:
   1. Current rate
   2. Current/noncurrent
   3. Monetary/nonmonetary
   4. Temporal
   In each case, treat the translation gain or loss as a single, balancing figure.

b. For each method, calculate:
   1. The accounting exposure
   2. The additional gain or loss that would result if the exchange rate one year hence was $3.50, assuming no change in the balance sheet accounts in mats.

P17-3

Kantor Corp. is a wholly owned subsidiary of Windsor Inc., and is located in the country of Zinnia. The currency of Zinnia is the zin (Z). At December 31, 19x9, the balance sheet accounts of Kantor Corp. appeared as follows:

Cash	Z 10,000
Accounts receivable (net)	20,000
Inventory	30,000
Temporary investments	40,000
Fixed assets	100,000
Accumulated depreciation	(30,000)
Long-term investments	40,000
Total assets	Z210,000
Accounts payable	Z 20,000
Long-term note payable	60,000
Deferred income taxes	10,000
Common shares	100,000
Retained earnings	20,000
Total equities	Z210,000

Additional Information:

1. The inventory is valued at current market value. It was purchased when the zin was worth $0.53.
2. The cash is all held in Zinnian banks, and the accounts receivable and payable are all denominated in zins.
3. The long-term note was signed on December 31, 19x7, and is due on December 31, 19x12. It is denominated in zins.
4. The initial investment (in the common shares) by Windsor Inc. was made on December 31, 19x6.
5. The fixed assets were purchased on March 31, 19x7, and are being depreciated over ten years on a straight-line basis.
6. The temporary investments are carried at lower-of-cost-and-market. They were purchased for Z50,000 when the zin was worth $0.65. At the end of 19x9, their net realizable value was less than cost.
7. The long-term investments are also carried at lower-of-cost-and-market. They

were purchased when the zin was worth $0.72. Their net realizable value on December 31, 19x9 was Z52,000.

8. The deferred income taxes arose as the result of timing differences between CCA for tax purposes and depreciation for accounting.

9. The Canadian dollar equivalent of the zin has been as follows:

December 31, 19x6	$0.80
March 31, 19x7	0.75
December 31, 19x7	0.70
December 31, 19x8	0.60
December 31, 19x9	0.50

The average rate for each year has been midway between the rates at the beginning and end of the year.

Required:

In columnar format, translate the balance sheet accounts of Kantor Corp., using each of the following methods. Treat the translation gain or loss as a single amount to balance the statement.

a. Current rate
b. Current/noncurrent
c. Monetary/nonmonetary
d. Temporal

P17-4

Refer to P17-3. Kantor Corp. had net working capital at January 1, 19x9, of Z60,000. Net income retained by Kantor Corp. for 19x9 was Z10,000.

Required:

To the extent possible from the information given, determine how the translation gain or loss should be incorporated into Windsor Inc.'s (the parent's) financial statements for 19x9, in accordance with the *CICA Handbook* recommendations, assuming that Kantor Corp. is:

a. a self-sustaining foreign operation.
b. an integrated foreign subsidiary.

P17-5

The income statement for 19x6 for Hilary Co., expressed in Coker francs (CF), is as follows:

Sales revenue	CF3,000,000
Cost of goods sold:	
Beginning inventory	CF 200,000
Purchases	1,000,000
	CF1,200,000
Ending inventory	400,000
	CF 800,000
Depreciation	300,000
Other operating expenses	900,000
Interest expense	200,000

Total expenses	CF2,200,000
Net income	CF 800,000

Hilary Co. is 100% owned by Bryan Inc., a Canadian corporation.

Sales revenue, purchases of inventory, and operating expenses (except depreciation) all occurred evenly through the year. Interest expense accrued throughout the year, but was all paid at the end of the year. The beginning inventory was purchased on October 1, 19x5, when the exchange rate was $0.72; the ending inventory was purchased on November 1, 19x6, when the exchange rate was $0.83. The depreciable assets were acquired when the exchange rate was $0.60. Other exchange rate information is as follows:

December 31, 19x5	$0.75
Average for 19x6	$0.80
December 31, 19x6	$0.85

Required:

Translate the income statement into Canadian dollars, using:

a.   the current-rate method.

b.   the temporal method.

P17-6

Refer to P17-5. The comparative year-end balance sheets for Hilary Co. were as follows:

	19x5	19x6
Cash	CF 500,000	CF 200,000
Accounts receivable	300,000	400,000
Inventory	200,000	400,000
Land	—	500,000
Equipment (net)	2,000,000	1,700,000
Total assets	CF3,000,000	CF3,200,000
Accounts payable	CF 400,000	CF 500,000
Bonds payable	1,800,000	1,800,000
Common shares	500,000	500,000
Retained earnings	300,000	400,000
Total equities	CF3,000,000	CF3,200,000

The common shares were issued when the exchange rate was $0.50.

The land was purchased at the end of 19x6. The bonds were issued at the end of 19x4, and mature at the end of 19x10. The exchange rate at the end of 19x4 was $0.60. Dividends are declared and paid at the end of each year. The retained earnings at the end of 19x5 were earned at an average rate of $0.65.

Required:

a.   Translate the 19x5 and 19x6 balance sheets, using the current-rate method. (Note that each year's balance sheet is translated at the current rate *at that year's balance sheet date.*)

b.   Translate the 19x5 and 19x6 balance sheets, using the temporal method.

c.   Calculate the net change in the cumulative translation gain or loss for 19x6, under each translation method.

d. Determine how the translation gain or loss would be shown on the parent company's 19x6 consolidated financial statements, assuming:
1. that Hilary Co. is self-sustaining.
2. that Hilary Co. is an integrated foreign operation.

Follow the *Handbook* recommendations.

P17-7

Parent Ltd. has a 100% owned subsidiary in a foreign country, Ruritania, and the subsidiary, Turic Inc., has submitted to you its financial statements in the foreign currency (SNATS). In your professional judgment, this is a "self-sustaining" subsidiary.

Turic Inc.
Balance Sheet
(in SNATS)
December 31, 19x5

	SNATS
Cash	340,000
Accounts receivable	410,000
Inventory	750,000
Fixed assets	1,200,000
Accumulated depreciation	(380,000)
	2,320,000
Current liabilities	210,000
Long-term liabilities	400,000
Common shares	200,000
Retained earnings, at January 1, 19x5	1,310,000
Net income for 19x5	200,000
	2,320,000

Turic Inc.
Income Statement
(in SNATS)
Year ended December 31, 19x5

	SNATS
Sales	980,000
Cost of goods sold	660,000
	320,000
Depreciation	30,000
Other expenses	90,000
	200,000

EXCHANGE RATES

December 31, 19x5	$1 = 82 SNATS
December 31, 19x4	$1 = 70 SNATS
19x5 Average	$1 = 76 SNATS

The following information relates to the financial statements and provides additional data:

1. The inventory is kept on a FIFO cost system. The opening inventory was composed of 246,000 SNATS at an applicable exchange rate of $1 = 65 SNATS and 304,000 SNATS at an applicable exchange rate of $1 = 68 SNATS. The purchases during the period were 360,000 SNATS at an exchange rate of $1 = 73 SNATS and 500,000 SNATS at an exchange rate of $1 = 76 SNATS. (The exchange rates listed are the exchange rates in effect at the date of the transaction. The subsidiary acquired all of its assets and incurred all of its debts within Ruritania.)
2. The fixed asset account is composed of land, 390,000 SNATS, purchased when the exchange rate was $1 = 55 SNATS and buildings, 810,000 SNATS, purchased when the exchange rate was $1 = 58 SNATS.
3. The long-term liabilities were issued at January 1, 19x5, and are due at January 1, 19x10.
4. The retained earnings of 1,310,000 SNATS at January 1, 19x5, would translate, using the *temporal method*, to $46,778.
5. The retained earnings accumulated at an average rate of $1 = 60 SNATS.
6. Parent Ltd. purchased the common shares of the subsidiary when the exchange rate was $1 = 52 SNATS.

Required:
Using Section 1650 of the *CICA Handbook*, prepare the Canadian dollar financial statements for Turic Inc. for the year 19x5.
[CGA-Canada]

P17-8

Dom Ltd. has a subsidiary, Tarzan Inc., in the country of Tarzania, which uses the Tar as its currency. Preparatory to consolidating this 100% owned subsidiary, the financial statements must be translated from Tars to Canadian dollars, but the person responsible for the translation has quit suddenly and left you with a half-finished job. Certain information is available but the rest you must determine.

Tarzan Inc.
(In Tars)
Financial Statements
For the year ended December 31, 19x6

Cash	T 100,000
Accounts receivable	200,000
Inventory (1)	400,000
Land	500,000
Buildings (2)	800,000
Accumulated depreciation	(300,000)
Total assets	T1,700,000
Accounts payable	T 250,000
Note payable (3)	400,000
Common shares	300,000
Retained earnings at January 1, 19x6	600,000
Net income — 19x6	150,000
Total liabilities and equity	T1,700,000

Sales	T1,000,000
Cost of goods sold	(600,000)
	400,000
Depreciation	(80,000)
Other expenses (4)	(170,000)
Net income	T 150,000

NOTES:
(1) The opening inventory was 500,000 Tars and the purchases during the period were 500,000 Tars. Tarzan Inc. uses a periodic LIFO inventory system. The opening inventory had an exchange rate of $1 Canadian = 3.1 Tars, and the purchases were made 30% from the parent and 70% from the local area. The local area purchases were made evenly throughout the year, and the purchases from the parent were recorded by the parent at $35,714.
(2) There were two buildings and one piece of land. The land and building number 1 (300,000 Tars) were acquired when Tarzan Inc. *was formed by Dom Ltd*. The exchange rate at that time was $1 Canadian = 2 Tars. Building number 2 was acquired when the exchange rate was $1 Canadian = 3.2 Tars. The depreciation expense is proportional to the purchase prices. The accumulated depreciation relating to building number 2 is 200,000 Tars.
(3) The note payable is due on January 1, 19x10, and was created on July 1, 19x6.
(4) The other expenses were incurred evenly throughout the year.

The opening Retained earnings translated into $181,818 Canadian.

Exchange Rates:

January 1, 19x6	$1 Canadian = 3.7 Tars
19x6 average, July 1, 19x6	$1 Canadian = 3.9 Tars
December 31, 19x6	$1 Canadian = 4.1 Tars

Required:
Assume that Tarzan Inc. is "integrated." Prepare the financial statements of Tarzan Inc. in Canadian dollars. Show your calculations in good form.
[CGA-Canada]

P17-9

Investco Ltd. is a Canadian real estate and property developer that decided to hold a parcel of land in downtown Munich, West Germany, for speculative purposes. The land, costing DM12,000,000 (deutsche marks) was financed by a five-year bond (DM9,000,000), which is repayable in deutsche marks, and an initial equity injection by Investco of DM3,000,000. These transactions took place on January 1, 19x6, at which time a German subsidiary company was created to hold the investment. Investco plans to sell the land at the end of five years and use the deutsche mark proceeds to pay off the bond. In the interim, rent is being collected from another company, which is using the land as a parking lot.

The 19x6 year-end draft financial statements of the German subsidiary company are as follows (assume that rental revenue is collected and interest and other expenses are paid at the end of each month):

Income Statement
For the year ended December 31, 19x6

		DM
Rental revenue		1,000,000
Interest expense	990,000	
Other expenses	10,000	1,000,000
Net income		0

Balance Sheet
December 31, 19x6

Cash	—
Land	12,000,000
	12,000,000
Bond (due December 31, 19x10)	9,000,000
Common stock	3,000,000
	12,000,000

Assume the following exchange rates:

January 1, 19x6	1 DM = $.45
December 31, 19x6	1 DM = $.60
Average, 19x6	1 DM = $.53

Required:

a. Prepare the translated 19x6 income statements and balance sheets at December 31, 19x6, following Canadian generally accepted accounting principles and assuming
   1. the German subsidiary is an integrated foreign operation as defined in Section 1650 of the *CICA Handbook*; and
   2. the German subsidiary is a self-sustaining foreign operation as defined in Section 1650.
b. Which translation method better reflects Investco's *economic exposure* to exchange rate movements? Explain.
c. Which translation method would Investco be required to use? Explain.
d. Assume that, instead of incorporating a West German subsidiary, Investco carries the investment (land, debt, etc.) directly on its own books. Some accountants would argue that it is inappropriate to reflect any portion of an unrealized exchange gain or loss on the bond in the 19x6 income statement because the land serves as an effective hedge. Explain the reasoning behind this position. Would this approach be acceptable? Explain.

[SMA]

P17-10

Sentex Limited of Montreal, Quebec, has an 80% owned subsidiary, Cellular Company Inc., which operates in Erewhon, a small country located in Central America. Cellular was formed by Sentex and Erewhon Development Inc. (located in Erewhon) on January 1, 19x4. Advantages to Sentex of locating in Erewhon are: easy access to raw materials, low operating costs, government incentives, and the fact that the plastics market of Erewhon is not well developed. All management, including the Chief Operating Officer, Mr. V. Globe, has been appointed by Sentex. Top management of Cellular is paid directly by Sentex.

Cellular makes plastic coatings from petrochemical feedstock purchased from Mexico. The process is automated but still uses significant amounts of native Erewhonese labour. The government of Erewhon has determined that this type of development is good for the country, and has underwritten 22,000 cuzos (local currency of Erewhon) of staff training expenses in 19x4 by reducing the taxes payable by Cellular. This employment assistance is not expected to continue in the future.

Approximately 75% of total sales by Cellular is made to Sentex, which uses the plastic coatings in its Montreal operations. These coatings are generally of a heavy grade and require special set-up by Cellular. The Sentex orders are handled directly by Mr. Globe and his assistant, Mr. A. Oppong, and the price is set on the basis of variable costs of manufacture, plus freight and a 30% markup, less applicable export tax incentives. The export tax incentive received by Cellular has been about 1,000 cuzos per order. Plastic coatings are also sold to both commercial and wholesale outlets in Erewhon, with commercial users constituting 20% of the total sales revenue of Cellular.

Cellular has agreed with the Erewhon government not to pay any dividends out of profits for two years. After that, it is anticipated that the majority of profits will be remitted by Cellular to Sentex and its other major stockholder, Erewhon Development Inc.

The opening balance sheet of Cellular Company Inc. at January 1, 19x4, was as follows:

(in cuzos)

Cash	30,000	Long-term debt	180,000
Fixed assets	350,000	Common stock	200,000
	380,000		380,000

All debt financing was provided by Sentex. The debt was incurred on January 1, 19x4, in cuzos, and is secured by the assets of Cellular.

Additional Information:
1. Raw material and labour costs were incurred uniformly throughout the year.
2. Sales were made uniformly throughout the year.
3. The fixed assets were acquired on January 1, 19x4, and are depreciated using the sum-of-the-years'-digits method over four years.
4. The note receivable is a 90-day non-interest-bearing note received from a customer in exchange for merchandise sold in October.
5. Land was purchased on December 31, 19x4, for 10,000 cuzos.
6. Cost of sales and inventory include depreciation of 98,000 cuzos and 22,000 cuzos respectively. See Cost of Goods Sold schedule below.

The following exchange rates were in effect for the 19x4 year:

Rate at January 1, 19x4	1 cuzo = $2.00 Canadian
Average rate for the year 19x4	1 cuzo = $1.82 Canadian
Rate at December 31, 19x4	1 cuzo = $1.65 Canadian

Cellular Company Inc.
Income Statement
For the Year Ended December 31, 19x4
(in cuzos)

Sales		600,000
Cost of goods sold*		400,000
Gross margin		200,000
Selling and administrative expenses	70,000	
Interest	20,000	90,000
Net income before taxes		110,000
Local taxes	33,000	
Less allowance for:		
Export incentive	6,500	
Training costs	22,000	28,500	4,500
Net Income after taxes		105,500

*Cost of Goods Sold Schedule (in cuzos)

Material purchases	300,000
Labour	70,000
Depreciation	120,000
Total	490,000
Less Inventory at Dec. 31x4	(90,000)
Cost of goods sold	400,000

Cellular Company Inc.
Balance Sheet
December 31, 19x4
(in cuzos)

ASSETS		LIABILITIES	
Current assets		Current liabilities	
Cash	25,000	Accounts payable	30,000
Notes receivable	100,000	Taxes payable	4,500
Accounts receivable	65,000		
Inventories (at cost)	90,000		34,500
	280,000	Long-term liabilities	
		10% Bonds payable due	
Fixed assets (at cost		January 1, 19x11	180,000
less accumulated			214,500
depreciation of			
120,000)	230,000	SHARE EQUITY	
Land (for future			
development)	10,000	Common stock	200,000
		Retained earnings	105,500
			305,500
	520,000		520,000

Required:

Sentex is in the process of preparing consolidated financial statements for the year ended December 31, 19x4.

a. Which method of translation should Sentex use, according to Canadian generally accepted accounting principles? Justify your selection, using the information from the question.

b. Translate into Canadian dollars at December 31, 19x4, according to Canadian generally accepted accounting principles, the following balance sheet accounts of Cellular Company Inc.
   1. 10% Bonds payable
   2. Fixed assets (net)

c. Calculate the translation gain/loss on the accounts of Cellular Company Inc. and show its disposition, according to Canadian generally accepted accounting principles.

[SMA]

18

Reporting Foreign Operations

hapter 15 discussed in general the problems of consolidating foreign operations and, in particular, the question of whether or not reporting for the domestic parent corporation is improved by consolidating its foreign subsidiaries. Chapter 17 discussed the various methods of translating the results of foreign operations, and the theoretical arguments in favour of each method. In this chapter, we focus on the technical problems and the mechanics of reporting the results of foreign operations. Primary concern will be with consolidation, although we will also look at equity reporting.

In Canada, internationally active corporations normally consolidate their foreign subsidiaries. Section 3050 of the *CICA Handbook* recommends that all subsidiaries should be consolidated, with few exceptions. The one explicit exception relating to foreign subsidiaries that is mentioned in the *Handbook* is when "the subsidiary is in a foreign country and there are significant restrictions on the transfer of funds" [para. 3050.07]. Another reason that would mitigate against consolidation would be impaired control, such as by restrictions or direct intervention by a host-country government.

In addition, foreign subsidiaries are sometimes excluded from consolidation on the grounds that the "subsidiary's financial statement components may be so dissimilar to those of the other companies in the group that their inclusion in the consolidated financial statements would provide a form of presentation which may be difficult to interpret" [para. 3050.13]. Some people would argue that the fact of operating in a foreign country, in a different economic and cultural environment, plus the arbitrariness inherent in selecting a translation method, renders all consolidated statements "difficult to interpret" when they include foreign subsidiaries. On the other hand, most foreign operations of Canadian companies seem to be in the United States, where the economic and cultural differences are not very great.

Notwithstanding the possible justifications for not consolidating foreign subsidiaries, most Canadian corporations do in fact consolidate their foreign subsidiaries. Any subsidiaries that are not consolidated are usually reported on the equity basis, as are any affiliated or significantly influenced foreign corporations.

When the results of operations of a foreign subsidiary or affiliate are reported either by consolidation or on the equity basis, the parent's earnings and net assets are affected by the translation method used. The remainder of this chapter will illustrate consolidation and equity reporting when each of two translation methods recommended in Section 1650 is used: the temporal method and the current-rate method.

This chapter provides only an introduction to the complex procedures involved in consolidating translated foreign operations. We will touch lightly on such issues as accounting for minority interest and intercompany transactions, and not deal at all with income taxes, changes in ownership, and other topics. The chapter is divided into two parts. Part A covers consolidation of subsidiaries that were founded by the parent corporation. Part B deals with consolidation and equity-basis reporting of subsidiaries and affiliates in which ownership was purchased in a business combination.

A.   CONSOLIDATING PARENT-FOUNDED SUBSIDIARIES

Temporal Method

Assume that on January 1, 19x1, Canapar, a Canadian corporation, established a subsidiary in the Republic of Litvak. The currency of the Republic of Litvak is the lit (L), and at the beginning of 19x1, the lit was worth $2.00 Canadian. The new subsidiary was named Litsub. Litsub issued 100 shares of common stock for L1,000 each. Sixty of the shares were purchased by Canapar, and the other 40 were purchased by citizens of Litvak. Thus Canapar held 60% majority interest in Litsub, acquired at a cost of $120,000 (60 shares @ L1,000 x $2.00).

Three years later, on December 31, 19x3, the trial balances of Canapar and Litsub appeared as shown in Schedule 18-1. Canapar wishes to consolidate the statements of Litsub when preparing its 19x3 consolidated financial statements. In order for consolidation to take place, Litsub's trial balance must be translated into Canadian dollars. Assuming that Litsub is an integrated foreign operation and therefore that Canapar's management uses the temporal method, the translation would be performed as shown in Schedule 18-2.

The temporal method translation is performed exactly as was described in Chapter 17. The monetary assets and liabilities are all translated at the rate in effect on the balance sheet date, while the nonmonetary assets and the shareholders' equity accounts are translated at the historical rates in effect at the times of the transactions. For greater clarity, the balance of Litsub's retained earnings has been broken down into its component parts, separately disclosing the earnings retained in 19x1 and 19x2 (with no dividends having been paid in either year), and the dividends paid in 19x3. The net income for 19x3 has not yet been closed to the retained earnings account.

The retained earnings for each year are not determined by applying any specific exchange rate to the net income for each period. Instead, the dollar equivalents of each year's earnings must be taken from the translated income statement for that year. A direct translation is not possible because the com-

SCHEDULE 18-1

Trial balances
December 31, 19x3
Dr. (Cr.)

	Canapar	Litsub
Cash and receivables	$100,000	L 60,000
Inventory	40,000	30,000
Machinery and equipment	600,000	200,000
Accumulated depreciation	(240,000)	(50,000)
Investment in Litsub (60%: at cost)	120,000	—
Accounts payable	(70,000)	(20,000)
Bonds payable (10-year; due January 1, 19x11)	—	(85,000)
Common shares	(100,000)	(100,000)
Retained earnings	(354,400)	(15,000)
Sales	(800,000)	(500,000)
Cost of sales	480,000	300,000
Depreciation	60,000	20,000
Other expenses	180,000	160,000
Dividend income (from Litsub)	(15,600)	—
	$ 0	L 0

Additional Information:

1. Exchange rates:

	average	year-end
19x1	$2.10	$2.20
19x2	2.30	2.40
19x3	2.50	2.60

2. Investment was made on January 1, 19x1, when exchange rate was $2.00.
3. Bonds and all common shares were issued on January 1, 19x1.
4. Litsub machinery and equipment was purchased in mid-19x1.
5. Litsub inventory details:
   Beginning inventory   L 20,000 (exchange rate = $2.40)
   Purchases   L310,000 (purchased throughout the year)
   Ending inventory L 30,000 (exchange rate = $2.55)*
6. Litsub's prior year's earnings (no dividends paid):
   19x1   L 10,000
   19x2   L 15,000
7. Litsub paid dividends of L10,000 at the end of 19x3 (debited to Litsub's retained earnings).

*Includes L10,000 purchased from Canapar.

ponents of revenue and expense that went into determining the net income are translated at various rates under the temporal method. Thus, Litsub's 19x1 net income of L10,000 translates to $21,500 (on the basis of information not given here) and the 19x2 net income of L15,000 translates to $40,000. The dividends paid for 19x3 are translated at the rate in effect at the time that the

SCHEDULE 18-2

Temporal Method Translation
Litsub Trial Balance
Dr. (Cr.)

	Per books	Exchange rate	Translated amounts
Cash and receivables	L 60,000	$2.60	$ 156,000
Inventory	30,000	2.55	76,500
Machinery and equipment	200,000	2.10	420,000
Accumulated depreciation	(50,000)	2.10	(105,000)
Accounts payable	(20,000)	2.60	(52,000)
Bonds payable	(85,000)	2.60	(221,000)
Common shares	(100,000)	2.00	(200,000)
Retained earnings:			
19x1	(10,000)	*	(21,500)
19x2	(15,000)	*	(40,000)
19x3 dividends	10,000	2.60	26,000
Sales	(500,000)	2.50	(1,250,000)
Cost of sales:			
Beginning inventory	20,000	2.40	48,000
Purchases	310,000	2.50	775,000
Ending inventory	(30,000)	2.55	(76,500)
Depreciation	20,000	2.10	42,000
Other expenses	160,000	2.50	400,000
Cumulative translation loss	—		22,500
	L 0		$ 0

*Obtained from previous years' translated income statements; not
directly calculable from balance in retained earnings.

dividends were paid in order to offset the equivalent amount received by the parent and credited either to income or to the investment account.

Once the Litsub trial balance has been translated, the consolidation process can begin. The *translated* trial balance is transferred to a consolidation worksheet, along with the Canapar account balances, as shown in the first two columns of Schedule 18-3.

The first adjustment that is made on the worksheet eliminates Canapar's investment account and Canapar's proportion of the Litsub common shares. Since Litsub is a parent-founded subsidiary, there is no need to worry about fair-value increments or goodwill:

(a) Common shares	$120,000	
Investment in Litsub		$120,000

The second elimination establishes the minority interest's share in Litsub's net assets:

(b) Common shares	$80,000	
Retained earnings	14,200	
Minority interest		$94,200

SCHEDULE 18-3

Consolidation Worksheet, Temporal Method
Dr. (Cr.)

	Trial balances			Canapar Consolidated
	Canapar	Litsub	Eliminations	trial balance
Cash and receivables	$ 100,000	$ 156,000		$ 256,000
Inventory	40,000	76,500	$(10,200)d	106,300
Machinery and equipment	600,000	420,000		1,020,000
Accumulated depreciation	(240,000)	(105,000)		(345,000)
Investment in Litsub	120,000	—	(120,000)a	—
Accounts payable	(70,000)	(52,000)		(122,000)
Bonds payable	—	(221,000)		(221,000)
Minority interest			(94,200)b (24,600)e 9,000 f	(109,800)
Common shares	(100,000)	(200,000)	120,000 a 80,000 b	(100,000)
Retained earnings	(354,400)	(35,500)	14,200 b (15,600)c	(391,300)
Sales	(800,000)	(1,250,000)	25,500 d	(2,024,500)
Cost of sales	480,000	746,500	(15,300)d	1,211,200
Depreciation	60,000	42,000		102,000
Other expenses	180,000	400,000		580,000
Dividend income	(15,600)	—	15,600 c	—
Minority interest in earnings and Litsub			24,600 e	24,600
Translation loss	—	22,500	(9,000)f	13,500
	$ 0	$ 0	$ 0	$ 0

The Litsub retained earnings on Schedule 18-3 are the sum of the components of retained earnings as shown on Schedule 18-2, or $35,500 ($21,500 + $40,000 − $26,000). The minority interest's share of this amount is 40%, or $14,200.

The third adjustment eliminates Canapar's dividend income from Litsub. This adjustment also eliminates the dividend payment from Litsub's retained earnings, since the minority interest share has already been removed by adjustment (b):

(c) Dividend income $15,600
      Retained earnings $15,600

The purpose of the fourth adjusting entry is to eliminate the intercompany sale and the unrealized profit in the inventory. The sale was downstream, so all of the unrealized profit must be eliminated. The gross profit percentage was assumed to be 40%, and can be verified from the ratio between sales and cost of sales on the Canapar trial balance. The dollar value of the intercompany sale is determined by multiplying the amount in inventory by the historical exchange rate when the transaction occurred: L10,000 x $2.55 = $25,500. If we assume that there were no other intercompany sales during the year, then the adjustment would appear as follows:

(d) Sales	$25,500	
Cost of sales		$15,300
Inventory		10,200

The last two adjustments record the minority interest's share in the 19x3 earnings of Litsub and *the minority interest proportion of the translation loss*. The translated net income of Litsub is the sum of the translated revenues and expenses as shown on the trial balance, which amounts to $61,500. The minority interest proportion is 40%, or $24,600:

(e) Minority interest in earnings of Litsub	$24,600	
Minority interest		$24,600

The cumulative translation loss is $22,500. Forty percent of that loss must be transferred to minority interest:

(f) Minority interest	$9,000	
Translation loss		$9,000

When these eliminations have been entered on the worksheet and the accounts crossfooted, the consolidated trial balance of Canapar will appear as shown in the last column of Schedule 18-3. The amount of the translation loss that pertains to the parent company is $13,500. We will illustrate the allocation of that loss after we discuss consolidation using the current-rate method.

Current-Rate Method

The translation of Litsub's trial balance using the current-rate method is illustrated in Schedule 18-4. All of the assets and liabilities are translated at the current rate of $2.60, while the revenue and expense accounts are translated at the average rate for the year. The shareholders' equity accounts are translated at the historical rate of the investment (for the common shares) or of the earnings (in the case of retained earnings). Since all of the income statement accounts are translated at the same rate under the current-rate method, the amounts of retained earnings can be determined directly by multiplying the net income for each year by the average exchange rate for that year. The dividends paid are translated at the exchange rate in effect when they were paid, just as under the temporal method.

Since the current-rate method results in a net asset accounting exposure, an increasing exchange rate (as in this case) will cause a net translation gain. For Litsub, the cumulative translation gain amounts to $71,500. This amount can be verified by computing the gain on the net investment (i.e., shareholders' equity) as follows:

Common shares: L100,000 x ($2.60 − $2.00) =	$60,000
19x1 net income: L 10,000 x ($2.60 − $2.10) =	5,000
19x2 net income: L 15,000 x ($2.60 − $2.30) =	4,500
19x3 net income: L 20,000 x ($2.60 − $2.50) =	2,000
19x3 dividends: L 10,000 x ($2.60 − $2.60) =	0
Cumulative translation gain	$71,500

SCHEDULE 18-4

Current-Rate Method Translation
Litsub Trial Balance
Dr. (Cr.)

	Per books	Exchange rate	Translated amounts
Cash and receivables	L 60,000	$2.60	$ 156,000
Inventory	30,000	2.60	78,000
Machinery and equipment	200,000	2.60	520,000
Accumulated depreciation	(50,000)	2.60	(130,000)
Accounts payable	(20,000)	2.60	(52,000)
Bonds payable	(85,000)	2.60	(221,000)
Common shares	(100,000)	2.00	(200,000)
Retained earnings:			
19x1	(10,000)	2.10	(21,000)
19x2	(15,000)	2.30	(34,500)
19x3 dividends	10,000	2.60	26,000
Sales	(500,000)	2.50	(1,250,000)
Cost of sales	300,000	2.50	750,000
Depreciation	20,000	2.50	50,000
Other expenses	160,000	2.50	400,000
Cumulative translation gain			(71,500)
	L 0		$ 0

The translated Litsub trial balance from Schedule 18-4 appears on the consolidation worksheet shown in Schedule 18-5. The eliminations that are necessary under the current-rate method for parent-founded subsidiaries are similar to those under the temporal method.

The first two adjustments eliminate the investment account and Litsub's common share account, and establish the minority interest at 40% of the translated net asset value:

(a) Common shares $120,000
    Investment in Litsub $120,000

(b) Common shares $ 80,000
    Retained earnings   11,800
    Minority interest $ 91,800

In this case, the translated sum of Litsub's retained earnings is $29,500 ($21,000 + $34,500 − $26,000) as compared to $35,500 under the temporal method, and the minority interest is affected accordingly. It is important to recall, however, that changing the minority interest on the Canapar consolidated financial statements does not affect the minority shareholders in any way. The interests of the owners of the other 40% of Litsub will be portrayed in Litsub's separate-entity statements, prepared in lits.

The third adjustment eliminates the intercompany dividends, and is exactly the same as under the temporal method:

(c) Dividend income $15,600
    Retained earnings $15,600

SCHEDULE 18-5

Consolidation Worksheet, Current-Rate Method
Dr. (Cr.)

	Trial balances Canapar	Trial balances Litsub	Canapar Eliminations	Consolidated trial balance
Cash and receivables	$ 100,000	$ 156,000		$ 256,000
Inventory	40,000	78,000	$(10,400)d	107,600
Machinery and equipment	600,000	520,000		1,120,000
Accumulated depreciation	(240,000)	(130,000)		(370,000)
Investment in Litsub	120,000	—	(120,000)a	—
Accounts payable	(70,000)	(52,000)		(122,000)
Bonds payable	—	(221,000)		(221,000)
Minority interest			{ (91,800)b (20,000)e 28,520)f }	(140,320)
Common shares	(100,000)	(200,000)	{ 120,000 a 80,000 b }	(100,000)
Retained earnings	(354,400)	(29,500)	{ 11,800 b (15,600)c }	(387,700)
Sales	(800,000)	(1,250,000)	25,500 d	(2,024,500)
Cost of sales	480,000	750,000	(15,300)d	1,214,700
Depreciation	60,000	50,000		110,000
Other expenses	180,000	400,000		580,000
Dividend income	(15,600)	—	15,600 c	—
Minority interest in earnings of Litsub			20,000 e	20,000
Translation gain		(71,500)	{ 200 d 28,520 f }	(42,780)
	$ 0	$ 0	$ 0	$ 0

The intercompany sale is eliminated in the fourth adjustment. However, a minor problem arises in eliminating the unrealized profit. The profit is eliminated from the income statement by the difference between the amounts of the sales and the cost of sales, both of which are in Canapar's trial balance in terms of dollars. The inventory, on the other hand, is in Litsub's inventory, and has been translated at the current rate of $2.60 rather than at the transaction rate of $2.55. The difference is the change in exchange rate ($2.60 — $2.55) times the inventory value in lits (L10,000) times the gross profit percentage (40%), or $200. The $200 represents an exchange gain that was recognized by translating the inventory at the current rate, but is being eliminated. Thus, the elimination entry for the unrealized profit also involves an amount for removing part of the translation gain:

(d) Sales	$25,500	
Translation gain	200	
Cost of sales		$15,300
Inventory		10,400

An alternative solution to the problem of eliminating unrealized inventory profits is to ignore the $200 impact of exchange rate movements since the date of the sale. Indeed, the AcSC prefers the alternative approach; para. 1650.59 of the *CICA Handbook* suggests that the exchange rate in effect on the date of the transaction should be used to compute the intercompany profit elimination. If this approach were used, the credit to inventory in adjustment (d) would be for $10,200, exactly the same as with the temporal method.

The difficulty with the AcSC preference is that it leaves the $200 of restated profit in the consolidated inventory, and the resultant inventory amount "does not fit in with any known asset evaluation theory."[1] On the other hand, this approach is easier to apply, and the resultant distortions will almost certainly be immaterial in the vast majority of cases.

The fifth adjustment accounts for the minority interest's 40% share of the Litsub 19x3 net income of L20,000 or $50,000:

(e) Minority interest in earnings of Litsub	$20,000	
Minority interest		$20,000

The last adjustment credits those holding minority interest with their share of the cumulative translation gain. The gain on the translated trial balance was originally $71,500. But adjustment (d) has reduced that amount by the $200 translation gain on the unrealized profit. Therefore, the adjusted gain is $71,300, of which 40% is $28,520:

(f) Translation gain	$28,520	
Minority interest		$28,520

Now that the consolidation procedure has been illustrated, we might briefly compare our results under the two translation methods. Schedule 18-6 shows the balance sheet and income statement under each alternative, with the translation gain or loss shown as a balancing figure in the balance sheet.

The consolidated monetary assets and liabilities are the same under both methods, because the current rate is used for translation of these items under both. The differences are in the nonmonetary items in the balance sheet and in cost of sales and depreciation in the income statement. The largest single difference (other than for the exchange gain/loss) is for the minority interest, which is $109,800 under the temporal method but is $140,320 under the current-rate method. That difference is primarily due to the cumulative translation gain/loss, 40% of which is charged or credited to the minority interest. In view of the size of the gain or loss, it is quite likely that the reported consolidated results for Canapar may be affected significantly by the way in which the gain or loss is reported. Therefore, we will now turn our attention to the alternative ways of reporting that amount, as we discussed in Chapter 17.

---

1 Dr. Pierre Vézina, *Foreign Currency Translation: An Analysis of Section 1650 of the CICA Handbook* (Toronto: CICA, 1985), p. 66. Dr. Vézina goes on to say: "In my opinion, the financial statements of a self-sustaining foreign operation should not be consolidated with those of the Canadian enterprise. If the foreign operation is self-sustaining, the only important items are the net investment and the dividends that can be derived from the operation."

SCHEDULE 18-6

Comparison of Consolidated Results

BALANCE SHEET	Temporal	Current Rate
Cash and receivables	$ 256,000	$ 256,000
Inventory	106,300	107,600
Machinery and equipment	1,020,000	1,120,000
Accumulated depreciation	(345,000)	(370,000)
Total assets	$1,037,300	$1,113,600
Accounts payable	$ 122,000	$ 122,000
Bonds payable	221,000	221,000
Minority interest in Litsub	109,800	140,320
Common shares	100,000	100,000
Retained earnings	498,000	487,500
Translation gain (loss)	(13,500)	42,780
Total equities	$1,037,300	$1,113,600
INCOME STATEMENT		
Sales	$2,024,500	$2,024,500
Cost of sales	1,211,200	1,214,700
Depreciation	102,000	110,000
Other expenses	580,000	580,000
Minority interest in earnings of Litsub	24,600	20,000
	1,917,800	1,924,700
Net income	$ 106,700	$ 99,800

Alternative Treatments of Translation Gains and Losses

Temporal Method

In the previous two chapters, we discussed several alternative ways of reporting the gains and losses that arise on translating monetary balances and foreign operations. Before attempting to apply these alternatives, we need first to ascertain the components of the net translation loss of $22,500 under the temporal method.

In general, it is useful to view the cumulative translation loss as being composed of two components: (1) the gain/loss from current monetary balances, and (2) the gain/loss from long-term monetary balances. In turn, each of those components consists of (a) gains/losses arising from the current year and (b) gains/losses arising from prior years. Schedule 18-7 shows the breakdown of the cumulative loss for Litsub as of December 31, 19x3.

The top portion of Schedule 18-7 shows the calculation of the net gain on the current monetary assets and liabilities for 19x3. The opening balance of the net current monetary items was assumed to be L20,000 (an amount that can also be derived by working backwards from the ending balance of L40,000). When the flows during the period are translated, a net gain of $7,000 is the result.

The centre portion of Schedule 18-7 summarizes the losses that arose from the bonds payable over the three years during which they have been

SCHEDULE 18-7

Components of Translation Loss
Temporal Method

	Per books	Exchange rate	Translated equivalent
CURRENT MONETARY ASSETS AND LIABILITIES:			
Net balance, January 1, 19x3	L 20,000	$2.40	$ 48,000
Flows from operations:			
Sales	500,000	2.50	1,250,000
Purchases	(310,000)	2.50	(775,000)
Other expenses	(160,000)	2.50	(400,000)
Dividends paid	(10,000)	2.60	(26,000)
			97,000
Net balances, December 31, 19x3	L 40,000	2.60	104,000
Net gain on current monetary items for 19x3			$ 7,000

BOND PAYABLE (L85,000):

Date	Exchange rate	Dollar equivalent	Translation loss
January 1, 19x1	$2.00	$170,000	—
December 31, 19x1	2.20	187,000	$17,000 for 19x1
December 31, 19x2	2.40	204,000	17,000 for 19x2
December 31, 19x3	2.60	221,000	17,000 for 19x3
Cumulative loss			$51,000

SUMMARY OF COMPONENTS:

Relating to current year:		
Current monetary assets and liabilities	$ 7,000 gain	
Bonds payable	17,000 loss	
		$10,000 loss
Relating to prior years:		
Current monetary assets and liabilities (plug)	$21,500 gain	
Bonds payable	34,000 loss	
		$12,500 loss
		$22,500 loss

	Prior years	Current year	Total
Net current monetary items	$21,500 G	$ 7,000 G	$28,500 G
Bonds payable	34,000 L	17,000 L	51,000 L
Totals	$12,500 L	$10,000 L	$22,500 L

outstanding. Originally issued when the exchange rate was $2.00, the dollar-equivalent of the bonds has increased from $170,000 at the rate of $17,000 per year, to a current balance of $221,000.

The final part of Schedule 18-7 summarizes the previous information, and shows that a gain of $21,500 is needed to reconcile to a cumulative loss of $22,500. Since the loss for the bonds payable has been determined for both the current year and prior years, and since the gain on the current items has been determined for the current year, the balancing figure must be the gain on the current items accumulated from the previous years. Therefore, another way of summarizing the cumulative loss of $22,500 is as follows:

	Prior years	Current year	Total
Net current monetary items	$21,500 G	$ 7,000 G	$28,500 G
Bonds payable	34,000 L	17,000 L	51,000 L
Totals	$12,500 L	$10,000 L	$22,500 L

Once the components of the cumulative loss have been determined, a decision must be made as to how to report these components. How much of the gains or losses should be recognized in income for 19x3? How much should be deferred for recognition in later years, and how much would have been recognized in income in prior years and thus should be included in retained earnings?

One alternative is to defer all gains and losses until realized by liquidation or partial liquidation of the investment. Under this approach, no part of the cumulative loss would be recognized in income currently. The net income for Canapar would then be $106,700 under the temporal method, as can be verified by reference to Schedule 18-6. This alternative does not seem to be consistent with the fact that the temporal method implicitly evaluates the results of foreign operations as though the parent had directly engaged in foreign currency transactions. Consequently, this approach is not feasible.

A second alternative would be to recognize the current year's gain from the current items, but to defer recognition of the loss on the bonds until the bonds are retired. Under this alternative, the exact disposition of the cumulative loss would be as follows:

Recognized in 19x3 net income	$ 7,000 gain
Included in retained earnings	21,500 gain
Deferred charge on balance sheet	51,000 loss
Cumulative translation gain or loss	$22,500 loss

Forty percent of these amounts would be charged to the minority interest, and thus Canapar's current year earnings would be increased by 60% of $7,000, or $4,200. The 19x3 consolidated net income for Canapar would then be $110,900.

The third alternative would be to recognize the current year's gain on the current monetary assets and liabilities, as above, and also to amortize the loss on the bonds over the periods remaining until maturity. Since the bonds have a ten-year term, the 19x1 loss would be amortized over ten years; the 19x2 loss would be amortized over nine years, and the 19x3 loss would be amortized over eight years. The cumulative loss would then be recognized as follows:

Recognized in 19x3 net income	$ 1,286 gain
Included in retained earnings	16,211 gain
Deferred charge on balance sheet	39,997 loss
Cumulative translation gain or loss	$22,500 loss

The amounts above are net amounts. The $1,286 is the $7,000 gain on the current monetary items less the amortization of the three years' losses on bonds of $5,714: $17,000/10 + $17,000/9 + $17,000/8. Similarly, the amount included in retained earnings is the sum of the current items' gain of $21,500 from prior years and the amortization of the loss on the bonds for 19x1 and 19x2, or $5,289: 2($17,000/10) + 1($17,000/9). Canapar's 19x3 net income would then be $107,472. Of course, the amount is subject to variation depending on the method of amortization used.

The fourth and final alternative is simply to take all of the current year's gain or loss into income immediately. The current year gave rise to a gain of $7,000 on the current items and a loss of $17,000 on the bonds. The net translation loss of $10,000 can simply be recognized in income, with the remainder of the cumulative loss ($12,500) incorporated into retained earnings. After deducting the 40% minority interest, Canapar's 19x3 consolidated net income would then be $100,700.

These four alternatives are summarized in the upper portion of Schedule 18-9. Of the four, only the first alternative, indefinite deferral, seems to be of doubtful viability. The third alternative is the approach that is recommended in para. 1650.31 of the *CICA Handbook*, but the second and fourth alternatives are not without their merits.

The second alternative is logical when the bonds are hedged by the non-monetary assets held in the Republic of Litvak. Earnings from the Litvakian operations will be used to generate the funds that will be used to retire the debt; therefore it makes sense not to recognize exchange losses on the bonds, because Canadian dollars will not be used to pay off the debt.

The fourth alternative is appealing because of its simplicity and the clarity of its meaning. If a note were used to disclose the composition of the current year's translation gain or loss, then the reader could adjust the statements if he or she felt that a different treatment would give better measurements.

While managements have shown some aversion to this approach, immediate recognition does have the virtue of simplicity, and should not cause concern in an efficient market or among sophisticated users. Indeed, while *SFAS No. 52* did reduce the emphasis on the temporal method by recommending translation approaches that are similar to those of Section 1650, the FASB still recommends immediate recognition of translation gains and losses when the temporal method is used.

Current-Rate Method

When the current-rate method is used, all of the assets and liabilities are translated at the current rate. Therefore, the cumulative translation gains and losses relate to the net investment as a whole rather than to specific groups of assets or liabilities. While it is mechanically possible to disaggregate the net gain or loss by specific classes or groups of net assets, as we do under the temporal method, there seems to be no logical reason for doing so. The cumulative gain or loss needs to be broken down only to determine the portion that relates to the current year and the portion that relates to prior years.

Schedule 18-8 shows the calculation of the translation gain for each year,

---

SCHEDULE 18-8

Components of Translation Gain
Current-Rate Method

Gain on net assets, 19x1:
Common shares: L100,000 × ($2.20 − 2.00) = $20,000
Retained earnings: L10,000 × ($2.20 − 2.10) = 1,000

$21,000

Gain on net assets, 19x2:
Common shares: L100,000 × ($2.40 − 2.20) = $20,000
Retained earnings:
19x1 L10,000 × ($2.40 − 2.20) = 2,000
19x2 L15,000 × ($2.40 − 2.30) = 1,500

23,500

TOTAL TRANSLATION GAIN RELATING TO PRIOR YEARS $44,500

Gain on net assets, 19x3:
Common shares: L100,000 × ($2.60 − 2.40) = $20,000
Retained earnings:
19x1 and 19x2: L25,000 × ($2.60 − 2.40) = 5,000
19x3 net income: L20,000 × ($2.60 − 2.50) = 2,000
− 19x3 dividends: L10,000 × ($2.60 − 2.60) = 0

TRANSLATION GAIN RELATING TO CURRENT YEAR 27,000

Total translation gain $71,500

---

using the net investment for each particular year. The total gain of $71,500 actually comprises $27,000 relating to 19x3 and $44,500 relating to the prior years.

The only decision that then needs to be made is whether to recognize the gain for the year in income (with the remainder shown as part of retained earnings), or to treat the entire cumulative amount as a separate component of shareholders' equity. The Canapar 19x3 consolidated net income under each of these two alternatives is shown in the lower portion of Schedule 18-9.

Deferral as a separate component of shareholders' equity is the treatment recommended by the *CICA Handbook* for self-sustaining foreign subsidiaries.

Summary: Parent-Founded Subsidiaries

The process of consolidation for a foreign subsidiary is not much different from consolidation of a domestic subsidiary. The consolidation is of the parent company's trial balance and the subsidiary's *translated* trial balance. First, the method of translation must be selected, then the subsidiary trial balance translated, and then the translated trial balance consolidated with the parent company's trial balance.

Minority interest is determined as the minority share of the translated balances, not on the basis of the foreign-currency balances. This is because the minority interest offsets those net assets that are included in the parent's

SCHEDULE 18-9

Alternative Consolidated Net Income Amounts, 19x3

	Adjustment	Net income
TEMPORAL METHOD		
1. Basic net income, without recognizing any translation gains and losses in income	0	$106,700 T1
2. Recognition of gain from current monetary items (60% × $7,000)	$4,200	110,900 T2
3. Recognition of gain from current monetary items and amortization of losses on bonds [60% × ($17,000/10 + $17,000/9 + $17,000/8)]	4,200 〕 (3,428)〕	107,472 T3
4. Full recognition of net translation loss relating to 19x3 (60% × $10,000)	(6,000)	100,700 T4
CURRENT-RATE METHOD:		
1. Basic net income without recognizing any translation gains in income	0	99,800 C1
2. Recognition of current year's translation gains (60% × $27,000)	16,200	116,000 C2

CICA Handbook recommended approaches: T3 and C1.
SFAS No. 52 recommended approaches: T4 and C1.

consolidated balance sheet *in Canadian dollars,* but that are not a part of the parent's share.

One balance emerges as the result of the translation that is not on the foreign-currency trial balance, and that is the cumulative net translation gain or loss. The gain or loss accrues to the parent only to the extent of the parent's ownership interest, and therefore the minority interest must be charged or credited with their proportion of the cumulative gain or loss.

Since the method of translation affects the values of the nonmonetary balances, it also affects the consolidated balance sheet. If the foreign operations make up a major segment of the parent's business, the parent's net asset value can be significantly affected, especially when long-term non-monetary assets form a large part of total assets.

Once the foreign accounts have been translated and consolidated, the disposition of the cumulative translation gain or loss must be determined. Under the temporal method, the major choices are (1) to recognize the gain or loss from the current monetary accounts but defer recognition of the gain or loss on long-term monetary balances, (2) to recognize the gain or loss from the current monetary accounts but defer and amortize the gain or loss on the long-term monetary balances, or (3) to recognize the full gain or loss for each year in that year's net income.

Since the temporal method yields results that are comparable to those that would be obtained from direct foreign currency transactions, it is logical to accord the same treatment to gains and losses arising from application of the temporal method as are accorded to gains and losses from foreign currency transactions in the particular company. The *Handbook* recommends the second alternative above, because the second alternative is consistent with the *Handbook*'s recommendations on gains or losses from foreign currency transactions and balances.

Where specific nonmonetary assets or revenue streams can be designated as implicit hedges of specific long-term monetary liabilities, however, the translation gain or loss on the liability can be deferred under the recommendations of Section 1650. The result of such deferral would be similar to the first alternative above.

When the current-rate method is used, there is no rationale for disaggregating each year's translation gain or loss into components relating to specific accounts or groups of accounts. Therefore, the only real alternatives for treatment of the cumulative translation gain or loss are either to recognize each year's gain or loss in income or to defer recognition of the entire amount until the investment in the subsidiary is reduced.

The *Handbook* recommends that the gain or loss be deferred as a separate component of consolidated shareholders' equity [para. 1650.36]. The cumulative deferred gain or loss would be recognized in income only if the parent's *net* investment in the foreign subsidiary declines. The net investment will decline if the subsidiary pays dividends in excess of its earnings for the year, or if the parent sells part of its interest in the subsidiary. In either case, a proportionate part of the accumulated translation adjustment would be transferred from the separate component of shareholders' equity to net income in the year of the reduction in the investment [para. 1650.38].

Whichever method is used for reporting the translation gain or loss, the parent company will report only its share of those amounts. The minority interest will be debited or credited for its portion of gains and losses, whether recognition is current or is deferred.

B.   BUSINESS COMBINATIONS AND FOREIGN AFFILIATES

In the previous section of this chapter, we reviewed the process of consolidation for subsidiaries that were established by the domestic parent corporation. In this section, we look at the procedures of consolidating the results of foreign operations when the foreign subsidiary was not founded by the parent but was acquired in a business combination.

A business combination may involve fair-value increments and goodwill, and thus this section examines the additional complications that arise when the process of consolidation is applied to fair-valued assets and goodwill of a foreign subsidiary. Only the parent-company approach will be discussed; pooling of interests and methods of purchase accounting other than the parent-company approach are beyond the scope of this discussion. This section is intended to provide only an introduction to the problems of consolidating a purchased foreign subsidiary.

A domestic company may carry out its foreign business through a significantly influenced foreign affiliate rather than through a subsidiary. Foreign affiliates are usually reported in the domestic corporation's financial statements on the equity basis. In addition, any unconsolidated foreign subsidiaries are normally reported using the equity basis. Therefore, this chapter concludes with a brief discussion of the equity method as applied to foreign operations.

In order to highlight the differences in consolidation procedure when a foreign subsidiary has been purchased rather than founded by the parent, we will use an example that is parallel to that used in the previous section. Let us assume that on December 31, 19x1, Canapar acquired 60% of the shares of Litsub, a corporation in the Republic of Litvak, for L120,000. To finance the purchase, Canapar borrowed L100,000 from the First National Bank of Litvak and used its own cash for the balance.

Temporal Method

Schedule 18-10 shows the book and fair values of Litvak's assets and liabilities on December 31, 19x1. The book value of the net assets was L110,000, of which Canapar acquired 60%, or L66,000. The fair values of the assets and liabilities were equal to their book values except for the machinery and equipment, which had a fair value L50,000 higher than net book value. The fair-value increment acquired by Canapar is also 60% of the total, or L30,000. Thus Canapar's share of the fair value of Litsub's net assets at the date of acquisition amounted to L96,000: book value of L66,000 plus fair-value increment of L30,000. Since the purchase price was L120,000, the pur-

---

SCHEDULE 18-10

Canapar Acquires 60% of Litsub
December 31, 19x1

Litsub Net Assets: Dr. (Cr.)

	Book value	Fair value		
Cash and receivables	L 10,000	L 10,000		
Inventory	20,000	20,000		
Machinery and equipment	200,000	240,000		
Accumulated depreciation	(10,000)	—		
Accounts payable	(25,000)	(25,000)		
Bonds payable	(85,000)	(85,000)		
Total net assets	L110,000	L160,000		
60% share acquired	L 66,000	L 96,000	× $2.20 =	$211,200
Purchase price		120,000	× $2.20 =	264,000
Goodwill		L 24,000		$ 52,800

chase transaction gave rise to goodwill of L24,000 (L120,000 — L96,000) relating to Canapar's 60% interest in Litsub.

The book and fair values, as well as the purchase price and the goodwill, are all expressed in the Litvakian local currency. If we assume that the exchange rate at the time of the purchase was $2.20, then Canapar's cost of acquiring control of Litsub was $264,000. Of the total purchase price in Canadian dollars, $211,200 was for the fair value of the net assets acquired and $52,800 was for goodwill. In all future translations of Litsub's statements for consolidation with Canapar, the historical cost of Litvak's assets acquired by Canapar will be the value in lits at the date of acquisition times the historical exchange rate at the date of acquisition, $2.20.

The translation of Litsub's trial balance two years after the acquisition, on December 31, 19x3, is demonstrated in Schedule 18-11, using the temporal method. The underlying assumptions about exchange rates and transactions are the same as were detailed on Schedule 18-1. To simplify matters, the trial balance shown in Schedule 18-11 is a post-closing trial balance; we will concentrate on consolidation of the balance sheet rather than on the full set of financial statements.

SCHEDULE 18-11

Post-closing Trial Balances
Temporal Method
December 31, 19x3
Dr. (Cr.)

		Litsub		
	Canapar	Per books	Rate	Translated
Cash and receivables	$ 176,000	L 60,000	$2.60	$ 156,000
Inventory	40,000	30,000	2.55	76,500
Machinery and equipment	600,000	200,000	2.20	440,000
Accumulated depreciation	(240,000)	(50,000)	2.20	(110,000)
Investment in Litsub (60%; at cost)	264,000	—		
Accounts payable	(70,000)	(20,000)	2.60	(52,000)
Note payable (L100,000 @ 2.60)	(260,000)	—		
Cumulative translation loss on note payable	40,000	—		
Bonds payable	—	(85,000)	2.60	(221,000)
Common shares	(100,000)	(100,000)	2.20	(220,000)
Retained earnings	(450,000)			
Prior to December 31, 19x1		(10,000)	2.20	(22,000)
for 19x2		(15,000)	—	(38,000)
for 19x3		(10,000)	—	(33,500)
Cumulative translation loss				24,000
	$ 0	$ 0		$ 0

The translation process is similar to that used in Schedule 18-2 for Litsub as a parent-founded subsidiary, except that the historical rate used to translate the machinery and equipment existing at the date of acquisition is the rate of $2.20 at the date of acquisition, not the rate in effect at the time that Litsub purchased the fixed assets. Similarly, the net investment at the date of acquisition (L110,000 shareholders' equity on December 31, 19x1) is also translated at $2.20 rather than at the rate that existed when the common shares were issued. The relevant amount is the cost of the assets *as acquired by Canapar*; all exchange rates prior to the date of Canapar's acquisition of the Litsub shares are irrelevant in the translation of Litsub's statements for consolidation with Canapar.

Since the machinery and equipment account is translated at $2.20, the depreciation expense on the translated income statement would also be translated at $2.20. The depreciation expense is L20,000 per year, and thus the translated retained earnings for 19x2 and 19x3 (that is, since the date of acquisition) are $2,000 less for each year [L20,000 x ($2.20 - $2.10)] than was the case in Schedule 18-2. In addition, note that the retained earnings prior to the date of acquisition are translated at the rate in effect at the date of acquisition, and are not derived from any translated income statements as are the earnings subsequent to acquisition.

The translation of Litsub's trial balance yields the translated *book* values for inclusion in Canapar's consolidated statements. The fair-value increments and goodwill emerge in the consolidation process, as a result of eliminating the investment account.

Rather than using a worksheet, we have prepared the consolidated balance sheet directly. Schedule 18-12 shows the Canapar consolidated balance sheet, with notes explaining the amounts. For the calculation of each account, the dollar figure shown first is the amount from Canapar's post-closing trial balance. This amount is then followed by a translation of the relevant Litsub book value, with any necessary adjustment or adjustments following that.

The cash is a straight-forward combination of the cash balance of Canapar with the cash balance of Litsub, translated at the current rate. The inventory is a similar combination, but at the historical rate for Litsub. The inventory requires an adjustment for the unrealized profit of $10,200, exactly as in Part A of this chapter.

The machinery and equipment amount is derived by taking the Canapar balance of $600,000 and adding to it the *net* book value of the Litsub machinery and equipment at the date of acquisition and translating that amount at the spot rate at the date of Canapar's acquisition. The fair-value increment is then added, also translated at the rate at December 31, 19x1. Accumulated depreciation is Canapar's balance of $240,000, plus the depreciation accumulated by Litsub since December 31, 19x1, plus two years' amortization of the fair-value increment, assuming that the appropriate straight-line depreciation rate is 10%.

The amount shown for goodwill on December 31, 19x3, is the original amount of L24,000 translated at the historical rate of $2.20, less two years' amortization, assuming that the goodwill is amortized over twenty years on a straight-line basis.

The consolidated liabilities consist of three items. The accounts payable is simply the combined balances of the two companies. The note payable is the

SCHEDULE 18-12

Canapar Corporation
Consolidated Balance Sheet*
Temporal Method
December 31, 19x3

ASSETS

Cash and receivables	
$176,000 + (L60,000 × $2.60)	$ 332,000
Inventory	
$40,000 + (L30,000 × $2.55) − $10,200	106,300
Machinery and equipment	
$600,000 + (L190,000 × $2.20) + (30,000 × $2.20)	1,084,000
Accumulated depreciation	
$240,000 + (L40,000 × $2.20) + (2)(L30,000/10)($2.20)	(341,200)
Goodwill	
[L24,000 − 2(L24,000/20)]($2.20)	47,520
Total assets	$1,228,620

EQUITIES

Accounts payable	
$70,000 + (L20,000 × $2.60)	$ 122,000
Note payable	260,000
Bonds payable	
L85,000 × $2.60	221,000
Minority interest	
$289,500 × 40%	115,800
Cumulative translation losses:	
Note payable	(40,000)
Litsub Ltd.	(14,400)
Common shares	100,000
Retained earnings	
$450,000 + .60($38,000 + $33,500) − $10,200	
− (2)(L30,000/10)($2.20) − 2(L24,000/20)($2.20)	464,220
Total equities	$1,228,620

*Prior to disaggregation and allocation of translation losses.

L100,000 loan of Canapar from the bank in Litvak, translated at the current rate of $2.60. Since the original dollar equivalent of the loan was $220,000, there is a cumulative translation loss of $40,000 on this balance. This liability balance and loss are not a part of Litsub's translated amounts; they are the result of a foreign currency transaction by Canapar and represent a liability of Canapar, not of Litsub. The bonds payable are also translated at the current rate. However, this balance is a liability of Litsub, not of Canapar.

Minority interest is 40% of the translated net assets of $289,500, from Schedule 18-11. This is the same as 40% of the translated shareholders' equity, *including* the cumulative translation loss. Thus 40% of the translated balances of the net assets includes 40% of the translation loss, and no further adjustment is necessary.

The cumulative loss from translating the trial balance of Litsub was $24,000 (from Schedule 18-11). Canapar's share of that loss is 60%, or $14,400. Thus, the consolidated balance sheet shows two cumulative translation losses, one relating to the foreign currency debt of Canapar, and another relating to the translation of Litsub's balance sheet.

The disposition of the translation loss relating to Litsub has already been discussed in the previous section and will not be repeated here. However, a new aspect has been added by the existence of the Canapar lit-denominated note payable. It would be possible to report the loss on the foreign currency balance in accordance with the alternatives discussed in Chapter 16, without considering how the Litsub translation loss will be reported. The two losses could be viewed as arising from two separate events: (1) purchasing an investment and (2) obtaining financing for Canapar.

The "pool of capital" concept of financial management holds that funds are raised at any point in time by the best means then available. What is available is partially a function of the methods used to raise capital in the past. Under this view, the sources of financing for a particular investment should not be linked to the investment itself in determining the profitability of the investment. Therefore, accounting for the cost of the funds (including the loss on the exchange rate) should not be dependent on the accounting method used for the investment itself.

However, the loss arising from the translation of Litsub is not a loss on the investment, but is a mechanical result of the translation method used and the resultant accounting exposure. Similarly, the loss on the note payable can be viewed not as a real economic loss because the loan will probably be paid by earnings generated in Litvak by Litsub and returned to the parent through dividends. Therefore, many people would argue that the accounting for the loss on the note payable should be consistent with the accounting for the translation loss relating to Litsub. If the Litsub loss is recognized in income, then so should the loss on the note be recognized. If the Litsub loss is deferred, perhaps as a separate component of shareholders' equity, then so should the loss on the note.

Since the temporal method yields translated results that are the same as would have been obtained if the parent had conducted its business directly by means of foreign currency transactions, the reporting of the translation gain or loss on the subsidiary should be consistent with the parent company's reporting of gains and losses on its direct foreign transactions.

The *Handbook* achieves the consistency by requiring the gain or loss from translating the long-term debt of an integrated foreign operation to be deferred and amortized, exactly as would the gain or loss on the parent's own foreign-currency-denominated long-term balances (of fixed maturity). Under the *Handbook* recommendations, therefore, each year's translation loss from Canapar's note payable and from Litsub's bonds payable would both be deferred and amortized over the remaining life of each. The *cumulative* losses shown on the 19x3 balance sheet relating to both liabilities would be disaggregated and distributed to retained earnings (for amortization relating to 19x2), to 19x3 income (amortization for the current year), and to deferred charges (to be amortized in future periods).

Consolidated retained earnings consist of Canapar's separate-entity retained earnings plus Canapar's 60% share of Litsub's earnings since the date of acquisition: 60% of $38,000 for 19x2 and of $33,500 (after dividends) for

19x3. Subtracted from retained earnings are the consolidation adjustments for unrealized profits in inventory ($10,200), amortization of the fair-value increment on machinery and equipment for two years ($13,200), and amortization of goodwill for two years ($5,280).

Current-Rate Method

When the purchased subsidiary's accounts are translated by the current-rate method, the general procedures of consolidation are similar to those under the temporal method. However, an additional complication arises from the fact that under the current-rate method, the fair-value increments and goodwill are translated at the current rate while the amortization included in prior years' earnings is translated at the average rate for each year.

Schedule 18-13 demonstrates consolidation of the balance sheet under

---

SCHEDULE 18-13

Canapar Corporation
Consolidated Balance Sheet
Current-Rate Method
December 31, 19x3

ASSETS

Cash and receivables	
$176,000 + (L60,000 × $2.60)	$ 332,000
Inventory	
$40,000 + (L30,000 × $2.60) − $10,400	107,600
Machinery and equipment	
$600,000 + (L190,000 × $2.60) + (L30,000 × $2.60)	1,172,000
Accumulated depreciation	
$240,000 + (L40,000 × $2.60) + (2)(L30,000/10)($2.60)	(359,600)
Goodwill	
[L24,000 − 2(L24,000/20)]($2.60)	56,160
Total assets	$1,308,160

EQUITIES

Accounts payable	
$70,000 + (L20,000 × $2.60)	$ 122,000
Note payable	260,000
Bonds payable	
L85,000 × $2.60	221,000
Minority interest	
(L135,000 × $2.60 × 40%) − $80	140,320
Cumulative translation gains (losses):	
Note payable	(40,000)
Litsub Ltd. (from Schedule 18-14)	50,100
Common shares	100,000
Retained earnings	
$450,000 + .6($34,500 + $50,000 − $26,000)	
− $10,200	
−(L3,000 + L1,200)(2.30)	
−(L3,000 + L1,200)(2.50)	454,740
Total equities	$1,308,160

the current-rate method. The calculation of each of the asset amounts is similar to that used in Schedule 18-12, except that the Litsub balances are translated at the current rate of $2.60 in every case. The adjustment for the unrealized profit in the inventory is for $10,400, since the unrealized profit is included in the inventory on the balance sheet at the current rate rather than the historical rate. The adjustment for the unrealized profit is exactly the same as it was under the current-rate method in Part A of the chapter, and causes a reduction of $200 in the net translation gain.

The consolidated liabilities are the same as under the temporal method, since they are all monetary liabilities and are translated at the current rate under both methods. The minority interest is 40% of the translated net assets of Litsub: L135,000 x $2.60 x 40% = $140,400. From this amount must be deducted the minority interest's share of the adjustment for the translation gain on the unrealized profit (40% of $200), yielding a final minority interest of $140,320.

The earnings of Litsub since acquisition must be translated at the average rate for each years' net income, less dividends translated at the rate at the date of payment. The Canapar share of Litsub's 19x2 earnings is converted at $2.30 and the 19x3 earnings are translated at $2.50. The dividends are translated at $2.60. The earnings of Litsub since the date of acquisition must be adjusted for the amortization of the fair-value increment on the machinery and equipment and of the goodwill (ten and twenty years, respectively). Canapar's separate-entity retained earnings of $450,000, plus the adjusted retained earnings of Litsub since the date of acquisition, amount to consolidated retained earnings of $454,740.

The translation gain relating to Litsub is most easily viewed simply as a balancing figure or plug on the consolidated balance sheet. However, it is possible to derive the amount of $50,100 directly.

Schedule 18-14 shows that the basic translation gain from translating Litsub's balance sheet is $50,500, of which Canapar's 60% share is $30,300. Three adjustments must be made to this amount. The first is the elimination of the $120 from the unrealized inventory profit. The other two adjustments relate to the fair-value increment and goodwill.

In Canapar's accounts, the investment account shows a balance of $264,000 (Schedule 18-15). This balance is the cost of the Litsub shares of L120,000 translated at the historical rate of $2.20, including the cost of the fair-value increment and the goodwill. On the consolidated balance sheet, however, the fair-value increment and the goodwill are translated at the current rate, not the historical rate. In making the worksheet elimination entry, the difference between the credit to the investment account at historical cost and the debit to the asset accounts at the current rate is credited to the translation gain account. The translated balance sheet already reflects the change in rate as it affects the book values of the assets; therefore, the extra adjustment is necessary only for the fair-value increments and goodwill. The net book value purchased was L66,000, and the excess of the purchase price over the net book value acquired was L54,000. The adjustment is for $21,600: (L120,000 — L66,000) x ($2.60 — $2.20).

The fair-value increment and the goodwill have been amortized for two years in preparing Canapar's consolidated statements. Since the increment and goodwill have been restated to the current rate, the amortization must also be adjusted to the current rate. The final adjustment shown on Schedule

SCHEDULE 18-14

Details of Computation of Litsub
Translation Gain, Current-Rate Method

(1) Gain resulting from translation of Litsub's
     balance sheet at the current rate:
     Net assets: L135,000 @ $2.60 = $351,000
     Net investment:
        Purchased at date of acquisition:
          L110,000 @ $2.20 $242,000
        Retained earnings for 19x2
          L15,000 @ $2.30   34,500
        Retained earnings for 19x3
          L20,000 @ $2.50   50,000
        Less dividends: L10,000 @ $2.60   (26,000)
                                                         300,500

     Translation gain $ 50,500

     Canapar share — 60% $ 30,300

(2) 60% of exchange gain on unrealized
     inventory profits   (120)

(3) Gain on excess of purchase price over net
     book value:
     (L120,000 − L66,000) × ($2.60 − $2.20)   21,600

(4) Difference between balance sheet valuation
     (@ $2.60) and dollar-equivalents charged to
     income for amortization of goodwill and fair-
     value increment:
     (a) for 19x2:
        L1,200 GW
        <u>L3,000</u> FVI

        L4,200 × ($2.60 − $2.30)   (1,260)
     (b) for 19x3:
        L1,200 GW
        <u>L3,000</u> FVI

        L4,200 × ($2.60 − $2.50)   (420)

Total translation gain relating to Litsub Ltd. (to Schedule 18-13) $ 50,100

18-14 makes this change. The result is that only the *unamortized* portion of the fair-value increment and goodwill appear on the consolidated balance sheet, translated at the current rate.

The net translation gain of $50,100 relating to Canapar's interest in Litsub is shown in Schedule 18-13 as a balance sheet amount. A decision must be made whether to carry the cumulative amount on the balance sheet or to recognize each year's gain or loss in income, as discussed in the previous chapter. If the gain is recognized in income, then the translation loss for the year that arises from Canapar's note payable should also be recognized in income. Conversely, deferral of the Litsub translation gain should be accom-

SCHEDULE 18-15

Consolidation Worksheet, Current-Rate Method
Dr. (Cr.)

	Trial balances Canapar	Trial balances Litsub	Eliminations	Consolidated trial balance
Cash and receivables	$176,000	$156,000		$ 332,000
Inventory	40,000	78,000	$(10,400)e	107,600
Machinery and equipment	600,000	520,000	78,000 a (26,000)b	1,172,000
Accumulated depreciation	(240,000)	(130,000)	26,000 b (15,600)c	(359,600)
Investment in Litsub	264,000		(264,000)a	
Goodwill			62,400 a (6,240)d	56,160
Accounts payable	(70,000)	(52,000)		(122,000)
Note payable	(260,000)			(260,000)
Bonds payable		(221,000)		(221,000)
Minority interest			(96,800)a (20,120)f (23,400)g	(140,320)
Common shares	(100,000)	(220,000)	220,000 a	(100,000)
Retained earnings	(450,000)		15,600 g	(434,400)
19x1		(22,000)	22,000 a	—
19x2		(34,500)	6,900 c 2,760 d 13,800 g	(11,040)
19x3		(50,000)	7,500 c 3,000 d 10,200 e 20,000 g	(9,300)
Dividends paid — 19x3		26,000	(26,000)g	—
Translation loss — note payable	40,000			40,000
Translation gain — Litsub		(50,500)	(21,600)a 1,200 c 480 d 200 e 20,120 f	(50,100)
	$ 0	$ 0	$ 0	$ 0

panied by deferral of the loss on the related debt. Consistency of treatment between the two types of translation gains or losses is generally preferred.

The *Handbook* specifically provides for deferral of gains and losses from a long-term monetary liability if the liability is a hedge of an investment in a self-sustaining foreign subsidiary [para. 1650.55]. Any gain or loss from the liability would be reported as part of the cumulative translation gain or loss account, which is a separate component of shareholders' equity. The recommended treatment of the gain or loss on the liability is not dependent upon a direct linkage between the loan and the investment, as there was in the Canapar-Litsub example above. The loan could be arranged later and still be designated as being hedged by the net investment in the subsidiary.

Worksheet Approach

In this part of the chapter, we have chosen to prepare the balance sheet directly, rather than by preparing a consolidation worksheet. The derivation of the balance sheet amounts may be clearer under the direct approach than under a worksheet approach. Nevertheless, some readers may prefer to see how the adjustments are performed using a worksheet approach. Therefore, Schedule 18-15 illustrates the consolidation worksheet, using the current-rate method. The facts are the same as were illustrated in Schedule 18-14. The elimination entries are summarized in general journal form in Schedule 18-16.

Reporting on the Equity Basis

Frequently, a domestic company will operate in foreign countries not through subsidiaries but rather through *affiliates*. The affiliates may be independent, but may nevertheless be significantly influenced by the domestic company. For example, Harry Rosen Men's Wear Ltd. (a subsidiary of Dylex Ltd.) began operations in the United States through an affiliate in which the Harry Rosen company owned only a 25% interest. Rosen had a hand in site selection for the new U.S. stores, as well as directing the store design, buying, merchandising, and promotion of the new chain. The 25% interest "is expected to bring in annual profit of $3-million (U.S.) to Harry Rosen Men's Wear Ltd. in five years from 30 stores."[2]

As with any such domestic affiliates, it is appropriate to report the income earned by the affiliates in the investor corporation's financial statements on the equity basis. The equity basis is also appropriate for any unconsolidated subsidiaries.

Equity-basis reporting is illustrated in Schedule 18-17. Assuming that Litsub is reported by Canapar on the equity basis rather than by consolidation, the schedule shows Canapar's equity in Litsub's earnings for each of 19x2 and 19x3, the balance of the investment account on the Canapar balance sheet at each year-end, and Canapar's reported retained earnings at the end of 19x3. The calculations are made using both the temporal and current-rate methods. The final retained earnings figures on Schedule 18-17 can be compared with the consolidated retained earnings shown on Schedules 18-12 (for the temporal method) and 18-13 (for the current-rate method).

Summary: Business Combinations

When a parent corporation is consolidating a foreign subsidiary that was acquired by purchase of a going concern, the problems of accounting for foreign currency operations are combined with the problems of accounting for business combinations. The added complications, as compared to consolidating a parent-founded foreign subsidiary, relate mainly to the adjustment of the fair-value increments and goodwill.

Under the temporal method, the nonmonetary assets are translated at the exchange rate in effect when the assets were acquired. In the case of a business combination, the assets of the acquired company are being acquired by the parent company on the date that the subsidiary's shares are acquired.

2 Paul Goldstein, "Dylex's Harry Rosen unit taking first step into U.S.," (July 28, 1983), p. B1.

SCHEDULE 18-16

Elimination Entries for the Consolidation of Litsub
Current-Rate Method

(a) Common shares $220,000
    Retained earnings (at Dec. 31, 19x1) 22,000
    Goodwill (L24,000 × $2.60) 62,400
    Machinery & equipment (L30,000 × $2.60) 78,000
        Investment in Litsub $264,000
        Minority interest (40% of $242,000) 96,800
        Translation gain (L54,000 × [$2.60 − $2.20]) 21,600
    (to eliminate the investment account, establish minority interest at
    40% of net book value at acquisition, record fair-value increment and
    goodwill at current rate, and record translation gain on increment and
    goodwill)

(b) Accumulated depreciation $ 26,000
        Machinery and equipment $ 26,000
    (to net the accumulated depreciation at the date of acquisition
    (L10,000) against the asset account)

(c) Retained earnings (for 19x2) $ 6,900
    Retained earnings (for 19x3) 7,500
    Translation gain 1,200
        Accumulated depreciation $ 15,600
    (to adjust for amortization of fair-value increment at L3,000 per year)

(d) Retained earnings (for 19x2) $ 2,760
    Retained earnings (for 19x3) 3,000
    Translation gain 480
        Goodwill $ 6,240
    (to amortize goodwill at L1,200 per year)

(e) Retained earnings (for 19x3) $ 10,200
    Translation gain 200
        Inventory $ 10,400
    (to eliminate unrealized profit from inventory)

(f) Translation gain $ 20,120
        Minority interest $ 20,120
    (to adjust minority interest for 40% of the cumulative translation gain:
    ([$50,500 − $200] × .40)

(g) Retained earnings (for 19x2) $ 13,800
    Retained earnings (for 19x3) 20,000
    Retained earnings (Canapar dividend income) 15,600
        Retained earnings (dividends paid) $ 26,000
        Minority interest 23,400
    (to credit minority interest with 40% of Litsub earnings since
    acquisition and to eliminate the intercompany dividends)

Note: These are worksheet entries only, and are not recorded on the
books of either Canapar or Litsub.

Thus, the appropriate exchange rate to use for that part of the subsidiary's
assets that were on the books at the date of the business combination is the
exchange rate on the date of the business combination. The same rate will

SCHEDULE 18-17		
Reporting Litsub on the Equity Basis		
	Temporal	Current rate
INVESTMENT ACCOUNT:		
December 31, 19x1 investment	$264,000	$264,000
19x2 earnings:		
Translated net income (60%)	22,800	20,700
Amortization of fair-value increment	−6,600	−6,900
Amortization of goodwill	−2,640	−2,760
	13,560	11,040
Balance, December 31, 19x2	277,560	275,040
19x3 earnings:		
Translated net income (60%)	35,700	30,000
Amortization of fair-value increment	−6,600	−7,500
Amortization of goodwill	−2,640	−3,000
Unrealized inventory profit	−10,200	−10,200
	16,260	9,300
Dividends received	−15,600	−15,600
Balance, December 31, 19x3	$278,220	$268,740
CONSOLIDATED RETAINED EARNINGS:		
Canapar Corporation retained earnings		
(excluding dividends received from Litsub)	$434,400	$434,400
Equity in earnings of Litsub (above):		
19x2	13,560	11,040
19x3	16,260	9,300
Balance, December 31, 19x3	$464,220	$454,740

also be used for any fair-value increments and decrements and for translating goodwill. The fair-value increments, decrements, and goodwill will be amortized in the foreign-country currency, translated at the exchange rate at the date of acquisition.

When the current-rate method is used in translating the operations of a purchased subsidiary, a disparity arises from the fact that the amortization of the fair-value increments and the goodwill will be at the rate in effect for the period for which income is being measured. On the balance sheet, the unamortized fair-value increments and goodwill will be reported at the current exchange rate, while the parent's investment account will carry the increments and goodwill at the historical rate at the date of acquisition of the subsidiary. The consolidation adjustments that are necessary in order to reconcile these different valuations all affect the cumulative translation gain or loss.

Unconsolidated subsidiaries and significantly influenced affiliates are usually reported on the equity basis. Equity reporting involves the same types of adjustments as those made for consolidation. As with domestic subsidiaries, equity reporting results in the same net income and retained earnings as does consolidation. The principle of "one-line consolidation" is just as valid for foreign as for domestic subsidiaries.

SELF-STUDY PROBLEM 18-1[3]

On February 1, 19x1, Horvath Ltd. (HL) established a subsidiary in the country of Daly. The subsidiary, Horvath (Daly) Inc. (HDI), issued 10,000 common shares to HL in return for an investment of $4,500,000. Expressed in Daly currency (the dale), the initial investment was D1,500,000.

Daly's inflation rate has been about 20% per year higher than Canada's. The differential has pushed the exchange rate down to $0.64 by the end of 19x7.

On December 31, 19x7, the balance sheet for HL and HDI are as shown below.

Additional Information:
1. The HDI bonds were issued early in 19x2, when the exchange rate was $2.40. They mature on January 1, 19x12.
2. The HDI fixed assets were acquired in 19x2 when the exchange rate was $2.20 and are being depreciated over ten years on a straight-line basis.
3. The inventory of HDI at the end of 19x7 was purchased when the exchange rate was $0.70, including D100,000 of goods purchased from HL. Total purchases by HDI from HL amounted to D500,000 during 19x6. HL's gross margin was 40% of the selling price. HDI's opening inventory contained no goods purchased from HL.
4. The earnings and dividends of HDI since its incorporation are as follows:

	Net income	Dividends paid
19x1	D 50,000	—
19x2	100,000	—
19x3	140,000	D200,000
19x4	200,000	200,000
19x5	300,000	350,000
19x6	360,000	400,000
19x7	400,000	300,000

Except for depreciation expense of D400,000 per year from 19x2 to 19x7, all revenues and expenses were accrued at the average rate for each year. Dividends were paid in midyear.

5. Exchange rates for the Daly dale were as follows:

Year	Average	Year-end
19x1	$2.80	$2.50
19x2	2.20	2.00
19x3	1.80	1.50
19x4	1.40	1.20
19x5	1.10	1.00
19x6	.90	.80
19x7	.70	.64

3 The solutions to the self-study problems are at the end of the book, following this chapter.

6. HL's current receivables include D200,000 due from HDI, converted at the current exchange rate of $0.64.

Balance Sheets
December 31, 19x7

	HL	HDI
Cash and receivables	$1,200,000	D1,900,000
Inventories	300,000	500,000
Fixed assets	2,500,000	4,000,000
Accumulated depreciation	(1,500,000)	(2,400,000)
Investment in HDI	4,500,000	–
	$7,000,000	D4,000,000
Accounts payable	$1,000,000	D 400,000
Bonds payable	–	2,000,000
Common shares	4,000,000	1,500,000
Retained earnings	2,000,000	100,000
	$7,000,000	D4,000,000

Required:
a. Prepare a consolidated balance sheet for Horvath Ltd. at December 31, 19x7, assuming that HDI is a self-sustaining foreign subsidiary and that the recommendations of the *CICA Handbook* are followed.
b. Prepare a consolidated balance sheet, assuming that HDI is an integrated foreign subsidiary, as recommended by the *Handbook*.

REVIEW QUESTIONS

18-1 Under what circumstances would it be appropriate for a public Canadian company *not* to consolidate its foreign subsidiaries?

18-2 When consolidating a parent-founded integrated foreign subsidiary, what rate is used to translate the subsidiary's previous years' retained earnings?

18-3 Why is part of the translation gain or loss credited or charged to the minority interest?

18-4 How is the amount of the minority interest in a foreign subsidiary measured when the parent's consolidated balance sheet is prepared?

18-5 When consolidating a parent-founded, self-sustaining foreign subsidiary, how is the subsidiary's retained earnings translated?

18-6 When eliminating unrealized inventory profits from downstream sales to a self-sustaining foreign subsidiary, why is the translation gain/loss affected?

18-7 How do the recommendations of *SFAS No. 52* for the disposition of cumulative translation gains/losses differ from the recommendations of Section 1650 of the *Handbook*?

18-8 When, if ever, would the translation gains/losses that are accumulated in a separate component of consolidated shareholders' equity be removed from that separate component and recognized on the income statement?

18-9 In a business combination involving a foreign company purchased in a foreign currency, is the purchase price discrepancy calculated in terms of domestic currency or the foreign currency?

18-10 When a corporation acquires a foreign subsidiary via a business combination, at what exchange rate are the subsidiary's fixed assets translated in subsequent years, assuming that the temporal method is being used?

18-11 What rate is used to translate the amount of fair-value increments resulting from a purchase of a foreign subsidiary, using the temporal method? Using the current-rate method?

18-12 How is the minority interest's share of the net assets of a purchased foreign subsidiary determined when a consolidated balance sheet is prepared?

18-13 Under what circumstances is it permissible (within the recommendations of Section 1650) to treat a long-term monetary liability of a parent company as a hedge of an investment in a self-sustaining foreign subsidiary?

18-14 If a foreign-currency-denominated liability is viewed as a hedge of the net investment in a self-sustaining foreign subsidiary, what treatment is accorded to the exchange gain or loss on the liability?

18-15 When is equity basis reporting appropriate for an investment in a company in a foreign country?

Video Displays, Inc. (Part C)   CASE 18-1

In early February, 1983, Reginald I. Axworthy, the controller of Video Displays Inc. (VDI) attended a meeting of the board of directors in order to present the draft financial statements for discussion. The statements for the year ended on December 1982 were the first statements to be issued externally since the company had established its subsidiary in the United States. There were no external shareholders, but the company was highly levered financially, and the company's bankers routinely received copies of the annual financial statements, plus whatever other information they wanted.

The board of directors consisted of four members—Alice, Bob, Carol, and Doug—all of whom were the founding partners of the corporation. The following conversation ensued between the directors and Reg, the controller:

CAROL: Well, Reg, what have you got for us today?

REG: Some draft statements for 1982. I thought that we should discuss how we want to present our California sub in the statements, since our approach will have a pretty significant impact on our reported results.

DOUG: What's so special about the California operation? Can't we just add it in with our domestic operations, using the same accounting policies as we've been using all along? There's nothing particularly arcane about our past policies.

REG: Unfortunately, it's not that simple. The California operation is all in American dollars, and we have to translate the results of those operations into Canadian dollars before we can consolidate the statements.

ALICE: Why is that a problem?

REG: Because the exchange rate keeps changing. In fact, the U.S. dollar was inordinately strong in 1982, and rose constantly throughout the year. We're seeing some correction of that upswing right now, and the dollar is falling a bit. But the problem is in choosing an exchange rate or rates to use for translating the U.S. transactions.

BOB: But we've had that problem since 1980, when we took out that $3,000,000 loan in New York.

REG: Well, actually we've been ignoring that problem. We've just been carrying the loan at $3,600,000 on our books and on our statements, which is the amount that we got in Canadian dollars when we took out the U.S.-dollar loan. We figured that we would be refinancing that loan when it came due on March 1, 1985, since there was no way that we could generate that much cash in earnings in five years. And since the bank indicated a willingness to take a longer-term position if we were reasonably successful in our first five years, we felt that we could ignore the effect of currency fluctuations on the real amount that we owed them. We may have to change that policy now, though, because of some new accounting rules that the CICA has laid down.

CAROL: What have the CAs been up to now?

REG: If we follow their rules, we have to show our loan on the balance sheet at its equivalent value in Canadian dollars, and spread the effects of any changes in the value since the beginning of the year over all of the years until maturity. In 1980, the U.S. dollar fell slightly, and we had a gain of $60,000. In 1981, we had another gain of $90,000. But in 1982, the strong U.S. dollar has given us a whopping loss of $750,000. Since there are only 38 months remaining from the beginning of 1982 until the loan is due, we have to show 12/38 of that loss, or $236,800, in the income statement for 1982. If we apply the new rules retroactively, as I have in the draft statements, we can reduce the 1982 loss a bit to $203,200 by offsetting portions of the previous two years' gain against the '82 loss.

DOUG: But that's ridiculous! I'll bet that's almost as much as we made all year, after taxes.

REG: Funny you should mention taxes! They get all involved here too. Since the loss on the debt isn't deductible for tax purposes, we have to set up an account for deferred taxes. In effect, we recognize now the impact of the loss on income taxes if we ever have to pay the debt at the high exchange rates.

BOB: It sounds so complicated.

REG: The concept is simple, although the numbers can get a little hairy. But it works to our advantage, since the effect is to reduce the impact of the loss on the financial statements.

ALICE: Now let's see if I've got this right: we have to show a loss that we may never suffer, offset partially by a tax benefit that we won't get if we don't have to pay the debt at high rates.

REG: You've got it! If the U.S. dollar goes down in 1983, which it shows every sign of doing, then we'll show a gain in the '83 statements that will offset the loss that we didn't really suffer in '82.

CAROL: We seem to have gotten sidetracked. You started out to talk about the California sub, and the problems of combining those operations with our home operations. Can we get back to that issue?

REG: Sure, but the issues with the sub are related to the issues with the U.S. note. What we do in one case may affect what we do in the other. Let's look at these draft statements (Exhibit 1). I've prepared two versions, one for each of the approved alternatives. There are major differences in the results, because 40% of our sales have been through the sub.

DOUG: Forty percent and rising. In a few years, we should be getting a good 75%-80% of our sales from the U.S.

ALICE: That's a bit high, I think. The big U.S. buyers are going to want to use U.S. sources, to protect their political position. But we should be able to increase our share of the market among the smaller manufacturers, especially as they try to undercut the prices of the biggies and we can supply them cheaper.

DOUG: Cheaper, as long as the U.S. dollar stays up. That high dollar gives us a real advantage in labour costs. Heaven help us if the Canadian and U.S. dollars are at par!

BOB: Sure; we'll have to squeeze our margins really tight if the U.S. dollar goes below $1.20 Canadian.

CAROL: Back to the draft statements! Reg, would you like to explain the differences between these two sets of figures?

REG: The first column is prepared by using what is called the *current-rate method*. To get the balance sheet figures, we just multiply the amounts on the Cal sub's balance sheet by the exchange rate at the end of the year, and add them to our own domestic figures. The income statement is similar, except that the rate is the average exchange rate for the year. The second column uses the *temporal method*. Under that method, we translate each amount of the statements at the rate in effect at the time of the transaction, except for monetary balances, which are translated at the closing rate for the year. The net result of the temporal method is the same as we would have gotten if we didn't have the sub, but conducted our U.S. business directly from here or through an agent, like we did in New England for a while.

CAROL: Can you explain the amounts for "loss from exchange rate changes?" There is quite a difference between the two methods.

REG: In the current-rate method, the loss is only the '82 portion of the accumulated loss on the long-term note that we were discussing earlier. Under this method, the CICA says that any exchange gains and losses from translating the subsidiary don't show up in income, but are shown in the balance sheet as a part of the shareholders' equity.

BOB: In effect, then, it's just a plug. It seems to me that the loss on the note is also just a plug. Why different treatment?

REG: Because the CICA says that the current-rate method should be used only for what they call *self-sustaining* subsidiaries—subsidiaries that function more or less on their own, generating their own revenue and incurring their own costs. They get cash in the foreign currency and pay cash in the foreign currency, and the parent doesn't get involved in the day-to-day financial transactions of the sub. Our own note, on the other hand, is an obligation that eventually will have to be paid, and it will be paid out of Canadian earnings.

CAROL: That might have been true when we took out the loan, but now it looks like the earnings from the sub are going to be what eventually pays off that loan. What about the other column?

REG: The loss in the second column starts out with the loss on the note, but is reduced by a gain on the translation of the sub.

DOUG: So the translation gain in the first column is a plug, but the translation gain in the second column is put into income.

REG: Yes and no. There actually is an overall translation loss of $47,500 under the temporal method; a difference of $95,000 as compared to the current-rate method. But we get to break that into two components, a loss of $200,000 on the sub's long-term note that is due on March 1, 1986, and a gain of $152,500 on the net current assets. We can take the gain on the current items into income, but we have to spread the loss on the note over the period of the note, just like we talked about for our own note. The result is that the income statement includes all $152,500 of the gain, but only $41,700 of the loss, for a net gain of $110,800 relating to the sub.

CAROL: And I gather that these amounts for deferred taxes are the non-tax effects of all these nontaxable gains and losses?

REG: Yes, calculated at 40%, our marginal tax rate.

DOUG: When are companies supposed to use the temporal method?

REG: When the activities of the subsidiary are integrated with those of the parent. I think that that is the case with us; the California operation is really just a sales agent for our VDUs. They pay us regularly for the shipments, and a lot of our cash flow comes from them.

BOB: But we haven't taken anything out in dividends, and we probably won't. We might supply the product, but the sub generates its own sales and keeps its profits and a lot of our product development ideas come from the sub. All those people have to do is to keep their eyes and ears open in silicone valley, and tell us what's going on.

CAROL: I can't say that I'm too impressed with either of your sets of statements, Reg. Nothing personal, but all these non-losses and non-taxes just seem to muck up the statements. As I see it, we made either $150,000 or $173,000, depending on the translation method. I don't mind going along with either translation method with those results, but I just don't understand what good all these exchange losses, deferred losses, and deferred taxes do. Do we really have to use one of these methods?

REG: We do if you want a clean auditor's opinion. But if you don't mind a

---

EXHIBIT 1

Video Displays, Inc.
Consolidated Income Statement
Year ended December 31, 1982

	Current-rate method	Temporal method
Sales revenue	$3,900,000	$3,900,000
Cost of sales	2,430,000	2,412,000
Operating expenses:		
Depreciation	375,000	370,000
Other	845,000	845,000
Loss from exchange rate changes	203,200	97,400
Income taxes — current	100,000	100,000
— deferred	(81,280)	(36,960)
	3,871,920	3,783,440
Net income after taxes	$ 28,080	$ 117,560

Consolidated Balance Sheet
December 31, 1982

ASSETS

Current assets:		
Cash	$ 95,000	$ 95,000
Accounts receivable	1,800,000	1,800,000
Inventories	700,000	688,000
	2,595,000	2,583,000
Furniture and equipment	4,860,000	4,790,000
Less accumulated depreciation	1,460,000	1,450,000
	3,400,000	3,340,000
Deferred foreign exchange loss	440,400	598,700
Deferred income taxes	63,840	19,520
Total assets	$6,499,240	$6,541,220

EQUITIES

Current liability:		
Accounts payable	$ 394,000	$ 394,000
Long-term liabilities:		
Notes payable ($4,000,000 U.S.)	5,600,000	5,600,000
Total liabilities	5,994,000	5,994,000
Shareholders' equity:		
Common shares	200,000	200,000
Retained earnings	257,740	347,220
Unrealized translation gain on U.S.		
subsidiary	47,500	—
	505,240	547,220
	$6,499,240	$6,541,220

little qualification here and there in the audit report, we can do something different.

CAROL: The bank was really understanding when we started out. They took a pretty big risk. Surely they wouldn't mind a qualified opinion, would they?

REG: I'll tell you what. Suppose I go back and have another go at this. I'll stick to the CICA recommendations where they seem suitable, but maybe I'll try treating the exchange gains and losses and the related taxes in a way that you'll be happier with. They're your financial statements; you should get what you want!

Required:

a. Reconcile the numerical amounts mentioned in the conversation, including the amounts shown on the draft statements for the exchange gains and losses and the deferred taxes, and including the disposition of the total translation gain or loss difference of $95,000 between the two translation methods.

b. Draft a new set of statements, as Reg indicated.

c. Draft a report to the board members in which you explain your revised draft statements, and reply to the concerns expressed by the board.

Local Brewery Limited

CASE 18-2

Local Brewery Limited (LBL) is a small, privately owned brewery incorporated under federal legislation. The brewery has been very prosperous and now wants to use its excess cash to go into other, diverse lines of business. A number of corporate acquisitions are being planned by the company's management, in addition to one that took place during the current fiscal year. On January 1, 19x4, LBL acquired a small hotel, The Airport Hotel Inc. (AHI), located in a foreign country. The shares of this foreign subsidiary were purchased for 1 million Canadian dollars. On that date, the subsidiary had common stock of 1,000,000 and retained earnings of 800,000 both expressed in local currency units (LCU). Condensed balance sheets at December 31, 19x4, were as follows:

	Local Brewery Ltd. (Canadian Dollars)	The Airport Hotel Inc. (Local Currency Units)
Current assets	6,700,000	1,400,000
Long-lived assets, net of accumulated depreciation	15,100,000	8,200,000
Investment in foreign subsidiary	1,000,000	—
Total assets	22,800,000	9,600,000
Current liabilities	4,900,000	2,000,000
Long-term debt	7,900,000	5,600,000
Deferred income tax	1,000,000	—
Shareholders' equity:		
Common shares	5,000,000	1,000,000
Retained earnings	4,000,000	1,000,000
Total liabilities and shareholders' equity	22,800,000	9,600,000

You are the newly appointed controller of LBL. The president of LBI wants your advice on matters related to the preparation of the 19x4 financial statements. The following conversation takes place:

President: "I am not an accounting expert, but I have some serious concerns regarding the consolidation of our foreign subsidiary. We are a brewery and I want the financial statements to portray our success as a brewery. I do not want a meaningless combination of results from two vastly different lines of business. I think we should use what you accountants refer to as the equity method."

Controller: "I think the CICA Handbook will require us to consolidate. I'll look into it for you and give you a report on the Handbook recommendations for further discussion."

President: "Fine. Include in your report a translated balance sheet for AHI prepared in accordance with Canadian generally accepted accounting principles. Do not prepare a consolidated balance sheet until we have discussed your report."

During the next few days you gather the following information:

1. Net income of the subsidiary for 19x4 was LCU 200,000, and no dividends were paid.
2. The local income tax rate for AHI is 40%. The company does not record deferred income taxes because it uses the taxes payable method to determine income tax expense. The cumulative timing differences, which relate entirely to fixed assets, are as follows:

	December 31, 19x3	December 31, 19x4
Excess of net book value over undepreciated capital cost for income tax purposes	LCU 300,000	LCU 350,000

3. On December 31, 19x4, equipment with an estimated useful life of five years was received and installed by the subsidiary. On the same day, the subsidiary signed a five-year, non-cancellable lease. The capitalization of leases is not required in the foreign country in which the subsidiary is located. Lease payments are due at the start of each year. The first of five annual lease payments of LCU 100,000 was made and charged to prepaid rent on December 31, 19x4. The subsidiary's borrowing rate is 8%.
4. The exchange rate for one LCU was $.40 Canadian at December 31, 19x3, and $.50 Canadian at December 31, 19x4. The rate changed uniformly over the year.
5. The subsidiary operates independently of its parent and the long-term debt (owed to a local bank) will be repaid entirely out of cash flows generated by the hotel. The subsidiary's total debt to equity ratio is typical of the hotel industry. The hotel has been very successful since its opening several years ago, and local management is confident that the long-term debt will be repaid according to schedule.
6. The long-term debt of LBL is owed to a life insurance company. The debt agreement contains the following condition with respect to LBL's audited financial statements, which are filed annually with the insurance company:

"... at the end of the fiscal year, if the total debt (excluding deferred taxes), to shareholders' equity ratio exceeds 1.5:1, the debt principal becomes due and payable."

The limit reflects leverage ratios typical in the brewing industry. For other companies, the insurance company has sometimes agreed to renegotiate conditions in debt agreements.

Required:
As newly appointed controller of Local Brewery Ltd., prepare the report to the President.
[SMA]

P18-1

The balance sheet accounts for Peter Corp. and its Butanian subsidiary, Caldwell Inc., are shown below. Caldwell's accounts are expressed in buttes, the Butanian currency. Peter established Caldwell when the butte was worth $0.60. The equipment was purchased when the butte was worth $0.70. The ending inventory was purchased when the rate was $0.54. The current rate for the butte is $0.50.

Required:
Prepare a consolidated balance sheet for Peter Corp. using:
a. The current-rate method.
b. The temporal method.

	Peter	Caldwell
Cash	$ 100,000	B 200,000
Accounts receivable	300,000	250,000
Inventory	400,000	400,000
Equipment	1,000,000	600,000
Accumulated depreciation	(400,000)	(150,000)
Investment in Caldwell	600,000	—
	$2,000,000	B 1,300,000
Accounts payable	$ 200,000	B 300,000
Bonds payable	800,000	—
Common shares	600,000	1,000,000
Retained earnings	400,000	—
	$2,000,000	B 1,300,000

P18-2

The trial balances at December 31, 19x7, for Gowan Corp. and Hewlett Ltd. are shown below. Hewlett is a subsidiary of Gowan that is located in Wolsley. The currency of Wolsley is the weevle.

Additional Information:
1. The original investment by Gowan was made on January 1, 19x5.
2. Gowan's long-term note was issued in order to finance the investment in Hewlett.
3. Hewlett's equipment was purchased on March 31, 19x5, and is being depreciated over ten years, straight-line.
4. Hewlett's ending inventory was purchased when the weevle was worth $2.18. Eighty percent of the inventory was acquired from Gowan.
5. Hewlett's opening inventory was W50,000. The exchange rate at the time of purchase was $2.00.

6. During 19x7, Gowan had sales of $2,400,000 to Hewlett. The sales occurred evenly throughout the year. Gowan's gross margin was 40% of the selling price.
7. Hewlett pays all earnings to Gowan as dividends at the end of each year.
8. At January 1, 19x7, Hewlett's cash balance was W80,000. Hewlett's accounts receivable and payable were at the same level at the beginning of the year as at the end of the year.
9. Hewlett had no transactions involving long-term assets or liabilities during 19x7.
10. Additional exchange rate information:

January 1, 19x5	W1 = $1.80
March 31, 19x5	W1 = $1.85
December 31, 19x6	W1 = $2.00
Average for 19x7	W1 = $2.10
December 31, 19x7	W1 = $2.20

Required:
Prepare a consolidated income statement and balance sheet for Gowan Corp., following the *CICA Handbook* recommendations, assuming that Hewlett Ltd. is a:
a. Self-sustaining operation.
b. Integrated operation.

Trial Balances
December 31, 19x7
Dr. (Cr.)

	Gowan	Hewlett
Cash	$ 100,000	W 110,000
Accounts receivable	260,000	150,000
Inventories	300,000	100,000
Equipment	2,000,000	800,000
Accumulated depreciation	(800,000)	(200,000)
Investment in Hewlett (at cost)	1,440,000	—
Accounts payable	(300,000)	(160,000)
Long-term note	(1,200,000)	—
Common shares	(1,000,000)	(800,000)
Retained earnings	(580,000)	—
Revenue from sales	(6,000,000)	(2,000,000)
Cost of sales	3,600,000	1,550,000
Depreciation	200,000	80,000
Other expenses	1,700,000	270,000
Dividend income	(220,000)	—
Dividends paid	500,000	100,000
	$ 0	W 0

P18-3

On January 1, 19x5, the Candoo Company, a Canadian company, acquires 100% of the outstanding shares of the Brazos Company for 11 million New Cruzeiros (NC). The Brazos Company is a merchandising company located in Brazil, and on this date the net identifiable assets of the Company had carrying values of NC10 million. Since the fair values of all of the Brazos Company's identifiable assets and liabilities were equal to their carrying values, the excess of the investment cost over book value was allocated to goodwill. In the consolidated statements presented by the Candoo Company, this balance is being amortized over a period of 40 years.

The income statement of the Brazos Company for the year ending December 31, 19x9 is as follows:

Sales revenue	NC2,500,000
Cost of goods sold	1,600,000
Depreciation expense	200,000
Other expenses	150,000
Taxes	220,000
Total expenses	2,170,000
Net income	NC 330,000

Additional Information:
1. The 19x9 cost of goods sold consists of NC700,000 for merchandise that was purchased on October 1, 19x8 and NC900,000 for merchandise that was purchased on April 1, 19x9. An additional NC600,000 in merchandise was purchased on this latter date and remains in the December 31, 19x9 inventories of the Brazos Company.
2. The 19x9 sales revenue consists of two large sales. On April 1, 19x9, merchandise was sold for NC1,000,000 and on October 1, 19x9, merchandise was sold for NC1,500,000.
3. All of the depreciation expense was recorded on assets that the Brazos Company owned when it was acquired by the Candoo Company.
4. Other expenses were accrued uniformly over the year.
5. Taxes were accrued and were payable on December 31, 19x9.
6. Exchange rate data is as follows:

January 1, 19x5	NC1 = $1.00
Average for 19x8	NC1 = $0.80
October 1, 19x8	NC1 = $0.75
January 1, 19x9	NC1 = $0.70
April 1, 19x9	NC1 = $0.65
Average for 19x9	NC1 = $0.60
October 1, 19x9	NC1 = $0.55
December 31, 19x9	NC1 = $0.50

7. On January 1, 19x9, the Brazos Company had net current monetary assets amounting to NC750,000.
8. Neither company declared or paid dividends during 19x9.

Required:
(Note: This question does *not* require the preparation of a consolidated income statement.)

a. The Candoo Company prepares consolidated financial statements that include the accounts of its subsidiary, the Brazos Company, translated by means of the temporal method. Prior to preparing the consolidated income statement, you are to prepare an income statement for the year ending December 31, 19x9, for the Brazos Company, expressed in Canadian dollars. Provide a separate computation of the 19x9 exchange gain or loss.
b. The Candoo Company reports its investment in Brazos Company on the equity basis. Prepare a schedule to calculate the earnings from Brazos that Candoo would report on its 19x9 income statement, using:

1. The temporal method.
2. The current-rate method.

[SMA, adapted]

P18-4

On December 31, 19x6, the Dore Company acquired 100% of the outstanding shares of the Benz Company. The Benz Company is a merchandising firm, located in Germany. The shares were acquired at a cost of 20 million deutsche marks (DM). The 19x7 income statements and the comparative balance sheets for the Benz Company are as follows:

Balance Sheets

	December 31, 19x6	December 31, 19x7
Cash	DM 2,000,000	DM 2,500,000
Accounts receivable	2,000,000	2,500,000
Inventories	15,000,000	20,000,000
Plant and equipment (net)	6,000,000	5,000,000
Total assets	DM 25,000,000	DM 30,000,000
Current liabilities	DM 5,000,000	DM 7,000,000
Common shares	10,000,000	10,000,000
Retained earnings	10,000,000	13,000,000
Total equities	DM 25,000,000	DM 30,000,000

19x7 Income Statement

Sales	DM 100,000,000
Cost of goods sold	80,000,000
Depreciation expense	1,000,000
Other expenses	16,000,000
	97,000,000
Net income	DM 3,000,000

Additional Information:
1. The Benz Company did not declare or pay any dividends during 19x7.
2. Purchases, sales, and other expenses were accrued evenly over the year. This would make translation at the average exchange rate the appropriate procedure.
3. On December 31, 19x6, the exchange was DM1 = $.40. By December 31, 19x7, the rate had increased to DM1 = $.50. The average rate for 19x7 was DM1 = $.45.
4. The December 31, 19x7 inventories were purchased when DM1 = $.47.

Required:
a. Prepare comparative balance sheets in Canadian dollars for the Benz Company as of December 31 for the years 19x6 and 19x7, using the temporal method.

b. Prepare an income statement in Canadian dollars for the year ending December 31, 19x7. Exchange gain or loss should be recognized in the year in which it occurs.

c. Make an independent calculation of the exchange gain or loss for 19x7. [SMA]

P18-5

Refer to P18-4. Prepare the information requested in that problem, using the current-rate method instead of the temporal method.

P18-6

The comparative balance sheet and income statement for the Dore Company (see P18-4) are shown below.

Balance Sheets
(Canadian dollars)

	December 31, 19x6	December 31, 19x7
Cash	$ 2,000,000	$ 2,500,000
Accounts receivable	4,000,000	3,000,000
Inventories	10,000,000	11,000,000
Plant and equipment (net)	8,000,000	7,500,000
Investment in Benz Company		
(at cost)	8,000,000	8,000,000
Total assets	$32,000,000	$32,000,000
Current liabilities	$ 5,000,000	$ 6,000,000
Long-term liabilities	10,000,000	10,000,000
Common shares	5,000,000	5,000,000
Retained earnings	12,000,000	11,000,000
Total equities	$32,000,000	$32,000,000

Income Statement
Year ended December 31, 19x7

Sales	$50,000,000
Cost of goods sold	30,000,000
Depreciation expense	500,000
Other expenses	18,000,000
Total expenses	48,500,000
Net income	$ 1,500,000

Required:
Using the information given in P18-4, prepare a consolidated comparative balance sheet and income statement for Dore Company for 19x7, using the temporal method. Recognize any exchange gain or loss in income.

P18-7

Refer to P18-6. Using the information given therein, prepare the consolidated balance sheet and income statement using the current-rate method. Show the translation gain or loss as a separate component of shareholders' equity.

P18-8

On January 1, 19x5, Parsley Ltd. acquired 70% of the outstanding common shares of Savory Inc. for U.S. $750,000 cash. Savory is situated in the United States, and conducts its business in U.S. dollars. To finance the purchase, Parsley negotiated a five-year loan of U.S. $600,000. Parsley expects that the earnings from Savory will be adequate to repay the loan in five years.

At the date of purchase, the net book value of Savory's net assets amounted to U.S. $800,000. The fair values of Savory's assets and liabilities approximated their book values, except for machinery that had a fair value of U.S. $100,000 higher than book value. The machinery had a remaining useful life of five years, and is being depreciated on a straight-line basis. Goodwill arising from the purchase will be amortized over thirty years.

On December 31, 19x5, the balance sheet accounts of the two companies were as follows:

	Parsley	Savory
Cash	Can. $ 20,000	U.S. $ 40,000
Accounts receivable	60,000	30,000
Inventories	120,000	80,000
Machinery and equipment (net)	1,200,000	750,000
Investment in Savory (at cost)	900,000	—
	Can. $2,300,000	U.S. $900,000
Accounts payable	Can. $ 70,000	U.S. $ 50,000
Note payable (U.S. $600,000)	720,000	—
Common shares	600,000	200,000
Retained earnings	910,000	650,000
	Can. $2,300,000	U.S. $900,000

The exchange rate for the U.S. dollar was Can. $1.20 on January 1, 19x5, Can. $1.25 through the year, and Can. $1.30 on December 31, 19x5.

Required:
a. Prepare a consolidated balance sheet for Parsley Ltd., in accordance with *CICA Handbook* recommendations, assuming that Savory Inc. is self-sustaining and that the note payable is a hedge of Parsley's net investment in Savory.
b. How would your answer be affected if the note payable was *not* designated as a hedge of the investment in Savory?

P18-9

On January 1, 19x5, Parent Limited, a Canadian-based company purchased 90% of the outstanding shares of Forsub Incorporated for 3,200,000 francs, which, at that date, translated to $1,333,333 Canadian. At the date of acquisition, Forsub Incorporated's retained earnings were 1,840,000 francs. At the date of acquisition, the book values of the net assets equalled the fair market values, and the only purchase price discrepancy was goodwill, which is amortized over twenty years.

The financial statements of Forsub Incorporated are presented below, and management has determined that the temporal method of translation is appropriate.

Forsub Incorporated
Balance Sheet
December 31, 19x6

Cash (Note 1)	F 340,000
Receivables (Net of allowance of 90,000 francs)	800,000
Inventory (FIFO) (Note 2)	1,400,000
Fixed assets (Note 3)	3,400,000
Accumulated depreciation (Note 3)	(1,060,000)
	F4,880,000
Current liabilities (due within one year)	F 200,000
Notes payable (Note 4)	900,000
Common shares (issued at date of incorporation)	1,000,000
Retained earnings at January 1, 19x6 (Note 5)	2,100,000
Net income	730,000
Dividends (Note 6)	(50,000)
	F4,880,000

Forsub Incorporated
Income Statement
For the year ended December 31, 19x6

Sales (made evenly throughout the year)	F1,900,000
Cost of sales (Note 2)	(800,000)
Gross profit	1,100,000
Depreciation	(220,000)
Other (incurred evenly throughout the year)	(150,000)
Net income	F 730,000

Other exchange rates:

January 1, 19x6	$1 = 3.1 francs
July 1, 19x6	$1 = 3.5 francs (average for 19x6)
December 31, 19x6	$1 = 3.9 francs

Notes to Financial Statements:
1. Cash is available for immediate withdrawal.
2. Details of inventory are:

	Francs	Exchange
Opening inventory	F1,100,000	$1 = 2.7 francs
Add: Purchase #1	400,000	$1 = 3.2 francs
Purchase #2	500,000	$1 = 3.4 francs
Purchase #3	200,000	$1 = 3.7 francs
	2,200,000	
Less: Cost of sales	(800,000)	
Closing inventory	F1,400,000	

3. Fixed assets:
Building #1 was purchased when the company was formed eight years ago (exchange rate was $1 = 1 franc), and building #2 was purchased on January 1, 19x6.

	Cost	Accumulated depreciation
Building #1	F2,400,000	F 960,000
Building #2	1,000,000	100,000
	F3,400,000	F1,060,000

4. Notes payable were incurred on January 1, 19x6, and are due on July 1, 19x11.
5. Retained earnings at December 31, 19x5, were translated, using the temporal method, to $868,628.
6. Dividends were paid in equal amounts on July 1 and December 31.

Required:
Ignoring income taxes,
a. Prepare the eliminating entry at *January 1, 19x5*, which is the date of acquisition.
b. For December 31, 19x6, prepare the Canadian dollar balance sheet and income statement using the temporal method, indicating the disposition of translation gains and losses to the extent possible from the information given.
[CGA-Canada]

P18-10

Jaguar Industries Limited (Jaguar) is a Canadian company whose shares are publicly traded. Jaguar designs and assembles integrated electronic industrial control devices. It relies on Serval Limited, a company situated in Austereland, to supply electronic processors used in the assembly of the devices. The currency used in Austereland is the aut (A). On January 1, 19x7, Jaguar purchased 80% of the common shares of Serval for $9,600,000 cash. On that date, the book values of Serval's common shares and retained earnings were A5,350,000 and A450,000 respectively. The fair values of Serval's assets and liabilities were equal to their book values except for the following:

	Net Book Value	Fair Market Value
Inventory	A2,100,000	A1,800,000
Land	1,400,000	1,500,000
Plant and equipment	5,750,000	6,500,000

The average remaining useful life of the plant and equipment was twenty years.
The pre-closing trial balances for Jaguar and Serval at December 31, 19x7, are shown in Exhibit 1. The following additional information is available:

1. The exchange rates were as follows:

		Auts		Dollars
January 1, 19x7		A1.00	=	$1.50
Average for 19x7		1.00	=	1.80
December 31, 19x7		1.00	=	2.00

2. Serval is considered to be a self-sustaining foreign operation.
3. The following information with respect to 19x7 intercompany transactions is given in Canadian dollars.
   a. Serval sales to Jaguar $5,000,000
      (translated at average exchange rate for 19x7)
   b. Profit on sale of machinery by Jaguar to Serval at end of 19x7 (Serval does not calculate depreciation on assets acquired during the second half of a fiscal year) (translated at December 31 rate) $250,000
   c. Profit on Serval sales to Jaguar still in inventory at December 31, 19x7 $500,000
      (translated at average exchange rate for 19x7)
   d. Amount still owing to Serval by Jaguar on December 31, 19x7 $400,000
      (translated at December 31 rate)
4. All dividends are declared at the end of the year. Jaguar has not recorded the dividend income or receivable from Serval.
5. Jaguar amortizes goodwill over twenty years on a straight-line basis. Fixed assets are depreciated on a straight-line basis over the estimated useful life. Inventory turns over approximately twice per year.

EXHIBIT 1

Jaguar and Serval pre-closing Trial Balances
December 31, 19x7
(in thousands)

	Jaguar Dr.	Jaguar Cr.	Serval Dr.	Serval Cr.
Cash	$ 3,400		A 765	
Accounts receivable	14,000		2,000	
Inventory (at cost)	15,000		2,335	
Investment in subsidiary	9,600			
Land	3,000		1,400	
Plant and equipment — net	28,000		5,900	
Accounts payable		$ 8,000		A 900
Dividends payable		4,000		350
Long-term debt		10,000		3,500
Deferred income tax		1,000		1,000
Common shares		29,000		5,350
Retained earnings		13,000		450
Sales		99,550		10,225
Cost of sales	77,100		6,000	
Depreciation	1,400		300	
Other expenses	3,500		2,100	
Gain on sales of fixed assets		450		
Income taxes	6,000		625	
Dividends	4,000		350	
	$165,000	$165,000	A21,775	A21,775

Required:

a. In accordance with generally accepted accounting principles, prepare the consolidated income statement for the year ended December 31, 19x7, and the consolidated balance sheet for Jaguar at December 31, 19x7. Ignore consolidation effects on income taxes. Show all calculations.

b. Discuss (without calculations) the effects that consolidation adjustments would have on the companies' income taxes payable and the consolidated income taxes provision.

c. Identify the circumstances under which it would not be appropriate to treat Serval as a self-sustaining operation.

d. Jaguar wishes to maximize reported net income in order to obtain financing for a planned expansion. The president asked if this could be accomplished by accounting for Serval using a method other than consolidation. Discuss.

e. In evaluating the acquisition of Serval, Jaguar considered a share exchange. Relevant market data at the time were as follows:

	Jaguar	Serval
Price per share	$24.00	$12.00
19x7 estimated earnings per share	$ 1.20	$ 2.00
Price/earnings ratio	20	6
Number of shares outstanding	10,000,000	1,000,000

Jaguar considered issuing 400,000 shares to purchase 80% of the shares of Serval. Comment on the reasonableness of this approach.
[SMA]

P18-11

On December 31, 19x7, Canadian-based Multinorth Ltd. acquired 83% of the outstanding shares of Sunbird Inc., a merchandising company located in a small underdeveloped country called Nawkland. The local currency in Nawkland is the nawk (NK, hereafter) and on the date that Multinorth acquired the Sunbird shares, the Canadian/Nawkland exchange rate was NK1 = $.60.

To acquire the Sunbird shares, Multinorth paid the equivalent of NK22,410,000. Of this amount, $7,446,000 was paid in cash and the balance was covered by issuing 100,000 Multinorth shares to the shareholders of Sunbird. On December 30, 19x7, just prior to this acquisition, there were 122,000 Multinorth shares outstanding and they were trading at $60 per share.

On December 31, 19x7, all of the identifiable assets and liabilities of Sunbird had fair values equal to their carrying values except for the following:

1. Insurance coverage on plant assets was acquired at a very favourable rate and, as a consequence, the fair value of the prepaid insurance exceeded its carrying value by NK102,000. The policy expires on June 30, 19x9.

2. Sunbird's plant and equipment was acquired on January 1, 19x3, at a cost of NK24,700,000. At that time, it was expected to have an economic life of ten years. On December 31, 19x7, it was estimated that the undepreciated cost of replacing this plant and equipment would be NK26,400,000. There was no change at this time in the original estimate of the economic life of the plant and equipment.

3. Sunbird was holding a parcel of undeveloped land that had a fair value that was NK223,000 less than its carrying value of NK813,000.

4. As the result of differing accounting principles in Nawkland, Sunbird had no carrying values for accounts receivable or deferred taxes. The fair value for accounts receivable was NK1,425,000. If interperiod tax allocation had been

used, deferred taxes would have had a credit balance of NK2,470,000, related entirely to Sunbird's plant and equipment.

The comparative balance sheets of Sunbird at December 31, 19x7, and December 31, 19x8, and the income statements of Multinorth and Sunbird are shown below.

Sunbird Incorporated
Balance Sheet
As at December 31

	19x8	19x7
Cash	NK 6,849,000	NK 1,876,000
Inventories (at market)	4,818,000	3,856,000
Prepaid insurance	325,000	975,000
Plant and equipment (at cost)	24,700,000	24,700,000
Accumulated depreciation	(14,820,000)	(12,350,000)
Land	4,973,000	5,786,000
Total assets	NK26,845,000	NK24,843,000
Current liabilities	NK 473,000	NK 562,000
Long-term liabilities	1,876,000	1,876,000
No-par common stock	10,873,000	10,873,000
Retained earnings	13,623,000	11,532,000
Total equities	NK26,845,000	NK24,843,000

Income Statements
For the year ended December 31, 19x8

	Multinorth Ltd.	Sunbird Inc.
Sales revenue	$24,022,000	NK23,331,000
Cost of goods sold	12,186,000	13,325,000
Depreciation expense	4,280,000	2,470,000
Insurance expense	420,000	650,000
Lease expense	0	518,000
Other expenses	3,566,000	2,618,000
Tax provision (all current)	1,428,000	1,244,000
Total expenses	21,880,000	20,825,000
Income before extraordinary items	2,142,000	2,506,000
Extraordinary loss	0	415,000
Net income	$ 2,142,000	NK 2,091,000

Accounting Principles:

Sunbird was incorporated in Nawkland and, as a consequence, its financial statements must comply with the Recommendations of the Nawkland Accounting Standards Authority (NASA). These generally accepted accounting principles (GAAP) that have been established by NASA are similar to Canadian GAAP. The differences between NASA and Canadian GAAP are as follows:

1. While NASA has issued a pronouncement dealing with accounting for leases,

its Recommendations do not require lessees to capitalize long-term leases. As a consequence, Nawkland lessees do not capitalize any of their leases.

2. The recognition of sales revenue is on a cash rather than an accrual basis. Sunbird's credit terms and the degree of uncertainty associated with the collection of receivables is not significantly different from those of Multinorth and other Canadian companies.

3. The use of interperiod tax allocation procedures for dealing with timing differences between accounting income and taxable income is strictly prohibited by NASA.

4. Nawkland companies are required to carry their inventories at net realizable value, regardless of whether that amount is higher or lower than cost. Multinorth values inventories at the lower of cost and market with market measured on the basis of net realizable value.

Other Information:

1. Sunbird's long-term liabilities were issued on January 1, 19x3, the same date on which the plant and equipment were acquired. On this date, the exchange rate was NK1 = $.35. These long-term liabilities mature on January 1, 19x18.

2. The Nawkland government assesses taxes at a 20% rate on all business income. With two exceptions, the tax rules for computing business income are identical to GAAP as established by NASA. One exception is that the full cost of plant and equipment can be deducted in the year of acquisition. The other is that the Nawkland government does not assess any tax on capital gains.

3. While Sunbird's sales revenues are recorded in its general journal on a cash basis, a subsidiary ledger is used to account for balances owed to the company by individual customers. On December 31, 19x7, this ledger contained balances in the total amount of NK1,425,000. The corresponding balance on December 31, 19x8, was NK1,642,000.

4. On January 1, 19x8, the cost of Sunbird's inventories was NK3,923,000. The corresponding figure on December 31, 19x8, was NK4,745,000.

5. On January 1, 19x8, Sunbird leased additional plant and equipment with an estimated economic life of ten years. The lease term is five years and its provisions call for annual payments on January 1, 19x8, through January 1, 19x12, in the amount of NK518,000. The fair value of the leased assets was NK2,160,008 on January 1, 19x8. Sunbird's incremental borrowing rate is 10%, and the lease contains an option that would allow Sunbird to purchase the plant and equipment on January 1, 19x13, for one dollar.

6. During 19x8, Multinorth had $732,000 in sales to Sunbird while Sunbird had NK1,470,000 in sales to Multinorth. Of the goods purchased by Sunbird from Multinorth, $270,000 remain in the December 31, 19x8, inventories. With respect to the goods purchased by Multinorth from Sunbird, NK410,000 remain in the December 31, 19x8, inventories. The goods that are in Multinorth's December 31, 19x8, inventories were purchased on October 31, 19x8. All intercompany sales are priced to provide the selling company with a 40% gross profit on sales price and there are no intercompany receivables on December 31, 19x8.

7. The NK415,000 extraordinary loss experienced by Sunbird resulted from the sale of a parcel of undeveloped land on December 31, 19x8, for NK398,000. This is the same parcel of undeveloped land that had the fair value that was NK223,000 less than its carrying value on December 31, 19x7, when Multinorth acquired Sunbird.

8. The December 31, 19x7, inventories of Sunbird were acquired on November 15, 19x7, while the December 31, 19x8, inventories of Sunbird were acquired on October 31, 19x8.

9. Assume that sales revenues, purchases (including intercompany purchases), and the other expenses of Sunbird occurred uniformly over the year ended December 31, 19x8.

10. Sunbird is considered to be an integrated foreign investee from the point of view of Multinorth.
11. No dividends were paid by Sunbird during the year ended December 31, 19x8.
12. Selected exchange rates were as follows:

January 1, 19x3	NK1 = $.35
November 15, 19x7	NK1 = $.55
December 31, 19x7	NK1 = $.60
October 31, 19x8	NK1 = $.41
December 31, 19x8	NK1 = $.38
Average for 19x8	NK1 = $.49

13. Multinorth carries its investment in Sunbird using the cost method.
14. It is the policy of Multinorth to amortize goodwill over a period of fifteen years.

Required:
a. Will Multinorth's acquisition of the Sunbird shares be accounted for by the purchase method or the pooling of interests method? Explain your conclusion.
b. Before being translated or incorporated into Multinorth's consolidated financial statements, the financial statements of Sunbird will have to be restated to reflect Canadian GAAP.
  1. Prepare the restated income statement of Sunbird for the year ended December 31, 19x8. The statement should be in Nawkland nawks. (Worksheet format is acceptable.)
  2. Indicate the accounts that would be added, eliminated, increased, or decreased in the December 31, 19x8, balance sheet of Sunbird by this restatement process. Calculate the amount of each change.
  3. Would you always convert a foreign investee's sales to an accrual basis when they are reported on a cash basis in the foreign currency financial statements? Explain your conclusion.
c. Before being incorporated into Multinorth's consolidated financial statements, the restated financial statements of Sunbird will have to be converted into Canadian dollars.
  1. Prepare the translated income statement for the year ended December 31, 19x8. The translation should be based on the restated income statement that was prepared in Part (b). (Worksheet format is acceptable.)
  2. If Sunbird had been classified as a self-sustaining foreign operation, any exchange gain or loss that arose during 19x8 would have been allocated to an accumulated exchange rate adjustment account. Explain why it appears that Canadian standard setters believe that this approach is more consistent with the objectives of financial reporting than would be the inclusion of such amounts in the income of self-sustaining foreign operations.
d. Multinorth will prepare consolidated financial statements using the restated and translated balances of Sunbird.
  1. Calculate the amount of goodwill to be recorded on December 31, 19x7, as the result of Multinorth's acquisition of Sunbird.
  2. Prepare the consolidated income statement for Multinorth and its subsidiary Sunbird for the year ended December 31, 19x8. (Worksheet format is acceptable.)
  [SMA]

Solutions to Self-Study Problems

SSP 6-1

Bunker Ltd.
Consolidated Income Statement
Year ended December 31, 19x3

Sales revenue	$14,000,000
Cost of sales	6,200,000
Other operating expenses income	4,200,000
	10,400,000
Net income	$ 3,600,000

Bunker Ltd.
Consolidated Balance Sheet
December 31, 19x3

Current assets:	
Cash and receivables	$ 320,000
Inventories	1,400,000
	1,720,000
Furniture, fixtures and equipment	3,700,000
Buildings under capital leases	9,000,000
Total assets	$14,420,000
Current liabilities	$ 1,620,000
Long-term liabilities	6,000,000
	7,620,000
Common shares	1,500,000
Retained earnings*	5,300,000
	6,800,000
Total equities	$14,420,000

*$2,100,000 + $1,600,000 + $3,600,000 − $2,000,000 = $5,300,000

Eliminations (Not required):

Common shares	$1,000,000	
Investment in Bunker Ltd.		$1,000,000
Sales	4,000,000	
Cost of sales		4,000,000
Current liabilities	280,000	
Current receivables		280,000
Dividend income	500,000	
Dividends declared		500,000

SSP 7-1

Analysis of the purchase transaction (both alternatives):

	Book value	Fair value	Increment
Net assets acquired	$12,400,000	$15,700,000	
Adjustment for mkt. res. costs	40,000		
	$12,440,000	$15,700,000	$3,260,000
Purchase price		20,000,000	
Goodwill		$ 4,300,000	4,300,000
Excess of purchase price over book value of net assets acquired			$7,560,000

Ace Corporation
Balance Sheet
August 31, 19x4

	a*	b
Current assets	$ 7,725,000	$ 4,625,000
Plant and equipment	32,500,000	32,500,000
Patents	810,000	810,000
Market research	190,000	190,000
Goodwill	4,300,000	4,300,000
	$45,525,000	$42,425,000
Liabilities	$ 4,750,000	$21,650,000
Common shares	34,950,000	16,200,000
Retained earnings	5,825,000	5,825,000
Treasury shares	—	(1,250,000)
	$45,525,000	$42,425,000

*Consolidated

The internal expenses relating to the merger have been charged to net income for fiscal 19x4. Ace's 19x4 net income therefore is $2,425,000.

SSP 8-1

Analysis of the purchase transaction, January 1, 19x3:

	Book value	Fair value	Increment
Net assets acquired:			
Cash	$ 80,000	$ 80,000	—
Accounts receivable	99,000	95,000	$ (4,000)
Inventory	178,000	195,000	17,000
Fixed assets, net	579,000	642,000	63,000
Current liabilities	(70,000)	(70,000)	—
Long-term liabilities	(201,000)	(201,000)	—
	$665,000	741,000	76,000
Purchase price		761,000	
Goodwill		$ 20,000	20,000
Excess of purchase price over book value of net assets acquired			$96,000

Par Ltd.
Consolidated Balance Sheet
December 31, 19x5

Current assets	
Cash (120,000 + 110,000)	$ 230,000
Accounts receivable (150,000 + 135,000)	285,000
Inventory (240,000 + 195,000 − 18,000 − 20,000)	397,000
	912,000
Fixed assets (890,000 + 706,000 + 63,000 − 18,900 − 200,000)	1,440,100
Goodwill (75,000 + 20,000 − 3,000)	92,000
	$2,444,100
Current liabilities (142,000 + 60,000)	202,000
Long-term liabilities (600,000 + 201,000)	801,000
Total liabilities	1,003,000
Common shares	500,000
Retained earnings (994,000 + 635,000 − 415,000 − 200,000 − 18,900 − 3,000 − 18,000 − 20,000 + 4,000 − 17,000)	941,100
Total shareholders' equity	1,441,100
	$2,444,100

Par Ltd.
Consolidated Income Statement
Year Ended December 31, 19x5

Sales (1,200,000 + 987,000 − 390,000 − 150,000)	$1,647,000
Cost of goods sold (800,000 + 650,000 − 390,000 + 18,000 − 150,000 + 20,000 − 12,000)	936,000
Gross profit	711,000
Other expenses (234,000 + 146,000 + 200,000 + 6,300 + 1,000)	587,300
Net income before income tax	123,700
Income tax (66,000 + 76,000)	142,000
Net income (loss)	$ (18,300)

Consolidation worksheet (not required), in thousands:

	Trial balances		Adjustments and eliminations			Consolidated trial balance
				Operations		
	Par	Sub	Acquisition	Cumulative	Current	
Cash	120.0	110.0				230.0
Accounts receivable	150.0	135.0	(4.0)	4.0		285.0
Inventories	240.0	195.0	17.0	(17.0)	(18.0)a (20.0)b	397.0
Fixed assets, net	890.0	706.0	63.0	(12.6)	(200.0)c (6.3)d	1,440.1
Goodwill	75.0	—	20.0	(2.0)	(1.0)e	92.0
Investment in Sub	761.0	—	(761.0)			—
Current liabilities	(142.0)	(60.0)				(202.0)
Long-term liabilities	(600.0)	(201.0)				(801.0)
Common shares	(500.0)	(250.0)	250.0			(500.0)
Retained earnings (Jan. 1, 19x5)	(894.0)	(520.0)	415.0	27.6	12.0 f	(959.4)
Sales	(1,200.0)	(987.0)			390.0 a 150.0 b	(1,647.0)
Cost of goods sold	800.0	650.0			(372.0)a (130.0)b (12.0)f	936.0
Other expenses	234.0	146.0			200.0 c 6.3 d 1.0 e	587.3
Income tax expense	66.0	76.0				142.0
	0	0	0	0	0	0

Comments:
- The FVI/D on accounts receivable and inventory have flowed through operations prior to 19x5 and require an adjustment to retained earnings under both the direct approach and the worksheet approach.
- The unrealized profit on beginning inventories requires an adjustment to beginning retained earnings on the worksheet but not to ending retained earnings in the direct approach.
- Beginning unconsolidated retained earnings was derived by subtracting the 19x5 net incomes from the ending balance sheet amounts.

SSP 9-1

Analysis of the purchase transaction:

	60% of Dakota Ltd.		FV
	Book Value	Fair Value	Increment
Cash	$ 6,000	$ 6,000	—
Accounts receivable	12,000	12,000	—
Inventory	18,000	18,000	—
Land	27,000	48,000	$21,000
Building (net)	60,000	78,000	18,000
Equipment (net)	30,000	6,000	(24,000)
Accounts payable	(24,000)	(24,000)	—
Bonds payable	(30,000)	(36,000)	(6,000)
	$99,000	108,000	9,000
Purchase price		150,000	
Goodwill		$ 42,000	42,000
Purchase price discrepancy			$51,000

Regina Ltd.
Consolidated Balance Sheet
January 1, 19x9

Current assets:	
Cash (50,000 + 10,000)	$ 60,000
Accounts receivable (70,000 + 20,000)	90,000
Inventory (80,000 + 30,000)	110,000
	260,000
Fixed assets:	
Land (0 + 45,000 + 21,000)	66,000
Building (260,000 + 150,000 − 50,000 + 18,000)	378,000
Accumulated depreciation	(40,000)
Equipment (175,000 + 130,000 − 80,000 − 24,000)	201,000
Accumulated depreciation	(70,000)
	535,000
Goodwill	42,000
Total assets	$837,000
Accounts payable (80,000 + 40,000)	$120,000
Bonds payable (0 + 50,000 + 6,000)	56,000
	176,000
Minority interest (165,000 × 40%)	66,000
Common shares (220,000 + 150,000 issued)	370,000
Retained earnings	225,000
	595,000
Total liabilities and share equity	$837,000

SSP 9-2

Statement of changes in consolidated retained earnings

Retained earnings, December 31, 19x8	$ 225,000
Net income	144,500
Dividends declared	(20,000)
Retained earnings, December 31, 19x9	$ 349,500

Consolidated balance sheet

	December 31	
	19x9	19x8
Current assets:		
Cash (30,000 + 10,000)	$ 40,000	$ 50,000
Accounts receivable (110,000 + 30,000 − 52,500)	87,500	70,000
Inventory (160,000 + 60,000 − 20,000 − 40,000)	160,000	80,000
	287,500	200,000
Fixed assets:		
Land (135,000 + 21,000)	156,000	—
Buildings (300,000 + 150,000 − 50,000 + 18,000)	418,000	260,000
Accumulated depreciation (45,000 + 60,000 − 50,000 + 1,800)	(56,800)	(40,000)
Equipment (200,000 + 130,000 − 80,000 − 24,000)	226,000	175,000
Accumulated depreciation (80,000 + 90,000 − 80,000 − 4,800)	(85,200)	(70,000)
	658,000	325,000
Goodwill (42,000 − 2,100)	39,900	
Total assets	$985,400	$525,000
Liabilities:		
Accounts payable (40,000 + 80,000 − 52,500)	$ 67,500	$ 80,000
Bonds payable (65,000 + 50,000 + 6,000 − 600)	120,400	—
	187,900	80,000
Minority interest [(40% × 165,000) + 28,000 − 16,000]	78,000	—
Shareholders' equity:		
Common shares	370,000	220,000
Retained earnings	349,500	225,000
	735,500	445,000
Total liabilities and shareholders' equity	$985,400	$525,000

Consolidated income statement

Sales (2,000,000 + 1,000,000 − 400,000 − 200,000)	**$2,400,000**

Operating expenses:

Cost of sales (1,000,000 + 600,000 − 400,000 + 40,000 − 200,000 + 20,000)		1,060,000
Other expenses (839,000 + 170,000 + 1,800 - 4,800 + 2,100)		1,008,100
Interest expense (2,000 + 10,000 − 2,500 − 600)		8,900
Income tax expense (45,000 + 110,000)		155,000
Minority interest in earnings of Dakota: 40% (110,000 − 40,000)		28,000
		2,260,000
Operating income		140,000
Other income (7,000 − 2,500)		4,500
Net income		$ 144,500

Consolidated statement of changes in financial position

Operations:

Net income per income statement		$144,500
Expenses not requiring cash:		
Depreciation and amortization:		
Buildings (5,000 + 10,000 + 1,800)	$ 16,800	
Equipment (10,000 + 10,000 − 4,800)	15,200	
Goodwill	2,100	
Bond premium amortization	(600)	
Minority interest in earnings of Dakota	28,000	61,500
Changes in current assets and liabilities:		
Accounts receivable (70,000 + 20,000 − 87,500)	2,500	
Inventory (80,000 + 30,000 − 160,000)	(50,000)	
Accounts payable (80,000 + 40,000 − 67,500)	(52,500)	(100,000)
Cash from operations		106,000

Dividends:

Paid to Regina shareholders	20,000	
Paid to Dakota minority shareholders	16,000	(36,000)

Financing activities:

Bonds issued	65,000	
Common shares issued to acquire 60% of Dakota's shares, less cash acquired	140,000	205,000

Investing activities:

Net assets of Dakota acquired (excluding current items):		
Land	66,000	
Buildings	118,000	
Equipment	26,000	
Goodwill	42,000	
Bonds outstanding	(56,000)	
Minority interest	(66,000)	
	130,000	

Other assets acquired:

Buildings	40,000	
Equipment	25,000	
Land	$ 90,000	(285,000)

Increase (decrease) in cash		$ (10,000)

Consolidation worksheet (not required):

	Regina	Dakota	Adjustments and eliminations Acquisition	Adjustments and eliminations Operations	Regina, Consolidated
Cash	30,000	10,000			40,000
Accounts receivable	110,000	30,000		(52,500)e	87,500
Inventory	160,000	60,000		{ (40,000)h (20,000)j }	160,000
Land	—	135,000	21,000 b		156,000
Buildings	300,000	150,000	{ 18,000 b (50,000)c }		418,000
Accum. depr. — building	(45,000)	(60,000)	50,000 c	(1,800)d	(56,800)
Equipment	200,000	130,000	{ (24,000)b (80,000)c }		226,000
Accum. depr. — equipment	(80,000)	(90,000)	80,000 c	4,800 d	(85,200)
Investment in Dakota	150,000	—	{ (99,000)a (51,000)b }		
Goodwill			42,000 b	(2,100)d	39,900
Accounts payable	(40,000)	(80,000)		52,500 e	(67,500)
Bonds payable	(65,000)	(50,000)			(115,000)
Premium on bonds			(6,000)b	600 d	(5,400)
Common shares	(370,000)	(100,000)	100,000 a		(370,000)
Retained earnings	(225,000)	(65,000)	65,000 a		(225,000)
Dividends paid	20,000	40,000		(40,000)f	20,000
Sales	(2,000,000)	(1,000,000)		{ 400,000 h 200,000 j }	(2,400,000)
Cost of sales	1,000,000	600,000		{ (360,000)h (180,000)j }	1,060,000
Operating expenses	839,000	170,000		(900)d	1,008,100
Dividend income	(24,000)	—		24,000 f	
Other income	(7,000)	—		2,500 e	(4,500)
Interest expense	2,000	10,000		{ (600)d (2,500)e }	8,900
Income tax expense	45,000	110,000			155,000
Minority interest			(66,000)a	{ 16,000 f (44,000)g 16,000 i }	(78,000)
Minority interest in earnings of subsidiary				{ 44,000 g (16,000)i }	28,000
	0	0	0	0	0

Explanation of adjustments and eliminations:

a. Elimination of Dakota's share equity.
b. Adjustment to fair values for Regina's share, and goodwill. The FVI for bonds could have been credited directly to Bonds Payable. The use of the premium account facilitates the preparation of the SCFP.
c. Elimination of Dakota's accumulated depreciation at acquisition date.
d. Amortization of fair value increments.
e. Elimination of intercompany loan and accrued interest.
f. Elimination of Dakota's dividends paid.
g. Adjustment for Minority Interest's share in subsidiary book earnings (40% × $110,000).
h. Elimination of upstream unrealized profits (gross profit margin = 40%).
i. Minority interest share of unrealized upstream profits (40% × $40,000).
j. Elimination of downstream unrealized profits (gross profit margin = 50%).

SSP 10-1

Regina Ltd.
Consolidated Statement of Income and Retained Earnings
Years Ended December 31

	19x10	19x9
Sales revenue (2,200,000 + 1,100,000 − 40,000 − 160,000)	$3,100,000	$2,400,000
Gain on sale of fixed assets	10,000	
Other income (12,000 − 5,000)	7,000	4,500
Total revenue	3,117,000	2,404,500
Cost of sales (1,300,000 + 660,000 − 40,000 − 160,000 + 32,000 − 44,000)	1,748,000	1,044,000
Operating expenses (826,000 + 362,000 + 1,800 − 4,800 + 2,100)	1,187,100	1,008,100
Interest and bond retirement expense (20,000 + 18,000 − 5,000 − 600)	32,400	8,900
Income tax expense	68,000	155,000
Total expenses	3,035,500	2,216,000
Operating income	81,500	188,500
Less minority interest's share of earnings of Dakota Ltd.	15,200	28,000
Net income	66,300	60,500
Retained earnings, January 1	365,500	225,000
Dividends paid	(25,000)	(20,000)
Retained earnings, December 31	$ 406,800	$ 365,500

Regina Ltd.
Consolidated Balance Sheet
December 31

	19x10	19x9
ASSETS		
Current assets:		
Cash	$ 12,300	$ 40,000
Accounts receivable (120,000 + 27,000 − 57,500)	89,500	87,500
Inventory (130,000 + 55,000 − 32,000)	153,000	176,000
	254,800	303,500
Fixed assets:		
Land (105,000 + 90,000 + 21,000 − 60,000)	156,000	156,000
Buildings (380,000 + 150,000 − 50,000 + 18,000)	498,000	418,000
Equipment (230,000 + 170,000 − 20,000 − 24,000)	356,000	226,000
	1,010,000	800,000
Accumulated depreciation:		
Buildings (56,200 + 70,000 − 50,000 + 3,600)	(79,800)	(56,800)
Equipment (68,000 + 47,000 − 20,000 − 9,600)	(85,400)	(85,200)
	844,800	658,000
Other assets:		
Future income taxes	15,000	—
Goodwill (42,000 − 4,200)	37,800	39,900
	52,800	39,900
Total assets	$1,152,400	$1,001,400
EQUITIES		
Accounts payable (82,900 + 77,500 − 57,500)	$ 102,900	$ 67,500
Bonds payable (145,000 + 50,000)	195,000	115,000
Premium on bonds payable (3,700 + 6,000 − 1,200)	8,500	5,400
Total long-term debt	203,500	120,400
Total liabilities	306,400	187,900
Minority interest in Dakota Ltd. [(40% × 310,000) − 12,800 − 18,000 − 24,000]	69,200	78,000
Shareholders' equity:		
Common shares	370,000	370,000
Retained earnings	406,800	365,500
	776,800	735,500
Total liabilities and shareholders' equity	$1,152,400	$1,001,400

Regina Ltd.
Consolidated Statement of Changes in Financial Position
Year ended December 31, 19x10

Operations:		
Net income, per income statement		$ 66,300
Adjustments for items not requiring cash:		
Depreciation (note 1)	$113,200	
Amortization of bond premiums	(900)	
Goodwill amortization	2,100	
Minority interest in Dakota's earnings	15,200	
Gain on sale of fixed assets	(10,000)	119,600
Adjustment for income tax paid on intercompany		
transaction (note 2)		(15,000)
Changes in current assets and liabilities:		
Accounts receivable	(2,000)	
Inventory	23,000	
Accounts payable	35,400	56,400
Cash from operations		227,300
Dividends:		
Paid to Regina shareholders	25,000	
Paid to Dakota minority shareholders	24,000	(49,000)
Financing activities:		
Bonds issued		84,000
Investing activities:		
Purchase of buildings	80,000	
Purchase of equipment (note 3)	240,000	
Proceeds from sale of equipment	(30,000)	(290,000)
Net increase (decrease) in cash		$(27,700)

Notes on the Statement of Changes in Financial Position:

1. Depreciation expense equals the change in the consolidated accumulated depreciation accounts plus depreciation written off during the year, as follows:

	Accumulated depreciation		
	Buildings	Equipment	Total
Balance, December 31, 19x10	79,800	85,400	165,200
Balance, December 31, 19x9	56,800	85,200	142,000
Net change	23,000	200	23,200
Written off		60,000	60,000
Sold		30,000	30,000
Depreciation expense	23,000	90,200	113,200

2. The intercompany land sale was eliminated in the consolidation, but the income taxes did require a use of funds during the year.
3. The change in the consolidated equipment account was $130,000. To this must be added the $60,000 that Dakota wrote off and the $50,000 that Regina sold.

Consolidation worksheet (not required):

Account	Regina	Dakota	Adjustments and eliminations			Consolidated
			Acquisition	Cumulative	Current	
Cash	9,800	2,500				12,300
A/R	120,000	27,000		(52,500)d	(5,000)h	89,500
Inventory	130,000	55,000			(32,000)f	153,000
Land	105,000	90,000	21,000 b		(60,000)e	156,000
Building	380,000	150,000	{ 18,000 b { (50,000)c			498,000
A/D-building	(56,200)	(70,000)	50,000 c	(1,800)d	(1,800)j	(79,800)
Equipment	230,000	170,000	{ (24,000)b { (20,000)c			356,000
A/D-equipment	(68,000)	(47,000)	20,000 c	4,800 d	4,800 j	(85,400)
Investment in Dakota	150,000		{ (99,000)a { (51,000)b			0
Goodwill			42,000 b	(2,100)d	(2,100)j	37,800
A/P	(82,900)	(77,500)		52,500 d	5,000 h	(102,900)
Bond payable	(145,000)	(50,000)				(195,000)
Bond premium	(3,700)		(6,000)b	600 d	600 j	(8,500)
Common shares	(370,000)	(100,000)	100,000 a			(370,000)
Retained earnings	(350,000)	(135,000)	65,000 a	54,500 d		(365,500)
Dividends paid	25,000	60,000			(60,000)i	25,000
Minority interest			(66,000)a	(12,000)d	{ 24,000 i { (15,200)k	(69,200)
Future income tax					15,000 e	15,000
Sales	(2,200,000)	(1,100,000)			{ 160,000 f { 40,000 g	(3,100,000)
CGS	1,300,000	660,000		(44,000)d	{ (128,000)f { (40,000)g	1,748,000
Operating expense	826,000	362,000			(900)j	1,187,100
Dividend income	(36,000)				36,000 i	0
Gain/FA	(10,000)	(45,000)			45,000 e	(10,000)
Other income	(12,000)				5,000 h	(7,000)
Interest expense	20,000	18,000			{ (5,000)h { (600)j	32,400
Income tax expense	38,000	30,000				68,000
Minority interest in earnings					15,200 k	15,200
	0	0	0	0	0	0

Explanation of eliminations and adjustments:

a. Elimination of Dakota's share equity at date of acquisition.
b. Fair value increments and goodwill as of date of acquisition.
c. Elimination of Dakota's accumulated depreciation at acquisition date, less the $60,000 in fully depreciated equipment written off in 19x10.
d. Amortization of FVIs and goodwill for 19x9; minority interest's share of unremitted 19x9 earnings; unrealized profits from 19x9, realized in 19x10.
e. Elimination of unrealized gain on intercompany sale of land, including tax effect. This will affect minority interest.
f. Elimination of intercompany (upstream) sale of inventory and related unrealized profit in inventory. Markup is computed from Dakota's trial balance as 40% of sales. Unrealized profit is $160,000 × 50% × 40% = $32,000. This will affect minority interest's share of Dakota's earnings.
g. Elimination of the downstream sale. The sale was at cost, and therefore no profit elimination is necessary.
h. Elimination of additional accrued interest (for a full year) on the intercompany loan.
i. Elimination of Dakota's dividends.
j. Amortization of FVIs and goodwill for 19x10.
k. Minority interest share of Dakota's adjusted earnings:

Net income, per trial balance	$ 75,000
Adjustments:	
Unrealized inventory profit, ending	−32,000
Unrealized inventory profit, beginning	+40,000
Unrealized land profit	−45,000
Dakota's adjusted net income	$ 38,000
	× 40%
Minority interest share	$ 15,200

SSP 10-2

a. IOR's equity in the earnings of IEE for 19x3:

70% of IEE's reported net income	$56,000
Less unrealized profits in inventory, end of year:	
Upstream: $12,000 × 30% × 70%	(2,520)
Plus profits in opening inventory realized during 19x3:	
Upstream (from Schedule 10-3)	3,150
Downstream (from Schedule 10-3)	1,800
Amortization (from Schedule 10-3):	
FVI on buildings and equipment	(7,000)
Goodwill	(1,750)
Unrealized profit on upstream sale of land: $20,000 × 70%	(14,000)
IOR's equity in IEE's 19x3 net income	$35,680

b. Equity-basis general journal entries:

Investment in IEE	$35,600	
Equity in earnings of IEE		$35,680
Dividends receivable	$16,800	
Investment in IEE		$16,800
(not required:)		
Cash	$12,600	
Dividends receivable		$12,600

BALANCE OF INVESTMENT ACCOUNT, DECEMBER 31, 19X3:

Balance, December 31, 19x2	$901,550
Equity in 19x3 earnings	35,680
Dividends received or receivable	(16,800)
Balance, December 31, 19x3	$920,430

SSP 12-1

Note: this is a downstream sale; minority interest is not affected, except by the gain from salvage in 19x16.

a. Excluding taxes

19x3:

Sales	$100,000	
Cost of sales		$60,000
Equipment		40,000
Accumulated depreciation	$ 2,000	
Depreciation expense		$ 2,000

19x4:

Retained earnings	$ 38,000	
Accumulated depreciation	2,000	
Equipment		$40,000
Accumulated depreciation	$ 4,000	
Depreciation expense		$ 4,000

19x8:

Retained earnings	$ 22,000	
Accumulated depreciation	18,000	
Equipment		$40,000
Accumulated depreciation	$ 4,000	
Depreciation expense		$ 4,000

19x15:

Accumulated depreciation	$ 40,000	
Equipment		$40,000

19x16:

Minority interest in earnings	$ 200	
Minority interest		$ 200

b. Including taxes

19x3:

Sales	$100,000	
Future income taxes	16,000	
Cost of sales		$60,000
Income tax expense		16,000
Equipment		40,000
Accumulated depreciation	$ 2,000	
Depreciation expense		$ 2,000
Income tax expense	$ 800	
Future income taxes		$ 800

19x4:

Retained earnings	$ 22,800	
Future income taxes	15,200	
Accumulated depreciation	2,000	
Equipment		$40,000
Accumulated depreciation	$ 4,000	
Depreciation expense		$ 4,000
Income tax expense	$ 1,600	
Future income taxes		$ 1,600

19x8:

Retained earnings	$ 13,200	
Future income taxes	8,800	
Accumulated depreciation	18,000	
Equipment		$40,000
Accumulated depreciation	$ 4,000	
Depreciation expense		$ 4,000
Income tax expense	$ 1,600	
Future income taxes		$ 1,600

19x15:

Accumulated depreciation	$ 40,000	
Equipment		$40,000

19x16:

Minority interest in earnings	$ 120	
Minority interest		$ 120

The equipment becomes fully depreciated in 19x13; thereafter, there is no unrealized profit and no income tax effect.

SSP 12-2

The $500,000 face value bonds were purchased by Passion for $479,000, a discount of $21,000. The discount will be amortized by Passion over the six years remaining to maturity at $3,500 per year. On Sweetness's books, the original issue discount (also $21,000) will be amortized over 10 years at $2,100 per year. The book values of the $500,000 bonds on both companies' books will be as follows:

	Sweetness	Passion
Original issue price, 1/1/x1	$479,000	
4 years' amortization	8,400	
Book value, 31/12/x4	487,400	
Purchase price, 31/12/x4		$479,000
2 years' amortization	4,200	7,000
Book value, 31/12/x6	491,600	486,000
4 years' amortization	8,400	14,000
Book value, 31/12/x10	$500,000	$500,000

The consolidation elimination must dispose of the difference between the carrying values of the bonds on the two companies' books. Assuming that the bonds are carried net of their discounts:

1. Agency method:

   DECEMBER 31, 19x4:

Bonds payable	$487,400	
Bond investment		$479,000
Gain on bond retirement		8,400
Minority interest in earnings (I/S)	$ 2,520	
Minority interest (B/S)		$ 2,520
(30% of the gain of $8,400)		

   DECEMBER 31, 19x6:

Bonds payable	$491,600	
Bond investment		$486,000
Minority interest (30% × $5,600)		1,680
Retained earnings		3,920
Interest income (include $3,500 amortization)	$ 63,500	
Interest expense (include $2,100 amortization)		$ 62,100
Minority interest [30% × (3,500 − 2,100)]		420
Retained earnings		980

   DECEMBER 31, 19x10:

Bonds payable	$500,000	
Bond investment		$500,000
Interest income	$ 63,500	
Interest expense		$ 62,100
Minority interest		420
Retained earnings		980

2. Par-value method:

   DECEMBER 31, 19x4:

Bonds payable	$487,400	
Bond investment		$479,000
Gain on bond retirement		8,400
Minority interest in earnings (I/S)	$ 3,780	
Minority interest (B/S)		$ 3,780
(30% of $12,600, the difference between face value and carrying value on Sweetness's books)		

DECEMBER 31, 19x6:

Bonds payable	$491,600	
Bond investment		$486,000
Minority interest (30% × $8,400)		2,520
Retained earnings		3,080
Interest income	$ 63,500	
Interest expense		$ 62,100
Minority interest (30% × $2,100)		630
Retained earnings		770

DECEMBER 31, 19x10:

Bonds payable	$500,000	
Bond investment		$500,000
Interest income	$ 63,500	
Interest expense		$ 62,100
Minority interest		630
Retained earnings		770

SSP 12-3

Power Company
Consolidated Income Statement
Year Ended December 31, 19x9

Sales ($2,000,000 + $900,000 − $400,000 − $250,000)	$2,250,000
Investment income ($1,000,000 + $100,000 − $32,000)	1,068,000
Total revenues	3,318,000
Cost of goods sold (see below)	1,143,000
Other operating expenses (see below)	712,500
Income tax expense (see below)	580,400
Minority interest in earnings of Spencer (see below)	35,760
Total expenses	2,471,660
Net income	$ 846,340

[Note: the extraordinary gain is from an intercompany transaction and is eliminated on consolidation.]

Purchase transaction (January 1, 19x5):	
80% of net book value acquired ($3,000,000 × 80%)	$2,400,000
Fair-value decrements:	
Building: $600,000 × 80%	−480,000
Long-term liabilities: $500,000 × 80%	+400,000
Fair value of net assets acquired	2,320,000
Purchase price	2,500,000
Goodwill	$ 180,000

Cost of goods sold:

As reported — Power	$1,300,000
— Spencer	500,000
Less intercompany sales, 19x9 — downstream	−400,000
— upstream	−250,000
Realized profit, beginning inventory:	
Downstream, $100,000 × 30%	−30,000
Upstream, $70,000 × 40%	−28,000
Unrealized profit, ending inventory:	
Downstream, $90,000 × 30%	+27,000
Upstream, $60,000 × 40%	+24,000
	$1,143,000

Other operating expenses:

As reported — Power	$500,000
— Spencer	200,000
Depreciation on unrealized loss on sale of machine:	
[$210,000 − 15/20($400,000)] divided by 15	+6,000
Additional amortization:	
FVD on building (10 years)	−48,000
FVD on long-term liabilities (8 years)	+50,000
Goodwill: $180,000/40	+4,500
	$712,500

Income tax expense:

As reported — Power	$460,000
— Spencer	120,000
Add taxes on realized profit in beginning inventories:	
($30,000 + $28,000) × 40%	+23,200
Less taxes on unrealized profit in ending inventories:	
($27,000 + $24,000) × 40%	−20,400
Less tax on realized portion of loss on intercompany sale of	
machine: $6,000,000 × 40%	−2,400
	$580,400

Minority interest in earnings of Spencer:

20% of net income before extraordinary items	$36,000
Inventory adjustments:	
Realized (beginning), $28,000 × 20%	+5,600
tax effect @ 40%	−2,240
Unrealized (ending), $24,000 × 20%	−4,800
tax effect @ 40%	+1,920
Machine: $6,000 × 20%	−1,200
tax effect @ 40%	+480
	$ 35,760

Check via equity-basis income (not required):

Spencer net income, 80%	$144,000
Downstream inventory profits, net of tax:	
($30,000 − $27,000) × 60%	+1,800
Upstream inventory profits, net of tax:	
($28,000 − $24,000) × 60% × 80%	+1,920
Depreciation on intercompany sale of machine, net of tax:	
$6,000 × 60% × 80%	−2,880
Fair-value decrements:	
Building	+48,000
Long-term liabilities	−50,000
Goodwill	−4,500
Equity in earnings of Spencer	138,340
Power net income	740,000
Less dividends received from Spencer	−32,000
Consolidated net income	$846,340

SSP 13-1

Essentially this problem requires that the balance of the investment account be determined at January 1, 19x5, prior to the sale of part of the investment. The FVI and goodwill (if any) must be determined at each of the two purchase dates. The fact that the purchases are in mid-year is not a problem; the year-to-date net income is simply included as part of the net book value (i.e., as retained earnings on acquisition). The two purchases can be analyzed as follows:

JULY 1, 19x3: 30% acquired for	$312,500
Subco net fair value acquired: $875,000 × 30%	262,500
Subco net book value acquired: $875,000 × 30%	262,500

Therefore, goodwill = $50,000, to be amortized over twenty years (at $2,500 per year). *Net* fair value increment is zero, but actually an increment offsets a decrement:

Inventory FVI = $50,000 × 30% =	$15,000
Fixed asset FVD = (50,000) × 30% =	(15,000)
	$ 0

The inventory FVI will flow through to earnings in two months (i.e., a "six times" turnover rate) and the fixed assets FVD will be amortized over ten years (at $1,500 per year).

SEPTEMBER 1, 19x4: 15% acquired for	$183,500
Net fair value acquired: $1,290,000 × 15%	193,500
Net book value acquired: $1,100,000 × 15%	165,000

FVI acquired amounts to $28,500:

Inventory FVI = $10,000 × 15% =	$ 1,500
Fixed asset FVI = $180,000 × 15% =	27,000
	$28,500

However, negative goodwill of $10,000 must be taken into account by reducing the FVIs assigned. Any one of three approaches could be used:

1. Eliminate the FVI on inventory and reduce the FVI on fixed assets to $18,500.
2. Reduce the FVI on both inventory and fixed assets proportionately, to 185/285 of their full fair value.
3. Leave the inventory FVI at $1,500 and reduce the fixed asset FVI by $10,000, to $17,000.

Each approach will yield a different result, but all will be "correct." The actual choice would depend on Parco's reporting objectives. We will use the third approach in the remainder of this solution.

INVESTMENT ACCOUNT:

July 1, 19x3 acquisition (30%)	$312,500
Subco earnings for remainder of 19x3, $100,000 × 30%	30,000
FVI on inventory	(15,000)
Amortization (1/2 year) of fixed asset FVD	750
Amortization (1/2 year) of goodwill	(1,250)
December 31, 19x3 balance	327,000
September 1, 19x4 acquisition (15%)	183,500
Subco earnings for 19x4:	
$125,000 × 30%	37,500
$ 30,000 × 45%	13,500
Amortizations:	
Inventory flow-through, 2nd purchase	(1,500)
Fixed assets: 1st purchase (FVD)	1,500
2nd purchase (1/3 year)	(567)
Goodwill, 1st purchase	(2,500)
December 31, 19x4 balance	$558,433

When Parco sells 4,000 of its 9,000 shares, the investment account must be reduced by 4/9. The difference between the sale proceeds and the carrying cost is the gain or loss to Parco:

Proceeds from selling 4,000 Subco shares	$300,000
Carrying value of shares sold: $558,433 × 4/9	248,192
Gain on sale	$ 51,808

SSP 16-1

a. December 2, 19x2:

Accounts receivable (DM100,000 × $.50)	$50,000	
Sales		$50,000

December 31, 19x2:

Accounts receivable (DM100,000 × $.01)	$ 1,000	
Deferred exchange gains and losses		$ 1,000
Unrealized forward premium	$ 1,000	
Exchange gains and losses		$ 1,000
(Recognition of one half of the premium on the forward contract)		

February 1, 19x3:

Cash (DM100,000 × $.525)	$52,500	
Deferred exchange gain	1,000	
Exchange gains and losses		$ 2,500
Accounts receivable		51,000
(To record payment by the customer)		
Cash	$52,000	
Exchange gains and losses	1,500	
Unrealized forward premium		$ 1,000
Cash		52,500

(The net effect on the income statement is to recognize $1,000 of the premium as an exchange gain in 19x2, and to recognize the remaining premium of $1,000 as an exchange gain in 19x3.)

b. December 2, 19x2:

Accounts receivable	$50,000	
Sales		$50,000

December 31, 19x2:

Accounts receivable	$ 1,000	
Exchange gains and losses		$ 1,000

February 1, 19x3:

Cash	$52,500	
Accounts receivable		$51,000
Exchange gains and losses		1,500

SSP 16-2

October 14, 19x7: no entries necessary.

December 7, 19x7:

Equipment (US$200,000 × $1.22)	$244,000	
Accounts payable (US$200,000 × $1.18)		$236,000
Deferred forward premium		8,000

December 31, 19x7:

Deferred exchange gains and losses	$ 2,000	
Accounts payable (US$200,000 × $.01)		$ 2,000

January 30, 19x8:

Accounts payable	$238,000	
Exchange gains and losses	10,000	
Cash (US$200,000 × $1.24)		$248,000
Cash	$248,000	
Deferred forward premium	8,000	
Deferred exchange gains and losses		$ 2,000
Exchange gains and losses		10,000
Cash		244,000

SSP 17-1

Income statements

	19x2 @ $1.70	19x1 @ $2.20
Revenue	$ 510,000	$ 484,000
Depreciation	102,000	132,000
Interest expense	68,000	88,000
Other expenses	204,000	176,000
	374,000	396,000
Net income	$ 136,000	$ 88,000

Balance sheets

	19x2	19x1
Cash	$ 45,000	$ 320,000
Accounts receivable	60,000	60,000
Temporary investments	300,000	—
Fixed assets	900,000	1,200,000
Accumulated depreciation	(180,000)	(120,000)
	$1,125,000	$1,460,000
Accounts payable	$ 15,000	$ 40,000
Note payable (long-term)	300,000	400,000
Common shares (1)	1,250,000	1,250,000
Retained earnings (2)	73,000	22,000
Translation loss (3)	(513,000)	(252,000)
	$1,125,000	$1,460,000

Notes:

(1) The original investment is translated at the historical rate of $2.50.

(2) The retained earnings is translated at the historical rate at which the subsidiary's earnings were included in the parent's net income:

	19x2	19x1
SF10,000 from 19x1 at $2.20	$22,000	$22,000
SF30,000 from 19x2 at 1.70	51,000	
Translated retained earnings	$73,000	$22,000

(3) The translation losses can be proved as follows:

19x1: loss on original investment, SF500,000 ($2.00 − $2.50)	$250,000
loss on earnings retained, SF10,000 ($2.00 − $2.20)	2,000
Balance, December 31, 19x1	252,000
19x2: loss on beginning of year shareholders' equity, SF510,000 ($1.50 − $2.00)	255,000
loss on 19x2 earnings retained, SF30,000 ($1.50 − $1.70)	6,000
Balance, December 31, 19x2	$513,000

SSP 17-2

(a) Translated 19×1 financial statements (temporal method):

Income Statement

Revenue	SF 220,000	@ $2.20	$ 484,000
Depreciation	60,000	2.30	138,000
Interest expense	40,000	2.20	88,000
Other expenses	80,000	2.20	176,000
	180,000		402,000
Net income	SF 40,000		$ 82,000

Balance Sheet

Cash	SF 160,000	@ $2.00	$ 320,000
Accounts receivable	30,000	2.00	60,000
Fixed assets	600,000	2.30	1,380,000
Accumulated depreciation	(60,000)	2.30	(138,000)
	SF 730,000		$1,622,000
Accounts payable	SF 20,000	2.00	$ 40,000
Note payable (long-term)	200,000	2.00	400,000
Common shares	500,000	2.50	1,250,000
Retained earnings	10,000		22,000*
Translation loss			(90,000)
	SF 730,000		$1,622,000

*Net income, per income statement	SF 40,000		$ 82,000
Less dividends declared and paid at year-end 19x1	30,000	@ $2.00	60,000
Retained earnings	SF 10,000		$ 22,000

(b) Translation loss:

(1) Loss on current monetary items:

Current monetary balance, January 1, 19x1	SF 0		$ 0
Additions:			
Investment by Var Corporation	500,000	@ $2.50	1,250,000
Funds from operations:			
Net income	40,000		82,000
Depreciation	60,000	2.30	138,000
Note payable	200,000	2.40	480,000
	800,000		1,950,000

Uses:			
Purchase of fixed assets	600,000	2.30	1,380,000
Dividends declared	30,000	2.00	60,000
	630,000		1,440,000
Derived balance, December 31, 19x1			510,000
Actual balance, December 31, 19x1	SF 170,000	2.00	340,000
Loss on current monetary items			170,000

(2) Gain on long-term note payable:

SF200,000 ($2.40 − $2.00) =	80,000
Net translation loss	$ 90,000

The loss on current monetary items of $170,000 would be deducted on Var's 19x1 income statement. The gain on the long-term (three-year) loan would be credited one-third ($26,667) to Var's 19x1 income statement and the remaining two-thirds ($53,333) would be a deferred credit on Var's balance sheet.

(c) Translated 19x2 financial statements:

Income Statement

Revenue	SF 300,000	@ $1.70	$ 510,000
Depreciation	60,000	2.30	138,000
Interest expense	40,000	1.70	68,000
Other expenses	120,000	1.70	204,000
	220,000		410,000
	SF 80,000		$ 100,000

Balance Sheet

Cash	SF 30,000	@ $1.50	$ 45,000
Accounts receivable	40,000	1.50	60,000
Temporary investments	200,000	1.90	380,000
Fixed assets	600,000	2.30	1,380,000
Accumulated depreciation	(120,000)	2.30	(276,000)
	SF 750,000		$1,589,000
Accounts payable	SF 10,000	1.50	$ 15,000
Notes payable (long-term)	200,000	1.50	300,000
Common shares	500,000	2.50	1,250,000
Retained earnings*	40,000		47,000
Translation loss			(23,000)
	SF 750,000		$1,589,000
*Balance, January 1, 19x2	SF 10,000		$ 22,000
Net income for 19x2	80,000		100,000
Dividends declared (at year-end)	(50,000)	@ $1.50	(75,000)
Balance, December 31, 19x2	SF 40,000		$ 47,000

(d) Loss on current monetary items for 19x2:

Current monetary balance, January 1, 19x1	SF 170,000	@ $2.00	$ 340,000
Additions:			
Net income	80,000		100,000
Depreciation	60,000		138,000
	310,000		578,000
Uses:			
Dividends declared	50,000	1.50	75,000
Purchase of nonmonetary investments	200,000	1.90	380,000
	250,000		455,000
Derived balance, December 31, 19x2			123,000
Actual balance, December 31, 19x2	SF 60,000	1.50	90,000
Loss on current monetary items			$ 33,000

(e) Cumulative translation loss:

Reconciliation of cumulative total:

	19x1	19x2	Total
Loss on current monetary items	$170,000	$ 33,000	$203,000
Gain on note payable	(80,000)	(100,000)	(180,000)
Cumulative loss			$ 23,000

Effect on Var Corporation's statements [Dr.(Cr.)]:

In retained earnings:	
19x1 loss on current monetary items	$170,000
Amortization of 19x1 gain on note payable	(26,667)
	143,333
In 19x2 net income:	
19x2 loss on current monetary items	33,000
Amortization of 19x1 gain on note payable	(26,667)
Amortization of 19x2 gain on note payable	(50,000)
	(43,667)
On 19x2 balance sheet:	
Deferred 19x1 gain on note payable	(26,666)
Deferred 19x2 gain on note payable	(50,000)
	(76,666)
Cumulative loss	$ 23,000

a. Self-sustaining operation

Translation of Horvath (Daly) Inc. (HDI) balance sheet:

Cash and receivables	D1,900,000	@ $ .64	$1,216,000
Inventories	500,000	.64	320,000
Fixed assets	4,000,000	.64	2,560,000
Accumulated depreciation	(2,400,000)	.64	(1,536,000)
	D4,000,000		$2,560,000
Accounts payable	D 400,000	.64	$ 256,000
Bonds payable	2,000,000	.64	1,280,000
Common shares	1,500,000	3.00	4,500,000
Retained earnings:			
19x1	50,000	2.80	140,000
19x2	100,000	2.20	220,000
19x3	(60,000)	1.80	(108,000)
19x4	—		—
19x5	(50,000)	1.10	(55,000)
19x6	(40,000)	.90	(36,000)
19x7	100,000	.70	70,000
Translation loss			(3,707,000)
	D4,000,000		$2,560,000

b. Integrated operation

Translation of HDI balance sheet:

Cash and receivables	D1,900,000	@ $ .64	$1,216,000
Inventories	500,000	.70	350,000
Fixed assets	4,000,000	2.20	8,800,000
Accumulated depreciation	(2,400,000)	2.20	(5,280,000)
	D4,000,000		$5,086,000
Accounts payable	D 400,000	.64	$ 256,000
Bonds payable	2,000,000	.64	1,280,000
Common shares	1,500,000	3.00	4,500,000
Retained earnings; annual earnings less dividends plus depreciation of D400,000 per year from 19x2			
19x1	50,000	2.80	140,000
19x2	500,000	2.20	1,100,000
19x3	340,000	1.80	612,000
19x4	400,000	1.40	560,000
19x5	350,000	1.10	385,000
19x6	360,000	.90	324,000
19x7	500,000	.70	350,000
Less depreciation	(2,400,000)	2.20	(5,280,000)
Exchange gain (loss)			
Gain on bonds payable:			
D2,000,000 ($0.64 − $2.40)			3,520,000
Loss on current transactions and balances [plug]			(2,661,000)
	D4,000,000		$5,086,000

Horvath Ltd.
Consolidated Balance Sheet
December 31, 19x7

	(a) Self-sustaining	(b) Integrated
Current assets:		
Cash and receivables	$2,288,000	$2,288,000
Inventories	594,400	622,000
	2,882,400	2,910,000
Fixed assets	5,060,000	11,300,000
Accumulated depreciation	(3,036,000)	(6,780,000)
	2,024,000	4,520,000
Total assets	$4,906,400	$7,430,000
Current liabilities:		
Accounts payable	$1,128,000	$1,128,000
Long-term liabilities:		
Bonds payable	1,280,000	1,280,000
Total liabilities	2,408,000	2,408,000
Deferred exchange gain on bonds	–	1,815,682
Shareholders' equity:		
Common shares	4,000,000	4,000,000
Retained earnings (deficit)	2,203,000	(793,682)
Cumulative translation loss	(3,704,600)	–
	2,498,400	3,206,318
Total equities	$4,906,400	$7,430,000

Integrated operation worksheet (not required):

	HL	HDI	Eliminations	Consolidated
Cash and receivables	$1,200,000	$1,216,000	$(128,000)b	$2,288,000
Inventories	300,000	350,000	(28,000)c	622,000
Fixed assets	2,500,000	8,800,000		11,300,000
Accumulated depreciation	(1,500,000)	(5,280,000)		(6,780,000)
Investment in HDI	4,500,000	–	(4,500,000)a	–
Accounts payable	(1,000,000)	(256,000)	128,000 b	(1,128,000)
Bonds payable	–	(1,280,000)		(1,280,000)
Common shares	(4,000,000)	(4,500,000)	4,500,000 a	(4,000,000)
Retained earnings	(2,000,000)	1,809,000	28,000 c	163,000
Translation loss		(859,000)		(859,000)
	$ 0	$ 0	$ 0	$ 0

c. Unrealized profit = D100,000 × 40% × $0.70 = $28,000.

Integrated operation, supporting schedules

Computation of deferred gain on bonds payable: Bonds issued early 19x2, maturing January 1, 19x12 (ten-year term):

Year	Total Gain	Years	Amount	Deferred balance at December 31, 19x7: 4 years' amortization
19x2	$ 800,000	10	80,000	$ 320,000
19x3	1,000,000	9	111,111	444,444
19x4	600,000	8	75,000	300,000
19x5	400,000	7	57,143	228,571
19x6	400,000	6	66,667	266,667
19x7	320,000	5	64,000	256,000

Deferred balance, December 31, 19x7	1,815,682
Total gain to date	3,520,000
Gain amortized to income to date	$1,704,318

Consolidated retained earnings:

HL retained earnings	$2,000,000
HDI translated retained earnings (deficit)	(1,809,000)
Unrealized profit in inventory	(28,000)
Amortized exchange gain on bonds (above)	1,704,318
Exchange loss on current transactions and balances	(2,661,000)
Balance, December 31, 19x7 (deficit)	$ (793,682)

Self-sustaining operation worksheet (not required):

	HL	HDI	Eliminations	Consolidated
Cash and receivables	$1,200,000	$1,216,000	$ (128,000)b	$2,288,000
Inventories	300,000	320,000	(25,600)c	594,400
Fixed assets	2,500,000	2,560,000		5,060,000
Accumulated depreciation	(1,500,000)	(1,536,000)		(3,036,000)
Investment in HDI	4,500,000		(4,500,000)a	—
Accounts payable	(1,000,000)	(256,000)	128,000 b	(1,128,000)
Bonds payable	—	(1,280,000)		(1,280,000)
Common shares	(4,000,000)	(4,500,000)	4,500,000 a	(4,000,000)
Retained earnings	(2,000,000)	(231,000)	28,000 c	(2,203,000)
Translation loss		3,707,000	(2,400)c	3,704,600
	$ 0	$ 0	$ 0	$ 0

c. Unrealized profit in inventory = D100,000 × 40% × $0.64 = $25,600.
   Unrealized profit in consolidated retained earnings = D100,000 × 40% × $0.70 = $28,000.

Index

G

To the Owner of this Book

We are interested in your reaction to *Canadian Advanced Financial Accounting* by Thomas H. Beechy. Through feedback from you, we may be able to improve this book in future editions.

1. What was your reason for using this book?

_____ college course

_____ university course

_____ continuing education

_____ other (please specify)

2. If you used this text for a program, what was the name of that program?

3. Which chapters or sections were omitted from your course?

4. Have you any suggestions for improving this text?

Fold here

- -

Society of Management Accountants of Canada Research Studies

- *A Practical Approach to the Appraisal of Capital Expenditures (Second Edition)*, by C.G. Edge and V.B. Irvine (1981)
- *Business Planning: Key to Profit Growth*, by P.H. Irwin (1969)
- *Selective Inventory Management*, by K.A. Lavery (1972)
- *Management Planning and Control of Information Systems*, by J.E. Cooke and D.H. Drury (1980)
- *Accounting Income Models: An Application and Evaluation*, by R.J. Hanna (1974)
- *Normative Models in Managerial Decision-Making*, by L.A. Gordon, D. Miller and H. Mintzberg (1975)
- *Impediments to the Use of Management Information*, by H. Mintzberg (1975)
- *The Canada Business Corporations Act: Implications for Management and the Accountant*, by R.W. Dickerson (1980)
- *Inflation Accounting: Implementation Issues and Some Empirical Evidence*, by S. Basu and J.R. Hanna (1976)
- *Business Combinations and Long-Term Investment: The Canadian View*, by C.E. Byrd (1979)
- *Inflation Accounting, Capital Market Efficiency and Security Prices*, by S. Basu (1977)
- *The Lease-Purchase Decision*, by W.L. Ferrara, J.B. Thies and M.W. Dirsmith (1979)
- *The Lease Purchase Decision — How Some Companies Make It*, by W.L. Ferrara (1979)
- *The Combines Investigation Act: Stage One Amendments and Implications for Management*, by G.E. Kaiser (1978)
- *The Distribution Channels Decision*, by D.M. Lambert (1978)
- *Data Processing Chargeback Systems: Theory and Practice*, by D.H. Drury and J.E. Bates (1979)
- *Research Methodology and Business Decisions*, by J.W. Buckley, H.H. Buckley and Hung-Fu Chiang (1976)
- *The Zero-Base Budgeting Process: A Practical Guide to Evaluation, Implementation and Use*, by H.C. Knight (1979)
- *The Pricing Decision*, by Lawrence A. Gordon, Robert Cooper, Haim Falk, and Danny Miller (1980)
- *The Make-or-Buy Decision*, by Anthony J. Gambino (1980)
- *Leasing Arrangements: Managerial Decision-Making and Financial Reporting Issues*, by S. Basu (1980)
- *Accounting Implications of Collective Bargaining*, by C.T. Lau and M. Nelson (1982)
- *Management Forecasts of Earnings: Issues and Practices*, by D.H. Drury (1982)
- *The Capital Expenditure Decision*, by Arthur V. Corr (1984)
- *The New Product Decision*, by Dale Flesher, Tonya Flesher, and Gerald Skelly (1984)
- *Management Control of Computer-Related Errors*, by John Cooke (1984)
- *Internal Control in Canadian Corporations*, by Lois Etherington and Irene Gordon (1985)
- *Linking Managerial Accounting Systems with Computer Technology*, by Howard Armitage (1985)
- *Canadian Corporate Social Performance: Status Measurement and Control*, by Len Brooks (1986)
- *Financial Reporting: Theory and Application to the Oil and Gas Industry in Canada*, by John Butterworth and Haim Falk (1986)